The Chronicle
of the
Hutterian Brethren

Volume I

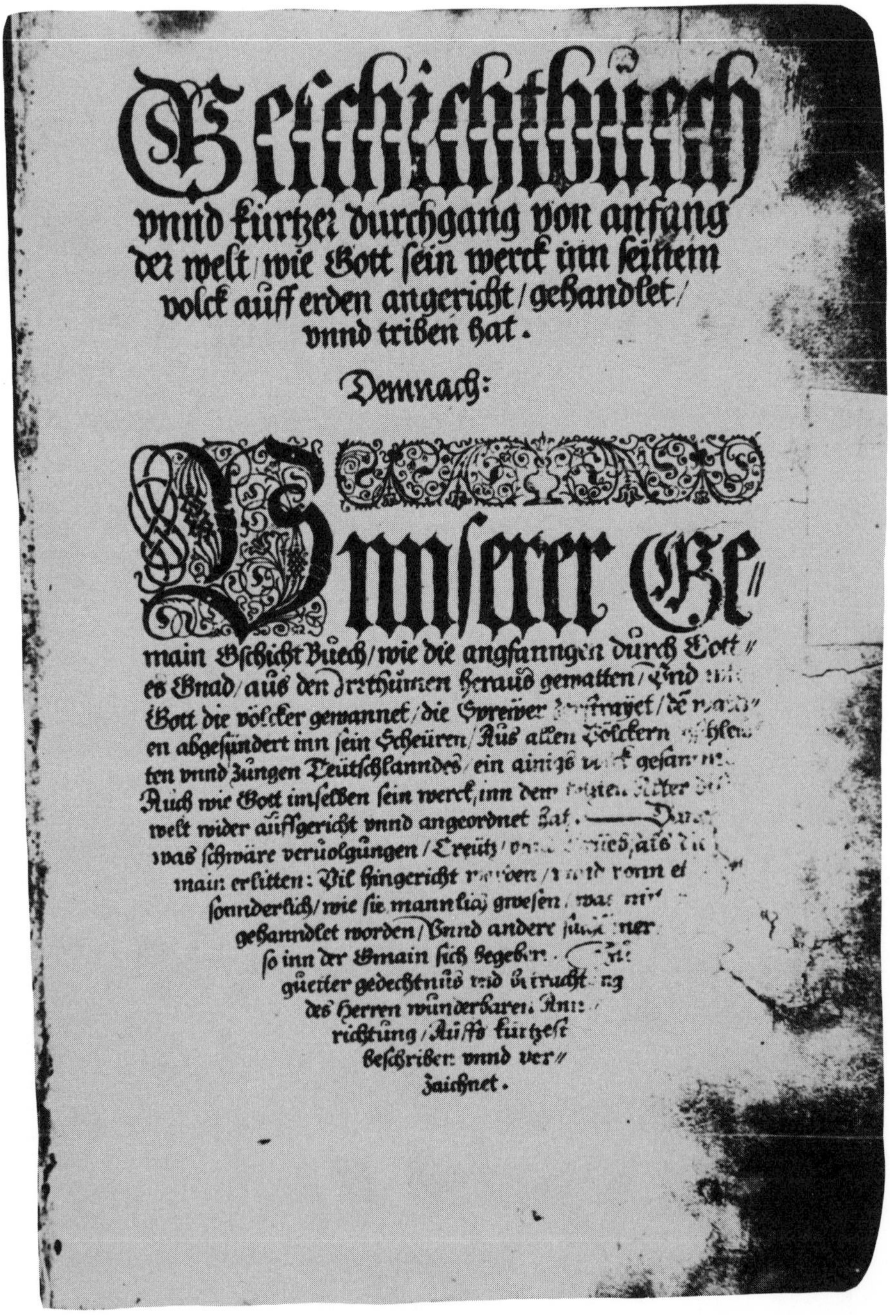

Geschichtbuech
vnnd kürtzer durchgang von anfang
der welt/ wie Gott sein werck inn seinem
volck auff erden angericht/ gehandlet/
vnnd triben hat.

Demnach:

Vnnserer Ge-
main Gschicht Buech/ wie die angfanngen durch Gottes Gnad/ aus den Irrthümen heraus gemallen/ Vnd [illegible]
Gott die völcker gemannet/ die Spreiwer [illegible]/ de[illegible]
en abgesündert inn sein Scheüren/ Aus allen Völckern [illegible]
ten vnnd Zungen Teütschlanndes/ ein ainigs [illegible] gesam[illegible]
Auch wie Gott imselben sein werck/ inn dem [illegible] Alter [illegible]
welt wider auffgericht vnnd angeordnet hat. — Du[illegible]
was schwäre veruolgungen/ Creütz/ [illegible] aus [illegible]
main erlitten: Vil hingericht [illegible]
sonnderlich/ wie sie mannlich gwesen/ [illegible]
gehanndlet worden/ Vnnd andere [illegible]
so inn der Gmain sich begeben. [illegible]
güetter gedechtnus vnd betrachtung
des Herren wunderbaren Ann-
richtung/ Auffs kürtzest
beschriben vnnd ver-
zaichnet.

Title page of the “1581” codex
(Translation, p.XXIII)

The Chronicle of the Hutterian Brethren

Volume I

known as
Das große Geschichtbuch der Hutterischen Brüder

Translated and edited by
the Hutterian Brethren

PLOUGH PUBLISHING HOUSE
HUTTERIAN BRETHREN
Rifton, New York, USA
Ste. Agathe, Manitoba, Canada
Robertsbridge, England

Hutterian Brethren
at
Rifton, NY 12471, USA
Ste. Agathe, Manitoba ROG 1Y0, CANADA
Robertsbridge, E. Sussex TN32 5DR, ENGLAND

Translated from

Geschicht-Buch der Hutterischen Brüder
Prof. Dr. Rudolf Wolkan, ed., Vienna, 1923
and
Die älteste Chronik der Hutterischen Brüder
A.J.F. Zieglschmid, ed., Evanston, Illinois, 1943

by the Hutterian Brethren at
New Meadow Run Bruderhof, Farmington, PA
Woodcrest Bruderhof, Rifton, NY

Forthcoming:
The Chronicle of the Hutterian Brethren, Volume II
known as
Das Klein-Geschichtsbuch der Hutterischen Brüder

Library of Congress Cataloging-in-Publication Data

Great chronicle.
The chronicle of the Hutterian Brethren.

Bibliography: v. 1, p.
Includes index.
Contents: v. 1. Das grosse Geschichtbuch der Hutterischen Brüder.
1. Hutterian Brethren—History. 2. Anabaptists—History. 3. Reformation. I. Hutterian Brethren (Rifton, N.Y.)
BX8129.H8G67 1987 289.7'3 87-2464
ISBN 0-87486-021-0 (v. 1 : alk. paper)

ISBN 0-87486-021-0
Printed in Canada
by Friesen Printers
Altona, Manitoba

Contents

Preface

The purpose of this translation is to share an invaluable treasure, a heritage of the Hutterian Brethren handed down for 450 years. This chronicle presents the background of the people whom men call Hutterian, the origins of a church built on the rock of Jesus Christ the Son of God, the Holy Spirit of Pentecost, the apostles who proclaimed the holy church of Christ, the community of saints, and his kingdom on this earth.

Though driven underground time and again for many centuries, the church of Jesus Christ surfaced powerfully in the sixteenth century under the fire of persecution and the shedding of blood. Its members were falsely accused of being heretics, seducers, and deserters. This chronicle is a testimony of true faithfulness at the cost of martyrdom. Believers in Christ Jesus were transformed and given the strength to die, a strength that came from the sacrifice of Jesus. They heroically accepted the way of martyrdom.

These historical testimonies witness to a way of life that can be lived today, led by the Spirit of New Testament Christianity, even if it costs great struggles. True discipleship, burning with the fire of love, can be a reality. Jesus calls men to a practical way of life—to love and brotherhood, to God's reign of unity and truth, which cannot be quenched or crushed. May this call shake the whole of mankind out of its sleep so that they may see the power of evil, which is driving the world into destruction.

This publication was made possible through many hours of dedicated service from the Hutterian Brethren at Woodcrest, NY, and at New Meadow Run, PA, and through the help and encouragement from the Hutterian Brethren in Canada. For their technical assistance and generous financial support for this publication, the Hutterian Education Committee wishes to recognize and thank Multiculturalism, Canada; Manitoba Culture, Heritage, and Recreation; and the Manitoba Intercultural Council's Community Support Fund.

February 25, 1986

Signed by the elders on behalf of all the Hutterian Brethren,

Jacob Kleinsasser
Crystal Spring Colony
Ste. Agathe, Manitoba R0G 1Y0
CANADA

Johannes Wipf
Rosetown Colony
Rosetown, Saskatchewan S0L 2V0
CANADA

Joseph Wipf
Lakeside Colony
Cranford, Alberta T0K 0R0
CANADA

Johann C. Arnold
Woodcrest
Rifton, New York 12471
USA

Acknowledgments

The task of translating and publishing this approximately 800-page chronicle would hardly have been possible without the encouragement of two well-known Mennonite historians, Cornelius J. Dyck, professor of Anabaptist and Sixteenth-Century Studies at the Associated Mennonite Biblical Seminaries, Elkhart, Indiana, and Leonard Gross, executive secretary of the Historical Committee of the Mennonite Church and director of its archives at Goshen, Indiana.

As our enthusiastic consultant throughout, Leonard Gross deserves special thanks. We are also indebted to him for giving us access to the invaluable collection of manuscripts, codices, and microfilms in the archives at Goshen, Indiana.

The staff of the Mennonite Historical Library at Goshen was of invaluable help, graciously putting their large collection of Anabaptist resources at our disposal.

Warm thanks are due to Jan Gleysteen, the Anabaptist Communicator of the Mennonite Publishing House at Scottdale, PA, for the loan of his maps of the areas covered by this chronicle, which form the basis of maps included at the back of this volume.

We wish to thank Jarold K. Zeman, professor of Church History at Acadia University, Wolfville, Nova Scotia, Canada, for his valuable work, in particular regarding the location of Hutterian communities in sixteenth-century Moravia, as well as for his encouragement in this undertaking.

And finally, a word of gratitude especially to Jacob Kleinsasser of Crystal Spring Colony and to all our brothers and sisters in Canada, the United States, and England, whose support made this effort possible.

Translators' Note

In translating we have aimed at a simple style that captures as much as possible of the frank, down-to-earth, heartfelt language of our sixteenth-century brothers. We used both the Wolkan and the Zieglschmid editions of this chronicle. Wolkan's edition is based on a handwritten copy made around 1890 by Elias Walter Jr. The "1581" codex (see Introduction p.xvi) is the basis of the Zieglschmid edition. As Zieglschmid was working directly from one of the early codices, we have used his text as authoritative, but we have inserted those phrases from Wolkan not included in Zieglschmid. Only the addenda in Wolkan's edition have been annotated. These are contained in the "1580" codex. Thanks to the loan of the microfilms of both codices, which became available to us shortly before the completion of this translation, we have been able to look at the originals to check some unclear passages. But a careful comparison of the two codices has yet to be made. Brackets have been used to indicate translators' explanations.

To help the reader keep the time frame in mind, we have divided the chronicle into sections (based on the historical divisions made by Josef Beck in *Die Geschichts-Bücher der Wiedertäufer*), added centered dates whenever the chronicle starts a new year, and added the current date at the top of the margin of each page to avoid constant repetition in the text itself.

The marginal notes have been translated from the Wolkan edition.

Unless otherwise acknowledged, Bible passages are translated from the text of the chronicle and may differ in varying degrees from those found in English Bibles. The brothers often quoted from memory. The Froschauer Bible, which was the edition most used by the Hutterian Brethren at the time of this chronicle, does not have verse numbers, so we have supplied appropriate numbers. Bible references in the margin are placed at the beginning of the passage to which they apply.

For the consistent spelling of proper names *The Mennonite Encyclopedia* was used as a guide, bearing in mind ease of pronunciation in English. The German form of place names is used, with current equivalents given in parentheses and in the index. An alphabetical list of current place names with their German equivalents is provided in an appendix.

The footnotes are based on both the Zieglschmid and Wolkan editions and edited for the English reader with some new footnotes added; paleographical and linguistic information has been omitted. References to German works have been partly omitted as they are to be found in Zieglschmid's footnotes and bibliography. Added citations of works, both English and German, are merely suggestive.

Introduction

The Vision

This chronicle is the story of an awakening in which thousands of people, and later tens of thousands, perceived God's truth with new clarity.

This chronicle is the history of a movement that converted hearts, reversed lives, created a new society, defied churches, and gathered a Christian brotherhood on earth.

This chronicle is the firsthand account of an act of God in human history.

God's Spirit seeks embodiment in people who voluntarily give themselves to him and who align themselves on his side in the battle to reconquer this earth for his reign, against Satan, the prince of this world. To this purpose God made a covenant with Abraham and gave his commandments to Moses, so that a people of his own would come into being, a society reflecting his will on earth.

But the history of the Jewish people, the descendants of Abraham, became one of alternating faithfulness and unfaithfulness. Again and again prophets called God's people back to him. Obedient remnants appeared, among whom the neighbor was loved, the widow was cared for, the stranger and the guest honored, the poor looked after, the slave freed, and justice held in respect. But a permanently dedicated people, ready to represent the image of God's kingdom on earth, did not come into being. Not until God's own Son had died on the cross and won a decisive victory over Satan was it possible for the Holy Spirit to be poured out upon a group of surrendered men and women. This outpouring gave birth to a visible church—a body of believers open and faithful to the leading of God's Spirit.

A.D. 33 The founding of the early church at Pentecost sparked an awakening unparalleled in history. Yet even this clear revelation of God's will was slowly blurred as compromise crept in and love and obedience were relinquished in favor of comfort and selfishness. When Christianity gradually became a state religion in the fourth century, the church was no longer exclusively a body of believers. Satan was thwarting God's purpose. But under the ashes of the first fire there were glowing coals: individuals were faithful, a remnant was preserved here and there. From time to time the fire was fanned by God's Spirit into bursts of flame among small groups of believers: the Waldensians, the early Franciscans, the Bohemian Brethren, the Brothers of the Common Life, and many others.

1500 Then in the 1500s, at the time of the Reformation, the ashes from the Middle Ages were blown away and the light of truth blazed forth with power. With the Bible newly opened to them through translations into the vernacular, men saw again a vision of God's will for his creation, and thousands were willing to sacrifice their lives for the embodiment of the true church on earth. In their search to realize that vision, these men and women enthusiastically and obediently put into practice the answers they found. They honored God's claim on their partnership in the fight for his kingdom, and they claimed God's promise for the whole earth. Satan was not to have the last word.

The Power

This new outpouring of spiritual power has been described by a twentieth-century historian:

> The amazing fact is that amongst the early Anabaptists (particularly among the Hutterites) there was this kind of inner kinship between them and the early church at Jerusalem, the apostolic church of the first century A.D., which is, for instance, so evident in the similarity of the Hutterite epistles and the epistles of the New Testament. . . . It is not only an imitation, but a real inner kinship.[1]

---

[1]Robert Friedmann, in Leonard Gross, "Conversations with Robert Friedmann," *MQR*, April 1974, 160.

The early Anabaptists pledged their lives to follow God's leading, and a spiritual battle began, focused on several questions of faith. One of these was the accepted practice of infant baptism and automatic membership in the church. After careful study of the Bible, Georg Blaurock, Conrad Grebel, and Felix Mantz concluded that Jesus had meant baptism only for adults who believe and confess their faith in him. Only people who voluntarily receive baptism should be members of his church. These three men, probably with several others, finally took action and baptized one another in January 1525, 1525
at Zurich, Switzerland. A movement came into being that could not be stopped in spite of the imposition of the death penalty for those who accepted baptism as adults. The name Anabaptists (or rebaptizers) was given them later by the Roman Catholic Church and by Luther's and Zwingli's state churches.

Another issue was nonresistance—should a disciple of Jesus use the sword?—a question that led to division even among the Anabaptists. Other points were the Lord's Supper, leadership in the church, marriage and divorce, swearing of oaths, and war taxes.

Linking all these issues was the question of the relationship of church and state and hence the deeper question of the nature of the church itself. Should the church be free of state influence? The Anabaptists said yes, there must be separation of church and state, otherwise the church is not genuinely the church whose Lord is Jesus Christ alone.

These became life-and-death issues, for which hundreds were burned at the stake. Through the power of the Holy Spirit men, women, and young people went resolutely and even joyfully to their execution rather than deny their faith. To some, God gave the strength to die for their faith. To others, God gave the strength to live on in their faith, making a brotherly way of life a reality. All things were held in common again as in the early church in Jerusalem. One of the groups who had rejected the use of the sword began to practice a form of community of goods. Some two hundred adults left Nikolsburg, the first Anabaptist center in Moravia (now part of Czechoslovakia), and in 1528 moved about thirty miles 1528
away to Austerlitz. On the way there, the spirit of brotherly love impelled them to pool their few belongings on a cloak laid on the ground—the actual beginning of full community

of goods. This practice became one of the most controversial points within the Anabaptist movement.

Several communities or Bruderhofs were then established in Moravia, which at that time was tolerant toward Protestantism, and in 1533 Jakob Hutter was asked to take on the leadership. On one of his mission journeys to Tirol, where the Roman Catholic Church tolerated no so-called heretics, he
1536 was betrayed, and on February 25, 1536, he was burned at the stake at Innsbruck in Austria.

The power to be faithful under persecution, the power to fulfill God's will of establishing brotherhood on earth, was exemplified in his life. His name was used to distinguish the brotherhood he had led—neither he nor his brothers chose this name—and it is his martyrdom that is commemorated by the publication of this chronicle for the first time in English 450 years later.

The Record

The writers of this chronicle had a vivid sense of history. From the title page on, the first chronicler makes it clear that he has no other wish than to record the works of God among men, starting with creation itself. After summarizing the Old and New Testaments and telling about some outstanding witnesses of the Spirit since early Christian times, the chroniclers record the beginning of the Anabaptist movement
1525–1665 in 1525 and the history of the Hutterian Brethren until 1665.

Seldom has history been written with so much frankness, a frankness reminiscent of the Bible. It is simply told, yet it has power and authority, written as it was by those who experienced it. The chroniclers were not glorifying themselves or their martyred brothers and sisters. They were simply stating facts. Not all the facts were complimentary. Men and women at the time of this chronicle were made of weak flesh and blood like any human being today. Some brothers, even servants of the Word, were found to have kept money hidden for their own use; others committed adultery. Jealousy and rivalry among the leaders were candidly reported. But these things were not condoned or gossiped about. They were confronted. Church discipline, based on Matthew 18 and 1 Corinthians 5, was practiced then in Hutterian communities, as it still is now: a repentant sinner finds God's forgiveness through the church by accepting discipline from his brothers and sisters.

This chronicle was begun in the late 1560s. Kaspar Braitmichel, one of the few who could remember the early years, began to bring the records together. He tells in his Preface to the Reader how he used the Bible and *The Antiquities of the Jews* by Josephus to give a short history up to the time of Christ. For the early centuries of the Christian church, he followed the New Testament and *The Ecclesiastical History* of Eusebius. For the period from Eusebius until the early sixteenth century, he quoted Sebastian Franck's *Chronica*, a history written at the time of the Reformation which includes accounts of so-called heretical sects. For the early years of the Anabaptist movement there were contemporary records available. His description of the first adult baptism in 1525 is probably the earliest known account of this event, thought by some scholars to be based on a report by Georg Blaurock, one of the participants.

The struggles of the new movement in the face of oppression and persecution by the authorities were written down by participants or eyewitnesses, often in songs recounting martyrdoms or in farewell letters from imprisoned brothers. These were preserved at the Hutterian archives in Moravia along with accounts of trials and disputations which show the brothers' stand against the Roman Catholic, Lutheran, Zwinglian, and Calvinist churches. Confessions of faith and regulations (*Ordnungen*) for the daily life of the communities were also preserved there. Many of these records Kaspar Braitmichel and subsequent chroniclers summarized or quoted in full, in this way preserving some documents which have not been otherwise traced.

Kaspar Braitmichel worked in a time of relative peace under the eldership of Peter Walpot. He completed the account to the year 1542. Hans Kräl and Hauptrecht Zapff, whose names appear below Braitmichel's at the end of his Preface to the Reader, carried on the work of recording the history and brought it up to date, that is, to around the year 1580. From this date until 1665 the text of the chronicle is a contemporary record. Hauptrecht Zapff made current entries until 1591. Other brothers continued.

The Book

It is a small miracle that this document has been preserved. For more than three hundred years since the last entry, made in 1665, the brothers managed to keep it safe in spite of repeated sacking or burning of their homes by marauding armies, in spite of enforced flights and other dangers, and in spite of efforts by representatives of the state churches to find and destroy their writings.

Kaspar Braitmichel's original handwritten chronicle is lost, however, and what has come down to us is the copy of it made by the elders' secretary-clerk Hauptrecht Zapff before he and Hans Kräl continued the work of recording. This record (referred to as the "1581" codex, from the date 1581 in the illuminated letter J on folio 89v; see plate #8) is in almost perfect condition: a book of over 600 leaves, measuring 3¾″ x 7¾″ x 11¼″, it is at present kept by the Hutterian Brethren at the Bon Homme Colony in South Dakota, United States.

Remarkably enough we have yet another, apparently earlier, copy to refer to, although this one had suffered considerable damage during a time when the Hutterian descendants were no longer living in full community. Only about two-thirds of it is preserved (referred to as the "1580" codex, from the date 1580 in the illuminated letter N on folio 16r; see plate #7). Today it is in the safekeeping of a Hutterian colony in Montana, United States.

The care and love the chroniclers gave to their task can be seen from the frontispiece and the plates at the back of this volume, photographed from pages of the two originals, which have been described as works of outstanding penmanship and artistic illumination.[1]

For centuries, however, the chronicle was lost to the world of scholarship. The schools of learning showed little interest in the various Anabaptist groups, which were considered
1883 heretical, until 1883 when Josef Beck published a collection of short Hutterian chronicles. He was aware that a comprehensive history of the Hutterian movement had existed; annotating a mention of it, he wrote, "The church's history

[1]Microfilms of both the "1580" and the "1581" codices are kept at the Archives of the Historical Committee of the Mennonite Church, Goshen College, Goshen, Indiana.

book must be considered lost. My most thorough research did not reveal any trace of it."[1]

In 1903 Rudolf Wolkan, professor of German literature at the University of Vienna, published a study of Anabaptist hymns.[2] This came to the attention of the Mennonite historian John Horsch in the United States in 1908, who immediately informed Wolkan that the Hutterites were still in existence there—and that they still had the original chronicle ("Unserer Gemein Geschicht-Buch"). It is not hard to imagine the astonishment of European scholars when they learned that descendants of Hutterian Anabaptists were still living out the faith of their forebears in the United States. Professor Wolkan contacted the Hutterian Brethren and was soon engaged in prolonged correspondence with Elias Walter Jr., nephew of the elder Elias Walter Sr. 1903

At that time Beck's collection of Hutterian chronicles, well known and much prized by the brothers in America, was out of print. Professor Wolkan's interest sparked a new hope in many Hutterites, Elias Walter Jr. in particular, that their chronicle would become available to every member of the Hutterian Church.

As a result, the first German edition was published in 1923 1923
by the Hutterian Brethren under the editorship of Professor
Wolkan in Vienna. In 1943 a second German edition was 1943
published by the Carl Schurz Foundation, edited by Professor A.J.F. Zieglschmid at Northwestern University in Evanston, Illinois, United States. He had access to the "1581" manuscript kept at the Bon Homme Colony, South Dakota, and brought out a diplomatic (letter-perfect) copy of the chronicle, especially for the world of scholarship. Both editions were a significant addition to the sources of Anabaptist history. It is hoped that the present edition will make a similar contribution for the English-speaking world.

The Testimony

Yet this book is not a period piece, irrelevant for our age and its cultural norms. The men and women in these records

---

[1]Dr. Josef Beck, *Die Geschichts-Bücher der Wiedertäufer in Oesterreich-Ungarn, 1526–1785* (Vienna, 1883, 1967), p. 286 n.1.

[2]Dr. Rudolf Wolkan, *Die Lieder der Wiedertäufer* (Berlin, 1903). See also *ME*, IV, 971.

grappled with the same problems that face Christian groups today. The brothers knew the same hard beginnings while struggling for discernment among a welter of unclear ideas. They knew the power struggles, the splinter groups, the painful separation from loved and long-known believers who chose a less demanding way. Through faith in God, a remnant always found the power to endure. They held firm to his purpose and guidance and with his grace were able to build a life of brotherhood. Each one loved and valued the other as a child of God. Each surrendered all possessions and devoted every ounce of strength to serve the others. All were supported by the community: the children and the weak, old, and sick received especial care. At the same time they felt the spiritual need of their contemporaries so keenly that they sent members throughout central Europe with the joyful message of redemption and new life. Nothing could stop them from seeking out fellow believers who hungered for the good news—neither the most arduous journeys nor laws nor punishment, even by death.

This translation was originally undertaken with all Hutterian Brethren in mind. Our communities are spread wide over English-speaking lands, from Washington State and British Columbia to Connecticut and England. The hope is that this record, made available in English, will have the same impact as that of the lost Book of the Law upon the Israelites (2 Kings 22—23). We who find discipleship difficult even in a time of peace and freedom of conscience can scarcely imagine what it cost to be loyal when death was the penalty for traveling to join the community or for attempting to spread the message. Thousands of men and women had the courage to hold to their faith and testify from their hearts under cross-examination and torture. Some endured years of crippling imprisonment; some were drowned, others beheaded, others burned at the stake.

May we, as descendants of the men and women whose lives are recorded here, take to heart the following words from this chronicle. They were written as a warning after a description of the hardships suffered by the brothers and sisters when they were driven from their homes between 1548 and 1552:

> All this is described and written down as a record, especially for you and us, their descendants living in times

> when God gives peace, so that we do not think there will always be peace. At the same time, when God does bless us in temporal matters, let us be thankful and remember that our brothers and sisters of earlier times would not have known how to praise and thank God enough if they had had only a half, a third, or even less, of what we have now. Indeed, anyone who cannot endure now, in these good times, has not stood the test as a true Christian. And if ever God should bring similar tribulation on us, their descendants, we should not be taken by surprise but should show the same patience and endurance to the end, to the praise and glory of God (p.314).

It is, however, not merely for us as Hutterian Brethren that this English edition is published. Its significance reaches far beyond the brothers known as Hutterian. This chronicle is the story of an awakening such as mankind needs today. This chronicle is the record of a movement of Spirit that still today can convert hearts, reverse lives, create a new society, and gather a Christian brotherhood on earth. Whenever men and women have surrendered their lives to God and allowed him to act, he has penetrated human history with his divine plan. This chronicle is a testimony to an act of God that was coupled with the response of a faithful people, a people that still survives today. Its message can give us hope and courage for our time.

February 25, 1986

THE EDITORS AT WOODCREST,
NEW MEADOW RUN, AND DEER SPRING
on behalf of the Hutterian Brethren

ABBREVIATIONS

Beck	Josef Beck, *Die Geschichts-Bücher der Wiedertäufer in Oesterreich-Ungarn, 1526–1785*.
LdHBr	*Die Lieder der Hutterischen Brüder*
ME	*The Mennonite Encyclopedia*
ML	*Mennonitisches Lexikon*
MQR	*The Mennonite Quarterly Review*. Goshen, Ind.: The Mennonite Historical Society.

The Chronicle

Chronicle

STARTING WITH A BRIEF NARRATIVE
of the beginning of the world
and of how God began
his work among his people on earth
continued it, and furthered it

Followed by

The Chronicle of our church community—how through God's grace our forebears fought their way through all error and how God winnowed the peoples, scattering the chaff and separating the wheat into his barns: he gathered a united flock from among all the peoples of the German lands. Further, how God has now reestablished his work in this last age of the world. Followed by the severe persecution, suffering, and cross borne by the church: great numbers were executed; about some a particular account is given of the trials they were subjected to and of their manly courage. All this, as well as other matters that happened in the church, has been recounted briefly so that the Lord's wonderful work may be remembered and taken to heart.

The Elders of the Hutterian Church

JAKOB HUTTER
came from Tirol in 1528
1533–1536

HANS AMON
from Bavaria
1535–1542

LEONHARD LANZENSTIEL
from Bavaria
1542–1565

PETER RIEDEMANN
from Silesia
1542–1556

PETER WALPOT
from Tirol
1565–1578

HANS KRÄL
from Kitzbühel in Tirol
1578–1583

KLAUS BRAIDL
from Hesse
1583–1611

SEBASTIAN DIETRICH
from Württemberg
1611–1619

ULRICH JAUSSLING
from Switzerland
1619–1621

VALENTIN WINTER
from Württemberg
1622–1631

HEINRICH HARTMANN
1631–1639

ANDREAS EHRENPREIS
1639–1662

JOHANNES RIEGER
1662–1687

REGISTER
CONTENTS OF THIS CHRONICLE OR HISTORY BOOK
where and on which page each item can be found
arranged in two parts

Part One lists all events and occurrences

Part Two shows where to find the accounts of
all those who suffered imprisonment
or gave witness with their blood
and were executed for the sake
of divine truth

Part One

Part Two

List of All Those
who suffered imprisonment or witnessed
with their blood as Christian martyrs
for the sake of divine truth by
fire, water, and the sword

Preface to the Reader

May Grace, Peace, and Joy in the Holy Spirit increase among you. This I wish from God to you who are chosen, holy, and dearly beloved in the Lord.

I once wrote a short but thorough history with dates, from the time of the beginning of all creatures to the end of the Babylonian captivity, based on the Bible. The account of the rulers after the Babylonian captivity until the time of Christ is based on Josephus. Almost all historians agree with Josephus that the scepter was then taken from Judah and given to an alien (an Edomite), Herod the Great, king in Judah, in the thirtieth year of whose reign Christ was born.

While writing the above history—and even earlier—the thought often occurred to me that God might at some time give a devout man the courage and zeal to trace the whole story of the dawning of grace, including the inception of God's church, and to continue the story up to recent times, embracing what has taken place within the church. As this has not happened till now, I have taken up this work myself, motivated by an earnest love. I seek no honor, for I am certainly the simplest and least suited for the task. I have worked with care and painstaking effort to make it useful for many people, as did those who wrote in the time of the Maccabees. 2 Macc. 2:23–32

There is another reason that led me to undertake this work. For a long time I have been hearing God-fearing people express a great longing for such an account. Some of these have passed away in peace, commended to the grace of God. And from those who are still living I hear daily the same eagerness to know in what shape and form God made the light of his truth shine out in recent times; how the church of God, in great fear and anguish of heart, was delivered from many errors; how it has grown in times of great tribulation; and finally, what events of importance have taken place within the church, and how they were dealt with.

Now I have spared no pains to inquire about these things in whatever way I could from reliable people, some of whom were there at the time. And I have compiled this information with great care, including all that I myself have been able to remember or verify—in all simplicity, without flowery words. But now, although I would gladly have continued the work, I am unable to complete it because of physical weakness and a problem with my eyes. I brought the story only to the year 1542, when the church was entrusted to brother Leonhard Lanzenstiel.[1] I still hope that through this beginning God will move others to carry on this work with even greater diligence, as completely as possible. (This is being done at the present time with the greatest possible care.)[2]

In my opinion, this work will be a valuable mirror in which many God-fearing people may examine themselves, so that they may guard against every division and error and everything that does not serve God's honor. And with this I lay the following on the hearts of all true believers in Christ: If anyone can improve on this book in truth and with good reason, I would be perfectly content with such changes. I ask too that whoever reads this book read it carefully, in the fear of God, so that it does not become a stumbling block but an inner strengthening for himself and his neighbor.

We will also find therein the zeal, joy, and valiant courage in God, demonstrated in the teachings and lives of those who have gone before us. They were faithful even unto death. Many of them suffered long, harsh imprisonment and death by fire, water, or sword. From these examples, each and every godly person has reason to be inspired and motivated to live a life of discipleship in steadfastness to the end. As the Apostle also teaches, we should remember how they died and walk in their faith.

[1]Leonhard Lanzenstiel, or Seiler (rope maker) after his trade, a native of Bavaria, was elder (*Vorsteher*) from 1542 to 1565.

[2]This parenthetical note was added c. 1581 by Hans Kräl and his scribe, Hauptrecht Zapff, the team of chroniclers who succeeded Braitmichel.

May God grant his blessing, so that his name may be praised, the whole church be strengthened, and many people find salvation through Jesus Christ our Lord. Amen.

Kaspar Braitmichel[1]
a servant of Jesus Christ and his church

Continued by Hans Kräl and his scribe
Hauptrecht Zapff of Sprendlingen

[1]On All Saints' Day (Nov. 1), 1538, Kaspar Braitmichel was appointed as servant for temporal affairs (*Diener der Notdurft*) at Schakwitz. In 1548 he was appointed as servant of the Word (*Diener des Wortes*). He died in February 1573 at Austerlitz, Moravia. According to the entry for 1548 he was a native of Silesia.

Creation to 1517: Pre-Reformation History

HERE IS A SIMPLE BUT THOROUGH SUMMARY OF HISTORY
from the beginning of the world until the present time
telling as accurately as possible how God began his
work and carried it out among
his people

THE ONE ALMIGHTY LORD, whose power is above all things, calls himself Shaddai, that is, one with complete authority and an abundance of everything good, a Father, and Creator of all things. With his all-seeing care and well-considered counsel, he has already established order for everything he has created, according to his eternal nature. He has appointed what should happen from the beginning of the world until the present time—even to the last day. To make known his great power and to show forth his glorious might so that all might truly acknowledge him, he let the Word of his mouth separate light from darkness and day from night, and he began to make a separation between the waters above and the waters beneath. Between them he spread out a vault on high and called it the heavens, and he gathered the water below into one place and set its limits, calling it sea. He drew the dry land from the water and called it earth. And God commanded this earth to bring forth grass, herbs, and many kinds of flowers, also fruit trees and every kind of shrub, each bearing its own seed. He adorned the heavens with sun, moon, and stars, by which time can be reckoned. Next he brought wonderful creatures out of the water, birds and fish that were to live in air and water; and out of the earth, many different four-footed and creeping animals that were to live on dry land.

Gen.17:1
Exod.6:3
Deut.6:1

Gen.1
2 Esd.6:38–54
2 Cor.4:6

Job 26
Ps.104
Prov.8:22–31

Through all this God showed his power: whatever his mouth commands, his Spirit can accomplish. His work stands there

Ps.33:9

perfect as soon as the Word leaves his mouth. With one Isa.43—46 command all he wills is carried out. What pleases him is done, as he says, "I am the Lord, I alone made all things, and there is none beside me." But God in his almighty power could not be sufficiently acknowledged by these creatures that he had Gen.2 made, let alone be honored and glorified in the right way. He therefore took a lump of earth, formed a man with all his limbs, and created him in his own image by breathing a living soul into him. And God endowed man above all other creatures with reason, knowledge, and the senses, so that man could acknowledge him as his Creator and God and honor him, love him, keep his commandments, and fear him all his life.

God set his created work like a book before this richly gifted Ps.8 man, so that he might learn of his great power and glory. And he placed man over everything as master, for man was to have everything in his power and use it. But above all he was to honor his God and Creator. And in order for man not to live too confidently or without cares, God gave him one very earnest command: that although he had power to rule over all created things, he must nonetheless beware of the fruit of the tree of the knowledge of good and evil in the middle of the garden, for on the day that he tasted its fruit, he would die.

As long as this man used his God-given authority properly, he turned with a joyful heart and open eyes toward the light, without fear of his Creator. But the woman who had been Gen.3 taken from his ribs followed the counsel of the serpent. She persuaded the man to do so too. As soon as he ate the forbidden fruit, he began to run away from the light and to hate it. The serpent received his punishment, and so did the woman and Adam himself. Yet God in his compassion with the human race promised that through the woman's seed they would once again be delivered.

Adam set his hope on this promise, and it was the light and comfort of his heart. He also directed his descendants toward Gen.4 this light, to the Word of divine promise. We can see this in his son Abel, who, through his service and offerings, was acceptable in God's sight. Others are named in the Bible who steadfastly hoped and longed to be enlightened by this light. Here is a list of them, from the beginning of time, given in order.

Gen.5 First Comes Adam (meaning "taken from the earth"),

the first man created, a son of God. When he was 130, he begot a son named Seth through his wife Eve, whom God had formed from his ribs. After this he lived 800 years and saw Lamech, the ninth in descent counting himself as the first, and died 726 years before the flood. Luke 3:23–38

SETH (meaning "a leader") was Adam's son. When he was 105, he begot Enosh, 235 years after the creation. At this time people began to call on the name of the Lord. Seth lived for 807 years after Enosh's birth and for many years of Lamech's lifetime. He died 614 years before the flood.

ENOSH (meaning "toiler" or "sorrowful man") was the son of Seth. When he was 90, he begot Kenan, 325 years after the creation. After this he lived for 815 years and died in the time of Noah, 516 years before the flood.

KENAN (meaning "he who has possessions") was the son of Enosh, fourth in descent counting Adam. When he was 70, he begot Mahalalel, 395 years after the creation. After this he lived for 840 years and died in the time of Noah, 421 years before the flood.

MAHALALEL (meaning "one who praises God") was the son of Kenan, fifth in descent counting Adam. When he was 65, he begot Jared, 460 years after the creation. After this he lived for 830 years and died in the time of Noah, 366 years before the flood.

JARED (meaning "one who is strengthened") was the son of Mahalalel, sixth in descent counting Adam. When he was 162, he begot Enoch, 622 years after the creation. After this he lived for 800 years and died in the time of Noah, 234 years before the flood.

ENOCH (meaning "a man dedicated to God") was Jared's son, the seventh in descent counting Adam. When he was 65, he begot Methuselah, 687 years after the creation. After this he lived for 300 years and God was well pleased with him. During Lamech's time, 669 years before the flood, he was taken away, so that he did not see death.

METHUSELAH (meaning "victor over death") was Enoch's son, the eighth in descent counting Adam. When he was 187, he begot Lamech, 874 years after the creation. After this he lived for 782 years and died in the year before the flood.

LAMECH (meaning "a man who has been humbled") was Methuselah's son, the ninth in descent counting Adam. When he was 182, he begot Noah, 1056 years after the creation, and he proclaimed his hope, saying, "This one will bring us relief in our work." After this he lived 595 years and died 5 years before the flood.

NOAH (meaning "a peacemaker" or "a comforter") was the son of Lamech, tenth in descent counting Adam. When he was 500, he begot Shem, 1556 years after the creation, and 100 years before the flood. He lived for 350 years after the flood and died when Abraham was 57.

All these mentioned above hoped to receive the promised salvation of God through the woman's seed. But because all peoples otherwise had turned their hearts from God to every kind of wrongdoing, God regretted that he had made men. Gen.6—8 Noah, however, found mercy because he obediently followed God's command and built the ark. Because of this, he and his whole household were saved from the judgment, along with all the creatures that went into the ark as God had commanded. Everything else living on dry land had to be destroyed because of men's sin and wickedness. In his fierce anger, God opened the windows of the sky and all the springs of the earth and let rain fall until the water covered all the mountains to a depth of fifteen cubits. And this flood, sent as a punishment to all sinners, lasted a whole year and several days.

The number of years from the beginning of the world to the end of the flood is 1656.

THEN IN HEARTFELT COMPASSION, even in the very midst of his wrath, God thought again of Noah and his household and all the living creatures in the ark. He put an end to his wrath and his punishment, drawing the earth once more out of the water and commanding all creatures to multiply.

But Noah, who acknowledged that he was saved by God, was quick to bring an agreeable offering to the Lord, chosen from all clean animals and birds. This splendid gift moved the mighty God so that he promised Noah never again to destroy Gen.9 men, animals, and birds by water. He made a lasting covenant with Noah and with all living creatures and promised to set his bow as a sure sign in the clouds to remind men of it forevermore. And by this sign, believers have always remembered the heartfelt compassion of God, as the following will show.

First SHEM (meaning "a renowned and mighty one") was the son of Noah who received the blessing from his father. Two years after the flood, when he was 103,[1] he begot Arpachshad. After this he lived 500 years and died in the time of Isaac, when Jacob was 48. Gen.11

ARPACHSHAD (meaning "a giver of delight who will heal all needs") was the son of Shem and second in descent [counting Shem]. Thirty-seven years after the flood, in the thirty-fifth year of his life, he begot Shelah. After this he lived 403 years and died in Abraham's time, when Isaac was 48.

SHELAH (meaning "sent as a vine or branch") was the son of Arpachshad, third in descent counting Shem. Sixty-seven years after the flood, in the thirtieth year of his life, he begot Eber. After this he lived 403 years and died in Isaac's time, when Jacob was 18.

EBER (meaning "a victor," "a comrade," "a companion," or "a follower") was the son of Shelah, fourth in descent counting Shem. When he was 34, he begot Peleg, 101 years after the flood, at the time when the earth was divided. After this he lived 430 years and died in Isaac's time, when Jacob was 79.

PELEG (meaning "a branch" or "a scion") was the son of Eber, the fifth in descent counting Shem. When he was 30, he begot Reu, 131 years after the flood. After this he lived 209 years and died in the time of Terah, when Abraham was 48.

REU (meaning "shepherd," "nourisher," "friend," or "neighbor") was the son of Peleg, sixth in descent counting Shem. When he was 32, he begot Serug, 164 years after the flood. After this he lived 207 years and died in the time of Terah, when Abraham was 78 and had been in Canaan 3 years.

SERUG (meaning "a vine," "a twig," "owner of a vineyard," "payer of his workers") was Reu's son, seventh in descent counting Shem. When he was 30, he begot Nahor, 193 years after the flood. After this he lived 200 years and died at the time of Terah, when Abraham was 101.

NAHOR (meaning "peace through light," "fire sacrifice") was the son of Serug, eighth in descent counting Shem. When

[1]Gen.11:10 has: "When Shem was a hundred years old."

he was 29, he begot Terah, 222 years after the flood. After this he lived 119 years and died when Abraham was 49.

TERAH (meaning "one who gives pasture, refreshes, or makes alive") was Nahor's son, ninth in descent counting Shem. When he was 70, he begot Abram, 292 years after the flood. After this he lived 135 years and died in Abraham's time, when Isaac was 35.

ABRAM (meaning "a mighty father") was Terah's son, tenth in descent counting Shem. When he was 75, he was called by God to leave his idolatry, his homeland and relatives—367
Gen. 12 years after the flood. Obedient to God's words, he journeyed
Acts 7 from Haran into the land of Canaan and became an alien.

From the flood until Abram was called was a total of 367 years.

ABRAM OF CHALDEA, A PILGRIM CALLED BY GOD into the land of Canaan, traveled to Egypt because of a famine. His wife Sarai was taken from him by the king but
Gen. 13 given back. He traveled a second time to Bethel in Canaan, called on the name of the Lord, and separated from his brother's son Lot. Following the divine promise, he went toward Hebron
Gen. 14 and lived by the oak tree at Mamre. He saved Lot and brought back the people and the plunder. He was fed and blessed by the king of Salem, and to him he gave a tenth of all his possessions.

Gen. 15 The Lord promised him unnumbered children. These would be mistreated for a long time in a strange land. Yet it was the Lord's purpose to lead them out with a strong hand and give
Gen. 16 them the land of Canaan as their possession. Ishmael was born
Gen. 17 to him by the handmaid Hagar. God changed his name and called him Abraham (meaning "a father of many peoples") and entered into an enduring covenant with him. He put the sign of it upon his body with blood, as a great promise that
Gen. 18 in him and in his seed all peoples would be blessed. He showed him too the annihilation that would come to the proud
Gen. 20 Sodomites because of fleshly lusts. Abraham journeyed from Canaan again and came to Gerar. Abimelech, the king, took his Sarah from him, and at God's command gave her back, along with a rich gift. Then Abraham prayed to God for the king, and the king and his wives were healed.

He was an alien for twenty-five years before the ninety-year-old Sarah bore him Isaac. When he was about to sacrifice his son according to divine command, God restored the boy to him with the pledge that the Lord's blessing would be given through him. Abraham gave Rebecca as a wife to Isaac and made Isaac the heir to all his goods; he died in the hundredth year of his pilgrimage, when Jacob was fifteen and Noah's son Shem was still living. Gen.21 Gen.22 Gen.24—25

ISAAC (meaning "joy" or "laughter") was the son of Abraham. When he was sixty, he begot Jacob, eighty-five years after his father was called [to go to Canaan]. God renewed his promise to him, which had been given to his father Abraham. Because there was a famine, he journeyed once more to Gerar to the king of the Philistines and afterward to Beersheba, where he called on the name of the Lord and blessed his son Jacob. When he was 180, he died, weary of life, 10 years before Israel went into Egypt. His sons Esau and Jacob buried him at the burial place of his father. Gen.26—27 Gen.35:28–29

JACOB (meaning "one who treads underfoot or vanquishes") was the son of Isaac, chosen and loved by God in his mother's womb. Through God's providence he received his father's blessing, and to him God renewed and strengthened the promise he had made to his forefathers Abraham and Isaac. On his parents' advice he journeyed to Haran in Mesopotamia to his mother's brother. There God gave him twelve sons, born of Laban's daughters Leah and Rachel and of their two serving maids. After he had tended his father-in-law's sheep for many years, he journeyed at God's command and with his full blessing into the land of Canaan. He wrestled with the angel and was reconciled with his brother Esau. He received the name Israel (meaning "a heart that God sees"). Therefore his sons' descendants were called the twelve tribes of Israel. Hos.12 Gen.29 Gen.32—33 35

Through God's wonderful providence, his most beloved son Joseph was given to the Ishmaelites. His brothers, who were envious of him and hated him, exchanged him for twenty pieces of silver, and he was sold to Pharaoh's steward in Egypt. Although he went through great fear and tribulation when he was imprisoned on account of his master's wife, God helped him out of it all and decreed that he become overseer for the whole land of Egypt. Gen.37 Gen.39

When a great famine came over the entire land of Canaan Gen.41

and Egypt, he provided bread for his own people and for many
Gen.45 others. His brothers, who had previously handed him over to
be sold, were filled with fear and grief when they found out
Gen.46 who he was. With their father Jacob and all their households,
they went to him in Egypt. The Lord promised Jacob at
Beersheba that he would be with him on the way down and
Gen.47 on the return. When Joseph presented his father to Pharaoh,
Jacob was 130 years old. After this, Jacob lived another
seventeen years and died in Egypt, and Joseph and his other
sons buried him with his forefathers in the land of Canaan.
Seventy souls went to Egypt with Jacob; their number
multiplied greatly.

Exod.1 Many years after Joseph's death a new king ruled in Egypt
who knew nothing of Joseph and his good works. This king
began to oppress the Israelite people with heavy burdens. He
ordered that the newborn baby boys should be killed and thrown
out, hoping in this way to destroy the child who was to be
Exod.2 born the savior of the Israelite people. But through God's
Acts 7:20–38 providence the Egyptians, in spite of themselves, had to care
faithfully for this child [Moses] and educate him in all their
own wisdom and learning.

When he was forty, he left Egypt, denied that he was the
son of Pharaoh's daughter, came into Midian, and herded
Exod.3 Jethro's sheep for forty years. When God wanted to open a
way for the promise he had made to Abraham, Isaac, and
Jacob, he called from the burning bush to Moses, who was
now humble and stripped of all his glory. He sent him to
Pharaoh, the Egyptian king, with the solemn command to let
Exod.7—12 the mistreated and overworked people of Israel go free. Moses
demonstrated God's glorious might to the king through some
powerful miracles, but nothing helped until the Lord killed all
the firstborn in Egypt, men and cattle.

Then the people of Israel were not only allowed to go, they
were commanded to go. After Israel had lived in Egypt for
430 years, the whole people (600,000 strong) left in one day.

Gen.12:1–3 The number of years from the time Abraham was called
until Israel left Egypt is 645. Some disagree with this
reckoning, counting it as only 430 years. They cite Josephus
Gal.3:17 and the patriarchs and Paul's Letter to the Galatians. But Moses
Gen.15:13–16 stated it quite clearly, saying, "The Lord spoke to Abraham,
'Your descendants will be aliens'"—he does not say in this

land where you now are, or in the land I have promised to you, but "'in a land that is not theirs; they will be held in oppression there and made slaves for four hundred years. But I, the Lord, shall be judge over this people whose slaves they are, and I shall lead them out, and the fourth generation will return here, for the sins of the Amorites are not yet ripe.'" The Lord also promised Jacob to go down with him and to bring him back. And it is quite plainly written in Exodus: "The Israelites had been settled in Egypt for 430 years, and the whole host came out in one day." Achior, the Ammonite leader, made the same statement before Holophernes [Judith 5],[1] and Stephen, a trustworthy witness, agrees with it.

Gen.46:3–4
Exod.12:40–41
Acts 7:6

MOSES (meaning "one drawn from the water") was called by God to be a ruler (as is described above), and he led the whole people of Israel out of Egypt. King Pharaoh pursued them with all his army to force the Israelites back into his service. Yet God helped his people, protected them with his angels through a cloud by day and a fiery pillar by night, and led them through the depths of the sea. He let Pharaoh and his hosts sink to the bottom like lead, and not one of them survived. In the desert he gave his people water to drink from the hard rock, fed them for forty years with bread from heaven, made the bitter water sweet for them, and led them safely on the course of their many wanderings. He gave them a strict commandment and a just law, to be a candle holder and a fiery, shining light. He also gave the discipline of punishment, which is the way of life. And through this the teacher of the Law [Moses] points them to the first Teacher of the Gospel. By divine command he appointed Aaron as priest, set up the tent of the testimony, and organized the entire order of worship.

God, however, who hates sin, punished those who were impatient, the grumblers, and the unthankful, all those who were great in their own estimation and had unbelieving hearts. Yet he had patience with their ways the whole time in the wilderness. Moses died at the age of 120. He had sung his song of testimony and had proclaimed his blessing to each

Exod.2:10
2 Esd.1:12–14
Exod.14
Exod.13:21–22
Num.9:15–23
Exod.15
17—20
Ps.78:12–16
Deut.4
32—33
Ps.19
Deut.18:15,18
Acts 7:37
Exod.4:14–31
24—25
Num.14
16
Heb.3:7–19
Deut.31—34

[1]In the Froschauer Bible, used at that time by the Hutterian Brethren, Judith 5:10 reads, in translation: "stayed there four hundred years." About the Froschauer Bible editions, see *ME*, II, 415–416.

tribe, had appointed Joshua leader of the people in his stead, as God had commanded, and had seen the promised land from Mount Pisgah. And the Lord buried him. The whole assembly of Israel mourned him for thirty days. He had ruled them for forty years.

Acts 7:36

Exod.24:13
Num.13:8,16
27:15–23

JOSHUA (meaning "a benefactor") was the son of Nun of the tribe of Ephraim and was Moses' servant. God chose him and promised that he would be with him as he had been with Moses. Through Joshua, God led all Israel across the Jordan with dry feet into the Promised Land. Joshua circumcised all those born in the wilderness and kept the Passover with them; he destroyed the inhabitants of the lands and allotted each tribe its portion of land by measurement. This same Joshua admonished Israel to keep all the ways and laws of the Lord, pointing out the severe punishment that would be theirs for not keeping them; he died at the age of 110 and was buried at Timnath-serah on his own land. Josephus says that he ruled for twenty-six [twenty-five] years.

Josh.1
3—5
Josh.11—15

Josh.19:49–50
23—24

Antiquities of the Jews, bk.V, ch.i,29

Judg.2

Israel served the Lord during the lifetime of Joshua and the elders who had seen all the miracles of God and had lived according to his counsel. But another generation arose which did not know the Lord their God. They began to take wives from the daughters of another country and to give their daughters to the sons of that country. In this manner they served strange gods, whored after them, and worshiped them. Then the Lord's wrath fell on all Israel, and he gave them into the power of Cushanrishathaim, king of Mesopotamia, for eight years.

Judg.3

OTHNIEL means "all my time is in God's hands." When Israel had sinned and then cried to the Lord, God gave them this man as a savior. He was of the tribe of Judah [son of Kenaz], Caleb's youngest brother. He conquered the king of Mesopotamia and ruled or judged Israel in great peace for forty years.

After Othniel's death Israel again did evil in the sight of the Lord. He gave them into the power of Eglon, king of Moab, for eighteen years.

EHUD (meaning "a gathering" and "a declaration") was a son of Gera, the son of Jemini, that is, from the tribe of Benjamin. Ehud brought a present to Eglon, the Moabite king, and took his life by cunning. Then Israel cried to the Lord, and he helped them through this Ehud, who ruled all Israel in peace for eighty years. After Ehud died, the children of Israel Judg.4 sinned gravely against the Lord, and he gave them into the hands of Jabin, king of Canaan, the commander of whose forces was Sisera; he had nine hundred chariots of iron and oppressed Israel harshly for twenty years.

DEBORAH (meaning "eloquent") was a prophetess and the wife of Lappidoth of the tribe of Ephraim. When the children of Israel cried to God because of their sins, he helped them through Deborah, through her commander Barak (whose name means "lightning"), and through Jael (meaning "one who is raised up"), a wife of Heber the Kenite, Moses' brother-in-law. Jael led the commander Sisera into her tent and did everything he wished, bringing food and drink and covering him. When he was asleep she took a hammer and drove a nail through his temple, so that he died. In this way all Israel was saved. And as long as Deborah lived she acted as a judge, and Israel was Judg.5 at peace for forty years.

After Deborah's death Israel sinned against the Lord. He Judg.6 gave them into the hands of the Midianites and Amalekites. They ravaged Israel for seven years. But God sent Israel a prophet when they cried out to him because of their sins, and he showed them how far they had gone from God and pointed out all the good things God had done for them ever since they had left Egypt.

GIDEON (meaning "one who cuts off or destroys") was the son of Joash from the tribe of Manasseh. An angel called him while he was threshing wheat and through a powerful sign showed him that he would be victorious over the Midianites. Then he utterly destroyed the Baals and the idolatrous worship of them. And because he was obedient to the mouth of the Judg.7—8 Lord, the Midianites and the Amalekites and everyone who helped them had to die by their own swords. So Israel was saved from the hands of its enemies. As long as Gideon lived, the people and the land were at peace—for forty years.

After Gideon's death the whole of Israel played the harlot, worshiping the ephod or robe that Gideon had made from his plunder, and this brought his whole household to ruin.

ABIMELECH (meaning "my father is king") was an Judg.9 illegitimate son of Gideon. After his father's death he slaughtered seventy of his brothers on one stone block. Yet he was chosen to be judge. When he was at Thebez, a woman threw part of a millstone at him, which crushed his skull. In this way God repaid Abimelech for what he had done to his brothers, according to the word of Jotham, his brother, who was the son of Jerubbaal (Gideon). Abimelech ruled in Israel for only three years.

Judg. 10 TOLA (meaning "a small worm" or "purple worm") was of the tribe of Issachar, a deliverer and judge in Israel, ruling peacefully for twenty-three years.

JAIR (meaning "a light" or "one who has received light") was a Gileadite from the tribe of Dan. He ruled Israel for twenty-two years. After Jair's death the children of Israel sinned very deeply against God. They worshiped Baals and the Ashtaroth and other idols. Then God, in fierce anger toward them, gave them into the power of the Philistines and the children of Ammon for eighteen years.

Judg. 11—12 JEPHTHAH (meaning "a key" or "an unlocking") was a Gileadite and a great warrior, an illegitimate son of Gilead. The people of Israel had cried out to God on account of their sins, and, although God reminded them of the alien gods they had chosen, he helped them—yet only after their many entreaties. Then the Lord, speaking through the elders in Gilead, called Jephthah to be a commander. Jephthah made a vow to God, freed all Israel from its enemies, and was judge in Israel for six years.

IBZAN (meaning "a father who has sufficient" or "a spring of waters") was from Bethlehem, of the tribe of Judah. For seven years he ruled Israel in peace.

ELON (meaning "an oak," "strength," "one who is amazed") was born in Zebulun. He judged and ruled Israel for ten years.

ABDON (meaning "a son of judgment, of servitude") was judge in Israel after Elon. He died and was buried in Pirathon in the land of Ephraim. He ruled Israel for eight years.

After Abdon's death Israel sinned still more deeply against the Lord. Therefore he gave them into the hands of the Philistines, and they were oppressed for forty years.

Judg. 13—16 SAMSON (meaning "a powerful sun" or "one who changes the name") was a son of Manoah from the tribe of Dan. His birth was promised by an angel of God. He grew in spiritual power in the sight of God and men and gave wonderful proof of God's help through his superhuman strength. And although it seemed that he had lost all his strength and his eyesight, he killed more enemies in his death than in his life and so freed Israel. He had been a judge for twenty years.

In the years after Samson's death, Israel had no judge or king. Each man did what he pleased, and no one knows for how long. Judg.18:1 21:25

ELI (meaning "my God" or "the Lord is God") was of the tribe of Levi, the high priest at Shiloh. He learned of his sons' wrongdoing, but he did not punish them with godly severity. So God sent young Samuel to warn him of impending punishment—that because of his misdeeds, he and his sons and his whole house would be destroyed. Therefore, Eli and his sons all met their death in a single day. He had served as judge over Israel for forty years. 1 Sam.1—2 1 Sam.3—4

SAMUEL (meaning "entreated of God") came from the hills of Ephraim. He was of the tribe of Levi, highly honored by everyone, and became priest and judge in Eli's place. When he was too old to perform his duties, he appointed his two sons as judges; but because they did not walk in his path, Israel wanted a king. Although Samuel advised against it, he obeyed God's command and anointed Saul, son of Kish, as king over all Israel. Josephus states that he ruled Israel for twelve years. 1 Sam.8—10 *Antiquities of the Jews*, bk.VI,ch.xiii,5

From the above account it seems that Israel was without a ruler for a long time after Joshua's death, and again the same after Samson's death—no one knows how long. Everyone should study carefully the length of Samuel's rule (as Josephus has it) and judge accordingly, for Samuel was but a young boy when Eli was well advanced in years, and after Eli's death Samuel ruled Israel for so long that because of his great age he appointed his sons as judges. This stirred the people to ask for a king.

Yet according to the reckoning given here, if forty years are allowed for Moses, twenty-six for Joshua, and twelve for Samuel, it comes to the 450 years of which Paul speaks in Acts. But the years between some of the judges, when Israel was under heathen rule because of its sins, belong in the reckoning too: all this together comes to 528 years.

SAUL (meaning "one who is desired," "the one appointed," and also "one who misuses") was a son of Kish, from the

tribe of Benjamin. Although Samuel heard the Lord say, "It
is not you, it is I whom they have rejected," he anointed Saul
as king over all Israel at God's command. As long as Saul
1 Sam.13 was humble, he was leader of his people. But when his heart
15 grew proud and he assumed the priestly office, he disobeyed
18—22 the Lord, hated his benefactor David, and ordered the priests
of the Lord to be killed. Then the Lord rejected him in wrath,
1 Sam.31 and he and his sons met a terrible death on a single day. Saul
had ruled all Israel for forty years.

1 Sam.16—19 DAVID (meaning "a beloved one, great in strength") was
the youngest son of Jesse, of the tribe of Judah. God took him
from herding sheep and commanded Samuel to choose him
from among his brothers and anoint him king at Bethlehem.
He played the harp to Saul, became his armor-bearer,
vanquished Goliath, made a bond with Jonathan, was commander
of a thousand, and married the king's daughter. He
won great victories yet had reason to flee from Saul. While
his master Saul was in his power, he spared Saul's life because
1 Sam.24 God had anointed him. He did no more than cut off the end
26 of Saul's robe and take his spear and jug of water while he
1 Sam.27 slept. Then he fled to Achish, king of the Philistines.

2 Sam.2 After Saul's death, when David was thirty, he came to
2 Sam.4—5 Hebron, where Judah anointed him as their king. When
Ishbosheth was killed, all the elders of Israel came to David
and they too anointed him. So he became king over the whole
of Israel.

He conquered Jerusalem, annihilated the Jebusites, and
2 Sam.11 dwelt in the stronghold. Although he sinned before God by
24 committing adultery, by commanding that the righteous Uriah
be killed, and by counting the people, he obtained grace
1 Chron.28 through true repentance. He drew up plans for the house of
God and established various divisions for service to God. He
gathered gold, silver, jewels, brass, iron, common stones, and
1 Chron.29 whatever was needed for the building. He confirmed his son
Ps.78:70–72 Solomon to be king in his place. David was a man after God's
heart and ruled Israel with devotion for forty years.

2 Sam.12:24 David's son SOLOMON (meaning "a peaceable man" or "one
who is rich in peace") was born to Bathsheba through the
1 Kings 1 providence of God. He was anointed king on Mount Gihon
1 Kings 2 by Zadok the priest and Nathan the prophet. His father taught
him how to organize worship and to order his household and

his whole life. After his father's death, Solomon offered a 1 Kings 3
sacrifice at Gibeon; there God gave him both the wisdom he
pleaded for and wealth. He dealt wisely in judgment, built the 1 Kings 4—6
temple at Jerusalem, and with great diligence established an
order for worship to honor the name of the Lord. All the kings 1 Kings 10—11
of the earth were eager to see how Solomon had organized his
household with all his officers and servants, and they wanted
to hear his great wisdom and gracious proverbs.

But Solomon broke the law and took heathen wives, who
turned his heart to idolatry. Then the anger of the Lord God 1 Kings 9
of Israel burned against him, for God had appeared to him at
Gibeon and in the temple, warning him and forbidding such
abominations. And God showed him how his kingdom would
be divided after his death. Solomon ruled over all Israel for
forty years.

Solomon's son Rehoboam (meaning "the people's folly") 1 Kings 12
destroyed the people with his tyranny. He was born to Naamah
the Ammonitess, and all Israel came to Shechem to anoint
him king in his father's stead. But he followed the advice of
young men and gave the people a cruel answer, so that ten of
the tribes of Israel turned against him and chose Jeroboam,
son of Nebat from Ephraim, to be their king; this was in
accordance with the words the Lord spoke through Ahijah the
prophet. Rehoboam remained king over Judah only, ruling in
Jerusalem. Then Shishak the Egyptian king came with his 1 Kings 14:25–26
army. He took the treasures from the Lord's temple and the
king's house, the golden shields made for Solomon, and
whatever else there was to take. Rehoboam ruled for seventeen
years.

Abijam (meaning "the Father is Lord") was Rehoboam's 1 Kings 15:1–8
son. His mother's name was Micaiah, a daughter of Uriel of 2 Chron. 13
Gibeah. After his father's death Abijam became king in Judah.
He fought against Jeroboam, the king of Israel, and because
he put his trust in the Lord, the Lord gave him the victory.
As soon as Abijam began to depart from the Lord and walked
in the sins of his father, he died, having ruled in Jerusalem
only three years.

Asa (meaning "a physician," or "one who restores health") 1 Kings 15:9–24
was the son of Abijam. His mother's name was Maacah, a 2 Chron. 14—16
daughter of Abishalom. Asa became king in Judah after his
father's death. For a long time he did what was pleasing to

the Lord; therefore God helped him to destroy the great armies of Ethiopians. He deprived his mother of her rank, suppressed idolatry, and restored the true worship of God. But when he asked the Syrian king for help against Israel and imprisoned the prophet Hanani, who rebuked him, and when he oppressed some of the people, his feet became diseased. Instead of turning to the Lord, he sought help from physicians. Therefore he died. He had ruled in Jerusalem for forty-one years.

1 Kings 22:41–50

JEHOSHAPHAT (meaning "the Lord's judgment" or "the Lord will judge") was Asa's son; his mother was Azubah, daughter of Shilhi. He became king in Judah, after his father Asa. Jehoshaphat did what was pleasing to the Lord and made great efforts to restore the worship of God. But he helped Ahab, the ungodly king of Israel, and went with him into battle. He was sternly rebuked by Jehu, Hanani's son, for loving those who hate the Lord.

2 Chron. 18—19

Jehoshaphat accepted the rebuke, and he and his people turned around and sought the help of the Lord. When the men of Moab, Ammon, and the hills of Seir attacked him, the Lord helped, as he had promised through Jahaziel the Levite, by making Jehoshaphat's enemies destroy each other.

2 Chron. 20

Finally, he made an alliance with Ahaziah, the wicked king of Israel, and joined him in building ships. Eliezer prophesied against this undertaking, and the ships were wrecked. Jehoshaphat ruled in Jerusalem for twenty-five years.

1 Kings 22:48–49

JEHORAM (meaning "the royal marriage is the Lord's" and "the Lord rejects") was Jehoshaphat's son. He was thirty-two when he became king of Judah. Like the kings of Israel, he did evil in the sight of the Lord; he murdered six of his brothers. Then the Lord stirred up the spirit of the Philistines and Arabs, as the prophet Elijah had foretold. They seized all they found in the king's house and carried off his wives and sons, except for Jehoahaz. And in accordance with the Lord's word Jehoram lay sick for two years, and his bowels fell from him, causing him great agony. He had reigned at Jerusalem for eight years.

2 Kings 8:16–24
2 Chron. 21

AHAZIAH (meaning "the one who takes hold of the Lord" or "the one who holds back the Lord") was the son of Jehoram and was twenty-two when he became king of Judah. His mother's name was Athaliah, daughter of Omri and Ahab's sister. Ahaziah followed in Ahab's footsteps and did evil in God's sight, for his mother encouraged his ungodly ways. He

2 Chron. 22

helped Joram, king of Israel, to fight against Syria and later visited him at Jezreel when he was sick. There Jehu, the son of Nimshi, attacked and killed him. He had reigned at Jerusalem for one year. 2 Kings 9

When Ahaziah's mother ATHALIAH (the daughter of Omri, king of Israel) saw that her son, Ahaziah, was dead, she set out to destroy every descendant of the royal house of Judah. But Jehosheba, Ahaziah's sister, the wife of Jehoiada the priest, kidnapped Joash and his wet nurse and hid them in the house of God. Athaliah was driven from the house of God and put to death with the sword, at the priest Jehoiada's command. She had ruled over Judah from Jerusalem for seven years. 2 Kings 11 2 Chron. 23

JOASH (meaning "fire of the Lord," "sacrifice of the Lord," and "not lasting" or "transitory") was Ahaziah's son. His mother was Zibiah from Beersheba. When he was seven, Jehoiada the priest anointed him and set him on the royal throne of Judah. Joash destroyed the Baals and all idolatry and diligently restored true worship in the house of the Lord. He reappointed all the offices assigned by David in accordance with the law of Moses. He carried out much-needed repairs to the house of God and made daily sacrifice there to please the Lord. As long as Jehoiada the priest was living, Joash did what pleased God. But after Jehoiada's death the leading men of Judah made obeisance to King Joash, and when he gave in to them, he and they turned away from God and worshiped idols. Although the Lord rebuked them through his prophets, they paid no heed to him. The king forgot all the benefits received from Jehoiada and killed his son Zechariah in the court of the house of the Lord. The Lord therefore gave him into the hands of the Syrians, and in the end he was killed by his own servants. He had ruled in Jerusalem for forty years. 2 Kings 12 2 Chron. 24

AMAZIAH (meaning "strength and might are with the Lord" and "one who leads the people away from the Lord") was the son of Joash. He became king of Judah when he was twenty-five. His mother's name was Jehoaddan of Jerusalem. He killed his father's murderers, he struck down ten thousand Edomites in the Valley of Salt, and he hurled another ten thousand from the cliffs. Then he chose the idols of Seir as his own, worshiped them, and despised the prophets God sent to him. He did not stop fighting against Jehoash, king of Israel, and was wounded and taken prisoner, robbed of all his treasure and his children. 2 Chron. 25

He fled to Lachish but was overtaken, killed, and brought back to Jerusalem, where he was buried with his forefathers. He had ruled over Judah for twenty-nine years.

2 Kings 15
2 Chron. 26
UZZIAH, also called Azariah (meaning "the Lord is helper," "the strength of the Lord," "help comes from the Lord"), was the son of Amaziah and became king when he was sixteen. His mother's name was Jecoliah of Jerusalem. Uzziah did what was pleasing to the Lord as long as Zechariah lived, who instructed him in the law. God helped him in wars against the Philistines, Arabs, Meunites, and Ammonites. Uzziah fortified Jerusalem. He had a strong army and his fame was great. But as his power increased, his heart grew proud, and he even dared to assume the priestly function. Because of this he became a leper, was isolated, and had to live in a separate house until his death. He was laid in the burial field next to the royal graves, after ruling in Jerusalem for fifty-two years.

2 Chron. 27
JOTHAM (meaning "the Lord will bring it to conclusion and bring about increase," "he is executor") was the son of Uzziah. He was twenty-five when he became king of Judah. His mother's name was Jerushah, daughter of Zadok. He did what was pleasing to the Lord, yet he did not enter the house of the Lord but built the gateway to it, the city wall, and many other buildings. He overcame the children of Ammon and forced them to pay tribute. He died and was buried in David's city after reigning in Jerusalem for sixteen years.

2 Kings 16
2 Chron. 28
AHAZ (meaning "possessor," "assailant," or "one who converts") was the son of Jotham and became king of Judah when he was twenty. He did what was evil in God's sight and committed the same abominations as Israel. He had metal images cast for the Baals, offered sacrifices on every green hilltop and in the valley of Hinnom, and burned his sons in the fire.

When Rezin, king of Syria, and Pekah, king of Israel, wanted to attack Jerusalem, the Lord spoke to Ahaz through Isaiah,
Isa. 7
saying that this would not come to pass. He said to Ahaz, "Ask for a sign, either in the valley or on the heights," but Ahaz would not put God to the test. Isaiah said, "It is not enough for you to offend men, but you offend my God too!" Then the Lord himself promised a sign, saying, "Behold, a maiden shall conceive and give birth to a son who shall be called Immanuel, that is, God with us." Because Ahaz put no

faith in the Lord, faith was not kept with him either. Rezin the Syrian came with Pekah, and these two kings fought a great battle against Judah, taking many prisoners. But Ahaz appealed to the king of Assyria for help and made his sin against the Lord still greater. He closed the doors of the temple, destroyed the true worship of God, and set up altars to idols in every corner of Jerusalem; then he died. He was not given burial among the kings, yet he had ruled in Jerusalem for sixteen years.

HEZEKIAH (meaning "the Lord takes hold," "my strength 2 Kings 18
and trust is the Lord") was the son of Ahaz and became king 2 Chron. 29—31
in Judah when he was twenty-five. His mother was Abijah, daughter of Zechariah. He did what pleased the Lord as his forefather David had done. He removed the filth from the sanctuary and made every effort to restore the true worship of God. He destroyed the sacred poles, smashed the bronze serpent that Moses had made, and held the Passover with great rejoicing, which had not happened since Solomon's time.

In the sixth year of Hezekiah's reign, Israel was led away to Assyria by Shalmaneser. But Hezekiah gave treasures from his own house and from the temple to King Sennacherib. And 2 Kings 19
because Sennacherib would not leave Judah in peace but 2 Chron. 32
blasphemed God in his sanctuary, God helped his people by sending an angel who in one night slew 185,000 men in Sennacherib's camp.

When Hezekiah became ill, the Lord heard his prayer, 2 Kings 20
comforting him through Isaiah and lengthening his life. The prophet had rebuked him when he showed his treasure to the Babylonian ambassadors, but the Lord was merciful to him because he humbled himself. He died with a true heart and was laid in the burial place of David's descendants. He ruled in Jerusalem for twenty-nine years.

MANASSEH (meaning "one who is forgetful") was 2 Kings 21
Hezekiah's son and became king when he was twelve. His 2 Chron. 33
mother was Hephzibah. He did what was evil in the eyes of the Lord, copying all the abominations of the heathen. He rebuilt the high places, erected altars to Baal, made Asherah poles, worshiped all the hosts of heaven, sacrificed his own son in the fire, practiced sorcery and divination, consulted mediums and spiritists, and put an Asherah pole in the house of the Lord. Therefore the Lord vowed to bring such disaster 2 Kings 24:3–4

on Judah that the ears of all who heard of it would tingle.

Manasseh was led captive to Babylon. When he humbly sought the Lord and prayed to him, God helped him and restored his kingdom. Then Manasseh restored the worship of God, destroyed the idols and all worship of them. When he died, he was buried in his house. He had ruled in Jerusalem for fifty-five years.

AMON (meaning "trustworthy," "loyal," "true," "of the sorrowing people") was Manasseh's son. He became king of Judah when he was twenty-two. His mother was Meshullemeth, daughter of Haruz of Jotbah. He did what was evil in the Lord's eyes and brought back idolatry. He offered sacrifices to all the idols his father had made. But he did not humble himself before the Lord as his father had done. He was killed by his own servants and buried in the garden of Uzza. He ruled in Jerusalem for two years.

2 Kings 22
2 Chron. 34

JOSIAH (meaning "the Lord will kindle a fire," "the Lord will make the sacrifice," "my rest is in the Lord") was Amon's son and became king in Judah at the age of eight. His mother was Jedidah, daughter of Adaiah of Bozkath. In everything he did, he pleased the Lord's heart as his ancestor David had done. His birth had been prophesied. (1 Kings 13)

2 Kings 23

In the eighth year of his reign Josiah sought the God of his ancestor David and made every effort to restore the neglected worship of God. In the twelfth year he began to purify Judah and Jerusalem, making a thorough purge in his land of idols and images and everything used for idolatry, with their priests, soothsayers, diviners, and prostitutes. And he burned the bones of their priests at Bethel, according to the Word of the Lord. He read the newly discovered book of the Law.

2 Chron. 35
1 Esd. 1

The prophetess Huldah foretold that great evil would befall Judah but that Josiah the king would not be touched by it. He had the book of the Law read out to the whole people and removed all the abominable things that had been introduced by Solomon and all the kings. He celebrated the Passover and all worship of the Lord with all his heart; no Passover like this one was ever held before or after. But he was killed at Megiddo by Pharaoh Neco, king of Egypt, because he refused to be turned back. He was given burial in his own grave at Jerusalem after reigning for thirty-one years.

2 Chron. 36

JEHOAHAZ (meaning "to the mighty one," "one who holds

strength in reserve," "an inheritor or landowner of the Lord," also called Shallum) was Josiah's son. He was chosen by the people as king of Judah when he was twenty-three. His mother was Hamutal, daughter of Jeremiah of Libnah. He did what was evil in the Lord's eyes. Therefore he was carried off to Egypt by King Pharaoh Neco and died there, according to the word of Jeremiah. He reigned in Jerusalem for three months.

ELIAKIM (meaning "God will arise," also "fortress of God") 2 Kings 24
was given the name Jehoiakim by Pharaoh Neco, who made him king over Judah when he was twenty-five. He was Josiah's son and Jehoahaz's brother. His mother was Zebidah, daughter of Pedaiah of Rumah. He too did evil in the sight of the Lord. As the book of the prophet Jeremiah was being read to him, Jer. 22
he cut it to pieces and burned it. Nebuchadnezzar, king of 36
Babylon, bound him with chains. He was killed, thrown outside the walls of Jerusalem, and like a donkey, left unburied. He had ruled in Jerusalem for eleven years.

JEHOIACHIN (meaning "the Lord will prepare," also called Coniah, and Jeconiah) was Jehoiakim's son. He became king in Judah when he was eighteen. His mother was Nehushta, daughter of Elnathan of Jerusalem. Like his father, he sinned greatly in God's sight. Therefore, according to the Word of the Lord, he and all his court were captured and taken to Babylon, with all the treasures—the gold and silver vessels—which were taken from the house of the Lord. After thirty-seven years of Jer. 52:31–34
imprisonment he was released by Evil-merodach, king of Babylon, and was accorded royal treatment for the rest of his life. He had ruled in Jerusalem for three months and ten days.

MATTANIAH (meaning "the Lord's gift") was the son of Josiah. The Babylonians made him king of Judah when he was twenty-one and named him Zedekiah. His mother was Hamutal, daughter of Jeremiah of Libnah, and he was a brother of Jehoahaz. He, too, did evil in the Lord's sight, as his forefathers had done.

Then, at God's command, the king of Babylon attacked 2 Kings 25
Jerusalem with all his power. The city fell; Zedekiah was captured at Jericho and was taken to the Babylonian king of Riblah. Nebuchadnezzar had all Zedekiah's sons killed before his eyes. Then he had Zedekiah's eyes put out, bound him with chains, and took him captive to Babylon. This was what the Lord had foretold through Jeremiah.

In this way Jerusalem was despoiled and the worship of God stamped out. Zedekiah's reign in Jerusalem had lasted eleven years.

As is shown above, the Lord cared for his people as long as they served him. He gave them godly priests and sent them his prophets. But since they did not heed any warning but turned their backs on the Lord, he gave them into the power of the Babylonian king to bring fear to their souls for seventy years.

Jer.25
29
Zech.1:12

Altogether the length of time from Saul to the end of the Babylonian captivity was 584 years 6 months and 10 days.

2 Chron.36
Ezra 1—2

AFTER THE CAPTIVITY IN BABYLON, God had great compassion with his people and liberated them as he had promised. Through Cyrus the Persian king God released them, letting them go in wonderful freedom to build up the city of Jerusalem and the temple. Cyrus gave them back all the vessels for the worship of God and all the gold and silver and other goods they needed, for it was God's work. He gave the people leaders: Zerubbabel; Ezra the scribe; Nehemiah, who was King Darius's cupbearer; and the prophets Nahum and Zechariah, who encouraged God's people to build up the city and the temple.

Ezra 6—7

Esther
Jth.
1 Macc.
2 Macc.

Even after this they had to suffer a great deal, for instance at the hands of Holophernes (Nebuchadnezzar's commander), and proud Haman, as well as with Ptolemy Philometor, king of Egypt, and Antiochus with the elephants. But God delivered them and overthrew the tyrants in his wrath.

Josephus writes the following account of what the people of Israel had to endure for 481 years after the Babylonian captivity.

Antiquities of the Jews, bk.XIII,ch.xi,1

ARISTOBULUS was son of the high priest Hyrcanus at Jerusalem. When his father died he crowned himself with the royal diadem and was called king and priest. Because he was ungodly, killing his brother Antigonus and committing other shameful sins, he was seized with unbearable pains and died after ruling only one year.

According to Josephus, God appointed JANNEUS (or Alexander), brother of Aristobulus, to be ruler and high priest. But he gave way to gluttony and became seriously ill, suffering from a fever until he died three years later. His reign in Judah had lasted twenty-seven years. On his advice, his wife Alexandra and her sons continued to reign.

SALOME, who was also called Alexandra, wife of Janneus, kept the throne with all the royal pomp, but the Pharisees had the authority. She did not ask what was right; however, she protected the peace in her country during the nine years she reigned. *Antiquities of the Jews*, bk.XIII,ch.xvi

HYRCANUS, a son of Janneus, was appointed by his mother to the office of high priest, which he held for nine years. After her death he reigned for three months and then was driven out by his brother, who was king and high priest for three years and six months. When Pompey took Aristobulus to Rome as a prisoner, he appointed Hyrcanus high priest. Hyrcanus led an honest and virtuous life, but he opened King David's tomb and took out three thousand talents of gold, which he presented to Antiochus Pius. Herod the Great ordered him to be killed. His reign and that of his brother lasted for thirty-four years after their mother's death. *Antiquities of the Jews*, bk.XV,ch.ii

HEROD, a son of the Idumean Antipater, was appointed king over Judah and Jerusalem by Augustus Caesar and the Roman Senate. His reign was a violent one. In times of need he was kind and lenient, but otherwise he ruled as a tyrant. He massacred all the innocent two-year-old boys in Bethlehem and its surroundings. He murdered his sons, his wife, his sister, and many other innocent people. But God punished him terribly. He was consumed by worms and suffered unbearable pain. He died after ruling for thirty-seven years. Christ was born in the thirtieth year of his reign.

A total of 582 years passed from the Babylonian captivity until the birth of Christ.

NOW IN THE FULLNESS OF TIME, when more than 4360 years had passed, God purposed to keep his promise to Adam and Eve and to make whole, in her seed, what Eve had shattered. He had sealed his promise through an oath sworn to Abraham, Isaac, and Jacob. He had confirmed it to the entire Israelite nation through Moses. He had made the same promise to David and renewed it again and again through his prophets. Gen.3 Deut.18:15–19

First God sent his angel to the priest Zechariah of the order of Abijah, to tell him that his wife Elizabeth would bear a son Luke 1

who should be called John. "Many will rejoice at his birth; in
the spirit and power of Elijah, he will make way for the Lord
and prepare a righteous people, turning the fathers' hearts to
their children." The birth of this child while his father was
Luke 3 dumb caused amazement throughout Israel. At the appointed
time he came forth like a shining light, a voice crying in the
wilderness.

At the same time God revealed to the angel Gabriel the
secret of his Word, which was from eternity, before the world
was made. It had been hidden from the eyes and ears of the
Heb. 2:16 forefathers. Because he wanted to gather to himself the
descendants of Abraham (not the angels), he sent Gabriel to
Isa. 7:14 the town of Nazareth in Galilee, to the virgin foretold by
Isaiah. Her name was Mary, of the line of David. The angel
Gabriel proclaimed God's peace to her: that she was blessed
(freed from the curse); that in the power from on high, through
the working of the Holy Spirit, she would conceive a son; and
Matt. 1 that the Holy One to be born to her would be called Immanuel,
Jesus, the Son of God.

This took place in the twenty-ninth year that King Herod
the Great reigned in Judah. He was an alien from Idumaea.
Gen. 49:10 This was to fulfill the patriarch Jacob's prophecy that the
scepter would not pass from Judah until a ruler was given in
Shiloh.

When the virgin received the angel's word in faith, it took
human form within her and became a living fruit. And so Mary
was received by Elizabeth as the mother of her Lord and was
joyfully acknowledged by John the Baptist while he was still
in his mother's womb.

Matt. 2 In the forty-second year of the reign of Caesar Augustus,
Luke 2 this child was born in the land of Judah in the city of David
called Bethlehem, as foretold by the prophet Micah. He was
proclaimed by the angels to the shepherds in the field,
circumcised on the eighth day according to Jewish custom,
and named Jesus. A brilliant star led the wise men from the
East to him, and they made his birth known to Herod and all
Jerusalem. He was presented to God and sanctified in the
Temple as a firstborn and accepted by godly Simeon and Anna
as their Savior while he was still an infant. Obeying God's
command, his parents escaped with him from Herod's massacre
of innocent children and fled to Egypt. When Jesus was twelve,

he sat among the teachers in the Temple. Then he went with his parents and was obedient to them. People were amazed at his knowledge of the Scriptures, although he had never studied them. And he increased in wisdom, years, and favor with God and men.

When Jesus, also called the Christ, the only begotten Son of God, reached his thirtieth year, he accepted baptism by John in the river Jordan—the sign of the new covenant and of submission—as an example for mankind. He suspended the old law according to the letter, with its pictures and symbols, all of which pointed to him as its fulfillment. This law had indeed required righteousness before God but could not achieve it because it had no power. And so when God wanted to make his promise abundantly clear to his heirs, he prophesied about Christ: "Sacrifices and offerings you did not desire, but you have prepared a body for me. Burnt offerings and sin-offerings you did not delight in. Then I said, 'See, I am coming. As it is written of me in the scroll, I desire, O God, to do your will.'" By this Christ lays aside the earlier law and takes up the task for which the Father sent him into the world; he brings forth light out of the dark shadow and brings forth the living word out of the letter.

Luke 3
Rom. 8:3–4
Heb. 6:17
Ps. 40:7–8
Heb. 10:5–7

For this purpose he chose twelve disciples, who were true witnesses of all the teaching and miracles he manifested—yes, of his whole life, suffering, death, and resurrection.

Matt. 10
Mark 3:13–19
Luke 6:12–16

The Pharisees and scribes were filled with envy and hate against him and kept trying to kill him. Then Judas Iscariot betrayed him to them for thirty pieces of silver. They came with a crowd of men armed with swords and cudgels and captured him, for their time had come and that of the power of darkness.

Mark 14
Luke 22
John 18

They led him to the high priest Annas, and from Annas to Caiaphas. They gave false witness against him, spat in his face, struck him in the face with their fists, bound him, and led him to the procurator Pontius Pilate. They vehemently accused him of claiming to be the Son of God, of misleading the people with his teaching, of stirring them up to revolt, and of forbidding them to give tribute to Caesar.

Luke 23
John 19

The crowd condemned him and shouted, "Away with him! Away with him! Crucify him! If you set him free, you will earn Caesar's wrath!" He was led from Pilate to Herod, who sent him back to Pilate. They put a white garment on him and mocked him. He was scourged, and the soldiers put a purple robe on him, a crown of thorns on his head, and a cane in his right hand for a scepter; they bent their knees to him and worshiped him. They took the cane and struck him on the head, and they mocked him unmercifully. They led him to Golgotha, crucified him with murderers and criminals, and gave him vinegar mixed with gall to drink. And even when he hung on the cross, the passersby still reviled him. They wagged their heads, wrinkled their noses, and screwed up their mouths at him and said, "So how are you going to tear down the temple and build it up again in three days? If you are the Son of God, come to your own aid and climb down from the cross." And the chief priests and the scribes jeered at him on the cross, saying, "He trusted in God, let God help him now if he pleases God." Even one of the criminals who was crucified with him jeered at him. In this way he suffered the most shameful death possible for mankind's sake, to redeem them.

Mark 15:29–30

Through his deep suffering, death, and the shedding of blood, he sealed the new covenant and so broke down the dividing wall and tore the curtain from top to bottom to reveal the hidden treasure. He brought light to all who turn to God from their sins in order to see, acknowledge, and experience the Father's perfect will. After his resurrection he appeared victoriously to his disciples for forty days, he who conquered and destroyed hell, death, and the devil. He spoke to them about the kingdom of God, commanding them, first, to preach repentance; second, to preach faith in what Christ did for men; and third, to baptize on confession of faith and to teach people to observe what had been commanded them. They should not leave Jerusalem until they were filled with power from on high, with the Holy Spirit that was promised to them.

Jer.31:31–34
Matt.27:51
Mark 15:38
2 Cor.3
Eph.2:14
Heb.8:8–13
10:16–17
Acts 1

Christ's instruction on baptism.
Matt.28:18–20
Mark 16:15–16

Luke 24:49

When the Lord Christ had ascended from his disciples into heaven, they continued to meet, being of one heart in fervent prayer. On the day of the glorious feast of Pentecost, they received the Holy Spirit. Tongues like flames of fire appeared, proclaiming God's great deeds. All who were assembled in Jerusalem were amazed and perplexed to hear these things, some saying one thing and some another. They began to talk about them with many opinions. Then the apostle Peter stood

Acts 2

Joel 2:28–32

up and gave public testimony that this was a work of God, promised of old by the prophet Joel.

Through this first proclamation of the Gospel, three thousand souls became believers in one day and were baptized and added to the number of the saints. They remained steadfast in the apostles' teaching, in fellowship, in the breaking of bread, and in prayer. But those who proved false or unfaithful were severely punished. Then fear came over all the people. Many marvels and signs were also brought about by the apostles. All who believed stayed together and held all their goods in common, but unbelievers were not allowed to join them. There were about five thousand men who believed, gathered together, united in heart and soul. They experienced great favor.

Acts 5

Acts 4

To promote this great work of God, seven God-fearing men were chosen to attend to the wants of the needy. As the Word of God spread and the number of disciples grew very large, some unbelievers took offense at Stephen, one of those chosen as deacon or servant for temporal affairs, but they could not withstand his wisdom and the Spirit. When he was brought before the council in Jerusalem, his face shone like an angel's, and he made a wonderful confession of his faith, based on divine witness. But it did not help; he was stoned to death.

Acts 6

Acts 7

Stephen stoned to death.

A great persecution arose against the Christians, brought about by the Jews; the church at Jerusalem was scattered over the lands of Judah and Samaria, so that Samaria, too, received the Word of God. This was clearly to be seen in many powerful deeds and signs.

Persecution of the church in Jerusalem.

Acts 8

The account of Paul's conversion, the calling of Cornelius and other Gentiles, and the many deeds of the apostles can be found in detail in the narrative about them. About this time James, the brother of John, was put to death with the sword at King Herod's command. The Christians had to suffer a great deal from the Jews. This Herod was struck down by an angel and devoured by worms.

James the apostle killed.

Acts 12

Afterward the first persecution of the Christians by the heathen was begun under the sixth Roman emperor, Nero, who had many of them killed for their steadfast faith. The apostles, too, had to endure many trials. But after all his tyranny, the emperor himself committed suicide.

First persecution of Christians by heathen.

The next persecution broke out under the twelfth Roman emperor, Domitian, son of Vespasian. It is written that he put

Sufferings of John the apostle.

Rev. 1

the apostle John into boiling oil and gave him a cup of poison to drink. When nothing harmed him, he was finally exiled to the distant island of Patmos, and there he received and wrote down his Revelation from the Lord. Later he left the island and came to Ephesus, where he is said to have passed away. This Domitian caused severe suffering to the Christians and then was killed himself.

All the apostles condemned to death by the world.

The apostles went out into all the world to fulfill their mission to preach the Gospel of repentance before God and say that whoever believed and was baptized would be saved. Old historians record how one after another they were all condemned by the world to terrible tortures and execution for the sake of the Gospel and the witness of Jesus Christ.

JAMES THE JUST, the apostle and brother of the Lord, as the Scripture calls him, is said to have been beaten to death with a dyer's rod.

THE APOSTLE PETER was crucified head downwards, and his wife Nela was buried alive.

THE APOSTLE PAUL was beheaded by order of the emperor Nero.

ANDREW, Simon Peter's brother, a fisherman from the town of Bethsaida and an apostle of Jesus Christ, was also bound to a cross and killed.

PHILIP, a brother of Nathaniel, was also nailed to a cross and killed.

BARTHOLOMEW, who came from a noble family, had his skin stripped off up to the neck, so that he carried his own skin in his arms, and was finally beheaded.

THOMAS the twin was stabbed with a spear by an idolatrous priest.

MATTHEW LEVI, the apostle and evangelist, was executed with the sword.

MATTHIAS, who was chosen by the apostles in place of Judas Iscariot, was struck and killed with a halberd, as some write; others say with a hatchet or ax.

SIMON THE ZEALOT, a brother of James and Judas, brothers of the Lord, was sawn in pieces.

JUDAS THADDAEUS, a brother of Simon and James, brothers of the Lord, was beaten to death with a cudgel.[1]

---

[1]Some sources say Simon the Zealot and Judas Thaddaeus traveled together to Persia, where they preached the Gospel and were martyred. Current Bible

MARK, the evangelist, had a noose put around his neck and was dragged away and strangled to death by idolatrous priests.

In this way the old historians of the early church describe how these men ended their lives in this world and had to witness with their blood to the teaching of Jesus Christ. At that time they were not called saints but heretics and evil seducers and rebels. They were all condemned by the world as the worst sectarians and seducers, which still happens today to those who witness to Jesus Christ and the truth.

In their time the apostles were not called saints but attacked as seducers by the world.

Under Trajan, the fourteenth Roman emperor, the third persecution of Christians began, instigated by malicious men, and many thousands of Christians were killed in horrible ways. This emperor soon died.

How Roman emperors cruelly persecuted and killed the first Christians.

The fourth persecution of the Christians arose under Marcus Annius Verus, the seventeenth Roman emperor, but was brought to an end by God through pestilence, war, locusts, and great earthquakes.

Under Severus Pertinax, the twenty-first Roman emperor, the fifth persecution of the Christians broke out, and many were killed, but it was stopped by grave times of danger and war.

Under Maximinus, the twenty-seventh Roman emperor, the sixth persecution of the Christians began. He took such pleasure in murdering others that he was soon murdered himself.

Under Decius, the thirtieth Roman emperor, the seventh persecution of the Christians took place. Since he was wreaking his malice in part on believers, he suffered the judgment he deserved and was drowned in a pond or lake and never seen again.

Under Valerian, the thirty-second Roman emperor, a very bad persecution arose against the Christians. It was the eighth one. But Valerian, too, was struck down by divine wrath and met a shameful death.

The ninth persecution took place under Aurelian, the thirty-fifth Roman emperor. After his decree had been written and sent out, he met divine judgment and was killed.

---

scholarship tends to question the assumption that Simon the Zealot and Judas Thaddaeus were brothers of the Lord; the word "brother" here may simply mean kinsman or relative. See *Harper's Bible Dictionary* (New York, 1973); *The New Schaff-Herzog Encyclopedia of Religious Knowledge* (Grand Rapids, MI, 1977), among others.

Under Diocletian and Maximian (the fortieth emperor), the tenth and most intense persecution arose against the Christians, so that many thousands were killed and a great number exiled to islands. But both these emperors received from God the full punishment they deserved.

Early Christians tortured and killed by grotesque methods.

This was the last of the persecutions raised by heathen emperors against the Christians, who had to endure great torture during these ten persecutions. Eusebius, the historian of old of the early church, records that they were put to death by fire, water, and the sword. They were stabbed, hanged, drowned, strangled, or murdered in many other ways. This happened at various times and places: in Asia, Arabia, Egypt, Palestine; and under the Roman emperors already mentioned. Some, both men and women, were bound hand and foot and hung over smoke, like hog's flesh, until they died. Some had nose and ears cut off; some had the fingers cut from their hands and the toes from their feet and then were let go. Some had hot lead and hot tar poured over their backs, sharp thorns pushed into their fingernails, or their teeth broken; others were cut to pieces with saws. A number were thrown down from high cliffs onto sharp rocks and thorns that tore their bodies. Others were burned, hacked to death with axes, or had their bones broken, their eyes put out, and were then killed. Others were led out in a great crowd to be slaughtered, so that the execution lasted all day and the executioners' swords grew blunt. They hurried to be numbered among the martyrs and willingly gave their necks to the sword. Others were roasted by being chained to gridirons and iron seats with fire burning underneath; others had their intestines unwound from inside their bodies; others were thrown to fierce wild beasts.

No one was spared, neither man nor woman, neither young nor old. Many were driven away from their own people to face privation with wife and children. They had to wander on the mountains in great danger, living in clefts in the rocks, so that some died of hunger or were devoured by wild beasts or lay dead from thirst, cold, and snow. And some were lost and never found again. This still happens to the faithful in the world today and has always been so from the beginning until our time.

How Christians of the early church were slandered.

They were much slandered and accused of such evil as secretly eating human flesh. They were reviled as swine, asses' heads, thieves who rob the gods, manslayers, child murderers, lascivious dogs, evil panderers who served heinous impurity with mothers and sisters and offered sacrifices of human blood and children, rebels, worshipers of a donkey and of the cross and the gallows. They were called enemies of the human race because they separated themselves from other people; enemies of God because they would not serve idols; useless people because they had no fellowship with robbers and corrupt men; desperate scoundrels because they let themselves be killed for their faith. All these misfortunes happened for one reason only. And true followers of Christ are still being treated like that by the world.

Popes sided with emperors, acquired great power, and forged the cross onto the sword.

At that time, however, the thirty-fourth pope, Silvester, testified to Constantine the Great, the forty-third emperor, and won him over with many flattering words, accepting him as a Christian through baptism. With the good intention of doing God a service, the emperor obtained peace throughout his kingdom for the pope, as the bishop of Rome, and for all those who called themselves Christians. Here the pestilence of deceit that stalks in darkness and the plague that destroys at midday swept in with force, abolished the cross, and forged it onto the sword. All this happened through the old serpent's deceit. Ps.91

In the course of time the Roman bishops took over. They gained full power over emperors and kings, becoming the Babylonian harlot, seated in power on the seven-headed beast, daring to rule over all peoples, giving them drink out of her cup, and daring to alter time and law. Anyone who ventured to speak against the Roman bishop or pope was soon judged a heretic and condemned to die by the sword, fire, or other cruel means. In this way the sheep took on a thoroughly wolfish nature. Almost all the Roman bishops, or popes, had worked in secret, but under Silvester their work was unmasked and the secret evil was revealed. And although they confessed the name of Christ with their lips, with their actions they denied it. Even though they won many followers, they still had much to fear from the antichristian emperors, like Julian the Apostate, the forty-fourth emperor. He used cunning to persecute the Christians, and his favors, flattery, and blandishments moved more people to deny Christ than persecution had done. Dan.7 Rev.17

Valentinian, the forty-seventh emperor, who had been

baptized according to the Arian custom, persecuted all those who called themselves Christians but would not be persuaded to his interpretation of scripture. If they were not willing to fight or to follow the customs of knighthood, he ordered them to be executed or exiled with a cruelty seldom equaled.

Those unwilling to fight or follow practices of knighthood were killed.

Meanwhile Donatus,[1] a learned bishop of Carthage, had begun to teach and write against the pope as the greatest abomination, saying that the pope and his followers were not a Christian church and had no true baptism, for there was only one baptism, Lord, God, faith, Gospel, and church. So when people from the Roman Church came to him, Donatus baptized them, not actually a second time, but for the first time with true baptism, for the pope as an archheretic had no divine mission—everything he did was against God.

Donatus, a bishop, wrote and taught against the pope. A.D. 224.

Then Arius, a bishop of Alexandria in Egypt and an outstanding scholar, came forward to attack the Roman Church for its errors because it did not rightly distinguish between God and Christ. A great many well-known men became his followers. These Arians used the sword and fought many battles against all who were not of their faith, and they were reviled by the pope as rebels and rebaptizers.

The Arians used the sword just as the pope did.

In this way the light of truth began to lose its brightness. Although a glimpse of it could be seen from time to time, the enemy, using the pope as his tool, was soon there to stamp it out. And although many groups split away on questions of faith, the popes gained the upper hand by their violence, and this abomination grew so great that it ruled wantonly over the emperor and all the kings of the Roman Empire. For this reason the emperor withdrew to Constantinople. The pope occupied the imperial throne in Rome, and there he remained.

At that time too, the Mohammedan belief and sect arose through Mohammed, a descendant of the tribe of Ishmael. He compiled parts of the Old and New Testament into a special lawbook called the Koran, and the Turks still use it today, by his order.

Islam
A.D. 610

But the popes were not content with the book of Moses or

Popes make their own lawbook: Decretals. 1145.

[1]This may refer to Donatus, fourth-century leader of the north African church, which followed a strong puritan tradition and broke with the Catholic Church in A.D. 312. He died c. A.D. 355. About Donatism, see *Schaff-Herzog*, III, 486–489.

with the Gospel of Christ or New Testament, and so they were not pleased with the Koran either and made another lawbook of their own, patched together from many bits and pieces. From heathen, Jewish, and Christian traditions, and from their own ideas, they made a mixture and called it the Papal Decretals. With this they threw out the Holy Scriptures and swept them out of sight; they destroyed the holy men of God, laid waste the church of Christ, and set up a new paganism, falsely bearing the name of Christ, the like of which had never existed before.

Instead of the church of Christ, which is the fellowship and gathering of the believers, they built stone temples and called them churches to deceive people. Instead of having saintly people made holy by God, they set up painted images in their churches, dumb statues of saints made of wood, stone, or silver. Then they worshiped them. So the living saints, called by God, were prevented from worshiping.

Stone churches.

Painted images of saints.

They refused to take on the suffering or cross which the church of Christ must bear here in the world. Instead, they put a cross on the top of their stone churches and wooden ones inside, and these were supposed to carry everything for them. And so they turned everything upside down, utterly scorning the name and truth of Christ.

Wooden crosses.

Many came forward to protest this abomination, but they were soon put to death by fire and sword. And there was a great silence in heaven from all believers, so that someone might well have exclaimed, he would like to see even one person who was truly dedicated to God; and one country could well have asked another whether justice had in fact passed that way.

Rev.8:1

2Esd.5:11

This ravaging horror reared up against everything that is God's, and still today speaks unbelievable words against the God of all gods. It will also succeed until its time comes. As a result truth is hidden and the land devoid of faithfulness. Righteousness has retreated and justice is neglected; truth has fallen down in the streets, and purity and clarity cannot be seen.

Dan.11

Isa.59:14–15

In such evil and corrupting times the popes devised quite new ceremonies—more and more of them as time went on—which opposed God's clear testimony: ordination, tonsure, and celibacy of priests; infant baptism (that is, baptism based on someone else's belief), blessing and christening of bells and

Popes invented many new ceremonies.

guns; falsifying the Lord's Supper and turning it into idolatry; and instituting many strange customs, including mass for the restless spirits of dead people in order to quench the fires of purgatory. Masses for the dead on the seventh and thirtieth day after the burial, and many other horrible, destructive practices were also introduced for greed of money.

Popes supported many sects and factions, many orders of monks and nuns.

Then, too, they supported innumerable factions, sects, and orders: Brothers of Our Lady, Order of St. James of Compostella, Brothers of St. Sebastian and St. Erhardt, Brothers of St. Loy, Brotherhood of Beggars and Lords, red Carthusians, Benedictines, Augustinians, Franciscans, Dominicans, Scapularies [Carmelites], red, black, and white Bethlehemites, Discalced Friars, Woodenshoes, Terminators, Gileans, Orders of St. Vitus, St. Lawrence, Quirinians, Marinians, Crantzians, and now the Jesuits, the dross of them all; and each division has its particular dress, rules, orders, ceremonies, and other customs and beliefs. There are countless orders of nuns as well. These and similar sects and their modes of existence were instituted and confirmed one after another by the popes. These are the true mystery of Babylon, the infamous harlot, dregs of abomination.

Rev.17

Some say, however, that within all this falsehood there have nonetheless always been devout people: the good offsetting the evil. This I leave in God's hands. He knows. If there was anything good, it must have had a glimmer of the truth. Yet from time to time there were men who protested against these evils, notably Adalbert the Gaul and Clement the Scot in France. They had a large following, for they preached that the teaching of the apostles should be practiced, but they were soon denounced and executed.

Adalbert and Clement testified against the pope and were killed.

These ungodly dealings were promoted by the emperor Charlemagne (who was chivalrous and pious in the world's eyes) and by his son Louis and their descendants. They swore fealty to the popes to the point that they willingly did whatever the popes wished. They gave the papacy power, wealth, cities, islands, and kingdoms, with their people. In addition they endowed religious foundations, universities and monasteries, to spread the papal religion. In fact, whatever His Holiness the Pope wished for, these emperors were willing to grant, promising all kinds of privileges.

The emperors were completely bound by oath to the popes.

And so the new "Christ" in Rome, supported by the emperor, sent out his apostles into all lands with his "gospel" of violence. He wanted to convert mighty kingdoms and strong nations by means of war and bloodshed. His realm increased so enormously as a gathering of the wicked that hardly anyone dared oppose it. So God the Almighty left these supposed Christians to their error of serving the creature rather than the Creator.

With much bloodshed t e popes forced the kingdoms to accept their faith.

The mad drive to be pope and to rule took on such proportions that one pope ousted the other, each with a following of evil men, murdering with violence and poison. In their wickedness they defied God by forcing their way into this office.

Peter of Aragon protested against this, saying that Christ came to prepare a way for the Holy Spirit and that Rome was a real Sodom and Gomorrah.

Those who spoke or taught against the pope condemned to death as heretics.

Dolcino of Novara[1] in Spain was taken prisoner with his wife, torn in pieces, and burned, and his persecutors gleefully flung the ashes in the air. In his church community there were about six thousand people who had all things in common. They were blamed for many evil deeds, just as even today many lies are told about believers.

Johannes Scotus Erigena and Berengar of Tours protested against this abomination, saying in particular that Christ's body is not in the bread and that Christ's words at the Last Supper were meant in the same sense as many other things he said: I am the vine, the way, door, light, rock, stumbling block, cornerstone; and he is none of these in a literal sense. After many people had joined them, they were outlawed and rejected by the popes and cardinals in council.

A.D. 740. [2]

[Peter] Waldo, an influential citizen of Lyons, France, at the time of Pope John XXII, held the same views. He divided

A.D. 1218.[3]

---

[1]Dolcino, a 13th-century leader of the Apostolic Brethren, born in Novara, Italy (not Spain); burned at the stake in Vercelli, Italy, on June 1, 1307. *Schaff-Herzog*, III, 478–479.

[2]Johannes Scotus Erigena is placed in the 9th century on the evidence of his writings, dated up to A.D. 877; A.D. 882 is considered the year of his death. *Schaff-Herzog*, X, 303–307; Rufus M. Jones, *Studies in Mystical Religion* (New York, 1970), 113–129.

[3]Peter Waldo's conversion and the beginning of his ministry are generally placed in the second half of the 12th century. He died before 1218. *Schaff-Herzog*, XII, 241. For a brief discussion of the movement bearing Waldo's name, see Eberhard

his possessions among the poor. The people known as Waldensians trace their origin to him. They lived in the kingdom of Bohemia, where they endured great suffering at the hands of Rome.

A.D. 1340.[1]

In Italy, Sicily, and other places the Fraticelli arose, also called the Poor Brothers. They believed in voluntary poverty, possessing nothing of their own but having all things in common, and their faith opposed that of Rome. The body of Hermannus, a founder of this group, was dug up after lying in the earth for twenty years, and his bones were burned to ashes—an act of pure stupidity. His followers were persecuted with fire and the sword at the time of Pope Boniface VIII.

Peter John.

Under Pope Clement VI there appeared a man by the name of Peter John, who interpreted the Revelation of John the apostle, saying the church at Rome was the real Babylon, a fleshly synagogue of the devil, and the pope was the antichrist. His followers were not tolerated. At the command of Clement his body was dug up and his bones burned to ashes.

A.D. 1394.[2]

Then there was a man in England named John Wycliff who taught that Christ is not in the bread of the mass, neither his nature nor his body; the mass is not instituted by Christ; university degrees are as much use in the church as the devil; the Decretals are nothing but a book of lies and those who study it are fools; the pope's election by the cardinals is of the devil, who deceives emperors, kings, and princes so that they increase the wealth of the church against the will of Christ. Because of this teaching Wycliff's body, too, was exhumed and burned to ashes.

At this time there was a teacher by the name of Piccard from whom the Piccards took their name.[3] They were also

---

Arnold, *The Early Anabaptists* (Rifton, NY, 1984), 9–14; Samuel Henri Geiser, *Die Taufgesinnten Gemeinden im Rahmen der allgemeinen Kirchengeschichte* (2nd ed., Courgenay, Switzerland, 1971), 64–77.

John XXII was pope from 1316–1334.

[1]The Fraticelli, Italian for "little brothers," grew out of the Franciscan order in the latter part of the 13th century and quickly spread in Italy, southern France, Flanders, and parts of Germany; see *Schaff-Herzog*, IV, 373. They were subjected to severe persecution throughout the 13th and 14th centuries and into the 15th century.

[2]John Wycliff, c. 1330–1384. His body was exhumed and burned in 1428. *Schaff-Herzog*, XII, 454–466.

[3]If the origin of the name "Piccards" was known to the chronicler, it is now obscure. It could be a corruption of "Beghards," a movement alive in the 12th

called hole-dwellers because they lived in gloomy caves and holes underground.

A man called Jerome of Prague returned from England with books and teachings that he passed on to John Huss[2] (named after the village of Huss). Huss accepted Wycliff's teachings as the truth. Nearly all Bohemia renounced the papacy and became his followers. Because of these articles of faith, the emperor Sigismund summoned Huss to a council at Constance, granting him safe-conduct both ways. But because he refused to follow the teachings of Rome, he was condemned to death and burned.

A.D. 1410.[1]

Those who protested against the pope's abominations put to death as heretics.

His disciple Jerome received the same sentence 140 days later.[3] The persecution of the Hussites in Bohemia was not small.

Johannes Bacius, another Hussite, was captured and hanged in Prague by order of the emperor Sigismund. Jacob Justus was walled up and starved for the sake of this teaching.

The Hussite teachers Bartholomew Fustii and Guillaume Giliberti were condemned to the stake.

Guillaume Albus, a doctor, said that priests should be allowed to marry, that it was not a sin to work on Sunday, that it was idolatry to encase the bones of the saints in gold or silver; he was soon punished.

Guillaume Sartoris declared that people should pray to God

A.D. 1422.

---

century, or a development from middle high German "begehart," a lay brother. They are also traced to a 12th-century priest of Liège, Lambert le Begue. The 15th-century belief was that they were founded by Begga, the canonized daughter of Pepin of Landen. Whatever its origin, the name "Piccards" became a term of derision applied to various heretical groups, including the Bohemian (or Czech) Brethren, into the 16th and 17th centuries. See *Schaff-Herzog*, II, 27–30; IX, 50; *Mennonite Encyclopedia* (Scottdale, PA, 1959), IV, 168. See also references to "Piccards" in J. K. Zeman, *The Anabaptists and the Czech Brethren in Moravia, 1526–1628: A Study of Origins and Contacts* (The Hague, 1969).

[1]In 1401 or 1402, Jerome of Prague (c. 1380–1416) brought Wycliff's teachings to John Huss in Bohemia. By 1410 Wycliff's teachings, carried on by Huss, had caused such upheaval in Bohemia that all his books and valuable manuscripts were burned. *Schaff-Herzog*, VI, 129–130.

[2]John Huss, c. 1370–1415, Bohemian religious reformer, burned at the stake July 6, 1415. His native village was Husinec, north of Prachatice not far from the border with southern Germany. *Schaff-Herzog*, V, 415–420.

[3]Jerome was condemned and burned at the stake on May 30, 1416, 328 days after Huss; see footnote above.

but not to saints or creatures; to worship any creature is idolatry. For this and other reasons he was condemned as a heretic at Lyons, France.

All the people now living on earth would scarcely equal those executed by the Babylonian harlot.

In such ways countless numbers witnessed to the truth against the evils of Rome, and their innocent lives were taken. Some believe that the present number of all the inhabitants of the earth would scarcely equal the masses killed by the Roman popes and their church.

From the beginning of the world, there has never been such tyrannical opposition to the truth of Christ among any nation, Jewish or heathen, nor such outrageous and unsated shedding of innocent blood. Therefore God will give them blood to drink, as John describes in his mysterious Revelation, saying: "The woman was clothed in purple and scarlet. Written on her forehead was the mysterious name, Babylon the great, mother of harlots and of every horror and atrocity on earth. She was drunk with the blood of the saints and the martyrs of Jesus." God will inflict terrible retribution for this innocent blood, as he has promised, and pour out double for her to drink. God deems it just to bring suffering on those who make the faithful suffer, for they deserve it.

Rev.16:3–6
17:4–6

Rev.18:6
2 Thess.1:6

2 Thess.2:3–8

The man who exalts himself above everything having to do with God and divine worship and who takes his seat in the temple of God, proclaiming himself to be God—this man is named by Paul the apostle as the antichrist, as the man of lawlessness and child of perdition. God will destroy him with the breath of his mouth and cast him and all his followers into the lake of fire.

1 Tim.4:3–5

Why is this man of lawlessness not yet revealed? He has turned every Christian practice into idolatry; for instance, forbidding the thankful enjoyment of certain foods that God created for man's nourishment.

Rev.18
Rom.1:21–25

All the kings and leaders on earth, together with their subjects, drank so greedily of the cup of all error and became so blind and besotted that they preferred the lie to the truth. So darkened were their foolish hearts that they were more intent on worshiping created things than on worshiping God the Creator, who is blessed forever. Sin and wickedness increased to such a point that one vile deed followed close on another. Yet people thought that there was nothing wrong, that everywhere things were in order, just as the world still thinks today. But God will avenge the evil as he has promised, for his Word cannot lie.

God loves the human race, however, and did not create it for destruction. In order to forestall the damage caused by the devil's deceit, God in his mercy began to fan the fire of divine truth and with great wisdom brought light out of darkness. His purpose was to show to many people the way of truth that leads to eternal life if they turn to God and leave their sinful and corrupt ways.

Pope Leo sent out messengers in Germany to sell the grace of God and indulgences for sin.

Pope Leo X [1513-1521] played no small part in this development. He spied on the emperor and all the kings and princes through their confessors. Then he sent his peddlers throughout Germany with authority to sell the grace of God and forgiveness of sins for money, in letters of indulgence authenticated with his own seal. This was against the teaching of Christ; besides, the apostle Peter had refused to accept money from Simon the Sorcerer. The pope's practices brought the abscess of the Roman court to a head; but it was Doctor Martin Luther, an Augustinian monk, who opened it and made it obvious to everyone.

Matt. 10:8
Acts 8:18–23

1517–1532: The Beginnings of Anabaptism

In the thirty-second year of the rule of the emperor Maximilian I,[1] Martin Luther began teaching and writing at Wittenberg in Saxony, warning people to be on their guard against such peddling and other Babylonian trickery. The pope summoned him to Rome, but instead he presented his views in writing to the legate of the pope at the Imperial Diet in Augsburg. When he did not receive an answer, he returned home on the advice of his well-wishers. Then Ulrich Zwingli at Zurich in Switzerland set out to storm the papacy.

Martin Luther. A.D. 1517.

Ulrich Zwingli. A.D. 1519.

About the time that the emperor Maximilian died (January 12, 1519) and Charles V became emperor, Zwingli began to teach and write against the loathsome evil of Babylon, the shameless harlot.

These two, Luther and Zwingli, exposed all the deception and villainy of the pope and brought it to the light of day as if they would strike everything to the ground with thunderbolts. But they put nothing better in its place. As soon as they began to cling to worldly power and put their trust in human help, they were just as bad—like someone mending an old kettle and only making a bigger hole. They left behind a shameless people, whom they had taught to sin. To speak in a parable, they struck the jug from the pope's hand but kept the broken pieces in their own.

And so it had to be as Jesus said, "A man that is not faithful in small things will not be trusted with great, but what he thought he had will be taken from him."

Luke 8:18
16:10
19:26

Now these two named above soon won a large following of those who accepted their teaching as the truth. Some gave their lives for it, believing that they had found salvation in

[1]Maximilian I (1459–1519), Holy Roman Emperor from 1493; 1517 was the 24th year of his rule.

Two young monks burned at the stake.

Christ. This can be seen in the two young monks, Johannes and Heinrich, who were burned at Brussels in the Netherlands in 1523.[1]

Kaspar Tauber executed in Vienna.

It was the same with Kaspar Tauber, a rich citizen of Vienna, Austria, who because of his faith was condemned and burned by his fellow citizens in 1524.[2]

Those executed for their faith at the very beginning. James 5:11

There were others besides, of whom nothing further is known, and we count them blessed according to Christ's teaching, for they suffered and fought a good fight. But however wonderful the beginning, Luther and Zwingli and their followers were soon divided into two wicked camps because of the sacraments, and they showed all the signs of a new Babel. There was no change in their lives, only boasting and the kind of knowledge that made them despise others. Eating meat, taking wives, and reviling popes, monks, and priests (who of course richly deserved it) was the extent of their service to God.

Luther's eucharist.

Zwingli's eucharist.

Luther and his followers taught that the body of the Lord Christ is in the bread of the Lord's Supper and that through it we have forgiveness of sins. Zwingli and his followers taught that the Lord's Supper was a memorial of the salvation and grace of Christ and not a sacrifice for sin, because that had been offered by Christ on the cross.[3]

---

[1]Heinrich Voes and Johannes Esch were monks from an Augustinian monastery in Antwerp that was destroyed in 1522. Their martyrdom is described in Martin Luther's song, "Eyn newes Lied wir heben an" (Let us sing a new song); see Philipp Wackernagel, *Das deutsche Kirchenlied von der ältesten Zeit bis zu Anfang des XVII. Jahrhunderts* (Leipzig, 1870), III, 3–4.

Literature regarding their martyrdom and the various types of tools used for torture at that time can be found in Josef Beck, *Die Geschichts-Bücher der Wiedertäufer in Oesterreich-Ungarn, . . . 1526–1785* (Vienna, 1883; Nieuwkoop, 1967), 13 n.1; Wolkan, *Geschicht-Buch*, 32 n.1; Zieglschmid, *Chronik*, 43 n.1. See also *ME*, IV, 232–234.

[2]A song about Tauber, "Nun hört, ich will euch singen ausz traurigklychem mut" (Hear now the song I sing to you with sorrowful heart), is in Wackernagel, *Kirchenlied*, III, 436–438. See also *ME*, IV, 684–685; Beck, 14; Thieleman J. van Braght, *The Bloody Theater or Martyrs Mirror of the Defenseless Christians* (Scottdale, PA, 1982), 414; for additional literature in German, see Zieglschmid, *Chronik*, 43 n.2.

[3]For the history of the Anabaptist movement in Switzerland, see Leland Harder, ed., *The Sources of Swiss Anabaptism: The Grebel Letters and Related Documents* (Scottdale, PA, 1985); George H. Williams, *The Radical Reformation* (Philadelphia, PA, 1962), and the revised and augmented edition (to date in Spanish only): *La*

Both of them baptized infants and rejected the true baptism of Christ, which is sure to bring the cross with it. However much they reviled the pope in other respects, they followed him in the practice of infant baptism, taking over from him the leaven that gives rise to all kinds of evil, the very gateway to false Christianity. The pope had just as little scriptural foundation for infant baptism as for purgatory, the mass, the worship of saints, letters of indulgence, and the like.

Both baptized infants as the pope did.

Luther and Zwingli defended their teaching with the sword, as they had learned from the antichrist, their father and chief, knowing well that Christian knighthood is not of the flesh but is mighty before God to destroy all human attacks. Therefore, faith cannot be forced but is a gift of God. Christ says to his disciples, "If any man wants to follow me (take note: if any man *wants* to, *desires* to), let him deny himself and take his cross upon him." He does not say the sword, for that has no place at the cross. Sword and cross are as much akin to each other as Pilate and Christ or a wolf and a sheep in the fold.

Like the pope, Luther and Zwingli defended their teaching with the sword.

2 Cor. 10:3–4

Eph. 2:8

Matt. 16:24

1525

BECAUSE GOD WANTED ONE UNITED PEOPLE, separated from all other peoples, he brought forth the Morning Star, the light of his truth, to shine with all its radiance in the present age of this world. He wanted in particular to visit the German lands with his Word and to reveal the foundation of divine truth, so that his holy work could be recognized by everyone. It began in Switzerland, where God brought about an awakening. First of all a meeting took place between Ulrich Zwingli, Conrad Grebel (a member of the nobility),[1] and

---

Reforma Radical, translated by Antonio Alatorre (Mexico City, 1983). See also Bibliography. For a listing of older German works on Swiss Anabaptism, see Zieglschmid, *Chronik*, 43 n. 1, or Wolkan, *Geschicht-Buch*, 33 n.

[1]About Conrad Grebel, the spiritual leader of the Swiss Anabaptists, see *ME*, II, 566–575; Harold S. Bender, *Conrad Grebel, Founder of the Swiss Brethren* (Goshen, IN, 1950); John L. Ruth, *Conrad Grebel, Son of Zurich* (Scottdale, PA, 1975); Hans-Jürgen Goertz, ed. (Walter Klaassen, Eng. ed.), *Profiles of Radical Reformers* (Scottdale, PA, 1982), 118–131. For Grebel's letters, see Harder, *Sources*.

1525

Felix Mantz.[1] All three were men of learning with a thorough knowledge of German, Latin, Greek, and Hebrew. They started to discuss matters of faith and realized that infant baptism is unnecessary and, moreover, is not baptism at all.

Two of them, Conrad and Felix, believed that people should be truly baptized in the Christian order appointed by the Lord, because Christ himself says, "Whoever believes and is baptized will be saved." Ulrich Zwingli (who shrank from the cross, disgrace, and persecution that Christ suffered) refused to agree—he said it would cause an uproar. But Conrad and Felix said that was no reason to disobey the clear command of God.

Georg from the house of Jakob, or Blaurock, a priest.

At this point a man came from Chur, a priest named GEORG FROM THE HOUSE OF JAKOB, later known as Georg Blaurock.[2] Once when they were discussing questions of faith, Georg shared his own views. Someone asked who had just spoken. "It was the man in the blue coat (blauer Rock)." So he was given this name because he had worn a blue coat. This same Georg had come because of his extraordinary zeal. Everyone thought of him as a plain, simple priest; but he was moved by God's grace to holy zeal in matters of faith and worked courageously for the truth.

Georg Blaurock, Conrad Grebel, and Felix Mantz discussed true baptism.

He, too, had first approached Zwingli and discussed questions of faith with him at length, but he had got nowhere. Then he was told that there were other men more on fire than Zwingli. He inquired eagerly about them and met with them, that is, with Conrad Grebel and Felix Mantz, to talk about

[1]About Felix Mantz, see John Allen Moore, *Anabaptist Portraits* (Scottdale, PA, 1984), 47–66; Harder, *Sources*, 311–315, 473–475; Heinold Fast, *Der linke Flügel der Reformation: Glaubenszeugnisse der Täufer, Spiritualisten, Schwärmer und Antitrinitarier* (Bremen, 1962), 27–35; *ME*, III, 472–474; *Martyrs Mirror*, 415; Beck, 17–20.

For Mantz's song, "Mit Lust so will ich singen" (I sing with exultation), see *The Mennonite Hymnal* (Scottdale, PA, 1969), #40; Wackernagel, *Kirchenlied*, III, 451–452; *Die Lieder der Hutterischen Brüder* (Scottdale, PA, 1914), 7–9; Rudolf Wolkan, *Die Lieder der Wiedertäufer: Ein Beitrag zur deutschen und niederländischen Literatur- und Kirchengeschichte* (Berlin, 1903), 8–9.

[2]About Georg Blaurock, a former Catholic priest, see Moore, *Portraits*, 69–93; William R. Estep, *The Anabaptist Story* (Grand Rapids, MI, 1975), 33–37; *ME*, I, 354–359; *Martyrs Mirror*, 430–436; Beck, 18–22, 79–81.

Two of Blaurock's songs are extant: "Gott fürt ein recht Gericht" (God's judgment is just), and "Herr Gott, dich will ich loben" (Lord God, how I do praise you); see Wackernagel, *Kirchenlied*, III, 447–450; *LdHBr*, 35–38. The latter was Blaurock's farewell song before his death. He was burned at the stake on September 6, 1529; see below, p.53.

questions of faith. They came to unity about these questions. In the fear of God they agreed that from God's Word one must first learn true faith, expressed in deeds of love, and on confession of this faith receive true Christian baptism as a covenant of a good conscience with God, serving him from then on with a holy Christian life and remaining steadfast to the end, even in times of tribulation.

1525

One day when they were meeting, fear came over them and struck their hearts. They fell on their knees before the almighty God in heaven and called upon him who knows all hearts. They prayed that God grant it to them to do his divine will and that he might have mercy on them. Neither flesh and blood nor human wisdom compelled them. They were well aware of what they would have to suffer for this.

They bent their knees before the most high God and called to him.

After the prayer, Georg Blaurock stood up and asked Conrad Grebel in the name of God to baptize him with true Christian baptism on his faith and recognition of the truth. With this request he knelt down, and Conrad baptized him, since at that time there was no appointed servant of the Word. Then the others turned to Georg in their turn, asking him to baptize them, which he did. And so, in great fear of God, together they surrendered themselves to the Lord. They confirmed one another for the service of the Gospel and began to teach the faith and to keep it. This was the beginning of separation from the world and its evil ways.[1]

Georg Blaurock the first to request baptism.

Georg from the house of Jakob baptized his companions at their request.

Soon after this, more people joined them, like Balthasar Hubmaier of Friedberg[2] and Ludwig Haetzer,[3] and other

Balthasar Hubmaier, Ludwig Haetzer, as well as preachers and others, accepted the faith.

---

[1]January 21, 1525, is generally accepted as the date of this first baptism. The above description is the earliest known written account of this historic event; see Heinold Fast, "Wie doopte Konrad Grebel? Overwegingen bij Meihuizens uitleg van de bronnen" (Who Baptized Conrad Grebel? Reflections on Meihuizen's Interpretation of the Sources), *Doopsgezinde Bijdragen*, new series IV (1978), 22–31. See also Harder, *Sources*, 341–342; Geiser, *Die Taufgesinnten*, 136; Williams, *Radical Reformation*, 120–127; Beck, 15–16; Fast, *Der linke Flügel*, 1–9; Fritz Blanke, "The First Anabaptist Congregation: Zollikon, 1525," *The Mennonite Quarterly Review* (Goshen, IN), Jan. 1953, 17–33; Blanke, *Brothers in Christ* (Scottdale, PA, 1961), 21–26.

[2]About Balthasar Hubmaier, see *ME*, II, 826–834; Harder, *Sources*, 550–551, and Index; Fast, *Der linke Flügel*, 35–58; Moore, *Portraits*, 165–242; Goertz, *Profiles*, 144–157; Sebastian Franck, *Chronica, Zeytbuch und geschycht bibel . . .* (Strasbourg, 1531), fol. 349v; Beck, 47–49; *Martyrs Mirror*, 465; Henry C. Vedder, *Balthasar Hubmaier: the Leader of the Anabaptists* (New York, 1905). For excerpts from Hubmaier's writings, see Walter Klaassen, ed., *Anabaptism in Outline: Selected Primary Sources* (Kitchener, Ontario, 1981), Index.

[3]About Ludwig Haetzer, see below, p.60 n.1.

1525

scholars of German, Latin, Greek, and Hebrew, well acquainted with the Scriptures,[1] as well as priests and preachers and other people. Soon they all gave witness with their blood.

Felix Mantz, one of the first believers, drowned at Zurich.

Felix Mantz was drowned at Zurich for the sake of the true faith and baptism, thus giving his life in steadfast witness to the truth.[2]

Wolfgang Uliman burned at Waldsee and ten others with him condemned to death.

Later, Wolfgang Uliman was condemned to death and burned at Waldsee, also in Switzerland. His ten companions, including his own brothers, were executed with him. Valiantly and resolutely they gave their lives as a witness that their faith and baptism were founded on divine truth.[3]

Melchior Vet burned at Ettach.

Melchior Vet,[4] Georg Blaurock's traveling companion, was burned at Ettach for the sake of his faith.

So the movement spread through persecution and great tribulation. The church increased daily, and the number of the Lord's people grew quickly. This the enemy of divine truth could not endure, so he used Zwingli as a tool. Zwingli began to write and preach with fanaticism that baptism of adult believers was false and should not be tolerated. This was contrary to his earlier confession, when he himself had taught that not one clear word from God justified infant baptism. But now, because he wanted to please men and the world rather than God, he opposed true Christian baptism. He persuaded the authorities to use the imperial law to behead as Anabaptists those who were truly dedicated to God, those who out of

Zwingli raged against believers' baptism.

---

[1]Among others: Wilhelm Reublin, a preacher at Wytikon; Johannes Brötli, a preacher at Quarten, later at Zollikon; Andreas auf der Stültzen ("with the crutches"), or Castelberger, of Chur; Simon Stumpf, pastor at Höngg, a suburb of Zurich; Wolfgang Uliman of Chur; Michael Sattler of Staufen. Beck, 19; Harder, *Sources*, 510, #10.

[2]The date of Mantz's death was January 5, 1527. For literature about Mantz, see above, p.44 n.1.

[3]This happened in 1530; see Heinold Fast, *Quellen zur Geschichte der Täufer in der Schweiz* (Zurich, 1973), 636. Wolfgang Uliman or Schorant (also called Uolimann or Ullman), son of St. Gall guild master Andreas Uliman, a former monk at St. Lucius, Chur, was won over by Conrad Grebel. He became an active propagator of Anabaptism around St. Gall and Appenzell. After escorting a group of believers to Moravia, he returned in 1528, and while gathering a second group, Uliman and his people were arrested in the Appenzell area. He and ten other men (including Johannes Brötli) were beheaded at Waldsee in Swabia (not Switzerland); the women were drowned; those who recanted were sent home. See Harder, *Sources*, 342, 568, 710 n.53; *ME*, IV, 787–788; Beck, 20; *Martyrs Mirror*, 427; Williams, *Radical Reformation*, 132.

[4]About Melchior Vet, see *ME*, IV, 819; *Martyrs Mirror*, 416; Beck, 20.

conviction had made the bond of a good conscience with him.

Finally Zwingli succeeded in having twenty men, widows, pregnant women, and young girls thrown into misery in a dark tower. They were shut up with only bread and water and saw neither sun nor moon for the rest of their lives. They were condemned to remain in the dark tower—the living and the dead together—to suffocate in the stench, die, and rot, until not one of them was left.[1] There were some who did not take one bite of bread in three days so that the others would have something to eat.

1525

In Switzerland men, women, and girls thrown into a tower to starve and rot for the sake of baptism. See preface to Balthasar Hubmaier's book on baptism.

At the same time severe mandates were issued at Zwingli's instigation: from now on, any person in the district of Zurich who was baptized should be thrown into the water and drowned without any trial or judgment. That shows the spirit Zwingli belonged to, and his followers still belong to it.

Ulrich Zwingli's tyranny.

1526

However, God's cause cannot be changed, and God's decisions are not controlled by human power. Therefore he inspired the men named above to go out to proclaim the Gospel and foundation of truth. Georg Blaurock went to Tirol; at the same time Balthasar Hubmaier went to Nikolsburg in Moravia[2] and began to preach. The people accepted his message, and in a short time many were baptized.

Georg Blaurock went to Tirol. Balthasar Hubmaier went to Nikolsburg, taught, and baptized.

Hans Hut[3] also went to Nikolsburg. Several servants were

[1]Their sentence and imprisonment is reported in *Martyrs Mirror*, 465, including a paragraph from "Balt. Hübmörs von Fridberg: gesprech auff Mayster Ulr. Zwinglens Tauffbüechlen von dem Kindertauff. gedruckt zu Nikolsburg 1526" (A Dialogue between Hubmaier and Zwingli on Infant Baptism). See George H. Williams, *Spiritual and Anabaptist Writers* (London, 1957), 287; Moore, *Portraits*, 256; Beck, 15.

[2]Nikolsburg (Mikulov), town near the Austrian border, on the main road from Vienna to Brno. *ME*, III, 883–886; J. K. Zeman, *Historical Topography of Moravian Anabaptism* (Reprint from *The Mennonite Quarterly Review*, Oct. 1966, Jan. and Apr. 1967), #101.

[3]Hans Hut, a native of Haina near Römhild (Thuringia, Germany), formerly a sexton at Bad Bibra near Meiningen, was an early defender of Anabaptism who traveled across Germany as a colporteur, particularly in Silesia, Franconia, Bavaria, and Austria; he is referred to as the "apostle of Anabaptism in Upper Austria." *ME*, II, 846–850; Williams, *Radical Reformation*, 162–165; Goertz, *Profiles*, 54–61; Fast, *Der linke Flügel*, 78–99. See also Herbert Klassen, "The Life and Teachings of Hans Hut," *MQR*, July and October 1959; James M. Stayer, "Hans Hut's Doctrine of the Sword: An Attempted Solution," *MQR*, July 1965, 181–191; Werner Packull,

1526
Several teachers appointed.

appointed to preach the Word of God, namely Oswald Glait,[1] Hans Spittelmaier, Christian Rodtmäntel, Klein Utz (Short Utz) and Gross Utz (Tall Utz), Hans Werner, Andreas Mosel, and Strützel, and others, some of whom had been preachers before. They all gathered at the castle in Nikolsburg to consider whether to wear and use the sword and whether to pay war taxes. They also discussed other problems, but they could not reach a common understanding and parted in disunity.

They met to talk about the sword.

But Hans Hut was held prisoner in Nikolsburg Castle because he would not agree with its lord, Leonhard von Liechtenstein, on retaining the use of the sword. One of Hans Hut's well-wishers, concerned for his safety, took a net meant for snaring hares and lowered him through a window and over the wall by night.

Hans Hut did not agree to using the sword.

The next day the people in the town protested loudly against Lord Leonhard and his followers for keeping Hut in the castle by force. Balthasar Hubmaier was moved to speak publicly in the hospice with his friends because they had previously been unable to agree about the sword and paying taxes.

During this time the movement grew rapidly, and people were gathering in such numbers that King Ferdinand was informed of it. He responded by summoning Lord Leonhard von Liechtenstein (who lived at Nikolsburg, had been baptized, and was called a brother) to appear before him in Vienna with his brother, Lord Hans, and all their preachers. And they complied. Straightaway Balthasar Hubmaier and his wife were taken prisoner and sent from Vienna to Kreuzenstein Castle.[2]

Balthasar Hubmaier and his wife taken prisoner.

In prison, Hubmaier remembered that he had unjustly opposed Hans Hut on several points. He realized that he was guilty of giving way too much to worldly freedom in regard

---

Mysticism and the Early South German-Austrian Anabaptist Movement, 1525–1531 (Scottdale, PA, 1977), ch. 3–5. For German literature, see Wolkan, *Geschicht-Buch*, 36 n.

[1]Oswald Glait, also called Oswald from Jamnitz (in Moravia, where he had lived last), was born at Cham, Bavaria; left the priesthood; went to Nikolsburg in 1525, and became Hans Spittelmaier's assistant minister. Well-versed in Scripture, Glait participated in the Nikolsburg disputation between Hubmaier and Hut, siding with the latter. In 1527 Glait baptized Leonhard Schiemer in Vienna; met Hans Schlaffer in Regensburg soon after. *ME*, II, 522–523; Beck, 160 n.1. For additional details about Glait's role in Hutterian history, see Zeman, *Anabaptists and Czech Brethren*, Index.

[2]Kreuzenstein Castle in Lower Austria, north of Korneuburg, now a ruin, was a state prison in 1527.

to retaining the sword. This moved him to write to Nikolsburg, particularly to his fellow worker Martin, provost at Kanitz,[1] asking him and the others to change in anything that was not right. He added, "If Hans Hut were here now, we would soon be united." Brother Balthasar Hubmaier was taken from Kreuzenstein back to Vienna to be questioned on many articles of faith. Finally he was condemned to death and burned, and a short time afterward his wife was drowned.[2] Two songs composed by Balthasar Hubmaier are still known in the church,[3] besides writings that show how powerfully he defended true baptism and opposed infant baptism with proofs from Holy Scripture. In the same thorough way he threw light on the Lord's Supper according to the truth and refuted the idolatrous mass and its great error and deception.

1526

Balthasar Hubmaier burned at Vienna, his wife drowned.

At this time Martin [Göschl], provost at Kanitz, was summoned to appear before King Ferdinand in Prague, Bohemia. When he appeared, he was taken prisoner and sent to the bishop at Kremsier in Moravia, where the priests left him to starve and rot in the dungeon.

Martin, provost at Kanitz, starved and rotted at Kremsier.

At this time two brothers came to Nikolsburg from around the Enns River. Their names were Jakob Wiedemann[4] and Philip Jäger. They heard Hans Spittelmaier's teaching and

Jakob Wiedemann came from the Enns Valley.

---

[1]Martin Göschl, of Iglau, entered Selan monastery around 1500; in 1507 he became pastor at Iglau; in 1509, Bishop of Olomouc; 1521, provost of the Himmelsrose Nunnery at Kanitz (Dolní Kounice), Moravia. The new Lutheran doctrine, introduced in Iglau by Paul Speratus, had long attracted Göschl, and by 1525 he had joined the Reformation. He married a nun from his convent and was defrocked. Göschl played a leading part in the Nikolsburg disputation of 1527 with Hubmaier and Hans Hut. He was arrested in 1528 and tortured seven times in prison at Prague, where he died in oblivion. *ME*, II, 546; Beck, 53–55; Zeman, *Anabaptists and Czech Brethren*, 179–193, and extensive footnotes.

[2]March 10, 1528, is the date generally accepted for Hubmaier's death, March 13 for that of his wife. They were married about 1525. Goertz, *Profiles*, 155.

[3]Only one of Hubmaier's songs seems to have survived: "Freut euch, freut euch in dieser Zeit" (Rejoice, rejoice, in this our time); see *LdHBr*, 23–25; for first and last stanza in English translation, see Moore, *Portraits*, 242.

[4]Jakob Wiedemann, called "one-eyed Jakob," came from Memmingen, Swabia. By 1527 he was in Anabaptist circles at Augsburg (where Hans Schlaffer made his acquaintance), and at Strasbourg from 1530 to 1531, the year he was expelled. This chronicle does not mention Wiedemann after the exodus from Austerlitz (1530); see below, pp.88-89. Yet Hieronymus Käls (burned at the stake at Vienna, 1536) writes in his letters that Wiedemann was executed at Vienna, in 1535 or 1536, "for the sake of baptism," although the judge maintained there were other reasons. *ME*, IV, 941; Beck, 50–51.

1526

tested the life there for several weeks, but they realized that this group was seriously lacking in the true order of brotherly discipline according to the Lord's Word. They could not agree to wearing or using the sword, paying war taxes, and other matters that were against their own convictions. They therefore admonished the group at Nikolsburg about all these abuses, because they were not in keeping with the life and teaching of Christ. These concerns and the rumor that the Turks were marching on Vienna led the elders of the church to hold a meeting at Pergen[1] to discuss the points mentioned above. They were unable to reach unanimity and parted in disunity, divided in their views as in Balthasar Hubmaier's time.

Dispute at Pergen.

Jakob Wiedemann withdrew from the group at Nikolsburg and began community of goods.

As a result, Jakob Wiedemann, Philip Jäger, and others withdrew from the group at Nikolsburg. They met from time to time in different houses, received the pilgrims, guests, and strangers from other countries, and began living in community.

Hans Spittelmaier wanted to retain war and the sword.

When Hans Spittelmaier discovered this, he spoke in the hospice at Nikolsburg and taught publicly that the sword, war taxes, and similar things should be retained. Thereupon Lord Leonhard von Liechtenstein sought out those who called themselves a community and had them come to him with their servants, Jakob and Philip, in order to find out why they had cut themselves off. They answered Lord Leonhard that in many areas they had found serious disorders in the way he and his congregation lived: they did not give hospitality to guests and strangers, affirmed the sword and war taxes, and did not live according to the Word of truth—which we considered to be sufficient reason.

Lord Leonhard summoned the community people and told them to leave.

Then Lord Leonhard said, "If you refuse to go to the worship services my preachers hold and meet separately, I cannot tolerate you in my domain."

The brothers replied, "With God's help we will wait patiently for whatever the Lord permits to happen to us." At the same time they earnestly warned Lord Leonhard to consider what he was doing, because he himself claimed to be a brother. Lord Leonhard responded that he personally did not object to their devout way of life but that he could not tolerate them because their presence would cause division among

[1]Pergen (Perná), German-speaking Catholic village north of Nikolsburg (Mikulov).

his brothers. However, the situation remained unchanged throughout the winter until the following Lent.

1526

In the first week of Lent King Ferdinand sent the provost[1] all over Austria to stir up indignation and persecution against the believers in Christ. Some he put in prison, those he caught in the fields or streets, he beheaded, and the villagers who refused to recant, he hanged on the gateposts. Therefore many people left Austria for Nikolsburg, and in the villages around Nikolsburg many left their houses and fled with wife and children up to the mountains. Then Lord Leonhard and Lord Hans von Liechtenstein warned the provost not to interfere within their boundaries or they would present him with a few bullets. At this the provost withdrew.

The provost of Austria arrested brothers, beheaded them on the streets or hanged them on gateposts in the villages.

Lord Leonhard threatened the provost.

At about the same time King Ferdinand sent a savage provost named Aichelin[2] into Swabia and the province of Württemberg. He shed much innocent blood and burned down the Mantelhof not far from the town of Aalen, killing about twenty people—men and youths, women and young girls, including their servant of the Word.

20 people burned in one house in the Riess region, Swabia.

The divine truth became known far and wide, and the words of Scripture were fulfilled throughout the Holy Roman Empire: God allowed his people, the sheep of his pasture, to be led to the slaughter. There was so much killing and bloodshed for the sake of divine truth that the whole of Germany was stained by it. An account of some who suffered is given here, but only of a few, as follows:

Ps.44:11

1527

In 1527 on May 21, several people were captured at Rottenburg on the Neckar, including brother Michael Sattler[3] of Staufen c.1490, a scholar in Hebrew and Latin with a wide

Michael Sattler, a servant of the Word, captured at Rottenburg on the Neckar.

[1]Dietrich von Hartitsch, governor of the Hungarian district and city of Ödenburg (Sopron, approx. 40 miles southwest of Bratislava) and provost of Lower Austria. See *ME*, II, 667–668, for details about the duties of a provost.

[2]Provost Berthold Aichelin from Wiesensteig (southeast of Stuttgart, Germany); see *ME*, I, 27; Beck, 27–28; Zieglschmid, *Chronik*, 54 n.1.

[3]Michael Sattler, born at Staufen c. 1490, had left the monastery of St. Peter in the Black Forest and joined the Anabaptists in the Zurich area in 1525. Expelled by an edict of November 18, 1525, he returned to Germany and founded several Anabaptist church groups around Horb and Rottenburg on the Neckar. All of these accepted the Seven Articles of the Schleitheim Confession agreed to at the conference held on February 24, 1527, at Schleitheim, near Schaffhausen. (About

1527

knowledge of the Holy Scriptures, a man who truly loved God. They were imprisoned because some points in their understanding of Christian faith were opposed to the pope's teaching.

1. Michael Sattler and his fellow believers had acted against the imperial mandate.
2. They set no value on the mass and did not believe that Christ's body and blood were present in it.
3. They set no value on infant baptism but believed in what they called the baptism of Christ.
4. They set no value on the sacrament of extreme unction.
5. They did not pray to or worship the mother of God or the saints.
6. They said people should not swear oaths.
7. They said Christians should not wage wars.
8. He, Michael, had left the monastic order and taken a wife.

Michael Sattler offered to dispute with the best scholars.

Michael Sattler asked them to send for their most learned men and for the Bible in any language and then let him dispute these things with them according to the Word of God. Wherever they could prove from Holy Scripture that the brothers were mistaken in their beliefs, the brothers would gladly recant and accept punishment for their guilt. If not, they were ready to suffer for the Word of God to their last breath. But Michael Sattler's accusers called him an infamous heretic and said, "We'll let the executioner argue with you." Then they

---

Schleitheim, often called Schlatten am Randen, see John H. Yoder, trsl. and ed., *The Legacy of Michael Sattler* (Scottdale, PA, 1973), 49 n.35.)

These seven articles became the basis of Anabaptist teaching: 1. Infants should not be baptized. 2. The ban, in three stages, should be used for members who have fallen into sin. 3. The Lord's Supper should be held as a remembrance of Christ's suffering. 4. The church must cut itself off, not only from the evil planted in the world by the devil, but from all abominations represented by popes and anti-popes. 5. Each congregation should have a shepherd, supported by the church, who carries out all spiritual tasks. 6. The sword is a tool of secular government outside the church, needed to punish evil and protect the good, but the church may only use the ban; therefore no member may hold office in the government. 7. All swearing of oaths is forbidden. For full text of the articles, see Yoder, *Legacy*, 34–43; John C. Wenger, *Glimpses of Mennonite History and Doctrine* (Scottdale, PA, 1949), 206–213.

For details about Michael Sattler, see *ME*, IV, 427–434; Williams, *Radical Reformation*, 185–188; Moore, *Portraits*, 97–121; Goertz, *Profiles*, 132–143 (esp. for further reading); C. Arnold Snyder, *The Life and Thought of Michael Sattler* (Scotttdale, PA, 1984). *Martyrs Mirror*, 416–420; Franck, *Chronica*, fol. 428r.

For songs written by or attributed to Michael Sattler, see Yoder, *Legacy*, 139–149. *Ibid.* 66–85 for first-hand reports about Sattler's trial and martyrdom.

condemned him and handed him over to the executioner because he would not recant. They took him to the place of execution and cut out his tongue, chained him to a cart, and twice gashed his body with red-hot tongs. Then they took him outside the gate, gashed him again five times with the irons, and finally burned him to ashes.

1527

His body torn with red-hot tongs. He was burned to ashes.

The brothers imprisoned with him also refused to forsake the truth, although they were strongly urged to do so, and they were executed with the sword. The sisters were drowned. His wife steadfastly withstood many efforts to make her recant. She was drowned several days later. Long and detailed reports about this can still be found in the church.

Michael Sattler's wife and the sisters drowned.

GEORG BLAUROCK was taken prisoner at this time at Gufidaun in the province of Tirol. He and another brother were tried near Klausen and condemned to be burned alive at the stake for the sake of their Christian confession of faith. The points against him were: he had abandoned the priestly office he had held under the papacy; he set no value on infant baptism and had rebaptized people; he set no value on the mass and did not believe that Christ's body was actually in the wafer after the priest had consecrated it. Further, he did not think that confession made to a priest was of any value or that the mother of Christ should be prayed to or worshiped.

Georg Blaurock, a servant, burned alive in Tirol.

For all these reasons he was executed, but first he spoke powerfully to the people, directing them to the Scriptures.[1] Brother Peter Walpot was present at this execution as a boy.

Peter Walpot was 8 years old.

In 1527 Thomas Herrmann,[2] a servant of the Gospel and of God's Word, was executed. Several people had been captured at Kitzbühel, where they renounced the truth after being tyrannized by the magistrates. Yet they were still taken to a public place in front of a great crowd of people and abused with blasphemous words to intimidate others. "Just see how wonderfully your teachers lay down their lives for you now," the crowd was told.

Thomas Herrmann, a servant, burned at Kitzbühel.

---

[1]Scholars agree on September 6, 1529 (not 1527), as the date of Blaurock's death; *ME*, I, 359b; p.82 below.

[2]Thomas Herrmann from Waidhofen, Bohemia, was executed on August 28, 1528. *ME*, II, 713–714; Beck, 55–56; Johann Loserth, *Der Anabaptismus in Tirol*, Archiv für Österreichische Geschichte, Vol.78 (Vienna, 1892), 469; *Martyrs Mirror*, 422.

1527

They could not burn his heart.

67 people executed after him.

The judge later utterly disgraced.

At this Thomas Herrmann pushed his way through the crowd of people, stood in front of them, and said joyfully, "It is the truth that I have taught you, and I will witness to it with my blood." He was immediately taken prisoner, tortured, condemned to die by fire, and burned. As he went to his execution he composed and sang a song which we still have.[1] They were unable to burn his heart. They threw it into a lake near the place of execution.

Sixty-seven people, his fellow believers, were put to death after him in the same place.

The judge at Kitzbühel, who helped condemn and execute many believers, said they were heretics for ever and ever because of their faith. God let him come into such terrible ill repute later that he himself was judged a heretic and called such by everyone, not on account of his faith but because God let him fall into such dishonor that he could not escape disgrace even in the world's eyes.

The clerk of the court at Kitzbühel, who had helped shed much innocent blood, was also struck by God's wrath. As he was driving round the town in his sleigh in winter, he tried to make a turn; the horse threw him against the wall at a street corner and his skull was shattered. So he came to a terrible end. Brother Hans Kräl and brother Christian Häring reported it.

Leonhard Kaiser condemned to be burned.

In this year of 1527 Leonhard Kaiser,[2] formerly a priest, was converted to faith in Christ and became a servant of the Gospel and of God's Word; he was later taken prisoner at Schärding in Bavaria. He was sentenced by the bishop of Passau and other priests and canons and given over to the flames on Friday [Aug. 16] before St. Lawrence Day in that year. He was taken to his death bound to a cart, and priests rode beside him to talk to him, though he refused to listen. He stretched his hand down from the cart and picked a flower from the wayside, held it in his hand, and said to the judge who was riding beside him, "See, I have picked a little flower;

---

[1]"O Gott ich tu dich bitten" (My God, I ask of you); see *LdHBr*, 27–28.

[2]For details about Leonhard Kaiser, formerly a chaplain at Waizenkirchen (west of Linz, Austria), see *ME*, III, 135; Beck, 25–26; Friedrich Roth, *Leonhard Kaiser, ein evangelischer Märtyrer aus dem Innviertel* (Halle, 1900); Franck, *Chronica*, fol. 428v.; *Martyrs Mirror*, 420–422.

1527

if this flower and I are consumed by the fire, then you have done right. But if not—if I and the flower are not burned and I hold the flower in my hand unconsumed—then think what you have done."

Brother Leonhard Kaiser could not be burned.

At this, many cords of wood were used to burn him, but he was not burned. Then they took as much wood again and set fire to it a second time, but it was impossible to burn him. Only his hair burned and his fingernails were a little scorched. He still held the flower in his hand, as fresh as when he had first picked it. When his body was washed and the soot came off, his body was still perfectly white underneath.

The judge no longer wanted to hold office.

Then he was cut in pieces and the pieces thrown in the fire, but they did not burn either. The executioner took the pieces and threw them into the Inn River. The judge mentioned above received such a shock that he no longer wanted to hold office. He resigned and moved away from the place. A man named Leonhard Mittermaier, born at Schärding, was at this execution and saw it all. He came to the church and became a brother.

1528

Leonhard Schiemer.

In 1528 brother Leonhard Schiemer[1] of Vöcklabruck was taken prisoner. He was a servant of the church of God, well versed in the Holy Scriptures, also in Latin. He taught the true baptism of Christ and his apostles, the true Supper of the Lord, and the other articles of faith; and he taught the Word of God. He gave testimony against infant baptism and the idolatrous mass and other abominations of the religion of the antichrist. For six years he had been a Barefoot Monk, but his experience

---

[1]Leonhard Schiemer, the first Anabaptist elder (*Vorsteher*) in Upper Austria, had studied at Vienna and other places; for six years he was a Franciscan monk at the Judenburg Monastery. For a biographical sketch of Schiemer, see *ME*, IV, 452–454; Beck, 59–62. For Schiemer's writings, including his confession of faith, see Lydia Müller, *Glaubenszeugnisse oberdeutscher Taufgesinnter*, I (Leipzig, 1938), 44–83; Williams, *Radical Reformation*, 167–169; Klaassen, *Outline*, Index; *LdHBr*, 18–20, for his song, "Wir bitten dich, ewiger Gott" (We pray, O everlasting God), and a list of his writings. The records of Schiemer's trial (described by Loserth, *Anabaptismus*, 452–460) are in the archives of the provincial government at Innsbruck, Austria. A diplomatic copy of Schiemer's letter dated November 25, 1527, to January 14, 1528 (the day of his execution), is published in A. J. F. Zieglschmid, "Unpublished 16th Century Letters of the Hutterian Brethren," *MQR*, Jan. 1941, 5–15. See also Robert Friedmann, "Leonard Schiemer and Hans Schlaffer: Two Tyrolean Anabaptist Martyr-Apostles of 1528," *MQR*, Jan. 1959, 31–36.

1528

of the impurity, hypocrisy, vice, and evil nature of the monks and priests made him realize that their life was not a godly one, so he left the monastery at Judenburg in Austria and went to Nuremberg. Here he learned tailoring and traveled in Austria, plying his trade until he reached Nikolsburg.

There he heard of Balthasar Hubmaier and his baptism and was told that people of the same faith were gathered at Vienna. He made inquiries about them, then went there and listened to them, and had himself baptized by Oswald Glait. Afterward he journeyed to Steyr, making his living by his trade, and was asked to teach and baptize there. He went on through Bavaria as far as Rattenberg, teaching and baptizing in the Inn Valley until he was taken prisoner for the sake of his faith. He was very harshly treated and put under pressure. During his suffering he made a request that if his faith was considered heretical, then scholars, doctors, monks, and priests should be brought to dispute with him. If, on the true foundation of the Scripture, he should be found in the wrong, he should be punished for it as an evildoer.

Leonhard Schiemer captured at Rattenberg on the Inn River.

To underline the truth still more, he offered in several speeches and writings that if any scholar convinced him by the truth of Holy Scripture that his beliefs were not right or scriptural, then they should let the executioner tear off one of his limbs for each time he was proved wrong, and when his limbs were gone, they should tear out the ribs from his body until he died. But if they refused to hear him in a disputation, if they condemned him and killed him without a trial, then he asked all those who heard his confession and all the bystanders to be his witnesses before God on the day of judgment. But he was condemned and handed over to the executioner on the strength of the imperial edict issued in Hungary and Bohemia. On January 14, 1528, he was beheaded and burned to ashes at Rattenberg for the sake of his testimony to Jesus Christ, which he refused to give up.

Leonhard Schiemer willing that each time he was proved wrong by Scripture, a limb be torn from his body and lastly his ribs too.

Leonhard Schiemer beheaded and burned at Rattenberg.

After him as many as seventy people witnessed with their blood in this place. Some of Leonhard Schiemer's writings still exist in the church.

70 people executed after him.

In this year of 1528 brother Hans Schlaffer[1] was also imprisoned, and brother Leonhard Frick with him, at Schwaz

Hans Schlaffer captured.

---

[1]Hans Schlaffer entered the priesthood in 1511; left the Catholic Church in 1526; traveled to Upper Austria, Augsburg (where he associated with Jakob Wiedemann

in the Inn Valley. Hans Schlaffer was at first a Roman Catholic priest but afterward a teacher of the Word and Gospel of Christ, a very gifted man. He was tried by torture and questioning, and they disputed with him about infant baptism. He used divine Scripture to testify by the spoken and by the written word (which we still have). He showed them that it was clearly commanded in the New Testament that first of all a man should learn the Word of God, that baptism should be given only to those who hear the Word and understand it for themselves, who believe it themselves and accept it themselves. That is the true Christian baptism and is not a second baptism. Nowhere has the Lord commanded that children are to be baptized. They in any case belong to the Lord; and as long as they remain in their innocence and simplicity, they are in no way condemned or excluded from the kingdom of God.

1528

Hans Schlaffer's defense and witness on baptism.

They asked him what was the foundation upon which sects like the Anabaptists stood. To this he answered, "Our faith and our act of baptism stand on no other foundation than upon the command of Christ (Matt.28:19,20; Mark 16:16), 'Go out into all the world and preach the Gospel to every creature. He who believes and is baptized will be saved,'" and he pointed to many other passages of Scripture.

They asked him what conspiracy lay hidden behind this pretext of rebaptizing, because many suspected that new disturbances were being stirred up. He answered that in all his days it had never entered his mind to cause a rebellion. Nor did he approve of others causing one. He had even fled from a house where people were living in disunity, and he would gladly prove this by the testimony of all those he had lived with. Rebaptism was only a sign that they wanted to amend their lives and reject the sinful life of the world. Among other things, he had always taught that not the least of God's commandments was obedience to the authorities in everything good. How could he then be accused of stirring up riot and rebellion?

Hans Schlaffer's answer.

---

and Hans Hut, among others), Nuremberg (Ludwig Haetzer, Hans Denck), and Regensburg (Oswald Glait). He witnessed the disputation between Hans Hut and Balthasar Hubmaier at Nikolsburg in 1527. Schlaffer joined Ulrich Moser on a journey to Matzen near Brixlegg (Tirol), and from there he visited Hall and Schwaz. He was arrested at Schwaz on December 5 or 6, 1527, and taken to Freundsberg Castle by Judge Gabriel Weisacher for a hearing. *ME*, IV, 457–459; Williams, *Radical Reformation*, 169–172; Geiser, *Die Taufgesinnten*, 250–251; Beck, 60–64.

1528
They asked him who were the leaders and originators of this sect.

They asked him who were the real leaders of such a heretical and riotous sect, as they falsely call it. He told them he knew of no leader except the Son of God, Jesus Christ the Crucified. He is the true Lord of our faith. It is not a new thing, however, for men to call it a heretical and riotous sect; the work of Christ himself and his apostles' teaching were called the same, as they can see in the Jews' accusation of Christ before Pilate and of Paul before the governor Felix.

Luke 23:1–5
Acts 24

What led him to resign his priestly office.

He was further questioned about his reasons for resigning his priestly office. He told them it was for the sake of his conscience. He had come to see that he had been a false prophet and that he had run ahead before God had sent him.

They also wanted to know who had told him to come to this district to plant such evil seeds of Anabaptism. He replied that he had no instructions, but since he had nowhere to live, he had to travel about as a stranger. He happened to be there because a friend had given him lodging. He had then gone on to Schwaz and had been taken prisoner there by God's will. As for the evil seeds they spoke of, he knew nothing of them; he had nothing evil in mind, only the pure, divine truth.

Hans Schlaffer executed with the sword at Schwaz in the Inn Valley.

When he had been in prison for some time and could not be made to waver by more questioning, they condemned to death both him and the brother captured with him. They executed them with the sword at Schwaz. These two brothers witnessed to divine truth with their blood, challenging us to follow on the way pointed out by Hans Schlaffer in his farewell prayer. Nineteen people were executed thereafter in the same place, giving testimony with their blood. Two songs Hans Schlaffer wrote are still in the church.[1]

19 people thereafter.

Hans Feyerer burned at Munich in Bavaria.

At this time Hans Feyerer,[2] a servant of the Christian church, was sentenced at Munich with five of his fellow believers.

[1]See *LdHBr*, 20–23, for a list of Schlaffer's writings and two of his songs: "Herr Vater, mein ewiger Gott" (Almighty Father, eternal God), with the acrostic "Hans Schlaffer," also in an Augsburg manuscript of 1528 published in *Zeitschrift des historischen Vereins für Schwaben*, 27 (1900), 33ff.; "Ungnad begehr ich nicht von dir" (Thy displeasure I do not seek); see Wackernagel, *Kirchenlied*, III, 479–480; Wolkan, *Lieder*, 11–12. For Schlaffer's farewell prayer, see Beck, 652. Schlaffer and Frick were executed on February 4, 1528; Loserth, *Anabaptismus*, 461–462; *Martyrs Mirror*, 425–426.

[2]The fate of Hans Feyerer and eight of his fellow believers is described in *Martyrs Mirror*, 428; *ME*, II, 327; Beck, 24.

They were burned for their faith. Three of their wives were drowned. Two men of noble birth named Bergwanger and a miller were beheaded. *1528*

In the same year, 1528, the brothers Thomas and Balthasar, both servants of the Gospel, and a companion named Dominicus were captured in the town of Brünn in Moravia.[1] They were sentenced to death and burned, remaining completely steadfast in their faith in divine truth. At the time they were captured, these brothers warned the council to beware of shedding innocent blood, for God would not let it go by unpunished. Then one of the council named Thoman Kürschner stood up and made the motions of washing his hands, saying, "That is how I would like to wash my hands in their blood." With that he supposed he was doing God a service. But God gave him a washing: a few days later God's judgment came over him, and he was found dead in his bed beside his wife. Sudden death struck him down at night, and he did not witness the death of the faithful. It was a great shock to many. Brother Bastel Wardeiner or Schlosser (a locksmith) had been well acquainted in Brünn with this Thoman Kürschner who died so suddenly. Brother Andreas Gauper knew about it too. We still have a letter from Thomas and Balthasar.

One of the council said he would wash his hands in their blood. One morning a few days later he was found dead.

1529

In 1529, brother Virgil Plattner, a servant of Jesus Christ, was captured at Schärding in Bavaria, and after great steadfastness he was condemned and executed. A song that he wrote is still in the church.[2]

Virgil Plattner executed at Schärding in Bavaria.

---

[1]Beck, 65, mentions "Thoman Waldhauser, a servant of the Word, one of three who were condemned to death at Brünn . . . ." Waldhauser, a native of Upper Austria (Waldhausen, north of Grein on the Danube) and former Catholic chaplain at Grein, managed the estates of the Lutheran lords von Hardegg at Bad Kreuzen, northwest of Grein. In 1527 he joined the Anabaptists in the town of Steyr, where he was known as "Thoman of Grein" or "Tall Thoman." Imprisoned at Brünn (Brno) in 1528, he was executed on April 10 (Friday before Easter), 1528. See *Martyrs Mirror*, 428; *ME*, IV, 876; Zeman, *Topography*, #23.

According to a letter from Johannes von Zwolle to Johannes Hess, dated April 15, 1528, one of the men executed on April 10 was the Bohemian brother Jan Cizek (Czech for the German Zeising). About Johann Zeising and the Bohemian Brethren, see *ME*, IV, 1021–1022; Zeman, *Anabaptists and Czech Brethren*, Index under "Zeising," esp. 197–198.

[2]Virgil Plattner, formerly a vicar at Rattenberg, Tirol, had been watched by the district judge for some time. For his song, "Wach auf, mein Seel, wann es ist an

1529
Ludwig Haetzer beheaded near Lake Constance.

In the same year, brother Ludwig Haetzer was executed with the sword after a long, wearisome time of imprisonment. He was one of a group of three who suffered at Constance on the Lake of Constance and was a servant of Christ, a scholar educated in Hebrew, Greek, and Latin, well versed in the Holy Scriptures. His parting words were filled with wonderful teachings, which amazed and moved many to weep with him. One, possibly four, songs are still left that were composed by Ludwig Haetzer.[1]

Hans Hut condemned to death in Augsburg.

Also in the same year brother Hans Hut, a faithful servant of Jesus Christ, was imprisoned at Augsburg in Swabia[2] for the sake of his testimony to God. They racked him in a tower. When they stopped questioning him under torture, he was left lying like a dead man; they went away, leaving a light standing in the straw in the prison, and the straw caught fire. When they returned, they found him dead. They put his dead body on a chair in a cart and drove to the court, where he was condemned and burned. All this was reported by his son Philip Hut, who died in the Lord as a member of the church. This Hans Hut wrote the "Thanksgiving" we sing at the Lord's Supper. He wrote one or two other songs as well.[3] He is the

---

der Zeite" (Awake, my soul, for now the time is coming), see *LdHBr*, 45–46; Wolkan, *Lieder*, 15. See also *ME*, IV, 189; *Martyrs Mirror*, 432–433; Beck, 33.

[1]Ludwig Haetzer (c. 1500–1529) is considered one of the outstanding writers of the early Reformation. About his translation of the Bible, in particular the Prophets (in collaboration with Hans Denck; Worms, 1527), see W. Fellmann, "Fünf alte Wormser Täuferdrucke," *Mennonitische Geschichtsblätter*, 2. Jahrgang, No. 1/2, Dec. 1937, 25–31.

About Haetzer's life and work, see *ME*, II, 621–626; Gerhard Goeters, "Ludwig Haetzer: A Marginal Anabaptist," *MQR*, Oct. 1955, 251–262; Ludwig Keller, *Ein Apostel der Wiedertäufer* (Leipzig, 1882), 211; Franck, *Chronica*, fol. 415v.; Beck, 33–34.

LdHBr attributes five songs to Haetzer (pp.29–35) of which one (p.32) yields the acrostic "Wilhelm von Zellach" and does not seem to be Haetzer's work. The other four are: "Die Lieb ist kalt jetzt in der Welt" (Love has grown cold now in the world); "Geduld sollst han auf Gottes Bahn" (Be patient as you walk with God); "Lug Herr, wie schwach ist mein Gemüt" (See, Lord, how weak and faint my soul) with the acrostic "Ludwig Hätser"; and "Erzürn dich nicht, o frommer Christ" (Beware of anger, devout Christian). The song on pp.28–29, "Sollst du bei Gott dein Wohnung han" (If you would seek to dwell with God), attributed to Leonhard Schiemer, is believed to be Haetzer's work. See Friedmann, *Die Schriften der Huterischen Täufergemeinschaft* (Vienna, 1965), 133; Wolkan, *Lieder*, 12–14.

[2]Augsburg is now part of Bavaria, Germany.

[3]For Hans Hut's songs, see *LdHBr*, 38–40. About Hut's death, see Beck, 34–35; *Martyrs Mirror*, 433. According to Johann Loserth and Robert Friedmann, Hans

Hans Hut who could not agree with Balthasar Hubmaier at Nikolsburg about the use of the sword.

1529

About this time too, Hans Langenmantel was imprisoned, a rich citizen of noble family in Augsburg.[1] As he had gout and could not walk, he was put on a chair, carried out of the city, and banished from the area. He reached Weissenhorn, where he proclaimed the Gospel as a faithful teacher of the truth, was captured again, condemned to death, and executed with the sword.

Hans Langenmantel executed at Weissenhorn.

In 1529 brother Wolfgang Brandhuber of Passau and Hans Mittermaier, both servants of God's Word and Christ's Gospel, were captured with many believers at Linz in Upper Austria and condemned to die for the sake of divine truth.[2] Altogether over seventy believers were executed by fire, water, or the sword. Wolfgang Brandhuber faithfully held and taught Christian community: in the church no one should be the steward of his own purse. The property of poor and rich should be distributed by the one chosen by the church, and everything should be held in common to serve God's glory whenever and wherever God granted it.

Wolfgang Brandhuber, Hans Mittermaier, and 70 others executed at Linz.

Brandhuber's teaching on community and other godly matters.

He led his people to reject worldly splendor, idolatrous images, buying and selling, taking vengeance, and doing

---

Hut died in 1527 (not 1529): "On December 6 he was found asphyxiated, and on December 7, 1527, his body was burned" (*ME*, II, 849a); Klassen, "Hans Hut," *MQR*, Oct. 1959, 283; Packull, *Mysticism*, 120–121. See also above, pp.47-48.

[1]Hans Langenmantel was the son of the mayor of Augsburg; *ME*, III, 289–290; Beck, 35–36; *Martyrs Mirror*, 429–430; Friedrich Roth, "Zur Geschichte der Wiedertäufer in Oberschwaben," *Zeitschrift des historischen Vereins für Schwaben* (1900), 1–45; Roth, *Augsburgs Reformationsgeschichte, 1517–1530* (Munich, 1901), 270, for a letter from Langenmantel to Matthias Metzger, dated Weissenhorn Prison, April 28, 1528. One of Peter Riedemann's songs has erroneously been attributed to Langenmantel: "Komb, gott vater von himel" (Come, God our heavenly Father); see *LdHBr*, 483–485; Wolkan, *Lieder*, 192; Wackernagel, *Kirchenlied*, III, 457–458.

[2]About Wolfgang Brandhuber, see *ME*, I, 404–405; *Martyrs Mirror*, 433; Beck, 88–89. For Brandhuber's letter to the church at Rattenberg on the Inn River, see Müller, *Glaubenszeugnisse*, I, 136–143. Prior to his activities at Linz, Austria, Brandhuber preached at Passau while working in his trade as a tailor in the parish of St. Nikola. He was imprisoned in December 1529 and executed in January 1530. Peter Riedemann took over Brandhuber's mission work in the fall of 1529. See also Grete Mecenseffy, *Quellen zur Geschichte der Täufer: Oesterreich, I. Teil* (Heidelberg, 1964), 207–209; Hans Wiedemann, *Die Wiedertäufergemeinde in Passau 1527–1535* (Passau, 1963), 268–269.

1529

military service. But governing authorities should be obeyed in everything not opposed to God. He held true Christian baptism and the true Lord's Supper, rejecting infant baptism, the mass, and other antichristian abominations, as we can still see in his writings.

Eucharius Binder burned in the Salzburg area.

Around this time a servant of the church of God named Eucharius Binder and several other believers were locked into a house in the Salzburg area and burned. The church still has a song by Eucharius Binder.[1]

Daniel Kropf executed in Styria.

Daniel Kropf, a servant of the truth, was captured with six others at Graz in Styria. He and two brothers were executed with the sword; the four sisters were drowned. They gave witness with their very lives. We still have three or four songs written by this Daniel, besides writings on baptism and other points.[2]

1530

Georg Grünwald burned at Kufstein on the Inn.

In the year 1530 Georg Grünwald was taken prisoner at Kufstein on the Inn for the sake of divine truth. He was a cobbler, a servant of God's Word and his children, full of zeal for God. He was condemned to death and burned and so testified valiantly to the Lord's teaching with his blood. Some days later a second brother was executed at Kufstein for the sake of divine truth. Brother Peter Voit knew them and was present when Grünwald became a brother and was appointed

---

[1]Eucharius Binder, a joiner by trade, was baptized by Hans Hut near Coburg (Thuringia, Germany), Binder's native town. The correct date of Binder's death appears to be October 25, 1527 (not 1529), when he and 37 fellow believers were arrested and locked up in a house at Salzburg. Their captors set fire to the house, and all 38 burned to death. *ME*, I, 343; Beck, 57. The song attributed to Binder, "Wir dancken Gott von Hertzen" (We thank God from our hearts), is in Wackernagel, *Kirchenlied*, III, 488–489; see also Wolkan, *Lieder*, 10. *Martyrs Mirror*, 433, names a Carius Prader, whose story is the same as Binder's.

[2]Daniel Kropf was not executed until 1534; *ME*, III, 249–250; *Martyrs Mirror*, 435, "Kopf"; Beck, 115; Johann Loserth, "Wiedertäufer in Steiermark," *Mittheilungen des historischen Vereines für Steiermark* (Graz, 1894), XVII, 131–132. Three of Kropf's songs are in *LdHBr*, 59–67: "Das Himmelreich sich nahet" (The heavenly kingdom is drawing near) with the acrostic "Daniel Kropf"; "Wer da christlich leben will" (Who would lead a Christian life); "Wohlauf, o Gott vom Himmel" (Rise up, O God in heaven). The fourth song seems to be lost.

to his service. This same Grünwald wrote the old song, "Come ye to me, calls God's own Son."[1] *1530*

1531

In 1531 Walser Mair and two others were captured at Wolfsberg in Carinthia; they witnessed steadfastly to the truth unto death and were executed with the sword. Walser Mair was a bookbinder by trade and a servant of the Gospel; a song he wrote is still in the church.[2]

Walser Mair beheaded at Wolfsberg in Carinthia.

In the same year brother Martin Maler, a servant of the Gospel and Word of God, was imprisoned with six others at Schwäbisch Gmünd for their faith in divine truth. They were put under great pressure and then told that if they recanted they would be completely free to return home to their wives and children. But they answered with a joyful no; they would willingly die rather than recant. After being in prison for almost a year, they were condemned to death. They were led to the town hall, and some of the articles from their indictment were read aloud to them. When the first article was read, brother Wolfgang Esslinger spoke: "As you judge us today, so God will judge you when you come before his face, but that will be a different, an eternal judgment."

Martin Maler and 6 others captured in Schwäbisch Gmünd.

The indictment read to brother Martin and his fellow prisoners.

As the second article was read, brother Bamberger spoke: "When you come to face God, he will certainly judge you as you have judged us today."

When the third article was read, brother Panj[3] said, "You defile your hands with our blood. God will assuredly not give it you freely but will require you to pay dearly for it."

When the fourth article was read, brother Melchior spoke: "We want to give witness this day with our blood that what we stand for is the truth."

When the fifth article was read, brother Wolfgang Esslinger spoke again: "Turn from your sins and repent, and God will remember them no longer."

---

[1]For this song, "Kommt her zu mir, spricht Gottes Sohn," see *LdHBr*, 47; Wackernagel, *Kirchenlied*, III, 128–129; Wolkan, *Lieder*, 17. About Georg Grünwald, see also *ME*, II, 607; *Martyrs Mirror*, 438–439; Beck, 104–105; Loserth, *Anabaptismus*, 496.

[2]The song by Walser (Balthasar) Mair seems to be lost. *ME*, III, 442; *Martyrs Mirror*, 440; Beck, 105.

[3]Also called "Pain"; *ME*, IV, 106; *Martyrs Mirror*, 439.

1531
The brothers commended themselves to God.

A youth 16 years old urged the people to repent.

Then all seven of them were led out to the place of execution under escort and with drums. Brother Martin Maler commended himself to the Lord, and they all did so, asking that he might grant them a blessed death and continue to care for his lambs. As they were taken across the water to the meadow, the miller's boy, who was sixteen years old, spoke to the bystanders, telling them to turn from their sins and be converted to God, for there is no other way to heaven except through our Lord Jesus Christ, who died on the cross and redeemed us.

A nobleman promised the youth lifelong support if he would recant.

When they were brought into the ring, a nobleman rode up to the boy, pleading with him: "My son, recant this error, and deny it. You are young. Hold on to your life! What has got hold of you? I will take you home with me, and you shall stay with me for always. You will be provided for in my house and have good things all your life. Just follow me, my son."

The boy's wonderful answer.

But the boy said: "God forbid! If I kept my earthly life and deserted God, I would be doing evil, and I refuse to do that. Your possessions can help neither you nor me. I await something far better if I endure to the end. I will yield my spirit up to God and commend myself to Christ so that the bitter death he suffered and accepted on the cross may not be in vain for me."

Martin Maler and 6 others executed at Schwäbisch Gmünd.

In this way all seven openly and joyfully confessed to God and his truth by giving their blood and dying. This is told in the song they wrote, which we still have. There are three other beautiful songs written by Martin Maler still in the church.[1]

Martin Maler said that no more of the faithful would be taken over the bridge; it was so.

When Martin was being led across the bridge, he had said, "No more of the faithful will be taken across this bridge."

---

[1]Martin Maler was also called Zehntmaier. According to one source, these seven brothers were executed at Gmünd, Swabia, on December 7, 1529 (not 1531); Geiser, *Die Taufgesinnten*, 249–250. See also *ME*, IV, 1021; *Martyrs Mirror*, 439–440; Beck, 37–39.

For Martin Maler's song—"Mit Freuden will ich singen" (With joy would I be singing)—and those about him and the brothers who shared his suffering, see *LdHBr*, 48–59; Wolkan, *Lieder*, 17–21. Co-authorship of songs by Hutterites in prison was not uncommon. The song, "Aus tiefer Not schrei ich zu dir" (From deep distress I cry to you), has seven verses and is introduced by the words: "This song was written by the seven brothers imprisoned at Gmünd, one verse each." Three songs were written in memory of the martyred brothers: "Wer Christo hier will folgen nach" (Those who on earth would follow Christ); "Kürzlich hab ich mich besonnen" (Not long ago I did reflect), said to be by Peter Riedemann; and "Aus herzlichem Mut und Eifer" (With joy and eagerness in my heart), by Andreas Ehrenpreis.

This came true, for only a little later there was such a violent storm and flood that the bridge was torn down and carried away. *1531*

I have heard more than once and from more than one person that on the day these brothers were executed, a wayfarer was approaching the city in the evening and passed by the place of execution. On that very spot he saw seven lights like burning flames and heard a wonderfully sweet and beautiful song, as if angels were singing. On reaching the city he asked what had taken place and what it was he had heard and seen. When this report reached the city council, they made a deal with him, and he consented to say nothing about it.

7 lights seen at the place of execution and beautiful singing heard.

Within a very short time, in every corner of the German lands a great number of servants and teachers of the truth had to seal their teaching with their blood.

In every corner of the German lands, witnesses shed their blood for the truth.

THERE WERE MANY OTHER BELIEVERS—WHO WERE NOT SERVANTS OR TEACHERS—who recognized the truth and were faithful to it, leaving the errors of false Christianity. They were also executed in those days, just like their teachers, and witnessed with their blood to what they confessed with their lips, as follows:

1527

In 1527 Georg Wagner of Emmering was one of them.[1] He was taken prisoner at Munich because of the following four articles:

Georg Wagner captured at Munich in Bavaria.

1. He did not believe priests could grant a man forgiveness of sins.
2. He did not believe a man could bring God down from heaven.
3. He did not believe that God or Christ was present bodily in the bread the priest had on the altar but that the loaf of bread belonged to the Lord.

---

[1]Emmering, town on the outskirts of Munich.

About Georg Wagner, see *ME*, IV, 869; *Martyrs Mirror*, 416; Beck, 22–24. For Wagner's song, "Den Vater wolln wir loben" (Let us all praise the Father), and the song about him, "Wer Christo jetzt wil folgen nach" (Whoever now would follow Christ), see *LdHBr*, 9–12; *Ausbund*, 201–205, 60–65; Wackernagel, *Kirchenlied*, III, 454–455; Wolkan, *Lieder*, 9; Klaassen, *Outline*, 88. Another song about him, "Nun merket auf, ihr Frummen" (Give heed, ye faithful people), is in A. Knöpfler, *Die Kelchbewegung in Bayern unter Herzog Albrecht V* (Munich, 1891), Appendix, 13–17.

1531 (1527)

4. He did not believe that baptism by water brought salvation.

The prince himself visited him in prison. Promised him a livelihood if he recanted.

He refused to recant on any of these points, although he was tortured so severely that the prince was filled with pity and came to him personally, urging him to recant and promising him a pension for the rest of his life. The prince's steward also urged him to recant, making many promises.

His wife and child brought to him.

Finally they brought his wife and child to him in the prison to make him recant. But he would not give way. He said that he would not sell his beloved wife and child to the prince for all the prince's lands, yet he would leave them for the sake of his God and Lord.

Monks, priests, and others came to persuade him, but he was steadfast in the recognition given him by God. He was therefore condemned to be burned alive. He was taken by the executioner and led to his death. When they came to the town, he said, "Today I will confess my God before the whole world." He had such a joy in Christ that his face did not grow pale nor did his eyes show any terror. He went to the fire with a smile on his lips. The executioner bound him to the ladder and hung a bag of gunpowder round his neck. At that he, Georg Wagner, said, "May this be in the name of the Father, the Son, and the Holy Spirit." With a smile on his lips he took leave like a Christian. Then the executioner thrust him into the fire, and he joyfully gave up his spirit. This happened on February 8, 1527. A song was written about him, which is still sung in the church.

Georg Wagner's joyfulness.

Georg Wagner burned at Munich in Bavaria.

The judge died a sudden death.

The local judge rode home from the burning with full authority and intention to seize others of like faith, but that same night God in his wrath took his life, and he died suddenly in his bed.

1528

Judge eager for the death of the faithful.

In 1528 three brothers and two sisters were imprisoned at Znaim in Moravia,[1] where the judge, by name of Lebisch, was a bitter enemy of the brothers. As time went by and the brothers and sisters were still in prison, Lebisch severely questioned the council as to what they were planning to do

[1] *Martyrs Mirror*, 428; Beck, 66–67. Znaim (Znojmo) is close to the Austrian-Czech border, approx. 35 miles southwest of Brno.

about the baptizer heretics, since in spite of the king's mandate they had not been brought to judgment. If they were not willing to do anything about it, he would go to the king himself and denounce their disobedience. But if they were ready to sentence them, his own horses would cart the wood for the burning. The council's answer was friendly: "Judge Lebisch, we leave it in your hands. Do what you like with them." Firewood was brought in Lebisch's own carts, and the three brothers and two sisters were burned. So they were condemned in this summary manner and gave themselves as a true burnt offering to God the Lord, fulfilling their baptism vows and faithful to death for the sake of the divine truth they had acknowledged.

1531 (1528)

Brothers and sisters burned.

This Lebisch, impelled by the old serpent's hate and envy, had not yet had enough of the blood of innocent believers. He went on until he brought his own judgment upon himself. He offered money to any who would inform him where the brothers met. When a certain house was pointed out to him, he set out across the square with constables and guards. In front of the house Lebisch accidentally stepped in a hole meant for holding a tavern sign. He hurt his foot, fell down, and cried piteously for the guards to pick him up and let the villains go. The brothers heard the screams and escaped from the house.

Judge planned to attack the brothers further; he had an accident.

After this, Judge Lebisch became dangerously ill. He lay as though unconscious but suddenly began to scream, "Oh, the baptizers, the baptizers!" That was all he said, but he said it again and again. Finally he bellowed like an ox and bit his tongue until blood and foam ran from his mouth and his wife and children could not bear to stay with him. Only his servant girl, a relative, remained at his side until he choked on his own blood. She told brother Bastel Wardeiner all about it. His relatives did not like anyone to speak of it, but it was common knowledge among the people that he had sinned against innocent blood.

The bloodthirsty judge became sick, cried out and bellowed like an ox, bit his own tongue, and died miserably, choked in blood.

Through such examples (many more than can be described in this book) God often puts fear into the wicked so that his work can grow among his people, to his honor and for the salvation of many who seek justice and a new life. Without God's continual strengthening of his work, the enemy would have extinguished it in no time. Not a spark of the truth would have been left.

1531 (1528)
9 brothers and 3 sisters captured at Bruck an der Mur in Styria.

In that same year, 1528, nine brothers and three sisters were taken prisoner at Bruck an der Mur in Styria. For the sake of their faith they were condemned to death, bound, and taken to the place of execution outside the town. But they were joyful and said, "Today we will suffer for the Word of God and offer him our sacrifice." They spoke earnestly to the lords of Bruck, reminding them that the blood of innocent souls would be on their heads.

They made their prayer to God.

As the people gathered around them, the condemned knelt down and prayed to God from their hearts. Then they stood up joyfully and prepared themselves for the sword. But the executioner was distressed because of what he had to do. The youngest brother encouraged the others to bear the pain willingly when their turn came. He kissed each one on the lips, saying, "God bless you, my beloved brothers; today we will be together in paradise." The nine brothers were beheaded in a green meadow. Their great courage was a miracle. They knelt down and shed their blood under the strokes of the sword.

The brothers beheaded.

The three sisters were drowned. They refused to turn away from God. Several people saw the youngest smile down at the water. Some thought she was hardened by the devil, but others were moved in their hearts, for they realized that this could only come from God. Their valiant witness to the divine truth is preserved in a song that was written about them.[1]

The 3 sisters drowned. The youngest smiled down at the water.

Johannes Bair of Lichtenfels imprisoned for 23 years at Bamberg in Franconia.

In this same year on Wednesday after All Saints Day [Nov. 1], brother Johannes Bair of Lichtenfels was captured. He was imprisoned for the sake of his faith, and because he remained steadfast, he lay in a dungeon at Bamberg in Franconia [Bavaria] for twenty-three years. He wrote a letter to the elders of the church, as follows:

Johannes Bair's letter from prison.

> Dear brothers,
>
> I received the writing tablet, the "Account of our Religion, Doctrine, and Faith," six candles, and some pens. But although the Bible was listed on the tablet, it was the one thing that did not reach me. If you still have it, I beg you to send it to me, God willing, for I would

[1]*Martyrs Mirror*, 429; *ME*, I, 444, "Bruck." Beck, 68. For the song, "Nun wollen wir aber singen" (Now let us sing together), see *LdHBr*, 25–27; Wackernagel, *Kirchenlied*, III, 467–468.

1531 (1528)

prefer that to anything else. Send it to me through brothers in the faith or any good-hearted person, if that is the Lord's will. I suffer greatly from the lack of God's Word these many long days and years. I pour out my grief over this to God and to you, his church, for I have had such a great hunger and thirst for the Word of the Lord for many long years. My days of distress in prison now add up to twenty years minus eight weeks, which will be completed on Wednesday after All Saints Day.

I, Johannes Bair of Lichtenfels, wretched of the wretched and forlorn of the forlorn, a captive of Jesus Christ our Lord, pour out my need to God and to all his angels and saints, as well as to you, his workers and church community. Most beloved brothers and sisters in the Lord, pray to God that he may deliver me from this perilous and great need, this unspeakable need. God knows it and so do I, poor wretch that I am. And you feel it with me too. Now God be with you.

Written in a dark hole at Bamberg
in the year 1548

Johannes Bair died in prison.

After this letter Johannes Bair spent three more years in prison, twenty-three years in all. In the year 1551, still in prison, he fell asleep in the Lord with a peaceful heart and has attained the victor's crown.

1529

4 brothers and 4 sisters captured in the Adige region.

In 1529 four brothers and four sisters were captured in Vill,[1] a village in the Adige Valley, and were taken to the castle of En. Their names were Wolfgang from Moos near Deutschnofen, Thomas Imwald from Aldein, Georg Frick from Wirtsburg, Mang Kager from Füssen, Christine Töllinger from Penon (a widow), Barbara from Tiers, Agatha Kampner from Breitenberg, and her sister Elizabeth. On November 16, the Tuesday after St. Martin's Day, each had a special hearing in

---

[1]Benedict Gampner, a former lay priest of Bruneck, baptized many people at Vill (northeast of Brixen) in the home of Philip Koffler. Koffler was arrested in 1530.

Deutschnofen, Tiers, Tramin, Aldein, are in the Adige Valley, northern Italy; Breitenberg, north of Ried in Upper Austria; Füssen, southern Bavaria near the Austrian border. *ME*, I, 12, "Adige Valley"; *ME*, II, 330, "Fill"; *Martyrs Mirror*, 435–436; Beck, 89–90.

1531 (1529)

front of the judge and nine jurymen. Each was questioned about certain articles of faith. It was all written down by the court, and we use this record to give the following account.

Brother Wolfgang's testimony.

BROTHER WOLFGANG from Moos testified that on the Sunday after the Feast of Our Lady [Sept. 8] a year earlier, a man named Michael Kürschner had come to Deutschnofen. This man was later sentenced at Gufidaun and burned to death for the sake of the cause and its witness. He had preached the Word of God to Wolfgang himself, to Martin Nauk, and to Strölen from Deutschnofen. Afterward he had baptized all three of them anew, according to God's command. Further, he said he did not believe in infant baptism; God had not instituted it, nor had Christ commanded it. He did not believe that Christ's body was in the host consecrated by the priests. He attached no more importance to feasts, Sundays, and other festivals than was given them in the New Testament.

Brother Thomas's testimony.

THOMAS IMWALD from Aldein testified that he had been baptized at Breitenberg on the Saturday before St. Ulrich's Day [July 4] by a former priest, Georg Blaurock from Switzerland. He denied the value of the mass, for it was invented by men and not commanded by God. He did not believe that the priests could bring Christ into the wafer by consecrating it. Christ must be received in the Word. The bread is only a symbol and a means of remembrance. Confession as made to a priest held no value for him either, as it was not according to God's command. To Our Lady he gave the honor for which God had chosen her: she was a virgin and the mother of our Savior. He was asked: if their numbers increased, would they not attempt to convert all the people on someone's land by force? He answered no, they did not intend to force anyone; God wants willing hearts. He himself had not been forced by any man—God had put it in his heart.

We force no one to accept our faith.

Brother Georg Frick's testimony.

GEORG FRICK from Wirtsburg, a tailor, testified that he was baptized by an elder of their faith called Benedict at Philip Koffler's place in Vill at the time of the most recent annual fair at St. Gallen. He did not believe that a priest could transform a wafer into the body of Christ. God had not instituted the mass; the bread at the Lord's Supper is only a symbol in remembrance of him. As to confession, how can a fornicator and an idolater forgive him his sins? Of Our Lady he believed that she had found favor in God's eyes and that she was a virgin before and after the birth. With God, that and more was possible. He would remain true to his faith and surrender to God's will.

1531 (1529)

MANG KAGER, a cobbler's apprentice from Füssen, testified that he was baptized that summer at Georg Kärtner's in Penon, around St. James's Day [July 25]. The man who baptized him was Georg from Chur in Switzerland [Georg Blaurock], a former priest who had recently been burned at Klausen. Mang did not believe in infant baptism or in the mass, nor did he believe that our Lord is present in the host. He believed in the virginity of Mary, the mother of Christ, but not in intercession through her or the saints, because Christ is the mediator between God and man. He set no value on private confession to a priest. About keeping the Sabbath, he said that God the Almighty created the world in six days and rested on the seventh day; that was the origin of Sunday, and he would leave it at that. Work is not forbidden and is not a sin; but men should rest from and break with their sins. He said that the priests practice idolatry in the morning and commit fornication in the afternoon. What he confessed with his mouth he wanted to witness to with his blood; he would not renounce his faith but remain true to it until the end.

Brother Mang Kager's testimony.

About keeping the Sabbath.

In the morning, idolatry; in the afternoon, fornication.

CHRISTINE TÖLLINGER from Penon, a widow, testified that brother Georg Blaurock had baptized her in her home with the true Christian baptism. About the mass, she did not believe at all that the priest could bring our Lord into the host; it is nothing but bread, and what the priests do only leads people astray. As for infants being saved without baptism, the Lord said, "Let the children come to me, for of such is the kingdom of heaven." The priests go to the trouble of needlessly baptizing innocent babies, but as the children grow up in this world of sin and vice, the priests make no efforts to turn them away from sin. She believed that Our Lady was the mother of Christ and a virgin. She did not believe in confession heard by a priest, but when a person acknowledges and confesses his sin, rejects it, and sins no longer—that, she thought, is true confession. About feast days and Sundays she said that in six days God the Lord created the world, on the seventh he rested; the other feast days were instituted by popes, cardinals, and archbishops. Since she was living in the world, she observed the feast days like other people, to avoid giving offense, but

Sister Christine Töllinger's testimony.

About confession.

About feast days.

1531 (1529)

no one would be damned for working. Besides, the priests practice idolatry in the morning and commit fornication in the afternoon. By God's grace and with his help she would die for her convictions.

Sister Barbara's testimony.

BARBARA FROM TIERS, the wife of Hans Portz, testified that she had been baptized according to true Christian command by a servant of the Word of God named Benedict. Her baptism had taken place around Michaelmas [Sept. 29] on a hill near Tramin on the Moos. She did not believe in the priests' idolatrous sacrament of the mass. The priests practice idolatry in the morning and commit fornication in the afternoon. She set no value on the way confession was made to a priest. About Our Lady she had nothing to say. About Sundays and feast days: God the Lord intended the seventh day for rest, and she left it at that. With the help and grace of God, she would remain faithful unto death, for this was the true faith and the only way in Christ.

Agatha Kampner's testimony.

AGATHA KAMPNER from Breitenberg testified that she was baptized the year before on the Sunday before Christmas at "the hollow" near St. Gall in Switzerland by brother Többich, a servant of the Word of God. She was against infant baptism, for if children die without baptism, they die in innocence and belong to the Lord. She was against the mass, for Christ did not tell his disciples, "Go out and hold mass," but "Go out and preach the Gospel." About the mass she said that since the confession of faith states that he sits at the right hand of his heavenly Father and will come from there to judge the living and the dead, she in no way believed that he allows the priests to bring him down into the host, handling and transforming him. About Our Lady, she believed that Mary bore Christ the Lord who redeemed us all and that through her the Word of God became man, who suffered for us on the cross. Concerning feast days she said that no day was more holy than another. The Sabbath was appointed for people to gather for preaching and discussing the Gospel, but now it is used for gluttony and immorality. With the help and grace of God, she would remain steadfast in her faith.

About keeping the Sabbath.

Elizabeth's testimony.

ELIZABETH, Agatha's sister, testified that she was baptized that summer at Breitenberg by brother Georg Blaurock in the name of the Father, the Son, and the Holy Spirit, according to Christ's command. She did not believe in the priests' sacrament and mass, since there is no evidence that God appointed them. About Our Lady, she believed that Mary was a virgin and bore Christ our Savior. Mary and the saints had to suffer just as much as she and many others were suffering now, but she did not believe that Mary was a mediator, because all power in heaven and on earth is given to Christ alone. As for feast days, she did not value one above another; we should watch at all times for the great day of the Lord and abstain from sin. She was determined to remain steadfast. After the hearing, these true lovers of God were executed.

1531 (1529)

In the same year, 1529, two sisters, Anna Maler and Ursula Ochsentreiber were sentenced to death for the sake of divine truth and drowned at Hall in the Inn Valley. They armed their womanly hearts with such manly courage in God that everyone was astonished at their steadfastness. Thus they witnessed to the truth in life and in death. This testimony is contained in the songs that were written about them and still exist.[1]

2 sisters executed at Hall in the Inn Valley.

In the same year there was a divine zeal among the people of the Palatinate, near the Rhine; they began to see the truth, which shone out so clearly that the priests appealed to the authorities and threatened violence. As a first measure nine brothers and several sisters were imprisoned in the town of Alzey[2] for their faith. These arrests were instigated by priests with the help of some noblemen, not by order of the prince. The brothers and sisters were kept in prison because no one knew what to do with them. The burgrave of Alzey asked his superior, the count palatine, for advice. The latter replied that the district court at Alzey should investigate the matter and decide. The burgrave complied and brought them before the court, which was unwilling to pass sentence, since the prisoners were held purely on grounds of faith; there was no charge against them warranting death.

9 brothers and several sisters imprisoned in Alzey near the Rhine.

The district court unwilling to judge the prisoners.

As the Imperial Diet was in session, the count palatine brought up the question: what should he do with the Anabaptists

---

[1]Only one song about these sisters is known: "An unsrer Frauentag das geschah" (It happened on Our Lady's Day); see Wolkan, *Lieder*, 15–17, and *LdHBr*, 46–47. *Martyrs Mirror,* 437; Beck, 90.

[2]Alzey on the Selz River, south of Mainz, Germany, mentioned as early as 1200 in the *Nibelungenlied* (a German epic poem), was the administrative center for Rhine-Hesse. See also *Martyrs Mirror*, 437; Beck, 29–31.

1531 (1529)

in his prison? The case was passed on to the four inquisitors (as they were called), who referred to the imperial mandate, in which exhaustive information on the statutes of the imperial constitution for such cases could be found. The constitution stated clearly that every Anabaptist, every rebaptized adult, man or woman, was to be executed by fire, sword, or other means, depending on the person. Under penalty of severe punishment, anyone who found them was to hand them over to the court to be accused and convicted. They should be judged and treated in this way and no other.

The brothers beheaded, the sisters drowned.

After this the imprisoned brothers and sisters were brought once more before the court, and the imperial mandate was read to them. Since they refused to recant, they were sentenced to death without further hearing, merely on the strength of the mandate. The men were to be killed with the sword, the sisters to be drowned in the horse pond.

While they were still in prison, a sister came in to comfort them. She encouraged them to be steadfast in the Lord and to accept this suffering because of the eternal joy that would follow. When she was discovered, she too was imprisoned and later burned to death because she had comforted and strengthened her sisters. The others were drowned.

A sister burned.

In this way the persecutors tried to put out the light of truth, but it burned more and more brightly. They took prisoner woman or man, servant or young girl—anyone who had embraced the faith and left the world and its idolatrous ways. In some places the prisons were full of them. This was done in an attempt to intimidate people. The prisoners responded with such joyful singing that their enemies outside the prison became much more fearful than the prisoners inside. They did not know what to do with them, especially since they were imprisoned merely for the sake of their faith.

They sang in prison.

The count palatine then acted on the imperial mandate, and in a short time more than 350 brothers and sisters were executed because of their faith. In particular Dietrich von Schönberg, the burgrave of Alzey, had many believers in that town beheaded or drowned. Many who lived in Alzey at that time and who later joined the church reported that believers were taken from any house known to shelter them and led to the place of execution like sheep to the slaughter. Not one recanted; they met death with joy. While brothers and sisters were being

Count palatine had 350 executed within a short time, many at Alzey.

While some were executed, the others sang.

executed or drowned, those who were waiting sang until the executioner took them too. They were all steadfast and firm in the faith they had received from God.

1531 (1529)

Some, instead of being executed, were cruelly punished. Their fingers were chopped off, their foreheads branded with a cross, or other terrible things were done to them. The burgrave of Alzey himself said, "What shall I do? The more I condemn and execute, the more of them there are."

Some had fingers cut off or were branded with a cross on the forehead.

This burgrave of Alzey, Dietrich, was punished for his tremendous guilt in the shedding of innocent blood. When he was visiting the count palatine in Heidelberg and was about to have a meal with him, he suddenly fell dead as he sat at table.

The burgrave of Alzey met a sudden death.

One of the last executions in the town of Bad Kreuznach was that of a man called Philip of Langenlonsheim.[1] As he was being beheaded, the people saw the executioner put up his hands to ward off something from his face, but they did not know why. Afterward people said that a black hen had flapped against his face, although only he had seen what it was. Some said the blood had spurted into his face. Later it was clear what it must have been, because his nose rotted away completely. That is how God made him suffer for the innocent blood with which he had stained himself, and this incident made people see the wickedness perpetrated against the faithful. Reports of this execution came from several brothers who joined the church from towns on the Rhine. Their parents had been eye witnesses of it.

The executioner's nose rotted away.

The count palatine was shocked and his heart was moved by these two events. Besides, he began to realize that his victims were innocent. In the end, although belatedly and after many incidents, he was seized with great remorse. He is supposed to have said that it cost him a large sum of money to have so many people executed, but now he would readily spend the same amount again if he could undo what he had done. A great deal could be written if all such stories were to be narrated in detail. After that, the executions gradually stopped, although persecution, expulsion, and hostility has continued up to the present.

The executions cost the count palatine a large sum of money. In the end he would have given as large a sum again never to have let it happen.

In the Palatinate at that time, all who renounced their popish

The Palatinate changed beliefs 4 times because of one man's opinions.

[1]Langenlonsheim, a village near Bad Kreuznach, southwest of Mainz, Germany. See also *ME*, III, 289; *Martyrs Mirror*, 438; Beck, 31.

1531 (1529)

beliefs were executed. A few years later the persecutors reversed their beliefs themselves and became Lutheran. Not long after, they left the Lutheran faith and became Zwinglian; a few years after that the whole Palatinate became Lutheran again—all this purely on the grounds of one man's opinion and within his life span—a miserable, tottering belief built on sand and diseased through and through with inconstancy. It was the same in other places: the people had to believe what their prince believed. In short, none of it was the true faith, built on a firm foundation. It was empty and hypocritical.

Brother Georg Baumann captured in Württemberg.

He recanted and agreed to obey.

About this time a brother, Georg Baumann,[1] was imprisoned at Bauschlet in Württemberg for the sake of his faith. The nobleman whose subject he was kept him in prison and tortured and racked him. He was pressured, questioned, and tormented so badly that he wavered and gave in to his interrogators. They demanded that he recant publicly in the church, which he did once or twice by going into the church and declaring his forced agreement. At the same time he was struck in his heart and reflected on the honor of God and his name; he realized what he had done and felt remorse. The third time he came into the church to recant, he told the priests and their assistants, "You scoundrels! You got the upper hand: you tortured and plagued me until I agreed to give up my faith and follow you. But now I am sorry I did it, and I repudiate it all." Then he restated that this was the divine truth and the true faith, yes, the way to life in Christ, that the idolatrous life and ways of the world lead astray and are opposed to God, and that he wanted to remain steadfast in his faith to the end. They immediately seized him again and sentenced him to death. He sang joyfully as they led him to the place of execution. It was very muddy in the village. His shoes got stuck in the mud but he walked straight ahead, leaving them behind, and hurried to the execution place, singing for joy that God had again given him such courage. And so he was beheaded.

The third time he came into the church to recant, he began to confess his faith anew.

He was condemned to death; sang as he was led away.

He was beheaded.

Afterward the nobleman who caused his execution lost his toes by gangrene and suffered great misfortune. All those who had judged and sentenced this brother came to a bad end. One went out of his mind and died a horrible death, bellowing like a cow. Another contracted leprosy. The only one who died a

All those who condemned him came to a terrible end.

[1]About Georg Baumann, see *Martyrs Mirror*, 438; Beck, 32–33.

normal death was someone who had not wanted to pass sentence. He was spared this torment, as was known to those who later joined the church from that locality. *1531 (1529)*

At that time God visited the German lands with his Word, and many hundreds of people were executed at different times for their faith, in many provinces, towns, and marketplaces. [The world could not tolerate them, because they opposed its works. They rebuked the world for sinning against God's Word by denying it and living in ways that flaunt all morality. They turned their backs on the ways of the world as impure and exposed the world's deceitfulness. The clergy feared them, afraid that they themselves and their practices would no longer be honored and upheld and that all their pomp and false doctrine would come to naught. That is why they brought imprisonment, martyrdom, and death upon these witnesses and lovers of God who, when suffering came their way, fought a valiant battle against pain and were not horror-struck, because they had prepared themselves for it beforehand. God gave them help that was greater than all the suffering their enemies were able to inflict. The things of this world were like fleeting shadows to their consecrated hearts. What they were leaving behind here seemed insignificant, since their hearts were filled with hope of greater things. They had lived this futile life long enough and were hastening toward life in heaven. That is why their endurance in suffering proved to be greater than that of their enemies in tormenting them, and their murderers were amazed to see the strength of their God-fearing souls. But the blood of these innocent ones will bring everlasting hellfire upon their enemies.][1]

Church *Ordnung* for a Christian life.

In 1529 the church community taught, practiced, and agreed to uphold the following *Ordnung*,[2] namely, how a Christian who stands within the apostolic faith should live:

1. Ask God for grace.

FIRST, when the church assembles, we should ask God from

---

[1]The bracketed passage (Wolkan, *Geschicht-Buch*, 695–696, errata and addenda) is from the "1580" codex of this chronicle, fol. 68v–69r. About this codex, see Introduction, p.xvi, and Appendix 6, plates 1, 3, 5, 7, 9.

[2]*Ordnung* (pl. *Ordnungen*), retained in the present translation, often rendered as "orders" or "discipline" (as in School Discipline, Barber-Surgeons' Discipline), is a charter or rule, both spiritual and practical, of the communal life among the Hutterian Brethren. See Robert Friedmann, "Gemeindeordnungen," *ME*, II, 454–455.

1531 (1529)

our hearts for his grace to make his divine will known to us. When parting from one another, we should give thanks to God and intercede for all brothers and sisters of the whole Christian church.

2. Proclaim the Lord's Word often.

SECOND, as Christians we should encourage one another from our hearts to remain steadfast in the Lord. We should meet frequently, at least four or five times a week if possible.

3. Practice discipline.

THIRD, when a brother or sister does wrong openly, it should be corrected openly before the church with loving admonition. If it was done in secret, it should be disciplined privately, but in accordance with God's command.

4. Keep Christian community.

FOURTH, every brother and sister should be fully surrendered to God and to the church, in body and soul. All gifts received from God should be held in common, according to the practice of the first apostolic church community of Christ, so that the needy in the church can be supported. Acts 2:44–45; 4:32–37; 5:1–11.

5. Care for the needy.

FIFTH, on behalf of the church, the servants chosen by the church community should look after the needs of the poor with great care.

6. Live uprightly. 1 Tim.3:1–13

SIXTH, brothers and sisters should be straightforward and not superficial in their speech and behavior, either to one another or to anyone else, inside the community or outside.

7. One to speak in meetings.

SEVENTH, in the meetings of the church community only one at a time should speak, and the others should listen and use good judgment about what is said; two or three should not stand up at once. No one should curse or swear or talk idly; this is to spare the weak.

Ecclus.23:1–15 Eph.5:4

8. Be moderate when meeting.

EIGHTH, when we meet we should not eat or drink to excess but give thanks and be moderate with what God created for our nourishment, serving one or two dishes. After the meal, the tables should be cleared.

9. Baptism.

NINTH, matters that are dealt with and put right among brothers and sisters in meetings are not to be made known outside the church. As for the sympathetic seeker, at the outset the Gospel should be proclaimed and explained to him. If that person accepts the Gospel with joy in his heart and is willing to live accordingly, he should be received by the church community as a member of Christ.

10. Be ready for the cross and suffering.

TENTH, we should be prepared for God's working and for the cross every day, for we have surrendered ourselves to be disciplined by him. Everything he lays on us should be received with thanks and borne with patience; we should not be swayed by gossip or frightened by every wind that blows.

1531 (1529)

ELEVENTH, all those who are of one body and one bread in the Lord and are of one mind should celebrate the Lord's Supper in memory of his death. At that occasion everyone should be challenged to be like the Lord in obedience to the Father.

11. Celebrate the Lord's Supper.

TWELFTH, as we have been taught and warned by the Lord, we should at all times be watchful and await his coming so that we may be worthy to go in with him and escape the evil that is to come upon the world.

12. Always be watchful in the Lord.

Let us now continue to tell how, from the beginning, the church was cleansed of those who were false and lukewarm. Especially here in Moravia a genuine gathering together and a true ordering of life emerged under great hardship. The king's provost in Austria stopped his persecution (described earlier), and the lords of Nikolsburg sent messengers into the mountains and hiding places in the woods where people had fled, to tell them all to return home and no longer be afraid.

1528

At that time several servants and their congregations settled in Moravia: in Znaim, Eibenschitz,[1] Brünn, and elsewhere. A certain Gabriel Ascherham came to Rossitz.[2] Born in Nuremberg, he had been a furrier in Schärding, Bavaria, then moved to Rossitz where he gathered the people and taught them.

Gabriel Ascherham from Bavaria.

Soon after this, Philip Blauärmel[3] came to him from Swabia

Philip Blauärmel from Swabia.

---

[1]Eibenschitz (Ivančice), town on the Iglau (Jihlava) River in Moravia; in 1529 the property of the lords of Lipé, who granted full religious freedom in the 16th century. Zeman, *Topography*, #34; *ME*, II, 166–167; Beck, 68–69.

[2]Rossitz (Rosice), market town in a coal mining area of Moravia, approx. 18 miles west of Brno; 1522 the property of the lords von Pernstein; 1549–1562 owned by the lords of Lipé; 1562 became the property of Johann von Zerotin whose son Karl inherited it in 1583 and sold it to Albrecht von Wallenstein in 1628. Until 1622, when the Anabaptists were driven out of Moravia, there were Anabaptist settlements as well as Bohemian Brethren at Rossitz. Zeman, *Topography*, #133; *ME*, IV, 362; Beck, 69; Zeman, *Anabaptists and Czech Brethren*, 282, 291, 297.

[3]Philip Blauärmel's family name was Plener. He came from Strasbourg and was a weaver, therefore also called Philip Weber. Since he wore blue sleeves, the sign

1531 (1528)

with several others. Gabriel took them into his community and laid down his service so as to give honor and precedence to Philip and his assistant. But soon Philip's actions no longer pleased Gabriel, so Gabriel assumed the leadership over his own people again and they continued living where they were. Philip moved away with his people and started another community. They still claimed to be brothers, but their hearts were disunited, and as a result two groups emerged, the Philippites and the Gabrielites; but more about this later.

Hans Spittelmaier at Nikolsburg broke away.

As we have just explained, the number of people in Nikolsburg kept growing, and the majority joined Jakob Wiedemann and Philip Jäger. Supported by his assistants and relatives, Hans Spittelmaier in a public sermon at Nikolsburg forbade his people to have anything to do with Jakob Wiedemann's people: they should ignore them because they were forming a separate group. All those who followed Jakob Wiedemann were called "the small group," or *Stäbler* ("staff-bearers").[1] But those at Nikolsburg retained the sword and were therefore called *Schwertler* ("sword-bearers") and now "Sabbatarians"; they have the spirit of the Münsterites. As a result, Lord Leonhard von Liechtenstein summoned Jakob Wiedemann, Philip Jäger, and other servants and stewards as he had done before. He ordered them to pack up and vacate his land because they were setting up a separate church. So they offered their goods for sale—some they sold, others they left behind—and they all moved away. Afterward, however, Liechtenstein's people sent on all the goods they had left behind.

Small group, staff-bearers. Sword-bearers now called Sabbatarians.

Jakob Wiedemann and his people were told to leave Nikolsburg.

200 people left Nikolsburg.

About two hundred people (not counting children) from Nikolsburg and Pergen and the surrounding area gathered outside the town of Nikolsburg. Out of sympathy a number of people came from the city to see them and wept with them, but others argued with them. They started on their way and encamped in a deserted village between Dannowitz and

---

of the dyers' trade, he was generally known as Philip Blauärmel. *ME*, I, 174–176; Beck, 69–72; Williams, *Radical Reformation*, 418 n.1.

[1]The *Stäbler*, meaning staff-bearers, "teach that a Christian cannot with a clear conscience and according to the Word of God bear a sword or any weapon or wage war but shall let a staff suffice. They are generally counted among the Anabaptists, who came into being in our time"; Caspar Franck, *Catalogus Haereticorum* (Ingolstadt, 1576), 495, "Stebler." See also *ME*, IV, 607; Beck, 73; Williams, *Radical Reformation*, 229–233; Estep, *Anabaptist Story*, 89–92.

1531 (1528) Jakob Wiedemann and his people appointed servants for temporal affairs.

Muschau and stayed there for a day and a night.[1] They took counsel together in the Lord because of their immediate need and distress and appointed servants for temporal affairs: Franz Intzinger from Leoben in Styria and Jakob Mändel, who had been treasurer to Lord von Liechtenstein in Nikolsburg, with Thoman Arbeiter and Urban Bader to help them.

They put all their goods together.

These men then spread out a cloak in front of the people, and each one laid his possessions on it with a willing heart—without being forced—so that the needy might be supported in accordance with the teaching of the prophets and apostles. Isa.23:18; Acts2:44–45; 4:34–35; 5:1–11.

Just as they were about to move on, Lord Leonhard von Liechtenstein came from Nikolsburg with several mounted retainers, asked them where they were going, and told them they could have remained at Nikolsburg. By way of answer they reminded him why he had not allowed them to remain. They certainly had not acted lightly, but only in the fear of God and for their conscience' sake, which did not allow them to go along with his (Leonhard's) brothers and the teachings and way of life of his preachers. Furthermore, they said, they held it as unchristian that he and his brothers had threatened the provost with force, for although the provost had been sent by a higher authority, Leonhard, incited by his preachers, had resisted him.

They then broke camp and went on. Lord Leonhard rode with them as far as Wisternitz, where he provided them with a drink and let them through toll-free. After crossing the bridge, they spent the night on the right bank by the old temple, the little hermitage, and stayed there for breakfast the next morning. They tried meanwhile to find wagons to move their sick people and children. They traveled that same day as far as Gross Niemtschitz near Nuslau (Nosislav). From there they sent four men to Austerlitz to request the lords to take them in and allow them freedom of conscience.[2] They mentioned

---

[1]The village was Bogenitz (Purkmanice), deserted since 1450.

Dannowitz (Dunajovice), a market town, in 1528 the property of Kanitz Abbey (Himmelsrose) whose provost, Martin Göschl, was at that time living with the Anabaptists at Nikolsburg. In 1574 Dannowitz belonged to the counts von Thurn. Zeman, *Topography*, #30; Beck, 74. About Muschau (Mušov), see below, p.368 n.2.

[2]Austerlitz (Slavkov, originally Nova Sedes; approx. 12 miles east of Brno) existed already in the 13th century. In the 16th century Austerlitz became the property of

1531 (1528)
The lords at Austerlitz allowed the brothers to settle.

several points such as war taxes and other similar things that in the fear of God they were unable to comply with. These lords agreed and were willing to accept them, saying that even if there were a thousand of them, they would take them all in. They sent three wagons to meet them so that they could travel more conveniently.

When they arrived near the town of Austerlitz, the lords gave them a burned out, deserted farmstead to live on, where they lived in the open for three weeks.

During this time the following lords visited them: Lord Jan, Lord Václav, Lord Oldřich, and Lord Petr, the lords of Kounice at Austerlitz, who showed them many kindnesses. The townspeople too were very helpful and asked the brothers whether they intended to build houses.

At the brothers' request, permission was granted for them to build on the potters' market. The lords gave them the wood they needed and in addition freed them from rent, taxes, compulsory labor,[1] and other obligations for six years. All this the brothers accepted thankfully as a blessing from God.

They sent brothers out to other countries.

As the members of the church began to increase in number, their zeal and divine grace moved them to send brothers out to other countries, especially to Tirol.

1529

Georg Blaurock went to Tirol and was executed.

As already mentioned, Georg Blaurock, one of the first three, had left Switzerland with another brother and was proclaiming the Gospel in Tirol. In order to bear fruit for the Lord through his gifts and bring salvation to many, the two brothers traveled in the Gufidaun area, where they were taken prisoner and killed, as has already been told above.

Many executed in Tirol.

After this, as the love of truth was kindled, many were killed in Tirol for their witness to it, especially in the following places: in the district of Gufidaun and at Klausen,

---

the lords of Kounice. The brothers Jan, Václav, Petr, and Oldřich of Kounice, all supporters of the Reformation, were the owners of Austerlitz, where their father Oldřich had given sanctuary to the "Piccards" (Bohemian Brethren) as early as 1511. *ME*, I, 192–193; Beck, 74–75; Zeman, *Topography*, #7. About the name "Piccards," see above, p.36 n.3.

[1]Compulsory labor (German: *Robath* or *Roboth*, from Slavic: *robota* = work) the corvée or unpaid labor due from a feudal vassal to his lord; here, a system that evolved from the earlier, more formal, feudal system.

Brixen, Sterzing, Bozen, Neumarkt, Kaltern, Terlan, on the Kuntersweg; similarly in the Inn Valley, at Steinach, Imst, Petersberg, Stams, Innsbruck, Hall, Schwaz, Rattenberg, Kufstein, and Kitzbühel. In these places a great number of believers witnessed steadfastly to the truth with their blood and were killed by fire, water, or the sword. In spite of all this suffering, the people of God increased from day to day.

1531 (1529)

Around that time a man named Jakob appeared,[1] a hatter by trade, born at Moos in the Puster Valley, half a mile from Bruneck. He accepted the covenant of grace, the covenant of a good conscience in Christian baptism, promising to live in true surrender and to go the way of Jesus. When after a time it was felt that he had abundant gifts from God, he was chosen

Jakob Hutter became a brother.

Jakob Hutter appointed to the service of the Word.

---

[1]Jakob Hutter (also Huter, Hueter, from middle-high German *huot* = hat, a hatter). Very little is known about Jakob Hutter before 1529. His birthplace was Moos, a hamlet just below St. Lorenzen (southwest of Bruneck in the Puster Valley, South Tirol). In the nearby town of Prags (Braies; not Prague, Bohemia) he learned the hatter's trade. Nothing certain is known about when and how he made contact with the spreading Anabaptist movement in South Tirol, nor about the place and date of his baptism. It is probable that he was a partisan of Michael Gaismair (b. between 1485 and 1490, d. April 15, 1532, leader of the Peasant Revolt in Tirol, 1525–1526), and descriptions of his person present a man of military appearance. It is therefore uncertain at what time in his life Jakob Hutter became a nonviolent Anabaptist. Following the failure of Gaismair's armed uprising in South Tirol, it is likely that Jakob Hutter gathered around him some of the surviving partisans and organized Christian community of goods, albeit embryonic, at Welsberg (Monguelfo, approx. 25 miles east of Bruneck) as their spiritual leader. When the Welsberg group was routed in the summer of 1529, Jakob Hutter was among the leaders who managed to escape, possibly just before the time he first appears in this chronicle.

Shortly before Gaismair's assassination, a warrant for Hutter's arrest was issued, dated March 10, 1532, with the following details: "Jakob Hutter of Welsberg, a person with a black beard, who wears a black woolen military coat, a blue doublet, white trousers, and a black hat," *und der ein hackl am arm tregt* (Loserth, *Anabaptismus*, 504; Mecenseffy, *Österreich*, III, 37, #26), or . . . *und der ein harkl am arm treget* (Hans Fischer, *Jakob Huter: Leben, Froemmigkeit, Briefe*, Newton, KS, 1956, 28), an expression that could be variously understood to mean that he had a birthmark on his arm or that he was carrying a hand gun or other weapon. One source specifies: . . . *so ein Püchsen tragen soll*, ". . . who is said to be carrying a gun" (Fischer, 29).

See Johann Loserth, "Hutter, Jakob," *ME*, II, 851–854; Mecenseffy, *Österreich*, II, 238, 263–265, 278; Beck, 84; Williams, *Radical Reformation*, 418–419; Leonard Gross, "Jakob Hutter," Goertz, ed., *Profiles*, 158–167; Fischer, *Jakob Huter; Allgemeine Deutsche Biographie* (56 Vols., Leipzig, 1875–1910), XIII, 460, which mistakenly gives Welsberg as Hutter's birthplace. About Michael Gaismair, see Josef Macek, *Der Tiroler Bauernkrieg und Michael Gaismair* (Berlin, 1965); Walter Klaassen, *Michael Gaismair, Revolutionary and Reformer* (Leiden, 1978); about Gaismair and Jakob Hutter, see Aldo Stella, *Genesi del comunismo evangelico hutterita: Storiografia e nuove interpretazioni*, reprint from *L'uomo e la storia: Studi storici in onore di Massimo Petrocchi* (Rome, 1983), 207–228.

1531 (1529)

for and confirmed in the service of the Gospel. Now the church in Tirol learned that at Austerlitz, in the Margravate of Moravia, God had gathered a people in his name to live as one heart, mind, and soul, each caring faithfully for the other. So they were moved to send Jakob Hutter with Simon Schützinger and some companions to the church at Austerlitz to make inquiries about all that had taken place.

After the church in Tirol had taken leave of them and commended them to the care of God, they went to Austerlitz. There they talked everything over thoroughly with the elders of the church, as the church in Tirol had said they should.

Jakob Hutter and Schützinger came to Moravia and united with the brothers at Austerlitz.

They found that both groups were of one heart and soul in serving and fearing God. Thereupon Jakob and Simon and their companions, in the name of the whole church, united in peace with the church at Austerlitz.

As they had now accomplished their mission and brought to a happy conclusion all that had been entrusted to them, they wished to report all this to their own people, so Jakob and Simon with their companions prepared for the road again.

Jakob Hutter returned to Tirol.

They were worthily sent off by the community at Austerlitz with peaceful hearts and in unity of spirit, commended to God and his grace for their return home.

Many brothers executed in Upper Austria.

Peter Riedemann arrested at Gmunden.

He was 23 years old.

In this year of 1529 many brothers were arrested in Upper Austria, and some were executed. Among those arrested was Peter Riedemann, born at Hirschberg in Silesia, a cobbler by trade, who was taken prisoner at Gmunden on St. Andrew's Eve [Nov. 29] in 1529. Although he was tortured through many and various means almost to the point of death, he remained faithful. Finally, after having lain in prison for over three years, he was freed by the providence of God.

Jakob Wiedemann and his assistants.

The most prominent teacher in the church at Austerlitz was Jakob Wiedemann, also known as one-eyed Jakob. His assistants were Franz Intzinger, Jakob Mändel, Kilian [Volckamer], and others, all appointed to the service of the Word at Austerlitz.

When Jakob Hutter was sent back to the believers in the mountains of Tirol, as just described, he joyfully told them about the community of saints he had seen and experienced at Austerlitz. He told how, in the name of them all, he had united with those at Austerlitz in peace and unity of soul and spirit and how they had sent him on his way home to Tirol in peace. God had opened the way for them with his blessing and care. The whole community was full of joy, giving praise and thanks to God with all their hearts.

1531 (1529)

At this time quite a few brothers were living at Böhmisch Krumau,[1] with Hans Fasser as their servant or elder. These had formed a group to express their unity in the Spirit. Their hearts were moved when they heard of the uniting between Jakob Hutter and the church at Austerlitz. All created things show that like cleaves to like, so they too enthusiastically sought out those who shared their beliefs and wanted to become one with them in Christ. They united with them in seeking a more perfect life. They were about eighty or ninety persons, among them Hans Amon,[2] Leonhard Lanzenstiel,[3] and Christoph Gschäl. All of them remained in the church at Austerlitz except their servant, Hans Fasser, who returned to Bohemia, making it appear that he had reason to do so. But he was caught in shameful fornication and was later severely disciplined by the church, excluded,[4] and delivered up to Satan.

Brothers at Böhmisch Krumau.

Ecclus. 13:15–16

Hans Amon, Leonhard Lanzenstiel, Christoph Gschäl, and 80 or 90 others came to Austerlitz.

1 Cor. 5:5
1 Tim. 1:20

Later on, since there was no place available in Tirol because of the excessive oppression, Jakob Hutter, with Simon Schützinger, sent people to the church at Austerlitz. He sent a servant of the Word, Georg Zaunring by name, along with

Jakob Hutter sent his brothers down to Moravia, Georg Zaunring with them.

---

[1]Böhmisch Krumau (Český Krumlov), in southern Bohemia; see Zeman, *Topography*, #68; *ME*, I, 382c, "Bohemia"; Beck, 86–87.

[2]Hans Amon, called Tuchmacher (cloth weaver), a native of Bavaria, worked with Jakob Hutter in Tirol 1530–1534 and succeeded him as shepherd of the church at Auspitz after Hutter's death, February 25, 1536. Amon died in 1542 at Schakwitz (Šakvice), Moravia; see below, pp. 213–214. Beck, 86–87.

[3]Leonhard Lanzenstiel, also called Seiler (rope maker), was born in Bavaria. He joined the Anabaptist movement and was sent out on mission to Meran in the Adige Valley and from there to Switzerland. Although closely watched, he managed to evade his pursuers until, on a mission journey in 1536, Lanzenstiel and Georg Fasser were captured and imprisoned at Mödling (near Vienna); see below, p. 153.

In 1539 Lanzenstiel was appointed to the service of the Word, and in 1542 he succeeded Hans Amon as shepherd of the church until his death in 1565; see below, pp. 186, 214, 385.

For his letters from prison, written together with Georg Fasser, see below, p. 153 n. 1. Lanzenstiel also compiled the "Schuster-Ordnung" (Shoemakers' Discipline) of 1562. See also *ME*, III, 292–294; Williams, *Radical Reformation*, 670–672; Friedmann, *Schriften*, 120–121.

[4]For the meaning of exclusion, see *Peter Riedemann, Confession of Faith: Account of Our Religion, Doctrine, and Faith* (Rifton, NY, 1974), 131–133; Harold S. Bender, "Excommunication, Procedure and Grounds," *ME*, II, 277–279.

1531 (1529)

them, and afterward he sent one small group after another with all their belongings to live in community with the believers.

Wilhelm Reublin.

At this time a man named Wilhelm Reublin came to Austerlitz, claiming to be a teacher or servant, but as nothing was known about him, he was not permitted to teach.[1]

1 Pet. 5:8

Meanwhile the devil—who does not rest but prowls around the house of God like a roaring lion, seeking every opportunity to cause division, destroy the unity of spirit, and stamp out what God gives—made an attack at the critical place, namely, at the elders of the church, who were responsible for the whole life of the people, as the devout Judith testifies in her book.

At that time they had no place where everyone could meet to hear the teachings, because it was winter and extremely cold. Therefore they decided to hold their meetings in three places, and for each place a particular servant was appointed to teach, exhort, and comfort his little flock.

The servants' teachings differed.

Their teachings differed, however. One taught this and another taught something different. One of them declared among other things that Christ had been a citizen of Capernaum and that therefore as citizens it was permissible to do civilian duties and swear oaths. Besides this, Jakob Wiedemann told several young sisters that if they would not follow his suggestions about marriage, he would have to give heathen wives to the brothers. He and some of his assistants alarmed the sisters with strange questions and gave them texts to learn. Those who could remember the texts and answer the questions clearly were highly praised, but the simple, unassuming sisters, although faithful and devout, were ridiculed and put to shame.

Jakob Wiedemann acted unwisely at Austerlitž.

Actions of Franz Intzinger and Jakob Mändel not in order.

As there were so many people and their number increased daily, they were not all able to live in one house. Some of the servants who had learned more than one language—Franz Intzinger, Jakob Mändel, among others—came to think highly of themselves and supplied food and drink to one another, which was not in order. As is generally known, arrogance goes before destruction and pride goes before a fall. In that spirit some self-seeking members who had kept money in their pockets went to market to buy what they liked for themselves.

Prov. 16:18

Some selfish and greedy.

[1]Wilhelm Reublin (also Räbel, Röubli), came from Rottenburg on the Neckar River, Germany. See *ME*, IV, 304–307; Beck, 86; Williams, *Radical Reformation*, 419; Goertz, *Profiles*, 107–117.

All these disorders, and more, were noticed by those who fought against avarice, and this caused a great deal of complaint among the people. Especially those from Tirol complained about the teachings and said they were not as comforting and instructive as they had been at home. Similarly, many were troubled and complained about church discipline and the children's education, saying that in these and related matters not nearly enough was done. *1531 (1529)*

They reported these things to their particular servant, Georg Zaunring, who also became very disturbed about it and began discussing it with some of his assistants and servants, who all agreed with him, especially Burkhard [Braun] of Ofen, Bohemian David of Schweidnitz, and Adam Schlegel.

1530

Early in 1530 Wilhelm Reublin began reading rather loudly one evening in one of the rooms. When people gathered around him to listen, he also expounded the Scriptures to them, although he had not been given the authority to teach. God cannot bear disorder in his church, so he seeks ways to change it even through unredeemed men, as we can see in this and other cases.

Wilhelm Reublin spoke against the offenses among the servants in Austerlitz.

Wilhelm Reublin began to speak openly in the church against all the offenses committed by the servants. As Jakob Wiedemann, who was entrusted with the care of the whole church, was not at home, his assistants sent messengers to him without delay. As soon as he came, he summoned all the elders, from wherever they lived, and placed the whole matter before them in the presence of Georg Zaunring and the other servants who supported him. This took place in private at first. Reublin, however, persisted in what he had said and by scriptural proof tried to convince Jakob Wiedemann and all his followers that they were neither teaching nor standing rightly. Jakob Wiedemann and his supporters did not accept this but called the church together. He told the people how, in his absence, Reublin had pushed himself forward, teaching things that were opposed to what Jakob and his assistants taught, which could not be tolerated. At the end of a long speech that Jakob made before the church, he said that whoever acknowledged his teaching to be right and had changed his

Division between the servants at Austerlitz.

1531 (1530)

life through it should come and stand next to him.

Wilhelm Reublin then asked them, for the sake of God, to give him a chance to answer. Likewise Georg Zaunring, Bohemian David, Burkhard of Ofen, and Adam Schlegel unanimously requested all the people to hear Reublin's reply, since they had heard Jakob Wiedemann's charges. The church could then decide which side was right and which was wrong, as would only be fair before God and man. But their request was rejected outright.

Jakob Wiedemann refused to hear the other side.

Now most of the people went over to Jakob Wiedemann's side, many of them without knowing why, since not all of them had heard Jakob's accusations. About forty or fifty persons remained standing with Zaunring and Reublin, eager to hear Reublin's reply in order to be fair. But the others would not give in.

Zaunring and Reublin with 40 or 50 people stood apart.

Thereupon Jakob Wiedemann called several of his followers and sent them to Georg Zaunring to inquire why they had gone over to the other side. They replied that, having heard Jakob Wiedemann's accusation against Reublin, their request now as before was for God's sake to let Reublin's answer be heard as well. This would enable the church to decide what was right before God, for no one should judge a matter that had not been given a hearing. But, as before, this was unjustly refused them. In other words, they attacked the flock with their horns.

Jakob Wiedemann refused to let the other side be heard.

Jakob Wiedemann warned his people that they should have nothing to do with the others. As a result, many who had previously followed Wiedemann now felt impelled to go over to Zaunring and Reublin. When the time came for Jakob Wiedemann's people to be called to a meal, the others were treated as though they were excluded. They had handed in what little they had, and if there had been fairness, they would have been glad to remain. But they had to leave empty-handed.

Zaunring and Reublin and their people gathered outside the house, sick at heart. Reublin shook the dust from his shoes as a testimony against the high-handed action of Jakob Wiedemann and all who stayed with him. Then they set out, first finding lodging for their children and sick people in the town and leaving a servant, Burkhard of Ofen, to care for them and comfort them.

Zaunring with 150 people moved from Austerlitz to Auspitz.

Zaunring and his assistants, with about 150 other people,

made ready to move to Auspitz. Once outside the city of Austerlitz, the servants named above spoke very earnestly to the people, saying that whoever wanted to go with them should be ready, with them, to face the poverty of Christ and possibly even death. All the money they had between them amounted to only a farthing per person. Therefore anyone who did not feel the courage to suffer hunger, great need, misery, and poverty for the sake of truth should rather return to the city or to his home. But all of them wanted to dare it, trusting in God. Not one turned back.

1531 (1530)

They were very poor.

It was in this way that God again brought about a purification, separating the true believers from the unbelievers. Those who remained with Jakob Wiedemann are therefore still known today as the Austerlitz Brethren.[1]

Origin of the name Austerlitz Brethren.

1531

All those who set out with Zaunring succeeded in reaching Auspitz as planned, although they traveled in great dread of highwaymen. They were housed and given refuge by the people there but had to suffer great need and hunger, for they were quite ignorant of the country and the work in the vineyards. Besides this, they had no provisions and often had to be content with water and a small piece of bread for a whole day, doing hard work. Yet they still cared for the sick and the children so far as they were able with their humble means. They brought their people from Austerlitz and lodged them at Steurowitz,

Poverty.

They lodged some of their people at Steurowitz.

---

[1]The split took place on January 8, 1531. On January 26 Reublin wrote a full account about it to his friend, the Tirolean Pilgram Marpeck, at Strasbourg (*ME*, III, 494); see J. C. Wenger, tr./ed., "Letter from Wilhelm Reublin to Pilgram Marpeck, 1531," *MQR*, Apr. 1949, 67–75. See also Williams, *Radical Reformation*, 419–420; Beck, 94–96. Several of the "Austerlitz Brethren," including Jakob Wiedemann, were executed in Vienna in 1536.

When the Austerlitz group was expelled from Moravia in 1535/1536 along with the Hutterian and Rossitz groups, some of them moved to Slovakia. Some, under the leadership of Ulrich Stadler, moved to Kraśnik, southwest of Lublin, Poland. A small remnant remained in the Butschowitz area. In 1536, according to this chronicle, Stadler's group and the "Austerlitz Brethren" from Slovakia united with the Hutterites. In 1537, after six elders (Hans Wucherer, Hans Hueter, etc.; see below, pp.160–161) from the Austerlitz group had joined the Hutterites, the latter started moving back to Austerlitz, at first living in Hans Hueter's house. By the time they built up their own community at Austerlitz in 1538, theirs was the only major Anabaptist group there. The former "Austerlitz Brethren" were by and large dispersed or had joined the Hutterites.

See also entry for 1536, pp.155–160.

1531

Were robbed.

half a mile away from Auspitz, hoping they would be safe there. But soon robbers came by night, took all they had, and beat some brothers so severely that one of them died. "Deep called to deep,"[1] which demanded great endurance on the part of the saints.

Were deceived.

There was a man named Kaspar who had a house at Auspitz. Some time previously he had come from the community at Austerlitz. He pretended to have a repentant heart and a wish to reunite with Zaunring and his people; but he went about with a false and deceitful front. He took the brothers into his home, pretending to be happy to give them lodging. He let them work in his vineyard with scarcely any food, until the time the vintage was gathered in. Then he revealed his treachery, gave up the idea of brotherhood, and ordered them out of his house empty-handed.

They bought a house at Auspitz.

Educated their children.

Throughout these hardships the believers cared faithfully for the weak and needy, supplying their needs. They brought them to Auspitz, where they had purchased a house near the horse market by agreement with the nuns at Brünn, who owned the land and lent them money. They began to gather in this house and to care for their children, with a God-fearing brother and several sisters to educate them in the discipline and ways of the Lord; but at night the children slept with their parents.

The church in Tirol received from both sides a report about the separation.

At this time two brothers from Auspitz, Hans Amon and a companion, and two from Austerlitz were sent to Tirol to report to the church about the division that had taken place. These four asked the church in Tirol to send brothers to look into the matter.

Ps.1:5

Wilhelm Reublin, too, proved unfit.

At that time, because God wished to purify his people and because sinners cannot remain in the church of the righteous, it happened that a servant of a little group in Swabia arrived in Auspitz to inquire about the faith, Ordnung, and teaching of the church of God. He spoke with Wilhelm Reublin about various articles of faith, but as they could not agree on one point, this servant from Swabia did not want to stay. The other brothers and elders asked him why he was leaving. When he told them how Reublin had explained one of the articles, the elders said, "But that is not the position of the church," and

[1] "How deep I am sunk in misery, groaning in my distress: . . . deep calls to deep in the roar of thy cataracts, and all thy waves, all thy breakers, pass over me" (Ps.42:5–7; NEB).

suggested that perhaps he had misunderstood. But the man insisted that that was how he had heard it from their teacher Reublin. The elders asked Reublin, but he denied it. The man from Swabia, however, still insisted on what he had said before and called upon God as witness. Reublin was severely admonished, but he, too, called on God as his witness. Finally others who had also heard him proved him wrong, and he had to admit his guilt and confess that he had spoken as the man had testified. The elders told Reublin that the matter was too serious for them to close. *1531*

Soon after, Reublin became extremely ill. Without the knowledge of the elders and the church and regardless of the great hunger among the people, he had hidden twenty-four gulden that he had brought with him from his home. In his illness he entrusted this money to a married sister named Katharina Loy, who immediately reported it. This made it even harder for the elders to close the matter.

Wilhelm Reublin was a miser and deceiver.

Around this time Jakob Hutter and Simon Schützinger arrived from Tirol. They examined Reublin's situation carefully and summoned him before the church. He was excluded as an unfaithful, malicious Ananias. He himself admitted that such a judgment was right.

Jakob Hutter came from Tirol.

Wilhelm Reublin excluded.

Jakob Hutter and Simon Schützinger had been asked by the communities at Austerlitz and Auspitz to go into the matter of the division and to administer discipline. They examined the matter thoroughly and considered it in the fear of God. They found those at Austerlitz most guilty, but when Jakob admonished them, they would not listen to him. Yet he showed them their error and rebuked them for their lack of discernment: In the first place they had acted unjustly in expelling the innocent; second, they had allowed freedom of the flesh, resulting in a return to private property; third, there had been marriages with unbelievers; and there were many similar points.

Jakob Hutter inquired into the division at Austerlitz.

The brothers at Austerlitz at fault.

No warning or punishment helped, however. One freedom of the flesh led to another, as the false teaching in their printed statement of faith still proves. It was impossible to distinguish them from worldly people. Although they still claimed to hold to their first calling, their lives showed next to nothing of it. But in a wonderful way the Lord gradually brought back to the church those at Austerlitz who were still devout, as will be recorded later.

1531

Jakob Hutter returned to Tirol.

When Jakob Hutter and Simon Schützinger had brought this matter to a satisfactory conclusion, as they had been asked to do, they entrusted the church to Georg Zaunring. Both of them were commended to the grace of God, and they set out for the church in Tirol, where God had been powerfully at work.

Matt.5:29–30

Adam Schlegel and Burkhard of Ofen excluded.

Around the middle of 1531 other things happened. Since God always seeks to advance the work he has begun, he was resolved to build up and purify his church. It will be told below how he gave his people, whom he called the salt of the earth, such zeal that they would not spare the eyes, hands, or feet that were hurting the body of Christ. Their servant Adam Schlegel misled some members into licentiousness and behaved in a scandalous manner. As soon as this was revealed, he was disciplined, his service was taken from him, and he was forbidden to teach. Others sided with him, including another servant, Burkhard of Ofen. These two looked for every excuse to find fault with the church (as people do who want to abandon their friends), but there was nothing they could truthfully bring forward. So both of them were excluded from the church as opponents of the truth.

Bohemian David excluded.

It also became clear that Bohemian David was not honest. Without the knowledge of the brothers, he had paid the judge at Nikoltschitz[1] for an escort to protect them from robbers on the way from Austerlitz to Auspitz. He was admonished for his faults in a brotherly way but was unable to honor God humbly, persisting in his own opinion. So he was disciplined before the whole church because of his stubbornness.

God, wanting to put his people to a severe test to find out whether they relied on him or on men, caused a great deal of talk and complaining to break out in the church. It came to light that Bohemian David and Georg Zaunring had agreed to settle in secret a corrupt matter which should have come before the whole church: Thomas Lindl had committed adultery with Georg Zaunring's wife, so David and Georg excluded them. Georg did separate himself from his wife during her exclusion, but as soon as David and Georg proclaimed the forgiveness of sin, Georg took back his wife. When it became known, the brotherhood could not accept such light punishment of

[1]Nikoltschitz (Nikolčice) near Auspitz (Hustopeče), Moravia.

1531
Matt.5:27–30
18:8–9
Mark 9:43–47

adultery, for according to the Word of the Lord it is better to enter the kingdom of God with one eye or as a cripple than to go to hell with corrupt members.

1 Cor.6:15

Georg Zaunring excluded.

The church had no servants.

It was Leonhard Schmerbacher, a servant for temporal affairs, who brought the matter before the church and told what Georg Zaunring had done. The whole church agreed unanimously that members of Christ should not be members of a harlot and therefore Zaunring and his wife should be excluded and separated from the church. Now the church was without a shepherd, teacher, or servant of the Word, but they were zealous for the truth, punishing wrong without regard of persons.

The servants for temporal affairs, with the whole church, immediately let those in Tirol know of their need by letter and word of mouth. They made a heartfelt plea for a servant to be sent to care for them with the Word of the Lord.

Jakob Hutter and Simon Schützinger sent from Tirol.

The church was entrusted to Schützinger.

Jakob Hutter and Simon Schützinger were sent off immediately, arriving at Auspitz around Easter. They consoled the church and praised them for acting so zealously against wrong, which pleased Jakob, although he said he wished it had not been necessary; but he was satisfied that everything had been handled in the right way. Simon Schützinger was appointed shepherd of the church in place of Georg Zaunring.

Gabriel and Philip united with us.

Jakob and Simon soon united with Gabriel Ascherham and Philip Blauärmel and their people at Rossitz and Auspitz. From now on the three groups were no longer to act separately in difficult matters but to seek each other's counsel as befits a united people.

Jakob Hutter returned to Tirol.

Since all the needs of the church had been seen to and all disorder put right, Jakob Hutter returned once more to the church in Tirol. Simon, Gabriel, and Philip looked after the three communities together, yet each remained at his own place with his community.[1]

Zaunring admitted his sin and said many times that his heartfelt wish was to change. He was taken back into the

---

[1]There were two communities at Auspitz (the Philippites and the Hutterites) and one at Rossitz (the Gabrielites), approx. 25 miles away; Beck, 102. The three communities lived in harmony for about two years, but in 1533 there was a painful division; see below, pp.98–110; *ME*, I, 174–175; Robert Friedmann, "The Philippite Brethren: A Chapter in Anabaptist History," *MQR*, Oct. 1958, 272–297; W. Wiswedel, "Gabriel Ascherham und die nach ihm benannte Bewegung," *Archiv für Reformations-Geschichte*, XXXIV (1937).

1531
Georg Zaunring repented, was reaccepted, became a servant again, and was executed in Franconia.

church with intercession to the Lord on his behalf. As his whole life continued upright, he was again entrusted with the service of the Gospel and later sent to Franconia. Not far from Bamberg, he was executed with the sword for the sake of divine truth.[1]

During this time the number of people in the church increased daily at all three places. From Silesia they came to Rossitz, from Swabia and the Palatinate they joined Philip's group, and Jakob Hutter sent many from Tirol to Schützinger. So the work of the Lord spread more and more.

1532

Soldiers robbed the church.

In 1532 a profane mob of soldiers on their way from Prague in Bohemia to Hungary attacked the faithful. At Rossitz they plundered Gabriel's people, using violence and making a lot of noise. Then they came to Auspitz, where they attacked Schützinger's people and carried off all they could. The brothers and sisters had to stand by and watch helplessly. The wanton rabble treated the elders of the church outrageously. They wanted money, but as there was very little, they beat the brothers and tore off their clothes. Then they turned on the sisters and neither respected nor spared their womanhood. In the middle of their attack, they found a little money in a small earthenware pot. But God, who hates robbery, caused them to fight over this small sum, each one hoping to get a large amount. During the struggle one of them shot and killed a fellow soldier. As Job says, robbery was "turned into the gall of asps within him." The soldiers were so shocked that they ran away. Although they attacked Philip's people too, they did not do as much harm there. The faithful left all vengeance to God, the righteous Judge, who rewards each one according to his deeds.

Peter Riedemann, a servant, came from imprisonment in Upper Austria.

Toward the end of 1532 a servant of the Word, Peter Riedemann, a native of Hirschberg in Silesia, came from Upper Austria. For more than three years he had been in prison there at Gmunden, subjected to great pain, hunger, and mistreatment. But he persevered in his faith and was released.

---

[1]For Georg Zaunring's story, see above, pp.85 ff.; *ME*, IV, 1018–1019; Beck, 91–102; *Martyrs Mirror*, 440.

Six brothers were imprisoned for the sake of divine truth at Sterzing in the Adige region in that year, 1532: Lamprecht Gruber, Hans Beck, Lorenz Schuster, Peter Planer, Peter [Hungerl] his manservant, and Hans Taler. They were cruelly tortured and stretched on the rack to make them recant, but they remained steadfast and were condemned to death and executed. All six witnessed valiantly to the truth of God with their blood. We still have letters they wrote to the church from prison.[1] *1532*

Kuntz Fichter and several others executed at Sterzing in the Adige region.

Brother Kuntz Fichter[2] was also captured in the same year at Sterzing for the sake of divine truth. He was tortured and stretched on the rack until even the ungodly executioners and the sons of Pilate thought he could not endure it. Several believers in Christ imprisoned with him had to go through great testing. Monks, priests, and others cunningly tried to get the better of them, using Bible quotations falsely. They tempted them by speaking to them of their homes, their wives and children, and life itself. When they could not make them deviate from the truth, they sentenced them and murdered them. The brothers gave steadfast testimony with their blood. A long letter Kuntz Fichter wrote to the church from prison is still in existence.

---

[1]Three letters are known: to the elders of the church; to the servants of God in the Adige region; and to the whole church, written at Sterzing (Vipiteno), 1532; see Friedmann, *Schriften*, 108, "Brüder, b)." See also Loserth, *Anabaptismus*, 505; Beck, 105–106; *Martyrs Mirror*, 440; *ME*, II, 602, "Lamprecht Gruber."

[2]About Kuntz (Konrad) Fichter, see *ME*, II, 327; Beck, 106; *Martyrs Mirror*, 441.

1533–1536: Jakob Hutter and the Emerging Brotherhood

1533

After Georg Zaunring was martyred in 1533, the church sent Peter Riedemann, a servant of the Lord, into Franconia. He and his companion Six Braitfus were soon captured and taken to Nuremberg. Braitfus was whipped out of town, but Peter was detained for over four years. The Nuremberg people and their priests tormented him and worked on him a great deal, but the Lord stood by him and after a long time delivered him from their hands, as will be recorded later.[1]

Peter Riedemann, a servant, sent to Franconia.

Imprisoned in Nuremberg for 4 years.

Brother Ludwig Fest,[2] a steadfast witness, was taken prisoner at Schwaz in the Inn Valley in 1533 and was executed because of his valiant testimony to Jesus Christ. He shed his blood for the sake of divine truth. We still have an epistle he wrote.

Ludwig Fest was executed at Schwaz.

Also in this year, seven brothers were arrested at Gufidaun in the Adige Valley. They were: Hans Beck, Walser Schneider, Christian Alseider, Waltan Gsäl, Wolf of Götzenberg,[3] Hans Maurer of Flaas,[4] and Peter Kranewetter. The many attempts

7 brothers executed at Gufidaun in the Adige Valley.

---

[1]About Peter Riedemann, see Robert Friedmann, "Peter Riedemann: Early Anabaptist Leader," *MQR*, Jan. 1970, 5–44; Williams, *Radical Reformation*, 426–429; *ME*, IV, 326–328; Beck, 40–41. He was released from prison on July 14, 1537; see below, p.163.

[2]Ludwig Fest from Pinegg north of Brandenberg, northern Tirol, had won people for the faith in the mines at Schwaz and elsewhere. He was arrested in the Freundsberg area and beheaded on July 3, 1533. For his letter to the church of God at Rattenberg on the Inn River, see Zieglschmid, "Unpublished Letters," *MQR*, Jan. 1941, 23–25. See also *ME*, II, 327; Beck, 107; *Martyrs Mirror*, 441; Loserth, *Anabaptismus*, 509.

[3]Götzenberg, a mountain near Niedervintl, district of Bruneck, formerly under the district court of Schöneck, Tirol.

[4]Flaas, a village about 8 miles north of Bozen (Bolzano).

1533

to make them waver and fall were unsuccessful, and the brothers remained steadfast in witnessing to the true faith. They were condemned to death by the sons of Pilate, who ordered their high priest the executioner to carry out the sentence. The brothers remained courageous and joyful, telling the people the divine truth and urging them to repent. They had written several letters from prison. In their last letter they indicated that Wolf had wavered and stumbled, but the other six brothers were determined to remain faithful unto death.[1] They invited Jakob Hutter and Hans Amon to be witnesses at their wedding feast. They bravely testified to the truth with their blood here in Gufidaun in the Adige Valley.

This Wolf was steadfast at the end and executed with the others.

Jakob Hutter was in the mountains of Tirol, proclaiming the Lord's Word and doing the Lord's work. He traveled around, visiting those who were eager to hear the truth, helping them, and setting them on the right path. He sent one group after another down to Schützinger in Auspitz since the intense persecution made it impossible for them to remain in Tirol. Everywhere they were spied on and betrayed, hunted down, and seized by the constables.[2]

Jakob Hutter came from Tirol with his people.

Not long afterward, Jakob Hutter, too, came to Auspitz with several others, arriving on August 11, 1533. The elders and the whole church welcomed him with great joy, and he himself

---

[1]Two letters from the brothers in prison are contained in Codex Hab. 17, fol. 686ff., and Codex Hab. 9, fol. 92, at the Bratislava City Archives. The first is addressed to Jakob Hutter and the church in Moravia, the second to the church of God in the Adige region. The latter mentions among other things that brother Wolf had stumbled. Faced with interrogation under torture, he had begged for mercy and promised to recant but then admitted he had done wrong. A postscript notes, "The waverer is keeping up his courage." Beck, 108–109; *Martyrs Mirror*, 444–445; Friedmann, *Schriften*, 108, "Brüder, c)."

[2]1533 was the time of the most intense persecution for the brothers in Tirol. Officials at Welsberg, Gufidaun, Michelsburg (not Michelsberg), and other places were untiring in their efforts to capture the brothers and pass speedy sentence. On Corpus Christi Day (Thursday following the first Sunday after Pentecost), 1533, the brothers in the Gufidaun district consulted as to how to get their followers to Moravia, "for in the whole country they no longer have a place of refuge anywhere." In July 1533 a group of brothers and sisters with twenty-five children left the Gufidaun district for Moravia and managed to reach their goal, even though the officials at Schwaz and Rattenberg had every path watched. Loserth, *Anabaptismus*, 498–521; Hartmann Ammann, "Die Wiedertäufer in Michelsburg im Pusterthale und deren Urgichten," *Programm des k.k. Gymnasiums zu Brixen*, XLVI (Brixen, 1896), 3–52; *ME*, II, 608–609, "Gufidaun"; *ME*, III, 668–670, "Michelsburg"; Ernst Correll, "Anabaptism in the Tyrol," *MQR*, Oct. 1972, 49–60.

1533

rejoiced from his heart that God had led him safely to them. He told Simon Schützinger and the other elders and brothers and sisters that he had not come to strangers but to his dear brothers, his little children. Schützinger and all the others echoed his words, asking Jakob to help them care for the people, and he promised to do so. Jakob had also brought them a temporal gift, a sweet sacrifice, a small sum of money to repay the nuns of Brünn (who owned the land at Auspitz) for their help in a time of need.[1]

Jakob Hutter passed on the greetings from those in Tirol and gave an account.

On the following Sunday, Jakob Hutter shared news of the church in distant lands, telling of the believers he had left behind in Tirol, who were suffering harsh persecution. He delivered their greetings and told about the wonderful deeds God had worked in spite of many tribulations. Then he announced publicly that he had heard there were some in Auspitz who hoped that when he came he would move with them to a different place. As far as he knew he had challenged and admonished all of them, making it clear that he had no such intentions. But he would help punish according to God's Word any fickle, selfish people who still wanted to go somewhere else. And since God had sent him to the church, he would put all his efforts into overcoming any faults he found in the house of God.

Jakob Hutter intended to correct all faults that came to light.

Now I want to tell further what happened in the church: the enemy always mixes weeds among the wheat; the Lord humbles the mighty; and nothing is so hidden that it will not be revealed. Each one can judge for himself from the following account how God separated the devout from the hypocrites. But this is how it began.

As reported above, Simon Schützinger and the elders had asked Jakob Hutter to help them care for the people, so a few days later Jakob was about to start improving certain things in the church. But Schützinger resisted and tried to stop him. Then Jakob wanted to know if he was wanted as a shepherd or not. He felt that he could not remain silent and fail to exercise his service. If he was not needed, he would move on and serve wherever the Lord led him. So he went to Rossitz and explained the situation to Gabriel [Ascherham], saying he

Simon Schützinger opposed Jakob Hutter.

[1]At that time the abbess of Queen's Cloister at Old Brünn held the estates at Auspitz and Gross Steurowitz, where the Anabaptists had settled. Beck, 103–104; Zeman, *Topography*, #146c.

1533

did not know whether the people wanted him or not. He said he was willing to bring the matter before the church and do whatever the people of God asked of him. Gabriel agreed but said, "Do it humbly."

While Jakob was at Rossitz, Schützinger spoke with the two servants for temporal affairs, Leonhard Schmerbacher and Wilhelm Griesbacher. He said he intended to continue in his service and not give Jakob much chance to speak. The two brothers were not in agreement but said he should remain in his service and Jakob should serve with him. But Simon did not want this.

Simon Schützinger did not want Jakob Hutter as assistant.

When Jakob returned home from Rossitz and wished to pass on greetings from Gabriel and his community to the church, Schützinger forbade it. He admonished Jakob and asked him what he was trying to do. Thus Schützinger revealed his own intentions against Jakob.

Jakob Hutter wanted to know whether the church needed him or not.

In reply Jakob told Schützinger and the elders, including Kaspar, a servant from Rossitz, that he wanted to know whether or not the church needed him. To sit around and not fulfill his service was something he was not free to do, and he would not know how to answer for it before God. Simon answered that through the drawing of lots God had entrusted this people to him and made him their shepherd and therefore he intended to continue in this service. If Jakob had anything to say, he should do so briefly, for he could not allow him to speak very long. Even though the elders who were present opposed him, he insisted on being the one to teach the people. The elders, including Kaspar from Rossitz, said they should both care for the people together, but still Simon wanted to be the only shepherd.

The elders wished to gather the church the very next day but had to postpone the meeting until Sunday, because a number of brothers were away. Meanwhile Simon sent to Rossitz for Gabriel, who set out immediately but stopped in at Philip's community.[1] Simon Schützinger joined them and complained to Gabriel and Philip that Jakob was pushing to be a shepherd over the church. So they sent for Jakob, who came without knowing what they wanted. Later in the night, Kaspar from Rossitz, Leonhard Schmerbacher, and Wilhelm

[1] Also at Auspitz; see above, p.93 n.

1533
Gabriel, Philip, and Schützinger against Jakob Hutter.

Griesbacher were also called. When they arrived, Gabriel accused Jakob of putting himself above Simon Schützinger in the shepherd's service. Jakob said that it was not so; he only wished to serve the church. "I have been sent here after earnest prayer to God. The people have been entrusted to me and to Schützinger. All I ask is to be able to continue in my service."

Philip retorted, "If you want to do that, Jakob, then you are the most wicked devil who has ever come into this country."

But Jakob stood firm, adding, "How would you feel if you had gone on a journey, entrusting the people to someone else, and then had to stand back when you returned home?"

After much talking, Philip said Jakob and Simon should work together, faithfully caring for the people, "Just as Blasi [Blasius Kuhn] and I do."

When he asked Jakob what he thought of that, Jakob replied, "I want nothing more than to serve with Schützinger. May God be praised."

Then Gabriel said, "No, I don't see it that way. I command you, Simon, to continue in your service as shepherd to this people. If you now were to lose courage for your service and allow it to be weakened because Jakob is more gifted and a better speaker than you, God would punish you. The same would happen to you as happened to me with the Swiss Brethren."

See the story of the thorn bush, Judges 9.

Simon quickly replied, "Yes, yes, my brother. Praise the Lord! It is true, my brother Gabriel, it is true!"

Leonhard Schmerbacher objected, "But Philip said first that both should care for the people together, and now Gabriel says something quite different."

Philip untruthful.

Philip replied, "I feel exactly like Gabriel. Even though what I said may have sounded otherwise, that is what I meant in my heart." After much talking (which does not need to be recorded here) Jakob again desired to hear what the church felt about him. This they could not refuse, but they told him to be willing to adapt himself and not push himself forward.

Jakob Hutter spoke to the church, saying what his task was.

On the following Sunday Jakob spoke to the gathered church, explaining the reason for his coming and that for a time he had had to stop the work God had entrusted to him. With restraint he told about his talks with the elders and with Simon, Gabriel, and Philip.

Simon Schützinger spoke to the church.

Then Simon spoke, reminding the people of his election

1533
Gabriel spoke to the church.

and saying that he was going to stand by it. Gabriel supported him in a long speech, describing how Simon had originally been chosen by lot. However, if they were going to insult him and preferred Jakob because he was a better speaker, or if they placed Simon and Jakob in the service together, then he, Gabriel, would have no part in it and would go back by the road he had come. He pointed out that in Jerusalem there was only one shepherd, namely James. Here Jakob contradicted him.

Nothing could stop Gabriel. He warned the people, using the terrible example of Korah: if they looked down on Simon's simplicity and preferred Jakob's fine speaking, God would punish them as he did Korah and his company. He warned the people to guard against making an idol of Jakob, who to him seemed proud and arrogant. After many words, he declared that Jakob did not have the gifts to serve the people as a shepherd but only as an apostle.[1]

The church was then asked to make a decision. Two or three spoke to the effect that Simon should continue in his service and Jakob should assist him. But Peter Hueter said that to him neither seemed higher or lower, greater or smaller; one seemed to him as good as the other. Schützinger cut him short, calling him a stupid man—he had thought him a great deal wiser. Gabriel spoke against him in the same way, but with little basis of truth. Then Leonhard Schmerbacher declared that he was unable to put one before the other, for the people had been entrusted to one as much as to the other, but for the sake of peace, love, and unity, Jakob should give the honor and precedence to Simon. Everybody said, "Yes, yes." However, one brother added that he had nothing against the decision, "but Simon would do very well without having Jakob there."

Gabriel asked Jakob if he would accept the decision to give Schützinger precedence. Jakob replied that he wanted first to consider it before God, taking counsel with the elders and servants. Gabriel retorted, "I have nothing more to say to you; I will be on my way."

The brotherhood separated in great anguish of heart. Some went to comfort Jakob, who was deeply distressed; others who

[1]That is, a person sent out on mission.

1533

saw this presumed that he wanted to win the people over and take them to a separate place. One said this, another that. In short, everyone was overcome with grief.

The church held a second meeting. Jakob Hutter gave his answer.

On the following Tuesday the brotherhood was again called together. Jakob announced to the church that he had taken counsel with God and talked with the elders, and he could only acknowledge that God, in his providence, had appointed him and sent him to this people. "But the brothers did not understand me," he added, "so there is nothing to be done. For the sake of love, peace, and unity, I will accept the decision of the church, but not for the sake of righteousness."

Gabriel retorted, "You say we did not understand you—but we speak German too. There was no need for you to say anything at all." The brotherhood, though very distressed, kept up their spirits and trusted that with God's leading everything would work out.

God intervened and Schützinger became seriously ill.

Two weeks later the Lord struck Simon Schützinger so severely that he lay seriously ill in bed. So Jakob Hutter proclaimed the Word of the Lord to the church, according to the grace he had been given.

Jakob Hutter held a meeting on true community.

The next Sunday, September 28, at the repeated request of the elders, he held a meeting in which he admonished and taught in the power of God, exhorting the people to the true community of Jesus Christ. At that point several began again to mutter against Jakob.

Just then Georg Fasser of Rattenberg in the Inn Valley placed his earthly goods at the disposal of the church. As head of the family, he ordered his wife and children to submit willingly to the Lord and his people by doing the same. They agreed, and he lost no time in bringing his bed and chests into the communal storeroom. The servants examined all his things and made careful inquiries, and it was found that without her husband's knowing, his wife had kept money that had belonged to her and the children and had hidden it. She was admonished and disciplined by the servants, her husband, and Schützinger.

Since this woman had deceived her husband and hidden money from him, it occurred to Jakob that Simon's wife, too, might turn out to be another Sapphira, for God had given Jakob the gift of discernment. He brought his concern before the elders and said, "If you will support me in the strength of God, we will take the matter up and look into it thoroughly."

1533
Jakob Hutter made a careful search into how each kept to community.

The elders readily agreed and told him he should simply do it; he should start with his own room and continue with the rooms of the elders, including Simon's.

When they came to Simon and asked him to let them take a look in order to set their hearts at rest, he was perfectly willing. As they were looking through a chest, they found a too-plentiful supply of bed linen and shirts and four pounds in Bernese money, all in small coins. Jakob pleaded with him in the name and power of the Lord, asking him to unburden his heart, to tell whether he knew anything about the money, and not to conceal anything else that was there. Simon then confessed that he had known about it. So saying, he reached under the roof and brought out forty gulden. Jakob and the other servants were appalled. They could hardly believe that he would knowingly have done such a thing: he taught full surrender and community to others and yet did not hold to it himself. Jakob pointed out his dishonesty and sent immediately for Philip [Blauärmel], but he was not at home.

Simon Schützinger had been avaricious and deceitful.

Since Simon had been found guilty of such great deception, they could not postpone dealing with it. Early the next morning, on October 5, they called him before the brotherhood, and Jakob informed them of his faithlessness, greed, and treachery of heart. The whole brotherhood was horrified. The brothers and sisters began to lament and weep loudly in pain and heaviness of heart. But, as was only right and just, he was excluded in the power of Christ, according to the Word of the Lord, and given over to Satan. He confessed before the whole brotherhood that he deserved this but longed for grace and mercy. Jakob faithfully urged him to repent, and he promised to do so with all his might. Georg Fasser's wife and other unfaithful members were also separated from the church.

Brothers and sisters wept and groaned. Schützinger was excluded.

The whole brotherhood had previously chosen Schützinger as elder in preference to Jakob. Now that Schützinger was found to be a deceiver, Jakob exhorted all the brothers and sisters to consider how they had talked and acted and what sort of decision they had made. Also it had been said that he, Jakob, did not have the gifts to be a shepherd to such a people; instead they had chosen Schützinger as shepherd, a man whose wickedness was now revealed. And so, he said, they were once more completely without a shepherd, for as they had had so little respect for the Lord's Word, he was no longer certain

Jakob Hutter said they should consider what they had said.

1533

about serving them. He challenged them, however, to pray earnestly, calling on God to raise up a faithful shepherd and servant for them.

The brotherhood asked God for a shepherd.

For eight days and nights they prayed earnestly to God. They sent two brothers to Gabriel [Ascherham] at Rossitz to tell him of their need and to ask his advice about what they should do. He, too, suggested Jakob Hutter.

Jakob Hutter became a shepherd.

As they persevered in prayer, God gave them all a united heart and mind. They accepted Jakob as a gift from God to be their shepherd, and were all united in great love.

On October 12 the whole church rejoiced in spite of all their troubles. They also confessed before God and to Jakob that they had done wrong in giving precedence and honor to the deceiver. They admitted that Simon had not been the servant of God they had believed him to be. But because he was known to God, who knows all hearts, he had been revealed to God's own people. They asked earnestly and unanimously for forgiveness for this sin of ignorance. God forgave them because this had been done in blindness, and he blessed them. The Word of God grew in power among them; peace, love, and the fear of God increased daily; the wicked were separated from the church and the devout were accepted.

The brotherhood confessed that they had chosen Schützinger as shepherd and asked for forgiveness.

But when love, justice, and true judgment according to God's commandment increased—when the entire church lived in true peace—the devil, that ancient serpent, could not rest. He strove day and night to destroy this work by his cunning and to tear apart the bond of love.

On October 26 of this same year, 1533, the church was gathered to hear the Word of God when Philip Blauärmel appeared with Gabriel Ascherham and his assistant Peter Hueter. They had slipped in quietly before dawn, like wolves in sheep's clothing. The people were very startled to see them and feared that the devil would bring disaster, and indeed disaster soon followed. Nonetheless the servants and elders received them in peace, for at first they gave the impression of being very friendly, but Jakob asked them to explain why they had come. In response, Philip began by asking, "On what grounds did you exclude Bohemian David? He received a good testimony among you earlier, and yet you refused to receive him back. Second, why did you exclude Bernhard Glaser?

Philip and Gabriel came into the meeting.

1533

Third, we understood you to say that the decision for Simon Schützinger's election did not come from God." Then Philip said it was and is from God and would remain valid forever in his sight. There was so much talk for and against on both sides that the brotherhood was unable to arrive at any clarity or true judgment.

Philip and Gabriel caused disturbance in the brotherhood.

After all manner of things had been said and one called the other a liar, the brotherhood was in deep distress. Many were heard to groan, and the faithful were shaken to the depths. No one knew what the outcome would be, who was right or who was wrong, and which side was to blame, until finally Philip and Gabriel came out with their malice, which could be concealed no longer. When Jakob Hutter spoke to them in the strength of God, saying, "You have made accusations against me and the brotherhood, and if your accusations were true, we would be the greatest scoundrels that ever lived," Philip shamelessly denied it and called Jakob a liar. But Jakob replied, "The lie will come back on you."

Philip told a lie in face of the whole brotherhood.

Then Philip said, "I have always said you are an idol and the people worship you. That is the plain truth." At this there was a great turmoil among the people, who cried out, "That's a lie!"

As soon as Philip was recognized as a liar by the entire brotherhood and was admonished for his blasphemy, he tried to gloss it over and take back what he had said. But after pouring out abuse for a long time, Philip and Gabriel stood up and said, "Dear brothers and sisters, we have nothing against you, only against your servants." They proposed that the brotherhood should delegate a few men, and they would do the same in their communities, and these brothers should judge the matter among themselves. As this was received in silence, they left.

On the following Monday the brotherhood appointed eight men to report to the other two communities what had taken place, informing them where the brotherhood stood in relation to them and their servants. The brotherhood sent four of these eight to Philip and his people to say, "We would like to come to you tomorrow or whenever it suits you to report about our brotherhood's actions."

Philip's wickedness.

But Philip received them as if they were children of the devil, not children of God. Because they represented the

1533

brotherhood, they were harshly accused of making an idol of Jakob and worshiping him, of excluding Simon Schützinger out of envy and hate, and of accepting Georg Fasser for the sake of his money. "And Bernhard Glaser," said Philip, "who was excluded by the church for lying, is more upright than any of you. I would rather believe him than I would all of you put together." The four men contested these accusations, but Philip and his followers reviled them on many other matters which are omitted here for the sake of brevity.

When the four men described the response they had received, their whole brotherhood was still more horrified. Philip had so recently acknowledged them as children of peace (as reported above), and now his heart was set against them.

Gabriel's community sent eight men to find out what had happened.

The very next day eight men came from Rossitz, saying that Gabriel and Peter Hueter, their servants, had brought news that distressed them very much. The brotherhood at Rossitz had therefore sent them to find out what had happened. They expressed the wish of the group at Rossitz that all three brotherhoods should meet while Jakob, Philip, and Gabriel were to stay outside. Then Jakob's brotherhood should give an account to the other two, who were not involved, and let them judge the matter.

Gabriel's people proposed that the brotherhood judge the matter without the servants.

Gabriel's people retracted their suggestion and consent

That same night, however, the enemy put a new idea into their minds. In the morning, when Jakob's brotherhood agreed to the Rossitz brothers' proposal, these eight brothers denied everything they had agreed to before and did not want Jakob's group to be present when the matter would be judged. (They thought no one would notice the reason for their change of mind.) But the answer was that Jakob's brotherhood wished to consider this before God and would let them know what they decided. At this the eight brothers went back to Rossitz, apparently in peace.

Jakob's brotherhood decided in great fear of God that they would prefer both communities to come to them and bring along Philip and Gabriel or anyone else they wished, and then they would give a full account. This decision was reported to the other two communities by the eight brothers from Auspitz, but it was rejected. The others wanted to know only one thing from Jakob's brotherhood: were they willing to meet without their servants or not? At this the brothers returned home and talked to Jakob and the other servants. They were all ready to

1533

Jakob Hutter's brotherhood agreed to meet without the servants and let the brotherhood judge, but Gabriel's people would not accept this.

stay away from the meeting, provided they were convinced through the Word of God and true testimony. The eight men conveyed this to Gabriel's representatives, who would not accept it but wanted an answer from the whole brotherhood. To avoid more trouble, it was agreed that they should meet with the brotherhood. They would be called the next morning when the brotherhood was gathered. But that same night they crept in secretly to listen while the brotherhood was meeting to discuss the matter.

As soon as Jakob Hutter noticed them, he announced them publicly. When they came forward, they were informed by the brotherhood of the same decision the delegates had told them before. But they refused to accept it, saying, "Dear brothers and sisters, dear children of God, we have no authority to accept it, and we undertake nothing outside our own brotherhood. We will part from you now in peace, as from brothers and sisters, and will announce your views to our people. Then we will let you know what our brotherhood thinks." With this they took leave of Jakob and Leonhard Schmerbacher and the other servants, embracing and kissing them. They gave the greeting of peace to the whole brotherhood, and everyone said, "Amen, Amen."

Gabriel's men took leave of the servants in peace, and kissed Jakob Hutter.

Everybody rejoiced, hoping that the Lord might still provide a peaceful way out.

After all this, just as they were leaving, one of them asked, "Did you exclude Gabriel?"

Jakob replied respectfully, "We do not regard him as a brother or as a servant of God." Now the wolf could no longer stay in sheep's clothing. One of them, Hans from Strasbourg, jumped up and called Jakob a liar and a false prophet. Although they had been hypocrites for so long and taken leave in peace, he now poured it all out with such a flood of slander that everyone could see what the devil was trying to do. But God would no longer tolerate such lying and hypocrisy.

Gabriel's men changed face completely and reviled Jakob Hutter terribly before they left.

The brothers and sisters were in great distress, and God in heaven might well pity them. Then Jakob Hutter asked the brotherhood to pronounce its judgment on these men—who they were and whether they had come seeking peace or not. One brother began to speak with deep feeling, saying that they had seemed to come in peace and had said in the hearing of many that they would not undertake anything without their

1533

brotherhood, and now they had undertaken without their brotherhood to slander, revile, and tell lies. They had made a lie of their peace and their kiss, like Judas. Since they had behaved with such deceit that a blind man could see it, he would consider them the same as Gabriel and Philip.

Gabriel and Philip no longer regarded as brothers.

When Gabriel's men heard this, they hurled abuse at this brother and rushed out of the door. But the brother continued to speak, comforting the brotherhood, for people stood trembling and full of pain but still trusting in the Lord. A few irresponsible souls, however, banded together and would gladly have made a commotion. Yet the Lord stood by his own and did not allow it.

Jakob's brotherhood warned Philip's people against him, but no one listened.

The following Sunday the brotherhood sent the same eight representatives to Philip and his community to tell what had happened and warn them about Philip. But no one would listen to them or let them speak to the people. They were treated harshly and sent away with many abusive words.

They warned Gabriel's community against him, but no one listened.

On Thursday the brotherhood sent six members to Rossitz to advise the brothers there to exclude Gabriel and other evildoers and to explain the reason. Here again no one would listen or allow them to have a meeting, for Gabriel had so bewitched his people that not one said, "For the sake of fairness we should hear them." The six messengers then said that if the brotherhood was not ready to banish evil, they would be treated like Gabriel.

Gabriel and his people excluded.

When the messengers returned to Auspitz, they told the brotherhood there was little hope of these people changing since they all agreed with Gabriel. May God protect the simple and innocent from suffering for this and redeem them from all error through Jesus Christ our Lord. Amen.

In the course of these discussions Gabriel had given his own opinion, as follows. He said a different way could have been found with Schützinger, without subjecting him to such humiliation and slander. (Actually Schützinger had rightly borne discipline for his greed and selfishness and had acknowledged that the discipline was just. All this had been brought to light before God.) Regarding Georg Zaunring, Gabriel said he and Philip could see no other way, since the name of God had been horribly blasphemed by what he had done. Actually Georg had always been faithful and had a good

1533

testimony before God and many people. He was disciplined at the time for the error he had committed on his wife's account. The church had prayed for him, had forgiven him, and reaccepted him as a dear brother, and from then on he had not been involved in any wrongdoing. Regardless of all that, Gabriel thought Georg Zaunring should have been excluded and given over to Satan as a sinner and fornicator. That would have had Gabriel's and Philip's approval. To this day they felt that would have been right. (Georg himself never believed or confessed that he had been such an evildoer, but Gabriel said he would not have listened to him or reaccepted him without such a confession.) Concerning Bohemian David, Gabriel and Philip felt it was wrong for the brotherhood to have pressed him into confessing that it was envy that made him treat Georg Zaunring the way he did (although it was well known and clear before God, and David himself had admitted it earlier). Let each one judge for himself whether those who condemn others have not themselves committed the same deed, thus bringing about their own condemnation, according to Paul's words.

Rom.2:1

Our church named "Hutterian."

This is a short but truthful record of what took place at Auspitz in Moravia when the three communities split apart, and of the great distress and hostility provoked by Satan, which the church named after its shepherd, Jakob Hutter, had to suffer.

Anyone who reads this report should take care lest reading of rebellion and false spirits becomes a stumbling block for him. There must be stumbling blocks to reveal the chosen people who withstand the test, but woe to those who make stumbling blocks. And you, innocent and honest reader, rejoice in the Lord your God.

Matt.18:7
Luke 17:2
1 Cor.11:32
1 John 2:19

The struggle ended on November 22, 1533, fulfilling the Lord's words that two-thirds of the people shall be wiped out while a third of them shall be refined by fire like silver and gold.

Zech.13:8–9
Mal.3:2–3
Wisd. of Sol.3:6
Ecclus.2:5

Jakob Hutter sent reports of all this in writing and by word of mouth to the church in Tirol, as can be seen in the following letter:

Jakob Hutter's letter to the church in Tirol, telling of the division.

JAKOB, A SERVANT of our Lord Jesus Christ and of his holy Christian church through God's grace and mercy, set apart by God our heavenly Father and called to proclaim his Holy Word, to reveal his mystery and magnificent riches in these last days before the glorious and awesome coming of our beloved Lord Jesus Christ. Praise and glory to him and honor and thanks from our whole heart on behalf of myself and all holy Christian preachers, shepherds, servants and overseers, and all faithful believers, wherever they may be, for all his love and faithfulness, the signs and miracles he has shown and is still showing us daily. His holy name be praised through Jesus Christ for ever and ever. Amen.

1533
Jakob Hutter's letter to the church in Tirol, telling of the division.

Grace, peace, love, faith, victory, and eternal mercy—these I wish you from the bottom of my heart. All the believers and children of God join me in wishing this for you, my dearly beloved and longed-for fellow members in the body of Jesus Christ, all of you in the Puster Valley, the Adige Valley, and the Inn Valley, or wherever you are scattered for the sake of the name of God. May he comfort and strengthen you all with the precious comfort of his Holy Spirit, through Jesus Christ. Amen.

Most dearly beloved brothers and sisters in the Lord, there is so much I would like to write to you and talk to you about, but I cannot. And no letter can reveal to you what is on my heart, nor can I really satisfy the longing of my heart. I would so much like to speak to you face to face. My heart is filled with an overwhelming longing for you, as God in heaven knows well and all the children of God who are with me here. I have written this to you twice before; this is the third time, and it will surely not be the last time.

Now I will let you know how it is with us here. We cannot fail to do this, out of true and deep brotherly love. On the Thursday after the Feast Day of Simon and Jude [Oct. 28] we sent our beloved brothers Kuntz Maurer and Michael Schuster to you. We took leave of them in a fitting manner, praying and calling on God earnestly with the whole church that he might speed them on their way to you and back to us with great joy. Through them we let you know in detail, both orally and in writing, how we were faring here and how much had happened in a

1533
Jakob Hutter's letter to the church in Tirol, telling of the division.

short time. We hope that through God's grace this message has reached you.

I will now give you a brief account of what has happened since and what God has revealed further. The brothers will tell you more in detail about everything. They will be our living letter to you, and you can ask them any questions.

The day after the brothers left, to our great joy Peter Voit arrived with all those you sent with him, for which we all praised and thanked God. Our hearts leapt with joy in the Lord, and we were flooded by his love.

I received the letters from Hans [Amon], Onophrius [Griesinger], and the other beloved saints with great joy, but they also brought me sadness, pain, and sorrow of heart. My heart was shocked and grieved, and I wept many tears, as God knows, when I read the letter from our dear brother Hans, my beloved and faithful assistant. And even now I am writing to you with weeping heart and eyes—God is my witness—for I have learned how violently you are being persecuted because God has allowed those villains to gain so much power over you that they have again imprisoned dearly beloved brothers and sisters. They took Valtin,[1] the faithful brother who was so dear to me, and the beloved children whom I bore with labor and great anguish through the grace of God— Gretel, Christina, Rüpel, Stoffel, and also Zentz and others who had been imprisoned before and had given a witness. God be praised.

1 Cor.4:15
Gal.4:19

Many, that is, nearly all the children of God who are here with me are also very much shocked at this news, for I lost no time in telling them my great sorrow. We also prayed to God our Father with earnest entreaties for you, and you can be sure that we will continue to intercede fervently for you—it is God's truth.

A few days later, more brothers and sisters and several children came from the Puster and Inn valleys. You know who they are; I cannot name them all. On the same day our dear brother Klaus arrived from Carinthia and brought

---

[1]Valtin Luckner from Taufers, South Tirol, approx. 25 miles north of Bruneck. For the official record of his confession of faith, dated October 6, 1533, see Loserth, *Anabaptismus*, 577–584; Mecenseffy, *Österreich*, III, 165–172.

seven people with him. They have all found the faith here, praise be to God. Soon after that, brother Peter Hueter arrived with twenty-four souls, and the day before, eighteen souls had arrived from Hesse. So we reckon that in the short time of three or four weeks the Lord added more than one hundred and twenty souls to the church of God, who were baptized and taken into the brotherhood. Everyone was welcome. Adults and children, all those who came from other lands as well as from your area, were welcomed here with great joy as we would welcome the Lord himself.

1533
Jakob Hutter's letter to the church in Tirol, telling of the division.

We thank God from our hearts for these new brothers and sisters, and we will continually praise him for making us worthy to receive his holy children and to shelter and serve them. That gives us a deep and heartfelt joy in the Lord. We also know how wonderfully God protected them on their journeys by water and by land, and we cannot stop marveling and praising the Lord for all the messages and letters and for all the beautiful, loving, and comforting greetings you have sent us by word of mouth and in writing. These I read and shared fully with the whole church of God.

Your letters are a great comfort to all of us, a joy and delight before God. We are all very eager to hear from you and to talk about you. I cannot tell you enough how our hearts praise God for all you write and all you do through God's grace and power and mercy. It is beautiful and pleasing to my heart; it is like a garland of gladness and delight to me and to all God's children, making us inwardly leap for joy. When you write or speak to us, we receive it as coming from God, which it truly is. It is almost as though the angel Gabriel had written it. This is how we have always felt and how we feel now again about the letters from Hans [Amon] and all of you dear brothers and servants of the Lord.

It has moved us deeply to hear of those who have overcome, those who have testified to God's Word, faithfully keeping their promise to the Lord and sealing with their blood the holy covenant they made with him. For this we all praise God and his holy name, extolling his majesty and giving him the honor and glory that belong

1533
Jakob Hutter's letter to the church in Tirol, telling of the division.

to him many thousand times more than we can ever give. His glory is great and unutterable! His name be praised for you and all the believers and for all the signs and miracles he has done and continues to do daily through Jesus Christ, for ever and ever. Amen.

We really needed this encouragement in our deep pain and sorrow. It was a timely help to us; the Lord truly came at the right hour. We are greatly grieved and distressed on your account, because you are being so terribly persecuted and destroyed and we are thus robbed of your fellowship. Yet we have to endure sadness and pain as long as body and soul are one, as we read in the book of Job.

Three suns in the sky.

My beloved children, I want to tell you that on the day after the departure of our brothers Kuntz and Michael, on a Friday, we saw three suns in the sky for a good long time, about an hour, as well as two rainbows. These had their arches turned toward each other, almost touching in the middle, and their ends pointed away from each other. And this I, Jakob, saw with my own eyes, and many brothers and sisters saw it with me. After a while the two suns and rainbows disappeared, and only the one sun remained. Even though the other two suns were not as bright as the one, they were clearly visible.

I feel this was no small miracle. It was a sign from God, and there was surely a reason why he allowed it to appear. This much I am able to tell you, but the Lord alone knows what he had in mind and wanted to show us by it. To him all hidden things are known, whether present or future, in heaven or below heaven, on the earth or below the earth. May the Lord protect us from all evil and keep us holy, pure, and blameless until the end. That is my prayer to God and my longing through Jesus Christ. Amen.

Further, my chosen and dearly beloved children of the truth and of the living God, I want to tell you what else happened among us here. On the first Sunday after the brothers started their journey to you, we assembled the brotherhood about two hours before daybreak. I wanted to speak the Word of God to them in view of the great

1533
Jakob Hutter's letter to the church in Tirol, telling of the division.

need that was among us and still continues. I challenged the brothers and sisters very seriously to be watchful and in all things maintain the right attitude toward God and toward all men, friends and enemies alike, so as not to fall into the error of rash judgments and hasty talk. This has happened often and still does every day, as we have noticed frequently. There was very good reason for this warning, but it would take much too long to tell you about it. I was greatly troubled, for through God's Spirit and wisdom I knew of a good many things that were going on in the community—things partially hidden, not to the extent that they could not have been discerned, yet they were not revealed in the church.

As there are so many single brothers and sisters here, I had in mind also to speak about marriage so that each one might know how to bear his situation better and how to take the right attitude. I was anxious lest in speaking plainly about the right foundation I might say too much for some and they might seek to entangle me in my own words and accuse me or something like that. I was especially afraid of Philip and Gabriel, and not without reason, yet I feared God even more. So I was prepared to speak the truth with prudence and modesty, trying to find the right and holy way in order that I could stand before God and let neither Philip nor Gabriel nor any other man intimidate me. The great need urged me on, and in the fear of God I felt compelled by his Spirit. And so with great earnestness I pleaded with the brothers and sisters to listen carefully to what I was saying so that they could give a witness if needed. I spoke in this way also for other reasons, which soon became evident to all those who were present.

Suddenly, after I had spoken and we were all about to fall on our knees in prayer before God, Philip and Blasius [Kuhn], also Gabriel and Peter Hueter from Rossitz, entered the room without our previous knowledge or agreement. We welcomed them as brothers, although for several reasons their arrival was a shock to nearly all of us. We had never experienced anything like this before. Nevertheless I asked them to say what they had on their minds.

1533
Jakob Hutter's letter to the church in Tirol, telling of the division.

Matt.7:15
Acts 20:29

They began by appealing to God and declaring that they had come for the sake of peace and unity and in true love, and words to that effect. They spoke like peaceful messengers and angels of God; they came in sheep's clothing and with the appearance of angels of light. But inwardly they were ravening wolves, who did not spare the flock, as Christ and the apostle Paul said. We easily recognized them by their fruits, their words, and their works. God revealed them with great power before I had spoken one word about marriage. For this I praise God from my heart and rejoice mightily, because otherwise they would have tried to attack me on account of my words. Others may have thought that I brought up the subject specially because of them, which was not the case. But God no longer tolerated their evil and cunning. He did not want faithful hearts to be deceived any longer, so he delivered them from the jaws of those whose poison had deceived them for so long.

That is why God allowed them to come before the whole brotherhood with envy and hatred in their embittered hearts: they had to reveal the poisonous feelings they had harbored for so long. And the entire holy church of God recognized that they were liars, slanderers, and false shepherds and prophets. Therefore they were excluded by the church and handed over to Satan in the power, Spirit, and truth of God.

1 Cor.5:5
1 Tim.1:20

Nobody should think that we acted lightly in this matter, nor did we give anyone reason to think so. We acted with great earnestness and in the fear of God, according to God's command and to what is right and good in his sight. We acted carefully and with wisdom and discretion, in true humility taking everything into consideration. We cannot help it that they take offense at what is good and right. That is exactly what the ungodly have always done to all the faithful since the beginning of the world. But woe to them for turning what is good into a reason for doing evil! Our conscience is free and clear before God and does not accuse us with regard to any part, large or small, of this whole matter. Nor did we deal with them rashly; on the contrary, we considered everything thoroughly, looking at it in the holy light of truth. For about five days we concerned ourselves with it in great pain and trembling before God, together with the whole brotherhood.

1533
Jakob Hutter's letter to the church in Tirol, telling of the division.

We did not deal with them in a prejudiced way either. We did not bring up the difficulties that had frequently arisen before and about which a great deal could be said. (But now God and we hold them accountable for these matters too, because there had never been repentance or a real improvement.) We spoke only of what we actually saw and heard, nothing more. And everything we accused them of we have been able to prove by many devout and truthful witnesses, in fact, by the whole church of God.

It would take too long to tell how the affair began, all the reasons for and details of what happened, everything that was said, and how it was finally settled—the brothers will report to you as much as they know and are able to tell. Besides, I hope it is not necessary, since I know you have a deep trust in me and in all of us. We all stand fully revealed to you in your hearts, and I hope you believe us as if God were speaking to you, which is right, for we do speak the Word of God.

Here is a summary of it all. We lived in great love, peace, and unity. The church of God grew in every Christian work and virtue ever since we separated from such evil and deceitful people as Simon and those who say what he wants to hear. These false brothers had slandered and defamed us; all peace and unity had come to an end, and this continued as long as this lax Simon had his way. It started as soon as I arrived here. In fact, without any fear of God they persecuted and slandered me and all of us more terribly than any unbeliever or cruel tyrant, any false prophet or false brother, has ever done. God knows this is true. Oh, what a big thorn in their flesh I am, even though from the bottom of my heart I have shown them nothing but love and stood by them faithfully as a true Christian. God knows this, but they talk and shout so terribly against me that it is dreadful to listen to or to tell about. They spread many horrible stories about me, saying that no greater rogue has ever come into the land. They all clamor for revenge and wish me

1533
Jakob Hutter's letter to the church in Tirol, telling of the division.

evil, and their greatest longing is that God may put me to shame.

Prov.26:2

They say that my coming brought division and disunity, that previously they had lived in true peace, and that I am the cause of their division. But I am comforted by the Lord, because an undeserved curse or evil wish does no harm—God does not hear the prayer of the unrighteous, and I have done nothing to deserve it. I am not guilty of anything, great or small. God knows I did not come to break the peace and the unity but to increase them. This I began to do faithfully, as I can testify with many other honest witnesses. God has kept my heart pure and undefiled. In this whole matter there has never been any falsehood or deceit in my heart.

All the things for which they hate and revile me have come about through the Lord's great mercy. He alone is the cause, and I will let him alone answer for it; they will have to acknowledge his strength and wisdom. He has done it through me, his weak and miserable vessel; I myself am quite incapable of it. Still, for the sake of the Lord and his holy people, I bear and suffer gladly the many evil lies they spread about me, and he helps me faithfully to carry it—otherwise I could not do so. They rage against me more terribly than words can describe. I think they would like to stir up the unbelievers against me if they could, and we have already heard something to that effect from the judge here and from other sources. They say I bribed the brotherhood with money and that is why they worship me. They spread wicked, devilish lies like this, such as I have never heard before.

2Tim.4:17

You can see that I am very much in need of your prayers, as we all are, so that God may protect me from their jaws. The Lord will surely do this; I trust fully in his great mercy. And even if he were to give them power over my flesh, and even if my soul were gravely threatened by them, still I am in God's hand. Christ and all the prophets and apostles were reviled and persecuted, so why should it be different for me? It is all for the sake of truth and divine justice alone!

They hate us all without any cause. And everything that Simon, Gabriel, Philip, and others had planned to

do to me has come upon them. They dug a pit for me *1533*
and fell into it themselves (as the Holy Spirit declares Ps.7:15
through David); the righteous judgment of God was
executed upon them, just as it was on wicked Haman; Esther 7
and while destroying others they themselves were de- 2 Pet.2:1
stroyed (as the apostle Peter points out). Their folly and 2 Tim.3:1–9
villainy is evident to anyone who is willing to see and
hear it. That is what the apostle Paul says about this end
time and about wicked people such as these. That they
are wicked has been brought to light; it is no longer hidden.

They wanted to uphold Simon and make him appear
to be a faithful brother. Me, however, they wanted to
destroy. They did all they could to support Simon with
human strength, but the Lord stood by me throughout 2 Tim.4:17
and helped me gain the victory. He does not forsake his
own. Yet right up to this day they believe Simon and all
other rogues and evildoers rather than all of us. They
welcome those whom we excluded for their sin and declare
boldly that these are more trustworthy than all of us put
together.

O brothers, what a tremendous struggle has come over
the church of God! How we have had to wrestle with 1 Cor.15:32
wild beasts! How much we needed to be armed with the Rom.13:12
spiritual weapons the Holy Spirit speaks of in the 2 Cor.10:3–6
Scriptures! And if God had not stood by us with his great Eph.6:10–17
power, we would certainly all have been driven apart,
scattered, and destroyed. But God has been our victory
and captain; he has held us together like a strong wall
and powerful fortress.

Several who were not deeply committed have left us. They had never been clear in any case and were never completely at peace with God's people. For a long time they looked for a reason to leave us, and now that they have found it we praise God they have gone. All slack and superficial souls must be eliminated from the church through trials and suffering, just as dross is separated from gold by fire, and chaff from wheat by the wind. But those who are faithful and God-fearing have all been kept together in love, faith, peace, and unity, through the power and grace of God. Many sincere Christian souls

1533
Jakob Hutter's letter to the church in Tirol, telling of the division.

have come to the church of God to take the place of the evil ones who left. This is a sure sign to us that God is with us and that the course we have taken is according to the will and Word of God. Indeed, we have been faithfully upheld by his mighty arm.

O what a mighty storm, what a great blow, has struck the house of God! These men had such a good reputation with most people that no one could oppose them; practically everyone had to bow and submit to them. Even though someone might have had an uneasy feeling about what they said and did, he would not have had the heart or the courage to admonish them; whoever dared was no longer their friend—that was quite clear. But anyone who flattered them and said amen to all they did, good or evil, was their brother and dear friend. I could easily have created this kind of unity with many of them, but it would not have been from God. I would have been committing a sin instead of doing good.

Rom.10:2–3

There are many who have a zeal for peace and unity, but it is a misguided zeal. They do not discern God's way of righteousness, which brings about unity. They want to set up their own righteousness and what is good in their own opinion, but they are unwilling to submit to the righteousness that is valid before God. What the apostle Paul said of the Jews is now true of many people.

Matt.15:13
Matt.9:16
2Chron.32:8

These plants are not planted by God and therefore cannot survive. However long we go on patching and mending, the end will be worse than the beginning, just like putting a new patch on an old garment, as the Lord has said. The arm that guided those people was a carnal one, but that which guided us was spiritual and powerful. God dealt with them with firmness, wisdom, and great power, with the result that they could no longer hide but had to reveal themselves and bring to light the deceitfulness of their hearts. Otherwise they would have continued to deceive us and to lead us by the nose.

But God could not bear to look on any longer. He opened up things before our eyes in a marvelous way and with glorious power, and for that we cannot praise him enough. The devil could no longer conceal himself. He showed himself in a very crude way. But that was God's doing. I think they themselves now regret to some extent that they went about it in such a blunt and unwise manner. Had they been more subtle, we would not be rid of them yet and would have to put up with them still longer. But they are hardening their hearts. The evildoers we excluded are comforting and supporting each other in their wrong, and I fear that many or at least some of them may never find true repentance. That is what I am afraid of, but I certainly do not want to deny God's grace to anyone. The way they have been so far, it is truly a lost cause; that is clear to me. Simon at first wanted to repent, but now he is worse than ever, maligning and abusing us like a wicked demon, a raging lion, or a bloated dog. Also [Bohemian] David, Gilg, Marx, and many others are in every way much worse than before. But that is the fate of evil and unfaithful hearts: they are bound to be led astray and become hardened. The Scriptures give many examples.

1533
Jakob Hutter's letter to the church in Tirol, telling of the division.

We tell you all this in true love and fear of God, as a word from the Lord. We owe you this report so that you can be on your guard against these people and against all evil. Accept this warning for the sake of God's love and mercy, and lift your hearts and heads up to God, because the hour of peril, the very last hour, is at hand, as Christ and all the prophets and apostles foretold. Therefore wake up, for the Lord will come with great power and is not far off. Let each one get ready and arm himself with love, faith, and patience, with righteousness, holiness, and truth, so that we may be found irreproachable before him and have free and sure access to him when he comes. Then we will have joy and delight in him with all the heavenly hosts. May God the Father help us toward this through Jesus Christ our Lord. To him be praise and honor forever.

1 Cor. 15

Rejoice and be comforted in the Lord, you holy children of the living God, for he is with us. He is our captain and watchman, our power, strength, and shield. Praise be to him eternally.

I want to let you know, my dear children, my fellow members in the body of Jesus Christ, that there is great love among us here; there is justice and truth and the peace and unity of the Holy Spirit. Love to God and to

1533
Jakob Hutter's letter to the church in Tirol, telling of the division.

our neighbor, the love we feel for one another, is increasing. The peace of God is flourishing and truth blooms, bringing forth many divine fruits. God's children here are blossoming like beautiful flowers in the fields, which bloom when winter and the dark time is past, when summer arrives, and when the gentle rains of May moisten the ground and make everything fruitful. As we wrote you before, there is continual growth and increase on all sides.

The Lord has taken away much power from the devil, who constantly tried to hinder us. God will root him out of his holy church, as we read in the Psalms of David. He is indeed doing this every day. Such thorns or devils as these men have always prevented the good seed from sprouting and bearing fruit. For the first time hearts and consciences are truly free from outward cares and human commandments, and the Lord has delivered them from bondage and heavy burdens. Many, not just a few, were bound by a human spirit and by the arbitrary commandments of men; their hearts and consciences had long been burdened, confused, and distressed by the false shepherds and other misguided people. All these Christ has set free. He took pity on them and led them out of bondage and is now walking ahead of them. And the lambs, the obedient children of God, all rejoice in his voice and his salvation, and they follow him faithfully. They refuse to listen to the voice of a stranger, for they know and obey the voice of their Shepherd and King, who is Christ. This hurts and infuriates the devil, making him roar like a raging, devouring lion.

John 10:3–16

1 Pet.5:8

My dearly beloved brothers, there is no doubt that the only freedom we can have is the freedom of Christ, not the freedom of the flesh. Only God can make us free, through Christ, and only the Holy Spirit can redeem our hearts. But our flesh, our outer man, can have no freedom, no peace or security anywhere. Still we are joyful and courageous, for we know that as our outer man diminishes and decays, our inner man grows and is renewed day by day. We also know that we have a dwelling place in heaven, made not by hands but by the power of the infinite God—a habitation that remains forever and can never be

2 Cor.5:1–10

destroyed like this mortal, bodily frame. And for this home we yearn with our whole heart; it is the goal of our longing, thoughts, and hopes. Toward this we strive, leaving behind this transitory life and everything that is of the earth.

1533
Jakob Hutter's letter to the church in Tirol, telling of the division.

Our hearts are full of joy. We exult in the Lord and thank him for his goodness, faithfulness, and compassion, and for his fatherly protection and redeeming presence. He satisfies our hearts, making us very quiet and still before him. For this we praise and glorify his most holy, all-powerful name and thank him unceasingly with our whole heart for his goodness to ourselves and to you. We want to magnify and praise his name and not pass over his wonders and deeds in silence but proclaim them to all the saints. Even among unbelievers as well as in the church we want to praise, thank, and honor the Lord and declare his wonders for ever and ever. His deeds are mighty, and he has done great things for us, for he is powerful and his name is holy. May his name be magnified and honored by us and by all the saints and all the heavenly hosts through Jesus Christ, from everlasting to everlasting. Amen.

Heb.2:12

Luke 1:49

You dearly beloved brothers and sisters in the Lord, I want to tell you what our greatest concern still is, what saddens our hearts deeply and causes us great pain and distress. There is great fear and anxiety in our hearts on your account, and we find no rest by day or by night (God is our witness in this and in all things) because you are being persecuted and tortured with utmost cruelty and secretly murdered or suppressed. May God in heaven have mercy! It wounds our hearts to the quick that you are being taken from us like this.

O dearly beloved fellow members, how we long for every one of you, how much we suffer on your behalf, and what deep compassion and grief we feel for you! Our hearts weep for you constantly; they are heavy and sorrowful because of your suffering. Sometimes it seems as if they will melt away with pain and great sadness and that they are about to break. Because of you our souls have no peace or rest in our bodies; we simply cannot

1533
Jakob Hutter's letter to the church in Tirol, telling of the division.

find enough words to tell you how we feel. And we hear one sad and pitiful story after another. When I think of it, I feel more like weeping and crying my heart out than writing.

All this time, that bloodhound the devil is destroying one child of God after another. Oh, dear brothers and sisters, this fills all of us with great pity and compassion! If my own person were all that is involved, I would rather die than hear such news. Every day and every hour we are in great fear for those of you who are still free, and every day we must expect to be told that you, too, have been captured. We know that our worrying does no good, and yet we cannot stop worrying, because of the childlike, brotherly love that burns in us. And though it helps neither you nor us and drains our strength and courage, it shows how deeply we love you and drives us to intercede for you by day and by night with earnest crying to God.

Well, I have written this to you twice already with my own hand, and now I am writing you for the third time with tears and a weeping heart: we all urge you to come out of that accursed and murderous land. Flee, flee away from those ungodly and wicked people! Surely God has given you enough reason to do so.

O that God might grant our prayers and protect you from their rage, those of you who are still alive and free! We long that he might send you to us. That would be our hearts' delight. If this were possible, we would all willingly endure hunger and thirst, cold and heat, and all kinds of suffering. For your sakes we would gladly be persecuted and driven out the next day, if it were God's will for you to come to us. Oh, would to God that our holy zeal for you might be rewarded and that he might find us worthy to bless us [by leading you to us]. May God's will be done according to his holy compassion and goodness, and may he fulfill your and our heartfelt desire, through Jesus Christ our Lord. Amen.

2 Cor. 13:1
Heb. 10:28

My dearly beloved children and fellow members, take heed of what I write to you and believe it, for truth is confirmed by the testimony of two or three witnesses. Therefore be watchful and pray to God diligently. He will teach you what is right if you will listen to him.

1533
Jakob Hutter's letter to the church in Tirol, telling of the division.

In conclusion, I commend all of you to the protection of God's mighty hand. May the Lord be your guard and captain, your shelter and shield, keeping safe your souls and bodies until the great day of the Lord's revelation, through Jesus Christ.

The entire holy church of God here, all servants and elders, all brothers and sisters, whether old or young, greet you from the bottom of their hearts a thousand times in a truly burning and brotherly love and with the holy kiss of our Lord Jesus Christ. We greet all of you and each one personally, especially from those of us who know you so well in the Lord and who have a special love for you. I cannot pass on with pen and ink every personal greeting the brothers and sisters here would like me to; it would simply take too long. But you know their hearts well, for they are wide open to you in the love of God. So please accept their greetings, each one of you, and know them to be a thousand times better than anything I have written here. All the brothers and sisters you know would have liked me to put down the name of each one, but I simply cannot.

And I, Jakob, your servant and brother in the Lord, an apostle and servant of God through his grace, greet every one of you a thousand times from the bottom of my heart with a holy kiss in the genuine, pure love of God. I think of you every hour and every moment. With my whole heart and mind and soul I am thankful for you. And I kiss you with my heart and mind, with the true kiss of Jesus Christ and of all the holy men of God. Although I am not with you in the flesh, my thoughts are completely with you all, and I cannot put into words how much my heart longs for you.

Give my greetings especially to all those whom I know and who truly love me for the sake of the Lord. They are particularly close to me, and I love them with my whole heart. Brothers and sisters, shepherds and sheep, in the Puster, Adige, or Inn valleys: greet each one of them. They are well aware of the faithful love I feel for them, even though I cannot mention each one by name. I wish I could still greet and comfort each one of them individually and kiss them with my own lips and heart.

1533
Jakob Hutter's letter to the church in Tirol, telling of the division.

I wish I could serve them with my own hands and show them love with all my strength. That would be my greatest delight and give me pure joy in God.

My heart and mind are with you forever; your heart, soul, and spirit are with me, and may God the Father be with us all through Jesus Christ, from everlasting to everlasting. Amen.

I, Jakob, wrote this with my own hand, but Klaus has copied it for me, and we are sending the copy to the Puster Valley. If there is anything else you should know, brother Voit will tell you personally. I greet you, Onophrius [Griesinger] and Hans [Amon], faithfully from my heart. Please also give my warmest greetings to the dear sisters Gretel Marbeck and Ursula Brähl and to all the others. We have received Georg Fasser's wife back into the church through God's mercy and grace, and she is doing very well, as Bärbel from Jenbach is also. Your hearts will rejoice about this news. Georg Fasser, our brother and servant of the Lord, and his wife, our dear sister, greet you all faithfully, and once again, greetings from all the brothers and sisters here. The Lord be with you eternally. Amen.

Sent from Auspitz in Moravia
to the Adige Valley
carried by brother Peter Voit[1]

Hans Both from Hesse.

In the middle of the affair described above, a servant named Gilg Schneider arrived and soon after him Hans Both, his fellow worker, with a group from Hesse. They acted as if they sought nothing but peace and unity, and for a time they proved peaceable, but in reality it was hypocrisy. The church accepted them in good faith, trusting in the good impression they made. But Hans Both was not honest at heart. It was soon clear that he wanted to increase his own little flock by snatching some of the faithful out of the Lord's hands. But he did not succeed,

---

[1]For the above letter, see also Jakob Hutter, d. 1536, *Brotherly Faithfulness: Epistles from a Time of Persecution* (Rifton, NY, 1979), Letter II, 13–47, and Appendix B, 205–218; Friedmann, *Schriften*, 118, "Huter, Jakob," #2; Williams, *Radical Reformation*, 421–423; Beck, 113–114.

About Peter Voit, see below, pp.131–132.

because the church looked to the Lord and not to Hans Both and his followers or to any other human being.

1533

Hans Both and his followers excluded. They no longer believed in devils or angels.

Hans Both and his adherents held the false opinion that there were no such things as angels or devils. They refused to be corrected, despising all sound teaching, so they and all who persisted in this error were excluded from the church of God in accordance with the Lord's Word.[1] They talked a great deal.

---

[1]Hans Both, a friend of the Thuringian Anabaptist leader Melchior Rink (*ME*, IV, 336–338), was a man inclined to mysticism and to a purely spiritual interpretation of the Scriptures. Hans Both was leader of a church group at Sorga near Kassel (Hesse, Germany); this group was forced to emigrate by Prince Philip of Hesse, who was generally lenient in dealing with Anabaptists. Early in September 1533, Hans Both and a large number of his followers moved to Moravia, where he spread false teachings. About Both's activities there, the brothers wrote a detailed account in August or September 1537 to one of the Anabaptist leaders named Matthias Hasenhan, who had remained behind in Hesse; see *ME*, I, 395–396, "Both, Hans"; II, 719–727, "Hesse"; Beck, 114. The following excerpt is taken from Karl W. H. Hochhuth, "Mittheilungen aus der protestantischen Sektengeschichte in der hessischen Kirche," *Zeitschrift für historische Theologie*, XXIX (1859), 206–207.

> Our dear brother Christoph Gschäl has come to you once more and has told you of our love, our life, and our work in Christ Jesus, which has moved many to join us here. But many of these, may God have mercy, left us again; they were taken away by the false servant Hans Both, who wanted to mix his false leaven among God's people. When we refused to allow this, he said we were trying to cut him off from the springs of living water. But we acted rightly and in the fear of God and replied that we could not tolerate such talk; but if he would agree to be silent, we would bear with him in love. Thereupon he insisted all the more that we were trying to keep him from the living springs.
>
> We replied that his was not the wholesome teaching of our Lord Jesus Christ, but a false leaven; he persisted, however, and said that Melchior Rink took the same position. Our answer was that even if Melchior Rink did say and teach this, it still was not right. We did not believe Melchior took this position, however, and thought Hans Both and his followers might have misunderstood him. They then said we were calling Rink a false prophet and were furious (that is typical of Hans Both). By influencing those who had recently joined us, they stole their hearts from us, with the result that they would no longer listen to us but went with Hans Both and Valtin Schuster, who drew the people after them and grew more and more hostile. Finally, in our pain, we laid it all before God and left it in the hands of him who knows us and sees us as we are.
>
> Our dear brother Jakob, servant of the Lord, has confessed the Word of God with gladness, and our dear brother Georg Fasser has given valiant witness with his blood, and so have Wilhelm, Hieronymus [Käls] our schoolteacher, and many other dear brothers. And now, by the gracious will of God, our dear brother Peter Riedemann from Gmunden has been released from prison in Nuremberg, and he is with us in the Lord, acknowledging the love and grace in which we live before God. . . . The Lord is richly among us, for which we praise and thank him, and because he so sustains us, we are deeply concerned for you and for all people everywhere who call upon our Lord Jesus Christ with pure hearts.

1533

Especially Hans Both admitted that Philip and Gabriel had acted wrongly and were therefore no longer his brothers; the treatment they had received was right. Yet as soon as those two were under church discipline, Hans Both went to Philip and was his good friend. This revealed his deceitful heart even more plainly. If he could have split the church with his hypocrisy, it would have delighted him greatly. He never came out clearly with what he was thinking. He said he knew the church and the brothers and the other communities very well, and he would not go to them. But his actions clearly belied his words. In this way God once more protected and rescued his own from these erring people.

Philippites poured abuse on our people.

After all this, the church suffered a great deal of abuse and slander from the renegades, especially from Philip and his people. Whenever a lord, citizen, or farmer needed help and employed brothers and sisters from both communities, the Philippites refused to work, sit, eat, or drink with those who sided with Jakob Hutter, despite the fact that their employers made the arrangement. This brought abuse and disgrace to God's name. Although Jakob Hutter's people would much rather have worked quietly by themselves, they accepted and enjoyed the food and drink of their employers and gave thanks to God for it, regardless of who worked with them.

The Philippites refused to give or return greetings in the streets.

In addition, Philip's people refused to greet anyone on the street. They neither gave nor returned any good wishes, and our people, who were innocent, often had to suffer for this.

Jörg Scherer and his people joined us.

To make matters worse, a servant named Jörg Scherer came

Would to God we could confer with you, my Matthias, and especially with Melchior Rink, and open our hearts to one another; but if it cannot be, we lay it in the Lord's hands. But we never made accusations against Melchior Rink, for why should we slander a man we do not even know? The Lord forbid! If someone quotes Rink in order to prove his own wrong ideas, we cannot agree with it but must say that even if an angel from heaven were to try to bring us an alien teaching, we would with God's help neither follow it nor weaken our position.

Melchior Rink will bear the responsibility for whatever he says or does, but we only hear about his integrity and constancy in affliction, for which we heartily rejoice and praise God in heaven. God grant we shall meet and speak with him in the Lord, but Hans Both's thinking is alien to us; we do not know his voice, and he will have to face judgment for spreading slander about us.

See Walter Klaassen and Frank Friesen, *Sixteenth Century Anabaptism: Defences, Confessions, Refutations* (Waterloo, Ontario, 1982), 98–102, for a translation of the complete text of the above letter, here dated 1538.

to Auspitz and brought a group with him. They inquired about everything that was done in the community and then united with Jakob Hutter and the entire holy meeting. But after a while they began to criticize many things in the church. As people always do when they want to break with their friends, they find fault even with the best things. They said it was not right that some wore gold or silken trim on their head coverings and that the thread for their cotton material and head coverings was spun much too fine.

1533

Ecclus. 11:7

In his compassion, Jakob Hutter offered to make changes and give up anything that was not good, for he desired greater perfection. He did not want to permit anything that was against the Lord. When they complained about the food because they were not used to it, Jakob said that he would put their cooks in the kitchen to cook according to their custom and that the community should eat what their cooks prepared. He was even willing to let them move to Schakwitz to live under the lord marshal of Mährisch Kromau,[1] where they had bought a house half a mile from Auspitz, if only they would remain in the Lord and in the church. But nothing helped. They only laughed and mocked us. When the church was informed of their contempt for every kindness, Jörg Scherer was excluded and separated from the church, and all his people with him.

First house bought at Schakwitz.

Jörg Scherer and his people excluded.

In Tirol, persecution increased day by day, and there was no place for the believers to go. Many were captured and killed for the sake of truth. The priests, too, thundered from their pulpits that people should watch out for them, seize them, and destroy them by fire and the sword. Again and again large sums of money were promised to anyone who would ferret out brothers and sisters and inform on them. The woods were searched and any house suspected of harboring them; every room was ransacked. Locked chests had to be opened, or else they were broken open and searched.

Persecution and suffering in Tirol.

Locked chests were searched for hidden believers.

There was a son of Judas named Prabeiger.[2] He set cunning

A traitor in Tirol.

[1]Schakwitz (Šakvice), a half mile south of Auspitz, in 1533 the property of the lords of Lipé at Kromau. Until 1622 the village of Schakwitz was the location of one of the main Hutterite communities. Zeman, *Topography*, #137.

[2]Such informers were recruited by the government of Tirol at the express command of King Ferdinand and were paid up to one hundred gulden for every Anabaptist they delivered up, depending on the importance of the person caught. See Loserth, *Anabaptismus*, 476, 492, 512, 576, 175. An official mandate of July 30, 1530, reads: "To anyone who denounces one or more Anabaptists who with certainty have joined the movement, the treasury shall pay 30–40 gulden" (Loserth, 492 n.1).

1533

traps to catch believers, then hurried to the magistrates and informed on them, bringing back constables and the children of Pilate with swords, spears, and clubs, going in front of them just like the traitor Judas. In this way they caught many and scattered and drove away the rest.

Jörg Früe a traitor and rogue.

Not long after, when they gathered again, another child of Judas, Jörg Früe, ran to the priests. If they would reward him, he would go after the brothers and not one would be able to hide from him. That race of scribes and Pharisees, the priests, soon provided him with a substantial reward and a letter besides. This deceiver hid his hypocrisy under an angel's likeness and visited people, especially those he suspected of knowing something about the brothers, inquiring up and down the Puster Valley where they might be. The scoundrel begged for help, pleading with ready tears and declaring that he would have no peace until he found them. In this way he deceived them and gained entry among them. He pretended to be sorrowful, humble, and virtuous, like someone seeking to repent and change his life.

A little later he said, "My brothers, be so good as to let me return home to fetch my wife and child and bring them here too." The servant did have misgivings and told him that if he was false-hearted and was planning evil, God would certainly know it, and he would have to bear hard punishment. But he answered, "Oh, no! May God protect me from any such thing. Come home with me to my house!" He left and hurried to the judge, priests, and magistrates, who came with swords and cudgels and took the brothers and sisters by force.

Many treacherous dealings.

There were other such deceivers, in particular one named Peter Lantz and another named Christel Pranger. Some went about at night, carrying staves and talking and acting like brothers. In order to find believers, they visited places and houses where they thought people would open their doors to them as brothers. But God has given them their recompense, striking some with great terror and a horrible death to make them realize what they have done, like Judas the betrayer of Christ. On God's judgment day their hair will stand on end. These deceivers will sweat blood and wish they had never been born.

Jakob Hutter wrote to those in Tirol to come.

Because the brothers there were so hard pressed that they were unable to stay in Tirol, Jakob Hutter and the church with him were moved to send messages by letter and word of mouth, telling them to leave Tirol as soon as possible and come to the church community in Moravia. In response, Hans Amon and several brothers and sisters set out and with God's help reached the church at Auspitz.

1533

Hans Amon left Tirol.

[1534]

Meanwhile brother Bastel Glaser and his people in Tirol were on their way to the church, but on arriving at Hohenwart, a village in Austria, they were arrested. Jakob Hutter wrote them a letter of comfort, which is still in existence.[1]

Bastel Glaser and several others captured in Hohenwart.

They were then taken to Eggenburg, where their cheeks were burned through, and they were released. This is the Bastel Glaser who wrote several songs, which we still have.[2]

Their cheeks were burned through, and they were released.

Another brother, named Peter Voit, was imprisoned at

Peter Voit imprisoned at Eggenburg in Austria.

---

[1]Hohenwart, parish in Lower Austria, located between Krems on the Danube and Meissau, where a number of Hutterites were imprisoned in 1534; Beck, 116.

The letter Jakob Hutter wrote from Auspitz to comfort the prisoners at Hohenwart is one of his most moving writings. A short extract is included here, taken from Codex I 87.708, fol. 161ff., Vienna University Library.

> Now I want to let you know how things are with us here. The Lord is with us, although we suffer much. Yet that is right and good, and we praise and thank God with all our hearts that in spite of it we live in great and holy love, in the joy and unity of the Holy Spirit, while all the time expecting trials and persecutions even greater than those we are suffering now. May God watch over us through his great mercy! With deep longing we wait for the deliverance of our bodies, for the Sabbath when we rest from all trial and labor and from all works of our own, when we leave behind this earthly tent and our soul and spirit may at last find rest and eternal peace. For this divine homeland we yearn, since we have no peace or rest in this wretched wilderness. We have no permanent home here but are awaiting one that is to come.
>
> Brother Onophrius [Griesinger] has arrived with many other brothers and sisters. We thank God for protecting them and bringing them safely to us. Their arrival gave us much joy, and we praised God for it. There are not many brothers and sisters left in Tirol now.
>
> Finally, dearly beloved children of God, the brothers Hans [Amon], Georg Fasser, Onophrius [Griesinger], Leonhard [Lanzenstiel], Wilhelm [Griesbacher], and all the servants of God here greet you, and so does the entire holy church of the Lord, every one of God's children. We greet you a thousand times in pure and holy love from the depths of our hearts and with the kiss of our Lord and Savior Jesus Christ.

For a diplomatic copy of the above letter, see Zieglschmid, "Unpublished Letters," *MQR*, April 1941, 118–129; translated in Jakob Hutter, *Brotherly Faithfulness*, Letter III, 49–64.

[2]See Wolkan, *Lieder*, 171; *LdHBr*, 71–74. About Glaser's second imprisonment and his execution, see below, entry for 1537, p.162; *ME*, II, 524.

1534
Mice carried away the toes from his feet.

Eggenburg.[1] Both his legs were so tightly clamped in stocks that gangrene set in and they rotted away; then the mice took the toes from his feet right before his eyes. By the time he was released from prison, his body was utterly ruined. He returned to the community, which had been driven from house and home and was living in open fields, and then he had both legs amputated. He lived for many years after this and fell asleep in the Lord at the age of seventy.

Onophrius Griesinger came to the church from Tirol.

Around that time Onophrius Griesinger,[2] a servant of the church, traveled from Tirol with other devout brothers and sisters and under God's protection reached the church of God at Auspitz. Somewhat later he was involved in sin on his wife's account, and because of this his service was taken away from him. His wife also received the punishment she deserved.

Abbess wanted to borrow money from the brothers at Auspitz.

She had the brothers put in prison at Auspitz.

About that time the abbess at Brünn, who was landowner of Auspitz, asked the elders of the church to lend her some money. When they refused because the church itself was in great need of the money, she had Jakob Hutter, Hans Amon, and other elders put in prison, also Hieronymus Käls, who was schoolmaster for the community children at the time. She tried in this way to force them to lend her the money, but when she did not succeed, she released them and ordered them off her property. She let them stay for a time, however, as will be described later.

Since Jakob Hutter himself was under attack as the cause of every evil and conflict, he asked Hans Amon whether he felt any special zeal to go to Tirol. Hans replied that he felt no special zeal but was ready to follow whatever the Lord showed to his people. But Jakob said, "I feel great courage and zeal for it, and I hope God will still grant it." Jakob announced this with many brothers present, and to a large extent they agreed to his acting on this urge, but they waited for the right time.

Jakob Hutter zealous to go to Tirol.

2 Esd. 16:74

God wanted his elect to be made manifest. They are revealed by great afflictions, as gold is proved in the fire. So he tested

---

[1]Peter Voit was captured in 1534, possibly after delivering Jakob Hutter's letter from Auspitz, Moravia, to the church in Tirol; see also Beck, 116.

[2]Onophrius Griesinger, born at Frasdorf (Bavaria, Germany), was clerk at a mine in Salzburg, Austria, until he joined the church community in 1532; *ME*, II, 579–580. About his imprisonment and death, see below, pp. 171–172.

the faithful but hardened the hearts of sinners and hypocrites. In any case, the devil begins all his work in the name of God and under the appearance of truth. Wherever God builds his church, the devil builds a new chapel alongside to confuse and blind people. He started the trouble in the Westphalian city of Münster, where several Lutheran preachers met in 1532. In 1533 they were joined by Jan van Leyden, a tailor from Holland, who used Scripture to testify that infant baptism was not commanded by God but that adults and believers should be baptized. A number of people joined him and raised a great outcry against those who held infant baptism to be right. They robbed them of their goods and made the citizens flee from the city. After this, in 1534, their own bishop laid siege to the city, and they resisted him. Jan van Leyden appointed the mayor as executioner, claiming that God had directed him to set the highest in the lowest positions.

1534

The devil played his hand through the Münsterites.

This Jan set up a government according to Jewish custom and a new religion, saying, for instance, that a man could take as many wives as he wished. Then he made himself king in royal splendor and in his folly believed that he would rule the whole world and possess the throne of his father David until the heavenly Father would claim the kingdom from him. When the ungodly were destroyed, the faithful alone would rule on earth. But after the siege had gone on for a long time, the city was at last taken. The evil king and two of his companions were captured and led around the country as a spectacle for the princes. After that they were tortured horribly with red-hot tongs and killed. Then they were placed in iron cages and hung from the highest tower of the city, the king in the middle, a man's height above the others. This took place on January 23 or 24, 1536.

The actions of these corrupt and ungodly people brought intense suffering to the church of God in many places. A great number of the faithful were imprisoned, tortured, and accused of belonging to this sect.[1] But the whole church and all devout hearts testified steadfastly, yes, some even with their death,

The church had to suffer because of the Münsterites.

---

[1]About the Münsterites, see *ME*, III, 777–783. How little the authorities knew about the true character of the Hutterites ("the quiet in the land") is borne out by a mandate dated as early as April 1, 1528, which describes the Anabaptists as a sect "that destroys the honor of God, despises the governing authorities, and breeds disobedience, war, corruption, bloodshed, and all manner of evil. . . " (Loserth, *Anabaptismus*, 481).

1534

against all this cruel abomination, this invention of the devil. The church of true believers will never have outward weapons, whether few or many, with which to fight their misguided enemies. Vengeance is the Lord's—believers do not thirst for it. The Lord knows how to repay each man according to his deeds.

1535

Matt. 16:6
Mark 8:15
Luke 12:1

Decision of the church to shun false prophets, monks, and priests.

2 John

In 1535 the whole church, wanting from the beginning to follow the best and perfect way and to abstain from the world and all ungodliness, unanimously decided in the fear of God to be on their guard against the leaven of the scribes and Pharisees, in accordance with Christ's teaching. This was because the pope, priests, monks, nuns, and all who preach for their belly's sake are the greatest cause of idolatry and of hypocritical, sinful, and corrupt living. They decided that from then on the church would not work for them, trade with them, eat or drink or have anything at all to do with them without a very specific and godly reason, because all their profits come from and are used in the service of idolatry—they call themselves preachers of the Gospel, yet they neither practice Christ's teaching nor bring it to others.

After this decision the church gave notice to the abbess of the Queen's Cloister at Brünn, the landowner of Auspitz, that they could no longer work in the vineyards or other places for her or for other people in the same position. This was not because of pride but because, in the fear of God, they were troubled that they might take part in serving idolatry, which would surely be against God.

The community had to leave Auspitz and moved to Schakwitz.

This declaration made the abbess furious, and she ordered the community off her lands. Since no other way was found, the community moved out of Auspitz on Ascension Day 1535, leaving their houses and going to Schakwitz on the lands of the lord marshal. There they made every effort to start building for themselves and their children, but this did not last.

Royal command that no brother be tolerated in the land.

The events at Münster already reported were now running their course and furthering the God-ordained work of testing the faithful. They caused the emperor, king, princes, and all the worldly leaders to oppose the gathering of believers. There soon came a stern command that no one belonging to the communities of true believers should be tolerated in the land.[1]

1535

In particular a strict order was sent to the lord marshal at Mährisch Kromau to expel the brothers without delay on pain of great disfavor and punishment. So he had to do it, however reluctantly, for he had a great love for the Lord's people. He instructed Jakob Hutter, that heroic Christian, to gather his people together again when these troubles were over. He sent his officers to summon all the neighbors from the villages round about. They soon came with drums beating, flags flying, and weapons in hand to the community at Schakwitz. Then the officers began by expressing the earnest request of their master that the brethren should spare him and not bring disgrace on him, for he, too, could not oppose the higher authorities but had to be obedient to them. They talked for a long time, taking counsel together, but there was no other way. The faithful had to leave their home, as it is written: They had to leave city or village and camp out in the fields.

With drums, flags, and weapons in hand, they came to us at Schakwitz to drive us out.

Mic.4:10

So Jakob Hutter took his bundle on his back. His assistants did the same, and the brothers and sisters and all their children went in pairs, following their shepherd Jakob through the crowd of ungodly, villainous robbers, who ground their teeth in rage, full of lust to rob and attack. They were unable to do so, however, because of the presence of the officers, which was in accordance with God's will.

Jakob Hutter took his bundle on his back. So did all his people. They moved out of Schakwitz onto the moor.

The little band of the righteous were driven into the open like a herd of sheep. They were not permitted to camp anywhere until they had left their lord's lands. Although they had only just moved to Schakwitz a few days earlier, they were driven out again. A very few of the sick people remained in the house, but not for long. This persecution took place in 1535.

After their move into the open country, while they were encamped on Lord von Liechtenstein's land at Nikolsburg, the Philippites, too, were driven out of Auspitz into the fields. They reached the hill near Lassling, singing joyfully, and set up camp there.[2] Their leading servants, Philip [Blauärmel] and

They lay on the heath under the open sky.

[1]About the mandate issued by the Provincial Diet of 1535 at Znaim (Znojmo), Moravia, at which King Ferdinand was present, see Loserth, *Anabaptismus*, 544–545; Beck, 116–117; *ME*, III, 448b.

[2]The Hutterites camped for some time at "Starnitz under Lassling" (Starnice), an abandoned village near Tracht (Strachotín), about 18 miles south of Brno. See Beck, 116–117; Zeman, *Topography*, #144.

1535
Philip, in exclusion, turned traitor and cheated his own people.

John 10:12–13

John 16:32

Luke 9:58–62
17:31–33

Philippites moved back to Württemberg and the Palatinate.

Some Philippites taken prisoner at Passau.

Rom. 1:21–22

Lord's people accused that they had armed themselves.

Governor's servants asked the church to write their intentions to the lord.

Blasius [Kuhn], mounted horses and set off from there, pretending to search for a place of shelter for their people. Not long after, a message came back that everyone should look after himself and find a place to live as best he could. These two are still searching to this day and have found no place. So they were like false shepherds and hirelings, who allowed the flock to be scattered among the wolves. Their judgment on Jakob Hutter, recorded earlier, now proved to be true for themselves. Their flock has indeed been scattered, and many have come to ruin. Some cannot return even today. In the beginning they surely followed God's command to leave country and family, but they looked back and loved the world again.

They separated into small groups, some to go to Württemberg and others to the Palatinate, but a large group was captured at Wegscheid and at Ilzstadt near Passau. About sixty people in all were taken to Passau, and some were in prison there for up to five years, suffering acute hunger and severe treatment besides. Many of them died while in prison. A few returned to the church of God after their release, but the rest went to utter ruin, their hearts perverted and bent on doing wrong.

While the Lord's people camped on Liechtenstein land near Tracht in Starnitz under Lassling, as told above, they were denounced to the authorities and falsely accused of carrying guns. The governor sent his couriers to the camp to find out if it was true, but instead of muskets and spears they found many children and sick people.

When Jakob Hutter pleaded with the governor's servants and told them the whole story, they requested that the community's ideas and intentions be conveyed to their lord in writing. So Jakob Hutter, who at that time was the leading servant and shepherd of the believers, wrote a letter to the governor and sent it by his messengers.[1] This letter was attacked and evilly misrepresented by Philip's and Gabriel's people and others, as if Jakob Hutter had called King Ferdinand a bloodhound and was put to death on this account and not for

[1]The governor's name was Jan Kuna of Kunštát. About this letter, see Beck, 117 n.3; Loserth, *Anabaptismus*, 547–548; Friedmann, *Schriften*, 118, "Huter, Jakob," #4. See also Jakob Hutter, *Brotherly Faithfulness*, Letter IV, 65–74; Müller, *Glaubenszeugnisse*, I, 160–165.

the sake of God's truth. For this reason the letter is included here, taken from the first copy, and each should judge for himself.

1535

Jakob Hutter's letter to the governor when the faithful were living on the open heath.

We are brothers who love God and his truth, we are true witnesses of our Lord Jesus Christ, and we have been driven out of many countries for the sake of God's name. We arrived here in Moravia, where we have been living together under the lord marshal through God's protection. To God alone we give praise forever.

This letter is to let you know, dear governor of Moravia, that we received the order delivered by your servants. We already answered you by word of mouth, as you know, and now want to do the same in writing. This is our answer: We have left the world and all its wrong and ungodly ways. We believe in God the Almighty and in his Son, Jesus Christ, who will protect us from evil forevermore. We have given ourselves to God the Lord in order to live according to his divine will and keep his commandments in the way Jesus Christ showed us.

Because we serve him, do his will, keep his commandments, and leave behind all sin and evil, we are persecuted and despised by the whole world and robbed of all our goods. The same was done to all the men of God, to the prophets, and to Christ himself. King Ferdinand, that cruel tyrant and enemy of God's truth and justice, has mercilessly put many of our innocent brothers and sisters to death. He has robbed us of our homes and all our goods and persecuted us terribly. But through God's grace we were able to move to this country, Moravia, and have lived here for a time, recently under the lord marshal. We have not troubled or harmed anyone and have lived faithfully in the fear of God. Everybody will confirm this. But now even the marshal has given us notice and forced us to leave our houses and property.

So we now find ourselves out in the wilderness, under the open sky on a desolate heath. This we accept patiently, praising God that he has found us worthy to suffer for his name. Yet we feel great pain of heart for you, that you treat God's faithful children so cruelly. We cry to him about your hard-heartedness and about the enormous

1535
Jakob Hutter's letter to the governor when the faithful were living on the open heath.

Isa.59:15
2Esd.16

Rom.8:17

Heb.12
Rev.3

injustice that increases daily. Day and night we plead with God the Lord to protect us from evil, trusting in him to lead us through, according to his will and mercy. And God will surely do so; he is our Captain and Protector and will fight for us. The prophets Isaiah and Esdras foretold that all who turn away from evil, all who love God from their hearts, who fear and serve him and keep his commandments, are bound to be robbed and driven from their homes. This shows that we are God's children, fellow heirs of his glory, that he loves us and is pleased with us as with all the saints. Therefore we suffer all this quietly, and our hearts are comforted by his Holy Spirit.

Deut.32:35–43
Joel3:21

But threefold woe to all who persecute, expel, and hate us without cause, simply because we stand for God's truth! Their condemnation and punishment is approaching and will overtake them with terror, here and in eternity. According to his holy prophets God will call the persecutors most terribly to account for the suffering and the innocent blood of his children.

Matt.10:16

Acts4:19
5:29

Now since you have commanded us to leave without delay, we give you this answer: We know of no place to go. We are surrounded by the king's lands. In every direction we would walk straight into the jaws of robbers and tyrants, like sheep cast among ravenous wolves. Besides, we have among us many widows and orphans, many sick people and helpless little children who are unable to walk or travel. Their fathers and mothers were murdered by that tyrant Ferdinand, that prince of darkness and enemy of divine truth and justice. He also robbed them of their goods. These poor and weak ones are entrusted to us by God the Almighty, who commands us to feed, clothe, and house them, and in every way to serve them in love. So we cannot leave them behind or send them away—truly, may God protect us from ever doing that! We dare not disobey God for the sake of man's command, though it cost our life. We must obey God rather than men.

We have not had time to sell our homes and possessions. They were earned by honest, hard labor, by the sweat of our brows, and rightly belong to us before God and men. We also need time because of the sick, the widows and orphans, and the small children. Praise God, there are not just few but many of these helpless ones among us, about as many as there are able-bodied people. Now, by God's will, we are out on the open heath, harming no one. We do not want to hurt or wrong anyone, not even our worst enemy, be it Ferdinand or anyone else, great or small. All our words and deeds, our conduct, our way of life, are there for all men to see. Rather than knowingly wrong a man to the value of a penny, we would let ourselves be robbed of a hundred gulden. Rather than strike our worst enemy with our hand—to say nothing of spears, swords, and halberds such as the world uses—we would let our own lives be taken.

1535
Jakob Hutter's letter to the governor when the faithful were living on the open heath.

As anyone can see, we have no physical weapons, neither spears nor muskets. No, we want to show by our word and deed that men should live as true followers of Christ, in peace and unity and in God's truth and justice. We are not ashamed of giving an account of ourselves to anyone. It does not trouble us that many evil things are said about us, for Christ foretold all this. It has been the lot of all believers, of Christ himself, and of all his apostles, from the beginning.

Matt.5:10–12
Luke 6:22–23
John 16:2
1 Pet.4:13–14

It is rumored that we took possession of the heath with so many thousands, as if we were going to war, but only a callow, lying scoundrel could talk like that. We lament to God that there are so few believers (which we truly are). We wish all the world lived like us. We would like to convince and turn all men to this faith, for that would mean the end of warfare and injustice.

Next we would like to say that in our present situation we just do not know how we can leave the country unless God the Lord in heaven shows us where to go. You cannot simply deny us a place on the earth or in this country. The earth is the Lord's, and all that is in it belongs to our God in heaven. Besides, if we promised you to go and planned to do so, we might not be able to keep our word, for we are in God's hands and he does with us whatever his will is. Perhaps God wants us to remain in this country to test our faith. This we do not know, but we trust in the eternal and true God.

Ps.24:1
1 Cor.10:26

On the other hand, it is a fact that we are being

1535
Jakob Hutter's letter to the governor when the faithful were living on the open heath.

persecuted and driven out, so we tell you that if the almighty God showed us enough cause to leave the country and move somewhere else, if he gave us good proof that this were his will, we would do it gladly, without waiting for any command from men. Once God's will about where we should go is clear to us, we will not hesitate. We will not and cannot disobey his divine will. Neither can you, even though you may think you can. God the Almighty may suddenly reveal to us, even overnight, that we should leave you. Then we will not delay but be prepared to do his will—either to leave or to die. Perhaps you are not worthy to have us among you any longer.

Therefore, threefold woe to you Moravian lords into all eternity! You have given in to Ferdinand, the awful tyrant and enemy of divine truth—you have agreed to drive those who love and fear God out of your lands. You fear a weak, mortal man more than the living, eternal, almighty God and are willing to expel and ruthlessly persecute the children of God, old and young, even the Lord's widows and orphans in their need and sorrow, and deliver them up to plunder, fear, great suffering, and extreme poverty. It is as if you strangled them with your own hands. We would rather be murdered for the Lord's sake than witness such misery inflicted on innocent, God-fearing hearts. You will have to pay dearly for it, and you will have no more excuse than Pilate, who also did not want to crucify and kill the Lord Jesus. Yet when the Jews threatened him (by God's plan), fear of the emperor made Pilate condemn an innocent man. You do the same, using the king as your excuse. But God has made it known through the mouth of his prophets that he will avenge innocent blood with terrible might on all who stain their hands with it.

John 19:6–12

Joel 3:2
2 Esd. 15:5–27
Jth. 8:18–23

Therefore you will earn great misfortune and distress, deep sorrow—indeed, eternal torment. They are ordained for you by God in heaven, in this life and forever. In the name of our Lord Jesus Christ, we declare that this will certainly happen, and you will soon see that what we have spoken is God's truth. This we declare to you and to all who sin against God.

> We wish you would turn away from evil and turn to the living God so that you may escape this judgment. How we long that you and all men may be saved with us and inherit eternal life. For the sake of God we plead with you to accept his Word and our warning and to take them to heart, for we testify to what we know and to the truth of God. We do this purely out of fear of God and because we love God and all men.
>
> Now we entrust ourselves to the protection of the eternal Lord. May he be gracious to us and dwell with us forever, through Jesus Christ. Amen. As for you, may God the Lord allow you to understand his fatherly warning and chastisement, and may he be merciful to you through our Lord Jesus Christ. His will be done. Amen.

1535
Jakob Hutter's letter to the governor when the faithful were living on the open heath.

John 3:32
Acts 4:20

The governor read this letter from the church, brought to him by his couriers, and immediately sent his servants back with strict orders to arrest Jakob Hutter. Thanks to the foresight and presence of mind of the faithful, they did not find him in the house at Schakwitz or among the people in the camp. So they arrested Wilhelm Griesbacher of Kitzbühel, a servant for temporal affairs, and Loy Salztrager of Hall in the Inn Valley and took these two to Brünn, where they racked and burned them, questioning them under torture about money or goods supposed to be in the possession of the poor fugitives.[1] The brothers told them plainly that they and their fellow believers had not been driven out of their fatherland and inheritance for the sake of money or earthly treasure but had come to this country for the sake of God's truth. On the basis of this confession, Wilhelm was sent, guiltless, to be burned alive. Loy gave way under the great agony of torture. Later, however, he repented deeply and in the end fell asleep in the Lord.

They tried to capture Jakob Hutter.

Wilhelm Griesbacher captured and executed at Brünn.

Loy recanted.

[1]From his prison at Brünn, Wilhelm Griesbacher sent a letter with Hans Donner from Wels, telling the church of his longing to die and exhorting the brothers to remain faithful to one another. He ended his letter asking that they intercede for Loy Salztrager "so that God may open the eyes of his heart and accept him once more in his mercy." Salztrager had recanted and was released on bail, having promised to remain in Brünn at the court's disposal; see Beck, 118–120. His official written recantation read as follows: "I acknowledge that I allowed myself to be seduced by the sect that represents Anabaptism and all that goes with it; that I did wrong and regret it wholeheartedly; that I herewith publicly recant and abjure this same Anabaptist sect of seducers; that I bind myself from now on to the unity of the Christian church and promise to remain faithful to it and not separate from it again, as long as I live" (Loserth, *Anabaptismus*, 473).

1535
Jakob Hutter sent to Tirol.

Since Jakob Hutter was in such great danger that he could no longer serve the church by teaching in public and could never let himself be seen, it was unanimously decided by the church of God that he should move for a time to Tirol, there to gather the saints of the Lord.

The church entrusted to Hans Amon.

Jakob Hutter entrusted the church to Hans Amon and advised them how to proceed in case they should need another servant. The church accepted this from God in great thankfulness. They commended Jakob to the grace of God with many tears and sorrowful hearts, and after a solemn leave-taking they sent him on his way with the prayers of the church.

Forbidden to draw the water they needed.

They divided into groups and parted from one another on the heath.

The people out on the open heath moved from place to place, unwilling to part from one another. But when they were refused all provisions and even water, they at last had to separate into groups of eight or ten. Each brother with the little group entrusted to him had it laid on his heart very earnestly that they should care for one another as God gave them grace and that no one should hold back from helping another. It was said in particular that nobody should leave Moravia without asking advice. This separation was quite pitiful; with many tears they set off like Abraham, not knowing where God would grant them a place to live.

In the time following, Hans Amon and his assistants carried out their service as well as they could, making every effort to visit the people wherever they were, up and down the country, and faithfully providing for all their needs as far as possible. The people wandered about the land in misery and suffering for almost a whole year.

Almost a year in distress, moving from place to place.

Leonhard Lanzenstiel found shelter in Steinebrunn in Austria.

As there was little hope then of finding a place in Moravia where they could settle, Leonhard Lanzenstiel, with those entrusted to him, took on harvesting and later other work for Lord Hans Fünfkirchen at Steinebrunn in Austria, not far from the Moravian border.[1] They remained there for some time.

In Tirol Jakob Hutter traveled about in great need and anguish of heart, sparing no effort to bring salvation to many.[2] He

[1]The lords of Fünfkirchen owned the parish and estate of Steinebrunn and Fünfkirchen Castle, Lower Austria, across the Austrian border from Nikolsburg (Mikulov). In 1539 the Anabaptist community at Steinebrunn was suppressed, and ninety members were carried off to the galleys of Andrea Doria; see below, pp. 188–196.

[2]Hutter himself described his activities in Tirol in a letter to the church in Moravia. The following excerpt is translated from Codex I 87.708, fol. 168ff., Vienna

visited the people with the Word of God and gathered them under great difficulty, for throughout the country strict mandates were issued against them. For example, the judge of Brixen rode into Lüsen,[1] summoned all the men, women, and children able to walk, and read out a brutal mandate

1535
Jakob Hutter traveled through Tirol in great sadness.

University Library.

> At the same time we are deeply pained and full of sorrow—godly sorrow—hearing how much evil opposition and injustice has been spreading and that many who had given themselves to God and were our brothers and sisters have lost the way because of this persecution and the temptations of the world. They have broken their covenant with the Lord and his people in an ungodly way. They go back on their promises and join the devil and the world again, becoming enemies of God and his children. . . .
>
> You should know that our presence here is no longer a secret. The wicked people know it and are very hostile, raising a great hue and cry. The ungodly, thieving clergy, those messengers of the devil, those cruel hellhounds, are already raving from their pulpits about us and warning people that we are in the country and up in the mountains and ordering them to attend their accursed church services, idol-worship, and mass. . . .
>
> The Lord is still daily adding those who are saved to his holy church. The harvest is ripe, and there is much work to do, but good laborers are scarce. We need to call upon the Lord of the harvest, as Christ says, pleading with him to send workers into his vineyard. Many of the people we were told about as having open hearts and seeking the truth do not amount to anything, and many we knew nothing about come forward, accept the faith, and join us. One disciple awakens another, and so one is discovered and led to God by the other. There is so much of God's work for us to do—work with the brothers and sisters, work with those still seeking God, work with children, work everywhere—that we cannot do it all at once, and some things have to be left undone. But we will do as much as we can and will not spare ourselves. We are really needed everywhere at once. The urgency and greatness of the task weigh heavily upon us. . . .
>
> As you know, Martin Nieder and Christel Bühler fell away from God and his people and are excluded; they are now up here in Sterzing. They are ungodly, wicked men, traitors in alliance with the devil. They have betrayed everything they know to the authorities at Innsbruck, telling many terrible lies, and they continue to do so. Devil's brood that they are, they slander and blaspheme the truth of God. Of their wickedness and sin quite a lot more could be said, but I will write about that to the servants. I will just say this: They plan to come to your area in a few days. They have no good intentions—they are only out to make trouble, and their designs are very evil. The enemies are planning to send them to you; but do not trust these men. They will come like thieves and murderers, sent out to rob, cheat, and kill. Beware!

For the complete text of this letter, see *MQR*, April 1941, 129–140; Fischer, *Jakob Huter*, Briefe 44–52; translated in Jakob Hutter, *Brotherly Faithfulness*, Letter VI, 103–118.

[1]Lüsen, a parish northeast of Brixen (Bressanone), South Tirol (now Italy), was Balthasar Dosser's birthplace (*ME*, II, 95); in 1525, Carlstadt's residence (*ME*, II, 519–521); in 1536, a stronghold of Tirolean Anabaptists, one of whose prominent leaders was Hans Grünfelder; see below, p.162; *ME*, III, 415.

1535 forbidding anyone to lodge or shelter us. If anyone did, he would be punished more severely than ever before and his house would be burned to the ground, for his lord at Brixen would not tolerate such people but would root them out. Soon after this he captured several brothers and sisters and took them to Brixen.[1]

---

[1]Conditions in Tirol and the dangers surrounding Jakob Hutter are described in his last letter to the church in Moravia, doubtless the source for this account. Here follows one passage taken from this letter (Codex I 87.708, fol. 356, Vienna University Library).

> Beloved brothers and sisters, about ourselves I can say that we are living in love and faith and in the peace and unity of the Holy Spirit. But in our hearts there is great pain and sorrow for your sake, and outwardly we, too, are suffering severe persecution. The horrible, raging dragon has opened its jaws wide to devour the woman robed with the sun, who is the church and the bride of Jesus Christ.
>
> After our meeting on Sunday, a beloved brother from Taufers was captured on his way home. Soon afterward, the judge of Brixen rode into the village of Lüsen, summoned all the men, women, and children able to walk, and read out to them a cruel mandate that forbade them to house or shelter any of us. If anyone did, he would be punished more severely than ever before, and his house would be burned to the ground. The judge said that this thing was spreading and getting out of hand, and his fiendish master, the prince-bishop of Brixen, would not tolerate it but would root it out. He has just been here and now threatens the people with big words, forbidding what is good and right and commanding what is evil. The believers, however, are still courageous and pay no attention to his threats but serve God eagerly and do his will.
>
> The judge would have held off for a while to see whether we would let ourselves be intimidated and take part in their blasphemous idol worship. As far as he was concerned, he would gladly have looked the other way, but his deputies would not leave him in peace. Our brothers and sisters are already known to everybody in the valley and round about.
>
> When the judge saw that his orders had no effect on the faithful, he set out and captured five or six of our brothers and sisters and took them to Brixen. On that occasion God protected the others, but we have just now been informed by an unbeliever that five more have been taken from Lüsen to Brixen. We have not heard anything definite, but there is good reason to worry about what is happening to them and how they are faring. At this point we do not know where they are imprisoned, but God in heaven knows. I immediately sent brothers to Lüsen and all around to visit the brothers and sisters and find out how they are. They have not returned yet, so I really do not know how matters stand. But it is very likely that all have been chased out and scattered and that wherever they are they are in great danger.
>
> So far, everything we have heard about the prisoners, and all the others, points to their steadfastness and faithfulness. May God comfort them with the Holy Spirit and strengthen them with his Word. May he keep them in his name and truth to the end. May he stand by their side through Jesus Christ to help and support them in his great mercy. Amen.
>
> Our brother Hieronymus will surely tell you what our situation is and whatever else there is to report. He is as well informed about everything as I am at the moment and knows what you need to be told. He is our living

Soon after these events, in the night of St. Andrew's Eve [Nov. 29] 1535, God allowed it to happen that Jakob Hutter was arrested. He was deceived and betrayed at Klausen on the Eisack River in the Adige region. They tied a gag in his mouth and brought him to Innsbruck, the seat of King Ferdinand's government. They tortured him and caused him great agony by all they did to him, yet they were not able to change his heart or make him deny the truth. Even when they tried to prove him wrong with Scripture, they could not stand up to him. Full of hatred and revenge, the priests imagined they would drive the devil out of him. They put him in ice-cold water and then took him into a warm room and had him beaten with rods. They lacerated his body, poured brandy into the wounds, and set it on fire. They tied his hands and again gagged him to prevent him from denouncing their wickedness. Putting a hat with a tuft of feathers on his head, they led him into the house of their idols and in every way made a laughingstock of him. After he had suffered all their cruelty and yet remained firm and upright, a Christian hero steadfast in faith, these wicked sons of Caiaphas and Pilate condemned him and burned him alive at the stake. A huge crowd was present and saw his steadfast witness. This took place about the time of Candlemas [Feb. 2], on the Friday before the first week of Lent, 1536.[1]

1535
Jakob Hutter captured.

Jakob Hutter cruelly tortured at Innsbruck.

Jakob Hutter burned alive.

---

letter to you and will answer all your questions. For the rest, let us all wait patiently for the Lord.

For the complete text of this letter, see Müller, *Glaubenszeugnisse*, I, 150–151; Fischer, *Jakob Huter*, Briefe 62–72; translated in Jakob Hutter, *Brotherly Faithfulness*, Letter VIII, 137–157, and Robert Friedmann, "Jakob Hutter's Last Epistle to the Church in Moravia, 1535," *MQR*, Jan. 1960, 37–47; see also Beck, 120 n.2.

[1]As he was being led to the stake, Jakob Hutter said to his executioners: "Come closer, those of you who would gainsay me! Let us test our faith in the fire. This fire will harm my soul as little as the fiery furnace harmed Shadrach, Meshach, and Abednego" (Beck, 123).

February 25, 1536, is the date generally accepted for Jakob Hutter's death, borne out by the following quotation from a report of the municipality of Innsbruck to the Provincial revenue office, dated February 26, 1536: "Since the Anabaptist Jakob Hutter, who had been brought to His Majesty's prison in the *Kreuterturm* here [at Innsbruck] on November 29, 1535, and on the 25th of this month of February was removed from prison and was executed according to the law, and since during this time the said Hutter. . . was provided with food and drink by our beadle, Martin Hayler, who demands 12 kreuzers per day, we therefore request that payment of 17 gulden and 24 kreuzers be made to said Martin Hayler." See Loserth, *Anabaptismus*, 558–564; *ME*, II, 851–854.

1535
For nearly 3 years Jakob Hutter had led the church with the Word of God.

Why we are called Hutterian Brethren.

Jakob Hutter had led the church for nearly three years and left behind him a people gathered and built up for the Lord. It is from this Jakob Hutter that the church inherited the name Hutterite, or Hutterian Brethren. To this day the church is not ashamed of this name. He stood joyfully for the truth unto death and gave his life for it. This has been the fate of all Christ's apostles.

When Jakob Hutter was captured, the brothers in Tirol immediately sent word to Hans Amon and the church at Auspitz in Moravia.

1536–1547: Growth of the Movement Despite Severe Persecution

1536

In the first days of 1536 the church sent brothers to Tirol: Hieronymus Käls of Kufstein, schoolmaster of the church community of God, and with him Michael Seifensieder from Wallern in Bohemia and Hans Oberecker from the Adige Valley. They reached Vienna in Austria, but already on January 8 they were taken prisoner while sheltering at an inn, a stopping place for the Neustadt wagons. During the evening meal the people there made efforts to get them to drink toasts, as is the devilish custom. The brothers told them plainly that they would not take part in that or in any other horrible practice. When the others noticed this and recognized who the brothers were, they began to slander and tell lies about the community, which the brothers refuted. After the meal one of the men at the table called for paper and ink and wrote a letter in Latin that said, among other things, "There are three persons here who I think are Anabaptists." He did not know that Hieronymus Käls understood Latin.[1]

Hieronymus Käls and 2 others captured in Vienna.

Hieronymus told the other brothers. They talked it over and agreed to wait and see what would happen. After two hours the judge's servants arrived, bound them, and took them to the judge. When he found out that they were from Jakob Hutter's church, he said they were undoubtedly the right men. They said, "Praise to God, we are indeed the right men!" He had them taken to his house and put in a common prison.

Hieronymus and the 2 brothers with him knew they were betrayed but decided to see what would happen.

A week later the judge summoned them to appear before his court and urged each of them individually to recant. They

They were tried and exhorted to recant.

[1]The above story is based on Hieronymus Käls's letter to Hans Amon, quoted by Johann Loserth in "Deutschböhmische Wiedertäufer," *Mittheilungen des Vereins für Geschichte der Deutschen in Böhmen*, XXX, Nr. 4 (Prague, 1892), 413–414.

1536

replied that with God's grace they would hold to the truth to the end of their lives. In turn they urged their hearers to change from their unbelief and no longer misuse the precious name of Christ. This made the judge furious with Hieronymus. Every time he told them they were not Christians, the judge called him a wicked scoundrel. When he questioned Hieronymus for the tenth time and received the same testimony, the members of the court said, "This evil man is not worthy of your honor's anger."

The judge enraged because Hieronymus told them they were not Christians.

After another week in prison, all three brothers were summoned by the judge. He had called three especially evil priests, who tried to talk with them, pouring contempt on our calling and slandering our faith. They claimed they were sent to show them their error. Hieronymus answered cheerfully, "We are on the right path, and our mission is from God, as Christ has taught us. We must not listen to an alien voice." He added, "We are ready to give all men an account of our faith and the foundation of our hope, but we have no desire to speak with monks and priests or anyone sent by the pope (who is the antichrist), for there are no greater scoundrels, fornicators, adulterers, deceivers, and corrupters than they."

Hieronymus and the 2 brothers questioned a second time.

John 10:5

Hieronymus told the priests that there were no greater scoundrels, fornicators, and deceivers than they.

At that the judge said, "No, no, my Hieronymus. You do not know these good lords."

Hieronymus said, "God is Lord, not they."

Next he was questioned under torture for two and a quarter hours on original sin, on infant baptism, on mission, and on the idolatrous mass. His interrogators implored him to think of his wife and children, to consider his own life, and to take their appeals to heart and pray to God. They would pray too. But he told them the truth and said he would stand by it, regardless of their attitude. After they had also failed to overcome the other two with their poison, the judge ordered them all back to prison. Here they composed songs (which we still have) and often sang them to each other, even at night.[1]

---

[1]Hieronymus Käls's three songs are in *LdHBr*, 67–71: "Ich freu mich dein, o Vater mein" (In you, O Father, is my joy; see below, pp.358–360 for complete translation), "Ich reu und klag den ganzen Tag" (All day long I sorrow and lament), and "Ich will dich, Herre und mein Gott, loben" (I will praise you, my Lord and my God). Wolkan, *Lieder*, 170; *Martyrs Mirror*, 445–446; *ME*, III, 139–140; Beck, 127–129. See also Friedmann, *Schriften*, 119.

Käls himself describes their singing in prison in a letter he sent to his fellow prisoners (Codex I 87.708, fol. 237, Vienna University Library).

. . . Praise be to God, I rejoice with all my heart to hear you sing in the

They were joyful in the Lord, and when they found they were able to hear one another, they shouted from their prison cells, greeting, comforting, and strengthening one another. The church still has in its possession letters they wrote to one another, full of love and burning zeal. They also wrote down their confession of faith and defense, fully supported by passages from Holy Scripture, and gave them to the judge and lords at Vienna.[1] *1536*

> Lord, especially you, my dear brother Michael, when you sing evening songs. I can understand almost every word if you are sitting right by the window and I listen carefully. Please, my very dear brother, wake me more often out of my sleepiness with your songs in the Lord Jesus Christ. I often woke early on Hans's account and began to sing, and then you both sang together. I love hearing each one of you, for I rejoice when I hear the Jerusalem song being sung, dear brothers. The very fact that it hurts Satan so much is a sure sign that it is pleasing to God; for they think they have prevented us from talking and comforting one another. So let us shout until we are hoarse! I sang two songs then and would have liked to give them to you, but the devil works harder than I would ever have imagined. I sang them in the Lord and not otherwise, for when the ungodly start their blasphemy and idle talk, I start making up songs as if I were deaf so that I don't hear their ungodly talk. May the Lord teach you to sing his songs! Amen.

[1]For the confession of faith, dated "Friday before Passion Sunday" (two weeks before Easter), see Müller, *Glaubenszeugnisse*, I, 206–210; Codex I 87.708, fol. 219–230, Vienna University Library. From fol. 228 we quote the moving farewell letter Hieronymus Käls wrote to his wife:

> My own dear wife, my most beloved Traindel, I, Hieronymus, wish you everything good from God our faithful heavenly Father through Jesus Christ, his beloved Son, our Lord. Amen. My beloved sister Traindel, I am sending you a Christian song, which I sang with a sincere heart in my prison through God's Spirit. May the Lord teach you, too, to sing it to his praise and glory. I am sending it out of heartfelt love to remind you of my loving plea and admonition when I last took leave of you: remain God-fearing, faithful, and steadfast in the truth. I hold nothing against you, my dear sister. I thank God for you; I thank my heavenly Father who in his grace gave you to me and united us through his faithful servants. Now I have given you back to him, my chosen gift from God, and with all my heart commend you to the Lord's keeping, along with the children whom he in his grace gave us both.
>
> My dear sister, praise and thank God with all your heart for making me—weak, poor, and unworthy creature that I am—worthy of being a witness to his divine truth in this cruel, sodomite city of Vienna. I pray more and more fervently that God may keep you among his holy children. May you always be obedient to the beloved sisters and brothers and be of a lowly and humble heart and always esteem another more highly than yourself. O dear Traindel, love the children of God dearly and be humble and respectful toward them. Never forget what God has done for you. I entreat you, set your heart on good and godly things so that you may see me and I you and that we all may see the Lord with joy on the last day. May God help us all in this. Amen. Greet all the saints for me, and where I have wronged you, forgive me for Christ's sake. This I ask of all God's

1536
A vision of the Lord's judgment day appeared 3 times to Hans Oberecker.

Three times, Hans Oberecker (mentioned above) had a vision of the day of the Lord that is to come over the whole world. We still have the letter he wrote from the prison where he saw with the inner eyes of his heart—as clearly as if he were seeing with the eyes of his head—certain things which words could not express. He saw how it is with the children of God, who have received God's abundant grace, and in contrast, with what overwhelming power and terror this day breaks in upon the ungodly. This made him pray, "O my God, let us never fall under your wrath, which is so great and terrifying for all the children of wickedness."

Hieronymus Käls and the 2 brothers burned at Vienna.

After all kinds of torture had been used against these brothers, during which they remained steadfast as valiant knights and lovers of God, they were condemned to death by these sons of Pilate and burned to ashes in Vienna on the Friday before Passion Sunday [2 weeks before Easter], Lent 1536. It was this same Hieronymus Käls who wrote the following prayers for the schoolchildren:

Before and After Meals

Our children's prayer at mealtimes in the school.

O Lord almighty, eternal, and merciful God, our Father, we your little children praise, honor, and thank you with all our hearts. We praise your holy, all-powerful, and glorious name for your great and unspeakable grace and mercy, which you have shown us through Jesus Christ. We thank you that you tend us as your little children at all times with your faithful and fatherly care and give us food and drink for body and soul and at all times graciously provide us with all we need. We praise and glorify you in your holy heaven and give thanks to you with all our hearts through Jesus Christ for ever and ever. Amen.

The Long Children's Prayer
before going to sleep in the evening
and after getting up in the morning

Our children's evening and morning prayer.

O almighty, eternal, and merciful God, you who have created all things in heaven, on earth, and in the sea and who

---

children. Greet my son David for me. Greet my dear brother Leonhard Lanzenstiel from me and ask him to teach you the tune; sing it for my sake. May the Lord comfort his people forevermore. Amen.

have made everything holy and good and through your grace have made us in your image—we thank you for it all.

1536
Our children's evening and morning prayer.

O holy Father, we praise your holy name for your unspeakable grace and mercy. We all ask you with our whole heart, O beloved Father, look down from heaven with your merciful eyes upon us poor, helpless little ones. May we be commended to your care. Grant us your blessing and your heavenly wisdom.

O gracious God and merciful Father, may we be planted according to your will. May we be brought up in fear and obedience to you, in your truth and righteousness. May we learn to serve you and to honor and glorify you together with your holy people, whom you have chosen from the whole world, from all nations, for which they are hated and persecuted by all men. O Lord, strengthen and comfort your people and uphold them in your truth so that we may be kept in your favor, holy and unstained before your countenance. O holy Father, we who are still very young pray to you with all our hearts for our parents, whom you have given us through your grace and set in authority over us. Give them grace and strength, understanding and wisdom, to bring us up according to your divine will, to keep us from evil and to teach us what is good.

O holy Father, we pray for our beloved brothers and sisters in prison the world over, who suffer torture, fear, and distress. O Lord, strengthen them and comfort them with the power of your Holy Spirit and uphold them in your truth, pure and unstained before your blessed countenance.

O holy Father, we entrust and give ourselves to you completely. Do with us what is pleasing to you, only let not your favor and your compassion be taken away from us or from your people. All this we ask of you, beloved and only Father, through our dear Lord Jesus Christ. Amen.

The Lord's Prayer.

O one true and merciful God, we also pray to you as your Son Jesus Christ has taught us: Our Father in heaven, your name be hallowed, your kingdom come, your will be done on earth as in heaven. Give us today our daily bread and forgive us the wrong we have done as we forgive those who have wronged us. Lead us not into temptation, but deliver us from all evil. For yours is the kingdom, the power, and the glory for ever and ever. Amen.

1536

Praise, honor, glory, and blessing be to you, within us and through us and in all your saints, together with all your heavenly hosts, through our Lord Jesus Christ. Amen.

Some found shelter and work at Böhmisch Krumau.

At the time I have just described, some carpenters and miners found both work and housing at Böhmisch Krumau and in the mines at Brimsitz; they also lived at the gold mine at Heroltitz half a mile outside Tischlawitz. Their steward was Onophrius Griesinger.

Onophrius Griesinger again entrusted with the service of the Word and sent to Tirol.

In early spring, Onophrius was summoned before the elders, and the whole church once more entrusted the service of the Gospel to him. Soon afterward he was sent to Tirol, commended to the grace of God by the prayer of the saints. On the way he was captured in Styria, but through God's intervention he was soon freed and continued his journey to Tirol as he had been instructed. There he visited all who belonged to the Lord. He sent his assistants with letters and messages to the Swiss Brethren in Switzerland in an effort to stimulate them to a more perfect life, but to no avail.

At Easter 1536 Hans Amon and the elders who assisted him summoned the people from Böhmisch Krumau, Brimsitz, Heroltitz, and wherever they were living up and down the country. They gathered the church in the pine forest between Nikolsburg and Pulgram and celebrated the blessed meal of remembrance of the Lord Jesus Christ in great joy. The local magistrates came upon them there and ordered them to leave the grounds. So after their meeting they commended themselves to God's care and returned to the places they had come from, joyfully praising God.

Lord's Supper held in the pine forest.

Georg Fasser, a servant, and Leonhard Lanzenstiel sent to Tirol.

Brother Georg Fasser, too, a servant of the Lord and his people, was instructed by the church to travel to Tirol. Leonhard Lanzenstiel was named as his companion. The church took farewell of them with earnest prayer as they set out to bring many zealous people to the Lord. On their way to Vienna, at an inn near Neudorf in Austria, they met a number of kindhearted people and spoke with them. There was a group of evil sodomites at the inn who took hold of a simple man by force and shamefully mistreated him. For the same kind of wickedness in the days of the judges, God destroyed 80,000 men.

When the brothers left Neudorf, they were followed, taken prisoner, and put in the stocks in the town. The next day the judge came from Mödling with his whole council and a number of other people and asked them why they had been imprisoned. "For the sake of divine truth and justice," they said. They were taken a short distance to the market town of Mödling, two miles from Vienna. All the way to the prison they joyfully testified to the truth and spoke at length about God's judgment, at which the judge and those with him were so terrified that they found no words to answer them.

1536
Georg Fasser and Leonhard Lanzenstiel captured at Neudorf near Mödling in Austria.

They gave witness all the way to the prison.

The brothers were put in a common prison where evil, ungodly men of all kinds were confined with them. This was a source of great distress to them every day, and they would rather have been in a stinking dungeon than witness their ungodly ways.

Georg Fasser and Leonhard Lanzenstiel would have preferred a stinking dungeon to the lewd company of a common prison.

While they were imprisoned they were frequently cross-examined about infant baptism and the mass and asked why we called our opponents "ungodly" and "unbelieving." But our brothers told them that they understood the mass and infant baptism very well and that those who called themselves Christians assumed the name falsely and did not come anywhere near what Christ taught and commanded. They should know that they belong to the devil and that if they did not repent of their sins, God would blot out their false claim. They would be cast out with all the worldly, just like the rich man, and thrown into the pit of hell. This would surely happen, even if they did not believe it.

The two brothers were held in prison for nearly a year. They were fully prepared to die and witness to the truth with their blood, unless God performed a miracle. We still have some wonderful letters they wrote to the church during that time.[1]

---

[1]Georg Fasser and Leonhard Lanzenstiel wrote nine letters from prison to the church in Moravia (of which five are in Codex A b 5, fol. 123–174, Budapest University Library), and Hans Amon wrote four in reply, (fol. 34–59). See Friedmann, *Schriften*, 48, 120–121; Beck, 129–130. Parts of their letters are quoted here. The first letter gives details of their capture:

> We set out on the Tuesday before St. Philip and St. James's Day [May 1], taking leave of you in the peace of the Lord. About two o'clock the following Thursday afternoon, we reached Neudorf without any incident and went to the inn. By chance we met our dear sister, Hans Schuster's wife, and others who seemed to be good people. In the same house was a group of grossly immoral sodomites, making it impossible for us to talk together in the Lord for any length of time. We looked around for another

1536
Released from prison, Georg Fasser and Leonhard Lanzenstiel returned to the church.

By God's special intervention they were released, their consciences wonderfully preserved from harm. They arrived joyfully at the village of Drasenhofen[1] and were received by the church with great rejoicing as beloved and honored guests.

> inn, and the wife of the customs officer promised us lodging. We were no sooner in the stable behind the house, talking together and wondering how things were in the Lungau region (Austria), than the very same indecent sodomites burst in and attacked us violently. How they treated us concerned us very little, but when we heard the name of God and his tabernacle blasphemed, we were struck in our consciences. For the sake of those who were seeking the truth, we spoke out from zealous hearts and showed these men their sin and their evil, ungodly ways. . . .
>
> After this we left the inn and parted from each other. We had gone a little beyond the village when we were overtaken and arrested, without Hans Schuster's wife or the others knowing of it. That, in short, is how our imprisonment started.
>
> We were put in the stocks at Neudorf for the night and until Friday noon. The judge from Mödling, a large market town nearby, came to us with the whole council and others besides. The judge asked us why we had been taken prisoner. We answered, "For the sake of divine truth and righteousness." Then we went with them to Mödling, and all the way to the prison we joyfully gave witness to the truth and told them about the terrible wrath and judgment of God.

The second letter, dated May 11, 1536, cautioned the brothers:

> We would like to write more to you, dear brothers and sisters, but we are always afraid our letters will be confiscated. At the beginning we wrote you many letters, but the ungodly judge confiscated them. I wrote to you, dear brother Hans, and to Blasi and Michael, Klaus Müller, Oswald and Balthasar Mair, as well as to the dear sisters in the kitchen, and three letters to other brothers and sisters. Now that some of your names are known to the judge, be all the more watchful so that nothing happens to you, for the judge is now at the Diet in Vienna.

The third letter, dated May 13, is one of inner encouragement. In the fourth, dated May 19, the two brothers say:

> Outwardly our prison conditions are quite good, but the Lord knows how much we suffer daily because of the shamelessness of our fellow prisoners. Truly we would rather be in a stinking hole than listen to their evil talk.

The fifth letter, dated Ascension Day 1536, is full of dark forebodings.

> I have the feeling that this will be our last letter to you because of the ungodly judge and his whole council. Earlier they had assured us that our case would end in our favor, but I never believed them, as I wrote before. Now they are beginning to threaten us with burning and other cruel and agonizing tortures if we don't recant. . . . O merciful God, make us worthy to die for the sake of your name, for our joy is great and we long to depart from this life. We now wait from one hour to the next and cannot count on living one more day. Georg and I are staying together for as long as it is God's will. Either they are going to try us further, or they realize we will never recant, as we told them at the beginning of our imprisonment.

About Leonhard Lanzenstiel, see also above, p.85 n.3.

[1]Drasenhofen, Austria, near the border with Moravia, formerly part of the Steinebrunn estate.

1536

At that time God provided his people with more places to live, as was told above. He moved the hearts of the population to have compassion for them and give them shelter. From a nobleman called Sturtzhauser, the elders in Austria secured a house at Drasenhofen, just outside Steinebrunn. There they once more built up Christian community. Now for an appointed time King Ferdinand had to tolerate in his patrimonial territory what he had been unwilling to tolerate in Moravia. This should be recognized as an act of God and not an accident.

The brothers lived at Drasenhofen in Austria.

Groups of believers started gathering also in the town of Kostel and at Rohrbach near Gross Seelowitz in Moravia.[1] The members of Christ's church met eagerly with great joy and courage. They came by day and night, walking many miles through wind, rain, snow, and mud to hear the Word of the Lord. Each cared for the other in a brotherly, Christian way, with warmth and tenderness, ready to serve each other in love. They had to make do with small, cramped dwellings, all moving closer together and putting up with many shortages and worries. Yet they wholeheartedly thanked and praised God for it all. They were all kind and patient, as befits the saints who say they are guests and sojourners on earth. They seek a better country, a heavenly one ruled by the Lord Jesus Christ, and that is why they bear with one another patiently, like guests in a foreign land.

They lived and gathered at Rohrbach and Kostel.

Zeal for God's Word in spite of wind, rain, snow, and mud.

Cramped living quarters.

Heb.11:13–16

Their children were brought up communally, entrusted to God-fearing sisters, who conscientiously took care of them and led them to the Lord through Christian discipline. And so the faithful continually praised God, who had provided dwelling places for them.

They educated their children together.

In those times of trial, when there was no place in Moravia for the brothers and sisters to settle, Ulrich Stadler and Leonhard Lochmaier (both servants of the Word),[2] Michael Kramer (a servant for temporal affairs) from Gangkofen, and

Ulrich Stadler and his people moved from Austerlitz to Poland.

---

[1]Kostel (Podivín), northwest of Lundenburg (Břeclav); property of the Liechtenstein family until 1553, when it was sold to the provincial governor Vaclav of Ludanice, who had defended religious freedom at the 1550 Diet of Brünn; Johann von Zerotin bought the property in 1559. See *ME*, II, 552, "Gostal"; Zeman, *Topography*, #63.

Rohrbach (Hrušovany u. Brna), south of Brno, west of Gross Seelowitz (Židlochovice); see Zeman, *Topography*, #132, #139.

[2]Ulrich Stadler, a former mining official at Sterzing, was born in Brixen, Tirol. In the early 1520s he became a Lutheran but soon joined the brothers at Austerlitz. When persecution set in, he moved with part of the community to Poland. One of

1536

a small group of brothers and sisters left the church at Austerlitz because of differences in their faith. They moved to Krasnik in the kingdom of Poland, where they went through times of fear and suffering, as the following letter shows:

Ulrich Stadler's letter to the authorities in Poland.

> The church of Jesus Christ, gathered in his name, addresses the following words to you, the two governors: God the Almighty knows the cruel way you treated his poor hunted children all winter. You held us by force, although we never intended to remain in this place. You carried off our faithful elders for no good reason, and to this hour we do not know whether they are living or dead; you took our brothers by force, without any justification.
>
> Now you are threatening to burn us all, though we have done no harm to any of your people. Your only reason is that we refuse to bow down before your idols (for you worship the work of your own hands) and to obey your Roman church. We obey the Lord Christ alone, in life and in death. You have no other complaint against us. We have lived among you as God-fearing people, working faithfully for you and spending only what we earned in Moravia by the work of our hands.
>
> You have put us in prison for contempt of the royal command to leave the king's land. (We heard this from the lord Wojewoda[1] himself.) But we were willing to comply with that order, and we did not refuse to obey the authorities, as people falsely report.
>
> So far you have always dealt crookedly with us. You have continually threatened to divide and scatter us as if we were prisoners you have captured in battle or criminals under arrest or slaves you have bought. You have not only threatened to do these things but have actually done

---

his epistles regarding original sin is dated 1536 at Ladomir (Vladimir-Volynskij), and addressed to the brothers at Kraśnik, southwest of Lublin, where there was evidently another community; see Müller, *Glaubenszeugnisse*, I, 228–232; (Codex I 87.708, fol. 28–35, Vienna University Library). Stadler died in 1540 at Butschowitz in Moravia. For Stadler's treatise on community, see Rudolf Wolkan, *Die Hutterer: Oesterreichische Wiedertäufer und Kommunisten in Amerika* (Vienna, 1918), 153–160; Williams, *Writers*, 274–284. See also Robert Friedmann, "Stadler, Ulrich," *ME*, IV, 607–608; Beck, 133; Fast, *Der linke Flügel*, 137–147; Friedmann, *Schriften*, 127–128.

About Leonard Lochmaier, see below, pp.169–172.

[1]*Wojewoda* (Polish), the military governor of a province or kingdom.

them to us. You were not willing to search your hearts and humbly consider that God, the protector of widows and orphans, knows how unjustly you are dealing with his poor, exiled children. Yes, in very truth, God the Lord, the righteous Judge, will bring upon each man's head whatever he did in this world, be it good or evil, for on the day of judgment it will be clearly shown to all. Strict judgment without mercy will be passed on everyone who has not been merciful to his neighbor in this world. You are misusing the power God gave you to protect the devout and punish evildoers. He did not give you power in matters of faith. Christ alone rules over our faith, not the pope or any worldly power. This Lord does not want anyone to be coerced for the sake of his faith, much less killed, as the world does today.

1536
Ulrich Stadler's letter to the authorities in Poland.

James 2:13

Rom. 13:3–4
1 Pet. 2:14

The Lord Christ himself will come to inflict vengeance on all who do not want to obey his holy Gospel in this time of grace. We fear you have done all these things and that you are not innocent. It is also not right that you call us to repentance, as if we did not know enough to discern whether or not your lives and deeds are of God. The apostle John says that the man who is of God does what is right. And Paul says, "Do not be deceived, dear brothers; evildoers will not inherit the kingdom of God."

2 Thess. 1:7–8

1 John 3:7,9
1 Cor. 6:9

So how can you challenge us, saying, "Repent, be converted, and become Christians," while you yourselves are not Christians but heathens? Therefore we say to you with one accord and in the fear of God, "Turn from your evil ways and your unjust deeds, or you will inherit eternal damnation." Consider carefully what we are writing. The time will come when you will acknowledge the truth of our words.

Next we remind you that we came here in peace and have lived with you peaceably, offending none. If you had not detained us unjustly, we would have moved on just as peacefully wherever God led us. Truly, God did not give the authorities their power in order to harm peaceful people but to protect them. But as you and we are not united in faith, you cannot help us. Therefore we must leave everything in Christ's hands, for in his own time he will judge between the sheep and the goats. He alone is the righteous Judge.

1536
Ulrich Stadler's letter to the authorities in Poland.

Therefore, if there is at least a little fear of God in you, you should take heed and stop sinning against poor, peaceful strangers. But if you will not stop your wanton cruelty to us, we will wait patiently for the Lord Christ, who will come in his own time to rescue us from your hands. If you insist on keeping us by force, we want you to know that we are here against our will—we are here only because you are intent on wreaking your violence and cruelty on us. If you have orders from your king to keep us here (which we do not believe), then direct us to some place where we can provide for ourselves like other free people who are not prisoners or purchased slaves; for in God's eyes we are free. You will see that we are ready to work for you and all men faithfully and diligently, as much as we are able—indeed, as if we were serving Christ himself, as the apostle Paul teaches us.

Eph.6:7
Col.3:23–24

If, however, you persist in threatening us and treating us harshly, we are willing to endure it, trusting that our gracious Father will grant patience to us and to all who trust him and believe in Christ. But you will not benefit from such a course. Unless you keep us in chains and fetters, we will not stay with you. You know very well that anyone held like that is unable to work joyfully and efficiently. Besides, your consciences will torment you for treating us so inhumanly, and everyone will see your injustice and brutality, for even in this place there are many people whose hearts are filled with pity for us, though they dare not say so for fear of you.

With this letter we want to make you aware of all this, and we pray that God's eternal punishment may not overtake you, as it surely overtakes all those who do not love and fear God with pure hearts. But all our wishes will not help you unless you wholeheartedly repent and change your lives.

Therefore, we sincerely warn you not to undertake further action but to fear God with all your heart. Since you have repeatedly challenged us: "Repent, repent, and be converted," it is only right that we also challenge you to repent in your turn. So we say in all sincerity, renounce your evil ways and then point out to us what we have done wrong while living among you. We are ready to

1536
Ulrich Stadler's letter to the authorities in Poland.

turn from any wrong that you know about us, yet at the same time we must truthfully point out your evil actions to you. Or do you think we can keep silent about what you are doing to us?

Among you, Christianity consists in fasting on Friday, according to your custom, and gorging at midday until your bellies can't hold any more. And when you have kept the Sunday, you think you have done all you should. Oh, you are very much mistaken! If only we spoke your language, we would mince no words in telling you and all men the sinfulness of such conduct.

We have written this to you in good faith. If the lord Wojewoda comes we will write to him, too, what God the Lord has shown us. This letter is written in the spirit of the whole church community of Christ. We hope it will challenge you and call you to repentance. We have also pointed out what you have done to us. May the gracious and compassionate God, the Father of all the devout, have mercy on you and grant you his understanding in Christ, if this is your longing. Amen.

If you are hurt by what we have written, remember this proverb: The truth gives rise to envy, and the truth stabs the liar. The Latin in which we have written to you is very simple; we were not able to express ourselves any better. In German we could have made it much clearer to you. To God be the honor.

On the strength of this letter, the brothers were allowed to leave the country. Some of them got as far as Slovakia but could hardly make their way to Moravia because of the many robbers.

These brothers then bought a house at Butschowitz.[1] Soon after, Ulrich Stadler, Leonhard Lochmaier, and Michael Kramer set out on behalf of their people to visit Hans Amon

[1]At that time, 1536, the manor and town of Butschowitz (Bučovice), just east of Austerlitz, Moravia, was the property of Anna of Ojnice and her husband, Count Václav Černohorský of Boskovice, after whose death it passed to his sons Albrecht Černohorský and Jan Šembera; see Zeman, *Topography*, #27. From Butschowitz the Hutterites founded communities at Bohuslawitz (Bohuslavice), Urschitz (Uhřice), Milonitz (Milonice), etc.; see articles in Zeman, *Topography*.

The first elder of the Hutterite community at Butschowitz was Ulrich Stadler, who advocated strong leadership by the servants of the Word; see his letter, Codex I 87.708, Vienna University Library, published in Müller, *Glaubenszeugnisse*, I, 215–227, in particular pp.220–221. Friedmann, *Schriften*, 61.

1536

and the church at Kostel and Drasenhofen. They spoke with the elders of the church of God about the articles of faith and other specific questions they had. After a thorough discussion with the elders, Ulrich, Leonhard, and Michael Kramer, as well as their people, became convinced; they gave all honor to God and openly admitted that they had done wrong earlier in supporting the group at Austerlitz against the church and that they had done wrong in other things too. Then Ulrich, Leonhard, and Michael, accompanied by the elders and other brothers, returned to Butschowitz and united with all the brothers and sisters there. About a hundred souls were added to the church on that day. So the devout started to gather at Butschowitz on the lands of Lord Václav Černohorský, and their number grew daily.

Ulrich Stadler and his people—about 100 souls—united with us.

We settled at Butschowitz.

Through God's leading, too, a lord in Slovakia—Nikoläsch of Slopnie and of Werschätitzi—sent a messenger to the church (at his own expense) to express by word of mouth and by letter his wish that the church send a servant or brother who could instruct his people in the true faith; this would be showing him very great kindness.

A lord in Slovakia asked the church to send a servant of the Word.

His request was granted, and Leonhard Lochmaier, a servant of the Word who had been a priest and knew Latin well, was sent with several others. He preached the Gospel in that place through an interpreter. A number of those who heard him accepted the divine Word, and after confessing their faith they were incorporated into the bond of grace and united with the church of Christ through Christian baptism. Among them were two blood brothers of noble birth, Jan and Peter Holba. Thus a community of believers started at that place too. Their lord gladly granted them land for this purpose, where they lived until the year 1540. In the drought that summer about sixty of them moved to the church of God in Moravia and stayed there.

Leonhard Lochmaier, a servant, sent to Slovakia.

About 60 souls came to the church from Slovakia.

1537

As the Lord had begun to gather his people and to free from error those who were still faithful, he moved the hearts of six former elders of the lapsed group at Austerlitz. Their names were Hans Wucherer, Hans Hueter, Hans Beer, Hans Lindner, Jörg Dräxler, and Urban Lintzer. Hans Wucherer was later

6 elders from the Austerlitz community united with us.

burned at Burghausen for the sake of divine truth, as will be told at the appropriate place. The others died in the Lord while in the community. *1537*

When these men united with the church, they publicly pointed out to the community at Austerlitz their shortcomings and error. This caused many more to leave the lapsed group and unite with the church of God, which began to live in Hans Hueter's community again. Because of this, those who had fallen away and lost all joy in the truth were angry, like a wounded bear or a lion robbed of its prey. They raged against the believers in their homes and on the street, wherever they met them. They attacked them with a flood of invective and blasphemous words. By this they showed plainly to what spirit they belonged, for, as they refused to obey the truth in love, God gave them over to profound error. Their actions show it to this very day.

Our brothers settled again in Austerlitz.

At this time Christoph Gschäl, a brother entrusted with the service of the Gospel, was sent by the church of God to Styria and Carinthia to search out those who were zealous for God and for the salvation of their souls. He converted many people and sent them to the church community, where they were received with joy.

Christoph Gschäl sent to Styria and Carinthia.

Another servant of the church of God, Georg Fasser, was sent by the church to Pöggstall[1] in Austria because of the fervent longing in a number of people. He did not know the alphabet, but he preached the Gospel with power. Even though he had just returned from prison in Mödling (near Vienna), he set joyfully about the Lord's work, gathered the believers, and established a church community in accordance with God's commands.

Georg Fasser, a servant of the Word who could not read, was sent to Austria.

But the enemy could not endure the Lord's work. After a time the devil stirred up a cunning man, Lord Roggendorf's bailiff at Pöggstall, who pretended that he wanted to learn about the true faith from Georg Fasser. He had posted constables nearby with the order to seize Georg Fasser when he gave the signal. They did exactly as they were told. In prison they set upon him and tortured him cruelly. He remained steadfast, however, and the sons of Pilate condemned him to death. He was executed with the sword, witnessing to the

Georg Fasser captured in Austria, cruelly tortured, and executed with the sword.

[1]Pöggstall, a market town below Roggendorf Castle, southwest of Krems, Lower Austria.

1537

divine truth with his blood. Those whom he had taught and gathered set out and traveled to the church of God.

Bastel Glaser and Hansel Grünfelder executed with the sword in the Inn Valley.

In this same year 1537 brothers Bastel Glaser and Hansel Grünfelder were taken prisoner at Imst in the Upper Inn Valley for the sake of their faith.[1] They were executed with the sword and then burned. They testified to God's holy Word and his truth with a joy so great that it defies description. About a thousand people were present at their execution. Hansel shouted as he spoke to them, challenging and warning them, and so did Bastel, right up to their death. The people were deeply shaken. It was impossible to burn their bones, so they were thrown into the water, and the heart of one of them did not burn. Such testimony was certainly not in vain.

Their bones could not be burned and one heart would not burn.

Hans Betz, a servant, and several others died in prison at Passau.

In 1535, as recorded above, Hans Betz,[2] a servant of the Gospel, and many other Christians had been imprisoned for the sake of divine truth at Passau, where the Inn River flows into the Danube. After a long time of suffering and harsh treatment, he and other witnesses to the truth fell asleep in the Lord while still in prison, enduring to the end with heroic steadfastness, as we can see from the many songs Hans Betz wrote while in chains.

Brothers began to live at Steinebrunn.

At the same time, as God carried out his work in a wonderful way, the church grew and spread, for he desired to make his glorious work manifest to everyone, to comfort and uplift his people, and to save many. So he provided his people with shelter and housing in several places, notably in Austria, where Lord Hans Fünfkirchen allowed them to settle at Steinebrunn. The believers received this from God with thanksgiving. They bought houses and altered them to make them suitable for their way of living.

They began to live at Poppitz.

In this year of 1537 a house was bought at Poppitz[3] on

[1]Hans Grünfelder came from Lüsen, Tirol, and was treasurer and later servant of the Word in the community at his home village, as well as in Michelsburg and Schöneck. The report given here is drawn from letters Onophrius Griesinger wrote to Hans Amon and Ulrich Stadler. See Loserth, *Anabaptismus*, 148–149; *ME*, II, 604.
About Bastel Glaser, see *Martyrs Mirror*, 446–447; Beck, 131–132.

[2]Hans Betz was a weaver from Eger (Cheb), northern Czechoslovakia, baptized near Donauwörth, Bavaria, by Georg Haffner. *ME*, I, 319; *Martyrs Mirror*, 447. About his songs, see Wolkan, *Lieder*, 31–35; *LdHBr*, 74–77; Beck, 132.

[3]Poppitz (Popice), a village southwest of Auspitz; in the 14th century famous for its vineyards; property of the lords of Lomnice in 1537; later, part of the Nikolsburg estate. See Zeman, *Topography*, #116.

behalf of the believers by brother Wolf Strobel, and there they began a Christian community. *1537*

About this time Peter Riedemann, a servant of the Lord, was released from the prison at Nuremberg, where he had been held for four years and ten weeks.[1] He traveled first to the Philippite brothers in Upper Austria, who complained to him about the split that had taken place at Auspitz. He told them that since God had helped him out of prison, he wanted, as far as the Lord permitted, to visit all who had been at peace when he left and to find out from both sides what had happened. Then he would act in accordance with whatever God showed him. Hearing this, the Philippites appointed two companions to go along and get a full report.

Peter Riedemann released from prison at Nuremberg.

Because of the division, Peter Riedemann wanted to visit each side before he decided which to support.

On September 14, 1537, Peter Riedemann arrived at the Feldsberg market in Austria,[2] where he met Leonhard Lanzenstiel, who had come with other servants for temporal affairs to make purchases for the community. They took Peter and his companions with them to Steinebrunn and then on to Drasenhofen. There, in the presence of his two companions, he talked with the elders of the church about all the tension and the split at Auspitz.

At that very point Peter Hueter arrived in Drasenhofen. He was Gabriel Ascherham's assistant in the service of the Word, and he had come to seek repentance. He blamed himself bitterly for his failures and mistakes and promised to improve. So in Peter Riedemann's presence he had to recount step by step the events that led to the separation from Gabriel [Ascherham] and Philip [Blauärmel].[3] It was clear, as Peter Hueter confessed, that Gabriel and Philip had no justified grievance against the church to excuse their own deviation. Peter Riedemann, drawing conclusions for himself, realized that

Gabriel Ascherham's assistant Peter Hueter arrived, seeking repentance. Peter Riedemann formed his judgment from this encounter.

Peter Riedemann stood with our people.

---

[1]Peter Riedemann's release from prison took place on July 14, 1537. The Nuremberg council's decree for that date reads: "Peter Riedemann, the Anabaptist fanatic in the tower, shall be released on his promise not to preach here or elsewhere in my lord's territory, but to go straight to his brothers in Moravia. He shall be given the essential items of clothing and one gulden for food." This shows the leniency of the council of Nuremberg compared with the terrible cruelty in Tirol. See Hochhuth, *Zeitschrift für historische Theologie*, XXVIII (1858), 536–644; XXIX (1859), 167–209.

[2]Feldsberg (Valtice), Czechoslovakia, approx. 18 miles east of Drasenhofen across the Austrian border.

[3]About these events, see above, pp.98ff.

1537

Gabriel and Philip were in the wrong and so decided to support Hans Amon and his community. His two companions returned home but had little enthusiasm for peace and unity.

Peter Riedemann did all he could by faithfully visiting the other Gabrielites and Philippites. Many of them, however, refused to listen. They attacked him and the church of God with malicious lies, as will be told later.

For good reasons, Peter Riedemann was unable to visit those living in Upper Austria. So they sent a messenger to inquire about the church. Peter Riedemann quickly sent him back with a letter warning the people against further harm and telling them of his recognitions and consequent actions in the Lord. The letter was as follows:

Peter Riedemann's letter to the brothers in Upper Austria.

John 15:2–5
Rom. 11:17–24
1 Cor. 1:3

> Peter, your brother and servant in the Lord, to the brothers living in various places in Upper Austria. I wish you true mercy in the grace of God the Father and of the Lord Jesus Christ. God has made him the salvation and eternal life of all those grafted into him through obedience to truth in the Holy Spirit. And I wish you pure, heartfelt love through Jesus Christ. To him be praise for ever and ever. Amen.
>
> Dearly beloved, from your letter I understood very well your longing that I should take time for you and visit you as soon as possible (as Wolf has expressed it too), to set right what is not in order. It cannot be fitted in at the moment because of other tasks God has put in my hands; but I appeal to you from my heart, as my dear children, to consider the grace you received from God when his Word was first brought to you by men whose teaching was pure, simple, and unfeigned. I along with others have cared for you as a father cares for his children, and I have labored hard with your servants Wolfgang Brandhuber[1] and Wolfgang Wimmer, those true witnesses of the Lord, that I might present you to the Lord Christ as a pure virgin; that you might not be deceived through the serpent's cunning but be protected against every delusion that leads away from salvation. As you know, such delusions became widespread among the group at Austerlitz

2 Cor. 11:2–3

[1]Wolfgang Brandhuber of Passau; see *ME*, I, 404–405; *Martyrs Mirror*, 433; Beck, 88; see also above, pp. 61–62.

while I was in prison, and many people were led onto a wrong path, but you were protected at that time and remained at peace.

1537
Peter Riedemann's letter to the brothers in Upper Austria.

In heartfelt love and concern for you, I remind you of the grace through which you then discerned what was false. What a fire God in his grace kindled in you at that time, what oneness of heart and mind he gave you when you were first shown the divine nature and the heavenly inheritance! And when you put your faith in the truth, how you were renewed through the Holy Spirit to serve the saints of God! I testify to the following about you: You would have torn out your eyes and given them to us if that had been possible. I say nothing of the food that you so willingly shared with us—beyond all our expectations—and begged us to accept. Yes, you even admonished us to take it as our own. Oh, how happy you were then, when such blazing fire from God was burning in you. That was a sure sign of your salvation.

Gal.4:15

2 Cor.8:3–5

Now, my dear children, when God kindled such fire in all his saints through the Holy Spirit, he wanted this fire to burn in his children with full effect. That is why he moved his servants to restore the zeal that had earlier burned in his children, encouraging them to demonstrate the fellowship of the Holy Spirit among themselves. You supported this work and were of one mind with all the chosen children of God in Moravia and elsewhere when I left, as you know. When I reached Nuremberg, I was put in prison, and during my time away Satan provoked division in the house of the Lord, which confused and hindered many simple-hearted brothers and sisters. Indeed, many were led away from their early zeal, even abandoning it and returning to their private homes, where they go to utter ruin, as was foretold long ago by the prophets. This is really happening now to many, because they look back after they have put their hands to the plow and thus leave God's work after it has been kindled in them.

Hag.1:4

Luke 9:62

The devil tries his hardest to mislead those who love the truth, causing havoc among God's servants in order to draw many people away from the kingdom of God. Whenever the devil wants to cause trouble, he has to do

1537
Peter Riedemann's letter to the brothers in Upper Austria.

it through rogues. But if some are misled only because of their simplicity and ignorance and otherwise belong to God, God will save them at his appointed time.

Now, my dear children, see what evil motives Satan put in a man's heart to wreak such destruction. To prevent his own falsehood from coming to light, Schützinger the thief tried to hinder Jakob Hutter, who was more devout than he, by withholding the service of the Word from him. Jakob (since he had the same service and had certainly borne more children in the truth than the other) would not give way to him. In the church action that followed, Philip and Gabriel and their followers declared that Schützinger was right, but the brotherhood did not agree with them. So Philip said, among other things, that Jakob was their idol. The brotherhood denied this. As a result Philip and Gabriel and their followers left the meeting. The brotherhood asked them to stay since there was more to discuss, but they refused and disobeyed the brotherhood.

Report on the course of the separation.

In the afternoon the brotherhood met again and condemned them rightly as disobedient. With flattering and smooth speeches Gabriel and Philip kept their followers, who supported them without hearing the whole story and then condemned the other group. Since I heard both sides together I learned the truth of it all and could judge the situation on the basis of the truth. Then, in front of Hans Amon and other servants, I listened to Peter Hueter, who at the beginning had been on Gabriel and Philip's side. From what Peter Hueter confessed it was clear to me that they had acted without any fear of God, and I did not want to spend any more time hearing about it.

Because you, too, were uninformed, you were hindered for a time and withdrew from the faithful with whom you and I used to consider ourselves united. As for this rogue Philip, who, while among you, slandered the whole brotherhood without any cause, God has exposed him as a thief so that many simple souls may perhaps open their eyes and not condemn the innocent with the deceiver. I am explaining this for your sake as briefly as I can, for I am aware that you have no exact knowledge of the matter; but there is no need at present to explain in full detail how one thing led to another.

Now what I want to tell you is this: Since God the Almighty gave me back to his people and I returned to you and then came to this brotherhood in order to learn the truth, I have discovered, through God's grace, about both the division and the life here. I have found this brotherhood in the same love and faith as when I left them, and they have not only held to it but have grown more fully in it. I am therefore compelled by the testimony of my heart to remain with them in this love, which God initially kindled in us, and we are determined to go forward in the Lord's service together. I beseech you from my heart to do the same faithfully and return to the children of the Lord, whom you deserted because you were fooled by words (which was not right) and led away from God's children by evildoers. Ask the Lord again for faithful servants who may lead you to find reconciliation with God's children. Certainly, it is necessary that you do this in absolute sincerity, otherwise nothing will come of it.

1537
Peter Riedemann's letter to the brothers in Upper Austria.

I heard from Balthasar Sattler (and the more I think about him the more it saddens me) that he no longer wants to put himself under the yoke of the children of God and, as he says, let them rule over him. Yet it is not at all our way to rule over anyone but rather to watch over one another as God's little children. And he tells me that you also, my Sigmund, are no longer willing to accept that yoke, those "bonds and chains." I wish that you, my Sigmund, would watch yourself a little more; and all of you, do not refer to what God first set alight in you as "human bonds and chains."

You know that God has urged his servants to carry out his work, to learn it, and to grow in it; therefore it is their duty to persevere and guide the brothers and sisters onward. He who falls away is putting his hand to the plow and then looking back; he is not fit for the kingdom of God.

Luke 9:62

I therefore appeal to you, who once took part in the work with all the children of God but have now deserted it, to turn back to it with all your hearts, so that your long race will not be in vain but will receive a full reward. When a brother leaves community and returns to private property, it is a sure sign that he has turned away from

2 John 8

1537
Rev.2:4
Peter Riedemann's letter to the brothers in Upper Austria.

God and left the first love. This is enmity to God and loss of all God's gifts.

In addition, what you have written to me about Balthasar and Gretel's marriage makes me somewhat afraid that you will take things too far and that perhaps lustful eyes have something to do with it. The same is true of Adam Schlegel. I let the matter rest, but you should watch where you are going. I do not know much more about it, except what I have heard from some of you. It is not reason enough for me to come to you now, and even if I came, I would not venture to deal with such a matter until I felt surer in my heart, for I cannot advise on a matter of which I am ignorant.

Although I had hoped to come and speak to you face to face, to remind you of the first love that God gave among you, this letter must suffice for the present. I cannot take so much time from the task. But if I hear that your hearts have wholly returned to your earlier love of God and his children, then I still hope to visit you at a fitting time through the grace of God. Then I will serve you with the gift God gave me and with my whole life. With all my heart I would lay down my life for you if you are living in love as you were when I knew you at the beginning. That is all. May the God of all grace turn your hearts to the love of Christ. Amen.

Carried by Wolf Wägerer
from Steinebrunn, Austria

Onophrius Griesinger returned from Tirol.

Toward winter of that year, Onophrius Griesinger returned from Tirol to the church of God in Austria and Moravia (after sending many devout brothers and sisters ahead of him) in order to support and comfort the believers with his service.

4 brothers chosen as servants for temporal affairs.

In the same year of 1537 the following brothers were appointed to the service for temporal affairs by the church in Steinebrunn: Matthias Legeder; Hans Gütten; Michael Planer, a shoemaker; and Michael Kramer from Gangkofen.

1538

Peter Riedemann sent to Upper Austria.

In 1538 brother Peter Riedemann was sent by the church of God to visit the scattered Philippites in Upper Austria. When they accepted his report, he restored brotherhood among them, appointed elders in the various places, set in order what was necessary, and then returned to the church at Steinebrunn. The elders of God's church very soon appointed a brother named Simon Waindel and sent him to Linz and Styria to advise the church in that region.

1538
Titus 1:5

Simon Waindel sent to Upper Austria.

In the spring of 1538 the assembly of God's children felt the Lord's leading to send Onophrius Griesinger and Leonhard Lochmaier, both servants of divine truth and preachers of the Gospel of Christ, to Tirol to gather the chosen of the Lord. The saints took leave of them by interceding for them and commending them to God's mercy. They then left for Tirol, where they carried out their service with the utmost dedication, in constant danger of persecution. They helped many to find eternal joy and salvation and, after a fitting farewell, sent them home to the church of God.

Onophrius Griesinger and Leonhard Lochmaier went to Tirol.

During that time Leonhard Lochmaier was captured and taken to Brixen.[1] Here a whole crowd of priests harassed him

Leonhard Lochmaier, a servant, captured at Brixen and caused to fall.

[1]Leonhard Lochmaier, a native of Freising, Bavaria, had been a Catholic priest for eight years before being baptized in 1526 by Jörg Krautschlögel (who was burned at the stake with his wife in 1527). He joined the brotherhood in 1527 and came to Moravia in 1528. For two years he was servant of the Word in Austria and Hungary. In 1538 he went to Tirol and gathered a community in the Upper Inn and Pitz valleys but was soon captured along with eight companions and imprisoned at Petersberg (castle and village in Tirol in the Inn Valley between Imst and Stams). He was taken to Brixen, where the court preacher Gallus Müller (see *ME*, III, 769–770) and Albrecht Bishop of Brixen succeeded in persuading him to recant; about to be pardoned, he repented of his unfaithfulness. The government at Innsbruck ordered him to be burned, but as a former priest he was executed with the sword. His letter to the church in Moravia is in Codex Hab. 17, Bratislava City Archives. See *ME*, III, 381–382; *Martyrs Mirror*, 448–449; Beck, 135–138. Lochmaier's three songs are in *LdHBr*, 82–85; see also Wolkan, *Lieder*, 171–172.

From prison in Brixen, Leonhard Lochmaier sent the following letter to his wife (Codex A b 5, fol. 245, Budapest University Library):

> . . . My dearest wife and sister in the Lord, I thank the Lord for you every time I think of you and of the love and faithfulness you have shown me all the time we were together. But now, dear sister and partner in marriage, if it pleases God and he wishes to chasten me, and if we should not see each other again, I urge you with all my heart and in the divine love that I have for you and all the saints to complete my joy in the Lord. Be devout of heart and God-fearing and serve the Lord faithfully all your life, as you have been taught by the gracious Word of God, which has often shown you how to live in a way pleasing to him. Trust him in faith, love, and godly patience, my dear wife and sister, and in this way overcome the world, for you know that the faithful have a great fight here. The Holy Spirit tells us that we have not only to believe in Christ but also to suffer for his sake;

1538 with wicked tricks until they brought about his downfall. They then asked him to travel round the country for a year to preach with Dr. Gallus Müller against divine truth and contradict it.

> the time of suffering and affliction for the sake of divine truth has certainly come over us along with the mighty struggle we have against our flesh here on this earth. . . .
>
> My sister, look to the Lord all the more and rejoice with me, for I hope to remain true to the Lord to my death and am in expectation of seeing you in joy once more on the last day. May the Lord our Father grant you and all God's children the strength to attain his kingdom and his great glory, in which all the chosen will have joy and eternal rest. . . .
>
> With this I commend you to the hands of our merciful God and Father and bless you from my heart in the Lord and take leave of you in loyalty, if it is God's will that I now witness to the truth with my blood. I have no other intention but to do this through the strength of God, and I greet you in the Lord, my Bärbel, with God's peace. I greet you, my sister, and all the children of God a thousand times with a loving kiss. I wish you God's eternal peace and commend you to the Lord. Give my heartfelt greetings in the Lord to the dear brothers and sisters, each and every one. With this letter I am sending you a handkerchief, and with it my whole heart. The Lord be with you eternally through his Spirit. Amen.
>
> O my most beloved brothers Hans and Ulrich, I send each of you many thousand heartfelt greetings in the peace of God, although I well know that I have grieved you deeply by my fall. I entreat you from my heart to forgive me, and I beg all the other children of God for forgiveness too. May the Lord in heaven be thanked forevermore, for he helped me up again and stretched out his generous hand to me. Blessed be he in all eternity for this. Rejoice with me once more, dear brothers, for I know that you and all children of God who heard it were in great pain and sorrow on my account.
>
> O my God, protect us from sorrow forever. Give all your saints your holy and eternal joy in your kingdom and in your great glory, which you will grant in blessing to your Son and your chosen ones on that great day when you will come to take us to yourself. To you be praise forever.

This letter was written for him by Onophrius Griesinger, who added a few lines of his own. Onophrius himself wrote the following letter to the brotherhood while he was in prison (Codex A b 5, fol. 384):

> We wish you the Lord's blessing; Leonhard and I send you many thousand heartfelt greetings in the Lord, . . . especially to Hans [Amon], my dear brother and friend in the Lord, to Ulrich and Peter and each of your servants for temporal affairs by name, and to you too, my dear Nickel, and you, my little son Hensel. Our heartfelt greetings to you all. I send you, too, my dear sister Anna, true and heartfelt greetings in the Lord. Your message brought me great joy. May the Lord be honored forever!
>
> O my Hans, please greet the dear brothers and sisters from me wherever you meet them, for I cannot name each one, although I would gladly do so. Please give my warm greetings to my brother-in-law and to dear brother Hans Plattner and to the dear schoolchildren with their school mothers. God's peace and love and his Spirit be with all of you for all time. Amen.
>
> My most beloved brother, may the Lord comfort you. Do not be sad for me. God the Lord will not forget your faithfulness. Ask the Lord if he may still let me be your helper, but if not, then come to my wedding feast, you and all your brothers and sisters. The Lord be with you always. Amen.

He refused, so they kept him in prison, since he had been a priest before he found the true faith.

1538
Refused to contradict truth. Repented for his fall.

In prison he felt deep remorse for his unfaithfulness; fear overcame him when he thought of God's judgment and condemnation. God saw his faithful heart and, to help him, opened a way through Onophrius Griesinger, who was arrested soon afterward for the sake of Christ's truth and taken to Brixen. There he was imprisoned close to Leonhard Lochmaier, so they were able to speak to each other. Leonhard confessed his fall to Onophrius and told of the tremendous pain, sorrow, and distress that he suffered in his heart because of his unfaithfulness. Finally, on the bottom of his plate, he wrote his request for forgiveness. Onophrius was in turn a great comfort to Leonhard. Seeing his faithfulness and genuine repentance, Onophrius pronounced forgiveness of his sin in the name of the Lord, restored him to the faith by interceding to God, and reaccepted him as a brother and member of the church.

Onophrius Griesinger also captured.

Onophrius Griesinger restored Leonhard Lochmaier.

Soon after this, Onophrius, faithful servant of God's Word and his church and writer of several fine letters we still have, was threatened with torture unless he would betray those of his brothers who were not yet dispersed, especially those who had done something to help him. To this Onophrius said, "Rather than betray my brothers, I will undergo this with strength from God. I have surrendered myself to suffer unto death as much pain and torture as a man can bear. I knew very well that this would happen to me. I am in your hands. Do with me whatever God allows you. If you want to ill-treat me, you may. God will find you out. I have nothing to say and no information to give."

Onophrius ready to suffer pain and torture rather than betray anyone.

Then they pressed him hard, telling him that if he loved the truth, he should speak and tell them the truth. Brother Onophrius said: "I know you well, you and your truth. You have heard what I said."

They even asked him whether, if we grew to be many in number, we would rise up against them and kill those who refused to join us. Onophrius answered, "If we did that, we would not be Christians, but only false Christians like you. If you were Christians, you would not mistreat, torture, or kill anyone."

Onophrius Griesinger was asked whether we would kill them if we became many.

They mocked him and pulled him up on the rack but soon

Onophrius Griesinger tortured.

1538

let him down again to threaten and coax him, asking him why he should want his limbs to be torn. He said to them, "I am in your hands. Do with me what God allows you. You cannot do more to me than take my life." So they gave up on him.

A week later they again pulled him up twice, without weights. He only said to them, "I have already told you all I can, and I know that God will find you out for your cruelty." They gave up a second time, left him alone, and stopped torturing him. He was ill from the torture and so spoke very little to them.

Monks from Bozen worked on Onophrius.

The following week, monks came from Bozen, and he was brought before them twice, but they did not stay long after he made their ears ring with their own wickedness and injustice.

Onophrius Griesinger burned alive.

After enduring great suffering, Onophrius Griesinger was condemned to death in Brixen by the sons of Pilate, thrust alive into the fire, and burned to ashes. Thus he witnessed valiantly to his faith and teaching with the constancy of a Christian hero and sealed this with his blood on All Saints' Eve [Oct. 31] 1538.[1]

Leonhard Lochmaier to be degraded from the priesthood, but the suffragan bishop died.

Leonhard Lochmaier beheaded at Brixen.

The tribe of priests prevented Leonhard Lochmaier from dying with Onophrius because he had formerly been a priest. They wanted to degrade him from their accursed orders first, but God foiled their plans through the death of the suffragan bishop, who was to do it. Leonhard Lochmaier was therefore executed with the sword a few days after Onophrius, giving his life like a true priest of God as an acceptable sacrifice and proving himself true unto death. A letter and some songs by him are still preserved.

Aichelin, the imperial provost, swore never again to condemn a brother.

These brothers were executed while Aichelin was provost of the whole empire.[2] Through the integrity and steadfastness of his servants, however, God overwhelmed Aichelin with such terror that in the end he raised his hand and swore that, as long as he lived, he would never again condemn a brother. Later he was stabbed to death while in Württemberg.

[Around this time brother Michael Widemann, or Beck, was

---

[1]Onophrius Griesinger's songs are in *LdHBr*, 77–82; see also Wolkan, *Lieder*, 171; *ME*, II, 579–580; *Martyrs Mirror*, 448–449; Beck, 136–141.

[2]The imperial provost, Berthold Aichelin from Wiesensteig (not to be confused with Josef Lauscher, alias Aichele, a regional judge on the estate of Lienz, Tirol, who had similar difficulties with Anabaptists in 1585); see Beck, 140 n.1. He is the same provost who had carried out the raid at the Mantelhof near Aalen in 1531 (see above, p.51).

captured with a group of other believers at Reutte in the Allgäu region. All except Michael were sent home, but he was put in prison and tortured and tormented for the sake of his faith. He was urged to recant but remained firm in his faith in Christ and said, "Formerly, when I lived a life of injustice, sin, and wickedness like the rest of the world, no one urged me to change. Everyone considered me a good Christian. But now that I have changed, repented, and amended my life, I am told I should turn around. I have already turned around and away from all evil. In this repentance I will remain to the end, and nobody shall move me, for the foundation on which I stand is the truth." After he had been in prison for six months, he was beheaded and then burned in this year of 1538.][1] *1538*

In this year of 1538 a man named Wendel Fürman gave the community legal possession of a house in Schakwitz, where he had settled from Württemberg.

The church was given houses at Schakwitz .

In addition we were given legal possession of a house in Schakwitz belonging to Valtin Häselwanter, who was received into the church; his wife Madel was also our sister. The house was next to the big house, and the smithy was built on a site where there had been no house before. So we made arrangements to live in Schakwitz again.

In that year of 1538 we built a house at Austerlitz on the grassland. Lord Jan Zischko, the owner of Austerlitz, gave us land to build on, and we paid him nothing for it. So we lived and gathered there.

House built at Austerlitz.

Around Bartholomew's Day [Aug. 24] of that year, 1538, Philip Blay from Flehingen, Württemberg, united with us. Previously a Philippite, he had been a brickmaker at Pausram.[2] He gave us legal possession of a house with a vineyard at Pausram, where we began to live.

House given us at Pausram.

---

[1]The bracketed passage (Wolkan, *Geschicht-Buch*, 696, errata and addenda) is from the "1580" codex of this chronicle, fol. 146r–146v. See also Beck, 141; *Martyrs Mirror*, 449.

"Reutte in the Allgäu region": town in northern Tirol on the Lech River, near the German border.

[2]Pausram (Pouzdřany), market town approx. 11 miles north of Nikolsburg (Mikulov); in 1538 property of the lords von Liechtenstein; in 1556 of the provincial procurator Ambroz von Ottersdorf; from 1574 to 1630 of the Zerotin family; after 1630 of the Dietrichstein family. Zeman, *Topography*, #106.

1538
Received houses at Pulgram.

In autumn of 1538 we were given houses at Pulgram[1] by brothers who had come to us from the Philippites and united with us. These buildings comprised the bakery, the large house where the school had been, the smithy, and a new house next to the smithy, which we built on new foundations, also the charcoal burner's house and the hatter's house, and there we lived.

5 brothers chosen for service for temporal affairs.

On All Saints Day [Nov.1] that year, the service for temporal affairs at Schakwitz was entrusted to brothers Hans Klampferer, Andreas Gauper (for the first time), Georg Han, Kaspar Braitmichel,[2] and Lorenz Schuster.

Hans Wucherer and one other captured at Mermos in Bavaria.

In the year 1538 Hans Wucherer was arrested. He had been an elder of the Austerlitz Brethren but later united with us. With another brother, Bärtel Synbeck or Weber (a weaver), he was captured in Bavaria and taken to Mermos. During their sixteen days' imprisonment they were questioned twice—once under torture—by the children of Caiaphas, that brood of priests. They were asked what they thought about the mass. They strongly opposed it, saying it was an abomination and idolatry in the Lord's eyes. They also could not believe that the body and blood of Christ as he hung upon the cross could be given out in the bread and eaten a hundred thousand times. No, it was rather a memorial of how Christ suffered and died and poured out his blood to redeem us. The believers, who are the members of his body and of his church, should hold the Lord's Supper to remember this and give him heartfelt thanks.

Asked what they believed about the mass. Their answer.

Next the brothers were asked about infant baptism and how they regarded the ungodly priests and their church. They confuted all these with the truth. They were questioned on what they believed about marriage and about the Ten Commandments. They gave answers in accordance with the Word of God.

Hans Wucherer and Bärtel Synbeck taken to Burghausen.

Afterward they were taken, bound, to Burghausen. Each was chained in a separate dungeon and brought out six times for interrogation. They were told that if they would recant and

[1]Pulgram (Bulhary), village and parish northeast of Nikolsburg, in 1538 property of the lords von Liechtenstein. Zeman, *Topography*, #124.

[2]About Kaspar Braitmichel, the first writer of this chronicle, see below, p.436.

deny their faith they would be shown mercy. But they were on no account willing to exchange God's mercy for the mercy of the world, for they felt assured that they were founded in true faith and in God's truth. *1538*

A seventh time the priests came to them in the prison, but they remained steadfast in God. They also tortured them cruelly. Hans Wucherer, who was ill, was pulled up on the rack, and brother Bärtel was pulled up twice, but the priests gained nothing by it.

Hans Wucherer and Bärtel Synbeck cruelly tortured.

The eighth time the judge came with two others and sentenced them to be burned to death after first being subjected to the most cruel and terrible torture, as Hans Wucherer wrote from prison to the church in a letter, which we still have.[1]

---

[1]On the eve of his death in 1537 (not 1538), Hans Wucherer wrote a farewell letter to his wife. The following excerpt is taken from Codex A b 5, fol. 236–245, Budapest University Library.

O my dearly beloved wife,

I want with all my heart to write to you so that when I am gone you will have something to remember me by for your soul's salvation. But God may not grant it. I am physically very weak from fever, imprisonment, torture, sorrow, and temptation, which the ungodly inflict on us for the sake of divine truth. The hour is at hand for me and for my dear brother Bärtel, a valiant fellow-fighter for the truth of God. Yes, the time has already come for us to lay aside this earthly frame. God our beloved Father wants to take us home to himself and bring us into his kingdom. . . . They have now sentenced us to death by fire this coming Wednesday. . . . But I plead with you in the name of the Lord not to lose courage. The Lord works in a marvelous way through his poor, weak vessels, even those of whom we would least expect it, for I do not count myself worthy in God's eyes. But I hope that his grace is not given me in vain. . . .

O my Bärbel, for the sake of God, his mercy, and your soul's salvation, I ask you to fear and love God with all your heart, keeping him always before your eyes. Serve him day and night in holiness and righteousness, in gentleness and humility, in kindness and patience, in love, faith, self-control, and wisdom. . . . Be quiet and chaste, leading a godly life in Christ, as befits a devout widow. . . . Stay with this people your whole life, as I told you when we parted. I have complete trust in the Lord that they will care for you and for the little orphans I am leaving behind. . . .

I could write a great deal about our arrest and imprisonment, but the time is too short. We faithfully carried out the task of encouraging the brothers and sisters as our dear brother Hans asked us to do. We stayed in a mill overnight, and at daybreak the ungodly rabble came to the house and shouted to be let in, saying they wanted flour. The miller's wife let them in, and we could not escape from our room. They opened the door and guarded it with spears while the constable came at us with his weapon drawn and arrested us.

The attack was cruel and terrifying. They bound us together and took us to the prison at Mermos. We were held there for sixteen days and questioned twice, once under torture. They asked us what we thought of their mass, and we spoke out clearly against it, calling it an abomination and idolatry

1538
Hans Wucherer and the other brother burned at Burghausen.

Finally they were burned to death for the sake of their faith. They valiantly witnessed to the truth until death and attained the crown of Christ's martyrs.

Martin from Villgraten and Kaspar Schuster executed with the sword in the Puster Valley.

In 1538 brother Martin from Villgraten and Kaspar Schuster were held in prison at Michelsburg Castle in the Puster Valley for the sake of divine truth. After making a courageous stand, they were condemned to death and executed with the sword and remained steadfast to the end. We still have their songs, which give us much to think about, for they show us how these brothers were comforted in their bonds and suffering and how the love of God burned in their hearts.[1] From this love nothing could separate them: neither tribulation nor fear nor persecution, neither hunger nor poverty, nakedness nor peril. No sword was too sharp, no fire too hot, no devil too evil, no man too active on the side of the devil. Nothing could turn them away from God and his truth, from their Lord and Savior Jesus Christ. What they confessed with their lips, they also testified to with their blood through the grace and power of God.

Growth of the church.

God the Almighty delighted in building up his house. In his mercy, and so that the Supper and the house of the Lord might be full, he brought back into the church some members from groups that had weakened or dissolved. It happened this way: The Philippites were now living in Württemberg, in the

---

in the Lord's eyes. Then they questioned us about infant baptism and asked us what we thought about their ungodly priests and churches. We refuted all these with the truth. Next they asked how we regarded marriage and the Ten Commandments.

We were bound and taken to Burghausen, where each was chained in a separate dungeon. Six times we were brought out and questioned. They would have pardoned us if we had recanted. The seventh time the vile priests came to us in the prison, but God mercifully gave us strength to hold out through everything. Praise and blessing and honor be to him in all eternity through Jesus Christ. Amen. They tortured us and stretched me on the rack until I was quite weak. They racked Bärtel twice. On the eighth visit the judge came and condemned us to die by fire. They were terribly cruel. I am not able to write anymore. I leave it in God's hands.

The above letter was evidently used as a source by the chronicler. See *Martyrs Mirror*, 447; Beck, 133–134; Friedmann, *Schriften*, 131.

[1]Martin from Villgraten (in the Puster Valley) and Kaspar Schuster each composed a song in prison: "Merkt auf und nehmt zu Herzen" (Now hear and take to heart), "Erzürn dich nicht, o frommer Christ" (Be not aroused to anger, O true Christian); see *LdHBr*, 86–87; *Ausbund*, 198–201; Wolkan, *Lieder*, 142; Wackernagel, *Kirchenlied*, V, 787–788; *Martyrs Mirror*, 449; Beck, 135.

Palatinate near the Rhine River, in the Margravate of Baden, and in Austria and Moravia. Some of them, longing for a more excellent way, wanted to visit the brotherhood of true believers, so they sent one of their servants, Hans Gentner, to the church community. He had many talks with the elders of the church; the godly, surrendered way of life that he found there convinced him that he and his people had been following a way that was not based on the truth. Then Hans and a few others came to the church of God and were completely united.

1538

A Philippite named Hans Gentner united with our people.

Others of the Philippites who had also given witness to the teachings of the church felt no desire to embrace the more perfect way, choosing private property and their own gain rather than patient surrender in Christian community. Many were lost in this way. Then Peter Riedemann, who wanted to protect them from further harm, did all he could to warn them, to seek contact, and to hold out a brotherly hand. We can see this from the following letter:

Peter Riedemann's second letter to the scattered Philippite brothers.

> Peter, a servant of Jesus Christ and his church, to the Philippite brothers wherever they are: grace and mercy from God the Almighty and from his beloved Christ, who was anointed and sent by God the Father. He is the source of righteousness that arises from genuine faith in him who unites all things into one body through the bond of love and peace. He leads together the hearts of all his beloved children, and their lives are spent in serving one another to his eternal praise. Amen.

Rom.1:4–5

Eph.4:1–3
Col.3:12–15

> Blessing, glory, and heartfelt praise be to God, the almighty and eternal Father. In his unfathomable mercy and in his love he has enlightened us by revealing the Word of his divine power. We had lost sight of it because darkness had blinded our hearts through the devil's doing. The evil one had sown weeds and deception in every human heart. He choked the glorious seeds of God by causing thorns to grow instead of wheat, and all flesh was corrupted. The Holy Spirit testifies: All men have become corrupt and worthless, strangers to the godly life; everyone has gone his own way, resulting in delusion and wickedness. God the Almighty declares war on such wickedness. In his grace and faithful love, he sends his divine light, that is, knowledge of the truth, so that the

Matt.13:24–30

Rom.3:10–12

Eph.4

2Cor.4:6

Ps.45:4

1538 darkness of sin is driven away and we may all walk as
Eph.1 children of the light. You have the same calling that we
5 have: to be one body of which Christ Jesus is the head.
Col.1 You know, dearly beloved, how God the Almighty
brought us into oneness of mind and faith in the Holy
Eph.4 Spirit; to the same love, community, obedience, and hope
of eternal life; to a united recognition of the Son of God,
that we should become mature in the perfect maturity of
Christ.

1 Pet.5:8 But the devil, that great enemy of our salvation, wastes
no time. He prowls around like a roaring lion, seeking
to devour those he can catch. He has never stopped
destroying and dividing, for he wants to reverse everything that gives honor to God's name. Thus he hopes to
lead men away from God's love and from serving one
another.

Dearly beloved, I cry to the Lord God with great pain
because the devil has started his sport among you. You
know that we parted in unity and peace, but now I find
you divided. I fear that at heart your servants never were
1 John 2:18–26 fully at peace with us. Their actions show that they never
Rev.2:2–5 truly belonged to us, for they did not remain with us.
Instead they were the devil's disciples, sent to mislead
into evil all who followed them. You know only too well
what confusion and distress they caused through their
wickedness. But because you still belong to God, he in
his mercy put an end to their wickedness, thereby
preventing you also from falling prey to the tempter.
Through the persuasion of evildoers you separated from
the faithful. Now open your eyes while there is still time
and return to peace, love, and unity in the Holy Spirit.
Hans Gentner (whom you had sent for this very purpose)
and I have been working tirelessly to this end, and God
the Almighty has brought us back to true peace, love,
and unity. In his mercy he has drawn us back to the first
love, to live and work in obedience to the Holy Spirit
and in community with it so that no one lives for himself
any longer but serves God and God's beloved children.

When they heard of the reconciliation, some carnal-minded people turned their backs on Hans Gentner and other brothers, even though they gave a different reason

1538
Peter Riedemann's second letter to the scattered Philippite brothers.

(of which I will speak later). But it was plain that Philip and others were such a stumbling block for them that they are now backsliders. Their actions show that they have lost their courage and zeal for God, and each one is returning to his own home. At this moment they are not ready to acknowledge their error. Greater disaster may bring it home to them.

So I am writing to warn you not to be corrupted with the corrupt nor to become angry with the angry nor to stumble with those who have already stumbled nor to fall still further among the fallen.

I want to tell you briefly the reason for the split. We can explain it more clearly later on when we visit you, as we plan to do if that is God's will, but I am writing now in love to encourage you to wait patiently until we come. Hold firm, and do not go further astray by associating with other groups. Be patient. You have sent a servant to seek unity and to find out what caused the division. He did this through what he experienced with me and other faithful brothers; he or another will come to you. Meanwhile do not let anyone mislead you.

Reason for the separation from Philip and Gabriel at Auspitz.

This is what happened:

FIRST, it seemed right that Jakob Hutter, who had been entrusted by God with the same service of the Word as Schützinger, should serve side by side with Schützinger without restrictions, instead of Schützinger having precedence, which was what Philip [Blauärmel], Gabriel [Ascherham], and their supporters wanted.

SECOND, against their consciences the people gave in to pressure from Gabriel and made the unjust decision to put Schützinger above Jakob. Now they have humbled themselves and confessed their error, praying to God the Lord to forgive their lack of wisdom.

THIRD, although the people made a wrong decision, that does not mean they belong to the devil, as Philip asserts. Even the devout make mistakes.

FOURTH, in evil talk, Philip and Gabriel called Jakob an idol and the people idolaters because they had humbled themselves before God and asked forgiveness for their mistake. In their opinion, the people were blasphemers and should be excluded.

1538
Peter Riedemann's second letter to the scattered Philippite brothers.

FIFTH, Philip lied. He reversed his position publicly. First he said they should part from one another as brothers and sisters. Then when he did leave, he turned around in the room and said he was separating from them as from strangers and fools.

SIXTH, Gabriel tried to justify the deceiver and condemn the faithful, saying, "Schützinger is being blamed for everything, but he will be reaccepted when someone else is excluded."

SEVENTH, they [Gabriel and Philip] despised a request of the brotherhood by leaving against the wish of the entire brotherhood, who wanted them to stay and talk further about the matter.

EIGHTH, it was unanimously decided in Upper Austria and in Moravia that they [Gabriel and Philip] deserved exclusion for their ungodly conduct. However, some carnal-minded people who had originally participated in the decision said afterward it was not done according to the proper order, since they [Gabriel and Philip] were not asked to appear once more before the brotherhood. They say this is their only reason for separating from their servants and all the children of God and for continuing in their sins. But we and all who want peace agree unanimously that, while it would have been good to call them before the brotherhood again, there was no sin or injustice in not doing this, since they had despised the request of the whole brotherhood and disobeyed. Since the unfaithful make this omission the only reason for their falling away, it is clear to us that they are simply shirking Christian obedience, love, and community. Nearly all of them have returned to private property, leaving the house of the Lord to go to rack and ruin.

NINTH, they admit too that they were wrong to believe those now in exclusion and to leave the community of God's children, refusing to heed their earnest warning. (So it was not unjust that the church of the Lord let you go your own way when you were unwilling to listen.) God the Almighty has shown them their fault. Now they feel moved to seek out all those whom they had hurt and be joyfully reunited with them in the Lord. They are hindered by others, however, who try their best to bring confusion.

1538
Peter Riedemann's second letter to the scattered Philippite brothers.

> Take this warning to heart. If such people come to you, do not be misled. Wait until the visit I told you about; then you can hear a more exact report about what I describe here in a few words. Pray to the Almighty to protect you from going further astray and to free you from your error. May he once more bring you to peace in the truth with all his holy ones, through Jesus Christ forevermore. Amen. May the God of all grace and mercy, who sent his beloved Christ to proclaim unity and peace, direct your hearts to the love of Christ and to true obedience and submission for ever and ever. Amen.

Hans Gentner, as a true shepherd of his people, had always been eager to send such a letter. Now that he was following the more perfect way, he thought he should visit his people again, those who had sent him to the church, and show them the more excellent way that leads to salvation.

However, the church and the elders felt that a different approach would be better at this point, and Hans Gentner readily agreed.

About this time Christoph Gschäl sent many God-fearing people from Carinthia and Styria to the church of God, and at the beginning of winter he himself came with some companions.

Hans Seidel and Hans Donner executed at St. Veit in Carinthia.

But two of them, Hans Seidel from Murau and Hans Donner from Wels, were taken prisoner for the sake of divine truth on the Wednesday before Christmas 1538 at St. Veit in Carinthia. After holding valiantly to their faith and to the truth of Christ, they were sentenced to death and executed with the sword. Joyfully testifying to the true way until the end, they sealed this witness with their blood. This is told in their song and in the letter they wrote from prison, which have been preserved until today.[1]

1539

Group in Hesse sent request to the church for help and advice.

In 1539 God awakened courage and zeal in Hesse among the people who had already taken their stand for the truth.

---

[1]The letter from the two brothers, Hans Seidel and Hans Donner, is in Codex A b 5, fol. 250–255, Budapest University Library; see Friedmann, *Schriften*, 111, 127. Donner's song, "Ich dank dir, lieber Herr, mein Gott" (I thank you, dear Lord, my God), is in *LdHBr*, 88–89; see also Wolkan, *Lieder*, 172; *ME*, II, 84; *Martyrs Mirror*, 450; Beck, 141–142; *MQR*, Oct. 1947, 238.

1539

Some of them had belonged to Hans Both's group. (As reported earlier, Hans had once been a member of the community at Auspitz.) This group now sent two of their members to Moravia and Austria to ask for teaching and for inner guidance.

Peter Riedemann sent to Hesse and to Württemberg.

The brotherhood considered their request and agreed to send brother Peter Riedemann, a servant of the Lord and of his church. He was to travel to Württemberg and to the place where they lived in Hesse to gather much fruit for the Lord and also to fulfill Hans Gentner's burning wish to visit his own people.

Peter Riedemann visited the people in Upper Austria.

Commended to the grace of God, Peter set out. First he went to the community in Upper Austria, doing all in his power to instruct them. He comforted them with the Word of truth and challenged them. He parted from them in peace and journeyed on to his appointed places in Württemberg and Hesse. You will learn what he achieved there when you read the following letter to Hans Amon, the servant of the Lord entrusted with the care of the church:

Peter Riedemann's letter to Hans Amon.

Peter, your brother and true friend in the Lord, to my dear brother Hans Amon: I wish you much compassion, strength, wisdom, and understanding from God our Father and his beloved Son Jesus Christ in caring for his flock and teaching them the right way. The grace of the Holy Spirit is given us to prepare a holy church without spot or blemish, beloved and pleasing to him.

My dear brother, I thank my God at all times for you, praising and honoring him because of the grace you have received to serve his children. You do all you can, working so eagerly that there is no need for me to spur you on, because God is at work in you. My constant prayer is that the Lord keep this zeal burning ever more brightly in you so that you will care for his people lovingly, carrying them in your heart as those who are precious in your eyes. Indeed I have always felt this to be so.

Out of love, dear Hans, my brother in the Lord, I cannot keep back my heart's concern. You asked me particularly to send news soon, so it troubled me that it has been delayed for so long. Blasi knows how much I wanted to write, and he will be able to tell you everything we have talked over. It was not possible to write earlier because we had nothing definite to say.

1539
Peter Riedemann's letter to Hans Amon.

Now that an opportunity has presented itself, I did not want to delay any longer in responding to your request and have sent this brother to you to report how we are doing and what the Lord has shown us on this journey. You probably know already how we set out for Upper Austria, commended to the Lord, and what took place there. Then we went to your brothers—for your mother's sake—and arrived about midmorning. But she and your brothers and their wives had all gone to the wedding. The farm hands said that no one would be home before night, so we did not wait. Since we were unsuccessful, Blasi plans to visit them on the way down, and if they want to come, he will bring them with him.

After this we came to Lauingen and were told about some brothers, but we did not know who their leader was.[1] We went to them and found out that they were Swiss Brethren. We inquired about Jörg Sattler and Matthias and were deeply shocked when told how badly things were going. All their servants of the Word had lost their services because of one man among them who declared he had received a revelation. He asked the servants if their service was from God, and when they said it was, he said it was not.

Almost all Swiss servants at Lauingen had lost their services through a man who declared he had received a revelation.

First he admonished Jörg Sattler and two others, saying that because they made decisions that were afterward changed, their service was not from God. The three accepted this and laid down their services. Next he turned to Matthias (whom you know), but Matthias opposed him. They quarreled, parted, and met again next morning. As the man was unable to do anything with Matthias, he confronted another servant and questioned him in the same way. This other servant replied that he believed there was nothing wrong in his passing on faithfully to the people what was given him from God. The man said he agreed, provided he did not claim that his service was from God. When Matthias heard that, he spoke just like that other servant, with the result that the two agreed. As

[1]Lauingen, Swabia, about 150 miles southeast of Stuttgart, where an Anabaptist group existed possibly as early as 1528, until the 1580s. Two brothers were put to death at Lauingen according to the table of martyrs (see below, pp.217–220), probably in 1530. See Claus-Peter Clasen, "The Anabaptists at Lauingen: A Forgotten Congregation," *MQR*, April 1968, 144–148.

1539
Peter Riedemann's letter to Hans Amon.

all of them were removed from their services, they asked what they should do now and whether they should stop meeting. The man said they should hold together more fervently than ever before. Although there was no one to exhort them and no one to intercede for them before the Lord, they should still meet and continue to pray in all earnestness, and God would send them faithful servants in his good time. All this happened soon after they had left Moravia, when they gathered the people to tell them what they had done there. They are meeting now to consider the matter, but I do not know the result.

Then we traveled on to the Philippites and spoke with them. They felt the same as those in Moravia concerning the division and the decision to exclude Philip, if it had indeed come about as we say. We have hope for them since they have come this far. But they were opposed to living in community, and as we could not agree with them, we took leave of them. We do not know their stand on marriage and other points. They brought forward several grievances against Hans Gentner, especially in connection with money; I believe if he had come to them they would have excluded him. As it would be too much for me to write it all down, Blasi will tell you about it when he comes. They also say that Adam was not telling the truth when he said that the brothers were willing to accept them.

We found the situation in Hesse very sad. There used to be a big group here, but they have nearly all gone astray, following false spirits. They are all being lured back to idolatrous temples, to infant baptism, to the idolatrous meal, to war, and other abominations. Nearly all of them have turned away from Matthias. Even those supposedly in unity with him have strong feelings against him. If we had not come as mediators, they would have removed him from the service of the Word. We found that both he and they had to be corrected. After we talked with them, the group split. The selfish and rebellious ones turned away, while the others made up their minds to follow the Lord—forty of them, I think—obedient, faithful souls.

If we were to go there to live, I imagine some from

1539
Peter Riedemann's letter to Hans Amon.

the Puster Valley might even return. If Matthias were completely of one mind with us, we would, I trust, be able to live together peacefully. There is a great deal lacking in him, however, which the brothers and sisters realize to a large degree. Yet I hope God will lead us together even if he [Matthias] wants no part in it. He is hot-tempered and speaks rashly and thoughtlessly. It would serve no good purpose if we were to treat him as he treats us. Now both he and the brothers and sisters can see clearly that the Lord is with us. Because the brothers and sisters are now all taking our side and testifying against him, one day he, too, will turn around.

The others gave us a lot of trouble. We had hoped to win them back and help them, but this was not possible. So I know nothing except that Matthias is self-willed and obstinate. All the brothers and sisters who hear of it are distressed that he opposes us in so many things he does not understand. Some of them will consider leaving if I go away. I am at a loss and need your advice in the Lord. I encouraged him to go to Moravia for a while, so he could experience the order and the life of the church, but I could not get him to go. All the brothers and sisters who were present thought it would be good, but he was not in the least ready to accept it.

I cannot with a good conscience leave the people, for they would not be cared for, and I am afraid that their last state will be worse than their first. But we [Riedemann and Matthias] can't both work and be fed here, as Blasi will tell you. I have asked him to hurry so that he can tell you personally in detail before the news gets around, and then you can decide what to do. Brother, it is urgent that something happens soon, for I will not go ahead with anything until I hear from the elders. I expect you have already sent me one or two devout brothers who have some knowledge and experience of the orders of the church so that we can move forward in the right way. Before taking any action, therefore, I am waiting for an answer.

So, my dear brother, I ask you and all the brothers to carry this situation in your hearts. I know you will. That is all I can think of to write for now. I commend you to

1539
Peter Riedemann's letter to Hans Amon.

the Lord. May he comfort, strengthen, guide, and sustain you in his grace forevermore. Amen.

And now, from your true friend and brother in the Lord, many thousand heartfelt greetings in holy love and with the blessed peace of our Lord Jesus Christ. Greet Hans Gentner, Ulrich, Leonhard [Lanzenstiel], both Michaels [Kramer and Planer, servants for temporal affairs at Steinebrunn], Oswald, and all the faithful children of God. Many thousand greetings in the Lord to your wife too. Brother Blasi also sends his greetings of love and so do all the saints here. May the grace of our Lord Jesus Christ be with you forevermore. Amen.

Carried by Kaspar Klaindopf
from Hesse to Austria

4 brothers appointed to the service for temporal affairs.

At the beginning of 1539, four elders were appointed by the church of God to the service for temporal affairs, to care for the believers and for those in want. They were Leonhard Lanzenstiel, a ropemaker by trade, who came from Niederalteich in Bavaria; Jakob Säckler from Schwäbisch Gmünd; Balthasar Maierhof the older, from Niedervintl in the Puster Valley; and Michael Matschidel, known as Klein Michael (Short Michael), from the Gail Valley in Carinthia.

Christoph Gschäl sent to Upper Austria and Carinthia.

Toward spring of the same year, the brotherhood decided to send Christoph Gschäl to visit the church in Upper Austria and then go back to Styria and Carinthia, which he did, but with little result.

Leonhard Lanzenstiel chosen for the service of the Word, confirmed, and sent to Tirol.

It was also unanimously decided by the church of God that Leonhard Lanzenstiel[1] (or Seiler) should be appointed to the service of the Gospel. Soon afterward he was confirmed in this service by the elders with the laying on of hands and was sent to Tirol where he brought blessing and salvation to many souls.

Christoph and Leonhard, with those accompanying them, were commended to God's grace with earnest prayer, and after the leave-taking they traveled to Linz. While meeting with fellow believers there, they received the letter quoted above from Peter Riedemann in Hesse. Then Leonhard went on to Tirol while Christoph visited the church in Upper Austria and then traveled to Styria as he had been instructed.

---

[1]About Leonhard Lanzenstiel, see above, p.85 n.3; Beck, 143.

All the devout were glad when this news from Hesse reached Hans Amon and the church. Soon the brotherhood asked Hans Gentner to go to Württemberg, to the group that had sent him to the church earlier. They prayed fervently to God as he started on his journey. He carried out his task with joy and in the fear of God and helped many to find salvation and eternal blessedness.

1539

Hans Gentner sent to Württemberg.

During this time the church in Austria and Moravia had no servants, teachers, or preachers to proclaim the Word of God except Hans Amon and Ulrich Stadler. These two, according to the grace given them, devoted all their powers to this task. As faithful shepherds they taught the believers to follow the way of truth and with upright hearts led them to God.

When Leonhard Lanzenstiel had visited as many God-fearing people as possible in Tirol and had worked hard to gather the saints for the Lord, he returned joyfully in the fall to the church community. He brought with him many who had surrendered their lives to God. But Leonhard's wife, Apollonia, was arrested and taken to Brixen. Because she held steadfastly to faith in Christ and refused to recant, she was drowned.

Leonhard Lanzenstiel's wife Apollonia drowned at Brixen.

A little later, around Martinmas [Nov. 11], Christoph Gschäl and his companions returned from Carinthia and Styria to God's church community. In the week after St. Nicholas Day [Dec. 6], Peter Riedemann returned from Hesse to Steinebrunn in Austria, not knowing that the provost had carried off the brothers. He found only sisters and children. There was heartbreak and great grief. Hans Gentner also came back from Württemberg into this overwhelming distress in God's church community.

Christoph Gschäl came home.

Peter Riedemann came home.

Hans Gentner came home.

The beginning of this time of tribulation is described in what follows. When God wished to increase his glory and the welfare of the believers, he put those who had joined together in his name to a rigorous trial, as gold is tried in the fire. This was to test what was in their hearts so that the steadfastness of their faith would be visible in them as God's children. At the same time the malice of the old serpent showed up in his false prophets, who beset the Roman king Ferdinand (in the same way that Satan beset Job), filling his ears with unjust accusations against the church of God. They goaded him on until he finally did as they wanted and dispatched his marshal

1539
The royal marshal and provost raided Steinebrunn. Took the brothers prisoner.

from Vienna with the provost and some mounted attendants, who arrived without warning at Falkenstein.[1] Taking a reckless mob with them, they attacked the Christian community at Steinebrunn in the late evening of December 6, 1539. They locked all the men they could find in one room, the women and girls in another. They posted guards and made a terrifying uproar, plundering whatever they could.

Their main purpose was to capture servants of the Word. God prevented this.

Most of all they wanted to capture the elders and servants of the church, hoping to get large sums of money and goods from them, thus robbing the poor without a thought that God would requite it with heavy punishment. Although the people they were after were in the house, God in his providence saved those brothers from the wanton rabble.

Unwilling to leave even a little food for widows and orphans, they searched every corner but could find nothing, for God frustrated all their plans and turned their efforts into sheer folly. During this infamous raid, the sick, the children, and the expectant mothers were overwhelmed with terror and fear for their lives. The brothers and sisters who were locked up prepared themselves to sacrifice their lives for God and die by fire or the sword.

Some Philippites came seeking unity. They were made prisoners too.

150 brothers taken to Falkenstein.

That same evening, in the midst of all the distress, several men arrived from the Philippites to find out on what basis the church community at Steinebrunn was living.[2] They were among the 150 brothers captured and taken under secure guard to Falkenstein Castle.[3] Among the captives were some who

---

[1]Falkenstein, northeast Austria (near the Czech border, southwest of Mikulov), seat of a county court and former estate; in the 15th century included the ancient fortress of Falkenstein; from 1529 to 1571 property of the lords of Fünfkirchen. See Beck, 144 n.2.

[2]On that fateful evening, December 6, 1539, a number of Philippites and Swiss Brethren had arrived at Steinebrunn, hoping to prepare the ground for a possible uniting with the Hutterites; see *Martyrs Mirror*, 450–453; Beck, 144–149; *ME*, IV, 624. In 1539, Steinebrunn was the property of the lords of Fünfkirchen. Cardinal Franz von Dietrichstein purchased it in 1637.

[3]An animated correspondence developed between the brothers who had been carried off to Falkenstein Castle and the church in Moravia. Four letters the prisoners wrote to the community are in Codex A b 5, Budapest University Library; see Friedmann, *Schriften*, 108, "Brüder d." Stoffel Aschelberger wrote four letters, three of them to his wife. Leonhard Roth, another prisoner, wrote three letters to the church. Hans Amon sent four letters in reply, and Antoni Erfordter also wrote to the prisoners; see Friedmann, *Schriften*, "Aschberger," 106; "Roth," 125; "Amon," 105 (10–14); "Erfordter," 113. The following extracts from these letters supplement the above report.

Of the four letters written in the name of all the prisoners, the first ends with

had not yet been baptized and others who had fallen away from the truth and were seeking repentance. *1539*

When they had all arrived at Falkenstein Castle, the brothers

---

some of their names: Nickel Schreiber, Christian Häring, Peter Schuster, Jörg Planer, Ulrich Gschäll (also called Ulrich Hofer), Stoffel Aschelberger, and the writer of the letter, Leonhard from Braunau. The second reports that four brothers were put in irons—Michael Oswaldt, Nickel Obster, Jobst, and Stoffel Aschelberger—and continues:

> We do not know what the Lord will allow and what more he has in store for us, but we think that they have sent for the executioners and will torture us again. The Almighty's will be done. Let them threaten us all they wish, we are not frightened by their abuse.

The fourth letter contains information about the way the brothers managed to send their letters home:

> The people to whom we entrusted this letter will certainly let you know how things are with us. They kept faithfully on our track and held their own lives cheap for the Lord's sake and for ours. We were taken in a long line, begging and suffering want, along the difficult paths through Wendish country [southern Austria] all the way to the sea. . . . We do not know what else they will do to us, except that we are told that another order has come from the king, and it is possible that at Trieste we will be separated and placed in different castles.

Eighty-one brothers were brought to Trieste, among them those who signed the above letter: Oswaldt, Nickel, Blasi Schneider, Christian Häring, Ulrich Gschäll, Casperle Schneider (Kaspar Braitmichel), and Liendl.

From Aschelberger's first letter we learn that about 136 had been taken as prisoners to Falkenstein.

Leonhard Roth, in one of his letters to the church addressed to Hans Amon, mentions Amon's activity in Tirol:

> I heard about your work in Tirol. When the news reached me that they had united with the Swiss [Brethren], I was afraid for you. I know the deceitfulness of the Swiss in Tirol. I thank God in heaven who saved me from them in my simplicity, for as soon as I entered the country I noticed that they lived in a way that would lead to their own ruin and collapse. May God in heaven help them to do his divine will. I hope all goes well. I had hoped that you would manage to do something about a number of people, such as Michael from Cinsen, Melchior Zimmermann, Hans from Elbrun, and some of those from Laymen and Malsch. May the Lord guide them so that his name is glorified.
>
> Dear brother, please take my Clara into your special care, and please send brothers to my mother at Dannowitz sometime to challenge her, but do it with my Clara's advice, for it should be done with discretion on account of my stepfather. He is a great hindrance. But for him, my mother would have found the right way long ago. My Clara will tell you all about her. I don't have time to write much. You will surely be wondering about the others who wanted to join us—like Hans Schneider from Gutenbrunn, Gilg from Rakwitz, Paulo Schumacher and his wife, and Anna from Pawlowitz—and who may have been discouraged because of this imprisonment and turmoil. . . . We heard that Galle, who came with me, has fallen away. I can well believe it, although we know nothing definite, but he and four other brothers are no longer with us. . . . Do not be grieved with me on his account; you

1539

They decided to count as brothers those fellow prisoners who were not members, provided they were ready to suffer for the truth.

met outdoors with those who were not committed to the faith and asked them what they were going to do in this predicament. With great love they explained that if for the sake of the witness they would put their lives in Christ's hands in this time of suffering, regardless of any fear or need they might have to face, the brothers would consider them as fellow heirs of God's kingdom, in the certainty that God would be merciful to them. The brothers added that if with God's help any one of them should regain his freedom and return to the community, then the church had the authority from God to consider the personal situation of each according to the church order. In the meantime the brothers would let the elders at home know what they all desired and then inform them of the church's decision. All the men expressed their heartfelt agreement. They were full of joy

---

> yourself know what he was like. He caused me a lot of trouble; thank goodness that I am rid of him.

In Leonhard Roth's third letter to Amon we read: "They marched us under arrest to a village called Kagran, about a mile outside Vienna. There we were allowed to rest for a day, but we are told we still have to go to the sea."

Hans Amon writes in his second letter to the prisoners at Falkenstein: "We have sent off some brothers to follow you and see where God the Lord allows you to be taken, and later we want to send others who with God's help and strength will search you out and comfort you." We learn too that three sisters were ready to join the brothers in captivity. Amon advised against it because he was afraid they would soon be separated from the brothers, especially "among the foreign dogs."

In a letter to the sisters and the sick people left behind at Steinebrunn, Amon thanks them for remaining faithful and steadfast, adding, "It is a fact that we were protected, for at Kostel and Pulgram our people were ordered to leave. The sick and the children were mercilessly driven out, and at Kostel there was an uproar when our people were unwilling to go."

Another of Amon's letters is addressed to the brothers who did not manage to escape from Trieste: Stoffel Aschelberger, Jörg Planer, Jörgel Maier, Valtin, Leonhard, Matthias, Michael from Viless, Jörg Geier, Martin from Elbogen, Kaspar Müller, Thoman Graber, and Melchior Stockner. (See below, p.195 for the story of the escape.) He tries to comfort them by reminding them of the many brothers who have been in prison for years—for instance, "One brother has been at Bamberg [Bavaria] for twelve years now, and some have been in prison seven or eight years, and God has kept them devout and faithful. Another is dear brother [Jörg] Liebich and a sister [Ursula Hellrigel] who have been in prison at Innsbruck for three years already." Amon goes on to report about conditions in Moravia:

> You know we are living in Moravia as before, but at Whitsun they decided to drive out all who want to live in community. But with God's help we are ready to die rather than give up community. . . . Thanks be to God, the dear brothers who were imprisoned with you have all returned to us, except for you and Christian. Lamprecht Creutztaller and Kaspar Braitmichel are still in Carinthia or Styria. We expect them any day and don't know what has happened to them. Michael Schneider and Hansel Koll are back in their own country; the two dear brothers are still imprisoned at Graz, and Nickel at Vienna. Jörgel from Salzburg, Bastel Beck, and Alt-Rupp were called to their last rest after they had come back. Our dear brother Leonhard

and thankfulness over the proposal and received it as a gift from God's grace. *1539*

Straightaway a written account was sent to the church, and a letter soon came back saying that all the believers agreed: Since those who had not yet become members of the church according to divine order (for reasons valid in God's eyes) were now of one mind with the church and ready to witness to the truth, to suffer with the brothers, and to endanger their own lives, they should be joyfully given recognition as fellow believers.

When the church's decision was made known to them, they readily entrusted themselves to the Lord and proved patient in all distress, giving good testimony in front of many witnesses, just as other believers did.

> Lanzenstiel is in his former place. Brother Peter [Riedemann] has gone to do the Lord's work in Hesse.

A last letter from Amon to the brothers "at Trieste or on the sea" asks for news about them: "We have inquired all around Trieste and Laibach (where the Lord has given us a few new brothers), but we have not heard anything certain about you." Later in the letter he describes conditions in Moravia:

> We are living in Moravia in the same places as before, especially the community at Schakwitz in the big house where we used to be. But every day we are threatened with persecution. Just now, for instance, there is an Imperial Diet at Regensburg, and some say a council will be held as well, which they believe will not tolerate us any longer. But we are in God's hands, and nothing will happen to us unless it is his will.
>
> Brother Hans Gentner is in the empire [Germany], and we have many brothers there too, the Lord be praised. Peter [Riedemann] was captured in Hesse. As you know, he was in prison earlier for eight years, and now it has been almost a year. Andreas Keller, who was left behind on your way down, is still in prison at Graz. At Innsbruck there are still Jörg Liebich and a sister [Ursula Hellrigel].
>
> Schuster's wife, the sister of your betrothed, dear Stoffel [Aschelberger], is with us in the Lord. Your wife, dear [Jörg] Planer, has died in the Lord. Your father, dear [Melchior] Stockner, and your mother, too, are with us in the Lord with all their children except their eldest son, and it is their prayer that you remain faithful to the Lord. Your sister, dear Kaspar Müller, has also died in the Lord. But these dear ones are still with us in the Lord: your Tilga, dear Stoffel; your Sophie, dear Matthias; your Agnes, dear Valtin; and your sister, dear Jörg Geier. They ask you from their hearts to remain faithful and not to worry about them. They are willing to give you up for the Lord's sake so that they may meet you in eternity among all the faithful. You, dear Jörgel Maier, beloved brother-in-law, your father Balthasar and his Justina ask you from the bottom of their hearts to fight valiantly for the truth. . . .
>
> Through our brother Peter we are sending each one of you a handkerchief as a sign of love and to remind you, as you wipe your eyes in your grief and misery, that God will one day wipe away all tears.

See also Beck, 146–148. For the confession of faith written down by the captive brothers, see Müller, *Glaubenszeugnisse*, I, 190–205.

1539
The royal marshal, scholars, priests, and an executioner came to question the prisoners in Falkenstein, some under torture.

Meanwhile King Ferdinand dispatched his marshal, several scholars and priests, as well as the executioner as their "high priest" and assistant. They used the Christmas days (a thing rarely done anywhere) to begin their malicious treatment of the captive witnesses for the truth. Some they questioned under torture regarding their basic beliefs and hopes and where they kept their treasures. The believers confessed unanimously that Christ the Savior was their only hope and dearest treasure, in whom they had attained the Father's mercy.

The host is a dumb idol.

Their tormentors questioned them about many other points, with the intention of teaching and converting them. They especially stressed the eucharist and exalted it, trying to get the prisoners to believe that the flesh and blood of Christ was present in it, that it was "our Lord God." The brothers answered that it was a dumb idol and that they had an entirely different conception of the Lord's Supper than the twisted one used by their adversaries to deceive the world. After hearing this and many other statements of faith, the royal emissaries returned to Vienna, and the brothers remained imprisoned in Falkenstein Castle.

1540

In 1540 the royal marshal came to Falkenstein accompanied by a mounted attendant known as Lang Hans (Tall Hans) and the provost and other armed riders. They questioned the imprisoned brothers one by one. All who refused to agree with them and held firm to the truth were bound in pairs with iron fetters, their hands chained together.

When the brothers were to be led away to the sea, many sisters came to the castle, knelt down together, and prayed.

When word got around that the prisoners were to be sent to the sea, many sisters in the faith came to Falkenstein Castle. Some of them were wives of the brothers, others were friends and relatives. They knelt down together and prayed fervently to their Father, the most high God, for protection from all sin and evil on land or sea and for steadfast hearts that remain faithful to the truth until death.

They took leave in tears.

After they had prayed, the marshal's attendant Lang Hans gave orders for everyone to make ready for departure. They took leave with many bitter tears, encouraging one another to hold firm to the Lord and to the truth. Each one commended the other to God's merciful protection, not knowing if any would ever see the other again on this earth. Let each one judge for himself what a hard struggle that was for husbands to be parted from their wives and for fathers to leave their little children behind. In truth, flesh and blood cannot do it, but God will seek out those who cause such great distress and punish them severely. *1540*

The marshal could not hold back his tears at their leave-taking.

The leave-taking was such a pitiful sight that the royal marshal and some of his men were unable to hold back their tears. When things were ready and the escort had arrived, the believers were marched through the gate two by two, firmly trusting that God would protect them. Ninety set out after being imprisoned for six and a half weeks.

90 brothers led from Falkenstein to the sea.

The sisters had to stay behind in the castle. They climbed on the wall and, heartbroken with grief, gazed after their brothers, to whom they were bound by divine love, until they could see them no longer. Then they were sent away from the castle to return home.

The sick and the young kept in the castle.

Those brothers who were not taken to the sea because they were weak or sick or too young were held in the castle. Several of the young boys were given into the possession of Austrian noblemen, but nearly all of them returned to the church. The other brothers remained in Falkenstein Castle until God in his mercy led them out.

There were never so many devout people at Falkenstein since it was built.

On that occasion the lord, Hans Fünfkirchen, vowed he would place an inscription above the castle gate, stating that since it was built, there had never been so many devout people in it as at that time, but it is likely that he forgot to do this. In spite of himself he had had to witness to the truth.

Reasons for our suffering.

This great distress came upon the faithful because they testified against pope and priests, against their sinful lives and the whole idolatrous system, saying that God will punish them severely for their abominations and let them die in their sins. That is why King Ferdinand had empowered the bloodthirsty mob of priests to do as they pleased with the prisoners. The priests were quick in deciding that the brothers deserved to die, that they could not be tolerated on land but should be sent to sea to waste away in great suffering as galley slaves. They were to be handed over to the high admiral Andrea Doria[1]

Like the Pharisees, the priests shouted, "Away with them!"

---

[1]In 1528, Andrea Doria (1468–1560), the famous Genoese admiral, had placed himself and his fleet at the service of Emperor Charles V, using slaves as well as convicts on his galleys.

From 1492 to 1559, with a brief interruption, Trieste and Fiume (Rijeka) belonged to Austria.

1540

Brothers told the royal officers beforehand that they would not row the galleys.

for use in his fleet of warships that fought the Turks and other enemies. Even as the brothers were being violently carried off and imprisoned, they warned the king's agents that they would not row a stroke to aid war and pillage. Whether on land or at sea, they refused to take part in evil and to sin against God because their hearts rejected all sin. God in his invincible power would protect them at sea as on the land and keep them in his grace.

They were allowed to pray morning and evening without interference.

Nevertheless the king's men received strict instructions that the prisoners be marched under guard from one courthouse to the next. So these witnesses to the truth were brought before the magistrates in towns and villages, where they had to suffer much hostility and hardship. But God always gives means of grace to his people. The brothers were able to pray to God every morning and evening without anyone stopping them. Any brother who was given words of solace or encouragement from God could speak without fear and so bring comfort to his brothers. The believers were deeply grateful for this special gift and mercy of God.

Their escorts told them to sing as they passed through the towns instead of walking in silence.

This among other things worked a change in people's attitude toward them in many places, with the result that they were regarded with sympathy instead of being taken for criminals as when they first arrived. As well as that, the soldiers who accompanied them frequently spoke on their behalf and encouraged them to witness to their faith in songs and other ways, instead of passing through the towns in silence.

Brothers' route to the sea.

In this manner the band of believers was driven like a flock of sheep through town and countryside to the sea at Trieste: first from Falkenstein Castle to Vienna, then to Neustadt, Schottwien, and over the Semmering to Bruck an der Mur and down to Graz, to Leibnitz and Marburg (Maribor) and so to Cilli (Celje), then to Stein (Kamnik) in Carniola, over the Sava River to Laibach (Ljubliana), on to Upper Laibach and finally to Trieste.

They suffered great hunger.

All this time, the brothers endured hunger and great hardship; they were fed with the bread of fear and the waters of distress.

That was the way God chose to reveal his truth to peoples who were still in ignorance, to be heard like the sound of a mighty trumpet. God has always provided means of grace to draw men away from evil, as in this case. When the believers passed through the different places where strange languages were spoken and people had never heard the truth, they found some in southern Austria, Carniola, and northern Italy who were moved by their witness to seek it. A number of people embraced the truth and are serving God with sincere hearts to this day.

1540
Contacts on the journey.

As for the ill-treatment the prisoners received in many places—how they were beaten and roughly handled, how they were tied to one another with ropes and chains—all this is unnecessary to describe. Everyone can imagine that what goes on in such places is far from pleasant. But although it was a dreadful experience, God always comforted the brothers in their hearts.

Even in times of greatest distress, God does not forget his own. He gave several of the prisoners inner promptings of hope and trust that God would show them a way to escape. They spoke of this together in the fear of God. Although they were determined to suffer and die for the truth rather than take part in wicked piracy, they had every reason to continue sighing and pleading that God might demonstrate his honor in them.

God gave the brothers hope of escape.

As they prayed, God showed them that they should agree among themselves how the strong were to take care of the weak and how one would help the other. Even though they had little food, they trusted that the Lord would provide for them so that they need not beg or search for bread. On the twelfth night in Trieste they all got free of their bonds. They walked out of the prison, and God showed them a place where within an hour they could all let themselves down from the city wall with ropes. The ropes that had bound them and by which they had been led into the prison now served for their escape. So whatever evil designs ungodly men have on the devout, God turns to good for his own people.

On the twelfth night the brothers escaped.

The ropes that had bound them served to free them.

Thanks to God's intervention they escaped from their enemies. With all the diligent watches the ungodly had posted on the city walls, God turned their precautions to folly: he showed the brothers a place right next to the sentry box on the wall. When all of them, sick and healthy, were over the wall, they knelt down to praise and thank him. The Lord also prepared the way for most of them to return to the church of the saints in Moravia, their hearts filled with joy and peace.

God helped them escape in spite of the strict watch.

At the foot of the wall they thanked God for their escape.

Twelve of them, however, were seized in the merciless

1540
12 brothers recaptured and led off to the sea.

pursuit that followed. They were handed over to Andrea Doria, the emperor's admiral for naval warfare, and taken to the galleys with the intention of using them at the oars. But the faithful were determined to risk their lives, to be flogged rather than to set their hands to rowing. We do not yet know exactly how each one met his end, but if they remained faithful to the Lord it is certain that they did not have many good days left.[1]

The brothers who escaped returned to the church.

The brothers whom God had delivered returned to the church in Moravia on the fourth Sunday of Lent in 1540. They were welcomed with great joy and thanksgiving as a gift from God.[2]

The church community had previously been forced to leave Schakwitz, but in this year 1540 they received permission from the lord marshal of Mährisch Kromau to start building again and to gather the believers there. At Candlemas [Feb. 2] of

---

[1]Brothers were sent to Trieste to search for the missing brothers, but without success; one of these was a Jörg Maierhofer. See Beck, 147. In his study, "Die ungarischen Wiedertäufer bei Grimmelshausen," *Zeitschrift für Kirchengeschichte* (1940), LIX, A. J. F. Zieglschmid establishes the theory that at least some if not all of the twelve reached the Mount Athos Republic in Greece and were taken in by the Athos monasteries. It is possible that the Athos monks, after hearing the brothers' account, sent three representatives to Moravia in 1540 to make contact and learn more about the basis of the Anabaptist faith. About Athos, see also *Schaff-Herzog*, I, 348–349.

[2]For the story of the brothers' deportation and escape, see also *Martyrs Mirror*, 451–453. This experience gave rise to a wealth of songs written by or about the prisoners; see the *Falkensteiner Lieder* in *LdHBr*, 89–115. Leonhard Roth wrote three songs: "Ach Gott im höchsten Reiche" (My God in the highest realm), "O Gott, Vater in Ewigkeit" (O God, eternal Father), and "Herr Gott, Vater vom Himmel" (Lord God, Father in heaven) with the acrostic "Hinzug der gefangenen Brueder" (Departure of the imprisoned brothers). Hans Amon wrote, among others, one song starting "Unbillig haben's gehandelt" (They acted criminally) with the acrostic "Und ihr Erledigung" (And their escape). Peter Hagen or Schuster wrote "Ewiger Gott vom Himmel" (Eternal God in heaven); Kaspar Braitmichel, among other songs, "Merkt auf, herzlieben Brüder mein" (Now hear, beloved brothers).

One song was written jointly by several brothers, each contributing one or two verses; first line: "O Gott, Vater vom Himmelreich" (O God, Father in the heavenly kingdom). The authors were Oswald Falger, Stoffel Aschelberger, Jobst from Villach, Bastel Beck, Blasi Schneider, Wolf Schwägel, Leonhard Roth, Hans Brigel, Kaspar Braitmichel, Georg Krel, Jörgel from Salzburg, Georg J. Schneider, Hansel Taurer, Peter Hagen, P. T., Klein Gilg P., Georg Schuster, Anthony Schuster, Jakob from Sternenfels, Martin Schuster, L. H., Matthias Schuster, Ulrich Gschäll.

Other songwriters: Antoni Erfordter (see also *ME*, II, 242–243), "Von Trübsal, Schmerzen, Elend gross" (Of suffering, pain, and misery great); Hansel Taurer, "Herr Gott, ich tu dich bitten" (O God, I do beseech you) with the acrostic "Hennsel Taurer"; Hans Brigel, "Herzliebster Vater in deinem Himmelreich" (Beloved Father in your heavenly kingdom) with the acrostic "Hans Brigl."

that year Michael Matschidel and Blasius Tischler (both servants for temporal affairs) bought the big house at Schakwitz on our behalf for the second time since the persecution of 1535, from a citizen of Brünn called Schleicher. They put it in order again, as well as two other houses that had come into our possession at that time when people from Schakwitz joined us. Later we were given legal possession of several other houses.

1540
They settled in Schakwitz a second time.

To build up the house of God with his chosen, God gave his servants the courage and eagerness to send brothers out in various directions. A burning zeal for the truth was now kindled among people through the witness given during the past trouble at Steinebrunn and drew them to the believers, who bore the cross as a sign of victory on their bloodstained banner. In the time of Pharaoh, who ordered all boys to be killed at birth, hoping to weaken the people of Israel, God circumvented his designs, and the Israelites increased until the land swarmed with their children. In the same way King Ferdinand's intention of wiping out the people of God by sending every male to the sea served only to increase their numbers.

King's action like that of Pharaoh in Egypt.

In this same year of 1540 the assembly of the Lord sent brothers out on mission journeys. Leonhard Lanzenstiel was sent again to Tirol, Christoph Gschäl to Styria and Carinthia, and Peter Riedemann to Hesse.[1] Hans Gentner was sent to

Leonhard Lanzenstiel sent to Tirol, Christoph Gschäl to Carinthia, Peter Riedemann to Hesse, and Hans Gentner to Swabia.

[1]Peter Riedemann had been commissioned to renew the earlier contacts between the brothers in Hesse and those in Moravia and to form as close a relationship as possible. The following letter from Hans Amon to the church in Hesse, which Riedemann must have taken on his journey, will have served the same purpose (Codex A b 5, fol. 97, Budapest University Library); see also Günther Franz, *Wiedertäuferakten, 1527–1626*, Vol. IV of *Urkundliche Quellen zur hessischen Reformationsgeschichte* (Marburg, 1951), 276–277 (excerpts).

> From the elders and servants and the whole church at Auspitz in Moravia, gathered in the name of our Lord Jesus Christ through God's Holy Spirit: Beloved brothers in Hesse, who have been driven hither and thither, suffering many trials, we wish you grace and peace from the almighty, compassionate God, our heavenly Father, through the pure, unadulterated knowledge of our Lord Jesus Christ. He is our hope, a God over all things, blessed in all eternity. Amen.
>
> Dear brothers, because of our overflowing love for you we have on several occasions sent brothers to seek you out and show you brotherly love, although they were actually much needed here at home. Those brothers have always given the same testimony of us, praise and thanks be to God, namely that God keeps us steadfast in his only Son.
>
> But now, dear brothers, we understand that you are having doubts because

1540

Lower Swabia and Württemberg. From all these places God led many people to his church, which spread widely throughout Moravia.

Hermann Schmidt and others rebelled. Demanded that the brothers return to prison.

Yet Satan is always at the right hand of the devout to prevent them from doing God's work [Ps.109:6]. Now he stirred up several of the believers themselves to turn in rebellion against the church, particularly one Hermann Schmidt and others like him, who maintained that the brothers had escaped from Trieste not through God's intervention but by being unfaithful and running away from God's discipline and that they should return to their prison. This faction tried to undermine the trust among

---

of a few unscrupulous people who have given you evil reports about us. It shocked and grieved us to hear that you allowed yourselves to be swayed and turned against us so quickly. When things went badly with you, we were deeply concerned on your account, and we rejoiced when it was well with you in the Lord. We visited you more than once to open our hearts to you, and you believed us at the time and sent some of your brothers and sisters to us. They are still among us and are glad to stay with us. They join with us every time we write and send messengers to you. Nevertheless, you so quickly allowed yourselves to be led astray by people whom we excluded for their sins.

O dear brothers, we are afraid you will get nowhere. As the Holy Spirit testifies, when men believe lies rather than the truth, God strikes them with such blindness and confusion that they grope their way from one darkness to another like a drunken man along a wall. We have come to you in love, in the fear of God, and with earnest prayer to the Almighty. Our brothers have always given you the same testimony about us, and we have not changed. But we understand that our enemies have made you unsure of us. It is a painful shock to us that you believe so easily when evil is spoken against us. Do you not know that people will speak evil of us falsely and unjustly, as Christ says?

Now, dear brothers, we love you more than we can say, and so we send our brothers to visit you again. They are a living letter to you, and you will hear from them what the truth really is, for we have told them all our heart's concern for you. They will explain it all to you, and you should believe them. Our brothers will tell you personally about Hans Both and Valtin [Schuster]; they are our living witnesses, since they experienced everything themselves. If you believe them, we will give praise to the Almighty. If you do not, this will bear witness on the day of the Lord Jesus Christ that we rendered faithful account to you and all your people, acting in a fair and godly way.

Those of us who have come here from Hesse enjoin you in the name of our Lord to believe the brothers and not to let your hearts grow further estranged. We experienced it all personally and have asked these brothers to visit you as a living letter to explain everything to you. We do not know what else to write. In heartfelt brotherly love we commend you to the grace of God. May he keep your hearts and ours in the peace and unity of the Holy Spirit through our Lord Jesus Christ, who called us to this way. Amen. We servants and the whole church greet you all from our hearts with the peace of God. May he be with you and us forevermore. Amen.

those people who had recently arrived and to cause a split in the brotherhood. *1540*

When the church withstood their attempt, they looked for other ways to make the people suspicious of their servants. Among other things, they said that the servants favored those sisters whose jackets had puffed sleeves (which they had brought with them from the world because it was the fashion at that time) and took them on journeys around the country. The servants answered that they did this only so that the people they met would rejoice with the church in the grace of God. Then in their foolishness Hermann Schmidt and the others thought that believers should not keep pigeons flying around their houses to be used for food. This was disproved by the divine testimony that God has created food for every creature. It is the custom in this country to eat pigeons, and there is nothing wrong in the devout enjoying them.

Hermann Schmidt and his followers protested against believers keeping pigeons.

The trouble-makers also criticized the brotherhood for providing their servants with special food and drink.

They talked about the servants' food and drink.

All this was clearly reported in a meeting of the brotherhood. As Hermann Schmidt and his followers were unwilling to accept any correction, they were all excluded for their rebellious disturbance.

Hermann Schmidt and his followers excluded.

Not long afterward another member, Hans Edelmair, began in the same way, though secretly, to gather a few irresponsible people around him and form an opposition to the church and her servants. He was soon recognized as an agitator, and he and his followers were excluded from the church.

Hans Edelmair started a faction against the church and her servants. He was excluded.

For this reason, as many brothers as possible met to confer without the elders—servants of the Word and servants for temporal affairs. Turning to Holy Scripture, they learned that those who serve the Gospel should receive their daily food by it. A threshing ox shall not be muzzled, and those with greatest responsibility are worthy of double honor. Since they faithfully serve the brotherhood with spiritual food, there should be no begrudging them the temporal food. So the brotherhood realized it was wrong to give way to envious malcontents. The brotherhood members affirmed that it was right to provide for their servants in love and brotherly care. Anyone who found fault with this should not criticize the servants but should go to the brotherhood for an answer.

The brotherhood members discussed the question of food and drink for the servants.

The brotherhood confirmed giving food and drink to the servants. Anyone against it should come to the brotherhood for an answer.

During this time Peter Riedemann was in prison at Marburg

1540
Peter Riedemann held in prison in Hesse in the dry summer of 1540. There he wrote our confession of faith which was printed.

and then at Wolkersdorf in Hesse.[1] When this Hermann (mentioned above) went to Hesse with his followers, who were also under discipline, one of them met a sudden death through God's wrath. At this, Hermann had a terrible shock and was filled with remorse. He went to Peter Riedemann in prison and disclosed what he had done. After much persistence and many tears, he moved Peter to send him to the church, comforting him with the grace of the Lord, and trusting that the church, too, would make peace with him again, which then took place. Besides this, Peter wrote an earnest letter from prison to the church, saying that they should regard him as unbiased, as he was still in chains and did not know if he would ever enjoy the blessings of the church again. He urged them all to show every concern for their servants, and the letter he sent at that time runs as follows:

Hermann Schmidt reaccepted.

Peter Riedemann's letter about what is due to the servants for their task.

From Peter, your brother and a prisoner of Christ as a witness to his name. To all in Hesse, Swabia, and Moravia who have found a common faith with us, my dear fellow members in the Lord:

May the blessing of heaven, where all the fullness of the Father's grace dwells, be with you always and refresh you like an evening shower and make your righteousness grow green and fruitful like a plant, to the praise and glory of our Father in heaven, the invisible and only wise One.

Phil.1:3–8

Dear brothers, I hold you all in my heart as my fellows in grace, even in my bonds. Because of my responsibility to represent the Gospel, I cannot neglect writing to you, in trust that you will do what I tell you, since you have already started to follow the Lord's way and actively live out his order.

It is God's will for you—and he has given you his Spirit for this purpose and sealed you as his chosen ones with this sign—that you should all be urged by the same Spirit to live before him with one heart and mind in the likeness of the Son of God, Jesus Christ our Lord, who showed by his whole life that he had community with the

[1]Riedemann did not return to the community in Moravia until 1542; Beck, 151. About the "Confession of Faith" or *Account of Our Religion, Doctrine, and Faith*, see below, p.294 n.

Father and the Father with him. This means that the Father lives in him and he in the Father. In the same way you should show that you have community with him, which means that he is living in you and you in him. As the Son does nothing except what he sees the Father doing or what the Father does in him, so you, too, should do nothing except what you see him doing or what he does in you. Then you will always be one in him; and no division, grumbling, malice, or anything of the sort will be able to rise up in you. Then Satan cannot harm you, because every access to you will be shut and barred against him.

1540
Peter Riedemann's letter about what is due to the servants for their task.

John 5:19

Be mindful, therefore, of the calling for which you have been chosen and accepted. Consider the worth of the precious treasure entrusted to you, through which you become a royal priesthood and divine heirs. Put every effort, then, into guarding this treasure well, for it is your life, your riches, your security. Do not lose heart in serving one another with love and joy, for then the God of love and peace will be with you. The more you put heart and soul into his work, the closer he comes to you; and the more you serve him, the more he bestows his grace on you. Therefore, anyone who wishes to be rich in God must not be niggardly in service. Let him throw off the laziness of his flesh, and he will be given a willing spirit that serves with joy, a joy that will increase the more he serves. Those who are ruled by that spirit will receive greater strength; they shall walk and not be faint, they shall run and not be weary.

1 Pet. 2:9

Gal. 6:2
2 Thess. 3:13

Isa. 40:31

Dear brothers, I am not writing this to you as if you did not know it. You already know it well since you are children of the knowledge of God. I am writing it with the sole purpose of reviving your clear understanding in Christ so that you can share more diligently what you know and thus let your light shine out more and more. Then you will not let yourself be frightened off by opposition, grumbling, and slander from those who are falsely called brothers, but instead will let them spur you on to greater zeal, more love, wholehearted obedience, and reverence toward one another, most of all to your servants, through whom God grants his grace to you.

1540
Peter Riedemann's letter about what is due to the servants for their task.

God is specifically telling you to do this, and because it is a pleasing service to him, the devil shrieks and rages against it all the more through those who serve him. He is trying to make you careless and suspicious of your servants so that you will dislike hearing the Word from them and the Word will bear no fruit in you. In this way the devil will be able to scatter you and drag you into his kingdom.

At what point could he attack harder than here? What better way is there to demolish a house than to dig out and remove the pillars that hold it up? Now the servants are called pillars of the house of God. As Paul says, "They were recognized as pillars." The devout Judith says, "You elders, on whom the lives of the people depend." So he, the devil, seeks out the best place to attack and says, "A true shepherd lays down his life for the sheep; but when troubles come, your servants run away from you, so they are hirelings and not shepherds." Furthermore: "They eat by themselves and of the best. They teach you community of goods but do not keep it themselves." With these and similar words the devil and his helpers try to deceive you and make you uneasy in your consciences and loath to do good. Woe to those who listen to them!

Gal.2:9

Jth.8:24

My dear children, I am not writing because I think you are negligent in this matter, for I know you yourselves are eager to do it. But to prevent any of you from being weakened by slander, I ask you, dear brothers, to consider God's severity to those people and his goodness to you, who have so far continued in what is good. Consider those who begrudged the servants what was given them by the church: is there a single one who has remained steadfast in the truth? Has God ever been pleased with a people who thought little of their servants instead of counting them worthy of the honor ordained for them by God? Haven't they all fallen into futility, and haven't some of them conformed to the world again? You who have held the servants in due respect have remained firm in the truth, and the Lord has been with you to this day. Why is that? It is because you have kept his ordinances and valued his gifts highly. The Lord, who knows this,

Rom.11:5

1540
Peter Riedemann's letter about what is due to the servants for their task.

gave you the best gifts (because you were worthier of them than many others), withdrawing them from those others who despised them and thus were not worthy of them. A man who prizes the gifts God grants him will be given more and more of them, but one who despises these gifts will have them taken from him because he is unworthy.

So, dear brothers, continue as you began. Do not be misled by unspiritual prattle, but honor your servants, and the Lord will be with you always, as he has been until now, and will increase your blessedness. If some take offense because they do not understand or are too simple, you will be able to teach them what is right, and they will be willing to learn and to follow the right way Where this is not so, know that their hearts are hardened and that no signs or wonders will help them any more than they helped Pharaoh; such people will come to the same end as he did. Then, like him, they must be left to go their way. But you must not let anyone hold you back from deeds of love to your brothers and sisters, especially to those who lead you, for that is the Lord's will. Therefore, think of the words from the Lord, spoken by the Holy Spirit: "This child is set for the fall and rise of many in Israel, and for a sign that shall be spoken against."

Exod.9
Rom.9:17
Luke 2:34

Is it not true, dear brothers, that a man who opposes the Lord's order opposes the Lord himself? And the Lord's order is: "You should count your servants worthy of double honor because of their work." Consider: Has the Lord ever given a task without appointing the wages so that the task can be fulfilled? If he has done this for other tasks, how much more for the task of preaching the Gospel? So Paul says, "If we have sown a spiritual crop for you, is it too much if we reap your material benefits?" He says as well, "Who tends a flock without getting some of its milk?" Do I say this from a human standpoint? Does not the Law say the same: "You shall not muzzle an ox that treads out the grain"? Is it for oxen that God is concerned? Is it not said mainly for our sake?

1 Tim.5:17
1 Cor.9:11,7
Deut.25:4

In all this, dear brothers, see to it that you care for your servants not only out of love but also because it is your duty. What if the slanderers say, "If they eat the

1540
Peter Riedemann's letter about what is due to the servants for their task.

same as everybody else, they are still enjoying the milk from the herd. It does not follow that we always have to give them the best." My dear brothers, I know how you think about it, but to help you answer the slanderers, I will show you the truth of these things. Just as it is our responsibility to defend you because you are inscribed in our hearts, so it is your responsibility to defend us. In this mutual trust I am all the more outspoken because you know me well and realize that my concern is only for your salvation, that you may be pleasing to God.

1 Cor.9:13

Paul shows in a clear and wonderful way that there is no validity in our opponents' interpretation. He says: "Do you not know that those who perform the temple service get their food from the temple, and those who serve at the altar get their food from the altar?" So the Lord commanded that those who preach the Gospel deserve their living from the Gospel. Look into what Paul shows us here, dear brothers.

Matt.10:9–10

Lev.7

Did not God ordain the best of the sacrifice for the servants of the temple and altar, instead of letting them eat the same as those who brought the offering? All the fat was the Lord's, and after the Lord's portion the best was the priests'. The people took the rest to eat with their households. It was the same with the tithe and firstfruits of their crops and flocks. This is the context for the Lord's words, "You shall not muzzle the ox that treads out the grain." It means, "You shall not withhold or stint what is due to those who serve." These words state plainly that the servants have rights in temporal things, rights that must be heeded, and that they should enjoy the freedom of the Gospel. As Paul says, "We should be given the same consideration as Peter and the other apostles." It was not wrong for them to use this right, which is said especially of Peter.

Num.18:12–14

1 Cor.9:9

1 Cor.9:4–5
1 Thess.2:6

Out of love, therefore—and not only out of love but also because you owe it, as the commandment says—show double honor and love, be obedient and give generously in temporal things, as Simon the tanner did to Peter. Who can claim that Peter did not eat by himself? The objection is frequently made that Paul did not make use of this freedom in a number of places in Achaia, but

Acts 9:43
10:5–6

2 Cor.11:8–10

that had its reasons, as he himself shows us. It does not follow, though, that he did not use it in other countries. Yes, I tell you, he certainly used it in other countries—the churches gave him temporal support both while he was with them and when he was far away. That was how zealously they cared for him, and he accepted it too, calling such service "a fragrant offering well pleasing to God." He says to the Corinthians, "In what way were you inferior to other churches except that I myself did not burden you?"

1540
Peter Riedemann's letter about what is due to the servants for their task.

Phil.4:18

2 Cor.12:13

From this, dear brothers, we see (if we are willing) that even if the servants themselves waive this freedom, you do not honor the church but dishonor it by accepting the situation, for that means you are neglecting the order and command of the Lord. Dear brothers, even if your servants are willing to give up this right, you ought not to let it happen, for it is a matter of your honor before God and his holy angels. I know well that your servants are willing to surrender not only what is due them but their very lives as well, for the sake of your salvation. How much more should you on your side, dear brothers, be ready to uphold them in their rights, for it is to your own benefit. Do not let the slanderers mislead you. Among yourselves do all you can to teach one another. Then your good deeds will be done with joy and zest and will be genuine and not hypocritical.

James 5:9

Gal.6:6

My dear brothers, I have written this to you because of the special love I bear you for the Lord's sake. I know that the dear brothers are afraid to broach this subject and would rather go without than say anything—in case someone should imagine they are self-seeking. Since I am away from you, a prisoner for the Lord, not knowing if I will ever see you again in this life or you me, no one can imagine I am writing this for my own sake or for any fleshly reason. I only want to carry out my service for you and show you the fitting way. As I have already explained to you, it is your duty to stand by your servants, whom you have acknowledged as faithful, defending them against all slanderers and opponents. Your servants are ready not only to forgo what is their due but to lay down their lives too, because all they seek is your salvation.

1540

They want nothing that is not given them by you, the church, and with all you may do for them, you owe them still more; for you owe them your very selves, as Paul tells Philemon.

Philem. 19

Peter Riedemann's letter about what is due to the servants for their task.

If you consider this rightly, dear brothers, it will make you all the more eager to carry out this service to the full. Then your love of one to the other will increase, peace will flourish, and righteousness will be foremost among you. Apart from this I do not think it necessary to write much, dear brothers, for you have no lack of godly admonition, the Lord be praised! Only, dear brothers, take seriously before the Lord what he himself commanded you: "You shall take these words to heart and keep them in mind when you sit in your house and when you walk along the way, when you lie down and when you rise." Therefore David says, "Happy is the man who delights in the Lord and who meditates on his law day and night. He is like a tree planted beside streams of water, which bears leaves and fruit in due season. In all that he does he prospers"; for the Lord his God is with him and prepares all his ways.

Deut. 6:6–7
11:18–19

Ps. 1:2–3

As I have said, be diligent, dear children, and serve one another faithfully for the benefit of the whole body of Christ. Be examples to one another in love and godly obedience. Honor one another, but above all honor your servants, and you will be honoring the Lord, for it is his command and a step in truth. Anyone who grumbles and argues against it is opposing truth.

Gal. 5:13–14
1 Pet. 4:8

So do not let yourselves be swayed from this service by our opponents and those falsely called brothers, who wormed their way in to spy upon the liberty we have in Christ and to steal it from you. Take heed not to yield to them or obey them; then the truth of God will endure through you.

The reason I felt compelled to write this to you, dear brothers, was the amount of gossip among our enemies. They bring up all kinds of unjustifiable slander against the truth and use this on the simple-minded to confuse their consciences. Many try to defend their folly with this, which then leads to quarrels and heated words. The Lord rejects such foolishness and brings it to light. Be

2 Pet. 2:1–3

warned, then, and do not imitate their folly of heart lest you come to harm with them. My only concern is for you, since I see how other churches, on losing their zeal, have perished or been corrupted. If you lose your eagerness to serve and grow indifferent, then Satan, having won you over on this point, will soon attack you harder in another and will not give up until he has done the same to you as to others. Anyone who neglects or violates the Lord's command in one particular will soon be unfaithful altogether.

1540
Peter Riedemann's letter about what is due to the servants for their task.

Therefore I feel bound to warn you, because I see what Satan is planning to do, and perhaps I can protect you from harm and keep myself guiltless of your blood. The Lord says, "If the watchman sees disaster approaching and does not blow his trumpet to warn the people and the disaster takes place, some will die in their sins; but I will hold the watchman answerable for their blood. But if he blows the trumpet to warn the people and they refuse to heed the warning and the disaster takes place, those who die in their sins will be answerable for their own blood. The watchman will then be free of guilt because he warned them and they would not take heed." Though I write thus, I expect something better of you, dear brothers, than a refusal to heed my warning. I trust you will do as I say.

Ezek.3:17–21
33:1–9

I wrote this letter also because I could not resist Kaspar's persistent urging that I do so. He says it is our duty as servants to step into the breach wherever division threatens and restore harmony by teaching what God says. Nowhere else is there more division, grumbling, ill will, and slander than in connection with that teaching, which is God's order and command. Kaspar felt we could not remain silent and fail to make God's order known and uphold it. If I had not written, he would not be at peace about it with me. He could not be at peace with the other servants either unless they made every effort to represent this matter to the church. He says that at first he himself took the same position, namely, that out of love the servants should drop the matter because of the offense it caused. Now that God has shown him that it is a wonderful order and God's express command, he no longer feels it

Ezek.13:5

1540
Peter Riedemann's letter about what is due to the servants for their task.

should be given up—they should rather hold firmly to it so that God's ordinance not be belittled and his wrath brought upon the whole church.

Phil.4:8

Further, dear brothers, strive for all that is honorable and of good report, all that the Lord values in you. Give love the chief place among you so that you benefit each time you meet one another. Do your utmost to have a blameless conscience on the day of the Lord's coming from heaven. May the God of all grace, who has power to make you steadfast and keep you blameless, who can make you abundantly rich in the work of Christ—may he nurture you as a plant of his kind, to his eternal praise. Amen.

As for us, dear brothers, we still wait patiently for the Lord and for what he intends to do with us. The works he does for the faithful are marvelous. He is angry with them for a moment, and then of himself he is reconciled with them and shows them his loving-kindness. He says to the raging sea, "Be still," and its proud waves subside. To the darkness of the dungeon he says, "Give up my sons and daughters to the light." The Lord has given us into the hands of tyrants to deal with us according to their whims, so as to reveal what is in our hearts and whether we love God or not. They took us and threw us into a dark hole, where they kept us in great privation, enduring hunger and thirst. But the Lord was watching them and

Deut.8:3
Matt.4:4

clearly showed us thereby that man does not live by earthly bread alone but by every word that comes from the mouth of God. In the Lord's time he said, "It is sufficient. Ease the heavy bonds of my children." As soon as he spoke, it was done.

Now our imprisonment has been so much eased for our bodies that it fills my heart with anxiety, as if I were on tenterhooks. Everything around us is so favorable and

Gen.39

pleasant that I am afraid it may be the daily allurement—such as Potiphar's wife used to lure Joseph—to make us forget the Lord's work, trusting their kindness until it becomes a snare. All our hope and will is to leave our garment (this body) with her, as Joseph did, and with him to flee away undefiled rather than to yield in the slightest way. I tell you, dear brothers, this freedom to walk about unchained has made me so afraid that I would not have accepted it had I not feared to be deprived of visits from brothers and sisters. I was afraid we would cut ourselves off from the brothers and sisters by refusing to accept it. Now, praise the Lord, we are no longer in prison nor are we robbed of you. So, with the Lord's help, we want to wait in patience for his will, which he will carry out according to his plan as he has done until now. We beg you, however, not to forget us but to remember us before the Lord in your prayers. We are sure that you do this, dear brothers, for we would not forget you either.

1540
Peter Riedemann's letter about what is due to the servants for their task.

Now, dear brothers, we take leave of you in the Lord and commend you to God the King of eternity. May he keep you in his truth, faithful and devout until the end, and protect you from the enemy's deceit, to the praise of his holy name.

Heartfelt greetings in divine love from me, your brother Peter, now a prisoner of Christ. Greet Hans [Amon] too, Leonhard [Lanzenstiel], and all your servants and elders. Also greet my wife, with all who love us in Christ Jesus. Greetings to all the dear brothers and sisters who serve in the school and the kitchen and to all the saints. Kaspar, my fellow prisoner in Christ, sends loving greetings to you all by name. Greet one another with the kiss of love. Dear brothers, may the grace of our God and the blessing of his Beloved be with you always and keep you united in the mind of Christ forevermore.

May my heart, soul, and spirit be one with you always and the Spirit of Christ be with us all eternally. Amen.

Written from prison
at Wolkersdorf in Hesse

When this letter was read aloud in the church, Hans Edelmair's heart was moved and he declared that if he had heard the teaching in this letter earlier, he would never have gone so far as to rebel against the servants and the church. Thereupon he began weeping and went on so long that the church had mercy on him and reaccepted him as their fellow believer. This lasted only for a limited time, as will be told later in the right place.

Hans Edelmair repented.

1540
Hans Zimmerauer executed at Schwaz.

In this year 1540 brother Hans Zimmerauer was put in prison at Schwaz in the Inn Valley for the sake of divine truth. As his captors could neither make him recant nor convince him by Holy Scripture, they commissioned their high priest the executioner to complete the task. He was executed with the sword, testifying with his blood to his faith in God. His songs, which are still preserved, give further testimony that he stood right with God.[1]

Ulrich Stadler passed away.

In 1540 brother Ulrich Stadler, servant of the Word of God and his church, fell asleep in the Lord at Butschowitz in Moravia after suffering much tribulation.

House purchased.

In 1540 we bought a house at Rakwitz[2] on a site towards Prittlach. We lived there after rebuilding most of it from the ground up.

1541

House purchased.

In 1541 we bought a house in Saitz, got it ready, and lived there in Christian community.

Cornelius, a teacher from Austerlitz, slandered the church.

In that same year a teacher named Cornelius from the Austerlitz group came to Schakwitz with some of his followers, and in front of the gathered church they did all they could to slander its order and teaching. They hoped to weaken some of the believers and make them fall away. But the believers remained unswayed.

A certain Pilgram wanted to unite all the groups.

Similarly, a man by the name of N. Pilgram arrived soon afterward, full of guile and intrigue. He claimed he had come to the country to gather and unite all groups that had split up over matters of faith, but he straightaway proved the opposite. His very presence seemed to cause disturbance and confusion, and his slanderous talk confirmed this. When the brothers and sisters met to seek comfort and strength in the Lord's Word and knelt with one accord to pray, this slanderer wanted to join them in prayer. The brothers and sisters did not permit this, because of his great lack of understanding—he had first poured contempt on them and now wished to pray with them.

---

[1]About Hans Zimmerauer's songs, see Wolkan, *Lieder*, 40. See also *ME*, IV, 1139; *Martyrs Mirror*, 455; Beck, 148–149.

[2]Rakwitz (Rakvice) and Saitz (Zaječi), parochial villages northeast of Nikolsburg (Mikulov), north of Eisgrub (Lednice), owned by the lords of Lipé. At both places Jan of Lipé ceded land and farmsteads to the Hutterites. Zeman, *Topography*, #128, #134.

He talked on and on. The brothers and sisters did not react but continued in prayer. He then became incensed and said openly that he would rather unite with the Turks or the pope than with this church, and he left in a rage.

1541
Pilgram said he would rather unite with the Turks and the pope than with us.

The church, however, withstood all Satan's onslaughts without weakening or losing heart. They stood firm, trusting in Christ, their rock and foundation of unshakable truth, and continued steadily with their work of spreading the Gospel.

Soon after, it was decided in the church council that Hans Gentner, a loyal servant of Jesus Christ, should go once more to Hesse and Württemberg, and so he was sent on his way. In the same way, the church took leave of Christoph Gschäl with the commission first to visit the believers in Upper Austria and then to go on to the Salzburg region and to Carinthia.

Hans Gentner sent to Hesse and Württemberg.

Christoph Gschäl to Upper Austria, Salzburg, and Carinthia.

As the church had few shepherds and servants at the time, Christoph Gschäl was instructed to tell the church in Upper Austria that all who did not have sufficient reason to remain there should move to the church community in Moravia so that they would not need a servant or teacher in Upper Austria. When this decision was reported, some of them rebelled, especially Simon Schneider, Andreas Kupferschmied, and Antoni Kupferschmied. These were heard grumbling and asking impatiently whether the group there was really so bereft that there was no one at all who could be entrusted with this service. The implication was that someone could be found among themselves.

Decided that the brothers in Upper Austria should move to the church community.

Other things besides were going on that the church could no longer ignore, things which showed that their way of life did not conform to Christ's life and teaching but opposed it, as listed here. First, the community had bought housing at Steinbach near Steyr and had put one of their members, Adam Fichter, in charge there as steward so that the believers would have someone to apply to for what they needed. At the same time all stewards were required by the magistrates to appear with weapons for inspection, as is done in the world. This same Adam Fichter presented himself at the appointed place, carried a halberd throughout the muster, and gave taxes for bloodshed in war.

Housing found outside the community.

Disorder among the brothers in Upper Austria.

Then Antoni and Andreas Kupferschmied promised in the town hall at Steyr to help when called on in wartime and on other occasions. And they gave their journeymen armed escort

1541 on their way out of town with large containers of wine.

When they realized that the brothers from Moravia wanted to admonish and punish them for this disorder, they, especially Simon Schneider, took it upon themselves to do the punishing and to exclude several, which they had neither the authority nor the right to do. When Christoph [Gschäl], with other brothers from the church in Moravia, wanted to investigate and punish these offenses, they put up a strong resistance, maintaining that they had already been punished. Thereupon, Christoph with his companions returned to Moravia and described the situation to the elders. The elders very soon sent Christoph back to Upper Austria with fourteen brothers to talk to the people there, find out what had happened, and use discipline where anything was wrong. They were also to say that if the brothers in Upper Austria considered themselves their fellows in faith and in obedience to truth, they should prove their obedience by doing what the elders and the whole church wished them to do, since the way they lived together was not conducive to their salvation. Those who wanted to remain faithful to the truth should move to the church community.

14 brothers sent to Upper Austria to administer discipline and to tell the people to move to the church community.

Except for a few who did move to the church, the majority deserted and became part of the world, for they refused to accept any warning or discipline from the brothers sent to them. The brothers from Moravia mentioned earlier continued their journeys, each to the country appointed him. In this way the church in Upper Austria came to an end.

Christoph Gschäl and his companions stayed with a group of believers not far from St. Georgen in Attergau and then went to the people around Salzburg. Those who desired to give themselves to the truth were brought to Gmunden, where brothers spoke with them and then sent them on their way to the church in Moravia.

Next, Christoph Gschäl went to Rattenberg in the Inn Valley, which did not please Hans Amon, shepherd and teacher of the whole church, as he would rather have seen Christoph return to the church. So he sent brothers from the community with a letter to him saying that unless he had especially important reasons for remaining up there, he should return. But Christoph talked to the brothers he had gathered in Tirol, and they felt it necessary for him to stay up there. He himself was not eager to return to the church, and he stayed there all winter.

1541

2 brothers imprisoned, then released.

Christoph sent Matthias Legeder and Christian Lissner over the Brenner Pass into the Adige region. They were both captured at Sterzing for the sake of their faith and were imprisoned there for a time. After enduring many hardships they were released by God's will, came unharmed out of prison, and were welcomed by the church with great joy. Christoph, however, who remained in Rattenberg over winter, fell seriously ill but recovered later.

A house purchased.

In this year of 1541 on the Thursday before the day of Paul's Conversion [Jan. 25] Hans Amon, servant of the Lord's Word, and Jakob Kircher, servant for temporal affairs, bought a house on our behalf in Gurdau[1] near Auspitz, and there we lived.

Leonhard Roth passed away.

In this same year brother Leonhard Roth, a God-fearing and highly gifted man whose writings and testimonies we have, fell asleep in the Lord at Schakwitz in Moravia. He was one of those who had been taken captive to the sea and who then returned.[2]

Terrible plague in Moravia.

Wolf Röschel and Blasius Tischler passed away.

In that year around St. James's Day [July 25], the plague broke out in Moravia and lasted throughout the winter into the year 1542, and God visited his people with the same sickness. Quite a number of the believers were taken to their last resting place, notably the brothers Wolf Röschel and Blasius Tischler, who had both been looking after the temporal affairs of the church.

1542

Hans Amon, our elder, passed away.

At Candlemas [Feb. 2] in 1542 the Lord released our dear brother Hans Amon from this world through the same plague. The entire church community had been entrusted to him. For six years he had tended it with God's Word and guided it in utmost faithfulness through God's grace. He had a good testimony from all believers and from unbelievers too, for God's blessing was abundantly visible in his work, as can be

---

[1]Gurdau (Kurdějov), northeast of Auspitz (Hustopeče), belonged to the lords of Lipé. Beck, 168 n.2; Zeman, *Topography*, #45; *ME*, II, 612.

[2]About Leonhard Roth as a songwriter, see Wolkan, *Lieder*, 173; Beck, 149.

1542

felt in the letters he wrote to those in prison and to the church communities. We still have many of these letters as well as some of his songs.[1] And so the whole church suffered deep grief and loss, now that they had to do without him.

Church entrusted to Leonhard Lanzenstiel.

But God, who comforts his people in all need and does not leave them without a leader, once again provided them with a faithful shepherd gifted with burning zeal. This was Leonhard Lanzenstiel, a rope maker by trade and a servant of God's Word, who accepted the care of the church because of its great need. Hans Gentner loyally assisted him. The two brothers at once sent word, first to Rattenberg on the Inn River in Tirol, saying that as Hans Amon had been called by God from this life, Christoph [Gschäl] should return to the church without delay. Second, they sent word to Peter Riedemann in prison at Wolkersdorf in Hesse that as God had eased his imprisonment and had in some ways opened a door for him and as the church needed him badly, it was the conviction and advice of the elders and the whole church that he and his fellow prisoner should return as soon as possible if they could leave with a good conscience.

Gschäl's impurity disclosed.

At this time deep called to deep even more, and the church's distress increased daily. A sister was struck in her conscience with great fear and terror of soul and compelled by God to reveal her heart. She disclosed that while she was still in Carinthia, before she came to the church, Christoph Gschäl, who was supposed to be a servant of the church, had touched and handled her in unseemly parts. The elders were shocked but kept the matter secret until his return.

As the arrival of brothers from abroad was delayed more and more, Leonhard Lanzenstiel and Hans Gentner called together the elders of the church and told them of the pressing need to provide the church with elders. After persevering in

[1]Hans Amon's songs are in *LdHBr*, 115–120; see also Wolkan, *Lieder*, 178 n.2.

Among Amon's letters are the following, written to his imprisoned brothers: 1) to the prisoners at Mödling, 1537; 2) to the brothers in captivity at Falkenstein, 1539; 3) to the missing brothers at Trieste, 1540; 4) to the brothers "at Trieste or at sea," 1540. Seventeen of Amon's letters are in Codex A b 5, fol. 1–122, Budapest University Library. See Friedmann, *Schriften*, 105; Beck, 150; *ME*, I, 99–100; see also above, p.188 n.3.

fervent prayer to God, the whole church unanimously appointed five brothers to a time of testing in the service of the Gospel. Their names were Peter Walpot, a cloth shearer by trade; Kaspar Seidelman or Bohemian Kaspar, a cutler by trade; Michael Matschidel also called Klein Michel (Short Michael), a shoemaker by trade; Jakob Kircher, and Simon Waindel.

1542
Peter Walpot and 4 others chosen as servants of the Word.

In the same way five brothers were appointed to the service for temporal affairs; their names were Andreas Stuck, Peter Hagen, Klaus Dreytzel or Müller (a miller), Paul Zimmermann, Christian Stöckel or Häring.

5 brothers appointed to the service for temporal affairs.

The church community rejoiced about these brothers and accepted them with deep gratitude as a gift from God.

After all this, Christoph with his companions returned from Rattenberg in Tirol and stayed first with the brothers living in Dannowitz, a mile from Nikolsburg. When the elders at Schakwitz heard this, they went there to meet them immediately but not very joyfully. The elders did not receive Christoph in peace but immediately called him aside and rebuked him for his sin and indecency. He told them that he would give an account if they would be patient with him. This was granted him. But that same day the brothers, including Christoph and his companions, returned to Schakwitz. That very night many of the elders came and met with others right away.

Christoph Gschäl returned from Tirol, but not received as a brother.

When Christoph was questioned, it turned out that what the woman had told about him was true. It was decided unanimously that he should appear before the whole church, and although he begged that out of mercy the matter be dealt with secretly, the united decision was upheld. The church assembled the next morning before daybreak, but he did not come when sent for. Instead he tried to make a secret escape, but daylight overtook him, and he had to stay.

During that day the brothers spoke earnestly with him many times, and he finally confessed that he had committed the sin of fornication with several women. He thought he would rather be damned than have to confess it. That evening, discipline was laid upon him with all earnestness in the presence of the whole church. He was placed under the ban and excluded. All those who had defiled themselves with him were also excluded without leniency and separated from the church.

Christoph Gschäl excluded.

1542

This event brought great sorrow and pain of heart to the church community, and they cried to God in their misery. But the false brothers were delighted; they reviled and abused the church all the more. The faithful, however, carried out the exclusions in holy zeal, without regard to persons, thus purifying themselves according to the Lord's command and Paul's words.

Peter Riedemann released.

Church entrusted to Leonhard Lanzenstiel and Peter Riedemann together.

Following these serious meetings Peter Riedemann was released from prison in Hesse, and the church was once again full of joy and lifted above her troubles. Just a few days later, all the elders of the church gathered and decided unanimously that the brothers Leonhard Lanzenstiel and Peter Riedemann should together care for the church, which they did with true dedication.[1] The Lord gave his blessing, the church grew, and the number of believers increased daily.

God's messengers and witnesses gave steadfast testimony in word and deed, speaking powerfully of God's kingdom. They urged people to change their lives, to repent and turn away from this world's sin, blasphemy, and injustice and to dedicate themselves to the living God, their Creator, and Jesus Christ, their Redeemer. God blessed them and gave them joy in doing his work.

Time of persecution in the German lands.

Wherever there were Christians, there were executioners as well.

This, however, was always at the price of great suffering and the shedding of much blood in many lands, towns, and marketplaces for the sake of Jesus Christ and his divine truth. God has especially visited Germany with the truth, but Germany has resisted it, just as blind and stubborn Jerusalem resisted the apostles and prophets sent to her. From the beginning of the church community to this day many hundreds of brothers and sisters in Christ have been condemned and put to death for their faith. Even those who had only just begun to recognize the truth and live by it, leaving behind the horrors of the antichrist, were made to suffer for it. As recorded, this was especially so in Austria wherever the royal provost went. If he encountered anyone in field or road who admitted that he was a brother and refused to recant, he ordered him to kneel down and beheaded him on the spot. In the villages he hanged

[1]About Lanzenstiel's eldership with Peter Riedemann's support, see Williams, *Radical Reformation*, 670–673.

believers on the gateposts, and some he consigned to prisons. *1542*
It was the same with Aichelin, the imperial provost, who traveled all over Swabia and Württemberg. Wherever brothers and sisters were found or searched out, he put them to death by fire, sword, or rope.

This bloodshed has not ceased yet but continues to this day. On the following pages an attempt is made to tabulate all that can be recalled for certain, though not all are known. We are not concerned with the exact total, which certainly was higher. Our concern is to show how, through the blood of martyrs, faith and divine truth were revealed by God in every corner of the German lands.

TABLE OF MARTYRS

how through the blood of the faithful
God testified to his truth
and made it known in every corner of the German lands

The householder sent his servants to the tenants of the vineyard to get his fruit. But the tenants took his servants, beat one and killed the others, etc. (Matt.21:33–39).

Babylon, the great harlot and mother of all the abominations on earth, is drunk with the blood of the saints and with the blood of the witnesses to Jesus (Rev.17:5–6).

Among the members of the church, the people who understand rightly will yet for a while fall victim to fire and sword, captivity, and pillage (Dan.11:33).[1]

---

[1]In both the "1580" and "1581" codices of this chronicle, the table of martyrs extends over nine sides, leaving blank spaces between regions and several blank columns at the end, perhaps for later additions. On each page a Bible verse (including these three quotations) runs vertically between the two columns.

1542

Table of martyrs, how through the blood of the faithful God testified to his truth and made it known in every corner of the German lands.

In Bohemia

Prague	11

In Hungary

Kirchschlag (Lower Austria)	3
Loren*	3
Nusel*	2

In Moravia

Brünn	4
Znaim	7
Olmütz	4

In Lower Austria

Vienna and many executed secretly	23
[Wiener] Neustadt	2
Kreuzenstein*	6
Melk	3
Grein	1
Lembach	45
Mödling	4
Pöggstall	1
Ybbs	1
Krems	3
Böheimkirchen	2
Ottenthal	4
Pottenhofen	4
Feldsberg	1
Falkenstein	5

*Places marked with an asterisk could not be identified.

Behold, I send you out like sheep among wolves (Matt. 10:16).
They will deliver you up to tribulation and kill you (Matt. 24:9; Mark 13:9).

In Upper Austria

Mauthausen	1
Gmunden	2
Enns	1
Kropfing	2
Steyr	30
Wels	10
Fesselsbruck*	4
Gramastetten	3
Freistadt	10
Falkendorf	1
Vöcklabruck	8
Weissenburg*	2
Linz	72

In Bavaria

Munich	9
Rosenheim	1
[Bad] Aibling	3
Wasserburg	1
Mühldorf	5
Altötting	7
Landshut	5
Lambach	22
Burghausen	7
Ried (Upper Austria)	4
Schärding	3
Passau	2
Vilshofen	1
Mermos*	1
Ingolstadt	2
Nüneburg*	9
Neuburg	3
Freyburg	2
Julbach near Braunau	1

In Styria

Graz	7
Bruck an der Mur	12
Unzmarkt	1
Griesbach	5

1542

Table of martyrs, how through the blood of the faithful God testified to his truth and made it known in every corner of the German lands.

The time is coming when whoever kills you will think he is doing God a service (John 16:2). Jerusalem, Jerusalem, killing the prophets and stoning those who are sent to you! (Matt.23:37).

In Carinthia

St. Veit	7
Kematen*	3
Göpingen*	5
Wolfsberg in the Lavant Valley	3

In the Puster Valley

Sillian	3
Taufers	1
St. Lorenzen	11
Kiens	5
Schöneck	4
Michelsburg	24

In the Adige Region

Brixen	16
Klausen	7
Kaltern	4
Kuntersweg	9
Bozen	11
Neumarkt	9
Terlan	3
Sterzing	30
Gufidaun	19
Rodeneck	4
Schlanders	2
Trient	1

In the Salzburg Region

Salzburg	38
Tittmoning	4
Berchtesgaden	18
Marklibat*	2
Kuchl in the Kuchl Valley	3
Abtenau	1

In the Inn Valley

Kufstein	16
Rattenberg	71
Schwaz	20
Hall (Solbad Hall)	2
Innsbruck	8
Landeck	1
Steinach	4
Kitzbühel	68
Stams	3
Petersberg	2
Imst	8
Rotholz	1

In Franconia

Ansbach	1
Bamberg	3
Kitzingen	20
[Bad] Frankenhausen	1
Fehelsbruck*	3
Würzburg	10

In Swabia

Augsburg	2
Landsberg	19
Lauingen	2
Dillingen	2
Höchstädt	2
Weissenhorn	1
Zusmarshausen	8
Nördlingen	1
Schwäbisch Gmünd	7
Günzburg	6
Mantelhof	20
Kaufbeuren	5
Sonthofen	1
Warthausen	1
Reutte	1

1542

Table of martyrs, how through the blood of the faithful God testified to his truth and made it known in every corner of the German lands.

In Wuerttemberg

Urach	1
Esslingen	3
Schorndorf	1
Tübingen	5
Weil	2
Stuttgart	2
Rottenburg on the Neckar	13
Rothenburg on the Tauber	24
Herrenberg	12
Schlüsselfeld*	1
Stätz*	18
Deutschnofen (Tirol)	1
Ulmerfeld*	2
Waldshut	5
Wilhelmsbruck*	1
Weiden	3
Königsberg	3
Kürchen on the Eck*	1
Illingen	10

In the Margravate of Baden

Baden-Baden	20
Pforzheim	2
Prethaim*	9
Bühl	2
Bruchsal	1
[Karlsruher] Durlach	12
Gernsbach	1

The Count Palatine

alone was responsible for the execution of 350

Behold, I send you prophets and wise men and scribes, some of whom you will kill (Matt.23:34). For your sake we are killed all the day long; we are accounted as sheep for the slaughter (Rom.8:36).

On the Rhine

Speyer	1
Pühelsberg*	1
Kislach*	1

In the Netherlands

Aurea*	1
Andorf*	5
Lagrentzen*	1
Brussels	2
Aachen	5

In Velschland*

Fuld*	18

In Alsace

Ensisheim	600
Mühlhausen	17

In Switzerland

Zurich	16
Basel	3
Bern	1
Schwyz	3
Appenzell	1
Constance on Lake Constance	3
Waldsee (in Swabia)	11
Ettach*	1
Baden	3

In Italy

Venice	3
Lavarone (near Trento)	3
Lechensteg*	4

These confessors of the faith—so many that they become like a new cloud of witnesses surrounding us, like a fiery pillar going before us in the night—these Christians, valiant for the truth of God, were condemned to torture and death in ways too numerous to describe. There were men and women, youths and girls, old and young, teachers and listeners. In them we see that God pours out his grace and strength in recent times as well as in days gone by.

1542
Heb.12:1

Condemned to every kind of death, with many kinds of torture and suffering.

Some were racked and stretched until the sun could have shone through them.

Tyranny and the shedding of Christian blood seen not only across the sea among the heathen.

Some were torn apart and died under the torture.

Some were burned to ashes as heretics.

Some were roasted on pillars.

Some were torn with red-hot tongs.

Some were locked into houses and burned together.

Some were hanged on trees.

Some were executed with the sword, strangled, or cut to pieces.

Many had their mouths gagged and their tongues fastened so that they could not speak or answer for themselves, and in that state they were taken to their death.

They witnessed with their blood to the testimony they made with their lips.

They were taken in droves like lambs to be slaughtered and murdered, as is pleasing to the devil, for he is a murderer from the beginning.

John 8:44

Some of the women were pushed into water, pulled out again, and asked if they would recant. When they persisted, they were sunk and drowned. In these violent ways Satan worked through his children. In many places the books of the Bible were strictly forbidden and even burned, as the ungodly king Antiochus had done. Some people were killed merely because books were found in their houses.

1 Macc.1:56–57

Some starved to death in gloomy dungeons where no light could enter.

Others were put in deep pits and suffocating prisons with bats, snakes, and vermin, where their feet rotted away and they watched the mice take the toes from their bodies. This had happened to brother Peter Voit. Some who were tightly fettered rotted away completely and perished.

Many were fed on bread and water for a long time before

1542

they were killed, and many were tormented with hunger and harassed in every way imaginable. Some who were thought too young to be executed were bound and cruelly beaten with rods. This had been done to brother Hans Mändel when he was still a youth and imprisoned at Sterzing. The same was done to Anna Tuchmacher in Tirol, a sister not even sixteen years old. Yet they all remained steadfast. None of this could make them waver from their faith or from the love of God in Christ Jesus our Lord. Here the truth of Christ's words in the Gospels can be plainly seen: "You will be hated by all men," and "They will ban you from the synagogue; the time is coming when anyone who kills you will think he is doing God a service."

Rom.8:35–39

Matt.24:9

John 16:2

Many were promised valuable presents and riches if they would recant: fat salaries to some and power and position to others. Many were implored to say just one word of what was wanted, and they would be let free. But they would not consent to a dishonest way out. Others were told they should curse just once, just one little curse, and they could go free. This was done to brother Christian, but he chose to suffer bitter death and was beheaded in the district of Mermos in Bavaria.

No great promises moved them, and neither sweet nor harsh tones.

Many were tormented day and night with unheard-of tricks and cunning. Monks and priests came with smooth words, and scholars of Scripture with false teaching; they insulted and threatened, stormed and abused, with lies and horrible blasphemy. But all this did not make the faithful lose heart.

Some of those who suffered such cruel imprisonment sang songs of praise to their God because they were full of joy.

Joyfulness of the martyrs and witnesses of God.

Some did the same when taken from prison to the place of execution. They sang joyfully, their voices ringing out as if they were going to meet the bridegroom at a wedding.

Before going to the place of death, many young girls put on their finest dresses and adorned themselves as for a day of rejoicing, like those who feel heavenly joy and are about to enter the gates of eternal bliss.

Others went with a smile on their lips, praising God that he found them worthy of the death of true Christian heroes, and they would not have exchanged it for a peaceful death in their beds.

Others spoke to the crowds of onlookers, urging them seriously to repent and change their lives. Others, who were captured before they had received baptism by water, hastened on to be baptized with the baptism of blood on the basis of their living faith. We could give the names of some, but this is not necessary.

1542
Some who had not been baptized with water received the baptism of blood instead.

Yes, there were many who never saw the church community, who had only heard and believed the truth, yet remained steadfast when captured. They let neither fire, water, sword, nor executioner terrify or persuade them. No human being and nothing on earth could steal the truth from their hearts anymore. They were such zealous lovers of God that his fire burned in them, and they would rather die the bitterest death, rather endure ten deaths, than forsake the truth they had recognized. They would accept neither glory nor kingdom nor all the world's pleasures and goods in exchange for their faith in Christ, in whom they had their foundation and assurance.

Christians arose from Christian blood.

From the shedding of such innocent blood, Christians arose everywhere. The number of believers increased in all those places. It bore fruit and was not shed in vain. These deaths moved many to think deeply and direct their hearts and minds toward the future. In the end, as happened in Tirol, many authorities stopped executing them in public. Instead, they executed them secretly at night so that few would see, hear, or know about it. It was no longer done in the usual places, since, though innocent, they were being condemned and killed and sometimes simply murdered without any sentence.

Enemies outside the prisons more terrified than the devout inside.

In some places the authorities filled all the prisons and dungeons (as was done by the count palatine on the Rhine), thinking to quench God's fire by violence. But the prisoners sang joyfully until their enemies outside (who had thought the prisoners would be terrified) were themselves more frightened than the prisoners and did not know what to do with them, for in many cases they realized that the believers were innocent. Many were kept in prisons and dungeons for a short time, some for many years, enduring every torture. Some had holes burned through their cheeks before being set free. Some obtained their freedom with God's help, often through his intervention in wonderful ways. They remained steadfast in faith until God took them to himself.

Persecution of God's children.

Those who escaped all this were hunted and driven from place to place and from land to land. They had to be like owls and night herons, not daring to appear by day, hiding among

1542

crags and crevices in the rocks, in wild woods, and in pits and holes. They were hunted by constables and dogs; snares were set to capture them like birds. All this without any offense on their part—they neither harmed nor wished to harm anyone.

Much grotesque and horrible slander about the believers.

Everywhere, evil and completely false stories were spread against them: that they had cloven hooves like goats or oxen; that they gave people a drink from a little bottle to make them imitate them; that they had their women in common, causing complete confusion; that they did away with children and ate them. They were accused of being kidnappers and divorcers because at times a believer would join the church and leave his unbelieving partner, if she was unwilling to follow him. They were called rebaptizers, tramps, seducers, sectarians, gangsters, gluttons, and other vile names.

Emperor, kings, and princes issued mandates.

From every quarter, emperor, kings, and princes issued mandates forbidding any toleration whatsoever: they were to be rooted out and destroyed, and no one should shelter them.

Unspeakable thousandfold punishment for the sons of Pilate.

Many of those cruel sons of Pilate who murdered the believers and made them suffer met with a horrible death, snatched away before their time by the master they served:

Some died a sudden death.

Some were struck by God with other calamities.

Others were seized with great fear, remorse, and despair.

Some never had another good or happy day as long as they lived.

One went out of his mind.

Another would have given any amount of money never to have done what he did.

Many wished the devout had never come into their hands.

Many resolved to have nothing more to do with persecution, for fear had come over them and their consciences were struck. We could name a considerable number, but there is no need.

Rev.21:8
Matt.13:42; 22:13
25:30
Rev.14:11
Isa.14:15
66:24
Mark 9:48

All those who do not honestly repent and find true conversion in this life can expect the fire of hell, the fiery lake that burns with sulfur; the outer darkness, the place of weeping, wailing, and grinding of teeth; the abyss of hell where the smoke of their torment rises up for ever and ever, and they have no rest day or night, their fire shall never be quenched, nor shall the gnawing worm ever die. There will be no redemption or help for them ever again. God says through the holy prophets, "Though I remit all sins, yet I will certainly exact justice for innocent blood and will not leave it unrequited" (Gen.9:5–6; Deut.32:43; Joel 3:21; 2Esd.15:8; Jth.8:22). *1542*

When our Lord Jesus Christ comes in blazing fire with many thousands of angels to bring justice on his great day, then all shall arise again, for the earth will yield up the blood it has swallowed and will no longer hide its slain. 2Thess.1:7 Isa.26:19,21

When the sea gives up its dead, when those who were burned to ashes rise and appear again, there will be a judgment that is different from that of the world today. Emperors and kings will be peasants, their mandates will be finished with, meaningless, their power of no account. The prince will no longer be a prince, nor the nobleman a noble. These men who now want to rule man's conscience, where God alone shall dwell, and his faith, which belongs to God alone, will see the One whom they have pierced. As the book of Wisdom tells us, they will lament: "Fools that we were, we held the life of these people to be madness and their end dishonorable. Look, they are now numbered among the children of God and assigned a place of their own among the devout."

The sea will give up its dead, those burned to ashes will rise again. Rev.20:11–15

God's judgment differs from the world's.

Wisd.5:3–5

The holy martyrs of God and those who have remained steadfast through all distress will receive a crown of splendor, a glorious kingdom, great joy, heavenly peace, everlasting life, eternal salvation—immeasurably great glory, far outweighing the sufferings of this present time. No eye has seen, no ear has heard, no human heart has conceived, no human tongue, however eloquent, has been able to tell the glory God has prepared for those who love him. This blessing is timeless and endures from eternity to eternity. Now enough of that; let us go on with our story.

Blessedness and a thousandfold reward for the martyrs of God. Wisd.5:16 Rom.8:18 2Cor.4:17

1Cor.2:9

In 1542, brother Ulrich Hofer, Hans Greckenhofer, Stoffel Niedermair or Spängler, and Bastel Schmidt were chosen for the service for temporal affairs and appointed at Schakwitz.[1]

4 brothers chosen for the service for temporal affairs.

About this time Burkhard Bämerle came and united with us in the Lord. He had been at Auspitz with the Philippites and had gone with them when they left us and united with the Swiss Brethren.[2] Burkhard was a servant of the Word in this

Burkhard Bämerle united with us.

---

[1]Ulrich Hofer, also called Ulrich Gschäll, was one of those who had escaped the galleys at Trieste. See also below, p.483; Beck, 274.

[2]According to Beck, 152 n.1, the name "Swiss Brethren" applies 1) to the Swiss Anabaptists settled in the Palatinate and near Bad Kreuznach, and 2) to the brothers

1542

group, and when he united with our church, he was allowed to continue in this service among us.

1543

A Swiss servant, Hans Klöpfer from Feuerbach, united with us.

In 1543 Hans Klöpfer of Feuerbach and four others united in the Lord with our brothers at Schakwitz. He was previously a servant of the Word among the Swiss Brethren and lived at Pollau, at the foot of the Mayberg.[1] He left the Swiss Brethren because of the following points of faith. (He had informed the Brethren about these earlier, when they were gathered at Tasswitz, and told them that he would not have had a good conscience before God if he had not first informed them.)

Downfall of the Swiss Brethren.

FIRST, they have given up true Christian community, so God has abandoned them and they go from one wrong to the next.

SECOND, they pay war taxes, thereby supporting war and bloodshed.

THIRD, their elders or teachers became unsure of their services and gave them up. Later they reinstated themselves and were allowed to teach more or less what they liked. To speak honestly, they make a mockery of God's working, and this will surely be disastrous for them.

FOURTH, at the devil's instigation they have brought about a real abomination by allowing all sin to be settled privately between brothers, whether fornication, adultery, theft, or anything of that sort. In this way they have gathered impure

---

at Nikolsburg, Moravia, who had been without a leader since Hubmaier's death, and who settled in Pergen, Pollau, Wisternitz, Voitelsbrunn, Tasswitz, Urbau, Jamnitz, etc. In the persecution of 1535 the Swiss Brethren congregations in Moravia had been all but wiped out. Strengthened by new arrivals from Germany, they gathered again at Pollau, Muschau, Znaim, Tasswitz, and other places, and gradually they merged with the Hutterites. Hans Klöpfer (see below) was an early Swiss Brethren leader at Pollau in 1543; in 1591 they still existed at Znaim; and in 1618 they still had a small community in a suburb of Eibenschitz, then a sanctuary for all free churches. See H. S. Bender, "Swiss Brethren," *ME*, IV, 669–671. For the various towns and villages mentioned, see Index and Zeman, *Topography*.

[1]About Hans Klöpfer, see *ME*, III, 206 (Feuerbach, a town northeast of Stuttgart, Germany); Beck, 153. Pollau (Pavlov), north of Nikolsburg (Mikulov), was part of Leonhard von Liechtenstein's estate.

The Mayberg (Děvín) is a mountain in the Pollau Hills (Pavlovské Vrchy), a ridge about 1700 feet high, in whose caves or "holes" the Hutterites found safe refuge during later persecutions. At the east end of the ridge stands the ruin of Maidburg Castle or Maidstein (Dívčí Hrady). Zeman, *Topography*, "Mayberg," #78; "Pollau," #114.

hearts and spirits among themselves and so have participated in the guilt. Even though the apostle John says, "All wrongdoing is sin, and some sins lead to death; I do not say that one is to pray for that," it should still be punished openly before the church so that it comes to the light, as Christ says. To prevent anyone saying later that ignorance or lies had made them twist the power of the ban and led them to tamper with judgment and discipline in the house of God, Hans Klöpfer pointed out ten or twelve incidents, naming those involved, where this had taken place among them and they had been well aware of it.

1543

1 John 5:16–17

John 3:20
Eph. 5:8–14

That was why he left them, and since he found things were different among us, he united with us. This Hans Klöpfer was later appointed to the service of the Gospel among us as well, was sent abroad to do the Lord's work, and finally fell asleep in the Lord, as will be recorded later.

In this year, 1543, we bought a house at Lundenburg[1] from Lord of Lundenburg's mother, got it ready, and settled there; also the shoemaker's house, where the bathhouse is.

A house purchased.

That same year we bought a burnt-out site at Saitz, built a new house, and moved in.

A house purchased.

In this same year there was dissension about Christ's incarnation. This is how it happened: Hans Gentner, a servant of the Word, was sent to Württemberg, and brother Michael Kramer, a servant for temporal affairs, was sent as his assistant. There was a little group who called themselves brothers, led by a certain Jörg Nörlinger. What they believed about Christ's incarnation was that he brought his flesh from heaven. They held that if he had received his flesh in Mary, it was not a virgin birth. These people wanted so much to unite with Hans Gentner and our brothers that Hans accepted them while he was still out on mission. Although he and Michael Kramer knew to some extent of their wrong belief about the incarnation of Christ, they let them continue in it because they were united on other articles of faith. They thought that when the group

Jörg Nörlinger and his group held that Christ brought his flesh from heaven.

[1]Lundenburg (Břeclav), town on the Dyje River near the Austrian border, owned by the lords von Zerotin until 1620. A provincial capital in the 13th century, it is one of Moravia's oldest towns. The Hussites settled at Lundenburg in 1426. Zeman, *Topography*, #76; *ME*, III, 414.

1543

came to the church community, they would be convinced on this point too, give up their own view, and accept the church's belief.

When they came to the church community, however, they held to their own opinion, even spreading it to some of the members. As soon as the servants learned of it, they challenged them about their false idea. It was certainly not what the church believed, nor was it in accordance with the truth and Christian faith, which states THAT CHRIST WAS CONCEIVED BY THE HOLY SPIRIT, BORN OF THE VIRGIN MARY. Christ was not conceived through a man by natural union, nor was Christ's mother stained like other women, who lose their virginity when they conceive a child. She was a virgin mother, a virgin before and after the birth.

Concerning Christ's incarnation: he did not bring his flesh from heaven but was born of a virgin.

Gen.2:22
17:16–17
Judg.13:3
1 Sam.1:1–20

When Adam's wife was taken from his side, when the barren gave birth, when women bore children in their old age—all this was a preparation to make it more believable that a virgin might bear, and did bear, a child. This miraculous conception and birth was foretold by the prophet, who said, "God will give you a sign; behold, a virgin is great with child; she shall conceive and bear a son." This would have not been a sign if he had been conceived in the normal way with the participation of a man, and she would not have been a maiden or virgin.

Isa.7:14

Matt.1:18–25
Luke 1:26–38

When the angel greeted Mary and told her she was to be a mother, she asked how it might come about, since she did not know a man. She would have had no need to ask this question if she had not known herself to be an untouched virgin. But the angel replied, "The Holy Spirit will come upon you; the power of the Most High will overshadow you; and the holy child to be born of you will be called the Son of God." It does not say "from the seed of Joseph" but from "the Holy Spirit" and "the power of the Most High." These were master workmen working in the pure and hallowed body of Mary. It follows that her pure flesh and blood was the human seed from which God and the Holy Spirit formed the noble and pure body of Christ. Therefore Joseph planned to leave her quietly, because she was great with child before they lived together, but the angel appeared to him and said, "The child that is born in her is of the Holy Spirit."

Gen.3:15
Gal.4:4

Accordingly, the Scriptures speak only of a woman and call him "seed of a woman." Paul speaks in the same way, saying,

"God's own Son, born of a woman." Other children are born of man and woman, but here the Scriptures tell only of a woman, not meaning a wife who knows a husband. *1543*

This is the promise made to Abraham: "In your seed shall all nations be blessed," for Mary, according to the flesh, is a descendant of Abraham and David, and Christ comes from Mary according to the flesh, so he is himself of the seed of Abraham. On her father's side Mary comes from the tribe of Judah, on her mother's from the tribe of Levi, and so John the Baptist's mother Elizabeth was her cousin, her relative. The virgin Mary, on her father's side, was of the same family as Joseph, her partner in marriage, and so the evangelists make the table of descent lead to him. Gen.22:18 Luke 1:5,36 Matt.1:1–17 Luke 3:23–38

In becoming man, Christ is the fruit of Mary alone (that is, of a woman and not of a man), born in a supernatural way. Here a new Adam had to be born in a new way, without spot of sin, because he was to take away the taint of the sinful birth of the old Adam, tread the serpent's head underfoot, and overcome death and hell. If he had been born in sin, the devil would have had power over him as he has over the children of wrath. But the devil, the prince of this world, had no hold over him. John 1:14 Rom.5 1 Cor.15:20–26 John 14:30

When he said, "I am not of this world" (from which some would have it that he received his flesh from heaven), he did not mean that he did not take his flesh from the virgin Mary. He meant that he had nothing to do with the evil of the world. Further on he said that the disciples were not of this world, but in spite of that they had flesh. And how could he be Abraham's seed if he had brought his flesh from heaven? John 17:14,16

Now this Nörlinger and his followers were spoken to about their false belief. He then asserted that Hans Gentner had taken the same position when in Württemberg, since he had not contradicted them. As they were unwilling to give up their opinion and accept what they were taught, they were excluded—Nörlinger and those who agreed with him—and twelve or more left with him. Every effort was made to find out who was similarly infected so that such false belief could be rooted out from the church. Jörg Nörlinger and those with him excluded.

Leonhard Lanzenstiel and Peter Riedemann, servants of the Lord and his church, with their assistants in the service of the Word, immediately prepared a letter admonishing and correcting Hans Gentner and Michael Kramer on this point and

1543

instructing them to return to the church without delay. (This letter from Leonhard Lanzenstiel is still preserved.) It was taken to Württemberg by another servant, Hans Klöpfer of Feuerbach, who had united with the church not long before.

When Hans Gentner and Michael Kramer arrived, it became clear that not only had they left those mentioned earlier in their wrong belief without trying to change it but they had even accepted them and sent them to the church community, where they had misled other members. Hans Gentner confessed his mistake and laid down his service of the Word. Later, when his service was recognized again, he was reappointed and continued faithful for the rest of his life. Nor did Michael Kramer remain without discipline, for he was actually the more guilty of the two, having persuaded Hans to ignore the matter, which Hans should not have done.

Hans Gentner's service of the Word laid down.

1544

Hans Mändel taken prisoner and tortured cruelly.

In 1544 brother Hans Mändel was imprisoned for the sake of divine truth at Landeck in the upper Inn Valley for twenty-two weeks. There he was cruelly tortured to make him recant. But he remained steadfast. Then he flattened the iron fetters around his ankles by hammering them with two stones and slid his feet out. He knotted together the ropes that had been used to lower his food to him as well as to torture him, and he let himself down from the top of the tower. So he was free, with his heart and conscience at peace.

He escaped from prison.

Hans Mändel's first imprisonment.

Some years earlier, he had been imprisoned as a youth for twenty-six weeks at Sterzing and had been severely beaten with rods. One day when the jailer had not locked the prison door properly but had left it partly open, he slipped away secretly. So by God's intervention he managed to escape both times.[1]

Jörg Liebich captured.

During this year 1544 brother Jörg Liebich was imprisoned at the Vellenburg near Innsbruck for the sake of divine truth.[2]

---

[1]Hans Mändel's first imprisonment occurred in 1537 (not 1536), right after his baptism; see Beck, 134–135. About his last imprisonment and his execution in 1561, see below, pp.372–375; *ME*, III, 454–455.

[2]Vellenburg Castle is now a ruin. About Jörg Liebich, see *ME*, III, 337; *Martyrs Mirror*, 466–467; Beck, 155–158; Mecenseffy, *Österreich*, III, 500–501.

This is known as a particularly horrible dungeon because it is haunted by gruesome spirits or the evil one, so this dear brother had to endure a great deal from the devil, who tempted him in visible form, particularly during the first year. He came to him in the guise of a young woman who tried to embrace him. When Jörg knelt and prayed, the devil in woman's form lay down in his bed, and he had a very hard time to drive him away or roll him off.

1544

Jörg Liebich much tempted by the evil one.

The devil tried to lift him as if to carry him off, but could not. He would come in the shape of a youth or a soldier and tried all kinds of tricks. When all attempts proved in vain, he vanished through the top of the dungeon, leaving such an evil stench behind him that the brother almost fainted.

The devil told him many things that were happening or had happened among the brothers in Moravia and about the kind of brothers he had. He reproached him about many wrong things he had once done, making mountains out of molehills and much out of little, saying, for example, that Jörg Liebich claimed he loved his neighbor as himself yet had cut off the heel of the loaf, which he enjoyed most, while his neighbor had to cut from the rest. Liebich responded that his brothers had already admonished and disciplined him about such things, and since he had then improved, he was not going to lose heart. Finally, the devil, unable to achieve anything, left him more or less in peace. Here we can see how the devil works.

How the devil can read a person the record of his faults.

Admonition and discipline give help in the house of God.

To provide more temptations, the devil worked through his children as well as in person. One of his brood came in disguise to visit Liebich in prison, calling himself Dr. Weber.[1] Once he came dressed as a brother and acted the part, saying, "The Lord be with us, my brother," and giving him the greeting of peace. This trickery was meant to mislead him, but Liebich asked him who he was and where he came from. When he replied that he came from the church of God in Moravia, Liebich inquired how things were going there. He told him the church community and all the brothers had been driven away and scattered, not one remained with another. It was all over with them. At this Liebich saw through the deception, reproved him for his dishonesty, now quite obvious, and sent

Dr. N. Weber also once attempted to mislead Liebich.

[1]Pseudonym of Dr. Gallus Müller, court preacher at Innsbruck; see also above, p.170.

1544

him away with earnest words of advice, which gave him enough to think about for a long time.

Over and above this, to fill up the measure of his temptations and omit nothing, the ungodly brood of Satan put a sister next to Liebich in the prison, chained her to his feet, and left them together for a long time. She, too, was imprisoned for her faith, a beautiful young woman named Ursula Hellrigel.[1] It is easy to imagine what the devil and his brood would have liked to see, but the two feared God and did not give way to temptation. It was this Ursula Hellrigel who wrote a song we still have. During his imprisonment Jörg Liebich, too, wrote several songs that are still known and sung in the church.[2]

Ursula Hellrigel also imprisoned.

Liebich knew in advance the day on which he would be released, but not which year. When that day passed by, he knew he would have to remain in prison another year. Later he was released on that very date and returned to the church. After a time he fell asleep in the Lord at Bohuslawitz near Gaya.[3] Ursula Hellrigel was later released through God's intervention, with her faith and conscience unharmed. She came to the church community and fell asleep in the Lord.

Jörg Liebich knew on which day he would be released.

In this same year of 1544 at Schakwitz, brother Walser (Balthasar) Maierhof the older (from Niedervintl), Hans Gütten, and Christian Häring were confirmed in the service for temporal affairs by the elders with the laying on of hands.

3 brothers confirmed in the service for temporal affairs.

---

[1]Ursula Hellrigel, a farmer's daughter from the Petersberg area in the upper Inn Valley, was seventeen in 1538, when she was imprisoned for her faith in the Petersberg tower. From there she was transferred to Liebich's prison in Vellenburg Castle, and finally to the *Kräuterturm* at Innsbruck. In February 1544, after six years of imprisonment, she was released when her guardian, Peter Müller from Silz, offered to pay the costs of the case. See *ME*, II, 695; Beck, 157–158; *Martyrs Mirror*, 466–467; Mecenseffy, *Österreich*, III, 377, 522.

[2]Ursula Hellrigel's song "Ewiger Vatter von Himelreich, Ich ruff zu dir gar inniglich" (Eternal Father in heaven, to you I call most fervently) has erroneously been attributed to Anna from Freiburg; see *Ausbund*, 209–211; Wackernagel, *Kirchenlied*, III, 487–488; Wolkan, *Lieder*, 178.

Of Liebich's songs only one is preserved; see *LdHBr*, 120–121: "Zum ersten preis' ich meinen Gott" (Above all I would praise my God).

[3]Bohuslawitz (Bohuslavice), a parochial village near Gaya (Kyjov), north of Göding (Hodonín), Moravia, part of the Butschowitz estate. In 1544, the estate was the property of the district judge, Count Václav of Boskovice; see above p.159 n.; Zeman, *Topography*, #16.

Liebich was released on April 24, 1544, and banished from Austria; Beck, 158 n.; Müller, *Glaubenszeugnisse*, I, 262–263.

1545

1545

In 1545 we bought a house and all the furnishings at Rakschitz[1] near Kromau, with Hans Greckenhofer, Melchior Kellner or Zimmermann (a carpenter), and Hans Klampferer acting on our behalf. We got it ready and lived there.

We bought a house.

On January 16 of that year Bärtel Riedmair or Schlesinger (the Silesian), Fabian Fitz, Martin Voyt, and Jakob Heusler talked with our brothers in the Lord and united with us.

Several Gabrielites united with us.

Bärtel Riedmair had previously been a servant of the Word among the Gabrielite brethren, but then he and the others had experienced the disorderly ways and dealings of Gabriel Ascherham, their servant (who had been excluded and put under the ban by our church community). Gabriel circulated a book among his people in which he wrote, "If anyone asks me whether infant baptism is wrong, I will answer no. If he wants to know the reason, I say there is none." He added that until the reason was known, infant baptism should be discontinued because of its misuse.

Gabriel even ceased to hold infant baptism as wrong.

At one point he paid the landlord a higher rent for a house so that if war came he could be exempt [from taxes].

He also had a cup made, and when they observed the remembrance of Christ in their false outward show, one of his elders carried this cup in papist fashion, with a cloth wrapped around it as if it were holy and could not be touched with bare hands, and gave it to each one to drink from. He even asserted that this bread and wine were spiritual food and drink.

The Lord's Supper according to Gabriel.

He once disciplined Bärtel Riedmair because of a fur coat and took his service away from him, although Gabriel himself had two better coats. According to Gabriel, no one ought to match him in this or that privilege, since no one matched him in gifts—as if these were his own doing and not gifts he had received. And yet he did not even have what he should have had.

Gabriel's wrong handling of church matters.

Now even though Gabriel had removed this Bärtel from his service, he had no true reason to exclude him. He had written to the group in Silesia, where Bärtel had been servant, telling

[1]Rakschitz (Rakšice) on the outskirts of Mährisch Kromau (Moravský Krumlov), southwest of Brno. M. Kromau was the center of a large estate owned for three hundred years (1320–1620, with brief interruptions) by the house of Lipé, who protected the Hussites as well as the Piccards and other groups both at M. Kromau and the neighboring town of Eibenschitz (Ivančice).

1545

them that at one time Bärtel had done something wrong and so had been removed from his service but that they must not inquire into the reason. This meant that a congregation had its servant taken away without being allowed to know the reason. If they asked, they were accused of having the spirit of Dathan and Abiram. All of this caused the brothers mentioned earlier and others to think more deeply and seek something better. The way these brothers from the Gabrielites united with us, being satisfied on the main articles of faith and godliness, was as follows:

Gabrielites who united with us.

First of all the four men, Bärtel Riedmair, Fabian Fitz, Martin Voyt, and Jakob Heusler, were sent to us by their people, who had already noticed from certain events that Gabriel acted dishonestly and without fear of God. These men came with instructions to find out the truth of what happened, whether they had been right in shunning us for so long and whether Gabriel had been justly excluded or not. When we found that they had a genuine zeal for the truth, for what was perfect, we rejoiced that the Lord had once more moved their hearts to seek what they had lost unwittingly, looking more to the bewitching charm of the crafty and deceitful person, Gabriel, than yielding to the clear, undeniable truth. In the fear of God we explained to them the whole course of events and told them quite openly what we hoped for, since we saw where we had done wrong.

Answer: Gabriel rightly excluded.

We told them that Gabriel's exclusion had been justly laid on him for the terrible blasphemy he had poured out publicly in front of the church. Gabriel had rejected this judgment as unjust and not in accordance with divine truth because the church had pronounced it in his absence, although in fact the whole church had pleaded with him to stay because they wished to speak with him. He had not listened to the church but pushed his way through the assembly of brothers and sisters and out of the door. We had continued to deal with him according to the truth because of his terrible blasphemy. We had sent brothers to explain the justice of this decision to his group, but Gabriel had already won them over, obviously telling lies, and they were no longer willing to listen to us. In the end there was nothing we could do. This had caused great pain to the whole church community, and we had felt deep compassion for this group which, after forming one loaf and body in Christ with the church, had been deceived by the spirit of dissension described above. *1545*

After hearing this report, the four men were convinced that the exclusion was justified. They expressed their deep pain that they had shunned us for so long without knowing the whole story and openly confessed their ignorance before God and his people. They also begged us for more instruction regarding our main articles of faith, so that they might see how far they had strayed from their original foundation. We saw that their longing for reconciliation was sincere and therefore gladly agreed to their request as follows.

Our uniting with the Gabrielites.

Concerning Baptism

We asked them whether, from the time when they first submitted themselves to baptism, they had remained firm and unwavering on this point. We found that they saw it clearly as we do, according to Christ's words. They told us, however, that Gabriel had recently written a booklet (and sent it around to be read in all the places where his group had settled) in which he condoned the terrible blasphemy of infant baptism. That had been the reason, they said, why they were inquiring more carefully into what he had done. They had not given their agreement, either in words or in their hearts, but had kept to the same single-minded conviction that we all had shared when we were still one people. In this, we were completely of one accord with them.

Matt.28:19
Mark 16:16

Concerning Community

Community, both spiritual and temporal, is a cornerstone and foundation of the entire Christian life of the believers, whose hearts grow together in mutual trust, bound one to another through grace. The inner community, attained through true surrender to God and his only Son Jesus Christ, is mirrored in their outward actions, in wholehearted, genuine service to all God's children, seeking not one's own advantage but that of the many. The whole life of Christ is our best example for this.

Yet, although the Gabrielites had claimed to be living in community, there was a great lack of mutual help in outward things. Their way of life had not stayed on the right foundation.

Matt.19:21
Acts 2:44–45
4:32–35

1 Cor.12
1 John 1:3

Matt.8:15
Luke 16:11
John 12:26
17:21
1 Cor.10:17
13:4–7
Heb.6:10–12
1 Pet.4:

1545 They confessed this before God and all his people and affirmed that from now on they would be more watchful. In regard to this kind of failure, they were ready to submit willingly at all times in genuine obedience to the whole church. We were fully satisfied in the Lord on this point.

Concerning Marriage

Matt. 19:3–9
Mark 10:2–12
Luke 16:18
1 Cor. 7:12–16

They held the same belief as ours: marriage partners must not divorce except in the case of adultery. However, they had not followed the whole teaching of the apostle Paul: "If any brother has an unbelieving wife and she consents to live with him, he should not divorce her. And if a wife who is a sister has an unbelieving husband who consents to live with her, she should not divorce him."

Here Paul makes it clear that, whether husband or wife, the believer is the head. If the unbelieving husband of a believing wife tries to hinder her faith and will not allow their children to be brought up in the fear of God, then he certainly should not have his way. In such a case the believing partner is not bound, for God has called us to peace.

Acts 4:19
Rom. 7:2–3

On this basis, therefore, we say that if a believing wife is pressed by her unbelieving husband to do anything against her conscience, she owes obedience to God rather than to her husband and may separate from him for this reason. But as long as her husband is living she must remain alone and may not take another. In this, they were in complete agreement with us. In this question as well as others they submitted in utmost obedience to the church of the Lord in order to make a radical improvement.

Concerning Governing Authorities

Matt. 17:24–27
22:17–21
Rom. 13:1–7
1 Pet. 2:13–14

We believe with the apostle Paul that the governing authorities are servants of God's wrath. Therefore we pay taxes and duties, do our share of compulsory labor, and anything else that is not against our consciences. But if the governing authorities require anything that destroys peace, such as war taxes, executioner's dues, or anything to serve bloodshed, we refuse to support it either by word or deed, for we know that vengeance belongs to the Lord alone. We are not to fight evil but to love our enemies.

Deut. 32:35
Matt. 5:44
Rom. 12:19

We do not try to deceive ourselves by paying more taxes than required in order to be exempt when war taxes are levied, nor do we use our work, or anything else that may be demanded, as a cover-up for blood taxes. We look to the Lord instead. He has the hearts of the overlords in his hand and will direct them as he pleases.

1545

Prov.21:1

Nor do we give our rulers the honor that belongs to God by bowing or kneeling before them and addressing them as "your Grace, Serene Highness, Wise and Provident Excellency," because we know that the Lord is a jealous God, who does not give his honor to another. Grace belongs to him alone, whereas all rulers are disgraced before God with their ostentatious conduct. God alone is serene, wise, and provident. Without him, men live carelessly, their hearts are blind, and they are ignorant of his truth. That is why no one should honor them by bowing or kneeling before them. It is at the name of Jesus Christ alone that every knee should bow.

Esther 3:2
Matt.22:21

Isa.48:11
Dan.3:17

Rom.1:21–25

Phil.2:10

On this point the Gabrielites who came to us had strayed far from the true foundation. Yet they acknowledged their failure and submitted themselves in lowly obedience to the church of God in order to amend their lives and make a new beginning.

Concerning Priests and False Brothers

We cut ourselves off from all ungodly priests, false prophets, and false brotherhoods and have nothing to do with them. We do no business with them, do not work with them, do not greet them or eat and drink with them, because by God's grace we know that their possessions come from sacrifices made to idols. That is why we do not support them by services, taxes, tithes, or any kind of work; instead, in the fear of the Lord, we avoid participating in their wickedness. We have every reason to guard against this, since they persuade many with their lying spirit, preventing them from following the way of true godliness.

1 Cor.5:9–11
2 John 10–11

What the priests own came from sacrifice to idols.

We approach with friendly words those heathen who are ignorant and do not have the audacity to rage against the truth; we wish that God may help them. And we do this in the fear of the Lord—the words on our lips are in our hearts too and God's name is not spoken in vain. We are not influenced by fear of men or by hypocrisy but look to God alone.

Exod.20:7

1545

We do not greet false brothers either. We do not eat or drink or have anything to do with them any more than with the priests, because they boast of the grace of God with their mouths but deny it with their actions. We shun them, not out of arrogance (for we wholeheartedly seek all men's salvation), but because the Holy Spirit warns us on this point, saying, "If anyone comes to you who does not bring this doctrine, do not invite him into your house or greet him—for anyone who greets him shares in his wicked deeds."

2 John 10–11

The men previously named acknowledged that this article of faith was in accordance with the truth. Although they had gone wrong on this point as on all the others, they now submitted to the judgment of the whole church. They strove to overcome all their failings, wanting always to remain obedient in the fear of the Lord.

In conclusion, we asked these men to submit their concern in godly obedience to the judgment of the church. (This obedience in a person embraces all that is pleasing to the will of God.) We longed to intercede with the Lord for them because they had gone astray thinking they were doing right, but now they admitted their unclarity before God and his people. Then, in peace with us, they could strive for what is perfect, and together we could correct the faults and errors that had taken hold among them. Then their way of life would be in harmony with God's order—in harmony with ours and ours with theirs, and we would be of one mind in pure love. After they had given their heartfelt consent to stand unwavering before God, united with God and his people, we called on the name of the Lord on their behalf and joyfully reaccepted them into the community of all the saints,[1] that they like us might be one people before the Lord, in holy obedience, in the Spirit with us, and we with them, to bear fruit for the Lord. To him alone be praise, honor, and glory in eternity. Amen.

Hans Gentner and Jörg Liebich went to Silesia to tell the people about the uniting.

After the uniting had taken place, Hans Gentner was sent as servant, with brother Jörg Liebich and all the brothers who had just united with us, to go to their three hundred people in Silesia and tell them about the uniting. They were welcomed

[1]The uniting took place on January 16, 1545; see Beck, 159. A splinter group of Gabrielites remained outside the union and barely managed to survive at Kreutz near Göding (Hodonín) until they, too, joined the Hutterian Church in 1565 (see below, p.391). From that time on, almost all Anabaptists in Moravia and Austria were Hutterian Brethren.

with gifts as bearers of good news. Brother Bärtel Riedmair, their servant, stayed behind for a time to experience the Lord's work in our church community. Early in the spring the Lord's Meal of Remembrance was held at Butschowitz. Bärtel stayed to take part and afterward traveled to Silesia. Then all three hundred of his people joined us in the unity of the Spirit and came to the church community here. There was great joy on both sides. This moved many other people in Silesia to follow the truth with great enthusiasm.

1545
Bärtel Riedmair remained among us.

The 300 people in Silesia left Gabriel and came to us.

In accordance with the Lord's will and the wish of the church, Bärtel Riedmair carried the service of the Word among us faithfully for many years and passed away in the Lord, as will be told later.

At Candlemas [Feb. 2] of this same year of 1545 we rented a house at Gobschitz[1] from Mathiasch (the landowner at Mährisch Kromau) and settled there.

We settled in Gobschitz.

On February 16 we moved into a house at Eibenschitz, which brother Leonhard Lanzenstiel, servant of God's Word, and Christian Häring, servant for temporal affairs, bought on our behalf.

We settled in Eibenschitz.

In the first week of Lent Leonhard Lanzenstiel and Peter Riedemann, both servants of God's Word, and Hans Klampferer [servant for temporal affairs] bought a house on our behalf at Bisenz.[2]

We settled in Bisenz.

That same year we also acquired the site of a burned-down house there. Bastel Schmidt, servant for temporal affairs, bought it on our behalf, and we built a house on the lower part of the site.

Lord Paul von Zerotin leased us two houses at Napajedl[3] on approval for a year. We moved in on St. George's Day [Apr. 23] but left again the following year at Michaelmas [Sept. 29].

We settled in Napajedl.

At Whitsun Jakob Säckler, our servant for temporal affairs,

We settled in Pawlowitz.

[1]Gobschitz (Kubšice) in the vicariate of Wolframitz (Olbramovice), part of the Mährisch Kromau estate, southwest of Brno. Beck, 164 n.3; Zeman, *Topography*, #42.

[2]Bisenz (Bzenec), ancient town northeast of Göding (Hodonín), famous for its wine-growing since the 1220s. Beck, 164 n.4; Zeman, *Topography*, #13.

[3]Napajedl (Napajedla) on the Morava River. Beck, 164 n.5; Zeman, *Topography*, #90.

1545

bought a house on our behalf at Pawlowitz.[1] Tall Matthias was steward there at that time.

We settled in Altenmarkt.

Shortly after Whitsun we bought two houses at Altenmarkt[2] near Lundenburg. They were next door to each other, almost in the center of the village.

We settled in Lundenburg.

That year we bought another house in Lundenburg, next to the lord's estate, where we lived under the protection of Lord Bartholomew von Zerotin.

We settled in Bilowitz.

On St. John the Baptist's Day [June 24] we bought a well-equipped house at Bilowitz.[3]

Later that year we bought another house in Bilowitz, next to the first, and built a bathhouse there.

We settled in Göding.

On St. James's Day [July 25] we bought a well-equipped house at Göding[4] and began a community there.

We settled in Tscheikowitz.

A week before Michaelmas we bought a house at Tscheikowitz,[5] got it ready, and moved in.

We settled in Boretitz.

At Michaelmas Jakob Säckler, our servant for the church's temporal affairs, and Thoman Schmidt, our interpreter, bought a house on our behalf at Boretitz.[6]

Later we bought another house next to the first and lived there in Christian community.

Brother Oswald taken prisoner in Vienna.

In that same year brother Oswald[7] was taken prisoner in Vienna, Austria, because of his faith in the divine truth. Many attempts were made to shake his faith. The townspeople visited him in prison and pleaded with him to recant, saying they otherwise would be forced to condemn him and drown him in

---

[1]Gross Pawlowitz (Velké Pavlovice), northwest of Lundenburg (Břeclav); in 1545 property of the lords of Lipé. Zeman, *Topography*, #107.

[2]Altenmarkt (Stará Břeclav = Old Lundenburg), now part of Lundenburg (Břeclav), where the Hutterian brothers had their tanneries and leather workshops. Zeman, *Topography*, #3.

[3]Bilowitz (Velké Bílovice), village approx. 20 miles west of Göding. From 1532 the village belonged to the Lundenburg domain of the Zerotin family. Zeman, *Topography*, #10.

[4]Göding (Hodonín), on the Morava River, southeast of Brno; property of the lords of Lipé from 1512–1594. Zeman, *Topography*, #43; *ME*, II, 534.

[5]Tscheikowitz (Čejkovice), southeast of Auspitz, in the administrative district of Göding; 1545–1624 property of the Víckov family. Zeman, *Topography*, #159.

[6]Boretitz (Bořetice), village near Tscheikowitz, southeast of Auspitz. Zeman, *Topography*, #18.

[7]Oswald Glait or Jamnitz; see above, p. 48 n. 1.

the Danube. But he said, "Even though you drown me, I will not forsake God and his truth. Christ died for me, and I will follow him and die for his truth rather than desert him." They could not make him recant, say what they would, honeyed words or harsh. Two brothers came and comforted him, and he entrusted his wife and children to them.[1] They embraced and kissed him and took leave of him, wishing him fortitude from God in the suffering he had to endure in innocence. After a year and six weeks in prison, he was led outside the town at midnight (so that no crowd would gather), thrown into the Danube, and drowned. There was no trial, no mention of any crime. He found strength to endure to the end, and on the last day God will crown him and will judge his enemies. There is a song written by this brother too.[2]

1545

Brother Oswald drowned by night in Vienna.

Brother Andreas Kofler[3] from the Adige region was imprisoned that same year at Ybbs on the Danube for the sake of divine truth. When he refused to recant or let the priests and false prophets lead him astray, he was condemned to death by these sons of Pilate. They handed him over to their high priest, the executioner, who satisfied the ungodly by executing him with the sword. Unto death, he bore valiant witness to the everlasting truth which is God himself.

Andreas Kofler executed at Ybbs.

In 1545 a brother named Hans Blüetel was also captured at Ried, Bavaria,[4] where he had been sent by the church community. The magistrates of Ried had promised a reward to anyone who caught him, and so a man called Gugelwein betrayed him. He spoke to Hans in a friendly way, as if he had been eager to meet him, and invited him into his house.

Hans Blüetel taken prisoner at Ried in Bavaria.

---

[1]The two brothers were Anthoni Keim from Guntzenhausen and Hans Staudach from Kaufbeuren. *ME*, II, 523c; *Martyrs Mirror*, 475.

[2]About Oswald Glait's songs, see Wolkan, *Lieder*, 179. An anonymous song served as basis for the above account; see *LdHBr*, 121. Glait's song, "Es redet Gott mit Mose" (God spoke to Moses) is in Wackernagel, *Kirchenlied*, III, 465–467. *Martyrs Mirror*, 472–473; Beck, 160.

[3]About Andreas Kofler, see *ME*, III, 212; *Martyrs Mirror*, 473; Beck, 163.

[4]Ried im Innkreis, Upper Austria.
About Hans Blüetel, see *ME*, I, 366; *Martyrs Mirror*, 473–474; Beck, 161–163. *LdHBr*, 123–128, has a song about Blüetel's suffering and death; the author is not known.

1545

The brother, thinking Gugelwein was concerned for his own soul's salvation, went with him. Once inside, the traitor locked the house and said, "Hans, you are a prisoner."

He refused to pay a ransom for his release.

Hans replied, "God forbid, for I came to you in good will!" Then this traitor demanded money for his release. When Hans refused, Gugelwein went to the magistrates and betrayed him. While the traitor was on his way, his wife, too, demanded money, saying the magistrates would take it from him anyway. If he gave her fifteen gulden, she would set him free. But brother Hans Blüetel refused to give a penny and said that with God's help he was ready for any tribulation.

Traitor arrested with the brother. They racked both.

Meanwhile the magistrates arrived with a crowd of armed men, arrested the brother together with the traitor and his wife, bound them securely with ropes, and set guards over them. When they arrived at the marketplace in Ried, they were racked terribly, the traitor as well as the brother; the magistrates thought Gugelwein had stolen Hans's money because so little was found on him. To make his wife talk, they squeezed her hands in a vise until they bled, although she and her husband had nothing. So their treachery brought them nothing but disaster. In the end this traitor hanged himself in his despair.

Traitor hanged himself.

Around St. John's Day [Dec. 27], when brother Hans had been in prison four or five weeks, he received the death sentence: to be burned alive. He was led to the place of execution, and the priests came to him, urging him to abandon his faith. But he told them, "You would do well to turn from your monstrous deception. I will neither agree with it nor listen to your false teaching. Today I have more important things to do than to listen to your false prophecies. I must follow the Lord my God, in Christ, and fulfill my promise to him." And he spoke to them in such a way that the priests drew back and left him in peace.

Hans Blüetel repulsed priests.

On the way to his execution, he met a man named Michael Dirk, or Kramer (a peddler), whom he knew very well. Hans Blüetel looked at him with a smile on his lips that was a witness of heaven to this Michael. He was amazed that Hans could smile on his way to death by fire. This struck Michael's heart deeply and his wife's too. She went three days without food and mourned and wept over brother Hans's innocent death. Later, both of them joined the church community and became believers, as did others too.

Hans Blüetel went to the place of execution smiling.

When this dear brother came to the place of execution, he thought of the church community of God and called out in a loud voice that could be heard by the whole crowd, "Oh, if there were someone here who could be trusted to send word to the church in Moravia that I, Hans Blüetel, have been burned to death at Ried in Bavaria for the sake of the Gospel." A man came forward who had encouraged many to embrace the faith, though he himself was unable to do it. He promised to inform the church in Moravia that Hans Blüetel had been burned to death at Ried for the sake of divine truth. This encouraged brother Hans to continue speaking to the people: "This faith of mine is the divine truth, and I want to make this clear to you. I tell you, unless you repent, change your lives, and leave your corrupt ways, God will visit your sins upon you and punish you with the everlasting torment that is prepared for all sinners. He will avenge the innocent blood you have shed and require it at your hands to the last drop."

1545
Hans Blüetel cried out to the people, "Oh, if only someone here would tell the church of God that I have been executed."

"God will punish you for shedding innocent blood."

When the fire was ready, they bound him to a ladder. All this time he went on telling them that this was the truth, the way of eternal life, and the true church of God; heaven and earth should bear witness. "This very day," he said, "God will give a sign in heaven that this is the way to eternal life." And so it happened. The sun in heaven grew pale and dim, as if it could no longer shed its light. Although the sky was clear and cloudless, the sun cast a shadow on the earth and was nothing but a pale yellow shape. Thus God affirmed this witness.

Hans Blüetel foretold a sign; the sun grew dim.

This lover of God, Hans Blüetel, was alive and singing in the fire for quite a long time. He praised Christ and prayed that all who were worthy might be enlightened by God. And so, like pure gold, he endured the fiery test and proved steadfast in faith.

Hans Blüetel sang in the fire.

He had foretold as a further sign that the smoke would rise straight upward and his spirit would rise up to heaven with it. It happened just as he said. The smoke from the execution went straight up to the sky. Several people told us that a snow-white dove circled in the fire and soared up into the sky. Praise be to God who stands so faithfully and powerfully with his own and himself bears witness to his divine truth by the miracles he performs for his saints.

He said the smoke would rise straight up and it did.

1545
Andreas from Villach plundered the community.

In the fall of 1545, Andreas from Villach plundered the communities at Schakwitz, Pulgram, and Rampersdorf,[1] taking especially cattle, horses, oxen, leather, and wine, which God allowed and the authorities condoned. He caused great damage to the church community because his own brother Stoffel, a former army captain, had joined the brotherhood and handed all his property over to the church. Andreas wanted to get it back. Up to that time the community had been free from severe troubles since the persecution in 1535.

Many came from Kaufbeuren.

The number of believers increased, with people coming from many countries, especially from Kaufbeuren and the surrounding area. Many joined the church, surrendering their lives to the Lord's will. More accommodations were needed, and so more houses were bought, as follows.

We settled at Bochtitz.

Before St. Gall's Day [Oct. 16] Stoffel Niedermair bought a house on our behalf outside Bochtitz,[2] and we moved in.

We settled at Hrubschitz.

On October 5 Hans Klöpfer from Feuerbach and Hans Mändel from the Adige region bought a house on our behalf outside the village of Hrubschitz,[3] near Eibenschitz, and we settled there.

We settled at Wessely.

At Martinmas [Nov. 11] Jakob Säckler bought a house on our behalf from a nobleman at Wessely. We moved in, but on June 2, 1546, it burned down, and we made a contract with the owner for the burned-out site.

On St. Catherine's Day [Apr. 30] Michael Matschidel, our servant of the Lord's Word at that time, bought another house on our behalf in Wessely.[4] This house, too, burned down in the fire of 1546. The lord at Wessely gave us another burned-out site in exchange, situated by the upper gate near the March

---

[1]Rampersdorf (Ladná), village north of Lundenburg (Břeclav); property of the lords von Zerotin; the brothers ran the mill and the farm. *ME*, IV, 249; Zeman, *Topography*, #129.

[2]Bochtitz (Bohutice), southwest of Brno, village and estate belonging to the family Kusý of Mukoděl, c. 1500–1620. Zeman, *Topography*, #14; *ME*, IV, 197.

[3]Hrubschitz (Hrubšice), village on the Jihlava River, near Eibenschitz (Ivančice); in 1545 the property of Wenzel of Hodic; after 1550 the village was part of the estate of Mährisch Kromau. Zeman, *Topography*, #51.

[4]Wessely (Veselí nad Moravou), a town on the Morava River approx. 17 miles northeast of Göding (Hodonín), at this time the property of Hynek Bilík of Kornice, a zealous "Piccard" himself. The Hutterites occupied a house adjoining the seigneurial zoological gardens in the Wessely suburb of Břeh. Beck, 165; Zeman, *Topography*, #171.

River. This location was more convenient for us, and we built a new house there in 1547. *1545*

On St. Andrew's Day [Nov. 30] we bought and moved into a house at Bohuslawitz near Gaya, which had a mill with three gears. The purchase was made on our behalf by Michael Matschidel, servant of the Lord's Word; Melchior Kellner, servant for temporal affairs; and Thoman Schmidt, our interpreter.

We settled at Bohuslawitz.

1546

In the year 1546, at Candlemas [Feb. 2], we bought another house at Bohuslawitz near Gaya. Hans Gütten, Paul Zimmermann, and Hans Klampferer made the purchase.

At Whitsun in that same year we bought a farmstead at Tscheikowitz, where we built a new house from the foundations up.

We settled at Tscheikowitz.

On July 29 we bought an undeveloped mill from Clement Pap at Sabatisch in Hungary,[1] made dwellings out of it, and lived under the protection of Franz Niáry at Branc. The purchase was made on our behalf by Abraham Schneider, Hans Klampferer, and Christel Stampfer. Later, Lord Franz Niáry bought two thirds of the mill, which left us with only one third of the mill as our property.

We began at Sabatisch.

---

[1]Sabatisch (Czech: Sobotište; German: Freischütz), Slovakian market town east of Lundenburg (Břeclav), between the Morava and Vah rivers. Freischütz was the German name used by the 16th-century Hutterites. "Freischütz" or "Freischutz," a place where freedom is protected, may derive from the Hungarian *Szabad* = freedom, thus Sabatisch or Sobotište. Another possible explanation of the name Sobotište is the derivation from the Slovakian *Chobot* or *Sobota*, the "Saturday fair." See Beck, 196 n.2.

Throughout this chronicle, the designation "Hungary" or "Hungarian" has been kept for that part of Slovakia which formerly belonged to the kingdom of Hungary and is now part of Czechoslovakia.

Sabatisch was partly owned by Franz Niáry of Bedek and belonged to the Branc (Branč) estate. (The ruins of Branc Castle can still be seen from Sabatisch.) In 1938, there existed 150 descendants of the early Hutterian brothers who had become Catholics in the late 1700s and were called *Habaner*; some of them were still living in the original thatched-roof houses. The origin of the name *Habaner* is uncertain: It may derive from the German *Haushaben*, meaning "communal households." Some scholars trace it to a Slovakian word that means "people who have lost all their possessions," and there are other conjectures (see also *ME*, II, 618–619). Robert Friedmann, *Die Habaner in der Slowakei* (Vienna, 1927); *ME*, IV, 557–558; Beck, 165 n.4; Zieglschmid, "Die ungarischen Wiedertäufer...," *Zeitschrift für Kirchengeschichte*, note 29, or an excerpt of the same in *Publications of the Modern Language Association of America*, LIV, No.4 (December 1939), 1031–1040, note 12.

1546
Hans Staudach and 3 other brothers captured.

That same year four brothers were taken prisoner in Austria with their wives and children. They were Hans Staudach from Kaufbeuren; Anthoni Keim, a tailor from Gunzenhausen; and Blasius Beck and Leonhard Schneider, both from Kaufbeuren.[1] They were on their way to the community here. On August 3 they were taken to Vienna. They were led through the city like criminals, chained two by two with shackles on their feet, their wives and children following them. A crowd gathered as if the king were coming. The brothers were taken to prison and left with their wives and children for four days. During these four days they were severely questioned again and again whether they wanted to hold to their faith. They gave their witness: yes, with God's help. Then the four brothers were moved to a different prison, where they were again questioned. Their wives and children were taken to the judge's house, and the brothers were prevented from speaking with them.

Hans Staudach and his fellow prisoners questioned.

On Sunday, August 16, a large number of people came to the brothers in prison to talk to them, wishing they would recant, also for the sake of their wives and children. But they were courageous and stood firm, even though threats were made to take their children from them. Meanwhile their wives were released and came to the church community here.

The wives were released.

Many cruel tricks were then tried on these brothers to frighten and confuse them and make them recant. They were taken to Vienna and had to appear four times before the authorities. This included monks, priests, and scholars, whom Christ rightly calls ravening wolves, warning us to be on our guard. Like wolves that eat their fill at their leisure only after they have killed every animal in the fold, the false prophets are not satisfied as long as one believer is left who has not been misled. That is why they torment them in so many ways, as they did these lovers of God; but they achieved nothing. They were only brought to shame, for no one can tear Christ's own from his hand.

False prophets are ravening wolves. They do everything to bring souls into the devil's power.

Then the royal mandate was read to the brothers. They were threatened with fire, water, and the sword; they would be kept on bread and water and separated from one another. To strike terror into them, brother Oswald from Jamnitz was drowned

The king's mandate read to the brothers.

[1]About the four brothers mentioned here, see *ME*, IV, 619; III, 161; I, 260; IV, 470, respectively; *Martyrs Mirror*, 475; Beck, 165–167.

by night, as already recorded.[1] But these heroes and knights of God's truth were not to be frightened. *1546*

On Thursday after St. Michael's Day [Sept. 29] they were again asked whether they were ready to deny their faith. If not, their interrogators had orders to take their lives by fire, water, or the sword. That was the last word.

Since all these threats were to no avail, the four were imprisoned separately: Anthoni Keim in the jail, Staudach back in the old prison, Blasius in the woodshed, and Leonhard in another, smaller prison.

On All Souls' Eve [Oct. 31] they were put together again. Through all this they remained steadfast, continuing to witness that this was the way of divine truth, which they would seal with their blood. On November 22, shortly after St. Martin's Day, they were condemned to death and handed over to the executioner. He bound them and led them to the place of execution at dawn so that the news would not be spread and a crowd gather.

They sang joyfully as they were taken to execution.

They sang joyfully as they were led to the slaughter block. As was the custom at executions, a circle was made and the brothers knelt down inside it and prayed fervently. The executioner was heavy-hearted and reluctant to carry out his work. The other sons of Pilate, too, would gladly have been innocent, but they had to do it because of the authorities and to protect their own positions. They wished they were miles away.

The youngest of the brothers was taken first. He blessed the others from his heart, telling them to be of good courage: "Today we will be together in our heavenly Father's kingdom."

They were beheaded.

So all four were beheaded. They valiantly and joyfully offered their necks to the sword for the sake of Christ's name. A song Wolf Sailer composed about them bears witness to this. So does the song written by Hans Gurtzham, who was in the same prison at that time. In addition, we still have some songs and letters by Hans Staudach and his fellow prisoners.[2]

---

[1]Oswald from Jamnitz = Oswald Glait; see above pp.240–241.

[2]For their letters, see Adolf Mais, *Jahrbuch des Vereins für Geschichte der Stadt Wien*, Vol. 19/20 (1963–1964), 137–152, 159–161, 161–162.

See Wolkan, *Lieder*, 179–185, and *LdHBr*, 128–138, for songs written by or about Hans Staudach and his fellow martyrs. Wolf Sailer, a servant of the Word

1546
Klein Michael and 2 others captured.

At this time Michael Matschidel, also known as Klein Michael, a servant of Jesus Christ and his church, was taken prisoner at Ortenburg in Upper Carinthia. Two others were captured with him, his wife Lisel and Hans Gurtzham,[1] a shoemaker. They were questioned in the presence of a dean and the parish priest of Villach, who tried to argue with them. But these brothers continued to answer until their questioners had to leave in shame, having accomplished nothing.

After this, the prisoners were put in chains and irons and led through Styria to Vienna. At the courthouse they were handed over to the warder, who said, "Come, I will take you to a dungeon where some of your brothers are." There they found Hans Staudach and the three captured with him. When they met, they embraced and kissed each other, praising God who had brought them together for the glory of his name. Later Hans Staudach and the three others were executed, as was just told. The others were kept in prison for almost three years, until 1549, when there was a fire in the city of Vienna. As was the custom when a fire breaks out, the city gates were closed and the prisoners were released. When the fire was extinguished, brother Michael and his wife Lisel—through God's providence—were helped by a townsman to escape from the city, and they returned to the church community. Thus God provided a way for them to escape unharmed and in peace. We still have epistles and letters written by this Michael.[2]

Klein Michael escaped from Vienna during a fire.

Hans Gurtzham was returned to prison and executed.

Hans Gurtzham, however, was returned to prison for another year, until 1550. Very early on a Friday morning, around June 27, he was drowned in the Danube. Some said that when they were getting ready to drown him, they took him into a warm room, where he passed away while sitting behind the stove, and that he thus died in the Lord, but then they threw his body into the river. We still have one or two songs that he composed in prison.

---

and cabinetmaker, died 1550 at Saitz in Moravia; see below, p. 315. *ME*, IV, 400; Zeman, *Topography*, #134; Beck, 167.

[1]About Hans Gurtzham, see *ME*, II, 612; *Martyrs Mirror*, 474; Beck, 167–168.

[2]About Michael Matschidel, see *ME*, III, 538. About his letters (in the Bratislava City Archives, Codex Hab. 17), see Beck, 168 n.1; Friedmann, *Schriften*, 121.

1547

1547

In 1547 at Gurdau, Hans Greckenhofer, Wolf Sailer, and Peter Hagen were chosen for the service of God's Word and appointed by the church for a time of testing.

3 brothers chosen for the service of the Word.

On March 18 the servant for temporal affairs, Bastel Schmidt, bought a house on our behalf at Fraitz[1] near Bisenz, and we settled there.

We settled at Fraitz.

On May 17 we bought another house at Bohuslawitz near Gaya. Peter Riedemann, servant of the Lord's Word, and Andreas Stuck, servant for temporal affairs, made the purchase.

Purchased house at Bohuslawitz.

---

[1]Fraitz (Vracov), southeast of Gaya (Kyjov), belonged to the lords von Zerotin until 1547, when it passed into the possession of Franz Niáry of Bedek, who allowed the brothers to settle there. Beck, 168 n.3; Zeman, *Topography*, #178.

The Five Articles of Faith

These five articles of faith are the reason for the great controversy between us and the world. All those of our church who have been executed by fire, water, or the sword were condemned because of these articles. All the tribulation, persecution, imprisonment, and death of believers in recent times has been on account of these articles on baptism, the Lord's Supper, community of goods, governing authority, and the separation of believing and unbelieving partners in marriage.

The 5 most controversial articles herewith introduced.

As the history recorded in our chronicle is closely related to these main articles of faith, we will state them here, giving their clear scriptural foundation, which shows that our faith was not invented forty years ago by Jakob Hutter or any other man but was established by our Lord and Savior Jesus Christ and by his holy apostles and their Gospels and writings.

Our faith was not made up 40 years ago or invented by Jakob Hutter but is grounded in the Holy Scriptures.

Concerning True Christian Baptism
as opposed to infant baptism

Matt.28:18–20

Christ says, "All power in heaven and on earth is given to me. Go therefore and teach all nations, baptizing them in the name of the Father and of the Son and of the Holy Spirit and instructing them to observe all that I have commanded you." He puts teaching first, baptizing second. So people must first be taught and believe, and be baptized only when they themselves gladly and willingly accept teaching, knowing what they do and confessing their faith. Otherwise baptism is meaningless.

Scriptural basis for the church's position on baptism, given briefly.

The church's position on baptism.

Mark 16:15–16

"Go out into all the world and preach the Gospel to the whole creation. All who believe and are baptized will be saved, but those who do not believe will be condemned." Here, too, we are told that preaching should come first, then belief, and third, baptism of the believers. Infants cannot have faith. They know nothing about God, about Christ, about the Gospel, or about the suffering and death of Jesus Christ. Therefore they should not be baptized in infancy. God does not demand that they have faith as long as they are infants, nor that they be baptized as long as they do not know what baptism is.

Matt.3:1–12; Mark1:4–8; Luke 3:3

John the Baptist first preached repentance and conversion. Those who were moved by his words, he baptized with the baptism of repentance and faith in the One who was to come after him. All this is not possible for infants, therefore John did not baptize infants.

Matt.3:13–17; Mark 1:9; Luke 3:21

Christ himself, who is our example, was not baptized until he was thirty years old and about to begin his ministry. Therefore, neither should we be baptized until we are old enough to understand and start doing God's will.

Matt.16:24

Christ said, "If anyone wants to come after me, let him deny himself, take up his cross, and follow me." Infants have no will of their own and cannot deny themselves, yet this is required in baptism. Therefore infant baptism is opposed to Christ on every point.

Luke 14:28

"Which of you, desiring to build a tower or fight a battle, does not first sit down and count the cost?" In the same way, any who desire to give themselves to God in baptism must be able to count the cost beforehand.

Luke 24:46–47

"It was necessary for Christ to suffer and rise from the dead on the third day and for repentance and forgiveness of sins to be preached in his name to all nations." Although only teaching and repentance are mentioned, baptism is not excluded, but teaching and repentance must come before baptism.

The church's position on baptism.

Acts 2:37–38

When the apostle Peter was preaching to the people, they were cut to the heart and said, "Dear brothers, what shall we do?" And Peter said to them, "Repent and be baptized, each one of you, in the name of Jesus Christ for the forgiveness of sins." That means one should be able first to seek God's will and repent and then receive baptism. Those who accepted Peter's words were baptized and added to the church.

Acts 8:5–12

The apostle Philip was preaching in Samaria. When the people believed Philip's words about the kingdom of God and the name of Jesus Christ, they were baptized, both men and women. Nothing is said about infants, since it was not meant for infants.

Acts 8:26–38

In the same chapter Philip spoke to the eunuch, a minister of Queen Candace of Ethiopia, and taught him the Gospel of Jesus. When the eunuch asked for baptism, the apostle asked him, "If you believe with all your heart, let it be done," as if to say, "If you do not believe, or do not understand, then it cannot be done." That is how baptism should be approached. One should first desire it, otherwise it is meaningless.

Acts 10:34–48

Peter proclaimed God's Word to the household of Cornelius and taught them what they should do. Then the Holy Spirit came upon all who were listening, and they spoke in tongues and glorified God. At this, Peter commanded them to be baptized. Infants can neither speak in tongues nor glorify God, and so they were not baptized.

Acts 16:14–15

"A devout woman named Lydia from the city of Thyatira, a seller of purple goods, heard Paul speak. The Lord opened her heart to heed what Paul said. And she and her household

The church's position on baptism.

were baptized." Here, too, teaching comes first, then faith, and third, baptism. Others in her household who were baptized had, like her, first heard the Word, given heed to it, and accepted it in faith.

Acts 16:29–34

"The jailer threw himself down before Paul and Silas and said, 'Masters, what must I do to be saved?' They said, 'Believe in the Lord Jesus, and you will be saved, you and your household.' Then they spoke the Word of the Lord to him and to everyone in his house, and straightaway he and all his family were baptized. He rejoiced with his whole household in his new-found faith in God." Infants cry. They cannot rejoice that they have found faith in God, as this jailer and his household did. If they ever do, then baptize them!

Acts 19:2–7

About twelve of John's disciples at Ephesus had received only the baptism of John. They had not received the Holy Spirit or even heard that there was a Holy Spirit. So they were then baptized in the name of the Lord Jesus. If baptism by John was not sufficient, the baptism of infants counts still less. Infants have never heard of the Holy Spirit and therefore know even less about him.

Rom.6:3–4

Paul said, "Do you not know that all of us who have been baptized into Jesus Christ were baptized into his death? We were buried with him by baptism into death, so that, as Christ was raised from the dead by the glory of the Father, we, too, may have new life." If little children understand that this is what baptism means, then let them be baptized; if not, it is nothing but a sham and an insult to true baptism.

Rom.6:13

"Give yourselves to God" (take note: *yourselves*) "as men who have been brought from death to life, and your members as tools of righteousness." Infants cannot give themselves to God. If others do it in their stead, it means nothing.

Rom.14:12

"Each one of us will have to give an account of himself to God," said Paul. So baptism, too, requires the personal consent and surrender of each one.

The church's position on baptism.

1 Cor.1:16

Among those baptized in Stephanas's household, infants are not mentioned. Paul said the household of Stephanas devoted themselves to the service of the saints. If babies in the cradle do this, then by all means baptize them.

1 Cor.16:15

1 Cor.1:17

Paul said, "Christ did not send me to baptize but to preach the Gospel." He also said, "I have given you birth through the Gospel." "I planted, Apollos watered, but God made it prosper." He does not mean that he was not sent to baptize at all, but that teaching, giving birth through the Word, and implanting faith should all precede baptism by water; and that this was the order the apostles kept, for the Lord had commanded them both to teach and to baptize.

1 Cor.4:15
1 Cor.3:6

Gal.3:27

"As many of you as were baptized have put on Christ." Infants cannot put on Christ. They do not know who Christ is. Therefore only rational, believing adults are meant here.

Heb.6:1–2

"Let us stop discussing the elementary teachings about the Christian life and advance to maturity. We should not be laying all over again the foundations of faith in God, repentance from dead works, baptism, teaching, laying on of hands, resurrection from the dead, and eternal judgment." Here he again describes the order that the apostles and their churches followed from the beginning.

Heb.10:38

"The righteous man shall live through his own faith." It does not say, "The righteous man shall live through baptism," but "through his own faith." Faith is given first place, to be followed by baptism. Thus it is wrong to put baptism ahead of faith.

The church's position on baptism.

1 Pet.3:21

"Baptism is not the washing away of the filth of the flesh but the sign of a good conscience before God, through the resurrection of Jesus Christ." Infants know nothing about a good conscience before God, so baptism is not required of them until they have gained understanding and faith.

Acts 2:42–46; 4:32

"The believers continued steadfast in the teaching of the apostles, in community of goods, in the breaking of bread, and in prayer." If any infants did this, then they also were baptized; otherwise they were not. Just as it would be foolish to think of infants in cradles breaking the bread at the Lord's Supper, so it is foolish to baptize them or even to consider it.

Rom.10:17

"Faith comes from hearing the teaching, and the teaching comes from the Word of God."

Eph.4:5

"There is only one faith and one baptism," said Paul. So there cannot be two faiths, one that is our own and one that is borrowed; there cannot be true baptism based on the Scriptures and infant baptism about which not one syllable is written.

Eph.2:8

"Faith is a gift of God"; it is not the gift of a godfather, who answers in the infant's name and believes on its behalf, which clearly shows that the infant cannot believe for itself.

Rom.4:3

"Abraham believed, and it was reckoned to him as righteousness." In the New Testament, unbelievers cannot be accepted into the covenant as children of Abraham.

Rom.3:21–24

If it were not for faith, the heathen could never enter into Abraham's covenant. It is through faith that God justifies the heathen, leads them to righteousness, and includes them in Abraham's covenant, not through infant baptism, which requires no faith. Therefore baptism must not be given or received without faith.

Heb.11:1

"Faith is the assurance of things hoped for" (RSV). Infants know nothing about assurance of things hoped for. How then should they have faith?

The church's position on baptism.

1 John 5:1

"Everyone who believes that Jesus is the Christ is born of God," said John. Infants do not and cannot believe that Jesus is the Christ. So they are not born again through God, and baptism, the bath of rebirth, is not meant for them.

John 3:3–5

Titus 3:5

Deut.1:39

"Infants do not know good or evil."

Jonah 4:11

The Lord spoke to the prophet about infants, who cannot tell their right hand from their left. It is right for infants to remain in their innocence and purity, as God created them. They belong to the Lord from the beginning, and God accepts them just as they are, unbaptized, because Christ has atoned for them too. It is blasphemy to say that unbaptized infants are damned and that the devil is in them and must be driven out.

John 15:15

Christ said, "All that I have heard from my Father I have disclosed to you." He has not told us one syllable about infant baptism. So we can be sure that he never heard it from his Father, for it is not a plant of his Father's planting but was planted by men and must be pulled up by the roots.

Matt.15:13

Acts 20:20

When Paul, the last apostle to be called, spoke to the elders at Ephesus, he avowed that he had kept nothing from them that would benefit them. He was therefore innocent of their blood, for he had declared to them the whole counsel of God. But he neither wrote nor said a single word about infant baptism; and so this is not God's counsel but comes from the antichrist, who twists the order of God.

Concerning the Lord's Supper Given by Christ
as opposed to the priests' mass

Matt.26:26–28; Mark 14:22–24
Luke 22:17–19; 1 Cor.11:23–25

Scriptural basis for the church's position on the Lord's Supper, given briefly.

On the night the Lord Jesus was betrayed, he took bread, gave thanks, and broke it, saying, "Take, eat; this is my body which will be broken for you." In the same way he took the cup, saying, "Drink of it, all of you. This is my blood of the new covenant, which will be shed for many. Do this in remembrance of me." Notice, he adds by way of explanation: we are to do it in remembrance of him.

He spoke of his body as bread and of his blood as wine only in a symbolic way, meaning the very body and blood that he poured out for our sake. So that we do not forget the source of our salvation, we are again and again to remind ourselves of it and take it to heart, giving him praise and thanks that he redeemed us who were lost.

John 15:1–6

Further, we declare that through God's grace we are members of Christ's body. Anyone who keeps the Supper of Christ should be a living branch, a green shoot growing on the true vine, living in community of goods as a member of the body of Christ, his church. We are shown this by the one loaf of bread made from many grains brought together and ground, and by the wine made into one drink from many bunches of grapes that have been crushed. That is why Paul says, "The bread we break expresses the unity of the body of Christ. We who are many are one loaf and one body, for we all partake of the one bread."

1 Cor.10:16–17

Matt.26:26–28
Mark 14:22–24; Luke 22:17–19

Christ's body was not in the bread when he held the Last Supper with his disciples. He remained seated among them at table and did not transform himself from one piece of bread into another. Much less does he do this now.

1 Cor.11:26

"Whenever you eat this bread and drink this drink, proclaim the Lord's death until he comes." If Christ were physically in the bread with the flesh and bones and hands and feet that

Matt.27:35–50

hung on the cross, the apostle would not have said "until he comes," for he would already be physically present.

The church's position on the Lord's Supper.

Luke 22:20; 1 Cor.11:25

Luke and Paul wrote that Christ said at the Last Supper, "The drink of the new covenant is in my blood." Then the wine would have to be in the blood, not the blood in the wine. And what about the cup, if we are to take everything literally and have no other explanation?

Matt.26:29

After he had held his last supper, Christ said, "I tell you, I will not drink again of the fruit of the vine until the day I drink it once more with you in my Father's kingdom." Here he still speaks of the wine as wine, and to make it even plainer he says, "the fruit of the vine," not actual blood, although the wine symbolizes it.

John 15:1

Christ said, "I am the true vine," but he is not a vine in the physical sense. He is called a lamb but is not one physically. He called Simon Peter a rock, but this did not make Peter an actual rock. He remained a man. Paul said of Sarah and Hagar, "These women are the two covenants." Were they actual covenants? No, they were only symbols. Christ said, "I am the door into the sheepfold and the way." And again, "Whoever believes in me, streams of living water shall flow from within him," which does not mean that there will be a brook. He said that the hypocrite has a plank in his eye. That does not mean there is a rafter or a hay pole in it.

John 1:36
Rev.5:12–13; 19:7
Matt.16:18
Gal.4:24
John 10:7
John 7:38
Matt.7:3–5

On the cross he said to Mary, "Woman, behold your son. Son, behold your mother." Then John would have been Christ's own brother, for these words are just as clear as those we spoke of above. No, John's mother was someone else.

John 19:26–27

The seed is the Word of God, the field is the world. The seven fat and seven lean cows are seven years. Many similar passages from Scripture could be given, and if they were all meant literally, many ludicrous things would result. So when Christ said of the bread, "This is my body," and of the wine, "This is my blood," he did not mean this in a literal sense but as a symbol.

Luke 8:11
Gen.41:26–27

The church's position on the Lord's Supper.

John 20:24–25

The fact that Thomas refused to believe that Christ had risen shows clearly that the disciples had not understood Christ's words, "This is my body," to mean that he gave them his body to eat in a physical sense. If they had thought they had eaten and would eat Christ physically in the bread of the Lord's Supper, then Thomas would have found it much easier to believe that Christ must rise from the dead and had in fact risen.

Acts 2:42

Luke said, "They continued steadfast in the apostles' teaching, in fellowship, and in the breaking of bread." Notice that he said, "in the breaking of bread," not "in eating his body."

John 6:35–63

Christ said, "I am the bread of life; he who comes to me shall not hunger, and he who believes in me shall never thirst" (RSV). Here "coming" means eating and "believing" means drinking. It is the same throughout the sixth chapter of John. Eating the flesh of Christ and drinking his blood simply means believing in him who suffered for us and reconciled us by his blood. There is no eating with the mouth, for he said, "the flesh is of no avail" (if eating is understood literally, as the Jews understood it) but "the words I speak are spirit and life."

John 4:32–39

When the disciples begged Christ to eat, he said, "I have food to eat about which you know nothing." By this he did not mean that he would eat the Samaritans who believed in him after hearing the woman's report. He was telling his disciples that his food consisted in the salvation of men and doing his Father's will. Just as a man hungers for food, so Christ hungers for the salvation of mankind. In the same way, when he said, "Take, eat; this is my body which is given for you," he did not mean that his flesh should literally be eaten but that the redemption he achieved for us on the cross is our food, if we believe in him. As men are sustained by nourishing food for their temporal life, so, if we have faith in Christ, we will truly be sustained by him for eternal life.

The church's position on the Lord's Supper.

Matt.24:23–24
Mark 13:21–22; Luke 17:23

Christ said, "If anyone says to you, 'Behold, here is the Christ!' or 'There he is!' do not believe it. False Christs and false prophets will arise and perform great signs and wonders in order to lead astray even the elect, if that were possible."

Matt.24:26–27

"See, I have forewarned you," said Christ. "If they tell you, 'Look, he is in the wilderness,' do not go out; or, 'He is in the inner room,' do not believe it." That is no different from their saying now, "He is here in the bread, he is there in the wine," or "He is in the tabernacle." We must not believe it. "For as the lightning comes from the east and shines as far as the west, so will be the coming of the Son of man" (RSV).

Heb.2:16

It was not the nature of angels he took upon himself, but that of the seed of Abraham. If the body of Christ were physically present in the bread, it would necessarily follow that Christ, and therefore God, had taken on himself the nature of bread.

Acts 1:9–11

"As they were watching, Christ was lifted up, and a cloud took him from their sight; and the angels said, 'Men of Galilee, why do you stand here looking into heaven? This Jesus whom you see taken up into heaven will return in the same way.'" He did not ascend to heaven in the bread; nor will he come into the bread or come down to us in the form of bread.

Furthermore, one of the articles of the Christian faith that we are to confess is that Christ ascended into heaven and sits at the right hand of his heavenly Father. From there he will come again to judge the living and the dead. He will not come into the bread. If Christ came into the bread, they would be eating the judge of the living and the dead.

Col.3:1

The apostle said, "Seek those things that are above, where Christ is sitting at the right hand of God." He does not tell us to seek him here below in the bread of the Lord's Supper.

The church's position on the Lord's Supper.

Ps.40:6–8; Heb.10:5–7

The apostle, echoing the words of King David, said, "You have prepared a body for me that I may do your will, O God." This speaks of one body that God had prepared, not of many hundreds of thousands of bodies, as the priests would have it when they speak of changing his body into bread.

John 1:30

John the Baptist said, "After me comes one who is stronger than I." If Christ is one, there cannot be as many Christs as the times the priests celebrate mass.

Matt.28:6

The Scriptures tell us that Christ's body can never be in more than one place at a time, even after the resurrection. The angels said to the women who sought him in the tomb, "He is not here; he is risen," knowing that he was true God and true man. Moreover, even though the angels and the women had met in his name, which meant that he was among them, still they said, "He is not here," as if to say, "He is not bodily in more than one place at a time." We are told the disciples went to him in Galilee; so it is beyond doubt that Christ, though he was in their hearts, was not with them in the flesh, or they would not have needed to go to him.

Matt.26:11; Mark 14:7

Christ said, "The poor you always have with you, but you will not always have me." He meant his bodily presence, which is what the priests are talking about.

Ps.16:10

David said, "You will not allow your holy one to see corruption." If the bread were Christ, he would be far more corruptible and perishable than men are, for what is eaten is digested.

Matt.15:17

"Whatever goes into the mouth passes into the stomach and in a natural process is discharged," as Christ told us.

The church's position on the Lord's Supper.

Rom.14:17

"The kingdom of God does not consist in eating and drinking but in righteousness, peace, and joy in the Holy Spirit." Now if Christ were literally to be eaten and this could bring salvation or help to bring in God's kingdom, then the apostle spoke too briefly about him here.

Heb.13:9

"Do not be led astray by strange teachings," said Paul, "for it is good to strengthen our hearts by grace, not by food and drink. Such things have never benefited those who are occupied with them."

1 Cor.15:50

The apostle Paul said, "The perishable will not inherit the imperishable." Men are perishable but the body of Christ is imperishable. A perishable body cannot eat or receive the imperishable body of Christ; earthly bodies cannot eat heavenly bodies.

Heb.1:5; 5:5

The apostle said of Christ that Christ was made just as any other man, except that he was without sin. If sinlessness, then, was the only exception, there could not be another exception that allowed him to be everywhere. Consequently it is obvious that he is not in many pieces of bread any more than he was in many places at once when he was teaching on earth. He walked from one place to another.

Furthermore, if the body of Christ is in many places, how is it received in a person's mouth? If it is received in completeness, then it is not in many places. If it is received in part, then it is not Christ in flesh and blood as he hung on the cross.

Eph.2:8

It is through faith that Christ dwells in our hearts. The apostle does not say, "through the food we eat."

John 14:23

"If a man loves me, he will keep my words, and my Father will love him. And we will come to him and dwell with him." It does not say, "through eating his body."

The church's position on the Lord's Supper.

2 John 9

"Anyone who strays from Christ's teaching does not have God," and he will not receive him in the host either. "Anyone who keeps to Christ's teaching has both the Father and the Son." It does not say, "Anyone who has eaten the host will receive Christ."

John 10:11

Christ said, "I am a good shepherd." So when they eat the host, they are eating the shepherd and claim to be sheep. Sheep indeed! It is the wolves that eat the shepherd. Sheep never eat their shepherd.

Wisd. of Sol. 13:10

"Men who give the name of gods to the work of human hands, artfully fashioned in gold and silver, are accursed, and their hope is with the dead." Those who worship bread or the host as though it were Christ are just as idolatrous and accursed.

1 Cor. 12:2

Paul wrote to the Corinthians, "You know that when you were heathen you went to dumb idols, as you were directed." Apart from Christ, who ascended into heaven, everything that is raised up and worshiped is an idol. So the false mass of the priests is nothing but a dumb idol, and it is a heathen practice to receive and worship it.

John 20:20
Luke 24:37–43

If anyone says it takes place spiritually and is a spiritual food, then Christ's body must be a spirit and not a body with flesh and bones. Is it then the body or the soul that receives food in the host? If it is the body, how can it eat spiritually? If it is the soul, how can it eat physically? Does the soul eat actual food?

1 John 4:2–3

If you say that since Christ's body was conceived through the Holy Spirit it can be everywhere in every form, you are denying that Christ came in the flesh and was made true man.

You say: He is now glorified, and so he is everywhere, for what else does it mean that he is glorified? Answer: He was not yet glorified when he instituted the Lord's Supper and held it with his disciples. And after he was glorified, just as before, he had only one body.

John 1:14

It is said that because the Word became flesh, wherever the

Word is, there is Christ too; that the Word cannot be separated from the flesh; and that he is not only in this place or that, but everywhere the Word is present through faith. Answer: It is true that the Word is everywhere if by "Word" we mean God, his nature, and his power. It is not true if we mean the Word accepted through faith for salvation, for that would include Jews and heathens. Likewise, the Word is not in the bread, for bread cannot hear or believe, nor is the flesh in it.

The church's position on the Lord's Supper.

Rom. 10:8

If you say that faith should not be discussed in such terms, but the simple words of Christ should be believed without brooding over the way it takes place, the answer is this: We must test the spirits and watch that the words are not misinterpreted and taken differently than they were meant by Jesus and understood by the apostles. We must understand them in the light of our faith in Christ. The Lord has commanded us to listen with discernment. Therefore we must test ourselves as to whether we are truly standing in faith.

1 John 4:1
Matt. 7:15–17

Mark 4:9

2 Cor. 13:5

Each year Israel, God's people in the Old Testament, killed the Passover lamb and ate it to commemorate how God had spared them, freed them, and led them out of Egypt. In the same way, Christ in the New Testament commanded us to take bread, break it, and eat it, holding the Lord's Supper in remembrance of his suffering, his death, and the shedding of his blood. By this he redeemed us and won grace and everlasting life for us. This is the meaning of the words, "Do this in remembrance of me."

Exod. 12

TRUE SURRENDER (*Gelassenheit*[1]) and Christian community of goods

Exod. 16:14–20

When God the Lord had led the children of Israel out of Egypt and they were in the Wilderness of Sin, he gave them bread from heaven, manna, which they gathered, some more and others less. When they measured it with an omer, those who had gathered much had nothing over, and those who had gathered little had no lack. But when some kept part of it for

Scriptural basis for the church's position on Christian community.

[1]*Gelassenheit* cannot be translated by one word. It denotes trusting yieldedness to God's will, abandonment of self, and joyful acceptance of suffering for Christ's sake. See Robert Friedmann, "Gelassenheit," *ME*, II, 448–449.

The church's position on Christian community. 2 Cor.8:14–15

the next day, it bred worms and stank. This is an example for us. Now that God has brought the Christian church out of the Egypt of the present time, the church in the wilderness of this world should be like the Israelites: the rich should have no more than the poor, and the poor no more than the rich, but everything should be given up for common and equal use. The apostle Paul explains this very point to us.

Lev.25:1–7; Deut.15:1–11

For six years each man in Israel was to harvest his produce, but the seventh year was to be a year of release, a year of rest for the land, kept as a Sabbath to the Lord. What the land bore in the seventh year belonged to everyone, to the head of the household, the men servants and maid servants, the day laborers, the household members and strangers, the cattle and the beasts. Likewise, a man who lent something to his neighbor could not demand it back in the seventh year but had to forgo the debt, for it was a glorious and festal proclamation of the year of freeing given by the Lord. This year of freeing pointed to the time of the new covenant in Christ, which is the true year of freeing, the acceptable year of the Lord of which the prophet spoke. That is why all the goods bestowed on us by God in this new time should be held in common in Christian love. We should enjoy them with our brothers, neighbors, and household members, and no longer amass them for ourselves as during the former six years. Now it is a much more glorious and festal proclamation of the year of God's grace than it was in the Old Testament.

Isa.61:2

Deut.15:4–5

The Lord commanded Israel: "There shall be no poor among you." How much more perfectly should we fulfill this in the new covenant by living in Christian community!

Num.18:20; Deut.12:12
Josh.13:14; Ezek.44:28

The Lord said to Israel, "The priest shall have an inheritance. Yes, I shall be their inheritance, and you shall give them no possessions among the people, for I am their possession." That applies to the whole people gathered in Christ Jesus, for they all are a royal priesthood of God and Christ. The earlier

1 Pet.2:5
Rev.1:6

priesthood lived from the sacrifices which, once they had been made, no longer belonged to those who brought them. So it should be in the Christian church today.

The church's position on Christian community.

Isa.23:18

When God was about to destroy Tyre, the prophet said, "All" (take note: *all*) "their merchandise and their gains will be dedicated to the Lord. It will not be stored or hoarded but will belong to the citizens of the Lord and supply food and lodging for the hungry and clothing for the old." This is a prophecy of the church gathered in Christ.

Isa.60:9

The Lord points to this when he speaks through the prophet, "The islands (namely, the heathen) shall gather to me, and above all, the ships of the ocean shall bring your sons from far, their silver and gold with them, for the name of the Lord your God, and for the Holy One of Israel, who has made you glorious."

Zech.14:21

The prophet said, "On that day (the time of the new covenant) there shall no longer be a Canaanite trader or merchant in the house of the Lord," as some translations read.

Luke 3:11

When the people asked John the Baptist what they should do, he answered, "Whoever has two coats, let him share with the one who has none; and whoever has food, let him do the same." See how clear that is!

Matt.5:3

Christ said, "Blessed are the spiritually poor, for the kingdom of heaven is theirs." These include the people who have given up all earthly goods for the sake of Christ and no longer own anything. When someone is urged by the Spirit to live in poverty and Gelassenheit (true surrender), he is one of the spiritually poor. He may expect heavenly riches and will be called blessed. But unhappy are those who do the opposite. 2Cor.6:4–10

The church's position on Christian community.

Matt.6:24; Luke 16:13

Christ said, "No one can serve two masters. Either he will hate one and love the other, or he will cling to one and despise the other. You cannot serve God and mammon," which means private material possessions or wealth. Here Christ tells us that it is impossible to cling to both. Therefore let no one say that it is possible, for no servant of mammon can be a servant of Christ. Whoever wants the one must give up the other.

Further, it is one of the main articles of Christian faith to confess one holy Christian church and one community of saints, which is not a partial community but a full community of both spiritual and temporal goods. Anyone who confesses the community of saints with his lips but does not practice it is a deceiver and not a faithful member of the church.

Matt.8:20

To one who wanted to follow him and become his disciple, Christ said, "The birds in the sky have nests, and foxes have their dens, but the Son of man has nowhere to lay his head," as much as to say, "That is how poor you must become if you want to be my disciple. You must give up your property and be free of it."

Matt.13:22

Christ said, "The seed sown among thorns represents the man who hears the Word but goes his way among the cares of the world and the illusions of wealth; these choke the Word and so it bears no fruit." The two cannot exist side by side. If a man wants to hold on to both, he is deceiving himself.

Matt.14:19–21; 15:36–38
John 6:10–13

Christ also taught Christian community by the example he gave, first among 5000 men (not counting the women and children), then a second time among 4000 who had come to him in the wilderness. He fed them with bread and fishes, and when the disciples were told to share it all out, they gladly distributed the small provision among all the people and gave to each what he needed. This is a lesson for us. Just like the disciples, we, too, have left our homes, our relatives, and our countries for the sake of God's Word, which we cling to in this wilderness. Like them we should also hold our temporal goods in common out of love for our neighbors.

The church's position on Christian community.

Matt. 13:44–46

"The kingdom of heaven is like a treasure hidden in a field, which a man found and covered up; then in his joy went and sold everything" (take note: *everything*) "he had and bought that field." And those who find the treasure of divine truth should do the same, and do it with joy.

"The kingdom of heaven is like a merchant searching for fine pearls, who on finding one pearl of great price went and sold all" (take note: *all*) "that he owned and bought it." When God has shown us his truth, we should do as the merchant did and gladly give up all temporal goods in exchange.

Matt. 19:20–24
Mark 10:20–25; Luke 18:21–25

The rich young man who asked where he still fell short was told by Christ, "One thing you still lack. If you wish to be perfect, go and sell what you possess and give to the poor, and you will have treasure in heaven; and come, follow me." Notice, he says perfection lies in selling everything (again take note: *everything*) and giving to the poor. Love is a bond of perfection; where love dwells, it does not stop halfway but brings about full community. Giving to the poor (understood as the spiritually poor) does not mean being saved by the poor. A man is saved by following Christ and his commandment.

Matt. 5:3
James 2:1–5

Further, Christ said, "How hard it will be for the wealthy to enter the kingdom of God. I tell you, it is easier for a camel to go through a needle's eye than for a rich man to enter the kingdom of God." It would not be hard for the rich to enter God's kingdom if Christ had not required Gelassenheit and community of goods in his church from all those who want to enter into eternal life and inherit the heavenly treasure. It would be just as simple as for the poor.

Further, every devout person should be able to say with Peter, "See, we have left everything" (take note: *everything*) "to follow you." The Lord said, "Everyone who has left houses,

The church's position on Christian community.

brothers or sisters, father or mother, wife or children, or fields for my name's sake will receive a hundredfold and inherit eternal life." This does not mean remaining settled in one's home, farm, or property.

Matt.21:12–13; Mark 11:15–17
Luke 19:45–46; John 2:14–16

"Jesus entered the temple of God and drove out all who were selling and buying in the temple. He overturned the tables of the money changers and the seats of those who sold pigeons. He said to them, 'It is written, "My house shall be called a house of prayer," but you have turned it into a robbers' den.'" Christ does not want any trading of goods in his house; he wants Christian community. This buying and selling is a sign by which one should recognize the false church, discerning the evil that Christ drove out on two occasions with a good whip.

Matt.22:37–39
Mark 12:29–31; Luke 10:27

"'You shall love the Lord your God with all your heart and with all your soul.' This is the most important commandment. The second (which follows from it) is like it, 'You shall love your neighbor as yourself.'" Anyone who wants to do this will have to share all things with his neighbor and brother; otherwise he does not love them as himself, and his love is only false and pharisaical.

Matt.25:34–46

On the day of the last judgment Christ will say to his own, "You gave me food; you gave me drink; you gave me clothing," meaning you did not keep them for yourselves alone. "What you have done for one of the lowliest of my brothers, you have done for me. Enter into eternal life." Those who did not do so will be put at his left hand and sentenced to eternal damnation.

Luke 12:33

"Sell what you have and give to the poor. Provide yourselves purses that do not grow old, a never-failing treasure in heaven, where no thief can get near it and where it remains forever."

He does not talk about charitable gifts such as the world gives. It is not wrong to be sympathetic and help a passing beggar who has wasted his goods and wrecked his life by gambling or drinking or such, or who is destitute because of his own laziness. He certainly is poor, yet as full of wickedness as any other man. But it cannot be said that this was done to Christ, because the man was not one of his members. Christ is speaking here of total giving in community with believers, of giving everything a man has in his power to give.

The church's position on Christian community.

Luke 14:33

"Whoever of you does not renounce everything" (take note: *everything*) "that he has cannot be my disciple." It should not happen that each one keeps his own possessions and is master and steward over them himself, for that is not renouncing them.

Luke 16:9–12

"Make friends for yourselves by means of unrighteous mammon so that when you lack they may receive you into eternal dwellings." These dwellings are the true church of God, which receives people in need and from that time on cares for their spiritual and temporal needs in brotherly love. It is right to make friends by this use of mammon, and those are true friends who put all their possessions at each other's disposal out of Christian love. "A man who is faithful in very little things is faithful in great; and a man who is dishonest in very little things is dishonest in great." The very little thing is the temporal. If a man is not honest in temporal things and does not practice Christian community within the church of God, then in God's eyes he is not worthy of what is great, namely, the things of the Spirit.

Rev.22:1–5

"If you have not been faithful with wicked mammon, who will entrust to you true riches? If you have not been faithful in what is alien to you, who will give you what is your own?" Jesus calls the temporal things alien. Therefore, a man who claims earthly possessions for himself does wrong.

Luke 21:1–4; Mark 12:41–44

"Christ looked up and saw the rich putting large sums into the temple treasury. He also saw a poor widow put in two copper coins. Jesus said, 'Truly, I tell you, this poor widow

The church's position on Christian community.

Matt.19:21

has put in more than all of them; for they all gave to God from their abundance, but she in her poverty put in all' (take note: *all*) 'she had to live on.'" God demands all our property and our whole heart for Christian community. About the rich he said (as he told the rich young man), they must give all they have, and to prevent the poor from saying, "I have little," he taught them to do the same. Therefore we should all practice Christian community.

John 13:34–35

"I give you a new commandment, that you love one another as I have loved you. By this everyone will know that you are my disciples, if you have love for one another." Christ loved us so much that he promised to share with us his inheritance in heaven, while here on earth he had community with his disciples. So we should share all things with our brothers here on earth, ready to bear together joy and sorrow, bad times and good. That will be the sign for all to see that we are of one faith in Christ, that we are his true followers; for love is the mark of faithful and dedicated people.

John 17:10

Christ says, "Father, all that is mine is yours, and what is yours is mine." That is how it should be among God's children in regard to their temporal goods.

John 12:6; 13:29

Christ, who went before us, practiced community of goods with his disciples. They had a common purse, and Judas was responsible for it.

Acts 2:44–45

When the Holy Spirit came, he established full community, and the three thousand and five thousand people at Jerusalem, "all who believed, were together and had all things in common. They sold their possessions and goods and gave to all whatever they needed."

Acts 4:32–35

"The company of those who believed were of one heart and one soul, and no one said any of his goods were his own, but they had everything in common. There was not a person in need among them, for those who had houses and fields sold them and laid the proceeds at the apostles' feet, and each man was given what he needed."

The church's position on Christian community.

Acts 5:1–13

"None of the others dared to join them." Ananias and his wife Sapphira sold their property and brought part of the money to the apostles but kept the rest (doubtless so that they would still have something in case they were unable to hold out; which shows that if members were unfaithful, they would not receive their property back). Both suffered sudden death because of their avarice and Satan's cunning.

Acts 2:41–42

"Those who accepted his message were baptized, and about three thousand souls were added on that day. They continued steadfast in the teaching of the apostles, in community, in the breaking of bread, and in prayer." Here we see that it is just as necessary for us to continue in Christian community as in the apostles' teaching, the breaking of bread, and prayer.

Acts 11:26–27; 13:1

The disciples gathered at Antioch for a whole year. Among them were prophets and teachers. They all met together as they had done in Jerusalem, and so they probably lived in a communal household as in Jerusalem. Those who had been driven from Jerusalem and scattered during the persecution of Stephen came down to Antioch and established a community there.

2 Cor.8:3–5

The church in Macedonia did the same. Paul himself praised this church: "They were willing to give to the limit of their means and beyond, earnestly begging us to accept their help and fellowship in supporting the believers. And their giving surpassed our expectations; for they gave their very selves, first to the Lord and then to us by the will of God." Is that not the same community as at Jerusalem? No one can deny it.

2 Thess.3:10–12

The church at Thessalonica also lived in community, for when Paul wrote to them about lazy, careless members who

The church's position on Christian community.

did not work but meddled in other people's affairs, he said such people should eat their own bread. This shows that they ate their meals in common, for Paul would not have written like this if each of them had always been eating his own bread.

1 Cor.10:17

"We who are many are one loaf," said Paul. Like grains of wheat, we have yielded up all we are and live together in Christian community.

Rom.12:4–5; 1 Cor.12:12
Eph.4:4; Col.3:15

The apostle taught us that we are one body and members one of another, and that is how we should live. Think what it means to be like members of one body. You cannot have a more powerful teaching of Christian community.

1 Cor.10:24; Phil.2:3–4

Paul taught us, "No one should seek his own good, but the good of his neighbor." In order to do this, we have to seek the same common good.

1 Cor.13:5

"Love does not seek her own good." Certainly, therefore, she seeks only community.

Phil.2:5–9

"Let this mind be in you, which was in Jesus Christ, who being in the form of God did not think it robbery to be equal with God, but emptied himself, took the form of a servant, and appeared in the likeness of men. And being found in human form he humbled himself. Therefore God has highly exalted him." In the same way he wants us, however splendid and rich we were in the world, not to think it robbery when we are deprived of these things but to empty ourselves and take on the form of a servant in the house of God. Even though we may have been masters when we were living in private property, we should now be like any other brother in Christ, humble ourselves, and remain obedient to God until death.

Then God will exalt us. Just for this reason it is hard for the rich to enter the kingdom of heaven.

The church's position on Christian community.

2 Cor.8:9

"You know the grace of our Lord Jesus Christ, that though he was rich, yet for our sake he became poor, so that through him we might become rich." This is the example he gave us, so that when we shed the old nature and put on Christ, we are willing to become poor for the sake of others and love one another as he has loved us. Eph.4:22–24

1 John 1:7

"If we walk in the light as he himself is in the light, then we have community with one another."

1 John 4:21

"We have the commandment from the Lord that he who loves God should love his brother also."

We have ample proof that Christ and his disciples taught community untiringly. In every country, in every place, wherever there was an opportunity, they gathered as many as possible to demonstrate life in Christian community. So we find that the church was in the house of Priscilla and Aquila, (Rom.16:3–5) and in Laodicea the church was in the house of Nymphas. (Col.4:15) Archippus, Paul's fellow fighter, had the church living in his house. (Philem.1–2) Paul writes from Corinth to Rome that brother Gaius is host to him and to the whole church there, (Rom.16:23) and in the same letter he urges those in Rome, "Receive one another as Christ has received you, for the glory of God." (Rom.15:7) Clearly, the apostle did not wish each disciple to look for a house for himself and maintain his own household. Paul himself did not do this. When he came to Rome as a prisoner and lived in his own rented rooms for two years, he welcomed all who came to him. Here is the fulfillment of the prophecy that men will say, "Move together and make room for me too!" (Isa.49:20) "Let us never give up gathering together, as has happened with some, but let us encourage one another, all the more as we see the Day drawing near." (Heb.10:25)

CHRISTIANS MAY NOT WAGE WAR
administer worldly law or use force and the sword

People in these positions cannot be considered Christians

Gen.9:5–6

Scriptural basis for the church's attitude toward governing authorities.

In the beginning God said to Noah, "I will require a reckoning from every beast for your blood, because the soul is in the blood, and I will require a reckoning for men's souls at the hands of men, each man's soul at the hands of the other. Whoever sheds the blood of man, by man shall his blood be shed, for God has made man in his own image."

Gen.49:10

Jacob the patriarch prophesied that the scepter should pass from Judah at the coming of the victor, who is Christ. Since the ruling power of the Jews (the people of God in those days) came to an end in Christ and was taken from them, it is plain that in Christ it should have no existence and that from now on the new people of God should not carry or use the worldly sword or rule by it. Christ alone will rule his people, governing them with the sword of his Spirit.

Judg.9:7–15

In the Book of Judges, a parable is given to the house of Gideon. Gideon said to Israel, "I will not rule over you, and my son will not rule over you; the Lord will rule over you" (RSV). [Judg.8:23] But Abimelech, the son of his maidservant, went out to the people and was made king. Then Jotham told them in a parable how the olive tree refused to be king when asked by the other trees and how the fig tree and the grapevine refused. But the thornbush accepted readily. From this we learn that a Christian (who is compared in many passages of Scripture to the grapevine, to the olive and the fig tree, or to other cultivated trees) should not participate in worldly government, for then he would no longer bear the Christian fruits of peace, gentleness, and humility but ally himself with the world to quarrel and scratch like a thornbush. But we should not be like that, dear brothers. Instead, as Isaiah said,

Isa.55:13

"Pines shall grow up in place of thorns, and myrtles instead of briers."

1 Sam.8:7

When Israel asked for a king such as the heathen had, to lead them in war, Samuel was angered. The Lord said, "They have not rejected you; they have rejected me as king over them." And he gave them a king in his wrath.

The church's attitude toward governing authorities.

1 Chron.17:1–15; 22:7–9; 28

King David wanted to build a house for the Lord, but the Word of the Lord came to him, saying, "You are a warrior and have shed blood and waged great battles. You shall not build a house for my name, because you have shed so much blood before me upon the earth. But the son who will be born to you shall be a man of peace, and I will give peace to Israel in his days. He shall build a house for my name." This shows that the house of Christ shall be a peaceful people, unstained by blood.

2 Esd.13:25–39

1 Kings 6:7

When Solomon built the temple (which was to symbolize the church of Christ in the New Testament), it was made of blocks of undressed stone, and no hammer or axe or any iron tool was heard in the house while it was being built. This shows clearly that the church of Christ should not be built up with tumult or be forced to believe but will exist of its own free will in the day of God's power.

Ps.46:9; 76:2–3
Hos.1:7; 2:18; Zech.9:10

David, in his prophecy about the church of Christ, said, "His tent is in Salem and his dwelling in Zion. There he has broken the arrows, shields, swords, and weapons of war."

Isa.2:3–4; Mic.4:2–3

The prophets Isaiah and Micah, of one mind, spoke about the temple and church of Christ: "The law will go forth from Zion and the Word of God from Jerusalem. He will judge among the heathen and rebuke many peoples, and they shall beat their swords into plowshares and their spears into pruning knives, sickles, and saws; one nation shall not lift up sword against another, neither shall they learn war anymore." These words are plain. That is how peaceful the people of Christ will be.

The church's attitude toward governing authorities.

Isa.11:6–9; 65:25

"The wolf shall dwell with the lamb, and the leopard shall lie beside the kid; cattle and lions shall be together, and a little child shall lead them. The cow and the bear shall feed side by side, and their young shall lie down together. The lion will eat straw like the ox, and none will harm the other. No one shall destroy another in all my holy mountain." So wherever there is beating, stabbing, shooting, and injuring one another; destroying, quarreling, killing, and bloodshed, there is the devil's ungodly mountain, the abode of Lucifer.

Hos.13:11

"I have given you a king in my anger, and I have taken him away in my wrath." What was given in anger will not submit to Christ's grace and blessing. No child of blessing and peace can be a servant of wrath.

Matt.5

Christ said, "Blessed are the meek. Blessed are the merciful. Blessed are the peacemakers. Blessed are those who suffer persecution for righteousness' sake." All this is opposed to the rule of force and the sword.

Further: "You have heard that it was said to the men of old, 'You shall not kill, and anyone who kills shall be liable to judgment.' But I say to you that anyone who is angry with his brother shall be liable to judgment." In the Old Testament it was said, "You shall not kill," which [is in the singular and hence] applied to the individual and his personal violence or anger. Killing was to be carried out by judges and magistrates. But here Christ says, "I tell you" [which is in the plural], meaning not certain individuals but all Christians without exception. Every Christian should act accordingly. That is why the worldly power of the sword is abolished in the house of Christ but retained in the world.

"You have heard that it was said, 'An eye for an eye and a tooth for a tooth.' But I say to you: Do not resist evil; instead, if anyone strikes you on the right cheek, turn the other to him as well." In other words, rather than avenging yourself by returning blow for blow, you should be willing to suffer even more. This is the only way for every Christian. Any magisterial office is in direct opposition to this, for its task is to serve revenge.

The church's attitude toward governing authorities.

"If anyone wants to sue you and take your coat, let him have your cloak as well." Since Christians should not go to court, legal proceedings and judicial power have no place in Christianity.

"You have heard that it was said, 'You shall love your neighbor and hate your enemy.' But I say to you: Love your enemies, speak well of those who curse you, do good to those who hate you." These words are addressed to all Christians. The government uses the sword and is therefore directly opposed to this. That is why no Christian can hold office in a worldly government.

Matt.6:12

Christ taught his disciples to pray: "Forgive us our sins, as we forgive those who have wronged us." It is clear that a Christian must not seek revenge, for if a man were to avenge injustice with imprisonment or the sword, he would be praying, "As I have done to my brother and neighbor, do you to me, O God."

Matt.7:1–2

"Judge not," said Christ, "that you be not judged. For with the judgment you pronounce you will be judged, and the measure you give will be the measure you get" (RSV). Therefore the sword, law courts, and revenge can never be tolerated in the church of Christ.

Matt.10:16

Christ told us, "Look, I am sending you out like sheep among wolves." A sheep is a peaceable and defenseless animal that can save itself only by running as fast as it can. The sheep are the Christians, who have as little place in government as the sheep among wolves or lions.

Matt.13:28–30

In the parable of the weeds, the servant asks, "Master, shall we go and pull out the weeds?" The master answers, "No, lest you root up the wheat as well. Let them both grow together until the harvest." Christ said this also because he wanted to

1 Cor.5:7
2 Cor.6:17

The church's attitude toward governing authorities.

prevent war and bloodshed. He did not forbid the casting out of weeds from his church through the power of the keys. He did, however, forbid his followers to put them to death.

Matt.16:24

"If any man would follow me, he must deny himself and take up his cross." It does not say the sword, for that has no place at the cross. They are as far apart as Christ and Pilate. Just as Christ can have nothing in common with Satan, so the sword of this world has nothing to do with the cross of Christ.

Matt.16:19; 18:18; John 20:22–23

Christ gave the keys to the apostles of his church community when he said to Peter, "I give you the keys of the kingdom of heaven." To them all, he said, "Receive the Holy Spirit. If you forgive the sins of any, they are forgiven; if you retain the sins of any, they are retained" (RSV). This is the power Christ gave to his apostles and to his church. He never entrusted the power of the sword to any apostle or disciple in his church. The ban (the power of the keys entrusted to the church) and the sword (the power given to the world) are as different as night and day. They are as different as life and death and cannot be mixed. The authority of the keys excludes from the church what is evil, but the evil can be repented of. The sword of this world removes the person from earthly life, depriving him forevermore of the chance to repent.

Matt.10:17–18; 24:9
Mark 13:9; Luke 21:12; Dan.11:33

The evangelist reported to the Christians what Christ had prophesied about them: "Men will deliver you up to their councils, they will whip you in the synagogues, and you will be brought before rulers and kings, for my sake. They will exclude you from their meetings. The time is coming when any who kill you will think they are serving God." Consider, then, whether such authority is Christian. The same is happening today as at the time of the apostles.

John 16:2

Matt.20:20–23

Zebedee's two sons begged Christ that they might sit one at his right hand and one at his left in his kingdom. They desired the most honored places, for they thought it would be an earthly kingdom. When they still did not understand, Christ pointed them to another way, challenging them to struggle and suffer, that is, to drink of his cup.

The church's attitude toward governing authorities.

Matt.20:25–26
Mark 10:42–43; Luke 22:25–26

Jesus called his disciples together and said, "You know that in the world the rulers lord it over the people, and their great men wield power. It shall not be so among you." Here he spoke of worldly authorities and rulers and added simply, "It shall not be so among you." He did not mean the twelve only but every Christian and member of his church.

Matt.26:51–52
Mark 14:47; Luke 22:49–51

When Christ was taken prisoner, Peter took a sword and struck the high priest's servant, cutting off his ear. The Lord rebuked him, saying, "Put your sword back into its place; for all who wield the sword will die by the sword." He completely rejected the sword, and his followers were to lay it down, as it had no place among them. The sword of the Spirit and the sword of this world each has its own sheath. The sword of the Spirit belongs in the church of Christ. The worldly sword belongs in the world with the evildoers. There is no record anywhere of Peter or any other apostle using the sword again. They left it in its place. John 18:10–11

Luke 9:52–55

The disciples went into a Samaritan village to find lodging for Jesus, but the people refused to receive him. Then his disciples James and John asked him, "Lord, do you want us to call down fire from heaven to consume them, as Elijah did?" 2 Kings 1:10
But Jesus turned and rebuked them, saying, "Do you not know what spirit you are of? The Son of man did not come to destroy men's souls but to save them." Not many words are needed. It is clear that revenge has no place in the kingdom of Christ and that a Christian may neither go to war nor seek revenge. Anyone who does has abandoned Christ and his way. Just as it was no help for the disciples to mention Elijah, it will not help you to say that David was a king and that many devout

The church's attitude toward governing authorities.

men have used the power of the sword and gone to war; for Christ said, "Do you not know what spirit you are of?"

Luke 12:13–14

"A man in the crowd said to Jesus, 'Master, tell my brother to divide the inheritance with me.' But he said to him, 'Man, who made me a judge or arbiter over you?'" Likewise no disciple of his who has the Spirit of Christ can hold judicial authority or judge in the affairs of the world.

John 6:15

"Jesus, being aware that the people would come and seize him to make him king, withdrew from them and escaped." He did this as an example for us, and we should follow in his footsteps. The apostle Paul said, "Those whom God has called, he ordained to be conformed to the likeness of his Son." This clearly proves that any man willing to hold office in the world does not have the Spirit of Christ. If he does not have Christ's Spirit, he is not a Christian. Therefore a Christian certainly cannot hold a position of authority in the world.

1 Pet.2:21

Rom.8:29

John 8:3–11

Christ refused to condemn the adulterous woman to death, although that was the law. Likewise, no member of Christ's body may do this today. Christ said, "As the Father sent me into the world, so I send you."

John 17:18
20:21

John 18:36

"My kingdom is not of this world," Christ said to Pilate. "If it were, my servants would stand with me and fight for me." It follows that the realm of Christians is not of this world; it is of Christ. Governmental authority is part of the world; its realm is of this world only. And these two kingdoms can in no way be reconciled.

Rom.12:17–19

The apostle Paul taught the Christians: "Repay no one evil for evil; do not be haughty, but humble yourselves. If possible, insofar as it depends on you, live at peace with all men. Beloved, never avenge yourselves, but withdraw from anger; for it is written: 'Vengeance is mine, I will repay, says the

Deut.32:35

Lord.'" This shows that no Christian is allowed to carry out revenge.

The church's attitude toward governing authorities.

Rom.13:1; 1 Pet.2:13–14; Titus 3:1

"Let everyone be subject to the governing authorities," said Paul. "There is no authority except from God." In such words, the apostles take pains to teach us that Christians should be subject to those in authority, but not that they should hold such authority.

1 Cor.5:12

"What have I to do with judging people outside?" asked Paul. So a follower of Christ cannot rule in the world.

1 Cor.6:7–8

"You are already at fault by going to law with one another," Paul told the Corinthians. "Why not rather suffer wrong? Why not rather be cheated? But you yourselves cheat and do the same to your brothers." From this it follows again that judging and law courts have no place in the church of God.

2 Cor.1:24

The apostle Paul said, "We are not dictators over your faith." And Peter urged the elders to tend Christ's flock with forbearance and without domineering over God's children.

2 Cor.10:4; Eph.6:13–17

"The weapons used in our fight are not of the flesh but spiritual. They are mighty before God to destroy everything that rebels against the knowledge of God."

Rom.12:5; 1 Cor.10:17; 12:12–13
Eph.4:4; Col.3:15

"The believers or Christians are one body in Christ; all are baptized into one body." It is preposterous for a body to take the sword against itself. To injure or destroy oneself is a desperate act. So the use of the sword has no place in the church of Christ, for its members are one body in Christ. Would it not be madness if the two hands of a body each had a sword to stab each other as enemies? It is just the same to say that Christians may wage war and use the sword.

The church's attitude toward governing authorities.

1 Cor.13:4–7

Love is patient and kind. The sword and its servants break into sudden bitter and violent conflicts. Love is not envious. The sword quickly takes revenge. Love is not contentious, neither is it puffed up; the sword and its servants oppose others and puff themselves up mightily. Love does not seek her own advantage; the sword defends its own interests. Love is not provoked to anger; the sword is nothing but anger and an instrument of wrath. Love is not resentful but seeks reconciliation; the sword is vengeful and exacts revenge. Love endures everything; the sword bears with nothing but returns blow for blow. That is why Christian love and the sword of the world do not belong together.

John 19:1–30
Rom.9:22–23

Rev.1:16; 19:15

In the book of Revelation, Christ appeared to the holy apostle John with a two-edged sword in his mouth. From this, we who are his disciples and believe in him learn that the sword belongs not in our hand but in our mouth, namely, that we are to wield the sword of the Spirit and not the sword of blood.

Rev.4:10

The twenty-four elders who appeared at the throne of God cast their crowns before the throne. Where will those men find themselves who are unwilling to cast away their crowns here on earth but want to be crowned and honored by everyone, who tear each other apart over a crown? Their place will not be among the elders at the throne of God. They will find themselves at the throne of Lucifer.

Rev.13:9–10

"If anyone has ears, let him hear: If anyone takes captive, he will be brought into captivity. If anyone kills with the sword, he must himself be killed with the sword."

If government comes from God and is his servant, why—one may ask—can there be no Christians in it? Here is the answer: If the name "servant of God" makes a ruler into a Christian, then the Roman emperors Claudius and Nero would have been Christians too, since Paul called them servants of God by virtue of their scepters. When the powers that be were called servants of God, did Paul mean that a Turk who is a

Rom.13:4

servant of God in this sense is therefore a Christian? Obviously not. The Lord spoke even of King Nebuchadnezzar and King Cyrus as his servants, yet they were pagans. Just as the Scriptures speak of two kinds of angels, good and evil, and both are called angels, in the same way God has two kinds of servants on earth.

Jer.43:10

Ps.78:49, KJV

The church's attitude toward governing authorities.

A Christian cannot be a ruler in this world; but a ruler may certainly become a Christian if, with Christ, he strips himself of his glory, humbles himself, lays down the sword, takes up the cross, and follows him. From time immemorial the power of the sword has been identified with the government of this world to make it clear that its functions cannot be reconciled with those of the Christian church.

We neither wish nor intend, however, to remove the governing authority of this world or to disobey it in what is good and just. There has to be government for the people in the world just as much as there has to be daily bread and the schoolmaster's rod for children. The masses refuse to be ruled by God's Word. They have to be ruled by the sword so that scoundrels and worldlings, who are not controlled by Christian morals, are compelled to abide by the grim morality of the world, in fear of the gallows. If they were not bridled and kept within bounds, no one would be safe from his neighbor, and the earth would be drenched with blood.

Government, therefore, is God-ordained, and we rightly respect its officials because of their position. We show them friendliness, obey them, and pay their fees readily and regularly. God gave us an order so that the servants of the Word in his church are provided for. In the same way, he gave an order so that government officials are provided for, in the form of tithes, rent, services, compulsory labor, and so on, since they are unable to take on other work. This, too, a Christian may do as long as it is not against his faith and conscience. He is not obliged to do anything that is against God and his faith. Peter and the apostles did not do this either. It is true that Peter taught, "Submit to every human ordinance," but when he was forbidden to do right and forced to do wrong, he said, "It is our duty to obey God rather than men." Shadrach, Meshach, and Abednego did just the same with King Nebuchadnezzar, and so did Maccabeus and his followers in the days of King Antiochus. We owe the emperor and the

1 Cor.9:4–14
1 Thess.5:12–13

1 Pet.2:13

Acts 4:19; 5:29
Dan.3:16–18

Matt.22:21

government what is theirs and give to God what is God's. So a Christian should be awake to this difference and not give
Rom.16:18 the heads of government the honor that belongs to God. He should not flatter them by calling them gracious, wise, or invincible as hypocrites in the world do, who bow and kneel
Dan.3:18 down before them. All honor belongs to God alone, who alone
Phil.2:10 is wise. It is to him that every knee shall bow. He gives his
Isa.48:11 glory to no one else, so neither should a Christian.

Concerning the Separation
of believing and unbelieving marriage partners

Gen.12:1

Scriptural basis for the church's position on divorce.

Abraham, a father of all believers, was called by God to leave his own country, his kinsmen, and his father's house. If his wife Sarah had refused to follow him, he would have had to separate from her or he could not have followed God. That is how it has to be if this should happen between married people.

Gen.19:14–16

Lot's sons-in-law did not believe him when he told them of the Lord's command to flee Sodom because he was going to destroy the city. They only laughed about it. Nonetheless Lot took his two daughters away from them and set out in obedience to the angels' command.

Rev.18:4–5

In the New Testament the voice from heaven gives the same command, "Go out of her [the great city], my people, lest you take part in her sins and are stricken by her plagues. Her sins have reached up to heaven, and God has remembered her wickedness." For the same reason the believing partner in a marriage has the right to leave so as not to become guilty of the sins of the world and of the unbelieving partner and thus receive the same punishment.

Deut.13:6–10

The Lord says, "If your brother, your mother's son, or your son or daughter, or the wife of your bosom, or your friend who is like your own soul, should secretly try to persuade you, saying, 'Let us go and serve other gods,' then you shall not consent. Your eye shall not grieve for him; you shall have no pity on him, but you shall put him to death. Your hand shall be the first to be raised to kill him, for he is trying to lead you astray from the Lord your God." Now if men had to stone and kill their wives if these tried to turn them away from God's law, how much more should we separate ourselves from them if they prove to be an obstacle to us.

The church's position on divorce.

Exod.34:12–16; Deut.7:3–4

In Israel, the people of the Old Testament, no man was allowed to marry an unbeliever, for the Lord spoke through Moses: "If you take the daughters of alien peoples for your sons or give your daughters to their sons, they will draw your sons away from the Lord and make them serve other gods. Then the Lord will be angry with you and will surely destroy you."

1 Kings 11:1–13

Solomon, the wisest of all kings, ignored this command, although it was well known to him. His foreign wives caused him to commit great folly and to suffer divine punishment, which brought about his downfall. In the same way King Ahab was led astray by Jezebel, his foreign wife, with the result that he followed the priests of Baal and allowed Baal worship. This shows that it is not right for the people of God to live with marriage partners of alien beliefs.

1 King 16:31–32

Ezra 9; 10:1–17; 1 Esd.9:1–17

In Ezra's time the people sinned against the Lord by taking foreign wives. When they turned again to the Lord, they had to separate from them and send them away, although they had taken them in marriage and had had children by them. Responsible men were appointed from the whole assembly to see to it that all those who had foreign wives separated from them.

Neh.13:23–27

There were Jews who had married women of Ashdod, Ammon, and Moab; half of their children spoke the language

The church's position on divorce.

of Ashdod, and they could not speak the language of Judah—the languages of other nations were heard among them. Nehemiah reviled and cursed them and beat some of them. He pulled out their hair and made them swear an oath in the name of God. He said to them, "Do not give your daughters to their sons, or take their daughters for your sons or for yourselves. Did not Solomon king of Israel sin in this way? There was no king like him among the heathen, and he was beloved by his God, yet foreign wives caused even this man to sin."

If the men of old treated this matter with such severity, regarding the covenant with God more highly than the bond with an unbelieving marriage partner, how much more should we Christians set the bond with God above the human bond of marriage. If we notice that the children's language is worldly and not Christian and they learn the evil ways of the world, we should advise separation from the unbelieving partner.

Matt.5:29–30; 18:8–9

Christ said, "If your hand or your foot causes you to sin, or your eye, tear it out and throw it from you; it is better for you to enter the kingdom of heaven maimed or lame or with one eye than to go with all your members into the eternal fire." He was not speaking of the members of our physical body. By hand, foot, and eye he meant those who are closest to us and important to us, and even if they are as essential as hands and eyes, still we must cut them off if they hinder our salvation. So if a wife hinders her husband and leads him into sin, or if a husband does this to his wife (for an unbelieving spouse can be a terrible stumbling block), and if no efforts help, then it is right for the believing partner to dismiss the unbeliever according to the Lord's Word.

Matt.5:31–32; 19:9
Mark 10:11–12; Luke 16:18

So that no one finds any cause to separate and leave [his marriage partner] except to preserve his soul, Christ also told us, "It was said, 'A man who dismisses his wife must give her a certificate of divorce.' But I tell you, if a man dismisses his wife for any reason other than adultery, he makes her an adulteress; and whoever marries a divorced woman commits adultery."

Matt.10:23

"If they persecute you in one town, take refuge in another. Truly, I tell you: you will not have gone through all the towns of Israel before the Son of man comes." A believer who is converted while living with an unbelieving spouse has this same freedom given by Christ. Such a believer has as much right as the partners in a believing marriage to flee from persecution and take refuge with fellow believers elsewhere.

The church's position on divorce.

Matt.10:34–38
Luke 12:51–53; Mic.7:6

Christ said, "Do not think that I have come to bring peace to this earth. I have not come to bring peace but a sword. I have come to set a man against his father, a daughter against her mother, a young wife against her mother-in-law; and a man's enemies will be the members of his household." Here we see that it is not our doing, but it is Christ and his Word that bring about such a conflict.

Then follows: "Whoever loves father or mother more than me is not worthy of me, and whoever loves son or daughter more than me is not worthy of me." Now the Ten Commandments tell us to love and honor father and mother as well as to uphold the marriage bond. It is just as natural to love one's children as to love one's wife. Yet he says, "Anyone who loves them more than me is not worthy of me. And anyone who does not take up his cross and follow me is not worthy of me."

Matt.19:6

Christ said, "What God has joined together, no man must separate." Here we must first consider whether a marriage was joined by God or according to the ways of the world. Many couples come together as fornicators; even if they are later married by a priest (who is usually of the same stamp), does that mean they are joined together by God? More often than not they are joined together by the evil one, who has power over such people. When people marry for money and possessions, are they joined together by God? Greed for money has brought them together. Be that as it may, when there is separation for the sake of faith in Christ and for the soul's salvation, then the marriage is not separated by man but by

Tob.6

The church's position on divorce.

Christ alone through his Word. In fact, although we speak of separation, the marriage is not dissolved when one partner leaves the other in this way. If after a time the other partner should follow and change his life, the marriage is then whole and unbroken. If it is not Christ's Word that brings about a separation but man, as often happens among the fornicators of this world, that is wrong. It is a sin also against the Ten Commandments.

Matt.19:29
Mark 10:29–30; Luke 18:29–30

Christ said, "Anyone who has left houses, brothers or sisters, father or mother, wife" (take note: *wife*) "or children, or fields for my name's sake will receive a hundredfold and will inherit eternal life." Take note: where in this passage is separation between marriage partners limited to adultery as the cause? In this case he does not even refer to adultery.

Luke 14:16–24

When Christ spoke about gathering his church, he said, "A man prepared a banquet and invited many guests. When it was time, he sent his servants to tell the guests, 'Come, the supper is ready.'" They began to excuse themselves—one because of his field, another because of his yoke of oxen, a third because of the wife he had just married—and said they could not come. What was the Lord's reply? He was angry with them and passed the terrible verdict that not one of them should taste his supper, let the world say what it will.

1 Cor.7:10–16

The apostle Paul wrote to the Corinthians, "For the married" (that is, if both partners are believers) "there is the command, not mine but the Lord's, that the wife should not separate from her husband. If she does, she must remain unattached or be reconciled to her husband. Nor should a husband divorce his wife."

And, as if speaking with sympathy and understanding for human weakness, since the problem may have arisen, he said, "I—and not the Lord—say to the others (not that I have a special command that the believing partner must stay with the unbelieving) that if any brother has an unbelieving wife who

The church's position on divorce.

is content to live with him, he should not separate from her." Paul (who claimed the Holy Spirit) was taught by the Holy Spirit that when one partner believes and the other does not, their situation is different from that of a believing couple—there may be some freedom allowed. Otherwise he would have held them to their marriage bond (as the Lord commanded for a believing couple) and would have said to the believer, "Since you have bound yourself to your spouse, you must remain together, come what may." But he did not say that. His advice makes the matter depend on willing consent. If there is such consent, the believer may remain. In other words, if the unbelieving wife wishes, her husband may remain with her as a believer, but he will be living a new and different life based on faith and following the Christian order for the education of their children and all areas of a Christian life. If she is happy with this and is not a hindrance to him, then, the apostle says, he should not leave her as long as there is a suitable place for them to live in the neighborhood of the church community. "And if a wife has an unbelieving husband, and he is pleased" (take note: *is pleased*) "to live with her, they should not separate." That is, as above, provided that the unbelieving husband is content to have his believing wife (who is now a sister) live with him according to her faith—that he allows her to listen to the Word of God, to remain among the faithful, to reject the world and whatever is against her conscience, to teach her children the way of God and not the way of the world (otherwise they would be impure), and whatever else her faith requires. If, then, the unbelieving husband is happy with this and does not mislead or oppose his wife, she should remain with him.

It follows that the believer is right in leaving her unbelieving husband if he does not show the willing consent of which Paul spoke, but tries in all kinds of deceitful ways to mislead his wife and make her lose faith—if he grumbles and storms at her, scolds her, slanders her, or mistreats her physically without respect or pity, or whisks their children off to be baptized and wants to bring them up in the ways of the world. Again, a spouse who is young in faith and is therefore not certain of standing the test (because of pressure from the authorities or for other reasons), and who does not have the courage to stay with the other spouse, is justified in separating. "In such cases,"

Paul said, "the brother or sister is not bound," as much as to say that the bond with God counts a thousand times more than the bond of marriage and our promise to God must be kept above all else. The bond of his peace must not be robbed of its strength. We must love God more than anything else, and neither heights nor depths nor any creature shall separate us from him. Therefore the apostle Paul speaks with great earnestness to a believing spouse who intends to live with an unbelieving one, saying, "Wife, how do you know if you will save your husband? Husband, how do you know if you will save your wife?" Are you sure that your patience and perseverance will win your partner for the faith? You might not only fail to win your partner but lose the way yourself, as has often been the case.

Isa.54:5
Matt.22:37
Luke 10:27

Rom.8:39

The church's position on divorce.

It is clear from all we have heard and from Christ's Gospel that the apostles and the early church also allowed separation from the unbelieving, resisting partner in a marriage. Therefore the present-day church, the little flock of Christ, is right in doing the same. Let the world and the false brothers criticize us all they want; that cannot be helped. A person who conforms to the world cannot be Christ's servant. A servant of Christ faces opposition on all sides. We are not in favor of one partner leaving the other, and we would never advise it without serious consideration. It is much better if both partners can submit to the Lord and together follow him in faith. But as faith is not granted to everyone, each person must do what he sees as right and let the other find his way. When Christ comes to judge the living and the dead, the husband will not be able to render an account for his wife, nor the wife for her husband. Each will have to answer for himself and carry his own burden.

James 4:4
Gal.1:10

Luke 1:6
Acts 28
1 Thess.3:2

Rom.14:12
Gal.6:5

2 Cor.6:14–18

Paul taught, "Do not work under an alien yoke with an unbeliever; for what does godliness have in common with ungodliness? What does light have in common with darkness? What understanding can there be between Christ and the devil? What can a believer share with an unbeliever? What similarity is there between the temple of God and idols? You are the temple of the living God, who said, 'I will live in them and move among them, and I will be their God and they shall be my people. Therefore come out from the other peoples and separate yourselves, and touch nothing unclean; then I will receive you, and I will be a father to you, and you shall be my sons and daughters, says the Lord Almighty.'" The believing spouse is certainly not excluded from this admonition to separate from unbelievers; it is addressed to him just as much as to other people.

The church's position on divorce.

If you say that this "coming out" is meant spiritually and not with the feet, you should know that anyone who leaves the world's wicked ways in spirit to become part of God's people will certainly not spare his feet; he will physically go to join them if he can. If he has made his choice in spirit and in truth, which is the greatest thing, he will surely not neglect the smallest, for they belong together. Just like Abraham, who left when he was called (though in his heart he had already left the Chaldeans and their idolatry), and like Lot, who left Sodom, so also the apostle left Ephesus because some were stubborn and did not believe but spoke evil of the way of the Lord. So he left them and separated his disciples from them. That is how it should be now so that God's people, the members of the body, remain whole.[1]

Gen.12:1–4 Heb.11:8
Gen.19
Acts 19

It seemed fitting to include above a thorough account of the chief articles of our faith, in order to show that it is not a new faith (a reproach frequently made against us by the world) but that this is the old faith and the teaching of Christ and his apostles, which the antichrist had twisted and suppressed. As a result, the so-called Christian world strayed further and further from the way and the truth in Christ Jesus.

The basis of our whole religion, teaching, and faith and all

---

[1]The above "Five Articles," *Die fünf Artikel des größten Streits zwischen uns und der Welt*, are generally considered to be the forerunner of Peter Walpot's work, the "Great Article Book" or *Ein schön lustig Büchlein, etliche Hauptartikel unseres christlichen Glaubens . . .*, written in 1577, possibly earlier. There is reason to believe that Peter Walpot was also the author of the above "Five Articles." For a discussion of both documents and the complete text of the "Great Article Book" in German, see Robert Friedmann, *Glaubenszeugnisse oberdeutscher Taufgesinnter, II, Quellen zur Geschichte der Täufer*, XII (Heidelberg, 1967), 49 ff.; Friedmann, *Schriften*, 129B, 143; for a translation of Article Three, see Friedmann, "A Notable Hutterite Document Concerning True Surrender and Christian Community of Goods," *MQR*, Jan. 1957, 22–62. See also *ME*, I, 173–174; Beck, 271 n.1; Leonard Gross, *The Golden Years of the Hutterites: The Witness and Thought of the Communal Moravian Anabaptists During the Walpot Era, 1565–1578* (Scottdale, PA, 1980), 200–204.

1547 the articles can be found in our *Confession of Faith*.[1] Therefore we now return to the history.

[1]*Die Rechenschaft vnserer Religion, Leer vnd Glaubens. P.R.*, the above-mentioned "Confession of Faith," was written by Peter Riedemann during his imprisonment in Wolkersdorf Castle (Hesse, Germany), 1540–1542. Part 2 is specifically noted as having been written in prison; Part 1 may have been written shortly after Riedemann's return to Moravia. See Gross, *Golden Years*, 196–197, 227 n.5.

While for many years scholars had merely assumed the existence of an early printing, in 1961 a copy of such an edition was discovered by J. ten Doomkaat Koolman in the Zurich Central Library (Sign. RP. 140, no date), printed before or around 1545 (originally belonging to the church historian Johann Heinrich Ott, 1617–1682); see *MQR*, April 1962, 169–170. A 1565 printing (British Museum, London, No. 3908a8) ends with the words: ". . .newly printed by Philips Vollanndt." The next edition appears in *Mittheilungen aus dem Antiquariat von S. Calvary*, Vol. I (Berlin, 1870). See Friedmann, *Schriften*, 91–92. The Hutterian Brethren published a semi-modernized German edition in 1902 (Berne, Indiana) and 1938 (England). An English translation was first published with the title, *Account of Our Religion, Doctrine, and Faith: Given by Peter Rideman of the Brothers Whom Men Call Hutterians* (London, 1950; 2nd ed. Rifton, NY, 1970, 1974; 3rd ed. in modernized English, in preparation). For further discussion of the *Rechenschaft*, see *ME*, IV, 259–261; Williams, *Radical Reformation*, 427–429; Franz Heimann, "The Hutterite Doctrine of Church and Common life: A Study of Peter Riedemann's Confession of Faith," *MQR*, Jan. 1952, 22–47; April 1952, 142–160.

1547–1553: The Second Great Persecution

That same year of 1547 the church had increased greatly in number. The Lord was gathering his people and giving them places of shelter—communities were established in Schakwitz, Poppitz, Pausram, Gobschitz, Bochtitz, Rakschitz near Mährish Kromau, Hrubschitz, Eibenschitz, Gurdau, Pawlowitz, Boretitz, Bisenz, Wessely, Bohuslawitz, Butschowitz, Austerlitz, Pulgram, Rakwitz, Saitz, Kostel, Bilowitz, Altenmarkt, Lundenburg, Göding, Tscheikowitz, and a few other places. Satan could not stand this for long. Out of the depths of his envy he made evil insinuations, just as he had done to Job, and said it was easy for believers to be godly because they lived together.

Where the believers were living before the great persecution.

So, since God permitted him, Satan continually inflamed that viper's brood of priests, who worked on King Ferdinand with their persistent complaints, while other ungodly folk came to him repeatedly with lying indictments. Roused to bitter anger, the king issued a stern mandate that his people were not to tolerate believers in the land but were to drive all of them out on pain of losing royal favor and incurring severe disgrace and punishment.[1]

The priests continually incited the king, fanning the embers to a flame.

---

[1]Regarding the numerous imperial and provincial mandates that affected the Anabaptists in Austria and Moravia, see Beck, 177–180; Johann Loserth, *Der Communismus der Mährischen Wiedertäufer im 16. und 17. Jahrhundert* (Vienna, 1894), 161–166. See J. Kühn, ed., *Deutsche Reichsakten unter Kaiser Karl V*, VII (1935), for a full discussion of King Ferdinand's persecution of Anabaptists in 1527–1529; *ME*, III, 446–453, for an extended but not complete list of mandates and decrees published against Anabaptists and other heretics; *Mennonitisches Lexikon*, I (Frankfurt am Main, 1913), 201–209, "Bestrafung der Täufer."

The Diet at Brno, Laetare Monday, March 16, 1545, yielding to pressure by Ferdinand I, decreed that all Anabaptists living in community had to leave Moravia by St. Kunigund's Day [March 3, 1546]. A subsequent Diet at Brno, May 19, 1545, and the king's decree of March 26, 1546, reinforced that decision and demanded the expulsion of all Anabaptists: those living communally, by St. James's Day [July 25] 1546, the rest, by St. George's Day [April 23] 1547. The lords had opposed these measures because they deprived them of their best workers, to the detriment of the country. Ferdinand was not swayed, however, and by an order issued from Augsburg on the Wednesday after Easter, 1548, demanded the immediate expulsion of all Anabaptists. By a further decree of May 5, 1548 (Zieglschmid, *Chronik*, 317 n., gives this date; Loserth and Beck note this or another mandate issued three

1547

Since the lords of Moravia had forfeited the freedom God had given to Moravia for the sake of his believers, they were no longer able to resist either king or emperor. The king had worked behind their backs, and at the Diet of Brünn in mid-Lent [March] 1545 the decision had been made that unless we gave up gathering in communities, we were to be expelled from Moravia. They said that only five to seven persons should live in one household. Because of our beliefs, however, we could not comply with that.[1] Their prohibitions were a cunning attempt to steal our hearts and make us their slaves.

Decision of the Diet that only 5 to 7 of us should live in one household.

However, matters did not become serious for us for a year or more, until 1547, when the emperor Charles [Charles V], King Ferdinand's brother,[2] gained control over the kingdom,

---

days later, May 8), the Anabaptists were expelled from the whole of Austria and fled to Moravia, where they hid in the caves of the Pollau Mountains (see above, p.226 n.). About two weeks before Easter, 1549, the authorities, aware of the Anabaptists' return, renewed the May 1548 order of expulsion, giving the refugees till St. John's Day [May 6] 1550 to leave Moravia.

The Moravian lords were thus compelled to take action against the Anabaptists, in some cases against their own better judgment. Nevertheless, there remained a large number of Hutterites in Moravia under the protection of individual lords and nobles. New Hutterite communities were built up: in 1550 at Damborschitz; in 1553 at Schadowitz and Gobschitz; see below, pp.315 and 318.

[1]Community of goods, as mentioned before in this chronicle, was one of the basic tenets of the Hutterian Brethren, based on John 1:32–51, 17:6–26; Acts 2:44–47, 4:32–37; Rom.8:6; Eph.4:4; etc. It is still practiced today by their communities in Canada, the United States, England, and Japan.

[2]The following diagram may help to provide some historical background.

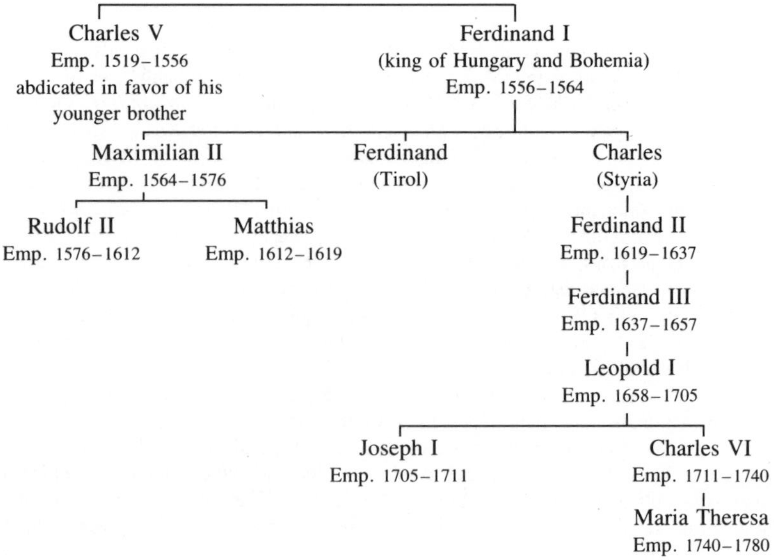

1547

and Duke Elector Hans of Saxony [John Frederick I] was taken prisoner. The lords had hoped the kingdom would win, as we would then have been left in peace. But as soon as Duke Hans was in prison, it was: Out! Out with us! Everywhere, the Moravian lords ordered us to leave their estates on short notice, taking with us the young and the old, the weak and the sick. We were not allowed to stay anywhere. We had to leave one place after another, until we were almost at our wits' end. There was great distress, misery, and need wherever we went. We called upon God and asked him, if his will was for us to remain together, to show us which way to go in our need and to care for those who trust in him but are deserted by everyone else.

Tribulation lasting 5 years began. Severe in Moravia and Hungary. In 1552 the people gradually began to gather again.

Then the Lord in his mercy showed us a way out, for we were accepted in Hungary (at that time this country was not well known to us), especially by Lord Franz Niáry of Branc Castle,[1] and we gradually moved onto his land. We were also received by Lord Peter Bakisch at Holitsch and Schossberg, with our sick people and children and all our belongings.[2] Communities were established at Sabatisch, Gunowe, Holitsch, Sdräse, Protzka, Egbell, Petersdorf, Toytsch, Senitz, Rabenska, Gätte, and Gutta.[3] Everything had first to be built and set up, and many wild stretches of land had to be cleared and plowed if the believers wished to live there and house their sick people

Moved into Hungary, but not for long.

---

[1]Count Franz Niáry of Bedek, manorial lord at Bisenz (Bzenec), Moravia, and co-owner of Branc-Sabatisch, Hungary (see above, p.245), had allowed the Hutterites to settle at Sabatisch in 1546, near Branc Castle. At Bisenz, where a community had existed since 1545 (see above, p.239), Count Niáry had become well acquainted with the brothers. See also Beck, 179.

[2]Within months Peter Bakisch de Lák, owner of Holitsch (Holíč) and Schossberg (Šaštín), was to become one of the fiercest opponents of the brothers, although at first he offered privileges to those who settled on his estates. In 1554 he divided his property with the heirs of Czobor, who are mentioned several times in this chronicle after 1616; see Index under Czobor.

[3]All places named were at that time part of Hungary, now Slovakia. Sabatisch (Sobotište); Gunowe (Kunov), south of Sabatisch; Holitsch (Holíč), southeast of Göding (Hodonín), Moravia; Sdräse (Stráže), on the Myjava River opposite Schossberg (Šaštín) (Schossberg and Sdräse are now one town: Šaštín-Stráže); Protzka (Brodské), north of Gätte (Kúty), on the Morava River; Egbell (Gbely), roughly halfway between Holitsch and Schossberg; Petersdorf (Petrova Ves) north of Sdräse; Toytsch (Dojč) on the Myjava River, west of Senitz; Senitz (Senica), east of Schossberg; Rabenska (Rovensko), halfway between Sabatisch and Senitz, where the community was burned down on November 21, 1623 (see below, p.704); Gätte and Gutta possibly the village and town with the same name, Kúty, near the confluence of the Morava and Myjava rivers.

1547

and children. These lords were well pleased to see the work of clearing, cutting, and building, and they were very obliging. But that did not last long, as will soon be seen.

1548–1549

Hans Greckenhofer and Hans Mändel taken prisoner.

In 1548 brother Hans Greckenhofer, a servant of the Word, and Hans Mändel, also called Klein Hansel (short Hansel), reached Rodeneck in the Adige region and were put in chains in a dungeon for eleven weeks. They were cruelly tortured and racked to make them reveal who had given them shelter, but they refused. They would betray no one, friend or enemy, so their torturers got nowhere and had to give up. The brothers were taken back to prison and told to think the matter over, for in two days they would be questioned further. But they commended their cause to God, determined to remain steadfast, whatever he might do with them. Meanwhile they escaped with the help of a wet nurse, who afterward traveled back to the church with them.

Hans Gentner passed away.

At this time, in 1548, brother Hans Gentner passed away at Schakwitz in Moravia. He was a faithful servant of God's Word and his church, and after suffering many tribulations and struggles for the sake of the Lord, he fell asleep in the Lord with peace in his heart.

4 brothers chosen for the service of the Word.

Not long afterward, at Holitsch in Hungary, the following brothers were chosen for the service of God's Word and appointed: brother Kaspar Braitmichel from Silesia, Hans Schmidt from Raiffach in Tirol, Hans Plattner (or Wimmer), and Kaspar Klaindopf or Schmidt (a smith). Fabian Fitz was also among their number, but his service did not last. He was soon revealed and excluded.

14 brothers appointed stewards.

At the same time fourteen brothers were chosen and appointed as servants for temporal affairs or stewards. They were:

Matthias Gasser	Kaspar Tischler
Christoph Lenck	Paul Schuster
Kaspar Ebner	Crisant Schuster
Jörg Ladendorffer	Abraham Schneider (or Ulstüber)
Thoman Schmidt	Valtin Hess or Schneider (a tailor)
Bastel Wardeiner	Hans Seckler
Andreas Gauper for the second time	Rupp Hess

1548-1549

As has been said, we were ordered to leave Moravia in 1548, while Leonhard Lanzenstiel was elder. Under King Ferdinand, the church of God in Moravia was severely persecuted and oppressed. And when the believers resettled in Hungary as described, this came to his notice, and he twice commanded the Hungarian lords sternly not to harbor the brothers but to expel them from the country.[1] These lords, fearing the king's disfavor, refused to let the brothers stay any longer.

King commanded the Hungarian lords to expel the brothers.

Peter Bakisch in particular wreaked his fury on them; he spared no one, neither the old nor the sick nor little children.[2] They were threatened and given short notice: in three days everyone had to be gone. Anyone still found there would see what would happen to him. Guards were posted to stop the believers from taking too much with them. They were ungodly folk, who day and night did everything they could to steal food from the faithful and anything else that took their fancy. They had no compassion.

Peter Bakisch's cruelty in Hungary.

Peter Bakisch sent peasants to cut wood, bring it in front of the brothers' houses, and build gallows right outside their doors as if about to hang them, especially those who did not move away fast enough. The brothers suffered much abuse of this sort.

Gallows built outside our doors.

Their persecutors did not even wait for the allotted days to end but used violence against the sick and old, the bent and crippled. The believers were forced into the forest, even in the cold of wintertime, to live like wild animals. If only they had been allowed to do this unmolested, they would have been happy. But there was no sparing of anyone, no mercy for the old and gray, for expectant or nursing mothers and their babies. They had to go out into the unknown.

No mercy shown to the old, to expectant or nursing mothers, or to little babies.

The treatment was so cruel that it would have been too rough for cattle, yet these people had not harmed anyone and were innocent of any crime. They were punished only on account of their faith and the truth of God and because they

---

[1]An edict dated May 16, 1548, prohibited the giving of sanctuary to Anabaptists fleeing from Moravia; a mandate of June 15, 1548, ordered the expulsion of all Anabaptists from Hungary; see Beck, 180–181; *ME*, III, 449.

[2]Such harsh measures as Peter Bakisch employed against the brothers were the exception in Hungary, where as a rule King Ferdinand's orders of 1548 received only slight attention.

1548-1549
Dan.3

We suffered much from plundering.

rejected the pope's ordinances and his idolatry and refused to worship the image of the Babylonian king.

The believers had to suffer in every way. People carried off their possessions. They were robbed and plundered on all sides. They had to abandon houses and farm buildings, vineyards and arable land, and whatever they had in field or village on Bakisch's estates. What was inside the houses was all stolen, including food and drink. No one hesitated to rob them—not a man or woman, old person or child held back. Their one aim was to lay hands on the believers' goods in village, field, and wood. They robbed them out on the highway, taking not only horses, cows, and other stock, but even their clothes.

It was on October 3, 1548, soon after Michaelmas, that all the believers were ordered out of Hungary. They had to leave everything—their land, a great deal of grain, wine, livestock, and tools. Yet, had it been a hundred or even two hundred times as much, they would not have thought twice about it and would have abandoned everything rather than forsake God and their faith.

They chased children from their meal.

They chased the infirm out of their beds.

The children had just sat down for supper and given thanks to God for food and drink when these ungodly men came and forced them from the table. The food stood there until the following day. The weak had to get out of bed or were thrown out. That was the mean kind of thing that was done. The believers begged them humbly and urgently to have some pity for the children, just till the next day, because it was already night. But no pleading was of any avail. The answer was, "Get out! Go! Get out of the house and leave no one behind. That is Lord Bakisch's order." They showed no more pity for them than animals might have done. They had lost all trace of human feeling. It hurts the name of Christ when such people call themselves Christians.

Food left on the stove, dough in the trough.

The people were just about to have their evening meal, but their enemies would not wait for them. The food was left standing on the stove and in the kitchen, the bread was left in the oven, the dough in the trough. Such was the violence and cruelty of these godless scoundrels, even a stone would have been moved to pity.

The cruel rabble even wanted to rob the believers of their

children, their own flesh and blood, guarding them so that none would be taken away. But the brothers managed to load the little children into two boats and tried to get them away by water in the dark of night. They had not gone far before the wicked crowd realized what was happening. They hurried after, turned the boats around, and brought them back to land. Then the poor children were left sitting on the bank a long time, suffering from the wind and the cold while their persecutors jeered at them, saying they ought to be sweating. Such was their cruelty. The night was bitter, and the children suffered terribly as they sat there together shivering, their teeth chattering with cold.

1548-1549
They even wanted to rob us of our children.

They mocked the children in the bitter cold.

Bakisch also sent hussars, who went into the house, took some brothers prisoner in front of their wives, and carried them off to the castle at Schossberg. All that Bakisch and his people did, all their cunning, lying, and cruelty, cannot be told. It was pitiable what suffering the believers had to go through on account of their little children.

Bakisch had some brothers arrested.

They all left together and reached the March River by night. They crossed over by boat and camped in the woods.[1] They were not left in peace there either. Robbers soon arrived, going up and down through the camp and taking anything that pleased their fancy. The believers had to look on, helpless, for the robbers were given the freedom of birds of the air to take what they wanted. So the believers set out once more. They had gone just half a mile further into the wood when the judge came in haste and told them to leave at once, since his superior, Lord Veldsberger, would not have them there.

No peace even in the wood.

Driven out of the wood too.

So they had no place to stay and no house to live in; their lot was distress, oppression, and violence. They were as worthless rubbish to everybody, continually on the move without knowing where to go. They put their hope in God alone, knowing he would help them in his own time if they held out.

Lord Franz Niáry of Branc, already mentioned, also sent his captain with strict orders in writing that in accordance with King Ferdinand's decree, he was to drive the brothers out of

Even Lord Franz Niáry of Branc expelled them.

---

[1]Near Rohatetz (Rohatec) on the Morava River, halfway between Göding (Hodonín) and Strassnitz (Strážnice). In 1548 Rohatetz was the property of the Zerotin family as part of the Strassnitz estate. Beck, 182.

1548-1549

all his estates in Hungary and Moravia. The captain called the brothers without delay, showed them the order his lord had sent, and said there was no choice: they all had to move out. He would help them by giving them an escort of mounted men and footsoldiers as far as the border to safeguard them on the way.

So these set out too, facing the same misery—old and young, adults and children, sick and well. They, too, were given no time to get ready but had to leave straightaway and traveled as far as the March River. The first night they camped out in the open near Strassnitz. Then the next day they crossed the March and joined their brothers, the other group already living in the woods a mile from Strassnitz on the Moravian border. Day and night, for five weeks, they lived in the woods with their wives and children, widows and orphans, the sick, the young and the old, like the animals that live in the wild. During this time they met with much violence and injury. Robbers stripped many of them naked, and one brother was even murdered in the woods.

Out in the woods for 5 weeks in wintertime.

Robbers stripped many naked.

The brotherhood sent many brothers abroad to see if they could find a home, but word came back saying they had found nothing.[1] Yet they could not remain in the woods; the bitter cold forced them to look for shelter.

Then the elders spoke comfortingly to the people and exhorted them to hold fast to God and his truth until death, as the saints had done from the beginning through all persecutions and hardships, for the world had treated them in the same way. This is what Christ said: "If they have persecuted me, they will persecute you." And: "You must be hated by all men for my name's sake." "If anyone wants to be my follower, let him take up his cross." And the apostle says, "All who desire to live a godly life in Christ Jesus must suffer persecution." "We must go through many troubles to reach the kingdom of God." In other words, persecution is the true

Heb.11:33–39

John 15:20

Matt.10:22; 24:9

Matt.16:24

2 Tim.3:12

Acts 14:22

[1] "They gathered in the woods near Rohatetz. . . . From there they sent four brothers to Poland. These were Hans Plattner (or Wimmer), Thoman Schmidt, Ott the older, and Leonard Stuck, who were to look for a place where the believers would find shelter. They traveled as far as Walachia [southern Romania], and could not find any place where the devout could settle. . . . Then they sent four brothers to the mountains—Bohemian Kaspar [Seidelman], Andreas Gauper, the old Hans Münich from Rotenburg, and Leonard Stuck—to search for a place where the believers could live, but they were unsuccessful." See Beck, 182–184, for more detail.

1548-1549

sign of the disciples of Christ and people of God. With these and many other comforting words the elders encouraged the people to put their trust in God.

They separated into little groups and left the woods.

When they could no longer maintain themselves in the woods, the elders divided the people into little groups of ten or twelve, as many as could find shelter in one house. Each group was entrusted to one brother, who was to go with them and look for work, and they had to find food where they could. So they had to part from one another and scatter. That was what caused them the greatest distress of all. If it had been God's will, they would rather have suffered death than scatter and go without meetings and the Word of God. But there was no other way, so they agreed and took leave of one another, many being unable to speak for weeping. The tears ran down their cheeks as they shook hands, blessed one another over and over again, put themselves in God's hands, and set out, each group in a different direction. Misery was their lot.

Separating was their greatest distress.

Returned to Moravia in little groups in great privation. Driven from one place to another.

They returned to Moravia, from where they had been expelled. They were in grave danger and suffered severely, fleeing as they were driven from place to place. There was great distress and misery on account of their sick and old people, their helpless little children, their lame and blind. They could find no place to stay but spent one night here, one there, always hungry and thirsty.

Nights spent under hedges in the snow.

Some had to spend nights under hedges in the snow. They would have been glad to be with cows and hogs in barns if only they had been allowed there. They would have lifted their hands and thanked God. But there was no place for them in field or village. They praised God, held to truth and godliness, and, though driven here and there, did not lose heart all that long winter.

House and shelter forbidden us in Moravia.

We were refused house and home because the governor of Moravia had forbidden the people to give us lodging, for King Ferdinand, incited by the priests, continued to threaten us severely. He intimidated the landed gentry and anyone else whose heart might otherwise have been moved to pity for our poor, needy people.

Heard abuse and contempt that cut us to the heart.

Over and above all this we had to endure a great deal from the world and from false brothers (comfortably settled on their property with house and farm), who also tried to make us waver. Wherever we went we had jeers and taunts shouted at

1548-1549

us. One said, "You wretches, who do you think you are? Do as other folk do, and then you can stay."

Another said, "Your suffering is not for God's sake—it is all because you are so stiff-necked and obstinate."

Others said, "There is no sense in what you do. It is just some idea of your own, and you have been misled."

Some abused us as hopeless heretics and scoundrels and said, "It serves them right—that is just how they should be dealt with. We have been waiting for this for ages. They should be beheaded, hanged, drowned, or burned."

Many said, "Where is your God that he does not come to help you?"

Some mocked when they saw us in great misery and said, "Where is your God; why doesn't he take care of you since you are so pious? Let him help you, let him get you out of this."

Others said, "Aren't you great fools? If you were in the right, wouldn't the emperor and kings and their scholars and other educated men agree with you?" In short, on top of our hardships we had to hear every kind of taunt.

Persecution did not slacken. Many discouraged and unfaithful.

Then many grew disheartened, weakened, and beaten down, and so they deserted God and the truth. They could not remain steadfast on the rough path in this wilderness but preferred the pleasures of sin and the world to the suffering of evil with God's people and bearing the shame of Christ. These were the ones who had been superficial and lax and had not served God in earnest while they lived in the house of the Lord during good times. They were unable to hold out and could not disguise it. They had to go, like chaff that cannot stay with the good wheat against the force of the wind. Of those whose hearts were impure, who had burdened themselves with sins, not one held out to the end. They grew weak and weary. The weaklings, those who were unable and unwilling to suffer for God's sake but who were ready to bring suffering on themselves for the devil's sake, let worldly happiness and the favor of the devil win them over. Their folly will bring them to a horrible end.

Yet many remained steadfast and were not moved from the way of truth, even though hardships of every shape and form put them to the test. They were robbed and beaten countless times, stripped of their clothing, and whatever they had was taken from them again and again. They were not safe anywhere. People whom they had trusted to keep things locked away for them seized what they pleased, even while the brothers were

Robbed and beaten countless times.

sheltering in their houses. This period of deep distress lasted several years without a break. Even then it did not end but grew worse, as follows.

1548-1549

1550

In 1550 a general Diet was held in Brünn in Moravia, to which King Ferdinand himself came from Vienna with many cavalrymen. When he heard that the brothers were still moving about the country like pilgrims, his orders were as ruthless as before. Anyone who did not comply and drive these people out of the land would incur serious punishment and the displeasure of the king. Petitioning would be useless; this sect must be driven out of all the king's lands. He gave them a short time—until St. John the Baptist's Day [June 24]—to prepare, but then they would have to leave.

King Ferdinand came to the Diet at Brünn.

This was proclaimed throughout the land. The following decree was nailed to town hall doors up and down the country: All Anabaptists (the dear brothers and sisters) were given notice to leave the country by St. John the Baptist's Day. By decree: His Majesty the Holy Roman Emperor.

By St. John's Day the brothers had to be out of the country.

When the time was running out, the lords started to evict any who were still on their land. So the persecution gathered force, and there were still fewer places where they could find rest or shelter. The foxes have holes and the birds of the air have nests, but the believers had no place at all in those days.

Now there was a wicked miller who had come to Moravia a short while before. His wife had become a believer and joined us there. When he saw that everyone was free to attack the brothers (for God had delivered them into their hands), he used his wife as an excuse for stopping any believer he met, robbing and beating him without mercy. So in him Satan gained a useful tool.

He roamed up and down the countryside, stealing wherever he could. He unharnessed horses from wagons, feeling sure that he would meet no resistance. He was not afraid to vent his fury, for no one raised a hand to help the believers. People looked on and tolerated it all. They were so godless that they allowed the man free rein. He continued like this for a long time, until he died.

A miller stole horses and anything he could.

The miller was allowed free rein to rob.

1550
The little groups had to divide still further.

Since the enemy now had the upper hand, people no longer tolerated large groups of believers in the houses. They were ordered to divide up still further and did so with great pain.

Everyone who gave them shelter put them to work for his own profit and exploited them in all possible ways. The believers would have borne it all thankfully, if only to find shelter for their children and their old and sick. But it was not enough; the persecution raged on. Houses were searched frequently to see if the believers were really out. People were strictly forbidden to harbor them lest they themselves be taken immediately to the lords and judges. To prevent the faithful from finding any place at all to stay, some householders were imprisoned or fined for sheltering them.

Houses searched to make sure the brothers had all left.

Some people put in prison for giving shelter.

Many of the believers then had to stay away from houses and flee to the woods and mountains in the cold of winter. They dug holes in the earth to live in, like foxes.[1] Hard as such conditions were, they would have endured it all thankfully if only they had been left alone. But even there they were soon hunted down.

They fled to the woods, mountains, and holes underground.

At Poppitz, where believers were living in holes underground, some godless men built a fire at the entrance and tried to suffocate them or smoke them out, but they were stopped and driven away. Thieving gangs would chase believers out of thickets and woods and force them to move on. Around the Mayberg[2] many lived with their children in holes among the bushes for a time. They also lived in rocky crevasses and caves in the Mayberg cliffs and in other similar places in Moravia, wherever they could.

Attempts made to smoke them out.

Around the Mayberg many lived in holes and among the rocks.

At Gätte in Hungary there were still about 250 children in one household, as well as sick and old, lame and blind. Their brothers in the area supplied them with food, sending them bread, in keeping with brotherly love. But the marshal there drove the brothers away, forbidding them to take anyone away by water or land; they should keep clear of the marshal's

[1]See *ME*, III, 382–384, for an article about these "holes," called *Lochy* by the Slovakian population. They form a maze of subterranean passages and rooms in large parts of southern Moravia and appear to have been built according to a unified plan, showing identical design and measurements. It can be assumed that many of these were made by the Hutterites. See Appendix 5; see also Beck, 184–186.

[2]See above, p.226 n.

estates.[1] It was proclaimed in the town square that none should have any dealings with us. Guards were set at the [town] gates to prevent any brother from entering. If a man identified himself as a brother, he had to stay out. All shelter in house or farm was barred to him, and there was to be no mercy.

1550
Publicly announced that we must leave.

A group made camp by the waterside and put up tents, but the marshal's men drove them away and set fire to the camp so that the faithful would have nowhere to go. The men even destroyed their oven to deprive them of bread as well. There was no end to fear and need for the poor little flock. Like owls, they could not go anywhere in the daytime. People shook their heads when they saw them. They were a laughingstock. Everybody shouted at them, mocked them, and chased them off.

Their camp set on fire.

Not allowed to travel by day.

When Peter Bakisch returned from Augsburg (where he had been at the time), he sent his hussars with the royal decree that every brother was to get ready to leave the community at Gätte in Hungary, where a number were still living. The king's men were coming to search the house, and so the brothers should soon be off with young and old, or else they would be forcibly evicted.[2]

At Gätte, Bakisch started persecuting them again.

Once again they faced fear and heartbreak. They were stopped at every turn. No one was allowed to give them shelter, although there were so many sick people and children. The ungodly crowd did not wait long. They came at night, surrounded the house, and drove old and young out into the cold. Their cruelty, violence, and malice knew no bounds; even a stone would have been moved to pity. They dragged sick people out of bed. They shrank from nothing and even took the clothes from a corpse. There was no end to the stealing.

The sick were dragged out of bed.

As already told, they came by night, drove the brothers out, caught some who were still in bed, chained their feet and necks with irons, and forced them to the courthouse. They locked

Several brothers arrested, locked up, and attempts made to burn them.

---

[1]Marshal Pertolt of Lipé, lord of Mährisch Kromau (Moravský Krumlov) and Göding (Hodonín), the latter including the villages of Gurdau (Kurdějov), Kobelitz (Kobylí), Pawlowitz (Pavlovice), Rakwitz (Rakvice), Saitz (Zaječí), Schakwitz (Šakvice), and others, where the brothers had settled. See Zeman, *Topography*, under the above names.

[2]A 68-verse song by Michael Kramer in *LdHBr*, 166–175, confirms the above account, in part word for word. Kaspar Braitmichel's song, pp. 175–178, refers to the same period.

1550

Sisters' hair pulled to make them carry the children outside.

some in a hen house and thrust fire in to burn them up. They used many torturer's methods, tied the brothers' hands behind their backs and racked them. They pulled the sisters' hair to compel them to carry the sick people and children outside, for they did not want a single one left in the house by morning, or they would all be burned. The sisters boldly refused. They said they feared God and would rather die than carry children and sick people out of the house in such cold weather—it might cost them their lives, and the sisters did not want to be responsible for their deaths. Their blood would cry aloud to God.

Children and sick carried out of the house.

Many of the sick died of cold.

An ungodly mob rushed in, only too eager to carry the sick and children out into the cold. Women and men came running and searched every corner of the house, each one keen to take away more than the next. So there they were, out in the open. The sick suffered so badly from cold and exposure that many died.

Sisters seized by the hair to force them to move the sick elsewhere.

As if that were not enough, even in the open they did not leave the sick in peace. They ran through the camp trying to set it on fire, drew their sabers and dealt hard blows with them, took sisters by the hair again and tried to make them carry the sick still further. Then the pitiable little flock of the faithful set out once again, although the night was very dark and they had to cross a deep river. This happened in the cold wintertime early in 1550.

Tribulation in Hungary and Moravia.

The devil could not have had better tools and servants to serve him.

So it was that God's people were terribly persecuted all over Hungary and Moravia. It is impossible to tell all that those who loved God had to suffer for the sake of righteousness. In his malice and envy the devil, that enemy of the truth, aroused those who were full of his spirit. There he found such ready tools, such violent and ruthless servants, that he could have wished for none more zealous than these, day and night, for they gave up sleep so as not to miss anything.

Lord von Liechtenstein at Nikolsburg hung a brother head downward from a castle window.

A certain brother wished to visit his wife at Nikolsburg. When he arrived at the castle, where she was nursing the governor's wife, he was taken to Lord von Liechtenstein, who angrily commanded him to renounce his faith and the brotherhood—their cause was in vain and had to be rooted out. But he was not intimidated. Even when they threatened to torture him, he refused to recant. So they threw him on the ground, tied his feet together, and hung him head down out of a high window—a heartrending sight.

He was in such intense pain that his only wish was that they would let him fall to the ground and put an end to his life, but he had to hang until he no longer even looked like a man. Then, before he was dead, they pulled him in. The lord in his rage ordered his servants (to express it with decency) to cut off the private member from the man's body. But one of his servants said he had never seen such a thing done. That was work for a hangman, not for them. At this the tyrant himself took the knife and would have cut and wounded this brother, but his nobles protested so much that he stopped. "It will bring disgrace to you throughout the country if it is talked about," they said. But what can one say? Such people know no shame.

1550

Inhuman, devilish behavior.

When this maniac learned that the brothers were living in caves and underground holes on his estates, he planned terrible things: to stab the brothers to death and to violate the women and rob them of their honor. But God in his might protected his people and foiled the tyrant's plans, for they heard of them and got away.[1]

Lord von Liechtenstein's vile and cruel plans.

1551

In 1551 all work was forbidden to the brothers in many parts of Moravia, with severe penalties for disobedience. No one was to sell them anything either. This was to hasten their departure. So they had to make do with what they had laid by in peaceful times, because they could not earn anything anymore.

Forbidden in Moravia to give us work or sell us anything.

In addition, prices rose. One peck of grain cost a gulden, in some places more, and this lasted into the following year. Now many were tested by hunger and distress; some had hardly one meal in a week or two or even longer. Even dry bread was hard to get. Yet they gave thanks to God and accepted it all. They raised their hands in praise to God that they had any food at all and clear water to drink as well. When they had bread and had water into which to break it, they were living well, and they were glad to work when they had work.

Prices rose as well.

Want and hunger. Gratitude of the faithful in tribulation.

In this time of want many people pretended to be friendly and promised good wages if the brothers would work for them. Then they would withhold the money earned and send the brothers away empty-handed.

Many who worked received no wages.

---

[1]See Beck, 186–189, for accounts of the above events.

1551

There was a place called Pulgram on the Nikolsburg estates where the believers were out of danger for a time, so those who were physically weak took refuge there: the lame, those with leprosy and other illnesses, also mothers and their newborn babies, who usually have everyone's sympathy. But it was not to last.

A scoundrel robbed the brothers at Pulgram.

That same year a butcher named Kontheer came from Austria. His wife, who was from Hesse, came with him, and he wanted to track down the brothers on her account, for her former husband had been with us in Moravia. He gathered a rabble round him, utterly ruthless like himself. All he wanted was to make himself rich at the expense of those who were poor. He had no justifiable cause, but the hate kindled in his heart by Satan drove him to do evil.

First he told lies to the nobles, passing on information with no truth in it. As a result he got permission and did not rest until he reached Pulgram with his followers and attacked the brothers' shelter there. None were spared. They stole from all whatever they wanted—from the sick, the children, and the infirm—not even the mothers with newborn babies or the crippled were spared. Neither friendliness nor entreaty had any effect. They took whatever they could. In the dark night they dragged the sick and bedridden out of bed and took away the sheets they lay on. They took bread and drove hogs and other livestock away. Nothing that was said to them was received with respect. In a short time all of the poor little flock were driven out into the woods, where they camped for some time.

Mothers with newborn babies not spared.

Took the bedclothes from under them.

Drove them into the woods.

More scoundrels soon arrived, planning to steal from the brothers. The robbers waited in the bushes during the day so as to get at their victims quickly when night came and no one could stop them.

Robbers drowned a brother in the Thaya at Pulgram.

The robbers met a brother named Jakob Binder not far from the camp. They treated him brutally, for his screams could not be heard and there was no one to see. They robbed him and threw him in the Thaya River. Then they went and robbed the others.

This was what happened to the poor, the infirm, the sick, and the mothers with newborn babies—to anyone who was weak.

In this time of deep suffering many of the faithful crossed over into Austria in little groups and tried to find work, food, and shelter. Some traveled a long way, north of Retz near the Danube. They went to many places, one group here, another there. In Austria they were occasionally given work and a place to stay. But the devil's envy did not let them prosper long. That year, 1551, a man called Lang Hans was placed in office and came as a provost in the name of the king. He rode around Austria and inquired where the brothers were. He searched in many villages and listed householders who had lodged them, threatening to report them to the king in Vienna. He scared them into giving him gifts, which became his profit. The faithful had no choice but to leave. Even in the woods they could not stay hidden for long.

1551
Many little groups went to Austria.

The provost drove them back into Moravia.

So again they were driven out of Austria into Moravia, since no one was ready to face danger and harm because of them. They left their belongings in many inns, but their trust was betrayed, and some things were stolen. Some innkeepers who had given them shelter kept things as a compensation in case they were punished for lodging them.

Two more men came in 1551 all the way from Upper Austria. They had previously wanted to become brothers, especially old Hans Bader's son. Now all they wanted was to rob. They went from one place to another, showing a letter of authorization from the king. With two companions to help them, they appeared before the judge and were well pleased when he gave them his support.

Many of our possessions had been given to a certain Festel to store in his house at Schakwitz. In broad daylight these rogues broke in and made off with it all. No one resisted them. The judge, who should have put a stop to it, was on their side. Most of the booty was put in his house overnight. But this thieving was stopped, for God would not permit it. He roused people in other places, who took the matter in hand when they heard of such injustice. One of the robbers escaped, but the others were arrested for their impudent wickedness and taken to the castle at Göding. There they were held for a long time, to their great annoyance. So they were put out of action and their spite counted for nothing. God prevented them from carrying out their evil intentions.

At Schakwitz they robbed us of goods stored in a house.

1551
2Esd.16:70–75

Certainly, the prophet spoke the truth when he said, "In all the neighboring places there will be a violent attack on all who fear the Lord. They will be like doves; not one will be spared. Their enemies will plunder and destroy all who fear the Lord. They will take their goods and drive them out of their homes. Then it will be known who my faithful people are, who have stood the test like gold in the assayer's fire. 'Listen, my beloved,' says the Lord, 'understand that the days of harsh suffering are here, but I will rescue you. Away with your fears and doubts, for God is your leader!'" And truly God rescued his people and led them, otherwise not one would have been left. They would have been swallowed up like water on dry earth. But God upheld them and protected their faith.

All who fear God will be plundered, destroyed, and driven out of their houses.

Wisd.of Sol.5:15–16

After this, the faithful still had to wander from place to place in want and suffering. Provincial Diets were held, and every lord made sure that the brothers left his land because the king had decreed it and they feared his threats. They had no wish to incur royal disfavor, and so they carried out the royal mandate, although they themselves had often said that this was a God-fearing people and what they believed was the truth. The lords feared no one but the king. They took no account of God in heaven. The more the rabble noticed what was happening, the more recklessly they began to plunder.

Many lords admitted that this was a godly people, but obeyed the king's will out of fear.

The faithful were driven out of Moravia into Hungary, out of Hungary back into Moravia, out of Moravia into Austria, out of Austria back into Moravia. In short, they had no home. They were forced to move hither and thither, and many of them were given no shelter, whereas the greatest villain in the country had no trouble finding lodging.

They had to move from one country to another.

It would take much too long to tell it all from the beginning, to recount the various things that happened to the faithful. Many know it only too well, for they went through it themselves. They were at everyone's mercy, a spectacle for old and young, for children on the streets, for rich and poor. No doubt about it, their way was straight and narrow.

It would take too long to recount everything.

In spite of this long and harsh oppression they did not waver. They thanked the Lord that they were found worthy to suffer for his name's sake. Although to their great sorrow many of their number did become unfaithful and returned to the world, the others held all the more firmly to God. Their only plea

The greatest pain was that many became unfaithful.

was that he might protect them from evil and keep them faithful, that he might lend them endurance and strength. This the Lord granted them, and they overcame everything through faith, the victory by which we overcome the world.

1551

1 John 5:4

Although the ungodly stormed and raved, the Lord often thwarted their plans, so their plots came to nothing. He lets men see his power from time to time to show that if we only trust him, no one can do anything if it is not his will.

The Lord brought plans of the ungodly to nothing.

The believers had to suffer all these things because they had accepted the faith and truth of God, of our Lord Jesus Christ, setting value not on the pope's infant baptism, but on the baptism of Christ alone. Nor did they believe in the idolatrous eucharist, where Christ bodily—in the same manner that he hung upon the cross with his flesh and blood, skin and hair, hands and feet—is supposed to be present in such a morsel of bread, on every occasion, a thousand times over. Instead, they believed that, as the Scriptures say, the Lord's Supper should be held in remembrance of his suffering and death, through which he redeemed us and made us members of his body.

Why we had to suffer.

Luke 22:20
1 Cor. 11:25–26

Because the believers had left the old, profligate church and had testified against it, Satan, envious from the beginning, worked on the pope, that antichrist, and the mob of priests and left them no peace until they made the king do what they wanted. The king forced the lords of estates to submit to his will and carry out the priests' wishes. Woe to them at the time of God's judgment, for then they will no longer be kings and lords with their priests. They will share the same lot and judgment as Pharaoh, the Egyptian king who oppressed the Israelite people; Sennacherib; proud Haman; King Nebuchadnezzar; King Antiochus, who also cruelly oppressed and tormented God's people in times past, wanting to bring all nations to his own faith; and bloodthirsty Jezebel and her four hundred false prophets, who had persecuted and killed the true prophets of God. All our persecutors will have the same punishment as these in eternal damnation if they die without sincere repentance and conversion. For this reason they are to be pitied and wept over, not envied. But innocent blood cries out from the earth to God in heaven and will not be forgotten.

The priests incited the king, and the king the lords of estates.

Woe to those who persecute the faithful.

Exod. 1:8–22
Isa. 37:37–38
Esther 3; Jth. 6:2
1 Macc. 1:29–42
2 Macc. 7

1 Kings 18:13, 19

Blessed are those who have endured faithfully to the end, for they will possess the kingdom of their Father in heaven,

Blessed are they who endure to the end.

1551

which has been prepared for them from the beginning of the world (Matt.25:34).

In times of tribulation many came to the church and changed their lives.

During these times of great tribulation, God added many to the church. People came from many places and believed, changed their lives, and took up the cross. More joined then than later in good times. They were not put off by great tribulation because they had true zeal, which led them to genuine Christianity and love of God.

All this is described and written down as a record, especially for you and us, their descendants living in times when God gives peace, so that we do not think there will always be peace. At the same time, when God does bless us in temporal matters, let us be thankful and remember that our brothers and sisters of earlier times would not have known how to praise and thank God enough if they had had only a half, a third, or even less, of what we have now. Indeed, anyone who cannot endure now, in these good times, has not stood the test as a true Christian. And if ever God should bring similar tribulation on us, their descendants, we should not be taken by surprise but should show the same patience and endurance to the end, to the praise and glory of God.

After these tribulations they lived in community as before.

After five years of great distress we gathered once more, determined to keep community as wholeheartedly as ever. We had every reason to give our heartfelt praise, honor, and glory to God in heaven, who sends times of tribulation and also frees us from them. It had seemed as if we would never be together again. The ungodly shattered our hopes again and again, and we thought, "If God should ever gather us again, how dear and precious would each one be to us, how we would love one another, and how we would thank God!"[1]

How wonderful it is when believers can live together!

Now God has granted it. Oh, let each one consider and realize what a grace, what a gift from God it is, when we can live together and do not need to be involved in the impure life of the world and its shameless people. Often one's heart weeps like faithful Lot in Sodom. It would be better to lie under the bench at a gathering of believers than to recline on one of Sodom's fine beds. The evil ways of the ungodly are a terrible example for young people. Every time a believer prays to God

---

[1]See also Beck, 189–193.

or gives thanks, the mockery of the ungodly is at its worst. Think how they would have railed at the Word of God and other holy things if we had had the chance to proclaim it! Now, praise be to God on high, he has given us every chance to hear it again.

1551

1550

In 1550, during those years of distress, our dear brother Wolf Sailer or Tischler (a cabinetmaker), servant of God's Word and his church, fell asleep in the Lord at Saitz in Moravia. He had brought us, his fellows in the faith, much wholesome teaching and comfort. He had put all the psalms of David into verse, and we still sing them in the church. He had also composed other beautiful songs of praise and comfort. He was a truly gifted brother.[1]

Wolf Sailer, a servant, passed away.

That same year we set up a community at Damborschitz and moved in.[2]

Community started at Damborschitz.

1551

In 1551 five brothers were chosen and appointed as servants of God's Word at Schakwitz near the swamp; these were Jakob Säckler, Matthias Legeder, Hans Mändel (also known as Klein Hansel), Paul Schuster, and Hans Spindler.

5 brothers chosen for the service of the Word.

At the same time five brothers were chosen and appointed as stewards, or servants for temporal affairs; they were Thoman Eppenstainer, Thoman Renn, Michael Kern, Gregor the Bohemian, and Gabriel Aichhorn.

5 brothers chosen for the service for temporal affairs.

That same year brother Peter Hagen, a servant of God's Word, fell asleep in the Lord at Pulgram in Moravia after much suffering. He was among those who had been marched down to the sea but had returned. We still have a song he composed about their imprisonment in the castle at Falkenstein.[3]

Peter Hagen, a servant of the Word, passed away.

---

[1]See *LdHBr*, 133–136, 161–164, 178–297, for fifty songs written by Wolf Sailer. Sailer's rendition of the Psalms is in the library of the Diocese of Esztergom, Codex III, 199. See also Wolkan, *Lieder*, 180–185; Beck, 195–196; Friedmann, *Schriften*, 125–126.

[2]Damborschitz (Dambořice), a market town southeast of Austerlitz (Slavkov), property of the Kounice family. Beck, 196 n.1; Zeman, *Topography*, #28.

[3]See *LdHBr*, 97–98.

1551
A servant passed away.

Brother Kaspar Klaindopf or Schmidt (a smith), a servant of the Word not yet confirmed, also fell asleep in the Lord with a peaceful heart at Freischütz[1] (Sabatisch) in Hungary.

A servant for temporal affairs passed away.

Brother Gabriel Aichhorn, too, fell asleep in the Lord. He was a steward or servant for temporal affairs at Poppitz near Tracht[2] in Moravia.

Michael Kramer passed away.

Michael Kramer, a servant for temporal affairs, fell asleep in the Lord at Popodin[3] in Hungary. He is the Michael who wrote the song about the suffering of the church in Hungary.

Hans Spindler passed away.

Brother Hans Spindler was freed from the service of the Word not long after he had been appointed for a time of testing. A short time later he fell asleep in the Lord with a peaceful heart.

Ott and 2 others resisted the church.

There were some who resisted the elders and servants of the church, grumbling against them: Ott (who later lived at Pergen), Anthoni Kürsner, and Hans Kürsner. They were excluded from the church as unserviceable members, but they never repented.

Bastel Schmidt passed away.

In this same year 1551 brother Bastel Schmidt, a servant for temporal affairs, fell asleep in the Lord at Fraitz in Moravia.

1552

Hans Schmidt and another brother confirmed in the service of the Word.

In 1552 at Gätte in Hungary, the elders confirmed brothers Hans Schmidt and Simon Waindel in their service of the Gospel with the laying on of hands.

4 brothers confirmed in the service for temporal affairs.

On the very same day and also at Gätte in Hungary, the elders confirmed with the laying on of hands the service for temporal affairs for the following four brothers: Christoph Lenck, Kaspar Ebner, Andreas Stuck, and Ulrich Hofer.

Hans Schluchter excluded.

In this year of 1552 Hans Schluchter grumbled and rebelled against the elders and servants of the church. With his flattering words he won the support of several brothers in the community at Hrubschitz. As a result he was excluded from the church.

---

[1]See above, p.245 n.

[2]Tracht (Strachotín), Moravia, a market town north of Nikolsburg (Mikulov); at that time under the jurisdiction of Maidburg Castle; see above, p.226 n.1; Zeman, *Topography*, #157.

[3]Popodin (Popudinské-Močidlany), village southeast of Göding (Hodonin). For Michael Kramer's song, see *LdHBr*, 166–175.

The situation of each of his followers was considered, and most of them found reconciliation. But Hans Schmidt[1] had gone too far in the matter and was lost to the church. Neither he nor Hans Schluchter ever repented. *1552*

A few days after the new year brother Hans Wimmer (also called Plattner), a servant of God's Word and his church, fell asleep in the Lord at the estate at Austerlitz after much suffering. We still have one or two of his songs. Hans Wimmer, a servant, passed away.

That same year, brother Matthias Legeder[2] fell asleep in the Lord at Pergen in Moravia. He was a servant of the Word of God, though still in a time of testing, and had gone through many tribulations for the sake of divine truth. He had spoken of his hope of release from this earthly frame a week before his end. Matthias Legeder passed away.

Brother Balthasar Maierhof the older, a confirmed servant for temporal affairs, fell asleep in the Lord at Altenmarkt in Moravia and after bearing much tribulation went to those who are at rest. Balthasar Maierhof passed away.

Brother Jakob Säckler, a servant of the Word still in a time of testing, fell asleep in the Lord at Sabatisch in Hungary. Jakob Säckler passed away.

Brother Melchior Kellner or Zimmermann (a carpenter), a servant for temporal affairs, fell asleep in the Lord at Sabatisch in Hungary. Melchior Kellner passed away.

Brother Hans Hess or Schneider (a tailor), a servant for temporal affairs, also fell asleep in the Lord at Alexowitz[3] in Moravia. Hans Hess passed away.

In this year brother Thoman Renn, a carpenter and also a Thoman Renn passed away.

---

[1]This Hans Schmidt is not to be confused with the Hans Schmidt or Raiffer whose confirmation in the service of the Word is recorded at the beginning of 1552 and who was executed in 1558 (pp.354–360 below).

[2]Matthias Legeder had been arrested at Sterzing in 1541. In December 1542 he was condemned to do galley service "against the Turks" the following spring but was able to escape and reach Moravia. See above, p.213; Mecenseffy, *Österreich*, III, 500, #706; *ME*, III, 312; Loserth, *Anabaptismus*, 180.

Of the two songs composed by Matthias Legeder and Christian Lissner, one is in *LdHBr*, 303–305; the other is in Codex Hab. 15, fol. 354, Bratislava City Archives.

[3]Alexowitz (Alexovice), formerly Oleckowitz or Olkowitz, southwest of Eibenschitz (Ivančice); in 1552 property of Heinrich Doupovsky of Doupowa. After the mandates of 1622, expelling the Anabaptists from Moravia, the Hutterite community at Alexowitz was given up, possibly in December 1622. See Robert Friedmann, "A Newly Discovered Source on the Transmigration of the Hutterites to Transylvania, 1621–1623," *MQR*, Oct. 1961, 312. Beck, 198, 407–408; Zeman, *Topography*, #2; see also below, p.674.

1552 servant for temporal affairs, fell asleep in the Lord at Schakwitz.

1553

Bärtel Riegel appointed to service of the Word.

In 1553 brother Bärtel Riegel from Gundelbach in Württemberg was chosen for the service of the Gospel and appointed.

Hans Mändel and Bärtel Riegel confirmed in the service of the Word.

At Sabatisch in Hungary two brothers, Hans Mändel (also called Klein Hansel) and Bärtel Riegel were confirmed by the elders with the laying on of hands for the service of the Gospel and Word of God.

Leonhard Klemp chosen for the service for temporal affairs.

On the same day at Sabatisch brothers Leonhard Klemp and Peter Dietrich were chosen and appointed to the service for temporal affairs.

Simon Waindel passed away.

In this year brother Simon Waindel, a servant of God's Word and of his church, fell asleep in the Lord at Popodin in Hungary.

We lived in Schadowitz and Gobschitz.

In 1553 the brothers began to establish communities at Schadowitz and at Gobschitz.[1]

Klein Michael passed away.

In this year brother Michael Matschidel, also called Klein Michael (short Michael), a servant of Jesus Christ and his church, fell asleep in the Lord at Altenmarkt in Moravia after enduring many trials and imprisonment.

[In this same year Gilg Federspil, Georg Rader, and many others from Tirol were brought to the faith through the witness of Hans Mändel.][2]

---

[1]Schadowitz (Žádovice), east of Gaya; in 1553 property of Zikmund of Zástřizl; Beck, 199; Zeman, *Topography*, #136. Gobschitz (Kubšice), see above, p.239 n.1.

[2]The bracketed passage (Wolkan, *Geschicht-Buch*, 696, errata and addenda) is from the "1580" codex, fol. 274r, of this chronicle. See also Beck, 199.

Georg Rader or Wagner was a cartwright by trade; his family name was Wyser.

1554–1564: The Good Years

1554

In 1554 brother Jörg Ladendorffer, a servant for temporal affairs, fell asleep in the Lord at Protzka in Hungary.

Jörg Ladendorffer passed away.

1555

In 1555 at Sabatisch in Hungary, brother Hans Klampferer[1] was chosen for the service of the Word of God, appointed, and confirmed by the elders with the laying on of hands.

Hans Klampferer chosen for the service and confirmed.

In this same year, brother Abraham Schneider was chosen and appointed to the service of the Word of God. Later that year he was confirmed in the service by the elders with the laying on of hands.

Abraham Schneider chosen for the service of the Word.

Two wealthy brothers from the same family, Remigius and Stoffel Heugen from Eyrs in the Vintschgau,[2] were driven off their estates on St. James's Day [July 25] for the sake of divine truth. Each had children and a wife with a baby of about five months at the breast. Because they had bound themselves to God through Christian baptism, they were in danger of being arrested in their own homes. They fled from the Vintschgau into the Puster Valley where brother Valtin Hörl was supposed to find shelter for them and their little ones for one or two days.

Remigius and Stoffel Heugen driven out of Vintschgau.

Brother Valtin was seized in the street by Paul Troyer, the judge at Niedervintl, and taken prisoner. On being asked whether he was an Anabaptist, Valtin replied that he was one of those to whom people gave this name. Then he was taken to the judge's house. The judge told his servant to put the prisoner in irons, but the servant refused. At this the judge

Valtin Hörl captured in the Puster Valley.

[1]Hans Klampferer, a tinsmith, is also called "Schlah-in-die-Pfann" (Strike-the-pan). Beck, 203.

[2]Vintschgau, the Upper Adige Valley, northern Italy.

1555

himself put Valtin's hands and feet in irons and brought him to Kaltenhaus, a mile away, where he handed him over to his officers. They were unwilling to take him but had to obey the judge because of their positions, so they took him without delay to Schöneck Castle. A midwife who had been attending a woman in childbirth at Kaltenhaus heard that a prisoner had been taken up to the castle, so she ran after them and said she did not agree with such a man being taken prisoner.

Valtin Hörl imprisoned in Schöneck Castle.

The officers carried out the judge's orders and took Valtin to the castle, where they locked him in a narrow cell in the deepest dungeon. But the lady of the castle felt compassion for him. She sent him a message through her cook that she would be glad to see him escape. As she was unable to help him herself, she sent her daughter with better food and drink than was ordered for him, for she knew that in a week's time the judge and his jurors would question him under torture.

The very day before they were to interrogate him, God prompted a compassionate servant girl to smuggle a tool to Valtin to take the iron door off its hinges. But as he feared he might dishonor the name of the Lord or stain his conscience if he did this, he turned to the Lord again and again in fervent prayer, asking God to speak to his heart and show him whether he should escape or remain in prison to await what would be done to him. When he was assured that he should try to open the door and found that it was possible, he prayed to God to direct him. The answer was always the same: to continue his efforts. He took the door off its hinges but was still unable to get out. Then he found a way to force the door, and the chain on the outside broke from the strain.

Valtin Hörl took counsel with God about escaping.

He opened the prison door.

He hurried out of the prison and hid under the stairs, afraid everyone would come running because of the loud crash in the dungeon. But no one came. He had been under the stairs two or three hours when he heard the lady talking to her servants about him, telling them that she believed him to be a God-fearing man.

The lady of the castle regarded the brother as a God-fearing man.

When everyone in the castle was asleep, Valtin risked going upstairs and out into the courtyard. The cook had warned him of the fierce dogs in the courtyard, so he had armed himself with plenty of bread to throw to them if they should try to attack him. But dogs and people had fallen so deeply asleep that not one of them made a sound. All this convinced Valtin that it was God's will and special intervention.

Following the cook's instructions, he got out of the courtyard by a little door into the keep and climbed over a low, broken-down wall. So with God's help he escaped from their chains.

1555
Valtin Hörl escaped from prison at Schöneck.

Now the judge had set Valtin's hearing for the following day, so he and his assessor came to the castle to proceed with the case. But the lady rushed up to the judge with loud cries of distress, clasping her hands above her head and pretending to be greatly upset by the escape, although she was actually glad.

When the people saw that the door had been broken open, they were astounded, for it seemed unbelievable that such a strong iron chain could have broken into pieces, and they could find no tool that Valtin might have used to break his way out. His friends reported to him afterward that everyone was saying they would really have liked to see a man so strong that he was able to break that chain.

Judge amazed such a chain was torn to pieces.

In fact, brother Valtin himself had thought it impossible to break the chain. His hope had been to twist the door instead (because he had lifted it from its hinges), although it had bands of iron running both ways. However, things did not turn out according to his plan, but according to God's will. So he felt clearly that God was helping him by making the iron as weak as a rotten piece of rope and thus sparing his life, granting him a longer time on earth. Praise be to God in all eternity for the many wonders he does for his saints.

God made the iron weak as a piece of rotten string.

Many years later, in 1571, as will be told in its place, Valtin was again taken prisoner and brought to this castle, but he was permitted to go free again.

In 1555 brother Hans Pürchner from Saalen was captured at Kortsch[1] in the Adige region and taken to Schlanders by the constables. There he was brought before the governor,[2] a cruel tyrant who was ready to stab Hans to death out of sheer fury. He had him interrogated under torture and put on the rack to make him tell who had given him lodging, and because he refused, they racked him again the same day. But to their great vexation their torture was useless.

Hans Pürchner taken prisoner.

There was a clerk in attendance named Grimm, who pulled

[1]Saalen, Tirol, southwest of St. Lorenzen; Kortsch, west of Schlanders (Silandro) in the Vintschgau (the Upper Adige Valley).

[2]Caspar von Monthanj; see Beck, 204 n.5.

1555

Hans Pürchner cruelly tortured until he could not stand or walk a step.

on the rope himself to rack and stretch this brother, though such work belongs only to executioners. They racked Hans again and again. They left him hanging on the rope several hours until he was so torn that he could neither stand on his feet nor walk one step nor bring his hands to his mouth to feed himself. Nevertheless he refused to give in and remained steadfast in the Lord.

Then they put him in stocks, hands and feet, in a dark, stifling dungeon and kept him there over six months.

Monks, priests, and noblemen pressed him.

Many educated people, priests, monks, nobles, and others, attacked his faith for two days and a night, trying to lead him astray. But he put them to shame by pointing out their errors. He was joyful and courageous and would not be intimidated.

Hans Pürchner beheaded.

Then they condemned him to death and led him to the place of execution. There he called the crowds to repentance. He could not kneel, because they had racked and tortured him so cruelly, so they supported him with a block of wood against his back and then beheaded him. A song written about him gives witness to his suffering.[1]

The constable who arrested him had told Pürchner that he would not let him go at any price. Later, however, he was overcome by remorse and would have been glad to pay any amount to undo what had been done.

One of the priests who had tormented Hans Pürchner in his eagerness to make him recant later became a brother and even a servant of the Word. His name was Leonhard Dax.[2] It was not unlike the prophecy: "Those who destroyed you will hasten to build you again; those who laid you waste will dwell in you." Leonhard Dax remained sincere and steadfast in his new life until the end, as will be recorded in its place.

A Bavarian nobleman and his group sent a request for a servant.

That same year a Bavarian nobleman by name of Taufkircher sent a message with some people traveling to Sabatisch in Hungary, asking Leonhard Lanzenstiel, servant of the Lord

---

[1]Hans Pürchner's companion Gilg Federspil and another brother were able to escape, as reported by Klaus Felbinger in his song about Pürchner, "Mit Freuden wollen wir singen" (With joyful hearts let us sing), in *LdHBr*, 441–446; also Sigmund Hosauer's song about Pürchner (ibid. 436–441), with same first line. See also *ME*, IV, 234; Wolkan, *Lieder*, 209 n.2, 229; *Martyrs Mirror*, 550; Beck, 204–205.

[2]About Leonhard Dax, see below, p.384.

and of his church, to send several brothers and a servant to establish a church community in Bavaria. Since Taufkircher and his group insisted, promising to bear patiently whatever might happen to them, cost what it may, and pleading with the brothers to risk it for their sake, the brothers were moved to agree. It was decided that Hans Mändel, a servant of the Word of God, should make the journey to Bavaria.

1555

As there had been a special request for brother Michael Veldthaler to come too, he went on ahead with several brothers, and after them came brother Christoph Achtznit and others. In spite of the danger that soon became apparent, they investigated the situation so that Hans Mändel would know where to begin when he arrived. They had thought that in Taufkircher they would meet a man on fire to talk about questions of faith. But Taufkircher had completely changed his mind, denied his earlier request for Veldthaler or the brothers to come, and said he did not want them to visit him and he was not going to meet them.

Michael Veldthaler and Christoph Achtznit sent to Bavaria.

The nobleman changed his mind.

He even tried to turn some against us who had once been Lutherans like himself but were now filled with love to our church, acknowledging our faith, teaching, and way of life as better than their own.

When Hans Mändel, a servant of the Lord's Word, arrived to take up the task for which he had been sent, there was a great uproar against the faithful because many eager hearts responded to him and received the Word of God. Anger and hatred flared up in Taufkircher. He spread lies about the zealous, who wanted to hold to the truth. He admitted that he had wanted to speak with Veldthaler and with the servant Hans Mändel, but that the zealous had acted impulsively and on their own had arranged for the visit of Hans Mändel and Veldthaler. This troubled the two brothers a great deal, and for more reasons than one.

Hans Mändel taught the Word of the Lord in Bavaria.

The zealous urged the nobleman to meet with the brothers.

Although this nobleman had agreed to their meeting in his castle at Guttenburg, he did not keep his word. Instead he arranged for it to take place in an extremely dangerous location: a farmhouse at Galbach, on the border between two jurisdictions, Kraiburg[1] and Mermos, where he assembled the worst enemies and defamers of the truth. When this became known,

[1]Kraiburg, Bavaria, a small town near the Inn River, east of Munich.

1555

the zealous regretted that they had arranged the meeting. But to avoid giving offense, the brothers attended, though in fear for their lives. Hans Mändel felt this so keenly that he said, in all the imprisonments and hardships he had endured since becoming a Christian, never had anything struck such fear into his heart as this. But they could think of no other solution and felt it was best to go ahead. They put their trust in the Lord and dared to go that night to the appointed place. The nobleman was there with his supporters, and the room was filled to overflowing. People were standing on benches and outside the windows. Veldthaler went first because he knew the nobleman, and as he and Hans Mändel entered the room, they wished everyone the grace of God through Jesus Christ. Then the brothers sat down with Taufkircher to hear what he thought and what he wanted of them. He started out with lies, saying he had not asked them to come, had nothing to discuss with them, and did not need their teaching. Then he said he was steward of what his Master and Lord had given him and Saint Peter could not take it from him, implying that, like Peter, the brothers forced their followers into community of goods, which Christ had not done. To these unfitting words Michael Veldthaler replied, "My Lord Taufkircher, you are going too far. It is presumptuous of you to speak against Peter in this way. You should not do that. Do you suppose that if Christ had given you something, Saint Peter would take it away?" Taufkircher's response was, "Oh, you serpent! You serpent!"

Hans Mändel and Michael Veldthaler met the nobleman.

Brother Hans Mändel, faithful servant of God that he was, tried to convince him on this point, but Taufkircher asked them to listen to his grievances against the brothers and not interrupt, as it would confuse him. Later he would listen for a whole hour to their point of view. But having lied about one thing, he was now lying about another. He started off by asking whether the Holy Spirit came to a person through the laying on of hands, to which Hans Mändel answered briefly, "Yes, but to varying degrees." At this, Taufkircher shot contemptuous questions at the brothers, venting his anger and malice. Then he broke off and said he had not come to be instructed by them. He had summoned them in order to expose them, to admonish them for leading others astray, and to protect good people from being misled.

The nobleman asked whether the Holy Spirit would come to a person through our laying on of hands.

At this a man named Pfenningmann, who had only recently

become a brother, spoke up in front of everyone present, saying he had not been misled, but "it is the very truth, Your Lordship." The nobleman got to his feet. He told them that there were spies everywhere, on land and sea, and if they were caught, they would have a hard time getting away—they were being too closely watched. They would have their heads cut off, which would be a good thing—after that the fires of hell were waiting for them. And he went off with his ungodly followers. The brothers reminded him of his promise to let them explain their standpoint, but it was of no use. The nobleman was so furious with them, without any cause, that they could only expect the district judges and constables to descend on them the moment he left, as a wolf snatches a sheep or a hawk takes a dove. But God did not let this happen. He protected them, mindful of his cause. All praise and honor be to him. This world is full of pitfalls for those who do the work of the Lord.

1555

The nobleman did not keep his word.

It was then decided that Hans Mändel, the servant of the Lord's Word, should go to several places on this side of the Alz, around Kraiburg, Mermos, Altötting, and Braunau,[1] to proclaim the truth to those longing to hear it. As soon as he started out and the four local courts heard of it, they opposed him with all their might. They sent spies, both secretly and openly, to find out what was going on. Some of these pretended that they wanted to hear what the faithful taught and were eager to become believers. But when this fraud failed to track Hans Mändel down, the officers of the law came out in full force, especially those from Mermos. The district judge with twenty-four men in armor, equipped with every kind of weapon, came on horseback and on foot to where the believers were gathered, since their meeting place had been betrayed. But God in his grace defeated the enemies' purpose. It was so cold that the ground crunched underfoot, and the moon was very bright. Besides, the brothers were keeping good watch. Their enemies knew all this but still set out, hoping to make a surprise attack. But the Lord made them lose heart. So halfway there they turned back, saying, "The devil tells them everything." They were furious because they had tried for eleven nights in vain.

Hans Mändel preached in a number of places in Bavaria.

Just as the sun causes turmoil among the bats, so does truth among the ungodly.

Judge from Mermos, with 24 men, searched for the brothers.

---

[1]Towns east of Munich; Braunau on the Inn River at the Austrian border. The Alz River flows northeast out of the Chiemsee into the Inn River.

1555
At Tittmoning, Trostberg, and Walt they searched for the brothers in houses, ovens, chests, and haystacks.

Similar attempts were made on the other side of the Alz, in the jurisdictions of Tittmoning, Trostberg, and Walt. Day and night, they worked for the devil: homes were raided in the hope of finding the brothers; every room was searched; they thrust their spears and swords into ovens and chests, through hay and straw, and everything was flung about. A farmer's wife suspected of sheltering the brothers was thrown down the steps into the cellar. The searchers acted like mad beasts.

Constant spying on the brothers.

When this proved fruitless, the enemies sent spies all over the place to listen by the houses, by walls and by windows. Everywhere they lay in wait for the believers. They crept into washhouses; they lurked at drop gates and gratings, at crossroads, behind woodpiles, by landing places, and wherever else they thought the brothers would pass; among ferrymen, sailors, and fishermen; among young and old—in short, everywhere. It was forbidden under penalty of death to shelter the brothers or ferry them across rivers. In cities, market towns, and villages careful watch was kept, in order to arrest them. If they attempted to escape or defend themselves, they were to be beaten down and shot dead. Such deeds would be considered worthy, and the duke promised a good reward.

Anyone who apprehended Michael Veldthaler would be rewarded with a life pension.

So the path was narrow and fraught with danger. This lasted for eleven weeks. Special efforts were made to hunt down Michael Veldthaler, and a pension for life was promised to anyone who delivered him up. This meant that he and brother Christoph Achtznit were not safe for one moment, since the magistrates had no intention of letting them escape. They wandered about in constant danger, but the Lord was their faithful protector.

Attempt to establish a community in Bavaria.

Nineteen brothers and sisters, who were young in faith and had just been baptized, were caught and taken to Mermos. Each was brought to a different court so that they would not be together. Michael Veldthaler and Christoph Achtznit tried hard to get them out of prison with the help of other believers, but it was all in vain.

Christel N., a brother, beheaded at Mermos.

Their enemies tormented and tempted them until, being young in faith, they all recanted except one, Christel,[1] who remained faithful. He testified to the truth and held to it, and because of his steadfastness, he was condemned to death and

[1]Last name not given; see *Martyrs Mirror*, 550; Beck, 204.

executed with the sword at Mermos in the early months of 1555. He had never lived in the church community, but once he had come to know and accept the truth, he defended it with his blood in the strength of God. One man said he should curse just once—just one little curse—and he would be set free. But he refused out of love to God and chose a bitter death instead.

1555

They would let him go if he cursed once.

Messages came from those in prison asking that their little children be taken into the brothers' care and sent to the church community. The brothers would have been glad to do this, but it was impossible. After some consideration, however, they sent for one brother's children who were at Grundt in the jurisdiction of Mermos. The children were to come to a place about a mile away, where the brothers were hiding for a day and a night in the straw. When the boy arrived with his little sister, the brothers considered what to do, explaining that the parents had asked them to help the children, but at that moment it was impossible to get them out of the country because the river was frozen and every highway and byway was being watched. They asked the children if they had any relatives in the neighborhood. Yes, they had a cousin. He, too, had received a message from their parents in prison to look after them. The brothers asked several times whether their cousin could be trusted if they were to approach him, and the children assured them there was no danger, they could trust him. So they sent the two children to this cousin, asking him to come that night to their house. The brothers would come too, but the children should give them a warning if they heard anything strange, which they promised to do.

Brothers did their utmost to care for prisoners' children.

After the children had explained it all to their cousin, he went straight to the judge at Mermos to inform him. The judge was delighted. Hoping to make a name for himself, he set out early with twenty-four well-equipped men, occupied the house, and had every path watched to prevent any escape. The brothers suspected nothing. The judge kept watch with his ungodly band until midnight. He got quite angry when time passed and the brothers did not come. Several times he seized the boy by the hair and called him a young liar. At the end he said it was a deliberate trick.

Judge from Mermos waited with 24 men to seize the brothers.

The boy replied, "My lord, they are sure to come." But the judge said, "The devil tells them everything," because the

1555

Orders given: if the brothers cannot be caught alive, they should be killed by any possible means.

same thing had happened to him several times before. He went away like a man who had been deceived, but to be on the safe side he left, from among all the servants of Pilate, the four most efficient rogues to watch the house. He gave orders that if the brothers came they should be taken alive if at all possible. If not, they should be killed by any available means: struck down, shot, or strangled. He promised that this would earn them a pension for life from his highness, the prince of Bavaria.

The men were going to do their best. They tried to plan it so that no one could escape. Time went by, and it was two in the morning before the brothers came and knocked a few times. The scoundrels in the house, figuring the moment had come, flung the door open and fell on the brothers with loud yells. They struck at them with their spears. The brothers fell over backwards in terror. The men attacked Christoph Achtznit and struck him down as if he were an ox, and his whole head was covered with blood. Then they bound him and took him away to Burghausen.

Brother Christoph Achtznit made prisoner and taken to Burghausen.

Michael Veldthaler escaped the constables.

Brother Michael Veldthaler fled in terror, not knowing which direction to take. He ran across the garden to the fence, which was high and covered with thorns, and flung himself over head first. The thorns tore his face badly, but in his terror he never noticed. He ran across a plowed field and on through the moonlit night in the bitter cold, until his feet were soaked from the snow and the mud. He reached a forest and fell on his knees to pray to the Lord. Soon after, he found himself at the inn from which he and Christoph Achtznit had set out earlier. He told the innkeeper his plight, but the man did not want him under his roof because the noblemen in Mühldorf had heard of their earlier stay at his place. So Michael had to leave the house, not knowing where to go. He was wet through and through, and it was snowing and raining. He went into the woods with no prospect of anything but freezing to death, for he dared not be seen. He stopped by a thicket and took the clothes off the upper part of his body to wrap around his legs against the frost and cold. While this was a help to the lower part of his body, the upper part froze. When he could stand the cold no longer, he thought, rather than freeze, he would go into a house, whether or not he was caught. Better to die an honorable death than to freeze to death so miserably. Trusting in the Lord, he risked returning to the man who had sheltered them before, since there was nowhere else to go.

Michael Veldthaler in great misery from frost and cold.

Soon a brother came to the house and asked through the window whether Michael Veldthaler and Christoph Achtznit were there. They did not know whether the two had been taken prisoner or not, he said. Michael was overjoyed—it was as if the Lord had sent him an angel. He set out again, and that same night he bade farewell to a group who were on their way to the church community [in Moravia], since Hans Mändel was [doing mission work] in Upper Austria. So Michael Veldthaler was somewhat encouraged, but for many weeks, right into Lent, he had to continue on his own, spreading the message among people who were eager to learn the truth. Then he traveled home with those who wanted to join the church community, and they were protected from the bloodthirsty lion. *1555*

Brother Christoph Achtznit was still in prison at Burghausen. He remained steadfast, yet the Lord enabled him to escape with a good conscience, thanks to his relatives. His sister Juliana brought him the means to set himself free. So he escaped and returned to the church community.

Christoph Achtznit escaped from prison at Burghausen.

All this happened in Bavaria, where the light of truth was breaking in among the people. God's messengers, who help others escape destruction, risk paying a high price in this world, and thus it has been from the beginning.

1556

In 1556 brother Valtin Hess, a servant for temporal affairs, fell asleep in the Lord at Schadowitz, and brother Leonhard Schuster, also a servant for temporal affairs, fell asleep in the Lord at Kostel in Moravia.

Valtin Hess passed away.

Leonhard Schuster passed away.

In this same year the brothers started building up a community at Nikolsburg.[1]

Nikolsburg.

A brilliant comet with a very long tail was seen in the sky that year.

Also in 1556, on the first day of December, our dear brother Peter Riedemann fell asleep in the Lord at Protzka in Hungary. He was born at Hirschberg in Silesia, a man inspired and highly gifted by God, a servant of God's Word and a *Vorsteher* (leading elder) of the whole church. His teaching and explanation of Scripture was of great value to us, his companions in the faith.

Peter Riedemann passed away.

---

[1]About Nikolsburg (Mikulov), see above, p.47 n.2.

1556

Peter Riedemann's imprisonments totaled 9 years.

He had served the church as servant of God's Word for twenty-seven years, including his imprisonments, which totaled nine years. The first time, he was imprisoned at Gmunden in Upper Austria for three years and four weeks. It was here that he got the name Peter of Gmunden. The second time, he was at Nuremberg for four years and ten weeks. The third and last time was at Marburg and Wolkersdorf in Hesse for about a year and a half.

The Lord delivered him from all the trials he endured for witnessing to Jesus Christ and his truth. There was no falseness in him: he stood firm and his heart and conscience were at peace, as told earlier in this book.

Peter Riedemann wrote many wonderful epistles, both from prison and from the community, to brothers and sisters who were imprisoned or living elsewhere.

He put together our printed confession of faith in 1540.

While in prison in Marburg and Wolkersdorf in Hesse, he wrote down the complete account of our religion, teaching, and faith. Both in prison and in the church community, he wrote many beautiful Christian songs, spiritual and biblical, for he was rich in all the secrets of God. The gift of God's Word flowed from him like running water and brimmed over.[1] All who heard him were filled with joy. He lived to be nearly fifty.

Peter Riedemann 50 years old.

As a farewell on his deathbed he wrote one more song, which begins, "From death's bonds Christ redeemed us, from the devil's might he freed us" (*Quitt, ledig, los hat uns gemacht Christus vom Tod des Teufels Macht*). This is still sung by the community.

The brothers and the people were in deep grief over his illness and full of anxiety about his leaving them, so he spoke these words from the book of Esdras [Nehemiah] to them in his last hour: "Go your way, eat the fat and drink sweet wine, and give gifts to those who have nothing; for this day is holy to our God. So do not be grieved, for the joy of the Lord is your strength." (Neh.8:10; 1 Esd.9:50–54). Then he passed away in the Lord.

Peter Riedemann's last words.

At this time, in the Palatinate by the Rhine River, a number

[1]Peter Riedemann was a prolific writer. About his *Confession of Faith*, see above, p.294 n. Forty-five of his songs are in *LdHBr*, 450–537; see Wolkan, *Lieder*, 185–206. An important source for the understanding of Anabaptist teaching are his numerous pastoral and other letters; see above pp.164–168, 177–181, 182–186, 200–209, for four of Riedemann's letters. See also *ME*, IV, 326–328; Friedmann, *Schriften*, 123–125; Beck, 206–207.

of people left the Swiss Brethren community near Bad Kreuznach because of the sin and offenses revealed there. They were Lorenz Huf, a servant from Sprendlingen, Rupp Gellner (also called Rupp Kern), Matthias Stroh, Wilhelm Henchen, and several other brothers and sisters.

1556
Lorenz Huf and his followers from the Palatinate left the Swiss Brethren.

FIRST, although they had been taught that a man should sacrifice himself with all he had to God and to his saints, their life was in opposition to their teaching. Everyone was allowed to keep his possessions and give the poor whatever suited him.

Swiss Brethren's faults and deviations.

SECOND, they taught that community meant that no one owned private property: each one's possessions belonged to all, to his neighbor as much as to himself. On the other hand, if anyone was in need he had to buy from others.

THIRD, they did not teach the truth about original sin.

They paid war taxes and sacrificed to idols. Church problems were dealt with unjustly, and wrongdoing was not punished in earnest. It was punished privately so that it would not be known among the people.

They did not keep a clear separation from other groups but mixed with them in many respects.

Their teachers were disunited and quarreled, and so did the people. There were also other reasons why these brothers and sisters left the Swiss Brethren and met with some of our brothers to ask them about the basis of the faith. They talked with Hans Schmidt, a servant of the Word, and his companions, who had been sent on mission from our brotherhood in Moravia. This meeting is described below, also the wonderful way God pulled away the mask of false piety and separated his own people from the hypocrites. How God was at work will be seen from the story that follows.

Swiss servants totally disunited.

Just as God has always provided a way for his work to go forward, so he did again in 1556, when division arose among the Swiss Brethren at Worms and Bad Kreuznach, especially between their leading elders, Theobald [Winter] and Farwendel. (Later we will see how God moved Farwendel in such a wonderful way that he was united with our church.) At that time the two started a dispute on original sin, and they clashed, so they met in Strasbourg[1] at a public inn to discuss

---

[1]The Strasbourg conference took place in 1557 (not 1556); see *ME*, IV, 642–643, "Strasbourg 3"; A. Hulshof, *Geschiedenis van de Doopsgezinden te Straatsburg van 1525 tot 1557* (Amsterdam, 1905), 224 ff.; John Horsch, "Strassburg, a Swiss Brethren Center," *MQR*, Jan. 1939, 26; Williams, *Radical Reformation*, 796.
About Farwendel, see below, pp.388–391.

1556

it further. So important was the question of original sin to them that they spent several hundred gulden during this discussion for the sake of their stomachs. There was great discord and quarreling between them. Theobald called Farwendel a false prophet and accused him of deserting the teachings of Christ and misleading his followers, leaving them without God. Another time Theobald said that the devil can disguise himself as an angel of light, so it is no wonder that the devil's servants pretend to preach righteousness. He and his followers repeatedly called Farwendel a liar. After this, without repenting, Theobald and Farwendel were reconciled in front of the people, saying everything was now clear between them and their divine gifts had not been taken from them. But since each of them was more concerned with his own honor than with God and his truth, they became disunited again, and so the whole matter ended with the separation of both themselves and their people.

Some of the people at Bad Kreuznach, however, who were aware of their ungodly ways and noticed that they tried to come to unity without any results, began asking about the true foundation of Christian faith and about those who practiced it. God used a man named Thomas Neuman to lead them in this search. He was a shoemaker from Wolfsheim who left because of the division. When he heard that there were people in Moravia who lived as brethren in unity and true community of goods, he determined not to give up until he had found them. So he left home and traveled about until he came to the church of God in Moravia and found the true basis of faith. Then he sent messengers back to his friends. The elders who had left the Swiss Brethren (Lorenz Huf, Rupp Gellner, Matthias Stroh, and Wilhelm Henchen) turned to these messengers, questioning them eagerly about the Christian faith. At first they got nowhere in their discussions, but they and especially their servant Lorenz did not give up their search for truth. When he and the other elders came to see that what Neuman had found was of God, the elders spoke with one another and then to all their people (who had left the Swiss Brethren with them). They wanted them all to hear the brothers from Moravia (who are called Hutterian) and inquire about the basis of their faith. This took place.

Lorenz Huf talked with our brothers.

Then they sent for the brothers from Moravia, that is, Hans Schmidt (a servant of the Word) and his companions, who were doing the Lord's work, traveling in Hesse and Württemberg in the area of the mountain called Bromberg. They begged them to explain the basis of divine truth, especially some points that puzzled them. The brothers from Moravia were glad to testify to the truth for the glory of God and for the salvation of their souls. They explained to them their tenets, in particular regarding the appointment and tasks of servants, mission, community of goods, the Ordnungen of the house of God, children's education, marriage, and separation from other groups. *1556*

After they had heard all these things, the Swiss Brethren urged their elders—Lorenz Huf and his assistants—to find out more from the brothers from Moravia so as to have greater certainty, especially about the following points:

Marriage
Taxes and blood money
Separation from other groups who also call themselves brethren
Food and drink for the servants
Serving idols
The purchase of houses for the church
Why one should move to Moravia

Lorenz and his assistants proposed that the people agree on whom to send to participate in these further talks, but the people thought the elders themselves should choose those they felt best suited. So the elders chose those who they knew had raised the most objections. After these men had listened to the brothers from Moravia and heard the reasons for their beliefs, they could not oppose them but were soon convinced and in agreement.

After they had gone thoroughly into each point, they were satisfied and asked our brothers from Moravia to write it all down for them so that they could make it clear to their group. Then they called a meeting of their people and read out the points and all they had talked over with the brothers. Hans Schmidt, a servant of God's Word, had written them down as follows:

FIRST, ABOUT MARRIAGE: The bond made with God (1 Pet.3:18) is the highest marriage (Eph.5:29–32). It lasts for all eternity and shall not be broken (Matt.24; Col.1; Heb.3). On marriage.

1556

Nothing must impair it (Matt.10:37; 1Cor.7): not the outward bond of marriage (Gen.3; 1Kings2:1–4), nor possessions, money (Matt.19:16–22; Mark4:19; Luke14:16–20), nor any created thing (Rom.8:35–39).

The outward bond of marriage (Ezra10:2,10; Tob.6:13–14) is not of God if it takes place in a human way and is not joined by the Holy Spirit (Gen.6:1–4; Matt.24:38; Luke17:27). But if the partners turn from sin and truly give themselves to God (Acts2:38; 16:31), their sins will be washed away (Acts22:16). Then the Spirit (2Thess.2:13) will consecrate their marriage (Heb.13:4); it will be in accordance with God's will, and what God has now joined together (Gen.24; Tob.7; Matt.19:6) no man shall put asunder.

On the separation of believing from unbelieving marriage partners, as Hans Schmidt wrote it for Lorenz Huf.

However, should one partner separate from the other, he must either remain unattached or repent and be reconciled (1Cor.7:10–11). Until he repents (1Cor.5:2–5; 2Thess. 3:14–15), the other partner should have nothing to do with him except for calling him to repentance, unless there should be some other godly reason.

If the partner who has separated himself joins another group who call themselves brethren but lead disorderly lives (2Thess.3:11–12), he should be shunned even though he claims the name of brother (1Cor.5:11; Ezra10:8,11). On the other hand, the separated partner may not be living in adultery, though conforming to the world, and out of need may long for the other, who is faithful to the Lord and wants nothing to interfere with his or her dedication. In spite of that, the latter still has the freedom to remain true to the Lord in his church, which is the safest way. He is then not bound to the unbeliever, for there is no express command to serve God at the side of an apostate (1Cor.7:15). But if he does join his unbelieving partner, it should be in the fear of the Lord.

It may also happen that a married couple comes from among the heathen and only one of the partners accepts the faith and enters into true community with Christ and the believers (Acts2:44), while the other is unable to grasp the faith. If the latter respects the other's faith and is willing to live with him and not interfere with the practice of his beliefs—whether it means attending meetings to hear the Lord's Word, raising their children in the right way (Eph.6:1–4), or serving the brothers and sisters (Luke8:2–3)—then they may live together in the hope that God will stretch out his hand to the unbeliever too (1 Cor.7:12). Under such circumstances the believer is not defiled by living with an unbeliever. Their children will be holy (1 Cor.7:13–14) because the Holy Spirit teaches them through the believer (Gen.8:15–18; Tob.4:12; Eph.6:1–3). *1556*

Should the unbelieving partner strongly oppose the one who believes and try to lead him away from God (Matt.10:34–39; Luke 12:51–53), then the believing brother or sister is not bound (Luke 14:26)—by the outward marriage, that is—if he parts from the unbeliever for God's sake and for the sake of his own soul. And if the unbelieving partner wants to separate, let him do so. How do you know, believer, whether you will win over the unbeliever? Take care that he does not win you over instead! The believer is called to live in peace with God. Let him remain at peace (1 Cor.7:15–16).

Government taxes.

SECOND, ABOUT TAXES or service due to the government (Matt.22:17–21; Rom.13:7; Titus 3:1; 1 Peter 2:13): We should give them in a right and fitting way, as God has ordained it. But a believer does not owe taxes destined for bloodshed, for fighting wars, for other unjust causes, or for things the government undertakes on its own account and not by divine order—things that are against his conscience (Acts 5:17–42). God commands him—and he has promised—to love his enemy (Matt.5:44; Rom.12:14). He should not make weapons of war (Isa.2:4; Mic.4:3) lest he be guilty of bloodshed.

Separation from and shunning of false groups.

THIRD, ABOUT SEPARATION from other groups: The believer shall have nothing to do with those who call themselves brothers (1 Cor.5:11) but lead undisciplined lives and do not live according to the Spirit (1 Kings 13:8–24; Ezra 10:11; Jer.16:11–13; 2 Thess.3:6; 2 John 10). Thus the children of God will not be lured away from God (Num.23; Deut.7:2–6; Josh.7:1; 23:6–13) by the hypocrites who try to mislead the devout (Eph.4:14) with their self-made righteousness (2 Cor. 11:3–15).

Regarding those from other groups who witnessed with their blood.

As for those who witness to the truth or die for the sake of their faith outside our community, we leave judgment to the Lord. They may not have found the full faith, but they longed for it. The Lord knows how each one stood and what he has suffered, and he can give them eternal salvation if they were

1556

seeking him with their whole heart. We must leave it in his hands and wait on his will, just as the sap or fruit of a young tree is appreciated only after it is harvested. I believe the Lord will give salvation to those who have truly sought the perfect foundation.

Food and drink for the servants.

FOURTH, ABOUT FOOD AND DRINK and daily necessities for the servants of the Word: The Spirit of Christ rules (1 Cor. 12) his church (Eph. 1:22–23) and uses all the members to build up the body (Eph. 4:11–16; Rom. 12:4–8), each supporting the other (Col. 2:19). Each member should devote himself to his appointed task, according to the Spirit at work in him. To say it with a parable: the hands serve the body and feed it (Matt. 9:10–15; Luke 5:30–35) through the spirit at work in them. The spirit continues to work in the body in such a way that energy and strength (John 15:1–6) are passed on to the feet, which carry the body. Similarly, in the body of the church, the hands, that is, the believers, serve the body and feed it (Acts 2:46; 1 Cor. 9:4–19) with a willing heart (Gal. 4:14–15; 1 Thess. 5:11) because they perceive the Spirit at work in the body through the feet, that is, the servants of the Lord, and because the Lord has commanded them (Deut. 26:11–12; Matt. 10:10) to honor their servants (1 Tim. 5:17–18). This is written in the Old and the New Testament (Num. 18:8–36; Acts 1:8; 1 Thess. 5:12–13).

Even though the spiritual hands (the faithful) provide food liberally for the body, yet the feet (that is, the servants) receive no more than what the Spirit in the body apportions to them (1 Cor. 12:14–26) and brings to fruition. The servants accept it with thanksgiving as coming from the Lord (1 Tim. 4:3) and in turn use the gifts they have received from God to serve the body, walking in the dirt, that is, suffering humiliation (1 Cor. 4:9–13). Out of their love for God (Gal. 4:13–15) and because he has commanded it, the believers respect their servants, and for the sake of his cause they consider them worthy of double reward.

About buying houses and land.

FIFTH, ABOUT BUYING HOUSES AND LAND: The devout must give up all earthly goods (Eccles. 2:1–11; Matt. 19:21; Luke 5:27–28; 12:15–34; 14:33) because God has called them out of private property. Furthermore, he has commanded them not to acquire goods in the future (1 Cor. 13:3) but rather to speak against taking created things as personal possessions (Gen. 3; 1 Cor. 10:24; Phil. 2:21). For believers to buy things for themselves is therefore out of the question. However, since God rules in the body through his Spirit (1 Cor. 12:4–7) and cares for his body by caring for his people (Rom. 12; 1 Pet. 5:10), giving each member a task to do (Eph. 4:11–13), it is up to the eyes (Num. 10:31) to look for a place where the body can live, wherever the Lord provides such a place (2 Esd. 16:55–60; Acts 2:44–47; 11:26; Rev. 12:6). *1556*

They are not looking for shelter for themselves or for their own benefit but for what benefits the body (1 Cor. 10:24; Phil. 2:4). God directs them (John 14:16–17; Acts 8:26–39) to meet the needs of the body. Therefore it is right for them to follow the leading of the Spirit and find housing for the believers, whether by purchase or some other arrangement that God may grant, so long as the one who does the buying does not do it for himself (1 Cor. 7:30–31).

Serving idols.

SIXTH, ABOUT SERVING IDOLS (Exod. 32; 1 Cor. 8): Idolatry leads away from God (Wisd. of Sol. 14); it is an abomination to him (Deut. 27:15; 2 Kings 10:18–28). All who take part in it serve not God but the devil (1 Cor. 10:20). It is therefore as clear as day that the apostles did not make any idols of wood, stone, silver, or gold; nor did they have any made for them. The same is true of temples. Indeed, they protested against them (Acts 7:39–43; 17:29), saying that God had no pleasure in them: he neither lives in them nor is worshiped in them.

It is clear that such temples are heathen in origin, devised by human ingenuity and built in false service of God. All this idolatry has continued to this day, since men still contribute to the building of temples with gifts or money (2 Cor. 2:17). And since the idolaters wrongly dare to take on the task of preaching the gospel (1 Cor. 12:2) and obtain their food from idols (Dan. 14:14–15; Bar. 6; 2 John 7), the believers rightly shun them as people who bring a false teaching. Believers do not listen to such men, for they are alien (John 10:5), and the Lord has not sent them (Jer. 23:11–21; Rom. 10:15). Believers refuse to partake of what they offer (1 Kings 13) and can have nothing to do with them. They neither work for them nor conduct business with them lest they take part in their sins.

1556
About gathering the believers in Moravia.

SEVENTH, ABOUT THE CALL TO CHURCH COMMUNITY: Through his Spirit, God has always led the believers (Num.9:15–23) according to his Word and will to the place that pleased him or that he had prepared for them to dwell in (Gen.12:1; Exod.19:4–6; Acts 11:4–18), and he still leads them and separates them from the world (Exod.12:51; Acts 2:40; 9:3–6; 2 Cor.6:14–18), for he wants to be their Lord and Ruler (Ecclus.7:29–31; 1 Cor.12) and has great joy when the faithful dwell together (Ps.26; 133; Ecclus.13:15–16; 25:1; Eph.4:3; Phil.2:2).

Therefore we see in the early church (Acts 2) how greatly the Lord delighted (Acts 4; 11) in gathering his own people from many tongues under the sun and establishing his heavenly rule on earth (Ps.48; Isa.2:1–5; Eph.4:1–16). It pleased him to prepare a place in the wilderness here on earth for his bride, where she would have a time of peace from the dragon and give birth to her children (Rev.12:6). This is why God's Spirit in the believers has the deepest desire to live in that very place (Ps.26:8; 42:4–5).

Since all the faithful apostles and true shepherds have done their utmost (John 21:15–17) and worked diligently in the sight of God (1 Cor.12) to keep Christ's lambs together (Acts 13; 19:1–20; Heb.10:32–34) lest they be torn by the wolves (John 10:11–12), the believers, too, were able diligently to make their way to the flock (Rom.12; 2 Cor.8:16–24; Eph.4:1). And that is how it still should be.

After Lorenz Huf obtained the above points in writing from the servant of the Lord and his Word Hans Schmidt, he read them to his people and asked each one personally to say whether he understood them and was in agreement. If anyone had an objection to any of these points or to the Hutterian Brethren, he should say clearly what it was. Nobody did, so another message was sent to our Brethren called Hutterian, saying they should hear for themselves that everybody was in complete agreement. This was confirmed at the appropriate time.

Hans Schmidt spoke to all of Lorenz Huf's group before uniting.

Before the decision was made, Hans Schmidt and the other brothers from Moravia challenged the group, emphasizing that each one must consider what he was undertaking. They must all recognize the error they had been led into and repent of it, confess and repent of anything else they had done against God and his truth, and humble themselves before God. Then each one was asked again individually, and a decision was made on the basis of his personal confession. Each person admitted his error and how much he had hurt God. Each one promised to change and from henceforth to surrender in obedience to God and his people and be of one heart and mind with them. Each one promised to accept good and bad times along with God's people, to shun all evil, and to let himself be used however God's Spirit directed in his church. *1556*

At that point Hans Schmidt, the servant of God's Word, turned first to Lorenz Huf (the teacher of the group) and his elders, who had been instrumental in bringing about the uniting. After he had accepted them [into the brotherhood], he took them aside and told them he would now talk with them and treat them as brothers. Since he was in a foreign country, as it were, he was not familiar with the group and did not know how each one stood. So Lorenz and the other elders, who knew them well, should now say of each one whether they felt he should be accepted or whether he should wait longer. They returned to the group, and on the basis of the elders' testimonies, they accepted into the church of God many of those who had requested it. Now they were all satisfied that the church community was firmly grounded in all points of Christian faith.

They were accepted individually on confession of their faith, after the brothers had prayed earnestly on their behalf that God might forgive their error and sin and send his Holy Spirit to lead them in true unity and community with God and his saints. With the laying on of hands as a sign of their covenant, they were received into the community of the saints and the body of Christ.

This took place on November 26, 1556. After this they moved to God's church community, where the brothers and the church asked Lorenz Huf to serve the brotherhood as a servant of the Word and Gospel of God for a time of testing.

Lorenz Huf chosen for the service of the Word.

1557

In 1557 four brothers, Kaspar Hueber, Andreas Arnolt or Bäck (a baker), Hans Zwinger or Gerber (a tanner), and a week later Sigmund Hosauer, were chosen and appointed to the service of the Gospel.[1]

4 brothers chosen for the service of the Word.

---

[1]Sigmund Hosauer is the author of four songs in *LdHBr*, 437–441, 446–450; see Wolkan, *Lieder*, 229–230. He died at Kostel, 1564; see below, p.384.

1557
4 brothers chosen for the service for temporal affairs.

Four other brothers were chosen and appointed to the service for temporal affairs: Charius Dreytzel, Peter Hörich, Paul Schnitzer or Schneider (a tailor), and Christoph Achtznit.

That same year the brothers started a big community at Kostel.

Driven out of Sabatisch in Hungary.

On September 1, 1557, Peter Diack[1] drove the brothers out of their place at Sabatisch in Hungary. He forced his way into the house, broke into rooms, and searched everything. He and his men carried off many of our belongings. He took three brothers prisoner, put them in chains, and set a guard over them. He insulted and threatened them and would have stabbed them. He told the peasants to guard the other believers so that nobody would escape. They searched for our provisions and stole whatever they found. They plundered everywhere, and no one was safe either inside or outside the house. They spared no one, neither the sick, the old, or the children. Everybody was pushed out and cast into exile. Oh, the villain and his men were ruthless. Our people lost house, home, and all their belongings. Their greatest grief was that he carried off some of their children by force, but most of these returned.

Communities.

In this year we began the communities at Pergen and Voitelsbrunn.[2]

Hans Kräl arrested.

In 1557, shortly before Ascension Day, brother Hans Kräl (called Kitzbühler after his birthplace) was taken prisoner for his witness to Jesus Christ and the divine truth. He was traveling for God's cause when he was captured at Taufers in the Puster Valley. About a mile from the castle he met a group of five men including the judge, Talhammer. The judge greeted him, since he did not know him, and rode past, and Hans acknowledged the greeting. Then the judge's clerk rode up to him and asked where he was from. Hans said, from Moravia. The clerk inquired about his business, and Hans told him he had been visiting his brothers. When the clerk asked him whether the Anabaptists were his brothers and Hans admitted they were, the clerk arrested him on the spot. The judge turned around, dismounted from his horse, and, taking brother Hans's

[1]Peter Diack was in the service of Januss Czobor.

[2]Voitelsbrunn (Sedlec), village southeast of Nikolsburg (Mikulov). The Hutterites operated a noted bathhouse at Voitelsbrunn. See *ME*, IV, 842; Beck, 208 n.2; Zeman, *Topography*, #166.

1557

own belt from his body, bound him as tightly as he could and led him alongside his horse. Hans had to run like a dog through the mud and puddles for a whole mile until they reached the castle. He was blue with suffocation from running and from the tight belt. He could hardly stand on his feet. The lord of the castle, named Füeger,[1] sharply reprimanded the judge for binding him so tightly.

Lord Füeger reprimanded the judge for binding Hans Kräl so tightly.

Then they searched him, took everything they found, and put him in prison for two days. The next day, a Thursday, they brought him out for a hearing. Lord Füeger and three others questioned him about his faith and his view on baptism and the mass. He witnessed to the divine truth and spoke about his beliefs, baptism, and the Lord's Supper. Then they stopped questioning him and pressed him to recant. When he told them not to expect him to abandon what he had acknowledged as the truth, they took him back to prison.

A week later Lord Füeger and six others questioned him again, but as they got nowhere, they returned him to the prison again.

Brother Kräl cross-examined.

Another week went by, and he was brought out for a hearing before the whole council. The judge called his faith heresy and the church of God a sect. Brother Hans said it was neither heresy nor a sect but the church of God. "The devil take you if you think you are the church of God!" the furious judge replied. He repeated it every time he heard Hans mention the church of God and said he would teach him not to say it again. But brother Hans persisted all the more. Then the judge told him that an order had come from Innsbruck demanding the names of the leaders who sent brothers out on mission and of those who gave them food and shelter. He answered, "We are not sent out to harm anyone. Our mission is the salvation of men, to call them to repent and change their lives." But this last question, he added, was not about articles of faith; they did not need to know and he would not tell them.

They wanted to know who sent us on mission and who gave us shelter.

Then the judge warned him sternly to consider his own safety. Unless he would tell who gave them shelter, food, and drink, they would use physical violence on him. So brother Hans asked the judge and the whole council how they would like it if he betrayed them after they had done him a good

[1]Hans Füeger, lord of the Taufers estate in South Tirol, now Italy.

1557

turn. The members of the council looked at one another and said they would not like it at all. The judge became angry. He asked him if he was trying to accuse an honorable council of making him betray someone and repeated his warning to take care, because they were going to deal with him in earnest. Since Hans refused to tell them what they wanted to know, he was sent back to prison. He had to go hungry, while they went to eat.

They took Hans Kräl to be tortured.

When they rose from the table, they fetched him back and led him to the torture chamber. He took off his cloak himself and sat down so willingly beneath the rope that the bystanders could not hold back their tears.

The torturer stretched him up by the rope, and the judge warned him again to spare himself and confess. But brother Hans said he would betray no one. He would wait on God's will. A big stone was brought. The judge was angry when he realized that he was getting nowhere and said, "You all swear that you won't betray or inform on one another."

Hans answered, "We do not swear; we betray no one, because it is wrong."

The devil's cunning in his children.

Then the judge said, "You are a scoundrel. I have already caught you telling a lie. Why do you allow yourself to be tortured? It is all over with you anyhow." (Mark well what the devil and his children can do. They know that a man who is not standing right cannot remain firm.) The brother protested: he was no scoundrel—what lie had they caught him in? The judge answered, "You said you were not a teacher, but we have learned that you are." Brother Hans replied that he was not a teacher, but if he were, he would not be ashamed of it, for it is honorable before God. So they left him hanging from the rope and went to the council room.

The torturer called him a fool for thinking God saw what they did to him.

The torturer remained with him and pleaded with him to give the information. "They will not stop until they have torn you apart." Hans answered that he would wait and see how far God would let them go. They could do no more than God permitted. The torturer scoffed, "Aren't you a fool to think God can see what we are doing to you in this hole!"

Then the council returned, saying the lady of the castle had asked them not to torture him and therefore they would stop. They sent him back to prison.

After that, Lord Füeger rode to Innsbruck, the seat of

government. When he returned, he had the priests interrogate Hans in his presence for two days running, Friday and Saturday.

1557
The priests talked with brother Hans Kräl for 2 days.

No matter what they tried, they got nowhere with their false teaching and insistent pleading. It would take too long to tell it all. Hans remained firm and, in a word, said he was standing in the truth and would remain in it with God's help. By that time Lord Füeger was furious. "You stubborn dog! I have tried everything with you, but I won't give up. I will send you to the stake, and then we'll see how you honor God."

Lord Füeger called him a stubborn dog.

Hans answered, "I will not be suffering because I did anything wrong but solely for the sake of the truth, and that will not dishonor God."

Three days later they put him in a deep, pitch-dark dungeon in the castle keep, where he could see neither sun, moon, nor light of day. He could not tell whether it was day or night but noticed it was night when the dungeon became somewhat cooler. During the day it was hot and steamy at the bottom of the dungeon, and he sweated. His clothes rotted away on his body until he was almost naked, and for a long time he had no shirt, only a rough blanket that had been let down to him. He wrapped it around himself, and there he sat in misery and darkness. His shirt rotted away until not a thread remained except the collar around his neck, which he finally hung on the wall. He could not stand the daylight and fresh air anymore. When the brood of Pilate hauled him up for a hearing to see if he would recant, the air and light were so painful to him that he was glad when they let him down into the dungeon again.

Hans Kräl put in the castle dungeon.

His clothing rotted to shreds on his body.

He could no longer bear fresh air and light.

He stank so terribly from the foulness of this dark pit that no one could stand being close to him. When they brought him out, they had to stand back. The councillors said they had never known even a carcass to stink so badly.

Terrible stench from the dungeon.

There he lay in the terrible dungeon that was so full of worms and vermin that he had to cover his head by wrapping it in an old rag someone had mercifully thrown down to him. For a long time no one had been in the dungeon; that was why the vermin had become so bad. Hans had a great horror of them until he finally got used to them.

Dungeon full of vermin.

The rats and mice even ate his food. When his meals were let down, he had to be sure to get hold of the bowl before it

Vermin ate his food.

1557

reached the ground, otherwise the vermin would be all over it before he had a chance. When he pushed the bowl away, they fought over it and bit one another, clattering the bowl around and cleaning it up in no time. He could not keep any food, because the vermin would have smelled it and eaten it off his very body. But there was no question of keeping food, for there was never any left over. They all but starved him. When he was well, he could easily eat the little he did get. When he was sick and could not eat, their attitude was, "Go without until you feel like eating."

Hans Kräl suffered hunger and want.

The vermin lifted the lid and drank from his water container until he got a heavy stone and placed it on top so they could no longer get it open.

Vermin drank the water from his container.

His greatest sorrow was that no messages got through to him from the church. At that time Hans Mändel, a servant of the Lord's Word, was in the mountains of Tirol. He had a great longing for news from Hans Kräl and got word to him in the dungeon, asking him to send some sign that he was still faithful to God and his church. If he had nothing else, he should send a little bundle of straw. Hans Kräl would gladly have done so, but he did not even have so much as a bundle of straw in the dungeon. That is how poor he was. Then he remembered the collar of his rotted shirt, which he had hung on the wall, and glad that he had it, he took it down and sent it to the brothers as a sign that he was at peace with God and the church. When they received the collar and saw how destitute he was, it went to their hearts and they wept out of pity for him. They sent a message back to him in the dungeon that they would be more than happy to send him a shirt or anything else, if only they knew how. But he did not want them to try, because if it were discovered he would be tortured again and those who brought it would have to suffer. So he let them know that they should not send him anything. He must clothe himself with the garment of patience.

No messages went between Hans and the church.

He had not so much as a bundle of straw to send as a sign.

He sent his collar as a token.

In this state he spent all summer in the dungeon, until Michaelmas [Sept. 29] in the fall, when they noticed that his feet were beginning to rot. They brought him to another prison, where conditions were so harsh that nothing could be worse. Here he was hung by one hand and one foot in the stocks for thirty-seven weeks. He had to sit on a tilted board and hang in the stocks in such a way that he could neither lie down nor sit properly, and he could not stand up at all.

Hans Kräl taken out of the dungeon but hung in the stocks for 37 weeks.

On top of all this misery, he was subjected to mockery from the godless folk who taunted him: "There lies a holy man. No one is as wise as he, and he alone knows it. There lies the chosen people of God!" This was because he testified steadfastly about the church.

1557
Abuse and mockery.

On the other hand, since he could receive no message of comfort from the church, on one occasion God gave him great comfort in secret through an unbeliever, a nobleman who told Hans to take courage and not be afraid: many people knew very well what was true and what was right, only they did not follow it and so would not tolerate it. This was a great encouragement.

An unbeliever comforted brother Hans Kräl.

It so happened that God prompted Hans to send for the clerk who had taken him prisoner. The clerk soon came, sat down, and asked why he had been called. Brother Hans said, "Because, as you well know, you are guilty of my imprisonment and of the great misery I am suffering, although I am innocent—I have to tell you this. Never in my whole life have I done you any harm." The clerk sat there, dumb with shock and unable to answer. All he could say was that he had no choice. Brother Hans said, "Indeed, it is God's judgment upon you that has been driving you. Because you have been so bloodthirsty against the believers, you will not be able to avoid bringing about your own judgment by this last deed. You have brought a severe sentence upon yourself. God will deal with you and punish you for your sin." The clerk was so terrified he could not say a word.

Hans Kräl sent for the clerk who had taken him prisoner.

Clerk terrified and unable to answer a word.

He left, and less than two weeks later he died in the night. He had been in good health, then within fifteen minutes he was dead. God brought him to his end in great fear. He howled and wailed and admitted that he had sinned. It is bound to be so with those who take pleasure in serving the devil and his henchmen. I omitted to say that his superiors were displeased and said he deserved a fitting reward from the devil. They told him (in Hans's hearing) that it must have been demonic possession that made him unable to leave Hans Kräl alone, and the devil should have carried him off for taking Hans prisoner. He hardly ever smiled again from that time on, because of what he had done, and in the end he had to pay for it.

The clerk who had taken brother Hans Kräl prisoner died a sudden death.

The clerk deserved the devil's reward.

It happened that on the night the clerk died, such great joy came over brother Hans that he prayed and gave thanks to God all night long, for he was given the certainty that he would

Hans Kräl knew he would return to the church.

1557
Isa.38:20

Ps.122:1–4

return to the church of the Lord. He was filled with joy and gladness, like the God-fearing King Hezekiah when he said, "Oh, what a wonderful thing that I should return again to the house of the Lord and his church." Yes, his joy was that of the king and prophet David, who sings in the Psalm, "I am glad that they say to me that I shall go into the house of God and my feet shall stand in the gates of Jerusalem, where the tribes of the Lord go up to give thanks to his name."

Never in his whole life had he experienced such a night. In the morning the jailer's wife came and told him about the clerk's sudden and terrible death that same night.

The lords were fearful and would gladly have got rid of him.

After what had happened to the clerk, the lords of the castle were very much afraid and tried to find ways to get rid of Hans. One evening about a week later, a farmhand who did field work for the castle came to brother Hans with the keys and asked if Hans would trust him to let him out. Hans said he would see what the man would do after he was out. The laborer tried to unlock the door but could not find the right key. Brother Hans told him not to try—it would get him into trouble. The man said that was for him to worry about. He looked for the right key but could not find it, so he had to give up. It was not to be this time.

The lady of the castle sent her servant to the dungeon to call down to brother Hans, "Her ladyship wishes to tell you she will send for the judge and jurors. If you will say just two words indicating that you are willing to be instructed or that you have been wrong, you will be released. If you are afraid to do it because you think it would be a sin, she is ready to take the sin on herself and you would be free of it."

Hans Kräl should say just two words to be released.

But Hans said, "Go and tell your lady she is already burdened with enough sin and should turn away from it. She does not need another's sin."

As a result he had to stay in prison for another winter. The following spring an order came from the government at Innsbruck, which the lords came and read to him. It said that because he was so stubborn and would not accept any correction, he would be sent to the galleys. They told him how he would fare on the ocean, that the prisoners were stripped naked and scourged. But he answered that he would trust God, his Lord, who was on the sea just as much as on the land, to help him endure.

Then he was taken out of the dungeon and allowed to go about the castle for two days to learn to walk, since he was completely crippled from the imprisonment, the stocks, and the fetters. He had been in prison for two years minus five weeks; for eighteen months of that time he had not seen the sun.

1557
They let him go about in the castle to learn to walk again.

A constable was made responsible for taking him to the galleys. Hans said farewell to everyone in the castle and called them to repentance. The lady of the castle sent a message telling him to come to her too, which he did. She let him come into her writing room, where he took leave of her and called her to repentance too. He asked her to let the faithful continue their work unhindered and not to imprison them anymore. She agreed and wept. With tears running down her cheeks she said, "As long as I live I will never again take a believer captive." Then she gave him some traveling money and dismissed him.

Planned to send brother Kräl to the galleys.

The lady promised never again to imprison believers.

The constable led him away. This was an ungodly man, who called brother Hans a scoundrel every time he spoke to him. One evening two days later, the constable got drunk in the inn at Niederdorf. They had given him so much wine that he fell across the table, and when he and Hans were taken to bed, the constable collapsed on the bed dead drunk. Then dear brother Hans opened the bedroom door, then the door of the house, closed it behind him, and was gone.

Hans Kräl escaped.

That was how God helped him escape that night early in 1559, and he returned in peace and joy to the church of the Lord, as is told in the song he wrote.[1] After he was entrusted with the service of God's Word, he made still more journeys in Tirol.

This story shows how God stands by a man who is upright and true—how much patience and strength he can give a man to endure suffering for the sake of his faith and God's truth, which would otherwise be impossible. All of this happened and is recorded here as an example of steadfastness so that we, too, may prepare ourselves with true devotion. No one

---

[1]Hans Kräl's song, with the acrostic "Hans Kral Gefenknuslied wie im Got beigestanden" (Hans Kräl's prison song of how God helped him), is the source of the story of his sufferings as told above; see *LdHBr*, 538–545; Wolkan, *Lieder*, 244–246.

Hans Kräl later became Vorsteher of the Hutterian Church (1578–1583); see below, pp.465, 492. *Martyrs Mirror*, 560–563, "Hans Brael"; *ME*, III, 231–232; Beck, 217–218.

1557
The lord of the castle, the clerk, the constable, and the judge died soon after.

who is not pure and upright can hold out under such torment.

While Hans Kräl was still imprisoned, Lord Füeger (the lord of the castle) died a terrible death. The same was true of the clerk who took Hans prisoner, as already told. The constable who was supposed to take him to the galleys died miserably too, while Hans Kräl was still in the mountains after his escape. Judge Talhammer died two years later. His was not a natural death either. That is how God destroys his enemies for their guilt toward his people.

In 1557 the brothers Michael Veldthaler and Paul Schnitzer were sent out on mission to the Rhine Valley. They had been traveling through Swabia, in the area called Ries, and were on their way over the Swabian Alps from Aufhausen[1] to Aalen when they were arrested right there on the road by Count Wolf von Öttingen with four mounted men. For years Veldthaler had feared falling into the hands of this man, who was well known to him and to his father. (Besides, he was a papist and had had brother Hans Schuster burned at Wasserburg.) One of the men rode up to the brothers and asked where they were from and where they were going. Without thinking, brother Michael said they were from Moravia, heading toward the Rhine. When the count heard this, he called them over. Furious, he thundered at Michael, asking what he was doing in his county. Was he planning to mislead the people as he had done in Bavaria? He threatened to send Michael to the prince of Bavaria. But Michael, pale with fright, pleaded with the count not to do it because he had already spilled enough innocent blood.

Michael Veldthaler and Paul Schnitzer captured.

The count answered, "There is no other way but to take you along as prisoners. That is the decision of the Augsburg Confession." He ordered two of his mounted men to take the brothers with them while he himself hurried to the village (which was not his) and urged the peasants there to accompany him. He acted as if he were a constable. He took the brothers to the inn, sat them down at a table, and ordered one of his men to keep close watch on them. The count left quickly and sent home for a cart with two horses, eight foot-soldiers, and

[1]Aufhausen near Neresheim, Swabia, approx. 22 miles southeast of Aalen. Count Öttingen was the administrator for the Bavarian district of Wasserburg. See *Theologisches Literaturblatt* (1916), 110.

three mounted men. They arrived fully armed and stood ready with muskets cocked. The cart was brought to the door and people lined the path on both sides so that the brothers had to pass between them. The constable went up to them and said, "Now, you fellows, out with you. I've got to tie you up. His Lordship has given me strict orders to take good care of you." *1557*

Brother Michael responded, "Do what God allows you to do." And so, with firm trust in God, the two brothers followed him to the cart. A large crowd of men and women had gathered. As the prisoners climbed into the cart, Michael told the people how the count had seized them, not because they were thieves or murderers—they had no wish to rob anyone or harm anyone—but simply because of their faith. The people were moved to sympathy, and the innkeeper even begged the mounted men on the brothers' behalf to spare them the terrible dungeon where no one remained alive.

Michael told the people why they were seized and imprisoned: because of their faith.

At that point the constable said, "I have orders from His Lordship to tie your feet together under the cart, but if you promise to sit still and behave, I won't do it." Michael Veldthaler replied that if he would trust them, they would make their own way to the castle. So the constable left them unbound, sat down in the cart, pointed a spear at them, and said, "If either of you moves, I'll run him through." He gave orders to start. Eight foot-soldiers surrounded the cart and three riders led the way. But as they left the village, the driver refused to go further unless the prisoners were bound, because that had been the count's order. So the constable bound the brothers' feet together under the cart, and they drove the rest of the way in this miserable manner.

The brothers' feet bound.

On their arrival at Flochberg Castle, near Bopfingen, the head steward of the estate, named Raming, exclaimed, "Oh, Michael, Michael, I am distressed to see you like this." He knew Michael well—they had once been friends.[1] He ordered the constable to untie the brothers and had them taken from the cart. Brother Paul was put in the keep with another prisoner.

The head steward, with a doctor and the bailiff, as well as

Michael Veldthaler interrogated.

---

[1]Michael Veldthaler came from the Bavarian nobility and had previously been a county administrator. After he joined the Hutterian brotherhood, he learned cabinetmaking (*Tischler*, not *Tuchscherer*, cloth shearer; this is according to Wolkan, *Geschicht-Buch*, 287 n., who disagrees with Beck, 216 n.1). He became a servant of the Word and died in 1587; see below, p.509; *ME*, IV, 804.

1557

a priest and a clerk with pen and ink, came to Veldthaler and began asking him what he was doing in His Lordship's county and what business he had there. Michael told them they were doing nothing; they were only passing through on their way to the Rhine to join their companions in the faith. Then the head steward asked him how he had come to the faith and how long ago that was. Michael said the steward must surely remember how he, Michael, had gone to Falkenstein in Austria and how the brothers working for the lord of the castle there had told him that a man who leads a worldly life cannot please God, much less obtain salvation. So he considered his soul's salvation and accepted the truth; that was about ten years ago. The head steward agreed that it was ten years ago and said approvingly that he had never known Michael to be anything but truthful. He went on to ask Michael who had baptized him, and Michael told him. Then he asked him what position he held—he had heard he was the leader—and what kind of work he did. Michael answered that he was the least of all the believers and that he worked as a cabinetmaker. The other asked, "Didn't you learn that before you joined the community?" Michael answered that he had learned that and other work in the community.

Head steward said he had never known Michael other than honest.

When he had answered all the questions, adding, "Even if you bring three executioners, I will not say anything different," they handed him over to the jailer, who put him in a deep dungeon. He was told it was sixty feet down and no one could remain alive in it for long. The jailer ordered him to hand over everything he had, made him sit on a wooden bar by the hole, and told him to watch out and hold tight to the rope so as not to fall. Then he was lowered down. The rope twisted and swung around as if there were no bottom.

Put in a dungeon 60 feet deep.

When he had reached the bottom and the jailer had shut the hole and left, Michael fell on his knees and, in his distress, prayed to the Lord as never before in his life. He prepared himself to yield up his life as a sacrifice to God. He prayed unceasingly, not for God to help him escape, for he had given up hope of that, but that he might be an honor to God and a joy to all the faithful.

Pitch-dark dungeon.

It was so pitch-dark in the dungeon that he could see nothing. Around midday for about half an hour a little light came in through a window nearly fifty feet above him. At night it was so damp and hot that he thought he would suffocate. He took off all his clothes except his shirt and would have been glad to strip this off too, if he had not felt shame, before himself, let alone before God. Food was lowered down to him, but he did not take much of it.

1557
It was so humid he had to undress.

The clerk came to the top of the dungeon and tried to persuade him to let himself be turned back to the old "Christian" faith, saying that his brother Paul was ready to listen, and that he too should recant. Michael said, "That I will not do, nor do I believe that my brother Paul has recanted." It was not the truth either. They did the same with Paul, telling him that his brother Michael was willing to change his mind and he should be willing too. That is how the devil tries to trap God's children by lies and deception. He and his children are not to be trusted or believed.

The devil tried with lies and other means to trap the believers.

The devil and his children cannot be trusted.

But the brothers continued praying to God. They knelt down, their hands lifted up to heaven, until they were too faint to go on. The Lord heard their prayers and changed the count's heart, for the head steward, the doctor, and the count's ladies pleaded with him for the sake of Michael Veldthaler's father, whom the count knew and liked well. Finally, after thinking it over, the count sent the head steward and the doctor to the prisoner. From the top of the dungeon the jailer shouted down to Veldthaler to get his things together and sit on the wooden bar. Michael thought, "O Lord my God, stand by me and help me endure. Now they will send me to the galleys." He sat on the wooden bar. The rope swung from side to side. The head steward encouraged him to hold on tight so as not to fall; he himself guided the rope through the narrow hole at the top.

God changed the count's heart, as he has power to do.

When Michael emerged, very pale, the head steward offered him his freedom provided he would make his way home without traveling any further. He must never set foot in the count's territory again. It had cost them a great effort to win the count over to this. But Michael replied, "That I cannot do. I thank you for all the trouble you have taken on my behalf, but I cannot go straight home and abandon the land that belongs to the Lord in heaven. It may well be that I never come back here again; but it may also happen that God gives me a reason for returning. That is something I do not know. The Lord may direct us to travel further or to go straight home. We will do whatever he shows us."

Michael Veldthaler would be released if he promised to leave the country forever and go home.

1557

At these words the head steward got angry and said, "Then all our pleading was in vain, and His Grace won't agree. So you may as well go back to the dungeon. We will report your obstinacy to His Grace. I am sure he will not let you go."

Then they left him, and in the presence of the clerk, Michael fell on his knees, asking God for protection against all evil and praising him for his great mercy. About an hour later they returned from the count and repeated the same stipulations, to which Michael gave the same answer. At this the head steward said, "God is showing you that you should go home and never come back here again. It is the devil who tells you to go on. Besides, this land does not belong to the Lord in heaven; it belongs to His Lordship. God has given it to him, and my lord does not want you in his land."

The head steward said the land did not belong to God: God had given it to His Grace.

As he got nowhere with Michael, he said that if the doctor, too, was willing to take the risk, they would take it on themselves to let him go. But Michael should be on his guard. Every place was watched, and if he did not go straight home and was seized again, he would not have a second chance. He should remember that.

Michael Veldthaler and Paul Schnitzer released.

So he was released, and they told him they had begged for his companion's release too. Shortly afterward they brought brother Paul to him at the gate. Before anything else, Michael asked Paul whether he was still true and steadfast. When Paul answered yes, they clasped hands, embraced, and praised God that he restored them to each other as faithful brothers. Then they were ready to go, but the jailer demanded his prison fees. They told him, "We owe you nothing and will give you nothing. We were unjustly imprisoned." The jailer shouted to the gatekeeper not to let them out and went to the count to ask what he should do. The message came back just to let them out.

The jailer demanded prison fees.

They traveled with joy and in the fear of God, again and again praising him who leads into prison and out again. They put their trust in the Lord, and after they had reached the Rhine and carried out their task in obedience to their mission from the church, they returned joyfully to the church community with good consciences.[1]

This story shows us how the world treats those who obey God and how much the world makes them suffer for the sake

How the world treats those who obey God.

---

[1]Michael Veldthaler's song about his experiences is the source for the above account; see *LdHBr*, 545–551, with the acrostic "Michael Veldtalers Lied."

of divine truth and faithfulness; how those who truly love God keep themselves unpolluted by the world and free before God, no matter what the cost. Therefore God stands by them and is their helper.

1557

Hans Arbeiter, one of the Swiss Brethren, came from the Netherlands.

In this same year, 1557, brother Hans Schmidt or Raiffer, a servant of Jesus Christ and his church, continued in the Lord's work, gathering the believers along the Rhine and in the Netherlands. There he met Hans Arbeiter[1] from Aachen, an elder for temporal affairs from the Swiss Brethren, and the two discussed the following points:

1. Surrender
2. Community
3. Services in the church
4. Original sin
5. Marriage
6. Separation from the world
7. The incarnation of Christ
8. Idolatry and priests
9. Church discipline
10. Food and drink for the servants
11. Raising children
12. Taxes
13. Greeting
14. Making promises or shaking hands on an agreement
15. Care of the sick
16. Widows
17. Trades and crafts

When Hans Arbeiter was satisfied that in all these points our stand was based on the Word of God, he united with our brothers and was accepted into the Lord's church.

Hans Arbeiter explained to the Swiss Brethren why he was leaving them.

Right there, in Aiffen, Netherlands, he spoke to the whole Swiss Brethren congregation in the presence of three brothers who were later executed with Hans Schmidt. He held another meeting in his home at Aachen and spoke to the elders of the Swiss Brethren about the faults and shortcomings he had seen among them and why he was leaving them. After that he traveled to the church community in Moravia, where he was certainly needed. This will be told later.

[1]For details about Hans Arbeiter's imprisonment, see below, pp.398–399.

1558

1558

In 1558 brother Hans Schmidt, a servant of the Gospel and an apostle of Jesus Christ, was sent by the church to do the Lord's work. He went out to gather those eager for the truth.

Hans Schmidt captured at Aachen with 11 others.

He felt called by the Lord to go back to the Netherlands, where he and eleven others were captured in the city of Aachen on January 9.[1] They had gathered in a house to speak of God's Word, praying to God in oneness of heart, when they were betrayed. The constables (that brood of Pilate) came by night with spears, halberds, ropes, and chains and surrounded the house with torches. They bound the brothers and took them

A mother and baby also taken prisoner.

to prison. They even took a mother and her baby who was lying in a cradle. But the prisoners were undaunted. They encouraged each other not to give way to fear, for they were being arrested for God's sake. So they began to sing with joy and confidence. Then they were separated and taken to prison. Even the sisters were cheerful and sang, which terrified other people.

Early next morning, the judge summoned the prisoners and spoke to each one individually, but finding them steadfast, he had them taken back to prison.

The following day, the servant [Hans Schmidt] was called before the lords again and asked how many he had baptized, where they were, and where the church gathered. He made it quite clear that he would lose his life rather than tell them and be a traitor.

Hans Schmidt racked and cruelly tortured.

So they racked him for fifteen minutes. He submitted willingly, unfastened his clothes, and took them off himself. At first they pulled him up without weights. As they did not get any result, they let him down again and left him, but they soon returned, saying, "You had better tell what we want to know, or we will rack you until you are torn apart."

His belief about infant baptism.

They also questioned him about infant baptism. He replied that it was a human institution and that was how he regarded

His belief about the mass.

it—not as true Christian baptism. Then they asked him about

---

[1]About Hans Schmidt (also called Raiffer after his native Raiffach in Tirol) and his activity in Aachen, see *ME*, IV, 462–464; Josef Hansen, "Die Wiedertäufer in Aachen und in der Aachener Gegend," *Zeitschrift des Aachener Geschichtsvereins*, VI, 295–338, which includes Schmidt's song about what befell him there: "Fröhlich so will ich heben an, Gottes Wunder erzählen tun" (I will sing with joy of the wonders God has worked); also in *LdHBr*, 557–564; see below, p.363 n.1.

the mass, and he said, "All I hear is a lot of quarreling about it, and the way the priests hold mass is not the true Supper of Christ but an idolatrous invention."

1558

Then they bound him again hand and foot and attached a large iron ball onto him, which weighed more than a hundredweight. They pulled him up until the ring in the iron broke, though the iron itself had not moved. Then they took a rope and put it in place of the broken ring, attached the iron again, and pulled him up. They left him hanging like that for some time, but they achieved nothing.

They hung a hundredweight iron ball on him to stretch him.

So they let him down again and returned him to prison until early Sunday, when the city governors came with two priests, who questioned him about his mission. He told them he himself had not chosen to do this task but had been appointed by God and his Spirit in his church. Just as God sent his Son, and as the Son sent his apostles into all the world, so he still sends out his servants through his Spirit, first of all to preach the Word of God. Then they are to baptize, not infants and young children, but those who hear, understand, and believe.

Priests questioned him about mission.

They also questioned him about those in government, whether he considered them Christians. He replied, "In the first place they are creatures of God, but they were misled by the priests and taught wickedness and never became part of the true Christian church." Then they asked him where governmental authority came from. He told them, "The office and the power is from God." To their question whether they were Christians, he said that if they denied themselves, surrendered everything, took the cross upon themselves, turned away from all their power and vainglory, and followed Christ, then they would be Christians. But they could not be Christians while maintaining their office.

About government.

Matt.16:24–26
Luke 14:26–33

Next they questioned him about swearing oaths, to which he replied that Christ had forbidden it. He said much more, but it is too long to report here, although they wrote it all down.

About swearing.

Another question concerned the incarnation of Christ. He said he believed that Christ was truly God and truly man but without sin.

About Christ's incarnation.

Finally they told Hans Schmidt that if he were ready to repudiate his baptism and confess that he had been mistaken, they would pardon him, and he could save himself and others too. But he answered that he had learned the pure truth of God

If Hans Schmidt repudiated his baptism, they would show him mercy.

1558

They feared the emperor, not God.

Case not closed with the death of the brothers.

and would stand by it. They said they were sorry but they could not help him. The king or the new emperor would punish them if they did not punish such beliefs, and they were afraid, being of the brood of Pilate. Brother Hans, however, told them how hard their lot would be, for although God forgave all sins, he would avenge innocent blood. They should not think that when they had killed the brothers the case would be closed. It would come before Christ, who would judge it on the last day.

They took him back to prison, and on Monday evening the judge returned with others, including a monk, to interrogate him; but they achieved nothing. The monk was red with shame as he left, glad to get away as quickly as possible.

Monks and priests did their utmost.

Repeatedly, monks and priests were sent to dispute with the prisoners, but they were totally discredited. They were unable to change the believers' minds. Many were the times the brothers were called up for questioning, and each time God put such wise and joyful answers into their mouths that their interrogators found no wrong, nothing in them worthy of death. Yet they were afraid of the emperor.

Brother Heinrich Adams silenced the scholar, who had to admit he was right.

One day they brought a cunning serpent of a flatterer to Heinrich Adams, saying that as he did not like churchmen, that is, monks and priests, they had brought a scholar of the world to instruct him. But brother Heinrich said he needed no instruction from him—he had received sufficient instruction from Christ and his Word and had no desire to seek life from among the dead. The learned man tried to prove that the apostles had instituted infant baptism. After Heinrich's reply, he was forced to admit that no infants were baptized in the apostles' time. Brother Heinrich also said that infants do not have faith. In the presence of the lords he wrote this on the table with a piece of chalk, saying it was to underline his testimony. His opponent was reduced to silence, and Heinrich said to the lords, "So will all your learned men be brought to shame by the Lord's Word." In response, some of the lords said to each other that if that man—meaning Heinrich—had his head cut off, they would like to have it on their own shoulders. They became quite friendly to him at that point.

Heinrich Adams took chalk and wrote on the table before the lords.

Once they were allowed to be together.

On one occasion the brothers were allowed to be in the same prison with the sisters from four in the morning until ten at night. Together they rejoiced in the Lord, prayed together, and praised God. Hans, as the servant, spoke the prayer for them in his loudest voice, so loud that people from all sides gathered to listen. As soon as the city magistrates heard of this, they sent an official to find out why there was such a noise in the town. The brothers said they had been praying and had finished just before he came. Brother Matthias [Schmidt] added, "We intend to lift our voices to God whether anyone else approves or not." When they were separated again at ten in the evening, they sang songs of faith as they were taken through the town.

1558
They prayed together. The servant led the prayer as loudly as he could.

Returning through the town, they sang songs of faith.

Some of the councillors wanted to kill them, but others opposed this because they had come to realize that the brothers were innocent. Five times the executioner came, ready to execute them, but the council could not reach a verdict.

Executioner came 5 times to execute them.

They had in mind to execute first the servant Hans Schmidt and one other, Heinrich Adams, because these two had opposed them the most, and they hoped that this would shake the others. When Hans heard he was to die, he began to sing for joy. He gave thanks to God and prayed with all his heart that God might protect his people.

When the servant heard he was to die, he sang for joy.

The date of the execution of Hans Schmidt and Heinrich Adams was set for August 13. Hans, the servant, was brought before the court, and then brother Heinrich was brought to join him under the arches by the pillory in the square, where a crowd had gathered. Some who felt sympathy for them and had sent them food and drink from time to time now came to offer their hand to Hans. He shook hands and smiled at them. Even when he had walked through the crowd in the square, there had been a smile on his lips. People had swarmed about him right and left, in front and behind, as he was being taken before the court, which made him exclaim, "What a wonderful wedding I am having, with so many people attending!" He was full of joy, for he hoped that evening to be in Paradise with his brothers and sisters and all the faithful, of whom he had known many on earth.

They wanted to execute Hans Schmidt and Heinrich Adams, but there was a delay.

Hans Schmidt said he was having a wonderful wedding.

At the place of execution, too, people had already gathered, men and women, young and old, to witness the brothers' end. At that point two monks came to dispute with them. For a while Hans answered them and pointed out their deceit, but then he refused to continue and said he was not going to forsake the truth, that his hour had come, and right now he had better things to do than to talk with them.

2 monks still came to argue.

1558

Now there was a delay in the proceedings because the seven jurors could not agree on the sentence. They told the brothers they would bring another scholar and that if they listened to what he said, they would postpone the whole matter. "Otherwise we will have to kill you, much as we dislike it." But Hans and Heinrich told them clearly that they held to their convictions and would not turn from the truth either to right or left. There was no reason for sparing them or for any delay on their account. But this much they should know: if they killed the brothers, no matter what they did, asleep or awake, their consciences would never be at peace again but would all the more accuse them like a gnawing worm.

The brothers said, "If you kill us, your consciences will never be at peace."

Then the lords put their heads together and told the crowd to disperse. When the brothers saw this, they were seized with fear at the postponement, for they were already quite prepared and thought they had overcome the serpent's cunning.

The brothers were alarmed when the execution was postponed.

So the people went away, each to his own affair, as if they had lost a battle. When evening came, the brothers had to return to the prison, grieved that they had been prevented from witnessing with their blood, and they were led back through the streets without chains. That gave people much to think about. Many were filled with fear because God was opposing and hindering this case.

A councillor informed the brothers of the decision to execute them in a week's time and not delay any longer, but this did not happen. Instead they were kept in prison until the fall and had to suffer many afflictions until they were condemned and executed.

Hans Schmidt sang as he was led to execution.

Because Hans Schmidt was a servant, they executed him first. As he was led through the town he sang the following song, written by our dear brother Hieronymus Käls,[1] who was executed for his faith in Vienna, Austria.

In you, O Father,
Is my joy,
Though I must suffer here!
Let me be scorned
By everyone
If your grace still is near!

[1]*LdHBr*, 67, "Ich freu mich dein, O Vater mein," with the acrostic "Jeronimus."

The world abhors it *1558*
That you love us.
Because we boast
Of your truth most,
They label us a heretic host.

Our thanks and praise
To you we raise,
While yet on earth we have a place.
May never need
Or suffering or hateful deed
Part us from your great love, we plead.

Our enemy
Is raging free.
But, O Lord, to do your will,
We, undeterred,
Will joyfully proclaim your Word
And with your strength our loins will gird.

Nothing has power
To make us stray
From you, our Strength and Tower.
For you are near
To comfort and bring cheer
Where hearts are faithful and sincere.

On this poor earth
There is no dearth
Of frivolous and wanton mirth.
Your children, though,
And loyal servants here below
In this blind world great sadness know.

And as, again,
Her time once come,
A woman bears her child in pain,
Then greets the new life
Full of joy and eagerly—
So we, too, suffer patiently.

1558

For all who dare
His cross to bear,
A crown of joy Christ does prepare.
Their grief shall be
Turned to pure bliss and ecstasy
By Jesus Christ eternally.

God Father, Son, and Spirit, too—
To them all praise and glory due
Be given by his people true.
Lord, lead your band
With gracious hand
Out of this world to your own land!

Hans Schmidt executed by strangling.

After this he said little more but went straight to the place of execution like a silent, patient lamb. There he was strangled with a rope, bound to the stake with a chain, and scorched with fire.[1]

Hans Schmidt had known how his end would be.

He had known the manner of his death because God had revealed it to him. He had told this to a man who used to bring him his food in prison. The man had said, "Hans, they say you will all be beheaded." Hans had answered no, he would not be executed with the sword. This had been made known to him in a vision the night before. For three days he did not eat but was found in constant prayer, for he said his end was approaching. Later he took food again and was cheerful, and soon afterward, on October 19, 1558, he was led to his execution as told above.

Three days later two others were taken before the court and then condemned to death. They were Heinrich Adams and his father-in-law Hans Weck.

One of the councillors at Aachen, Councillor Pock, was constantly maligning the brothers. Once, when they picked on brother Heinrich with their questions and could not move him, Councillor Pock shouted, "Into the fire with him! Let him die! It's no use. They don't deserve to be shown any more mercy."

Brother Heinrich foretold councillor's death.

Brother Heinrich (undoubtedly through divine prompting) told Councillor Pock he would not live until the day of execution,

[1]See A. Keller, C. Calvert, and A. W. Gruner, eds., *A Hangman's Diary: Being the Journal of Master Franz Schmidt of Nürnberg* (New York, 1928), regarding symbolic burning by scorching.

nor would he see the brothers die. And that was what happened. He died three days before Heinrich's end, on the day the servant Hans Schmidt was executed. On his deathbed he tore at his beard with both hands and was beside himself, which convinced many people that this bloodthirsty man had surely sinned and was being punished by God.

1558

The councillor's terrible end.

Brother Heinrich Adams, with the other brother, was led to his death without giving any sign of wavering. The executioner bound his hands so tightly that his fingers turned black, but Heinrich lifted up his hands in thanks to God for considering him worthy of such suffering. He slid the ropes off his hands so they were freed.

A miracle: however tightly brother Heinrich Adams was bound, the ropes loosened.

They tied his hands as tightly as before so that he could not free them again, but it was useless. As soon as he lifted up his hands, the ropes fell off. This miracle happened several times, and many witnessed it.

The judge was furious and gave orders to bind him again, but the executioner said, "Can't you see that it is useless to tie him up?" The last time it happened, brother Heinrich threw the ropes out over the crowd and no one could find them. He said, "It is not God's will that I should be bound," and added, "You see that God with his power and miracles is against you. Yet you are still enraged, and there is no repentance among you. God will certainly call you to account."

Heinrich threw the ropes over the people's heads.

Then these two brothers, Heinrich Adams and his father-in-law Hans Weck, were executed in the same way as Hans Schmidt, the servant. They were strangled with a rope, then bound to the stake with an iron chain and scorched. This took place on October 21, 1558, in the presence of a large crowd from the town.

Heinrich Adams and his father-in-law executed.

Later, about January 4, 1559, the brothers Matthias Schmidt and Tillman Schneider suffered the same death at Aachen. So five brothers witnessed steadfastly and valiantly to the truth with their blood, even though some of them had never lived in a church community or even seen one.

Matthias Schmidt and Tillman Schneider executed.

Hans Schmidt wrote many fine letters[1] during his imprison-

---

[1]Thirty-six of Hans Schmidt's letters are preserved in different manuscripts, giving us a remarkable picture of this brother. Here we can only include a fraction of what is contained in Codex I 87.708, Vienna University Library. See Friedmann, *Schriften*, 126 ("Thirty-seven letters").

The "Letter to the brothers and sisters in the communities and schools and in the services of the church of God" (fol. 43) tells of the sufferings Hans Schmidt

1558 ment, giving guidance and comfort to the church and his fellow prisoners. He also wrote many beautiful spiritual songs. Some

---

endured in prison at Aachen. Another letter, dated April 26, written to the church in Moravia in his own name and that of the brothers and sisters with him (fol. 80), continues the story of their imprisonment. Both letters may have been the source of the above account. Extracts of Hans Schmidt's farewell letter to his fellow prisoners (fol. 83) are given here as an example of the absolute Gelassenheit and trust in God with which these brothers faced death.

Beloved and faithful brothers and sisters in the Lord,

It may be that in a few days our loving Father in heaven will chastise us further, take some of us to himself, and keep some here on earth to do his work; or he may take us all to him, or provide some other way of release. The love of God compels me to write to you because I have a strong feeling that God is preparing my end through Maier of Butschet. It seems he intends to execute me in accordance with their emperor's mandate (though it is still in God's hand), while the rest of you may be beaten with rods, if God allows it.

Now, beloved brothers and sisters, I hope the Lord has upheld you and will continue to do so in your every need so that you may overcome everything that opposes the truth or tries to hinder what is of God. I do not think I need to write more about this, for by God's mercy you have often been a comfort and strength to me while I lay in bonds for his sake. Eternal praise and glory to God in heaven. May he keep you faithful, holy, and pure and bring you with joy before his countenance. And since you have already received comfort and strength from him—praise be to God—I know of nothing else I can add to encourage you except that God has made me determined to remain obedient to him in all suffering. All I know is that I will witness to his truth until I die, and so it is likely that I will not see your faces again on this earth or be able to write much more to you.

With this letter then, my beloved brothers and sisters, I already take farewell of you as if we were parting from each other. I do it with pain and tears. I know of nothing else on earth that can part me from you and from the faithful, with God's help, except the Lord himself, our greatest good. With his help I hope to obey him. Even though he may separate us in the body, he draws our hearts together and will lead us together to his eternal kingdom. So I bless you and offer you the hand of my heart. I embrace you in true godly love as my children in the Lord, sisters and brothers by the grace of God, whom I bore for him in travail. And now I am distressed because I must leave you. But I hope that the Lord will give me strength to be faithful through all suffering, and that he will take you, too, straight to himself. Then I will embrace you once more in eternal joy and glory. May the Lord be with you and protect you as the apple of his eye; may he care for you as a nurse cares for her little ones so that not one of you is harmed. God be praised for all the love you have shown me and for your obedience to him. May the Lord shed his eternal joy upon you. Amen.

Now from the depth of my heart I greet you a hundred times in the living love of God and the inward peace of Christ; and if God should bring you back to the believers and take me away, give them my heartfelt greetings too, especially the servants of the Word, and say farewell in my name to all who love Christ. Remember me before the Lord, and I will do the same for you. I commend you to God and to his mercy. Written on Monday, June 4, 1558. Out of love to you I have written this now, since I may have no time left. And you know that I am not always able to get messages through to you. May you continue well in the Lord, with God's help. There is joy

of the songs his fellow prisoners wrote are also still in existence.[1] *1558*

The sixth brother caught with them, whose name was Werner, gave way and recanted under all the torture; but not long after, he arrived at the community and found repentance.

After long imprisonment and cruel treatment, the six sisters were beaten with rods and set free. They returned to the church in the peace of God.

6 sisters beaten with rods. They returned to the church.

The endurance of these brothers and sisters so shook and convinced the people of Aachen that they stopped hunting them and left them unmolested. They felt a deep remorse for what they had done, especially those who were directly involved. Without doubt they must have suffered many pangs of conscience.

From this time onward, many people from the Netherlands, Aachen, and the Rhineland were filled with zeal, wanting to change their lives, and they joined the church.

During this year communities were begun at Neumühl and Tracht.[2]

Neumühl, Tracht.

---

in store for us soon, either with the believers on earth or in eternal rest. Amen. The end.

See also *Martyrs Mirror*, 588–590; Beck, 230–234; *ME*, IV, 462–464.

[1]*Die Lieder der Hutterischen Brüder* includes sixteen of Hans Schmidt's twenty-four songs (551–611), four by Heinrich Adams (611–619), and two by Matthias Schmidt (619–623), all of which are possible sources for the account in this chronicle.

Of special interest are the various acrostics. The stanzas of Schmidt's fifth song yield the sentence: "Gott ist mit euch, ihr lieben Brüder und Schwestern und Kinder Gottes und darum gehabt euch wohl" (God is with you, you dear brothers and sisters and children of God, and therefore fare you well); his eighth song: "Hansl, Heinrich, Matthias Schmidt, Tilman, Hans, Werner sambt unsern liben Schwestern täten euch zu wissen wie es uns geht in dem Herrn" (Hansel, Heinrich [Adams], Matthias Schmidt, Tillman [Schneider], Hans [Weck], Werner, and our dear sisters want to let you know how we are in the Lord); his twelfth song: "Mein Gott, gross Barmherzigkeit hast mir getan und viel Lieb durch deine Kindlein, darum so will ich dich preisen bis in Tod" (My God, you have shown me great mercy and love through your children, wherefore I will praise you until death). Heinrich Adams takes leave of his wife with the acrostic of his third song: "Heinrich Adams, meiner eelichen Schwester Marien" (Heinrich Adams, to my wife, Marie).

See also Wolkan, *Lieder*, 210–228. According to Wolkan, 211, and *ME*, IV 463d, "Hymns," Schmidt's "song number three" was not written by him but about him.

[2]Neumühl (Nové Mlýny), northeast of Nikolsburg (Mikulov). In 1558 there was only a mill belonging to the owners of Eisgrub (Lednice), the lords von Liechtenstein, who leased it to the Hutterites. The mill was rebuilt, and Neumühl

1558
Konrad Haintzeman captured.

Bastel Binder captured.

Bastel Binder unfaithful.

Also this year Konrad Haintzeman, a young brother and a cobbler by trade, was taken prisoner at Stein near Krems on the Danube while traveling from Swabia with a little group of believers.[1] A few days earlier Bastel Binder,[2] another brother, had been traveling here with a group from the Adige Valley and had also been captured at Stein. Bastel Binder renounced his faith because he was so badly mistreated. Konrad Haintzeman knew nothing about the others when he was arrested. He did not find out until he was brought before the magistrates. There, in front of the magistrates, the priests baptized a newborn baby with their useless, misleading infant baptism. The judge asked the unfaithful Bastel whether that was true Christian baptism. Bastel said it was.

Bastel Binder made a terrible recantation.

"Bastel, you are speaking against God and your own conscience," said brother Konrad, contradicting him in front of the magistrates. The judge was furious with Konrad and shouted insults at him. Seeing this, Bastel denied the truth again in such a terrible way that the magistrates said they would never forget it.

Bastel was then released. He made his way to Pergen in Moravia as if he wanted to repent. Suddenly he died of the plague, cut off by the wrath of God without having found repentance.

Brother Konrad Haintzeman taken to Vienna.

He suffered intense hunger.

Brother Konrad was taken to Vienna and handed over to the magistrates there. For the sake of his faith he was imprisoned in the courthouse for a year and several weeks. Along with sixty others—ungodly thieves and criminals—he had to endure terrible hunger and misery. They got nothing to eat except what other people shared with them or brought

---

became an important Hutterian center; Zeman, *Topography*, #95. It was at Neumühl that Kräl and Zapff continued this chronicle; see below, p.492 n. See Adolf Mais, ed., Elizabeth Bender, trsl., "The *Hausbuch* of Neumühl 1558–1610: The Oldest Land Register of the Hutterian Brethren," *MQR*, April 1974, 215–236; *ME*, III, 854–856; Beck, 209.

For Tracht, see above, p.316 n.2.

[1]For Konrad Haintzeman (or Schuster, after his trade), see *Martyrs Mirror*, 573–574, "Konrad Schumacher"; *ME*, II, 630; Beck, 219–220. According to Th. Wiedemann, *Reformation und Gegenreformation im Lande unter der Enns* (Prague, 1878, 2 vols.), a certain Mayerle, vicar of Krems, is said to have joined this "little group of believers."

[2]Bastel Binder (Sebastian Leutner) a native of the Adige region, by trade a cooper (a maker or repairer of wooden barrels or tubs: German, *Binder* or *Faßbinder*). See Beck, 219; *ME*, III, 240a.

1558

them. On top of this, when the criminals had been tortured by burning, as was commonly done, their burns ran with pus, and he was nauseated to the point of being unable to eat for a long time, even when there was food. So he had to endure much distress as well as cruelty and imprisonment.

The bishop of Vienna wanted to execute Konrad.

At this time, Emperor Ferdinand was attending the great Imperial Diet at Augsburg.[1] The bishop of Vienna[2] had Konrad brought before him twice in the dark of night, or at any rate before daybreak, for he wanted to have him executed in secret. The first time Konrad was brought in, he was ordered to state briefly whether he was ready to renounce his faith. He answered that they would wait in vain for him to do that: he was ready to stake his life that this was the truth and the way to eternal life, and he would confess it with his lips as long as he could. The Lord frustrated their plan, because their talk that day came to nothing, though they cross-examined him from early morning until noon. Then he was taken back to prison and given three days to decide what he wanted to do. Three days later, again in the dark before dawn, he was brought before the bishop and his monks and priests once more, and once more he faithfully defended the truth.

The Lord frustrated the bishop's plan.

Konrad Haintzeman brought for another hearing.

The executioner was already at his post outside, waiting to behead him in the early hours before anyone was around. Such are the ways of the devil, who fears that the truth might come to light and people become aware of the injustice. Again the Lord intervened. Konrad was taken back to prison, where the priests argued with him incessantly, giving him no peace.

The Lord prevented it again.

After that they constantly threatened to leave him to rot in the dungeon, which had not been used for eight years. But he was prepared; he had set his hope on the Lord, who would be able to free him from the dungeon and from all the power of his enemies. He rejoiced greatly that the Lord had accepted him as a witness to the truth. He was so upright and undaunted that many were alarmed; some said they wished they had never met him—he made them quite uneasy.

They threatened to put him in the dungeon.

---

[1]This may refer to the Imperial Diet at Frankfurt, 1558, when King Ferdinand I assumed the imperial crown abdicated by his brother Charles V in 1556.

[2]In 1558, the bishop of Vienna was Anton Brus, born 1528 at Müglitz (Mohelnice), northwest of Olomouc, Moravia. He is said to have spoken five languages and was known as a zealous "defender of the truth." He died in Prague, 1580. See Beck, 220.

1558
Konrad Haintzeman released.

Meanwhile, the baker to the court of King Maximilian had heard of the bishop's evil intention. He told Pfausinger, the king's Lutheran chaplain, who informed the king, putting in a good word for the prisoner. He said Konrad was young and it would be a pity to execute him like this. King Maximilian commanded them to stop tyrannizing him and to release him. This was done.

When brother Konrad was told how his release had come about, he went to these men and thanked them for the freedom God had given him through them. Then, with unsullied heart and a good conscience, he traveled back to Moravia and to the church community, who rejoiced at his coming. He was soon given a service, as will be told in its place below.

Boretitz.

This year the lord of Tscheikowitz expelled the brothers. They moved to Boretitz and set up a community there.

2 brothers confirmed in the service of the Word.

That autumn at Kostel the elders confirmed Kaspar Hueber and Hans Zwinger or Gerber (a tanner) in the service of the Gospel with the laying on of hands.

2 brothers confirmed in the service for temporal affairs.

2 brothers chosen for the service of the Word.

On the same day the elders confirmed Matthias Gasser and Leonhard Klemp in the service for temporal affairs with the laying on of hands. And two brothers, Christoph Lenck and Klaus Felbinger[1] or Schlosser (a locksmith by trade), were chosen for the service of the Gospel and appointed.

5 brothers chosen for the service for temporal affairs.

Five brothers were also chosen and appointed to the service for temporal affairs: Walser (Balthasar) Maierhof the younger, Lorenz of Schwaz, Leonhard Lungauer, Kuntz Herrlich, and Bärtel Gutscher.

Gregor the Bohemian passed away.

In this year brother Gregor the Bohemian, a servant for temporal affairs, fell peacefully asleep in the Lord at Bilowitz in Moravia.

Across the mountains.

The same year, the brothers moved out of Deutsch-Nussdorf,[2] a town on the other side of the Little Carpathians.

1559

Moved from Klein Niemtschitz to Polehraditz.

In 1559 the brothers were forced out of Klein Niemtschitz[3]

---

[1]About Klaus Felbinger, see below, pp.369–372.

[2]Deutsch-Nussdorf (Dolné Orešany), northwest of Tyrnau, Hungary, at the foot of the Little Carpathians.

[3]Klein Niemtschitz (Němčičky), village east of Auspitz; in 1558 property of Zdeněk Sobek of Kornice. Beck, 210; Zeman, *Topography*, #99.

near Boretitz, so we set up a community in Polehraditz.[1]

1559

That year brother Paul Schuster, a servant of the Gospel and the church, fell asleep in the Lord in Württemberg.

Paul Schuster passed away.

The same year, six brothers were chosen and appointed to the service for temporal affairs: Hans Kräl, Gilg Federspil, Blasi Harer or Ötztaler (from the Ötz Valley in Austria), Jörg Rack, Georg Grüber, and Wendel Münchinger.

6 brothers chosen for the service for temporal affairs.

Two more brothers, Andreas Maierhofer and Jobst Lackern or Säckler from Schwäbisch Hall, were chosen and appointed to the service for temporal affairs.

2 brothers chosen for the service for temporal affairs.

The same year, two brothers, Wolf Mair and Wolf Huber, were arrested in the Salzburg area because of their belief in divine truth. They were taken to Tittmoning and on to Salzburg, where they were handed over to the magistrates and imprisoned. At both places they were cruelly tortured and suffered greatly.

Wolf Mair and Wolf Huber captured.

Wolf Mair was questioned under torture twice. He was repeatedly racked and had to endure terrible pain, but he would not say anything against his conscience. The clerk of the court said, "You must tell me who gave you shelter, food, and drink, or else you must die on the rope."

Cruelly tortured.

He must give information or else die.

Wolf replied, "Then I must die, for I will not speak against my conscience or denounce those who showed me kindness." So they left him. Later the priests tried various tactics, some gentle, some brutal, to make the two recant. They used all kinds of threats and attacked their faith with blasphemous words, which the brothers rejected, vigorously defending the truth. The Lord gave them strength; they held their lives cheap for the sake of divine truth.

There were many discussions, especially among the priests, who decided at one point to sentence them to life imprisonment. But God frustrated their plan.

Decision to keep them in prison for life. God frustrated the plan.

Then monks, priests, and others tried once more to seduce them from their faith, but it was in vain. The brothers put them to shame through God's Word. In their steadfastness, they proved that their faith was the way of divine truth leading to eternal life in Christ Jesus. With God's help, they would remain true to it, whatever the priests and the devil might do, sing, or say.

---

[1]Polehraditz (Boleradice), market town on the estate of Záviš Prusinovský of Víckov. Beck, 210; Zeman, *Topography*, #113.

1559

The indictment read out to them.

They were then taken back from Salzburg to Tittmoning (whence they had been sent) and condemned to death. When the indictment was read out to them, they bravely spoke against every untruth in it, saying that their faith was in no way heretical or seductive.

Some women wept, but the brothers sang.

As they were led through the city, some women wept with pity that they were to be killed for their faith, but the brothers said, "You should not weep for us. Weep for yourselves and for your sins." They sang joyful songs because their end and deliverance was so close at hand.

Wolf Mair wanted to present a true burnt offering to God.

Both beheaded and burned.

When they were brought to the place of execution, brother Wolf Mair cried out to the people, "Today I will offer my God the true burnt offering, fulfill my vow, and witness to divine truth with my blood." They were executed with the sword and then burned. With courage and joy they surrendered their earthly lives for the sake of eternal life, as they testified in the song they wrote.[1]

Those guilty had their lives cut short.

Some of those who were responsible for the imprisonment and death of the brothers met with God's judgment and died soon afterward. Others died an unnatural death: God put an end to their lives in such a way that it was obvious his wrath was at work.

Melchior Waal, a servant from the Swiss Brethren, united with us.

Around this time, Melchior Waal, a servant of the Swiss Brethren and a cobbler by trade, came to us from Muschau[2] in Moravia. When he saw that the Swiss Brethren were not living according to the truth but were contaminated by the evil ways of the world and that they did not set to rights or punish the wrongs and errors he pointed out to them, he separated from them. After talking with our brothers, he united with us and later served the church well.

1560

3 brothers chosen for the service of the Word.

In 1560 three brothers were chosen and appointed to the

[1]Two songs by Wolf Mair are in *LdHBr*, 623–626, with the acrostic "Wolf Mair." About Wolf Mair and Wolf Huber, see *Martyrs Mirror*, 617; *ME*, III, 442–443; Beck, 221.

[2]Muschau (Mušov), formerly a village north of Nikolsburg (Mikulov), in the area of the confluence of the Dyje and Svratka rivers, which is now the site of a lake; see also Zeman, *Topography*, #88.

service of the Gospel: Hans Kräl, Michael Veldthaler, and Konrad Haintzeman.

1560

Brother Abraham Schneider or Ulstüber, a servant of the Word, fell asleep in the Lord at Neumühl.

Abraham Schneider passed away.

That same year, brother Klaus Felbinger or Schlosser, a servant of God's Word who was still in a time of testing, was arrested while traveling near Neumarkt in Bavaria together with another brother, Hans Leutner. On the Tuesday after Judica [Passion Sunday, two weeks before Easter], during Lent, they were taken to Neumarkt for the sake of their faith. There the prison warden and his guards cross-examined them twice, especially about infant baptism. The brothers proved that Christ had commanded only the baptism of adults who could hear, understand, and believe the Word of God. So, early on Palm Sunday they were chained to two carts and sent to Landshut with a guard of riders and foot soldiers. There they were put in separate cells, and Klaus was put in chains.

Klaus Felbinger and Hans Leutner arrested.

The warden cross-examined them, then sent them to Landshut.

Early the same week, the lords of Landshut, the captain, the old prison warden, the chancellor, and all their attendants summoned the brothers. They talked with them but could not get anywhere.

The lords at Landshut summoned Klaus.

Two deans from the city were sent to speak with the brothers about the mass, infant baptism, and their reasons for leaving the popish church. But the brothers gave such a good testimony, founded on divine witness, that they had to give up.

2 deans disputed with Klaus Felbinger.

The prisoners were then cruelly tortured and racked twice to make them tell where they had been going and who had given them shelter. But brother Klaus replied, "We have no obligation to tell you, and it does you no good to know."

They were terribly racked.

"Why?" they asked.

"Because you hound the people and torment them. You rob them and sin against them. Far be it from us to betray those who have done good to us. We do not betray our enemies, much less our friends."

"Very well," they said, "then we're not going to spare your skin."

They would not stop unless he told where they found lodging.

They left him hanging in agony until at last the torturer put in a word for him, saying, "He has hung there all day and won't tell anything."

The chief justice was malicious, calling him a vile scoundrel and accusing us of damning them. Klaus replied, "We do not

1560

damn anyone. But your sins will damn you if you do not repent. We are telling you nothing but the truth."

The judge asked, "What is truth?"

"What is truth?" asked the chief justice.

Klaus answered, "You won't understand, even if I tell you." So the justice knew no more about truth than Pilate, who asked the same question (John 18:38).

2 deans tried to sway Klaus.

The chancellor and ruling lords came to Klaus.

After this, two deans were sent out from Munich (about nine miles away), and they tried in many unusual ways to confuse and dissuade them, but they had no success. The chancellor and ruling lords at Landshut often came to pester them too. But they always found the brothers steadfast in their faith and had to go away leaving them unwavering. It was impossible to win them over with false teaching and tempting suggestions.

2 priests and a doctor questioned Klaus.

Two priests and a doctor of theology came and argued heatedly with them about infant baptism. But brother Klaus powerfully confuted them from Scripture, so they left him alone.

The magistrate and officials visited Klaus.

After all this, the magistrate and several officials came and tried to win them with friendliness. But they stood unflinching against all the gates of hell and trusted in God's truth, faithfully defending it on a sure foundation. They vowed they would remain true in the simplicity of Christ. The chancellor finally said to brother Klaus, "I don't believe you are so simple. I don't believe one in a hundred could defend himself like you. I don't take you for a fanatic, like those others who don't know what they are talking about." For the Lord himself gave Klaus words and wisdom, as can be seen in the letters he wrote to the church from prison and in the songs he made while in chains.[1]

The chancellor said, "I don't believe that you are simple."

---

[1]While in prison at Landshut, Klaus Felbinger wrote a letter to Leonhard Lanzenstiel (Seiler), found in the Olomouc University Library, Codex 180, fol. 147; printed in Johann Loserth, "Zur Geschichte der Wiedertäufer in Mähren," *Zeitschrift für allgemeine Geschichte, Kultur-, Litteratur- und Kunstgeschichte*, I (1884), 451–454; see also Friedmann, *Schriften*, 113–114. We quote the following excerpts.

> O you beloved brother Leonhard, beloved because of your God-ordained task of helping those who are to inherit salvation to find joy and redemption. Before God I must bear you witness that you have worked zealously with those young in the faith, bringing understanding to the ignorant—all honor be to God. I must write to you to tell you what has happened to us so far, since through a kindhearted servant girl God has provided me with paper and ink and there is still enough light in this cell. If sometime a messenger should come by, he can bring you this letter. I know you long to hear from us. Dear brother Leonhard, God has given us inner strength, praise be to

He also wrote a confession of our faith addressed to the lords and governing authorities in Landshut, and the church still has a copy.[1] *1560*

> him! But physically Hans has grown very weak, although he is treated better than I am. He has a large window in his cell and is free to move about in the prison, whereas I am chained up in a dungeon all the time. Praise God who makes me worthy to be his witness! When I think about it, I am filled with an inward joy, for I recognize God's great love in it.

Then follows the description of their tortures, of which this chronicle includes a summary. The letter continues:

> They are certainly at a loss about us. I hope they have now had enough of us. They seem to think killing us is too light a penalty. They cannot bear us, because we shatter their very foundation. People say, "Don't worry. They won't kill you. But they might whip you out of the town and forbid you to come back to this area." They may be right, but I leave it in the Lord's hands. Here it is completely popish, with plenty of priests, a show of harlotry and pride. Some say, "The prince has now gone to Vienna to deal with matters of faith because his brother-in-law the king has asked him to help straighten things out between him and his son Maximilian. And so now you just have to wait in prison until he returns." I am convinced that if they do not strangle us, they will punish us severely, unless we promise to stay out of the country, which we could not do. They may even mark us in some way. Only God knows. . . .
>
> Greet the other dear brothers for me, especially Peter Scherer (Walpot) and Hans Feuerbacher (Klöpfer), the servants of Jesus Christ, who faithfully minister to the church of God. Greet your assistants, Christel [Christoph] Lenck, Siegel [Sigmund] Hosauer, Kaspar Ebner, Hans Kitzbühler [Kräl], Konrad Schuster [Haintzeman], and all the devout in the house of God, Jobst Säckler, Hans Arbeiter, Remias, and your Lora, with her faithful daughters in the weaving room at Kostel, Bilowitz, and elsewhere. All my love to those in the kitchen, Margret with her dear sisters, all the brothers and sisters who carry services in the church, and each child of God in all the communities, Christoph Achtznit, my very dear brother and all his relatives, Jobst and Maria and the others in the sewing room. Give warm greetings to the two mothers. Dear Leonhard, give my heartfelt greeting to Hansel Schneider, and especially to Paul Schneider and his Anna, to Martel, to Bärtel Gutscher, Martin Klemp, Christel Schmidt, Leonhard Dax, to Schönlercher, and to our dear old brother Hans Eberle.

Three of Felbinger's songs are in *LdHBr*, 647–649; a fourth song, about the death of Hans Pürchner, is on p. 441; see also Wolkan, *Lieder*, 228–229.

[1]In a second letter addressed to the church of God in Moravia, Felbinger gives a detailed account of their capture and of the hearing that followed (Olomouc University Library, Codex 180, fol. 153–181). In the same manuscript we find (fol. 115–145): "[This is] a declaration of my faith, which I, Klaus Felbinger, wrote down for the lords, also on behalf of Hans Leutner, who is imprisoned with me."

This declaration or confession of faith was copied by Felbinger as part of his letter home to the brotherhood in Moravia. See Robert Friedmann, "Claus Felbinger's Confession of 1560," *MQR*, Apr. 1955, 141–161; "Confession of Faith, 1560" by Claus Felbinger, in *Brotherly Community: The Highest Command of Love*, Hutterian Brethren, ed. (Rifton, NY, 1978), 91–133.

About Klaus Felbinger, see *ME*, II, 320–321; about him and Hans Leutner, see *Martyrs Mirror*, 643–644; Beck, 234–236.

1560
They were executed with the sword.

The brothers' courage.

After this they were condemned to death by the sons of Pilate. Brother Klaus had his tongue bound to prevent him from speaking to the people at his execution, but in the end his tongue was freed long enough for the two brothers to speak to each other. Brother Hans Leutner, who was to be first, said to Klaus, "Now, brother Klaus, if my death will terrify you, then you go first and I will wait till last."

Brother Klaus replied, "No! Oh, no! I will not be terrified."

So Hans gave his neck to the sword, and Klaus looked on undismayed. He did not even turn pale. Anyone who did not know would have thought it did not concern him. Then he, too, stepped forward, knelt down, and gave his head for the sake of faith and divine truth. Both brothers witnessed valiantly with their blood. They were executed on July 19.

Servant of the Word chosen and confirmed.

Lorenz Huf passed away.

Bochtitz.

3 brothers chosen for the service for temporal affairs.

That year, 1560, brother Thoman Eppenstainer was chosen and confirmed in the service of the Gospel.

Lorenz Huf, a servant of God's Word from Sprendlingen on the Rhine, fell asleep in the Lord at Stiegnitz[1] in Moravia.

The community at Bochtitz was reestablished.

Around that time three brothers, Stoffel Heugen, Johann Schuster, and Hans Schneider from Kaufbeuren, were chosen and appointed to the service for temporal affairs.

Hans Mändel, Jörg Rack, and Eustachius Kotter captured.

On the Friday after St. Martin's Day [Nov. 11], 1560, Hans Mändel, also called Klein (Short) Hansel, was taken prisoner near Rosenheim in Bavaria because of his belief in divine truth. He was a servant of God's Word and his church and had been sent on mission into other lands many times. Arrested with him were Jörg Rack, a servant for temporal affairs, and Eustachius Kotter, a vinedresser. They were taken to Innsbruck and handed over to the authorities.

Hans Mändel lay among bats and vermin.

Because Hans Mändel was a servant, he was imprisoned in the Vellenburg, in a deep dungeon. He wrote that it was full of worms and vermin. The bats flew around him until the dungeon whirred with them, and the mice carried away his food and ran around him in great numbers.

---

[1]Stiegnitz (Trstěnice), northeast of Znojmo, under the jurisdiction of Wischenau (Višňové), and at this time owned by Zikmund of Zástřizl. Zeman, *Topography*, #147.

A song written by Lorenz Huf is in *LdHBr*, 626–629, with the acrostic "Lorentz Huf von Sprendeling."

The spirits whom God sends to terrify the ungodly at night were now sent to serve and help him. The Lord forewarned him through such a spirit when the noblemen were coming to question him. It called him by name and told him to prepare himself and to be ready to suffer. (Jörg Liebich had been imprisoned several years earlier in the same dungeon and had suffered many attacks of the evil one, which has already been reported.) The other two brothers were put in the *Kräuterturm* at Innsbruck. All three remained in prison until the following year, 1561.

1560

A spirit told him when his case would be heard.

On January 2 [1561] the authorities questioned Hans Mändel, using both friendliness and cruelty. Then they questioned Eustachius and Jörg Rack, each separately. The brothers faithfully defended many points of their belief. Minutes were made at the hearing and sent to Vienna and elsewhere for examination. The most relevant parts of their confessions were selected, and we have them in writing word for word in the church.[1]

Hans Mändel and his fellow prisoners questioned with both friendliness and cruelty.

After their trial they were returned to their dungeons and stayed there until June 13, the Friday after St. Vitus Day, when they were condemned to death.[2]

A great crowd was present at their execution. The brothers spoke sharply of God's judgment that the authorities were bringing upon themselves: shedding innocent blood would cause their own damnation, even though they said they had to judge according to the imperial mandate.

They warned the lords of judgment.

But Hans Mändel told them, "You blind world, judge each according to your own conscience, so that you can answer for it before God! If you judge and condemn according to the imperial mandate, how can you answer to God?"

Hans Mändel rebuked them for their false judgment.

Brother Eustachius also said, "What do we care about the imperial mandate you read out to us? Read out our confession of faith, based on Holy Scripture. It is God's truth for which we must suffer today." They spoke joyfully and called the people to repentance.

When brother Jörg Rack and Eustachius were led out of the

Jörg Rack called out to the people.

---

[1]These confessions are in Codex I 87.708, fol. 48–71, Vienna University Library; see Friedmann, *Schriften*, 121–122; Beck, 222 n.2.

[2]The date of the brothers' execution seems to have been June 10 (not 13), 1561; see Mecenseffy, *Österreich*, III, 685, lines 24–29; 697, lines 5–12; Loserth, *Anabaptismus*, 207; *ME*, III, 455. See also Beck, 223.

1560 (1561)

courthouse, Jörg began to call to people all along the streets till they reached the place of execution. He urged them to repent and follow the way of truth, for it was for truth's sake that he was being executed that day.

Leonhard Dax took leave of them.

Then the servant Hans Mändel was brought to the place of execution, and the brothers met in great joy and praised God. Brother Leonhard Dax[1] came too. They shook hands and took leave of one another, joyfully praising God that they had seen another believer.

Hans Mändel called to the people to repent.

Hans Mändel spoke to the people, calling them to repent of their sins and follow the truth of God so that they would not be damned but might find salvation in Christ Jesus. Yes, he raised his voice valiantly, saying, "What I have taught and confessed is divine truth, and today I will witness to it with my blood." And he did not stop proclaiming repentance.

So the judge said several times, "Now, Hans, listen a moment!" Then he was quiet for a while, but afterward he went on speaking until he was almost hoarse. Right up to their death, the brothers exhorted the people to turn away from the unjust life of this world. They were not cut short but given ample opportunity to speak.

They were given time to speak.

Hans Mändel and his brothers prayed together.

They were also allowed to pray together. So they brought their earnest prayer to God, praising and thanking him for keeping them steadfast in faith all this time and asking that he continue to do so until their death, now so close upon them. They commended their spirits into the Lord's hands when body and soul should part.

Indictment read to them.

Their indictment was read out to them, and the following points were stressed:

FIRST, they did not believe that the blessed body of Jesus Christ is present in the host but believed in celebrating the Lord's Supper just as Christ held it with his disciples.

SECOND, they set no value on infant baptism, valuing only the true Christian baptism that Christ commanded his disciples to practice.

THIRD, they upheld marriage—they acknowledged this and did not contradict it. Other articles of faith were read out. For each point they first stated the Roman Catholic position and then that of the brothers. The clerk who had put the record

---

[1]About Leonhard Dax, see below, p.384.

1560 (1561)

together had great understanding for the brothers and did not want to give it a slanderous and blasphemous slant as is usually done.

Brother Eustachius beheaded.

After that, the brothers were taken to their execution on the hog meadow near the huntsman's shed. There Eustachius, who was sickly and weak, was beheaded first. Next Jörg Rack went joyfully up to the executioner, spun around on one foot, and cried out, "Here I forsake wife and child, house and home, life and limb for the sake of divine truth!" He knelt down, and the executioner beheaded him too.

Jörg Rack spun around on one foot. Was beheaded.

Hans Mändel was last. When he saw the two lying there beheaded, he said to himself, "My brothers, he who overcomes will inherit all things." The executioner took him, bound him to the ladder, kindled the fire, and pushed him in. Then he put the two beheaded bodies on the pyre as well and burned them all to ashes.

Hans Mändel burned alive at Innsbruck.

In this manner, the three brothers[1] courageously sealed their witness to the true faith in Christ with their lives and their death, their words and their blood, and God gave them the

---

[1]All three brothers came from Tirol: Hans Mändel, or "Klein Hansel" (short Hans), from the village of Albeins in the district of Gufidaun; Eustachius Kotter, a vinedresser from Sellrain in the district of Axams; and Georg Mair, known as Jörg Rack, from Pfons in the district of Steinach. The last two wrote a letter from prison "to the vinedressers in the church of God in Moravia." This letter as well as the others following are in Codex I 87.708, fol. 43, Vienna University Library, from which the following passage is taken; see also Friedmann, *Schriften*, 121–122.

> We are writing to you out of pure, heartfelt love, since we have reason to believe that our lives here on earth may end soon and we may not meet again on this earth. May God help us all to enter his perfect kingdom and see one another again with joy. Beloved brothers, may God grant this to you and us. We praise him for the great love and faithfulness you have shown us, your unworthy brothers. May he reward you in eternity.
>
> We want to let you know that we are to be executed on [June 13, 1561] the Tuesday after Corpus Christi. We will suffer death joyfully with God's help and not be sad, for this day is holy to the Lord. My beloved brother Stachius [Eustachius] is very sick; he may not live to see that day.
>
> We wish we could do something to show our love for you dear brothers, but you will have to accept this short letter instead. For all I know it will be the last letter I ever write unless, God willing, I write another; he alone knows. With this letter we greet each one of you a thousand times in the pure love of God. We take leave of you all and bless you with the peace of our Lord Jesus Christ, also in the name of our dear brother Klein Hansel. He is not with us, but he is here in Innsbruck, and we cannot send messages or write to him. I heard that no one is allowed to visit him. So we are eagerly waiting for Tuesday, when our indictment will be read, for then we will have the joy of seeing one another. Afterward we will go in the Lord's name through the city and out to the place of execution, and there we will fulfill

1560 (1561)

victory. Brother Stoffel Schneider, who was present, saw and heard how courageous they were.

---

our promise to the Lord. You may expect that of us, all you beloved members in the Lord. God be with you all. Amen.

Dated: Corpus Christi, 1561

In a letter dated Sunday before Whitsun 1561 (fol. 88), Klein Hansel wrote to the church in Moravia:

> Every day I expect to be led out to the slaughter. For now, on the Sunday before Whitsun 1561, the jurors have been summoned once again on our account. And so I think God may change our predicament or end it altogether. Whether it means life or death, on water or on land, or remaining in prison all my life, I have complete peace of heart about it and am resolved to suffer joyfully. . . . Besides, there is no doubt in my heart that God's purpose is for our good, however wicked the plans of the ungodly may be. It is said that the emperor has written many times stating his power to condemn us to the galleys without sentence. Another time we were supposed to have been sentenced to death by burning. But God's time had not yet come. You can well imagine what awaits us now, after they have gone into our case a third time with the jurors. They spent four days on me, and there were about sixty points that I had to answer, apart from those the priests went over with me in the course of seven days. But praise be to God for ever and ever! He was with me in everything and granted it to me to confess his name, whether the questioning was considerate or harsh.

From another of Klein Hansel's letters to the "brothers and sisters living in the Adige region" (fol. 208):

> Further, beloved brothers and sisters, I want to let you know that I have now heard definitely (though it is not completely new) that people are well informed about you and that you can at any moment expect to be persecuted and imprisoned. This grieves me for your sakes. Yet I know that no believer can expect to be spared. That is what I have taught you, and the devout are promised nothing better here on earth.

In the defense or confession of faith made by the three brothers (fol. 48ff.), we find many interesting details about their lives. The brothers were asked "whether they were rebaptized, who had deceived them and talked them into joining this fanatical sect, and how and where it had happened." They answered:

> That it was no sect but the divine truth and they had not been deceived. They had been rightly baptized only once, for they knew nothing about their infant baptism. They had come to this faith in the following way: Several times brothers came and explained the Word of the Lord to them so simply and clearly that, when in addition to hearing their teaching they saw the brothers' lives, they acknowledged it as true and godly. So they surrendered themselves to God and renounced their sinful lives. In deep remorse for their sins, they received the baptism testified to above.
>
> Jörg, for example, before he came to the faith, had heard that a man named Jakob Hutter, who was burned at the stake here at Innsbruck, was gagged on the way here to prevent people from hearing the truth he proclaimed. Jörg had also heard that at Klausen, Ulrich Mulner, who was well liked by the people, was executed because of this same faith. Finally he, Rack, had seen with his own eyes how others of the same faith were burned at the stake in Steinach. Jörg had taken all this to heart, thinking that it must be a powerful grace and strength that enabled them to remain firm in their faith until death. This first prompted him to inquire about those people and to listen carefully to what they said. Then he realized that life

There still exist letters to the church, written by the brothers in prison, and songs they made up and sang in their bondage and suffering. *1560 (1561)*

---

in the world was very unlikely to lead him to salvation.

Mändel himself had received baptism twenty-four years ago last fall. He was baptized in 1537 in a forest called Weissenbach, two miles below Sterzing, by Onophrius Griesinger, who was burned at the stake at Brixen in 1538. Kotter had received baptism in the fall of 1540 in a meadow on the Jauffenberg; he had been baptized by Leonhard Lanzenstiel. Jörg Rack had also been baptized by Leonhard Lanzenstiel about fifteen years earlier at Schakwitz in Moravia.

They were asked "where they held their meetings for baptism, Lord's Supper, and preaching, and whether the authorities in those places had any knowledge of them, and where they had settled in Moravia." Answer:

> They held their meetings at night in the fields and in barns. By day they met in the woods to preach the Word of God and to teach one another the way of salvation. They did not think the authorities knew about them, because otherwise they would have been searched for, which was what happened when Kotter was captured again. His first imprisonment had been in the summer four or five years earlier, when he was captured in an open place near a wood in the Puster Valley. He was taken to Neuhaus Castle and lay in chains for a day and a night. The autumn of the following year he had gone into the Adige region and the Vintschgau and had been captured down in the valley, but once more, thank God, he had escaped. Mändel himself had been captured three times before. The first time was in the year he had come to the faith. He was imprisoned at Sterzing and severely beaten with rods, but that time God helped him to escape. The second time was about eighteen years ago. He had been captured at Landeck, held for twenty-two weeks and cruelly tortured, but had again escaped from the dungeon with God's help. The third time had been about twelve years ago when he was captured at Rodeneck and kept in prison for eleven weeks and again cruelly tortured. Finally he escaped with the help of a servant woman whom he had converted. And now he was in prison for the fourth time. He was awaiting what God had in mind for him and was prepared to die at any time if that was his will.
>
> The brother called Jörg had been in prison once before on account of his faith. That had been at Auspitz in Moravia, but he had been released and not tortured. In addition he said that they had been driven from one place to another in Moravia too and were scattered over several miles. Just before they left Moravia, their brothers and sisters had been at Kostel, but they did not know whether they were still there or not.

To the question "who was the head and real ringleader of their accursed sect, and who was responsible for misleading them into clinging to the brotherhood and being baptized and seduced into such error," the brothers answered the following:

> He, Mändel, had been appointed by his brothers and the church to be a teacher and shepherd. The other two had never baptized anyone, nor had they preached in the formal sense of the word, for it was not their task. But all three of them had loyally helped one another and with steadfast hearts, as far as God gave them grace, had persevered in teaching the truth and shown it by their example to all. . . . Mändel alone had converted and baptized about four hundred men and women.

About all three brothers, see *Martyrs Mirror*, 645–646 (where Hans Mändel is called John Korbmacher). Hans Mändel was among the most significant Hutterites

1560
Niemtschan.

In this year, 1560, a community was begun at Niemtschan[1] on the other side of Austerlitz.

1561

2 brothers chosen for the service of the Word.

In 1561 at Kostel in Moravia, two brothers were chosen for the service of the Gospel and appointed. They were Melchior Waal[2] and Ambrosius Pfeiffer. Melchior Waal had previously been a servant among the Swiss Brethren, as has been told earlier.

2 brothers chosen for the service for temporal affairs.

On the same day two brothers, Simon Putz and Adam Eppenstainer, were chosen and appointed to the service for temporal affairs.

Jakob Kircher passed away.

This same year, brother Jakob Kircher, an old servant of God's Word and his church, fell asleep in the Lord at Schadowitz in Moravia.

2 brothers confirmed in the service of the Word.

Two brothers, Hans Kräl and Konrad Haintzeman, were confirmed in the service of the Gospel by the elders with the laying on of hands.

Thoman Schmidt passed away.

Brother Thoman Schmidt, a servant for temporal affairs, fell peacefully asleep in the Lord at Damborschitz in Moravia.

Lorenz Schuster passed away.

At Urschitz[3] near Damborschitz brother Lorenz Schuster, another servant for temporal affairs, passed away in the Lord.

Michael Planer passed away.

At Alexowitz near Eibenschitz in Moravia, Michael Planer also passed away. He was a cobbler and a servant for temporal affairs.

Michael Kern passed away.

In the same year brother Michael Kern, a servant for

---

of his time and, like Peter Riedemann, one of the most frequently imprisoned: in 1537, his first year as a Hutterian brother, 26 weeks at Sterzing; in 1544, 22 weeks at Landeck; in 1548 at Rodeneck; in 1560 at Rosenheim, Bavaria.

The songs by Mändel, Kotter, and Rack, and a song about them by Andreas Ehrenpreis (1662) are in *LdHBr*, 629–647; about Mändel's and Kotter's songs, see Wolkan, *Lieder*, 228. See also Loserth, *Anabaptismus*, 194–210; Christoph Andreas Fischer, *Der Hutterischen Widertauffer Taubenkobel* (Ingolstadt, 1607), 9; Beck, 222–225. About Mändel, see *ME*, III, 454–455; Kotter: *ME*, III, 229–230; Rack: *ME*, IV, 241–242.

[1]Niemtschan (Něměany), northeast of Austerlitz, property of Jan of Kounice. Zeman, *Topography*, #97.

[2]Melchior Waal was a shoemaker by trade; Beck, 212.

[3]Urschitz (Uhřice), village southeast of Austerlitz. With the help of Oldřich of Kounice, the Hutterites had established a community here, generally known as "Taufarsky" (probably from middle high German *toufære* = *Täufer*, baptizer, hence "the baptizers' place"). Zeman, *Topography*, #165.

temporal affairs, fell asleep in the Lord at Pausram in Moravia.

1561

At this time Gütten Hans,[1] an old and confirmed servant for temporal affairs, fell asleep in the Lord at Protzka in Hungary.

Gütten Hans passed away.

Brother Franciscus von der Sach, who had come from Italy, was chosen for the service of God's Word and appointed to this office.[2]

Franciscus von der Sach chosen for the service of the Word.

---

[1]See Beck, 213, where he is called Hanss Gutenhenn.

[2]Among the Italian Anabaptists who joined the Hutterian communities in Moravia in the mid-sixteenth century, the following were outstanding: Francesco della Sega or Franciscus von der Sach (from Rovigo), Giulio Gherlandi (from Treviso, called Julius Klampferer or Trevisano), Antonio Rizzetto (from Vicenza, called Antonius Wälsch, meaning "the Italian"), and Gian Giorgio Patrizi (from Cherso). They may have been part of, or at least influenced by, the anti-Trinitarian circles in Venice and Vicenza, but they must have rejected the more radical theological elements of this influence, possibly even before seeking unity with the Hutterian Brethren. (Less than ten years later, and again in the seventeenth century, anti-Trinitarianism or Socinianism became a serious obstacle to an attempted uniting of the Hutterian brotherhood with the Polish Brethren; see below, pp.410–412 and 764–765.)

The determination of the Italian Anabaptists to lead a life of discipleship in brotherly love and ordered Christian community must have been stronger than any theological differences they may have had with the Hutterian Brethren, to the degree that when they joined, they were able to embrace Hutterian beliefs. On March 5, 1559, della Sega wrote to a fellow believer in Vicenza that he and other Italians who had joined the community in Moravia wished to share with their brethren in Italy the peace they had found, adding that only those would be welcome in the brotherhood who "were not contaminated with false doctrines about the nature of Christ" (Henry A. DeWind, *MQR*, July 1954, 167). Quoting Prof. Aldo Stella of the University of Padua:

> It was above all Francesco della Sega who strove to overcome the rather profound doctrinal differences. He was confident of being able to reconcile the basic Hutterian requirement, that is, church community, . . . rejecting any sectarian exclusiveness and . . . intolerance . . . for the sake of freedom of conscience and thought, so as to encourage and promote dialogue and brotherly love.

In his long letter to the brotherhood in Moravia, of 1563 (for details, see below, p.384 n.1), della Sega underscored his own and the brothers' indifference to theological dogmas by declaring that

> they did not care in the least for "subtlety, curiosity, or mysteries, which are unnecessary and of no use for a good and Christian life," and that just for this reason he was firmly and solely determined to "live according to Christ." The main part of his letter was therefore dedicated to emphasizing the need to be together as true brothers in the church community of the elect or saints.

A complete overcoming of former influences is also borne out by the fact that in 1561 Francesco della Sega was appointed to the service of the Word, and that soon afterward the Italian brothers were sent on mission journeys to their homeland. All four of the above-named were captured, tortured, and executed at Venice by drowning: Gherlandi in October 1562 (p.383 below), Rizzetto and della Sega in

1561
14 brothers chosen for the service for temporal affairs.

At Kostel, the following fourteen were appointed to the service for temporal affairs:

Wendel Holba, a Slovakian, a miller by trade
Hans Kircher from Hesse
Jobst Westeburger or Schneider (a tailor)
Christoph Sändteller, a carpenter
Lorenz Pürchner
Valtin Maier
Melchior Gasseroler or Oberecker
Veit Denniffel
Melchior Runcker
Bastel Hueber
Peter Klemp
Hans Klemp, his brother
Hans of Cologne, a mason
Bastel Rausch from Hesse

February 1565 (pp.386–388 below), and Patrizi in December 1570 (he is not mentioned in this chronicle; see *Martyrs Mirror*, 703, "John George, 1566").

The following testimony of another Italian brother, Girolamo Perosino (from Istria), in his letter to a friend, written at Lundenburg, April 13, 1570, shows the enthusiasm of the Italian Anabaptists who had joined the Hutterian Brethren in Moravia:

> I would wish for you and the whole world to be in the company and brotherhood in which I now find myself. I cannot deny that this congregation is the true church, showing her marks and signs, namely, the frequent preaching of the pure Word of God, the administration of the sacraments (baptism and the Lord's Supper), and church discipline with brotherly correction, excluding the erring and receiving back the penitent—no immoral or disorderly person is tolerated among us. Since you are zealous for your own and others' salvation, I beg you not to balk at spending three ducats to come here sometime to see for yourself, making up a group of some whom you know to be desirous of extracting themselves from the servitude of sin and the tyranny of their nature to do the will of God, invoking his holy name in Christian freedom. And when you reach Vienna, ask for directions to Bilfisdorf and then to Cruta and from there to Lundenburg, where the houses of the brothers are and where I, Geronimo Peroscino, live. . . .
>
> You could ask me, "Why did you leave so praiseworthy a company four years ago?" I answer: For no other end than to gather Italians together—on account of the difficulty of the German language—that they might live in the established orders we have learned from them [the Hutterian Brethren]. However, since nobody came and I by myself could not make up a company, I have returned to the brothers, where by God's grace I live at peace with my heart and conscience to the praise and glory of God, in great charity and simplicity of life and in complete mutual peace and love. We labor with our hands to supply our bodies with food and clothing, for there are among us all the suitable or necessary trades for our benefit and that of the people. . . .
>
> I understand that you are afraid that when you come to us, there will be

This same year, brother Hans Arbeiter from Aachen was also chosen and appointed to the service of the Gospel.

1561
Hans Arbeiter chosen for the service of the Word.

1562

In 1562 two brothers were chosen and appointed to the service of the Gospel: Valtin Hörl, a purse-maker by trade, and Hans Langenbach.

That same year we set up the community at Klein Niemtschitz[1] near Prahlitz.

Klein Niemtschitz.

Two old and much respected servants of God's Word and his church, Hans Greckenhofer[2] and Hans Klöpfer of Feuerbach, fell asleep in the Lord within a short time of each other at Nikolsburg in Moravia.

2 servants passed away.

Brother Valtin Mager, a Silesian, was appointed to the service for temporal affairs.

Valtin Mager chosen for the service for temporal affairs.

---

no place for you to teach Greek, Hebrew, and Latin. Do not seek this but seek first the kingdom of God and his justice, and everything else will be added unto you! Other qualified persons have come to us and have adjusted to trades that are suitable and honorable, and the church makes use of them. A little is sufficient unto the wise.

Quotations are from Prof. Stella's address, "Influssi e Sviluppi dell'Anabattismo Hutterita in Comunitá Eterodosse Italiana," (Influences and Developments of Hutterian Anabaptism in Italian Nonconformist Conventicles), given at the symposium "Täufer in Tirol anläßlich des 450. Todestages von Jakob Hutter," Sankt Lorenzen, Pustertal, September 4–6, 1986.

For additional reading, see Williams, *Radical Reformation*, 559–577, and *Reforma Radical*, 573 ff.; Henry A. DeWind, "Italian Hutterite Martyrs," *MQR*, July 1954, 163–185; Robert Friedmann, "Christian Sectarians in Thessalonica and Their Relationship to the Anabaptists," *MQR*, Jan. 1955, 54–69; *ME*, II, 513–514 (Gherlandi); IV, 346 (Rizzetto), 495–496 (della Sega); Beck, 211–212, 241–243.

About anti-Trinitarianism or Socinianism, see George H. Williams, "Stanislaw Budziński (c.1530–c.1595): The First Historian of Unitarianism," *The Proceedings of the Unitarian Universalist Historical Society*, Vol. XX, Part II (1986), 77–88; Williams, *Radical Reformation*; Fast, *Der linke Flügel*, ch. IV; *ME*, III, 455, "Manelfi"; Robert Friedmann, "Encounter of Anabaptists and Mennonites with Anti-Trinitarianism," *MQR*, July 1948, 139–162; *Schaff-Herzog*, X, 488–492.

[1]Klein Niemtschitz (Němčičky; not to be confused with the other "Klein Niemtschitz," p.366 n.3), village near Prahlitz on the eastern bank of the Jihlava River just south of Kanitz (Dolní Kounice), owned at the time by Zikmund of Zástřizl, lord of Kanitz, who ceded the farm, a mill, and several gardens to the brothers; Beck, 214. In 1578 Zikmund's son Jan sold the Kanitz estate to Governor Zdeněk Lev of Rožmitál, in whose family it remained until 1588. Both families were protectors of the Hutterites. In 1588 the brothers rented further fields from Maximilian and Zdeněk of Rožmitál. See Zeman, *Topography*, #100.

[2]Hans Greckenhofer was a joiner by trade; see Beck, 214.

1563

1563

4 brothers chosen for the service of the Gospel.

On Three Kings' Day [Jan. 6], 1563, four brothers were chosen and appointed to the service of the Gospel: Kaspar Ebner, Andreas Maierhofer, Klaus Braidl or Schuster (a cobbler),[1] and Gilg Federspil.

4 brothers chosen for the service for temporal affairs.

On the same day four more brothers were chosen and appointed to the service for temporal affairs: Ulrich Plattner, a carpenter; Nikolaus Geyersbühler, a miller;[2] Erhard Sattler; and Hans Heidelberger or Bäck (a baker).

Moved from Polehraditz.

That same year Lord Säbisch[3] drove the brothers and sisters out of Polehraditz.

Moved to Gallitz.

So we started a community outside the town of Gallitz.[4]

1564

Group in opposition. Some were disunited and excluded on question of divorce.

In 1564 several members—Christel Schmidt, Jörg Knofloch, Hans Neuhöfel, and others—who opposed the servants and elders on the church's attitude to divorce were excluded. Later some repented, but the others went the way of the world, and they bear their own judgment. They died soon after in their sins. On their deathbeds they lamented bitterly and were full of fear and remorse, especially Knofloch and Neuhöfel. They had longed for repentance and peace with the church but did not experience it.

Andreas Stuck passed away.

At Neumühl, brother Andreas Stuck, a confirmed servant for temporal affairs, fell asleep in the Lord.

Matthias Gasser passed away.

In Altenmarkt brother Matthias Gasser, a confirmed servant for temporal affairs, also fell asleep in the Lord.

Hans Langenbach confirmed.

At Niemtschitz brother Hans Langenbach was confirmed in

---

[1]Klaus Braidl was confirmed in the service of the Word at Niemtschitz in 1564 and was immediately sent out on mission along the Rhine River; see *ME*, I, 401–402. In 1583 Klaus Braidl was to succeed Hans Kräl as Vorsteher of the Hutterian Church; see below, pp.493–494.

[2]About Nikolaus Geyersbühler, see below, pp.394–395.

[3]Lord Säbisch: Záviš Prusinovský of Víckov, lord of Polehraditz; see above, p.367 n.

[4]Gallitz (Skalice), southwest of Brno between Hosterlitz (Hostěradice) and Stiegnitz (Trstěnice) in Moravia; see Beck, 214; not to be confused with Skalitz in Slovakia (Hungary at that time). The communities at Skalitz, Tschermakowitz, Wischenau, Teikowitz, and Alexowitz were called the "upper communities." Zeman, *Topography*, #143; *ME*, IV, 536.

the service of the Gospel by the elders with the laying on of hands.

1564

At Göding in Moravia Hans of Cologne, a servant for temporal affairs, fell asleep in the Lord.

Hans of Cologne passed away.

Brother Hans Schneider from Kaufbeuren, a servant for temporal affairs, fell asleep in the Lord at Stiegnitz.

Hans Schneider passed away.

In the same year a community was started at Turnitz.[1]

Community at Turnitz.

Brother Julius Klampferer[2] from northern Italy was imprisoned at Venice for the sake of divine truth. He was interrogated many times. His examiners argued with him to make him recant, but he answered every question with the simple truth. In the end, after he had shown great steadfastness, he was sentenced to be thrown into the depths of the sea. On hearing this he said, "I am not surprised. From the very beginning of my commitment to God, I have been aware that I would have to die for the sake of his truth. But what concerns me most is that the lords of Venice consent to this and forget that on the last day they will have to render an account before God for such a crime." The lords replied that they were not one bit afraid.

Brother Julius Klampferer captured at Venice.

At Venice they were not afraid to kill believers.

Displeased at what Julius Klampferer had said, they did not allow him to speak further but hurried him back to prison. They were planning to carry out the sentence as soon as possible. Since he had almost been a priest, they unfrocked him according to their custom. Then one evening they fetched him as if for a hearing, took him out, and drowned him without giving him any warning, although he had been expecting no other outcome.

They unfrocked him and drowned him.

He remained joyful and sang all the time, praising God until he won the crown of the martyrs of Christ and of the faithful witnesses to the truth. This story is told in a letter Franciscus

---

[1]Turnitz (Tvrdonice), east of Lundenburg (Břeclav), Moravia. Zeman, *Topography*, #162.

[2]Julius Klampferer (a tinsmith and lantern maker) was Giulio Gherlandi, or Julius Trevisano (from Treviso). He was imprisoned several times, last in October 1561 (not 1564), and was drowned on October 15, 1562. See *ME*, II, 513–514; see *Martyrs Mirror*, 652; Beck, 239–240; Karl Benrath, "Wiedertäufer im Venetianischen um die Mitte des 16. Jahrhunderts," *Theologische Studien und Kritiken*, I (1885), 37–67 (Gherlandi's confession, pp. 58–64); see also above, p.379 n.2.

1564

wrote from Venice.[1] Although he was drowned secretly by night, this crime will be brought to the light and severely punished on the great day of the Lord.

Michael Veldthaler confirmed in his service.

That same year, brother Michael Veldthaler was confirmed in the service of the Gospel by the elders with the laying on of hands.

Leonhard Dax chosen for the service of the Word.

Brother Leonhard Dax[2] was chosen and appointed to the service of the Gospel. He was formerly a priest and had celebrated the mass for thirteen years in Bavaria and Tirol. When he saw how abominable it was, he came to the church, surrendered to the Lord, and learned to work.[3] For several years he lived at Klein Niemtschitz near Prahlitz before he was appointed.

Sigmund Hosauer passed away.

Brother Sigmund Hosauer, a servant of God's Word, fell asleep in the Lord at Kostel in Moravia.

2 brothers confirmed in the service of the Gospel.

At Niemtschitz, brothers Valtin Hörl and Klaus Braidl were confirmed in the service of the Gospel and God's Word by the elders with the laying on of hands.

---

[1]This is included in Francesco della Sega's very long letter of 1563 to Leonard Lanzenstiel and the whole brotherhood; Codex III, 124, Episcopal Library at Esztergom. See Friedmann, *Schriften*, 125, #1.

[2]Leonhard Dax, native of Munich, had been a Roman Catholic priest in Bavaria and other areas (Tirol). See above, p.322, for the account of Pürchner's interrogation, in which Dax had participated as a priest. In 1558 he joined the Hutterian Church, was imprisoned for several months in 1567/1568 (see below, pp.395–396), and died in 1574 (see below, p.440). See Gross, *Golden Years*, 123–149; *ME*, II, 21; Beck, 223, 265–266.

[3]The emphasis on manual labor indicated by the chronicler is characteristic of the German Reformation. It comes to expression in contemporary literature: Hans Sachs, *Vom Schlauraffenland*, and *Der Müller mit dem Esel*; or Johann Fischart, *Glückhaft Schiff von Zürich*. In contrast, the idleness and prosperity leading to immorality among the clergy of that time are portrayed in Ulrich Hutten, *Gespräche*, and Burkart Waldis, *Der verlorene Sohn*, Neudrucke deutscher Literatur-Werke, Vol. 30.

1565–1591: The Golden Years

1565

In the year 1565, dear brother Leonhard Lanzenstiel became ill and fell asleep in the Lord on March 3 at Klein Niemtschitz near Prahlitz. He was a servant of Jesus Christ and as Vorsteher had led the whole church, which had been entrusted to his care by Hans Amon at the beginning of 1542.

Leonhard Lanzenstiel, the Vorsteher, passed away.

For twenty-three years he faithfully cared for the church, enduring much suffering and many struggles and enriching us, his brothers in the faith, with his teaching and explanation of the Scriptures. He also wrote comforting letters to those of us who were suffering or in prison. When he himself was in prison, suffering for the sake of divine truth, he wrote similar letters to the church. The story of his imprisonment is told earlier in this book.[1]

Soon after Leonhard had passed away, brothers from many communities met with the elders, and after taking counsel in the fear of God, they named brother Peter Walpot to take Leonhard's place. Peter Walpot had been faithfully carrying out the service of God's Word for twenty-three years. They entrusted the church of the Lord to him, to look after its needs and keep watch over it, to care for it in every way. From this time on he carried out this task with utmost diligence and trustworthiness until he departed from this world, as is told later.[2]

Peter Walpot entrusted with the care of the church.

[1]About Leonhard Lanzenstiel, see above, p.85 n.3; Beck, 216–217. For the story of his imprisonment, see above, pp.153–154.

[2]See below, pp.463–465. As Vorsteher, Peter Walpot spoke to the schoolmasters assembled at Niemtschitz (Němčice) on November 15, 1568. His address became the basis for the well-known Hutterian School Discipline (Schulordnung). See John A. Hostetler, Leonard Gross, and Elizabeth Bender, *Selected Hutterian Documents in Translation, 1542–1654* (Philadelphia, PA, 1975), 5–12; Friedmann, *Schriften*, 130 C) 1,2.

1565
Franciscus von der Sach and Antonius Wälsch captured.

About this time two brothers were put to death in Venice after having been in prison for almost two years. They were Franciscus von der Sach, born in Rovigo, Italy, who was a servant of the Word still in a time of testing, and his companion, brother Antonius Wälsch. They had been on their way to Moravia with a small company of travelers and had reached Capodistria, about one hundred miles from Venice. The others in the group were not arrested but allowed to continue on their way. The man who betrayed the two brothers and caused their imprisonment was a certain Alexius Schweitzer.[1] Franciscus's feet were chained like a criminal's, and the brothers were taken to separate cells in Capodistria. There, as we see from Franciscus's letters, they battled with and overcame many attacks from Satan, who at such times tries to make a mountain out of a molehill in order to make men lose their trust in God and fall.

At such times Satan tries to make a mountain out of a molehill.

Taken to Venice.

Their testimony was heard in Capodistria. Three days later they were sent to Venice, their hands and feet in chains. The sea passage took three days because of the stormy waves, but they encouraged each other to be steadfast, and their chains became less painful, whereas before they had suffered greatly, day and night.

They had arrived in Venice on September 1, 1562, and were straightaway separated and put in the pitch-dark prisons of the ten most prominent councillors.

Franciscus interrogated.

After the two brothers had been in prison about a month, they were brought before three Venetian lords and several worldly and unspiritual priests, who sat in state and splendor, gorgeously robed. Franciscus was asked whether he stood by what he had answered in Capodistria when he was questioned about his activities and whether he still declared it to be the truth. He answered yes, he believed it to be the truth, and it was the truth.

Next they asked if he had ever been in Moravia. They went on to ask if he believed what the holy, catholic, apostolic,

---

[1]Francesco della Sega had been traveling in Italy with Antonio Rizzetto, or Wälsch, from Vicenza; Antonio's son; Nicolo Buccella from Padua, a physician, who recanted in December 1564; and their betrayer, Alexius Schweitzer or Alessio Todeschi, a Swiss from Bellinzona. The arrest had taken place in August 1562. See *ME*, IV, 346, 495–496. The rest of the group were pursued as far as Trieste but apparently not caught; it may be assumed that they reached Moravia. Capodistria (Koper), Yugoslavia, is just south of Trieste across the Italian border.

Roman Church believes. He replied that in regard to faith he believed all the articles of the apostolic Christian confession. Then he was questioned about baptism, the mass, confession, and a great many other points of dispute. When he had spoken his mind, they heaped abuse on him, calling him a renegade and a sophist, one possessed by the devil. Then they sent him back to prison. They gave the other brother, Antonius, a similar hearing, and he, too, gave a good testimony.

1565

Venetians called him a confounded sophist.

Not long after, they again questioned Franciscus about the same articles, especially about infant baptism, but they accomplished nothing.

Franciscus interrogated a second time.

They had him brought several more times to dispute with him. They even sent monks to him who, once he had answered their questions, continually heaped abuse on him, saying he was a heretic and opponent of church councils and if he did not recant he would have to die. So back to prison he went.

Frequently brought for interrogation.

Soon after, the lords sent another monk to prove his heresy to him. This man was an inquisitor or examiner in questions of faith at Vicenza. He asked the brother if he came from the Moravian church. Franciscus said yes. The monk said, "That is the first error." Then he asked, "Haven't you broken bread with them?" When the brother acknowledged it, the monk said, "That is another error." He continued asking questions, and to every answer Franciscus gave he said, "You are a heretic."

Monk from Vicenza disputed with Franciscus.

The monk also said, "Tell me this: Who is the head of the church?"

Franciscus replied, "It is Christ."

"That is another error," said the monk.

Then Franciscus told him, "You are the heretic, not I. Christ is the head of his church."

Franciscus told the monk, "You are the heretic, not I."

The reply came, "Well, in the first place he is, of course. But the pope is head here on earth."

Franciscus said, "A body with two heads is a monstrosity."

But the only reply was, "Heretic! Heretic!" and he was told to recant. Brother Franciscus said no, he would not recant, because he had not been convinced through Holy Scripture. His questioners said, "We are not obliged to convince you by Scripture." After further interrogation they sent him back to prison. He wrote down his defense and confession of faith and sent it to them.

"Heretic! Heretic!"

1565
Drowned in the sea.

When he remained steadfast through many disputations, holding to the truth he had acknowledged and embraced, he and brother Antonius were condemned to death. As mentioned above, they were cast into the sea and drowned at Venice.[1]

Rev.20:13

But the sea will give up its dead on judgment day. Then those who have murdered the faithful will wring their hands as they begin to realize what is happening. They will be seized with dread and their repentance will be too late. From his prison in Venice, Franciscus wrote one or two letters to the church, which we still have.[2]

Farwendel united with us.

This same year, 1565, Farwendel, an old servant or teacher among the Swiss Brethren, united with us at Neustadt in the Haardt near the Rhine River. It happened as follows. He had been imprisoned for holding the beliefs of the Swiss Brethren.

Farwendel's heart disturbed.

While he was in prison at Oggersheim, a village two miles from Worms, God brought him into great distress, which he said he could hardly describe. After several weeks in prison, he was summoned to a hearing by the priests. He answered them quite well and was not distressed by their questioning. But back in his dungeon, he was seized with terror and doubts and such physical pain that for three days he did not eat, drink,

In prison Farwendel lost heart.

or sleep. He cried out day and night, pleading to the Lord without finding relief. Then he became very fearful. He thought that it was all over with him, that he had lost everything, and that he would have to deny the truth when the priests came.

He had searched his heart and examined his whole life in case there was anything that might have offended God and might therefore be the reason for his distress. But he could find nothing. He asked the Lord in prayer if it really was his will to let a man go to pieces so miserably that he blasphemes God's name and denies the truth, even though to do so is the greatest anguish. He was in such agony that he thought, if his pain were to last one or two days longer, he would die from it, humanly seen.

God gave Farwendel self-recognition.

As he pleaded with God to show him if he had done wrong,

---

[1]Antonio Rizzetto was drowned on February 16, 1565; Francesco della Sega, ten days later on February 26; see *Martyrs Mirror*, 664.

[2]See above, p.384 n.1. See also Benrath, 64–67, for a German transcription of della Sega's appeal of July 18, 1564, to the Inquisition, pleading for release. Letters of della Sega's are also found in Codex 305, Bratislava Academy of Sciences.

Farwendel suddenly realized, as clearly as if someone had spoken to him, that he had still been clinging to his own will. Besides, he was still living in private property and therefore had not yet truly died to himself. He was horrified and immediately remembered the stand the Hutterian Brethren took. Dumbstruck, he thought, "True, there were several articles of their faith I was never able to agree with." He thought about these points and prayed about them, and God gave him such enlightenment that he could no longer oppose our basic beliefs. As soon as his heart turned toward us, he was filled with such comfort and joy in the Lord that he was no longer afraid but full of courage and absolutely decided to witness to our faith until death. He would confess to everyone that ours is the true church of God.

1565

When Farwendel thought of us he found joy and courage.

He had also made up his mind that if God helped him out of prison, he would not go to any of his brethren before he was united with us [the Hutterian Church]. He had prayed for eight weeks that God might grant him peace with us.

In this year brother Klaus Braidl, a servant of God's Word and his church, had been sent to the Rhineland with Ludwig Dörker and Bastel Rausch to accompany him. The day they arrived, Farwendel and other Swiss Brethren sent two of their number to seek out our brothers with the message that he, Farwendel, was anxious to see them, and it did not take them long to find our brothers.

Farwendel sent for our brothers.

Klaus Braidl, Ludwig Dörker, and Bastel Rausch granted Farwendel's wish and visited him in prison. He told them everything he had experienced, which we have already reported, and he expressed his fervent longing to be united with us. The brothers were not willing to grant this at once but first questioned and reproached him because they had heard that he had opposed our brothers. If only he had been more open beforehand and had not willfully fought against the truth, his situation would be different now. It was a very serious talk. They pointed out to him that he bore heavy guilt, having been a stumbling block to many. There were other concerns too for which they reproved him.

Klaus Braidl visited Farwendel in prison.

Then he began to open his heart and told them everything. With a good conscience he could say that he had never opposed them willfully, since until now his eyes had not been opened. His deepest sorrow was that in his blindness he had misled so

Farwendel lamented having turned many away.

1565

In his ignorance he had thought us a detestable group.

many and caused their destruction. He felt great pain that he might never be able to bring them back. In his ignorance he had thought we were a detestable group that lacked the true apostolic foundation of faith, because we took a different stand from them on some points, such as taxes, separation of married couples, exclusion [church discipline], and food and drink for the servants. He said he had been so blind at that time, considering us to be so deep in error, that when Lorenz Huf of Sprendlingen (also a Swiss servant) and several others had come to us,[1] he, Farwendel, had separated or excluded himself because he thought he had not put up a firm enough resistance; he should have kept better watch over his flock. He thought he had been too soft, allowing his people to be led astray. And that was why he then went so far that he gleefully repeated anything he heard that would make his people suspicious of us.

Farwendel begged to unite with us.

But he asserted that he had never deliberately opposed the truth when he knew better. After the servant Klaus Braidl had talked almost all night long with him, with the result that neither of them so much as closed his eyes, Farwendel pleaded that he might be united with us if possible. He was afraid he would be taken to another place (which then did happen), and he did not know if he would ever see any of our people again with his mortal eyes.

Farwendel intended to confess our faith even if we did not accept him.

Even if we could not yet decide to accept him, he was resolved, with God's help, to stand with us on the same foundation and never break faith. But if now in his great need he could be united with us, he would praise God and feel more confident. He was determined never to bring disgrace on the church of the Lord by being unfaithful.

Farwendel united with us.

The brothers felt the urgency of his situation. There in the dungeon they took counsel in great fear of God, wanting to do neither too much nor too little. They agreed in the Lord to grant Farwendel his wish then and there in the prison, for he told them of the fear and distress he had been in for nearly eight weeks, pleading that God's will might be done.

Some of his congregation united with us.

Thus he and his wife were received into the church, and also many other brothers and sisters from his group, including his two sons. At Farwendel's request our brothers spoke to

---

[1]About the uniting of Lorenz Huf and other former Swiss Brethren with the Hutterian Brethren, see above, pp.332–339.

his church, and many were moved to unite with us. We accepted them, and they came to join us here. *1565*

But some, although they saw the truth, were unable to overcome themselves. They knew they would have to give up their possessions and their self-will in surrender to God and the Christian community. What was still harder, they would have had to reveal the sins they had committed since they had entered into the covenant of baptism. They therefore remained in the Swiss brotherhood, where this was not required of them.

Farwendel was later released from prison. He moved to the church and after some years fell asleep among us in the Lord. Others who had come with him also remained steadfast. It was for their sakes as well as for Farwendel's that the Lord had intervened. But Farwendel was relieved of the service of the Word and did not do this service among us, which he accepted willingly since he was well advanced in years.

Farwendel and some of his people moved to the community.

This year we brothers founded the community at Pribitz[1] in the domain of Gross Seelowitz, building from scratch on a green meadow with the permission of Lord Friedrich von Zerotin.

Community at Pribitz.

This year several Gabrielite brothers from Kreutz, including old Georg Weber and his sons, became one with us in faith and joined the church community. So our brothers joined them at Kreutz and established community in accordance with true Christian faith.[2]

Some Gabrielites united with us.

This year we also began the community at Landshut.[3]

Landshut.

---

[1]Pribitz (Přibice), a parish southeast of Pohrlitz (Pohořelice) on the left bank of the Jihlava River. In the 13th century Pribitz was owned by the Sovereign Order of the Knights of Malta. In 1565 it was part of the Gross Seelowitz (Židlochovice) domain, acquired by Friedrich von Zerotin, who was a benefactor of the Hutterites like the previous owners of Gross Seelowitz, Jan and Jaroslav of Zástřizl. Until 1623, Pribitz was one of the largest Hutterian communities. See *ME*, IV, 218–219; Zeman, *Topography*, #120; Beck, 247 n.2.

[2]After this uniting of the last Gabrielites with the Hutterian Church, there were predominantly Hutterites and a small number of Swiss Brethren groups in Moravia and Austria. See Zeman, *Anabaptists and Czech Brethren*, 282–283; see also entry for 1545 above, pp.233–238.

Kreutz, west of Göding (Hodonín), a village no longer in existence; 1561–1567 the property of Pertolt of Lipé; burned down in 1605 (see below, p.584). *ME*, I, 740, "Creutz"; Zeman, *Topography*, #67; Beck, 248.

[3]Landshut (Lanžhot), a small market town in southern Moravia, southeast of Lundenburg (Břeclav), between the Dyje and Morava rivers; in 1565 owned by

1565
Peter Dietrich passed away.

This year brother Peter Dietrich, a servant for temporal affairs, fell asleep in the Lord at Austerlitz.

1566

3 brothers chosen for the service of the Gospel.

In 1566 three brothers were chosen and appointed to the service of the Gospel: Blasi Harer from the Ötz Valley, Leonhard Reuss or Schneider (a tailor) from Württemberg, and Georg Wyser or Wagner from Tirol.

Bohemian chancellor wanted to attack the faith in Moravia.

At this time the following incidents took place in Vienna, Austria. The Bohemian chancellor from Neuhaus spitefully intended to destroy our faith. He begged the emperor Maximilian II for permission to drive the brotherhoods out of Moravia with the support of the bishop. If everything had gone as he wished, it would have caused great distress for the church of God. As soon as the emperor yielded to his persistent requests and gave him a letter to that effect, he set out. He took leave of the lords in Vienna, saying, "If God helps me cross this ditch (the Danube), you'll hear some news." He started out, but as his carriage drove onto the bridge, a beam gave way under him. The bridge fell into the Danube, taking horse, carriage and all with it, and the chancellor and two others were drowned. Only his servant boy managed to keep afloat. When the boy saw that his lord was dead and was being carried away by the current, he seized him by the beard and shouted for help. Both of them were pulled out of the river and brought to the emperor. The emperor took the dead chancellor's golden chain from his neck and put it on the boy, then had the dead man carried back to Neuhaus. This was the news of which the Bohemian chancellor had spoken, not knowing what it would be.

He drowned. The bridge broke under him.

Hard to kick against the goads.

The emperor and everybody else saw it as a judgment of God. It is hard to kick against the goads, or to fight against God and attack the faith. This is how God deals at times with those who plan evil and want to spill innocent blood or slaughter the son before his father's eyes.

Zech.2:8
Isa.8:10

God says through the prophets, "Whoever touches you touches the apple of his eye" (NEB). He lets them take counsel, but he brings their counsels to naught. Therefore David sings,

---

Johann von Zerotin at Lundenburg. See Beck, 247; *ME*, III, 284; Zeman, *Topography*, #70.

"The kings of the land rebel, and the rulers take counsel against the Lord and his anointed, but he who dwells in the heavens laughs, and he will mock them and terrify them in his fury." "He lets them dig a pit, but it is they who must fall into it." He lets them throw a stone in the air, but it is made to fall on their own heads. God's judgment falls upon those who plan such evil, and men can see what their attempts really are: glass striking at the rock, and the withered leaf or the dry straw rebelling against the devouring fire. And although God often lets the plans of such men succeed for a time as a test for the faithful, making the believers take the first sips of the cup, yet the adversaries must drain it to the dregs and eat the broken pieces as well.

1566
Ps.2:2–5
Ps.7:15
Ecclus.27:25
If glass strikes the rock it will break.
Ezek.23:32–34

This same year we started the communities at Tscheikowitz and Pruschanek.[1]

Tscheikowitz
Pruschanek.

A big army marched into Hungary in 1566.[2] The soldiers caused heavy damage to the communities in many different localities. Other communities were protected from the soldiers' violence by the lords and counts who had come from foreign countries. But some of the lords of Moravia took our horses and other things during the invasions.

Big army came through Hungary. Harassed the church.

Four brothers were confirmed in the service of the Gospel by the elders with the laying on of hands. They were Christoph Lenck, Kaspar Ebner, Andreas Maierhofer, and Leonhard Dax.

4 brothers confirmed in the service of the Word.

1567

In 1567 brother Burkhard Bämerle, an old servant of the Word and of the Gospel, fell asleep in the Lord. Previously he had been in prison with Bärtel Riegel of Gündelbach because of his faith. There they had racked him terribly. It was not merely a heavy weight that they had hung on him, but the whole earth, tying him to a ring fixed in the floor and pulling him up until the sun could have shone through him. Yet he

Burkhard Bämerle, terribly racked when in prison, passed away.

[1]Pruschanek (Prušánky), a parish between Göding (Hodonín) and Kostel (Podivín); in 1566 property of Záviš Prusinovský of Víckov. See Beck, 248; *ME*, IV, 224; Zeman, *Topography*, #123.

[2]These expeditions were directed against the Turks and their protégé Johann Sigismund Zápolya (prince of Transylvania since 1540), who was pressed on all sides by the imperial commanders Lazarus Schwendi and Andreas Bathory. Friedrich von Zerotin was one of the Moravian nobles in Schwendi's imperial army. See Beck, 248.

1567

Swiss Brethren drew up a letter. Asked for our answer.

remained true to the Lord and firm in his faith, and after his great suffering he passed away at Tracht in Moravia.

This year the Swiss Brethren wrote a letter to our brothers on behalf of their whole brotherhood, both at home and abroad, asking us for an answer on seven points:[1]

1. Community of goods
2. About those who have to leave us empty-handed
3. The servants [of the Word] and others who have special tasks in the church
4. Separation of believing and unbelieving marriage partners
5. The place of young people in the community, their duties, and how to discipline them
6. Taxes for government and executions
7. Why we shun the Swiss Brethren

We wrote them an answer, carefully explaining these points on the basis of Holy Scripture and pointing out their errors and shortcomings in these and other matters. They paid little or no attention to our answer, however, nor did they have it read to their congregations. Instead of leading to their improvement, it will be a judgment on them on the last day. A copy of our answer is still preserved.

Hans Mang imprisoned at Sonthofen.

This same year, brother Hans Mang or Huter,[2] a hatter by trade, was held in the prison infirmary at Sonthofen in Swabia for the sake of divine truth. He suffered severely from the cold in winter, for the irons made his feet so cold they could not get warm all night, as he wrote in the letter we still have. But he said that on the last day these chains will give him warmth and comfort and be a better adornment than the gold chains around the necks of the ungodly. He remained steadfast throughout all the cruelties the ungodly inflicted on him and fell asleep in the Lord in the prison infirmary.

He passed away in prison.

Nikolaus Geyersbühler captured.

In this year brother Nikolaus Geyersbühler or Müller (a miller),[3] a servant for temporal affairs, was imprisoned at

[1]For a discussion of the seven articles of 1567, see Gross, *Golden Years*, 168–185 and notes.

[2]About Hans Mang see *ME*, III, 456; *Martyrs Mirror*, 703; Beck, 252.

[3]Nikolaus Geyersbühler, originally from Geyersbühl in the Kitzbühel district, had lived in the village of St. Johannes. He was baptized by Peter Riedemann "at Freischütz [Sabatisch] on the Hungarian border." See *Martyrs Mirror*, 703–704;

Innsbruck for the sake of his faith and the divine truth. There the Jesuits and others set upon him, using both subtle and violent means as Satan, the tempter, does. But nothing could shake his faith. He stood firm like a Christian hero.

1567

Undaunted in his trust in God, he was condemned to death by the sons of Caiaphas and Pilate. The priests, like Herodias's daughter, had done their utmost to have his head, and they achieved their end. Nikolaus was beheaded and then burned. With his blood he gave valiant witness to the way of divine truth that leads to eternal life, and in this noble battle he defended the field in Christ.

He was beheaded.

That same year we founded the community at Wostitz[1] under Lord Albrecht Černohorský of Boskovice, who also owned Pürschitz.[2]

Wostitz.

On Sunday before St. Martin's Day [Nov. 11], brother Leonhard Dax and six others[3] were arrested because of their witness to Christ. Leonhard Dax (as was told earlier) was a former priest who had loathed and persecuted us because of our way of life. After thinking things over, he was converted and abandoned the priesthood. He joined the church community and proved himself as a brother. Later, he was chosen and confirmed as a servant of God's Word and sent out on mission to the lands along the Rhine, where he was captured. The prisoners were taken to the town of Alzey[4] in the Palatinate.

Leonhard Dax captured.

When they had been there two weeks, the superintendent of Alzey (a Zwinglian preacher) and several others came to question him. "Weren't you formerly a priest?" they asked Dax. He admitted that in his blindness and ignorance he had

A Zwinglian preacher questioned Dax.

ME, II, 512; Loserth, *Anabaptismus*, 213–214; Beck, 249–251. About his defense or confession of faith, see Leonard Gross, "Nikolaus Geyersbühler, a Hutterite Missioner to Tirol," *MQR*, Oct. 1969, 283–292 (NB notes 1 and 2); Gross, *Golden Years*, 57–63, 220 n.3.

[1]Wostitz (Vlasatice), north of Dürnholz (Drnholec), northwest of Nikolsburg (Mikulov). According to Beck, 252 n.1, the property was sold to Count Franz von Thurn the following year, 1568 (or possibly 1574; see Zeman, *Topography*, # 177).

[2]Pürschitz (Prštice), southwest of Brno, east of Eibenschitz; see *ME*, IV, 235; Zeman, *Topography*, #125.

[3]Dax's companions included Ludwig Zimmermann (also called Ludwig Dörker), Jakob Gabriel Binder, Jörg Schneider, Dax's wife Anna, and Bärbel from Teikowitz (Tavíkovice), near Mährisch Kromau, where the brothers occupied the "new farmstead," called "Taufarsky." See Beck, 252.

[4]Alzey, see above, p.73 n.2.

1567

served the idolatrous church of the pope in Bavaria and in Tirol. Leonhard Dax gave a powerful answer based on Scripture when asked about his mission, the basis of his faith, the reason for our separating from people like themselves, community of goods, and infant baptism. Then he was taken back to the dungeon and advised to think it over; they would take serious measures.

Leonhard Dax interrogated again by the Zwinglian preacher.

On January 12, 1568, he was again brought out for a hearing. The Zwinglian preacher spoke with him about the church, saying there had never been a church without blemish. Magistrates, he said, are Christians and as such may use the sword. He also spoke about separation of believing and unbelieving marriage partners, but brother Leonhard confuted all he said, and the superintendent was unable to uphold any point. He urged Leonhard to accept his advice and follow the Zwinglian religion. Then the noble lord and sovereign of this country, the count palatine, would provide him with a splendid position and he could live wherever he liked in his country.

But Leonhard told him that he could not show him Christ's truth if he did not live it. Besides, he said, his beliefs were no error but were founded on the true grace of God, and with God's help he would be faithful. Nobody should expect anything else of him.

He was taken back to prison with the threat that he would soon see how serious his situation was. But Leonhard replied that God's will should be done. He was ready to defend his faith and the people of God, not only with words but with his life, if it was God's will. And with God's help no one was going to stop him.

Leonhard Dax and fellow prisoners released.

He and his fellow prisoners were held in prison through the winter but then released on February 25, 1568. A written record of Dax's defense and some of his songs are still preserved.[1]

1568

Ambrosius Pfeiffer passed away.

On New Year's Day, brother Ambrosius Pfeiffer, a servant of the Word, passed away at Klein Niemtschitz near Prahlitz.

[1]To date, the songs by Leonhard Dax have not been found. His defense or confession of faith is in the Olomouc University Library, Codex 180, fol. 60–130, and at Esztergom, Codex III, 124, fol. 311–397; English translation in *MQR*, Oct. 1975, 293–334. See Christian Hege, *Die Täufer in der Kurpfalz* (Frankfurt, 1908), 106–111; Friedmann, *Schriften*, 110; Beck, 265.

On January 25, the three brothers Blasi Harer, Georg Wyser, and Leonhard Reuss were confirmed in the service of the Gospel by the elders with the laying on of hands.

1568
3 brothers confirmed in the service of the Word.

The same day, also at Klein Niemtschitz, four brothers were chosen and appointed to the service of the Gospel: Balthasar Maierhof the younger, Peter Hörich from Silesia, Ulrich Plattner or Zimmermann (a carpenter) from the Ötz Valley, and Hans Schlegel from Württemberg, a tailor by trade.

4 brothers chosen for the service of the Word.

On the same day, eleven brothers were chosen and appointed to the service for temporal affairs or steward's service:

11 brothers chosen for the service for temporal affairs.

Gall Perger
Valtin Preundel
Veit Hagenpühler or Lavanttaler[1]
Christian Lärch
Thomas Häring
Leonhard Stuck
Hansel Schneider from Rottenburg
Remigius Heugen from Tirol
Simon Päntzel
Bastian Foltz, a carpenter
Kuntz Kuenfelder

Brother Konrad Haintzeman or Schuster (a cobbler), a servant of God's Word, crossed the Hungarian mountains to the thermal springs to get help for his ailments.[2] Later he returned to Sabatisch and there fell asleep in the Lord after much suffering.

That same year, 1568, brother Hans Zwinger or Gerber (a tanner),[3] a servant of God's Word, fell asleep in the Lord at Wostitz.

Hans Zwinger passed away.

We reestablished the community at Urschitz where we had lived previously.

Community at Urschitz.

---

[1]Veit Hagenpühler, a native of the Lavant Valley in Carinthia; the Lavant is a tributary of the Drava River in Carinthia. See Beck, 253.

[2]The "Hungarian mountains" were the White Mountains (*montes albi*); today the "White Carpathians" and the "Little Carpathians." In the 16th century, no difference seems to have been made between these two ranges. The thermal springs are at Teplitz (Trenčianske Teplice), northeast of Trenčín. Beck, 253.

[3]Two of Hans Zwinger's songs are in *LdHBr*, 663–669 (under "Garber" and "Zwinger" respectively). See also Wolkan, *Lieder*, 230.

1568
Hans Arbeiter taken prisoner.

On July 18, a servant of God's Word and his church, Hans Arbeiter from Aachen,[1] and another brother, Heinrich Schuster, were captured at Hainbach on the Rhine in the bishopric of Speyer. The village mayor told the constable to chain them, but he refused, for he did not want to share the guilt. He said to the mayor, "You cannot order me to chain these men, who are much more devout than I am. Had I known they would be put in prison, I would have warned them."

Constable refused to chain them.

So the mayor bound them himself and brought them to Kirrweiler. This took place on Sunday night. The next day the mayor went to a market at Neustadt in the Haardt Mountains. On Tuesday he fell ill, and on Wednesday they buried him. Everyone said he must have sinned. After that, the constable said, not even for a hundred gulden would he make himself guilty of imprisoning the brothers. But Hans Arbeiter was put in a dark dungeon, cut off from the light of day, and Heinrich was put in the Kirrweiler jail.

The mayor died 3 days later.

After two weeks the bishop sent his sheriff and nine others to give each of the two prisoners a separate hearing, asking why they had entered their lord's estate and misled his people. Hans Arbeiter said he had neither misled nor deceived anyone—his intention had been not to mislead anyone but to teach the divine truth.

The sheriff gave them a hearing.

Hans Arbeiter also answered their questions about infant baptism: There is not one word in Scripture to prove that infants should be baptized. Baptism should be only for those who hear and believe the Lord's Word and obey it, who understand what Christian baptism, teaching, and life is and know what they commit themselves to. Then he was taken back to prison.

Questioned on infant baptism.

Ten or twelve days later the deputy official questioned him, and the bishop sent the dean of Speyer Cathedral, a Jesuit named Lamprecht, to speak with him about infant baptism, but he achieved nothing except his own disgrace and the contempt of all present. Arbeiter was taken back to prison with the threat that if he refused to submit, he would soon see what would happen. They treated the other brother in the same way.

A Jesuit priest came to him.

[1]Hans Arbeiter, formerly a member of the Swiss Brethren, had lived in the area around Worms and Bad Kreuznach. See *ME*, I, 145–146; Beck, 229–230, 268. Gross, *Golden Years*, 68–88.

This Jesuit returned to question him again about infant baptism, but Arbeiter answered in such a way that he was no more able to defend his stand than before.

1568
Jesuit came again.

He came a third time to defend infant baptism, and he lost again. Then he began asking strange things: How many evangelists were there? Did John die? and other irrelevant questions, but he did not achieve what he wanted. He told Arbeiter that since he had visited him three times and he still refused to obey, he would be drowned in the Rhine; the executioner would soon come for him. But Arbeiter was not intimidated. He was taken back to prison with the threat that if he did not recant, he would be given nothing to eat or drink and left to starve to death. Accordingly his food was reduced and he suffered great want.

Came a third time.

The Jesuit from Speyer came a fourth time to tempt Hans Arbeiter. He was as crafty as the devil himself. He left all Scripture aside and begged the brother to recant and return to the faith of his childhood. He pleaded with him to recant for the sake of Christ's sufferings. He even fell on his neck and kissed him, begging him to recant. Such a serpent of a man! But Hans Arbeiter said, "That is the kiss of Judas," and told him in no uncertain terms to leave, and he never returned. The dear brother had to go back to his prison. That shows how the devil's brood do all they can to lead a believer astray, trap him, and make his soul fall prey to the devil. That is their aim.

Came a fourth time.

Many attempts by the ungodly.

Finally the chief bailiff came twice, saying that if the brothers would promise never to enter the country again, they would be released. The brothers refused, saying they had to go wherever God sent them at any time and could not promise to stay out of any area.

The brothers should forswear reentering the country.

In the end, after twenty-nine weeks in prison, they were released without any conditions. They returned to the church, steadfast and in peace and joy, and the church rejoiced and praised God. We have their confession of faith as it was written down by Hans Arbeiter, which is an account of the questions put to them and the answers they gave.[1]

Hans Arbeiter and Heinrich Schuster released.

---

[1]Hans Arbeiter's confession of faith is in the City Archives at Brno, Codex 559, fol. 236–322, from which the following extracts are taken.

On July 18, 1568, I, Hans Arbeiter, and Heinrich Schuster were captured at Hainbach in the bishopric of Speyer. The mayor and those who had

1569

1569

4 servants of the Word chosen.

On January 9, 1569, four brothers were chosen for the service of God's Word and appointed at Klein Niemtschitz near Prahlitz: Matthias Binder or Schneider (a tailor), Ludwig Dörker or Zimmermann (a carpenter), Wendel Holba or Müller (a miller) from Slovakia, and Rupp Gellner from the Rhineland.

---

captured us started talking, some commending us, others insulting us, as Paul says. The mayor wanted us to give our word and shake hands on it or else pay for two or three rounds of drinks for those guarding us overnight in the town hall so that it would not be necessary to take us to the castle at Kirrweiler that night. We said it was against God to promise them anything and shake hands on it, for a man who pledges himself is a fool in God's eyes (Prov.17:18). Nor would we pay for their wine, not a single penny. If we were to reward those who kept us prisoners, we would be imprisoning ourselves. We also warned the mayor and the others that to treat the faithful with such wanton malice has never brought good to anybody, for it has often happened that the man who digs another's grave falls into it himself.

The constable and several others intervened on our behalf and asked the mayor to let us go, but he refused and ordered the constable repeatedly to carry out his lord's wishes and tie us up. The constable did not want to be guilty of putting the faithful in prison. He said to the mayor, "You cannot order me to chain these men, who are much more devout than I am. Had I known they were to be put in prison, I would have warned them." The mayor bound us himself and sent us to prison on Sunday night. On Monday he went to the market at Neustadt, on Tuesday he was taken ill, and on Wednesday he was buried, which made people say he had sinned against God. The constable said he would not for any amount of money be guilty of imprisoning us. We entrusted the matter to God, who knows what each man needs, and said we hoped God would hold nothing against him on our account.

When we got to Kirrweiler Castle, Heinrich was put in the common prison, and I, with many threats and insults, was shut in a dark dungeon deprived of all daylight, an experience familiar to many believers. Two weeks later the high bailiff of the bishopric came with several others and had us brought before him one at a time for interrogation, and the same later before the priest.

Then follows the interrogation, from which we quote Arbeiter's answer regarding the organization of the church in Moravia:

My lord, I take it that you do not know much about our faith, teaching, and way of life, and since you have asked me, I will gladly give an account. Please listen to what I have to say. You may not have heard much good about us, for the ungodly spread lies about God's people. I ask you, my lord, not to believe the lies. In Moravia we are subject to the local authorities and live on the land of lords who know very well what we do and who are on good terms with the emperor. The emperor himself knows we live there, as he often visits that area. If the slander about us were true, do you think they would tolerate us? And God would not protect us either. The lords are well acquainted with our way of life; they often bring other noblemen and ladies to look around our places, to visit our schools and our homes and see how and what our children eat and how they are looked after. Many are amazed at the high standard of our child care and at the good order they see everywhere. Let me add that if the authorities by the grace of God were to

That same year brother Georg Han, an old servant for temporal affairs, passed away at Pergen.

1569
Georg Han passed away.

Another servant for temporal affairs, Remigius Heugen, fell asleep in the Lord at Gross Seelowitz.

Remigius Heugen passed away.

In that year, in the time our dear brother Peter Walpot was elder and shepherd of the church, a period of great scarcity began. It became so severe that in the following year one peck of wheat cost two talers and was difficult to get even at that price. A loaf of bread cost forty-five kreuzer. Never in people's memory had there been such a famine in Moravia. Hunger and distress came upon them as a heavy punishment for their ingratitude and their sins.

Time of famine.

Conditions improved a little in 1571, and in 1572 grain was available again. Throughout this long and difficult time, God so mercifully provided for his people that on the whole no one suffered severe privation in the true sense of the word, considering the serious conditions at that time.

God provided for his people during the famine.

God provided through the diligence and foresight of the elders, servants of the Word, and servants for temporal affairs, who faithfully cared for his people. They were constantly trying to find ways to support and feed his church community, with its widows and orphans. They challenged the people to be grateful and shared out the church's resources faithfully, giving help and advice in a loving and brotherly way. And God gave us such a blessing and sufficiency that we were able

In the time of want, God blessed us so we could help others.

> allow us to live under their jurisdiction according to the teaching and order of Christ, we would render to them what God ordains and permits for the exercise of their office: We readily pay taxes and tolls on our goods and render services required of us. We wish to give everyone what we owe him before God. We help to build or improve the roads, and we will do anything that is not opposed to God and love of one's neighbor.

There followed weeks of hearings conducted by a Jesuit, who achieved nothing whatsoever, after which Arbeiter wrote:

> Then I was taken back to prison. They treated Heinrich in the same way. Twelve days later the executioner came. He had orders to beat us with rods, but since we had not been sentenced, he did not want to do it. But he did want the six gulden and would have done it, and while he haggled with the warden over the fee, some soldiers who had been encamped for a time in the bishopric tried to get into the castle. The executioner ran away, and we were left in prison for another four weeks. Then one night four men led me out through the garden behind the castle into a field. They asked me again not to return to their country—their lord had shown me mercy this time, but if I returned I would be treated differently.

Three songs by Hans Arbeiter, *LdHBr*, 652–663, describe his experience, as do the two songs by Hans Zwinger, 663–669.

1569

to help other poor people in Moravia outside our communities. But we had to live very frugally compared with those times when we were certain to have bread on the table. In these difficult years the church was almost drained of its resources, and if the shortage had lasted any longer, there would have been great distress, since there were so many of us living together. But the Lord, who knows the right time, mercifully intervened. Praise and thanks be to him for all his help.

Description of the church.

God gave his people peaceful days.

During these years God gave his people quiet times. In honor of his name we must record this in detail, for after the Lord had purified his church in various ways, allowing it to experience all kinds of tribulation and poverty for years (as can be found above in this book), God granted his people quiet times and rich blessings, as he did to the devout Job after his temptation. This he did to see how they would prove themselves in such times and to make sure that his work and plans would be publicly carried out and become known to all people far and wide. God did this and gave his people peaceful times, contrary to the intentions of the whole world, with the result that for twenty years or more there was no general persecution (as will be seen in this chronicle), except for a few incidents now and then.

Acts 4:26

However, in these times many accusations were made and decrees issued by the emperor and the king at the Imperial Diets, as well as in the Provincial Diets, which were made up of various Estates and faiths. Although they were otherwise quite disunited, in this they all agreed: that these people should be exterminated and not tolerated anywhere. But the Lord prevented this in many ways and at many times. On one occasion he gave the persecutors something else to worry about. Another time he made them lose courage to carry out their plans, for he can trim the sails according to his own wind.

Isa. 8:5–15
19:1–4

Ps. 33:10
The Lord often thwarts the counsels of the mighty.

The Lord destroyed those who sought to do evil.
Jer. 2:3–19

Many resolved not to lay their heads on a pillow until they had expelled and exterminated God's people, and they received power (but not from God) for this purpose. But the Lord destroyed them before they could begin. Many intended to inflict suffering on our people but only brought harm to themselves.

There was a great deal of discussion. One counseled that they [the believers] should all be hanged; another wanted to burn them; a third to seize their elders, thereby destroying them at the roots. A fourth wished he had the power to deal with them as he pleased and wipe them off the face of the earth. But most of these people did not live long, and the years of their lives were cut short by death. This we have experienced. We could even give names.

1569
God punished those who planned evil. He cut their lives short.

As usual, wherever possible, the tribe of priests kept stirring up the powers that be. But the Lord our God stood in the way. The Archangel Michael stood watch over his people; otherwise they would long since have been swallowed up and devoured like bread. But as a hen gathers her young under her wings, protecting them by pecking at all that want to attack her own—indeed, as an eagle hovers over its young—this and much more God did for the sake of his people. Even the unbelievers often had to acknowledge that God refused to let this people be driven away or annihilated.

Ps.124
Dan.12:1
God gathered his people like a hen her chicks.
2 Esd.1:30
Matt.23:37
Deut.32:11

They lived in the land God had provided especially for them. They were given the wings of a great eagle and flew to the place God had prepared for them, and they were sustained there as long as it pleased him. Thus they gathered in peace and unity and preached the Word of God publicly. Twice a week, sometimes more often, they held meetings in which the communal, united prayer was offered to God, asking him for all the needs of the brotherhood and giving joyful thanks for all the good things they enjoyed. Likewise, intercession was made for emperor, king, princes, and worldly authorities, that God might make them think about the office entrusted to them and conduct it properly, so as to govern peacefully and protect the faithful.

Rev.12:14
Meeting to hear the Word of God and for communal prayer.
Heb.10:23–25
1 Tim.2:1–2

Furthermore, the Christian ban was used against the wicked when they were discovered in the brotherhood. The brotherhood banned and punished, each according to his sin. When they showed true repentance, they were reaccepted into the church.

Exclusion and reacceptance.
Matt.18:15–18
1 Cor.5:9–13

In accordance with the Lord's command and the practice of the apostles, Christian baptism was given to adults who could hear the Word of God and could understand, accept, and believe it, infant baptism being the complete opposite and totally false.

Christian baptism.
Matt.28:18–20
Mark 16:15–16
Acts 2:38–41
8:12–13, 36–39
10:47–48
16:15, 30–33
19:4–5

The people met and celebrated the Lord's Supper to remember and continually refresh the holy memory of the

The Lord's Supper.

1569
Matt.26:26–29
Luke 22:14–20
Acts 2:42,46
20:7
1 Cor.10:16–21
11:23–26

suffering and death of Jesus Christ: through his death he redeemed us who were otherwise lost and brought us back, making us of one mind as members of his body. It was a celebration of thanksgiving for his love and unspeakable kindness in what he has done for our sakes; this we in turn should do for his sake in thanksgiving. Such a celebration of the Lord's Supper is the opposite of the idolatrous sacrament of the priests.

Christian community.
Matt.19:21–29
Luke 14:26–33
John 13:29
Acts 2:43–47
4:32–37; 5:1–13

They practiced Christian community of goods as Christ taught it and lived it with his disciples and as the first apostolic church practiced it. No one else dared to join them. Those who earlier had been rich or poor now shared one purse, one house, and one table—the healthy with the healthy, the sick with the sick, and the children with the children.

Sword and spear reforged.
Matt.23:8
5:9,21–26
Rom.12:14–21

Swords and spears were forged into pruning knives, scythes, and other tools. There was no musket, saber, halberd, or any other weapon of defense. Each was a brother to the other. They were a thoroughly peaceful people who never took part in any war or bloodshed by paying war taxes, much less by active participation. They did not resort to revenge—patience was their weapon in all strife.

Obedience to authorities.
Rom.13:1–7
1 Pet.2:13–17

They were subject to the authorities and obedient to them in all good works, in all things that were not against God, their faith, or their conscience. They paid their taxes, annual dues, interest, tithes, and customs, and they did their compulsory labor. They honored the governing authorities because of their divinely ordained office, which is as much needed in this wicked world as daily bread.

In conclusion, all twelve articles of the Christian apostolic faith and all things founded on Holy Scripture were confessed and observed.

Mission.
Matt.10:1–23
28:18–20
Mark 16:15
John 20:21
John 15:16

Christian mission was carried out according to the command of the Lord: "As my Father has sent me, so I send you." Also: "I have chosen and appointed you that you go out and bear fruit." Therefore each year servants of the Gospel and their assistants were sent out into the lands where there was a call. They visited those who wanted to change their lives, who sought and inquired after the truth. These they led out of their land by day and by night at their request, heedless of constable and hangman, with the result that many lost their lives for the sake of this cause. Thus they gathered God's people in a manner befitting good shepherds.

2 Cor.6:14–18

They separated themselves from the world and its evil, unjust life. They shunned especially the false prophets and false brothers.

1569
They left the world.
Rev.18:4; 1 Cor.5
2 John 7–11

The kind of cursing and profanity without which the world cannot speak was never heard among them. No oaths were sworn or promises made. There was no dancing, gambling, or carousing. They did not make fancy, slashed, fashionable, or immodest clothes; such things were done away with. They did not sing shameful, immoral songs, which the world is full of, but Christian and spiritual songs and songs of Bible stories.

Ungodly life given up.
Matt.5:33–37
James 5:12
Eph.5:1–20
Col.3:5–17

Leadership was entrusted to the elders, men who guided the people with the Word of God by reading, teaching, and exhorting them through Scripture. They practiced admonition and reconciliation, putting right any mistakes and wrong-doings.

Servants of the Word.
1 Tim.4:6–16
5:17
Titus 1:5–9

Some men were carefully chosen to take charge of the management of temporal affairs. They made and received payments, provided for food and supplies, and did the buying and selling.

Servants for temporal affairs, or stewards.
Acts 6:1–6

Others were in charge of organizing the work and sending each one to the job he knew and could do well, in the fields or wherever necessary. These were the work distributors.

Work distributors.

There were brothers charged with serving at table. The meals began with prayer and thanksgiving to God, and thanks were given at the end before returning to work. Thanksgiving and prayer were offered at bedtime and again in the morning before going to work.

Table servers.

Certain brothers were responsible for the school. Together with the sisters, they looked after the children and their needs in all areas.

Schoolmasters.

There was no usury, no buying and selling for gain. There was only honest labor to earn a living through the daily toil of those who worked as vinedressers and farmers in the vineyards, fields, and gardens. Carpenters and builders went out within Moravia and as far as Austria, Hungary, and Bohemia to build many large mills, breweries, and other buildings at fair wages for the lords, nobles, and other citizens. A brother was especially assigned for this purpose, an experienced builder who organized the carpenters, accepted work, bargained, and made agreements on behalf of the brotherhood.

Earning a living by various trades.
Eph.4:28
2 Thess.3:7–12

Many buildings constructed for the landowners.

1569
Mills were run for landowners.

Many of the brothers were millers, and there were many mills in that area whose owners asked the brothers to take them over and look after the grinding for a third or a fourth share, which was a fair deal according to current practice. So the brotherhood appointed a brother to oversee the mills. With the advice of the elders, he made all the agreements, assigned the millers, and saw to it that the mills were staffed and functioning well.

Employment on farms.

For a long time the lords and noblemen (especially those on whose land we lived) employed our people to run their farms and other work departments, some for a third share, some for wages, or whatever was acceptable to both parties. A brother was responsible for taking on such farms as the community could manage, often after repeated requests by the landlords. He made the arrangements and saw to it that enough people were available to staff them.

No one was idle.

In short, no one was idle; each did what was required and what he was able to do, whatever he had been before—rich or poor, aristocrat or commoner. Even the priests who joined the community learned to work.

Trades practiced in the community.

All sorts of honest, useful trades were represented: those of mason, scythesmith, blacksmith, coppersmith, locksmith, clockmaker, cutler, plumber, tanner, furrier, cobbler, saddler, harness maker, bag maker, wagon maker, cooper, joiner, turner, hatter, cloth maker, tailor, blanket maker, weaver, rope maker, sieve maker, glazier, potter, beer brewer, barber-surgeon, and physician. In each work department one brother was in charge of the shop, accepted orders and planned the work, then sold the products at their fair value and handed the proceeds over to the church.

Work done for the common good.

Everyone, wherever he was, worked for the common good to supply the needs of all and to give help and support wherever it was needed. It was indeed a perfect body whose living, active members served one another.

It resembled a clock.

Comparison with bees.

Think of the ingenious works of a clock, where one piece helps another to make it go, so that it serves its purpose. Or think of the bees, those useful little insects working together in their hive, some making wax, some honey, some fetching water, until their noble work of making sweet honey is done, not only for their own needs but enough to share with man. That is how it was among the brothers. So there has to be an order in all areas, for the matters of life can be properly maintained and furthered only where order reigns—even more so in the house of God, whose Master Builder and Establisher is the Lord himself. Where there is no order, there is disorder. There God does not dwell, and the house soon collapses.

1569
Good order essential to everything.

The brotherhood became widely known through those servants of the Word and other brothers imprisoned in different places for the sake of their witness to Jesus Christ and his truth. In many different ways, they were closely questioned about the basis of their faith. This happened all over the German-speaking lands, wherever brothers were imprisoned, some for long periods of time. In word and deed, by their life and their death, they testified that their faith was the truth.

Brotherhood became known through those in prison.

Moreover, emperors, kings, princes, lords, and those at their courts, especially in the German-speaking lands, became acquainted with the brotherhood's religion, teaching, faith, and life. They often came to see for themselves, and commoners came too, and learned that the communities were harmless and that the evil reports about the brothers were untrue. Many were convinced and praised them as a devout people that must have been established by God, otherwise it would have been impossible for so many to live together in unity, whereas among them, when only two, three, or four live together in one house, they are constantly in each others' hair and quarrel until they have to part company.

Nobles and commoners came to see for themselves.

Some preferred to have brothers rather than anyone else working for them and serving them, so there were not enough brothers in the land, since—because of their reliability—everyone wanted them for his own benefit. But because of their religion they were always thought to be too many.

For work's sake never enough brothers; for faith's sake too many.

It was a remarkable situation: Some lords were angry and ill-disposed toward the brothers because of their faith, and they did not want them to be tolerated in the land. Others were angry that not more brothers were assigned to work for them, although they had kept asking for many years. In short, some wanted to have them accepted, others wanted to have them expelled. Some said the best about them, others the worst.

The world did not want to tolerate them but had to. God divided the sea—the raging nations of this world—so that people could be gathered from all lands and dwell together in great numbers, fearlessly doing the work of the Lord against

The world would not tolerate them but had to.
Isa.11:10–16
49:8–13

1569

the devil and the world. Indeed, it is a wonderful handiwork of God, when you think about it. Some people thought it was right for those who had the strength. Others wished they, too, could live like that. Still others, the majority, in their blindness saw it as error and seduction or as a human undertaking.

All the world hated and reviled us.

Yet all the world so hated and envied them that they might have said with David, "We have more enemies than hairs on our head." As soon as they stepped outside the door, they were abused and called Anabaptists, re-baptizers, new baptizers, schismatics, agitators, and all kinds of insulting names. People everywhere disparaged them and taunted them with gruesome lies, accusing them of eating children and other horrible things that would have shocked us deeply had we even dreamed of them, much less done them. Many slanderous accusations of things that are not human, let alone Christian, were brought against the brotherhood to lay it open to suspicion and hatred.

Ps.69:4

Matt.5:11–12
Luke 6:22–23

2 Cor.6:4–10
1 Pet.4:12–19

The world hated us solely because we reject its ways.

The world hated and persecuted us solely for the sake of Christ's name and his truth, because we followed him, and for no other reason. And this was a sure sign: If someone traveled with only a staff in his hand to show that he did not mean to harm anyone, or if he prayed before eating, he was called an Anabaptist, a heretic. Such is the stupidity of the devil. But if someone became unfaithful and walked according to the ways of the heathen, a sword at his side and a musket at his shoulder, from that moment on he was welcome to the world and "a good Christian" in their eyes.

Outward signs by which the world recognized believers.

A man who wore no ruff round his neck or other signs of vanity in his attire, who declared that gambling, haughtiness, gluttony, drunkenness, and carousing are evil and against God, and conducted himself in a quiet way with patience and other qualities befitting a disciple of Christ—such a person was reckoned by the world to be a heretic, a sectarian, a deceiver, or a fool. He was hated and despised by people who had never seen him before and could accuse him of no wrongdoing, since he had harmed no one and had no wish to do so. This just shows what the world has come to.

What makes for popularity in the world.

But as soon as someone was unfaithful, returned to the world, and stepped into the inn saying, "Boys, let me treat you to a drink," singing immoral songs, drinking wildly with others, and sticking a plume in his hat like a fool; as soon as he indulged in gambling and dancing, wearing a huge ruff round his neck, baggy breeches, and clothes with ornamental slits, making a show of their thousand and one much-honored sacraments, spreading syphilis and other dreadful diseases, and swearing and blaspheming God—from that moment on such a person was befriended by the world and acknowledged again as one of them. They approved of him and said, "Well done! You were right to leave the brothers and be converted and become a good Christian. Now that you have the true faith never let yourself be led astray from our church again. You did well to leave the brothers and separate yourself from their sect"—as they call us. Wherever he went, he found good friends. People liked him and accepted him, even if they had never seen him before. They could see all his wicked deeds and vices, and still he was liked by the world because he had forsaken the truth of God. From all this it is clear that they hate and persecute us simply because we are zealous for God. Envy, stemming from the old serpent, is behind their hatred of God's truth. No one wants to admit it, but there is no denying it.

1569

Friendship with the world is enmity with God.

Eventually even the people living in our area began to hate and envy us, as Esau envied Jacob, on account of the blessings God poured out on us over and above what we earned with the toil of our hands. We had what we needed in house and home and—thank God—food, while they for the most part had to make do with very little because they spent it all on drink. They wasted their time and often squandered their money on drinks before they had even earned it. They loved to be idle and lazy.

Neighbors' hatred because of God's blessing on us.

What shall we say, then, about the false brothers and communities who complained about God's brotherhood more than about anyone else? They found fault with the brotherhood on every point. They hated us and resented it when we admonished them about their deviations. That verse in the Gospel is indeed true where Christ says about his own, "You will be hated by everyone for my name's sake." Because the Lord's Word truly applies to us, all this simply reassures and strengthens us all the more.

False brothers' hatred against the church.

Matt. 10:22
24:9

The Lord also strengthens us, his church, through those who forsake the truth and return to the world. Many of them—however long they live outside—have no peace in their hearts

Unpeace of unfaithful members is a proof.

1569

day in, day out, waking or sleeping. No matter what they set themselves to do, their consciences smite them constantly and their hearts pound with fear because of their unfaithfulness. They return deeply convicted, and in tears they repent and confess their sins, seeking peace with God and his church, ready to die rather than forsake the truth again.

Further proof seen in their belated remorse when dying.

Indeed, the number of such experiences gives us a deep certainty. It caused us great pain and shock to see for ourselves the despair of those backsliders who had once confessed and accepted God's truth but then deviated from it. Then God struck them down with sickness, and death hovered over them (a time when all things are revealed to a man). But too late and in vain they were overcome with remorse because they had turned away from the truth and had to die in their apostasy.

Some saw their punishment before their very eyes and carried on frightfully, crying out, "Woe is me!" and seeing themselves as beyond help. Others said that with their own feet they had kicked the door of heaven shut in front of them. Still others admitted that if only they had remained brothers and had repented, they would gladly die and part from this life. Many prayed in fear and trembling and pleaded with God to restore their health just once more. Then they would repent and return to what they had forsaken. Those who recovered did just that without a moment's hesitation. Many, however, were never able to experience such a reconciliation but, as already stated, died with a burdened conscience and in deep dread because they had mocked God too many times. When God had called them, they did not want to listen. Now, when they pleaded, the Lord turned a deaf ear.

Ps.81:8–13
Jer.7:13–15
24–29
Prov.2:22

Here we will end this part of the account and return again to the description of other matters.

Fruitless zeal in Poland.

A fervent seeking for truth arose in Poland in 1569, but with such lack of understanding as to be fruitless. People were given a light in their lamps, but not the oil the Lord speaks of in the Gospels, so it could not burn properly and was bound to go out. They gave up the unscriptural, ungodly baptism of infants. They rejected it as the antichristian teaching it is and wrote against it in no uncertain terms, teaching that baptism was for those who believed the Word of God.

In their writings they vehemently opposed the doctrine of

the Trinity as held by the pope and made a distinction between the rich Christ and the poor Christ.[1] When they asked for a visit, the church found their request reasonable and sent Ludwig Dörker, an appointed servant of the Gospel, to travel with three brothers to Poland. They were warmly welcomed, and as a result of their visit, four young men were sent to get to know the church community. They stayed through the winter. But in their worldly wisdom they looked down on God's work as too simple and would not submit to serving the poor and crucified Christ.

1569
Ludwig Dörker sent to Poland.

1570

On January 25, 1570, others from Lithuania and Poland arrived at Neumühl, where the elders were meeting: a Polish lord named Janckowsky, three preachers, and an apothecary from Kraków named Simon Ronemberg.[2] They came to learn about our church and faith. They brought a letter from their church, highly praising our church discipline and order and asking to unite with us. They admitted that the discussions among themselves had led to little improvement. They regretted having baptized people too hastily, and because shameful things were happening among them, they wanted to discontinue baptizing for the time being.

Polish lord came from Lithuania with 3 preachers.

They believed in baptism by immersion and considered baptism by pouring on of water as insufficient.

Tenets of the Polish Brethren.

They rejected the belief that the Son of God was with the Father from the beginning of the world as creative power.

They did not believe that the Word became flesh, but that the Son's beginning was when he entered the flesh at birth. Although he had long been promised by God, he had not been at work earlier in the creation.

---

[1]See Williams, *Radical Reformation*, 716, where George Blandrata, a leader of anti-Trinitarianism and physician at the Polish court (1563) is mentioned as making the distinction between "the *Christus dives* of orthodoxy" and "the *Christus pauper*, whom the pious poor, despised by the world, follow."

[2]About the Anabaptist community at Raków, Poland (established 1569), and their relationship with the Hutterian Brethren in Moravia, see Williams, *Radical Reformation*, 698–703. See also Leonard Gross, "The Hutterian Brethren and the Polish Brethren: Rapprochement and Estrangement," *The Proceedings of the Unitarian Universalist Historical Society*, Vol. XX, Part II (1986), 46–53; Gross, *Golden Years*, 150–163.

1570

They did not accept the Father, Son, and Holy Spirit as one united God.

They ridiculed the belief that the Word was made man and became flesh in Mary. They said that since God himself is the Word, it cannot be true to say that he became a man, or that he clothed himself in flesh, or that he became a child who cried and needed human help.

The Polish Brethren talked with us.

Ezek.43:10–11

We had a friendly discussion, from which we could see that their purpose in coming was not to learn about the true structure of the house of God but to impart their wisdom to us (which we could not regard as wisdom). They criticized various points without valid reason, yet at the same time they acknowledged us as God's people and the closest to the apostolic church.

When we came to the article in which we confess to God the Father, the Son, and the Holy Spirit, they rejected our printed confession of faith because they were unable to grasp parts of it. A few of them wanted these passages revised, which we refused to do. We certainly would not abandon our confession of faith for the sake of worldly people who are still unredeemed.

At this point God stopped us. He made us change our direction and put an end to further talks for the time being. So we told them that we had no leading from God to continue talking with them about a true uniting, unless God gave them a change of heart. Nonetheless, we urged them to visit some of our communities at our expense, to see what God had done, and to consider it carefully. Maybe that would convince them more than our talking. But they decided to return home, admitting that they could see that God was not bringing about a union through them at this point and perhaps their sins against God made them unworthy for the fulfillment of such a task. We left it at that and parted as friends, trusting that God would show us the right time if it was his will. The four young men who had come earlier went home with them.

Soon after, the little Polish flock sent three other men to get to know our community. They brought the following letter to our church:

A short letter from the Polish Brethren to our church.

Grace and peace from God the Father and from the Lord Jesus Christ, the Crucified.

Divinely blessed men, we thank God that he has

1570
A short letter from the Polish Brethren to our church.

awakened our hearts by your letter, in which you challenged us in a Christian way. We are sending two men from Raków, John Baptista [Święcicki, from Lithuania] and John the Italian, to visit you in Moravia. After considering the matter, we prayed that God might prompt someone in our little group to accompany them and return to us with strength and comfort (may God grant it). God prompted our fellow believer Järish Müller to offer, and we humbly prayed for God's blessing on their journey. We have the earnest request that you let them share in the gifts God has given you through the holy discipline you maintain, and we have no doubt you will do so, for we know you are a people of God, gracious and God-fearing. Out of your love to the believers you will joyfully do all that belongs to God's praise. We commend you to God the Lord.

Dated: Olkusz, May 25, 1570[1]

These men traveled around for a time with cold hearts, had soon seen enough, and returned to Poland. They were not in earnest, so their visit bore little fruit.

After this visit, in which they did not find unity with the church, brother Peter Walpot sent the following letter to some of the Polish Brethren who had shown good will:

A letter from Peter Walpot to some people in Poland.

I wish you grace and mercy from God the Almighty for a renewed Christian life, for a genuine love which surpasses all understanding, and for all that may serve your salvation in Jesus Christ our Savior. Amen.

Beloved ones who are zealous for the truth, Bartholomew, John the Italian, Lukas Delphinus, Adam Mendicus, Simon Ciechanowski (Tschechonofius), and Jacob Livius, and all who long for divine righteousness and seek to save themselves from the coming wrath of God in heaven: I have to write to you, as it is my longing and prayer that you may find peace of heart, and I am eager before God

[1]The writer of this letter was Daniel Bielinsky. See George H. Williams et al., *Stanislas Lubieniecki, the History of the Polish Reformation (Amsterdam, 1685) and Related Documents, Harvard Theological Studies*, XXXIV (1987), plate 30, commentary.

Olkusz: town northwest of Kraków, Poland.

1570
A letter from Peter Walpot to some people in Poland.

to accomplish as much as I can for your sakes. First of all, I must tell you that the joy we had hoped for in meeting the people you sent to talk with us was turned into sadness. We thought they wanted to learn about and accept the life and discipline of the Lord's church, but this did not really seem to be their purpose. They seemed rather to want to teach the church and have us pattern ourselves after them, which we, who are not built on sand, could never do. We will not adjust to those who have never completely rejected the worldly life, who have no baptism, no true submission to God, no Christian discipline, and lack what belongs to a people of God. Knowledge alone is not enough. You can find plenty of people who are not lacking in knowledge.

They accused us of being afraid of losing our authority (which is not so) if we gave in to them. Perhaps they think they are cleverer than we are and consider us inferior because we do not know Latin or other languages (though this would not disturb us). Be that as it may, we receive proof and confirmation from God for our cause. Even if we should relinquish our authority, they should not think the church would accept or even prefer them for their many languages or so-called wisdom, which they may suppose gives them an advantage over us. They must first be tested and proved by troubles, imprisonment, and hard work, as we have been.

We say farewell to the four men, leaving everything in God's hands. To you, however, who perhaps are more sincere about your salvation, I make an earnest appeal. If any one of you longs to live in such a way that his soul may be saved and he can stand before God's approaching judgment, he should come in a different spirit and prove it in his work and life, not contenting himself with mere knowledge, for that will only bring a heavier judgment.

I say this to you as a word from the Lord, because you know well that the life you and the world live deserves damnation. You also know a good deal about the way to salvation but do not live according to it, nor do you try to fulfill the whole of Christian righteousness, as Christ says to John concerning baptism. If you continue like

Matt.3:15

that, you will find it terrifying when you have to answer for yourselves on the day of judgment, and you will not be able to plead ignorance.

1570
A letter from Peter Walpot to some people in Poland.

So, you beloved men, and all you others who are so zealous, you know that human life is as transient as the passing night, but since God has given you time, turn around. Do not delay! Do not miss your chance like the five foolish virgins, who arrived with empty lamps and were rejected and shut out by the Bridegroom. Let this be a warning to each one who is concerned about God and his truth. I admonish you solely for the sake of your blessedness. If you listen, all will go well. But unless you are more serious than your messengers were about seeking a better foundation, you will find out that God does not uphold you. You will collapse, and your last state will be worse than your first. As you are now, you cannot expect to remain steadfast in tribulation and suffering. You will go to ruin and be the laughing-stock of your enemies. For each of you who longs for it, I wish a better way, that is, a greater earnestness to seek and find God's kingdom and his righteousness first of all, through Jesus Christ, our Lord and Savior. Amen.

Matt.25:1–13

This prophecy was fulfilled.

Peter Walpot
a servant of God and his church

Later [in 1571], Peter Walpot wrote in reply to Simon [Ronemberg], an apothecary in Kraków, one of the Polish believers. The contents of Simon's letter can be gathered from Peter Walpot's answer, which is included here.[1]

God, the eternal, great, powerful, and awe-inspiring God, mighty in counsel, infinite in thought, whose eyes behold all the ways of men, rewarding each one according to his ways and the fruit of his works: May he grant you and all who seek it the grace to deny your self-will, your flesh, and your life and bring your reason captive into the obedience of Christ. Then you will not run in uncertainty or fight as one who merely thrashes in the air. You will discipline your body, bringing it into true

Jer.32:18–19

Peter Walpot's letter to Simon the apothecary and his fellow believers in Kraków (Poland).

2Cor.10:5

[1]See also Robert Friedmann, "Reason and Obedience: An Old Anabaptist Letter of Peter Walpot (1571) and Its Meaning," *MQR*, Jan. 1945, 27–40.

1570 (1571)

Matt.7:13–14
Luke 13:24

Ecclus.2:5
1 Cor.3:13

submission, and, through self-restraint, enter in at the narrow gate and walk the narrow path leading to life. Few find it. Many strive for it in vain. But men are tested in the furnace of Gelassenheit as gold is tested by fire, which in due time will test and purify everything. Through Christ our Lord and Savior, his dearly beloved Son, may the merciful God grant you a heart and spirit to seek his truth and honor alone, for the salvation of your souls. May you be his true disciples and followers without shrinking back from the cross. This is my heartfelt wish for you.

My dear Simon, I have received your letter of November 1, 1570, and have read it carefully. I have understood that you wish me to think of you and of your situation and point of view and that of your fellow believers, but I was not sure what to make of your letter. On the one hand you praise us and wish to learn from us, asking for admonition and expressing your willingness to give up anything that might stand in the way of your salvation. On the other hand you speak highly of yourselves as God's children, whom God has also taught and whom he leads, who possess God's Spirit, and so on. Last, there is a strange tone to your letter that puzzles me and makes me say that your words sound hollow and empty, like tinkling cymbals.

Nor does it please me that you praise me so highly in your letter. I am no more impressed than Christ was by the Pharisees when they called him "Master" and said,

Matt.22:16

"We know that you are an honest man and teach the way of God truthfully, not caring what others think or seeking men's approval." But the question is whether they had

Matt.19:16–22
Luke 18:18–23

honest hearts and were eager to obey his teaching. In the same way, the young man familiar with the Scriptures approached the Lord saying, "Good Master, what must I do to have eternal life?" and declared that he had kept all God's commandments from his youth up. The Lord told him that to be perfect he must go, sell all he had, and give to the poor, and he would have treasure in heaven. He should come, take up his cross, and follow him. But the young man went away sorrowful and discouraged.

If, therefore, in the name of Christ I should tell you the truth you need to hear (and you call me a noble instrument of the living God), I would have this to say: If you desire to be saved and declare that you, too, fear God, know him, love him, and want to serve and please him alone; likewise, if you say you do not have the greedy and money-seeking heart you are reputed to have; if therefore you strive for perfection and want to gain treasure in heaven, then sell everything and free your heart of earthly riches and have done with them. You cannot seek both at once; one stifles the other. I am afraid you will soon tire of my telling you all this, but that would be a test of your sincerity as disciples of Christ, if you do indeed make room for the Spirit of Christ within you and let him rule over you, as you apparently think you do. I urge you to be diligent in fervent prayer (which, as you write, should be your true weapon and victory) to conquer your flesh and set your spurs into it.

1570 (1571) Peter Walpot's letter to Simon the apothecary and his fellow believers in Kraków (Poland).

Matt. 13:44–46
Luke 14:33

If you acknowledge me as the ark-builder Noah[1] and if you are not hypocrites, tempters, or stubborn rebels against the truth (it must be one of these), why do you not let yourselves be gathered in this ark, outside of which there will be no salvation? God has indeed invited you often enough, and as you say yourselves, the door is still open. But believe me, it may be shut and barred against you in one moment of great terror.

Think about it: are you not like Lot's sons-in-law, whom he asked to flee with him from Sodom? But they did not believe punishment would fall on them and scorned it. As it was in the time of Noah and Lot, so it will be in the days of the Son of man. Alas for those with child and for those with babies at the breast in those days! With whom shall I compare this generation? It is like children who sit in the marketplace and shout at their companions, "We have piped for you, but you would not dance; we wept and wailed, but you would not weep."

Gen. 19:14

Matt. 24:19, 37–39

Matt. 11:16–17

[1]With these words Peter Walpot is simply referring to the fact that earlier Simon Ronemberg had likened the Hutterian Church to the ark and Walpot to the ark builder; see George H. Williams, "Anabaptism and Spiritualism in the Kingdom of Poland and the Grand Duchy of Lithuania: An Obscure Phase of the Pre-History of Socinianism," Ludwika Chmaja, ed., *Studia Nad Arianizmen* (Warsaw, 1959), 250; Williams, *Radical Reformation*, 702.

1570 (1571)
Peter Walpot's letter to Simon the apothecary and his fellow believers in Kraków (Poland).

My dear Simon, examine yourselves and learn to know yourselves better. You admit that you have neglected the most important thing on earth, and therefore you have never taken the first step toward doing God's will, namely, surrendering to him and being united with his people. How do you want to carry it out? You must start out differently, following the footsteps of Christ on his narrow way. For if the first portion of dough is not holy, how can the whole lump be holy? But if the root is holy, so are the branches.

Rom. 11:16

Surely, if God's Holy Spirit had been poured out in your hearts and dwelt in you, he would not leave you to choose your own ways outside his gathered church but would lead you to the church in Christ's truth and unity. God's Spirit and the mind of Christ do not tolerate division. Therefore it is clear that you do not partake of God's Spirit. You lack it.

John 16:7–14

From the beginning, the multitude of believers was of one heart and one soul; they were united. Though they could not all gather in one place, they were ruled by one Spirit, one mind, and one faith. They wanted to hold steadfast to their Christian calling and be blameless in the eyes of God and his apostles, teaching these truths: one baptism, one Spirit, one Lord, one God and Father of us all, one mediator between God and man; also one community of saints, and one door into the sheepfold, of which Christ says, "Whoever climbs in some other way (not through me, not through my body, my church, to which I have entrusted my powerful Word and the authority to bind and to loose), he is a thief and a murderer." Whoever wants peace and unity with God and forgiveness of his sins must be freed through the intercession of the one church gathered and established by God and through the church's true servant. Otherwise his sins will be held against him like sealed packages. Indeed, a man can never forgive his own sin or set himself upright before the Lord.

Acts 2:42–44
4:32
5:12
Phil. 3:15–16
Eph. 4:4–6
Rom. 12:5
1 Cor. 12:12
John 10:1–8
Matt. 16:19
18:18
John 20:23

The example of Saul, later called Paul, shows that this is the true meaning of Christ's words when, after his resurrection, he delegated authority to his church and thereafter did not hinder it: When the Lord had struck

Acts 9:3–6

him down on the road, Paul asked what he should do, and he was told to go into the city to Ananias, who was to lay his hands on him and baptize him. And even though he had been set apart before his birth and chosen by God to spread the Gospel and establish obedience of faith among the Gentiles, he went up to Jerusalem to meet with the elders of the church, Peter, James, and John. When they saw the gift entrusted to him by the Lord, they all agreed to give him and Barnabas the hand of fellowship so that—since Paul was called by God and established in the faith through Ananias and incorporated into the body of Christ—his service for the Gospel might not remain outside the order of the church and its apostles, and his race might not be run in vain. It was similar with Cornelius, the God-fearing centurion: Though an angel came to him, saying, "Your prayer is heard by God," yet he was told he must send to Joppa for the apostle Peter, hear from him the words of salvation, and consent to be baptized by him in obedience to the truth. We learn the same from the apostle Philip's meeting with the eunuch who was a high official under the Ethiopian Queen Candace: after the resurrection, the Lord directed those foreordained and called to a life of faith to go to the church he had founded and to its messengers. That happened each time.

1570 (1571)

Gal.1:15–16

Gal.2:1–10

Rom.1:1–6

Acts 10

Acts 8:26–38

What Christ said to his apostles is still valid today: "Whoever listens to you listens to me, and whoever despises you despises me. If anyone will not listen to what you say, then leave that place. I tell you in truth, it will be easier for Sodom and Gomorrah than for such people on the last day." If anyone wants a different way, then I say that he is not upright but is one of the thieves and murderers who climb in at the wrong place.

Luke 10:16
1 Thess.4:8

Matt.10:14–15,40
Mark 6:11

Dear Simon, I am not writing this so that you or any one of your people should look to me or to us in a human way. On no account! If you do not acknowledge the truth and the apostolic foundation on which we must build and if you cannot accept our word as God's Word (which it truly is), then leave it alone and stay where you are.

I am writing to you at your request and for the sake of my conscience and God's honor, to exhort and warn you.

1570 (1571)
Peter Walpot's letter to Simon the apothecary and his fellow believers in Kraków (Poland).

It is not my intention to persuade you to pledge yourselves to the Lord as members of our church on the strength of my words (although they are not my own). That is each person's decision. If the Word of God and the testimony of a man's conscience do not compel him, nothing will help.

We force no one, though you might think so. And if we knew of anyone in our midst who only pretended to give of himself freely but in his heart felt differently, he could not last among us. Even if he concealed it from us, God would find him out and blot him out of the register of his people, the members of his household, and the Book of Life. The Lord desires a new heart and a voluntary church, which of its own free will separates itself from all evil and all taint of sin both within and without. And not only that—every faithful, zealous believer and friend of God is responsible in the love of God to testify against all evil and unrighteousness, against all works of darkness, and against the ungodly life of the world. He must witness against the unbelievers, reprove them, point out their transgressions to them, and use the sword of the Spirit, lest he be a hypocrite in the eyes of God and man.

Eph.5:3–14

John 7
16:8–11

I readily believe that you do not want to damn anyone because, as you say, no one can save a man but God alone. And even people who are foolish and ignorant before God know that the power of damnation is given to Christ. It is common knowledge that no man can damn another. But all traitors, false believers—in short, hypocrites—sit under this umbrella to shade them from the heat of the fiery test in store for them. That is why they have to use it as a protection for themselves.

1 Pet.4:12

Nor do we damn anyone. No man can do this (we would rather save a man if we could), but each man's own evil works condemn him. It is as the apostle Paul says: When Noah built the ark to save his household, he condemned the world through the ark. Even today, all those who follow Christ and the church of believers (which bears the likeness of the ark) condemn this world by separating from it, giving testimony that its works are evil and that if men do not repent, they will not become

John 7:7

heirs of salvation. Let yourselves be weighed in the balance and see whether you are not found wanting. Undoubtedly it is highly convenient for the comfort of your flesh that you do not clearly point out to the ungodly, the sinners, and the world (who have you right in their midst) their evil and condemnation; if you did, it might lead someone to amend his life. Indeed, your little spark of light looks like a burnt-out cinder. Is that what you call being ready to challenge, discipline, and improve yourselves and others? Oh, you will have no need to worry about being driven out. You have every hope for a permanent place in the world where you can live among your own possessions. But Christ tells us something different about his followers, namely, "You are the salt of the earth and will be my witnesses in Jerusalem, in Judea, and Samaria, and to the ends of the earth." If you were to practice this, instead of speaking or keeping silence to please men while harming God's truth, you would soon learn otherwise.

1570 (1571)
Dan.5:27

Peter Walpot's letter to Simon the apothecary and his fellow believers in Kraków (Poland).

Matt.5:13
Acts 1:8

Only a man with the discernment born of faith and a good conscience knows how long he can continue to associate with the world without hypocrisy and sin damaging his conscience (especially in the practices customary among you and your companions). But it seems to me that you can swallow and digest all kinds of bread. I am writing you this as a warning in the fear of God and in accordance with the truth and not, as you may think, out of ill-will or arrogance. May the Lord be our witness, for I know myself free from what you so lightly accuse me of. I hope, and God be my witness, that my brothers and I strive to work out our salvation in fear and trembling and that everything else is banished from our hearts.

1 Tim.3:9
James 1:5–8

Phil.2:12

We must say with Paul that our knowledge and prophecy are patchwork and that we have not reached perfection but press on, hoping to take hold of that for which God and Christ Jesus once took hold of us. Yet we have no doubt whatsoever about the foundation we stand on and the grace and truth we live by. With complete certainty we know that this is the perfect foundation of the apostles and prophets and that Jesus Christ is the cornerstone on which we build and are built. Of this we

1 Cor.13:9
Phil.3:12

Eph.2:19–21

1570 (1571)

2 Thess. 2:15

Peter Walpot's letter to Simon the apothecary and his fellow believers in Kraków (Poland).

have assurance and certainty from the Holy Scriptures, the prophecies, and the cloud of witnesses around us. We simply hold fast to this until death takes us. But the Lord knows our hearts, and if through God's Word we are shown failings and mistakes, we would not think of stubbornly continuing in our error against him. Rather (as we beseech God in all our meetings), we turn from them and change. Whether one person or several are involved, we punish the evil and put it out of our midst according to the Lord's Word. But you hypocrites dare to interpret even the appearance of the sky. Why do you not judge for yourselves what is right?

1 Cor. 5

Matt. 16:2–3

Luke 12:56–57

You seem to believe that we think too highly of ourselves, as if no one were good enough for us. You say (and obviously you are not worried about yourselves) that it is your own affair how you stand before God. But if we should bring your self-esteem (the like of which we do not have so far ourselves) into the light and examine it, I fear it would be much too great and would even surpass our own.

Frankly, if we are to tell the truth before God, we cannot believe that you truly are what you claim to be. What is more, we cannot acknowledge you as a people of God or as brothers, let alone our brothers, for you lack the fruits of righteousness that mark a genuine Christian. Where is your true surrender to God in baptism, your new birth? Where is your renunciation of the world, of sin and the devil, of your own flesh and self-will? Indeed, you lack what is most essential, which shows that your boasting that God is at work among you is not in good taste.

1 Cor. 5:6

Just ask yourselves: Are you not rather like one of the day laborers who stand idle in the marketplace? Ask your own heart why you are not already in the vineyard and employed by the householder. You have never made a decisive cut with the world, with the unbelievers and their futile works of darkness. What has become of your community, which no one should leave, as some have done? It is in disorder, and nothing is built up, while you sit in your well-built houses looking after your own interests, not those of your neighbors and brothers. The

Matt. 20:1–16

Eph. 5:3–14

Heb. 10:25

prophet's words may well be applied to you: "Is it a time for you to live in your paneled houses while the Lord's house lies in ruins?" The Lord does not draw near to such people, nor does he love them as his own children, as you suppose. Consider in your hearts the way you are going!

1570 (1571)
Hag. 1:4

Peter Walpot's letter to Simon the apothecary and his fellow believers in Kraków (Poland).

Where among you is the love to your neighbor as to yourselves, even though you say that what you own is for your neighbor's use and benefit? I would have to inquire from your servants, neighbors, or brothers how far your possessions are available to them. I would like to see proof that your righteousness in this respect exceeds that of the unbelievers and the rich (who also put large sums into the collection plate); that out of your faith grows the love that does not seek its own good but that of its neighbor, as you claim.

Mark 12:41–44
Luke 21:1–4

1 Cor. 13:4–7

How do you practice proper Christian discipline and exclusion among yourselves—putting out evil and the sinner from among you—to say nothing of godly and brotherly admonition for lesser offenses between brothers and sisters? This befits a people of God. Where it is lacking, we live as in a tumbledown house with no one repairing it. Unless the Lord builds the house, everything is in vain. To be sure, if I am to go on holding the mirror before your eyes, I will have to sharpen quite a few more quill pens.

Matt. 5:29–30
18:8–9
15–17
1 Cor. 5

Ps. 127:1

You still do not see yourselves as you are. You are quite pleased with yourselves. If you were not so stuck up, you would be able to see yourselves. You should worry about yourselves and not just about others! Pray for God's compassion, and ask him to lift up your hearts in his grace. Then you may rightly be concerned about other blind, foolish people in the world and ask God to have mercy on them.

You keep writing we should pray to God on your behalf that our hearts may be united in the Lord. That is our hearts' longing. We are continually praying for you and for all the zealous who hunger and thirst after righteousness. But what good will that do you unless you yourselves seek the prayer and intercession of God's church, which is our only source of help? You are not eager to seek the

1570 (1571)
Peter Walpot's letter to Simon the apothecary and his fellow believers in Kraków (Poland).

Job 13:5
Prov. 17:27–28

Luke 18:9–14

Lord with your whole hearts, but without this you will never find the true help. What am I to say? You imagine that God has filled you with such a marvelous fire that you wonder how he wants to use you. (If only you would be silent, you might perhaps be accounted wise.) What is still worse, you imagine that you need no longer fear God's countenance, but you dare to step into his presence lightly. You are just like the Pharisee who stood so boldly before God, saying, "I thank you, O God, that I am not like other men, thieves, evildoers, adulterers, or like this tax-gatherer. I fast twice a week; I give tithes of all I have." There is much still lacking in you. First you have to stand at the door with the acknowledged sinner in the temple of the Lord's church, truly beating your breast and not daring to raise your eyes to heaven, let alone to the countenance of God. Then you may be vindicated and God may be merciful to you.

1 Cor. 6:19–20
7:23

Rom. 1:11–17
16:17–20

You certainly write as if you had already yielded yourselves to God, taking your thoughts captive in obedience to him. To this I say, it is all very well to be obedient when you are lords, rulers, and stewards over your own possessions, acting according to your own will and wishes. This is not being one whom Christ has bought with a price. This is not rebirth. It is being devoted to oneself rather than to God. This is not the obedience Paul and the apostles strove to establish among the Gentiles.

It was Lord Johann von Zerotin at Lundenburg.

You may be able to reconcile this with holding forth about obedience and the poor Christ, dear Simon. What you write is true: so far life has been good to you. But I will tell you a different story, a sad one; I cannot hide it from you. A powerful lord over here has just ordered us to leave his lands. There were more brothers and sisters living there than on any other estate: about a thousand adults and three or four hundred children. The parents of some of these children had passed away while in the church community. Other parents had been imprisoned and tortured to death by persecutors outside Moravia because they stood for the truth. Still others were in the power of the same enemies of truth and were kept in chains for the sake of the Gospel. Unless God intervenes, we may be forced to move out to the fields and woods

1570 (1571)
Peter Walpot's letter to Simon the apothecary and his fellow believers in Kraków (Poland).

under the open sky and suffer privation—it certainly would not be the first time. If you should happen to be with us at such a time with one or two children, hardly able once in three days to provide the bread you need, that would be a different story. That would call for greater fortitude. Then you would be pushed into the furnace, and your hearts would be revealed. This is what you have to be ready for if you want to be a true disciple of Christ and a member of his church. But then you would have to put aside some of your learned disputations and look to God alone, leading a watchful life and holding fast to him with a humble and resolute heart.

Further, you should know that it was not your wolf's pelts (as you seem to think) that made us give up hope of your becoming members of Christ when you were here. You could have become sheep despite your outward appearance; that would not have hindered you. Nor were we offended by your eating and drinking; we did not begrudge you anything. If you had been immoderate and taken more than necessary, we would not have offered it to you. But what did disturb us is that you resisted the church and held on to your own opinions. You continued in your own ways with no good fruit or change for the better to this day, as though you expected the brotherhood to model itself after you and learn from you. But you yourselves are not yet founded in God and need to be taught the most elementary lessons in the Word of God (Heb.5:12—6:3) so as to lay the foundation of repentance from all dead works: faith in God, baptism, teaching, the laying on of hands, the resurrection of the dead, and eternal judgment.

Therefore, if we find that you profess to be brothers when in truth you are not, we have reason, and divine reason at that, to separate ourselves from you and to shun you. Paul commands: If anyone professes to be a brother (1 Cor.5:11) but is avaricious or represents a different teaching that (1 Tim.6:3–5) does not conform to the healing words of our Lord Jesus Christ and his message of salvation, and if he is admonished once and a second time, we should have (Titus 3:9–11) nothing to do with him. We should not even eat with him or greet him but avoid him. From such a person we do (2 John 10–11) not accept any greeting until we can see a real repentance and understanding of the truth.

1570 (1571)
Peter Walpot's letter to Simon the apothecary and his fellow believers in Kraków (Poland).

All this I am writing in answer to your letter, dear Simon, without holding anything back. I thought you should know everything I have on my heart, without prejudice for or against anyone. Please accept it with an open heart. Supposing your words were true, anyone who showed me what I was really like when I was blind to it would be my dearest friend. If you could understand this, I would rejoice with you as much for your eternal salvation as for my own. But you would have to turn around and change your direction just as if you had been born anew. And since no man knows when the Lord of the house is coming—at evening, at midnight, or at cockcrow—make sure that you are prepared, lest the hour find you asleep, catching you like a bird in a snare.

John 3:3
Mark 13:35–37
Luke 21:34–36

It is not enough to say, "I do not want my own way. May the Lord do with me as he pleases. Here I am; use me according to your divine will." When a servant knows his master's will, he should go and do it and not stand around, lest he get a beating. What a man's heart tells him should not be questioned and examined from all sides. Hear the words of Elijah, a man of God: "How long will you waver between two opinions? If the Lord is God, follow him; but if Baal, then follow him." I tell you—God is my witness—if the Lord comes and finds you no better prepared than this, you will not be able to hide among the seven thousand who were spared in Elijah's time because they had never bowed to Baal.

Luke 12:41–48
1 Kings 18:21
1 Kings 19:18
Rom. 11:4

Therefore, bear the fruits of repentance for all your wrongdoings and unredeemed life so that you may be preserved and may receive grace in your hour of need.

Luke 3:8

This is an invitation: I invite you to the wedding feast and great supper that the King of heaven is preparing for his Son. If you remain outside, the guilt is yours and your blood is upon your own heads. Behold, the Bridegroom comes. Go out to meet him. "The Spirit and the bride say, 'Come, Lord Jesus.' And let him who hears say, 'Come.' And let him who is thirsty come; let all who desire take the water of life freely."

Matt. 22:2–14
Luke 14:16–24
Matt. 25:6
Rev. 19:7
Rev. 22:17

May the grace of our Lord Jesus Christ be with all who seek it with a sincere heart. Amen. Yea, amen.

Peter Walpot
a servant of Jesus Christ and his church

That same year, 1570, the elders of the church decided to send brother Jörg Raber to Tirol, Hans Langenbach to the Rhine, Klaus Braidl to Württemberg, and Peter Hörich to Silesia, all to do the Lord's work among the people. This was carried out.

1570
4 servants sent out into other countries.

Before brother Peter Hörich left, he was confirmed in the service of the Gospel by the elders with the laying on of hands. This took place at Klein Niemtschitz near Prahlitz.

Peter Hörich confirmed in his service.

In the same year brother Thoman Eppenstainer, a servant of the Word, fell asleep in the Lord at Altenmarkt.

Thoman Eppenstainer passed away.

Soon after, brother Hans Klampferer or Schlahindiepfann, an old servant of God's Word, also fell asleep in the Lord at Boretitz.

Hans Klampferer passed away.

Later that year three brothers were confirmed in the service of the Gospel by the elders with the laying on of hands: Balthasar Maierhof [the younger], Ulrich Plattner, and Hans Schlegel.

3 brothers confirmed in the service of the Word.

Around this time communities were started at Nikoltschitz near Krepitz[1] and at Neudorf.[2]

Communities.

1571

On April 10, 1571, at Tracht, brother Bärtel Riedmair, known as Bärtel Schlesinger (the Silesian), fell asleep in the Lord. He was an old and highly gifted servant of the Gospel or preacher in God's church, who had brought us much Christian teaching.

Bärtel Riedmair passed away.

That same year the elders confirmed two brothers, Matthias Binder and Ludwig Dörker, in the service of the Gospel with the laying on of hands.

2 brothers confirmed in the service of the Word.

At Schärding in Bavaria, a brother named Wolf Binder was taken prisoner for the sake of his faith. He was on a journey

Wolf Binder imprisoned.

---

[1]Nikoltschitz (Nikolčice), southeast of Gross Seelowitz (Židlochovice) (not to be confused with Mikultschitz (Mikulčice) near Lundenburg). In 1570 Nikoltschitz belonged to Friedrich von Zerotin; see Beck, 255; Zeman, *Topography*, #102; #66, "Krepitz (Křepice)."

[2]Identification of Neudorf (Nová Ves) is complicated by the existence of several villages with the same name. Following F. Hruby, *Die Wiedertäufer in Mähren*, reprint from Archiv für Reformations Geschichte (Leipzig, 1935), 108–110, and Zeman, *Topography*, #94, it appears reasonable to place this Neudorf near Ungarisch Ostra (Ostrožská Nová Ves), northeast of Wessely (Veselí nad Moravou).

1571

A citizen betrayed the brother.

with a sister who was bringing her children from Bavaria, and on their way back to the community they took a riverboat. On the same boat was a man named Kurz, a citizen of Mühldorf. When they reached Schärding, this man betrayed them to the chancellor of Burghausen, who just happened to be at Schärding. The chancellor came in person to take brother Wolf prisoner and tied him up in the usual way. The sister (whose name was Margret) escaped, but she had to leave her children behind, which was a grief to her for the rest of her life.

The chancellor took the brother prisoner.

Brother Wolf was taken to Burghausen, where he was assailed by the rabble of false prophets, priests, and other worldly-wise men who put pressure on him to renounce his faith and accept their teaching. They spared no efforts and used all their cunning to make him recant, first with smooth, gentle words, then with false teaching, and even with coarse threats. But he would not be turned aside from the way of truth God had led him to know.

Wolf Binder racked so cruelly that the sun could have shone through him.

When the priests' efforts failed, it was the executioner's turn. He seized brother Wolf and tortured and racked him so brutally that the sun could have shone through him. His hands were so badly swollen that they looked as if they were cut at the joints. He was so torn and mistreated that he could not stand on his feet, let alone walk. That is how brutal and merciless the brood of Satan were, revealing their father's nature, which is full of wrath. Satan is determined to turn believers against the Lord through those instruments who carry out his work.

2 priests came to brother Wolf.

Two priests visited the brother and one of them urged him to turn from his error. But though in agony from the torture, brother Wolf answered him courageously, saying, "You priest, you are the one who needs to repent of your sinful life and distorted teaching! You are a false prophet, one of those scoundrels who go about in sheep's clothing, hiding their deceit under their long cassocks. Inwardly you are ravening wolves, and the Lord Christ has cried woe upon you many times." The priest repeated these words to a man who had been very kind to Wolf. The man told Wolf it had gladdened his heart to hear that the priest was told the truth for once. So the priests and other lords at Burghausen brought disgrace on themselves.

He told them they were hiding their deceit under their cassocks.

They sent him back to Schärding.

Finally, when they achieved nothing with this faithful brother who loved God, they sent him back to Schärding, where he

1571

had been captured. In both places they had seen enough of him but did not know how to get rid of him. As he was not willing to be instructed in the false teaching of the priests, he had to die. They appointed a day and in the early morning took him without warning to his execution. There had been no legal process and no verdict. Brother Wolf pointed this out to them, adding that it was no wonder: since there was nothing to accuse a believer of and no reason to kill him, there could be no verdict and no justice.

Wolf Binder beheaded.

The executioner took him and turned back the collar from his neck, but he did it in fear and trembling. Brother Wolf knelt down and commended his spirit to the Lord his God. The executioner had great difficulty beheading him; he just could not strike accurately. He had to finish cutting off the brother's head on the ground as best he could. He was afraid, and his own life was endangered by the mob. This experience made him say later that he would never execute another brother as long as he lived. Many people were present and saw how steadfast Wolf had been. This was soon after Candlemas [Feb. 2] 1571. Brother Wolf had been in prison all through the winter since fall. He had never studied the Scriptures and could not read, but God taught him abundantly through his Spirit.

Executioner in distress. Said that as long as he lived he would never execute another brother.

So it happened that Wolf was executed with the sword at Schärding. Without wavering, he endured to the end and shed his blood for his faith in Jesus Christ.

O God, look down from your heavenly throne, and see what is happening to your children. If they refuse to go along with the deception of the antichrist, they must give their heads to the sword. We still have a short song that tells the story of Wolf Binder.[1]

His betrayer went mad and died in chains.

But Kurz, the man who betrayed him, fell under God's wrath and met with disaster. Things went so far that he had to leave the country. He went insane and had to be chained up. And like this he died. Everyone said he had sinned in taking the life of a God-fearing, innocent man.

Chancellor who made the arrest was to be executed but died beforehand.

The chancellor of Burghausen, who had taken brother Wolf to prison, soon met with disaster too. He was a thief, an ungodly scoundrel. Because of his disloyal conduct, the prince,

[1]This song is in *LdHBr*, 691–693. About Binder, see *ME*, I, 344; *Martyrs Mirror*, 874–875; Beck, 257–258.

1571

who had placed great trust in him, was about to have him executed, but the chancellor grew sick and died; his good days were cut short.

Traitors never prosper.

That is what happens to such Judases who attack the believers and thirst for their blood: God does not allow it, and disaster is their lot. God's wrath falls on them sooner or later. This happened to Absalom, who sought the life of his God-fearing father David. He was hanged on an oak. Ahithophel, the adviser who sought David's blood, hanged himself. Haman, who was eager to shed innocent blood, was hanged on the very gallows he had built for the devout Mordecai. The traitors who caused devout Daniel to be thrown to the lions were themselves devoured by them. Judas, who betrayed the Lord Christ, was driven to despair and hanged himself. None of these came to a good end.

Ezek.

Valtin Hörl captured.

In this year, 1571, brother Valtin Hörl, a servant of God's Word, and several other brothers were sent to Tirol. The church sent them to look for people who longed for God's truth, people who were repenting for their sins and desiring to seal their surrender to God with the covenant of grace. Valtin was captured when he and three brothers were traveling by night in the Puster Valley. A constable accosted them and asked who they were. Three of the brothers slipped away, but Valtin, who was unable to escape, answered that they were honest and God-fearing men. The constable arrested him and took him to the attorney's house in the village of Kiens, shouting outside until he woke the attorney and others. At this point Valtin escaped from his grip, but not knowing which way to run, he fell over a wall in the dark. The constable grabbed at his coat and chased him about the village until he had hold of him again. Then he took him back to the attorney's house, where they kept guard over him all night. In the morning the attorney put thumbscrews on both hands, screwing them hard and fastening them with a lock. He took him to the castle at Schöneck, where Valtin had been imprisoned sixteen years before but had escaped through God's help, as has been told earlier.

Valtin Hörl taken to Schöneck Castle.

Attorney asked if Valtin escaped before.

The constable reminded the attorney that years earlier another Anabaptist (also called Valtin) had escaped from Schöneck. So the attorney asked the brother again and again if he was that man. Brother Valtin said he should not ask; there was no need, and it would be better for him not to know. But the attorney kept asking and promised on his honor not to tell anyone else, insisting that Valtin could trust him. Then Valtin told him he was the same man and the Lord in heaven had freed him. At this the attorney would not put him back in the same dungeon but chained him in the top of a tower that had many prison cells, where the winch for racking prisoners was kept. *1571*

The following day the attorney came with the jury and clerk of the court to ask where he had come from and what he had been doing. He replied, "God in his grace allowed us to see the sinful and demonic life that we, like the rest of the world, were leading—it was not leading to salvation. So we acted on what he showed us and changed our lives through true repentance. We left the corrupt and ungodly world. We no longer pull with them on the yoke of sin. God has commanded us to seek out and warn others as we have been sought out and warned, so that is our duty." He said that was why he and his companions were sent by the church to search out others who were struggling for the justice that God will acknowledge and who longed to change their old life. They were to help such people with counsel and trustworthy guidance.

Valtin Hörl questioned about his actions.

As we were sought out and warned, we should seek out and warn others.

He said that one of his brothers had been traveling through the Upper Inn and Ötz valleys while he had been visiting various places in the Adige. After that, their plan was to travel together, but they had not met, so he continued down the Puster Valley, looking for his brother. Then he met him on the road to this village, so they turned back, heading for Sterzing. They felt that they had traveled so far and met so few people interested in the truth that they had lost all hope of finding anyone who was ready to be obedient and surrender to the truth. So they had decided to leave the area rather than spend their money for nothing. But just as they were about to leave the Puster Valley for Sterzing, the constable seized him, Valtin, on the open road.

The clerk of the court wrote all this down and presented it to the royal judges at Ehrenburg. Two days later the constable came to the tower, showed Valtin an order to bring him to the attorney's house, and set out with him, unchained. About

Valtin Hörl went unchained with constable.

1571 halfway there, they met a woman panting with haste, bringing a letter for the constable. He let Valtin read it. It was an order for Valtin to be kept in the tower until further notice. So they turned back, but the constable let him walk free beside him. Back in the tower, the constable put the fetters on Valtin's feet without fastening them, so for two days he could walk up and down inside the tower. Take note—the reason they kept him was that they were ashamed to release him in broad daylight. That would have meant admitting that they had wronged him and that he had been imprisoned unjustly.

At midnight two days later, in the midst of a violent rainstorm, the judge arrived at the tower with the attorney and the clerk. They explained to Valtin that they had gone to great pains to persuade the magistrate to release him, and he had agreed. However, Valtin must promise never to return to this area. He replied that he could not make such a promise. He had surrendered himself to God, and now it was in God's power to send or use him wherever he willed. As Valtin did not know where or how God would wish him to meet his end, it was not for him to refuse to go to any place. He added, "Look at yourselves: Can you promise that you will never, in your whole life, go to Turkey? You know as little as I do where you will die." They admitted he was right, but they said if he refused to give them his word, they could not release him. He told them he could not make a promise he would not be able to keep. It was not his wish to make his own decision, but he wanted to be obedient to God and his church, even at the cost of his life. The judge repeated that if he would not promise, they could not release him. "God's will be done," Valtin answered.

Valtin Hörl refused to leave the area.

Then the attorney said, "Well, my lord, we could release him without the promise." So they took the fetters off his feet and brought him down to the attorney's house. "If the magistrate found out that you escaped from this prison once before, we'd have the devil after us. And if he discovered that you are a teacher, he would immediately send word to the government, and they would order us to hand you over to the bishop at Brixen. That is why we were in such a hurry to get you out of here."

Valtin Hörl released.

When Valtin asked for his money, knife, and purse that they had taken from him, they said they had used the money for his expenses and had divided the other things among themselves. And so they let him go on his way empty-handed. *1571*

The judge, however, was unable to go to his home a mile away because he had some business to transact the following day. Since his wife had been troubled about Valtin, the judge asked him to go to their house that night and reassure her that he was released from the tower. After this, Valtin continued his journey. The constable, however, was severely taken to task for arresting him in the first place.

Judge asked Valtin to show his wife he was free.

How wonderfully God works! He can bring sorrow or joy. He holds everything in his hands. Man has no power in the face of God's plans. Everything must yield to the Lord's will, however impossible it seems. Praise, honor, and glory be to him forever. In manifold ways he shows that he sustains and leads his own.

Everything must go according to the Lord's will.

On November 19, Rupp Bidmer, a weaver at Teikowitz, incited by Satan, rebelled against the church. He believed that anyone who used the expression "with all my heart" was a sinner and fool or else blind. He insisted that it was a forbidden oath, as serious as swearing by one's soul, and that whoever used it did not have the Holy Spirit but opposed him.

Rupp Bidmer insisted it was swearing to say "from my heart." Left the church.

Because of this, Rupp Bidmer left the church. However, he acknowledged he had been wrong and attempted to return. But then he gave up seeking repentance and joined the Gabrielites, even though they, too, disagreed with him on this point. In the end he was a ruined and useless man. In such outlandish ways Satan snares those who harbor false and presumptuous spirits.

In this year brother Hans Missel or Weber, a weaver who was still a young man, was taken prisoner at Langenschemmern in Swabia, a village in the jurisdiction of Warthausen. He had read and sung with the people who had sheltered him, for they wished to hear his witness to the truth of God. But then he was betrayed. The lady, a widow, sent for her scribe Felix, who came with the constables (those sons of Pilate) and attacked Hans, drawing his sword and several times hitting Hans hard over the heart with the hilt, then striking him with the flat of the sword. He reviled him cruelly and said he could kill him then and there if he wanted to. But Hans was not

Hans Missel captured.

1571

afraid, nor did he turn pale. With the best of intentions, he admonished the scribe not to lose control of himself or do anything rash. What was meant to happen was bound to happen.

He was taken to Warthausen.

Then the scribe Felix bound Hans and took him to Warthausen at night. There they kept him in a house overnight, while they ate and drank and had a gay time, making him the butt of their jokes. When day came they brought him to a dungeon in the castle.

Priests kept on trying.

Many priests came in the following days. They tried hard to persuade him, but none of them got any joy out of it, and they always left disappointed.

The priests tried everything, but he would not stray one step from the way of faith in divine truth. Then the lady of the castle asked them for advice, for she was a widow and did not know what to do with him.

Priests performed as Herodias's daughter did to gain John's head.

She had found the right ones to give her advice. Just as the daughter of Herodias had danced for the head of the God-fearing John, the priests began their dance. They told the lady that by imperial mandate this brother must die. They condemned him to death, just as their fathers did when they gave counsel against Christ, crying, "Away with him; he deserves death. We have a law, and by that law he must die."

A few members of the court would not agree to his death, but they were outnumbered. His execution was set for the following morning, but his friends came by night to help him escape from the dungeon. They dug until they had almost reached him. When he heard them, he sternly reproved and warned them not to continue. He wanted to go out by the same hole by which he had come in. So they had to leave it.

His friends wanted to dig a way out for him, but he refused.

Before his execution he was offered a good meal, but he did not want to eat. Knowing his last hour had come, he asked for a quiet place where he could be alone for a while. They did not know why he made this request, but they granted it and set a guard, who crept after him to see what he would do. Hans Missel raised his hands to heaven in earnest prayer, praising God for counting him worthy of this hour and for giving him strength and courage to die the death of a steadfast and public witness to God. He thanked God for all the goodness he had shown him again and again. He prayed that in this his last hour God would help him to the end, and he gave himself

He prayed earnestly.

into God's hands. The executioner said, "This man is more devout than any of us." When Hans had finished praying, he met the people with a smile on his lips and went willingly to his death.

1571
Executioner said, "This man is more devout than any of us!"

When they read out his sentence—that he was to be executed with the sword and burned—he told them that the Gospel says, "You shall not kill." How did they interpret this, since they too claimed to be Christians? But Felix the scribe reviled him and said, "Just hand him over to the executioner and take him to the marketplace."

The priest from Warthausen accompanied Hans on the way, still hoping he would recant and save himself. But Hans Missel told him it was they who should recant and repent of their adulterous and wicked lives.

Priest still urged him to recant.

When they arrived at the place, the executioner told Hans that he could still spare him if he recanted. But Hans refused, saying he would testify to his faith with his blood then and there. The executioner should do what he had to do.

Executioner also urged him to recant.

Then he was beheaded and burned. Because he did not burn quickly, they cut him in pieces and burned the pieces. He had still remained kneeling with his hands uplifted in prayer after his head was lying on the ground. Only when the executioner pushed him over with his foot did he fall.

Hans Missel beheaded but remained kneeling.

Before his execution, Hans had foretold that wonders would occur and that his blood would be seen in the sun. This came true three days later. At noon the sun turned bloodred, shining through people's windows and onto their tables, so red that many thought a fire had started and ran into the streets to look. We heard about this from people who had been eyewitnesses of his execution.

Hans Missel said his blood would be seen in the sun. This came true.

We were also told that his head and hair would not burn—they were found unharmed among the ashes and had to be buried.

His head did not burn.

This took place on December 13, 1571. He had been in prison only ten days and had been cruelly racked, but he remained steadfast.

The lady who had him imprisoned and executed was horrified and filled with remorse at what had happened. She could never be happy again. Everybody admitted how terrible it was that innocent blood had been shed.[1]

Lady received little joy from it.

---

[1]A song about Hans Missel's death is in *LdHBr*, 693–697; see Wolkan, *Lieder*, 233–234; Freiherr R. von Liliencron, *Zur Liederdichtung der Wiedertäufer* (Munich,

1571
Passed away:
Crisant Schuster.

This year brother Crisant Schuster, an old servant for temporal affairs, fell asleep in the Lord at Watzenowitz.[1]

Christoph Lenck.

The same year, brother Christoph Lenck, a servant of the Gospel and God's Word, fell asleep in the Lord at Watzenowitz.

1572

2 brothers confirmed in the service of the Gospel.

At Pribitz, on February 17, 1572, Wandel Holba and Rupp Gellner were confirmed in the service of the Gospel by the elders with the laying on of hands.

4 brothers chosen for the service of the Word.

On the same day four other brothers were chosen and appointed to the service of the Gospel and God's Word: Thomas Häring; Joseph Doppelhammer or Schuster (a cobbler); Andreas Lorengi, an Italian; and Hans Hueber, a wheelwright from the Ziller Valley.

Bärtel Riegel passed away.

On December 8, brother Bärtel Riegel from Gündelbach fell asleep in the Lord at Neumühl, having suffered a great deal [in his life]. Earlier he had been imprisoned with Burkhard Bämerle and had also been tortured and racked for the sake of his faith.

Bastel Rausch.

That year, brother Bastel Rausch or Hess (from Hesse), a servant for temporal affairs, fell asleep in the Lord at Tracht.

Stoffel Niedermair.

Stoffel Niedermair, another servant for temporal affairs, passed away in the Lord at Kostel.

1573

Kaspar Braitmichel, compiler of this book, passed away.

On February 27, 1573, brother Kaspar Braitmichel, an old servant of God's Word and his church, fell asleep in the Lord at Austerlitz in Moravia. He had suffered much for the sake of truth. He was one of the brothers who were taken from Falkenstein or Steinebrunn to Trieste but returned. Later, in the church community, he suffered persecution with the rest. We still have a few of his songs. He was the brother who began writing this chronicle, as told in the Preface.[2]

1875), 49–51. See also *ME*, III, 708; Gross, *Golden Years*, 56; *Martyrs Mirror*, 893–894; Beck, 258–259.

[1]Watzenowitz (Vacenovice), north of Göding (Hodonín). In 1571 it was owned by the lords von Zerotin. Zeman, *Topography*, #167.

[2]About Kaspar Braitmichel's writings, see Robert Friedmann, "The Oldest Known Hutterite Codex of 1566," *MQR*, April 1959, 96–107; Friedmann, *Schriften*, 107–108, also 69 #3.

Braitmichel's songs are in *LdHBr*, 98–100, 101 (verse 10), 175–178, 697–702

1573
Jobst Lackern and Hansel Schneider passed away.

This year two servants for temporal affairs fell asleep in the Lord: Jobst Lackern from Schwäbisch Hall at Tracht and Hansel Schneider from Rottenburg at Niemtschan on the other side of Austerlitz.

3 brothers chosen for the service of the Gospel.

To provide for the church, as several servants had passed away and others were nearing the grave, three brothers were chosen for the service of the Gospel and appointed at Pribitz on April 19, 1573: Stoffel Bach or Gerber (a tanner) from the Allgäu; Christian Zwick or Dietel from Tirol, who had once been a priest; and Hans Landman or Kitzbühler.[1]

Kaspar Hueber passed away.

On July 18, brother Kaspar Hueber, an outstanding teacher and servant of God's Word, fell asleep in the Lord at Alexowitz in Moravia.

Poppitz.

In the same year we bought a house at Poppitz, set it up, and moved in.

Marx and Bernhard arrested.

In 1573 two brothers, Marx and Bernhard, both tinsmiths,[2] were taken prisoner in Vienna, where they had gone to buy tools for their trade.

A young brother had traveled with them and visited his sister, who was employed in the lord marshal's[3] household. When the two tinsmiths were ready to return, they called at the lord marshal's house for their companion. The lord marshal of Austria demanded they be brought to him. He asked them if they came from Moravia and belonged to the Hutterian Brethren whom people called "staff-bearers" (*Stäbler*), but should more appropriately be called Anabaptists, a sect that slinks around in the dark. The brothers replied, "We have to bear that name patiently, but what people say about us is not true."

Summoned for a hearing before the marshal.

He called us "staff-bearers."

The marshal asked among other questions what made them

The marshal asked why baptism is denied to children.

(with the acrostic "Casper Breitmikhel Katharina nicht aus Leichtfertigkeit gemacht"), 702–703 (with the acrostic "Judit Breitmichl"). See also Wolkan, *Lieder*, 231; *ME*, I, 402; Beck, 261.

[1]Hans Landman should not be confused with Hans Kräl, who was also called Hans Kitzbühler (p.340 above). Beck, 264.

[2]The modern German word for tinsmith or plumber, *Klempner*, was *Klampfer* in middle-high German. *Klampferer* seems to have been used as their family name; see *ME*, III, 190.

[3]This lord marshal was Hans Wilhelm, Baron von Roggendorf, a zealous Lutheran (Beck, 261).

1573

deny Christian baptism to children—were they not entitled to it just as much as adults?

They answered, "We cannot find one word in the Bible about infants being baptized, so we do not baptize them. Neither Christ nor his apostles ever did it, nor did they leave any such command. We believe only what Scripture tells us. It would be foolish to ignore what Christ and his disciples clearly commanded and to build on an alien foundation with no Scripture to support it.

Origin of infant baptism.

"For even in our day there are plenty of records in the books of Roman decretals and councils to show that infant baptism was instituted by the popes. Augustine, who lived many years after the apostles' time, introduced it to the Roman Church.

"What is more, this tradition of baptizing young children was abolished by several councils as an unfounded human institution. But at some later point there was a pope who revived it, until at last it took root.

Proof that baptism is for believers, not for infants. Deut.1:39 Acts 2:37–38,41

"With God's help we can prove from Holy Scriptures that only believers should be baptized, not babies who cannot tell right from left. When the apostles proclaimed the Word of God, the people were cut to the heart and asked Peter and the apostles, 'Beloved brothers, what shall we do?' Peter did not straightaway say, 'Be baptized.' Even though he had already preached to them, he said, 'Repent, and let each of you be baptized in the name of Jesus Christ for the forgiveness of sins.' Later it says, 'Those who received his words with joy were baptized.' Little children cannot do any of this."

He did not believe it was written as the brothers said.

"I don't believe that is what is written," the marshal said.

"My lord," they replied, "if it is not written like that, you are right and we are wrong."

He said to his head steward, "Run and get the Bible. We want to see if he is right." The Bible was brought, and the marshal laid it in front of the brother, saying, "Now, my friend, show me where it is." The brother showed him.

The marshal read it in a blustering tone and said, "Yes, indeed, that is what it says," and left it at that. However, he still continued talking and tried to prove that children have a faith, but confronted with the Word of God and the brothers' answer, he could get nowhere. They said it was nonsense to declare that an infant has faith and then assert that an unclean spirit must be driven out of him by baptism.

An infant cannot have faith and at the same time a devil which they conjure out of him.

1573

The marshal told the two brothers that they should go but he wished to see them again the following day, which was Saturday. There was no way out. They feared still worse would happen if they did not comply, and so on Saturday they came back. This time he had brought his preacher with him and began again to argue about infant baptism. But he could not match the brothers and had to give up.

Marshal brought his preacher with him.

Then the preacher asked, "Why don't you preach in public, instead of in hidden corners?"

They asked why we did not preach in public.

The brothers answered, "Our teachers preach in public too."

"Yes," he said, "in your own meetings."

"We are not allowed to preach publicly everywhere, which is your fault, because you will not let us teach salvation. You cannot blame our preachers, for one does not often hear of a Lutheran preaching publicly in a Catholic town. Nor can you deny that Christ had to hide because of the ungodly Jewish scribes who tried to kill him."

On August 1 the marshal and the provost ordered that both men be chained and kept in prison.

They were put in irons.

On August 26, the Wednesday after St. Bartholomew's Day, the lord marshal sent a preacher from Krems[1] down to them to discuss the question of infant baptism. But he was silenced in his own foolishness, unable to stand his ground one hairsbreadth better than the marshal and his preacher, for lies cannot hold out against the Word of God. At last he said to brother Marx, "Of course, you are one of those fine fellows who mislead people! Oh yes, your leather apron is only a pretense. You probably made a lot of purchases in town, and your clever trick passed unnoticed." The brothers bravely withstood his lies, and he left in a temper. On October 23, after eleven weeks in prison, they were released. They returned in peace to the church.[2]

Preacher from Krems sent to them.

They were released.

---

[1]This was the Protestant clergyman, Magister Gangolf Wanger, preacher at Krems, 1568–1574. His patron, David Chytraeus (1531–1600), was later commissioned under Maximilian II to draw up Protestant church orders. See Beck, 263 n.1; Schaff-Herzog, III, 116–117; *Allgemeine Deutsche Biographie*, IV, 254–255.

[2]The "defense made by brother Marx and brother Bernhard, tinsmiths, in prison at Vienna for the sake of truth, 1573," is in the State Archives in Brno, Codex 798, fol. 231v–248v. See Friedmann, *Schriften*, 46,47; Gross, *Golden Years*, 93–96, 221 n.8; Beck, 261–264. It begins as follows:

> On Friday, the last day of July, when the marshal first summoned us for a hearing, he asked us if we were from Moravia, from the Hutterian Brethren

1574

1574

Wendel Münchinger passed away.

On May 15, 1574, brother Wendel Münchinger, a servant for temporal affairs, fell asleep in the Lord at Teikowitz.

Leonhard Dax passed away.

On August 4, brother Leonhard Dax, a servant of God's Word and his church, fell asleep in the Lord at Damborschitz. His imprisonment at Alzey on the Rhine is described earlier in this book.[1]

Hans Plattner captured.

That same year at Rotholz[2] in the Inn Valley, brother Hans Plattner or Passeier, a tailor, was imprisoned for the sake of

---

> whom people call staff-bearers but would do better to call Anabaptists, a sect that slinks around in the dark. I, Marx, replied that we must bear patiently with being called such names but what people say about us is not true. After commenting briefly on my word, he said it was a sin that we had so shamelessly seduced a fine young man. I told him I did not believe the young man would say the brothers had seduced him or taught him anything evil but I wanted to hear what he himself said. The marshal retorted, "I have questioned him, and he does not know the catechism or the Lord's Prayer and cannot recite the Ten Commandments. What do you teach your young people? I'll wager you don't know the Ten Commandments." And he asked me quite seriously if I knew the catechism.
>
> I answered, "There are many catechisms. Almost every group has its own: the papists, the Lutherans, the Zwinglians. Even Johannes Brenz (Lutheran preacher, 1499–1570; see *ME*, I, 418–420) has his own, and I could tell you of still others. We do not use such Latin and Greek terms much—we use our mother tongue. I know quite well, though, what the word 'catechism' means, for I am a catechumen, since I need daily teaching."

Now follows the marshal's cross-examination:

> When he saw he could get nowhere, he asked me what I was doing or looking for in his house. I answered, "I was not in your house but only in the courtyard to call for my brother and companion, who was visiting his sister." Then I continued, saying, "My lord, I hope you will not be angry with me for asking a boy whether our companion was ready to leave. You yourself would think it unbrotherly, I am sure, if we were to go on our way without him and leave our brother in an unfamiliar place. If I had known it would offend you, I would not even have entered your courtyard. I would have stayed outside, for we don't want to annoy anyone."
>
> He retorted, "Yes, I know well who you are: you seduce people with deceitful words."
>
> I said, "My lord, no one can truthfully say we teach evil. On the contrary, we witness against evil. . . ." On Wednesday after St. Bartholomew's Day, August 26, the marshal sent a preacher from Krems to us, a shrewd fellow, whose beard was already gray. (Why the marshal did not send his own preacher to us, I do not know.) But his pompous words got him nowhere, and he went off in a huff.

Added in a different handwriting: "On October 23, 1573, they were let out of prison and given back their freedom. Amen."

[1]See above, pp.395–396.

[2]Rotholz, village below the ruins of the Rottenburg Castle in the lower Inn Valley, northeast of Schwaz.

divine truth. He valiantly resisted the many attacks of the clergy and others, with God's help holding fast to the truth until the end. He was condemned to death and taken out to the place of execution. There he urged the people to repent and turn from their sins.

1574

Hans knelt down, turned his face to the east, and raising his hands up to heaven in front of the crowd, cried aloud to his heavenly Father and to the Lord Jesus Christ in heartfelt prayer. He praised God for his grace and kindness and prayed that God might give repentance and a new life to all men worthy of it. Finally he commended his spirit to God. With God's grace, he wanted to return the body and life he had received from God and for the sake of his truth remain faithful to the vow he had made in Christian baptism.

At the place of execution he made a heartfelt prayer to God.

The executioner found his prayer too long and wanted him to stop, but other officers said he should be allowed to pray all he wished. After his last prayer, he stood up and went joyfully to the executioner. He knelt down again without growing pale. Hearing his prayer and seeing his joy, the executioner was frightened and hesitated to carry out the sentence.

Executioner had to let him finish his prayer.

Executioner frightened by Plattner's lack of fear.

As he pushed Plattner's collar down before striking his neck, he asked him again if he would recant, but Plattner refused. So the executioner carried out the sentence: beheaded and then burned him. As a valiant Christian, Hans Plattner gave his blood in steadfast witness to the truth. He had refused to let anything on this earth separate him from eternal life in Christ, and so he attained the crown given to Christ's martyrs.[1]

Beheaded and burned.

There was a woman present who had the falling sickness [epilepsy] and had heard that she could be cured by drinking the blood of an innocent person. She pushed her way forward to get as close as she could, refusing to be driven off, and watched where the blood fell as the executioner struck off the head. Then, as the crowd dispersed, she went to the spot, gathered the blood in her hands, and drank it right there. She was freed from her sickness, as brother Stoffel Ziegler heard from the woman herself.

A woman drank the blood of the beheaded brother and was cured.

If a man will not accept the deceit and blasphemy of the antichrist, he must give his head to the sword.

[1]Hans Plattner wrote two songs; see *LdHBr*, 703–705. A song about his death, with the acrostic "Hans Blatner aus Passier ein Schneider," in *LdHBr*, 705–707. See *ME*, IV, 188–189; *Martyrs Mirror*, 993–994, "Hans Peltner"; Beck, 266–267.

1575

1575

Leonhard Klemp passed away.

On March 2, 1575 at Pribitz, brother Leonhard Klemp, an old confirmed servant for temporal affairs, fell asleep in the Lord.

3 brothers chosen for the service of the Word.

On April 17 three brothers were chosen and appointed to the service of God's Word at Pribitz: Christian Steiner or Passeier; Johannes Rath or Sichelschmid, a sicklesmith from Hesse; and Thomas Neuman, a cobbler from near the Rhine.

5 brothers confirmed in the service of the Word.

On May 23 at Pribitz, five brothers were confirmed in the service of the Gospel by the elders with the laying on of hands: Stoffel Bach, Thomas Häring, Joseph Doppelhammer, Christian Zwick, and Hans Hueber from the Zillertal.

Hans Arbeiter passed away.

Our dear brother Hans Arbeiter[1] from Aachen in the Netherlands, a loyal servant of God's Word and his church, traveled that year from Wessely to Sabatisch in Hungary to preach the Word of God to the brothers and sisters there. While he was there, he became ill and fell asleep in the Lord on July 21.

Kaspar Ebner suffocated in the smoke.

On October 21 at Kostel in the Podax,[2] brother Kaspar Ebner, a servant of God's Word and his church, was suffocated by smoke as he was burning off the old grass in a meadow.

Peter Klemp passed away.

The same year, brother Peter Klemp, a servant for temporal affairs, fell asleep in the Lord at Tracht.

Ludwig Dörker and two others seized.

The same year, brother Ludwig Dörker, a servant of God's Word, was sent by the church to Switzerland to visit people who were eager to learn about God's truth. He and brothers Melchior Platzer and David Falch were captured at Zurich.[3]

Questioned on infant baptism.

The lords and their Zwinglian preachers cross-examined them,

---

[1]About Hans Arbeiter, see entries for the years 1557 and 1568 (pp.353 and 397–399 above, respectively).

[2]Podax, possibly an obsolete name for the area around Kostel (Podivín); see also Zeman, *Topography*, #111; p.692 below.

[3]Ludwig Dörker, from Berbrunnen near Frankfurt am Main, who had been sent to Poland in 1569 to contact the Polish Brethren (see above, p.411); David Falch (in some sources Hieronymus Falk) from St. Gall, who had joined his father three years earlier, leaving his wife and child behind; and Melchior Platzer (or Melcher Blatz) from the Adige region.

According to documents in the State Archives at Zurich, the arrest of the three occurred in 1574, and the hearing took place on September 15 of the same year; see Cornelius Bergman, *Die Täuferbewegung im Kanton Zürich bis 1660* (Leipzig, 1916), 46. About Platzer, his second imprisonment, and his martyrdom in 1583, see below, pp.494–496.

questioning them about the basis of their faith and about other points, for instance, why they rejected infant baptism. The brothers answered in accordance with divine testimony: In all the many accounts of Christian baptism contained in the Word of God, there is no reference at all to infants or children being baptized. Only those should be baptized who are old enough to believe in God and Christ, surrender themselves to God in a new life, reject the devil and the world, and understand what baptism means. The brothers proved their point with references from Holy Scripture. *1575*

They were also asked why men holding government office cannot be Christians. Brother Ludwig pointed out that Christ had fled when the people had wanted to make him king and that he had refused to be a judge or divide an inheritance when someone asked him to. His followers should do as he did. God ordained that his chosen ones should conform to the likeness of his Son, and what is more, Christ says to his own, "In the world, princes rule over the people, but it shall not be so with you." "Indeed, they are not to resist evil, though the men of old had authority to do so by the law of Moses." When Jesus' disciples wanted revenge by calling down fire from heaven as Elijah had done, he said to them, "You do not know to what spirit you belong" (NEB). Concerning government officials. John 6:15 Luke 12:13–14 Rom. 8:29 Matt. 20:25–26 Luke 9:46–48 22:24–27 Matt. 5:39 Luke 9:54–55

Just as Christ did not use either worldly authority or outward force, no more can a Christian. A man does not belong to Christ unless he has Christ's spirit, and so no Christian can be a magistrate in the world. But a magistrate may well become a Christian if he humbles himself and flees from his high position, as Christ did, giving his whole life to good works as the apostle teaches. Rom. 8:9 No Christian may be a magistrate, but a magistrate can become a Christian. Titus 3:8

After further questioning, they were set free, and they returned in peace to the church. From this we can see that the time has come of which Paul spoke, when people cannot stand sound teaching of the truth but follow their own fancies and set themselves up with teachers who say what they want to hear, calling them Christians and assuring them of salvation in spite of their ungodly life. But they close their ears to the truth; they lock it up; they banish it from the face of the earth, driving it away from their land as the Gadarenes drove out Christ the Lord. Set free again. Jer. 23:32 2 Tim. 4:3–4 Jer. 9:3–6 Matt. 8:28–34 Luke 8:26–37

1576

1576

Valtin Preundel passed away.

In 1576 brother Valtin Preundel, a servant for temporal affairs, fell asleep in the Lord at Pribitz.

Hans Landman confirmed in the service of the Word.

This same year at Neumühl, brother Hans Landman was confirmed in the service of the Gospel and God's Word by the elders with the laying on of hands.

Hans Klemp passed away.

Brother Hans Klemp, a servant for temporal affairs, fell asleep in the Lord at Rampersdorf.

Turnitz and Altenmarkt burned down.

In this year our communities at Turnitz and Altenmarkt were burned down within a short time of each other by fires that started elsewhere in the village.

Ott Niederländer declared he no longer had inclination to sin.

In this year Ott Niederländer, a man whose high opinion of himself led him to spiritual pride and opposition to the church, wrote a letter in his own hand to the servant of the Lord and his church, Peter Walpot. He maintained that through his faith in Christ not only the depravity of sin was taken from him, but even the inclination to sin, for the Scriptures tell us that sin can no longer rule in believing members.

Yet in the church's confession of faith and in some of our teachings, he maintained that exactly the opposite was taught, namely, that sinful inclinations will not harm a believer as long as he does not follow them but fights against them to the end. When he heard that a person must fight against the flesh, he, too, had taken up the fight, but the more he strove, the more those evil inclinations rose up in him, which is what defiles and corrupts a man—according to him. Therefore, when in meetings the attempt was made to point out to him his sinful nature, this produced the opposite effect, and since he was being told that this inclination does not harm a person, it actually weakened his determination not to give in to his Adamic nature. That, he said, provides an excuse for the weaker members within the church.

All hypocrites and would-be communities can live according to the Scriptures, he continued, but their hearts are not pure. That is why they agree on these points as though speaking with one voice.

What made Christians any different from other people then, Ott asked, if they still had the inclination to evil and must overcome it in order to attain salvation? They would be just like the philosophers who teach that to conquer oneself is the

highest virtue. But Paul warns against such teaching, he said, *1576*
for if they can live rightly by their own efforts, without God, they count the power of Christ as nothing.

Ott objected that men were urging others to be baptized, saying that anyone who is baptized is at peace with God, while one who is not baptized is not at peace or devout; this often results in someone coming to baptism without good reason and then leaving without good reason.

He claimed that we baptize people in other places, people who have never seen the church community. They are told how wonderful everything is among the brothers and sisters. But when they join the community, they find just the opposite. They meet irresponsible and unredeemed people just like themselves, whose corrupt nature has not yet been sanctified. They seek peace among those who have no peace. What they find is quarreling, anger, envy, backbiting, covetous looks (as if the person who did such things in the community would not be found and punished). Now, since such people do exist, Ott claimed that the church must be at fault. But that is a wrong conclusion.

As he refused to be corrected by the elders and turn from his error, he was called before the brotherhood and his letter was read out in his presence. The brothers pointed out his recent whoring and fornication, for which he had only just repented. This and other things showed clearly to what extent he had indeed been freed from the flesh and the inclination to sin. He answered that he had not long been in this new state, but had only recently entered it.

He found a different interpretation of passages in the apostles' letters where they deplore their weakness: Paul says 2Cor.12:7–9
that Satan's messenger had boxed his ears to keep him from becoming too proud and that he had prayed three times to God, receiving the answer, "Let my grace be sufficient for you, for my power is made strong in weakness." This passage, Ott said, should be understood in this way, that ungodly people had struck Paul on the head and these were the messengers of Satan. A brother challenged him about this in front of the brotherhood, but Ott said the brother was more in the wrong than he was.

His ideas, moreover, were opposed to the Holy Scriptures, in which the great apostle Paul says, "I know that nothing Rom.7:18–23

1576

good dwells in me, that is, in my flesh, and I find another law in my members that opposes the law of God in my inmost self," and there are similar passages elsewhere. As Ott was immovable and his heart and mind were already alienated from the church, he was excluded and separated from the church. This took place at Neumühl.

Ott Niederländer excluded.

This is recorded so that we can see in how many ways the devil prowls around the house of God, how slyly he seduces those he finds and then devours them. All of us should know what to watch out for, and particularly the watchmen on the walls of Jerusalem should be on guard against the devil's guile and unexpected onslaughts.

1 Peter 5:8

Lord at Lundenburg took our horses for war.

On St. Andrew's Day [Nov. 30], Lord Johann von Zerotin at Lundenburg ordered the burgrave and judge to take our horses away: eight from Kostel, four from Turnitz and Rampersdorf, and four from Neumühl. The horses were to be used down in Hungary for war and other things we could not support, and so they were taken by force. Later some of them were returned, but in poor condition.

Veit Uhrmacher, Matthias Binder, and Paul Glock released from prison in the same year.

This year, three brothers were released from a long imprisonment, returning in peace to the church. They were received with great joy. One brother, a clockmaker named Veit Grünberger (or Uhrmacher after his trade) had been imprisoned at Salzburg. Paul Glock and Matthias Binder or Schneider (a tailor), a servant of God's Word and his church, had been in prison in Württemberg.[1]

Brother Veit Uhrmacher was the first to return to the church, arriving on August 9. He had been in his seventh year of imprisonment in the prince's castle at Salzburg for his faith in divine truth.

Veit Uhrmacher taken prisoner.

Together with a brother named Veit Schelch, he had been captured at Wald in the Pinzgau. A price had been set on their heads, and spies were on the watch, especially for Veit Schelch. Some peasants saw them, but as they were not quite sure if they were the right brothers, they followed them into the inn. When they saw the brothers say grace before their meal, the

Recognized by praying before a meal.

[1] Veit Uhrmacher (or Grünberger) and his companion Veit Schelch had been arrested in 1570. See Gross, *Golden Years*, 63–68; Loserth, "Grünberger, Veit," *ME*, II, 603; *Martyrs Mirror*, 841–842, "Veit Greyenburger"; Beck, 255–257, 269–270. About Paul Glock and Matthias Binder, see below, pp.450–455 and 455–458 respectively.

traitors put their heads together, convinced that these were the right men. As if praying were wrong! So rudely does the devil make his presence known! So the brothers were held at the inn, and a message was sent to the warden at Mittersill Castle. He came with constables and foot soldiers, shackled the brothers' hands behind their backs, and imprisoned them in Mittersill Castle. They were soon interrogated and then returned to the prison. *1576*

About five weeks later the Salzburg court clerk came and took them to Salzburg Castle, escorted by two constables and two men-at-arms. The brothers were put in chains in the dungeon.

Veit Uhrmacher taken to Salzburg.

The priests did not come until two and a half years later: the chaplain from the Salzburg cathedral, the Catholic judge, and other rogues. There they sat in their four-cornered hats, each with paper and ink, and cross-examined the brothers. When they summoned Veit Uhrmacher and demanded answers, he said, "What am I to say? You are the plaintiffs and the judges. What you cannot do is taken on by the constables and executioners. You instruct the prince, the prince instructs the judge, the judge the constable, and the constable the executioner, who is left to finish off your work. The executioner is your high priest, who wins the field for you."

Priests questioned him.

Executioner is their high priest who has to complete the process.

Brother Veit Uhrmacher also told them, "The Spirit says clearly who you are. You are those of whom Paul writes that in the last days some will fall away from faith and follow false teachings of the devil. Their consciences will become seared and stained through their hypocritical lies—forbidding marriage and avoiding food that God has created to be enjoyed with thanksgiving." At this a priest said they did not forbid marriage and that he had eaten meat that very day. Veit replied, "For sure, everybody knows that you forbid marriage but permit fornication."

Priests forbid marriage but permit fornication.

One of the priests said to him, "Do you not know what Christ said: 'The scribes sit on Moses' seat. Do everything that they tell you'?"

Priest told Veit they are the scribes spoken of in Matt.23:3–4.

"Do you think you are scribes?" asked brother Veit.

The priest replied, "Yes, God willing; that is what we are."

Veit said, "It is good you admit it. Several times Christ proclaimed woe over them and called them serpents and a brood of vipers, hypocrites, fools, and blind leaders. And that

1576

is exactly what you are, as you yourselves have just said." The priests were horrified, and one said if he had only known a few days earlier, he would have found out more about the Anabaptists.

Brother asked the priests if they thought Paul an Anabaptist too.

Then Veit Uhrmacher asked the priests if they thought Paul was an Anabaptist. They said no, so Veit asked why, then, had Paul said that those twelve men should be baptized who had already received the baptism of John, whose baptism was certainly from heaven and yet was not enough for salvation. How much less sufficient is infant baptism, which is only from men! At this they were silent.

Priests were left dumb as dogs that cannot bark.

Brother Veit asked them, "Why do you allow old women to baptize? Where is that written?" They could not answer and were like dogs that cannot bark.

Next they asked him if he belonged to the Hutterites. "Yes," he said, "we belong to the Hutterian Church, in which Hutter was a teacher."

Priests asked whether Jakob Hutter was our Messiah.

"Is he your Messiah?" they asked.

Priests disavowed pope and bishop of Salzburg.

"Christ is our Messiah, but I am not ashamed of Jakob Hutter. He was burned at Innsbruck for the sake of divine truth. You have a fine messiah and father at Rome, and one here in this city." The priests answered that the pope was no concern of theirs. Veit said, "But you have one here in this city." The priests declared he was not their father. Brother Veit told them, "You yourselves asserted only just now that your father had sent you." They did not know what to say, which happened several times, to their shame.

God gives his people courage and wisdom.

Matt.10:17–20
Luke 12:11–12
21:12–15

Here, valiant Christians, children of faith, and obedient disciples, we have another encouraging and living example which supports Christ's word in his promise: "When they bring you before synagogues and councils, magistrates, rulers, and educated people, do not be anxious how or what you are to answer, for I will give you words and wisdom which none of your adversaries will be able to contradict. Indeed, the Holy Spirit will teach you what to say in that hour, for it is not you who speak but the Spirit of your Father speaking through you." In the same way, the children of the world and of the devil do not speak themselves, but their father's spirit speaks through them, as he once spoke through the serpent to Eve. He is the false spirit in the mouths of his prophets. This is the way the devil works, maintaining his place on earth by working through

Gen.3:1–5
1 Kings 22:21–23

men. Yet they are powerless when faced by the Word of God, the pure truth. No Hebrew, Greek, Latin—in short, no kind of learning—will help. *1576*

Finally these priests at Salzburg openly admitted to brother Veit Uhrmacher that the Turks were also devout, maybe more devout than they, but it depended on what each person believed in.

Priests themselves say the Turks more devout than they.

Veit said, "If the faith is good, the works will be good too. But you are the kind of Christians that have to admit that the Turks are better than you, and I won't contradict that." With that they took him back to prison.

Veit Schelch, however, succumbed to the devil's cunning temptations, and he recanted. But he returned to the church and repented earnestly and for a long time, with deep remorse and weeping. He was then reaccepted and fell asleep in the Lord soon afterward.

But Veit Uhrmacher was kept in prison a long time, until the year 1576. Finally he made a rope from old clothing in the prison to let himself down from a high window. He climbed over the wall and escaped with God's help, for it would have been impossible any other way, as even the people in the castle admitted. They said he could have escaped only through supernatural powers, meaning through evil arts. But it was through God's intervention. For God, nothing is impossible. So Veit Uhrmacher returned to the church with peace and rejoicing. His defense refuting the priests at the hearing is still preserved, and so are other things he wrote from prison to the brotherhood.[1]

How Veit Uhrmacher escaped.

People in the castle said he got out by supernatural means.

---

[1]The "defense made by Veit Uhrmacher, imprisoned for divine truth in the castle at Salzburg" is in Codex 798, State Archives at Brno. The prisoners were in their third year of imprisonment before a hearing was granted. When it finally took place, Uhrmacher was first asked for his confession of faith. He replied, as he wrote to Peter Walpot in a letter dated "in the castle of Salzburg, February 16, or the second Monday in Lent, 1573":

> Your lord, the prince, has heard enough about our confession of faith. He knows it very well, for the warden at Mittersill told us he had sent our books to the governor. He can easily learn about our faith from these, since two of our teachers were executed: Klaus Felbinger at Landshut in Bavaria and Hans Mändel (who was executed with two other brothers) at Innsbruck. They were both teachers of our faith, and I could not make a better confession. Besides, your prince knew all about us before he was prince at Salzburg, because many have been murdered in Tirol and elsewhere. Let him do with us what he wants—we will endure it with God's help. I have read the confession of faith made by Klaus Felbinger and Hans Mändel more than

1576
Paul Glock imprisoned 19 years.

Paul Glock put to much torture and testing.

Brother Paul Glock, also called "young Paul," was in prison for nineteen consecutive years, mostly in Hohenwittlingen Castle in Württemberg.[1]

At first he was cruelly tortured, and many attempts to win him over were made by magistrates, nobles and commoners, learned doctors, Lutheran ministers, as well as by false brothers and all kinds of rabble. They were mainly concerned with four points: infant baptism, the eucharist, the state and its use of the sword, and the swearing of oaths. Paul always based his defense on the undeniable truth of divine Scripture, so his opponents came off badly. He exposed their ungodliness and depravity, making their ears tingle and their consciences smart.

He wrote down his confession of faith and his defense for them. They tried both harsh and lenient imprisonment.

For six months Paul Glock was not locked in.

During the year 1566 his cell was left unlocked for a full six months, and he was even allowed to go several miles away, as long as he promised not to leave without their knowledge. But then there was further cross-examination by the prince's court chaplain and others. As Paul was still firm in his faith, refusing to admit that magistrates, the sword, or war were Christian, these warmongers said they did not want him to associate with other people, and they would keep him in prison until he died or admitted that they were good Christians. This makes it clear why the world cannot tolerate believers. But Paul was undaunted and suffered everything for the sake of God and his truth.

In prison again until he would say they were good Christians.

---

once, enough to know with certainty that it is fully based on divine Scripture. If people do not want to believe, we cannot force them to do so. They know the truth well enough, and if they want to live accordingly, they need not ask us. . . .

My beloved brother Peter, I have a great deal to tell you, but I cannot write much and never have been able to. I just thought I should let you know that we are well. I believe that if they could find a good reason to let us go free and not lose face, they would pretend they never knew us. The warden told me we need not fear for our lives. They only want to keep us in prison for a long time. So we wait on God to provide for our release. No one wants to wash his hands in our blood, for they know very well who we are. I know of nothing else I need to write, other than to ask you never to cease interceding for us in prayer—which we also want to do. Have complete trust. Since God has put us in this place, we will serve him and his church faithfully, as all believers do. As far as I know, unworthy as I am, I have always tried to do my best in everything and to do it with all my heart.

[1]Hohenwittlingen Castle just outside Urach, South Germany, is now a ruin. Paul Glock was captured in the summer of 1558. See Gustav Bossert, *Quellen zur Geschichte der Wiedertäufer*, I (Leipzig, 1930), 172; *ME*, II, 525–526; Gross, *Golden Years*, 97–122; *Martyrs Mirror*, 1024–1026.

During the year 1567 he was ill from Easter until St. John's Day [June 12]. He suffered terribly from stabbing pains and crippled knees and hips, and his mouth was so sore that he could no longer eat bread. He gave up all hope of recovery. When his enemies heard of this, they thought: "Since God has struck him down with disease, now is the time." They sent two ministers to question him on infant baptism and the eucharist and win him over to their beliefs.

1576
He fell ill in prison.

Paul answered, "If you can show me one little flock of Christ that is a fruit of your preaching, I will join them, and I will lay down whatever is against God in me and accept what is better." The two ministers said that the Christian church is not something visible; you cannot point to it. Brother Paul said, "This shows what false prophets you are, for Christ pointed to his church and his disciples when he stretched out his hand toward them and said, 'Here are my mother and my brothers. Whoever does the will of my Father in heaven is my mother, my brother, and my sister.' He also said, 'You are to be a light to the world. A city set on a hill cannot be hidden.' And further, 'Love one another as I have loved you, that all may recognize you as my true disciples.' And Peter says, 'Lead such good lives among the heathen that they may be won without words,' and clearly points to the Christian church when he says of his brothers, 'You are the chosen race, the royal priesthood, the holy nation, God's own people.' Paul says the same: 'You are the temple of the living God,' and, 'You are the seal of my apostleship in the Lord' (RSV). You false serpents," he continued, "look how God points to his church. But as you cannot do it, you are still children of darkness, not members of the body of Christ. If you were members, you also would be able to point to the body. Am I to submit myself to you so that you can make me a Christian, when you have not yet made a single Christian in your church? You are like the four hundred false prophets of Ahab. Just as with them, a false spirit speaks out of your lying mouths to mislead the whole world. Yes, you are the thieves and murderers of whom Christ says that they come only to destroy and steal. All you are after is to make my soul the devil's prey."

Ministers said the Christian church was not something visible. His answer.

Matt.12:49–50

Matt.5:14

John 13:34–35

1 Pet.3:1

1 Pet.2:9

2 Cor.6:16

1 Cor.9:2

A member of the body can point to his body, his "temple."

1 Kings 22:6,21–23

John 10:10

He answered the cruel scoundrels with such confidence that they understood perfectly well and were horrified that he could give these answers while he was ill. After that they left him alone for a long time so as not to get involved.

1576
Even if our cause were good, it could not be tolerated.

They had also told him that even if his cause was right and good, it never had been and never could be tolerated. Paul Glock had replied, "Yes, ungodly and worldly men could never tolerate Christ, his apostles, or his true followers. And neither can you, for what are you but ungodly, miserable, evil people?"

In 1572 the prince's chancellors came to him in the castle for the third time and did a lot of talking as usual.

Prefect, prince's court chaplains, and chancellors interrogated Paul.

In 1573 Paul Glock was brought to Urach to appear in the chancellery before the prince's two court chaplains, the town preacher, and four other chancellors, as well as the prefect of the prince's household, who was next in rank to the prince. They began the interrogation with infant baptism, declaring that children have faith because of Paul's words: "Without faith it is impossible to please God." Therefore they demanded infant baptism.

Clergy said children have faith.

Heb. 11:6

Paul Glock replied, "In speaking to the Hebrews, the apostle is not talking about or to infants but to adults, as the entire chapter shows. It says expressly that anyone who wants to come to God must believe that God is God and will recompense those who seek him. Show me an infant who has this much understanding and faith, then baptize him, and you have won your point." They argued that an infant had no need to understand, to which Paul Glock replied, "Then neither does he need to be baptized." That silenced them.

Paul Glock said, "Bring me an infant who has faith, and you have won."

About government.

Rom. 13:4

Next they spoke about the governing authorities: These were Christians, they said, because Paul had called them servants of God. Paul Glock responded, "Paul calls them servants of wrath. Wrath belongs neither to the house of God nor to Christ, but to hell." They insisted that it did. Paul Glock challenged them: "Then show me worldly government in the church of God. The apostle appointed all the offices in the house of God, but tell me where he appointed constables, princes, or worldly kings and their functions."

1 Cor. 12:28
Eph. 4:11–12

Ministers mentioned Cornelius and Sergius Paulus.

The ministers continued, saying there was indeed worldly authority in the house of Christ. They mentioned Cornelius, a centurion with soldiers under him, who had become a Christian, "and you cannot prove that the apostle told him to lay down his office." They also referred to Sergius Paulus, saying he had been a proconsul.

Paul Glock answered, "Do you not believe the apostles had

to preach the Gospel to these men so that they could come to faith? And was not the apostle Paul a true follower and teacher of Christ?" They said yes. He asked further, "Did the apostle Paul hold jurisdiction in this world or carry a sword?" *1576*

They answered, "No—he used the sword and judgment of the Spirit."

Ministers admitted Paul neither wielded a sword nor exercised worldly authority.

"So," said brother Paul, "in this same way, the apostles taught the Gospel to Cornelius and Sergius Paulus. John writes that Christ fled when the people wanted to make him king. And it says in the Gospel: 'Princes in the world rule the people, and their great men use force, but it shall not be so with you.' Further: 'To the men of old it was said, "An eye for an eye, a tooth for a tooth, a hand for a hand, a foot for a foot, and a blow for a blow." But I say to you: Do not resist evil or fight back.'

John 6:15

Matt. 20:25–26

Matt. 5:38–39

"From all this and more, Cornelius and Sergius Paulus and all Christians will see that they cannot remain princes, lords, or constables in the world if they want to follow Christ and the apostle Paul, who said, 'Follow me as I follow Christ.'" At this the ministers fell silent.

Paul Glock's attitude to governing authorities.

Then the ministers spoke of evildoers. They said that God forgives all sinners, however great their sin.

Clergy said God forgives all sinners.

Paul replied, "Yes, I believe that too, if the sinner truly repents." He asked them if they also forgave sinners, regarding them as their dear brothers. The ministers said yes.

"Then why do you hang your wrongdoers on the gallows as thieves and murderers if you forgive them and they are your brothers?"

Paul Glock asked why they do not forgive wrongdoers, but hang them on gallows.

In their folly, they all laughed and said, "That is why authority is given to the government—to punish evil."

"And is it evil to repent?" asked Paul Glock.

The ministers said no, it was good.

Paul Glock said, "Where in the Old or New Testament is authority given to magistrates to kill a repentant and devout man—and you say that anyone who has taken part in the eucharist is a Christian?" The ministers said such a man would still find forgiveness, even though his body had to suffer as a warning to others. Brother Paul went on to ask: "When you convert such an evildoer in the dungeon by your preaching about infant baptism and the eucharist and he accepts those points, do you then acknowledge him as a Christian?" This

1576
Ministers said that when a criminal takes the eucharist he becomes a Christian and his body a temple of God.

the ministers affirmed. Paul continued, "Then if he has found faith, as you assert, he has also been sealed with the Spirit of God, in accordance with Paul's words." Again the ministers agreed. Paul Glock said, "So his body should be a temple of God, because the Holy Spirit dwells in him."

"Yes," they said.

Paul Glock said that if their view were true, they hang God's temple on the gallows.

"Then see what you are doing: desecrating the temple of God by hanging it on the gallows. Do you not know what Paul says: 'If anyone dishonors or destroys the temple of God, God will dishonor and destroy him'? For it is written that anyone hung upon a tree is accursed. Just look at what fine Christians you and your magistrates are! If it really is as you say, you strangle those who repent and you desecrate the temple of God."

They looked at each other as if to say, "We are not defending our Christianity very well."

About the Lord's Supper.

The next point was the Lord's Supper, and they asked Paul what he thought of it. He said, "I set great value on it when it is celebrated as Christ ordained it, but I don't think much of the way you do it. Through the bread and wine Christ shows us true Christian community, where all should be who want to keep the remembrance of his suffering and death. We who are many become one body, members one of another to help where another has need: the rich not having more than the poor, nor the poor less than the rich. But this directly contradicts your greedy nature. So it is useless to say much to you about it." And they were silent.

Would be freed on promising never to reenter the country.

Then the prince's prefect talked to the court chaplain in Latin, and when they were through, the chaplain asked Paul if he would leave the country and never return, for in that case His Lordship would release him from prison.

Paul replied, "If you give me a sealed letter to make sure that wherever else I go I will be accepted, then I will promise never to enter your country again." They said they could not do that. Paul told them, "Then neither can I promise never to come back. But I am willing to leave, and if I return and any action of mine deserves the sword, then use it. I will make no other promises." They were not pleased with this answer.

He could go if he stopped misleading others.

The prince's prefect spoke again with the chaplain in Latin and then said to Paul, "If you will agree to keep your faith to yourself and not lead others astray, we will let you go."

Paul Glock replied, "Use the sword if I am wrong. You are appointed to use it. But if I am right, others should have the right to learn the truth from me, and that is my aim." *1576*

The chaplain said, "We do not want to force any beliefs on you. We are keeping you in prison to stop you from misleading more people." And Paul was taken back to prison.

This uprightness was characteristic of our fellow believers in times when God was testing them like gold in the fire. They kept firmly to the way of truth, not letting the natural desire to be released from prison sway them. When given the chance of saying just one word to secure their release, they refused, for they held God's truth and honor and their souls' salvation high above their own deliverance. They sacrificed their earthly tabernacles—their bodies—for divine truth and courageously endured great suffering and privation. For their descendants and all true believers, this stands as a noble example of integrity and valor.

How our brothers kept clearly to the truth.

In 1574 this same Paul Glock had to take up a new fight on account of false brothers, the Swiss Brethren, two of whom were in prison with him.[1] They accused and slandered him and the church without any reason—all their information came from hearsay and a worldly approach. But he remained unshaken.

Paul Glock put to the test by false brothers.

Brother Matthias Binder or Schneider[2] was captured with another brother, Paul Prele,[3] at Neuffen on April 15, 1573. Matthias Binder was a servant of God's Word and his church and had been sent by the church to carry out the Lord's work in Württemberg.

Matthias Binder and Paul Prele captured in Württemberg.

After they had been held in prison a few days, the prince's chief inspector came with the warden and three ministers, a nobleman, a few councillors and citizens, plus a crowd of others. Matthias was brought to the town hall and asked first

Matthias Binder cross-examined.

[1]See Leonard Gross, "Dialogue Between a Hutterite and a Swiss Brother, 1573," *MQR*, January 1970, 45–58, and Gross, *Golden Years*, 185–193, for a description of the encounter between Glock and Leonhard Sommer in prison at Hohenwittlingen. See also Bossert, *Quellen*, 362–367, 412.

[2]About Matthias Binder, see *Martyrs Mirror*, 1026. Two songs by him are in *LdHBr*, 734–737. See also Beck, 264–265; *ME*, I, 343–344; Gross, *Golden Years*, 109–110.

[3]Beck, 265 n.1 calls this brother Paul Pretten; see also *ME*, IV, 214.

1576 of all why he had come and how God had called him to faith. Next they asked about his calling and appointment to the service of the Gospel. He told them he had been chosen by his community in accordance with God's will and had been sent out to show people the will of God in all simplicity.

Then they questioned him on four points: infant baptism, the eucharist, whether those in government office could be Christian, and the swearing of oaths. They were exhausted and stunned by his answers and said, "We will not gain a thing, no matter how long we sit here. They are all one and the same."

The warden said, "I've never heard of a Hutterian brother in this country who has forsaken his faith." This he had to admit, which also served to comfort the prisoners, and Matthias was taken back to prison.

Paul Prele refused to stay out of the country. He was released.

On May 15 they were again taken to the town hall, where the warden first told Paul Prele of the prince's command: Paul should promise to leave the country and never come back. He refused to make such a promise, but later they released him all the same, and he got away unharmed in his faith and conscience. He begged them to free his brother Matthias too, but it was useless. The warden said, "Matthias, I have orders to take you to Stuttgart; you have to preach there too."

Matthias Binder taken to Stuttgart.

But this was all in accordance with God's will. So two armed men took him to Stuttgart. On the way they were so struck by the Word of God given to Matthias that they both wept as they parted from him.

Doctors and ministers cross-examined him.

After a few days in the Stuttgart prison, he was taken into the chancellery, where Doctor Kaspar Wild was sitting with several ministers and a clerk. They asked him about his calling and again about the four points, just as they had done at Neuffen. Matthias answered them on the basis of the Holy Scriptures.

He should promise to shun the country.

Then they made a proposal, asking him to promise never to reenter the country. He refused and told them why it would be wrong: Christ taught us in the Lord's Prayer, "Your will be done on earth as in heaven." He could not make this promise since he did not know whether it might not be God's will for him to return to this country in the future. As a result he was taken back to prison.

A few days later the warden had him brought to his house

to ask if he had changed his mind, to which Matthias replied that he should not expect him to change his mind; with God's help he would stand by the truth until death. They put him back in prison.

1576
The warden questioned him in his house.

A week later he was told to get ready quickly, as he was going to be taken to Maulbronn. This took place with an escort of three armed men. As Matthias was led through the town gate, a crowd was waiting to see him. He told the people why he had been arrested, called them to repentance, and went on to Maulbronn. Here he was imprisoned and his feet put in chains, and when winter came he suffered severely from the cold.

Matthias Binder taken to Maulbronn.

The abbot came and asked him about his faith and where he was from. After the sermon on the following Sunday the abbot sent him a book containing slanderous accusations against us. Some of the people showed Matthias where he was to read, as if conducting a trial, but he told them, "I cannot defend myself against a book; I have enough people slandering me." And he sent the book straight back to the abbot. The abbot visited him twice after that with other clergymen and spoke about questions of faith.

Abbot at Maulbronn questioned Matthias.

Sent him a book that slandered us, but he sent it straight back.

Abbot visited him again.

Noblemen and courtiers also came to see him. They persuaded the abbot to go with them and make another attempt. As soon as they arrived, the abbot began by speaking about infant baptism and the Lord's Supper. Using the Bible, Matthias pointed out the fruits of their beliefs and ungodly lives, whereupon their only thought was to get away. An old nobleman said to him, "I can see your concern is for your soul's salvation. If only you were on the right path!" With that they left him.

Princes, courtiers, and the abbot made a further attempt.

After that all kinds of people tried to convert him, for the devil is a spirit that never rests, and his children get no holiday.

All kinds of people tried to make Matthias recant.

Some time later, Matthias was unchained and led to the council chamber where the warden and administrator were seated with the abbot and his pupils. The warden once more tried to make him promise never to return to that area unless he let himself be converted. Otherwise, things would take a turn for the worse. The abbot started talking about the four points: infant baptism, the eucharist, government, and the swearing of oaths. Matthias responded by witnessing once more to his convictions. So he was returned to prison.

Abbot, warden, and others summoned him.

1576
The abbot and warden came again.

About half a year later, on June 3, 1574, the abbot came with the warden and three others to ask him if he had changed his mind. For more than two and a half hours they tried to trap him with every kind of argument, without any result. Once again he was put in chains in the tower, where he stayed day in and day out, year after year.

After a considerable time, seeing that Matthias would not recant, they took him to Hohenwittlingen Castle, where brother Paul Glock had been imprisoned for a long time. This was where prisoners were kept indefinitely without any hope of release.

Means of their release.

In 1576, however, after the brothers had spent two years at Hohenwittlingen, God did prepare the way for their release. Through the carelessness of some women who were drying hemp, a fire broke out in the castle, and it burned down. The two brothers helped more than anyone else to rescue people and put out the fire. They did not take the chance to escape, but afterward they asked to be released. They had never harmed anyone and were willing to promise never to avenge their imprisonment.

Before the wicked clergy could intervene, a report was sent to the prince, who gave orders that they should be released and given provisions for their journey. That is how both Matthias and Paul were able to return joyfully to the community with unburdened consciences, arriving about New Year's Day 1577.[1]

The letters and songs they wrote in prison, especially Paul Glock's, show in greater detail what they experienced during their long imprisonment, how they confessed and defended their faith, and what they suffered for the sake of divine truth.[2]

---

[1]Oral tradition has it that when Paul Glock returned home, probably to Neumühl, the community happened to be preparing for some weddings. One of the brides was his own daughter, who had been born just before his departure nineteen years earlier. See A. J. F. Zieglschmid, ed., *Das Klein-Geschichtsbuch der Hutterischen Brüder* (Philadelphia, PA, 1947), 104.

[2]The songs of Paul Glock, Matthias Binder, and Veit Uhrmacher are in *LdHBr*, 709–737; the song on pp. 723–726 has the acrostic "Mathias Binder Paul Glock Veit Uhrmacher"; the song on pp. 729–731 has the acrostic "Paul Glohk auf Witling gfangen um Gottes Wort." See also Wolkan, *Lieder*, 231–233.

Paul Glock's confession of faith and his letters to the church are in Codex 587, Brno State Archives. See also Friedmann, *Schriften*, 116; Klaassen and Friesen, *Sixteenth Century Anabaptism*, 120–169. For the letters extracted below, see Bossert, *Quellen*, 1078–1102, 334–350.

1577

1577

On January 3, 1577, brother Ulrich Plattner, a devoted servant of God's Word, fell asleep in the Lord at Stiegnitz.

Ulrich Plattner passed away.

On February 17, Paul Glock and Veit Uhrmacher were chosen for the service of the Gospel and appointed at Neumühl.

Paul Glock and Veit Uhrmacher chosen for the service of the Gospel.

The first letter, dated Hohenwittlingen, June 7, 1563, signed by Glock and his fellow prisoner Adam Horneck, is addressed to Leonhard Lanzenstiel and the brotherhood:

> O beloved brothers, what thanks and praise we owe our God . . . for your message and letters, which brought great joy to us, God be praised forevermore. Your letters and gifts reached us just on Whitsunday of this year and we learned from them how you all are. Dear brothers in Christ—Leonhard and all fellow fighters in the Gospel—with us too, everything is still well in the Lord. God upholds us wonderfully in the midst of our enemies. . . . We can see from your letters, dear brothers, your eagerness to write and comfort us. Beloved brothers, we know what is in your hearts as you write: if it were at all possible to help us, you would not spare any effort. But as that cannot be, we are happy with the gift of your message. . . . We understand from you too that fewer and fewer are turning to the truth. The message seems to be getting lost, and faith has grown cold. But we must leave that in God's hands. See how he has struck evil Lutheranism with harsh punishment: famine and hailstorms, just as Egypt was struck. And there is witchcraft, burning, and great distress throughout Württemberg. This must be true, as we have heard about it from my own sister and from Melchior Waal. Be assured that we ourselves are not suffering privation, for we still get bread and water, porridge, and soup, as much as we need. . . . The lady and lord at Urach do all they can for us in our bondage, may God reward them according to his will. Besides, even the unconverted people at the castle allow us to meet almost every day outside of our prison cells, but at night each must return to his own cell.

The following letter, dated September 30, Monday after Michaelmas, 1566, is addressed to Peter Walpot and his assistants. Paul Glock writes:

> In this year of 1566 I have received many signs of God's faithful love, as is written in the song, for God gave the warden of the castle, a man of the world, such a heart for me that simply on my word he trusted I would return, no matter how far he sent me. This lasted six months, during which time he never locked me up by day or night, praise God. I can't count the number of times I have been to Urach, and I often ate with the lady and lord there, and then planted a beautiful vine by their house. I went twice to their property in Dillingen to fetch fruit. I helped with the harvest at Hohenwittlingen and earned nine batzen [silver coins]. Once I was sent three miles from the castle to the town of Blaubeuren, where I stayed overnight with the lady's daughter and washed my hands in the source of the Blau River. I have worked in and around the castle: carted manure, made a fence around the garden, mowed, made hay and helped turn it, besides going on many errands to market for the warden of the castle. . . .
>
> I should also tell you that the goldsmith who was in prison with me has been released. But the poor poacher, whose home is in Herfeldt, was kept in Adam's prison, near where I am, for more than a year. Some people outside got a saw and a hatchet through to him, and he broke his way out. I heard it all. The man's name was Hans Seng. He came from Eglingen,

1577
Hermann Schmidt's preposterous ideas.

That same year Hermann Schmidt, a brother from Hesse who had been a member of the church for thirty-five years, wrote a statement to the elders at Neumühl declaring that he could not believe that an angel in heaven had sinned. Just as on earth Adam's one sin penetrated into all mankind, so if an angel had sinned, it followed that sin would have penetrated into all angels and in that case all angels would be sinners. On the contrary, he believed that the angels in heaven could never sin because they are of divine nature and the nature of God cannot change.

Hermann Schmidt argued that we do not rightly understand

> not far from Nördlingen in the Ries region. He has a wife and many children. We often talked about faith, for he is a papist and was surprised to hear that the world will not be saved. He often said that if ever God helped him to regain his freedom, he with his wife and children would try to find the church and become a fellow believer. . . . Dear Peter, greet all my good friends, my cousin Hans Egen from Rommelshausen, and Agnes, young Anna Reifer, and my neighbor Judith . . . as well as Bärtel Haugen and his wife, Jörgen and his Dutch wife, my brother-in-law and his Ottlig, and the daughter of my father's brother.

Next, Glock writes on June 11, 1567, to Peter Walpot:

> I have been ill since Easter of this year, 1567, until now, St. John's Day. There is no hope of improvement or of recovering my health. May God grant what is best, to comfort you and to bring me salvation. My whole body is sick and wretched, crippled in the knees and hips with stabbing pains, and my mouth is so sore that I can't eat any bread. I have lost a lot of weight and am quite thin. I no longer have the strength to dress and undress and cannot even make my own bed.

A letter written in the Easter week of 1569, again to Peter Walpot and his assistants, informs them of Paul's recovery, thanks to the care he was given in prison.

> They warm my room every day, and I cannot complain of being cold at all. I am given good food and drink, meat twice a day, with fish or something baked, two courses at every meal and two meals a day, and with each meal a cup of wine. I have no lack of clothing or blankets, and they leave me in peace with their beliefs. If they do come here, it is only to speak with the priest who is in the cell next to me, for he also opposes them on questions of faith. . . . I should also tell you that in 1568 both princes died: young Duke Eberhard and his father Christoph, Duke of Württemberg. At first everyone thought that all prisoners would be released, which would apply to me too, but nothing has come of it. . . .
>
> I am enclosing a song I wrote two years ago. I sent you a copy before but never heard whether you got it. . . . I sing, I read, I write; I braid cord for people in Urach, so I earn a kreuzer every now and then, and anything I need is lovingly supplied by the brothers outside, God be praised. . . . Dear Peter, if possible, don't forget the loyal people who have done so much for me for so long and still do. As you did before, send them two sets of knives.

In the letter of August 24, 1569, also to Peter Walpot, Paul Glock rejoices that "all of you are well, growing in Christ and living in peace, love, and unity, as befits the children of God." He writes in detail about the views of a priest imprisoned

the passage in Scripture where Christ said he saw Satan fall from heaven like a bolt of lightning. Christ was not speaking of the natural heavens, but of the church of God. *1577* Luke 10:18

Nor was Peter speaking of heavenly angels when he said that God did not spare the angels who had sinned. 2 Pet. 2:4

Jude the apostle, too, was speaking only of messengers and servants of God who abandoned their proper sphere. Jude 6

Eliphaz, one of Job's friends, was wrong in saying that there had been pride and disobedience among the angels and that man born of woman must therefore be even more guilty before God. Job 4:18–19

---

with him, who could not agree with everything in the Hutterian Brethren's *Confession of Faith*. Paul Glock had given him this book to read after he had had it bound in Urach.

On March 12, 1571, Glock addresses Christoph Achtznit "at Stiegnitz, Moravia," thanking him and his wife Elsa for their letter and informing them that he was free again to move about the castle as before. He continues:

> I still have good food and drink, clothing, and a small allowance; what more can I ask? I cannot describe the goodness God shows me above all other prisoners in the castle. How then can I complain, even if I do get some pair in my back—for the Lord also cleanses one through fever and other troubles.

He ends with greetings to acquaintances in Wischenau (Višňové) and Teikowitz (Tavíkovice).

On March 14, 1571, he writes once more to Peter Walpot. Paul thanks him and his wife for the money they sent and speaks of the famine in Württemberg:

> A measure of corn is worth a gulden and more. A full bushel is eight gulden and more. The common people are starving. The shortage of food that began this year, 1571, is getting worse and worse. . . . In spite of widespread famine, I have not felt it yet. Instead, they have increased the allowance the warden gets for my food. . . . From time to time I am able to earn a little money by my work. How can I doubt God's goodness? . . . I also want to tell you that in 1570 I earned a good sum with my cord-making. I bought thread for a few coins and made nine hundred yards of cord to send you. So my request to you, dear brother Peter, is that you give one length to each of your weaving rooms at Klein Niemtschitz and at Kostel. If Ursula Würmen from Kaufbeuren is still living, she should have a share, even if only one yard, as a greeting. The other lengths should go as greetings to your Maria and to all the servants' wives (both the servants of the Word and the servants for temporal affairs), for I have nothing else to send. The remaining seven lengths are for you (Bossert, *Quellen*, 338–343).

On March 7, 1572, Paul Glock writes from Urach to his "dear sisters in the spinning room at Klein Niemtschitz in Moravia." He reports about the famine:

> I want you to know that my time of distress seems quite short to me, except that I have to be cut off from the church and from hearing the Lord's Word. But since it pleases God for it to be so, I will submit to it.

On "the ninth day of autumn [Sept. 9], 1572," Glock writes again to Peter Walpot, telling about the continuing famine in the country and about the possibility of escape which he was offered, but which he was not willing to accept because it would have endangered his benefactor.

1577
Hermann Schmidt's false teaching.

All this led Hermann to reject the belief that an angel had become a devil. He claimed, therefore, that there is no devil other than the one born of woman. Adam and Eve agreed to commit the sin, and that was the origin of the serpent's seed.

Adam did not commit sin in connection with any tree, only in connection with the woman, herself a forbidden tree.

Wisd. of Sol. 1:14 2:23

Hermann questioned the truth of the Scripture as translated, that God created man for immortality and that there is no poison of corruption in him.

He also declared that Christ had not yet trodden the serpent's head underfoot; that was still to come. But it had bitten his heel when Pilate condemned him.

Hermann Schmidt represented that the serpent embodies human power: the serpent's belly is rulership, its entrails are all its subjects, its head is human cunning and the lust of the flesh born of woman. He made no distinction between the curse laid on the serpent and that laid on the woman.

Matt. 26:36–42

Hermann Schmidt claimed that on the Mount of Olives Christ had pleaded with his Father that if possible, the cup of wrath might be given to the sinners who deserved wrath through their own guilt, which amounts to praying for revenge. Christ's flesh begged to depart this world without the suffering of death, and he was mindful of his own righteousness and innocence. Therefore, it must have been the devil who tempted him. But the pleading of both, that of Christ's flesh and of the devil, was in vain.

Matt. 8:28–32

He compared Christ's body to the herd of pigs that had to die in order for men to be healed. The pigs, to wit, his body, had to suffer the agony of the demons. These had to die amid a great storm in the sea of the cross, through which men were freed from sin (which is the devil).

Matt. 4:3–11

Schmidt represented that Christ's righteousness and innocence in the flesh tempted him to think that as the Son of God, he had the power to eat the stones of his adversaries as though they were bread. But Christ answered the demon of his human righteousness that man did not live by bread alone even if he were to eat his enemies' stones by virtue of his righteousness and power.

Hermann Schmidt excluded.

Because of these terrible errors, Hermann Schmidt was called before the church, which, greatly shocked, excluded him and separated him from the church. As a result, he reconsidered his beliefs and sought repentance. *1577*

He spent fourteen weeks in a time of repentance, but he still held on to three points of his statement. He insisted that it was blasphemy against God to believe that the angels in heaven could ever have sinned.

He still maintained that the angels do not have the freedom of will to do wrong. They were one body with Christ before he came on earth, so they could not sin either before or after Adam. Therefore, if we say that the angels sinned, we will bring severe judgment on ourselves and on the church.

Finally, when he was rebuked on account of his errors, he broke away from the church in anger. He turned his back on repentance and died in 1580, still holding on to his false beliefs. Earlier in this chronicle he was mentioned as someone with strange ideas. May God protect every believer from such ideas and from the thousand wiles of the devil with his manifold ways of misleading us.

On December 4, 1577, brother Andreas Arnolt fell asleep in the Lord at Stiegnitz. He was a venerable servant of God's Word and his church, who had held this service in the church for twenty years.

Andreas Arnolt passed away.

In November of the same year a remarkably bright comet appeared in the heavens and was visible for several weeks. It was first observed in the evening of November 13, the Wednesday after Martinmas, and set at about eight o'clock. For six weeks it rose higher and stayed longer every night, although less brilliant.

1578

On Sunday, January 26, 1578, about the time this comet faded, dear brother Peter Walpot, a faithful servant of Jesus Christ and his whole church, fell ill. (He was also known as Peter Scherer because earlier he had been a cloth-shearer by trade.) At seven o'clock in the morning of the 29th, shortly before his end, he gathered all of us elders around his sickbed and spoke to us for the last time. He warned and encouraged us, speaking with warmth and clarity, although it was hard in

Peter Walpot's illness.

1578

his extreme weakness. After he had been raised a little in his bed, he spoke as follows:

Peter Walpot's last words to the elders.

"Dear brothers, as far as I know, I have always feared God and served the church faithfully and my conscience is free from all sins. Even though I, like everyone else, have always been saddened at my weaknesses, in good conscience I have always wanted to live faithfully and uprightly.

"Now, as I sense that my life may be ending and the Lord may call me home, it is to you dear brothers that I entrust the church, asking you to make sure that it is in good hands. I do not need to suggest a brother to you. The one shown to you by the Lord and his church will bring you more assurance and joy than any man suggested by one individual.

"In any case, watch faithfully over the church, for you know that it is no small task, but a mighty one, that the Lord has laid upon you. Therefore, seek always to make sound judgments and decisions in the church's affairs. Do not be too soft in disciplining one person while being too hard on another, or disciplining one while closing your eyes to another, lest you destroy the people of God.

"Let your special care be for the needy and the young and for the widows and orphans. Since there are many ungodly people round about who are hostile to us, take care not to get too involved with them or become too compliant, but keep your relationship on the right basis.

"If I have ever hurt or offended anyone in any way, I ask for forgiveness. Whatever I said or did on the many occasions when we had to talk matters over was meant well and done out of a zeal for God.

"I can hardly speak anymore, I am so weak, but I am fully confident that the Lord will not abandon his church. He will continue to provide and will raise up another dedicated brother to care for you. Only persevere in the teaching and be a good example to the people. The Lord will give you his blessing, grace, and strength. And pray the Lord for me that he will take me home soon."

The brothers bore him witness that he had faithfully served the church, and he asked them to take leave of all the faithful in his name and give them his blessing.

Those were his last words, and at about a quarter to five in the morning on the next day, January 30, he fell asleep in the Lord. He was fully conscious to the end and often expressed the wish that the church be under God's protection.

1578
Peter Walpot passed away.

Peter Walpot was almost sixty years old, and the church had been entrusted to him for thirteen years, after brother Leonhard Lanzenstiel had departed this life. He had carried the service of the Word for thirty-six years.

His age and time of service as elder.

He was a faithful shepherd, an outstanding teacher, and a godly leader of the whole church; a man with much experience in all matters, who got along well with people, friendly and humble toward everyone, but stern when necessary. Above all, he was richly gifted by God with his Word and teaching, bringing great joy and strengthening to the church. His passing was a great pain and loss to the church.[1]

In the days following our dear Peter Walpot's death the whole church asked God in earnest prayer that he show them by unanimous testimony another devout and dedicated man, one whom he himself wished to have as a shepherd of his people, so that the church might be cared for in these troubled times. Thus, on February 5, almost all the servants of the Word and servants for temporal affairs, as well as many brothers from all the various church communities, met at Neumühl to take counsel in the fear of the Lord. They all gave the same witness that in answer to their united prayer, God showed them that brother Hans Kräl should lead the church.

Election of a brother in Peter's place.

Hans Kräl.

Then the assembled brothers (with earnest intercession for God's help and grace) laid upon Hans Kräl the care of the whole church, to watch over it and lead it in the Lord. They, in turn, would be obedient to him in accordance with God's will and with God's help. The church gave praise to God for this. And though brother Hans begged to be spared this burden if at all possible, it could not be. So he declared himself ready

[1]Peter Walpot from Tirol, who had witnessed Blaurock's martyrdom as a child (p.53), led the church as Vorsteher from 1565–1578 (p.385), a time considered the "golden period" of Hutterian history; see Gross, *Golden Years*. For a detailed list of Walpot's writings, see Friedmann, *Schriften*, 128–130. Two of his songs are in *LdHBr*, 737–739, and one by Offrus Sebold, addressed to him, with the acrostic "Gottes Geist sei mit dir, herzlieber Bruder Petrus Waldbot," on p.739. See Beck, 270–271; Robert Friedmann, "Peter Walpot," *ME*, IV, 880–882.

About "The Great Article Book" attributed to Peter Walpot, see above, p.293 n.

1578

with God's help to do his utmost in all faithfulness. Everyone then went back home, pleased with the outcome.

Charius Dreytzel passed away.

On February 10 brother Charius Dreytzel, an old and much respected servant for temporal affairs, fell asleep in the Lord at Neumühl.

4 brothers confirmed in the service of the Gospel.

On February 23 at Kostel, four brothers were confirmed in the service of the Gospel by the elders with the laying on of hands. These were Christian Steiner; Johannes Rath; Thomas Neuman, a cobbler; and Andreas Lorengi, an Italian.

Kaspar Seidelman passed away.

On March 13 brother Kaspar Seidelman, an old and faithful servant of the Gospel, of God's Word, and of his church, fell asleep in the Lord at Klein Niemtschitz near Prahlitz, after having endured struggles and tribulation. He had been chosen for the service of the Word in 1542, together with Peter Walpot, and had served as a preacher for thirty-six years.

3 brothers chosen for the service of the Gospel.

On Easter Day of the same year, three brothers were chosen for the service of the Gospel and appointed at Neumühl: Sigmund Pühler from Tirol, Wenisch Keller or Schmidt (a smith) from Wolframitz in Moravia, and Christoph Gschäl or Hueter (a hatter).[1]

7 brothers chosen for the service for temporal affairs.

That same day seven brothers were chosen by the church and appointed to the service for temporal affairs, or steward's service:

Christoph Riegel
Hans Baldauf from Bavaria
Martin Hänig from Silesia
Balthasar Hasenfelder from Silesia
Hans Lückel from Hesse
Matthias Geyersbühler from Kitzbühel
Wolf Gasteiger from Bavaria

Christoph Riegel passed away.

On April 13 Christoph Riegel, a servant for temporal affairs, fell asleep in the Lord at Protzka in Hungary.

Andreas Schlosser and Adam Schneider arrested.

Around St. Margaret's Day [June 10] two young brothers, Andreas Schlosser (a locksmith) and Adam Schneider (a tailor), were betrayed and arrested at Altötting in Bavaria as they were traveling down the Inn River with a small group from Tirol.

[1]Christoph Gschäl, also called Geschwendter (Beck, 273), should not be confused with the missioner Christoph Gschäl who was excluded in 1542 (pp.214–215 above).

The very first day of their imprisonment the warden, the counsel, and the priests started their interrogation and spoke with the brothers twice that day. They were chiefly concerned with baptism and why the brothers rejected the first baptism, meaning infant baptism, for Christ had said, "Let the children come to me." The brothers replied that Christ did say this, but he did not baptize them or command that they be baptized. There is no mention of baptism in this passage. In another place, however, Christ said clearly, "Whoever believes and is baptized will be saved." Belief in the Gospel comes first, which infants are not capable of. The others maintained that children who were not baptized would be damned in all eternity. The brothers denied this and proved with many examples how far it was from the truth.

1578

Asked why they disavowed the first baptism.

Their interrogators tried to make the brothers recant, but without success. So they took them to be tortured and racked, each of them twice, with a priest standing by as they were pulled up. With upraised hands he pleaded with them to turn around, not to let their young bodies be ruined in this way but to recant and submit. But they refused, saying they were founded in the truth of God and would remain firm. Finally, as nothing had been achieved, they were let down from the rack.

They were racked.

One of those present at the hearing said, "Well, if you are men like the apostles, why aren't you freed from your prison and chains like the apostles? Why doesn't God help you as he helped Daniel in the lions' den?"

One man said, "If you are like the apostles, why do you not leave the prison?"

In the afternoon the priest returned, pretending to come in love. He wanted to have a friendly talk with them about each point in turn. But they told him, "We have seen your kind of love today. You love us as a wolf loves sheep." Once more he was unable to accomplish anything and had to leave.

Our enemies love us as a wolf loves a sheep.

A week later a member of the Burghausen government, supposed to be a very learned man, was sent to them. Accompanied by the warden and others, he went to talk to the brothers. He approached one of them with a greeting, and the brother, not knowing who he was, thanked him. At this he asked the brother why he didn't say, "God thank you."

Someone was sent from Burghausen to deal with the brothers.

The brother replied, "It is not for God to thank men, but for men to thank God."

When the man realized that he, too, would get nowhere, he

1578

said, "These two are already hardened. They won't change their minds, and they are so young. I'm sure they are already baptized." When he heard that they were, he crossed himself ostentatiously as if to protect himself from some great evil.

"Away with them!" Pharisees sing the same song as of old.

But the priest said, "Away with such people!" The brothers told him that these same words had been shouted against Christ.

The brothers were cross-examined for three hours as to why they had left the Roman Catholic Church and joined this devilish sect and faith. They replied that it was neither a devilish sect nor a false faith, but the true people of God who taught, believed, and lived in the truth. Those who said it was of the devil showed as much discernment as the people who said Christ had a devil.

"We have already been converted and stand firm in our belief."

The warden urged them to recant and be converted, but they told him, "We have been converted once, and we hold firmly to this conversion, as we told you when you arrested us."

The warden said to one of the brothers, "Your companion is just as obstinate as you are," to which he replied, "I am glad to hear that, for what you call obstinacy is steadfastness in God."

Then the warden said, "Let me tell you, fire and burning will be your end if you don't give in."

The man from Burghausen said, "I will speak plainly to you. The executioner (in whom they all put their faith) is coming soon." And the brothers were put back in chains.

God, however, wanted to help them escape, and it occurred to Schlosser, the locksmith, that if only he had a nail he could undo both of his locks. Then if the outer door, which separated him and his fellow prisoner Adam and had a huge lock, was left unfastened just once, he could free his brother as well.

When God wants to help, everything works out.

Now it so happened that the wardress changed the locks on his chains. She put the stronger lock (which he needed both hands to open and had not been able to reach) on the chain around his feet. The one from his feet, which he could unlock with one hand, she put on the chain that ran through a hole in the door. Her intention was to make sure he would not escape since she did not trust him with the other lock (previously on his feet). But she achieved the opposite. In fact, she was doing him the best service she could have done.

Then it happened that he found a nail sticking out in the prison wall, and that same night the wardress forgot to shut the outer door. Seeing that things were falling into place, he prayed to the Lord to help him if that were his will and pleasure. If not, he would gladly bear his punishment and cross. Then he tried and was able to open both locks. He went in to his fellow prisoner Adam, saying, "Pray to the Lord while I work at your locks and see if I can open them too." For a long time he could not open them and was almost in despair, telling his brother Adam, "I will never be happy again if I have to leave you behind." Finally he said, "I will try once more, and if it is God's will for us to escape, the lock will open. If it is not his will, it will not open now either."

1578

Adam Schneider prayed. The other worked at the lock.

While he worked on the lock, the other prayed, and before long it opened. He had opened four locks, three of them with two bolts each. The brothers came out on the town wall just by the prison. There they prayed, asking God for further help since he had already given them so much. They climbed down as well as they could, clambering and falling. At the bottom they praised God for his wonderful help at every turn. At that very moment the heavens opened with a brilliant flash of lightning.

Andreas Schlosser and Adam Schneider escaped from prison.

By these means God showed them as well as their enemies that he can still release his own from prison as in the days of the apostles. Their enemies had intended to make short work of them and take their lives, but God had a different plan and, to the enemy's great amazement, freed them from their grasp. Joyfully the brothers returned to the church, still faithful and with good consciences. Praise the Lord!

On November 3, 1578, brother Melchior Waal, a servant of Jesus Christ and his church, fell asleep in the Lord at Schadowitz. He had come to us from the Swiss Brethren, where he had been a servant of the Word.

Melchior Waal passed away.

1579

In the year 1579, on the Tuesday before All Saints Day [Nov. 1], brother Martin Hänig, a servant for temporal affairs, fell asleep in the Lord at Damborschitz.

Martin Hänig passed away.

That same year, the Jesuits, that evil brood of vipers or locusts foretold in the Revelation of John, found their way to Nikolsburg too, under Lord Adam Count von Dietrichstein of Nikolsburg, Chief Master of the household of His Majesty the

Jesuits came to Nikolsburg. Matt.3:7; 23:33 Rev.9:3–11

1579

Our people suffered much at the hands of the Jesuits.

Holy Roman Emperor. They had the impudence to bring the whole district of Nikolsburg to the popish faith, to reinstate the mass and all the antichristian abominations and idolatry.

Our brothers on the Nikolsburg estates suffered greatly because they would not take their hats off to these Jesuits, who had made a point of demanding it, so insolent were they in their pride. Many brothers were knocked to the ground for not taking their hats off to the Jesuits. They even put our schoolmaster from Pergen in the stocks for two and a half days. His hands and feet were put in irons and in his mouth they tied a gag smeared with a bitter substance, because they had heard him say, "They don't act like the religious people they claim to be."

Our steward at Pergen was put in the dungeon in Nikolsburg for several days, in the cold of winter, on account of a boy who had joined the brothers and whose father was at Pergen, although the steward had no part in it. These Jesuits were always trying to find something against us and bringing complaints to the count. They threatened his subjects with imprisonment and fines, forcing them to take part in their abominable idolatry, mass, and ungodly practices. But we in no way gave in against our wills.

4 brothers captured at the Polish border.

They vowed to harass the brothers so as to deter others.

In this year four brothers, Joseph Schlosser, Matthias Wagenknecht, Bärtel Rader, and Bärtel Schneider, were taken prisoner at Kaibel in the kingdom of Poland. They were betrayed, and officials and nobility with their servants surrounded the house, arrested them, and led them away, vowing in their fury that they would make an example of them as a warning to others.

Their captors were pleased to have finally laid hands on the brothers—they had wanted to do that for a long time. And now they behaved as if they had a fortune. They put the brothers in the stocks with iron fetters. But it was not long before the wind changed, and their captors began to feel uneasy, wishing they had never set eyes on the brothers, for they were struck in their consciences as these prisoners answered fearlessly and were obviously without guilt.

6 guards watched them during the night.

The lord ordered the chief magistrate to keep a good eye on them and set a guard of six until the following day. So the magistrate armed six men with spears and guns and told them

1579

on pain of death to watch the brothers well. The next day the local official and the nobleman returned and spent the whole day arguing with them, cursing and swearing at them.

The nobleman quoted the words of Christ: Beware of false prophets who come to us in sheep's clothing but inwardly are ravening wolves. He told the brothers, "That is what you people are." They replied, "Have you ever heard of sheep tearing wolves? That would be a new one! Everybody knows that wolves tear sheep. Since you hunt us down, torture and kill us, it should be obvious to you that you are the wolves at heart, claiming to be Christ's sheep. No sheep has ever killed a wolf." The nobleman was silent and acted as if he did not understand.

No one ever heard of sheep tearing wolves.

The brothers were never given a proper hearing, as was otherwise customary. The nobleman told them, "I am not going to dispute with you. The executioner can teach you." The priest should have come to them, but refused.

The nobleman wanted the executioner to teach them. He is their best doctor.

They asked the brothers why they had entered the country where entry was forbidden them and they were not wanted. They poured abuse on us and said the brothers were not fit to be given even one night's lodging and ought to be wiped off the face of the earth. But the brothers told them, "We fear God, and no one can point to anything wrong we have done. We must suffer innocently."

He called us unfit for one night's stay.

The nobleman said, "I am glad I have you here in Poland, where Anabaptists are not tolerated. It is in my power to send you to the capital. Once you are in the castle, you are there for life. I intend to obey the king's order that anyone who gets hold of someone like you must report it and keep him in custody or pay a large fine. So I am not going to let you go. You take people out of the country, and we cannot tolerate that." The brothers reminded him of God's judgment: when he died he would have to leave his riches behind; though he was now a great lord, that made no difference in God's eyes, for God was not a respecter of persons. The nobleman should therefore consider what he was doing.

The Polish king had commanded that captured brothers be held in custody.

Then the lord demanded that the brothers hand over everything they had on them, including letters and provisions. They refused, so he told the chief magistrate to search them and take everything. But the magistrate and court officers were not willing to do so.

1579
Magistrate unwilling to search the brothers or take anything from them.

They said, "Dear sir, we find it difficult to take belongings from God-fearing people who only confess their faith and have done no harm to anyone." The nobleman and the officials were infuriated at the magistrate and his men and gave them such a tongue-lashing that they were intimidated and went to the brothers, begging them to hand over their things.

Magistrates trembled as they searched the brothers.

But they told him, "You have heard that we refuse. We are innocently being held in prison, simply for the sake of God's truth. Since we owe no one anything, we will not give you anything. If you take it by force, we must submit, leaving judgment to God. We will not take revenge." So the magistrate and his men set about their task in fear and trembling, asking the brothers for forgiveness—they were doing it only because their lord forced them. The brothers told them they were acting against their consciences and in the fear of men, which is not Christian. Every man, lord or servant, must bear his guilt himself when he faces the judgment of God. It will be useless to make excuses by blaming the nobleman or others. Therefore they should see to it that they repent and change their lives if they wanted to escape hell.

The lords and magistrates were harsh toward the brothers, but the common people mostly had compassion. Many came daily, shocked to see them so cruelly chained in the stocks; many wept about it.

They refused to pay money to avoid the cross.

A clerk was sent to ask if they would give in or pay for their release, or if they wanted to die for their faith. They answered, "You should know that we will pay nothing. It is not Christian to avoid the cross by paying a sum of money. We will endure the cross out of fear and love of God; for his sake we will suffer whatever he permits. You can read in many places that the faithful have always met with persecution and death, and it cannot be any different for us."

Official said, "Your fate is decided."

On the fifth day the official who had betrayed them came as if he had orders from his lord to keep the brothers in safe custody. He gave this order to the chief magistrate and told the brothers, "Believe me, it is all over with you. You could easily have gone free, but you delayed too long and refused. No pleading will help you now. We have already seen to your sentence, and you cannot avoid it now even by paying a large sum of money."

He began to speak about the Scriptures and the Christian

church but was soon confounded and said in front of everybody that he did not know anymore which was the Christian church, and he ran off in shame. "You have fine leaders!" the brothers said. "They are supposed to teach you, but almost any old woman in this village could tell us more about what being a Christian means. See what sort of Christians you are!" *1579*

Twice that day the chief magistrate was ordered to keep the brothers in safe custody. The hope was that another lord would come and take harsher measures. But this did not happen. The same lord came, and no one had anything to say, which pleased the jurors.

Twice that day chief magistrate ordered to keep 4 brothers in safe custody.

When this lord saw the brothers' prison, he spoke kindly to them and ordered their release, saying, "You are also Christian people. I know you and what you stand for. I will neither despise nor condemn you, for it would be no use just to call oneself a Christian."

This lord said, "I know you and what you stand for. I will not despise you."

The brothers told him, "True, it is no use. You can compare it with a man who is called king or emperor but has no kingdom and is nothing but a poor man. It is just the same when someone is called a Christian but does not lead a Christian life. It won't do any good to pay only lip service to Christ."

Then the lord said that God did not only dwell with us in Moravia.

God is not only in Moravia.

"Oh, no," they replied, "he is not only there; that is not what we teach. God and his Word are not confined to any one place but dwell with any person who renounces sin. But it is also written: 'With the holy you will be holy, with the pure you will be pure, and with the perverse you will be perverse.'" He made no answer and stopped arguing.

Answer.

This shows how God strengthens his own who trust in him, often through ungodly men who only want to rob the faithful of all hope. But sometimes the ungodly have to admit publicly that the faithful are right and even have to bless them instead of cursing. Soon afterward all four brothers were released and allowed to go on their way.

The 4 brothers released.

They had not gone far, however, before one of the brothers, Joseph Schlosser, was recaptured at Attendorf. There was an official who had made repeated inquiries among people he knew to be serious Christians, saying he wanted to hear the brothers speak and they should let him know when any of

Joseph Schlosser soon recaptured.

1579

them were in the area. So as soon as he was told they had come, he hurried there. For a time he listened to brother Joseph (who noticed from his manner that something was amiss); then he went out, sent for the constable, and had Joseph arrested. The people at Attendorf begged the constable to let him go free, but the constable said no, not for any amount of money. His superior had ordered his arrest in a towering rage, and he, the constable, had sworn to carry it out.

Slanderers then came with all kinds of horrible lies about us, but Joseph refuted them: "No honest man can prove them true. You ought to be ashamed of such lies. These things you accuse us of are just what you do. Sin and shame are simply rampant among you. How can people be led more astray than they are already by your teaching, or live worse lives than they do now in cursing, arrogance, gluttony, drunkenness, deceit, and every wicked walk of life that is apparent among you men and women here?"

What they falsely accuse us of often found among them.

At this, one of the officials called him a seducer whose head would be cut off. The brother replied, "I am ready to endure whatever God permits. You have come so far as to persecute believers. If someone teaches you what is good and admonishes you for evil, he is insulted, but if he engages in every kind of wickedness, you call him a good Christian."

He who teaches good and reproves evil will be persecuted as a seducer.

For a week Joseph Schlosser was imprisoned where people could visit him, and many who were eager to hear the truth came to talk with him. But the lords heard of this and were told that many would leave the area if they were allowed to speak with Joseph so freely. So there was an order that he should not be left there, and he was taken into a barn and put in the stocks. Two guards were set to prevent anyone from speaking with him. Frequent orders came to tie him hand and foot, for he was to be transferred and eventually face the death penalty.

They put him in the stocks and let no one speak to him.

After two weeks, the official who had captured him came and asked if he would not like to be released soon. He replied, "It is not up to me to choose that time. I will wait for God and entrust everything to him. I will bear whatever he permits. Even if you torture my body, you cannot rob me of my faith, joy, and hope in God." Then the official advised him to send two men to the lord to ask humbly for mercy. Joseph's answer was: "It is not right to give a man that honor belonging to

Official advised him: Send two men to the lord to beg for mercy.

God, for mercy is with God alone. As I have no guilt and have done no one any harm, I have no reason to appeal to him. If you ask me to witness to my faith, I will do it in front of everyone, for I am not ashamed. But if you take my life unjustly, without a hearing, you and your lord will bring heavy guilt on yourselves." *1579*

Noblemen and others approached him about the mass, insisting that the bread is the body of Christ, who had fully redeemed them. Therefore they had no doubt that even if the sin of the whole world lay upon them, they would be forgiven through the power of their priests. But Joseph explained why this was contrary to Scripture. Christ says, if a man gains the whole world but forfeits his soul, he can do nothing to redeem his soul. It is equally impossible, as Scripture says, to be made pure by the impure or to find life among the dead. Since the priests are themselves ungodly, steeped in heavy sin, God does not listen but withdraws himself far from them. The priests mislead people simply for the sake of money and their own stomachs. They give sinners free rein and encourage them in their sin instead of helping them to turn away from it. They promise peace where there is no peace. But the devout who renounce sin are cursed and killed. If it went according to the priests, all the ungodly would belong to Christ and the devout to the devil. Murderers, thieves, and all kinds of villains, who have served the devil all their lives and been his pawns, are blessed by the priests when they die and called children of eternal life once the priests have sold them their sacrament.

Even if the whole world's sin burdened them, the priest could forgive them through the mass.
Matt. 16:26

According to the priests, Christ must have the ungodly, and the devil the godly.

That is such a terrible delusion that many are deceived and live unconcerned in their sins, thinking, "It will cost me a little money to buy the Lord (as they put it), and the priest will absolve me—then I am forgiven." But Christ commanded that his Supper be kept by the pure-hearted alone, the newborn who have turned away from sin as children of God and members of Christ's body. Therefore Paul warns each one to examine himself, for anyone who eats and drinks unworthily, eats and drinks judgment on himself, for he has not discerned the body of Christ. And that is why their mass is a horrible error that misleads the people.

Christ gave the Lord's Supper to be held by the pure-hearted.

When they asked what he thought about infant baptism, he told them it was a human institution. Christ never spoke a single word commanding it. He does not want his words made

Asked about infant baptism.

1579

into child's play. Baptism is appointed for those who believe what is taught and are old enough to understand why they receive it. They do not falsely call themselves Christians as the world does but have renounced sin, the devil, and the world—a thing impossible for an infant.

The priests said, "You are wrong! What would happen to an infant who dies unbaptized? It is damned, for infants come into the world burdened with sin from birth. But through baptism, they are cleansed from original sin and born anew, and the wrath of God is appeased."

They claim that Christ has done enough yet doubt it: they say an infant is damned if not baptized.

Then the brother told them, "Usually you proclaim that Christ the Lord has done everything for you and redeemed you. But I notice that you yourselves have doubts, for you believe that an infant will not be saved unless you pour water on it. And so you put infant baptism in place of Christ, which is idolatry. There is no Scripture which says that an unbaptized infant is damned, for such infants have never committed sin." The priests were silenced.

A clerk came who slandered the church of Christ and spitefully accused Joseph of being a knave and seducer. The brother contradicted him, saying that his accusations were nothing but lies and that such things were not tolerated among us. They could certainly not be proved.

The clerk said, "If you weren't in the stocks, I would slap you in the face."

But the brother said he would not let lies go uncontradicted: "If what we stand for is seduction, convince me from the Scriptures. Your priests know I am here; they would be happy to have a reason for condemning me."

The clerk said, "You are not worth any priest's time. The devil speaks through you."

The clerk said, "You are not worth any priest's time. You have the devil speaking through you."

Joseph replied, "The devil is neither in me nor in anyone who lives a Christian life, but he is the father of all liars and blasphemers. These are his willing servants." This infuriated the clerk.

Joseph to find guarantors that he would not reenter the country.

He said Joseph should find someone to stand security for him and swear never to reenter the country. Otherwise, he threatened, Joseph would be handed over to the governor, and once in the dungeon he would certainly die. But Joseph refused, even though people came three times that same day, wanting him to find a sponsor. One of the jurors told him he had only to say the word and half the parish would vouch for him. Joseph replied, "Oh, no! When I say a word I keep it, which counts as much as a thousand of your sponsors." *1579*

They took him out of the stocks and brought him to the lord for a hearing. The lord told him that he had been put in prison because he had deceived so many in the country, and he added, "Your faith is one big error."

The lord had him brought for cross-examination.

Joseph replied, "I will testify that our faith is no deception but founded on truth. Here I stand: If you do not believe it, I will witness with my life, God willing. You have gone so far that you call those people Christians who are sunk in every kind of sin, who blaspheme God and insult him and whose lives totally oppose him. On the other hand, you call a man a deceiver if he teaches people to turn away from sin and live according to God's will. Him you persecute. Christ said that his followers would be persecuted and handed over to the authorities to be killed."

After this, the lord refused to hear him or to let him talk anymore, because so many people had gathered to listen. The lord said, "If you are so God-fearing, stay in your own country. Don't come here misleading people."

Joseph replied, "We do not mislead anyone. We go out at God's command to call people to repentance and help those who want to amend their lives."

Christ commands us to go to all lands. Matt.28:18–20 Mark 16:15 John 15:26–27 20:21

At this a clerk said, "Your faith is not founded on Holy Scripture."

Joseph answered, "It is founded on Scripture, and I can witness to that."

But the clerk said, "You should not be allowed to talk at all," and again demanded that he find sponsors and swear an oath. Joseph pointed out that sponsorship had been instituted by unbelievers, not by believers. Their words were yes and no, for they kept to the truth. His hearers then acknowledged that sponsorship indeed came from unbelievers, so the clerk dropped both this matter and that of the oath. He offered his hand, intending to trick Joseph, but the brother told him, "It is written: A man who shakes hands in a pledge is a fool." The clerk felt insulted because he was put in the wrong.

Sponsorship originated with unbelievers, not with believers.

Prov.17:18

When the clerk realized that he was getting nowhere, he ordered Joseph to leave the place before sunset, saying that if he were to catch him again, it would cost him his life.

He was released.

1579

Joseph told him, "I can't promise anything. If it pleases God, I might come here again"—something he could not know. So after three weeks of imprisonment, he set off and returned to the community. This shows how the world waits for believers on every side with bonds and chains, dungeon and prison.

New tax. As we did not pay, had our stock confiscated.

In this year of 1579 the community went through much suffering because of a new tax of four groschen imposed on every person over sixteen years of age.[1] We could not pay it as it was for war purposes, which is not in accord with our faith in Christ, who demands a peaceful people. So we were the object of much hostility from the lords in Moravia, who sent their servants to count the people in our houses and took the tax accordingly in oxen, cows, sheep, and other livestock. Some took it from what they owed us for our work. We could only lay it all before the Lord our God and rather suffer robbery than willingly give anything and defile our consciences.

Lord at Lundenburg in fury ordered us out within two weeks for not paying unjust taxes.

In the weeks after Michaelmas [Sept. 29], Lord Johann von Zerotin at Lundenburg furiously ordered us to leave all his estates within two weeks. Anyone still found there would see what would happen. This came about because we refused to pay the tax he had placed on everything we made, large or small. Depending on the product, we were expected to pay yearly four, three, or two gulden or less, in all communities on his property. Every brewery had to pay a certain sum too. We could not do this, for we were already paying the usual taxes on our houses besides doing excessive compulsory labor. We chose rather to move away, leaving behind houses, lands, and goods. While we were preparing in earnest for the move and had some houses almost emptied except for the people, Lord Johann asked us to stay.

Hans Zuckenhammer and Wolfgang Rauffer captured.

In the week before St. Gall's Day [Oct. 16] in this year, two brothers, a smith called Hans Zuckenhammer and a tailor named Wolf, were captured in the diocese of Salzburg.[2] They

---

[1]About the taxation of Hutterian communities, beginning in 1570, see Hruby, *Wiedertäufer*, 52–70; Loserth, *Communismus*, 200–205.

[2]Hans Zuckenhammer, born in Gangkofen, Bavaria (approx. 140 miles northeast of Munich), was also called "Redbeard." A bold man, he repeatedly went on mission to Bavaria and Tirol in spite of great danger. *ME*, IV, 1040; Friedmann,

were with a smith near Polzing when two constables entered the house with drawn weapons, seized the brothers, and struck Zuckenhammer so hard that blood flowed. After binding the brothers so tightly that Zuckenhammer's hands turned black, these constables brought them to the next village on the way to Fridolfing.[1] Here Wolf's ropes fell off, and the constables had to refasten them.

1579

Wolf's bonds dropped off.

Two priests came hurrying to try their skill. They talked and disputed with the brothers, especially about baptism and the mass, claiming that infant baptism removes original sin and that men must become sanctified through the mass. The brothers replied that this was a wicked lie, through which men are deceived and misled. Evidence proves that their infant baptism does not remove original sin and their mass does not sanctify, for all kinds of sin and blasphemy are in them, and every kind of sin and depravity comes from them, even following their infant baptism and mass. From day to day they grow more ungodly, running from one sin to the next. So they are wrong and what Solomon says is true: "There are those who are pure in their own eyes but are not cleansed of their filth" (RSV). True baptism and the Lord's Supper, as commanded by Christ, are very different; and the brothers kept firmly to Christ's way.

Priests asserted that people must be purified from sins through infant baptism and the mass.

Prov.30:12

Then they were taken from Fridolfing to the town of Tittmoning, where they were first brought to the judge's house. Here they were cross-examined the very same day, which was a Thursday. As they would not give the answers their questioners wanted to hear, they were taken to the castle. Brother Wolf was taken to a cell, and both his feet were put in the stocks. They were fastened with nine locks to make sure he was secure. The same was done to Zuckenhammer, who was secured with seven locks.

Wolf Rauffer was put in the stocks.

On Friday they were cross-examined again. The warden was furious with brother Wolf and wanted to give him a beating. (Wolf used to live in this warden's district and had moved away.) He threatened to burn him with hot irons,

---

Schriften, 131–132. See also below, pp.538–543.

Wolf Rauffer or Schneider (after his trade); *ME*, IV, 256. About his second imprisonment and his martyrdom, see below, pp.501–503. See also Beck, 274.

[1]Fridolfing (Bavaria), near Tittmoning on the west bank of the Salzach River bordering Austria.

1579

wanting to find out where the brothers preached and taught, where they stayed, and who sheltered them; but the brothers would not tell, so they were put back in prison.

Government at Burghausen accused the brothers but did not want to proceed with the case.

Three weeks later they were again summoned for a cross-examination. Four papers had arrived from the government at Burghausen and other courts with orders for the officials to proceed with severity against the brothers and to execute justice—Pilate's justice, which is false justice. So the people at Tittmoning offered to transfer the two prisoners to Burghausen, to be dealt with there. But Burghausen did not want them. Then Tittmoning wanted to send the brothers to the prince bishop of Salzburg, as they had been captured in his district, but the bishop did not want them either.

Bishop did not want them either.

The town priest (or whatever they call him), the deacon of Tittmoning, was also supposed to come to the hearing, but he declined. He was afraid they would rub it in that he kept whores, which everyone knew.

Warden wanted them racked; his wife prevented it.

The warden threatened them with torture, fire, and the sword if they did not recant—of that they could be sure. He would have had them tortured and racked then and there, but his wife, who was Austrian and knew very well what our brothers represented, pleaded on their behalf, asking why he wanted to torture such people.

"In our country," she said, "these people are the most skillful, hardworking, and faithful, the most liked and trusted workers in the house and on the farm." And God used her pleading to save the brothers from the rack.

Warden threatened to bring scholars.

When the warden threatened to bring scholars from Salzburg, they replied, "Let a whole city-full of priests come, it will make no difference; they will not be able to turn us from the truth or from the way of salvation God has shown us." And there in front of the warden, the ropes fell from brother Wolf's hands of their own accord for the second time.

Ropes fell off a second time.

The following day the provincial judge came to the prison to question them, saying death by fire would be their lot unless they recanted. If they did not reveal where they had stayed and who the people were who had taken them in, the executioner would come to question them next. But the brothers told him, "You will never find us betraying anyone, even if you tear our limbs from our bodies."

They refused to betray anyone, even if all their limbs were torn from their bodies.

Later that week they cross-examined brother Wolf alone,

hoping to find out from him who had sheltered us. But they did not succeed, so he was taken back to prison. *1579*

In the tenth week a doctor of theology came from Salzburg with the provincial judge, the town deacon of Tittmoning, and the treasurer. They summoned the brothers for a cross-examination and talked about many subjects. But they could not even stand up to the brothers, much less convince them.

A doctor of theology disputed with the brothers.

They looked upon the Ten Commandments and the creed as prayers, but the brothers said they were not written as prayers; the Ten Commandments are commands by which we should live, and the creed is a confession of faith.

Commandments and creed seen as prayers.

They also tried to persuade the brothers to believe in infant baptism and to acknowledge it as the truth. But the brothers said it was an abomination, a contradiction in every way to the true baptism of Christ.

Baptism.

The priests wanted them to believe that the bread contains Christ's body in flesh and bone, just as he hung upon the cross. The brothers told them it was a lie and against God and that no one should believe it. No one can prove that Christ has as many bodies as the priests have hosts to distribute. Christ ascended into heaven and sits at the right hand of his heavenly Father, whence he will come to judge the quick and the dead. This the brothers believed, and not that the Judge of the living and the dead is to be eaten physically in the bread. Christ appointed the Lord's Supper to be held in remembrance of him, and his death and our redemption to be proclaimed with thanksgiving. Finally, the above-mentioned doctor of theology ordered that brother Wolf be freed from the stocks and held in prison like the others.

Lord's Supper.

Three weeks later the brothers were summoned again, this time by the bishop's chaplain and the suffragan bishop who came from Salzburg (the latter, however, refused to attend the hearing), and the provincial judge and the deacon from Tittmoning. When the subject came up again, the bishop's chaplain agreed that the creed and the Ten Commandments are not prayers but statements of faith, thereby admitting that the brothers were right. He added that he was sent because his gracious prince the bishop considered it his duty, as minister to their souls, to instruct them. So the chaplain began to question them on several points, that is, on government,

Bishop's chaplain from Salzburg came to cross-examine them.

1579

baptism, the mass, marriage, servants of the Word, community, mission, and then about church fairs, original sin, and swearing of oaths. Their answers were written down and given to the prince bishop.

Bishop's chaplain said their testimony was all right.

Afterward the chaplain said, "Now, everything you said would be well and good, except that my lord the bishop cannot tolerate your coming into his country and taking people away with you."

The brothers answered this too, and brother Wolf said, "If I knew of a more devout people, I would not hesitate to go to them, even if it were a harder life. But I know of none better in the whole world than those with whom I now long to be, regardless of all tribulations."

Bishop's chaplain praised brother Wolf.

The chaplain said, "I commend you for the way you fight for the kingdom of heaven."

Brother Wolf's ropes fell for the third time.

Meanwhile, in front of them all, the ropes on brother Wolf's hands fell off of their own accord for the third time; he picked them up and put them on the bench beside him. The bishop's chaplain, the provincial judge, and the others saw it happen and fell silent. At the end of the hearing, the judge picked up the ropes and took them away.

Hans Zuckenhammer and Wolf Rauffer released.

After three more weeks in prison, an order for their release arrived from the bishop of Salzburg, and they were given their freedom on the Saturday before Candlemas [Feb. 2], 1579. After sixteen weeks of imprisonment and mortification of their flesh through hunger, they walked out of the town in broad daylight.

Most of the people in the town were glad for the brothers' release, because they believed in their innocence and remembered how God had punished those who had executed the two brothers Wolf Mair and Wolf Huber at Tittmoning. Almost all who had been responsible for their imprisonment and death had soon come to a terrible end. Thus Hans and Wolf were set free, since no reason for putting them to death could be found. That they were released was like a miracle from God in that place—no one could have foreseen that the authorities would release them of their own free will; this had never happened before in that area. It was an intervention from God, who can rob princes of their courage, hold their hearts in his hand, and break the fangs of the wicked. Two songs were written about this story, to be sung to God's honor, for they witness to what God has done.[1] Praise be for all the wonderful things he does for his people. *1579*

1580

On the last day of January, the Sunday before Candlemas, 1580, brother Ulrich Hofer fell asleep in the Lord at Neumühl. He was a confirmed and very old servant for temporal affairs who had been among those told of earlier who were taken prisoner at Steinebrunn, Austria, in 1539 and sent to the galleys at Trieste. When God helped him and the others to escape, he returned to the church, where he suffered a great deal in the persecutions that followed. He had been a brother for more than fifty years, having come to the community at its beginning.

Ulrich Hofer, an old servant for temporal affairs, passed away.

On Oculi Sunday [the third Sunday in Lent] brothers Paul Glock, Veit Uhrmacher, Sigmund Pühler, Wenisch Keller, and Christoph Gschäl were confirmed in the service of God's Word by the elders with the laying on of hands.

5 brothers confirmed in the service of the Word.

At the same time at Neumühl, brothers were chosen and appointed to the service of the Word for a time of testing: Balthasar (Walser) Hasenfelder from Silesia, Paul Iltzmüller or Schuster (a cobbler) from Bavaria, Gilg Molt from Württemberg, and Hans Zuckenhammer from Bavaria.

4 brothers chosen for the service of the Word.

On Saturday, April 9, dear brother Peter Hörich, a servant of God's Word and his church, fell asleep in the Lord at Klein Niemtschitz below Kanitz.

Peter Hörich passed away.

On May 24 brother Hans Hueber from the Ziller Valley, a servant of the Word, fell asleep in the Lord at Wischenau.[2]

Hans Hueber passed away.

In the same year, dear brother Thomas Neuman, who came from Wolfsheim on the Rhine, a cobbler by trade and a servant of God's Word, was sent to the Rhine to visit people who were seeking God's truth. He went to teach them the way of

Thomas Neuman passed away.

---

[1]There are four songs, three by Zuckenhammer and one by his companion Wolf Rauffer, in *LdHBr*, 741–752; see Wolkan, *Lieder*, 237; Friedmann, *Schriften*, 131, #2.

[2]Wischenau (Višňové), a village and castle about 2 miles northeast of Znaim (Znojmo), Moravia. In 1580, both village and castle belonged to Jindřich Zahrádecký of Zahrádky whose son Karel enabled the Hutterites to settle in the district of Trentschin in 1622 by writing a letter of commendation to the owner of the Trentschin estate, Caspar Illésházi; see below, p.676 n.3. See also Beck, 275; Zeman, *Topography*, #173.

The Hutterites ('Taufari' or baptizers) living around Wischenau, Stiegnitz, and Gallitz were renowned for their wine growing.

1580

the Lord and to tell them how to find salvation. Taken sick on the journey, he fell asleep in the Lord on July 1 at Appenheim, a mile away from Bingen.

He had been the first to come to the church from the Rhine area, having heard that there was a people in Moravia living in Christian unity and community like the first apostolic churches, moved by love for their neighbor to give their goods for the use of all and to surrender self-interest. He had resolved to keep searching until he found these people who were living according to the will of God. Thus he came to our country, which was foreign to him. Unperturbed that no one knew him and that he knew no one, he inquired how to get to our community. He asked to unite with us, which he did. He had previously belonged to the Swiss Brethren.

Veit Denniffel passed away.

On August 6 brother Veit Denniffel, a servant for temporal affairs, passed away at Wostitz in the severe epidemic which had begun about St. James's Day [July 25]. The illness started with coughing, sore throat, and headache. Many died, and hardly any were spared. This was happening in all the German lands.

Hans Landman passed away.

This year brother Hans Landman the younger, a servant of the Word, fell asleep in the Lord at Neumühl on August 28, the Sunday following Bartholomew's Day.

Christian Zwick passed away.

On September 18 brother Christian Zwick, a servant of the Word with a good knowledge of Latin, fell asleep in the Lord at Pausram.

New tax increased: stock confiscated in lieu of taxes.

This same year, the new tax was increased, so everyone who stayed in one place for more than ten years had to pay one gulden. This is against our faith and conscience, because a Christian should not knowingly support anything that takes men's lives in war and vengeance. It makes little difference whether we fight with our own hands or support someone in our stead by paying taxes; to help by handing over money would be the same as going in person—in God's eyes it is the same thing. Therefore, to keep our consciences free of blood guilt and other terrible crimes and to avoid participating in the sin of another, we do not pay such taxes. So again this year in many places the lords came and seized our oxen, horses, and other livestock, or they deducted the tax amount from our wages. We had to let them rob us of what was ours; but God will judge it.

On Saturday before Christmas, Joseph Doppelhammer fell asleep in the Lord at Pribitz. He had been brought up in the community, lived there all his life, and later was a servant of God's Word. So including him, six servants of the church passed away in one year.

1580
Joseph Doppelhammer passed away—the sixth servant to die in one year.

1581

At the beginning of the year 1581 we had to leave Wostitz, where we had lived for eleven years, because Count Franz von Thurn[1] at Pürschitz ordered us off his estates. It all started because our brothers and sisters at Wostitz, who owed him service as his tenants, refused to help at a wedding banquet he gave, to which many noblemen were invited. The housekeeper, who was one of our sisters, refused to go and prepare the hens and geese or have anything to do with it.

We had to leave Wostitz.

We have to refuse such service because it goes against our faith. It would burden our consciences to assist at weddings and banquets where there is no thought of God, only indulgence in the lusts of the flesh, luxurious living, ostentation, and excessive eating and drinking. What God has created is abused. The people celebrate with dancing and every kind of wild gaiety, altogether unchristian and opposed to God.

Reason for not helping at weddings.

Therefore we do not help at such occasions but avoid them, in order not to become coguilty in the sins and evils of others but keep our consciences pure and unblemished. Not that we despise marriage, but we cannot tolerate the sinful conduct that accompanies these occasions. The count was roused to fury by this, and the countess said, "Do I have to put up with servants who do not obey me? I won't have it. I would sooner not be called mistress!" Thereupon he promised on his honor that he would not put up with us.

Moreover, he was worked up by his chaplain, who warned him to heed his own conscience and the thought of divine punishment and not to tolerate us on his estates. Looking for further reasons to expel us, they accused us of teaching our people not to acknowledge any magisterial authority.

Chaplain incited the count to drive us out.

---

[1]Count Franz von Thurn, father of Heinrich Matthias Thurn (well known from the Thirty Years War; see below, p.633 n.), owned the Wostitz and Pürschitz estates from 1574 to 1622, having acquired them from the lords of Boskovice; see above, p.395 nn.1, 2; Zeman, *Topography*, #125d, #177d.

1581

We were accused of preaching against the Ten Commandments, the Lord's Prayer, and the Christian faith, and against Christian baptism and the Lord's Supper. They even maintained that we were fellow believers with the Münsterites.

We made our defense to the count in writing and orally. The following is a summary.

We acknowledge government as a good and divine order for the world.

To begin with, governmental authority is God's servant in the world in accordance with the words of the apostle in Romans 13. It is a good and necessary order given by God to punish the evil and protect the good, for which reason it is right to respect it insofar as it does not encroach on the honor of God, the Most High. That is our stand, and we teach our people nothing else.

We came here to live in accordance with the Ten Commandments, the Lord's Prayer, and the Christian faith.

We do not teach against the Ten Commandments, the Lord's Prayer, or the Christian faith; on the contrary, we have come from many places in order that in the fear of God and through his grace alone, we may diligently conform our lives to the Ten Commandments, the Lord's Prayer, all articles of the Christian faith, the Gospel of our Lord Jesus Christ, and the saving teaching of the apostles. Therefore, if any among us act against this, we discipline them and exclude them.

We do not preach against Christian baptism.

We certainly do not preach against the Christian baptism ordained by Christ (Matt.28:19–20, Mark 16:15–16), practiced by his apostles (Acts 2:38–41; 8:26–37; 10:47–48; 16:31–33; 19:1–7), and amply witnessed to in the New Testament. This is what we teach and practice. We cannot practice infant baptism, as we find nothing written about it either in the New Testament or in the entire Bible.

We teach and keep the Lord's Supper as Christ appointed it.

Neither do we teach against the Lord's Supper. We celebrate it in the fear of God, as Christ appointed and held it with his disciples (Matt.26:26–28; Luke 22:19–20; Acts 2:42,46; 1 Cor. 11:23–26). We cannot celebrate the mass as the priests do all over the place, for they do it quite differently from the way Christ held his Supper.

Not fellow believers with the Münsterites.

To the accusation that we are fellow believers with the Münsterites, we declare that not a single person, no matter who he is, can prove that our church was involved in such an evil undertaking or ever helped in any form of bloodshed, war, or destruction. We are not such people and have never been their fellow believers. With God's help, may no one ever suffer the least bit of such rioting and bloodshed at our hands, whether enemies or friends, whether magistrates or subjects. Therefore we declare before God that in their ungodly action the Münsterites were never our associates but those of Satan. *1581*

Our words were of no help, however, because the count had already said too much. So we moved out of Wostitz—old people, widows, orphans, and little children. We had to give up our houses, farm buildings, fields, vineyards, and property, which we had built up with the sweat of our brow. All this had to be sold with considerable loss in order for us to get it off our hands and leave before the date set by the count. And so we left.

The count, however, regretted his actions soon enough. Even as our people were leaving, the countess was suddenly taken ill, and three weeks later she was dead. She refused to receive the eucharist from her chaplain, who had prompted our persecution, which shows how hostile her feelings were toward him for inciting the count against us. So much misfortune plagued the count with the new servants on his estate that we really pitied the old man. Several of his horses and other livestock died, and people said nothing would prosper again on the estate because of the guilt incurred toward us.

On Oculi Sunday (the third Sunday in Lent) at Neumühl the church chose and appointed four brothers for a time of testing in the service of the Word: Hans Baldauf from Bavaria, David Hasel from Württemberg, Heinrich Sumer or Müller (a miller) from Switzerland, and Wastel Anfang or Schmidt (a smith) from Tirol.[1]

4 brothers chosen for the service of the Word.

At the same time five brothers were appointed as servants for temporal affairs: Bärtel Gaiber from Silesia, a buyer for the shoemakers; Matthias Mair from the county of Tirol; and Adam Prucker, Hans Franck, and Georg Maier from Bavaria.

5 brothers chosen as servants for temporal affairs.

His Imperial Majesty Emperor Rudolf II had been suffering from a dangerous disease for a long time, unable to make any recovery, although many famous medical doctors from Italy, Spain, and other countries attended him. Finally in that year of 1581 he sent for our doctor, brother Georg Zobel, to come to him at Prague in Bohemia. The emperor listened to his advice, accepted the treatment he suggested, and recovered.

Emperor Rudolf sent for our doctor. Through God's blessing he helped the emperor to recover.

---

[1]Beck, 275–276, names five brothers; the fifth was Balthaser Grueber, a smith from Kanitz, who was relieved of this service at his own request that same year.

1581

Through God's help he grew well and strong. Our doctor Zobel, who attended him for six months, was then sent home with a friendly farewell. Some nobles said the emperor would have died if our doctor had not come.[1]

Hans Kircher passed away.

This year brother Hans Kircher from Hesse, a servant for temporal affairs, fell asleep in the Lord at Watzenowitz.[2]

Pohrlitz and Frischau.

Difficulties forced us to leave Sabatisch.

We started communities at Pohrlitz[3] and Frischau.[4] Later that year we had to leave Sabatisch in Hungary, where we had been for thirty-five years. We had to leave without being able to sell our dwellings, farm buildings, and fields or our one-third share in the mill. This was because of the many problems that made it impossible for us to live there any longer. The lords of the place owed us a great deal of money for our work, but we could never obtain payment; it was put off again and again. We waited a long time but nothing changed. Each of the many lords wanted our craftsmen to work exclusively for him. If we were not ready to work for credit, their other servants grew angry, beat us, and took the jobs themselves without pay. So we moved out. In the end we were allowed to take most of what we had in the houses, but at the last moment the lords imprisoned several brothers to make them promise to move back. Then they beat them severely to force them to work as prisoners. The brothers refused because they were innocent and unjustly imprisoned. They were held all winter, about twenty weeks, and then released.

Refused to do compulsory labor while imprisoned.

---

[1]Georg Zobel was one of several Hutterite barber-surgeons who possessed considerable pharmaceutical knowledge and medical skill; see Loserth, *Communismus der mährischen Wiedertäufer*, 275–278.

For more about Hutterite medical practices, see Wolkan, *Die Hutterer*, 94–96; *ME*, III, 553–555; John L. Sommer, "Hutterite Medicine and Physicians in Moravia in the Sixteenth Century and After," *MQR*, April 1953, 111–127 (quoting extensively from the *Schul-Ordnung* of 1578 as the best source of information about hygiene in the early Hutterian communities); Robert Friedmann, "Hutterite Physicians and Barber-Surgeons (Additional Notes)," *MQR*, April 1953, 128–136.

[2]Beck, 276, gives May 7 as the date of his death.

[3]Pohrlitz (Pohořelice), market town on the Jihlava River, approx. 14 miles northwest of Nikolsburg. In 1581 Pohrlitz belonged to the Seelowitz domain, owned 1569–1598 by Friedrich von Zerotin. Zeman, *Topography*, #112.

[4]Frischau (Břežany), village approx. 13 miles east of Znaim. The owner at that time, Peter Certorejsky of Certorej, allowed the Hutterites to settle in the abandoned villages around Frischau (Rohoteř, Rochtitz, Libitz, and Drzkowitz) that had been devastated long before 1581. His son Bernhard was less favorably disposed to the Hutterites; see entry for February 5, 1597, pp.535–538 below. See also Zeman, *Topography*, #39.

That same year Simon Putz, a servant for temporal affairs, fell asleep in the Lord at Nikolsburg.[1]

1581
Simon Putz passed away.

1582

In the year 1582 we bought the large house at Schakwitz again and for the third time began a community there.

House at Schakwitz was bought a third time.

In the first weeks of September of this year, our dear and faithful brother Heinrich Müller was captured at Zurzach in Switzerland; he was an appointed servant of God's Word, still in a time of testing. With him was brother Jakob Mändel. Both were arrested for the sake of their faith. They were taken to the town of Baden and given a public hearing by the governor and court of justice in the town hall. In the presence of many people, the brothers were questioned about their faith, to which they witnessed with constancy. Heinrich and Jakob were beset by twenty-four ministers who tried to make them waver in their faith and recant, but even with their combined efforts, they made no headway against the brothers, nor could they convict them of any wrongdoing, much less find any just reason to put them to death.

Heinrich Müller and Jakob Mändel captured.

24 ministers at the cross-examination.

These brothers were steadfast in their faith. Through God's Word they clearly testified that they were on the right and narrow path of truth, the way to eternal life in Christ Jesus; they would not be moved from it, cost what it may. The ministers gave up and told the councillors they did not know what else to do—it was up to the councillors to deal with them according to their judgment. So the councillors decided to sentence the brothers, but they could not agree on a verdict. Several of the judges did not want to make themselves guilty of the death of these brothers, because they would be sentencing them for their faith while knowing them to be God-fearing men. However, since most spoke for the death sentence, they decided to carry it out.

Could not agree on the verdict.

When the dear brothers heard that their hour had come, they rejoiced and were undismayed, saying it was an even greater joy to them than celebrating a wedding. Yes, they were of such courage because God made them worthy to die for the truth in praise of his name, like many servants and saints of

Death a greater joy to them than a wedding.

[1]Beck, 276, gives December 4 as the date of his death.

1582

God before them who attained the heavenly crown.

As they were led out, they sang together with all their hearts.

When they were led out, they spoke courageously to the great crowd that had gathered, admonishing them to repent from their sinful life and turn to God. The two brothers began to sing with overflowing hearts, lifting their voices in a lovely song of praise to the Lord. Those present told us that the people were startled and shaken to hear them sing together so joyfully. Many of that great gathering wept as they heard the singing; it touched their hearts that the brothers should have such an inner joy and peace in the very moment of meeting death. Eternal joy had already blazed up in them because they were to be with Abraham, Isaac, and Jacob; with the patriarchs and all the holy ones; with all the prophets and apostles of the Lord; with all the faithful brothers and sisters already departed; yes, with Jesus Christ himself, their Redeemer for ever and ever. They sang until they came to the edge of the water where they were to be drowned. Then Heinrich said, "My brother Jakob, we have traveled long and far together. So now, together still, let us pass through this temporal death into the life of the world beyond."

Eternal joy filled them while still on this earth.

They sang right to the edge of the water.

Jakob Mändel drowned.

The executioner took brother Jakob Mändel first and pushed him under water. When he was dead, the executioner pulled him out and laid him right in front of Heinrich, saying, "My dear Heinrich, take a look at your brother, who has lost his life. Recant, or you must die too. There is no other way."

But Heinrich said, "I will never recant and desert the divine truth. I will remain firm, even if it costs my life."

Minister asked Heinrich to give up this sect.

One minister pressed him especially, saying, "Oh, Heinrich, give up this new belief, this sect."

His answer.

Brother Heinrich turned to him and said, "What? A sect? I believe in God the Almighty Father, in Jesus Christ our Lord and Savior, in his holy Word and divine command. I stand firmly by this. Do you believe that this is a sect? Do you dare to call the true Christian faith a sect? What kind of faith do you have? If you believe in anything else, it is you who are part of a sect with a new belief. Reject it and leave your sinful, blasphemous life." The minister was covered with shame and reduced to silence. Seeing that Heinrich remained steadfast, the executioner drowned him as he had Jakob. This took place at Baden in Aargau in Switzerland on October 9, 1582, after the brothers had been in prison four and a half weeks.

Heinrich Müller drowned.

1582

While still alive, these dear brothers had sent the Christian greeting from prison—first to the elders and then to the whole church of God—by word of mouth through a friend of ours who had been with them. They said we should have full confidence in them, for they were determined to remain loyal and would not turn away from the divine truth. Even if it cost them their lives seven times over, they would still give up everything through the grace and help of the Lord. For the sake of God's name, they entrusted to our care their wives and children, whom they must leave, however dear and precious. Finally, they said a loving farewell to the whole church community, because they might never see us again on this earth; each one should remain steadfast and true so that we might meet with joy in the other world, where thousands of the faithful await us. This story was also put into song.[1]

They refused to recant even if it cost their lives seven times over.

They sent a farewell message to us.

In 1582 brother Christian Häring fell asleep in the Lord at Pribitz.[2] He had been in the church a long time and was a confirmed servant for temporal affairs for almost forty years. He was among those taken as a prisoner from Falkenstein to the sea at Trieste for the sake of his faith. But God devised means to set them free, and they returned to the church in peace. Later he suffered much persecution, which he endured steadfastly for the sake of God's truth.

Christian Häring passed away.

In this year of 1582 brother Jakob Klemp, a servant for temporal affairs, fell asleep in the Lord at Wessely.

Jakob Klemp passed away.

1583

On Oculi Sunday [3rd Sunday in Lent] 1583, brothers Balthasar Hasenfelder, Paul Iltzmüller, Gilg Molt, Hans Baldauf, and David Hasel were confirmed in the service of the Word by the elders with the laying on of hands.

5 brothers confirmed in the service of the Word.

On Misericordia Sunday [2nd Sunday after Easter] brother Matthaeus Porst or Zimmermann, a carpenter from the Ötztal, and Stoffel Küenhuber[3] from the Puster Valley were chosen

2 brothers chosen for the service of the Word.

---

[1]Three songs were written about Heinrich Müller and Jakob Mändel, two of which are in *LdHBr*, 752–756. See *Martyrs Mirror*, 1057–1058; Wolkan, *Lieder*, 234; Beck, 281; *ME*, III, 455; IV, 656.

[2]Beck, 282, gives December 1 as the date of his death.

[3]Küenhuber was a harness-maker; see Beck, 282.

1583

Andreas Maierhofer passed away.

Hans Kräl's farewell words to the brothers.

Hans Kräl passed away in the Lord.

for the service of the Word to meet the need of the church and appointed at Neumühl for a time of testing.

On March 28 of this year, during Holy Week, brother Andreas Maierhofer, a servant of God's Word, fell asleep in the Lord at Klein Niemtschitz.

On Saturday before Martinmas [Nov. 11] of the same year, dear brother Hans Kräl, who was entrusted with the care of the whole church, was taken sick. When he realized he might be nearing his end (which he was longing for), he called for the elders, who had come to visit him in his illness. He asked them to take faithful care of the Lord's church—of the widows and orphans and all the believers. The Lord had bought them at great cost, so the brothers should hold them equally precious, always doing their utmost to give sound judgments. They should hold zealously to Christian community and not abandon the Ordnungen of the church. He asked them to give his last greetings of love in the peace of the Lord to all the faithful and say farewell to the whole church. He commended the church to the almighty God, because he must now leave this world.

Whoever might be shown by the Lord to take his place would also be given grace for this task. Hans Kräl also asked them to give that brother this message from him: that no one should hold anything against him; for to be sure, anyone in his position often has to act as need or urgency requires and is not always able to please everybody. His longing was for us all to remain faithful to the divine truth until the end. So having said these last words in the night, and remaining conscious and clear until the end, he fell peacefully asleep in the Lord between five and six in the morning on Thursday after Martinmas, November 14, at the age of sixty-three. The whole church had been entrusted to his care for six years, but he had been a servant of the Word for twenty-three years. He was very warmhearted and devout and had suffered greatly for the sake of his faith in divine truth, as recorded earlier.[1]

[1]Hans Kräl died at Neumühl (Nové Mlýny), Moravia; see Beck, 286; Codex Dreller, fol. 108r. As noted in the Introduction, Kräl and his secretary Hauptrecht Zapff had continued the work on this chronicle, begun about 1570 at Austerlitz by Kaspar Braitmichel, who recorded events up to 1542. Kräl and Zapff worked at Neumühl (Zapff up to 1591), after which unidentified writers continued at Sabatisch, Hungary, up to 1665, where it breaks off.

About Hans Kräl, his imprisonment and suffering, see *ME*, III, 231–232, and

After dear brother Hans Kräl's departure, the whole church implored God (who knows the hearts of men), now that he had taken this brother from us, to show us another brother in his stead who was pleasing to him and whom we would acknowledge unanimously. On November 19 all the elders in the service of the Word, the servants for temporal affairs, and many other brothers from all the communities of the whole church, assembled at Neumühl. They took counsel together in the fear of God to consider which of the elders should be given the burden of leading the Lord's church. It is indeed so heavy and great a task that the Lord Christ himself asked the apostle Peter three times whether he loved him before entrusting the guarding and feeding of his flock to him. After the assembled brothers had considered it seriously before God, the Lord gave them a united, joyful testimony for brother Klaus Braidl. He had been in the service of God's Word for twenty years, and it was felt the Lord had been with him. The care of the whole church was laid on him, entrusted to him as from God the Lord, so that as a shepherd he should promote the honor of God's name and the welfare and blessedness of God's people. He was to work for justice and righteousness,

1583

Council to find a brother in Kräl's place.

The church entrusted to Klaus Braidl.

---

pp.340–348 above.

David Hofer, servant of the Word at James Valley (Manitoba, Canada) from 1902 to 1941, wrote down the following account, which has been passed down by word of mouth among the Hutterian Brethren:

> There is a story told about this Hans Kräl, which I heard from my father, who said Martin (Mertel) Roth had told it in Alwinz (Vintu de Jos, Romania). This is the story:
>
> When Hans Kräl returned home to the community, he did not make himself known but went into the house where beggars were received and asked for alms. His own wife was in the kitchen. She put some soup in front of him, but she did not give him a spoon [expecting him to have his own]. When he asked for a spoon, his wife said to him, "Do I have to give my spoon to every fool?" She had not recognized him but thought he was just another beggar, which is understandable, considering what he must have looked like.
>
> After the meal he wrote on the plate: "The one who ate here was brother Hans Kräl." Then he went away and hid in the straw in a barn. Meanwhile someone had discovered the writing, and soon quite a crowd had gathered. They went to look for him and found him.
>
> It is said that his wife was disciplined for the way she had spoken to him: even if she did not recognize her husband, it is wrong to call anybody a fool, even an unbeliever.

A letter Kräl wrote on July 4, 1583, to encourage the imprisoned Melchior Platzer before his martyrdom (see below, pp.494–496), was published by John Horsch, "Ein Sendschreiben Hans Kräls an einen Märtyrer," *Familien-Kalender*, XLV (1914), 32–35; see Friedmann, *Schriften*, 120.

1583

yes, for divine truth in the church, to guard and to watch against all corruption. He and his assistants should intervene wherever the abomination of desolation attempted to break in. Through the Word of God he was to direct the church that the Lord had purchased through the precious blood of Christ; he was to keep the elders and the people of Israel gathered in love, peace, unity, Christian community, and all divine commandments, as the one who must give account to God.

Deut.33:10

Brother Klaus was dismayed at being named, for he did not consider himself equal to such a great task. He would much rather have been spared the burden of it, but it was laid upon him by the whole church, in the presence of God, and this he could not oppose. Therefore he offered himself in obedience to the Lord to do all he could until his death, with the help of God in heaven.

He earnestly requested the church to pray for him that the almighty God might clothe him with grace and gifts for the task and be with him always. The church interceded fervently for him. Afterward the elders and assembled brothers shook hands with him, accepting him as a special gift of God, whom they praised as they returned home under his protection.

Melchior Platzer captured.

On Friday after Whitsun 1583, brother Melchior Platzer, a former apothecary, was taken prisoner for the sake of his faith at the village of Rankweil (belonging to Innsbruck though in the jurisdiction of Feldkirch, the domain of Count Hannibal[1]). Melchior was immediately put in irons at Rankweil and taken to a deep dungeon in the castle at Feldkirch, from where he was repeatedly brought before the officials and priests. He was always prepared to witness to his faith, steadily opposing their false teaching.

A priest brought to him.

One priest in particular, supposedly a very wise and learned man, was brought from the town of Bregenz to dispute with brother Melchior in public. He hoped to increase his fame in this way but was soon so obviously put to shame that he said, "It was the devil who brought me here to be tricked by this Anabaptist."

---

[1]Jakob Hannibal von Hohenems (1530–1587), after 1560 imperial count, after 1568 chief magistrate of the four Vorarlberg domains (western Austria), was a son of Clara de Medici, thus nephew of Pope Pius IV. See Beck, 283 n.1; *Allgemeine Deutsche Biographie*, XIII, 509–511.

Since the priests could do nothing with him (this was a Catholic area), they sent for Lutheran ministers to set him straight, but to no avail. He proved that both parties were sunk in injustice, untruthfulness, and false teaching, which kept the whole world bound in corruption. That was why the world was in such an evil condition, with every kind of vice and idolatry, the clergy being the greatest scoundrels of all.

1583
When the papist priests could do nothing, they sent for Lutheran ministers.

As they could not convince him with subtle arguments, they handed him over to the authorities with the false accusation that he was a seducer who deserved the death sentence. Nonetheless, if he would ask for mercy and swear an oath to leave their jurisdiction, they offered to let him return home. But he answered, rather than swear or even make a promise, he would await God's will, even if it should cost him his life. He said repeatedly that he was neither afraid of nor worried about death. Then the lords at Feldkirch were even more horrified to think of staining their hands with his blood.

He would rather give up his life than ask for mercy and swear to leave the country.

They thought to wash their hands of his blood, like Pilate, by sending him back to Rankweil, where he had been captured. On arriving in Rankweil, he was brought before the court by Count Hannibal, for the prince in Innsbruck had handed the case back and left it up to him. The verdict was death, to be carried out immediately.

Sent back to Rankweil.

When brother Melchior heard he was to go to the everlasting heavenly Father, he praised God from his heart for this great gift and rejoiced to be found worthy of witnessing to divine truth with his blood. Soon afterward, the executioner led him to the usual place of execution. The people were greatly troubled and full of pity for him. But brother Melchior began to warn them all with great ardor to consider the sinful, ungodly lives they were leading while falsely claiming to be Christians, saying, "Eternal sorrow and pain awaits those who murder an innocent Christian on the grounds that he has renounced the shameful life of the world. But I will put this in the hands of the most high God in heaven, who will requite such lip-service Christians."

Melchior Platzer called the people to repent.

The priests came along as he was led out, attempting to comfort him. But he said, "You priests are the snakes and scorpions Christ warned us of. Inside you are full of sin, abomination, and depravity." He was ordered to be silent. Then he sang in a clear voice until he reached the place of

Rejected the priests.

He sang in a clear voice up to the place of execution.

1583

execution. Here he warned the people again to be on their guard against the false prophets, who had promised them freedom (though they themselves were slaves of destruction) and had flattered the people in order to bind them to their own evil ways.

He spoke to the people till the sweat poured from him.

He continued to speak to the people until the sweat ran down his face. The executioner took a cloth, wiped Melchior's face, and said, "Say all you want to say. I'm not going to stop you."

Executioner asked him again if he wanted to obey.

The executioner said to him again, "If you consent to do what the lords want and admit that they are right, I still have the authority to release you even now."

Melchior Platzer beheaded and burned.

Brother Melchior replied, "I will not do it, so do what you are ordered." At this, the executioner raised his sword and struck off Melchior's head. Then he put him on a pile of wood he had prepared nearby and burned him.

Melchior held to the truth of God as long as he had life in his body. He was executed after twenty-six weeks of imprisonment, on the Wednesday before Martinmas, which was November 6, 1583.[1]

1584

Wastel Anfang confirmed in the service of the Word.

On Sunday, February 23, 1584, brother Wastel Anfang was confirmed in the service of the Word at Neumühl.

3 brothers chosen for the service of the Word.

At the same time the following brothers were chosen for the service of the Word and appointed for a time of testing: Georg Planer, a clockmaker; Adam Neyffer, a barber-surgeon; and Wolf Hungermüller.[2]

10 brothers chosen for the service for temporal affairs.

Ten brothers were appointed as servants for temporal affairs: Hans Seidler or Schweizer, Paul Hörer, Hans Janes, Martin Wolf, Georg Leicke, Wolf Wentzel, Leonhard Maurer, Christel Kircher, Bärtel Rebner, and Matthias Pühler.[3]

---

[1]Melchior Platzer was an apothecary; see *ME*, IV, 189; Beck, 283–284; *Martyrs Mirror*, 1058–1059. A song about him is in *LdHBr*, 756–760. About his previous imprisonment, see above, pp.442–443.

[2]Wolf Hungermüller was also called Schönberger, presumably after his birthplace; see Beck, 288.

[3]Hans Seidler had been one of the first Swiss Brethren to join the Hutterian Church; see Beck, 352. Georg Leicke came from Hesse (Germany), Wolf Wentzel from Znaim (Znojmo, Moravia), Bärtel Rebner from the Rhine Valley, and Matthias Pühler from Swabia; see Beck, 288.

On July 13 taxes were abated by the Diet at Olmütz. Lord Hynek von Waldstein at Birtnitz, governor of the margravate of Moravia, and all the nobles and representatives assembled for the Diet decided these taxes should not be demanded of us but should be abated.[1] We heartily thanked God for his intervention. The church community had long been troubled by conscience questions over these taxes. We had explained this many times to the lords and stated clearly that we could never consent to pay. We were ready to give notice on their estates and suffer hardship rather than let them continue taking these taxes from us as they had been doing—because we refused to pay, they had been deducting them from what they owed us.

1584
Tax abated for a time.

On October 12 brother Stoffel Bach, a servant of God's Word, fell asleep in the Lord at Protzka.

Stoffel Bach passed away.

On May 26 the dear, faithful brother Andreas Pürcher, a tile-maker by trade, was captured in Latsch, a village in his native Vintschgau, and taken to Goldrain.[2] Here he was brutally racked three times to make him reveal where he had lodged and in whose house. But from the first he staunchly answered that, come what may, he would not be like Judas and betray people who had treated him kindly. He would rather lose his life, one limb after another. Besides, not a single article of faith was involved. Where faith was concerned, he would gladly give them a full account, making no secret of what he did for the sake of his belief. He had made a vow to God in Christian baptism and intended to remain true to it. Rather than make himself a liar before God, he would suffer death if there were no other way. It was enough for him if just one poor soul were converted to the truth through the shedding of his blood.

Andreas Pürcher captured.

Racked 3 times.

He would keep his vow to God.

Priests were also sent to dispute with him, but they soon gave up because they could achieve nothing. He challenged

[1]Hynek Brtnicky von Waldstein succeeded the Catholic Hans Haugwitz of Biskupice as governor of Moravia. Lord Hynek allowed Hutterites to live on his estates. He was known as an educated man and is said to have been sympathetic to the German Reformation. See Hruby, *Wiedertäufer*, 56.

[2]Latsch (Làces), town near Schlanders (Silandro, west of Merano) on the Adige River. Goldrain with a castle, and Schantzen (mentioned in Pürcher's story) were in the parish of Latsch. See Beck, 289 n.1.

1584

their life full of sin and lechery, asking them how they could show others the way while they themselves were stone-blind. He told them to think of their own actions and turn their backs on their sinful lives. He cited several chapters and sayings of the Old and New Testaments. Their attempt failed completely, and he remained steadfast in his faith.

Priests soon defeated.

Many others spoke with him, either secretly or in front of everybody, imploring him to give up his faith, for otherwise he must certainly die. He answered that all who want to live a godly life in Christ Jesus must suffer persecution. That is what the Scriptures say, and he believed it. Every day he asked God in the Lord's Prayer that God's will be done—God's will could set him free. If it were not God's will, he wanted to accept death patiently.

Begged him again and again to recant.

They asked him to renounce his faith just this once, and then they would let him go. But he answered that he could not and would not do that—God protect him from breaking his vow. Lying to God would be like a dog returning to its vomit. What he had long confessed as the truth and the will of God, he would have to deny and call it all lies. It might be a long time before he found repentance, and who knows if he would ever find it again? Therefore, he would not recant but would rather die, and he hoped he would remain a living witness to God's truth.

Asked him to recant just once. Then he could go free.

He could not and would not recant. He would rather die.

He was then taken from Goldrain to Schlanders and sentenced to death under the old imperial and royal mandates. He was handed over to the executioner, who took him to the place of execution at Schantzen. As he was led there, he spoke with a joyful heart, praising God for coming so near. He wanted to die patiently and joyfully since it was God's will. He addressed the people, expressing his great thankfulness and instructing them in the Christian faith.

He rejoiced in his end.

Then he knelt down. The day had been overcast, but just then a bright ray of sunlight shone full on his face. He rejoiced and said, "God be praised, thou dearest sun, that I may see you once again before my end." The executioner had drawn his sword and raised it for the first blow when the people shrieked at him to stop and implored Andreas to recant and save his life. But he refused and courageously laid his head on the block. The executioner beheaded him and he gave up his spirit peacefully.

Andreas Pürcher executed with the sword.

1584

His body was then singed a little with a straw fire as a symbol of burning. So in patience and constancy he ended his course with a smile on his lips. This took place on October 19, 1584, in the jurisdiction of Schlanders, after he had been in prison for twenty-two weeks.

Before his death, brother Andreas wrote a short message to us from prison. He sent the holy Christian greeting of the church, asking especially that all believers be greeted from him in the peace of Jesus Christ. We should have no anxiety about him, for he wanted to remain devout and faithful, in the Lord's hand, to the end. As reported, he held to this.[1]

Andreas Lorengi passed away.

On December 23, the Sunday before Christmas 1584, brother Andreas Lorengi fell asleep in the Lord at Kostel. He came from Padua in the state of Venice and was a servant of God's Word who spoke both Italian and German.

1585

Paul Glock passed away.

On January 30, 1585, the faithful and beloved brother Paul Glock, a servant of God's Word, fell asleep in the Lord at Schadowitz. He had been imprisoned continuously for almost nineteen years in the land of Württemberg for the sake of the faith, suffering much tribulation during this time, as told above. Then through God's providence he was set free again and returned to the brotherhood.[2]

3 brothers confirmed in the service of the Word.

On February 24 three brothers, Hans Zuckenhammer, Stoffel Küenhuber, and Matthaeus Porst were confirmed in the service of the Word at Neumühl. Three other brothers, Daniel Hellrigel, Abel Ockershauser, and Hans Neumair[3] were appointed to the service of the Word for a time of testing.

Leonhard Summerauer captured.

In the same year, four brothers were in prison at Burghausen in Bavaria for the sake of their faith. The first, Leonhard Summerauer from the region of Salzburg, was arrested about

---

[1]A song about Andreas Pürcher's death is in *LdHBr*, 760–763; see Wolkan, *Lieder*, 235. About his trial and death, see *Martyrs Mirror*, 1059–1060; *ME*, IV, 234; Beck, 289–291.

[2]About Paul Glock's release and return home, see above, p.458.

[3]Daniel Hellrigel was a saddler, Abel Ockershauser a tailor, and Hans Neumair a weaver of fustian; see Beck, 291.

1585

eight days before St. Martin's Day [Nov. 11] in the year 1584. He was traveling and had boarded a boat at Tittmoning. The crew was drunk, and when they got to Burghausen, the boat crashed into the bridge and was badly damaged. As Leonhard was leaving the ship on a ladder let down for him, the sailors cried out that they had an Anabaptist on board who had brought them bad luck. A chancery clerk who was standing by went straight to the chancellor to report about the Anabaptist at the landing place. The chancellor had Leonhard imprisoned and immediately questioned under torture. He was racked five times and stretched twice on the ladder. But they could get nothing out of him. During his imprisonment Leonhard suffered great pain and distress, going through much struggle for the sake of his faith, because he refused to give in to the sinful life of the world.

Summerauer racked severely 5 times.

After more than half a year in prison, he was led out to his execution. Four priests went with him, urging him to renounce his faith. He told them he had already renounced his unjust life twenty years ago.

Taken to the place of execution and pressed to recant.

As he was taken through the city gates, they again pleaded with him to recant. He answered, "Shall I turn away from God? Christ said, 'Whoever denies me before men, him will I deny before my heavenly Father.'"

They wanted him to bow before a statue of our Lord.

They led him before a stone figure and said, "Here is a statue of our Lord," and wanted him to bow before it. He answered that it was useless; they should move on.

When they had almost reached the place of execution, the priests reproached him for leaving the Christian church and joining heretics, as they called us. He told them, "It's not true. I left the ungodly and idolatrous, the harlots, blasphemers, and drunkards, and all impurity, and I gave myself to the devout, to God and his people." But they said a devil was speaking through him, just as the Jews had said of Christ.

Priest adjured him by the last judgment to recant.

On reaching the place of execution the priest adjured him three times by the will of God to recant, but he refused. So the priest adjured him by the last judgment and all that was highest, but Leonhard said, "Oh, please be quiet! Don't ask such a thing, but go on and do what you will. I want to die as a devout Christian. I stand in the true faith and on the right foundation. I will not forsake Christ, my Master."

Realizing that nothing was of any avail, the executioner

turned back the collar on Leonhard's neck. But the priest began again, saying that if he would renounce just two articles of faith, they would let him go free. But he said, "Leave me in peace and carry out your purpose. If that is what you want, I am ready to die for my faith."

1585
He should renounce just two articles of faith.

To this the executioner said, "I don't want to execute you, but if I don't do it, someone else will." He waved the sword before his eyes to frighten him, but Leonhard did not flinch. And so they beheaded him and buried him at the place of execution. Thus on July 5, 1585, at Burghausen this lamb of the Lord was brought down by the ravening wolves.[1]

Leonhard Summerauer beheaded.

On the Wednesday after Easter of the same year, the other three brothers, Wolf Rauffer, Georg Bruckmaier, and Hans Aichner, were captured for their faith in Christ while on a journey to the mountains. They were at the inn in Geiersberg, half a mile below Ried in Bavaria. At this inn they had some soup and a drink, praying before and after their meal. The innkeeper straightaway sent for the constable with the message that some kind of Anabaptists were at his house. While he was counting the money the brothers had given him for their meal, the ungodly band arrived, took all three brothers prisoner, and brought them to Ried.

Wolf Rauffer, Georg Bruckmaier, and Hans Aichner captured near Ried.

From Ried they were taken to the castle at Burghausen, a journey of several days. Here the priest of the town and other so-called learned doctors were sent to see if they could win the brothers over and make them relinquish their faith. But they got nowhere, and especially with brother Georg, neither doctor nor priest could achieve anything.

Taken from Ried to Burghausen.

Meanwhile, as told above, at about eight o'clock on Friday morning brother Leonhard Summerauer had been led to his execution and beheaded. After that the priest and several noblemen went to the castle to tell the other brothers about it, adding that if they did not renounce their faith, they would suffer the same fate. They answered that they were ready to die, to suffer whatever God laid upon them.

When they had been about fourteen weeks in prison at

Taken from Burghausen back to Ried.

---

[1]A song about Leonhard Summerauer and the three other martyrs (Rauffer, Bruckmaier, and Aichner), is in *LdHBr*, 763–768; see also Wolkan, *Lieder*, 235. About his imprisonment and death, see *Martyrs Mirror*, 1060; *ME*, IV, 656; Beck, 291–292.

1585

Burghausen and could neither be won over nor intimidated, they were each put in a cart and taken back to Ried on the Wednesday before St. Lawrence's Day. At four o'clock in the morning the following Tuesday, August 13, they were brought out of prison and taken to the town hall. There the prince's command stating what was to be done with them was read out. Accordingly, the judge commanded the executioner to take these persons in charge, lead them out to the usual place of execution, and there turn life into death with the sword. Afterward, he was to burn their bodies. "Not life into death, but death into life eternal!" responded brother Wolf.

The three brothers taken to place of execution.

Not life into death, but death into life eternal.

Then Georg and Wolf said, "Since we must die in any case, we want to die for the sake of divine truth alone. We have done no one any evil or injustice. Let any man whom we have harmed come forward! Though we will lose our lives for the sake of our faith and the Word of God, we shall find them again in eternity, as the Holy Gospel promises." They told the authorities that from now on they had better beware, for their innocent blood would cry out against those who were guilty of shedding it. But as it was God's leading, they were willing and ready to die, for the Lord Jesus Christ himself suffered death at the hands of this world.

"Come forward, any man we harmed or treated unjustly!"

Brother Wolf spoke, "Now, dear Georg, we take leave of each other, and of you too, dear Hans. Let us be joyful, for the Lord is with us." Then with deep feeling brother Hans took leave of Wolf and Georg. Brother Georg asked the executioner to lead him to Wolf so that they could clasp hands and take leave of each other, which the executioner was glad to do. The brothers were very joyful. Meanwhile the assistant priest approached, urging brother Wolf to recant. Instead, Wolf gave him the short reply that the priest was the one who should renounce his fornication and his ungodly life. Wolf had had enough of him; so the priest left.

Wolf said, "Be joyful, the Lord is with us."

He could no longer bear the priest.

They began a resounding song in the marketplace. Brother Wolf praised and thanked God that the time had come for them to be tested. He added, "Would to God that there were one trustworthy man in this crowd who could travel to our country [Moravia] and report to our brothers about us! How thankful I would be to God if he would send someone to let them know, personally or in writing, what it is that fills my heart with joy." His wish was later granted, for which we thank God.

Brothers began to sing.

1585

Wolf said, "My heart is not heavy," and laughed.

Wolf spoke once more to the executioner: "Christoph, sir, I want to be manly and suffer courageously. My heart is not the least bit heavy, not the very least," and he laughed. "If my brothers and my wife and children knew of this, they would rejoice for our sake, even though they might weep and mourn in the flesh. I pray that God will send someone to our community to convey our heartfelt farewell to all brothers and sisters, to our wives and children, and to all those we know." As he said this, brother Wolf walked to the place of execution. Georg and Hans were already inside the enclosure. He joined them, and all three said a final, heartfelt farewell to each other, praying together in the enclosure. After the prayer they were beheaded, first Georg, then Hans, and lastly Wolf. Their bodies were then put on the pyre and burned.

The 3 took leave of each other inside the barrier and said a prayer.

Wolf, Georg, and Hans beheaded.

When the executioner had finished, he said, "These people would not renounce their faith or have anything to do with a priest. Their faith was stronger than mine or anybody else's. I would rather have executed thirty or forty robbers. May God have mercy."

These dear brothers witnessed to the faith in Christ with their blood. For this God gave them the strength and power, praise be to him in all eternity.[1]

On May 15 of this same year brother Wastel Anfang, a servant of the Word, was captured in Switzerland not far from Bern together with two brothers, Heinrich and Uhl.[2] They were taken to the city of Bern, where the ministers questioned Wastel three times in the first two weeks and asked why he had entered their country. Wastel explained that it was for the sake of divine truth. They talked with him about the Lord's Prayer, government, and infant baptism. God stood by him as he answered, and so they did not care to continue the discussion, even though they had other points in mind.

Wastel Anfang and 2 brothers captured at Bern in Switzerland.

---

[1]Bruckmaier's songs are in *LdHBr*, 768–785, among them the well-known "Väterlied," with a few stanzas about each shepherd or Vorsteher of the Hutterian Church. Bruckmaier was the author of verses 1–76, up to 1583; it is not known who wrote verses 77–105, up to 1639; see also Wolkan, *Lieder*, 237–238.

About Bruckmaier and the other two brothers executed with him, see *Martyrs Mirror*, 1060–1061; Beck, 293–294; *ME*, I, 445.

[2]Beck, 295, has "Wastl Schmidt, Heinrich Schweitzer, a vinedresser, and Uhl Schuster."

1585

2 brothers racked.

Four weeks later they questioned the brothers under torture to find out where they had found lodging. The two other brothers were racked, but they bravely endured all the torture, and no answers could be wrung from them. Brother Wastel was bound and hung on the rope but not pulled up, because he had only just entered the country and did not know anybody. They realized that questioning and torturing him would be in vain. So they unbound him, demanding that he promise to leave their country and not preach there. Such a promise, however, he was neither able nor willing to make, and he told them why.

After the brothers had been in prison for twenty weeks, a plan was made to execute them, since most of the councillors were in favor of the death sentence. The brothers were completely prepared for this and thought there was no other way, since they had been given the hangman's meal [their last meal on earth]. But in the meantime those citizens who had a voice in the case had assembled to make a final decision. The majority were in favor of letting the brothers live, and that settled it. The two brothers Heinrich and Uhl were left tied to the whipping post for a time and then, after having their ears branded, were driven out of the town with rods and thus released. None of this was done to Wastel, the servant of the Word, who was returned to the prison instead, where he stayed until the other two were dealt with. Then he, too, was set free. All three returned to the church in peace and joy and with good consciences, praising God who had made them worthy to suffer for the sake of their faith and his name.

2 brothers branded through the ears and beaten with rods.

The 3 brothers released.

Severe famine.

In 1585 there was a great scarcity of food, for the grain crop had failed in this country (Moravia). In several communities where they had sown up to eight bushels of grain, they gathered only eight pecks at threshing time, or scarcely six pecks from six bushels sown.[1] On many fields that had been sown, neither sickle nor scythe was swung. There was not even old grain to be had in the country; they had to buy grain and cart it all the way from Austria, a bushel costing from twenty-six to thirty gulden. The drought was so severe that the water dried up. In many places the livestock died of

[1] A peck (*Metze*) could be from 1/30 to 1/6 of a bushel (*Muth*), depending on the area.

thirst and lack of pasture, fodder, and straw. In our communities in Hungary they took the straw out of mattresses and used it for the cattle. Many people stripped the thatch from their roofs and cut up the straw to keep their cattle alive through the drought. *1585*

This famine hit the church hard and was a time of testing, because our grain crop failed completely and everything had to be bought for cash. But God sustained us and brought us through. In the following year, 1586, there was a plentiful grain harvest. Praise be to God!

1586

On February 3, 1586, brother Balthasar Maierhof [the younger], a servant of the Word, fell asleep in the Lord at Altenmarkt. He had been in the church a long time, since his youth. He passed away after commending all the faithful to God's grace and giving thanks again and again for all they had done for him.

Balthasar Maierhof passed away.

On March 17 brother Veit Uhrmacher, a servant of the Word, fell asleep in the Lord at Schadowitz.

Veit Uhrmacher passed away.

On the Friday after Whitsun, May 30, brother Christian Gasteiger or Schmidt (a smith), was imprisoned at Ingolstadt in Bavaria. That very Sunday, two Jesuits and the city priest arrived to question him on his faith, but they soon stopped as the answers were not to their liking.

Christian Gasteiger captured at Ingolstadt.

Nine days later the two Jesuits came again to talk with him and started by abusing the [Hutterian] church at great length. Christian reproved them. They talked for more than an hour, and then the two left in anger. One of the Jesuits said they would block all the roads in order to catch us. The brother replied, "I always knew you were the ones who betrayed us."

Jesuits put him to the test.

Three weeks later two more Jesuits arrived to indoctrinate him, but as he would not sing to their tune, they left.

After another two days the parish priest came with a doctor of theology. They spoke about infant baptism and said that a child was damned if not baptized. Brother Christian replied that infants were not damned, and he referred them to Scripture. At this they called him a heretic and declared that an infant has a demon in him and therefore must be baptized. He asked, "How does the demon get into the child?"

They said a child is damned if not baptized.

1586

The chief justice came to brother Christian.

They told him, "It comes from the mother." But he contradicted them.

The following day the chief justice and his cohorts arrived, and they said, "You know very well why you are in prison. You have been here quite a time now, and the priests have visited you, but it has profited you little. I had to report about you to the court, and the order came that I should talk to you. Unless you return to the faith of your parents, you will be burned at the stake. Then we shall see whether you are an honor to God."

The brother replied, "I am already prepared to die at any time. I trust that God in heaven will keep me faithful until my end. I will not waver from the truth. May God's will be done always."

Again two Jesuits came.

The next day two more Jesuits came to dispute with him, and they claimed that his faith was wrong. Again they spoke of infant baptism and insisted that a child must be baptized, otherwise it would be damned. They talked for about three hours, and Christian answered when necessary, pointing out their false teaching; then they withdrew.

He would hold to the truth though it cost his life.

He wrote to us from prison in Ingolstadt that he had been imprisoned for the sake of divine truth and would not waver from it, even though it cost him his life. We should have full confidence in him, he would fight valiantly for the eternal crown. He felt clearly that God was standing faithfully by him in his bonds, for which he gave thanks to God day and night, asking that he be kept devout and faithful until death. At the end he sent greetings in Christ to us all.

Taken from Ingolstadt to Munich.

On August 25, when he had been in prison in Ingolstadt for more than twelve weeks and all the priests and Jesuits there were at their wits' end because they had achieved nothing, he was chained to a cart and taken from Ingolstadt to Munich. After he had been in prison in Munich for over two weeks, he was to be sentenced on September 13. Since the prince was away and the chief justice had just died, the assistant justice was to pronounce the sentence, but he refused, saying it was not part of his office. The mayor and others judging the case were also unwilling to give their consent, but the Jesuits insisted and forced it through. So they had their way.

Christian Gasteiger sentenced to be executed.

Christian was brought to the steps in front of the town hall and there sentenced to die by the sword. When led to his death,

1586

he was so joyful and unafraid and spoke so powerfully that the Jesuits were beside themselves. They spat in his face, and the executioner himself wiped it for him. The Jesuits gave him no peace, even holding their idolatrous crucifix in front of him, but he spat on it and said they should lock it up. The people were outraged that the Jesuits spat in his face.

Jesuits spat in his face.

When he reached the place of execution, he was so full of confidence in God that he leaped for joy, for he saw that the crown he was fighting to win was now very near. The executioner stood before him with naked sword, joining the Jesuits in their efforts to make him recant. But brother Christian spoke resolutely to the executioner, saying that he should fulfill his duty toward him. He told the Jesuits to go, for even if there were thousands of them or even tens of thousands, they would not win him over. Then he put his head down and the executioner beheaded him. He remained steadfast and joyful to the end.[1]

He leaped for joy at the place of execution.

He was beheaded.

This same year, several hundred people from Switzerland joined the community.[2] Many had been forced to move because of the famine, but they wanted to accept the faith and change their lives. We took them in with this same hope and agreed to try it with them.

Many Swiss came to the church.

On December 30, 1586,[3] brother Georg Planer or Uhrmacher (a clockmaker), who had been chosen for the service of the Word but was still in a time of testing, fell asleep in the Lord at Pribitz.

Georg Planer passed away.

1587

In the year 1587, on February 21, brother Hans Schlegel,

Hans Schlegel passed away.

---

[1]Christian Gasteiger's martyrdom is commemorated in the song "Himmlischer Gott und Herre, lass dich's erbarmen schier" (Lord God in heaven, have pity on us), *LdHBr*, 763–768 (verses 34–44). See *ME*, II, 440; Wolkan, *Lieder*, 235; *Martyrs Mirror*, 1062; Beck, 296–298.

[2]Beck, 296, "1586 f.," reads in translation: "In this year 1586 many people from Switzerland came to the church community." Christoph Erhard, *Gründliche Historia*, 1589, 41v, notes the following about migrations around that time: "It is no small matter that according to reliable sources, . . . between Easter and St. Michael's Day [Sept. 29], 1587, 1600 persons from Germany and Tirol were brought to Moravia."

[3]Other codices give different dates for Planer's death: January 2, 1587, and February 2, 1587; see Beck, 298.

1587

a servant of the Word, fell asleep in the Lord at Moskowitz.[1]

5 brothers confirmed in the service of the Word.

On Oculi Sunday [third Sunday in Lent] of this year, five brothers were confirmed in the service of the Word at Neumühl by the elders with the laying on of hands. These were Wolf Hungermüller, Adam Neyffer, Daniel Hellrigel, Abel Ockershauser, and Hans Neumair.

3 brothers chosen for the service of the Word.

At the same time the following brothers were chosen for the service of the Word and appointed for a time of testing: Andreas Kleesattel, Peter Trier, and Jakob Kitz [or Hinnen].[2]

Hans Baldauf and Wandel Holba passed away.

On March 26 brother Hans Baldauf, a servant of the Word, fell asleep in the Lord at Schadowitz.

On May 11 brother Wandel Holba, a servant of the Word who knew both Czech and German, fell asleep in the Lord at Stiegnitz.

Michael Fischer captured in Bavaria.

About Whitsun 1587, brother Michael Fischer was taken prisoner for the sake of the faith at Ingolstadt in Bavaria. For twelve weeks he was chained in prison while monks, Jesuits, and others tried their utmost with him, but he would not listen to their false teaching and idolatry. On the contrary, he courageously persevered in the way of God's truth. In the end he was condemned to death. If he refused to recant, he was to be executed on Friday, August 7. But he would not waver from his faith, for he knew that a better and eternal life awaited him. So on that Friday, August 7, shortly after eight o'clock in the morning, he was taken out of prison and brought to the front of the town hall in Ingolstadt. Here the indictment was read out to him: Since he had held firmly to rebaptism (as they called it) for twenty years and had misled others and since, moreover, he now absolutely refused to yield, he must die. The imperial mandates commanded that this should not be tolerated but should be punished by death through fire or the sword. After this he was taken to the place of execution, to which he walked willingly and unafraid with a quick step. A

Indictment read to him.

---

[1]Moskowitz (Mackovice), village near Frischau (Břežany), approx. 12 miles east of Znaim (Znojmo). In 1587 Moskowitz was a branch of the community at Frischau, which had been established on the site of the devastated villages of Rohoteř and Bransudice through the kindness of the owner, Peter Certorejsky of Certorej; see above, p.488 n.4; Zeman, *Topography*, #87.

[2]These three brothers were, respectively, a joiner, a bookbinder, and a tanner. Beck, 298, names a fourth, Georg Lackhorn or Säckler, who was relieved of this service a few days later.

Jesuit priest and a monk went along, still trying to persuade him, but he paid no attention and asked them to leave—he did not need them.

1587

At the place of execution they told him he had to die, there was no other way, and he should prepare himself. They held out a pole bearing a crucifix with its idolatrous image and said he should look at it and see the one who died for us. Such was their folly. But Michael—who knew his Redeemer to be at God's right hand in heaven and had long been prepared to die for him and his Word—shook his head, laughed at their idolatry, and said to the executioner, "Take that thing away! It is worthless. I will hold to the truth and die for my faith." He stepped forward and knelt down fearlessly, as if he did not care. His undaunted courage completely unnerved the executioner, who almost despaired of being able to behead him. He could not do his work properly and in the end had to cut off the head as best he could. It got him into great trouble—just as they had escorted the brother out, so they took the executioner back to town, weapons in hand, and put him in prison. This was told us by a man who had been present and had seen and heard it all.

Idol of the crucifix held out to him.

Michael Fischer executed.

God gave this dear brother strength and power to remain steadfast to the end on the way of truth that leads to eternal life in Christ Jesus. To him be all praise and glory.[1]

On August 21[2] of this year, brother Michael Veldthaler, an old servant of the Word, fell asleep in the Lord at Tracht.

Michael Veldthaler passed away.

On October 25, five brothers were chosen for the service of the Word and appointed at Neumühl. These were Nikolasch Holba or Müller (a miller), Hans Eberle or Sailer (a ropemaker), Sebastian Dietrich, Lamprecht Jänko or Schuster (a cobbler), and Andreas Lehner.[3]

5 brothers chosen for the service of the Word.

1588

In the year 1588, on Oculi Sunday [third Sunday of Lent],

3 brothers confirmed in the service of the Word.

[1]There is a song about Michael Fischer's death in *LdHBr*, 785–786; see Wolkan, *Lieder*, 335. See also *Martyrs Mirror*, 1063; Beck, 299–300; *ME*, II, 333.

[2]Sources vary as to the date of Veldthaler's death: August 19, 20, or 21; see Beck, 300.

[3]Sebastian Dietrich, a barber-surgeon, became Vorsteher in 1611; see below, p.594. Andreas Lehner was a locksmith. See also Beck, 299.

1588

at Neumühl, three brothers were confirmed in the service of the Word by the elders with the laying on of hands: Nikolasch Holba, Andreas Kleesattel, and Hans Eberle.

Nikolasch Holba passed away.

On July 3 Nikolasch Holba, a servant of the Word, fell asleep in the Lord at Klein Niemtschitz.

Peter Saimer captured in Bavaria.

This same year brother Peter Saimer was captured at Freiburg, a market town in Bavaria. He had stayed for a night at an inn, and in the morning when he was about to continue on his way, he was met by the constable, who took him prisoner. He was taken to Burghausen and given a hearing. When it became obvious that he would remain steadfast, he was sent back to Freiburg. Three days later the warden sent for him from the prison and told him to recant. But the brother answered, "I am not going to recant. If I did, I would be renouncing my God, the Christian faith, and the Ten Commandments."

When sentenced to die, he shouted and leaped for joy.

When the death sentence was pronounced and the judge's staff had been broken above his head,[1] he gave a glad cry and leaped for joy. He praised God the Lord in heaven and said he had only one head, but even if he had two or three, he would rather offer them all than renounce his faith.

A great crowd was there at the execution. They wept bitterly, and many said it was a shame that he should die. But he told them they had no need to weep, for there was a whole people who would weep for him. As he was led to the block, he sang with joyful and confident heart. He did not want either the priest or the clerk of the court to accompany him. A distinguished man came up and urged him, "My good Peter, recant."

Sang on the way to his death.

He replied, "Be quiet. You know nothing about it."

Executioner beheaded him while he was praying.

Then he knelt and made his last prayer to God in heaven, and while he was kneeling in prayer, the executioner beheaded him. As the head fell to the ground, it turned in a remarkable way so that the face was upward, and the people were filled with wonder. Peter Saimer witnessed valiantly to the faith and divine truth with his blood. This took place on July 8, 1588.[2]

---

[1]It was the custom for the judge to break his staff or mace above the head of the accused and throw the pieces at his feet to signify the death sentence.

[2]Peter Saimer wrote the first eight verses of the song in *LdHBr*, 786–787, which was continued by an unknown writer; see also Wolkan, *Lieder*, 238. About Saimer's death, see *Martyrs Mirror*, 1069; *ME*, IV, 400; Beck, 301–302.

In this year we began the community at Velké Levàre in Hungary.[1]

1588
Community at Velké Levàre.

1589

On St. Gall's Day [Oct. 16], 1589, brother Valtin Hörl, an old and faithful servant of the Word, fell asleep in the Lord at Klein Niemtschitz.

Valtin Hörl passed away.

About this time Stoffel Schenck, from Rehag in the Bern area, Switzerland, became our brother. Formerly a servant of the Word among the Swiss Brethren, he joined our church community with his people.

Stoffel Schenck and his group joined the church.

This year we had to leave Boretitz, where we had been living for many years. The lady of the estate would not pay us for the work we had done in her vineyard and wanted to deduct the war taxes from our wages. In the end she ordered us to leave and took our house away from us.

Moved away from Boretitz.

These taxes (mentioned several times before), which we could not pay for reasons of conscience, had been remitted for a time by the Provincial Diet but this had lasted only six months, up to a certain date. After that our supplies were confiscated again. In some places wine was taken, three barrels from Austerlitz and two from Lettonitz, for example. This happened just at a time when wine prices had risen to forty talers a barrel, even up to fifty-five talers, higher than anyone in Moravia expected. In several places our oxen were taken, as happened on the Nikolsburg estate; in 1590 sixteen oxen, fattened over the winter, were taken from the four communities there. In other places we were robbed of hogs, cows, and

Stock confiscated in lieu of taxes.

---

[1]Velké Levàre (Gross-Schützen) in present-day Slovakia, town southeast of Lundenburg (Břeclav), near the Austrian border. On June 26, 1588, the owner of Velké Levàre, Lord Hans Bernhard von Lembach, issued a deed of conveyance, inviting the Hutterites to settle on his domain; see A. J. F. Zieglschmid, "An Unpublished 'Hausbrief' of Grimmelshausen's Hungarian Anabaptists," *Germanic Review*, XV (April 1940), 81–97.

The descendants of these Hutterites, who in the 18th century (like those from St. Johannes and Sabatisch) chose Catholicism rather than fleeing to Transylvania (1725–1763), are still living in homogeneous congregations. At Velké Levàre they numbered about 150 members (in 1945; Zieglschmid, *Chronik*, 552 n.2). Called *Habaner*, they now speak Czech, with only the older generation still speaking some German.

About Velké Levàre and the Hutterian settlements, see *ME*, IV, 804–805. Beck, 302.

1589

horses. We have had to bear with this robbery to this very day. Who knows when it will end![1]

1590

Blasi Harer passed away.

On March 1, 1590, brother Blasi Harer, a servant of the Word, fell asleep in the Lord at Alexowitz.

5 brothers confirmed in the service of the Word.

On Invocavit Sunday, March 11, 1590, five brothers were confirmed in the service of the Word at Neumühl by the elders with the laying on of hands. These were Jakob Hinnen [or Kitz], Peter Trier, Lamprecht Jänko, Sebastian Dietrich, and Andreas Lehner.

3 brothers chosen for the service of the Word.

On the same day three brothers, Kaspar Uhle, Seyfried Geiss, and Georg Acker,[2] were appointed to the service of the Word for a time of testing.

Consultation about paying a yearly contribution.

For conscience' sake we could not pay the usual taxes insofar as they were levied for war or frontier posts, so the authorities had confiscated livestock, wine, and other chattels instead. After this had gone on for some years, they themselves grew tired of it and of our protesting and complaining. Several lords who had asked us this question before asked now again that we on our part tell them what we could do that was not against our conscience. They said we would surely realize that since we enjoyed the benefits of the country and could practice our trades, they could not exempt us completely. If a large group such as ours were to pay nothing at all, that would place the burden on the Provincial Diet. We should think it over.

Since we had been asked many times to do something for the country that would not be against our conscience, we considered what to do, as we did not want to be a burden to the Provincial Diet. There were many more of us living in Moravia now, and we made much more of a difference to the country than in previous years when we were fewer in number. Now we had to buy large quantities of grain and wood, as well as other things. We knew this made a considerable demand

[1]Other sources report that "the little flock was ordered to move to Kobelitz" (Kobylí, approx. 7 miles east of Auspitz), and that a community was established there that same year, 1589. See Beck, 302; Zeman, *Topography*, #61.

[2]The three brothers were, respectively, a shoemaker, a cooper, and a bookbinder; Beck, 303.

on the Provincial Diet. Therefore the elders and brothers from all our communities met to consult whether we could not give something for the good of the country that did not go against our conscience. It was unanimously felt that it was only fair, as we benefited from the country, that we should also contribute something to the Provincial Diet, with the reservations, however, stated in the following letter to Lord Friedrich von Zerotin at Seelowitz, who had brought the matter forward on behalf of the Provincial Diet. *1590*

Letter about the annual contribution.

We wish His Lordship now and always everything good from the almighty God! His Lordship realizes our difficulties in regard to paying taxes, and other lords on whose land we live are troubled (like His Lordship himself) at having to take our horses, oxen, and other things instead, as has been happening for some time. They see this as lamentable, which it certainly is, and have requested us to find some other way to help the country that is not against our conscience. We considered this seriously, for we do not want to be a burden, but for the good of the country we will gladly do something that is not against our conscience.

Our greatest fear, however (and we beg His Lordship not to take it amiss), is that only the name but not the tax would be changed, so that we would be led into it before we could turn around. If we then discovered that it was used for war or for other purposes we oppose, this would distress us greatly. If it should come to this, we would prefer to have our goods and chattels taken as hitherto rather than in any way support deeds of vengeance and so stain our conscience. We say this in the fear of God, for we pay no taxes for vengeance, nor do we give anything as substitute for such taxes.

We can only give what would benefit the country in some other way, as we realize that we enjoy the benefits of the country and are allowed to buy the grain we need wherever it is available. We cannot buy enough in the marketplaces because the people would protest. Further, we would be glad if the lords would graciously allow us to continue to brew beer for our own use, as before. In order not to encumber the country, we would like to

1590
Letter about the annual contribution.

support ourselves by our own trades and live off the land.

We would be willing to pay an annual sum on each house where we have a communal kitchen, as long as we can be assured that the money will be used profitably for the country and for people in need. God knows that we would do whatever we can to avoid being a burden to anyone. Yet we would ask that the sum not be higher than we can afford to pay and that it not be increased, because we have among us many sick, weak, and disabled people to care for.

We must expect times of distress, not knowing what God may allow to come upon us as a test of our faith. As we may have to move out of our houses or be driven from them into destitution, we cannot bind ourselves to make these payments. But since we are so often reproached with enjoying the benefits of the country without being willing to do anything for it, we thought it necessary to write our answer to His Lordship in all good faith. We are not opposed to doing our part if it can be done in God's name and without damage to our conscience. We wish to offer our help in whatever serves a good cause, to the best of our ability and as long as God grants it.

It is our humble request that His Lordship will not be displeased at our simple statement but will present our case to the Diet on our behalf. Plead with them on our behalf to have patience with us, for we have been driven into this land as strangers for the sake of our faith. We want to be patient, remaining hopeful and praying without ceasing that God will grant peace to our governing authorities and to Moravia, so that we, in their peace, may also experience peace. May God grant it. With this we wish His Lordship happiness and well-being.

Dated Neumühl, May 14, 1590.

From the elders of the Church
that men call Hutterian

Yearly sum imposed by the lords.

As a result, the Provincial Diet imposed a yearly tax of twelve gulden on each of our houses with a communal kitchen. Half the sum, six gulden, was to be paid on Bartholomew's Day [Aug. 24], and the other half on St. Nicholas' Day [Dec. 6], beginning in the year 1590.

Later, in 1593, the Provincial Diet demanded an extra eight gulden, making twenty gulden for each house with a communal kitchen.

1590
Yearly sum increased.

On August 1, 1590, brother Balthasar Hasenfelder, a servant of the Word, fell asleep in the Lord at Moskowitz.

Balthasar Hasenfelder passed away.

1591

On January 18, 1591, Hynek Šlach of Hřivice evicted us from his property, Schenkhof,[1] even though he had let us have his farm for a fixed annual rent, which we had always paid on time. This happened before our contract year expired, because the contract was destroyed through negligence on the part of the farm manager. But the responsibility really lay with Šlach for carelessly giving such an important document to a man who could not read and who understood nothing of what it was all about. So he made us pay for one person's stupidity by evicting us from the farm, though we were blameless and could do nothing about it. Our people could not even take clothing or bedding with them; these had been stolen from us for the most part. All the horses, cows, sheep, and other stock we had reared during the previous six years were taken. And not only that: Šlach even took the one-third share of livestock and grain that our people had earned as hard-won wages on the lord marshal's two farms. Household goods, kitchen equipment, wagons, harness—everything that had belonged to us, including the fields we had sown—were taken. Not yet content, he took horses and wagons and twenty beehives from the brothers at Kreutz. We estimated that the losses we suffered came to over 5000 gulden. We had to bear with this and leave it in God's hands.

Driven from Schenkhof and robbed.

On February 15, brother Paul Iltzmüller, a servant of the Word, fell asleep in the Lord at Moskowitz.

Paul Iltzmüller passed away.

On Friday in the first week of Lent, March 8 of this year, brother Leonhard Boltzinger, a clockmaker by trade, was executed for his faith in Christ. This took place at Julbach, a market town not far from Braunau in Bavaria, after twenty-three weeks of imprisonment. He had been captured at Julbach

Leonhard Boltzinger captured in Bavaria.

[1]Schenkhof, an estate farm near Tscheitsch (Čejč), northwest of Göding (Hodonín); see Beck, 304; Zeman, *Topography*, #138, #160.

1591

on the Tuesday before Michaelmas [Sept.29] of the previous year, then he was taken to the town of Braunau and put in a dark dungeon. In an effort to make him deny his faith, he was tortured by being racked, the first time without weights, the second time with a stone hung on him. Yet he always answered the same: he would not recant.

Finally he was taken from Braunau back to Julbach, where he had been captured, and that same Friday he was led out to his death. Crossing the bridge over the Inn River, he began to sing a cheerful song and went thus all the way to the place of execution. Although he was still harassed and pressed to recant, he said quite simply that he would not. He knew he was grounded in the true faith, and if he had ten heads, one on top of the other, they would all have to be cut off before he would renounce his faith.

He was executed.

The executioner then beheaded him and afterward burned him. Brother Leonhard remained steadfast in the faith, holding to God's love until his end and letting nothing sever him from it. Praise be to God who gave him the strength and the courage.[1]

Georg Maier passed away.

On March 9 of this same year, brother Georg Maier, a servant for temporal affairs, fell asleep in the Lord at Altenmarkt.

6 brothers chosen for the service of the Word.

On Oculi Sunday [third Sunday in Lent], six brothers were chosen for the service of the Word and appointed for a time of testing at Neumühl. These were Franz Moritz, Hans Schmied, Leonhard Schmidt, Stoffel Rath, Konrad Glasser, and Stoffel Schenck.[2]

On May 7 our two communities had to move from

---

[1]A song about Leonhard Boltzinger's death, with an acrostic of his name, is in *LdHBr*, 788–790; see Wolkan, *Lieder*, 235–236. See also *ME*, I, 385; *Martyrs Mirror*, 1080; Beck, 304–305.

[2]The first five of these brothers were, respectively, a tanner, a vinedresser, a carpenter, a shoemaker, and a linen weaver. The sixth, Stoffel Schenck, was a shoemaker and former servant of the Word among the Swiss Brethren; see above, p.511. Beck, 305.

Hans Schmied from Rommelshausen, Württemberg, became an Anabaptist in 1581, joined the Hutterites in Moravia, and was sent on mission to his native country in 1590. There he was arrested and held in prison from mid-August to December 4 of the same year. After his release he wrote a long account of his experiences to the church community in Moravia; see Bossert, *Quellen*, 652–665; English translation in Klaassen & Friesen, *Sixteenth Century Anabaptism*, 175–186. He died in Moravia in 1602 (p.555 below). *ME*, IV, 466; Friedmann, *Schriften*, 127; Beck, 303.

Voitelsbrunn and Pergen, where we had been living for more than thirty years. Lord Sigismund von Dietrichstein had inherited these two villages as well as others upon the death of his father. He ordered us to leave his estates, purely because of our faith, and we were obliged to go, entrusting our cause to God. He gave us eighteen weeks to move out. We were allowed to sell what we could of the property that did not belong to the buildings, though not without loss.

1591
Had to move out of Voitelsbrunn and Pergen.

We had to leave the houses and fields of grain without any recompense.

We also had to move away from the farm at Pulgram, where we had served the lords of Nikolsburg for more than thirty years, but we were allowed to take our belongings.

That same year there was a famine, especially in Bohemia, and as a great deal of grain was exported from Moravia, there was a shortage in this country too. In the week before John's Day [May 6], wheat flour was sold for two talers and four groschen at Auspitz, and rye for two talers. But God had thought of his people and had given their elders such prudence that their bread supply was never low enough to cause actual want.

Famine.

As there was a good stand of grain in the fields, after reaping time the situation improved.

This year we moved back to Sabatisch in Hungary and also to Wostitz, which we had been forced to leave ten years earlier. Now the landowners begged us to return.[1]

Moved back to Sabatisch and Wostitz.

On August 5 of this year, brother Georg Wenger, a tailor, was executed for his faith at St. Lorenzen in the Puster Valley in the county of Tirol. He had been in prison for more than a year. He was captured on St. James's Eve [July 24], 1590, and taken to the common jail in the courthouse in St. Lorenzen. The next day he was summoned by the lawyer, the warden, the clerk, and a priest. They wanted him to tell them who had been traveling with him and where they had been given shelter. He replied, "God forbid that I commit such evil. We do not betray our enemies, who have wronged us. Am I to betray those who have done us good, or even my dear brothers? With God's help, no man will get that out of me, for that is against love to my neighbor."

Georg Wenger captured at St. Lorenzen.

---

[1]Other sources add: "The same happened at Dannowitz"; see Beck, 306; Zeman, *Topography*, #30c.

1591

Then they pressed him to recant and ordered thumbscrews to be brought. The warden said, "If kindness will not move you, here is the instrument."

Georg answered, "And here am I. God gave me healthy limbs, and to him I will sacrifice them. If I cannot escape with a good conscience, neither will I leave with a defiled heart."

Taken to Michelsburg Castle.

After he had been kept a month in St. Lorenzen and cross-examined three times by the magistrates, he was taken to Michelsburg Castle to be tortured. Since he would not satisfy their evil demands (against God, against his conscience, and against love to his neighbor), they racked him twice. The second time they hung on him the heaviest stone they had and racked him so cruelly that the mark of the rope on his hands could still be seen after thirteen weeks.

Taken to Brixen.

Scorpions crawled near his head.

After two weeks in Michelsburg Castle, on September 15, he was transferred to a dungeon at Brixen and chained to a wall that was full of vermin. The scorpions crawled up the wall by his bed and filled him with such horror that he had to cover his head. In the nine weeks of his imprisonment at Brixen the death sentence was twice pronounced on him, and he was urged to recant. He answered, "It was neither the good life nor curiosity that drew me to this people, but among them I changed my own life and have seen improvement in the lives of others who previously would not be changed by anyone. So I see in them a work of God, not a sect. I will hold to the vow I made to the Lord in the covenant of baptism, so that my soul may be saved." The priests at Brixen pestered him countless times in the prison and also summoned him for hearings—the curate four times, the provost of the cathedral twice, the chaplain more than ten times, as well as monks, priests, noblemen, and others. They all wanted to lead him back, as they said, to the true church. He told them that he had never left the faith and teaching of the true church of Christ; rather, through God's grace it had been shown to him and he would hold to it.

Priests pestered him at Brixen.

Taken back to St. Lorenzen.

After ten weeks in Brixen he was brought back to St. Lorenzen to be executed before Christmas, but this was prevented. After nearly four weeks at St. Lorenzen he was taken back to the Michelsburg Castle, still before Christmas. His execution was then planned for March 1, but as the bishop of Brixen died four days before, it did not take place. So he remained a prisoner in the castle until August 5, when (as recorded above) he was brought back to the courthouse at St. Lorenzen. There the priests brought him to trial and spent two hours trying to make him recant, but they could not. Consequently, he was sentenced to death according to the emperor's mandate. His indictment was read out, giving the reasons for which they claimed he ought to die, namely, that he had left the Roman Catholic Church, submitted to baptism a second time, and then tried to bring other people to this so-called heretical sect. Brother Georg told them it was not a heretical sect, as they called it, but the divine truth and the right way to God's kingdom. They led him to the place of execution, where the parish priest of St. Lorenzen still made a last, desperate attempt, with friendly words, to make him recant. The priest said he would provide for him for the rest of his life and be his sponsor at the last judgment if what he did was wrong. But Georg said, "Supposing I did accept you as my sponsor for the last judgment, what would happen if the devil carried off the sponsor first? Where would I find another sponsor?" The priest was put to shame and left him alone.

1591

Priests did their utmost.

The priest offered to sponsor him at the last judgment.

There were many people there, and some wept, but Georg said they should not weep for him but for themselves. As he was led out, his hands were freed sufficiently for him to lift them up to praise God, who had given him grace and strength until now. He asked God to protect him in his last half hour from false prophets and false spirits. Then he commended his spirit into the hands of God. He was beheaded for the sake of God's word, for the faith and the divine truth.[1]

Georg Wenger executed at St. Lorenzen.

On June 19 Jakob Platzer, a locksmith, was captured at Sillian in the Puster Valley, Tirol.[2] He remained in fetters in

Jakob Platzer captured at Sillian.

[1]Georg Wenger's letters to Stoffel Küenhuber, to Klaus Braidl, and to his wife Anna, as well as his farewell song, are part of an unnumbered codex in the library of the Evangelische Kirchengemeinde A.C., Bratislava, fol. 516–520; see also Friedmann, *Schriften*, 130. A song about his death and that of Jacob Platzer (see below) is in *LdHBr*, 790–792; Wenger's song "to my wedded sister, Änndl," is on p.792; Wolkan, *Lieder*, 236. See also *ME*, IV, 917; *Martyrs Mirror*, 1080–1081; Beck, 306–308.

[2]Sillian, near the Italian border on the Drau River. Jakob Platzer was born at Prad on the Stilfser Joch, 8 miles west of Schlanders. See *Martyrs Mirror*, 1082; *ME*, IV, 189; Beck, 308–310.

1591

the prison for eight weeks, until August 7. His adversaries could not alter his convictions; he held to them resolutely as given him by God and refused to deviate from the truth. Therefore he was sentenced to die by the sword, according to imperial mandate. He went to the place of execution with an inner peace, unperturbed that he was about to die for his faith.

He was beheaded.

He made his prayer to God, and the executioner beheaded him and then buried him. Thus he gave an upright witness to the divine truth. Praise be to God, who granted him the needed grace and strength.

Leonhard Reuss passed away.

On Wednesday, November 20, brother Leonhard Reuss, a servant of the Word, fell asleep in the Lord at Moskowitz.[1]

Gall Perger passed away.

On September 18 brother Gall Perger, an old servant for temporal affairs, fell asleep in the Lord at Neumühl.

[1]This is the last entry in Hauptrecht Zapff's handwriting, in the "1581" codex. The name of the next writer, who continued the chronicle to the end of 1592, is not known.

1592–1618: Renewed Persecution

1592

On May 12 in the year 1592, brother Thoman Haan was captured and put in prison at Freiburg in Bavaria for the sake of his faith. He was cruelly racked and questioned under torture to make him give the information they wanted and recant. They left him hanging on the rack from eight o'clock until eleven.

Thoman Haan captured at Freiburg in Bavaria.

His answer was, "You have power over my body, so do what you will to it. You cannot take my soul. You will not get from me what you want to know. I will betray no one. Even if you tear one vein after another from my body and cut off a strip of my skin every day, I will not recant or waver from the divine truth."

They reviled him and called him a seducer who had led many people to this sect of rebaptizers. But he told them it was true Christian baptism and not rebaptism; if he could convert the whole world by dying three times over, he would gladly do so (if only that were possible).

After he had been in prison for six weeks and showed no sign of recanting, he was brought out on Thursday, June 18, and the judge's staff was broken over his head. At this he turned to the people and cried three times in a loud voice, "Praise and thanks be to God that this moment has come at last," for he had waited a long time.

Led to the place of execution.

The executioner bound him and intended to put him in a wagon, but Thoman said he wished to walk to his death just as Christ had walked to his, and he began to sing. The constable told him to be quiet, but the executioner said, "Let him sing."

He began to sing.

As he was led out, a priest and others came up to him. The priest asked if he was willing to be corrected or if he thought only he and his fellow believers were righteous and all others

1592

were damned. Brother Thoman answered, "We strive to obey God and to avoid sin. We tolerate no one who lives in sin—we do not allow him to remain with us. We do not condemn anyone, but every sinner stands condemned by his evil deeds."

"We, too, punish sin," the priest replied.

Brother Thoman responded, "How can you punish sin? The more you punish, the worse people become. If the shepherd isn't good, how can the sheep be? You are false prophets." Then he said to the priest, "Out of my sight, you false prophet!"

Then the priest started praising their mass. He said that the Catholics have the benefit of the real body and blood of Christ and we have none of it. Thoman answered, "You sell your mass for money, just like Judas when he betrayed and sold Christ. But we eat and drink the Lord's Supper in remembrance of him, as he commanded." Then he asked the priest where he got that from, about the mass.

They sell their mass as Judas sold Christ.

The priest became silent, for he did not know. But then he said, "It is written in the Bible."

Brother Thoman asked, "Where?"

The priest said, "Paul wrote about it in the fifteenth chapter."

"Not so!" the brother answered. "Go away! You are a false prophet."

The priest did not know where Scripture speaks of the mass.

When Thoman entered the enclosure, the executioner asked him if he wished to pray but was told, "I have finished my prayer, so go ahead." He chose a spot and knelt down. The executioner drew his sword and begged him three times for God's sake to recant and then he would let him go, for he did not wish to execute him. The brother answered that he would not recant. "Get on, get on! It has to be."

Executioner again asked him to recant.

So Thoman was beheaded and gave up his spirit in peace. Then the executioner placed the body on the woodpile, pushed the hands into the pile, and lit the fire. After the body had been burning for a time, the head moved close to the body and the hands raised themselves up. Although a strong wind was blowing that day, the smoke rose straight up to heaven, as eyewitnesses have told us. Thus brother Thoman Haan testified valiantly with his blood to the divine truth at Freiburg in Bavaria.[1]

He was beheaded.

[1]Two songs about Haan's death are in *LdHBr*, 792–798. The second song, with the acrostic "Thoman Haan Mateus Mair," also relates the death of Matthias Mair (see below); see Wolkan, *Lieder*, 236. See also *ME*, II, 614; *Martyrs Mirror*, 1089; Beck, 315–316.

In this same year on July 1, brother Michael Hasel, a weaver, passed away in prison at Hohenwittlingen in Württemberg. Because of his faith in Christ he had been in prison for over four years. He had remained firm, faithful, and confident in the Lord and suffered great misery during his imprisonment. He was resolved (as he wrote to us) never to turn from the divine truth even if he had to stay in prison to the end of his life. And God bore him witness—glory be to God!

1592
Michael Hasel died in prison in Württemberg.

Even unbelievers had to give brother Michael a good testimony. The warden in the castle said he had been a devout man, and if this brother did not get to heaven, he himself would not even dare to knock at the gates. He would rejoice in advance if he knew he would end his life like Michael.[1]

On Mary Magdalene Day [July 22], brother Matthias Mair was taken prisoner at Würenlos near Baden in Switzerland. He was captured because a priest, coming from church, noticed him. At once he told his cook to follow Matthias out of the village and get into conversation with him. She was to pretend that she was eager to go [to Moravia] and that others were coming to talk with him too. She kept him talking until the priest had time to send peasants after him, who seized him and took him to Baden. Six days later, on July 27, the ungodly band of priests brought about his death because he refused to renounce his faith as they had wanted. But they kept quiet about their interrogations and his answers.

Matthias Mair captured in Switzerland.

As he was led to his death, his brothers-in-law and several other relatives who had made a petition for him and offered money were standing nearby. Their request had not been granted, and they had not even been allowed to speak with him alone.

He was led out to his death.

On the way to his execution, he asked the crowd where his

---

[1]A very small, beautifully handwritten book with the initials M.W. (Michael Hasel was also called Weber, a weaver) and date 1582 embossed in the leather binding, was found among his personal effects after his death. Possibly written by himself, it contains writings by Peter Walpot and Hieronymus Käls, as well as numerous songs, collected in this volume as a source of inner strengthening. Such collections, small enough to be tucked in the leg of one's boot, were frequently made for brothers sent out on mission journeys. The "Michael Hasel Book" is now in the State Library at Wolfenbüttel, Germany, Codex 3844; see Friedmann, *Schriften*, 63–64 for a detailed description.

Two songs by Michael Hasel are in *LdHBr*, 798–802; see Wolkan, *Lieder*, 238–239. About his death, see *ME*, II, 675; *Martyrs Mirror*, 1088–1089; Beck, 316.

1592

relatives were, and when they came to him, he told them to ask his brothers and sisters, who were a devout people, to care for his wife and child. He said this very loudly in the middle of the crowd.

Encouraged not to give in.

One of his relatives in the crowd encouraged him not to waver, but to be courageous, for he would soon overcome. At these words the relative received a blow from someone behind who shouted, "This man is a heretic too! He should be treated just like the other." The man to whom it happened told us this himself.

Executioner drew him out of the water four times to ask him to recant.

The executioner pushed brother Matthias into the water and pulled him out three or four times to ask him if he would recant. He answered no for as long as he could speak. He was drowned on July 27, only six days after his arrest. Through God's power and might he remained steadfast in faith until his death.

There was much talk about his death among high- and lowborn alike. They said it was murder, and they cried out for vengeance on the treacherous, Judas-like priest and on the town of Baden, for brother Matthias was known to be a truly God-fearing man. This was why God had given him fortitude to endure to the end.[1]

Hans Franck passed away.

On November 3 brother Hans Franck, a servant for temporal affairs, fell asleep in the Lord at Kostel.

1593[2]

Convent bought.

At Martinmas [Nov.11] in the year 1593 we bought the convent building at Göding.

4 brothers confirmed in the service of the Word.

In the same year on March 21, four brothers were confirmed in the service of the Word at Neumühl. They were Seyfried Geiss, Georg Acker, Kaspar Uhle, and Franz Moritz.

24 brothers chosen for the service for temporal affairs.

On the same day the following twenty-four brothers were appointed and given to the church as servants for temporal

---

[1]A song about Matthias Mair's death is in *LdHBr*, 797–798 (stanzas 12–20). Würenlos, town just southeast of Baden. He was probably drowned in the Limmat River (which flows through Baden in Switzerland, a town northwest of Zurich). See *ME*, III, 442; *Martyrs Mirror*, 1089–1090; Beck, 317–318.

[2]The grammatical peculiarities of the German text beginning with the year 1593 seem to indicate that at this point a new writer continued the chronicle to the end of the year 1613.

affairs: Martin Kirsch, Abraham Laub, Georg Zobel, Peter Hasel, Hansel Hoffman, Michael Albrecht, Michael Oberacker, Marx Ehle, Thoman Pruckner, Johannes Haan, Hans Dorn, Henoch Westfal, Jakob Käpel, Jakob Märkel, Friedrich Samsun, Wolf Steudtel, Martin Hederich, Wilhelm Moldt, Bärtel Hentaler, Nickel Stain, Bastel Vorher, Georg Lackhorn, Hansel Adamer, and Hans Pommersummer. *1593*

On April 4 brother Hans Lückel, a greatly respected servant for temporal affairs, fell asleep in the Lord at Neumühl. Hans Lückel passed away.

On May 6 brother Wenisch Keller,[1] servant of the Word, fell asleep in the Lord at Velké Levåre in Hungary. Wenisch Keller passed away.

On May 17 brother Thomas Häring, an old servant of the Word, fell asleep in the Lord at Altenmarkt. He had been a brother in the church for fifty-three years. Thomas Häring passed away.

On May 23 brother Abel Ockershauser, a servant of God's Word, fell asleep in the Lord at Austerlitz. Abel Ockershauser passed away.

On September 21 brother Matthias Binder, an old servant of the Word, fell asleep in the Lord at Altenmarkt. Matthias Binder passed away.

That same year Lord Stanislaus Rakowsky at Piskowitz sent the judge and his men to give notice to our millers (who had worked faithfully for him for some time), and particularly to the head miller, that he, Lord Stanislaus, had hired a new miller. Our brothers were asked to leave the mill. The head miller handed over all that belonged to the mill and gave an account of everything to the judge and his men. In return they gave him the freedom to remove without interference anything that belonged to him. Millers dismissed at Piskowitz.

As the miller was loading the wagons with the intention of taking his belongings by daylight, the mistress came and forbade him to take any more. But twelve brothers from Teikowitz went to the mill without consulting anyone and without the knowledge of the elders took everything that was ours and drove away. They were brought to account and admonished by the brotherhood, and some were excluded for daring to act independently and causing the community a great deal of trouble and scandal. Mistress forbade them to take everything. Several brothers excluded.

The lord at Piskowitz had made an untruthful complaint to the emperor against the brothers and obtained an order for Klaus Braidl, to whom the entire church community was Klaus Braidl ordered to appear before the Diet at Brünn.

[1]A song by Keller is in *LdHBr*, 802; see also Wolkan, *Lieder*, 233.

1593

entrusted, and several other brothers to appear before the Diet at Brünn on March 11, 1594. Klaus Braidl was summoned to give an account to the lords although he had nothing to do with the mill affair, since it had taken place entirely without his knowledge.

However, Lord Hynek von Waldstein, the chamberlain, and the lords Friedrich von Zerotin at Seelowitz and Georg Christoph Teufel of Teikowitz[1] were each given a written copy of the brothers' defense. They could see that the brothers had been unjustly accused and took it upon themselves to give their opinion to Rakowsky. Lord Georg Christoph Teufel at Teikowitz in particular spoke on behalf of the brothers living on his land. In addition, the lords found it inappropriate that the brothers were summoned to the Diet. They said that if anyone had an accusation to bring against the brothers, according to custom he should turn to the lords under whom they were living. Upon this the brothers were sent home, and Lord Teufel pronounced their acquittal in the assembly room. So God helped us through once more.

Lord Teufel spoke on behalf of the brothers.

1594

On January 8, 1594, brother Jakob Hinnen or Kitz, a servant of the Word, fell asleep in the Lord at Pribitz.

Jakob Kitz, a servant, passed away.

At Neumühl, on March 9, the three brothers Stoffel Schenck, Konrad Glasser, and Leonhard Schmidt were confirmed in the service of the Word.

3 brothers confirmed as servants of the Word.

Brother Hauptrecht Zapff[2] was appointed and also confirmed as a servant of the Gospel.

Hauptrecht Zapff also confirmed.

On the same day also at Neumühl, four more brothers,[3] Martin Gotzman, Georg Haan, Rudolf Hirzel, and Joseph

4 brothers chosen for the service of the Word.

---

[1]This lord of Teikowitz (Tavíkovice), Georg Christoph Teufel, is mentioned in the travel diary (*Raisbuch*) of Hans Georg Ernstinger (Bibliothek des Literarischen Vereins Stuttgart, CXXXV, 113) in an entry for the year 1602: "Teikowitz includes a castle and village that belong to Lord Georg Christoph Teufel, as well as an Anabaptist community." See Zieglschmid, "Die ungarischen Wiedertäufer. . . ," note 59; Zeman, *Topography*, #153.

[2]Hauptrecht Zapff, one of the seven writers of this chronicle, copied Braitmichel's entire original manuscript (now considered lost) and continued the entries up to November 20, 1591 (p.520 above), under the eldership first of Hans Kräl, then of Klaus Braidl. See also above, p.492 n. For samples of Hauptrecht Zapff's handwriting, see plates at the back of this volume.

[3]The first three brothers were, respectively, a clothmaker, a barber-surgeon, and a saddler; see Beck, 319. About Hauser's mission to Prussia, see below, pp.561–563.

Hauser were chosen for the service of the Word and appointed for a time of testing. *1594*

Shortly afterward, Georg Haan was relieved of his service at his repeated request, because he suffered severely from some trouble with his head. Georg Haan relieved of the service.

On April 2, 1594, brother Matthias Geyersbühler, a servant for temporal affairs, fell asleep in the Lord at Klein Niemtschitz near Prahlitz. Matthias Geyersbühler passed away.

On April 24 the ninety-two-year-old brother and servant for temporal affairs, Andreas Gauper, fell asleep in the Lord at Protzka, Hungary. Andreas Gauper passed away.

On September 14 brother Martin Kirsch, a servant for temporal affairs, fell asleep in the Lord at Altenmarkt. Martin Kirsch passed away.

1595

On February 5, 1595, brother Matthaeus Porst, a servant of God's Word, fell asleep in the Lord at Watzenowitz. Matthaeus Porst passed away.

On March 30 brother Andreas Lehner, a servant of the Word, fell asleep in the Lord at Austerlitz. Andreas Lehner passed away.

On Laetare Sunday [fourth Sunday in Lent] at Neumühl, brother Valtin Miglitzer was chosen for the service of the Word and appointed for a time of testing. Valtin Miglitzer chosen.

That year the Diet at Brünn decided we should pay ten gulden in addition to the twenty which we had agreed to pay for each house with a kitchen. Also, whether our millers were employed in the lords' mills for wages or under contract, or whether they worked at our own mills on large or small streams, they had to pay one gulden for each mill wheel. Taxes increased.

Wherever we worked a mill for a third or quarter share, the tax was seven silver pennies for each mill wheel. We were unable to pay these mill taxes because they were imposed in wartime and we knew they would go toward the war.

The above-mentioned twenty gulden tax that we had agreed to pay on our houses, on the other hand, had been required for the benefit of the Provincial Diet in peacetime.

That same year we had to leave Welka where we had lived for many years.[1] Lord Arckhleb of Kunowitz, our Hungarian The landlord ordered us out of Welka.

[1]Welka (Velká nad Veličkou), east of Strassnitz (Strážnice). According to Beck, 320 n.2, the Hutterites settled there around 1560. Zeman, *Topography*, #170.

1595 landlord, ordered us to move, only because for various reasons we could not fulfill his request to send shoemakers to Welka. We had to obey, commending ourselves to God.

He confiscated all the building timbers and firewood we had there, about a hundred cartloads.

He took our buildings and some ninety-four morgen [roughly seventy acres], some already prepared and sown with winter grain and the rest with summer grain still standing in the fields. He appropriated everything, meadows, vineyards, and much more; and we had to bear the loss.

1593

Beginning of Turkish war.

Brother from Neumühl shot.

The elders bade us persevere in prayer as the only help.

In 1593, when the Turkish war[1] began in Croatia, many soldiers passed through the country, taking horses, oxen, and other things. In Neumühl a brother called Heinrich, a smith, was shot to death through the gate. That was the beginning of a time of great tribulation. Therefore the elders of the church exhorted us in this time of need to persevere in prayer more fervently than ever. They agreed that whenever the servants

[1]The following historical sketch may help to give a framework for this extended period, about which the chronicle repeats year after year, in effect: "Oppression and hardships caused by soldiers." It may also supply some background for the turmoil and persecution of vast segments of the population in Moravia and Hungary, in large part occasioned by the almost constant fighting in that part of the world in the 16th and 17th centuries, including the religious wars between Catholics and Protestants.

In 1526, the Turkish Sultan Suleiman the Magnificent (1520–1566) occupied Buda (on the west bank of the Danube, till 1872 an independent town, now part of Budapest) for the first time and made Hungary into a vassal state under the Transylvanian prince Johann Zápolya. In 1538, after twelve years of war, the secret pact of Grosswardein (Oradea or Nagyvárad) secured him the southern part of Hungary. In 1541 he started a new war, conquering Hungary as far west as Buda, Esztergom, and Stuhlweissenburg (Székesfehérvár), and making this part of the country a Turkish province. (Transylvania and the lands east of the Tisza River had come into the possession of Zápolya's widow and son after Zápolya's death in 1540.) The Hapsburg territories included western and northern Hungary and a small part of Croatia. Thus the Kingdom of Hungary was divided into three parts, a division that gave rise to endless conflicts and led to an almost permanent state of war. To these Turkish wars was added the unrest inside Hungary due to the insubordination of the nobles and the conditions within the churches.

Ferdinand I (king of Bohemia and Hungary after 1526, and Holy Roman Emperor, 1556–1564) was a sworn enemy of all Protestants, particularly of the Hutterites. In Hungary, the nationalist party had placed Johann Zápolya on the throne as rival king, while Sultan Suleiman the Magnificent had led his troops to the outskirts of Vienna in 1529 and to the Austrian border in 1532 and 1541. It was after 1551 (the year Ferdinand I opened a Jesuit college in Vienna in the interest of the Counter-Reformation), that the war over Transylvania began, which lasted until 1562.

of the Word could arrange it, any time of day or night, we should unite in prayer, humbly asking God to remember us and help us, for there is no one in the whole world upon whom we can rely; that even if we should suffer loss of temporal goods, he might keep our souls from harm and our people from suffering violence and dishonor; that he might protect us all—the widows and orphans, the many inexperienced young people, and our wives and children—from the bloodthirsty tyrant, the enemy of Christ; that he might keep us from being dispersed or sold among the heathen, from being drawn into their blasphemous and unchristian way of life. And if God uses the bloodthirsty tyrant to punish those who call themselves Christians (but whose lives are opposed to Christ through their shameful sodomy, terrible sins, and blasphemy), we should pray that he might give his people, who fear him and hope in him alone, special help such as he alone can give—and has given wonderfully from the beginning of the world. *1595 (1593)*

In short, we should pray that God might rescue us unstained from all enemies of divine truth and not let his people suffer punishment for the ungodly life these enemies lead. Therefore

---

Transylvania, however, remained in Turkish hands.

Under the mild rule of Maximilian II (1564–1576), Ferdinand I's successor, the Reformation was allowed to spread unhindered. Under Maximilian's successor, Rudolf II (1576–1612), however, the persecution of Protestants set in again. In October 1604, after Rudolf II had added to the 21 constitutional clauses of the Provincial Diet a 22nd clause seriously threatening the religious freedom of Hungarian Protestants, Stephen Bocskay (1556–1606) made common cause with Bethlen Gabor and other Hungarians to stir up a successful rebellion in Hungary. The imperial troops had to withdraw. In 1605 Sultan Ahmed I confirmed Stephen Bocskay as Prince of Transylvania, who concluded a peace treaty with the emperor in Vienna on June 23, 1606. The 22nd clause of 1604 was rescinded, and Protestants were granted freedom of religion, provided it was without detriment to the Roman Catholic Church.

Emperors Ferdinand II (1619–1637) and Ferdinand III (1637–1657), intent on re-catholicizing Hungary, were supported with fanatical zeal by the archbishop of Esztergom, Peter Pázmány (1570–1637). (About Peter Pázmány, see *Schaff-Herzog*, VIII, 424–425.) The Protestants found protectors in the princes of Transylvania, Bethlen Gabor (d.1629) and George Rákóczi I (1593–1648). The latter concluded a peace with Emperor Ferdinand III on December 16, 1645, at Linz, which was meant to insure religious and political freedom in Hungary. Under Emperor Leopold I (1658–1705), however, there was renewed suppression, leading to a major conspiracy in 1667 among the nobility, headed by Wesselényi, Zrinyi, Nádasdy, and others.

For Hungary's history during the Turkish era (1526–1711), see Dominic G. Kosary, *A History of Hungary* (New York, 1971), 92–137; Robert A. Kann, *A History of the Habsburg Empire*, 1526–1918 (Berkeley, 1974, 1977), ch. II, IV; C. A. Macartney, *Hungary: A Short History* (Edinburgh, 1962), ch. 4.

1595 (1593)

the brothers and sisters were enjoined to look to God and sigh to him in prayer, not only together in meetings but whenever they could, individually.

God heard his people's prayers.

We experienced that God heard his people's prayers and restrained the bloodthirsty enemy, for when this country's troops had fled as far as Raab, if the enemy had pressed their advantage in swift pursuit, they would have found the neighboring lands in a state of terror and flight and could have destroyed them all and brought them under their power.

Even the authorities had to acknowledge that it was God who prevented this. That same winter there would have been another opportunity for the enemy. In all this we give all praise and honor to God alone.

1596

5 brothers confirmed as servants of the Word.

On January 18,[1] 1596, at Neumühl, five brothers were confirmed in the service of the Word by the elders with the laying on of hands. They were Hans Schmied, Stoffel Rath, Martin Gotzman, Joseph Hauser, and Rudolf Hirzel.

Robbers attacked Neumühl.

On Monday, August 26, a wicked band of robbers—Poles, Italians, and others—raided our community at Neumühl. They blocked all the doors and rushed about with torches, ripped off the locks and chains from the horse stable, hauled sixteen wagon horses into the yard and harnessed them, ready to take when they had finished.

Then they broke into our homes, forced open doors, chests, and coffers, searching for gold. But they found none. They carried on like this for about two hours, until nine o'clock at night. By that time, news of their violent attack reached the two nearest villages. The alarm bell was rung, and people came running. The robbers, warned by their watchman, took fright and made off as if pursued, taking the sixteen harnessed wagon horses. Two horses broke loose, and we got them back again, but the robbers drove the other fourteen to Vienna.[2]

---

[1]Beck, 321: February 18.

[2]See Beck, 321–324, for a documented account of this raid, drawing on official records of the imperial supreme court, dated September 20, 1596, which state that the leader of the band, one Alexander Ciconia who claimed to be a count, was arrested with his companions on their way to Vienna and Vösendorf (now a suburb of Vienna). The booty was returned to the Hutterites, but this incident marks the

They caused such a commotion when they arrived with the horses that the lords in Vienna set out after them and imprisoned all twenty-four as robbers and felons.

1596
Robbers imprisoned in Vienna.

We got our horses back through the lords in Vienna and in particular through the governor of Moravia (on whose lands the raid had taken place), and he wrote a letter on our behalf. So God in his goodness helped us once again.

Also in 1596, the emperor sent an official letter to the governor of Moravia,[1] the county court judge, and the vice-chamberlain, summoning our elders (particularly those from Neumühl) to appear before them. The emperor wished to repay money he had borrowed from the free cities and other sources. This amounted to several thousand gulden, and we were supposed to loan the emperor this amount or put it at his disposal.

The emperor demanded money from the church.

So the above-mentioned lords, as commissioned, ordered brother Klaus Braidl as elder of the church and six other brothers to appear in the castle at Gross Seelowitz. They laid the emperor's letter before us and demanded that we lend the emperor the money. If we did not, the emperor would turn a blind eye and refuse to protect us in the event of further raids.

Klaus Braidl and other elders summoned to the castle at Seelowitz.

Five or six times the brothers were sent out and then called back again. Each time they answered every point explicitly and declared it wrong to think that we possessed such wealth. The church had nothing to lend the emperor.

Brothers dismissed five or six times.

As the lords heard this answer from us every time, they asked us to write down exactly and in detail what we had told them. So, as they requested, we presented the following document on October 25, 1596, at the castle at Gross Seelowitz, trusting them to lay it before the emperor.

Lords demanded that the brothers write down their answer.

---

beginning of the repeated demands Rudolf II and Ferdinand II made on the Hutterites to place part of their supposedly large amounts of money at the emperor's disposal.

This pseudo-count Alexander Ciconia, however, is not the Count Alexander Cicognia who was sent by the emperor to Moravia in 1621 to seize the Hutterites' available cash; see below, p.685.

[1]Friedrich von Zerotin (d. 1598), who on October 14, 1596, tried to convince the imperial supreme court of the financial insolvency of the Hutterites; see Loserth, *Communismus*, 202. Friedrich von Zerotin was probably the most distinguished among the Moravian nobility in the second half of the 16th century. Toward the end of his life he became governor, thus representing the crown in Moravia. The Hutterites spoke of him affectionately as "our Fritz." See Hruby, *Wiedertäufer*, 38, 47; *ME*, IV, 1024d.

1596
Brothers' written answer to the emperor's demand.

At His Majesty the Emperor's Request

his representatives, the governor, the county judge, and the vice-chancellor of the margravate of Moravia, summoned our brothers from Neumühl and other places in Moravia for repeated interrogation. We gave a fitting and humble answer each time verbally and now wish to submit it in writing.[1]

It is a new and painful experience for us to be suspected, by people who are not well disposed toward us, of having large sums of money at our disposal. This is not according to the truth and should not be believed as such. The following is sufficient evidence:

First, everybody knows that we have nothing to do with commerce and usury or any unproductive occupation. We earn our bread with hard manual labor. It is impossible to accumulate great wealth like that.

Second, it happens that out of ten people in the community scarcely one is able to earn anything, however little. This is true especially of those who have come recently and are not used to this country; many of them become ill and are incapacitated for a long time. We also have many weak and needy people, to say nothing of the old, the many helpless little children, the widows, and the orphans. The healthy brothers and sisters have to care for these and do the daily chores as well, without earning a penny.

Third, it was impossible for us to bring our goods and chattels into this country when we were driven here from other lands for the sake of our faith. For nearly seventy years we have been living here like pilgrims and have been told categorically that an imperial mandate was issued at that time, strictly prohibiting the entry of our goods. So we had to leave our homes with empty hands.

Someone did occasionally bring a little property. But for each one who brought something, a hundred poor, ragged people joined us, including the old and helpless

---

[1]The original version of this letter, like the one below, pp.569–571, was once kept in the Imperial Court Archives at Vienna, Austria; since 1922 it has been in Czechoslovakia (location not known to the editors).

Robert Friedmann lists both letters among the writings of Vorsteher Klaus Braidl; see *Schriften*, 107, #4 and #5 respectively; 115, #16 and #18 respectively.

as well as many young children. Before long the little that came was used up, and then all of us were left with nothing.

1596
Brothers' written answer to the emperor's demand.

Even in this country a lord may accept us on his land and later drive us off again. Then, without any compensation, we have to abandon land we have worked and houses we have built.

Many of us never see the wages we have earned by our hard work. Large amounts that we have no hope of ever receiving are being withheld.

Moreover, what we pay the Diet through all kinds of impositions and various taxes is no small matter; it amounts to a substantial sum.

FOURTH, over the years other people have burned down some of our houses, either deliberately or by accident. It cost a great deal to rebuild them.

FIFTH, it is obvious that over the years we have suffered great loss at the hands of soldiers. When they discover the location of a community, they go there even from far away with a plan of action all prepared. We are expected to meet the soldiers with obliging words and give them fodder, food, and drink. In order to give them the best of everything in abundance, we can hold nothing back for our own use. We even have to deprive our sick (as well as those who do hard and dedicated work) to feed the soldiers, or we would have the misery of seeing them pillage our houses and carry off every last thing.

SIXTH, in the years of famine, many came to us from German-speaking lands and wanted to live with us. They came with good intentions, and although we were poor, we shared with them the little we had. Besides, we ourselves have many poor communities in this country that could not manage to feed themselves and survive (and there can be no doubting this) if we did not do all we can to help one another with the slender means God in his mercy provides.

SEVENTH, our neighbors all saw what injustice and violence we suffered over and over again from people with grudges against us, who looked for an excuse to rob us of our goods and take them for themselves. We have never sought revenge; nor did we wish to cause trouble

1596
Brothers' written answer to the emperor's demand.

for the authorities or the lords (and do not want to do so now). We have not accused anyone or got involved in any lawsuit. We prefer to suffer everything, following the example and commandment of Christ and committing everything into the hands of God, the righteous Judge, let come what may.

We conclude with our humble request to the lords that they present all necessary information to His Majesty in a detailed and true account. Since His Majesty, in his kindness, has never before made intolerable demands on us (for which we pilgrims and strangers are deeply grateful), we have complete confidence that he will not require the impossible from us in the future. It is simply impossible for us to lend money in order to please His Majesty; we ourselves owe several thousand gulden.

It is our further petition that His Imperial Majesty not take our refusal and our simplicity amiss.

We in our lowliness will continue to pray in our meetings to our faithful God, as we have always done, asking for peace and well-being for His Majesty and all in the government.

Soon afterward, on October 29, 1596, all the elders in the service of the Word and the service for temporal affairs from all our communities, big and little, were called together at Neumühl for the godly purpose of dealing with church affairs.

Our dear brother Klaus Braidl read out the above answer to all the brothers and elders so that they could be fully informed and coresponsible in case there were further talks or incidents.

All the brothers were in complete agreement that the lords had been given a true report in reply to the emperor's demand. They said they would rather accept whatever God might allow to happen than give away what belonged to widows and orphans. It was clear to us that we could never do that in the name of God. This was the best answer we could give before God and men.

In 1596 on November 19, brother Franz Moritz, a servant of the Word, fell asleep in the Lord at Kostel.

Grain and wine tax imposed.

In this year a new tax was imposed on us: a silver groschen

for each cask[1] of wine and a half groschen for each sheaf of grain in the field. *1596*

As this tax was levied in wartime and we knew it would be used for bloodshed, for conscience' sake we could not pay it.

Because we could pay none of these taxes nor the ten gulden added as house tax, at various places the lords once more confiscated some of our oxen, sheep, or pigs, also wine and other things. We suffered great loss during those years.

Stock confiscated in lieu of taxes.

1597

On January 19, 1597, at Pribitz six brothers were chosen for the service of the Word and appointed. They were Hans Staindel, a saddler; Georg Wöller, a weaver; Hans Jakob,[2] a cobbler; Franz Walter, a barber-surgeon; Augustin Graf, a scythe-smith; and Georg Riedel, a vinedresser.

By 1597 we had been living at Frischau for nearly sixteen years, always thanking God for his goodness. On February 5, however, Lord Bernhard of Certorejsky at Frischau forced us to leave, although we had built up this community in 1581 at his request.[3] We had built it on an open meadow according to our needs and paid the high cost of it ourselves. At the time he set his seal to the following terms and gave his word to keep them: If the brothers did as much compulsory labor as his other workers (and he would not overburden them) and if they paid the required yearly rents and tithes, neither he nor his heirs would make any further demands on them. He would be just and protect them from any disturbance or violence.

If, however, he could no longer keep them because of imperial orders or if they decided to move for reasons of faith, then they had the freedom and the authority to sell their dwellings, fields, meadows, gardens, and vineyard for their

[1]*Eimer*, or bucket, used as a liquid measure, roughly 22 gallons; see Alfred Götze, *Frühneuhochdeutsches Glossar*, 61.

[2]Hans Jakob's last name was Wolf; see Beck, 324; about Hans Jakob Wolf's fate during the Thirty Years War, see below, pp.649–652.

[3]Lord Bernhard's father Peter Certorejsky of Certory had been favorably disposed to the Hutterites; see above, p.488 n.4. On April 1, 1598, however, the Hutterites moved back to Frischau.

1597

true value and accept the money without hindrance. Furthermore, they were free to move their goods and people in peace, with help or escort. They could go wherever they wished and for whatever reason, and neither Lord Bernhard and his heirs nor the overseers would hinder them under any pretext. He promised on his honor, both by word of mouth and in writing, to keep to this agreement and not take the liberty to get more out of us by underhand means.

Lord Bernhard, however, did not keep his word but, as the years went on, oppressed us so harshly with excessive compulsory labor and other unfair arrangements that we were unable to cover the needs of our community or maintain our fields. But not only that—our people were often badly beaten and even unjustly imprisoned, and in wartime their horses were taken. Once a brother had his teeth knocked out and was treated so badly that he suffered from it all his life.

We made frequent complaints to Lord Bernhard, telling him it was impossible to live there and endure such mistreatment. He declared he would improve matters and treat us well again, so we waited patiently, hoping things would change. But we had to wait many years.

Injustice and tyranny of the lord of Frischau.

Conditions became even harder, and we had to do more compulsory labor than ever. In the end we had only two free days in twenty-one weeks. Our brothers would take our oxen and horses to work on the lord's land—sometimes to fields so far away that they could not come home for three days—but he gave them nothing to eat. They had to drop their own work in the fields to work for him.

On top of this, Lord Bernhard took two horses from us. He returned one of them, but it had been so badly mistreated that it was only once in harness again. More than once, while the wagoners were out doing compulsory labor, eight others had to do manual labor at the lord's command. We had to cut and deliver firewood for the lord's brewery. In fact, we had to do the compulsory labor for almost the whole village. The farmers of the village were so worn out, they could hardly work anymore, and it fell on us.

All year long we hoed and tended the lord's vineyards, but for a long time he did not pay us a penny. Besides that, the farmers who worked for him got no fodder for the livestock, and the herds were too large. When the animals grew thin, the lord berated the brothers as if they were to blame.

If an animal died of old age or some deficiency, Lord Bernhard demanded that the brothers pay for it. When the farm brothers had to go on a journey for him, up to four nights away, he scarcely gave them provisions for one night. With all this, they had to endure terrible scolding and threats of beatings and imprisonment as well. They never got the wages or the food and drink due to them; so the lord ended up owing them a very large sum. *1597*

For these and other reasons, we saw that the longer we stayed the worse it became. So we decided to tell him well in advance that we simply could not live under him any longer. But before giving notice we wanted to take the best things out of the house as a precaution, since we did not know what would happen in the end.

Lord Bernhard, however, found out about our plans and appeared at our place with his lady and servants. No pity was shown to the old, the expectant mothers, or babies at the breast; they were driven out of the house by force and had to leave everything behind.

Lord drove us out of the house with violence. Not even infants were spared.

Two mothers with tiny babies only two weeks old had to go, as well as eleven other children with their mothers. Any baby that happened not to be in his cradle had to be carried by his mother; the cradle was left behind. The mother was not allowed even a diaper for her child, let alone a cradle or anything else.

If the sick did not leave their beds, they were thrown out. One married couple had been bedridden for twenty-one weeks, but even they were not spared. One brother was beaten to the ground like a dog and lay as if dead.

The sisters in the laundry in their old, worn-out clothes were driven out with violence and not allowed to fetch other clothes. Those who did not leave fast enough were beaten as well. No pleading helped.

They were driven out of their own houses with drawn swords, muskets, and clubs, accompanied by rude cursing.

Had to abandon nearly everything in Frischau.

They had to leave their houses and farm buildings, their fields, meadows, gardens, and the stock, which included twenty-three cows in milk, fifty-one dry cows, sixteen suckling calves, nine draft oxen, three oxen for fattening, three hundred and five sheep that would lamb later, seventeen fattened hogs, and sixty suckling pigs.

1597

They had to flee with their own horses, otherwise Lord Bernhard would have taken them too.

Grain was left behind, in particular about seventeen bushels of oats, as well as flour, wine, lard, salt, kitchen spices, all kinds of tools and household implements, clothes and bed linen, and thirty morgen of winter wheat [over twenty acres], already sown. We got no wages for work we had done for him, nor the money and grain owed to the dairy workers, which was no small amount. All this, to the value of 5000 gulden, we had to leave behind and commend everything to God.

Even this was not enough. Soon after, the lord stole one of the brothers' horses. He unharnessed it in the open field, knowing it was one of the Frischau horses. He threatened to take the other horses too, for, he asserted, everything we had bought with our own money to furnish the houses was now his property, and he meant to get it from us.

We bear this devastating robbery in patience for God's sake (though not without many sighs from our widows and orphans, who lost everything). We do not seek revenge for the evil done to us. We know him who has said, "Vengeance is mine. I will repay." And the Lord says, "In due time their foot shall slide. For the day of their downfall is near, and their doom is fast approaching." We leave it in God's hands, as faithful Job did when the Arabs and Chaldeans robbed him of his cattle, oxen, donkeys, and camels. A better and eternal possession in heaven shall be our comfort.

Deut.32:35
Heb.10:30
Job 1:13–21 (Froschauer)
Heb.10:34

But sorrow upon sorrow will come to our adversaries. These goods they have swallowed must be spewed out again (as told in the Book of Job). God himself will force the booty from their stomachs. The Book of Wisdom says an even greater horror will descend on those who have oppressed the God-fearing and have stolen the fruits of their labor.

Job 20:15
Wisd.5:2–13

Hans Zuckenhammer crisis.

On March 4, 1597, Hans Zuckenhammer, who had been a servant of the Word for seventeen years, was excluded in front of the whole church at Protzka in Hungary in the presence of brother Klaus Braidl, the elder, and Ludwig Dörker, Christian Steiner, Johannes Rath, David Hasel, Stoffel Küenhuber, Daniel Hellrigel, Hans Neumair, Sebastian Dietrich, Peter Trier, Lamprecht Jänko, and Hauptrecht Zapff, all of them servants of the Word.

Also present were fourteen or fifteen brothers from Velké Leváre (some of them responsible for work departments), who knew Zuckenhammer and his methods.

1597
Hans Zuckenhammer crisis.

This is what had happened: Several complaints had been brought to brother Klaus about Hans Zuckenhammer's inconsistent and even unjust judgments—some people he had not punished seriously enough, others he had treated much too severely, using coarse insults and showing them the door.

For these and similar things, brother Klaus had called him to Neumühl and rebuked him in the presence of the elders. He was told that unless he changed, he would no longer be trusted with the care of the community but would be placed under another brother. This was later decided at Kostel with several elders present, and Zuckenhammer was told to move to Protzka, where Christian Steiner was the servant of the Word. Someone else was given the responsibility for Velké Leváre.

As soon as Zuckenhammer heard that he was to move, he went posthaste to see the administrator at Jedenspeigen[1] on the pretext of wanting to settle accounts with him and set things in order, but actually to let the administrator know that he had to leave Velké Leváre.

The administrator was very angry. Zuckenhammer had turned to him often and been on very familiar terms with him. He sat down and wrote an urgent letter to the elder of the church, Klaus Braidl, asking him not to remove Zuckenhammer and threatening that if Zuckenhammer were sent away from Velké Leváre, he was afraid the whole brotherhood would have to follow.

Zuckenhammer gave his wagon to Friedrich Kellner (who was living at Velké Leváre at the time) to take the administrator's letter straight to brother Klaus in the middle of the night, thus hoping (so it seemed) to prevent the move from Velké Leváre.

Brother Klaus could not accept Zuckenhammer's unfitting conduct. He wrote to him that he did not believe such behavior would bring him any joy or comfort and that he had never heard of a servant of the Word who dared to approach the

[1]Jedenspeigen, a village in the district of Zistersdorf, Lower Austria, near the Czech border.

1597
Hans Zuckenhammer crisis.

authorities in order to gain influence and prevent his being moved to another place. Would Zuckenhammer let the elders know if it was right or fitting for one in his service to ignore his steward and take over completely, with the result that no one knew how things stood or what was happening? He had paid little heed, though warned about it repeatedly and with loving concern in the name of the Lord, that servants of the Word should avoid too familiar a relationship with the authorities. It was obvious that these warnings had not carried much weight, since Zuckenhammer had continued to go his own way regardless of what he (Klaus Braidl) or the other elders had said. He would not say more about it at that point.

The matter would be brought before the elders and discussed in the light of the truth, so that neither Zuckenhammer nor anyone else would be unjustly treated.

Another meeting of the elders was therefore called at Neumühl, and Zuckenhammer's case was considered. So many serious complaints were brought up that all the elders were horrified and grieved.

For instance, he used to abuse the person he was admonishing. He had railed at one brother, calling him a rogue and a villain, until the brother himself said, "Not even a Turk would rave the way you do. You have no right to speak like that!"

In the meeting of the elders already named and other brothers [at Protzka], all the above-mentioned complaints about Zuckenhammer were heard, and he was found to be in the wrong.

He defended himself instead of recognizing his sins. He tried to smooth everything over, just as he had done previously with the elders [at Neumühl].

In the evening after this confrontation, he was told to come before the brotherhood the next day. Zuckenhammer replied that he would be glad to do so. But late that same evening he asked to see the elders, and they agreed. He said he wanted them to give him an admonition then and there because he feared it would not be strong enough in front of the brotherhood. The elders should give him a sharp admonition. That was why he was standing before them—he certainly deserved it, and he admitted his guilt. He was told, however, that since it had been decided that he come before the brotherhood, this decision should stand.

1597
Hans Zuckenhammer crisis.

The next morning the whole matter was brought before the church, and the brotherhood was asked to decide whether such a man could remain in the service of the Word or not. Two or three voices spoke for relieving him of the service, as he had not proved fit for it.

One brother, out of sympathy, said he would be satisfied if Zuckenhammer continued in his service and prayer was made to the Lord on his behalf. It turned out that he had been approached by Zuckenhammer beforehand and had been swayed by his pleading. And he was not the only one—there were two or three others. Several more spoke in the same direction, although some very hesitantly.

At this point brother Klaus Braidl (speaking for all the elders) warned that everyone should speak in the fear of the Lord, instead of looking to one another; that each one is personally accountable to God and men. Since several had spoken for relieving Zuckenhammer of his service, everyone should ask himself seriously how effective Zuckenhammer's word and teaching would be from now on, for instance, when he disciplined others. A united testimony should be given in the fear of God.

After this many spoke. One after another they were in full agreement that it would be right for Zuckenhammer to lay down his service because he had not lived up to it and had made many unjust judgments and decisions. Even those brothers who earlier had spoken in favor of Zuckenhammer's service now expressed their agreement with all the others, namely, that this was the right and just course of action and that he deserved to have his service removed.

Brother Klaus Braidl then told Zuckenhammer about this decision and asked him to tell the brotherhood how he saw it. Zuckenhammer said he would accept it because it had been decided. Brother Klaus repeated the question, "How do you see it yourself?"

He replied, "I can't say. I will accept it," adding, "Don't question me so closely." When brother Klaus asked him once more, he flared up: "I tell you straight, I cannot agree. I am being accused of too much. But I realize that nothing I say or ask will make any difference. There is no mercy for me. As long as you are here, I'm always getting into trouble, I'll always be your whipping boy. I'm being treated as if I were

1597
Hans Zuckenhammer crisis.

the lowest kennel boy or swineherd." He repeated this angrily and continued, "Believe me, never in my life have I held to the faith as firmly as I do now.

"And you, Klaus, have been so hard on me—I would even say malicious—in this business. I could also say a thing or two if I wanted to."

Brother Klaus replied, "If you know something against me and don't say it, you will receive no thanks from me." Zuckenhammer was so angry he would gladly have spoken against the elder, but he did not know of anything to say.

(Later, on the day Zuckenhammer was reaccepted into the church, he wrote to brother Andreas Kleesattel, wanting him to ask brother Klaus Braidl not to hold his great foolishness and stupidity against him but to forget about it.)

Among other things he said he had not known he was like that, and why had no one admonished him when he had been in the wrong?

At this brother Ludwig [Dörker] stood up and rebuked him, saying he was only trying to make excuses; he knew very well that he had often been admonished. Zuckenhammer retorted, "Aha, my fine fellow, I know all about you!" and refused to listen to Ludwig.

Next, brother Johannes tried to help him, saying he would never have expected Zuckenhammer to react in such a wrong way. The latter responded, "Johannes, you may speak. I will listen to you. I know you are an upright, honest man." But when Johannes had too much to say, he interrupted: "Johannes, tell me later, when we are alone."

Seeing that Zuckenhammer would not listen to the others, brother Klaus Braidl told brother Johannes (whom Zuckenhammer had singled out) to take over the meeting and ask the brotherhood what to do with Zuckenhammer, as he would not admit his guilt but argued and rebelled.

The brothers began to speak again and came to the united decision that he should be excluded because he did not listen to the church or admit that his life had been superficial and without fear of God.

He argued back, saying, "Brothers, I hope you don't all speak. I can't take it from everybody!"

When the first one stood up and spoke for his exclusion, Zuckenhammer looked around and said, "Who is that? Is that you, Kürschner? You be quiet. I'm just as devout as you, that I know."

1597 Hans Zuckenhammer crisis.

The brother answered, "If I were no more devout than you, I should be standing there next to you."

Another said it would be right to exclude him. Zuckenhammer replied, "Oh, hold your tongue! Aren't you my son? I brought you to the church, and this is the thanks I get."

This brother said, "Yes, a fine father you are, giving me a fine example!"

A third brother agreed that Zuckenhammer should be excluded because he did not accept discipline the first time. "Let me remind you of a judgment you passed yourself," he said. "You once put a sister under discipline and she did not agree. Then you told her that because she did not accept it, she should receive a sharper discipline. That was the way you handled it, so it is right for you too."

Yet another brother said Zuckenhammer deserved the exclusion because he showed such contempt for the elders, who are as fathers to us. They should be all the dearer to us because they want to punish evil without respect of persons.

After Zuckenhammer had opposed the first ten brothers and could no longer contradict each one, he said, "I don't agree, even if you all speak. I still can't see it. That's all I can say." He did not even ask to stay in the community but told brother Johannes just to bring the affair to an end. So his exclusion was pronounced, and he left the meeting.

Later he thought it over and begged to be allowed to live in the community; he was willing to bear his discipline and repent. The church granted his request.

Because of all that came to light about him, Zuckenhammer accepted the exclusion, repented, and was reaccepted. He fell asleep in the Lord at Protzka on April 29 of the following year, 1598.[1]

On Monday, April 14, 1597, we were driven out of our community and farm at Bochtitz, where we had lived for forty years, praise and thanks be to God. Lord Jan Kusý forced us to go with our old people, widows, orphans, and little children,

Driven out of Bochtitz.

[1] About Hans Zuckenhammer's imprisonment and release, see above, pp. 478–482.

1597

leaving behind everything we had. His father, Lord Štěpán Kusý of Mukoděl (formerly at Bochtitz), had welcomed us on his land. We had lived under him for thirty-six years and under his son for four years. Now this son began to oppress us and inflict many hardships on us.

He took the pipes we had laid at our own expense—put in to carry water from the well to our place—and installed them in his own house. His servants came armed and took the hay from our barn by force. When his wagoners lost or broke their bushel baskets, they took our sisters' baskets. Many similar things had happened.

Exorbitant demands by the lord at Bochtitz.

The lord and lady had made all kinds of unjustifiable and unheard-of demands, expecting us to spin and bleach and weave certain amounts of cloth by weight. Our weaver could not manage to do our own weaving because of working for her ladyship, yet she would not give him even half wages. In addition, the lord was already heavily in debt to us, as he had not paid for our loyal services. When we asked for our wages, he was furious.

He did not protect us either. In the end, he just looked for more accusations against us. Although he knew the brothers would not help, he wanted them to haul several loads of stone for a church he was planning to build. All he wanted was a reason to blame them. When they refused to do it (for it would not have been right), he flared up in anger and threatened them.

On April 13 he had sent his men to our community at night. They behaved outrageously, forcing doors open and stealing meat and other things. All night long they gorged and drank, railed and blasphemed. The next day they forced everyone out of the house and drove our people off the lord's lands empty-handed. They beat several brothers severely and stole whatever they could—food, drink, and kitchen supplies: seven bushels of flour, eleven bushels of grain, forty bushels of oats, four bushels each of peas, barley, buckwheat, groats, lentils, millet, and linseed, as well as other things.

Our people forced from their homes empty-handed.

All our goods, livestock, and other things left behind.

Seventeen cows were stolen, four calves, ninety full- and part-grown hogs, seven fattened hogs, four oxen, forty sheep, forty-one lambs, two horses; seven hundredweight of fresh and dried meat, a considerable quantity of salt and lard, seven barrels of sauerkraut, thirteen casks of wine; various utensils and crockery, and many other things not listed here. They robbed us of house and home, of our seeded fields and vineyards. *1597*

They also drove us out of the mill we had bought at Klein Seelowitz.[1] With all that belonged to it, it was worth four hundred gulden.

Mill at Klein Seelowitz seized as well.

Lord Kusý had hired some of our people on his dairy farms for a fixed wage, but for over a year he had neither paid them nor given them the food and drink he owed. He owed these farm workers 527 gulden, so we lost that money too.

The losses we incurred amounted altogether to about 5200 gulden. This included robbery and damage to house and farm (all the movable and immovable goods with which God had blessed us), the seizing of the mill at Klein Seelowitz, plus the money owed to the farm workers. We commit all this into the hands of God, who told us through the prophets that such attacks will come upon those who keep their eyes on him. All who fear God will suffer harm, have their goods taken away, and be driven out of their houses. "Then it will be known whom I have chosen."

Loss amounted to about 5200 gulden.

Therefore we submit patiently to all such robbery and injustice. In both the Old and the New Testaments, devout and believing people have suffered these things. It cannot be otherwise in this world as long as we follow in the footsteps of the faithful; indeed, as long as we stand in the grace of God, all the world will be our enemy, as Christ says to his disciples, "You must be hated by all men for my sake."

On June 5 brother Georg Wyser or Rader fell asleep in the Lord at Kostel. He was an old and faithful servant of God's Word who had served the church for nearly thirty-one years. Before he passed away, he commended all the devout to the grace of God, thanking them again and again for all the kindness shown him.

Georg Wyser, a servant, passed away.

On Peter and Paul's Day [Jan.25] in this year, the brothers bought two houses at Budkau[2] from the knight Václav Hrubčický and set up community living there.

We began living at Budkau.

[1]Klein Seelowitz (Malé Zelovice), village near Wolframitz (Olbramovice), approx. 18 miles southwest of Brno. The mill, driven by spring water, was still standing in the 1880s. In 1597 the village belonged to the family Kusý of Mukoděl; see Beck, 324; Zeman, *Topography*, #140.

[2]Budkau (Budkov), village approx. 22 miles northwest of Znaim (Znojmo), northeast of Jamnitz (Jemnice). In 1597 the knight Václav Hrubčický of Čechtín was lord at Budkau. Beck, 325 n.1; Zeman, *Topography*, #24.

1597
Robbery and violence from soldiers.

That same year the church communities in all parts of the country suffered much oppression, terror, and loss from cavalry and foot soldiers who passed through, seizing great numbers of horses, sheep, and other things.

A servant for temporal affairs passed away.

On October 17 brother Lorenz Pürchner, an old servant for temporal affairs, fell asleep in the Lord at Tracht.

A servant passed away.

On All Saints' Day, November 1, brother Gilg Federspil, an old and faithful servant of God's Word, fell asleep in the Lord at Nikolsburg. He had served the church for nearly thirty-five years.

Further confiscations for taxes.

That year another tax we could not pay for reasons of conscience was imposed on us. As a result, oxen, sheep, hogs, wine, grain, and many other things were confiscated in different places, and the church suffered great loss.

Underhand dealings of Pisker Löw, a Jew.

Pisker Löw, a Jew from Nikolsburg, and Hans Parth, chief official in the town, had the audacity to involve us in a mean affair. They, especially the Jew, spoke as if they had an important imperial command which they wanted to pass on to us secretly, but only if brother Klaus Braidl, the church elder, came in person. So on November 2 brother Klaus went to Tracht with several elders, among them Ludwig Dörker, Johannes Rath, David Hasel, Andreas Kleesattel, Sebastian Dietrich, and Georg Zobel.

The Jew gave them a document demanding a large sum of money from the brothers; it was allegedly written in the name of the emperor. Georg Zobel was the only one mentioned by name—the elders were only referred to in one word.

As the document lacked the imperial signature, the brothers showed it to the governor, and he, too, doubted that it came from the emperor. He immediately sent the document to the court at Prague with other letters addressed to the emperor. Answers to these letters came back, but all that was said about the Jew's document was that it was not convenient at the moment for the emperor to reply.

The Jew insisted that he had verbal instructions from the emperor to get a list of all the servants of the Word in the church, and he whipped out his tablet to write them down himself, and also where each one lived. But we did not think it right to give him our names.

Our impression was that there were others involved in this

affair who were using the Jew and to whom he would betray us in a shameful way.

1597

A meeting of all the elders and many others from the church communities was called in order to decide how to proceed. They came to the conclusion that even if we had the means (which we neither had nor saw the possibility of having), our consciences would never allow us to sacrifice what belongs to the church community and to squander the little we have. They agreed not to give an answer to the emperor, but only to the lord under whom we were living.

Elders' response to the emperor's demand.

Nevertheless, even though we had not agreed to pay a single penny, the emperor was informed that we had consented to give 10,000 gulden and were eager to start paying.

Emperor led to believe we were willing to give 10,000 gulden.

Just then Zobel was called to Prague by a certain prince. This was an opportunity. Before setting out, he notified the lords von Dietrichstein of Nikolsburg of his intention to travel to Prague to take up his own defense because he was being so hard pressed by the Jew. The lords von Dietrichstein responded by summoning the Jew and obliging him to free Zobel from any further demands. So the Jew's attempts were foiled.

The Jew, Pisker Löw, had to release Zobel from any further demands.

When he saw that his deceitful plan would not succeed, the Jew began to excuse himself and begged the brothers not to take revenge, saying he had been urged to it by certain persons.

This time, too, the almighty God came to our aid and thwarted the plan the Jew and his accomplices had devised.

1598

On April 1, 1598, we moved back to Frischau and Bochtitz because the lords persistently requested our return. We had been driven out of these communities and had not lived in either of them for over a year.

Moved back to Frischau and Bochtitz.

On June 30 Lord Maximilian von Dietrichstein of Nikolsburg ordered us to leave his estates at Nikolsburg and Tracht. He gave us eighteen weeks and three days to turn our assets into cash and move out. He had wanted us to take over his three mills, two farms, and five gardens (each one separately) for a fixed yearly rent totaling 4988 gulden. The rents were so exorbitant and unreasonable that we could not possibly pay them. So we humbly asked Lord von Dietrichstein not to make

Lord of Nikolsburg gave us 18 weeks and 3 days notice to leave.

1598

such demands, but it was of no avail. However, on our request he allowed us to take our belongings by day or night and go wherever we could. If we could not move within the given time, he would give us three or four more weeks.

When he saw that rather than accept his demands, we really were taking our goods, moving away, and giving up our houses and farm, he sent his overseer to talk about a new proposal.

Lord of Nikolsburg offered good conditions.

We came to an agreement by which Lord von Dietrichstein promised to let us stay on good terms as before and to grant us protection, provided we were good tenants. So we moved back and stayed.

Stock confiscated in lieu of taxes.

Again that same year, on account of taxes we could not pay for conscience' sake, a great number of oxen, cattle, and hogs and large amounts of wine and grain were confiscated.

Trouble from soldiers.

In addition, many horses were stolen by soldiers in different parts of the country. The great damage and the many expenses drained our resources. We were being harassed and plagued to such a degree that were it all written down, it would make very painful reading.

Lord Oldřich of Kounice at Austerlitz ordered eight oxen to be taken from the brothers who were his tenants at Damborschitz. The oxen had cost 35½ gulden a pair. His only reason was that 150 soldiers were quartered at Damborschitz. The captain reserved the brothers' house for his own quarters, which cost the brothers a further eighty gulden. They had to submit to this robbery and leave it all in God's hands.

Lord of Austerlitz's injustices.

Lord Oldřich also took ten bushels of oats from the brothers at Damborschitz, paying ninety gulden for them, while the brothers had bought them for twelve or thirteen gulden a bushel. So they lost thirty-five gulden on the ten bushels.

1599

Moved back to Boretitz.

In 1599, on the Day of St. Paul's Conversion [Jan.25], Lord Václav Hrubčický of Budkau allowed the brothers to occupy the house at Boretitz again; he had evicted them nearly ten years before. So now they set it in order and moved back.

Six brothers confirmed in the service of the Word.

On March 14 six brothers were confirmed in the service of the Word at Neumühl by the elders with the laying on of hands. They were Hans Staindel, Augustin Graf, Georg Wöller, Franz Walter, Hans Jakob Wolf, and Georg Riedel.

1599
Three brothers chosen for the service of the Word.

On the same day at Neumühl, three brothers, Darius Heyn, Hansel Summer, and Ulrich Jaussling[1] were chosen for the service of the Word and appointed for a time of testing.

Damage done by soldiers.

Marauding soldiers unharnessed and stole about fourteen horses in all from the church community that year. Great damage and hardship was caused by cavalry soldiers on their way to Hungary.

David Hasel passed away.

On September 2 brother David Hasel, a faithful servant of the Word, fell asleep in the Lord at Pribitz.

Wolf Hungermüller passed away.

On October 3 brother Wolf Hungermüller, a servant of the Word, fell asleep in the Lord at Austerlitz.

Taxes increased.

In this year the lords in the Provincial Diet decided that on every house with a communal kitchen the brothers should be taxed ten more gulden over and above the additional ten mentioned before. In other words, twenty gulden more than the twenty they were already paying to the Diet on each house.

As our conscience did not allow us to pay this tax or the taxes on grain and wine and on the mill wheels (mentioned several times already), the lords took oxen, grain, wine, hogs, cows, and sheep during that year.

The lord cardinal expected us to work for him as for any other lord in Moravia.

In 1599 Lord Franz von Dietrichstein returned to Moravia from Rome, where the pope had made him a cardinal and bishop of Olmütz. When he arrived at Nikolsburg, he asked us to continue working for him as we did when he was only lord of Nikolsburg. He did not wish to demand anything against our conscience. He had previously treated us well and would continue as he had been doing when he was only a lord in the land.

So brother Klaus Braidl called together all the servants of the Word and the servants for temporal affairs (who were about to meet in any case) and laid the matter before them.

They considered it carefully in the fear of God, concerned to avoid any wrong involvement with the priests (which we have always had a horror of and have every reason to shun). Yet they recognized the difference between Cardinal von Dietrichstein and the other bishops of Kremsier before him,

---

[1]The three brothers were, respectively, a vinedresser, a furrier and clerk, and a coppersmith; see Beck, 329. Ulrich Jaussling became Vorsteher in 1619 and died in 1621; see below pp.646, 680–681; *ME*, III, 99.

1599

between the regime at Nikolsburg and the regime at Kremsier.[1] The lord cardinal had been and still was our lord at Nikolsburg, and he and his brother, Lord Maximilian, were drawing their revenues from there. The two communities, Nikolsburg and Tracht, were under his jurisdiction, and it was to him that we had to turn for advice in any questions that might arise from day to day.

Elders' response to cardinal's request.

Therefore it would be out of place for us to refuse him our service in his capacity as lord of Nikolsburg. The assembled brothers carefully considered whether we should continue to acknowledge his lordship and authority over us or move out of those communities on his land.

We could not find sufficient reason for moving out and refusing to serve under him, however. To do that would only cause unrest in the area, and it would not serve to God's glory or the welfare of the faithful.

Decision to work for the lord cardinal at Nikolsburg and build the mill at Kremsier.

It was unanimously decided that we work for the lord cardinal himself and his retainers at Nikolsburg as we would for any overlord in the country, but not on lands he held as bishop. Payment for our work would come from the revenues of the Nikolsburg estate. Further, we agreed to build the mill at Kremsier (which the lord cardinal had promised to build with revenues from the Nikolsburg estate), since the mill was needed by many for common use.

Priests should still be shunned.

We made no further commitments, nor did we say this agreement would apply to any future bishop, with whom there might be a completely different relationship than with the lord cardinal, but we should continue to shun bishops, priests, and false brothers as strictly as we did from the beginning.

Written statement, how far we would serve the cardinal.

A letter was then written to the lord cardinal containing our answer: If His Lordship approved, we would be glad, in a private capacity, to serve him and his retainers too (except for the priests) by making boots, shoes, knives, clocks, or other articles they might need.

The same would apply to any work done on the Nikolsburg

---

[1]Kremsier (Kroměříž) on the Morava River was the summer residence of the bishops of Olmütz (Olomouc). When Franz von Dietrichstein became bishop, the situation grew difficult for the brothers, who agreed to work for him as their manorial lord but not as representative of the Catholic Church, in accordance with the decision of 1535 (p.134 above). See Hruby, *Wiedertäufer*, 33–34; Zeman, *Topography*, #64; see also below, pp.564–567; Robert Friedmann, "Dietrichstein," *ME*, II, 59–60.

estate, provided we were paid out of the revenues of that estate, as we understood had been offered us by the lord cardinal. We would act toward His Lordship and work for him as before, just as for any lord in the country. *1599*

We would take on the mill at Kremsier if the lord cardinal or the ruling family at Nikolsburg would agree and give assurance that all expenses would be paid from the Nikolsburg estate (as mentioned above). We would do this (even though we did not consent to build it for the previous bishop) because we realize that the mill is of importance to the lord cardinal and will be useful to many people. Besides, no one, including ourselves, can manage without it. Should the lord cardinal die (though we hope his life will be preserved), we trust that payments would not be delayed and that we would not be referred to the clergy for payment, but that everything would be handled according to the contract agreed on. In that case we would come to a verbal agreement that would be acceptable to the carpenters.

As before, we refuse to become involved in anything to do with Kremsier and the bishop's estates by working for them, whether in building, farming, or anything else, such as making the priests' clothing—in short, doing any work for them. We and our whole community have a horror of accepting payment for our hard work from revenues accruing to the episcopal estates. Just as it defiles the believer's conscience to have any part in idolatrous sacrifice, so accepting such payment would be offensive to believers.

We cannot consent to do anything that goes against God and our conscience. We would rather await whatever hardship God may allow than cause brothers and sisters to twist their consciences by doing something that does not accord with our faith and that we have never done before.

The lord cardinal took the brothers' answer very badly.

On receiving this well-meant letter, the lord cardinal flew into a rage and threatened to show this "insulting" letter to His Imperial Majesty (insulting, because we had not addressed him by his proper title). He declared, among other things, that we would wring our hands before we were through. Then he recovered himself a little, tore up the letter, and said we were not to write to him anymore. If we ever did so, we should hand the letter to his servants to present to him. Then he once more promised us good conditions if we would serve him like

1599

any other lord in the country. However, he soon changed his mind again.

1600

Further taxes imposed by the lord cardinal, Lord Karl von Liechtenstein, and other lords.

About Candlemas [Feb.2] of the year 1600, a Diet was held at Znaim, Moravia, that imposed further taxes. The men behind the imposition were the above-mentioned lord cardinal; his brother, Lord Sigismund von Dietrichstein, deputy chamberlain in Moravia; Lord Ladislav Berka, head chamberlain for the province; and in particular Lord Karl von Liechtenstein, provincial judge in Moravia, who even boasted of having pushed the hardest.[1] A hundred gulden tax was imposed on every community belonging to the brothers, whether large or small. A tax of one gulden was imposed for every brewing of beer in addition to all other duties on wine and grain, which reached a considerable sum.

We could not pay the heavy taxes.

We took counsel before the Lord about these impositions, and we came to the conclusion that we were completely unable to pay them. It would be better to give up some of the poorer communities, even letting them stand empty, and move together until, should the situation become more serious, God would show the church a way out. This was agreed to by all the brothers in the fear of God.

A servant passed away.

On April 6 brother Christoph Gschäl, a servant of the Word, fell asleep in the Lord at Niemtschitz.

Moved out of Niemtschan.

About Easter time, the brothers had to sell the house and farm buildings at Niemtschan and move away because of the high taxes and harassment from soldiers, which became unbearable.

That same year there was a steep rise in food prices throughout Bohemia, Moravia, Austria, and Hungary, because an acute shortage in neighboring countries resulted in large grain exports. After Whitsun, wheat sold at a hundred gulden a bushel at Brünn.

---

[1]The following may be considered originators of the ensuing oppression: Cardinal Franz von Dietrichstein, bishop of Olomouc from 1599; his brother Sigismund, named deputy chamberlain in 1599; Ladislav Berka of Duba, head chamberlain from 1598; the future prince, Karl von Liechtenstein (who converted to Catholicism toward the end of the 16th century), provincial judge from 1599.

About the increase in taxation, see Hruby, *Wiedertäufer*, 59–60; Loserth, *Communismus*, 203; Beck, 331.

Not only grain was scarce at that time but everything else as well, owing to a disease that killed vast numbers of cattle, the like of which was almost unheard of. This epidemic had begun in October 1598, continued into the following year, and persisted with great severity during the summer of 1599. In many of our communities almost all the cows and oxen died, up to forty, fifty, and sixty head. This happened not only in Moravia, but also in Transylvania, Hungary, Austria, Bohemia, and other neighboring countries. In some places a hundred head sickened and died.

1600
Great shortage of grain.

Large number of cattle died.

100 head of cattle perished in places.

In this acute shortage and famine, God the Almighty (who always cares for his people and never leaves them) faithfully provided for his people and blessed them above many others, thanks also to the diligence and foresight of loyal elders. He distinguished between his own and other people in the world.

In previous times of famine (though it had never been so severe) the church of the Lord had been quite hard hit. Yet in this unusually serious situation we felt no marked effects, God alone be praised. For a short time we went without the mid-afternoon lunch; that was all. Otherwise our daily needs were provided as before. Compared with the suffering of others this was no privation.

God provided for his people during famine.

Some communities did not have enough to tide them over until the harvest, but brotherly love and Christian community were practiced through the elders' devotion and foresight—other communities stretched out a helping hand by contributing grain, flour, and other things.

Thus the Lord, to whom be praise for ever and ever, mercifully helped his people in their troubles: namely, the confiscations by the authorities in lieu of taxes and the robberies committed by soldiers, as described above. All the faithful pulled through together, and no one in the church community suffered real want.

We were even able to help many others in need and so felt deeply how God's mercy and his strong hand were with his people. We can never thank him enough.

Help given to many people outside the church during the famine.

In this same year of 1600, while we were going through a time of acute shortage, and hardly any flour or bread was to be had, the church of the Lord was again harassed by soldiers coming from Transylvania. They encamped in Moravia for fourteen weeks, waiting for wages and discharge.

Soldiers harassed the church communities.

1600

Meal of Remembrance could not be held at Kostel.

All this time the soldiers caused a great deal of trouble and anxiety for the brothers. At Kostel we could not celebrate the blessed Remembrance of the Lord, which had been held at twelve other places that year under the protection of the All Highest. The communities' supplies dwindled rapidly because we had to provide the soldiers with food that our brothers and sisters had toiled for with the sweat of their brow. To get any payment, however, proved bitterly hard, to say nothing of the other harassments, damage, and wilful misconduct which the God-fearing had to bear during those many weeks.

Cavalry soldiers stole many horses.

Besides, cavalry troops were recruited and mustered in Moravia for an advance into Hungary.[1] They seized many of our horses. Even though they did not behave as viciously to us as to others, their presence was a source of trouble, to say nothing of the amount of food, drink, and fodder that went to supply them.

A servant passed away.

On June 14 brother Peter Trier, a servant of the Word, fell asleep in the Lord at Watzenowitz.

A servant passed away.

On August 4 brother Hans Neumair, a servant of the Word, fell asleep in the Lord at Nikolsburg.

Livestock, grain, wine, and other things taken in lieu of taxes.

At the beginning of the year a heavy tax had been imposed, which we were quite unable to pay, as described above. From then on, the lords sent their underlings, judges, and officials into one or another of our communities to collect the taxes by taking away oxen, fattened hogs, grain, wine, and sheep.

1601

Andreas Kleesattel, a servant, passed away.

On Saturday July 14, 1601, brother Andreas Kleesattel, a faithful servant of the Word, fell asleep in the Lord at Neumühl.

Taxes slightly abated.

That same year the Provincial Diet at Brünn decided to reduce slightly the heavy taxes imposed in 1600. Instead, the brothers were to pay thirty gulden in addition to the twenty-gulden tax on each house with a kitchen, to which we had already agreed. As before, we were to pay one gulden on each brewing of beer, two groschen on every cask of wine, and one groschen on every stook of winter or summer grain.

As this money was to be used for war purposes, for

---

[1]Such mobilizations and advances were directed against the Turks and Tartars, who were devastating the countryside between the Ipel and Vah rivers as far west as the Little Carpathians, threatening Moravia with their incursions. Beck, 331–332.

conscience' sake the church could not pay it. That is why from time to time sheep, hogs, oxen, horses, grain, and other things were confiscated from different communities.

1601

This same year the church of the Lord was hard pressed and the communities suffered greatly because of the soldiers, as described several times already.

Soldiers again caused hardships.

A whole infantry regiment, about 8000 men, was ordered to muster at Ungarisch Ostra in Moravia. Most of them marched the whole length and breadth of the country and had almost got there when the mustering point was changed to Znaim, so the soldiers marched back through the country, and for six weeks they were on the move or billeted throughout Moravia. The church was hard pressed, and many communities suffered a great deal, since the soldiers consumed large amounts of food and drink. On top of this, cavalry and infantry soldiers marched through Moravia to Hungary, and in the fall a number returned to Moravia. They caused us great loss and hardship and stole more than a few horses.

1602

On February 24, 1602, at Neumühl, three brothers—Darius Heyn, Hansel Summer, and Ulrich Jaussling—were confirmed in the service of the Gospel by the elders with the laying on of hands.

Three brothers confirmed in the service of the Word.

That same day, also at Neumühl, three brothers were chosen for the service of the Word and appointed for a time of testing. They were Heinrich Schalcher, a clothmaker; Niklas Kuenzin, a vinedresser; and Hansel Metzger, a cobbler.

On July 1 brother Hans Schmied, a servant of the Word, fell asleep in the Lord at Stiegnitz.

Hans Schmied, a servant, passed away.

In this year more than in any other previous year, the church of God was again terrified and plagued by soldiers marching to Hungary, who were billeted across the country and requisitioned large amounts of food, drink, and other things. Many communities suffered more than ever before. One evening at Sabatisch a mob raided our community and stole horses and whatever else they fancied, a loss amounting to 350 gulden.

Soldiers harassed the church.

The Diet at Brünn again increased the taxes sharply that year. Eighty gulden were added to the twenty we had agreed

Taxes increased again.

1602

to pay, as well as five groschen on each barrel of beer brewed. There were also (as before) two groschen on every cask of wine, one groschen on every stook of summer or winter grain, and other impositions.

This year and preceding years, not all the lords had collected the taxes in full. Because some had taken only part of what was due, large amounts were outstanding in many places, and we had to expect great losses in the future. But lambs, sheep, oxen, hogs, grain, and wine were taken in payment this year too.

Stock confiscated in lieu of taxes.

That same year, the brothers at Gobschitz (who had lived there for forty-nine years) moved out with the lord's consent. We also moved out of Budkau, because the heavy taxation and the hardship caused by soldiers had become too much. However, several shoemakers and barber-surgeons remained at Budkau at the lord's request and lived in a rented house.

Moved from Gobschitz and Budkau.

Beautiful Hebrew writing was found on the grapes in many places. It was so skillfully done that no one could have painted it better, and each one was different from the others.

Hebrew writing on grapes.

On December 3, brother Wastel Anfang, a servant of the Word, fell asleep in the Lord at Nikolsburg.

Wastel Anfang, a servant, passed away.

1603

In 1603 the three communities at Austerlitz, Damborschitz, and Herspitz[1] (under Lord Oldřich of Kounice at Austerlitz and Steinitz) made preparations to move out. Most things had already been moved from those communities, and at Damborschitz very little remained. They were leaving because the lord and his officials had caused them all kinds of trouble over a long period of time, until they could endure such conditions no longer. But before everybody moved, the older servants of the Word and servants for temporal affairs decided after much careful thought to write a detailed letter to the lord of Austerlitz explaining the main reasons for the move:

Plan to move from Austerlitz and Damborschitz.

His Lordship was not to think that he could force his injustices on us by threatening us with prison or the loss of

Injustices of the lord of Austerlitz.

[1]Herspitz (Heršpice), southeast of Austerlitz (Slavkov), was part of the Austerlitz domain; see Zeman, *Topography*, #48.

our houses (which we had built on his land at great expense). It would be no small thing for us to leave so much property behind, since it would mean a considerable loss, but we had almost no hope that we could continue living under him, because of the injustice with which he was accustomed to treating us in many ways. The longer it continued, the more unbearable it was becoming and things had been done which His Lordship should readily admit were intolerable for us.

1603
Injustices of the lord of Austerlitz.

For instance, when ninety of his sheep died through accidents or cold weather (through no fault of the brothers), he unjustly deducted a hundred gulden from the account he owed to the brothers at Damborschitz.

When cattle died on His Lordship's farm at Nasselowitz (and cattle were dying all over Moravia in an epidemic), he deducted forty measures of lard from the farm workers' wages.

His Lordship ordered ten bushels of oats to be taken for his own use from the brothers at Damborschitz, paying them only nine gulden a bushel when they had bought it at twelve and thirteen gulden for the community's needs. They were also put under great pressure to buy salt from His Lordship.

Again, when many cavalry soldiers were billeted at Austerlitz, their captain told us that His Lordship had ordered fifty of them to be billeted with us. As our brothers opened doors and stables to them and led their own animals into the yard, the soldiers saw that although the brothers were willing to let them use their stables there was simply not enough room. So of their own accord the soldiers billeted the rest of their company in the surrounding villages. They had more sympathy for our people than His Lordship had.

When soldiers were billeted at Damborschitz, as His Lordship was informed in writing, the captains were quartered at our place. Although they did not stay, but came and went, they cost the brothers over sixty gulden. Yet His Lordship used this as an excuse to take eight oxen from the brothers. On another occasion soldiers came to the market at Damborschitz with no friendly intent toward the townspeople. The brothers found it necessary to intervene, and they appeased the soldiers with their good will. The soldiers declared publicly that if it had not been for the brothers, they would have burned down the whole marketplace.

On one occasion, the soldiers stole sheep from His Lordship

1603
Injustices of the lord of Austerlitz.

at Nasselowitz because he did not take the trouble to protect his property or his workers. When too many sheep had been stolen, he tried to get even by deducting ten gulden from his workers' wages. In fact, he took it into his head to make the brothers pay for all his losses. And there were many other hardships and injustices.

His Lordship controlled the work of the craftsmen at Austerlitz and Herspitz, such as weavers, barber-surgeons, and tailors, forbidding them to earn money by working for others.

He forced the craftsmen to make whatever he fancied, without any agreement or contract. Once the article was made, he paid what he wanted—their pleading was useless—and deducted a great deal from the price of finished work.

There were countless ways in which His Lordship made life hard for us. It would take too long to recount it all, but we could no longer put up with it.

What we wrote to the lord of Austerlitz.

If His Lordship was willing to act fairly and buy our property at a reasonable price or sell it and give us the proceeds, we would accept that with gratitude. But if not, we would have to move nonetheless and trust in God.

If His Lordship would not let us move away peacefully but tried to keep our property or use violence—by throwing our stewards and others into prison, for instance, as he had been doing—then we would have to inform His Lordship that none of the people working on his farms or elsewhere would complete their year of service. They would leave regardless of losing their wages.

Lord of Austerlitz's order to imprison the elders.

When this letter was presented to the lord of Austerlitz (who was at the thermal baths at Trentschin) and his wife and officials informed him that the brothers were moving out with their belongings, he flew into a rage. Immediately he ordered his men to stop the brothers from taking anything with them by intimidating them with threats. They should take the elders and stewards by the neck and throw them in prison. They were not to let them out until everything was returned. And if they saw anyone trying to remove anything by wagon, on horseback, or on foot, they were to take it from him. These instructions were carried out, the stewards imprisoned, and our possessions taken to the castle at Austerlitz. The outlook was very bad.

Our stewards imprisoned.

But before the lord of Austerlitz came home, he changed his mind and hastily sent a letter to the elders asking them not to go ahead with their plans. As soon as he was back home, they should send brothers to him to talk things over and reach a satisfactory settlement. His men also turned around and stopped the harsh treatment. They let the stewards go and told them that their lord was offering to treat the brothers well from now on and they should have no further cause for complaint.

1603
The lord of Austerlitz changed his mind.

Stewards released.

At this kind offer from the lord of Austerlitz, the elders met to give serious consideration to his written and verbal proposals. Several brothers were appointed to go to see him. The servants of the Word were Gilg Molt, Hans Eberle, Adam Neyffer, Hans Jakob Wolf, and Niklas Kuenzen; the stewards were Friedrich Samsun, Bastel Gilg, Jakob Rosenberger, Bärtel Knöringer, and Christian Mang, the carpenter. Before they left, they were instructed by all the elders first to listen to His Lordship's proposals and then to tell him plainly the brothers' answer and further complaints. To keep our letter short, we had not written about all the many other instances of unjust treatment we had endured from His Lordship over a long time, but in their talk with him the brothers had told him about some of them.

Several servants went to the lord of Austerlitz.

After much deliberation the brothers visited the lord of Austerlitz a third time, with the intention of informing him that they would not wait anymore but vacate the three communities on his estates because His Lordship had acted so unjustly for so long. His Lordship, however, made many concessions and persisted in his request, supported also by the helpful advice of other lords who did not like to see us move away. On May 21 the brothers were therefore sent to His Lordship for the last time to agree that they would try once more to live under him at Austerlitz and Damborschitz.

Brothers were sent for the third time to the lord.

Then in the presence of Lord Georg Tchechetschausky (whom he had expressly summoned), the lord of Austerlitz made verbal offers to improve conditions and remove all grounds for complaint.

After this verbal agreement, the brothers informed him that the elders would trust his given word and were willing to try staying in the two communities at Austerlitz and Damborschitz. If His Lordship kept to his agreement, the brothers hoped, God willing, to continue living under him.

1603
Lord of Austerlitz thanked the brothers.

The lord of Austerlitz thanked the brothers for trusting him and declared that he would keep his word as surely as if he set up a written agreement.

The brothers at Herspitz made preparations and, except for a very few, moved out in the summer of 1603.

Stoffel Rath, a servant, passed away.

On Philip and James Day, May 1, 1603, brother Stoffel Rath, a servant of the Word, fell asleep in the Lord at Kostel.

Georg Zobel, a servant for temporal affairs and physician, passed away.

On June 27 brother Georg Zobel fell asleep in the Lord at Nikolsburg. He was a servant for temporal affairs and an old and distinguished physician, who had served the medical needs of the church communities for a long time. His services had been used by many prominent lords as well.[1]

Dry summer.

A bushel of wheat cost a gulden and forty groschen.

The summer of 1603 was very dry. There was hardly any rain between springtime and harvest. Only the water retained in the soil since winter kept the winter wheat growing. Wheat became so expensive that you had to pay one gulden for a bushel of wheat, later, a taler and forty groschen a bushel. But God, to whom alone be the honor, provided his people with just enough to get by until the following year's harvest without suffering lack. In 1604 there was a specially good crop throughout the land, and conditions improved, thanks be to God.

Soldiers pillaged the communities.

Groups of soldiers broke into communities.

In 1603 as in other years, all communities of the church of God suffered a great deal at the hands of soldiers, especially roving cavalry and foot soldiers who were on the move daily from one place to another. Cavalry and infantry, especially from Bohemia, Silesia, and neighboring provinces, moved through Moravia to mustering places near Marchegg and to Raab in Hungary, causing great fear in many of the communities. They banded together, forty, fifty, and sixty strong, with about two hundred horses. In various places they forced their way into the community and consumed large amounts of food, also taking goods from our craftsmen. They promised to pay but left without doing so. From some places they took horses.

Stock confiscated in lieu of taxes.

In 1603 livestock, wine, grain, and other things were again confiscated from some of our communities because, as in the

[1]About Georg Zobel, see also above, pp.487–488.

beginning, we had refused for conscience' sake to pay the very heavy war taxes already mentioned. Some of our communities were hard hit, for in many places the value of two or more years' taxation was taken from us. *1603*

In 1603 Joseph Hauser, a servant of the Word, and five other elders were sent to Prussia. They found many Mennonites split into groups: Strict Frisians, House-Buyers, Flemish, Mundauer, Concerned Frisians, Waterlanders, and Separatists.[1] They all take their name from Menno Simons, yet do not consider one another brothers and sisters.

Joseph Hauser, a servant, sent to Prussia with five others.

Varying opinions among the Mennonites.

Brother Joseph Hauser, Michael Grossmann, and Karl Schneider were on the way from Danzig to Denmark. Their ship was captured at sea and taken to Sweden by subjects of the Swedish king. The brothers prayed earnestly and after four days were released, for which they gave heartfelt praise to God. They visited several people in Denmark, but not knowing the language, they returned to Danzig and in the fall went home to Moravia.

Brother Joseph and two others captured at sea.

Brothers were released. Returned to Danzig.

1604

In the year 1604 Joseph Hauser again traveled to Prussia with seven brothers and their wives. Darius Heyn, a servant of the Word, was also sent to Prussia.[2]

Two servants with several brothers and sisters sent to Prussia.

---

[1]Ziegelschmid, *Chronik*, 612 n.1, lists forty Mennonite groups known at the time. See also *ME*, II, 337–340, 413–414; III, 586–587. Horst Penner, "West Prussian Mennonites Through Four Centuries," *MQR*, Oct. 1949, 236.

[2]About Hauser and Heyn's unsuccessful attempt to found a Hutterian community at Elbing, East Prussia, see L. Neubaur, "Mährische Brüder in Elbing," *Zeitschrift für Kirchengeschichte*, XXXIII (1912), 447–455, from which the excerpts below are taken; see also Zieglschmid, "Die ungarischen Wiedertäufer," note 8; *ME*, II, 680–681; Beck, 337.

Joseph Hauser and Darius Heyn, representatives of the brotherhoods in Moravia, contacted Klaus Philip, a Mennonite lacemaker from Elbing. Having heard of the freedom of religion in Prussia, they were interested in settling in or near Elbing and asked the city for permission. At an audience on October 7, 1604, attended by the burgrave and other members of the city council and presided over by the burgomaster, the brothers said that in Moravia even the lords of estates sometimes listened to their sermons and watched how they broke bread together. The record continues:

> They said they did not believe that the actual body and blood of the Lord was received but that the bread and wine were taken in remembrance of the Lord. Their custom was for about five communities to meet at one place on a Sunday, approximately two thousand people. First of all the elders would warn the brothers that each one consider carefully how he stood. If anyone

1604
Mennonites sent two of their number to the church.

Sebastian Dietrich sent to Prussia.

The Mennonites sent two of their number, Peter of Hasel and Wilhelm Peters, to visit the church community [in Moravia]. They returned [to Prussia] with the report that all was well with the church. Our brother Darius then returned to the church community and was replaced by brother Sebastian Dietrich.

---

was burdened with conscious sins, he should speak up; he would not be permitted to take part. The others would meet again on a Monday. Long tables would be set with jugs of wine and with bread leavened in the usual way, rye or wheat, whichever was available, and cut in large slices. First the elders would declare that they had carried out their services according to the will of the brotherhood and that they intended to continue to do so, which they would confirm by partaking of the bread and wine. Then the other members of the church in turn, sitting or standing, would take the sliced bread, break a piece off, and give it to the next brother, who would pass it on. They would do this in remembrance of the Lord. A week later another five communities would gather, and this would continue throughout the year. But it would not be taken to the sick who were unable to come to the church meeting. If someone did not want to break bread, he would at once be asked the reason, whether it was due to hate, envy, or another cause.

They held their goods in common. Anyone who wished to join them had to hand in everything he owned. He was not compelled to do this immediately, however, but was given time to consider it for six months to a year, whatever seemed best. If during that time he decided not to stay, he was quite free to leave and his property was returned. But if someone wanted to leave after he had declared his intention to stay, the property he had brought would not be returned to him; it would be kept as an offering for the upkeep of the brothers.

If a bachelor or widower among them wished to marry, he could not just pick whom he wanted but must turn to the elders. They would go to the sisters and ask among the widows and unmarried women if any wished to get married. They did not mention names or put pressure on the sisters, who they felt should rather remain unmarried. If a sister responded and was suggested to the brother and if he accepted her gladly, the two would be married; but there was no compulsion. There was no courting among them; but if this should ever happen, the elders would decide, according to the situation, whether the two involved might be married.

The children were raised separate from their parents. There were two schools, the little school and the big school. In the little school the younger children (two years and over) were taught and looked after by certain sisters, who also washed them and who cared for them day and night. In the big school the older children were brought up more strictly in the fear of God by the schoolmasters. They were taught their mother tongue, but no foreign languages, and they were not sent elsewhere to study. The lords of the area and others often came to see how the children were raised.

The brothers were asked whether there was anyone in Elbing who wanted to join them. They answered, "There are some in and around the city as well as in Marcushof and Wengeln" (two villages in the Marienburg district belonging to Poland). Four days later, on October 11, the brothers' envoys, Darius Heyn and Christoph Stolz (a tailor representing Hauser during his absence), were informed that the city had refused permission to settle in Elbing. They appealed this with a new petition to the city on October 16, but on October 28, after their return from Danzig, they were notified that the council upheld its original decision.

The two Mennonite families were supposed to move to the church community, but Peter of Hasel never came. Wilhelm Peters and his wife did make the journey but soon returned to Prussia.

1604

Peter of Hasel did not move to the church.

Our brothers took over a farm from an unbeliever named Andreas Kämmerling. They rented it on a ten-year lease for 533 gulden and an annual ground rent of 266 gulden, with 790 gulden for all the household equipment, livestock, and grain.

Brothers took over a farm for 533 gulden.

We intended to start a community on this farm, but the new members who had formerly been Mennonites caused difficulties.

Mennonites caused difficulties.

Brother Joseph Hauser traveled back to the church community [in Moravia] and delivered the message that brother Sebastian Dietrich had given him. Then brother Rudolf Hirzel, a servant of the Word, went to Prussia for the winter, and Sebastian Dietrich returned home.

Servant Rudolf Hirzel sent to Prussia.

The ungodly prefect of Marienburg, a supporter of Kämmerling, used his position to harass the brothers and demanded the money still owing on the farm (but held in a trust), threatening to punish them severely for not paying. It was a wretched business, and the brothers were badly cheated.

Prefect of Marienburg harassed the brothers.

At the same time about a hundred apprentices, incited by their masters at Elbing, swore to burn down the farm the brothers were renting, because the guilds had the authority to exclude other craftsmen from their neighborhood.

Apprentices wanted to burn down the brothers' farm.

Sebastian Dietrich and Joseph Hauser were sent back to Prussia to get rid of the farm, but they could not get it off their hands for a long time, not even by handing it over to the treasurer.

Brothers Sebastian Dietrich and Joseph Hauser sent back to Prussia.

At last through God's leading they met a distinguished German nobleman who took over the farm and relieved the brothers of it. They thanked God with all their hearts in spite of the heavy losses they had suffered through it.

Freed of the farm with God's help.

When the Mennonites were expected to move to the church community, Peter of Hasel and his wife were unwilling to go. He was excluded by the church at Wengeln because, although he had spoken highly of the church a few weeks before, he now spoke against it. He slandered and cursed it bitterly, calling it a den of cutthroats and making malicious accusations, for instance, that neither young nor old were given the food they were used to and so died before their time.

Peter of Hasel's slander.

1604

Wilhelm Peters contradicted him.

He claimed that the Mennonites were nearer salvation than we, the church of the Lord. At this, Wilhelm Peters, who later became unfaithful himself, told him in the church meeting to open his eyes and see the pride, usury, cheating, and fornication among the Mennonites and their making of gunpowder and muskets.

Great loss for the church.

The move [to Prussia] and the attempt to establish a community there had cost the church a great deal in the way of goods and money but had borne little fruit for God. The people had certainly helped us to use up our supplies and at the same time had expected us to put up with their vanity, quarrels, and complaints.

Brothers and sisters from Moravia despised.

In short, the dear brothers and sisters from Moravia had had a miserable time among them. Some who were supposed to be united with us had mocked our brothers and sisters for their simple clothing, saying they looked like gypsies. At the same time they had reviled the other Mennonites and said that their pride and arrogance were worse than ever.

These new members were certainly no credit to us, although their community with us should have been an example to their former brothers. Our brothers and sisters from Moravia, who had been living in Prussia and understood what had happened, thanked God with all their hearts when they were free of them.

Brothers and sisters thanked God they were back in the church.

Mennonites a burden to the church.

A small number of these former Mennonites joined the church at different communities [in Moravia], but they were more of a burden than a help to the church. All they wanted was to argue and eat and drink, and there was much impurity among them.

Warning to the God-fearing.

The church of the God-fearing, who glorify none but the crucified Christ, must guard against accepting such people without serious testing and must give them time to prove themselves.

73 people had moved to Prussia.

The number of our people both young and old who had been in Prussia was about seventy-three.

Dear brother Peter Walpot had also visited the Mennonites in Danzig earlier but had soon realized that this group would be of no service in the Lord's church.

Meeting concerning our attitude to priests.

On January 27, 1604, a large meeting was called at Neumühl attended by all servants of the Word and stewards from large and small communities. Many brothers of different trades were also there. The concern was raised that some brothers had become too familiar with people holding false beliefs, especially priests. These brothers did not avoid them as they should have done.

1604

Some craftsmen were making stoves and large clocks at Kremsier castle; locksmiths and carpenters were working there too. It was said that a few were even employed in the cloisters, a place where we had never worked before.

Some craftsmen worked in Kremsier castle.

Therefore the brothers decided to take a thorough look at what was going on. Those concerned were reprimanded and charged to go to Lord Cardinal Franz von Dietrichstein to put the matter in order where necessary. They were to take the blame on themselves and put right what they had done wrong.

Craftsmen told to apologize to the cardinal.

But things took such a turn, as will be told later, that this was no longer felt to be possible, nor did the cardinal make any further demands.

These craftsmen took as their precedent for such work the building of the mill at Kremsier, as recorded under the year 1599.[1] At that time Lord Franz von Dietrichstein was made bishop at Kremsier, and he had begged us, as a lord, to build the mill for him. We had been very reluctant to do so because of the danger of setting a bad precedent, which might be a stumbling block to future generations.

After building the mill, craftsmen had assumed they could work for the cardinal.

Because of the pressing need, the elders had considered the matter thoroughly and in the end consented to building the mill. But they had stressed the fact that this was an exception, as has already been told.

When the mill was completed, the builders should not have gone on working there. They should have stopped altogether, but they had become too absorbed in the work. Some did not even know about the agreements that had been made, and others had forgotten. They started to take on other work, which was paid for from idolatrous sources, even though we had previously felt that this was wrong and refused to accept such payment. In our contract with the lord cardinal for the mill, we had been promised that we would be paid from the revenues of the Nikolsburg estates and not from idolatrous sources.

Craftsmen had not taken warning seriously enough.

Because the brothers were working without consulting anyone, the lord cardinal used this as an opportunity to try to

[1]See above, p.550.

1604

Cardinal required us to haul 7 or 8 wagonloads of marble from Vienna.

get us under his thumb or even bring about our downfall, to see whether we still held to our faith. He had his secretary write to brother Klaus Braidl, as the church elder, that he, the lord cardinal, required the brothers from Neumühl to haul marble from Vienna to Nikolsburg in seven or eight wagons, each with four strong horses.

Cardinal's demand refused.

We wrote a note to the secretary asking for time to consider this demand, after which we wrote humbly refusing the request. We said we could not serve the bishopric as it was against our conscience.

Cardinal threatened to take revenge.

The cardinal broke out in a rage and threatened brother Klaus and the others, swearing that he would deal with them. He told the locksmiths, clockmakers, and builders that he would propose to the Provincial Diet that we pay five groschen on every barrel of beer. He complained to Christian Mang about our craftsmen and accused them of not working reliably and of taking advantage of people.

Cardinal glad we had refused his request.

Now he was glad, he said, that we had rejected his request and refused to serve him as bishop, adding that he had heard we would not put one more nail in his wall.

Cardinal threatened we would have to loan the emperor money.

Among other things, he said that the emperor was sending three commissioners, of whom he was one. We would have to lend the emperor twenty thousand gulden as security. He made other threats to keep us on his estates, but in order to keep a clear conscience we could not let ourselves be intimidated. So he had the audacity to hold up the brothers' wagons that were being used for the compulsory labor we were doing for the lord at Gross Seelowitz. He even began to have the brothers attacked and imprisoned, but then he realized that all this would only harm him. Finally he threatened to have the brothers shot.

Imprisoned the brothers.

The cardinal relented.

When he saw that we were prepared to suffer and would await whatever God permitted, he relented again. But he still wanted us to admit some guilt toward him. We would gladly have done this, as we had seen that we did have some guilt, but for the sake of God's honor and our own conscience, we could not do so. He would have used it to disgrace us and to say, as he had done earlier, that we were no longer as steadfast and God-fearing as before. On one occasion at Kostel he had really slandered us.

Cardinal's brother intervened.

Finally his brother, Lord Maximilian von Dietrichstein of

Nikolsburg, took up the matter and told us that everything would have been settled if we had come to him. But now we should present our views in a short letter so that the lord cardinal would not falsely assume that we were no longer willing to serve him at all. *1604*

So we wrote briefly to Lord Maximilian that as we had previously agreed, we still wished to work for the lord cardinal and serve him in everything that was not opposed to our faith and conscience. But we could not do anything that went against our faith and conscience. We would rather suffer hardships.

We had to obey our conscience.

Lord Maximilian accepted the letter. He took it to his brother, the lord cardinal, and acted as mediator for us. The troubles described above were settled, and the lord cardinal said he would let bygones be bygones. We give all honor to God in heaven, who holds men's hearts in his hand and can incline them as he wills.

The cardinal agreed to forget the matter.

We have written this report as a warning to our descendants, so that as long as we live we do not deviate from this clear direction. Satan does not rest but continually tries to distract us from our goal and rob us of our heavenly crown.

On February 1, 1604, at Neumühl the three brothers, Niklas Kuenzin, Heinrich Schalcher, and Hansel Metzger, were confirmed in the service of the Gospel by the elders with the laying on of hands.

3 brothers confirmed in service of the Word.

On the same day at Neumühl, two brothers were chosen for the service of the Word and appointed for a time of testing. These were Michael Grossmann and Simon Stadelman, both cobblers. In the fall, however, Simon Stadelman was relieved of the service at his own request.

2 brothers chosen for a time of testing.

In January 1604 the lord cardinal at Kremsier had angrily told the brothers that we would have to lend the emperor twenty thousand gulden. Nothing was done about it until August 8, when a letter for brother Klaus Braidl came from Lord Karl von Liechtenstein, governor of the margravate of Moravia. Brother Klaus was to send Christoph Hirzel, Christian Mang, and another responsible elder to Tschernahor immediately, to receive important orders.

Governor summoned 3 brothers.

When the three brothers arrived, Lord Karl informed them of an imperial document from Prague affecting the Jews and

1604

He informed them of the emperor's demand.

the brothers. He, as provincial governor, and several noblemen were to summon brother Klaus and a number of elders and tell them that the emperor commanded them to help him in his plight with the enemy by supplying either horses and wagons or money.

Elders to talk over the emperor's demand.

The three brothers were to report this to brother Klaus by word of mouth so that he could think it over and talk the matter over with the elders. Then they could give the provincial governor and other lords their answer and he could let the emperor know what help they were willing to give. This was duly reported to brother Klaus.

Governor and military officers came to Neumühl.

On August 26 the governor himself came to Neumühl with several military officers, some of whom had come ahead and were waiting for him in the house. There were so many distinguished people as well as noblemen that the brothers began to suspect something serious was in store for the elders. They were relieved, however, that they were not called before all these people, but only before the provincial governor and the imperial procurator, Jakub Vojska, the first lord of Wessely.

Elders appeared before the governor.

The brothers appearing before them were Klaus Braidl (the church elder), Ludwig Dörker, Hans Langenbach, Johannes Rath, Gilg Molt, and Hans Eberle, all older brothers responsible for communities, as well as other brothers and servants of the Word.

The brothers' spoken answer.

The provincial governor began by telling us in an unassuming way about the imperial letter and the demands it made, showing us the document signed by the emperor himself. We brothers answered briefly that we did not feel the need to make a long speech, as we had known of the request beforehand and had written a detailed answer. That letter explained our need and complaints, how hard hit we had been by the war. Yet in spite of our severe losses, the Provincial Diet still took so much from us that we did not have enough to feed ourselves. Even after all this, rumors were spread abroad that we had large reserves of money. It troubled us deeply that no one believed we were in need. We knew that the governor himself did not believe it, so we had prepared a written answer. We had brought it along, in case he wished to see it.

Governor given a written answer.

The governor was willing to see our letter. He read it out carefully to the imperial procurator and all elders present and said he would accept it as our answer if that was our wish.

Then he included it with the imperial letter, and we assume that he sent it to the emperor or else used it to report from, since he had accepted it as our answer. We told him we were satisfied and knew that the whole church would be in agreement. That was as far as the matter went, and then we had to wait for the outcome, which we knew was in God's hands. Our written answer follows here, word for word: *1604*

At the Emperor's Request
a short report to the lords commissioner

We humbly ask Your Lordships not to receive our answer unfavorably. We are not exaggerating but write briefly in our pressing need. Brothers' answer to the emperor's demand.

We are deeply distressed that you think we are able to contribute toward the war, for we are only craftsmen and day laborers who must work hard and earn our bread with the sweat of our brow. Everyone knows that a craftsman does not earn any more than he needs in order to provide his daily bread.

We do not engage in any trade that might bring in extra profit.

People usually refuse to pay the debts they owe us or any small inheritances due to us, with the excuse that we are not entitled to such monies as other people are. We bear with such refusals (since we know they occur for the sake of our faith), and we never take anyone to court.

We also have many widows, orphans, sick people, and little children, who cannot earn their own bread. Others must do the hard manual labor to provide for them.

We ask the lords to realize, therefore, how impossible it is for us to contribute [to the war] by supplying horses, wagons, or money, even if we were to disregard our consciences, which we cannot do.

Though we already pay the Diet twenty gulden on each community, an additional eighty gulden has been imposed on every community, however poor it may be.

A tax of five groschen on every barrel of beer has been imposed on us as on people who sell it for a profit, although we brew it only for those who do heavy work and for the old and sick. We have to give what is left to

1604
Brothers' answer to the emperor's demand.

the soldiers and whoever else comes along, and we cannot charge them anything. They think beer is not worth paying for—they want to be served wine as well, which is very expensive for us.

All other dues, such as those on grain, wine, or anything else, are imposed on us as on all subjects in the country.

In the fear of God we cannot help in any war, and for conscience' sake we are unable to pay dues levied for the purpose of war, yet their equivalent or even more is confiscated from us. Some take outrageous amounts of the grain, oxen, and sheep we have purchased. The wine we have made ourselves or purchased, not for resale but for our own needs, is taken every year for taxes. Though it amounts to a large sum, we have to put up with it. As far as we can see, we will not be able to bear it much longer.

In addition, we notice every year how the soldiers drain our supplies. They have been on our necks for several years now and suck us dry, gorging themselves on the food and drink that our people have to do without. Because we continually have to reduce the food for our own people, we will have to find other ways to live in order to survive at all.

Hardly anyone else has to lodge the soldiers. We are the only ones, and they make straight for our houses. As soon as a group of them has come and gone, another group arrives. In this way, several thousand soldiers have been to one community in one year. They refuse to move on unless we give them something.

In the one year 1602 alone, the estimated loss to our communities was nearly seven thousand gulden. This was taking the lowest estimate, not even counting all the communities—though all the important ones were included. This amount includes what we gave the soldiers in food and drink plus articles they took from our craftsmen, pretending they would pay for them, which they never did. It does not include the losses sustained in the twelve years of trouble before and after 1602, nor does it include the annual taxes we pay to the Diet (as described earlier), which represents a large sum every year, quite apart from everything listed above.

1604
Brothers' answer to the emperor's demand.

Even after we have given the soldiers lodging, food, and drink, we only need to turn our backs and they unharness our horses and take them. Since the war began, two hundred horses have been stolen by soldiers, and we have not got one of them back, nor any money. We cannot even estimate the number of oxen, sheep, wagons, and other things taken during these troop movements.

We realize that however much we complain of our need, no one wants to believe it—our complaints are ignored and people even claim we are rich. So we would not mind giving up our poorer communities and sending some of our people out of the country—in the long run we cannot continue the way things are—but we are refused permission to abandon any places. Under these circumstances, if we were to send some of our people abroad, we would be worse off than ever before. We could no longer work for the lords or attend to our own needs, because our numbers would be reduced and very few useful people would come to us. In many places our people have to work for the lords, and we have to trust strangers to work for us.

On top of that we are expected (as mentioned above) to help [the war] by supplying horses, wagons, or money. That we cannot do. Rather, we would hope that those who rob us so outrageously (because for conscience' sake we cannot pay) and who want to take still more and ruin us completely will be horrified about it and consider it before God.

We are confident that if the emperor is told of our need (even though he has heard a contrary report), he will have pity on us and will not expect further help. Still less will he order more to be taken, over and above all we have suffered year after year, until we are robbed even of our food.

Stock confiscated in lieu of taxes.

We have already described how in this same year, 1604, sheep, oxen, hogs, wine, horses, and grain were taken from the brothers at various times in lieu of taxes which for conscience' sake we could not pay. The full value of these things would come to a large sum, apart from robberies and damage done by soldiers. In this year roving soldiers took many horses from the brothers.

1604

Detailed reports have been given of the violence and hardships that soldiers inflicted on the church at one community or another in other years. In this year too we suffered repeated attacks and raids from infantry and cavalry soldiers advancing to Hungary. There were several mustering points in both Moravia and Bohemia, and soldiers would come through our communities both before and after mustering. Supporting them was a great drain on the church community, apart from what they took by force.

In December 1604 a great comet with a long, wide tail appeared about midnight, red as the morning star. In Moravia it was visible low on the horizon for about an hour and a half, from eleven until half past twelve in the night.

1605

Marx Eder and Hansel Poltzinger captured in Bavaria.

On April 24, 1605, the two brothers Marx Eder, a cartwright by trade, and Hansel Poltzinger, a tailor, were captured for the sake of divine truth at Mehrnbach. They had been traveling through Bavaria and were betrayed.

Early on Monday, April 25, they were taken to the market town of Ried and held in prison for fifteen weeks. During this time various methods were used to make them renounce their faith. Two Jesuits were brought from the town of Altötting to convert them, but the brothers remained unshaken in their faith and refused to listen to alien voices.

Jesuits tried to convert the brothers.

Priest from Ried tried to persuade them to his faith.

The parish priest at Ried made a point of coming often to persuade them to accept his belief, which is one of idolatry and fornication. Its fruits show how sinful and blasphemous it is. But the brothers were not to be swayed. They always answered according to the truth and simplicity of Christ, that with God's help they would remain true until the end to the faith he had shown them; even if enemies took their lives, they could not harm their souls.

Brothers severely tortured twice.

The false teaching of the priests was of no avail, so the executioner was ordered to try his skill. The brothers were severely racked twice and questioned under torture about who had given them lodging and whom they were intending to visit, but they refused to tell the priests, saying there was no need for them to know.

Brothers to be executed with the sword.

Because the brothers would not be dissuaded, an order finally came from the government at Burghausen that they were to be executed with the sword, then burned.

At the place of execution, brother Marx asked the executioner to behead brother Hansel first, and he did so. Then brother Marx said to all the many people present, "God be praised, my brother has overcome!" Marx was also executed, and afterward both were burned. This took place on August 5, 1605.

1605
2 brothers beheaded and burned at Ried for the sake of divine truth.

The executioner had been told that if he noticed one of the brothers wavering, he should stop at once, even if his sword was already drawn. But such hopes came to nothing.

Executioner told to stop if he noticed wavering.

So as heroes of faith these two brothers gave witness to the truth, sealing it with their blood. Eternal praise be to God for giving them the strength.[1]

Brothers remained steadfast until death.

On May 12, 1605, brother Lamprecht Jänko, a servant of the Gospel, fell asleep in the Lord at Stiegnitz.

Lamprecht Jänko, a servant, passed away.

On October 19 brother Kaspar Uhle, a servant of the Gospel, fell asleep in the Lord at Alexowitz.

Kaspar Uhle passed away.

On November 21 brother Henoch Westfal, a servant for temporal affairs, fell asleep in the Lord at Alexowitz.

Henoch Westfal passed away.

On September 12 brother Hans Seidler, a servant for temporal affairs, fell asleep in the Lord at Klein Niemtschitz near Prahlitz.

Hans Seidler passed away.

On October 19 brother Wilhelm Moldt, a servant for temporal affairs, fell asleep in the Lord at Niemtschitz.

Wilhelm Moldt passed away.

On October 30 brother Christoph Heugen, an old servant for temporal affairs who had done this service for forty-five years, fell asleep in the Lord at Neumühl.

Christoph Heugen passed away.

Description of the Great Troubles More Terrible Than Ever Before
which the church of God along with other people had to suffer at the hands of the Hungarian rebels[2]

It so happened that the imperial troops in Hungary, who were on their way to fight the Turks (having already been at war with them for twelve years), clashed with the Hungarians,

---

[1]A song about Marx Eder and Hans Poltzinger is in *LdHBr*, 812–814; Wolkan, *Lieder*, 236. See also *ME*, II, 147–148; *ME*, IV, 201; *Martyrs Mirror*, 1103; Beck, 351–352.

[2]For a better understanding of the political situation of that time, the following may be helpful.

The Italian commander of the imperial troops in Hungary, General Georgio Basta, instead of supporting the Hungarians in their fight against the Turks and

1605
The great calamities that befell the church.

and there was violence on both sides. In the end, Hungarian troops reinforced by Turks and Tartars attacked Moravia and Austria in great numbers, robbing, murdering, burning, and carrying off prisoners, and leaving a trail of misery and destruction.

The blessed Meal of Remembrance held in peace.

Just before all this began, the church had held the Meal of Remembrance of the Lord Jesus Christ in all communities in the peace and protection of the Almighty. Through the grace of God this celebration was held in peace and without any interruption, and wholehearted praise and thanks were given to the Lord for his protection. Soon afterward the troubles began. Frightening reports followed one upon another that the Hungarians, Turks, and Tartars were gaining ground.

Rebellion began.

The towns of Tyrnau and Skalitz[1] surrendered, and so did many Hungarian lords, on some of whose estates our brothers were living. The enemy drew closer and closer, and the burning, murdering, and pillaging began. The church had to undergo great privation and terror and untold anguish of heart, such as they had never heard of or suffered before.

Sabatisch plundered. 2 brothers pitilessly murdered.

It began when the enemy made a night raid on Sabatisch on May 3. Through God's providence our people had fled into the woods, but two brothers who were still in the house were horribly tortured. One in particular was dreadfully burned and racked, and his tongue was torn from the back of his throat; then both were hacked to death.

4 people killed and 3 deported.

Our people left the forest, where they were not safe, and fled to the castle at Branc.[2] Three brothers and a sister were overtaken by the enemy and killed, and three others were carried off as prisoners.

Velké Leváre plundered. Many brothers and sisters mistreated and 42 people carried off.

On May 4 a great mob of Hungarian soldiers came and raided our community at Velké Leváre, mistreating and

---

Tartars, used his troops to force the Hungarians to return to Catholicism. Thereupon the Hungarians joined forces under the command of Stephen Bocskay (leader of the Hungarian revolts together with Bethlen Gabor against Emperor Rudolf II, 1604–1605; elected prince of Transylvania in 1605) and with the Turks and Tartars turned against Basta, who had to flee Hungary and suffered considerable losses. Moravia was among the areas repeatedly devastated by Bocskay in retaliation. See Polisensky, J. V. (Robert Evans, trsl.), *The Thirty Years War* (Berkeley, 1971), ch. 3; Kosary, 117–119; Beck, 337–349.

[1]Tyrnau (Trnava), approx. 30 miles northeast of Bratislava. Skalitz (Scalica), Hungary, approx. 10 miles east of Göding (Hodonín).

[2]Branc Castle near Sabatisch (Sobotiště); see above, p.245 n.

wounding many brothers and sisters so severely that some died. Then they flung into wagons everyone who had not escaped—wounded and unwounded, old and young—forty-two people in all, including Matthias Pühler the steward, and took them away. This brought deep grief to all the church elders and all the children of God. Those who had escaped in the woods and bogs were so scattered that it was impossible to tell who was still living and who had been carried off. *1605*

But God provided a wonderful means of freeing—without ransom—all those who had been carried off, and they returned to the church community. It happened like this: At this very time a brother named Hans Zwinckeberger, a barber-surgeon, was in the town of Tyrnau. From a sister (who as one of the prisoners had been given to the commander) he learned where our people were. He pleaded with the lords of Tyrnau to help his unfortunate brothers and sisters who had been deported. Hans Zwinckeberger convinced the lords to accompany him straightaway to the camp of Ferencz Redey, Bocskay's colonel-general, to ask for a letter in his own hand and with his seal, stating that all those people should be released without ransom.

All prisoners released.

When the lords of Tyrnau had gathered our people, they provided a strong escort as far as the March River. The brothers could not thank the lords enough, but above all they thanked the great and merciful God in heaven, source of every good gift. Nearly all from Velké Leváre returned to the church community. One brother, who wanted to reach the community before the others, was killed on the way.

Lords of Tyrnau escorted our people to the March River. One brother killed.

That same night there was a raid on Protzka. Although our people were still in the house, God prevented the enemy from entering until nearly all had escaped. Later, when the brothers and sisters were camping beside the March River, waiting for the ship to take them across, the enemy tried again to get them. But God frustrated their plans a second time. As the soldiers attempted to ride over the bridges, both by the mill and further upstream, they could not make a single horse cross over, however hard they tried. It was bright moonlight, and right in front of their eyes were the people they wanted to murder or carry off in their usual barbaric way.

Protzka attacked. Enemy could not enter our house until our people escaped.

Enemy could get no horse over the bridges.

Just as he opposed Balaam, the almighty God in heaven blocked the way of these enemies. All praise be to him! Although they did their utmost to force their horses over the

God frustrated the enemy's plan.

1605

bridges, they could not fight against the Lord God. They had to turn back, furious at having to abandon the pursuit.

1 brother cut to pieces, 2 brothers badly wounded, and several sisters abused.

When they returned to our place, they plundered and despoiled it and badly wounded two of the three brothers they found there. The third they killed when he reproached them for their wanton cruelty. They horribly mistreated some sisters, even one who had given birth only two hours before.

St. Georgen, St. Johannes, Gopschän, Neusorg, and Egbell plundered.

On May 5 the enemy attacked in force, plundering and burning at St. Georgen, St. Johannes, Gopschän, Neusorg, and Egbell,[1] as well as a number of farms and mills where our people were, and many neighboring villages.

At St. Georgen they arrested the steward, Matthias,[2] and two other brothers, but these also were released by the intervention of the lords at Tyrnau. With God's help they returned to the church. Praise be to him for ever and ever!

Landshut and Bilowitz burned. 4 brothers killed.

On May 7 the enemy made their first raid in Moravia. They burned Landshut and Bilowitz. In both places our communities were completely destroyed by fire, bringing great suffering and loss to the church. At Bilowitz four brothers were struck down and murdered.

3 brothers killed.

On May 9 the enemy raided a second time, plundering and burning Strassnitz[3] and killing three brothers.

3 brothers murdered.

On May 27 and 28 the enemy entered Austria, ruthless as ever, robbing, murdering, and burning until twenty-four fires could be seen at once. At Rabensburg three brothers were killed and cut in pieces.

Neudorf burned, 4 people killed, and 3 captured.

On May 30 the enemy returned to raid Moravia with fire, pillage, and murder. They plundered our community at Neudorf, killed four of our people, and carried off three as captives.

The same day the enemy stormed the town of Wessely and burned the brothers' smithy there.

2 brothers murdered, 3 people captured.

In this raid two brothers were murdered at Welka and one at Swetlau,[4] and three people were carried off.

---

[1]St. Georgen (Borský Sv. Jur.), northeast of Velké Leváre; St. Johannes (Moravský Sv. Ján), north of Velké Leváre; Gopschän (Kopčany), south of Holíč; Egbell (Gbely), approx. 6 miles south of Gopschän.

[2]Matthias Pühler, see Beck, 340–341. It is possible that this was the same Matthias Pühler who was captured the day before, May 4, and then released.

[3]Strassnitz (Strážnice), Moravia, approx. 10 miles northeast of Göding (Hodonín). Zeman, *Topography*, #148.

[4]Swetlau (Světlov), northwest of Göding. The brother murdered there was Hans Gärtner. Beck, 342 n.1; Zeman, *Topography*, #151.

1605
Watzenowitz burned, 4 brothers killed. Schadowitz, Göding, Kreutz, Jermeritz, and Tscheitsch plundered.

On June 2 there was an attack on Watzenowitz. Our community was burned to the ground and four brothers were knocked down and beaten to death. Our three communities at Schadowitz, Göding, and Kreutz were pillaged the same day; so were the farms at Jermeritz,[1] Tscheitsch, Grünwies,[2] and the surrounding areas.

10 brothers murdered. 6 people carried off captive.

At Kreutz, Mistrin,[3] and Milotitz[4] ten brothers were cruelly killed by the enemy. Four people from Grünwies and two from Kreutz were taken captive and carried off.

Enemy force, 2000 strong, repulsed.

On the same day the enemy, two thousand strong, gathered outside Rohatetz to make further raids into Moravia. But God did not allow it, for when they were coming by way of the Luschitz dam[5] near Göding, three hundred German cavalry soldiers put them to flight in terror. They left many dead.

Enemy force, 4000 strong, repulsed.

Then four thousand of the enemy, with many wagons and siege ladders, advanced against Uhersky Brod, but they were driven off by Lord Hodicky, and three hundred of them were killed. They lost cannons and all their siege ladders. So God, to whom all praise belongs, again drove the enemy back. By human reckoning this would have been impossible with so few men.

Turnitz burned, 16 people murdered, 112 carried off.

On June 28 the enemy again advanced, crossing the March River between Hohenau and Rabensburg. They took the Austrian guards by surprise and killed nearly a hundred men. Then they headed toward the forests by the March River, plundering and burning Turnitz and other villages. It was at Turnitz that our people suffered the most. Sixteen people were murdered without mercy, and 112 people—brothers, sisters, and children—were carried off into foreign parts. The church of God was in great anguish of heart. As a true mother sorrows

---

[1]Jermeritz (Jarohněvice), an abandoned village, site of the Jarohněvice farming estate, located between Gaya (Kyjov) and Göding (Hodonín). Beck, 342 n.2; Zeman, *Topography*, #56.

[2]Tscheitsch (Čejč), east, and Grünwies (Krumvíř), northeast, of Auspitz. Zeman, *Topography*, #160, #44.

[3]Mistrin (Mistřín), approx. 8 miles north of Göding. Zeman, *Topography*, #82.

[4]Milotitz (Milotice), town and castle approx. 8 miles north of Göding; seat of the Milotitz domain that included Mistrin and Watzenowitz (Vacenovice). Beck, 342; Zeman, *Topography*, #81.

[5]This dam with a road along it formerly extended from the Morava lowlands past Göding (Hodonín) to Luschitz (Lužice) and Bojanowice. Beck, 342 n.5.

1605

for her children, so the faithful felt the pain and suffering of these captives as if they themselves were in captivity. Just at this time a brother was seized by the enemy at Teinitz, murdered, and cut in pieces.

4 persons murdered, 25 taken captive.

The same day the enemy burned Altenmarkt and the farm at Birnbaum.[1] Fifteen people were carried off from Altenmarkt and ten from Birnbaum. At both places, four people were murdered and many injured.

At Rampersdorf one brother was murdered, and three people were taken prisoner.

On July 12 the enemy again crossed into Moravia near Luschitz. They set fire to about eight villages, and both our communities at Pruschanek and Tscheikowitz were burned to the ground. Four brothers at Pruschanek and two at Tscheikowitz were cruelly murdered.

6 brothers murdered, 35 people captured.

From Pruschanek thirty-five brothers and sisters were seized and carried off by the tyrant. This deeply grieved all the members of the church, and they faithfully prayed to God for them.

2 brothers killed.

On July 14 the enemy plundered Göding, Jermeritz, and Tscheitsch, and murdered two brothers at Jermeritz.

Enemy repulsed.

On July 15, in the course of the same raid, a mob of Hungarian soldiers, Turks, and Tartars arrived at Milotitz, took the castle, and plundered several nearby villages. In Bisenz about fifty people (not from our communities) were taken prisoner. At Schadowitz several brothers and sisters were still in the house when the enemy was repulsed by some Cossacks who had only just arrived there.

2 brothers killed.

On July 16 the enemy raided as far as Damborschitz but were soon driven off by the peasants. Two brothers who were in the fields, however, were surprised by the enemy and wounded so severely that one of them died shortly after. Another brother was knocked down and murdered at Watzenowitz.

Enemy reached Neumühl. God turned them back.

That same day, strong enemy forces advanced into Moravia as far as Ochsenberg near Auspitz and even to the cherry orchard at Neumühl. Neumühl was threatened many times, even by some Hungarian lords (so we heard) on whose estates our brothers were living. But God stood in their way, making them panic and take flight. After the war some Hungarians

[1]The Birnbaum farming estate is now part of the village of Birnbaum (Hrušky), approx. 8 miles northeast of Lundenburg (Břeclav). Zeman, *Topography*, #11.

who had been there told our brothers that when they rode into Neumühl, the streets were full of people on horseback and on foot; yet everybody knows that there was no one in the streets at all. Let us give all honor to almighty God in heaven, who heard the prayers of his faithful, confused the sight of the enemy, and drove them back.

1605

That same day the enemy burned down Kobelitz, Boretitz, Kostel, and many neighboring villages. Praise God, our people were spared except for three boys who were carried off and two brothers who were mercilessly slashed to pieces in Kostel and Rakwitz.

3 people taken prisoner, 2 brothers murdered.

On the same day the whole country was thrown into a panic when the enemy gathered four thousand strong near Bilowitz, with the intention of invading Moravia. If they had succeeded, they would have wrought havoc with their plundering, murdering, and burning, for almost everyone had fled, even the soldiers.

Terror in the land.

Through God's intervention, this large enemy force was put to flight by a mere seven hundred and fifty cavalrymen,[1] who killed three hundred men and took two hundred horses. By human reckoning it would have been impossible for a single one of that small number to escape alive, let alone to rout the enemy and inflict such heavy losses.

Enemy driven back.

The captain of these cavalrymen, who was billeted in the brothers' house at Altenmarkt, said it had seemed impossible, but God had done the fighting. The same captain asked the brothers to hold zealously to the Word of God and to be diligent in prayer; then they would be doing their part, for during the battle he had thought of the brothers' prayers and had been greatly encouraged.

Cavalry captain urged brothers to persevere in prayer.

In two more raids on July 28, our houses at Altenmarkt, as well as anything left standing in the neighborhood, were burned to the ground. This time not one of our people was killed or taken prisoner. The one brother who was captured was released by the lords of Tyrnau.

1 brother captured, then released.

On August 1 the enemy made the twelfth and last raid into Moravia. They plundered Bisenz by night, taking eighty horses from the soldiers billeted there.

Enemy made last raid.

After that they turned against Austria and Styria, robbing,

[1] Their commander was Ladislaus Velen von Zerotin, at the time lord of Bilowitz on the Lundenburg domain, later governor of Moravia (1619–1621). Beck, 345.

1605 murdering, burning, and carrying off captives, as they had done in Moravia. It would take too long to describe it all.

Church lost 16 communities and 11 schools.

The brutality and terror lasted three months and is described in a short outline here. Sixteen communities, large and small (including eleven schools), were destroyed. All were robbed, torn down, and burned by the enemy, which caused great damage and loss of property to the church. In the course of these raids the enemy took fifty-six horses and other animals from the fields and buildings, while marauding soldiers robbed the church of forty horses. So we suffered violence from both sides.

Church lost 96 horses.

Soldiers quartered in the country greatly burdened the church.

It was not only the enemy who caused the communities fear and anxiety but also the soldiers mentioned above, who were all over Moravia, both on horse and on foot. Many simply moved into our houses, burdening us greatly. Nearly every time the enemy advanced, these soldiers fled and robbed the refugees of whatever they were carrying with them on their flight. They robbed the brothers, not only on the roads but in our houses as well. Worst of all were the thousand horsemen of Lord Teufel, who harassed other people as well as our brothers and sisters.

Sorrow and need.

The situation in Moravia was desperate. Behind us was the enemy, devastating and murdering, and around and ahead of us were the soldiers, who were supposed to protect the country but in reality plundered at will.[1] And when our brothers fled before the enemy, the peasants, including our neighbors, would break into our houses and plunder them.

Our people were maligned and refused passage.

In some places the brothers were in great difficulties when no matter how great their need, our widows and orphans, women and children, were refused passage, as well as the food and drink they needed. Malicious lies, stemming from envy and hatred, were told against the church as if it were our fault that the enemy was attacking the country. People said we should be driven right into the enemy's path, or we should all be seized by the neck and strangled.

Priests denounced us from the pulpit.

The priests in other countries shouted the same story from

[1]See *Speculum Vitae Humanae*, Neudrucke Deutscher Literatur-Werke, Vols. 79–80, pp.13–14: "Neither did [the officers] learn anything but to dishonor God, to blaspheme, to gorge and drink, to gamble, and to commit fornication, robbing the very people they were supposed to protect, violating women and girls, and bringing distress on the poor."

their pulpits, as if these calamities had happened only because of the brothers. They declared that because the people would not root out the Anabaptists (which they, the priests, had long been hoping for), God had used the Turks to destroy them all. *1605*

After hearing the priests' lies, many people believed that the brothers had all been exterminated. Actually these miseries befell not only us and not only the country of Moravia. Austria and Styria suffered likewise, and we heard that many people had been deported, especially from the area around Vienna. Many thought we had been exterminated.

It is impossible to recount all the untruthful accusations that hostile people circulated against us, even though we would never harm anyone, we who hate war and rebellion with all our hearts and seek only peace.

Let us never forget those who were carried off into foreign parts, but continually remember them before God and daily bemoan their suffering.

About 240 brothers, sisters, and children were taken from us as prisoners. Through God's wonderful intervention, about ninety, both old and young, were later released and returned to the church, some as late as 1614. There was great rejoicing in the church, where they were received as a gift from the Lord, with praise and thanks. About 240, old and young, carried off. 90 returned to the church.

But there are about 150 of whom we heard no more. We have never found out whether they are still alive or where they may be scattered. 150 not accounted for.

The number of people murdered in all that terrible violence came to about eighty-one. 81 murdered.

Three of those killed were stewards: Bärtel Hentaler from Tscheikowitz, Jakob Käpel from Neudorf (both appointed servants for temporal affairs), and Hansel Wiedemann, the steward from Watzenowitz. Konrad Ritter, the steward at Turnitz, was taken captive and deported. 3 stewards killed, 1 deported.

This, then, is a brief description of the terrifying and heartrending times we went through. Our dear brother Klaus Braidl was filled with such pain, care, and sorrow that he wept, as did all the elders in the church. Disastrous news kept coming—tragedy after tragedy, endless suffering and pain—as deep called to deep. The faithful were in anguish about the atrocities committed by ungodly heathen against God-fearing, innocent people. It was appalling how they treated mothers Grief of the faithful because of ruthless tyranny.

1605 with newborn babies, expectant mothers, and unmarried sisters. Most terrible of all was the way they ruthlessly carried off innocent little babies, thrown on the horses' backs with feet bound together and head hanging down. Many mothers had to witness that. There was much weeping and heartache for all the brothers and sisters and boys and girls who were carried off. Husbands were separated from their wives, wives from their husbands, parents from children, and one friend from another. Some had been born in the community, but some had come from other countries for the sake of faith and Christ's name. Now they were carried off to foreign lands and sold into slavery to cruel, sodomitic people—the Turks and Tartars.

Every believer should always remember their misery as if he himself were suffering with those who were tortured and imprisoned, hungry and destitute, or driven with whips to heavy labor. We cannot describe the great inner pain and distress they suffered because they were deprived of hearing God's Word and deprived of the communal life. We know of this from dear brothers and sisters whom God in his mercy has freed from all that misery and brought back to the church. Honor, praise, and glory be to him in all eternity!

Now, dear brothers, whom God out of pure grace has called from many places in the world to be his people in these last, evil days, let each one of you cherish this precious time of peace (once more granted through God's mercy) and this life together in love, beyond comparison with anything on earth. Here the zealous can receive teaching, the hungry bread, the thirsty drink, the sick a doctor, and the weak care and a place to rest. Here we can work in the light of day and are not locked up in darkness.

Each one should make good use of his time and not waste even one hour, for we do not know what the almighty God still has in store for us. If one day any one of us should be deprived of his brothers and sisters, he will be able to draw strength from this time to help him overcome the mountain of sorrows and so attain the eternal crown of glory. Amen.[1]

---

[1]The suffering and hardship described in the preceding passage is told in the three "Bocskay songs," one of which is in *LdHBr*, 804–812 (158 stanzas); see also Wolkan, *Lieder*, 239; *ME*, I, 377.

1605
Ludwig Dörker's actions questioned.

That was the year (1605) when the greatest number of brothers and sisters were deported from Turnitz, Birnbaum, Altenmarkt, Pruschanek, and Tscheikowitz. Questions concerning this were brought to Ludwig Dörker (an old servant of the Word who had been responsible for these communities), to his assistants who were with him at Altenmarkt, and to the servant for temporal affairs. They were asked if they had shown enough concern for their communities. When the people from the upper communities had fled, would it not have been right to tell those at the lower communities[1] also to flee? They could not claim to be innocent of all the guilt for the distress of the deported brothers and sisters.

Ludwig Dörker before the church.

Ludwig, however, refused to take any of the blame and appealed to the church. In response, he was called before the brotherhood at Altenmarkt, and the whole matter was considered. He then asked the brotherhood to forgive him, which they did on March 1, 1606.

Further concern regarding Ludwig Dörker.

Later, as there were more tears and complaints from those whose loved ones had been carried off, he was again questioned. As he still refused to admit his guilt, he was called to Neumühl for another meeting with all the elders. They talked with him for about nine hours, but he still would not see his guilt and give God the honor. In the evening the matter was brought before the church, and he was excluded. He asked to stay at the community, however, and since he acknowledged the church's judgment as right and said he sought genuine repentance, he was allowed to do so. After his repentance he was received back into the church and forgiven but was no longer used in the service of the Word. He fell asleep in the Lord a few years later.

Ludwig Dörker excluded.

Kornelius Harb, the servant for temporal affairs at Pruschanek, had at that time sent his people from Pruschanek, Tscheikowitz (whence many had fled to Polehraditz by way of Wostitz), and Polehraditz back to Tscheikowitz for the harvest, against the strong advice of brother Klaus [Braidl, the Vorsteher]. Without consulting anyone, Kornelius had sent twenty-three strong young sisters there. He should have brought them back without delay when Klaus told him to get

---

[1]For "upper communities" see above, p.382 n.4. The "lower communities" were those mentioned here.

1605

them off the fields. But acting on his own, he sent scouts down to the March River to see if the enemy was approaching. The scouts ran into the enemy and were barely able to escape, much less bring back news. The enemy surprised the sisters from Pruschanek who were harvesting in the Tscheikowitz fields. They ruthlessly carried off almost all of them, and several were cruelly mistreated. For this Kornelius Harb was excluded along with Ludwig Dörker. He accepted and bore the church discipline of exclusion and was reaccepted.

Kornelius Harb excluded.

Question about ransoming the prisoners.

After this, persistent pleas were made to free the prisoners by paying ransom, coming especially from their relatives, who repeatedly went to the elders. The question was seriously considered whether this was God's will. Finally, on February 27, 1607, this was discussed in a large meeting at Pribitz. Soon afterward there was another long discussion to consider whether this was in accordance with our faith, and not against God.

Decision to ransom the prisoners.

The wretched plight of the captives was taken to heart. Because they were not taken captive for the sake of their faith (which had happened to us here in Moravia before), their situation was very different from anything we had ever experienced. Therefore it was agreed to help the prisoners by paying ransom or by doing whatever could be done. We could not desert them. The Turks or Hungarians set high prices. They might value one sister at a hundred talers, another at two hundred, another at as much as two hundred ducats, according to how young or good-looking they were.

Stock confiscated in lieu of taxes.

In this year, 1605, livestock, grain, wine, and other things were again confiscated from us in lieu of the taxes that we could not pay for reasons of conscience. This was done without taking into account the extreme damage and loss the church had suffered that year at the hands of the enemy through robbery, murder, arson, and deportation, also harassment by the soldiers who had been stationed in the country all that time.

A fire.

On June 12 of this year a fire was started in the village of Kreutz, and on June 20 the same happened at Wischenau, where the fire was ignited by a shot. In both places our houses were burned down and the church suffered great damage.

1606

1606

On January 10, 1606, at three o'clock in the morning, the deeply respected servant of the Gospel, brother Johannes Rath, fell asleep in the Lord at Pribitz.

Johannes Rath, a servant, passed away.

On February 5 at Pribitz, brother Michael Grossmann was confirmed in the service of the Gospel by the elders with the laying on of hands.

Michael Grossman confirmed.

On the same day, also at Pribitz, twenty-two brothers were appointed and recognized by the church as servants for temporal affairs. These were Jakob Schlegel, Bastel Gilg, Kaspar Hasel, Benjamin Elsasser, Brosig Schmidt, Noah Weiss, Kaspar Brecht, Matthias Zucker, Hansel Sanhammer, Uhl Joss, Jakob Rosenberger, Christoph Hirzel, Bastel Maier, Christian Mang, Tobias Lackhorn, Hansel Scharm, Michael Ritter, Philip Ferber, Bastel Haan, Hansel Kleger, Georg Schachtner, and Hans Nägele.

22 brothers chosen as servants for temporal affairs.

On March 30 brother Noah Weiss, a servant for temporal affairs, fell asleep in the Lord at Pausram.

Noah Weiss passed away.

On April 2 brother Georg Acker, a servant of the Word, fell asleep in the Lord at Moskowitz.

Georg Acker, a servant, passed away.

On October 4 brother Georg Schachtner, a servant for temporal affairs who had overseen the smithy work for sixteen years, fell asleep in the Lord at Kostel.

Georg Schachtner passed away.

In 1606 the community was again overrun and harassed by the soldiers who marched into Hungary and back again. They stayed in Moravia a long time, especially in our communities.

Soldiers harassed the church community.

On September 14 a treaty was made with the Hungarian rebels, who had caused the church untold distress and grief through robbery, murder, burning, and deporting many God-fearing members. On November 11, peace was concluded with the Turks, which lasted for twenty years.

Peace made with Hungarians and Turks.

That year much wine, grain, livestock, and other things were again confiscated in lieu of taxes.

Stock confiscated in lieu of taxes.

1607

In 1607 there were further complaints from the sisters in captivity at Ofen (Buda) about the brothers who had been responsible for the people at Pruschanek. One of them had

New complaints from prisoners.

1607

spoken with a brother, Salomon Böger, a miller, who had been at Ofen. Salomon had made three or four dangerous journeys far into Turkey for the sake of the poor captives and especially for his own wife and child.[1] The sister had told Salomon Böger that the brothers were to blame for their distress and would have to answer for it at the last judgment.

Sigmund Pühler had to see his guilt toward the prisoners.

Brother Klaus Braidl brought this before the elders. They realized that brother Sigmund Pühler was not without guilt; he should have taken better care of the sisters and sent a servant of the Word to them. The sisters from Pruschanek complained that at the time they were captured they had not been sufficiently protected.

When the brothers met to consider this, they came to feel that there had been gross oversight and lack of care. They realized that it could be dealt with only in the church. From the beginning Sigmund said that he was willing to accept whatever was seen to be right.

He submitted to the church's recognition.

On May 25 he was called before the church for a decision on the matter. After a unanimous testimony he was forgiven out of compassion for his age and infirmity, and the brotherhood prayed to God for him.

The church forgave his offense.

Hans Langenbach, a servant, passed away.

On July 13, 1607, brother Hans Langenbach fell asleep in the Lord at Damborschitz. He was an old servant of the Gospel who had faithfully carried out this service for nearly forty-five years.

Bastel Haan, a servant for temporal affairs, passed away.

On November 11 Bastel Haan, a metal engraver and a servant for temporal affairs, fell asleep in the Lord at Kostel.

---

[1]Salomon Böger, a Hutterian miller from Altenmarkt, Moravia, had lost his wife and child to the Turks. In an attempt to find and ransom them and the many other sisters who had been deported, he traveled extensively through Hungary and Turkey between 1607 and 1610. In 1608 (his fourth journey) Böger was invited by Balthasar Goller, a Hutterian physician from Nikolsburg who was accompanying the imperial embassy to Constantinople (Istanbul) as the ambassador's physician, to accompany the party as a butler. About letters Böger and Goller wrote home to Moravia, see Friedmann, *Schriften*, 106, 117.

In 1610, on his fifth journey to Turkey, Böger traveled in the company of a young Turkish prisoner given him by the imperial colonel Kollonitsch to offer in exchange for the wife of Konrad Ritter, steward of the community at Turnitz. (Kollonitsch owned the Velké Leváre estate in Slovakia, where Hutterites enjoyed particular freedom.) Böger was last heard of at Levice, Slovakia (approx. 70 miles east of Bratislava), and then all traces of him disappeared. For a detailed account of Salomon Böger's travels, see Robert Friedmann, "Adventures of an Anabaptist in Turkey 1607–1610," *MQR*, April 1943, 73–86. See also *ME*, I, 381–382; Beck, 349.

In 1607 the communities were overrun several times by soldiers who were on their way back from Hungary after the peace negotiations of the previous year. In particular, the foot soldiers of the Gaisberg regiment plundered our community at Austerlitz. They broke open all the storerooms and took whatever they fancied—all kinds of cloth, clothing, underwear, and bed linen—to the value of two hundred gulden.

1607 Soldiers raided the church communities.

This year the government again confiscated oxen, sheep, hogs, wine, grain, and other things from some communities in lieu of the heavy taxes.

Stock confiscated in lieu of taxes.

1608

On March 17, 1608, brother Rupp Gellner fell asleep in the Lord at Frischau. He was an old servant of the Word, who had been unable to preach for some years.

Rupp Gellner, a servant, passed away.

On February 24 four brothers were chosen for the service of the Gospel and appointed at Neumühl. These were Michael Kocher, a cutler; Simon Lorcher, a bookbinder; Albrecht Seyl, a shoemaker; and Burkhard Braitenstainer, a barber-surgeon.

4 brothers chosen.

On the same day, twelve brothers were appointed to the service for temporal affairs: Thomas Hasel; Paul Arter; Dietrich Pfingsthorn; Konrad Gerber; Klaus Wältzer; Hansel Schnuerl; Simon Stadelman; Leonhard Baume; Hansel Stam; Uhl Tobel, an engraver; Hans Holgans; and Michael Klug, a buyer.

12 brothers chosen for service for temporal affairs.

On April 27 brother Michael Klug, a buyer and servant for temporal affairs, fell asleep in the Lord at Stiegnitz.

Michael Klug passed away.

On May 13 brother Friedrich Samsun, a servant for temporal affairs, fell asleep in the Lord at Kostel.

Friedrich Samsun passed away.

On May 30 lightning started a fire at Klein Niemtschitz near Prahlitz, and the wheelwright's, cooper's, and furrier's workshop burned down completely.

Lightning.

On November 8 brother Heinrich Schalcher was excluded at Klein Niemtschitz. He had been nearly six years in the service of the Gospel but had not lived up to it. He was deeply repentant and was reaccepted on September 16, 1609. A month later he fell asleep in the Lord at Niemtschitz.

Heinrich Schalcher excluded and reaccepted. Passed away.

On December 20 brother Jakob Schlegel, a servant for temporal affairs, fell asleep in the Lord at Neumühl.

Jakob Schlegel passed away.

On December 24 brother Johannes Haan, a servant for temporal affairs, fell asleep in the Lord at Schakwitz.

Johannes Haan passed away.

1608
Intended to move from Nikolsburg and Tracht but made new agreement.

That same year, 1608, preparations were again made (as in 1598) to move from the estates of Lord Maximilian von Dietrichstein because of additional burdens imposed on our brothers at Nikolsburg and Tracht. These included too much compulsory labor, impossibly high rents, and refusal to pay our wages, introduced mostly by his overseer Hans Parth. However, when we had given a full report of our grievances to Lord Maximilian and told him we could not continue on his estates under such conditions, he offered to look into the matter and to make arrangements that would be tolerable. So this time too we agreed to try again and did not move away.

Great danger to the church.

In the spring of 1608 the church was in great danger. At that time the provincial governor of Moravia was a papist nobleman named Ladislav Berka of Duba and Lobkowitz at Meseritsch. There were signs that the country would be overrun in a surprise attack to bring the whole population to the papist faith. Several troops of horsemen, recruited for this purpose under the leadership of two counts, arrived unexpectedly and noiselessly at Moskowitz. For two hours they surrounded our community and the entire village on their horses, expecting word from the said Lord Berka to begin the assault. Berka was away at Brünn and with his followers planned to attack the members of the Provincial Diet. The soldiers could hardly wait and thought this was the day for them to sate the malice of their evil hearts at the expense of poor widows and orphans. They made no secret of how they intended to deal with us and how they would lord it in our houses. The faithful were thrown into an agony of grief, for death and destruction seemed to stare them in the face. In deep humility they called upon the Lord in heaven to have mercy on his people (who trust in him and have no other help), to comfort and rescue them in their great need.

Cavalry surrounded the village.

Soldiers' glee.

The almighty God in heaven heard their sighing and pleading and came to his children with wonderful help. He frustrated the purposes of these ungodly men, for they received a message that was different from the one they had hoped for. They heard that all their plots had been betrayed and were known to the Provincial Diet at Brünn. Lord Berka, the provincial governor, was arrested, and their commander Count Monfertili with his four hundred cavalry soldiers turned tail and fled from Brünn.

This news thoroughly alarmed the horsemen at Moskowitz, so they forgot all their eagerness. They were so terrified that they no longer wished to hurt anyone and, leaving food and drink untouched, fled headlong as if pursued and rode several miles that same day to the Bohemian border. With swiftness beyond all human comprehension, the almighty God rescued his people from the imminent danger and showed his might and power against the enemies of Israel.

1608
Soldiers fled, seized with terror.

When the archduke Matthias of Austria marched into Bohemia in 1608 with a large force, intending to win the Hungarian crown, the church was not spared this time as before.[1] Several thousand cavalry and foot soldiers from Hungary moved across Moravia. Most of them came to our communities, and we had to provide food, drink, and fodder for them, or they took it by force. In addition, five hundred cavalrymen and one infantry regiment were recruited in Moravia and billeted in many of our communities. So this year again the community was put to great expense.

Soldiers burden the community.

In 1608 again, oxen, sheep, hogs, grain, and much more was confiscated in many communities in lieu of taxes.

Stock confiscated in lieu of taxes.

1609

On February 12, 1609, brother Matthias Pühler, a servant for temporal affairs, fell asleep in the Lord at Pribitz.

Matthias Pühler passed away.

On October 26 brother Gilg Molt, a steadfast servant of the Gospel, fell asleep in the Lord at Kostel.

Gilg Molt passed away.

On November 21 brother Hansel Hoffman, a servant for temporal affairs, fell asleep in the Lord at Rampersdorf.

Hansel Hoffman passed away.

In the evening of December 21, the Sunday before St. Thomas's Day, our farm buildings at Altenmarkt were set on fire. Our stables, hay barns, cow and oxen stalls were burned, and so was all the unthreshed grain, bringing loss and damage to the church community.

Fire broke out.

In 1609 the provincial governor, Lord Karl von Zerotin,[2]

---

[1]For a more detailed account of these incursions, see Beck, 355–356; Kann, *Habsburg Empire*, 43.

[2]About Karl von Zerotin, Governor of Moravia (1608–1615), see *Allgemeine Deutsche Biographie*, XLV, 208–212; *ME*, IV, 1025b.

1609

on behalf of the whole Diet, asked the elders of the church for a loan of ten thousand gulden, offering adequate securities and a certified document. He wrote to brother Klaus Braidl in his own hand. But when the church's poverty was explained and details given in writing, he offered to report this to the Diet and to speak in our favor.

Elders decided to give notice at 4 farms at Austerlitz.

That same year all the elders and servants for temporal affairs, taking counsel in the Lord, decided to give notice to Lord Oldřich of Kounice at Austerlitz and Steinitz at his four farms worked by our people at that time (Austerlitz, Krenowitz, Damborschitz and Nasselowitz). Despite the great promises the same lord had made to the elders in 1603 (when we had ample reason to move from his estates), in 1609 he made so many unjust demands that it was impossible to put up with them any longer.

He tried most unjustly to reduce the very low wages of our workers, which had been fixed with his predecessors sixty years earlier, when everything was much cheaper. But not only that—he also brought great hardship to the two communities under him at Austerlitz and Damborschitz by imposing new and unprecedented burdens, the worst being that he demanded an annual fixed sum of money instead of compulsory labor. He still made the brothers do the labor, however, whenever he demanded it. If they refused, he would throw the stewards in jail.

Injustices of lord at Austerlitz.

He had the cheese brought to their community in early summer before it was ripe, even though they did not want it. The same with the fish. When the brothers could not accept this food, he ordered it to be tipped out in the yard, and they had to pay the price he fixed, or else he would take the money by force.

In ordering work from craftsmen such as locksmiths, he refused to make the usual agreement but took the finished work and paid what suited him.

Incited other lords against us.

These and similar intolerable practices were inflicted on our people by this lord at Austerlitz. He even urged other lords on whose lands we were living to treat us in the same way. He knew how to treat us, he said, and they should do the same.

Lord at Austerlitz would neither let the brothers go nor improve wages.

So great was our distress that, as mentioned above, we were forced to give notice on his farms and look for another place. But the lord at Austerlitz refused to make the slightest concession. He would neither let our people go nor increase their wages, which were too low for anyone in those times of high prices. He remained as hardhearted as ever. *1609*

So in the end we were ready to give up any claim to the two communities [Austerlitz and Damborschitz], and everything in them was prepared for the move, since there was no sign of fairness or pity on the landlord's part. Prepared to move.

Meanwhile the provincial governor, Lord Karl von Zerotin, took the matter up himself and persuaded the lord at Austerlitz to promise better wages in money and provisions for our workers. In general he urged him to offer favorable conditions to the elders who had been sent to him and remove the causes for the communities' complaints, so that our relationship would be improved in the future. So the differences were once more resolved and did not result in our moving away. Provincial governor gave help. Suggested favorable conditions.

Likewise in 1609, at Tscheikowitz, everything was ready for the community to move away from Lord Arkhleb of Víckov's estates. The school had already been transferred to Kostel. The heavy taxes and other injustices caused us such great difficulties and poverty that we could not face living there any longer. Just at this time young Lord Jan Adam of Víckov returned from Italy. He had become heir to the estate on the death of his cousin Lord Arkhleb, who had oppressed us so harshly. This young lord offered to treat us well. So when other lords appealed to us on his behalf, we decided to try once more under a new contract. Intended to move from Tscheikowitz, but made new agreement.

At Velké Leváre in Hungary we began to rebuild the community, yielding to the persistent requests of Lord Seyfried of Kollonitsch.[1] Rebuilding was undertaken on the burned-out site at Pruschanek (Moravia).[2] Lived at Velké Leváre and Pruschanek again.

Again that year, oxen, sheep, hogs, grain, wine, and the like were confiscated from different communities in lieu of the taxes we could not pay for conscience' sake. Stock confiscated in lieu of taxes.

---

[1]The contract between Seyfried of Kollonitsch and the Hutterites, signed in 1609 (as well as those signed in 1601 and 1646) is based on the original deed of conveyance of 1588; see above, p.511 n. See also Zieglschmid, "An Unpublished 'Hausbrief,'" 83; Beck, 357.

[2]According to Beck, 357 n.2, the Hutterites agreed to return to Pruschanek (Prušánky) in 1609, after the head steward of the Tscheikowitz estate (to which Pruschanek belonged) had lodged a complaint with the provincial court to the effect that the Hutterites refused to rebuild the Pruschanek community, allegedly for lack of people.

1610

1610

4 brothers confirmed in the service of the Word.

On February 21, 1610, four brothers were confirmed at Neumühl in the service of the Gospel by the elders with the laying on of hands. They were Simon Lorcher, Michael Kocher, Albrecht Seyl, and Burkhard Braitenstainer.

3 brothers chosen for a time of testing.

On the same day three brothers were chosen and appointed at Neumühl for a time of testing in the service of the Word: Konrad Blossy, a brewer; Hansel Hartmayer, a vinedresser; and Valentin Winter, a tailor.

8 brothers chosen for the service for temporal affairs.

Eight brothers were asked to take on the service for temporal affairs: Walser Fybich, Martin Hagen, Hans Egle, Simon Traxler, Jobst Neckerauer, Melchior Brecht, Karl Goller or Zimmermann (a carpenter), and Rudolf Kuesser.

Fire at Neumühl.

In the night of April 1, between eleven and twelve o'clock, a fire broke out in our buildings at Neumühl. The brewery, storehouse, and wheelwright's shop were burned to the ground with great loss to the church community.

5000 men recruited in Moravia.

In 1610 Emperor Rudolph II wished to subdue Moravia and Austria with the sword and bring them under his rule again. For this purpose he ordered several thousand men to be secretly recruited in the bishopric of Passau and about five thousand cavalry and infantry in Moravia. Since the greater part were stationed in the towns and on the borders, the church was spared to a large extent. The almighty God was our guard against the imperial troops from Passau, who caused great damage in the Enns region, at Prague in Bohemia, and at other places. He prevented them from entering Moravia, however keen they were to do so, and they had to take a route other than the one they had planned. For all this we must give praise to the Lord in heaven.

Stock confiscated in lieu of taxes.

That same year a great quantity of our movable goods—livestock, wine, grain, and so on—were once more taken from the community at various times and places in lieu of taxes we cannot pay.

1611

Klaus Braidl passed away.

On January 21, 1611, the Friday before Paul's Conversion, our dear and faithful brother Klaus Braidl fell asleep in the Lord at Neumühl between seven and eight o'clock in the morning in great peace of heart. Before his end he spoke to several of the elders, servants of the Word, who were with him during his illness and said the following:[1] *1610*

Klaus Braidl's last words.

My dear brothers, I feel that my end is drawing near, and I may become so weak that I cannot talk with you anymore. So I will speak now, while I am still able.

First of all I would like you to know that my heart is at peace and that I am in complete unity with all of you.

If there are any among you whom I have hurt, I beg you not to hold it against me but to forgive me.

Dear brothers, I plead with you to keep watch against disunity, for you can well imagine the terrible disasters that would come in its wake and what great suffering would befall many widows and orphans.

Watch that you keep firmly to the fine old church Ordnungen and follow them without moving the old boundary stones.

Hold firm to Christian community, and fight with all your might against stinginess and selfishness, for covetousness is the root of all evil and destroys everything good. Guard against innovations or starting on a new course. Take special care, my brothers, not to compete against or take advantage of one another, for that is not right. I appeal to you before God the Lord to give fatherly care to the widows and orphans and to concern yourselves faithfully with the needs of the church.

Always act in the fear of God, following truth, justice, and righteousness.

My brothers, I am very weak and do not know if all the elders will get here in time to see me, so I lay it on your hearts to tell them all that I greet them warmly as a farewell.

I thank you and all the devout for all the kindness and faithfulness you have shown me.

I am also thankful to the elders for the loyal support they have given me, thus for the Lord's sake showing their obedience to me.

Tell the elders as a last request that I urge them before God

[1]Klaus Braidl was an outstanding Vorsteher of the Hutterian Brethren. About Braidl's defense (written 1604) against the false accusations made by the Jesuit priest, Christoph Andreas Fischer, in his *Der Hutterischen Widertauffer Taubenkobel*, see Loserth, *Communismus*, 196–200; "Fischer, Christoph Andreas," *ME*, II, 332–333. Verses 75–77 of the "Väterlied" (*LdHBr*, 778) are dedicated to Braidl. See also Beck, 359–360.

1611

to be wholehearted in taking on the responsibility for the Lord's church and giving all their strength to its care.

My heart is at peace, and I have a clear conscience before God.

I say farewell to the whole church community, to all the faithful, young and old, as I have told you before.

I commend you to the protection of the almighty God. May he care faithfully for his people, bless you, keep you in peace, uphold and preserve you. Amen. Amen.

After this, on the day recorded above and at the age of eighty-two he passed away in peace and under the Lord's blessing. He had been a brother for more than sixty years, and the whole of the Lord's church had been entrusted to him for nearly twenty-eight years. A servant of the Word for forty-nine years, he had been used a great deal for the Lord's work abroad.

Church community entrusted to Sebastian Dietrich.

On January 27, soon after our dear brother Klaus passed away, all the elders in the service of the Word and the service for temporal affairs, as well as many trusted brothers from all places, met at Neumühl, and after earnest prayers to the Lord and in great fear of God, they committed the care and guidance of the whole church to dear brother Sebastian Dietrich.

Three brothers chosen for the service.

On March 20 three brothers were chosen and appointed to the service of the Gospel at Neumühl. They were Joseph Würz, a tailor; Georg Bieberstein, a saddler; and Heinrich Hartmann, a harness-maker.

Ludwig Dörker, a servant, passed away.

On June 8 brother Ludwig Dörker passed away peacefully at Nikoltschitz in his eightieth year. An old servant of God's Word and his church for forty years, he had made many journeys abroad for the Lord's work.

Stoffel Küenhuber, a servant, passed away.

On the last day of August at about six o'clock in the morning, an old brother, Stoffel Küenhuber, fell asleep in the Lord peacefully at Nikolsburg. He was more than seventy years old and had served the church faithfully for twenty-eight years in the service of the Word.

Hans Pommersummer passed away.

On September 23 brother Hans Pommersummer, an old servant for temporal affairs, fell asleep in the Lord at Pausram.

Christian Steiner, a servant, passed away.

On November 5 brother Christian Steiner, who had been in the service of the Word for thirty years, fell asleep in the Lord at Moskowitz.

In 1611 the brothers and sisters at Schadowitz packed up to leave the estate of Lord Albrecht Sedlnicky of Choltice, because of his tyrannical, unchristian treatment of our people. He had thrown the steward into prison more than once for no reason at all—an old brother who was white-haired, bent, and ailing. There this brother had been put in the stocks with a chain round his body like a criminal. He was publicly mocked by being put in the pillory, where he was nearly strangled.

1611
Intention to move from Schadowitz.

Lord Albrecht had maliciously struck one of the elders, a servant of the Word, inflicting three wounds on his head. This was Adam Neyffer, then about seventy-seven years old and scarcely able to walk for age and weakness.

Brother's head struck 3 times.

The cellarer, an old gray-haired man, had also been beaten, as were other brothers working for Lord Albrecht, including the head smith. Lord Albrecht had burdened the community at Schadowitz beyond all reason, although it was already impoverished and unable to provide for itself. Because he refused to hear our complaints, we could endure it no longer but felt compelled to leave and take flight.

When most things were moved and Lord Albrecht saw that we were in earnest, ready to leave house and home and risk everything rather than endure such oppression, he thought the matter over. He asked us not to move and said he was still a stranger in the country and did not know much about the brothers. In future he would live with us on better terms and no longer treat us so unjustly. He made very favorable offers and asked to be forgiven for what had happened; it would not happen again.

Lord Albrecht offered favorable terms.

After meeting many times to consider Lord Albrecht's good offers, which included a new contract, we agreed to try again to live at Schadowitz.

New contract made.

Again this year livestock, grain, and wine of considerable value were confiscated from various communities in lieu of the taxes often mentioned.

Stock confiscated in lieu of taxes.

The communities also had to eke out their small means to provide for soldiers, five thousand of whom were stationed in Moravia several times that year because of the forces from Passau mentioned above.

Burdened by soldiers.

1612

On February 10, 1612, brother Hansel Scharm, a servant for temporal affairs, fell asleep in the Lord at Watzenowitz.

1612
3 brothers confirmed in the service of the Word.

On February 19 at Neumühl, three brothers, Hansel Hartmayer, Konrad Blossy, and Valentin Winter, were confirmed in the service of the Gospel by the elders with the laying on of hands.

3 brothers chosen for a time of testing.

On the same day, also at Neumühl, three brothers were chosen for the service of the Word and appointed for a time of testing. These were Joseph Nägele, a cobbler by trade; Lorenz Putz, a miller; and Hansel Hueber, a vinedresser.

Abraham Laub passed away.

On April 8 brother Abraham Laub, an old servant for temporal affairs, fell asleep in the Lord at Polehraditz.

Christian Mang passed away.

On July 1 brother Christian Mang fell asleep in the Lord with a peaceful heart at Schakwitz. He was a servant for temporal affairs and had been head carpenter of the community for many years.

Tobias Lackhorn passed away.

On the last day of December brother Tobias Lackhorn, a servant for temporal affairs, fell asleep in the Lord at Lundenburg.

This year (after Rudolph II had died and his brother Matthias became emperor) the fighting stopped in Moravia, God be praised. On St. John the Baptist's Day [June 24] the Provincial Diet at Olmütz lifted the tax on beer—five groschen on every barrel. The sheaf, wool, and wine taxes were also discontinued as well as the excessive tax of eighty gulden on the mill and tannery at Tschermakowitz that had been levied for several years.

Beer, sheaf, wine, and wool taxes stopped.

But the heavy taxes on our houses were still enforced (eighty gulden for each community), which we could not pay for reasons of conscience, likewise the twenty gulden on each communal kitchen, which we had agreed to pay the Provincial Diet annually to show our good will. Oxen, sheep, hogs, wine, and grain were taken instead, as in other years.

Heavy tax on houses continued. Oxen, sheep, etc. confiscated.

That same year we began to rebuild and occupy the cobbler's shop at Landshut and the convent at Göding.

Landshut and Göding reoccupied.

In the same year, Count Hieronymus Wenzeslaus von Thurn at Wostitz allowed us to establish a community in Weisstätten[1] near Muschau for a yearly rent and use his house and farm with the gardens, fields, and meadows belonging to them.

House rented at Weisstätten.

[1]Weisstätten (Pasohlávky), northwest of Nikolsburg (Mikulov). Zeman, *Topography*, #169.

Brother Konrad Blossy, a servant of the Word, was traveling in Switzerland that year with three other brothers. In keeping with the task of the brotherhood, they were sent to gather God's people for his church. They were on their way back to the community, but brother Konrad had not taken to heart the warnings they had been given, and the brothers were captured in Swabia on the open road near Binzwangen, a village between Mengen and Riedlingen. From there they were taken to the town of Vöhringen (the residence of Count Ernst Georg von Hohenzollern), and all four were held in custody in the town hall.[1]

1612
4 brothers captured in Swabia.

The first evening, the count's clerk and several other men came to the brothers in prison, gruffly demanding what business they had in the gracious lord's domain. They ordered someone to search them immediately and take whatever was found.

Count's clerk visited the brothers.

This first search was not enough, however, and they were searched a second and a third time. Each brother had to strip to his undershirt, and every part of their clothing was carefully searched—even the seams. The soles of their shoes were also searched for money, for these wicked men were only out to rob, and they stole whatever they found on our brothers.

Brothers' clothing and shoe soles searched.

They said to the brothers, "Listen, one of your people who recanted from your heretical beliefs and returned to the old Catholic Church told us all about the money you take out of this country every year."

Brothers were told that a renegade Hutterite had betrayed them.

The informer was Klaus Prändtel, a brewer from Kobelitz, who had been captured that year in his native village of Markdorf in the bishopric of Constance. The false prophets had induced him to recant and so misled him that he not only dared to blaspheme the divine truth (against his own heart and conscience) but also to betray brothers, especially those who were then in Switzerland and Swabia. He also gave information that led to the imprisonment of five other brothers, two at Pfullendorf and three at Stockach (both in Swabia). All that was wanted of them was money, so when none was found on the brothers, even after a thorough search, they were released.

Klaus Prändtel recanted and betrayed the brothers.

5 more brothers captured.

At that time there were spies in Swabia watching out for the brothers day and night, particularly in all the districts under

Spies in Swabia watching for brothers.

[1]Mengen and Riedlingen, on the Danube, southwest of Ulm. Vöhringen, south of Ulm.

1612

the jurisdiction of the bishop of Constance. One of our doctors had been in the city of Zurich and in Swabia for over a year. God had blessed his work, and he had rendered good service to many prominent people with his medicines, especially during the epidemic in Zurich when eight thousand people died within a short time. He had made a lot of money. In addition, his faithful care had prompted the lords at Zurich to allow more than usual of the money inherited [by the brothers from Switzerland] to go out of the country to the church [in Moravia]. As a result brother Konrad Blossy had a large sum of money for the church. But all this was betrayed by the renegade Klaus Prändtel and taken from the church by robbery and violence.

Lords in Zurich allowed transfer of inherited money.

The four brothers were held in prison at Vöhringen for ten days. The priests came almost every day to the prison and did their utmost to convert the prisoners to their own false beliefs.

Priests wanted to convert the brothers.

Their efforts were fruitless, however, and they had to leave in shame, for the brothers showed the priests what sinful and ungodly lives they were leading and refused to listen to their alien voice. The clerk, the magistrate, and a doctor of theology also summoned the brothers several times and tried to confuse them and make them waver in their faith.

They said to brother Konrad, "You are completely confused and perverted in your beliefs. We'll send you another priest who can teach you a better faith."

Brother Konrad replied, "I am neither misled nor confused, as you think, but have a sound faith and know without a doubt that I stand in God's grace; therefore you need not trouble yourselves any further on my account. I will not accept your teaching.

Konrad unwilling to accept different beliefs.

"If you want to make converts, there are plenty who need it: fornicators, adulterers, drunkards, idolaters, blasphemers, liars, and the like. Convert those. But that is impossible because you yourselves are burdened by the same sin and blasphemy." The men were silent. They ordered the brothers to be returned to prison but warned Konrad to think things over, for they would be back again.

Several days later they summoned brother Konrad by himself and asked him what he now thought. He told them, "What I have said, I still say. I will not renounce my faith."

"Since you are so stubborn and refuse to be corrected," they said, "we have orders from His Lordship, our gracious count, to burn you at the stake as a heretic. If you will only take our advice, we will show you mercy and spare your life, and we will take the consequences."

1612
Threatened to burn him at the stake.

Brother Konrad replied, "I have told you many times that I will not renounce my faith, which is the true and right one, but will hold to it. I am in your power, and you can do with me whatever God allows. You can burn me, cut my head off, and tear my limbs apart, as you wish, but with God's help I will not weaken in my faith."

Konrad said he would not recant.

They said, "Then you must promise that if we should set you free, you will never return to the lands of our gracious lord."

He should promise never to reenter the country. He refused.

Brother Konrad answered, "I cannot promise never to come back, for the earth and all that is in it belongs to the Lord in heaven."

The clerk railed at him, "You cannot convince me. The devil take you." He sent for the executioner and in fury ordered him to rack the brother until he was ready to obey.

Clerk ordered him to be racked.

The executioner (who already had his tools out) took charge right away and bound brother Konrad's hands behind his back. He was about to take him to be tortured, but brother Konrad told them earnestly that he was unjustly imprisoned: he had harmed no one. He urged them to consider what they were doing. "If you tear and destroy my body even though I am innocent, you will burden your souls with a heavy guilt, and on the last day you will have to account for it before God, who is a strict Judge. Truly, that will be very bitter."

Konrad warned them and they did not rack him.

After this warning, the clerk ordered the executioner to release the prisoner and let him go on his way. But he warned brother Konrad, "If you are ever caught again in my lord's territory, you will be treated very differently." And with that he let him go.

Clerk ordered his release. Other brothers also answered with the truth.

The other three brothers were treated in a similar way. They defended their faith simply and truthfully, as God gave them wisdom, and refused to be frightened by the threats of ungodly men.

So after ten days at Vöhringen they were released and escorted through the city in broad daylight, and they returned to the church community with good consciences. But they were forced (as said above) to leave behind all they were

1612
Brothers had to leave behind all they had. Not a penny for provisions.

bringing to relieve the church's poverty, for it was stolen by ungodly men. They continued their journey empty-handed, with not so much as a penny to buy bread. But the Lord in heaven graciously provided for them so that they did not have to go hungry. He helped them return to the church in peace, praise be to him forevermore!

Count began to regret his actions.

Count Hohenzollern, however, was not getting much pleasure from his robbery of poor widows and orphans, recounted above. His cruelty and oppression caused so much talk among prominent people (including the Zurich Council, the imperial college of knights in the Hegau region, and other noblemen), who considered him grossly unjust, that in the end he was heard to say he would gladly pay a large sum of money just to be rid of their insults. Such regrets are not enough, however. He will feel far greater shame and remorse when the Judge of the living and the dead, who is no respecter of persons, gives him his reward with all who have oppressed the faithful and stolen the fruit of their work. So we will leave everything in God's hands.

2 brothers captured near the Rhine.

On May 9 of this year two other brothers were captured for their faith at St. Lamprecht on the Rhine in the bishopric of Speyer. These were Wendel Hueber, a clothmaker, and Georg Gramm, a tailor, who were traveling in their work for God's cause. From Lamprecht they were taken to the castle at Kirrweiler.

Magistrate used harsh language toward them.

Here they were brought before the district magistrate, who was just then at Kirrweiler. He stormed at them, asking where they came from and why they had come to his gracious lord's territory to deceive and mislead people.

The brothers replied that they had not come to mislead anyone, but rather to show the way to turn from evil to good.

"You're a fine pair!" The magistrate said, "I can tell from your feathers what kind of birds you are; it's a good thing we've got you. I know just how to deal with you." And he had them locked up separately right away.

2 Jesuits tried to convert the brother.

A few days later two Jesuits came, cunning serpents who expected to gain great honor through dealing with the brothers. They summoned brother Wendel first and had a chair brought for him, as he looked haggard from the dark, damp, and filthy prison. With affected kindness, they asked him how things were going, what his name was, his trade, how he came to this sect, and whether he had a wife and children. He was still a young man, they said, and it was a great pity that he was living in such error. *1612*

Wendel told them his name, that he was a clothmaker, and that his only reason for coming to this faith was his despair of finding salvation in the world's sinful life. He was not in error, he said, but was in Christ's true church, where people lived according to the teaching of Christ and his holy apostles.

Brother said he was not in error.

The Jesuits said, "To be sure it is a good thing if people live such godly lives. But you can also live godly lives here with us; we also like devout people."

To which Wendel replied, "That's not true. You yourselves are not devout, and your lives contradict the Gospel of Christ. The Holy Scriptures show that among the godly a man becomes godly and with the evil he becomes evil."

The Jesuits talked in Latin for a while and then asked brother Wendel if it were true that there were no drunkards, fornicators, adulterers, or such depraved people in our community. Brother Wendel said, "If there are, we discipline them with the Christian ban and separate from them as the holy apostle Paul directs us: 'Put out from among you what is evil.' Such people can have no community with us until they feel remorse and earnestly repent.

Jesuits asked about evildoers among us.

"But among you it makes no difference. A person can live as shamefully as he likes, and he is still regarded as a good Christian."

They asked him next what he thought of infant baptism. "I don't believe in it; it was ordained neither by God nor by Christ and has no foundation in the Holy Scriptures."

Asked about infant baptism.

At this they said, "Oh, infant baptism was commanded by St. Cyprian."

Wendel replied, "I know nothing about Cyprian; he was neither an apostle nor a prophet, still less Christ. Christ's command was to baptize those who believe, not children."

They also wanted to know what he thought about the mass. He replied, "I do not believe in it at all, for you claim that what you eat and drink is the actual body and blood of Christ. I acknowledge the Lord's Supper or breaking of bread. This was instituted by Christ and celebrated in the first church at Jerusalem in remembrance of his bitter suffering, when he

About the mass.

1612

Jesuits tried to convince the brother that Christ's body is in the host.

sacrificed his body and shed his blood for us on the cross."

The Jesuits tried to convince him, with a lot of high-sounding, empty talk, that Christ was physically present in the eucharist with his flesh and blood, as when he suffered on the cross. Brother Wendel refuted them with the truth and refused to listen any longer to their worthless talk. He told them he would not be misled and that he had a sure foundation for his faith; they had best leave him in peace.

Jesuits promised to make him a respected person.

Highly annoyed, the Jesuits called him a perverted and obstinate man who would not listen to sense. If only he would be converted to their beliefs, they would make a respected man out of him and help him to get a house and good food. He could send for his wife, and they would be welcome among them.

Brother pointed out that they had imprisoned innocent men.

"A fine Christian I would be if I followed your ways!" answered Wendel. "My brothers and I have done no harm to you or anyone—we have not so much as made a child unhappy—but you have thrown us into a dungeon as if we were the vilest thieves and murderers. When did Christ and his apostles ever do such a thing or command it to be done? They suffered imprisonment themselves and submitted to this kind of persecution from the world."

At this the Jesuits had him returned to prison. As he was being taken from the castle over the bridge, he met brother Georg (whom he had not seen for eleven days) being brought to the castle. Wendel told him in a few words what he had been through and encouraged him to hold out courageously, for the Lord would be at his side and give him strength.

Jesuits also tested Georg.

The Jesuits treated brother Georg in the same way, trying to trip him up first with smooth, gentle words and then with rough, angry ones. They got nowhere with him either and had to leave defeated, for in his simplicity and with God's help he answered them very well.

Executioner took charge of brother Wendel.

The next day the magistrate came again to Kirrweiler to hold a court session, because several people were in prison for various offenses, and he brought the executioner with him. After the offenders had been summoned in turn and all released without any punishment, he sent for the two brothers, first brother Wendel. The executioner immediately took charge of him and led him two floors higher in the castle. There he found the same two Jesuits. They took him into a separate room and asked him how he felt after the previous day's talk. Wendel's answer was, "I still hold to what I said yesterday, and with God's help I will continue to do so for better or for worse." *1612*

They warned him sternly to listen to them and accept their correction, or he would be sorry, for he did not know what his brother had promised them the day before. He said, "If my brother has promised anything, if he has allowed you to mislead him, he must bear the consequences. But I don't believe it. I have complete trust in him."

Jesuits warned him to obey and accept correction.

As they were powerless to move him, they took him back to the magistrate, who asked brother Wendel in his rough manner why he refused to listen to the Jesuit priests' well-meant advice. The Jesuits said, "He is very stubborn. He would sooner lose his life. These heretics are willing to suffer. Many have let themselves be killed for their faith, but they were heretics all the same."

Jesuit said, "Even heretics endure suffering."

"But you," said Wendel, "don't seem to be willing to lift a finger for your faith, let alone die for it."

The magistrate railed furiously at him, repeating many untrue accusations he had heard against the church. Wendel said they were not true and gave a good witness for the community.

Then the magistrate ordered the executioner to come and stand next to the brother, who should then tell who sent them out to mislead the people. Wendel said that as this was not an article of faith, there was no need for the magistrate to know; and he had not been sent out to mislead anyone but to help people turn from evil to good. The magistrate called him a clever scoundrel, saying, "I'll have you racked so badly that you'll have to come out with it."

Magistrate wanted to know who sent them on mission.

Magistrate threatened to call on the executioner.

The brother answered, "My body is in your power. I hope to suffer in patience whatever God allows."

He added that brothers were continually going out for one purpose or another. They would help anyone they met who regretted his sins, wanted to change his life, and wished to join the community of God-fearing people.

At this the magistrate said to the others, "Now you can see what sly fellows they are." To the brother he said, "If you had not told me that, I would have had you racked so that you would really have felt it. I can believe that you haven't yet dragged anyone in by force." And he ordered the executioner to take him back to the prison.

Magistrate had the brother returned to prison.

1612
Georg was also threatened.

Next they had brother Georg fetched again and urged him, too, to recant, saying he probably did not know what his brother had agreed to. They also threatened him with torture, while the executioner stood by with his instruments.

Brother Georg, however, was of good courage. He was not to be shaken in the least but determined to be true to the recognition once given him through God's grace. So he, too, had to go back to prison.

Order that the brothers be beaten.

A little later the executioner brought both brothers out of prison and took them before the magistrate, who told them he had received orders from his superior, the bishop of Speyer, to have them beaten with rods and banished from the country. In front of him on the table lay a letter which, he said, contained these instructions. He said he would show mercy, however, and take the responsibility for releasing the brothers from the beating. He handed them over to the executioner to be put in the pillory for three hours, after which they were to be expelled from the country. He also told the executioner that since he knew the brothers would not swear oaths or confirm promises with a handshake, he should not force them to do so.

Executioner put the brothers in the pillory.

So the executioner took charge of them. He bound their hands and fastened a heavy rope around their waists. Then he led them from the castle down to the courthouse and put them in the pillory in the public square. There they had to stand for over an hour.

The brothers were courageous.

A great crowd of people had gathered. Some wept, full of sympathy because they realized the brothers had done nothing to deserve this. But most of them enjoyed the spectacle and mocked them. The brothers bore it all patiently and praised God that they were found worthy to suffer contempt for his name.

Brothers released.

After thirteen days of imprisonment, they were released, taken to the border of the Palatinate, and allowed to go their way. The bailiff escorted them and told the brothers how the Jesuits and the seneschal had begged the magistrate not to have them beaten with rods. Earlier the brothers had seen the rods the executioner carried under his cloak, ready to beat them.

The 2 brothers returned to the community.

Thus God, whose ways are wonderful, can use the most wicked men for the good of the faithful, as clearly happened on this occasion. These two brothers returned to us, the Lord's church community, at peace and with clear consciences. The Lord's name be praised in all eternity. *1612*

1613

On February 10, 1613, brother Adam Neyffer, a servant of the Word, fell asleep in the Lord at Nikoltschitz at the age of eighty years. He had been in the church community for about sixty years and in the service of the Gospel for twenty-nine years.

Adam Neyffer, a servant, passed away.

On March 17 at Neumühl three brothers—Joseph Würz, Georg Bieberstein, and Heinrich Hartmann—were confirmed in the service of the Gospel by the elders with the laying on of hands.

3 brothers confirmed in the service of the Word.

On St. George's Day [Apr. 23] we moved back to Sabatisch, Hungary, at the urgent request of the lords at Branc and their promise of favorable terms.[1] In contrast to other Hungarian lords, they had proved loyal to our people during the terrible attack of 1605. So we set up our community at Sabatisch again after almost eight years.

Started again at Sabatisch.

On May 25 brother Georg Wöller, a servant of the Word, fell asleep in the Lord at Niemtschitz near Prahlitz.

Georg Wöller, a servant, passed away.

On September 12 at eight o'clock in the evening, brother Sigmund Pühler, an old servant of God's Word and his church, fell asleep in the Lord with a peaceful heart at Altenmarkt. He was seventy years old and had worked faithfully in the service of the Gospel for thirty-five years.

Sigmund Pühler, a servant, passed away.

On September 23 brother Philip Ferber, a servant for temporal affairs, fell asleep in the Lord at Pausram.

Philip Ferber passed away.

At Michaelmas, September 29, four brothers were chosen for the service of the Gospel and appointed at Neumühl. They were David Stainer, Stoffel Ruecker, and Isaak Baumann, all tailors, and Jakob Bössler, a locksmith.

4 brothers chosen for the service of the Word.

1614

On July 9, 1614, two brothers—Heinrich Bühler, a vinedresser, and Joachim Arter, a brewer—were captured at

2 brothers captured at Zurich.

---

[1]See Beck, 363 n.2, for the terms of the contract concluded on April 23, 1613. The owners of the Branc estates, acting "on behalf of the Tardy lords as well as the Niáry lords," were Johann von St. Georgy, Stefan Hedervåry, Ludwig Niáry, Sara Niáry, Georg Maytheny, Stefan Amady, Franz Nagy-Michaly. The Hutterite representatives were Sebastian Dietrich, Joseph Hauser, and Daniel Hellrigel.

1614

Zurich in Switzerland and imprisoned there for fifteen weeks.

On the third day several lords of the council came to them in prison and summoned each brother separately. They asked them what they were doing in the country—had they come to mislead the people?

The brothers replied that they had letters and messages to deliver in Zurich and other places, but the main reason for their coming was that both had an inheritance to claim.

Brothers to be released on promise never to return to that country.

A week later the warden of the dungeon was sent to the brothers with a message that the lords would release them if they promised to leave the country at once and never return.

The brothers said that on no account could they do this as it was against their faith and conscience.

After a few days the lords came once more to them in the prison and first rebuked them for obstinately refusing to see that they, the lords, wanted only the best for them.

Brothers' answers to three points.

Then they accused the brothers of misleading people, despising governmental authority, and rejecting the Christian church, which meant that they were an evil sect and could not be tolerated in the country. The brothers told them quite simply that they had no intention of misleading anyone. They were sorry that so many people were already misled and imprisoned in sin.

They said they wished to respect governmental authority, as God commands, and be obedient in all that is right, besides paying their rents, taxes, and tithes. But in anything that would be against their faith and conscience, they would obey God rather than men. Regarding the Christian church, they said they valued it so highly that they had left home and fatherland in their desire to join the true church.

Brothers threatened with the galleys.

These answers so enraged the lords that they refused to listen any longer. They withdrew in indignation, threatening to send them to the galleys, put them in the pillory, or beat them with rods.

The town clerk and the town constable in particular sought out the brothers and urged them to abandon their plans and obey the lords if they ever wanted to see their wives and children again.

The brothers answered that their wives and children were in good hands, so they were not worried about them even if they were never to see them again in this life. They would wait patiently for whatever God ordained.

1614

For quite a long time after this, the lords neither came to the brothers nor did anything further about them.

Terrible storm struck 3 times in Zurich.

On the last day of the month of July, a violent and terrifying storm broke over the city of Zurich. The Wellenberg tower where the brothers were imprisoned was struck by lightning in three different places. The cathedral and the Spitalkirche in Zurich were struck too.

Brothers unharmed.

This event filled many people with great fear. They believed the storm was a punishment for their sins and for letting innocent men be kept in prison, because the brothers imprisoned in the Wellenberg were completely unharmed. Some encouraged the brothers by saying that these happenings might lead to their release.

Ministers said God was displeased with this sect.

Many others, however, especially the band of Calvinist ministers (before they knew that the great cathedral and the Spitalkirche had also been struck) put the worst interpretation on it, saying that in the storm God showed his displeasure with that sect—he was obviously punishing it, since the authorities were unwilling to do so.

Within the next few weeks the lords came twice to the brothers in prison, each time with the question whether they had thought it over—were they ready to promise never again to enter the country?

The brothers said they could not give such a promise, for the earth and all that is in it belongs to the Lord of heaven.

Brothers threatened with the galleys, the pillory, and beating with rods.

They were again threatened with the galleys, the pillory, and beating with rods. One of the lords told them how terrible it would be in the galleys—they would certainly regret not having listened. The brothers replied that they would trust in God, whose eyes penetrate even into the depths of the sea.

Try as they might, the lords could make no headway, for Heinrich and Joachim refused to give in. The brothers were taken from prison to the town hall, where the court official pointed out how extremely vexed the lords were by their obstinacy and their refusal to accept instruction.

Brothers released.

However, on account of the long imprisonment and the lightning that had struck the tower, it had already been decided that the brothers should return home to their people.

Since the prisoners would neither swear nor even make a promise instead of an oath, the lords swore that if they were ever caught in their jurisdiction or territory again, they would receive very different treatment.

1614
The 2 brothers returned to the church with clear consciences.

Through God's intervention, the two brothers were released on Friday morning, October 24. After fifteen weeks in prison they returned to the church of the Lord with clear consciences and completely at peace. Let us praise God for this!

Ulrich Marggraf imprisoned, defended himself, and was set free.

On July 12 at Kürchen on the Eck in Württemberg, brother Ulrich Marggraf, a vinedresser, was captured for the sake of his faith. He was put in prison by the sons of Pilate and enemies of truth. They tried in many different ways to make him waver in his hope and certainty in Christ, but he gave a straightforward account of his faith according to the truth and would not let himself be swayed from the truth God had shown him. After four weeks in prison he was released, returning completely at peace to the church of the Lord. Praise God!

100 gulden taxes plus tax on beer imposed on us.

On July 10, the Thursday after St. Kilian's Day, the Diet at Olmütz again imposed heavy taxes on us: eighty gulden from every community besides a consumer's tax on every cask of beer and the twenty gulden we had been paying voluntarily to the landlords for some years. As in previous years, livestock, wine, grain, and other things were confiscated in lieu of payment.

Konrad Glasser, a servant, passed away.

On August 8 a servant of the Word, Konrad Glasser, fell asleep in the Lord with a peaceful heart at Altenmarkt.

Matthias Zucker passed away.

On August 23 brother Matthias Zucker, a servant for temporal affairs, fell asleep in the Lord at Nikolsburg.

Hansel Metzger, a servant, passed away.

On August 29 brother Hansel Metzger, a servant of the Word, fell asleep in the Lord at Watzenowitz.

3 brothers confirmed in the service of the Word.

On Sunday October 12 at Neumühl, three brothers—Joseph Nägele, Lorenz Putz, and Hansel Hueber—were confirmed by the elders in the service of the Gospel with the laying on of hands.

Moravian lords held a meeting about us.

At the Diet in Brünn on St. Kunigund's Day (September 9) the lords of Moravia, especially those on whose lands we were living with our widows and orphans, decided to meet at Nikolsburg on our account.

Lords wanted to set conditions for workers.

They wanted to reach an agreement to pay the same wages to all our people in their employ—farm workers, cellarers, treasurers, gardeners, and other servants. The lords would decide how much to pay us, regardless of the contracts we had signed.

It was to be the same with the mills: the lords would lay down the conditions under which the various mills around the country would be leased to us. *1614*

We were told to send several of our brothers to the meeting at Nikolsburg.

At that meeting, some of the lords tried hard to push through their plan. Especially Lord Karl, Prince von Liechtenstein, but others as well, gave their full support.

Prince Karl pressed the assembly.

But God the Lord (who had no place in their council but who can foil the plans of men) frustrated their intentions and let other things come in between.

A number of lords were friendly toward us and would not agree to such an arrangement, among them Lord Karl von Zerotin at Rossitz and Jindřich Zahrádecký at Wischenau. They tried instead to prevent it, with the result that our opponents' plan failed—praised be God alone. May God the Almighty in his grace continue to protect his little flock.

Some lords refused to let the measure go through.

At the same time, Lord Franz, Cardinal von Dietrichstein and heir to Nikolsburg, was furious with us because we would not let our tile-makers build a stove in the castle at Kremsier. He was not willing to accept our explanation that it was against our conscience to work for the bishopric.

Cardinal's anger.

Then the elders were told that the stove which the lord cardinal desired us to make was not to be in the bishop's apartments but in the council room at Kremsier, where the nobles and prelates met (as they did at Olmütz and Brünn). The elders decided, in the presence of the brothers in charge of tile-making, to build the stove at Kremsier. But they were not to undertake any work for the bishopric. The lord cardinal was satisfied and agreed.

Brothers consented to build a stove.

In 1614 in response to a request from Lord Ladislaus Velen von Zerotin at Lundenburg, we again took over the burned-out place at Bilowitz, where we had lived earlier for a long time. We began by building a vinedressers' house.

Vinedressers' house built at Bilowitz.

1615

On February 27 in the year 1615, brother Michael Ritter, a servant for temporal affairs, fell asleep in the Lord at Pribitz.

Michael Ritter passed away.

On April 3 at Nikolsburg, brother Daniel Hellrigel, an old brother who had been a servant of the Word for thirty years, fell asleep in the Lord with a peaceful heart.

Daniel Hellrigel, a servant, passed away.

1615
Stoffel Schenck, a servant, passed away.

On August 13 brother Stoffel Schenck from Rehag in Switzerland, a servant of the Word, fell asleep in the Lord at Frischau with a peaceful heart at the age of seventy. A former servant in the church of the Swiss Brethren, he with several others had left them because of the many abuses among them, and then he was a servant of the Gospel among us for twenty-four years.

Leonhard Baume passed away.

On October 4 brother Leonhard Baume, a servant for temporal affairs, fell asleep in the Lord at Tschermakowitz.

Lord Albrecht von Wallenstein's injustice.

In 1615 our people in the community at Watzenowitz were greatly oppressed by the landowner Lord Albrecht Wenzel Eusebius von Wallenstein[1] at Milotitz, suffering extreme cruelty at the hands of the lord and his officials. Many of their horses were ruined by the excessive compulsory labor, and some even died, so the brothers were obliged to leave some of their own fields untilled. What is more, year after year the workers were not paid their hard-earned wages, nor were the craftsmen's bills paid, although they were long overdue and the lord and his administrator had repeatedly promised to pay. By this time the debts amounted to a considerable sum.

Besides owing them large sums of money, Lord von Wallenstein also wanted several hundred gulden cash from the brothers in Watzenowitz for goods like cheese, fat, and wool. He had promised to supply them with these commodities as part payment of their wages but had postponed delivery for a long time.

Steward and storekeeper imprisoned.

When they insisted that it was impossible for them to pay in cash when such large sums were owed them, he put the Watzenowitz steward and the storekeeper in prison at Milotitz. A prominent lord in Moravia wrote to Wallenstein urging him to release the brothers, but it was several days before this took place.

No complaints or appeals had any effect on this hard-hearted lord, nor had he the least pity. To him the brothers were nothing but thieves and rogues. In his arrogance he told the

[1]About Albrecht Wenzel Eusebius von Wallenstein (Duke of Friedland, 1624), the famous commander of the Thirty Years War, see below, p.712 n.2. As owner of the Milotitz domain, which included Mistrin and Watzenowitz, Wallenstein must have signed various lease agreements with the Hutterites; see Zeman, *Topography*, #81, #82, #167.

1615

steward at Watzenowitz that the brothers would not be safe from him in heaven!

The servants of the Word had gone to Schadowitz because of all the oppression at Watzenowitz, but the overlord sent his men after them and promised the judge at Watzenowitz a reward if he would get hold of the elders for him.

Servants of the Word were pursued.

When the elders sent a brother to him with a letter, he had the brother's beard cut off out of sheer malice, and he did other spiteful things.

Brother's beard cut off.

It went so far that we were ready to give up living at Watzenowitz, and every day we thought we would have to leave.

Finally we informed Lord von Wallenstein—and made it very clear to him—that we could not and would not continue to live under such conditions. We would sooner risk losing everything that was ours on his property. He then relented a little, offered us better treatment, and promised to settle the huge debts. So we decided to try once more and did not move out at that time.

Promise that all would be well.

In 1615 we were also prepared to move out of Nuslau (Nosislav) on the Seelowitz property. There, too, our people suffered from scarcity of food, heavy demands on their labor, and confiscation when they refused to pay their taxes. They had to put up with so much unpleasantness and hostility from the landowners that they could bear it no longer. They had already moved a number of people as well as the school and the furriers' shop. But in the end, since the lord pleaded with them and offered to give the community the use of some fields to help them with their food, they decided to stay.

Plan to move from Nuslau.

In 1615 livestock, grain, and other things were once more confiscated, since it went against our conscience to pay the heavy taxes.

Stock confiscated in lieu of taxes.

1616

On January 13, 1616, brother Karl Goller, a servant for temporal affairs who had been head carpenter in the church community, fell asleep in the Lord at Schakwitz.

Karl Goller passed away.

On January 26 at six o'clock in the evening the carelessness of a coachman at Kobelitz caused a fire in the nobleman's courtyard adjoining our community. It burned down some of

Damage through fire at Kobelitz.

1616

our buildings where the coopers, masons, carpenters, and storekeepers were living, causing the community several hundred talers worth of damage.

Five days later, at nine o'clock in the evening of January 29, our community at Alexowitz also suffered great damage, through arson. Our barn was burned down with twenty-four bushels of top quality grain and nearly all the straw and feed for the livestock.

4 brothers confirmed.

On Oculi Sunday, March 6, four brothers were confirmed in the service of the Gospel at Neumühl by the elders with the laying on of hands. They were David Stainer, Jakob Bössler, Stoffel Ruecker, and Isaak Baumann.

3 brothers appointed.

Three brothers—Christel Kisselbrunner and Kilian Walch, both tailors, and Kuntz Porth, a cobbler—were chosen and appointed at Neumühl to the service of the Gospel for a time of testing.

5 brothers chosen for the service for temporal affairs.

At the same time five brothers were appointed to the service for temporal affairs. Their names were Hansel Ruecker, Valtin Kallenbacher, Joseph Seyer, Felix Biliad, and Hansel Wartburger.

Lord Oldřich's injustice to an old brother.

On March 21 Lord Oldřich of Kounice at Austerlitz and Steinitz (already mentioned several times) quite unjustly and arbitrarily arrested an old, God-fearing brother named Jäckel and had this innocent man put in the Austerlitz jail. For thirty-three years this brother had faithfully served him and his father as shepherd on the Nasselowitz estate but had been discharged five years earlier.

He was kept in prison for several weeks without any reason given either to him or to the elders.

Spiteful man had accused the brother.

Meanwhile, one of Lord Oldřich's servants reported that an evil person, a backslider, had shamelessly lied to the overlord about Jäckel, accusing him of raising weaker, less resistant sheep for the lord so that the brothers would profit from the good wool. Lord Oldřich thought he had suffered great loss in this way and wanted to punish this old, crippled man. Yet Lord Oldřich had always been satisfied with Jäckel's work. He had often inspected the sheep himself and had never given him any instruction as to what breed he should raise. In short, he had never found Jäckel to be untrustworthy.

The elders appealed for the brother.

Convinced of his innocence, brother Sebastian Dietrich and the elders wrote several letters to the lord at Austerlitz, carefully pointing out that the shepherd was innocent and had faithfully served Lord Oldřich and his father for a long time. The elders also warned him not to sin further against this devout and innocent man. In the end, after Jäckel had been in prison eight weeks and after many appeals, Lord Oldřich grudgingly released him.

1616

Brother Jäckel had been very courageous in prison. He had entrusted his cause to the Lord in heaven and borne whatever God allowed to befall him in his innocence. Therefore, God graciously delivered him.

Brother courageous when imprisoned though innocent.

On April 1 God the Lord took a heavy burden from his people through the death of Georg Riedel. But it is a terrible thing when God allows a man—who for a time proclaimed the Word of truth to others and should have been a pillar in the house of the Lord—to fall so far that he becomes an intolerable burden. Here is a brief account of what happened.

Georg Riedel affair.

Georg Riedel was elder at Klein Niemtschitz [near Prahlitz] and should have been concerned with his duties in the service of God's Word. Instead, in spite of many serious warnings from the older brothers, he engaged in the evil, seductive art of alchemy and cared all too little for his community. That was why, in 1610, he was relieved of his responsibility by brother Klaus Braidl with the agreement of all the elders and placed under brother Konrad Glasser at Kostel.

Riedel removed from leadership because of alchemy.

Riedel shook hands with brother Klaus in front of all the elders, thanked him, and praised the Lord for taking the burden from him, saying he was glad to be free of it.

But as soon as he returned home to Niemtschitz, he called some of the foremen and told them what Klaus had done, saying Klaus had treated him unjustly. He added that he had in mind to admonish brother Klaus and ask if he did not feel guilty—if Klaus had acted deliberately, he had double-crossed him worse than any Jew.

Shortly after this, brother Klaus became sick and fell asleep in the Lord. But before his death he told the elders to take Riedel to task very severely for his irresponsible dabbling in alchemy. He was also to be admonished for letting the two communities entrusted to his care, Niemtschitz and Bochtitz, suffer loss because, unlike other elders, he had not bought grain at the right time, as he had been advised to do, but had

1616

delayed until it had to be bought at double the price.

Peace restored with Riedel.

When Sebastian Dietrich became elder in Klaus Braidl's place, he appointed several brothers to take up this matter. Riedel promised to change completely, hand over his books, and have nothing more to do with alchemy, so peace was restored.

However, Riedel did not keep his promise. He did not hand over his books, but that very day he turned to his alchemy again.

Peace restored a third time.

Therefore, in 1611, he was called to account at a very serious meeting with all the elders, which lasted three hours. Finally, he was forgiven, since he solemnly declared he was ready to change if they would only trust him.

Some time later, toward the end of 1611, there was again disunity with Riedel. It came to light that on his move to Kostel he had taken with him certain confidential books (handed down by our beloved forefathers and regarded as great treasures), which brother Klaus Braidl had kept in a safe place in the community at Niemtschitz.

Riedel took a wrong and unhealthy interest in these books, using them in a misleading and untruthful way.

The Lord let Riedel fall from one folly into another.

In this as well as in other matters, Riedel had too little fear of God and despised the loving advice of the elders. He caused deep distress to several old and God-fearing brothers who had faithfully served the church for many years. He scorned and despised them in his heart. Therefore the Lord let him sink deeper and deeper into folly and deprived him of true zeal in attacking evil. In the end he was no longer able to keep to the truth in making judgments.

At Tscheikowitz, for instance, Riedel did something very stupid. A man who had been unfaithful had drunk away any sense or wits he ever had. He had cursed and slandered the elders and the whole church like any ungodly soldier, had left the community of his own free will, and was living outside in [the village of] Tscheikowitz. Riedel sent for this man, but he could not come that evening, because he was too drunk.

Riedel, in opposition to the church, invited a slanderer to the community to repent.

When this man arrived the next morning, Riedel assembled the brotherhood on his account. Most brothers pointed out that anyone who slandered in such a terrible way (and not for the first time) should remain outside the community, just as the man of his own accord had chosen to do. Although Riedel had first stated in the meeting that he agreed with what the brothers said, he then said the opposite and told the man in front of everybody that he was to seek repentance while living in the community. So Riedel's statement that he agreed with the brothers was not true, since he acted in direct opposition to them and had even been heard to say the opposite when he had entered the meeting, namely, that he was not going to put the man out—a man who had obviously turned his back on the community with slander and blasphemy. *1616*

Through his unreasonable action in this matter, through his misuse of the above-mentioned books, and because he had broken his promises to give up alchemy, Riedel was put under church discipline at Neumühl and the service of the Word was taken from him. Riedel was disciplined.

When his exclusion ended, he gave thanks before the church, praised the Lord for cleansing him, and said the church had not laid too much on him.

That same evening, however, right after leaving the meeting, he spoke quite differently to brother Sebastian Dietrich in front of several servants of the Word. He said he felt unjustly treated. He had not been able to defend himself adequately: once a man was in that position, he had to take on more than he was guilty of.

That very hour, when he had scarcely left the meeting, he began a new dispute. Yet the next day he was forgiven at his request in the presence of many brothers, and they let the matter pass. On their strict command, however, he promised never to bring the affair up again. Riedel started another dispute, but was forgiven.

After all that, in 1612, when Georg Riedel was already steward at Polehraditz, some people in Moravia were arrested for forging money. Then the executioner at Brünn and his wife, who knew some of our brothers, warned them that we should take care not to get into trouble; there were also people among us who were trying to make gold and silver, which was considered no better than forgery. In particular, they named Georg Riedel of Polehraditz, previously elder at Niemtschitz, saying he had asked them for something they would not have given to anybody else. Disturbing reports about Riedel.

As was his duty, as soon as he heard of this, brother Sebastian Dietrich summoned Riedel from Polehraditz before all the elders who were meeting at Neumühl. He asked him in a humble and kindly way how much he knew of what the

1616

executioner and his wife had reported about him, and how much guilt he had in it.

Riedel exploded in front of all the elders, shouting spitefully, "That is a lie! Why do you listen to it?" and other angry words.

Riedel's retort when questioned in a brotherly way.

Brother Sebastian humbly and lovingly told him not to talk like that—they were only asking, not accusing him, and would be happy to hear he was innocent. Riedel defiantly answered brother Sebastian, "Watch out that you don't get into a worse temper than I." Whatever they said, he contradicted them rebelliously.

However much the elders pleaded and admonished him, they were unable to induce him to humble himself. He was still angry and presumptuous, interrupting and contradicting almost every brother. In short, he accepted no advice.

Riedel opposed the church and was excluded.

Finally, he was brought before the whole brotherhood because he had despised, not only two or three, but all the elders. He had even rebelled against the brotherhood with arrogant words and refused to listen. Therefore, as a quarrelsome, spiteful man, he was excluded and separated from the church on July 16, in accordance with Christ's teaching.

Riedel spoke insolently to the church.

Several times he arrogantly said to the brotherhood, "I am more devout than the whole lot of you. You want to take a splinter out of my eye, but you have a plank in your own. You are not one hairbreadth better than I am. Everyone who excludes me excludes himself and is excluded by God."

To brother Sebastian, who pointed out how God had let this man fall into terrible blindness, he said, "You are the one who is blind." He spoke before the brotherhood with such contempt and insolence toward the elders and other brothers that any God-fearing person would have been horrified. Many brothers could hardly refrain from rushing forward to get him out of the room. In the end he had to be taken out because he continued to slander and blaspheme.

After exclusion Riedel still wanted to be steward.

In his blindness and obstinacy, he went to Polehraditz the day after his exclusion, wanting to take over the stewardship there as before. As this was not allowed, he assumed a false appearance of repentance. The next Sunday he walked unannounced and without permission into the meeting at Neumühl. For one who had formerly taught others, this was another sign of his great blindness.

Because he began his repentance in the wrong way and not under God, thinking he could force his way back by cunning, the Lord opposed him, denying him divine understanding and the grace of repentance. *1616*

For a time he confessed his guilt, especially in letters he wrote with his own hand, saying he had grieved brother Sebastian unjustly and slandered the elders and the church. He admitted that he deserved the discipline of being excluded and was willing to bear it until God and the believers were satisfied. But he was never willing to acknowledge his guilt clearly before the whole brotherhood. Soon he was again saying the opposite: before God we were doing him an injustice, and God would punish us for how we were treating such a devout man as he was. He had done nothing wrong—had never insulted brother Sebastian, the elders, or the church, and had never lied (though he had in fact done plenty of lying). In God's eyes he was not excluded; his covenant remained unbroken.

Riedel's wavering repentance.

He said he was being treated like the godly Susanna, the prophets, and the Lord Christ himself. With many more words he mixed sweet and sour, white and black, truth and lies.

At times he openly admitted in speech or in writing that the elders and the church were in the right, that brother Sebastian had not treated him unfairly, and that his suspicions came from a wicked mistrust in his own heart.

Immediately after, he likened the elders to false prophets, false judges, and children of hell, crying woe to them. With his envious and poisoned heart he tried to lay all the blame on those who had pointed out his wrong course.

Riedel justified himself and blamed others.

To sum up, it was clear that the Lord had turned away from him and a spirit of Lucifer had entered in; therefore (as said at the beginning) he became a terrible burden to the church of the Lord.

So he went back and forth. First he reviled and opposed the brotherhood as told above, arrogantly declaring himself more devout than any of us. Then he acted for a while as if he wanted to repent. He wrote a so-called confession that he had done wrong and that in God's eyes he had rightly borne discipline, but he had not been honest.

Next, he slandered us again, both in speaking and in writing, worse than ever before. He did not know why he should

1616

Riedel fell deathly ill and was allowed under our roof.

repent—he had done nothing wrong. But to us he cried, "Woe!" Last of all, he again said he wanted to repent (but by now it was too late). He was driven to it by the hand of God, which lay heavy upon him, for God punished him with physical illnesses that grew more and more severe. He could see clearly that death was waiting at his door, and he begged for God's sake to be taken in by the community, otherwise he would perish. Because of his sickness and misery he was given a small room in our community at Kostel.

After a while he moved to Pribitz. Although he was very weak, on his arrival he sent a message to be given to the elder Joseph Hauser when he came home, asking Joseph to have patience with him and trust him. As soon as he recovered, he would earnestly seek repentance and hoped he would find it.

Riedel did not repent but died in his sins.

But God did not grant him time for repentance. Riedel had been only two nights at Pribitz when on April 1, 1616, as already recorded, he died in his sins without finding repentance. He had been in exclusion for over three years, time enough to repent, but there was no sign of remorse. He therefore met the fate about which the brotherhood had warned him: he was rejected by God, just as Saul had been.

Martin Hederich passed away.

On May 1, 1616, brother Martin Hederich, a servant for temporal affairs, fell asleep in the Lord at Pribitz.

Zacharias Gartner's foolish action.

On May 27 the church was once more involved in a very distressing affair through the thoughtlessness of a brother working for a lord.

This is what happened. A prominent Austrian nobleman, Christoph Seifried Breuner at Staatz,[1] was extremely angry with his treasurer and suspicious of him though he had valued him highly until then. All of a sudden he removed him from office and put him in prison.

Zacharias Gartner took 300 gulden from the treasurer into safekeeping.

The treasurer had just given a brother named Zacharias (Zächerle), Lord Breuner's gardener at Rohof in Austria, a sealed packet of about three hundred gulden to keep safe until he asked for it. Zacharias had very unwisely accepted the money (never thinking that it would bring him into trouble) and took it home. On the way it occurred to him that perhaps something was not aboveboard with the money and decided to return it to the treasurer the next day.

[1]Lord Christoph Seifried Breuner, a confidant of the emperor.

Zacharias had no chance to hand the money back, however. Lord Breuner discovered that the treasurer had given it to him and immediately sent for Zacharias and the money. The brother was put in prison as if he had been in conspiracy with the treasurer.

1616

Lord Breuner arrested Zacharias and threatened to execute him.

Then Lord Breuner wrote to the elders at Neumühl in Moravia that Zacharias, whom we had placed in service with him, had been caught in serious theft and dishonesty. Since such an act called for the death penalty, the executioner would punish him as he deserved.

Brother Sebastian Dietrich, elder of the church, responded by sending two brothers to Lord Breuner and to the imprisoned Zacharias to find out what had actually happened with the money and whether Zacharias had been deliberately dishonest, or what the real story was.

Two brothers went thoroughly into the matter and found that Zacharias had only acted thoughtlessly and foolishly and had been tricked into taking the money from the treasurer.

No deceit found in Zacharias.

But Lord Breuner was not at all willing to acquit Zacharias; instead, he threatened to rack and hang him. He asked the brothers whether our brotherhood would vouch for Zacharias. If we were willing to take the responsibility, he would spare the brother's life provided we paid him three hundred gulden.

Lord Breuner demanded 300 gulden for the brother's release.

The elders sent Lord Breuner the following in writing:

The elders replied we could not pay for Zacharias's release.

> If it is proved that Zacharias Gartner has been dishonest and has taken the money from the treasurer with the intention of using some of it for his own profit, we cannot vouch for him but must let him face the consequences.
>
> Such a betrayal would have been contrary to the faithfulness and honesty we have taught him from his youth.
>
> But if Gartner is innocent of any deceit or evil intention, if his conscience is clear and he neither cheated Your Lordship nor intended to use the money but took it from the treasurer in pure foolishness, then it would not be right for us to pay bail for an innocent man.
>
> In this situation, we know of no other way than to encourage Gartner to remain firm in his innocence and suffer patiently whatever God the Almighty allows.
>
> As far as we know, Gartner has served Your Lordship

1616

> and his father faithfully for thirty years and, like other brothers, was allowed to be absent from the community only to oblige Your Lordship. It is therefore our humble request that Your Lordship take all this into account and not take Gartner's blunder for deceit and dishonesty but release him from prison and allow us to discipline him. We will punish him as an example to others for any negligence in regard to his work contract.
>
> It was not in place for Gartner to accept money from the treasurer for safekeeping, even while the treasurer was still high in his lord's esteem, much less after he had fallen into disgrace.

Lord Breuner made no reply to the elders' letter.

Lord Breuner did not answer the letter, and since he did not return home, it was not possible to speak with him personally as we had done earlier.

Zacharias Gartner was in prison at Aspern [near Vienna] for four weeks, and because his conditions had been eased, we were daily awaiting his release, when a totally unexpected order came from Lord Breuner: Zacharias was to be brought at once to the provost in Vienna without any further explanation and sent to the lowest fort to work on the city moat like a Turkish prisoner.

Zacharias taken to Vienna.

The command was obeyed immediately. On John the Baptist's Day [June 24] 1616, to the humiliation of the church, Zacharias was bound and taken to Vienna like a criminal.

Zacharias declared he was innocent.

Several brothers who came to visit and comfort Zacharias Gartner saw how pitiful his situation was. He wept as he took leave of them, assuring them that he was completely at peace with the Lord, with no deceit or disloyalty in his heart. With God's help he hoped to bear whatever God the Lord decreed for him, not wavering from the truth though it cost him his life. He also asked the church to care for his wife and children and always remember him in prayer.

After Zacharias Gartner had been in Vienna a few days, Lord Breuner saw that he was prepared to suffer and that we were not going to pay a ransom for his release (which seemed to be Lord Breuner's main interest). He must also have realized that Zacharias was innocent. So he changed his mind, and as soon as he returned to Aspern from Vienna, he sent for the brother in charge of the milling at Rohof. He told him that he intended to release Zacharias but keep him in service for the rest of his life as a gardener on his estate at Aspern and pay him fair wages. In addition, he asked the brothers for another gardener to take Zacharias's place at Rohof.

1616

Brother Franz Walter, elder at Nikolsburg, and his steward were sent to tell Lord Breuner in all humility that Zacharias could not serve him under the present circumstances. Lord Breuner should first release him and let him come home to the community. We would then consider whether to send His Lordship another gardener or not.

Lord Breuner had Zacharias brought back from Vienna.

Lord Breuner consented and immediately sent a messenger to the poor imprisoned brother in Vienna, but he persisted in his request to have Zacharias as gardener at Aspern and another gardener for Rohof. He explained that if he kept Zacharias in his service, any disgrace would be removed. He wanted to restore Zacharias's honor and show him more respect than ever.

He made it all sound very good to the brothers who were sent to him and spoke as if he were sorry for how much he had wronged Zacharias.

Yet when Zacharias returned from Vienna, Lord Breuner kept him to work in the garden at Aspern and did not send him home as he had promised. Soon afterward, however, Zacharias became seriously ill and was allowed to come home to Nikolsburg. Later, at Lord Breuner's urgent request and with his fair promises, we let Zacharias go back into his service.

Zacharias gave the church an account for his foolishness.

But before he went, Zacharias Gartner had to stand before the brotherhood and confess his irresponsible behavior in taking the money and causing the church so much trouble. Otherwise, everyone knew Zacharias as a faithful and honest person; even Lord Breuner's treasurer, who had brought him into that situation, cleared him of all blame. From prison he testified in writing that Zacharias had not joined him in anything dishonest and that he knew him to be a good person.

Thus the Lord in heaven graciously helped us out of this trouble and disgrace. Praise be to him alone!

Dangers of serving nobles.

We met with a number of similar unfortunate experiences within a short time. Despite their diligence and honesty, our people employed by the lords were often unjustly accused by ill-wishers and brought under suspicion through the ancient serpent's envy and hatred. This finally caused us to avoid the risk of entering such service as much as possible, since we

1616

could hardly do it in good conscience. We asked the Lord in heaven to show us what would best serve the praise of his great name and the good of his people.

Began living at Protzka.

On June 4, at Lord Michael Czobor's earnest request, we signed a new contract with him and began to build on his land again, on the burned-out site at Protzka in Hungary.

Joseph Hauser, a servant, passed away.

On September 3, shortly before eleven o'clock at night, brother Joseph Hauser[1] fell asleep in the Lord at Pribitz, with his heart at peace. He was a servant of the Word who had a good command of several languages, a man richly gifted by God.

On December 1 brother Hans Stam, a servant for temporal affairs, fell asleep in the Lord at Pribitz.

1617

Why we moved from Wostitz.

On January 3, 1617, Count Veit Heinrich von Thurn at Wostitz had twelve barrels of wine delivered to our community at Wostitz against our brothers' wishes. This count owed the brothers in his service at Wostitz and the carpenters from Schakwitz five hundred Moravian gulden for the previous year, 1616. He intended the wine as payment, but it was inferior, nine-year-old wine and hardly worth twenty gulden a barrel at that time, while he had assessed it at forty-five gulden.

Since the brothers could not accept the wine, also because in reckoning the debt the count had deducted fifty gulden, the barrels were left lying in the yard where they had been delivered.

The brothers complained, protesting that they could not accept it. In their desperate poverty, they could hardly provide enough food for themselves. They pleaded with him not to demand this of them since it would result in material ruin and shortage of food.

Three days later, on January 6, the count and his men, armed with cudgels, forced their way into the community and set guards at every door so that no one could go in or out.

Count of Wostitz's tyranny.

Then he raged through the houses like a madman and struck

[1] Joseph Hauser, known for his negotiations with the city council of Elbing, East Prussia, in 1604 (see above, p.561 n.2), was well-versed in Hebrew, Greek, Latin, French, and German. A song by him is in *LdHBr*, 814–815.

1617

the cellarer a blow with a heavy club. He threatened to burn the place down unless we accepted the wine. Some brothers gave way and took the twelve barrels of expensive but poor-quality wine into the cellar, even though the elders had forbidden anyone to touch them. They had to give an account to the brotherhood for this.

That same day the count wrote to the elders at Pribitz, among other things, that they were not to make the slightest complaint about the wine to him. If they did, not a single brother would remain on any property of his, especially not at Dannowitz.

Before this, we had complained about his refusal to honor the agreement drawn up between his father and our people at Weisstätten.

Count sent us a slanderous letter of expulsion.

He wrote the brothers at Pribitz a horrible, abusive letter ordering all brothers to leave his property at a day's notice, taking nothing but what they were wearing.

In addition, the count had tried to force the brothers at Wostitz to work beyond their strength in caring for his vineyard (near the castle), although they had given him due notice according to local custom. He had ignored the fact that the brothers had been unable to work their own vineyard and had burdened them with additional heavy work, giving them neither food nor fodder. For example, the brothers were allowed a certain time to drive three heavily laden wagons to Vienna. The weather was so bad that it took them several days and cost them fifty gulden. The steward did not have the money and had to borrow it in order to carry out the count's unreasonable demands.

For all these reasons we found that in the long run it would be impossible to live on the count's land. Even the most urgent appeals and complaints had no effect.

Decided to reduce the communities.

In January, therefore, all the elders took counsel before the Lord God and decided to reduce the size of the three communities on the count's lands—Wostitz, Dannowitz, and Weisstätten. (The place at Weisstätten had been leased from His Lordship's father, Count Hieronymus, at a yearly rent.) Should there be no improvement on the count's side, but a continuation of violence and injustice, a move would be more easily undertaken with smaller communities.

To carry out that decision, however, took time. So brothers were sent to the count to speak about the wine mentioned

1617

above, the vineyard, and all our other complaints.

In response, the count said he was ready to lower the assessment of the twelve barrels of old wine to thirty-six gulden each. He would not go lower than that, even though very good new wine was thirty gulden a cask at this time. He refused to give in to their request regarding the vineyard near the castle. He said it must be worked—they had been too late in giving notice. This was not the case; they had let him know a full three months beforehand. The brothers could not agree with the count about the wine and the vineyard because it would have set a bad precedent, and besides, the brothers at Wostitz simply could not afford it.

Count ordered the steward, his assistant, and the work distributor to be taken prisoner.

The count sent the following brothers to the constable at Wostitz: the steward and his assistant; the work distributor, because of the vineyard; and the storekeeper, because he refused to accept the wine. Then he imprisoned them in the castle and threatened to keep them for a whole year.

Now that the four brothers who had been responsible for the community at Wostitz were in prison and there was no hope that the count would relent, a further meeting was held at Pribitz on Easter Tuesday, April 28. The countess was heard to say that her husband could drive us all off his estates within the hour, and the count himself threatened to drive us to hell.

All elders decided that we should leave Wostitz.

The elders and other brothers took counsel in the fear of the Lord and decided unanimously to move all the children quietly that very night, as well as most of the people and our goods and chattels. Then we would have saved something at least. Once the count was informed of the move, he would probably carry out his threat to refuse to let us have our belongings. We could not expect anything good from the count of Wostitz.

The move from Wostitz took place that Tuesday night. No effort was spared to bring most of the people, goods, and livestock quietly to Pribitz and Pohrlitz.

Brother Sebastian Dietrich and the other elders, however, had decided that all brothers with special responsibilities remain behind, including all those in charge of work departments (forty-six brothers and sisters in all, not counting the four held in prison). We had no intention of giving up our home, farm, goods, and all the bitter toil and sweat of our faithful people without protest.

Our intention was to notify the count of our move. We

wanted to ask him to allow us to sell our belongings, collect the proceeds (in accordance with our contract for Wostitz), and let us go in peace, since he had so very little liking for us.

1617

But the count gave us no chance. The very next day, Wednesday April 29, he and the countess came to our community at Wostitz and ordered the forty-six remaining brothers and sisters to leave straightaway. He threatened to whip them out if they did not clear out immediately. He would not even allow two sick people to remain in the house overnight, however humbly we begged. He insisted that they be carried out before his very eyes.

Count expelled the 46 people from the community.

That same hour he sealed all the rooms in the community. In defiance of all justice, he took possession of our homes, farm buildings, and all movable property, the fields already sown, gardens, vineyard, and meadows, a total value of sixteen thousand gulden (at the very lowest estimate), to say nothing of the five hundred he owed our people for work and services faithfully rendered.

Homes, farm buildings, and all goods at Wostitz worth 16,000 gulden.

On the count's orders, all 350 old and young sheep belonging to the brothers at Wostitz were taken by force from the farm at Pohrlitz on the estates of Lord Adam of Waldstein, chief steward of Bohemia.

Our people at Dannowitz and Weisstätten heard how the count had treated the brothers and sisters at Wostitz and that he was threatening to treat them the same way. So they decided (without the elder's advice) to move part of their goods away.

When the count heard about it, he ordered all the livestock from the brothers at Weisstätten to be slaughtered, including their two fattened hogs.

On count's orders all livestock from the brothers at Weisstätten slaughtered. Steward put in irons.

He had the steward at Weisstätten put in irons. The work distributor from Dannowitz was thrown into jail (since the steward was sick). Besides this he forbade the brothers from Pribitz and Pohrlitz to come on his land, under threat of heavy penalties. Because of all this unjust treatment, an urgent letter signed by all the elders was sent to the count. After describing all the above injustices, they requested first that he allow us to sell the houses, farm buildings, and goods (all paid for and rightly ours) at the value stated in the contract the count's father had made with us and to collect the money; second, that the innocent brothers be released from prison. If the count refused, thus depriving our widows and orphans of what the

Elders wrote to the count.

1617

brothers had earned by the sweat of their brow, it would be hard for him to stand before God, the righteous Judge who is no respecter of persons and who knows the need of his oppressed people.

Cardinal von Dietrichstein freed the brothers.

Meanwhile Lord Cardinal von Dietrichstein visited the count at Wostitz. He freed the four imprisoned brothers and cancelled the prohibition against our entering the count's estate. The cardinal was not concerned, however, about our property, movable and immovable, which the count had unjustly taken from us by force. When the elders' letter arrived after that visit, the count was furious and threatened to answer in his own good time in a way the brothers would not like.

2 brothers sent to the count. Dismissed contemptuously.

After four weeks went by without an answer from the count as to whether he would return what belonged to us, two brothers were sent in the name of all the elders to speak with him about our property at Wostitz. They asked him not to withhold it any longer but to let us sell our property (on the terms agreed by his father) and collect the proceeds.

In all humility, the brothers delivered this message and earnestly pleaded with the count for what was rightly ours. They warned him in all kindness not to continue robbing the poor widows and orphans of their property, for he would have to give an account to God.

The count replied scornfully that he was not going to return any of our property at Wostitz, not a single penny of it. He was only sorry that we had carried off so much stuff and that he had not laid hands on the eighteen loaded wagons we had driven out of Wostitz in one night.

He said with much swearing and abuse that we had moved purely to spite him, adding that we had done it to show our determination not to let the lords take advantage of us. Besides, he claimed that, no matter what we said, fewer people had remained at the place than we had told him. So the end was no different from the beginning, as described in our record. The count did exactly what he accused us of—he said whatever he felt like and what suited his violent and unjust ways.

But without seeking revenge, we entrust everything to God in heaven, the righteous Judge, who is no respecter of persons but punishes all crime and violence in his own time. Although we must be hated by all the world, he rescues his little flock from oppression. Like the God-fearing in times past, we are ready to accept joyfully the robbery of our goods.

On October 9 that same year, 1617, brother Hans Nägele, a servant for temporal affairs, fell asleep in the Lord at Dannowitz.

1617
Hans Nägele passed away.

On December 11 an ungodly man named Erasmus von Landau, an Austrian lord of Lutheran faith, imprisoned a brother [David Wälsch] and his wife and children. In the previous year, Lord von Landau had obtained this brother's services as cellarer at Ebenthal after making many good offers over a long period. A few days earlier, on December 5, a brother from Velké Leváre [Hansel Krämer] had also been imprisoned; he had been helping the cellarer for a time without pay. The cellarer, his wife, and his children were put in the stocks like criminals. Lord von Landau declared they had ruined the wine and so caused him great loss. This ruthless treatment was intended to force the community to reimburse him for the loss, which he estimated at several hundred or a thousand gulden. No such guilt could be fixed on the brothers in prison. Besides, Lord and Lady von Landau had given written assurance with their own handwriting and seal that neither the community nor the cellarer himself was to be held responsible for any damage in the course of his service. The wine had been spoiled before this cellarer's appointment, and he was given far more wine to care for than was defined in his contract and was possible for him to manage. He was in charge of 4290 casks in twenty-four wine cellars at five different places, castles, or market towns.

Lord Erasmus von Landau's ill treatment of David Wälsch and his wife, imprisoned with a brother from Velké Leváre.

Cellarer had to oversee 24 cellars with 4290 casks of wine.

It did not seem right to pay for a release from such injustice and oppression. We came to the conclusion that if we bought several casks of wine of inferior quality from Lord von Landau, forced by his injustice and by the poor prisoners' plight, we would set a bad precedent for the entire community. It could even happen that when a lord whose cellarer was a brother did not like the taste of his wine, he would say it was spoiled and make us pay heavily for it.

In the end, we would have preferred to do without this employment, if that were possible, even though it provided our daily bread and we would lose what we had won by our bitter sweat and toil. So we encouraged the poor, innocent prisoners to be patient and steadfast in their faith, holding true to God in heaven, who would help them in his own time. Many devout before them had done the same when they had

Prisoners encouraged to have patience while efforts were made on their behalf.

1617

to suffer innocently. But dear brother Sebastian Dietrich, Vorsteher of the whole church, and other elders did not spare any efforts in their appeals to princes and many prominent lords to release these innocent prisoners from the tyrant's hands. Even the Holy Roman Emperor Matthias heard about it. In addition, they wrote and spoke repeatedly to Lord von Landau and his wife, humbly begging them to honor their promises and contracts and free the prisoners. But it was all in vain. This merciless and unchristian lord had no compassion and was not moved by any appeals, spoken or written, from great princes and lords. In his arrogance he said that he would not release them even if the emperor commanded it. So the poor, innocent prisoners had to remain in prison until God the Lord would bring about their release.

Lord von Landau said he would not free prisoners at emperor's command.

We humbly laid the grief of this great violence and injustice before God in heaven, the Judge of all. We prayed constantly for his fatherly compassion on their misery, as on all the wretched and oppressed. We implored that they be helped and sustained in accordance with his divine will and given patience in suffering, to the praise of his glorious name.

1618

Darius Heyn, a servant, passed away.

On February 6, 1618, brother Darius Heyn,[1] a servant of the Word, fell asleep in the Lord at Schadowitz.

4 brothers chosen for the service of the Word.

On Oculi Sunday, March 18, four brothers were chosen and appointed at Neumühl to the service of the Gospel. These were Bärtel Kengel, a saddler; Georg Geher, a tanner; Thoman Wilhelm from Bregenz; and Hans Lang, a cooper.

Jost Wilhelm imprisoned for his faith.

On May 24 Jost Wilhelm, a well-to-do, God-fearing man, was sentenced to death and executed with the sword at Au in the Bregenzer Wald for the sake of his zeal and true Christian faith. Because he refused to turn from this faith that God had given him, he was cruelly imprisoned for almost a year, and so was his wife, who was also devout and longed to join the church.

During that time the ungodly priests and false prophets tried

[1]In 1604 Darius Heyn, together with Joseph Hauser, had tried unsuccessfully to obtain permission from the Elbing city council to start a Hutterian Bruderhof in Elbing, East Prussia; see above, p.561 n.2.

in many ways to turn the prisoners away from their good intent in following the narrow way of life. They wanted them back on the broad road to hell, which the whole world follows.

1618

When they could achieve nothing despite all efforts and persistence, they called their high priest, the executioner, to help them. He had brother Jost Wilhelm brutally racked twice, once leaving him stretched for an hour. After letting him down they brutally shoved him into a wooden shackle in the prison and did not come back till the following day.

Jost Wilhelm racked twice so severely that he could not put his hand to his mouth.

They tore and crippled his limbs so badly that he could no longer get his hand to his mouth. They wanted to know who else in Bregenz shared his faith and conviction, but he refused to give any information.

He willingly endured the agony of torture, saying that Christ the Lord had suffered much more for mankind's sake.

Jost said Christ had suffered far more.

As they were about to pull him up on the rack, he warned his torturers that they should show the same mercy they wanted God the heavenly Father to show them on judgment day. He also said he believed that if Christ the Lord were to come again on this earth in the same form as before, they (who claim to be Christians) would treat him worse than the Jews had done.

He admonished the priests so severely about their shameful and ungodly lives—their deception, fornication, and idolatry—that they all left and did not want to speak with him again.

Jost Wilhelm admonished the priests for their adultery and idolatry.

Jost told them openly that if they released him, he would testify more zealously than ever against their false teaching and depravity and witness publicly to the divine truth.

Just as he was being condemned to death and the rod was being broken over his head, all because of the ancient serpent's spite and envy, a terrifying hailstorm suddenly arose, and many people thought the last day had come. Almost all the people present wept that this innocent, God-fearing man should die.

Hailstorm arose as he was sentenced.

This valiant Christian and true fighter for God remained unshaken. He said he was glad to suffer for Christ's sake and bear his cross in patience. He told the people that they should also be prepared to face the same death. He praised God with all his heart that he could give his life for the divine truth and die the death of an upright man.

Jost Wilhelm encouraged the people to be ready for such an end.

When he reached the place of execution, he told the

1618
Jost told the executioner he was ready.

executioner to get his work done. The executioner said he was not yet ready. Brother Jost Wilhelm replied, "But I am ready," and he thanked God again from the depth of his heart that his end was so near.

He went to his death smiling.

When the moment came to kneel and meet his death, he looked with a smile on his lips toward one of his friends standing by him, thus conveying his joyful courage, steadfast faith, and trust in God.

Priest responsible died within 10 days.

The priest from Au in the Bregenzer Wald (who had brother Jost Wilhelm imprisoned and so was responsible for his death) was at the execution. On returning home he was taken sick and died within ten days. This, many people believed, was God's punishment for the death of a devout and innocent man. The priest died in his sins.

Priest from Egg had pleaded for the brother's life. Wanted him buried in his churchyard.

Another priest from the parish in Egg, where brother Jost Wilhelm was executed, had often visited him in prison. He had learned so much of Jost's faith and had been so convinced in his heart by it that he not only pleaded against his execution but after he was executed wanted him buried in his churchyard. He said no other man there had been as devout as Jost. The priest was grieved by this innocent man's death.

Councillor said the brother was as surely in heaven as the Lord Christ.

After the execution, a prominent member of the council who had been one of those to condemn Jost to death said that no one should grieve for Jost Wilhelm, for he was in heaven as surely as the Lord Christ himself.

Jost Wilhelm had never seen the church community nor received baptism by water, but he did receive baptism by blood.

Brother Jost Wilhelm had never seen the Lord's church community with his own eyes. He had only heard of it—this spiritual Jerusalem and true church of Christ—through its witnesses. Yet through God's grace, he was filled with an unshakable faith and confidence, and he fought to gain the blessed end: the baptism of blood and the martyr's crown of the faithful witnesses to Jesus. And Christ Jesus himself, the heavenly King, will crown him with this glorious crown upon Mount Zion. He will put a palm branch into his hand, the sign of victory, and receive him into the Father's heavenly kingdom, prepared for the faithful from the beginning of the world.

But those who shed innocent blood will be punished by Christ with his terrible wrath and vengeance. They will be cast into the pit burning with fire and sulphur, where their tormented consciences will not die and the fire will never be quenched.

1618

Although Jost Wilhelm was never able to receive the baptism of water he had longed for, he gained the baptism of blood that was his wish. Therefore he is united with the community of the chosen people of God, accepted into the lineage of all the saints, patriarchs, kings, and prophets, and written into the book of eternal life.

The almighty God in heaven, strong and never-failing, be praised in all eternity for his faithful help, for through Jost a powerful testimony to divine truth was given—a comfort to the God-fearing and a greater condemnation to the ungodly.

Christine Brünner, a zealous woman ready to join the community, betrayed, imprisoned, and racked 6 times.

This year, a woman in Bregenz named Christine Brünner, also on fire for the truth, had prepared to travel to the community where her daughter was. She was about to leave her house when the constable and the executioner's assistant arrested her unexpectedly. They took her to Egg, a village about two miles from the town of Bregenz. There she was severely racked six times to make her abandon her good resolve and betray those who had sheltered the brothers and shown them kindness. This she refused to do. She armed her woman's heart with manful determination and held faithfully and firmly to the truth God had shown her, even though she had not been baptized by water and had never seen the church community of the Lord with her own eyes.

Christine Brünner sentenced to death and executed with the sword.

So, because of Satan's bloodthirsty hatred and envy, she, too, was condemned to death by the brood of Pilate, those enemies of the truth. She was executed with the sword on August 4 of this year, 1618.[1]

The Lord proved his great power in this weak woman.

So powerfully did God the Lord show his might and grace in this simple woman that she reckoned all temporal suffering as of little account. Neither torture nor the gates of hell could separate her from God.

Like the wise virgins with burning lamps, she went joyfully to meet her Bridegroom, the Lord Jesus Christ. He will lead her to the eternal wedding feast and invite her to the glorious Supper of the Lord, which no eye has seen nor ear heard nor heart of man conceived. Her short suffering will be repaid with everlasting joy.

---

[1]About Jost Wilhelm and Christine Brünner (or Brenner), see Johann Loserth, "Vorarlberg," *ME*, IV, 854b; "Bregenzerwald," *ME*, I, 413a. A song about them is in *LdHBr*, 817–821; see Wolkan, *Lieder*, 236–237.

1618

But woe, woe to those who shed innocent blood; for God through his prophets says that he will forgive all sins, but he will not leave unavenged the innocent blood of his holy ones. He will bring terrible requital and punish with eternal torment. Then they will see whom they have pierced.

3 brothers confirmed in the service of the Word.

On October 4 at Neumühl the three brothers Christel Kisselbrunner, Kuntz Porth, and Kilian Walch were confirmed in the service of the Gospel by the elders with the laying on of hands.

Bärtel Kengel freed from the service.

At the same time, Bärtel Kengel, who had been six months in a time of testing for this service, was relieved of it at his own urgent request, partly because he found it hard to speak [in public].

On November 29, 1618, around four o'clock in the morning, an extraordinary comet appeared.[1] It was brilliant and had a very long tail such as is rarely seen. After that, it appeared each morning a little earlier until it rose exactly at midnight. The time when it rose changed gradually from morning to midnight and from midnight to evening. This covered a period of four weeks, namely from November 29 until the end of December. It was watched with great awe and terror and was last seen close to the North Star, where it faded away. In the years following we were to learn, with much suffering and sorrow, what it had signified.

---

[1]About this comet, see *Theatrum Europaeum*, I, 116–118; Beck, 367–368.

Theatrum Europaeum: a German chronicle of events, forerunner of the newspaper, in 21 volumes published in Frankfurt am Main, 1633–1738, that covers events from 1618–1718; see *Der Große Brockhaus*, XVIII (1934), 603.

The Thirty Years War
1618–1622: Tribulations in Moravia

This same year, 1618, fierce agitation and revolt broke out in the kingdom of Bohemia, developing into terrible war and bloodshed between the [Roman Catholic] emperor and the Lutheran Estates in Bohemia.[1] Because of this, on John the Baptist's Day [June 24], the Provincial Diet at Olmütz decided to recruit 5,000 men—cavalry and foot soldiers—for the defense of Moravia. The decision was carried out immediately. As a consequence, on top of the heavy annual tax of one hundred gulden on each community, a tax of fifty gulden was added on every house. So this year a sum of 150 gulden was taken from every community in Moravia, large or small, regardless of the fact that many of them could not support themselves. But it did not even stop at what the Diet imposed:

50 gulden added to the tax.

---

[1]The Bohemian Revolt of May 1618, which was to develop into the Thirty Years War.

Count Heinrich Matthias von Thurn (1567–1640), a prominent leader of the Protestant Estates, had succeeded in forcing Emperor Rudolf II in 1609 to issue the Letter of Majesty granting religious freedom in Bohemia. In May 1618 Count von Thurn called a meeting of Protestant Estates at Prague University to discuss threats to that freedom: Two Protestant churches had been destroyed, at Braunau (near the Silesian border) and at Klostergrab (Hrob) near Teplitz (near the border with Saxony). Complaints made to Emperor Matthias were denounced as rebellion. The meetings ended on May 23 with the famous Defenestration of Prague, when von Thurn himself threw two Catholic councillors, Jaroslav of Martinitz and William of Slavata, and their secretary, Fabricius, from a window of the Hradschin into the moat. This act of violence marks the beginning of the Thirty Years War. Under the leadership of Count Matthias von Thurn, the Bohemian Protestants (by far the majority in the country) set up their own council and appointed thirty Directors.

For details of the Thirty Years War, as also described in this chronicle, see *Theatrum Europaeum*, I–VI (1635–1652); Polisensky, *Thirty Years War*, 98–132; J. V. Polisensky and Frederick Snider, *War and Society in Europe, 1618–1620* (Cambridge, 1978), 36–65; J.P. Cooper, ed., *The New Cambridge Modern History*, IV: *The Decline of Spain and the Thirty Years War, 1609–48/59* (Cambridge, 1970), 306–357.

1618
Stock confiscated in lieu of taxes.

In many places livestock, grain, wine, and other goods were taken in lieu of the tax at a much lower valuation than our selling price. In addition, several communities had to quarter soldiers for many weeks in summer and winter. On their marches back and forth, the soldiers often overran our communities, and we had to give them food, drink, and fodder—as much as they wanted. When they were billeted in other places, we still had to supply them with provisions and fodder. Through this heavy consumption, our food supply was greatly diminished.

1619

Emperor Matthias died. King Ferdinand continued the Bohemian War.

In the year 1619 we still had the hope and the great longing that the war between the Holy Roman Emperor Matthias and the Bohemian Protestants would come to an end, not only to save the church community and the whole country from further harm, but also to bring relief from the heavy taxes which (as already recorded) were imposed on us in the year 1618. On March 20, 1619, however, the emperor Matthias I died, and King Ferdinand continued the Bohemian War that had started under Emperor Matthias.[1] Through his generals Count Buquoy[2] and Count Dampierre[3] (who had also served under the previous emperor), he acted with a brutality never known before in the kingdom of Bohemia. Therefore no reconciliation was found—the war only continued all the more intense and widespread—and the Bohemian Estates tried to get the Moravians to support their side (while the king thought Moravia was on his side).

---

[1]Archduke Ferdinand of Styria (king of Bohemia, 1617; of Hungary, 1618) was elected Holy Roman Emperor (Ferdinand II) at Frankfurt am Main, Aug. 28, 1619. His intolerance is illustrated by these words ascribed to him: "I prefer a wilderness to a country full of heretics."

[2]Charles Bonaventure de Longueval, Baron de Vaux, Comte de Buquoy, born 1571 in Arras, France. In 1618 he became commander-in-chief of the imperial troops in Bohemia, and played a leading role in the Battle of the White Mountain (Prague, Nov. 8, 1620). In 1621 he defeated Bethlen Gabor in Hungary; he fell on July 10, 1621, in the siege of Neuhäusel (Nové Zámky), Hungary.

[3]Henri Duval, Count Dampierre (1580–1620), Austrian general; at the outbreak of the Bohemian Revolt, 1618, he led an imperial army corps into Bohemia; came to the aid of Emperor Ferdinand II, who was being pressured by the Protestant Estates in Vienna; advanced into Moravia and Hungary with 10,000 men against Bethlen Gabor; fell on October 8, 1620, in the storming of the fortified castle at Bratislava; see *Allgemeine Deutsche Biographie*, IV, 719–720.

As a consequence, Count Heinrich Matthias von Thurn, lieutenant general to the Crown of Bohemia, marched into Moravia in early spring with a large number of cavalry and infantry. He succeeded—although not without opposition—in convincing the Moravian Estates to support Bohemia as allies. Most of this support came from the non-Catholic lords. The Catholic lords, who held the power and the chief positions in Moravia at that time, were deposed from office, and the most important ones were imprisoned. Just as in Bohemia at that time, directors or provincial governors were elected from the three remaining Estates[1] (after the fourth Estate, the prelates, had been ousted), and within three days they expelled the Jesuits forever from Moravia. All of this gave rise to King Ferdinand's fierce hatred toward this country. *1619*

Catholic lords in Moravia removed from office. Jesuits expelled from the country.

Now Count von Thurn (mentioned above), who had marched from Moravia to Vienna in Austria with his Bohemian troops and a good number of the Moravian forces, had to leave Vienna and return to Bohemia because enemies were vandalizing his country. As Moravia was now without soldiers, King Ferdinand sent in several thousand men under General Dampierre to force Moravia to submit to his rule again.[2] Those who had deserted him and who still refused to return and beg for his mercy would be punished with the sword, and their lands and property would be burned to the ground.

Count Dampierre marched into Moravia to punish those who had disobeyed the king.

This terrible and remorseless punishment—beyond doubt by divine decree for the chastening of God's people—fell most heavily on the church communities of the Lord, although they were innocent of all that was going on. They suffered incalculable damage and unspeakably great sorrow, trouble, and anxiety from robbery, murder, and fire at the hands of Dampierre's soldiers, and even more from the ungodly Hungarians. Some of these had been sent by Catholic lords in

---

[1]About the Bohemian Estates and their role in the Bohemian Revolt and the Thirty Years War, see Kann, *Habsburg Empire*, 125–129; Polisensky, *Thirty Years War*, 98–132; Polisensky and Snider, *War and Society*; "Estates, general," *Encyclopaedia Britannica*, Vol. 3, 850d.

[2]See Friedrich von Schiller's report about this expedition in his *Geschichte des Dreißigjährigen Krieges*: "And now the emperor, too, began to show more serious activity: Buquoy and Dampierre entered Bohemia with two armies and started their brutal rampage. . . . With each new advance the opposition increased. The excesses of their troops (mostly Hungarians and Walloons) caused their allies to desert and their enemies to despair." See also Beck, 373–380.

1619

Hungary to help King Ferdinand and others whom King Ferdinand himself had hired from the border forts. There had not been such suffering even in the earlier Hungarian Rebellion of 1605 (apart from the suffering of those who were carried off into Mohammedan slavery). A brief summary follows, describing first the damage done, and then the great distress.[1]

On July 10, 1619, Dampierre and his troops arrived at Retz [in Austria], moved on to Joslowitz (Jaroslavice), seized the castle, and encamped there. On July 22 Moskowitz was plundered for the first time, and from then until October 15 it was raided thirty times. Everything found there was stolen: besides other movable property, large amounts of grain, flour, several barrels of wine, four horses, twelve oxen, and an entire herd of pigs were taken. Two brothers were arrested and brutally racked. One had his ear cut off to make them tell where the money was and give other information.

Moskowitz plundered.

On July 30 the community at Frischau was plundered twice, and on August 2 it was burned to the ground.

Frischau burned down.

On July 31 Tracht was plundered, and on August 6—the day following the battle at Wisternitz—the community with all its property was burned down.

Tracht burned down.

On August 1 Gallitz was plundered; on August 3 it was set on fire, and two brothers were fatally wounded.

Gallitz burned down.

On August 1 Bochtitz was ruthlessly plundered.

Bochtitz plundered.

On August 2 Stiegnitz was plundered for the first time, and an old brother was killed. Samuel, the brother who did the buying, was brutally racked to make him tell where the money was. Then there was another raid: cloth, linen, leather, and shoes were stolen, as well as quantities of clothing and bed linen and eleven fattened oxen. A sister in the advanced stages of pregnancy was raped.

Stiegnitz plundered with great cruelty.

On August 9 the house at Weisstätten and our mill at Eibis[2] were plundered.

Weisstätten plundered.

On August 15 Dannowitz was plundered and on the 16th burned to the ground.

Dannowitz burned.

On August 19 Polehraditz was plundered for the first time.

Polehraditz plundered 11 times with great brutality.

[1]The suffering of the Hutterites during the events of 1619 and 1620, chronicled in the following pages, is described in the two "Pribitz Songs"; see *LdHBr*, 821–827, 835–838.

[2]Eibis (Ivaň), west of Auspitz, Moravia, at the confluence of the Jihlava and the Svratka rivers; see Beck, 374 n.1; Zeman, *Topography*, #35.

Later it was attacked and robbed ten more times, and all the horses and much equipment were taken. Six sisters, three married and three single, were seized and raped in the forest where the brothers and sisters had made their camp. *1619*

On the night of August 28 our houses at Bilowitz were burned down. Bilowitz burned.

On September 18 and 24 Damborschitz, Urschitz, and Nikoltschitz were plundered: windows, doors, cupboards, and chests were hacked to pieces, and the rooms were broken into and ransacked. The soldiers made off with whatever they pleased. At Damborschitz they shot an unmarried brother dead. Besides everything else, eight fattened oxen were stolen, and the houses were set on fire, as were the market places in different villages, but the greater part was saved, God be thanked. At Nikoltschitz all the brothers' cattle were driven away. Damborschitz, Urschitz, and Nikoltschitz plundered.

On September 19 Dampierre moved from the Seizer Berg to the Lundenburg domain, where he burned down both our upper and lower houses in Kostel. Kostel burned.

On September 19 and 20 Rampersdorf, Altenmarkt, and Lundenburg were plundered. All the horses were stolen, along with some other animals and many goods, and then the houses were set on fire. The taking of Lundenburg Castle meant a serious loss for us because we had taken all kinds of things there for safekeeping. What hurt us most deeply was that twenty brothers and sisters were shot or struck down and murdered, among them old Wolf, a steward; Hans Kammerman, a cellarer; and Philip Phasant, who had served at table. We grieved, too, for the forty who were imprisoned; but by God's intervention these were nearly all set free and they returned to the church with a clear conscience. Rampersdorf, Altenmarkt, and Lundenburg burned.

On September 20 Landshut was plundered for the second time and then burned down. The cellarer and another brother were seized and cruelly tortured. Three sisters were raped. One of them had a baby at her breast, and she lifted her hands in desperate entreaty to spare her baby, but nothing deterred them; they tore the baby from her breast, flung it aside, and violated her. Landshut plundered a second time.

On September 21 Watzenowitz was plundered for the first time, after which it was raided countless times more. One brother was murdered. The cellarer was tortured with Watzenowitz plundered.

1619

thumbscrews[1] to make him tell what the community had. All the grain, flour, wine, cloth, linen, cheese, lard, salt, tools, and other things were carried off—in short, everything above and below the ground, a great quantity of goods. Neighboring farmers came in their wake and looted to the last item whatever the enemy had left and then on September 30 burned the plundered houses to the ground.

Watzenowitz burned by peasants.

Tscheikowitz, Pruschanek burned.

On September 23 Tscheikowitz and Pruschanek were completely ruined and burned to the ground.

People from Pribitz attacked by Dampierre on their way home.

On September 24 a tragic thing occurred. Our fugitives from Pribitz, trying to return home, had put their nursing mothers, their old, their sick, and all the children from both Austerlitz and Lettonitz into the twelve wagons in which they had fled. Not far from the little village of Tillnitz (Telnice) on the other side of Menitz, they fell into the hands of the enemy, who shot down the three brothers in charge of the wagons. They scattered the sisters and children and hounded some into the swamp where they had to remain all night, not knowing in their terror how to escape. They were scattered so far and wide that they found their way together again only after three or four days. Four sisters were raped by the enemy. About forty horses were stolen along with the wagons and most of the household goods.

There was such distress and terror among this poor little group, such heartrending weeping from young and old, that even a stone would have been moved to pity.

Our people from Herspitz and Tracht robbed in the wood.

On September 24, when the enemy burned down several villages around Austerlitz, they also came to Herspitz and fell upon our people from that community and from Tracht, who had already been plundered and rendered destitute. There in the wood, where they had made their camp and thought they were safe, they were attacked and robbed and two horses were stolen.

Those from Tracht fell into Dampierre's hands.

On October 3 those from Tracht who were in the Herspitz wood (no longer feeling safe from the enemy or the peasants) were trying to reach Pausram with three wagons filled with sisters and children. Between Mautnitz (Moutnice) and

[1]Torture with thumbscrews: A soldier would remove the flint from his pistol and jam his victim's thumbs in its place. See H. J. C. von Grimmelshausen, *The Adventurous Simplicissimus*, English translation by A. T. S. Goodrick (Lincoln, NE, 1962), 9.

Neuhof they were surprised by the enemy, who took all their horses and the best of the goods and carried off two wagoners to the camp at Lundenburg. But God intervened, and a few days later the wagoners found a good chance to get free. *1619*

On October 10 the community at Schadowitz was ruthlessly plundered by the enemy and the peasants for the fifth time, and a great quantity of goods was carried off.

Schadowitz plundered for the fifth time.

On October 11 and 12 the enemy plundered Kobelitz for the sixth time and ransacked the houses with unrestrained vandalism. They smashed doors, cupboards, and chests to pieces in nearly all rooms. They hacked open several large wine barrels to let the wine run out and go to waste. They took the brewing vats and built-in cauldrons, the great clock with its bell, the bellows and all the tools in the smithy, cloth, linen, clothing, bedclothes, and many other things. In those two days alone they rode off with seventy wagons filled with booty. They killed a poor brother who was deaf. They set the school on fire at two places, and together with several other houses in the village, it burned to the ground.

Kobelitz plundered for the sixth time. 70 wagon loads carried off.

Kobelitz school burned down. Brother killed.

On October 14 Wischenau was plundered: rooms were broken open; doors, cupboards, and chests were hacked to pieces; cloth, linen, clothing, boots, shoes, and whatever could be found was carried off; even the clothing was stripped off our people in the houses.

Wischenau plundered.

On October 18 the poor community at Nikoltschitz (plundered twice before) was raided by three hundred Hungarians. Every last possession was carried off.

Nikoltschitz plundered.

On October 19, when the enemy [Dampierre] withdrew from Lundenburg into Austria, all Moravian and Hungarian troops at Neumühl struck camp and marched by way of Nikolsburg and Feldsberg into Austria.

Moravian troops withdrew from Neumühl.

The Moravian forces, numbering twelve thousand cavalry and foot soldiers, had encamped at Neumühl for almost two months, from August 25 to October 19, and the Hungarians of Bethlen Gabor, who numbered ten thousand or more, encamped there for a week. Anyone can imagine the amounts of the community's meat, wine, fat, beer, bread, flour, oats, hay, and many other things too numerous to list, that were consumed.

Great numbers of soldiers at Neumühl: first 12,000, then 10,000.

Our community at Neumühl, which had been such a beautiful

1619
Our community at Neumühl vandalized.

home for the brothers and sisters, was ravaged beyond belief. The gardens were devastated, the trees cut down, the fences torn up and burned, the whole year's produce from field and garden carried off, not to mention the great damage done secretly in the houses to the beds, the rooms, and the cellars—all this was done by those who should have been friends and protectors of our country.

300 shots fired at our community at Neumühl.

The enemy did not rest either but kept up the firing against us, louder and heavier than ever before. During the two months referred to above, they fired over three hundred rounds of iron cannonballs weighing eighteen and twenty-four pounds, some red-hot. These were aimed at the roofs in Neumühl and were meant to burn down the houses. But God the Lord protected us in his mercy: not only was nothing burned down, but not the slightest harm came to any of the brothers in Neumühl (although many were there the whole time), whereas it cost some of the soldiers their lives.

All provisions from Schakwitz consumed. Livestock taken.

While the Moravian camp was at Neumühl and Dampierre's camp was at Pulgram, almost all our food supply at Schakwitz was used up: everything in house, cellar, fields, and vineyard. Two people were killed by the enemy. Twenty-four horses and all the sheep were taken.

Nikolsburg plundered.

On October 19 our community at Nikolsburg was raided by the Hungarians. Brothers, sisters, and children were stripped of their clothes. The steward was shot (though not fatally), and the soldiers did other terrible things. The mother of a two-day-old baby was robbed and stripped, and the bedclothes were taken from under a mortally sick brother.

Soldiers plundered our community.

Before and after the Hungarian raids, the Catholic soldiers and townspeople from Nikolsburg pillaged our community there, taking twenty-two bushels of flour as well as meat, lard, salt, sixty hogs, thirty wagonloads of wood, and much valuable medicine. They seized anything they wanted and took it to the castle.[1] On September 5 brother Balthasar Goller[2] was murdered in Nikolsburg by an ungodly townsman, Elias

Brother brutally murdered.

[1]See Hruby, *Wiedertäufer*, 80–81, summarizing two reports dated September 12 and November 13, 1619, from Castellan Henry Bruss to Cardinal von Dietrichstein (in the historical archives of Nikolsburg Castle).

[2]The same Balthasar Goller, a physician who traveled with the imperial embassy to Constantinople (Istanbul) in 1608 and took Salomon Böger with him on the latter's search for deported Hutterian brothers and sisters (p.586 n.). See also *ME*, II, 539–540; Friedmann, *MQR*, Apr. 1953, 129–130; Beck, 378.

Schadner, who brutally attacked him, shooting and stabbing him. Balthasar had been entrusted with the oversight of all our barber-surgeons. He had gone to great lengths on behalf of the church and had often exposed himself to danger.

1619

On October 23 the community at Velké Leváre was plundered twice—first by fifty hussars and then by four hundred. A brother was fatally wounded and a young unmarried sister raped. Seven horses were taken. After the first raid the brothers and sisters fled into the wood, but the hussars pursued them on the roads, scoured the woods, and stripped and robbed them.

Velké Leváre plundered.

On November 3 our community at Velké Leváre was plundered outrageously by a mob of peasants. They took all the flour, meat, salt, cheese, fat, wine, cloth, linen, utensils and tools, clothing and bedclothes, as well as doors, tables, chairs, benches, windows, cupboards, chests, and bedsteads. In short, they carried off whatever they were able to move, until only the walls were left. Besides the tremendous damage, several brothers were severely injured. The ungodly Hungarian peasants pillaged with such uncontrolled violence and cruelty that for a few days none of the brothers dared to be seen at Velké Leváre.

Velké Leváre plundered worse by peasants than by soldiers.

On November 10 Dampierre's soldiers joined the townspeople from Nikolsburg in a raid on Lundenburg and attacked the brothers who had gone back after the fire to sow a little grain. They stripped the brothers of their clothes and stole four horses and eight oxen. They also plundered the castle, mill, and brewery and captured and carried off the estate manager.

Lundenburg plundered; great damage to the church.

The terrible arson, assault, and slaughter described above lasted for several weeks, from August 2 to September 19, but the shameless pillaging did not end until November 10.

Time of trouble.

In these hard times, twelve of our communities were burned down and completely destroyed, including six schools. This count does not include the newly built house at Bilowitz and the communities in Kobelitz and Damborschitz, which were also damaged by enemy fire. Seventeen communities were desolated through plunder. But our greatest heartache was that forty men and women were cruelly murdered and that many God-fearing sisters, both married and unmarried, were raped.

12 communities and 6 schools destroyed.

Two hundred horses and many oxen, cows, hogs, and sheep were stolen from the church, both at our communities and on the roads.

Over 200 horses stolen.

1619

The tremendous loss and damage to the church of the Lord in this year is beyond all description.

No safety from the enemy anywhere.

In the end, the misery and terror in this country exceeded anything in human memory. There was no safety anywhere. The enemy attacked us in the north, then in the south, and finally all over the country. We had to flee from our houses, and we were not safe on the roads or footpaths, not even in the woods. We were in danger not only from the enemy but from the peasants, and in some places, when the enemy was gone, the peasants were even worse. Everyone was out to rob. There was no sparing of the old or sick, the mothers with newborn babies, or the young children. For many weeks we went with them from place to place through the woods and villages, suffering want, misery, and death. Reports of disaster followed thick one after another, and one depth of terror called to the next. It is impossible to overstate the depths of the need and pain we suffered. Many God-fearing people wished they might die rather than see the great misery of our poor little flocks or hear of the shameful violation of our women and girls. Many said they would be content with bread and water and would never stop thanking God if only they could remain peacefully under one roof.

Because of the suffering many believers longed for death.

Truly it seemed as if God the Lord had sent the Destroyer over Moravia. Although thousands had already been slain, the enemy continued to rob, burn, and slaughter, and no one had power to oppose them.

But from the beginning of the world, the almighty God has always helped his people in times of greatest need, when all human hope is gone. He faithfully did so now, and in his holy heaven he heard the unceasing, fervent pleading of his people. More than once he threw the enemy into such panic that even though no one was after them, they fled as if pursued by a great army—just as the Assyrians did, who were also a dreaded scourge to God's people. So the Lord put a bit in the enemy's mouth and a hook in their nose and led them back on the way by which they had come. In spite of great tribulation, we were very much aware of the many ways God opposed the enemy or changed their fury to kindness toward the devout. Let us all the more thank the Lord as long as we live for his deliverance and the good he has done to us. Let our lives be more dedicated and holy so that he has no need to bring still harsher punishment on us (as he can do sevenfold, and then sevenfold again).

God's help felt in many ways.

On January 31 of this year 1619, brother David Wälsch fell asleep in the Lord in prison at Zistersdorf, where he had been for two years and several weeks. As recorded earlier,[1] Lord Erasmus von Landau had kept him and his wife and brother Hansel Krämer in severe imprisonment for things of which he was innocent, connected with his cellarer's service. Before he died, he assured us that he was at peace with God. He had never to his knowledge spoiled or embezzled a single cask of Lord von Landau's wine, and he grieved that he had never been given an opportunity to make his defense.

1619
David Wälsch passed away in prison.

His last words were, "O Lord von Landau, O Lord von Landau, what have you done to us innocent people!"

All this was still not enough for Lord von Landau. When David was dead, he ordered the constable to bury him under the gallows (as a shame and disgrace to the church). The constable refused, since he knew David was innocent, and two night watchmen had to do it, but they buried him a few steps beyond the gallows.

Lord von Landau ordered that David be buried under the gallows and his wife be put in irons.

Lord von Landau even put David's widow in irons again and threatened to have the two children registered as orphans and made his serfs. He also gave orders to throw Hansel Krämer (who at this time was in irons in Zistersdorf Castle) back into the terrible Ebenthal dungeon, where he and David Wälsch had been imprisoned together for a long time.[2]

Brother Krämer and David's widow wrote their sad news in grief and trembling to the church and pleaded that we remember them in their great need. In response, all the elders in the service of the Word and some in the service for temporal affairs met at Kostel to consider in the fear of God what else could be done to free the poor prisoners.

They considered whether or not it would be right before God to send Lord von Landau a sharp and serious letter, warning him of God's judgment, which was already pronounced against him. Lord von Landau had treated David with great cruelty (even after his death), and his wife and children and Hansel Krämer were still suffering in prison for things of which they were innocent.

---

[1]See above, pp.627–628.

[2]They were imprisoned in 1617. Zistersdorf and Ebenthal, two towns northeast of Vienna, Austria, near the Czech border.

1619

It was feared, however, that such a sharp letter, instead of appeasing Lord von Landau, might lead him to vent his fury more violently on the poor prisoners. Up to now, the more letters and petitions we had sent him, the more spitefully and cruelly he had treated our people. So it was decided to give up the idea of writing to Lord von Landau and to lay before God, who will judge it, all the violence and injustice suffered at his hands and the outrage of David's burial. That is how our Teacher the Lord Jesus Christ suffered and overcame with great patience. We should leave all vengeance to the Lord God, the righteous Judge.

Prisoners encouraged to patience and steadfastness in faith.

We decided to write to the poor prisoners, and especially to our sister, David's widow, to comfort her in her bereavement and grief. We wanted to encourage them to be patient in all misery and temptation, to hold faithfully to the divine truth of the Lord in heaven to the end. Whatever happened to the body, if they kept a good conscience and their souls remained unharmed, the Lord would reward this short suffering with eternal joy; he would free them from this misery sooner than they expected. Only they should not set times and limits to his mercy but wait patiently for his help and redemption as the faithful have always done. They would not be tested beyond their strength. This letter, with many wonderful examples of comfort, was sent to the poor prisoners, for at that time we had no other way to console them.

Hansel Krämer released from his imprisonment.

On June 20, 1619, brother Hansel Krämer was released through the intervention of God. He returned to the church after two and a half years in prison without just cause. But our sister Bärbel remained in prison with her two little children, suffering innocently.

Benjamin Elsasser passed away.

On May 13, 1619, Benjamin Elsasser, a servant for temporal affairs, fell asleep in the Lord at Wischenau.

Kaspar Hasel passed away.

On May 14 Kaspar Hasel, a servant for temporal affairs, fell asleep in the Lord at Tscheikowitz.

Kaspar Brecht passed away.

On September 1 Kaspar Brecht, a servant for temporal affairs, fell asleep in the Lord at Neumühl.

Sebastian Dietrich passed away.

Between eight and nine o'clock in the morning on Sunday, December 8, 1619, our dear, faithful brother Sebastian Dietrich, Vorsteher of the whole church, fell asleep in the Lord with peace in his heart and a good conscience.

Three days before his passing, when the elders came to visit him in his sickness, he spoke the following words: *1619*

Brother Sebastian Dietrich's last words to the elders.

My dear brothers, as I am rather weak and do not know what God has in store for me, I ask each one of you for forgiveness where I have hurt you or been clumsy (since a brother in my place cannot always find exactly the right way).

I am completely at peace with you and all brothers and sisters and have a good conscience. To the best of my knowledge, I have tried to serve the church faithfully and to the best of my ability. I do not ask to lay my cross down yet if it is the Lord's will for me to continue.

I praise the Lord in heaven, my dear brothers, for all the kindness, love, and trust you and the church have shown me and that out of love, you have been obedient to me. Tell all the devout in the church that I take leave of them with the greeting of peace and thank each one of them for all their kindness. Hold zealously to the old Ordnungen of the church and to everything good until you are taken from this world. May the church be entrusted to your faithful care in all things. Regarding another brother to take my place, should the Lord take me away from this world, do what God shows you unanimously. Do not act on what just one or two may say, but act on what you are shown unanimously by God, for that gives you greater certainty. And now I commend you to God in heaven to guard and keep you. May he be your help, comfort, and strength on all your ways.

Elders testified to his devotion.

Then the elders assured him they were at peace with him and had nothing against him. They witnessed to his dedication: how he had cared for the church and looked after widows and orphans and others in need in the church. They told him the Lord in heaven would richly reward him. They wished that God might grant him a longer time in his church and thanked him for all the good advice, teaching, admonition, and zealous care he had given them and the church.

The following day, December 6, our dear brother Sebastian Dietrich once more took leave of the elders, assuring them that he was at peace with God.

Among other things, he said that since he wanted to be a joint heir with Christ, why should he not suffer with him? He

1619

Brother Sebastian passed away.

was very patient throughout his illness and the need of his last hour. He was completely alert until he passed away between eight and nine o'clock on Sunday, December 8, as reported.

He had been in the service of the Word for thirty-two years, and the eldership for the whole church had been entrusted to him for nine years. He was sixty-six years old.[1]

Since it was the will of God the Almighty to take our dear brother Sebastian Dietrich from this world, we followed the old, praiseworthy custom of the faithful. On December 18 of this same year, 1619, there was a meeting at Damborschitz of all the elders in the service of the Word and in the service for temporal affairs as well as all buyers and storekeepers and many other trusted brothers from all communities. In the fear of the Lord, these brothers laid their great need before God (as is right) to appoint another faithful shepherd for the church in this extremely dangerous time.

Church entrusted to Ulrich Jaussling.

After long and careful consideration, they came to the joyful, unanimous decision to entrust our dear brother Ulrich Jaussling with the leadership of the church and the responsibility of caring for her in every way with divine zeal. Brother Ulrich trembled in the face of this most important service and lamented his simplicity and inadequacy. But since he did not want to refuse to do this service, he submitted obediently and asked them all to pray that God might grant him the blessing, grace, and heavenly wisdom needed for such a task. This was done with deep faith, and then the elders appointed him, thanking God for this gift. They said they would do their best to support him.

Michael Oberacker passed away.

On December 10 Michael Oberacker, a servant for temporal affairs, fell asleep in the Lord at Wessely.

Dietrich Pfingsthorn passed away.

On December 16 Dietrich Pfingsthorn, a servant for temporal affairs, fell asleep in the Lord at Pohrlitz.

1620

Bohemian War intensified.

In the year 1620 the terrible war continued to spread. It had begun in 1618 and what happened in that year has been partly

[1]About Sebastian Dietrich, a barber-surgeon, Vorsteher from 1611 to 1619, see *ME*, II, 58; Friedmann, "Hutterite Physicians," *MQR*, Apr. 1953, 130; *Schriften*, 110–111.

described already. During 1620 it grew worse and worse until nearly all kingdoms and countries were in revolt. The emperor Ferdinand II, who had come to power on the death of Emperor Matthias, grew more and more hostile because the Bohemians, Moravians, Silesians, Upper and Lower Lusatians, with the help of the Hungarians, had chosen and crowned Frederick, the elector palatine of the Rhine, as king of Bohemia.[1] In order to crush this rebellion, Emperor Ferdinand II recruited bands of cruel men from distant countries: Poles, Croatians, Frenchmen, Walloons, Spaniards, and Italians. He enlisted them to fight against Frederick and his allies, who were relying too heavily on their own strength and good fortune. The duke of Bavaria and the elector of Saxony,[2] two powerful princes, also brought large forces to Emperor Ferdinand's support.

1620

Emperor Ferdinand brought many cruel men into the country.

In 1620, because of this terrible war, the communities again suffered incalculable loss of property. But much worse was the unspeakable grief and misery—worse than anything the church had endured before. A short account follows.

On February 7, while Frederick was at Brünn in Moravia receiving tribute from the Provincial Diet, about a thousand Polish soldiers made a surprise raid through Moravia into Austria.[3] They moved so rapidly that no one could hold out against them, and they took great quantities of loot on the way. They plundered three of our communities—Schadowitz, Watzenowitz, and Göding—seriously injuring about twenty brothers and sisters. At Schadowitz one brother was shot and

Poles plundered Schadowitz, Watzenowitz, and Göding.

[1]Frederick V (crowned 1619), who was defeated in the Battle of the White Mountain (Prague, November 8, 1620). On his travels through Bohemia, Moravia, and Silesia to receive the tribute of the people, the Hutterites living on the Mährisch-Kromau estates had presented him with an ornate wrought-iron bed, several finely crafted knives, lined gloves, and pottery dishes for the queen. See Hruby, *Wiedertäufer*, 81–82.

[2]Duke Maximilian of Bavaria and Johann Georg Prince of Saxony. Commander Johann von Denné of Nikolsburg Castle informed its owner, Cardinal von Dietrichstein, in a dispatch of August 7, 1619, that the prince of Saxony, who had been wounded in the battle of Unterwisternitz near Nikolsburg Castle, was quartered with the Hutterites and that although a room in the castle had been put at the prince's disposal, he chose to stay with the Hutterites, where he was receiving good care. For the German original of von Denné's report, see the official records for 1619 at the Nikolsburg Historical Archives; Hruby, *Wiedertäufer*, 80, n.4.

[3]See C. V. Wedgwood, *The Thirty Years War* (New York, 1961), 116; *Theatrum Europaeum*, I, 324; Beck, 380. King Sigismund of Poland had placed wild hordes of Cossacks and Poles at the disposal of his brother-in-law, Ferdinand II.

1620

killed, and a sister was raped. They took forty-one of the community's horses with them as they charged through.

Moskowitz plundered and set on fire.

At three o'clock in the morning of March 24, the imperial garrison from Laa an der Thaya raided our community at Moskowitz with both mounted soldiers and foot soldiers. They pillaged the whole place, taking all our cows, sheep, and hogs, and then they set fire to the buildings, reducing most of them to ashes. The attack came while everyone was asleep in bed, and in their shock and terror the brothers and sisters were not able to get one simple-minded girl out in time, and she was burned to death.

Kobelitz, Pruschanek, Lettonitz plundered. 6 people murdered.

On March 25 about three hundred Poles made a surprise raid from Austria into Moravia. They pillaged Kobelitz and Pruschanek, stealing seven horses from Kobelitz, and then swept on to Lettonitz,[1] where they treated us with great brutality. They murdered five of our brothers, shot a baby in its mother's arms, injured many brothers and sisters, plundered the house, and took six of our horses.

Velké Leváre plundered.

On July 17 the Poles raided our community at Velké Leváre; they pillaged the house, raped a sister, struck a child dead in its father's arms, and cruelly tortured several brothers in an effort to get money, maiming and burning them so severely that some of them died.

Polish soldiers raided Pribitz.

On July 28 a most tragic and horrible incident took place at Pribitz, worse than anything that had happened so far in this war and worse than anything ever heard of before.[2] At three o'clock that morning, when everyone was peacefully asleep in bed, a force of 1500 cavalry and musketeers (imperial troops, but for the most part Poles) made a sudden and violent attack on Pribitz. They were so unrestrained, ungodly, and savage that within two or three hours they had murdered fifty-two brothers as well as a sister and her child. Fifty-four people had to be buried at the same time, among them many fine and much-respected brothers, including brother Georg Bieberstein, a servant of the Word; Felix Haushalter (a steward) from Weisstätten; Valtin Kellner (a cellarer) and his assistant Kaspar Tischler; Hans Ausgeber (a storekeeper); Martin Schultes from Neumühl; Hansel Stainer, the schoolmaster; Heinrich Schuster

54 people murdered in 2 to 3 hours.

---

[1]Lettonitz (Letonice), village northeast of Austerlitz (Slavkov). Zeman, *Topography*, #74; Beck, 381.

[2]See Beck, 382–389; see also p.636 n.1 above.

(head cobbler); Uhl Schneider (head tailor); Jähne Gerber (head tanner); Peter Schmidt (head smith); Christoph Messerer (a cutler); and many others.[1]

1620

To get money, the Poles tortured some brothers terribly, particularly Heinrich Schuster, who was burned with a red-hot iron; wounds were cut in his thighs, then gunpowder poured into them and ignited, and finally he was so ruthlessly cut up that he scarcely resembled a human being. Kaspar, the cellarer's assistant, had hot grease poured over his naked body and was burned on his belly with red-hot pans. Abraham Messerer's fingers were pinched off with tongs, and then he was cut in pieces. Peter Schmidt was badly tortured and killed after he valiantly told the marauders that even if he knew where a bushel of money was, he would not show them. One brother's head was twisted until his face was over his back, and other atrocities were committed.

Poles' inhuman savagery.

The attackers seriously injured about sixty more people—shooting, stabbing, beating, and slashing them so badly that many died afterward. They shamelessly abused countless married and single sisters and even ten- or twelve-year-old girls.

About 60 people injured.

After wounding Hans Jakob Wolf severely because he was the main servant, they carried him away as prisoner with seventy people, mostly sisters. They also took great quantities of loot and all the horses, cows, draft and fattened oxen, and many provisions. In short, the way they treated the young and old, the crippled and sick, pregnant women, and mothers with new-born babies was so gruesome, devilish, and inhuman that such brutality had never happened in our land before. Even Turks and Tartars, who do not claim to be Christians, would have said it was too much. It was heartbreaking, more than human nature could stand, for a wife to see her husband struck down and murdered before her eyes, for a husband to see his own beloved wife violated, for mothers to have their innocent children torn from their arms and flung aside, and for people to see their relatives carried off. Every kind of shameful sodomy was practiced. It is impossible to put it all into words—even a stone (to say nothing of a human heart) would have been moved to compassion. Oh, the weeping, the suffering,

70 people taken captive.

[1]Beck, 387–389, lists the names of all who perished, a total of 71.

1620

and the terrible heartache that God the Lord allowed to come upon his people! And others in Moravia, highborn and lowborn alike, suffered the same.

Pohrlitz plundered. Two brothers murdered.

Pohrlitz was also raided by these wicked men. Two brothers were murdered, one at least eighty years old, and three were fatally wounded. The community was plundered and all the horses taken away. At Schabschitz (Žabčice), on the lord of Seelowitz's farm, two more brothers were shot.

Hungarians defeated Poles. Freed the prisoners.

God the Almighty, however, could not let such terrible violence continue unpunished. After all the reckless evil they had done, the wicked men started back for Laa (where they had come from), taking with them the poor brothers and sisters they had captured and all the loot from Pribitz and the surrounding villages. Between Höflein (Hevlin) and Grafendorf (Hrabětice) they were attacked and put to flight by Moravian cavalry and Hungarian soldiers, who had heard of their vicious raid on Pribitz. Such horrible shooting and slashing followed that the captives could scarcely describe it all. Many of the Poles abandoned their horses and hid in the water and reeds to save their lives. But it did not help them much. The musketeers threw their muskets and weapons away, held their hands above their heads, and in God's name pleaded for their lives. But no more mercy was shown them than they had shown to the innocent. When some of them saw that our people were spared (for no harm was done to the captives), they dressed themselves in the clothing they had stolen from us and pretended to be captured brothers. But they were recognized by their hair (since the Hungarians were keenly observant on this point) and by their military bearing, so they were killed. What happened was so dreadful that our people believed these soldiers were being repaid for having treated others the same way. It was estimated that six or seven hundred men were slain; one hundred and sixty people were taken prisoner, and twenty wagonloads of booty and all the livestock [they had stolen] were taken from them. About fifty of our people were rescued from their brutality and sent back to the community. Everyone had to acknowledge how God the Lord punished their terrible atrocities immediately, even before the sun went down. God avenged the evil of these ungodly sodomites, these men possessed by the devil, for he deems it just and right to repay with affliction those who afflict his people.

The rest of the Polish musketeers escaped to the town of Laa on the Thaya River (Lower Austria) with twenty-one of the sisters they had captured and brother Hans Jakob Wolf, who had been cruelly beaten and had severe head wounds. The Polish captain who had taken Hans Jakob prisoner had had to stand up to his neck in the swamp water for several hours. When he arrived in the town toward evening long after the others, wet and on foot, he was in a raging temper and immediately sent for brother Hans Jakob, who had asked to be with our people in the mill. That same night the captain had brother Hans Jakob terribly tortured on the rack and with the head mill[1] to make him tell where the money was, which he absolutely refused to do. Then the captain demanded a ransom of one thousand imperial talers for Hans Jakob. The citizens of Laa offered to pay this sum on Hans Jakob's behalf (though without his full consent), and early next morning they borrowed the money from the German commander in the town and presented it to the Polish captain. Hans Jakob, however, wanted the money to be used to free two sisters whom the Polish captain intended to take with him. The wicked Pole was infuriated. He flung the money back, and when he left the town, he took with him both Hans Jakob, who was very weak from the torture and from his head wounds, and a very good-looking young sister named Susanna, the daughter of Hans Ausgeber (the storekeeper) who had been murdered. He took them on horseback to the Polish camp at Krems.

1620
Hans Jakob Wolf and 21 sisters brought to Laa.

Hans Jakob terribly tortured. Ransom set at 1000 imperial talers.

Hans Jakob taken to the Polish camp.

They were held in prison there for several weeks, and especially brother Hans Jakob was cruelly mistreated. He suffered hunger, having nothing but unripe fruit to eat most of the time. As the church community was unable to send money or anything else to help him, he became ill and began to waste away. But the Pole refused to release him unless a thousand imperial talers were paid on his behalf. The priest from Laa who had been at Pribitz during the atrocities there demanded an additional two hundred talers because, he claimed, he had saved Hans Jakob's life and prevented the community from being burned down after the ungodly soldiers had set fire to it in several places. Prince von Liechtenstein summoned Hans Jakob to the camp to tell him about these demands.

Priest from Laa demanded 200 talers.

---

[1]Torture with the head mill: "They put a cord round a man's head and with a piece of wood twisted it so tight that blood gushed from his mouth, nose, and ears." Grimmelshausen, *Simplicissimus*, 9.

1620

In his great need, Hans Jakob wrote to the elders, begging them to give the money for the sake of all the prisoners and because not everyone at Pribitz had been killed. But the elders could not see that it would be right, for it would mean rewarding those who had so horribly maltreated our people. (For instance, more than one sister had been raped by many soldiers. They would gag a sister, and one after the other would wreak their lust on her.) Therefore, a letter from all the elders was sent to Hans Jakob, explaining that for many reasons the money could not be paid and that not one of them would ask such a thing in similar distress. Hans Jakob should put himself in God's hands and be prepared to suffer patiently for Christ's sake, since everything a believer suffered innocently was Christ's own suffering, and so it would not be right to buy freedom from it. But as Hans Jakob's sickness became more and more serious, the priest mentioned above had him transferred from the Polish camp to Vienna. There he lay for several days at the house of Christoph Roll, an ironmonger who, together with a barber-surgeon from Nikolsburg, nursed him until he fell asleep in the Lord on September 19 of this year of 1620. He was buried in the Lutheran cemetery. Before his end he said that he knew he was a weak man but nothing burdened his soul that merited exclusion.

Hans Jakob was encouraged to be patient.

Brother Hans Jakob passed away at Vienna.

Sister Susanna, to her great distress and agony of heart, had to stay even longer among the ungodly soldiers, who wreaked their lust on her. Finally God sent help, and she was released at Pilsen in Bohemia after it was proclamed in the Polish camp that all Germans must be set free on pain of severe punishment. Her great longing was realized, and on November 5 she returned to the church community. So, in the end, all the captured sisters returned to the church. The other twenty had been taken no further than Laa an der Thaya, where our brothers, the millers, were helped by the citizens to free the prisoners and return them to us. With tremendous joy and thankfulness we received all those who had been released. After the severe trials they had suffered, we counted it a great mercy of God that not one of those captured was missing except brother Hans Jakob Wolf, to whom the Lord had already granted merciful release from his suffering, as recorded above.

Sister Susanna returned to the church.

Throughout the summer, the two great armies of Ferdinand II and Frederick V were encamped opposite each other in Austria without any decisive move. It was during this time that the above-mentioned raids into Moravia took place. In the fall the duke of Bavaria took possession of Upper Austria, and the elector of Saxony invaded the margravate of Lusatia. Then the duke of Bavaria and the imperial general Count Buquoy marched on Bohemia.[1] Although their enemies followed close behind, the imperial troops took one town or hamlet after another, until the two forces reached Prague and engaged in battle at the White Mountain on November 8. Frederick's forces were ignominiously defeated and his whole army put to flight. Frederick and his wife and courtiers, with many prominent lords and officers, had to leave Bohemia, since the city of Prague betrayed him. As a result of this battle, the emperor brought almost the whole kingdom of Bohemia into subjection within a few days. So in the cold of winter, a new danger, an appalling distress, loomed over the church community, and deep called to deep.

1620

Battle of the White Mountain. Great distress for the church.

Through many agonizing experiences we had learned how the brutal foreign troops would treat our people, who because of their faith were hated more than others. It seemed quite impossible, however, to attempt flight in the middle of winter with such a needy little group, who would certainly perish miserably from the cold, so we decided to entrust ourselves to God and remain in our homes to await what he permitted. We turned to God constantly, early and late, praying earnestly for the protection of our poor widows and orphans during the bitter winter.

Brother Ulrich Jaussling, Vorsteher of the whole church, therefore agreed with the other elders to send a brother with a letter addressed to the imperial commanders General Lord von Teufenbach,[2] General Lord Maximilian von Liechtenstein,[3] Lord Adam von Waldstein (the chief administrator of Bohemia), and other lords of Moravia who were known to us. In all humility we explained that we had no guilt in this terrible

---

[1]See Wedgwood, *Thirty Years War*, 123–129; *Theatrum Europaeum*, I, 458–463; Beck, 385.

[2]Rudolf von Teufenbach (1582–1653), imperial field marshal under General Buquoy. *Allgemeine Deutsche Biographie*, LIV, 682–685.

[3]Maximilian von Liechtenstein, of the aristocratic Austrian family Liechtenstein-Nikolsburg; see Falke, *Geschichte des fürstlichen Hauses Liechtenstein* (3 Vols., Vienna, 1868–1883).

1620

Imperial troops entered Moravia. Committed many atrocities.

war and begged them to use their God-given power to protect our poor, defenseless people, who had never raised a hand against anyone. But the imperial vanguard advanced at great speed with its freebooters, the very worst of all. Spaniards, Neapolitans, French, and Poles at once started their usual atrocities in places to the east. The estates of lords who had imperial protection were spared no more than the others. They even attacked the lords commissioner who had been sent to the emperor with letters from the Provincial Diet—they shot at them, murdered them, and took some of them prisoner. No one could travel in the direction the soldiers were coming from; everybody had to flee. So the above-mentioned brother was unable to present our petition and returned home. (Later he was again sent out, though just as unsuccessfully, with a petition to General Buquoy.)

Teikowitz plundered and set on fire. A little girl abducted.

Meanwhile the imperial army was advancing further and further into Moravia. On December 14 the Walloons raided Teikowitz for the first time, plundering and burning part of the community. They wounded several brothers, raped some of the sisters, and abducted a twelve-year-old child, Benjamin Rieker's daughter, who to this day has not come back to us. So great was his grief for her that he died of a broken heart.

The terrible happenings at Teikowitz were a tremendous shock to us, giving a foretaste of the evils to come. Yet we still hoped (while the other upper communities,[1] as far as possible, were preparing for flight) that things would improve as soon as the generals came, for people said that the emperor had taken Moravia under his protection and that the freebooters who had acted so atrociously were acting without orders.

On December 17, however, Teikowitz was again raided, also Stiegnitz and Wischenau, and Tschermakowitz soon after. All kinds of evil raiders came: Walloons, Frenchmen, Croats, Poles, and Count Fugger's German musketeers, who were among the worst. They plundered the four communities for several days and carried off whatever they pleased. When one band left, another arrived, subjecting us to their violence and sodomy. In order to get our money, they relentlessly tortured some brothers and killed three of them. They burned and tortured the steward at Wischenau with such cruelty that he

[1]"Upper communities": see above, p.382 n.4.

died in great pain.[1] At Stiegnitz, they treated the cellarer's wife in the same way. She was a dear old sister, well advanced in years, who had fallen down some steps and broken her arm. Because she was the cellarer's wife and they wanted her to show them where the money was, they assaulted her, struck several gashes in her head, and burned the soles of her feet until she could no longer walk. After all that, they raped her, and she passed away a few days later. Many respectable women, young girls, and even little eight- or nine-year-old girls and boys were brutally violated.

1620

At the mill in Tschermakowitz several sisters hid behind the mill wheels in the water to save their honor, not caring how cold it was in the bitter, wintry weather. But the wicked soldiers found them and wreaked their lust on them.

Sisters sought safety in the water behind the mill wheels.

On December 19 the two communities at Alexowitz and Bochtitz were plundered.

Alexowitz and Bochtitz plundered.

Such dreadful things happened, just as in other places (already recorded), that all the elders and the whole church were seized with fear. They evacuated some of the communities, including Pribitz, which had already endured great suffering at the hands of the emperor's Polish troops, and also Pohrlitz, Klein Niemtschitz [near Prahlitz] and Bochtitz. They fled before the vicious soldiers reached them, for no one cared to risk such danger, and there was stark terror throughout Moravia among rich and poor alike. There was no one in the country to turn to for advice or help. Everywhere, the soldiers satisfied their lust and did what they pleased. He who acted most brutally and could boast of the greatest vileness and depravity was admired the most.

Pribitz, Pohrlitz, Niemtschitz, and Bochtitz evacuated before the enemy came.

Those able to escape from the upper communities fled down to Alexowitz and the lower communities.

The people from Pribitz, Pohrlitz, Nuslau, Klein Niemtschitz and Moskowitz fled to Pausram, Austerlitz, Damborschitz, Kobelitz, and Nikolsburg. Within a few days it was necessary to abandon Schakwitz, Neumühl, Damborschitz, Kobelitz, Schadowitz, Kostel, and Altenmarkt and flee toward Göding and Wessely. The people from Neumühl and Kostel took refuge at Eisgrub, where the lords allowed them to shelter in the castle.

On December 28 the large community at Klein Niemtschitz

Klein Niemtschitz burned down.

[1]The steward's name was Ule; Beck, 385–386.

1620

was completely plundered and the best buildings burned down. Whatever the soldiers left underground was later dug up and taken by the lord of Kanitz and his men—the same lord who was supposed to protect the brothers. So everything was lost.

Pohrlitz plundered and set on fire.

On December 29 the community at Pohrlitz was plundered and some of the buildings burned down.

Austerlitz and Herspitz plundered. 3 people drowned.

Before daybreak of the same day, several hundred imperial cavalrymen made a surprise attack on the communities at Austerlitz and Herspitz and hastily seized some booty. In their terror, many brothers, sisters, and children ran into the pond, which was not yet frozen over, and two sisters and a child were drowned. The villains were driven off by shots from the town and were not able to sate their malice against us.

General Buquoy and the imperial army now advanced to Eibenschitz, Gross Seelowitz, and Auspitz, with the terrible vanguard always ahead, plundering, burning, and killing wherever they went. Great numbers of our people from the communities at Göding, Wessely, Neudorf, Strassnitz, Ungarisch Ostra, and other nearby places were forced to cross into Hungary and make their way down to Sabatisch. Brother Ulrich Jaussling, brother Hauptrecht Zapff, Seyfried Geiss, Rudolf Hirzel, Franz Walter, and other servants of the Word traveled with them into a strange country with a very poor and needy flock.

Elders came to Sabatisch with large groups of people.

By now over three thousand of our people were at Sabatisch. It was impossible to support such a large number in the little community, especially as Bethlen Gabor's mercenaries—Hungarian footsoldiers—were also quartered there during this period. The imperial forces were a danger too; some way out had to be found. In these straits, our people were forced to make their way over the Little Carpathians (no matter how sad and painful it might be) to find shelter on the Schächtitz and Echtlnitz[1] estates, the property of the Counts Nádasdy[2] and Erdödy.[3] God in his wonderful intervention had prepared

Crossed the mountains.

[1]Schächtitz (Čachtice) on the Dudvah River, village and estate south of Neustadt (Nové Mesto n. Váhom).
Echtlnitz (Chtelnica), west of Pieštany on the Vah River.

[2]Count Franz Nádasdy of an old Hungarian family; he was beheaded in Vienna on April 30, 1671, by order of Leopold I, for his participation in the conspiracy led by Franz Wesselényi.

[3]Thomas Count Erdödy (1558–1624), imperial general until 1596, prominent in the Turkish wars; provincial governor of Croatia, Slavonia, and Dalmatia; successful statesman 1595ff. *Allgemeine Deutsche Biographie*, VI, 194.

a place where they were received with respect and great sympathy for their plight and could buy food and drink at a reasonable price. But it was not what they were used to in the community; there was great lack of clothing and bed linen. As a result of the terror, hunger, and cold they had suffered because of those wicked people, and perhaps still more as a result of God's hand lying heavy on us, the Hungarian sickness broke out among the fugitives. So many were lying ill that they were unable to take proper care of one another. Consequently, five hundred people died within a short time at our various places on the other side of the Little Carpathians. *1620* 500 of our people passed away.

1621

The distress and misery already described continued into the year 1621. It was an evil year, full of anguish.

Right at the very beginning of the year, on January 2 or 3, a dreadful thing happened. A sister from Teikowitz who had been in the hands of the Walloons there had fled and was in the mill at Ungarisch Ostra, when she heard that the imperial army was advancing from Auspitz to Ungarisch Ostra and surrounding places. Overwhelmed with fear and despair, she cast her little baby into the March River. She was on the point of leaping in herself to escape from falling again into the hands of these sodomites, but she was held back and admonished for her lack of faith. A sister's terror.

On January 5, our two communities at Pribitz and Nuslau were plundered and burned to ashes. At Pribitz, in particular, the loss was great. Pribitz and Nuslau burned down.

On January 6 the community at Kobelitz was plundered first once, and then countless times, until nothing was left. All their livestock was taken as well. Kobelitz plundered.

On January 8 our community at Watzenowitz, which had become more valuable since its rebuilding, was burned to the ground by imperial soldiers. Watzenowitz burned down.

On January 12 Hans Walmann, steward at Pruschanek, was killed by the Poles; everything in the community was plundered by soldiers and peasants. Steward killed.

On January 23, as the imperial army reached the Hungarian frontier and the Hungarian army made its way over the Little Carpathians, our two communities at Wessely and Neudorf were burned to the ground. There were a few at Wessely who Wessely and Neudorf burned down.

1621

were too sick to flee, and with no one able to help them, they died an agonizing death in the fire.

Schadowitz plundered.

On January 24 what was left of the community at Schadowitz was ransacked and robbed by the Guritschän lords.

Nikoltschitz plundered.

On January 28 and many times afterward, the community at Nikoltschitz was looted, until nothing was left. Leather, salt, fat, wool, copper pans—in short, everything—was carried off.

2 brothers killed at Herspitz.

On February 2 the Poles raided Herspitz. Georg Fückel, the steward, was shot dead inside the house, and the gardener was racked and burned to death.

Damborschitz plundered.

On February 2 the Poles also attacked Damborschitz. They found and emptied all the walled-in cellars and hidden vaults. They tortured and burned to death Hansel Scherer, an old, white-haired brother, and cruelly tortured the steward from Urschitz and other brothers with the rack, head mill, and burning.

Protzka, Velké Leváre, and St. Johannes plundered.

On February 6 our community at Protzka was plundered by the Poles, while Velké Leváre and St. Johannes were plundered by imperial troops from Marchegg.

20 barrels of wine stolen from Polehraditz.

On February 8 Saxonian cavalry pillaged the community at Polehraditz and among other things stole twenty barrels of the best wine.

Kostel and Altenmarkt plundered.

On February 14 about two thousand Hungarians crossed the frozen March River at Landshut, ransacking Kostel and Altenmarkt. They stole twenty-four horses and carried off five people, some of whom soon returned. At Kostel a brother was shot to death.

Polehraditz set on fire.

On February 19 the buildings at Polehraditz were set on fire again.

Alexowitz plundered.

On February 22 the community at Alexowitz was again heavily plundered and robbed of the four horses they had been able to save till then.

Klein Niemtschitz plundered.

On March 13, when we had just begun to make the burned-out site at Klein Niemtschitz livable again, the soldiers returned to attack it, looted the little that was there, and raped two sisters.

On March 23[1] brother Valtin Säliger from Schakwitz was sent to Göding with Jakob Trochsler, the head miller, and with the brother who helped supervise all the milling in the

[1]Beck, 401: March 30.

communities. Near Bilowitz, they fell into the hands of the Polish soldiers. All three were brutally murdered and later buried at Kostel.

1621

3 brothers killed.

On April 17 the ungodly Poles camping at Strassnitz made a sudden attack on Sabatisch, plundered the houses, and brutally murdered five brothers: Sadrach,[1] the head barber-surgeon; the head miller; Hans Gerber, the swineherd; and a potter from Damborschitz. A sister was raped until she died.

Sabatisch plundered and brothers murdered.

Also on April 17 a dear brother named Lorenz,[2] work overseer for Prince von Liechtenstein at Auspitz, was shot to death in the vineyard at Steurowitz by the Walloons stationed at Auspitz.

A brother shot.

On April 23 the entire Polish army, which had committed such wicked atrocities in Hungary, arrived at Schakwitz from Strassnitz. They numbered over three thousand men. For ten days they made themselves at home in our community and in the village. They consumed almost everything we had in the community and took what they pleased. But in spite of their fiendish, ungodly behavior elsewhere, they had some compassion on us when they saw our honesty and goodwill. Their commander in particular (though not staying in our community himself) gave us enough protection to prevent anyone from being assaulted or injured, and even allowed most brothers and sisters to continue living in their own homes. The soldiers also told some of us that if they had known what kind of people we were, they would not have treated us so cruelly at Pribitz. While they were quartered in the village at Schakwitz, a fire broke out and the Polish soldiers ran straight to our community to help put the fire out as diligently as if the house had been their own. They even sent a brother and one of their soldiers to ride full speed to Neumühl, asking for brothers from there to help save the building. So everything is possible for our God.

Poles quartered at Schakwitz for 10 days.

Poles helped to extinguish a fire.

On April 28 and 29 at Kostel, however, the marauding Poles were ruthless. They plundered everything in the community, stealing all the livestock and whatever else they found. Seizing four brothers, they flung them from the bridge into the lake. Two saved their lives by swimming, but the devilish Poles

Kostel plundered. 2 brothers drowned.

[1]Sadrach Hueber; see Beck, 401, where twelve brothers are mentioned.

[2]Lorenz Hauer; Beck, 401.

1621

pushed the other two under water with long staves until they drowned. Three sisters were raped.

Neumühl in great danger.

At that time our community at Neumühl was in greater danger than ever. The soldiers not only made fearsome threats about what they would do once they got into our houses, but some (who were only out to get the plunder) made several attacks and tried to force their way in. But God prevented it in a wonderful way, so nothing happened and they had to leave empty-handed. The Lord alone be praised for protecting his children from the ravening lions and for helping our brothers and sisters at Neumühl in their terrible plight.

On May 22 the imperial army had advanced toward Neuhäusel,[1] and almost all the soldiers had been ordered out of Moravia to join them. At the same time, General Hans Breuner had come down to Pausram with a complete regiment of infantry and several detachments of cavalry. They had seized whatever they wanted from our workshops and from other places in the community. The general himself had given away the brothers' wine as booty. There were seven barrels of it, all of which was drunk in half a day, and as a result there had been considerable mischief. From Pausram these soldiers had made for Neumühl to work off their wild spirits and make a big raid. They and their prostitutes had said publicly that the general was going to let them plunder Neumühl all they wanted. They had been so eager to get to Neumühl that they did not even take time to eat or drink on the way, and the people at Neumühl had been in terror of their coming. But when the general arrived in advance with some of the cavalry and found the people friendly and respectful, God changed his heart. At once the general sent orders to the approaching infantry to turn off behind the Neumühl cherry orchard and march through the corn fields to Saitz. His soldiers were disgusted at the order. They accused the brothers of giving their general a large sum of money to make him change his mind. We had not given him a penny; we had only sent him some provisions—wine, beer, bread, and oats. So once more God averted disaster from our community at Neumühl.

Breuner threatened Neumühl. God averted the danger.

[1]Neuhäusel (Nové Zámky, district of Nitra), city on the Nitra River, approx. 55 miles southeast of Bratislava; built by Friedrich von Zerotin (d. 1598).

On July 15, when foreign soldiers stationed in Moravia moved into Hungary, our community at Schadowitz was plundered again. On the same day, foreign soldiers from the garrison at Brünn raided the impoverished and burned-out community at Klein Niemtschitz. They hauled away thirty-five wagonloads of booty—everything they found, including grain.

1621
Schadowitz and Klein Niemtschitz plundered in one day.

On August 7 a large number of Hungarians penetrated as far as Landshut. They plundered our communities at Kostel and Altenmarkt and took all their livestock, including their horses. They took several people away, but most of them soon returned.

Kostel and Altenmarkt plundered.

On August 8 the Walloons plundered our community at Göding, as well as the town and the mill.

Göding plundered.

On August 10 and 16 Kobelitz was also plundered several times by Walloons. They took thirteen horses from there and at the same time took three from Tscheikowitz.

Kobelitz plundered.

On August 10 the Walloons plundered Schadowitz. They raped several sisters, especially two who were sick, and kicked one sister so brutally with their boots that she vomited. Then they stole all three horses and twelve oxen.

Schadowitz plundered again.

On August 18 the Walloons raided Damborschitz, plundering and committing many atrocities. They burned the upper house to the ground as well as the oxen mill below.

Upper house at Damborschitz burned down.

On August 22 the foreign troops entered Moravia again and passed through Lundenburg after their defeat by the Hungarians at Neuhäusel, where their general Count Buquoy had been killed. There was again widespread terror, and people fled from the communities in the south. The soldiers did not remain long, however, but retreated to Hradisch (Uherské Hradiště) and Brod in Hungary (Uherský Brod). The rest of the imperial forces, with Lord Maximilian von Liechtenstein now appointed general, encamped on the Schütt Islands.[1]

Imperial army returned to Moravia.

A few days later, on August 27, a mob of these ungodly Walloons came to Schadowitz and made a surprise attack on our community. It was appalling how they assaulted sisters, married and unmarried, and raped even little girls eleven and

Schadowitz ruthlessly attacked.

[1]Schütt Islands, southeast of Bratislava: *Grosse Schütt Insel* (Velký Žitný Ostrov) on the Czech side; *Kleine Schütt Insel* (Malý Žitný Ostrov, or Szigetköz) on the Hungarian side of the Danube, enclosed by two arms called Malý Dunaj and Mosoni-Duna respectively. These are large areas of land formed by alluvial deposits on both sides of the river.

1621

twelve years old. Everyone was driven from the houses. For several days no one dared return because the ungodly marauders were plundering everywhere. In all this misery, a sister died and had to be left unburied. When our people returned to bury her, the dogs had eaten all but her head. It was a time of utter horror, when they could not even bury their dead.

General Wallenstein threatened the communities.

On September 2 General von Wallenstein came to Lundenburg with cavalry and infantry to defend the pass against the Hungarians. He set up camp between the Thaya River and the marketplace, and many people from the villages as well as some from our communities had to help throw up barricades. The general ordered us to do this, threatening death by hanging and the destruction of our houses. So besides having to deliver supplies to the camp, we lived in terror; no one was safe on any road. They took whole herds of livestock from the pastures and villages.

On October 8, the Friday before Dionysius Day, General Maximilian von Liechtenstein (mentioned above) came up from the Schütt Islands with the imperial army. They advanced with eight cannons and a large troop of baggage carriers through Lundenburg to Göding, Bisenz, Ungarisch Hradisch, and other places in the area against the armies of Bethlen Gabor and the Margrave of Jägerndorf. The latter moved north on the other side of the March River along the Moravian border and seized several places to set up camp.

Kostel plundered. A brother shot.

The imperial army utterly pillaged our poor community at Kostel. Our brother Heine, who was in charge of the tools, was shot to death, and an old sister was tortured so cruelly that she died the next day. Some of the houses, which had been set on fire before, were burned down. At Altenmarkt the houses were under the general's protection, but everything outside was stolen. At Rampersdorf they killed the head miller's wife, and she was not found until some days later, in the water.

On October 8 the community at Kobelitz was pillaged, and several sisters were raped. The soldiers remained a number of days and found all the hidden vaults and cellars. They took all the horses, oxen, and other livestock. For days no brother dared to be seen.

Everything hidden underground dug up at Kobelitz.

Schakwitz plundered.

On October 9 they pillaged Schakwitz and took eight horses.

They began plundering Neumühl the same day, but it did not get too bad. *1621*

On October 11 about three hundred cavalry and musketeers pillaged Damborschitz and shot a young lad and a little boy three or four years old. Several people were fatally wounded. The little boy in his childlike way wanted to take his coat off and give it to the soldier so he would not hurt him, but the wicked man shot him all the same. There was no mercy for anyone.

2 brothers shot at Damborschitz.

On October 12 these ungodly people plundered Kobelitz again. When they got hold of a brother, they burned and tortured him. In the yard they shot Klaus Prauer, a brother who tried to stop them. They looted without interruption for seven days.

A brother shot at Kobelitz.

On October 16 the Walloons again pillaged Schakwitz, stole their wine, and tortured a brother with the head mill. They stripped a sister naked.

Schakwitz plundered.

On October 19 the poor people at Klein Niemtschitz were robbed of their last three horses as well as two oxen.

On October 20 they returned to Damborschitz, seized two brothers and racked one of them three times, the other seven times, to find out about money and other things. They scoured the woods for people and took whatever they wanted from the houses.

2 brothers tortured at Damborschitz.

On November 2 and 3 these depraved men raided Lettonitz and Damborschitz yet again. At Damborschitz they stripped many brothers and sisters and raped ten sisters. After completely stripping a young seamstress, they raped her until she lay as though dead.

Outrages committed at Lettonitz and Damborschitz.

On November 5 a detachment of Spaniards came to Austerlitz from Vienna, pretending to be a convoy with money for Kremsier. When General von Teufenbach's guards stopped them from entering our community at Austerlitz, they forced their way in and shot at the guards. In the tumult they shot our brother Sadrach Ochsenmüllner and spread terror throughout the community. Finally, because they had to obey the general, they managed to come to terms, and the uproar was settled before the whole community was totally plundered.

Brother shot at Austerlitz.

On November 9 the community at Damborschitz was plundered again and four oxen taken, as well as the clock and the bells (which we had been able to keep until then).

Damborschitz plundered.

1621
Steward at Damborschitz brutally tortured.

On December 9 fifty cavalrymen and many musketeers arrived at Damborschitz from Wischenau. The people fled to the woods, but the steward, who was fatally ill, and an old sister who was nursing him stayed behind. The marauders found them. They took the sick man from his bed and tortured him with the head mill and thumb screws to make him show them where treasure was supposed to be buried in the yard. When the steward would not and could not reveal it, they left him alone. They went to the Damborschitz peasant who had told them about this treasure when they were at Wischenau. The peasant showed them a big stone outside the bedroom, almost in the middle of the yard, under which the treasure was supposedly buried. After the stone had been raised with much effort and they had dug a long time without finding anything, they realized that they had been deceived. The peasant got a severe beating as a reward, and then the soldiers abused the old sister, mistreating her with their ungodly lust.

Peasant received what he deserved.

So this year of 1621 ran its course of misery and cruelty, which cannot even be fully described. During this year one third of the people in the communities met their death. The nightmare continued into the following year.

1622

The new year began with the same misery with which the previous year had ended. A brief account is given in what follows.

Hungarians raided as far as Damborschitz during peace talks.

On January 2, while the peace treaty with the Hungarians was being negotiated at Nikolsburg, about a thousand Hungarians carried out a raid that went through Strassnitz and on by night to Damborschitz. The soldiers came with such blood-curdling yells that people fled in terror from their houses out into the bitter cold. After plundering the community of all they could find, including two horses, the soldiers left. Even though they caught up with many of our people, they did not beat them or carry them off. From the marketplace, however, they carried off three people, and at Watzenowitz they found Abraham Gerber and forced him to go with them (but he was soon released through the help of brothers from Sabatisch).

Peace made with the Hungarians.

At ten o'clock on Monday January 3 in Nikolsburg, a fanfare announced the conclusion of peace with the Hungarians after three months of negotiations. But this peace only brought greater distress to the church. *1622*

On January 4 the imperial army—consisting of Walloons, French, Spaniards, Neapolitans, Croatians, Fugger's Swabians,[1] and all kinds of scoundrels—came from Kremsier and turned toward the communities, while the armies of Bethlen Gabor[2] and the Margrave of Jägerndorf[3] returned to Hungary. The imperial army was more ungodly and brutal than ever.

Both armies moved on.

On January 5 they sacked Bochtitz. Everyone had to flee—the brothers, the peasants, and even the lord of the place. Our community was set on fire, though most of the buildings remained standing. The same day, they plundered the upper house at Klein Niemtschitz. A relative of General Buquoy was quartered in the lower house, which gave the people some protection until the whole army had passed through Klein Niemtschitz and gone on its way.

Bochtitz burned down.

On January 6 the depraved soldiers fell on Moskowitz. They stripped brothers and sisters and even schoolchildren to their undershirts—some even stark naked—and drove them out of the house into the cold of winter. All the horses were taken and whatever else could be found. Some brothers were wickedly tortured to make them reveal anything that was hidden. The plundering and robbery went on for several days until a French cavalry captain arrived, who took our people

Imperial soldiers raided Moskowitz. Committed outrages.

---

[1]"Fugger's Swabians," troops probably under the command of Count Otto Heinrich Fugger (1592–1644), founder of the now extinct Kirchheim branch of the Fuggers, the famous German family of merchants and bankers going back to the 14th century. In 1617 he had fought with the Austrian-Spanish army against Venice, had risen to the rank of captain, and at the outbreak of the Bohemian Revolt supported the emperor with his mercenaries. See *Allgemeine Deutsche Biographie*, VIII, 184–185.

[2]Bethlen Gabor (1580–1629), the noted descendant of an old Hungarian family who possessed great wealth in Hungary and Transylvania and who had sided with the enemies of the Hapsburgs from the time of Ferdinand II. Elected King of Hungary in 1620, he was forced to relinquish the crown at the Peace of Nikolsburg (December 31, 1621, or January 1622), in a compromise which secured him several districts in Upper Hungary besides Transylvania. Through his marriage to Katharina von Brandenburg in 1626 he became brother-in-law to Gustav Adolf II, King of Sweden. *ME*, I, 318; *Schaff-Herzog*, VIII, 424d.

[3]Johann Georg, Margrave of Brandenburg, Duke of Jägerndorf; in 1621, placed in the imperial ban for siding with Frederick V, King of Bohemia. Until his death on March 2, 1624, he fought unsuccessfully on the side of Bethlen Gabor for the possession of the margravate Jägerndorf (Silesia). In 1611 Johann Dionys von Zerotin had ordered the Hutterites to make a gilded coach for the margrave; see Hruby, *Wiedertäufer*, 27.

1622

under his protection so they could continue living as they wished and even cook and bake. Before this no one had dared be seen. The soldiers shamelessly mistreated any sister they caught, Fugger's musketeers being the most ungodly of all.

Devilish acts at Stiegnitz.

On January 6 and 7, for two days and two nights, our people in the community at Stiegnitz were subjected to violence and outrage. The impious band raped many sisters and young girls, stripped them, and led them naked through the streets. Any brother they laid their hands on was racked and burned to get money. They plundered the whole community, destroying and digging up everything. Even if something was worth only two pennies, they took it, along with all the brewing vats and cauldrons, all the livestock, the lard and the flour, and grain from the underground stores. In short, everything they could find, they took. The robbery went on for days. They hanged one brother, Christoph the school master, but he was cut down again by a Spaniard stationed in the house as a guard. Our people, scattered in all directions, could neither help nor advise each other. An old brother called Walser Maier was tortured to death. They put him naked on hot coals, and he had to end his life in agony. One brother was murdered. An old brother and sister, both of whom had been in the sickroom, were in such fear that they fled out into the cold and froze to death. The same happened to a little girl. After all this cruelty, the soldiers set the house on fire and most of it burned.

Wischenau and Teikowitz cruelly attacked. No help anywhere.

At Wischenau and Teikowitz the looting was almost as bad, and most of the people had fled into the forest with those from Stiegnitz. The marauders caught the steward at Teikowitz, however, and tortured him terribly. There was nothing but distress and misery upon misery. We could not turn for help or advice to the lord cardinal, who governed the district, or to any other man. The soldiers were so lawless that they did not respect any authority. All we could do was commit everything to God, including the outrage and violence we suffered. Often at times of greatest fear and need, God provided a merciful way out, beyond all human comprehension. He prompted generals completely unknown to us—generals of foreign nations and languages—to take us under their protection. When they saw how inhumanly we were treated despite the fact that we were people of goodwill, they gave us protection in preference to many of our countrymen. Many

Foreign generals won over by our kindness.

were amazed at our ordered way of life and were full of sympathy for the ordeals and losses we suffered.

1622

On January 15 two cavalry detachments came from Austria and looted our houses at Altenmarkt, taking six horses, two oxen, and other things.

Altenmarkt plundered.

On the same day the community at Bochtitz was set on fire once again, and our people were driven out. After this the place was completely abandoned.

Bochtitz plundered again.

On January 30, when we had tried again to live in Stiegnitz and places nearby, the Neapolitans stationed at Znaim made a surprise raid on Stiegnitz at night, took what they found, stripped many brothers and sisters, and violated several sisters. They threshed the grain that was still in the straw and carried it off. The robbery continued for two consecutive days. Three horses and four oxen just brought back from Jaispitz were also stolen.

Stiegnitz plundered.

On April 22 Colonel Löbel's cavalry invaded Moskowitz. Five hundred of them were stationed at Mährisch Kromau and Eibenschitz for the whole year, and Moskowitz and Alexowitz had to give them a heavy contribution every week. In the attack on Moskowitz, they pillaged our community and hauled the booty away in eighteen wagons, brought just for this purpose.

Moskowitz plundered.

Besides these, there were many other imperial cavalry and infantry forces scattered throughout the country, who harassed and terrorized us on every side and robbed us of our food. This was in addition to the weekly contribution most of our communities had to give by order of the cardinal's commissioners. And we still had to provide the soldiers quartered in our houses with provisions worth many thousand gulden within a few months. Petitions and complaints were no help. When we protested vigorously, saying we simply did not have the means, they threatened to allow the soldiers to loot our communities and let them take what they wanted. In short, it was an evil and fearful time.

It is impossible to record all the inhuman savagery vented on us and other people during this ungodly, cursed war waged by Spaniards, Walloons, Poles, and the German imperial troops, and how many honorable and faithful older sisters, expectant mothers, mothers of newborn babies, desperately ill sisters, unmarried sisters and little girls eight and nine years

Inhuman savagery of this war.

1622 old, even young boys (which is completely contrary to nature) were shamelessly raped in public. Men and boys were hung up by their private parts and burned with red-hot irons and pans. Their feet were put in the fire until the toes burned away; wounds were cut and powder shaken in and set alight; fingers and ears were cut off. They were tortured with the head mill until their eyes started out of their heads, and they were hanged by the neck like thieves. These and other unheard-of things that cannot be told for very shame were publicly committed by the imperial soldiers (who believed themselves the best of Christians). Anyone who has not himself known the anguish of hearing and seeing it all would not believe that a man who claims to be a Christian can commit acts so vile and devilish. It would have been no wonder if heaven itself had paled, if the earth had shaken, and if the elements had trembled. Even the devil might have shown greater fear of God's power and majesty than these devil-possessed men. May God, into whose hands we entrust all judgment, open their eyes.

In spite of all the oppression and grinding misery, now lasting four years, we never lost hope of a little relief. But the longer the war continued, the worse grew the hardships. We had thought ourselves at our very poorest, since (as mentioned above) our money was almost gone, many communities burned down, others sacked, and our food supplies eaten up by

Unjust tax imposed.

soldiers. Yet an impossibly heavy tax was imposed on us in July 1622 (much more than others in the country had to pay). For five months our communities (half of them not lived in anymore by this time) were to make a monthly contribution of fifteen hundred talers cash, as well as twelve bushels of rye and twelve of oats. In five months this would total 7500 talers cash and sixty bushels each of rye and oats.

It was not within the church's means to hand over such a large amount of money and grain, for if the taxes were levied for a year (and such taxes usually lasted a long time), the quantity of grain required was more than all of us brothers in Moravia could grow. Our income was far too small to supply the 18,000 talers cash per year. Besides, it was against our faith and conscience to contribute money for the war, and our forefathers had never done so.

A letter, therefore, was sent to the cardinal telling him how much the church had suffered in this war, how many

1622
Letter to the cardinal. Poverty and conscience prevented us from paying taxes.

communities we had lost, and how many others had been pillaged and their stores consumed by soldiers; that our cash had already gone to the emperor and that all the communities put together did not earn enough to pay a contribution instead of giving provisions for the soldiers. Such a heavy imposition would mean starvation and ruin for our people, since even before this, the income of most of our communities had not been enough for their daily bread.

We wrote that many communities were so poor that for over a year they had not been able to give even one measure of wine to mothers of newborn babies or to the dying. In some places, no matter how hard our people worked, they had to go without meat for two months. Many were without underwear or bed linen. Even though in one year we spent a large sum of money (which we prefer not to name) on hides, wool, linen, salt, lard, and various grains, it was all plundered by the soldiers. There was scarcely one community with enough food for the next three weeks. Some communities reaped only enough to provide seed to sow when God granted us peace.

We had gone through times of such need and distress that it would have been better to die than to live. Our wives' and children's best clothing had been taken off their backs for money to buy bread. Therefore we poor and oppressed people begged the lord cardinal most humbly to have compassion on us.

Yet come what may, for reasons of conscience we could not and would not do what was asked of us (as far as money was concerned) any more than our forefathers had done. We were prepared, instead, to suffer and wait patiently for whatever God would allow to happen. With regard to the grain (since men must be fed and it is not a direct levy for the war), we would wish to do the same as our countrymen, as far as we were able.

Cardinal's answer.

In response to our letter, complaints, and humble petitions (which we had made to other Moravian lords as well), the lord cardinal informed us that the mandate was already made public and he could not alter it without the emperor's consent. We could see that nothing lay ahead but great calamity.

Moravian Estates protested the heavy taxes.

All the Estates as well as the towns of Moravia protested the taxation and appealed to the emperor, even though none

1622

of them were taxed half as heavily in proportion to their income as we were. The matter was therefore postponed. In the meantime the cardinal (a bitter enemy of the devout) went to Vienna. He swore an oath that on his return to Moravia he would no longer tolerate us in the country. Once in Vienna, he and his sworn supporters and the council of priests falsely represented to Emperor Ferdinand and his chief councillors that we were rebels, enemies of His Majesty, and had caused him nothing but trouble during the war.

Emperor gave cardinal authority to persecute us. Began on his own estates.

Through this false accusation the cardinal gained the power his malicious heart desired; he received authority from the emperor to drive our whole church out of Moravia. He wasted no time in carrying out his commission—and even more. Two days after his return from Vienna he made a start on his own properties at Nikolsburg, Tracht, and Klein Niemtschitz near Prahlitz. Without warning, he sent his officials and soldiers to these three communities on one day and had all the rooms, cellars, grain lofts, flour lofts, attics, and bedrooms sealed off, so no one could enter his own room. Soldiers were set to watch the houses. Then the people were called together and an imperial document was read to them: Neither they nor their fellows in faith were to be tolerated any longer, not only in Moravia but in any country under the emperor's power. Even in Transylvania they would not be safe but would be a people marked for death. Those, however, who would renounce their error and let themselves be taught by the priests and Jesuits were to remain in their homes, have the use of their property, and like all other subjects in the country, receive the protection and favor of emperor and cardinal.

230 weak people renounced their faith and followed the devil.

Following this, each of our people had to declare individually whether or not he would comply. Already at that point 230 people, young and old, from those three communities on the cardinal's land shrank back from Christ's bitter way of suffering. These were for the most part loose and disorderly members who had already been a burden to the church, since they loved the pleasures of the world more than God and listened to the voice of the old serpent. Their names were at once written down.

But most declared that theirs was the right faith, the truth, and the way to eternal life; come life, come death, they would not give way. With all his might, the cardinal tried in person to get several brothers, especially Jakob Braitenstainer, the steward from Tracht, to renounce their faith, but Jakob told him to his face in front of many others that he would never trust in salvation through the papist faith, which let people burn our houses, slaughter our men, and rape our wives and daughters. They were considered good Christians even if they behaved worse than the Turks; and yet God-fearing people who did honest work to support themselves and injured no one were forced to leave the country. After this and more, the cardinal was silenced and did not know what to answer.

1622
Steward Jakob told the cardinal that he set no hope of salvation in the papist faith.

Nevertheless, all who would not follow the advice of the false prophets or worship the image of the beast were driven out and robbed of their homes, land, and goods, according to God's Word spoken long ago by the prophet, that those who fear God will be driven from their homes, robbed, and destroyed. Thus will his chosen be made known. On all three places our people were forbidden to take even the little they could carry, and no tools at all. All livestock and whatever was in the houses, fields, or vineyards had to be left behind. They also stripped some brothers and sisters, especially at Wisternitz. The lord cardinal's servants searched for money in garments and shoe soles. The adz was withheld from the carpenter and the shears from the tailor. The faithful service we had given the cardinal, all the hard work over many years, was repaid with crass ingratitude.

The cardinal's servants searched even in shoe soles.

The elders wrote humbly to the cardinal, asking him, even if he no longer wanted our people on his estates, to let them at least take their livestock and the goods they had earned with the sweat of their brow. He should not sin by robbing God-fearing people, for God would not let it go unavenged. The cardinal had been heard to say that he alone was responsible for our persecution and was the only one from whom we could get help, so we begged him repeatedly, both verbally and in writing, to show us some sympathy as a man in authority. We begged him to provide shelter in Moravia during the winter (already practically upon us) at least for the old and sick, whom we wanted to gather in two or three places. He should remember that we had lived in Moravia over eighty years and had faithfully served many lords.

Cardinal warned not to sin by taking the goods of the God-fearing. Warning ignored.

But our petitions fell on deaf ears, for his heart was hardened against us. On another occasion our brothers tried again, in

1622

all humility, to approach him with an urgent petition. Besides the written petition, some brothers went to plead directly with him for mercy and understanding for our suffering people. With a smile on his lips and mocking words he told them, "You brought me only a handwritten petition from your elders, but I will give you a printed answer." Then the cardinal had a printed mandate sent to them through his servant, as at the emperor's command and in his name, dated from his residence at Brünn, September 28, 1622.[1] It read as follows:

Cardinal issued mandate from emperor ordering us to leave Moravia within 4 weeks.

Mandate.

> Whereas His Majesty the Holy Roman Emperor, having won the victory known to the whole world, intends to restore order in his hereditary kingdoms and above all to promote the honor and service of God; whereas, however, the Anabaptists, or Hutterian Brethren, though tolerated nowhere in the whole Holy Roman Empire, travel abroad and mislead people to accept their errors, deny baptism to infants, and refuse to submit to governmental authority as God has commanded, besides teaching and practicing many other accursed errors; whereas, moreover, they aided and abetted the enemies of His Imperial Majesty and of the archduke of Austria in the recent uprising through communications and help based on their knowledge of the countryside,
>
> Therefore it is His Majesty's firm intention and strict order that every person, male or female, who confesses to the Hutterian faith must leave the Margravate of Moravia within four weeks of this date and must never be found there again on pain of death. Those, however, who allow themselves to be turned from their error and led to the true way shall be given every assistance.

Winter was already upon us, and we did not know where we could possibly house our needy flock of so many thousands

[1]Orders of expulsion were issued on September 8, 17, and 28, 1622, but large numbers of Hutterites, on pretext of converting to Catholicism, continued to live at their Bruderhofs, encouraged by their patrons among the Catholic nobility (e.g., the lords Karl, Maximilian, and Grundaker von Liechtenstein; Count Zdeněk Žampach of Potnštejn at Göding; or the chief steward of Bohemia, Adam von Waldstein, who owned the Gross Seelowitz estate). Thereupon the cardinal issued further orders of expulsion on November 27, 1622, and April 13, 1623. See Beck, 416 n.2, for a summary of the latter. Both edicts were aimed at the total suppression of the Hutterites. See Hruby, *Wiedertäufer*, 95–100.

of souls. After this harsh imperial mandate, we humbly approached the cardinal again. We also turned to Prince von Liechtenstein, Lord Breuner, the lord marshal, the governor of Austria, and other distinguished lords. Finally, in our extreme need, we approached the emperor himself. We begged him to hear our desperate, humble plea and sincerely apologized for disobeying the imperial mandate to leave the country and go into suffering and misery. But we were denied all mercy by the emperor and given the answer that His Majesty would leave the matter to the discretion of Cardinal von Dietrichstein.

1622
Appeals for shelter in winter and hospital for our sick written to cardinal and other lords, even to the emperor.

Thereupon the persecution for our faith and witness to Christ intensified. The cardinal took over the Moravian estates of several lords who were in prison and then drove us empty-handed from Austerlitz, Damborschitz, Alexowitz, Moskowitz, Kostel, and Altenmarkt, just as he had done from his own property. All our horses, oxen, cows, sheep, and hogs, all the grain and other provisions—a large amount of valuable goods—had to be left behind. But in several places people managed, even with the help of some soldiers, to get away secretly with some clothing and bed linen. A few lords, knowing we were innocent, wanted to show us sympathy and allowed us to take some of our goods. But often the transport cost almost as much as the things were worth, for we had to hire wagons and an escort of soldiers—without them it was unsafe to travel—and there was hardly a community in Moravia that had been allowed to keep its horses and draft oxen. A wagoner's pay for two or three miles was fifteen or sixteen talers, and each member of the escort required up to ten gulden. Everyone wanted to grow rich at our expense, no matter how poor it made us.

So, as described above, we were persecuted and driven out of Moravia in October of this year, 1622, by an order of Emperor Ferdinand II instigated by Cardinal von Dietrichstein. A large amount of the church's movable and immovable property and a great deal of wine and grain produced in this year were left behind in the twenty-four communities in Moravia. Most communities had already sown their winter rye. The damage the church suffered for the sake of truth in this persecution is beyond all description, but part of the tremendous loss is recorded here for posterity: over 800 bushels

Expulsion from 24 communities. Church lost over 300,000 talers.

1622

of wheat, 114 bushels of barley, 478 bushels of oats, 133 bushels of buckwheat, over 300 barrels of wine; 130 head of cattle, 70 oxen, 150 horses, 655 hogs; in addition, all kinds of household goods—copper pans, cloth, wool, linen, salt, lard, and similar things—as well as tools and stores of material for the craftsmen. At the lowest estimate (by values then current in Hungary and Moravia) the total value exceeded 364,000 talers. This did not include the twenty-four communities[1] and their property, the vineyards, gardens, fields, and meadows, which would raise it to an immense sum.

Left Moravia.

We had to leave Moravia and go into Hungary practically empty-handed. Winter was approaching, and it was a difficult time, when everything was very expensive. Because of our great poverty, many of our people suffered. A large number had gathered, and there was very little food. Yet the elders, and especially Valentin Winter, Vorsteher of the whole church, did not spare any effort but did their utmost day and night to obtain bread and shelter. God moved the hearts of many Hungarian lords, with the result that they were glad to take our people in. They were even upset if we did not settle on their estates.

Great famine in Hungary.

Yet the great famine in Hungary, worse than any ever recorded in history books or chronicles, hit the church of God especially hard. A peck of wheat cost ten talers; a peck of rye, eight; a peck of barley, seven; a peck of peas, ten; a peck of millet, nine; and a peck of buckwheat, five talers. A loaf of bread cost one gulden; a barrel of salt, two talers; a pound of meat, nine groschen; a jug of beer, eighteen kreuzers; and one of wine, forty-two kreuzers. Lard was priced at half a Hungarian taler, a hundredweight of tallow at fifty talers, a hundredweight of wool at one hundred and thirty talers, a

---

[1]By the end of 1622, the 43 or more Hutterian communities existing in Moravia in 1619 had been reduced to 24 through the ravages of the war. Those 43 communities were located in an area roughly circumscribed by the cities of Brno, Znojmo, Břeclav, Uherské Hradiště, and Slavkov. See Hruby, *Wiedertäufer*, 107–109, for a listing of the 43 communities and the corresponding estates.

According to Codex Dreller, fol. 152r, the 24 communities given up in 1622 were: Neumühl, Tscheikowitz, Kobelitz, Tracht, Pausram, Pribitz, Nuslau, Pohrlitz, Austerlitz, Herspitz, Kostel, Göding, Schadowitz, Damborschitz, Urschitz, Nikoltschitz, Klein Niemtschitz, Alexowitz, Stiegnitz, Wischenau, Teikowitz, Tschermakowitz, Moskowitz, and Altenmarkt. See the respective entries in Zeman, *Topography*; Beck, 408–410.

hundredweight of hemp at nine, and two untanned oxhides at sixteen talers. In short, all basic commodities were extremely expensive, and to make matters worse, money had lost value both in Hungary and in other countries.[1] 1622

Hardly anyone would sell anything unless paid in the old currency (imperial talers and ducats), but we earned none of these, and no one in our whole church had any income. So for the church's needs we had to fall back on the little our forefathers had put by in good years against times like these and which our elders had painstakingly saved from being taken by the cardinal. This had to be used to cover the people's most urgent needs. Yet in these days of famine the peasants in our areas provided bread for the people of God's church, and so (thanks be to God) no one had to starve. Through God's grace, in the midst of the misery and distress we were far better off than our enemies would have expected. The Lord in heaven, who never abandons his children, mercifully helps us through, even in the greatest fear and need.

Many could not stand the test.

The Lord had sent this distress to his people as a test and purification to reveal the proven ones. Many could not stand the test, particularly the superficial and insincere, even though they had left Moravia. They were just like the children of Israel, who left Egypt, but as soon as they were faced with suffering, disaster, hunger, and cold, thought about Egypt (where they had had bread in plenty) and turned back, abandoning the Lord and his church. Many did not even leave the country but left the church in Moravia (most of these being people from the cardinal's estates, as mentioned above). Therefore the Lord punished us further with the plague and

[1]See also Beck, 410–411. About the monetary inflation of the years 1620–1622 (the so-called *Kipper- und Wipperjahre*), when debased coins were circulated, Codex Dreller, fol. 153v (1622), reads:

"You should also know, dear reader, that at that time good money had a very high price. One ducat was worth twenty gulden in the new, inferior currency, and one Reichstaler was worth ten. As far as small coins were concerned, they were very low in weight and fineness. And when the price dropped again and better coins were minted, not only the church communities, but the lords and everybody else as well, suffered great losses. For what had earlier been worth ten kreuzers was then sold for one kreuzer, and small change was called 'long money.' That is why everything was so expensive." Gustav Freytag, *Bilder aus der deutschen Vergangenheit*, Vol. II, reports that "the new money" of that time "was almost pure copper, which was boiled and whitened. After about a week it turned fiery red." The expression "not a red cent" (*kein roter Heller*) may have originated at that time.

1622
3 servants of the Word moved to Transylvania with their people. Some went to Croatia, most to southeastern Hungary.

took many of our people from us through death. Most of those from the two communities at Moskowitz and Alexowitz set out with the three servants of the Word, Michael Kocher, Thoman Wilhelm, and Albrecht Grob (who was still in a time of testing), and traveled in very bad weather to join our people in Transylvania. A little group with a servant of the Word was also sent to Croatia in response to Lord Batthyany's request and favorable offers. These were mostly in a position to serve him at good annual wages as cellarers, storekeepers, work managers, farm overseers, gardeners, millers, carpenters, and barber-surgeons. So this considerably reduced the numbers in the communities settled on the manorial estates of Branc, Velké Levåre, Schossberg, Schächtitz, Trentschin, and Schmalenz, as well as at Kesselsdorf[1] (under Lord Hans Palffy) and at Farkeschin, a mile from Schindau (under the count palatine).[2] At Velké Levåre we moved back into the houses we had built. At Egbell we rented the small castle from Lord Emmerich Czobor for three years at four hundred gulden annually. At Rabenska and at two places in Senitz, as well as at Tschätschowe (Častkov) on the Branc estate, we found winter lodging for a certain rent. At Schächtitz, too, they let us use a few rooms in the castle over the winter. At Soblahof on the Trentschin estate[3] we bought a house with gardens, fields, and meadows for 150 imperial talers, each one equal to four talers. On this same estate, we rented two other houses for a year, namely at Dubnitz and Teplitz, each at one hundred

[1]Schossberg (Šaštín-Stráže), southwest of Sabatisch (Sobotište); Schmalenz (Smolinské), just north of Schossberg; Kesselsdorf (Kostolné), southwest of Trentschin (Trenčín). About Kesselsdorf, see also *ME*, III, 168.

[2]Farkeschin (Vičkovce), a village on the Dudvah River southeast of Tyrnau; in 1622 it belonged to the Hungarian palatine Stanislaus Thurzo; Beck, 410; *ME*, II, 301. Historically, "palatine" designated the highest dignitary of the kingdom, elected by the Estates from four candidates proposed by the king. At the same time the palatine was both the king's legal representative and the mediator between the king and the nobility.

[3]The seat of the Trentschin estate was Dubnitz (Dubnica). In 1622 the owner, Count Caspar Illésházi (d.1648), gave shelter to the brothers and sisters, who had letters of recommendation from their Moravian lord, Karel Zahrádecký of Wischenau. Illésházi settled them first at Dubnitz, then at Teplitz (Trenčianske Teplice) and Soblahof (Soblahov), all near Trentschin (Trenčín); see Beck, 410 n.2; Zieglschmid, "Die ungarischen Wiedertäufer. . . ," note 46.

In 1651 Gabriel and Georg Illésházi (sons of Caspar) renewed the Soblahof contract. In 1652 Georg transferred half the property "Holgasovska" at Soblahof to the Hutterites as a gift; see Beck, 484.

imperial talers. At Farkeschin we took over the farmstead and mill for three years from the count palatine, the farmstead for three hundred gulden a year and the mill for a quarter share. We were to work the fields at our own expense and sow the seed on the lord's three-quarters and our one-quarter of the land, with three-quarters of the yield going to the count palatine and a quarter to us. These were very harsh terms, but we were willing to do our utmost and more for the count palatine, who as ruler in the land had admitted us into Hungary (against the emperor's wishes) by written letters patent at a time when we were being persecuted. *1622*

Thus in the cold and near-famine conditions of that winter, in spite of poverty and many obstacles, our communities began anew in Hungary. But Emperor Ferdinand, urged on by Cardinal von Dietrichstein, tried to continue persecuting us. He was like Satan, who was not content even when Job had lost his sons and daughters, his camels, sheep, and cattle, and all his goods and property, but persisted until he had power over Job's body as well and brought him to the dung heap. At the year's end, in December 1622, he sent letters patent to the Hungarian lords. Through God's special providence, however, they had safeguarded their freedom of religion with military strength and refused to comply until the emperor summoned a general meeting of the Diet.

Cardinal tried to persecute us even in Hungary.

The above was a description of the three consecutive years of misery and suffering the church of the Lord endured during the terrible days of devastation and war until the expulsion from Moravia. Now we will record the deaths of our brothers in the service of the Word and the service for temporal affairs during these three years of 1620, 1621, and 1622, as well as all other notable events of that period.

1620

First, on February 7, 1620, brother Hansel Kleger, a servant for temporal affairs, fell asleep in the Lord at Neumühl.

Hansel Kleger passed away

On February 12 brother Hansel Ruecker, a servant for temporal affairs, fell asleep in the Lord at Stiegnitz.

Hansel Ruecker passed away.

On February 19 brother Ulrich Jaussling, Vorsteher of the whole church, was summoned to Brünn with other elders to

1622 (1620)
Ulrich Jaussling, elder of the church, summoned to Brünn with other elders to discuss war aid.

appear before several prominent lords from the three Estates of the Moravian Diet. The lords reminded the brothers of all the benefits granted to the church and that we had lived under their protection for many years. Now, as there were skilled people of all nationalities among us, they entreated us to help in this time of dire need by supplying money and people for the war. In the end they asked us for only a few thousand gulden, with a firm promise of adequate security and a written agreement. Because it was against our faith and conscience, we refused outright, both verbally and in writing. It pained us that the lords should make such a request when we had lived so long on their estates in Moravia and they knew very well that we had never given any help during the Turkish wars. They accepted the elders' answer and declared that they did not wish to require anything of us that was against our faith and conscience.

Melchior Brecht passed away.

On March 6 Melchior Brecht, a servant for temporal affairs, fell asleep in the Lord at Velké Leváre.

Bärbel Wälsch released from prison.

On March 14 sister Bärbel Wälsch, the widow of David, the cellarer of Ebenthal (whose story was told earlier in this book[1]), was released from prison at Zistersdorf through God's wonderful intervention. She and her two young children had been unjustly imprisoned for over two years, and during this time many attempts had been made to bring her to recant. She returned to the church community with great joy.

Michael Albrecht passed away.

On March 16 brother Michael Albrecht, a servant for temporal affairs who had been a steward for thirty years, fell asleep in the Lord at Kobelitz.

Bastel Gilg passed away.

On March 21 brother Bastel Gilg, an old steward and servant for temporal affairs, fell asleep in the Lord at Schakwitz.

Celebrated Lord's Supper.

In June 1620, through God's protection despite the ever-present ravages of war, we were able to celebrate the Lord's Supper at thirteen communities in peace and with great thanksgiving.

Mission continued safely.

This year, too, we followed the example of our forefathers by sending out several brothers to various places in Germany. They went to seek those on fire for the truth and to call people to repentance. It amazed many people in Bohemia (where both hostile armies were encamped) as well as in Germany that our

[1]See above, pp.627–628, 643–644.

defenseless members set out in a time of such terrible danger, when scarcely anyone, whether of high or low estate, could travel in safety. But the Lord was their protector, and they relied on him alone. When their task was completed (through the intercession of his people), he led them home again in peace and safety.

1622 (1620)

On July 22 we began to rebuild the community at Tracht on the Nikolsburg estates, especially the upper house where the potters had lived. The lords of Nikolsburg had sworn allegiance to Frederick, the count palatine at that time, and had accepted him as overlord.

Began rebuilding potters' house at Tracht.

On December 8 brother Valtin Kallenbacher, a servant for temporal affairs, fell asleep in the Lord at Austerlitz.

Valtin Kallenbacher passed away.

1621

On January 31, 1621, brother Leonhard Schmidt, a servant of the Word, fell asleep in the Lord at Nikolsburg.

Leonhard Schmidt passed away.

On February 4 brother Augustin Graf, a servant of the Word, fell asleep in the Lord at Stiegnitz.

Augustin Graf, a servant, passed away.

On March 15 brother Stoffel Ruecker, a servant of the Word, fell asleep in the Lord with a peaceful heart at Sabatisch in Hungary.

Stoffel Ruecker, a servant, passed away.

On March 20 brother Hans Staindel, a servant of the Word, fell asleep in the Lord at Pausram.

Hans Staindel, a servant, passed away.

On March 29 brother Joseph Seyer, a servant for temporal affairs, fell asleep in the Lord at Damborschitz.

Joseph Seyer, a servant, passed away.

On April 1 a large group was forced to move from Hungary to Transylvania by Bethlen Gabor, prince of Transylvania: brother Franz Walter, a servant of the Word; Konrad Hirzel, a steward; and 183 brothers, sisters, and children. They had been living at the Schächtitz and Echtlnitz estates, where they had fled from the inhuman savagery of the imperial forces. Brother Franz wrote a farewell letter to all the elders and to the whole church (for there was no time to see them face to face). He told them he was at peace with God and all brothers and sisters and was determined to remain faithful to the true faith unto death. Prince Bethlen had the group taken all the way to Transylvania in his wagons and under his own escort. Through God's providence, they were treated with much

Franz Walter and 183 others taken to Transylvania.

1622 (1621)

kindness by people who were strangers to them, both on the way and in Transylvania.[1]

Cardinal demanded 10 wagons for the imperial armory at Vienna.

On April 2, when the imperial army was about to besiege the fortress of Neuhäusel in Hungary, Cardinal von Dietrichstein as governor of Moravia wrote a letter to Ulrich Jaussling at Neumühl. But Jaussling, elder of the church, was at that time still on the flight into Hungary. In the name of His Imperial Majesty, ten strong wagons were to be at the imperial armory in Vienna within a few days. Each wagon was to have four good horses and forty gulden for a months' supply of food and fodder, as well as brothers who would care for the horses as their own. There were to be no exceptions, on pain of imperial displeasure and punishment. Although this did not promise well for us, it turned out better than we expected. We complained to the cardinal and the imperial commissioners that we could not comply for reasons of conscience and that all our communities together had scarcely as many good horses as were required; we humbly begged them to have understanding. So we were freed from this obligation and ordered instead to transport foodstuffs within the country. But eventually even this order was quietly dropped, and it looked as if the whole thing had just been a malicious test.

Ulrich Jaussling passed away.

At six o'clock in the evening on Maundy Thursday, April 8, 1621, our dear and loyal brother Ulrich Jaussling fell asleep in the Lord with a peaceful heart and a clear conscience at Branc Castle in Hungary. He was a devout and zealous man, a faithful Vorsteher of the whole church, who left us many sound teachings. He departed from this vale of tears after

[1]Bethlen Gabor, king of Hungary (see above, p.665 n.2), compelled 185 Hutterites to move to Alwinz (Vintu de Jos) just southwest of Karlsburg (Alba Iulia), Transylvania (Romania), after the persuasive powers of his commissaries had failed. See Friedmann, *MQR*, Oct. 1961, 309–314; "Alwinz," *ME*, I, 83–84; Beck, 393.

A song in *LdHBr*, 827–835, tells of their departure for Transylvania. The acrostic forms the following prayer (in translation):

> Lord God, you have taken us from your church and its shepherds and led us afar into a strange land, where some of us do not have your Word and your comfort. O Lord, let us not perish, give us courage through your power. Let us not be faced with great temptation; uphold us with your Word. We will praise you and honor you from now on for all your goodness and praise your name through Jesus Christ our Lord. Amen.

About the letter of safe conduct for the Hutterites that Gabor issued at Karlsburg in August 1625, see Zieglschmid, "Die ungarischen Wiedertäufer. . . ," note 47, where the Latin document appears in a diplomatic edition; also Beck, 427 n.1.

1622 (1621)

enduring many hardships and anxieties that attacked him and the Lord's church in this time. As he neared his end, he often asked that in these sorrowful and evil days the Lord might take the church all the more closely into his faithful care. Brother Ulrich was forty-eight years old and had been a servant of the Word for twenty-two years; for over a year he had led the church of the Lord in the midst of turmoil and disaster.

Niklas Kuenzin, a servant, passed away.

On April 25 brother Niklas Kuenzin from Velké Leváre, a servant of the Gospel, passed away with a peaceful heart and a clear conscience at Nikolsburg.

Nikolsburg schoolmaster and a boy imprisoned for 17 weeks.

On May 6 Josef Händel (the schoolmaster from Nikolsburg) and a ten-year-old boy were put in jail by Lord Cardinal von Dietrichstein and kept there until September 24 because of a writing against the papacy. The previous schoolmaster Wilhelm Mändel had had it copied quite unnecessarily from a printed tract, and Händel from Nikolsburg had foolishly given it to the boy to learn from. Since neither schoolmaster nor schoolboy could be found guilty of any offense, they were released on September 24.

Church entrusted to brother Rudolf Hirzel.

At that time the Lord's church was without an elder for four weeks, since the danger from soldiers was too great for the elders to gather. But on Laudate Sunday, May 9, the entire brotherhood gave unanimous testimony for brother Rudolf Hirzel to lead and faithfully care for the church of God, and he was earnestly entrusted with this task by dear brother Hauptrecht Zapff. The enormous damage and slander brought on the church shortly afterward by this Rudolf will soon be fully told in all its pain and distress.

3 brothers confirmed in the service.

On May 16 the three brothers Georg Geher, Thoman Wilhelm,[1] and Hans Lang were confirmed in the service of the Gospel at Neumühl by the elders with the laying on of hands.

5 brothers chosen.

On the same day, five brothers were chosen for the service of the Word and appointed by the church at Neumühl: Jakob

[1]After Thoman Wilhelm's service was confirmed, he left Moravia with the brothers and sisters from Alexowitz and Moskowitz and moved to Transylvania. Because of unbrotherly behavior, he was excluded and after repenting returned to Sabatisch, from where at his request he was sent on mission to his homeland, the Bregenz area (northwest Austria). A widower, he remarried and left the Hutterian Church to join the Swiss Brethren. See Beck, 396.

1622 (1621)

Litzenbucher, a vinedresser; Andreas Ehrenpreis, a miller;[1] Albrecht Grob, a tailor; Ulrich Amssler, a cutler; and Uhl Müllner, a harness-maker.

David Stainer, a servant, passed away.

On June 2 brother David Stainer, a servant of the Word, passed away at Pausram.

Konrad Blossy, a servant, passed away.

On August 26 brother Konrad Blossy, a servant of the Word, fell asleep in the Lord at Bochtitz.

Franz Walter, a servant, passed away.

On October 6 brother Franz Walter, an old servant of the Gospel, fell asleep in the Lord with a peaceful heart at Alwinz in Transylvania. Before his end, he testified to his peace with God and all the faithful and to a clear conscience. He also expressed his thankfulness for all the kindness shown him and sent a loving farewell to the church in Moravia.

Since most of the soldiers had left Moravia for Hungary and the church now had an elder once more, our people were hoping that the sunshine of peace would show itself again after the violent storm. But just at this time, in the eventful year of 1621, an unexpected and very distressing event took place in the church, beginning on June 2, the Wednesday after Whitsun. A summary of what happened now follows.

Cardinal demanded several thousand gulden under false pretext.

In the evening of Whit-Tuesday, June 1, Cardinal von Dietrichstein sent his servant, Allanz, to Neumühl. Allanz was a Spaniard by birth but had been raised at Nikolsburg, so we had known him since his youth. He brought a sealed letter addressed to the elders at Neumühl, requesting in the emperor's name that our church pay altogether several thousand gulden (the exact sum was not named). The letter added that all inhabitants of Moravia living under the protection of His Imperial Majesty, regardless of their rank, would have to do the same. Allanz delivered this letter and then went into a long and wordy explanation of his own.

---

[1]Andreas Ehrenpreis (1589–1662) was confirmed in the service of the Word at Sabatisch in 1623 (see below, p.699); became Vorsteher in 1639 (see p.736). He was a prolific writer of epistles, sermons, and Ordnungen, as well as songs. About his life and work, including a list of his writings, see *ME*, II, 165–166; Friedmann, *Schriften*, 111–113. For the "Bader-Ordnung," or "Barber-Surgeon Discipline" of 1654, written during his eldership, see John A. Hostetler et al., *Selected Hutterian Documents in Translation*, 157–160. Beck, 485 n.1; Songs written by or attributed to Ehrenpreis are in *LdHBr*, 13–18, 55–59, 639–647, 851–864, 867–870, 873–877; Wolkan, *Lieder*, 243. See also Ehrenpreis's "Epistle on Brotherly Community as the Highest Command of Love," in *Brotherly Community*, 1–77, Introduction by Robert Friedmann.

As elder of the church, brother Rudolf Hirzel, with the advice of his assistants, said he would call the elders together within five days, read out the emperor's request, hear their opinion, and then send an answer as soon as possible. To all appearances Allanz was satisfied. At that point we did not see through the deceit and perfidy of it all. *1622 (1621)*

On the Wednesday mentioned above, June 2, the officials responsible for Prince von Liechtenstein's people—lords of manors, administrators, captains, and treasurers—arrived at Neumühl with their wives and children, pretending they were on a friendly visit, happy to see how well we were doing. They did not give the slightest indication of their deceitful intentions.

They were about to sit down for an early meal at 10 o'clock in the morning when Allanz arrived from Nikolsburg, unannounced, bringing twenty-three cavalrymen and seventeen musketeers. His story was that the city of Brünn had again rebelled and the lord cardinal was in great danger: as he had been driving through the streets the previous day, somebody had fired into his carriage and through his hat. Allanz had received hasty orders to escort the cardinal back with these cavalrymen and musketeers. He demanded to be provided immediately with a coach and pair to take him to Auspitz. Captain Senat acted as if startled by Allanz's sudden arrival and bad news, pretending to know nothing of it.

From the moment the cavalrymen and musketeers came into the community, they blocked every door and exit. Although brothers were let in, no one was allowed to leave. Then it was plain enough what was afoot. Rudolf [Hirzel], however, had to sit down at table with the leaders of that Judas-like crowd, who took greatest care that no one could warn him, much less call him away from the table. It was in any case too late, and there was no way of escaping.

At the end of this meal—a sad one for the faithful but highly enjoyed by those sons of Judas—Allanz asked Rudolf to call some of the responsible brothers, since he had a message for them. As soon as a few brothers appeared, Allanz told Prince von Liechtenstein's captain the reasons why he had been sent by His Gracious Prince the lord cardinal. He took out an imperial letter which said, in effect, that since His Majesty the Holy Roman Emperor had received trustworthy Emperor's letter.

1622 (1621)

reports that the Anabaptist leader was actively supporting by word and deed and in all kinds of practical ways the uprising against His Imperial Majesty, especially in Hungary, His Majesty gave strict orders to lay a snare for this leader and when they caught him, to take him to Nikolsburg Castle.

Captain Senat's false apology.

At this, Captain Senat apologized profusely, saying he had known absolutely nothing of all this and would gladly have taken Rudolf under his protection as his subject in His Gracious Prince's stead, but he would not and could not oppose the imperial command and authority. Nothing would happen to Rudolf, however; it was simply a matter of giving an account. Rudolf readily consented to go with them to do this.

Rudolf Hirzel and 2 brothers taken away.

Allanz requested that Rudolf take along one or two of the elders closest to him. The two chosen were Christoph Hirzel (Rudolf's cousin) and Hans Bencker (his assistant).

Right outside the room, while many of our people looked on and wept, they had to climb into the coach that Allanz had ordered on pretext of a journey to Auspitz. They were taken away, escorted by the twenty-three cavalrymen and seventeen musketeers (though not one of them was actually needed). One can easily imagine the anxiety and distress among our people. There was great grief and mourning.

The 3 brothers were searched at Pulgram.

When these Judases had crossed the Thaya River near Pulgram and reached the cardinal's estates, Allanz clearly revealed himself as an enemy. He searched all three brothers twice and took from them whatever he found, especially letters and writing tablets. Then they were brought to Nikolsburg Castle amid the jeering of the soldiers, who said they were bringing the king of England [*Engel landt*: land of angels]. Immediately the brothers were put into separate cells in the prison (Rudolf in the darkest and worst). In Nikolsburg Castle the coachman was also searched for letters—boots and all.

For six days they were given food and drink from our community at Nikolsburg, and the brother who brought the food was allowed to speak with them through the door, but always with a guard to hear what was said. On the sixth day, orders came from the cardinal at Brünn for the castle to provide the brothers' food and to allow no more brothers to visit them on pain of severe punishment. This order was strictly kept.

Brothers no longer allowed to visit the prisoners.

Many petitions for the prisoners' release.

For five weeks they remained in prison without further measures being taken. During this time appeals were made by letter and by word of mouth to the cardinal and other important nobles, humbly begging for the brothers' release.

1622 (1621)

On July 10 the cardinal arrived at Nikolsburg with Lord Christoph Seifried Breuner (residing at Staatz in Austria) and a foreign count from Vienna, unknown to us by name or family.[1] These three lords reprimanded the three prisoners in a private hearing. The cardinal reported in stinging terms that the brothers had sided with Bethlen and other enemies of His Imperial Majesty and contributed money for the war. Moreover, His Majesty had received trustworthy reports that we had amassed great treasure, as much as one million in gold. Since our elder Rudolf lived in a small village at Neumühl, it could easily happen that the rebels would seize him and get the money from him by torture, they said. It might thus come into the hands of the enemies of His Imperial Majesty to strengthen their war effort.

Cardinal and 2 lords reprimanded the 3 brothers. Explained emperor's intentions.

Therefore His Imperial Majesty wished to have information about our resources, not with the intention of taking them, but rather to keep them safe and prevent them from falling into the hands of His Majesty's enemies.

The cardinal and the other two lords appealed especially to Rudolf, exhorting him to tell them where the money was, since he was elder of the church and would know. The cardinal swore to them by God's honor and truth and as surely as day was day that the money would not be taken. At the same time he threatened terrible consequences if His Majesty's word was not trusted and the whereabouts of the money not revealed. He already had imperial command to exterminate our entire church: he would slaughter the men and send the women and children as bondservants to towns throughout Moravia. If we did not believe it, he would start the very next morning at Nikolsburg and Neumühl.

Cardinal swore that the money would not be taken from us.

These threats reduced Rudolf to a state of terror—for he did not trust the Lord in heaven enough in this affair—so he said he could not deny that he knew something about the money and asked to speak with the two brothers alone. The cardinal

Rudolf asked to withdraw to consult his brothers. His request refused.

[1]Count Alexander Cicognia, later referred to as "the Italian count." Emperor Ferdinand II, in a letter dated Vienna, March 22, 1621, asked Cardinal von Dietrichstein, who was familiar with Hutterian ways, to support Cicognia's efforts to find money in Hutterian communities. About the correspondence between Ferdinand II and Cardinal von Dietrichstein regarding Hutterian money, see Hruby, *Wiedertäufer*, 139–142; also 83–85; Beck, 396–397.

1622 (1621)

refused his request and said he should discuss the question in front of the lords, who were also good and honorable people. Thereupon Rudolf asked his cousin Christoph Hirzel, whom he credited with more discretion than himself, whether he should disclose what he knew. But Christoph (who the day before their imprisonment had hinted to Rudolf that they should do something for the emperor by giving him some money) was not firmly enough founded to be able to give Rudolf the advice he needed, namely, that it would be quite wrong to betray the sweat and toil of the church and that we cannot buy our way out of the trials God may send us.

Instead, he gave Rudolf the feeble answer that since the lords had made such great promises to take nothing, it might not be wrong to let them know.

Rudolf told them of all places where he knew money was hidden.

Then they pressed Rudolf still harder to tell where and in what places there was money, and he admitted that he knew of five places where money was buried, shown him in trust: one at Neumühl, Kostel, and Tracht, and two at Pribitz. The cardinal at once asked for a detailed description of where the money was, and he learned from Rudolf the names of other elders who might also know something.

After this, the cardinal, Breuner, and the Italian count rode back to Brünn. For several days we heard nothing, and the brotherhood could get no news of what had happened to the prisoners. No one in the castle knew anything, and we could get no message to them or they to us.

The whole affair was kept very quiet until July 22, when Breuner and the Italian count returned to Nikolsburg and sent for Burkhard Braitenstainer, then elder in Nikolsburg. With smooth, deceptive words they told him that the time had come to release the three brothers in prison. There was only one point left to clear up, which had to do with brother Sebastian Dietrich [no longer living]. Since Michael Kocher, elder at Moskowitz, was Sebastian's cousin, Burkhard should urgently send a letter by special messenger telling Michael to come immediately to Nikolsburg to answer in place of his deceased cousin. Burkhard believed their lies and wrote from the castle, asking brother Kocher to come as soon as possible. Brother Kocher, however, saw through their treachery and did not appear. So they took Burkhard prisoner, transferred Rudolf to the cell where Bencker had been, and put Bencker in with

Burkhard Braitenstainer also imprisoned.

1622 (1621)

Christoph. (Bencker was not asked many questions and came out of the affair quite blameless.) Burkhard was put in the dark cell where Rudolf had been before.

The following day, July 23 (the Friday before St. James's Day), the deceit of the cardinal, Breuner, and the Italian count became plain enough. Accompanied by several cavalrymen and musketeers, Breuner rode unannounced to Pribitz, taking Rudolf with him in the wagon. Rudolf was to show him first where the money was at Pribitz. In one place here they found it already the first day, but in the other place only after a week of searching.

Money found at Pribitz.

At nine o'clock on Saturday evening, July 24, these Judases took Rudolf to Neumühl, on July 26 to Tracht, and on July 27 to Kostel. At each place they managed to get their hands on the money that our poor people had toiled and sweated to earn, and breaking their promises, they took it away. So in the most shameful and treacherous way the church community of the Lord lost nearly all its ready money, saved over many years to provide for needs in times of hardship. And this happened because of Rudolf, in whom everyone had felt great trust.

Money found at Neumühl, Tracht, and Kostel.

After Rudolf had shown all he knew, it was Burkhard's turn. The cardinal summoned Burkhard to appear before him and his supporters. He tried to win him over with smooth and sanctimonious words as well as with harsh ones. He said the collapse and ruin of the church could be avoided only if all hidden money was revealed and handed over to His Majesty. If not, the church would surely be destroyed.

Burkhard brought the elders into great danger by referring the cardinal to them about the hidden money.

Burkhard thought he could handle the matter with greater wisdom than Rudolf, for while Rudolf was in prison, Burkhard had heard of the elders' opinion that someone who calls himself a brother could not disclose where the church's money was. So he replied that one man could not decide this on his own but only with the consent of all elders and the whole church. As a result, the cardinal rode with Breuner and the Italian count to Austerlitz, taking Burkhard, Rudolf, Christoph, and Bencker with them. From there, on August 5, he issued a sharp letter to the elders at Neumühl as well as to all elders in our communities. It ordered all servants of the Word to appear with all the stewards at Austerlitz early on August 7 on pain of the loss of all our possessions and the extermination

1622 (1621)

of our whole church. At such short notice, it was impossible for the brothers to reach Austerlitz on the day and hour set by the cardinal; but out of responsibility to all our people, a few brothers were appointed to go and appear before him. These brothers, however, were seized by Hungarians who were on a raid about half a mile from Auspitz. They were robbed and beaten and so were unable to get to Austerlitz.

The cardinal refused to accept the attack of the Hungarians as an excuse for the brothers' failure to appear. He set a second and third deadline for all the elders to assemble at Austerlitz. Even Burkhard himself wrote, pressing for the brothers to come and not leave him in the lurch, for no questions of faith were involved. He would agree to whatever they decided when they came.

Of course, everyone knew very well what it was all about: the cardinal and his men wanted all the church's money, and if the elders appeared and refused their demands, the cardinal would seize those entrusted with the community's property and throw them into prison too. Therefore many brothers with services decided—because of their love to the church and to the elders—that the elders should not appear, but that all the members should await what God might have in store for his church. Nevertheless, the elders from Austerlitz and Damborschitz with their stewards and some of the heads of the work departments set out once more to see the cardinal, Lord Breuner, and the Italian count at Austerlitz. But this did not satisfy the cardinal. He said he had not asked for tailors and shoemakers but for the elders.

Many brothers decided that the elders should not go.

It was therefore clearly necessary to write a letter to the cardinal in the name of all the elders. They made it amply clear that neither now nor later could they come, because what he was demanding was directly opposed to their faith and conscience.

Letter to the cardinal to say brothers could not appear.

Furthermore, the very little money we still had was urgently needed to support our poor people, the sick, and the old. No elder had the authority to break faith with widows and orphans by giving away their property. Anyone who did would never be able to justify it before God, nor could we acknowledge him as a brother.

Contents of letter.

We did not acquire our money by financial cunning, usury, or profiteering but by the toil and sweat of our brows, and we saved it (as already explained) to provide for people in need. Scripture says: "Bread is life to the destitute, and it is murder to deprive them of it. . . . And the man who cheats a worker of his wages sheds blood" (NEB).

1622 (1621)

Ecclus.34:21–22

Yet, still following Holy Scripture, we brothers wished to honor those set in authority over us, showing due submission and giving to the emperor what is the emperor's and to God what is God's. It would be a grievous thing, which would make us cry out to God, if His Imperial Majesty should further defile himself with our innocent blood for the sake of a small sum of money that is justly ours before God and men. The blood of the righteous, like that of the godly Abel, would cry out from earth to heaven. And God says through his prophets that though he forgives all sin, he will not let innocent blood go unavenged.

Elders' letter to brothers at Austerlitz and Damborschitz.

In all seriousness and in the fear of God we wrote to the cardinal. A separate letter was written to the elders at Austerlitz and Damborschitz, requesting that the four brothers in prison be allowed to read it too. The contents were as follows: The brothers were neither to demand that the elders appear nor in the slightest way to support or advise such a thing. They knew very well that the only concern was to get the church's money (of which the cardinal had already taken the greater part) and that not one of the elders had the right to give any of it away. Moreover, Rudolf would have to give an account for his lack of responsibility. If disaster was what God had in mind for the church, he would not be appeased by money—it would only provoke his displeasure. And should God destine one or more of the elders to be imprisoned and become their fellow sufferers, it would be every brother's duty to remain steadfast and true.

Cardinal enraged by brothers' failure to appear. Burkhard angered about it too.

The elders' failure to appear not only angered the cardinal, Breuner, and the Italian count, but was also taken very badly by Burkhard. In front of Breuner and the Italian (by that time the cardinal had already returned to Brünn), Burkhard complained to the brothers from Austerlitz and Damborschitz that he would never have expected the elders to stay away and leave him in the lurch.

Until that day Burkhard said, the church had been under the elders' authority and had obeyed their direction. If the elders had come and consulted about the money in the fear of

1622 (1621)

Burkhard said God had shown him he should reveal the money.

God, the church would not have opposed it. During his imprisonment he had intensely concerned himself with God, praying and fasting, and God had shown him that he did not have to withhold the money he knew to be buried, because as long as it stayed in the ground, it was of no use to our neighbors. Since the money was a gift of God, it should be used and not left to rot in the ground. Rather, it should go to His Imperial Majesty as the highest authority, under whose forefathers our people had lived many years in peace. If the money remained in the earth, it would only be a sacrifice to the devil.

Burkhard asked brotherhood at Austerlitz if he should reveal the money.

Burkhard then requested brother Michael Grossmann, the elder from Austerlitz, to ask the brotherhood whether he should reveal where the money was hidden. Brother Grossmann replied that in their brotherhood's understanding, it was not their business to advise him whether to reveal the hiding place or not, since they had not been asked when it was entrusted to him. But Burkhard was not satisfied with this. With the help of the Italian count he forced the matter until the brotherhood at Austerlitz had to assemble on his account. There in the presence of the count, he began to speak at great length of how the church had enjoyed the protection of the revered House of Austria for many years and lived in peace under His Imperial Majesty's predecessors. Now that the emperor, head of all countries, offered to take the church under imperial protection, he, Burkhard, felt in his heart that it was right to give him the church's money; if the emperor should demand the coat off his back, it was his duty to give it. Finally, he asked for an explicit answer from the brotherhood at Austerlitz as to whether he should reveal the hiding place of the money or not.

Burkhard received answer that anyone who revealed the money was not a brother.

Several brothers stood up and gave testimony to the brotherhood, most of them with the feeling already stated: that they had not been asked for advice when the money was entrusted to him, so he did not need their advice now about revealing it. One brother added that a man who disclosed where the church's money was kept was not to be reckoned as a brother, no matter who he might be. But the count got impatient. Realizing how much in earnest these brothers were, he used threats to try to coerce them. He represented to the brotherhood that the emperor was immensely great and powerful, that he was the head of this government, and that it was right for everyone to submit to him. To this the brotherhood said nothing, but they let him talk until he had had his say. 1622 (1621)

Burkhard, however, understood from both their words and their silence how painful this sad affair was for the brotherhood. There were many sobs and groans. So he left again, deeply disturbed, with nothing settled.

After this, Burkhard and the other three prisoners were taken from Austerlitz to the cardinal at Brünn, who had this evil business in hand. He talked a long time with them and then promised to release Rudolf, Christoph, Bencker, and finally Burkhard too, but only on condition that Burkhard would tell where the money was hidden. The cardinal added that he already had three elders to take their place in Nikolsburg Castle, namely brothers Hauptrecht Zapff, Heinrich Hartmann, and Joseph Nägele. He was quite certain of this, since he had given orders to Captain Senat at Feldsberg, who was an excellent tool for such business, to spare no efforts to get hold of the three brothers. The captain had no qualms about using deception for his purpose. He wrote a friendly letter to the elders at Neumühl, saying it was clear that Rudolf, Christoph, and Bencker would be released and that he had received orders from his gracious prince [the cardinal] in the name of His Imperial Majesty to ask the elders how they would like to be treated and how their rulers could be of service to them in the future. Because of the many Spanish soldiers encamped in the neighborhood, he was unable to leave home for long or travel very far, and therefore Hauptrecht, Heinrich, and Joseph should come to him at Eisgrub, where he would gladly talk over their needs face to face. But the three brothers were advised not to go to the captain, since it was plain enough that he was lying. So, contrary to his expectations, the cardinal's ungodly plans did not succeed this time.

4 prisoners taken to Brünn.

Captain Senat expected to catch Hauptrecht, Heinrich, and Joseph by some ruse.

On August 21 the Italian count and the Spaniard Allanz returned from Brünn to Nikolsburg with the four prisoners. All four were put in one room in the castle and allowed to stay there and have their meals together.

4 prisoners were returned to Nikolsburg. Put in a room together.

On Monday August 23 the moment came for Burkhard to show the place where he had known that money was buried. The Italian count and Allanz, bringing four wagons, fifteen mounted men, and thirty musketeers, went with him to Kostel,

Burkhard tried to show where the money was. None found.

1622 (1621)

since he had known of something in the Podax vineyard. From there they went on to Neumühl, where he and other brothers had known of two places. But he found no more money at Neumühl than he had at Kostel, for it had been removed by the time they arrived. Burkhard soon noticed that something had changed and told them nothing was there. Nevertheless, peasants had to dig in Podax and in two places at Neumühl for a long time until it was obvious to everyone that they were digging to no purpose.

Italian count spoke to the brothers at Neumühl.

When the count and his Judas band came to the community at Neumühl, he gathered the brothers in the yard outside the meeting room. In Burkhard's presence, he made a long and bombastic speech about how many nations, kingdoms, and lands contributed taxes to His Imperial Majesty as the highest authority after God, adding that even His Holiness the pope annually paid His Majesty a large sum of money. Why then did we brothers refuse to do the same, as we were living in His Imperial Majesty's domains, under his protection, and in great need of his favor? His Imperial Majesty was not asking for what we needed for our day-to-day existence but for the money hidden underground in order to take it into custody, so that it would not fall into the hands of His Majesty's enemies.

If we entrusted our money to His Majesty, well and good. If not, we were heading for disaster, since he was under orders from His Imperial Majesty to kill all our people, young and old, and burn down our houses. His Majesty had reliable reports that we had given a large sum of money to Frederick and Bethlen Gabor and, what is more, that there had been an understanding between Bethlen and our previous elder.

Brothers' answer to the Italian count's high-sounding speech.

In reply, the count was told in Burkhard's presence that most of the church's money was already gone, and we had no more than would cover our most urgent needs, since our communities had been plundered and burned down. Besides, it was neither for the oldest nor the youngest to give away—it belonged to the poor widows and orphans.

As to the accusation that we had given money to Frederick and to Bethlen Gabor and had made an agreement with them, that was an attack and an injustice before God. We had done nothing of the sort; at no time had we given either Frederick or Bethlen a single taler, far less a large sum of money. For reasons of conscience, we had never paid war taxes at any

1622 (1621)

time during the Turkish Wars but had put up for many years with confiscations instead, which had meant suffering great losses of property and food supplies. How much less fitting it would have been for us to contribute to this war in our own locality! For reasons of conscience, therefore, we could not give His Majesty the little ready money that remained. Let God send what he would—we set our trust and hope in him alone.

When the count heard this reply and saw that the brothers were not intimidated by his threats, he changed his manner and became quite friendly. He stayed overnight at Neumühl and ordered the digging to continue the next day, but they found nothing. He came back to the house to take leave, shaking hands with many brothers and thanking them for the night's lodging and hospitality. He showed no sign of anger at not finding the money. He set off for Nikolsburg with a very unhappy and frightened Burkhard, who bitterly regretted his own folly.

Burkhard bemoaned his folly.

Three days later, on August 26, the wicked Allanz arrived, hoping to win great acclaim by discovering money. He appeared unannounced at Stiegnitz with four wagons and several mounted soldiers and musketeers but without any of the prisoners. He and his rabble had stopped at the priest's house in Stiegnitz, but they came to our community for supper. Here he invented another lie: he had wanted to go to Trebitsch (Třebíč) but had lost his way in the fields and had found himself at Stiegnitz. Early next morning he made his real purpose clear to the brothers. He presented letters with orders from the emperor to dig up money at Stiegnitz, and through the captain at Wischenau he had ordered peasants to come and dig. So he went with the peasants into our farmyard at Stiegnitz, where many years before a woodcutter's hut had stood and there still remained an earthen floor and a walled-up window. There the peasants were set to dig as part of their compulsory labor service.

Allanz looked for treasure at Stiegnitz. Had to leave amid mockery.

When they had dug down about a man's height, they came on a piece of wood or a board. Allanz was overjoyed. He had the wagon brought to the spot and had someone clean out the chest he intended for the money. But his joy was short-lived; there was nothing but the one wooden board. The peasants had to dig deeper, because Allanz said he had been told that

1622 (1621)

money was sure to be there, so it must be there unless the devil had made off with it. After they had dug and searched for a long time, they finally hit an iron wedge that had somehow got into the ground. That was all the treasure any of them found. So that liar Allanz went away empty-handed, to the delight of many of our neighbors.

4 prisoners released with instructions to be reinstated in their offices.

The four men, Rudolf, Burkhard, Christoph, and Bencker, were kept in prison until Monday, September 20, when at five o'clock in the evening they were released and accompanied to our community at Nikolsburg by Allanz and the burgrave. Allanz told the four that His Majesty was determined to destroy the community unless all four, especially Rudolf and Burkhard, were reinstated in their respective services. They were not to be punished, for they had proved themselves obedient subjects of His Imperial Majesty. If the elders complied, His Majesty would protect our people. Allanz added that he had with him a letter to General von Wallenstein (encamped with his troops in the pass at Lundenburg), instructing him to take the brothers under his protection and spare their communities. All this was nothing but lies. Even before Rudolf, Burkhard, and Christoph had been judged and disciplined by the church, we found to our grief what kind of protection His Majesty was giving us. This is described further on.

Rudolf, Burkhard, and Christoph given task of inducing the cardinal to let them lay down their services.

Just at this most difficult time, there was no shepherd overseeing the whole church, so when the released prisoners arrived at Neumühl the next day, a few elders gathered. To begin with, they listened to the whole miserable story of Rudolf, Burkhard, and Christoph. Since none of them could be given back his former service, they were given the task (especially Rudolf and Burkhard) of telling the cardinal that they wished to lay down their services, so that the church could not be held accountable for this step. Then, at a suitable time, the whole matter would be taken up again. They willingly accepted this decision, and Rudolf and Burkhard went to the cardinal at Brünn. But the cardinal was adamant. He insisted that both be reinstated in their former position; anything less would mean contempt of His Imperial Majesty and would not go unpunished. He made such threats a number of times. Later, when several brothers were sent to him at Nikolsburg at his request, he showed them a short letter, written in the emperor's own hand and sealed with the emperor's signet ring, and let

Cardinal showed them emperor's letter requiring their reinstatement.

them read it for themselves. It said that those persons informing them where money was hidden should be restored to their former position and authority, since they had won His Majesty's favor. *1622 (1621)*

It was impossible for the church to accept orders in such a matter, because it was against divine justice. There were, however, sufficient reasons for postponing the matter until February 21, 1622. On that day, at Pausram, a meeting was held of all servants of the Word, all stewards, buyers, storekeepers, and many other trusted brothers from all communities, for it had become urgently necessary to elect a new shepherd. At this time Rudolf, Burkhard, and Christoph's actions (which had already been described to the whole brotherhood) were laid before the meeting at Pausram. All three were excluded and separated from the church completely for being so irresponsible, for bringing contempt from the world outside and even from those who call themselves brotherhoods, and for causing opposition and indignation among our own people. They saw that this decision was just, acknowledged their guilt, and begged for compassion. Rudolf was sent to Göding for a time of repentance but never completed it, for he died there on April 27 the same year. Burkhard was sent to Pohrlitz and Christoph to Schakwitz. After earnestly repenting, Christoph was reaccepted on May 25, and Burkhard on June 3, 1622.

Rudolf, Burkhard, and Christoph excluded.

Rudolf died during his time of repentance.

1622

To return to February 21, 1622: Once this miserable business had been concluded, the meeting at Pausram turned to the very important matter of electing a new shepherd, since there had been no shepherd in the church for nine months in this dangerous and evil time. All the assembled brothers gave joyful and unanimous testimony in favor of laying on our dear brother Valentin Winter the task of directing and caring for the church with godly zeal in these troubled days. May the Lord in his grace strengthen this brother, and may he give his people wisdom and the ability to comfort and rebuild the church so that what is broken may be raised and what is lost may be restored.

Elder Valentin Winter.

It brought much comfort and joy to the church to have an elder and Vorsteher once more. Since there was no other way,

1622

dear brother Valentin obediently accepted the burden of this highly important service. With all his strength he strove to oppose the greed, arrogance, and disorder that had crept into the church during this odious war and to restore the cornerstones of God's church, for which many of our dear forefathers had shed their blood. The other elders loyally supported him in this. Then God granted such grace and blessing that we could celebrate the Lord's Supper in remembrance of our dear Savior Jesus Christ. This was not possible in the previous year, quite apart from the fact that soldiers were swarming through the country, making travel unsafe. On June 12, 20, and 26, at ten of our communities we celebrated the Lord's Supper under God's great and merciful protection, in peace, and with joy and great thanksgiving, and everyone was able to return safely home. The Lord alone be praised!

Meal of Remembrance held at 10 places.

But the Lord's church was to be tempted in every way by Satan and his children. The ugly affair with Rudolf, Burkhard, and Christoph caused several members of the community to turn against the elders with abuse and contempt. Puffed up with pride, they imagined themselves wiser and more devout than anyone else. They declared that saving money was nothing but mammon and avarice and showed a lack of trust in God, that the elders and the whole brotherhood had broken their covenant and forsaken the right way, and that the church was no longer the same as in Jakob Hutter's time. They wanted to return to the first vision, restore the old boundary stones, and rebuild the Hutterian Church from its ruins. Those who took the lead were three tailors and two weavers, chief among them Peter Kaufman, a tailor and a native of Lothringen. An obstinate and difficult person, he had been excluded several times for his irresponsible, self-indulgent life.

Peter Kaufman and his irresponsible followers slandered elders and church with many impudent falsehoods. Excluded.

Peter Kaufman had claimed to understand secrets of the Scriptures and prophesied from strange books, especially against the papacy, foretelling its fall in the year 1620, when there would be a Lutheran emperor. He also warned us that our church was in danger of collapsing and dissolving. He and his supporters had the audacity to say that the only God we believed in was the Holy Roman Emperor, something that not even unconverted Jews say of us. Out of the malice of their hearts, they attacked the church and the elders with many other lies and senseless accusations which they could not possibly prove.

1622

Finally they were excluded from the church because they refused to be corrected by godly instruction. They wanted to establish a church of their own, but because they had so many false and confused ideas, they could not even agree with one another, especially about communal living. They finally decided to put off this question for the time being as the devil might be deceiving them about it. In their folly and disunity, they expected their cause to prosper, but it was not founded in God and therefore came to nothing. Death by the plague overtook the said tailor, Peter Kaufman (an impudent, malicious blasphemer), and shortly afterward his main supporter, Uhl Lips from Switzerland (previously responsible for the weaving at Schakwitz), and another tailor of the same stamp. The rest disappeared one after the other. Some scattered in this direction, others in that, and although they had been so great in their own eyes, in a very short time nothing more was heard of them. That was how the Lord brought their pride to a fall, and their foolish undertaking soon came to an end.

Peter Kaufman, Uhl Lips, and Hans Poner died of the plague.

The Lord can bring low those who are arrogant. He has no pleasure in the proud.

On February 2 brother Hansel Sanhammer, a servant for temporal affairs, fell asleep in the Lord at Klein Niemtschitz.

Hansel Sanhammer passed away.

On April 5 brother Konrad Gerber, a servant for temporal affairs, fell asleep in the Lord at Altenmarkt.

Konrad Gerber passed away.

On September 2, at his repeated request, brother Konrad Hirzel was relieved of the service of the Gospel for which he had been chosen by the brotherhood in Transylvania and confirmed by brother Franz Walter.

Konrad Hirzel relieved of his service.

On December 9, while traveling to Transylvania, brother Michael Kocher, a servant of God's Word, fell asleep in the Lord with a peaceful heart at Grosswardein in northern Hungary.[1] Before his end he testified that he was completely at peace with God and all brothers and sisters and had nothing burdening his soul. He was deeply thankful for all the kindness shown him and sent a loving farewell to all the faithful.

Michael Kocher, a servant, passed away.

---

[1]Grosswardein (Oradea or Nagyvarad), northwestern Romania, near the Hungarian border.

The Thirty Years War
1623–1650: Tribulations in Hungary and Transylvania

1623

On January 7, 1623, brother Hans Jakob Hegeler, a fuller by trade, was chosen for the service of the Gospel by the church at Alwinz in Transylvania. Their elder, brother Albrecht Seyl, was desperately ill with no hope of recovery. In spite of brother Albrecht's extreme weakness, he confirmed brother Hans Jakob in his service with the laying on of hands.

Hans Jakob Hegeler confirmed in his service at Alwinz in Transylvania.

Five days later, on January 12, brother Albrecht Seyl, a servant of the Gospel, fell asleep in the Lord with peace in his heart. Before he passed away he testified to the servants of the Word who had gathered around him that his conscience was clear. He encouraged them to go on teaching and using discipline with strict faithfulness and thanked them from his heart for all the kindness to him. Brother Joseph Nägele was appointed elder in his place. He set out for Transylvania with several others on February 18.

Albrecht Seyl, a servant, passed away.

At two o'clock in the afternoon of April 28, a fire that started in the smithy at Protzka burned down not only the smithy but half the buildings. Three people died in the flames. Several head of cattle and a number of hogs were burned, besides things like clothing and bed linen. It was a great loss for the church, which was already very poor.

Fire broke out at Protzka. 3 people burned to death.

On April 30 Jakob Rosenberger, a servant for temporal affairs, passed away at Feldsberg.

Jakob Rosenberger passed away.

On February 10 of the same year, Felix Biliad, a servant for temporal affairs, passed away at Alwinz, Transylvania.

Felix Biliad passed away.

On Sunday June 11 at Sabatisch, five brothers were confirmed in the service of the Gospel by the elders with the laying on of hands. They were Andreas Ehrenpreis, Jakob Litzenbucher, Ulrich Amssler, Albrecht Grob, and Uhl Müllner.

5 brothers confirmed.

1623
Martin Fischer passed away.

On October 7 Martin Fischer,[1] a servant for temporal affairs, passed away at Echtlnitz.

Beginning of war this year.

During October and November of 1623 the imperial army, which had been a cause of anxiety to us the whole year, moved into Hungary against the enemy. This proved a disastrous time for the church as well as for other people in the country. Several farmsteads and houses we were occupying were burned to the ground by foreign troops, and most of the others were pillaged. In several places where we had taken flight to the woods, the local people stole from our houses and fields anything the soldiers had left. The ravages of this war reduced many of our people to destitution and cost many their lives, as will be recorded below.

Farkeschin burned down.

On October 14, when Prince Bethlen and his army were encamped at Tyrnau and neighboring villages, the lord palatine's farmstead and mill at Farkeschin (on which we had a three-year lease) were burned down, and some of the community's goods were lost.

Tschäskowitz plundered.

On October 15 Hungarian mercenaries made a night raid on Tschäskowitz[2] on the Schächtitz estates. They plundered our buildings, stripped several people, and stole six horses.

Albrecht Grob, a servant, passed away.

On October 16 brother Albrecht Grob, a servant of the Word, passed away at Alwinz, Transylvania.

Velké Leváre plundered first time.

On October 19 our community at Velké Leváre was raided by a gang of robbers said to be from Gross Magerndorf on the Schütt Islands, south of Pressburg. They plundered almost everything, taking a great deal of movable property and seven horses.

On October 21 Lord Januss Czobor of Schossberg dealt a blow to our trust in him. Our Protzka community was on his estate, and we had expected good treatment from him. But he listened to the advice of some malicious and irresponsible people and committed an act of great injustice by plundering our community at Velké Leváre with his hussars and the neighboring gentry. They began by forcing their way into our community, yelling loudly and shooting. Four brothers in the yard were fatally shot and three more gravely wounded, one

[1] Beck, 416: "Martin Hagen, also called Fischer"; probably the same Martin Hagen appointed servant for temporal affairs in 1610 (p.592 above).

[2] Tschäskowitz (Častkovce), a village south of Čachtice on the Dudvah River.

of whom died a few days later. The outlook was black. Just at this point a servant of Bethlen's arrived with a letter from his prince, which made Januss Czobor give up his cruel plan and withdraw immediately. Nevertheless, the raiders had taken the lives of five brothers and had stolen a lot of goods as they rushed off.

1623

On this Saturday, October 21, at ten in the morning, a new tragedy befell the church. All our people from Sabatisch, with the old, the sick, and the children, had fled to the mountain on which Branc Castle is situated, because on that day a great horde of Turks and Tartars were crossing the Little Carpathians toward Senitz and Skalitz. Some makeshift huts and shelters that had been erected on the mountain for people and animals were set on fire through the carelessness of a slovenly neighbor from Sabatisch, Urban Jorga, who had his hut right next to ours outside the palisade. The church lost all kinds of commodities, such as cloth, linen, wool, salt, lard, and other expensive items to the value of several thousand gulden, but above all thirty-one of our people met an agonizing death in the fire. Because the flames blazed so fiercely, driven by a tremendous wind, they were not able to help each other or to save anything from the fire. Within fifteen minutes everything was alight, and almost everything was destroyed. The pain and shock was greater than any the community had ever known. We laid the misery of our plight before the Lord in heaven, who brings true comfort to souls that trust in him.

Sabatisch camp, below castle, caught fire. 31 people and goods and stores burned.

That same day, the Turks and Tartars who were moving through the country set fire to the buildings on the Senitz estate, where our people lived, and also burned down Lord Emmerich Czobor's castle at Egbell, which we had rented on a three-year lease. We had lived in the castle for less than a year, and the church suffered great losses there, yet poor as we were, we had to pay a year's rent of three hundred imperial talers.

Senitz property and fort at Egbell burned down.

On October 24 the place we were renting at St. Johannes was pillaged by the Turks and Tartars. Several brothers were stripped and severely beaten, and a poor, ailing sister named Eva was dragged from the sick room and carried off.

St. Johannes plundered.

On October 25 there was another raid on Velké Leváre. An ungodly crowd from Bösing and Moder[1] (who should have

Velké Leváre plundered a second time. Nearly all the livestock taken.

[1]Bösing (Pezinok) and Moder (Modra), approx. 12 and 24 miles, respectively, northeast of Bratislava on the main highway.

1623

been good neighbors) came on foot and horseback, plundering our community at will and stealing our copper pots and pans and almost all our livestock: two horses, seventeen oxen, the old and young cows and sheep. They stripped many brothers, sisters, and children down to their undershirts and drove off with five wagons piled high with all kinds of stolen goods. Not a single person opposed this outrage or had pity on the innocent victims. But God is able to save his own and to bring the ungodly to judgment.

Protzka burned down.

On October 28 our community at Protzka was plundered, all the livestock driven off, and the buildings set on fire. Anything left standing after the fire in the spring (recorded above) and all we had built up during the summer was reduced to ashes—a great loss to the church.

Sabatisch set on fire. 2 of our people led away. Very dark prospect.

On November 1, All Saints' Day, while the imperial army was under heavy siege from Prince Bethlen at Göding and most of the Turks and Tartars were encamped on this side of the March River, a great number of these barbarians attacked Sabatisch. In spite of all our kindness to them, they tried to force their way into our houses. They rode around our place for two hours with wild shrieks and bloodcurdling yells, then set fire to the village close by. Those who ran from the house in terror of the flames fled with their belongings up a stream to a neighbor's garden and were robbed there by soldiers. The soldiers carried off two fourteen-year-old girls and stole three horses. To this day we have heard nothing about these young girls.[1] There was intense fear and distress, piteous sobbing and wailing from young and old, for the enemy and the fire on all sides was like a nightmare. But the almighty God, who can do all things, intervened, so the outcome was far better and more merciful than we expected, since those who remained in the house were not harmed in the least. All honor be to God alone.

St. Johannes plundered. 26 people captured.

On November 4, during the siege of Göding described above, our people at St. Johannes suffered the worst disaster of all. They were encamped in the wood, hoping they were safe from the enemy, when a band of Turks and Tartars suddenly broke in upon them. They not only robbed them but seized twenty-six people—by far the greatest grief to us. Sisters and children

[1]They were "Susanna Gibolitz, the cloth-shearer's daughter, age fourteen; and Sara, an orphan from our school, also about fourteen." Beck, 422.

were ruthlessly carried off,[1] weeping and crying out in distress. *1623*

We did all we could to get them released. At the risk of our lives, we approached Prince Bethlen and his councillors and even the Turkish Pasha himself, offering ransom as we had done previously, but there was no way at all to free them from the power of these barbarous people. Only two sisters escaped from the Turkish camp at Skalitz with intense danger to their lives. One of them, to her intense pain, had to leave her child behind. They returned to the church in peace, with unblemished consciences. The other twenty-four captives, including sister Eva (who also came from St. Johannes and whose story has been told), had to endure the anguish of going into slavery among the Mohammedans. It is our hope that the Lord will have released many of them from this great misery, letting them die from lack of food and the bitter cold of winter. During the attack, one brother was also killed and several seriously injured when they tried to protect their families from being captured.

A brother killed.

The Turks and Tartars from Bethlen's camp at Göding made raids all over Moravia, covering many miles, especially towards Neumühl, Wisternitz, and even as far as Rossitz or further. They captured a brother and a sister from Neumühl, another sister from Wisternitz, and three brothers from Rossitz, brickmakers in Lord Karl von Zerotin's service. Through remarkable circumstances, the two from Neumühl gained their freedom during a skirmish near Neuhäusel, and the head brickmaker from Rossitz found freedom before he reached the March River. But (may our grieving be heard by God) the other three, with thousands of other captives, were taken from Moravia to Turkey.

6 people captured; 3 escaped.

In the troubled days of this terrible war, a brother named Kaspar was on the road between Göding and Neumühl. With the community's agreement, he had been employed for some time in the oxenmill at Brünn and had been home on a visit. On the way back he was lost, but we never found out what happened to him, whether he was killed or abducted.

A brother lost.

As a result of this wicked war, the church lost altogether sixty-nine souls in October and November of this year of 1623. They were taken captive or killed by fire or the sword. Thirty

The church lost 69 people.

[1]See Beck, 422–423, for the names of these 26 women and children.

1623

souls, young and old, are still missing, most of them women and girls. We entrust them to the Lord in heaven, who can free them from all distress and turn their days of sorrow into everlasting joy.

Rabenska burned down.

On November 21, during the unexpected withdrawal of Bethlen's forces from Göding, the property at Rabenska, which we had taken on for three years, was burned to the ground. So the church—already desperately poor—suffered immense and irreplaceable losses in many communities through pillage, robbery, fires, and other ordeals that have been only briefly recorded. Then, as if that were not enough, at a time when we had little housing or food for man and beast, there came an extremely severe winter with some forty snowfalls, the worst in living memory. The first snow stayed on the ground for over three months. There was so much snow in the whole country that all the ditches and deep lanes were filled and the fences covered. The result was one level expanse, and in some places it was impossible to travel. At this time one peck of rye cost a ducat, the Hungarian equivalent of 2¼ talers. Toward the end it was impossible to buy anything in imperial currency—twenty shillings were worth no more than twenty kreuzers.[1] Very little Hungarian money was coming in to any community, and just as in the previous year, everything was very expensive.

Cold winter with about 40 snowfalls.

Yet the Lord in heaven always provided for us, so we cannot thank him enough for his gifts.

Slander against the faithful.

Besides all the loss and misery described, we had to suffer slander and all kinds of untrue accusations from the world and from those within the church who were envious of us, just as ungodly people always have abused the faithful. They heaped lies and insults on us, calling us traitors who had brought the perennial foe[2] into the country and saying we were the cause and perpetrators of every evil. Quite apart from the fact that such treachery would have brought us into extreme danger, we could never have allowed ourselves to be used in even the

---

[1]About the inflation during those years, see above, pp.674–675.

[2]The German word *Erbfeind*, designating the Turks, is translated in this chronicle as "perennial foe." From middle-high-German *erbevint*, meaning the devil, it was first applied to the Turks in the 15th century, and from 1513 until the Second World War to the French by the Germans. It signifies a nation that for generations has been regarded as hostile and is continued to be feared as such.

1623

slightest way to bring injury or destruction upon anyone. But Christ's words have to be fulfilled: "They will say every kind of evil against you. Rejoice and be glad when they tell their lies, for your reward is great in heaven."

Our people served some Moravian lords.

In this year of 1623 a few of our people moved back to Moravia at the request of several prominent lords (such as Prince Karl von Liechtenstein and Lord Adam von Waldstein) who employed us on their farms, mills, and wine cellars and promised us escort and protection, as well as freedom of religion. Most of the local inhabitants were pleased and hoped things would improve in Moravia.

Many people said God had led us out of Moravia.

After we were expelled, the Margravate of Moravia had been burdened with all kinds of excessive taxes and terrorized by great numbers of soldiers, Poles, and other wicked people, worse than ever before. So not only our own people realized it, but also many prominent and knowledgeable lords in Moravia said that God had shown his special love and care for us when he led us out of Moravia and saved us from this oppression, since we would have been hit the hardest. The Lord in heaven knows what is best for us and will not desert us if we remain true to him, keep his commandments, and do not forsake him.

1624

No particular attacks on the church this year.

Several thousand Poles on Moravian border.

In 1624 the evil, oppressive war, which had lasted for six years, was still dragging on. As described earlier, it had begun in Bohemia in 1618 and engulfed many lands and kingdoms. Yet the Lord's church did not suffer any particular attack, because for the time being the Hungarians were quiet and no foreign armies invaded their country. In April, May, and June, however, several thousand Poles, the most infamous soldiers, were encamped on the Moravian border this side of the March River in Hungary, a day's journey from Sabatisch.

People from Sabatisch homeless for about 9 weeks.

Everyone living between the March and the Little Carpathians of Hungary was terrified of the Poles. So it was not just our people at Sabatisch who had to flee with their wives and children, leaving home just at the busiest time for spring work, which meant a great loss and setback in their food supply. In many villages there were no people or livestock left. These brutal Poles were a serious threat to Hungary, partly out of

1624

old enmity because of the harm they had suffered earlier from the Hungarians, and partly because the emperor had not paid them and they could not find much more to steal in Moravia, where they had been stationed for a whole year with devastating results. So they made a number of raids into Hungary, as on June 5, when they attacked the Hungarian town of Neustadt (Nové Mesto nad Váhom) near Schächtitz and in a few hours massacred over four hundred people.

More than 400 people massacred at Neustadt.

On June 12, six days later, in the middle of a pitch-dark night, they fell on the Sabatisch camp below Branc Castle, where our needy flock—sick and old, children, and mothers of newborn babies—were taking refuge along with neighbors from a number of villages on the Branc estates. They came with such strident yells, shooting, and loud clatter that it seemed as if everybody would be slaughtered. The screams of the fugitives and the bellowing of the terrified cattle in the dark night cannot be described. Yet bad as things looked, the church suffered far less harm than many of our neighbors, who before the above raid on Neustadt had always said that it was because of us that they would have to suffer at the hands of the Poles, whose threats were directed only against us. Through God's providence—for he always finds a way to help his children—not one of our people was hurt, apart from the shock and terror (though some cows and about forty sheep were stolen along with the neighbors' livestock).

Poles made a night raid on peasants' camp with piercing yells.

Although at this time the Polish raid caused relatively little harm to our communities and there was no particular danger from the war, yet the year 1624 was not without its troubles, for the hate and envy of the ancient serpent against the faithful continued to grow. In March, Cardinal von Dietrichstein, that enemy of the faithful, issued yet another strict mandate in Moravia in the name of Emperor Ferdinand II: Since several Moravian lords (as was mentioned above under the year 1623) had again taken our people into service as farm workers, millers, cellarers, gardeners, carpenters, brickmakers, and so on, and since the great shortage of food in Hungary had resulted in many of our people returning in small groups to Moravia, all who declared themselves members of the Hutterian brotherhood were once more ordered, on pain of death, to leave the Margravate of Moravia within two weeks of the date

Cardinal issued another mandate expelling us from Moravia.

on which the decree was issued. Anyone caught after the appointed time was to be killed without trial—hanged on the nearest tree or burned to death.

1624
Anyone who caught our people was to slaughter or burn them.

Since most of the lords could not resist such a strict mandate, a good number of our people were forced to move out. As they returned to Hungary, where God the Lord still had a place prepared in the wilderness for his little flock, they were in great danger and lost much property because of the imperial soldiers. This expulsion from Moravia brought further separation between the faithful and the unfaithful. Many who loved their stomachs and the pleasures of the world more than God and his righteousness deserted their faith and their brothers and sisters rather than return to Hungary. But those who were faithful and upright willingly submitted, praising God that they still had a place where they could serve him.

Our people returned to Hungary. Many stayed behind.

Several Moravian lords, among them Prince Maximilian von Liechtenstein, Lord Adam von Waldstein (chief steward of Bohemia), Lord Karl von Zerotin, and others, paid little heed to the above mandate. They let the cardinal write and make his commands but kept our people in service because of their industry, loyalty, and honesty. So this year, in spite of the cardinal's strict orders, it was impossible to drive all our people from Moravia and Austria, whereas toward the end of the same year, when the Lutheran and Calvinist pastors became the main target of strong religious persecution, they all had to leave the country.[1]

Some lords ignored the mandate.

Just as in the preceding years (and as was briefly mentioned at the end of 1623), the heavy, long-lasting snows and the severe winter ruined the beautiful winter grain, especially the rye. In many places both in our own and other areas there were wide fields with nothing to cut, and only in a very few could enough be gathered for seed.

Famine brought great hardship to the church.

As a result the price of wheat rose to 4 talers a peck at that time and rye to 3½ talers in the former, good currency of imperial talers and ducats.

Price of grain.

The faithful would have suffered greatly from hunger and lack of bread if the almighty God, who knows best in

Many summer crops thrived. All kinds of grains ground for bread.

[1]Some of the Hutterites expelled from Moravia moved to Lower Austria, where several manorial lords gave them shelter. This led to the General Mandate issued by Emperor Ferdinand II on March 3, 1625; see Beck, 425 n.1.

1624

everything, had not allowed the summer crops, grapes, and other fruit to grow plentifully in this ill-fated year of 1624. We ground barley, millet, oats, buckwheat, peas, and lentils together to bake bread.

It would have been quite impossible for the communities to buy so much expensive rye with the very small income they had in Hungary at that time.

Thanks and praise to God for his care.

We have every reason to thank God our life long for graciously helping us through the long, lean times and providing us with our humble share, so we did not have to dishonor his holy name by begging bread at other people's doors. May he continue mercifully to shield us from such misery and heartbreak, as long as we live on this earth.

1625

Hansel Summer, a servant, passed away.

In the year 1625 on September 5 at midnight, brother Hansel Summer, a servant of the Word, fell asleep in the Lord with a peaceful heart at Velké Leváre.

Joseph Nägele, a servant, passed away.

Isaak Baumann replaced him.

Between seven and eight in the evening of October 17 brother Joseph Nägele, a servant of the Gospel, fell asleep in the Lord with a peaceful heart at Alwinz in Transylvania. Brother Isaak Baumann, who had been his assistant, was appointed in his place as an elder of the church at Alwinz.

Klaus Wältzer passed away.

On November 2 brother Klaus Wältzer, a servant for temporal affairs, fell asleep in the Lord at Sabatisch.

Lord Januss Czobor's unjust demands on brothers at Protzka.

In this year 1625, Lord Januss Czobor at Schossberg, mentioned earlier in this book, made unjust demands on the brothers at Protzka. He wanted two hundred imperial talers, a length of cloth, and several knives, not as a loan or against surety, but as a free gift, without any cause or reason at all. But the community at Protzka had been burned down twice in three years, and Lord Januss Czobor had charged them excessive sums for their refuge in Schossberg Castle during the Turkish disturbance. They told him they were too poor to comply with his impossible demands. As a result, he ordered his captain to arrest two old brothers, the steward and the buyer, bring them to the castle at Schossberg, and hold them until they delivered the money, cloth, and knives. If we wanted to free the brothers, we would have to face not only the danger

Steward and buyer imprisoned.

but also the effort and expense. So we had to send a servant of the Word with two companions several miles beyond Kaschau[1] to Lord Czobor, and as a result of their strenuous efforts the two brothers were released after two months under arrest. *1625*

That was not the end of the affair, however; the worst was still to come. In December, when Lord Januss Czobor returned to Schossberg from the Hungarian Diet at Ödenburg, he summoned the elders from Protzka and Sabatisch to come to Schossberg, claiming his purpose was to settle the debt once and for all.

Lord Czobor summoned the elders.

The brothers he had summoned met twice with him, and the last time brother Valentin Winter, the shepherd of the church, came himself. It turned out to be a peculiar kind of settlement. Lord Czobor owed us 313 gulden, and by rights we owed him no more than 80 gulden rent for the two places. He wanted to let the debts cancel each other, and we were to have no further claims on him. In addition, Lord Czobor demanded two thousand talers for protecting our brothers and sisters at Protzka during the Turkish disturbance (although he had taken all their hogs at the time) and to compensate him for his one-ninth share (seventeen pecks) of the grain from the brothers' fields which had been stolen by the Turks along with ours.

Demanded 2000 imperial talers.

The brothers rejected these demands as unchristian and completely unjust, at first with pleading and finally in plain, simple words, saying they could never agree, no matter what the consequences. By now it was evening, time for the lights. It was bitter cold and snowing hard. In the elders' presence, Lord Januss Czobor sent for his hussars (about fifty stationed in the surrounding villages) to come immediately to the castle, with the intention of letting them raid our community at Protzka.

Lord Januss Czobor wanted our house at Protzka plundered.

They were ready to go, prepared to plunder our place at ten o'clock that night. But in the end, kindly people persuaded Lord Czobor to give up his cruel plan.

Since Lord Czobor's only concern was money and without it we could come to no settlement with him, the brothers

[1]Kaschau (Košice) in western Czechoslovakia, approx. 200 miles northwest of Bratislava.

1625

The brothers offered to buy grain from Lord Czobor.

consulted together and finally offered to pay him a hundred gulden for one year's rent at Protzka and for his ninth share of all grain harvested. In addition, so as to make some money available to him, we would buy a quantity of grain (which we actually needed very badly) and would pay ten shillings a peck in cash.

The unhappy affair was settled.

This would be on condition that the contract for Protzka made with the old lord his father (which he had wanted to change completely) should be honored by him and its terms left unaltered. In the end Lord Czobor agreed to this offer. So finally, after many earnest discussions back and forth, this difficult affair, which had posed such a threat to us, was settled.

2 sisters escaped from the Turks.

That same year, 1625, through God's wonderful intervention, two sisters who had been taken captive by the Turks returned to the church. These were Traudel Ochsenfuhrmann, a married sister, and Sarah Nähter, a single sister, both from St. Johannes. They had been in captivity at Ofen (Buda) for two and a half years, during which they endured brutal treatment and abuse against their will. They came back to the church with unharmed consciences. Praise and thanks be to God Almighty in all eternity for freeing them from this Mohammedan bondage and keeping them firm in faith. May he, the Lord, whose eyes see into every corner of the earth, take into his loving care all faithful souls still held in such severe bondage and slavery. May he soon free them from these depths of misery, according to his divine and holy will.

Another strict mandate to leave Moravia and Austria.

The year 1625 was not to close without its share of brutality. Satan's servants were to fulfill his designs in every way. In the last quarter of the year, at Cardinal von Dietrichstein's instigation, a new decree and strict mandate was issued in Moravia and Austria in the name of Emperor Ferdinand II. It stated once again that anyone belonging to our church and brotherhood who refused to become Roman Catholic was to leave these countries and not be seen there after the given date on pain of death. At the same time, the government in Vienna sent a sheriff (instead of a provost) to different places in Austria, particularly to those lords who still had our people in their employment and were giving them lodging on their estates (for instance, the three princes von Liechtenstein, Karl,

Maximilian, and Gundacker), with imperial orders to remove our people from their estates. The sheriff gave a description of each brother and sister in that lord's service and threatened to put in irons any such people he found on his return and send them to prison in Vienna. *1625*

So against their will, the lords von Liechtenstein, whose estates we had never left since the great troubles of 1556, turned us out of their farms, mills, and all other services. In Moravia Cardinal von Dietrichstein forced his policy through relentlessly. He abducted two children of our people in service with the lord of Marowitz (Moravice), Lord Hans Jakob of Magno, who was a loyal servant of the emperor and had given his word of honor, verbally and in writing, to return all our people and their belongings safely to the church. One was the little three-year-old son of the daughter of Hans Schnuerl, cellarer to this same lord; the other was Hansel Gartner's son, about ten years old. The cardinal, like a Turk, abducted them with cunning, deceit, and violence, baptized them according to papist rites, and gave them different names. The poor parents suffered the anguish and heartbreak of being robbed of their dear children, but God the Lord in his own time will bring heavy punishment on such outrageous presumption.

One lord took two children.

The lord cardinal, this bitter enemy of the faithful, had arranged a meeting of the Provincial Diet at Olmütz and wanted to aim his arrows with all their force against the church and all who would neither worship the image of the beast nor receive its mark. Then the Lord God let him hear the tumult of his enemies, the storm of approaching war, and immediately he had to postpone the persecution he had planned. The Diet broke up with nothing decided, for it was the will of the Lord our faithful God, who does nothing without good cause, that this evil against his people should be frustrated and Ahithophel's counsels against the God-fearing David should become mere folly.

In November 1625,[1] when Ferdinand Ernst etc., son of Emperor Ferdinand II etc., was elected and crowned king of Hungary, mention was made of us brothers in the minutes of the Provincial Diet at Ödenburg.

Duke Ferdinand Ernst crowned king of Hungary.

Since taxes had been imposed on the whole country in order

Taxes imposed on the church.

[1]*Allgemeine Deutsche Biographie*, VI, 665, has December 8, 1626.

1625

to pay the keepers of the crown, the brothers were not to be exempt but were likewise to pay the keepers of the crown whatever amounts the district judges and their jurors would decide in the course of their duties. So an assessment of one hundred gulden a year in Hungarian currency was made for the whole church on the estates of Trentschin, Neutra, and Pressburg, the three estates where we lived.

Church decided to pay the taxes.

As the money was not for war purposes but for the support of the keepers of the crown, the servants of the Word and of temporal affairs decided that we should pay the hundred gulden. We could not very well be exempt, since we were living under the Hungarian crown the same as other people who were subject to the tax and (as mentioned earlier) it had been imposed by the Provincial Diet. So we paid it from that date on until the Provincial Diet made another decision.

1626

Unexpected advance of imperial army into Hungary.

During the spring and summer of the year 1626 the church community had quite a long respite from the dangers of war and other troubles. All kinds of summer crops thrived and provided plenty of food. This lasted till fall.

In September the imperial general Albrecht von Wallenstein, Duke of Friedland, advanced unexpectedly into this country of Hungary with a great army of about fifty thousand infantry and cavalry and many large pieces of artillery. He encamped along several miles of the road on this side of the Waag River, from Hungarian Neustadt down to Schella.[1] (Prince Bethlen was encamped on the other side, also with a very large force of Hungarians, Turks, and Mansfeld's Germans.) Apart from the raiding done by Bethlen's soldiers, little more arose from this confrontation.[2]

Imperial army encamped opposite Prince Bethlen.

---

[1]Hungarian Neustadt (Nové Mesto nad Váhom) on the Vah River, north of Trnava. Schella (Šala), on the Vah River, southeast of Trnava.

[2]In 1625 Wallenstein became supreme commander of all imperial troops. On April 25, 1626, he defeated Ernst von Mansfeld at the bridge of Dessau. Mansfeld fled to Brandenburg, where he mustered reinforcements for the march through Silesia to Hungary to join Bethlen Gabor, who was planning a fresh attack on the imperial forces of Ferdinand II. Wallenstein pursued Mansfeld through Lusatia, Silesia, and Moravia to Hungary, but as Bethlen Gabor was then negotiating peace with Austria, the two opposing armies remained encamped opposite each other without action, as the chronicle tells. The plundering reported for the year 1626 and earlier was universal during the Thirty Years War. Wallenstein set up his army on Mansfeld's

It lasted four months, however, right into the cold of winter, and most of our places on both sides of the mountains were again sacked by imperial soldiers. Much of the food that we had sweated to grow and harvest was carried off. *1626*

Our community at Tschäskowitz was the first to suffer. On September 9 it was ransacked, and many of our people were stripped of their clothing. Tschäskowitz plundered.

On September 11 a large band of cavalry made a raid on Dechtitz and plundered our houses from top to bottom. A particular loss was the oats they hauled away, twelve bushels by Tyrnau measure. They caught many brothers and stripped them of their clothing. Dechtitz plundered.

On September 12 several hundred cavalry came to Dechtitz and once more searched every corner, taking whatever they found. Not one of our people was caught there, for most of them had escaped to Gutwasser Castle[1] with other people from that region. Several thousand fugitives camped near the castle with their wives and children, their livestock, and the best of their movable goods. Dechtitz plundered again.

That same day a few hundred of the cavalry soldiers and a large number of dragoons made a raid right into the village and even as far as Gutwasser Castle. They ransacked the whole village, including the rented house where our people had put all the supplies they had brought with them on their flight from Dechtitz. Our chief loss was twelve barrels of flour, but many other goods were stolen as well. Everything stolen.

Not yet satisfied, the raiders left the village and approached Gutwasser Castle, meaning to capture and plunder it. But since they were only on a raid and had no artillery with them, the fortifications prevented them from taking the castle. Castle attacked too.

In the end they invaded the camp where the local people had taken refuge, shooting and yelling wildly and making a horrible din. Six people were murdered and many women and young girls were raped and violated quite shamelessly in the open. It is a dishonor to the precious name of Christ that such people call themselves Christians.

---

principle: the war should "pay for itself" by levying war contributions and plundering at the cost of the countries where his troops happened to be. Beck, 428; *New Cambridge Modern History*, IV, 322–324; Polisensky, *Thirty Years War*, 181–184; *Allgemeine Deutsche Biographie*, XLV, 582ff.

[1]Gutwasser (Dobrá Voda), market town and castle approx. 7 miles northwest of Dechtice, southeast of Sabatisch.

1626

As already recorded, our people from Dechtitz had fled to the castle along with other country folk and taken shelter behind some ancient walls, also known as the old fortress. So this ungodly rabble fell on them too, filling them with dread, for most of our people expected nothing but death. But there can be no doubt that God the Almighty heard their fervent prayers and helped them to escape. Not one life was lost and the sisters' honor was saved. All praise to the Lord in heaven, who rescued them from their enemies' hands. God's help was powerfully felt when so many of our sisters jumped from the high walls to save their honor and not one of them was hurt, which is incredible from a human point of view.

They leaped over the walls.

All the belongings they had brought that far, however, were left inside the old wall and stolen, and on top of all this terror and looting, the soldiers stole nine of our oxen, two horses, and a yearling colt. Added to this was the damage done by the country folk, who were sure the soldiers had come only because of our people. Yet the calamity hit them the hardest. One brother witnessed a woman telling a soldier, "The brothers are over there," and the soldier turned around and shot her. Intending to bring disaster on others, she brought it on herself, even losing her life.

9 oxen and 2 horses stolen.

A woman intended to betray the brothers. She lost her life.

On September 21 about fifty imperial cavalrymen came from Nikolsburg in Moravia to Protzka [in Hungary]. We gave them as much food and drink as we could afford, but afterward they became violent and robbed us of all our cattle (cows and calves).

Protzka plundered.

On October 17 Dechtitz was pillaged again, and the new stables, which we had built in spite of our extreme poverty, were burned to the ground. For a long time no brother dared be seen there because of the marauding soldiers. The house was a shambles; all the stoves, doors, benches, and window shutters were broken to pieces.

Farm buildings at Dechtitz burned.

It was the same at Kesselsdorf and Farkeschin, where for three months our people had been unable to return home. All eight draft oxen and two horses were stolen from the brothers in Kesselsdorf, the barn was burned, and their living quarters were badly damaged.

Kesselsdorf plundered.

The people from Farkeschin lost four oxen, some calves and hogs, several bushels of grain, and other movables.

Farkeschin plundered.

On October 20 at eight or nine in the morning, several

hundred Turks raided Schächtitz and Tschäskowitz. Many imperial soldiers were killed, as well as two brothers—Hans Sutter (the work distributor) and a young tailor named Joseph N.[1] A young sister from Tschäskowitz and many people from the neighborhood were carried off; but through God's intervention our sister was released from the hands of the Turks without ransom and returned in peace to the church.

1626
2 brothers murdered. A sister carried off but she returned.

On November 9 at seven in the evening, a mob of nearly three hundred imperial cavalry—Croatians, Walloons, Frenchmen, and all kinds of villains—broke into our community at Velké Leváre and spent all night ransacking it, eating and drinking and stealing whatever they could find. They raped many sisters and wreaked their lust on them. In the morning they moved on to St. Johannes and plundered our house there, too, taking whatever they found. They put thumbscrews on the steward to make him tell where the money was and beat several brothers severely.

Velké Leváre and St. Johannes plundered.

In December 1626 at Pressburg, Bethlen and His Imperial Majesty sent delegates to establish a truce between both sides, which was to last until St. George's Day [Apr. 23], 1627. We feared the prospect of the imperial troops' withdrawal, but through divine providence they left the country without much disturbance. Most of them went through Senitz, Velké Leváre, and Schossberg to Skalitz in Hungary, and so by Strassnitz into Moravia.[2] Since the peasants had fled from nearly all the villages, we had to provide most of the food, drink, and fodder, so our supplies were considerably reduced during this period.

Truce established.

Soldiers withdrew from Hungary.

So, as recorded above, the weeks from early September until the end of the year were full of fear and misery. The entire community had to flee from one place to another during those four winter months—women and children, the old and

Community had to seek refuge for 4 months.

---

[1]According to Beck, 431, he was called Nägele. (Not to be confused with Joseph Nägele, the servant of the Word who died on October 17, 1625; p.708 above.)

[2]After General Ernst von Mansfeld's death (Nov. 1626, at Rakovica, Yugoslavia) and the rebellion caused by hunger and cold among the Turks and Hungarians, Bethlen Gabor agreed to a truce. The imperial troops under Wallenstein withdrew, desperate and defeated, via Skalitz toward Hradisch (Uherské Hradiště) on the Morava River, where they set up winter quarters. Rain, cold, starvation, and sickness wiped out whole squadrons; hundreds died at Hradisch. Reinforcements from Prague, however, made up for the loss, and a few months later Wallenstein appeared in Silesia with 40,000 troops ready for action. See Beck, 432.

1626

the sick. We did not have enough food or drink. We suffered cold and privation and even death. Yet we were glad and deeply thankful to God that our houses were left standing, which meant that we did have shelter from the bitter winter [when we returned]. In other ways, too, we felt God's bountiful help, for however savage and tyrannical the soldiers were elsewhere—to the extent that even some lords and nobles dared not risk being seen—they were often friendly and even protective toward us. All praise to the Lord in heaven!

1627

Uhl Müllner, a servant, passed away.

On January 6, 1627, at nine o'clock, brother Uhl Müllner, a servant of the Gospel, fell asleep in the Lord with a peaceful heart at Farkeschin.

Protzka plundered.

On February 20 the brothers' house at Protzka was raided by forty Croatian marauders. Apart from the terror they aroused, they ransacked our place, drove off six oxen that we never got back, and caused a great deal of damage, especially in the shoemakers' and tailors' workshops.

Jakob Bössler, a servant, passed away.

On February 23 dear brother Jakob Bössler, a servant of the Gospel, fell asleep in the Lord with a peaceful heart at Soblahof.

A secretary passed away.

On February 27 Heinrich Boxler fell asleep in the Lord with a peaceful heart at Sabatisch. He had been a secretary for the elders for eighteen years.

Seyfried Geiss, a servant, passed away.

On March 11 at two in the morning, dear brother Seyfried Geiss, a servant of the Gospel, fell asleep in the Lord with a peaceful heart at Sabatisch. He was seventy-eight years old and had been a servant of the Word for thirty-seven years.

3 brothers appointed to the service.

On March 21 three brothers were chosen for the service of the Gospel and appointed at Sabatisch—Georg Leopold, a shoemaker from Württemberg; Abraham Scheffer, a tailor from Hesse; and Jakob Mathroner, a miller from Tirol.

St. Johannes plundered.

On April 6 at about ten in the evening, thirty or forty cavalry—Croatians and other ruffians who had been stationed in Moravia—made a surprise attack on our community at St. Johannes in Hungary. They robbed us of a great deal of cloth, linen, and clothing, hauling away whatever they could lay hands on. They wounded the head shoemaker so severely that he died.

On April 11 at two in the afternoon, brother Hans Schnuerl, a servant for temporal affairs, fell asleep in the Lord with a peaceful heart at Tschäskowitz.

1627 Hans Schnuerl passed away.

On April 15 several mounted Croatian soldiers on a foray from Moravia raided our community at Gätte. They stole four of our horses and a yearling foal as well as other things.

Gätte plundered.

On May 14 the church suffered another blow when fire broke out in our community at Tschäskowitz. It did not spread from any particular fireplace, and no one knew how it started. The brothers' house was completely destroyed, and eight barrels of flour and a horse were burned. Twenty-four houses in the village were also burned down, and the brotherhood was more concerned about the peasants' houses than about their own great loss.

Fire at Tschäskowitz.

On June 10 brother Walser Fybich, a servant for temporal affairs, fell asleep in the Lord at Aichhorn in Moravia.[1]

Walser Fybich passed away.

As mentioned before, the imperial forces withdrew from Hungary, and during the summer of 1627 some were stationed in Moravia and some in Silesia. At the beginning of September most were moved back to Lundenburg, Landshut, and Strassnitz on the Hungarian border, causing renewed alarm to the church. For nine to ten weeks, for example, we had to support (at great expense) a number of German musketeers stationed as guards at Sabatisch.

Soldiers stationed again at frontier.

The brothers at Protzka (which is in that area) were in such acute danger that they fled with their wives and children to Schossberg for several weeks, but thanks be to God, the community was unharmed.

These imperial troops were stationed along the border because in September of that year the envoys of the Hungarian lords and the emperor were negotiating a peace treaty with the Turks. For this reason, representatives of the Hungarian authorities set up camp near Schindau[2] and met a number of

---

[1]Aichhorn (Veveří), Moravian fortress on the Svratka River, approx. 8 miles northwest of Brno; in 1627 property of Sigmund von Teufenbach. Despite all mandates of expulsion, the Hutterites succeeded in staying on in Moravia, individually or in small groups; final expulsion was not effected until 1650; see entries for the years 1628 (p.718) and 1650 (p.761); *ME*, I, 27–28; Beck, 433 n.1; Zeman, *Topography*, #1.

[2]Schindau (Šintava), market town west of Nitra on the Vah River. See Beck, 434–435.

1627
25-year peace agreed on.

times. Our community at Farkeschin suffered considerable losses as a result. When a peace of twenty-five years had been agreed on, the Hungarian representatives and the imperial forces withdrew from the border, though the treaty was not yet signed and sealed. So this eventful year of 1627 ended happily, with heavy yields of grain and low prices for all field crops. Only the grape harvest was poor, and wine became quite expensive.

Fruitful year.

1628

Lord Czobor's widow demanded 40 gulden for her husband's funeral.

On February 12, 1628, the widow of Lord Januss Czobor sent her chief official Ferencz Diack to the brothers at Protzka. She demanded forty gulden for the funeral of her husband, who had died in northern Hungary the year before. As we owed her nothing and for reasons of conscience could never assist in such pomp, the said official from Schossberg had the four best oxen forcibly taken from our community the very same day.

That same year Prince Cardinal von Dietrichstein, as governor of the margravate of Moravia and on behalf of His Majesty the Holy Roman Emperor, issued a letter from Kremsier, dated December 17, once again ordering any lord who still had brothers in his service to dismiss them within six weeks, on pain of incurring His Majesty's displeasure and severe punishment. Because of this, our brothers and sisters still employed in various places in Moravia were sent away, and most of them joined the church in Hungary.

Solemn decree to dismiss our people in Moravia.

1629

Unusual matter at Velké Leváre.

During the first week of the new year 1629, an unusual matter arose at Velké Leváre, the like of which had never happened before. It began with ten people, mostly men, and soon spread to other places as well. Therefore the elders had to look into it straightaway.

Peculiar way of praying.

To tell it briefly, this group separated itself from other brothers and sisters and adopted a peculiar way of praying. They chose unusual times of day to meet for prayer in corners or secretly in the woods, regardless of whether or not their work allowed time for it. They let nothing stop them but insisted that they owed obedience and service to God rather than to men. Three millers at Marchegg held the same opinion *1629* and often followed this strange practice instead of running the mill responsibly as they should have done. When they were rebuked, they answered that they had to hold their worship service. They were told that there was a time for prayer and a time for work and running the mill, and besides, it was not necessary for all three to go and pray together. But they were not willing to give up their practice. This going off together and separating themselves from their fellow workers caused division and quarreling, not only at Marchegg but also among those working at Velké Leváre, some of whom had similar ideas.

Since their strange practice was hypocrisy and no service to God at all, the whole question was laid before dear brother Valentin Winter, who came immediately with other elders and summoned the three millers and those involved at Velké Leváre. He appealed to them in different ways and pointed out that while prayer in itself is good and useful, yet everything has its time. As the wise preacher in Ecclesiastes 3 says, "Everything under the sun has its right time." So it is with prayer too. If instead of working side by side, someone leaves his brother with all the work and goes off for an hour or two into a corner or into a wood, apparently to pray, and in so doing burdens and annoys his brother, this is no worship of God but a curse.

After all this and more, which cannot all be told, enough had been said to wean these people from their wrong ideas, but not one of them would give in. They all persisted in their opinion and said that God had revealed it to them, that they had had a vision, and that the last day was soon to come. Soon their belief would be proved right. Brother Valentin and the other servants of the Word and many trusted brothers appealed to them in an earnest and kindly way with words from Scripture and many sound arguments, but to no avail. So the men were dismissed and given the night to consider the matter.

Next morning they were summoned again and addressed both gently and sharply. They were asked what conclusion they had come to—whether they were ready to change their minds, so as not to bring disruption to the church, which was founded on the true cornerstone, Jesus Christ, and established through the blood of many faithful witnesses and martyrs. If

1629

so, the matter could be considered with them. But good advice was lost on them. They persisted in their wrong beliefs.

As they would not accept brotherly correction, the church in Velké Leváre was called together. When they would not listen to the church either but stubbornly held to their wrong ideas, they were excluded and separated from the church. Jakob N., a hatter, and David N., a miller, had the most guilt in this matter and were chiefly responsible for misleading the others. None of them found repentance but went further astray. Their community soon broke up because they were not founded on the true rock, Jesus Christ. And then, as they had to earn their own food and clothing, their hours of prayer soon came to an end.

The leaders: Jakob N., a hatter, and David N., a miller.

This story shows how clever Satan is at contriving ways to sow confusion among the faithful. Here in a very subtle way he attacked them through the question of prayer and what appeared as worship to bring about the fall of these poor souls, dragging them overboard from the ship of Jesus Christ. Therefore every Christian needs to be firmly grounded in faith in order to resist the cunning attacks of Satan and to obey Christ's words in Luke 21:8: "Take care that you are not misled. For many will come in my name, saying, 'I am he,' and, 'The time is drawing near.' Do not follow them."

3 brothers confirmed in the service.

On April 1 three brothers—Georg Leopold, Abraham Scheffer, and Jakob Mathroner—were confirmed at Sabatisch in the service of the Gospel by the elders with the laying on of hands.

2 brothers chosen for the service.

On the same day two brothers, Georg Gaul, a weaver, and Hans Albrecht, a cobbler—both Swiss—were appointed for a time of testing in the service of the Gospel.

1630

Flood at Sabatisch.

On April 15, 1630, nearly all the brothers and sisters from Sabatisch had gathered at other places for the Lord's Supper, when about midday a sudden downpour caused a huge flood at Sabatisch. At our community there the workshops of the ropemaker, binder, potter, and hatter—mostly new buildings—became so sodden that they collapsed. Other buildings were badly damaged, and the walls were undermined by the water.

The damage cost the church hundreds of gulden. The people who were left at home were terrified. One old brother was crushed under a falling building and killed. Imagine how many would have lost their lives if the flood had occurred at night, since it would hardly have been possible to escape from such an unexpected downpour in time. Many household goods were swept away and not found again. May the almighty God protect us in the future from such disasters. *1630*

On May 25 at six in the morning, our dear brother and servant of the Gospel Hauptrecht Zapff fell asleep in the Lord at Sabatisch with a peaceful heart at the age of eighty-four. He was a zealous worker for the Lord, a member of the church for about seventy years, and for nearly thirty-seven years a servant of the Gospel. He was also the elders' secretary for more than thirty years.[1]

Hauptrecht Zapff, a servant, passed away.

On September 1 a fire broke out at the mill in Dechtitz, where our miller was employed by the lord. Our people were at the Sunday morning meeting. The roof and all the barns were burned, a great loss for the church, as we had to rebuild it all for the lord at great cost. We also had to pay damages to the Slovakian clothmakers who had some lengths of cloth in the mill for fulling and storage—everything was burned and we had to pay for it. One miller even lost a child in the fire. So let us be careful with fire.

Fire at Dechtitz.

1631

On March 16, 1631, two brothers—Georg Gaul and Hans Albrecht—were confirmed at Sabatisch in the service of the Gospel by the elders with the laying on of hands.

2 brothers confirmed in the service.

On the same day three brothers were chosen for the service of the Gospel for a time of testing: Balzer Rost, a cobbler from Meissen (Saxony); Andreas Hiller, a tailor from

3 brothers chosen for the service.

---

[1]It is generally accepted that the "1581" codex of this chronicle, on which Prof. Zieglschmid based his 1943 edition, is in Hauptrecht Zapff's handwriting up to but not including the last entry for the year 1591 (p.520 above). The initials H. Z. and the year 1581 in the illuminated letter J on folio 89v of this codex (see plate #8) seem to indicate that Hauptrecht Zapff, as secretary to the Vorsteher, was writing this copy of the chronicle in 1581. He was working under the direction of Hans Kräl and must have entered current events from 1581 to 1591. Zapff would have been about 35 years old in 1581.

Zapff also wrote songs, three of which are in *LdHBr*, 846–849. See Wolkan, *Lieder*, 241; Beck, 437–438; *ME*, IV, 1017.

1631

5 brothers appointed to the service for temporal affairs.

Switzerland; and David Lachner, a coppersmith from Moravia.

Five brothers were chosen and appointed to the service for temporal affairs: Hans Kern; Hans Gebhart; Hans Pheler; Felix Schweitzer, a head miller; and Dietrich Weinitz, a buyer.

Valentin Winter passed away.

At Sabatisch on November 29 at four in the morning, dear brother Valentin Winter, a faithful servant of the Word and Vorsteher of the church fell asleep in the Lord with a peaceful heart at the age of fifty-two.[1] He had declared his good conscience to the elders who had visited him during his illness, and he had thanked them repeatedly for all the love he had received from the church. He asked them to say farewell to the whole church on his behalf and to give them the Lord's greeting of peace. He had been a servant of the Gospel for nearly twenty-one years and for ten years had been entrusted with the oversight and leadership of the church.

Length of his service.

What he and the other brothers and sisters went through when the church in Moravia suffered persecution, acute shortage of food, and the unrest of war can be understood apart from this chronicle. Any sensitive person can well imagine the hardships and struggles that result from such severe persecution.

When through God's loving will dear brother Valentin Winter was peacefully taken from this vale of tears, there was a meeting at Sabatisch of all servants of the Word and servants for temporal affairs, stewards, buyers, and storekeepers, as well as many trusted brothers from all communities. They met before God to choose a new shepherd for his church. After thorough consideration, in which a unanimous and joyful testimony was given, they laid this service on dear brother Heinrich Hartmann. On December 3, 1631, he was asked to care for the church of the Lord faithfully in all things.

Heinrich Hartmann elder.

1632

Joseph Würz, a servant, passed away.

At Sabatisch on March 5, 1632, brother Joseph Würz, a servant of the Word, fell asleep in the Lord with a peaceful heart.

[1]Valentin Winter, Vorsteher 1622–1631. For his song, "Von Gottes Lieb und Fürsorg viel" (Of God's great love and care), see *LdHBr*, 850–851; see also Wolkan, *Lieder*, 242; Beck, 439.

That same night, March 5, when everyone was fast asleep, a mob of newly recruited Hungarian and Croatian soldiers pillaged our community at Protzka, stealing a large amount of linen, clothing, and other things. When this was reported to the old lord, Emmerich Czobor, he summoned his hussars, nobles, and some of his retainers and sent them after the robbers. When they had caught them, they took back most of the plunder and returned part of it to the brothers. The hussars and nobles did not forget their own interests but paid themselves in good measure for their trouble. So the brothers at Protzka suffered a great loss. It can be appreciated, however, that the lord was loyal to the brothers, took their part, and scared the raiders away.

1632
Community at Protzka plundered.

On July 16 between three and four in the afternoon, brother Lorenz Putz, a servant of the Word, fell asleep in the Lord with a peaceful heart at Gissing. He had served the church by preaching the Gospel for nine years on the other side of the Danube in Croatia.

Lorenz Putz, a servant, passed away.

On August 6 brother Hansel Hartmayer, a servant of the Word, an upright, zealous brother, fell asleep in the Lord with a peaceful heart at Velké Leváre.

Hansel Hartmayer, a servant, passed away.

On November 7 at Sabatisch, three brothers were confirmed in the service of the Gospel by the elders with the laying on of hands. The brothers were Balzer Rost, Andreas Hiller, and David Lachner.

3 brothers confirmed in the service.

On the same day two brothers, Hans Maier and Johannes Born (both vinedressers), were chosen for the service of the Gospel and appointed for a time of testing.

2 brothers chosen for the service.

On December 17 at ten in the evening, brother Hans Egle, a servant for temporal affairs, fell asleep in the Lord at Sabatisch. He was a venerable steward and a zealous, devout brother.

Hans Egle passed away.

1633

Around Easter 1633, a sad affair for the church arose at Alwinz, Transylvania, under Prince George Rákóczi.[1] It came about through their elder, Isaak Baumann, who, reporting about Alwinz in a letter to a friend in Croatia, wrote something

Sad affair for the church.

[1]George Rákóczi I, Prince of Transylvania (1630–1648), secured religious freedom for the Hungarian Protestants at the Peace of Linz, 1645.

1633

against the authorities. As the letter was left with a judge, who did not send it on right away but kept it for a time, it was found by one of the prince's servants. He opened it and brought it to the court. This was a shock and a great blow to the church at Alwinz. It not only caused serious losses but endangered the brothers' and sisters' lives. The matter was set right, however. Baumann was excluded for his negligence, but he repented and found the right way again. He fell asleep in the Lord about a year later.

Isaak Baumann, a servant, passed away.

Georg Geher entrusted with the care of the church at Alwinz.

Following Baumann's death, Georg Geher was entrusted with the care of the church, to proclaim the Word of God and to keep the right order and Christian community in the church. May he receive much understanding and wisdom from the Lord to lead the church for the honor of God and the strengthening of the believers.

Esaias Weih chosen for the service.

On June 5 brother Esaias Weih, a tailor, was chosen for the service of the Gospel at Alwinz and appointed for a time of testing.

A wretched affair.

That same year a very ugly affair was started at Sabatisch by Lord Franz Nagy-Michaly,[1] one of the lords of Branc. He had come on December 18 of the previous year to demand that the brothers take him over the mountains to Ziffer[2] with six horses. We could not do it, for we did not wish to set a precedent—he was not the only lord of Branc. There were others (and there would be more in the future) who would want to ask the same of us, contrary to the contract and privileges given us by their predecessors. This made him furious, and with some of his hussars, assisted by the foresters, he tried to take our horses from the stable by force and struck several brothers who were in the yard. At this, our people came running from all sides with flails, forks, sticks, and hoes to stop them, but our people did not attack them. The lord with his hussars rode away in a passion. Next he sent his head steward from Rabenska with a number of hussars to take our pigs from the field. Our swineherds ran home, shrieking.

Wanted to take horses by force.

Our pigs taken from the field.

[1]Franz Nagy-Michaly, one of the signatories of the contract concluded at Sabatisch in 1613 (p.605 above). A detailed account of this affair is also included in Beck, 442–454.

[2]Ziffer (Cífer), market town and castle, approx. 5 miles southwest of Tyrnau (Trnava).

Several brothers gave chase, along with neighbors and some servants of Lord Ludwig Niáry, and got the pigs back. The raiders fled, wounded and bleeding. This enraged Lord Franz Nagy-Michaly even more, and he swore to take revenge. Dear brother Heinrich Hartmann sent a written account of the whole matter to all the lords of Branc. At this the lords from both the Niáry and the Tardy families[1] reassured us, telling us not to be afraid, we had done nothing wrong in protecting our property in the face of such injustice and violence. But soon after, some of the lords claimed the opposite. *1633*

On August 22, all the lords of the Tardy family came to Senitz, and with their assistance Franz Nagy-Michaly set up a court with twelve noblemen acting as jurors. The lords Ludwig and Bernhard Niáry were called too, but they were not willing to come. Our brother Heinrich and the brothers assisting him were also summoned to appear in court, but they refused because our contract stated that we were not required to appear before any court or lord and that we do not go to law as the world does. If someone had just cause against us, it could be settled with the lords without going to court.

Brothers brought before the court.

Brothers accused in Latin.

It was no use, however. Our brother Heinrich was forced by the hussars to appear in court with four other brothers. The prosecutor indicted the brothers in Latin and his indictment was written down in Latin. It described how they had run at the lord of the manor with pitchforks, flails, hoes, sticks, and other tools, with intent to kill him. The jurors translated the indictment for the brothers and demanded an answer, although from the written report the brothers had sent to the lords, which had been read to the court, they knew quite well that the brothers were innocent.

Brother Heinrich answered respectfully and humbly: "My dear nobles of the jury and other lords present, you all know well how my brothers and I have respectfully asked to be exempt from going to court, since we are not instructed in the legal practices of the world or in Hungarian law, and it is against our conscience to go to court with our manorial lord. As we have been brought here by force and are pressed for an answer, I ask humbly that if I say something that is not quite correct according to law—which could happen to

[1]The lords Franz Nagy-Michaly, Ludwig and Bernhard Niáry, and Caspar Tardy and his paternal relatives were co-owners of the Branc estates; see above, p.605 n.

1633

anyone—that this is not held against me, as I have never learned the art of rhetoric." They told him to speak freely.

Brother's answer.

So he said, "Dear lords, you know that we have some twelve or thirteen manorial lords in Branc, and each one wants to have sole authority. Therefore, instead of doing compulsory labor for so many lords, we made a contract to pay a fixed yearly sum in addition to the rent for our houses. All the lords agreed to this and made a contract with us. My lord jurors can find in the copy here to hand what they had promised and committed themselves to. Now, however, contrary to this agreement, we have been ordered to do compulsory labor by Lord Franz Nagy-Michaly, who even tried by force to take our horses from the stables and our pigs from the field.

"He himself caused the excited uproar at our place because of the blows he dealt, and this in spite of our telling him that our steward had died the night before and lay in the house as yet unburied. I myself was sick in bed, and therefore nothing could be arranged with Lord Franz. So along with my brothers here, I have absolutely no guilt in that uproar, and I have seriously disciplined those who were involved. If what happened has upset our manorial lord, I humbly ask for pardon on my own behalf as well as that of my brothers." But nothing helped; our pleas fell on deaf ears. The jurors asked all the lords (including Franz Nagy-Michaly) and the brothers to withdraw. The brothers were carefully guarded.

A settlement sought between parties before passing sentence.

After long consultation the jurors commanded the brothers to reappear alone and explained to them that under Hungarian law it was the custom for the parties to seek settlement before judgment was pronounced and carried out. They advised us not to wait for a verdict but rather to seek a settlement with Nagy-Michaly. Brother Heinrich answered, "It has always been our wish to avoid going to law. Since we ourselves are innocent and since Lord Franz started the trouble himself and struck several of our people who were quite innocent, it would be difficult for us to see them punished. But in order to find an agreement, we would be willing to accommodate Lord Franz in some manner. Since the lords of the Niáry family also have part interest in our community, we would like to confer with them."

Brother Heinrich and one other were allowed to do this. They went to the Niáry lords, who were also at Senitz, and reported the jurors' advice to offer a sum of money to Lord Franz by way of settlement. The Niáry lords did not want us to pay anything, but for the sake of peace they agreed to an offer of forty imperial talers, and that also pleased the jurors. This was told Franz Nagy-Michaly and the lords of the Tardy family, but they would not be satisfied. The sentence should be pronounced and carried out. So the sentence was read out and explained to the brothers. The prosecutor read it out in Latin, and it was translated for the brothers. It read: According to present impartial judgment, it is understood that the brothers wanted, in their community, to strike their manorial lord dead, and therefore it is decided that all of them—men, women, and children—are liable to the death penalty. However, the court will show them mercy by having only twelve leading brothers beheaded or taking a fine of forty gulden from each male person over twelve years of age. This sentence, signed and sealed by all jurors, was delivered to Franz Nagy-Michaly.

1633

Hungarian law.

The brothers were afraid that they would also be severely punished because of the hussars who were wounded when trying to drive the pigs from the field. But the jurors said the hussars got what they deserved and no one had committed a crime by that. Violence may be met with violence, but no subject has the right to rebel against his manorial lord. With that the case was closed.

Our brother Heinrich, brother Jakob Mathroner, and Hans Scheuffel were delivered to the judge at Senitz to be imprisoned. He had them heavily guarded day and night by soldiers, as though they were criminals. Paul Wenzel, head potter, and Elias Ottwinowsky, head rope-maker, were set free, but they did not want to leave the other imprisoned brothers. The Tardy lords and Franz Nagy-Michaly were pleased that the judgment (more properly the misjudgment) was in their favor. Next day these lords sent some of their number to record all male persons over twelve years of age and reckon forty gulden for each one, which came to a large sum. The brothers, however, refused to pay anything, and the church was in great anxiety. Every day they pleaded in prayer that God through his grace might deliver them from their plight.

Brothers delivered to the judge.

All males over twelve years written down.

The Niáry lords were enraged. In indignation they rode from Senitz to Sabatisch and promised that they would soon end the brothers' imprisonment. They wrote a stern letter to the

1633

lords of the Tardy family, but it had no effect; they only became enemies. The lords of the Tardy family were afraid that the Niáry lords, with the help of Lord Bernhard Niáry's brother-in-law, Lord Sigmund Lony, would use force to take the brothers from the Senitz prison, for Lord Sigmund had just arrived from Upper Hungary with forty hussars and had also written a stiff letter to the Tardy lords. Therefore they took the brothers four days by wagon over the mountains to the mill of Lord Franz Nagy-Michaly at Koczknowa.[1] All the Tardy lords and Franz Nagy-Michaly went along and had the brothers accompanied by armed guards so that none should escape. At the mill, the five brothers were put in a cellar where dogs had been kept before, and they were securely locked in every night. Franz Nagy-Michaly came frequently with lords from other areas to show them the brothers, mocking them by saying that he had captured the king of the Anabaptists and his councillors, who had tried to kill him. That was why under Hungarian law they had been handed over to him as his prisoners. So besides being innocent, the brothers were mocked and intimidated. At one point, Lord Nagy-Michaly threatened to put them in chains and force them to do heavy labor while in the chains. Another time he threatened to flog them. If they were not ransomed, he would sell them for a good price to a Hungarian captain at a border fortress. He brought this captain in so the brothers could see him, as though he was going to conclude the sale.

The palatine gave orders to free the brothers. Nothing happened.

Meanwhile the lords of the Niáry family continually tried to secure the brothers' release. They wanted to open a fresh lawsuit against the Tardys but did not succeed. They went to the lord palatine, who gave them a written command for Franz Nagy-Michaly to set the brothers free, but even this was of no avail. Instead, Nagy-Michaly haughtily said that neither the king of Hungary nor the lord palatine had any authority in a matter that had already been decided in his favor by a Hungarian court. But he was still anxious lest the brothers be taken by force from the mill and so get free.

After they had been three weeks in prison, Nagy-Michaly came early one morning with the judge and asked brother Heinrich Hartmann whether he did not want to make an

---

[1]Koczknowa: probable location between Modra and Cífer, northeast of Bratislava; see Beck, 449 n.

agreement with him. Heinrich answered that he had told the lord many times he owned nothing but the clothes on his back and therefore had nothing to give. The judge had in his hand two chains used for hobbling horses at pasture. Franz Nagy-Michaly ordered that one be put on brother Heinrich's feet and the other on brother Jakob Mathroner's. When Hans Scheuffel asked that brother Heinrich be spared on account of his age, he was made to wear the chain himself. Then brother Heinrich, brother Jakob, and Hans Scheuffel were taken by wagon to the judge at Wystock,[1] who put them into a dark room for four hours. It made the brothers' flesh creep. They had no idea where they would be taken next, after all the threats they had heard. Franz Nagy-Michaly left them in the hands of the judge, hungry and thirsty and guarded by a few hussars, while he rode to Bibersburg Castle[2] to ask Burgrave Stefan Palffy to take the brothers into custody in his castle, and this was granted. On his return, Nagy-Michaly told the judge, and the judge secretly told the brothers, who were relieved. *1633*

After the lord had eaten, he commanded the judge to take the brothers to the castle. When they got there, they had to wait at the gate for a long time, and everybody came running out of the castle to see the sight. The brothers were embarrassed but took comfort in the knowledge of their innocence. The burgrave roared at them, threw a pair of heavy iron chains down in front of each and said, "Now you are prisoners and in my hands. His Grace, my lord, has given me orders to have you put in chains, and you will have to work in them carting rock and limestone and carrying water, wood, or anything else that is needed."

Brothers taken to the castle.

Such was their reception. As there was no smith to put the chains on them straightaway, the burgrave had them put in a stinking dungeon. The brothers began to feel faint from the stench and filth, for they had had nothing to eat all day. The steward from [our community at] Kesselsdorf happened to be at the castle, and when he saw how they were treated, he was

Steward from Kesselsdorf saw the brothers' plight.

---

[1]Wystock (Vištuk), a Croatian settlement just east of Modra.

[2]Bibersburg (Červený Kameň), castle north of Modra on the southeast slopes of the Little Carpathians; since the 17th century owned by the Palffy family of Hungarian nobility. See Beck, 450 n.2.

1633

filled with pity and asked the burgrave and Lord Franz Nagy-Michaly to take the brothers out of the stinking dungeon. And because he persisted, he finally succeeded. He also brought them food and drink, which refreshed and strengthened them a little. He took leave of them with a sad heart. When he got home, he told of their plight, and there was heartfelt sorrow on their account.

That night those dear brothers had to lie on the bare ground outside the prison, but they found this a great mercy, for at least they were out of the filth and stench.

The next day the burgrave put them in the guardhouse, where they were still in their hobbling chains (perhaps by order of Lord Nagy-Michaly). About midday, the burgrave came with the smith, bringing two heavy iron fetters to fasten on the brothers. He gave up the attempt, however, because it was so difficult, and he said the brothers would not escape him.

Until this time, Paul Wenzel and Elias Ottwinowsky had been in prison at Koczknowa. These brothers had been falsely accused of writing to Lord Niáry saying that Franz Nagy-Michaly had forced them into dancing and other vices. Even though the brothers denied it, saying they knew nothing of it, Franz Nagy-Michaly had them mercilessly flogged with a flagrum and then thrown into an even filthier dungeon than before. The burgrave's wife, who realized that the brothers were innocent, pleaded on their behalf, but nothing was done.

2 brothers beaten although innocent.

When brother Heinrich and his companions heard about this, they were terribly afraid that in his rage Nagy-Michaly would do the same to them. But God be praised, this did not happen. Brother Simon Lorcher, the elder at Kesselsdorf, appealed so persistently to his manorial lord, Burgrave Hans Palffy, that the burgrave wrote a letter advising Lord Franz Nagy-Michaly to send Paul Wenzel and Elias Ottwinowsky to join the other brothers at the castle and unshackle the two who were there in irons. This was done immediately. So all five brothers were brought together, and they thanked God for it.

All the elders did their utmost, making journeys and sending messages wherever they thought something might be achieved toward freeing the brothers. But little came of it because the Niáry lords were against a settlement with the Tardy lords and constantly reassured the brothers that it could all be settled by law without costing us anything. But they could not achieve this, and it was not possible to wait for the end of their legal process, as Hungarian law proceedings often take many years. So in the end there was no other way than to make an agreement with the Tardy lords and Franz Nagy-Michaly. *1633*

After various efforts on the part of the Niáry lords and the elders, the prince palatine finally ordered Burgrave Stefan Palffy as chief of the district to settle the matter. The burgrave sent for Lord Franz Nagy-Michaly, who came with his mother, and Burgrave Palffy urged them to accept a settlement. When they demanded a large sum of money, brother Heinrich Hartmann flatly refused, saying he would not buy his own release.

The wife of Burgrave Stefan Palffy also took up the brothers' cause, making pleas and writing letters to other lords and ladies, leaving no stone unturned in an effort to reach a settlement. Some brothers, seeing that nothing else would help, also took up the matter. Because Lord Franz Nagy-Michaly asserted that the costs of the law case and the care of the wounded hussars had been high, the brothers offered to forgo the little he owed those who worked for him and to pay a sum of money in addition. He and the other lords were satisfied with this, and the matter was settled. The Lord be praised!

The matter settled.

Two identical contracts were drawn up, which Burgrave Stefan Palffy and Lord Franz Nagy-Michaly endorsed with their own hands and sealed with their ancestral seals. One was given to Lord Franz Nagy-Michaly, the other to the brothers. This took place on October 8, 1633, at Bibersburg Castle in the presence of many eminent and noble lords. So the brothers returned to the church with unblemished consciences, and in great joy all the faithful praised and thanked God. One can see in all this what great problems there are when a subject incurs even the smallest guilt toward his manorial lord and what a Hungarian court can do, even if many high-ranking, honorable people acknowledge our innocence and testify to it. In the end, the Lord Franz Nagy-Michaly and his supporters earned more shame and dishonor than praise and profit.

Brothers returned to the church.

1634

On April 4, 1634, at five o'clock in the morning, our brother Michael Grossmann, an old and faithful servant of the Gospel, fell asleep in the Lord at Sabatisch.

Michael Grossmann, a servant, passed away.

1634
Simon Lorcher, a servant, passed away.

On August 22 between eight and nine in the morning, our brother Simon Lorcher, an old servant of the Gospel, fell asleep in the Lord at Dechtitz. He was seventy-one years old.

1635

Felix Schweitzer passed away.

On April 14, 1635, our brother Felix Schweitzer, a servant for temporal affairs, fell asleep in the Lord at Sabatisch. He had been head of the millers and carpenters in the church community for several years.

Esaias Weih, a servant, confirmed.

In August[1] of this year, brother Esaias Weih from Alwinz in Transylvania was confirmed in the service of the Gospel by the elders with the laying on of hands at Sabatisch.

2 brothers confirmed in the service.

On May 2 of this year, also at Sabatisch, two brothers—Hans Maier and Johannes Born—were confirmed in the service of the Gospel by the elders with the laying on of hands.

Brother chosen for the service.

In addition, brother Klaus Messner, a shoemaker, was chosen for a time of testing in the service of the Gospel.

1636

Fire at Sabatisch.

On March 27, 1636, at eight in the morning, a fire broke out at Sabatisch in the house of our neighbor Thomas Misslick, opposite our threshing yard. More than sixty houses in the village, ours included, were burned to the ground. In spite of every effort to control the fire, within fifteen minutes everything was in flames because of the wind. Not a roof was left to shelter so much as one person. Fire fighting was of no use. Because of the terrible wind, people could not escape fast enough, and nine lost their lives. Some were so badly burned that almost nothing of them remained.

9 people burned to death in our house.

Even with the greatest haste, we were barely able to rescue the children from the school. We suffered severe losses of grain and flour, household utensils, livestock, and all kinds of tools and provisions. It was beyond description—nothing was left.

Proposal to leave Sabatisch.

The elders were in great distress and took counsel how to find shelter for their people. They thought to divide them among other communities and even wanted to leave their land and the site of the fire to go elsewhere.

---

[1]The exact date is uncertain. Beck, 455, has June 5 in one source, May 20 in another.

Dear brother Heinrich Hartmann sent to all the lords of Branc, telling them of the terrible situation and the terrible damage. He asked them to release us so that we could care for the people elsewhere, since everyone considered it impossible to rebuild the community to its former state. The lords had great sympathy and offered help and materials, such as wood for building; they did not want us to leave. Lord Ludwig Niáry was particularly compassionate. The fire had not spread to his castle, and in the moment of our greatest need he sent to the field where our people and children, who had fled from the fire, were out in the cold wind, not knowing where to go. He had them brought to the castle and opened all the rooms to them, putting up as many as possible until enough rebuilding had been done to provide housing for them. The nobles and the entire neighborhood at Sabatisch also helped as much as they could, taking our people into their houses and providing for them as long as there was need. In neighboring villages, particularly at Senitz, great sympathy was shown. Some of the nobility and others sent bread and food from their kitchens and showed us kindness in many ways. *1636*

Nobles and others sent us bread.

We saw it as a special grace of God that we could still count on our neighbors to such an extent. The elders heard the generous offer of the lords and their promise to help us with wood and other building materials, and they saw the neighbors' friendliness and help. They also took into consideration that we had lived at Sabatisch for more than ninety years, and although these years had not been without difficulties with the lords, the church had met with much kindness and often been given shelter, for example, when we moved from Moravia to Sabatisch on the Branc estate and when we fled in wartime.

Church had been at Sabatisch for 90 years.

With all this in mind, the elders decided that if the lords would help us and relieve us of all compulsory labor, taxes, and other demands for two or three years, we would undertake to rebuild at the site of the fire. As a result, the lords made a new agreement with the brothers and drew up a new contract, freeing them from all taxes and compulsory labor for two years.[1]

---

[1]See Beck, 457 n.2 for the terms of the new contract signed on June 28, 1636, in all likelihood based on the one signed in 1613 (Beck 363 n.2; p.605 n. above).

In 1938 Prof. Zieglschmid discovered at Sabatisch a document dated August 8, 1640, confirming the previous two contracts (of April 1613 and June 1636), which

1636
Rebuilding begun.

Building was begun. The old, the sick, and the children were divided among the other communities. Most of those who were strong and in good health were needed for the building. So much building was done that summer with the help of other communities that by winter almost all could be accommodated. May God in his grace protect us in times to come from such misfortune and damage.

1637

Klaus Messner confirmed in the service.

On March 8, 1637, at Sabatisch, the elders confirmed brother Klaus Messner in the service of the Gospel with the laying on of hands.

Dry summer.

The summer of 1637 was very dry. Very little grain grew, and most of the fruit and vegetables dried up. Because of the drought, nothing matured, and there was a famine, which caused great suffering for man and beast. Little fodder was harvested. On the Göding estate, Kobelitz Lake, half a mile

---

reads as follows:

> I, Georg Maytheny the older, of Adelsberg, baron of Branc and Butschän, declare herewith before all men, in particular those concerned, out of good will and consideration, on behalf of myself and my heirs and descendants, to the brothers at Sabatisch whom men call Hutterian, that is, to their representatives, Elder Andreas Ehrenpreis, Georg Gaul, and Hans Scheuffel, in response to their humble petition, that I herewith pledge to uphold the new contract which the lords of Branc on behalf of the lords Tardy as well as the lords Niáry concluded after the great fire of March 27, 1636, in which the brothers suffered severe loss. I endorse every point and clause of this contract without exception, and reaffirm in this letter every word of the original contract.
>
> Neither I nor my heirs and descendants shall seek to change any part of it but will uphold it in its entirety and allow it to remain in full force, provided the brothers fulfill their side of the contract by paying the fees due to us, the lords of Branc, since I myself along with the other lords of Branc spared no effort, through traveling, to ensure that in 1613 the brothers move back and settle in Sabatisch upon the request of all the Branc lords, on the basis of the original contract concluded on April 23, 1613, which I with my own hand and seal have endorsed and helped to uphold along with the other lords.
>
> And because the new contract is based on the old one in all points, confirming them and more, I pledge (as said above) myself and my heirs or descendants to reaffirm both the old and the new contracts, promising in no way to change or increase their terms, but to uphold them faithfully without any evil intent.
>
> As witness thereof and to give it full validity, I have personally signed this letter with my own hand and sealed it with my patrimonial privy seal, at my own house in Sabatisch on the 8th day of August, 1640.
>
> Signed: Georgh Maytheny

long and about as wide, was said to have dried up from the drought, but this was largely because the lake had been opened up and allowed to drain.[1] Moreover, the ponds on other estates which fed the lake were also drying out. *1637*

1638

On October 1, 1638, Simon Stadelman, an old servant for temporal affairs, fell asleep in the Lord at Velké Leváre. Simon Stadelman passed away.

This summer again there was such a drought that the fields of grain, the orchards, and the gardens yielded hardly anything. Because the fodder was virtually gone, many people had to get rid of their animals. There followed a severe famine, and man and beast went hungry. It continued into the next year, 1639, making the price of a peck of grain rise to five or six Hungarian talers before the crops could be harvested. The need was so great that when spring came, many kept themselves and their children alive for several weeks with wild herbs and roots that they cut up and boiled. Some mixed white clay with their flour for baking. But our Lord and faithful God, to whom be everlasting praise, blessed his church so much through the foresight of the dedicated elders that the faithful suffered neither hunger nor want but were even able to help others in need. Some communities gave alms and shared their bread with fifty to sixty people, in some cases even up to eighty adults and children.

Dry summer.

Severe famine.

Communities helped other poor people.

The grape crop, on the other hand, was so plentiful that year that in Hungary, especially on the other side of the Little Carpathians, a cask of wine sold for seven or eight shillings (that is fourteen or sixteen Bohemian groschen), and the Hungarian half-liter cost one kreuzer. If someone brought two empty casks, he could get one filled in exchange for the empty one. Our almighty God can help in every need. To him be eternal praise! Abundant grape harvest.

1639

At six o'clock in the morning on September 29, 1639, our dear brother Heinrich Hartmann fell asleep in the Lord at The elder Heinrich Hartmann passed away.

[1]It was reported that Zdeněk Žampach of Potnštejn, lord of Göding, drained the lake and after seven weeks both the lake and the streams that fed it were dried up. See Beck, 458–459.

1639

Sabatisch. He had been a faithful servant of the Gospel and shepherd of the whole church. He declared his good conscience to the elders who visited him during his illness, testifying that he was at peace with God and all the faithful. He thanked them for all the love shown him and asked them to give his greetings of peace to the brothers and sisters in farewell. Then he fell asleep with a peaceful heart. He was sixty-three years old and had led the church for only two months short of eight years.

After the peaceful passing of our dear brother Heinrich, all servants of the Word, servants for temporal affairs, stewards, buyers, and storekeepers and many other trusted brothers from the whole church gathered at Sabatisch on October 3. In earnest prayer they considered the matter, asking God to give them another faithful shepherd and elder for the church. The choice fell on dear brother Andreas Ehrenpreis, who received a unanimous and joyful testimony from the brothers. This service of caring faithfully for the church of the Lord was laid on him on October 4, 1639.

Andreas Ehrenpreis chosen elder.

On November 1, two brothers—Georg Schultes, a cobbler from Bohemia and Moses Rapertshauser, a glazier from Moravia—were chosen for the service of the Gospel and appointed at Sabatisch for a time of testing.

2 brothers appointed to the service of the Gospel.

On December 13 brother Abraham Scheffer, a servant of the Gospel, fell asleep in the Lord with a peaceful heart at Kesselsdorf.

Abraham Scheffer, a servant, passed away.

1641[1]

On April 13, 1641, brother Jakob Mathroner, a servant of the Gospel, fell asleep in the Lord at Farkeschin.

Jakob Mathroner, a servant, passed away.

On May 8 three brothers were chosen for the service of the Gospel and appointed at Sabatisch for a time of testing. They were Hans Friedrich Küntsche, a cutler from Württemberg; Hans Blesing, a schoolteacher from Switzerland; and Joseph Forher, a cloth maker. Joseph Forher, however, was relieved of the service at his request because of his weak eyesight.

3 brothers chosen for the service of the Gospel.

1642

On June 22, 1642, two brothers, Georg Schultes and Moses Rapertshauser, were confirmed in the service of the Gospel by the elders with the laying on of hands at Sabatisch.

[1]No entry was made for the year 1640.

In 1642 around Whitsun, terror swept these lands when the imperial general Duke Franz Albrecht of Saxony and the Swedish field marshal Lennart Torstenson confronted each other in Silesia and fought a disastrous battle.[1] Duke Franz Albrecht was mortally wounded. The imperial army fled in panic. They crossed the March River at Ungarisch Hradisch into Hungary and came down [the valley] on our side. Then to the great alarm of our people, they suddenly arrived at Velké Leváre and stayed there for two days, until Count Piccolomini[2] took over the command and led them back across the March near Drösing.[3] No particular violence took place at Velké Leváre this time, although we had to bear the cost of putting them up. So God in his grace faithfully helped us through our troubles. Since the Swedes had won the field in Moravia, they advanced on Olmütz as fast as possible. Everyone was seized with terror, and the city surrendered without much resistance to the Swedes, who installed themselves and fortified it more strongly. They took a considerable amount of loot to their fort. Then both forces marched into the area of Meissen [Saxony]. The Swedes took the city of Leipzig after a hard battle, in which they suffered considerable losses.

1642
Swedes against imperial army in Silesia.

Swedes conquered Olmütz in Moravia and Leipzig in Meissen area.

To the Church of God in Alwinz

To our most beloved brothers and sisters, fellow members and friends in Christ Jesus our Lord, we wish you grace, peace, and mercy from God, the Father of our Lord and Savior Jesus Christ, and his blessing on you in time and in eternity.

Dearly loved brothers, we will not neglect to write you a heartfelt, brotherly letter after our dear brothers and yours have returned to us under God's protection. To our joy we heard from them that thanks to the Lord things

Epistle to the church at Alwinz from Andreas Ehrenpreis.

[1]Duke Franz Albrecht of Saxony-Lauenburg, born 1598, fell in the battle of Schweidnitz (Świdnica), Silesia, 1642.

Lennart Torstenson, count of Ortala (1603–1651), was commander in chief of the Swedish army in Germany from 1641 to 1646. In 1642 he advanced through Bohemia right into the heart of Austria, which until then had not seen the Protestant enemy. See Beck, 467.

[2]Ottavio Piccolomini, duke of Amalfi (1599–1656), replaced Wallenstein as general of the imperial armies in 1633.

[3]Drösing, Austria, northeast of Velké Leváre on the other side of the Morava River.

1642
Epistle to the church at Alwinz.

are going fairly well with you. Our hearts rejoice about this and give praise and thanks to the almighty God. We hope to receive another such reassuring message from you soon.

At the same time we understand that you have lost many capable people whose help was badly needed for your livelihood. If it were possible, we would gladly supply your need. But you know very well that unfortunately there are fewer and fewer believers from day to day, not only among you there, but here too. Recently we even had to send gleaners into fields and vineyards, and we have to be thankful and content with what the Lord provides. It is all the more necessary for each of the devout to see to it that order is kept for the sake of our subsistence. Each one must be prepared to do all he can in his work, instead of wasting half his time and doing less than half the work, with the result that a penny diligently earned in one place is wasted in another. Besides, whatever is saved and kept is safer than what has yet to be earned. Since it is God's order that man should earn his bread by the sweat of his brow, we should do this not only for twenty, thirty, or more years, but until we return to the dust from which we were taken. Lastly, Paul points out that he always taught that the weak must be supported by the work of the strong. It is more blessed to give than to receive.

Mic.7:1

Since there are all kinds of people in a community, it is necessary to give all kinds of teaching and admonition so that each one may see himself in the mirror of righteousness and be reminded of faults and shortcomings that have to be overcome. As some have occupations demanding that they work early and late, others too should show their diligence. Yet it would be quite unfitting for people to spend themselves to the utmost and then spare the horses and other animals, for these cost much in fodder and care. This should receive our careful attention and should be changed where necessary.

Likewise there should be proper moderation and order in the use of food. It should be remembered that when we work outside, we have to do strenuous work, but that does not mean we should indulge in an extravagant

1642
Epistle to the church at Alwinz.

consumption of food and drink, which does take place, according to hearsay. Since we are brothers and one people, it would be good if we did things the same way. Among the Israelites, who measured with the omer, he that gathered much had nothing left over, and he that gathered little had no lack; so we also should not neglect to share in an orderly way. If we forget this, bad thoughts and discontent may arise and cause grief and damage in the church. After all, we know that summer with its harvest provides for us in winter, and if we eat everything up in summer, we must starve in winter.

In the same way, if our dear forefathers had not thought of this and made good provision, the church would most certainly have died of starvation in times of war or persecution. Many of us know that in spite of great thrift and in spite of what the community laid by, there were times of acute shortage and hunger. Therefore it is right that we remember our forefathers, consider the fruits of their lives, and follow their faith.

It is generally known that the dear brothers who first went to live at Alwinz still led a poverty-stricken existence for quite a long time as part of the church in exile, in spite of considerable help from the church (according to its means and even beyond them). Just think how impossible it would have been to pull through if there had been no help from the church. So you must not only think how you can find means of subsistence but also remember that we may need your help in difficult times if God the Lord should visit us with poverty and allow us to suffer persecution. Therefore you should think ahead about ways of helping the church.

Added to this, we know man's earthbound nature, which breeds dissatisfaction and thanklessness in some who do not fear God, no matter how much is shared with them. Even if more is spent than has been earned, there are still complaints, just as in Israel. But many devout, warmhearted people who are thankful to God the Lord will understand our intention, that is, to honor God and to care for the well-being of the church. This is nothing but a brotherly service so that our children and descendants will not have to complain after we are gone that in good

1642
Epistle to the church at Alwinz.

times we neglected them and did not provide for them and set them a good example. We should also consider how bitter and painful it would be if, when times change and misfortune and famine come, we have to suffer want.

Many of you know how our life was in Moravia, with strenuous, hard work. The wagoners certainly worked early and late, and much work was done in field and vineyard without anyone receiving any money. Very much depends on the faithfulness of those who lead the work and on the direction given by them. We trust that all the faithful are willing to be led in their service to the church, without complaining or resisting.

We appeal first and foremost to each brother and sister appointed to a service in the church to give their utmost for the honor of the Lord and the welfare of the church, making every effort to keep good Christian order and carrying out the appointed tasks responsibly. They should be faithful in their life and conduct and in directing and distributing all the work. They should always be ready to serve the church and the faithful, particularly the old and the needy. Think how soon the time will come when each will be asked: Give account of your stewardship—how faithful, reliable, and prudent you have been in carrying out your service.

And now we ask each of the devout in the whole church to show faithfulness and diligence in all things and to be thankful and content. Seek peace and true unity and avoid all strife and disunity. Help each other to build the spiritual house of God and plant the garden of the Lord Sabaoth. Offer each other the hand of fellowship, and be an incentive to each other toward devotion and blessedness. Help each other on the way of peace, for the Administrator, who will give us our pay and reward, our Lord Jesus Christ, Judge of the living and the dead, stands at the door.

He will reward each one a hundredfold for his faithfulness, zeal, and honesty and bid him go in to our heavenly Father's kingdom, prepared by the Father for his own from the beginning. There, with inexpressible joy and in great glory, we shall receive the crown of everlasting life. None will regret whatever good he did,

1642
Epistle to the church at Alwinz.

but each one will think, "If only I had done more, if only I had been more faithful and zealous!" The ground and truth of Holy Scripture points to this alone: "Open the gates so that the righteous people may enter in, the people who are faithful" (take note: *faithful*) "and who keep the truth." Only to them will Christ the Lord say, "O you good and faithful servants of the Lord, man or maid, you have been faithful over a little. I will put you in charge of much. Enter into the joy of your master!" If there are any who have buried the talent of God's grace in a cloth, become tired and halfhearted, grown lame and cold in love, these still have time to wake up, to search again for the buried and lost talent, and to spend the rest of their lives following the gracious will of God before the Judge appears and demands a reckoning. By so doing they may yet escape and save their souls.

The apostle of the Lord surely means to advise such weak and tired hearts when he teaches, "Raise your drooping hands and your weak knees, and keep your feet on the straight path," so that none among us may be left behind and fail to find eternal rest but may reach the appointed goal in peace and joy with one another. Moreover, we exhort all the faithful to whom God has given children, if they truly love them and value their welfare and purity, to bring them up in the fear of God. They should stand against the evil in them while they are young and break their self-will, not letting them grow hardened in it by neglecting discipline and punishment. Afterward it will be too late to correct the evil, and they may have to suffer many reprimands and punishments that will then be of no help. It is not enough for father and mother to care for their children physically, providing them with food and clothing. They must attend to the children's discipline too, which is as necessary for them as daily bread; for the right way of love is to lead them to blessedness and eternal life and protect them from eternal punishment and damnation.

Similarly, all the school teachers, the heads of work departments, and all those responsible for the young are urged to be good builders in the house of God. The young

1642
Epistle to the church at Alwinz.

people (including those who may already be members of our covenant) should not be left to run free and unsupervised. Order and obedience should be expected of them on Sundays just as during the week. They should be brought up to follow God's way and his will, so that after we are gone they remain an upright people who uphold the honor of God. We must look at the example of Abraham, who received the blessing and praise of God, whereas Eli the priest, though himself devout and righteous, was too lenient with his sons, and he was put to shame and despised, and he died a sudden death. Not only he but the whole people of Israel were smitten with fear and distress and overcome by their enemies. The glory of the Lord and the ark of the covenant of God were lost to them. The whole house of Eli was removed from the priesthood and died out. This is an example for all the devout, so that their children's blood will not be upon their heads: for the word of the Lord shall not fail.

In spite of my limited gift, I felt compelled to write this to you in the name of your elders. I am writing as briefly as I can, with special love, in trust and warm affection. I have full trust and hope that all the devout who love God from their hearts will take this letter as it is meant and realize that its goal is the honor of God alone and the well-being of all the faithful. "Now may the God of peace who brought again from the dead our Lord Jesus, the great shepherd of the sheep, by the blood of the eternal covenant, equip you with everything good that you may do his will, working in you that which is pleasing in his sight, through Jesus Christ; to whom be glory for ever and ever. Amen" (RSV).

With this I greet the whole church of God, all those scattered here and there, each of the faithful, personally and many times, with the peace of our Lord and Savior Jesus Christ. All the elders and many of the faithful greet you from their hearts. May you be under God's protection at all times, and may he bless you and us in every good thing. Should we not see each other here again with mortal eyes, may the almighty God help us so that it may happen in that other world of eternal joy and splendor. This I wish all the faithful a thousandfold through Christ Jesus to all eternity. Amen.

Dated: Sabatisch, June 30, 1642

1642
Epistle to the church at Alwinz.

Your brother and servant in the Lord
Andreas Ehrenpreis

1643

On April 19, 1643, two brothers, Hans Friedrich Küntsche and Hans Blesing, were confirmed in the service of the Gospel by the elders with the laying on of hands at Sabatisch.

2 brothers confirmed in the service.

On May 9 at about one o'clock in the afternoon, a fire broke out in a neighbor's house in the marketplace at Sabatisch. Our place burned down again along with the whole marketplace, except for the church and a few small houses. Because of the fierce wind and the smoke and dust, no one could put out the fire or save anything. It is not hard to imagine what a great loss this was for the church. We accepted it in patience and put ourselves in God's hand.[1]

Sabatisch burned down.

---

[1]Following is a translation of the deed of purchase concluded at Sabatisch on June 18, 1643, between the Hutterian Brethren and George Sigethy the older; see also Zieglschmid, *Chronik*, 837 n.1.

> I, George Sigethy the older, resident of the town of Sabatisch, herewith acknowledge for myself and my heirs and descendants before all men, in particular all whom it may concern, that in the year 1623 in a case of urgent need I leased to the brothers at Sabatisch, that is, to Valentin Winter (their elder) and Martin Hämpel (their steward) as their representatives, the land on the towpath above the pond belonging to the honorable lord Ballan Jänuss, which adjoins the property of Lord Niáry on the lower side and runs along the vineyard at Rabenska on the upper side. The sum named was eighty (80) gulden of good money, reckoned at one hundred (100) Hungarian pennies to the gulden. Upon receipt of said sum in full from the brothers, in good currency of that time, I made over the aforesaid property (being my own land to which no relative had any claim whatsoever) to the brothers, for them to use until such time as I might pay back to them the total sum of eighty (80) gulden in good money.
>
> Inasmuch as the brothers have already enjoyed the use of the above-mentioned property from 1623 to 1643, and since it is now clear that I am unable to redeem it and the land no longer has the value of what I received for it, I have come to the agreement with the brothers Heinrich Habereuter (their steward) and Hans Scheuffel, as their representatives, that they pay me two (2) gulden in addition and that I will transfer the land to them as their property. These two (2) gulden I have now received from them. Therefore I herewith transfer and convey to the brothers and their heirs forever this property for them to enjoy, free from any impediment or hindrance from me or from my descendants and relatives, in the same way

1643
Imperial army at Olmütz. Swedes repulsed them and captured other places.

In June the imperial troops moved in again on Olmütz in Moravia to free it from the Swedes. But the Swedes sent forces too, and this made a bad situation worse, as they occupied not only Olmütz and places already conquered but also took possession of Kremsier, Prossnitz, Wischau, Rausnitz, Tobitschau, and the fortified castle of Eulenberg, and everywhere they took considerable booty.

His Imperial Majesty came to Skalitz in Hungary.

On September 2 His Imperial Majesty came to Skalitz in Hungary with the elector palatine Nikolaus Esterházy,[1] the Hungarian nobility, and thousands of Hungarian troops. They formed a league to resist the enemy [the Swedes] in Moravia. Again the church suffered no particular harm, through God's gracious help and faithful protection.

1644

Imperial army's movements in Hungary.

In February 1644 great fear gripped the land when Count von Buchheim reached Skalitz, Schossberg, and Senitz with the imperial army. Through God's help and faithful care, Sabatisch was fairly well protected.

On March 18 he crossed the mountains with his large army. Many froze to death because of snow and bad weather. A colonel with several hundred cavalrymen came unexpectedly to Dechtitz and stayed three days. They used up a great quantity of our supplies, and we had to give our two best horses to prevent them from plundering. Then they went down into Hungary to attack Prince Rákóczi.

On April 9 the imperial army came four thousand strong from Freistadt to Buchau[2] and descended on our community at Soblahof. They stripped many of our people of their clothes and stole whatever they could find, including all thirteen horses.

---

that I have enjoyed its use in the freedom of my high estate.

In witness and affirmation whereof I set my hereditary seal upon this deed and my signature in my own hand. In further affirmation I have caused the illustrious lord Ballan Jänuss to set thereto the seal of his rank and to sign the same with his own hand. Given at Sabatisch, June 18, 1643.

[1]Nikolaus Esterházy (1582–1645), the first of this ancient Hungarian family to become famous as palatine of Hungary (1625). During the Counter Reformation, he was a zealous partisan of the Catholic Church.

[2]Buchau (Púchov), a town on the Vah River, approx. 28 miles northeast of Trentschin (Trencin).

On August 6 some Hungarians from Transylvania fell on Schächtitz, plundered the marketplace, the castle, and our community at Tschäskowitz, and shot a brother. From there they turned back and burned the outskirts of Betzkow.[1] There was terror everywhere, and many fled to the castles. Then things became a little quieter, and most of our people returned home to Velké Leváre from Sabatisch and Branc.

1644
Schächtitz and Tschäskowitz raided.

1645

About March 6, 1645, the Swedish field marshal General Torstenson won a decisive victory against the imperial forces near Tschaslau in Bohemia, in which General Götz was killed.[2] Torstenson returned to Moravia and came as far as the March River, spreading his forces out everywhere.

On April 7 they crossed the bridges at Angern [into Hungary] in pursuit of Croatians who were fighting on the side of the imperial army. At ten o'clock that night they raided our community at Velké Leváre, plundering and taking whatever they found. Most of our people from Velké Leváre fled again to Sabatisch in great fear and terror.

Velké Leváre plundered.

Between April 15 and April 20 Nikolsburg, Göding, Skalitz, Strassnitz, Ungarisch Ostra, and other places came under Swedish domination.

About April 30 some Hungarians from Transylvania came down along the Waag River, plundered Schächtitz and Neustadt again, stole two horses and the wagon at Tschäskowitz, and spread great fear.

Schächtitz and Neustadt plundered.

On April 30 the Swedish army took the castle of Rabensburg after a hard battle.[3]

On May 10 the Transylvanian general Bakos Gabor crossed the bridges at Trentschin with eighty-six companies of Hungarians to join the Swedish major general Douglas.[4]

---

[1]Betzkow (Beckov), approx. 11 miles southwest of Trencin near the Vah River, with the ruins of Beckov Castle; seat of the Stibořic family, who owned the Vah Valley. See Beck, 469.

[2]Count Johann von Götzen, imperial general, fell in March 1645 in the battle of Jankov, approx. 35 miles southeast of Prague. *New Cambridge Modern History*, IV, 351.

[3]Rabensburg, village in Lower Austria, near the confluence of the Dyje and Morava rivers.

[4]General Gabriel Bakos was ordered by Rákóczi to the Moravian border with 6000 men to join the Swedish major general Douglas.

1645

Around midnight on May 19 several thousand Swedes advanced unexpectedly on Sabatisch. The officers came into the houses; the others remained in the fields. They left before daybreak without doing any particular harm. Nobody knew where they came from or what they had in mind.

At this time the Swedes crossed the Little Carpathians and took Tyrnau without much effort.[1] There was great misery throughout the land. The Swedish bodyguards were quartered in towns, castles, or market villages, and this also put the church to considerable expense.

On May 20 the imperial troops raided Velké Leváre. They captured a Swede and one of the Hungarian bodyguards. It cost us a large sum of money because in order to satisfy the Hungarian general, Bocskay,[2] we had to give him six horses and a wagon, as well as many knives and other things, in compensation for the Hungarian soldier and his horse and musket.

Velké Leváre, St. Johannes, and Protzka plundered.

In the beginning of June the thieving peasants took possession of our houses at Velké Leváre, St. Johannes, and Protzka. They opened up the holes where things were hidden underground and took away everything they found. This plundering continued for a number of weeks, and no brother could show himself during that time. At St. Johannes they brutally murdered two brothers, and at Velké Leváre they burned down the school and the workshops of the tailors, cobblers, and cutlers.

On June 24 Christel Kisselbrunner, an old servant of the Gospel, fell asleep in the Lord at Sabatisch.

On June 29 Major General Douglas went through Sabatisch with five thousand Swedish soldiers and stayed a night in the fields by a stream, the Schwebelbach. No harm came to us, through the mighty protection of God, to whom we must give heartfelt thanks.

Sad affair with Benjamin Kengel.

In June 1645 a problem arose with Benjamin Kengel, a

[1]Under Douglas's leadership, the city of Tyrnau (Trnava) was taken "without much effort," as the imperial troops had left only a small garrison there and retreated to Bratislava. The Swedish soldiers intended to loot Tyrnau, but Douglas drove them back and saved the town; the Swedes made outrageous requisitions in compensation. Beck, 470.

[2]General Bocskay, probably from the family of Stephen Bocskay, prince of Transylvania (1604–1606).

tailor at Sabatisch. He withdrew from the communal worship meetings. When spoken to, he replied that the righteous have no need of instruction, since the Holy Spirit will teach them, and that the common prayer is only a human custom, not prompted by the Holy Spirit. He also maintained that baptism is useless and unnecessary and nothing but a means of coercion to bring about human obedience, which is against the freedom of Christ. He considered all servants and teachers as serfs under contract and their work as ungodly. He completely rejected their authority to bind and to loose sin, saying that no man can be of any help to wash away another's sin. *1645*

In the same way, he said about the Lord's Supper that outward ceremonies and Ordnungen are not necessary for a true Christian. Likewise marriage and what it involves is not fitting for a Christian; because of that he had remained a widower for some years.

In short, the church in his opinion had never been right but in error about these and many other things. On the basis of truth—the teaching of Christ, the example of the first church in Jerusalem, and the work of the Holy Spirit—Kengel was admonished many times to give up his wrong ideas. When this had been said enough and he still arrogantly persisted in his own ideas, he was excluded and separated from the church. Was excluded.

He made a passionate plea to be allowed to stay in the community and live according to his own beliefs, but as he was an evil root and harmful weed, this was quite out of the question. He sought for true repentance yet did not find it, although he continued seeking for a long time, coming before the church and confessing openly that he had been in error. He said he had imagined that he understood something, and now he was heartily sorry and for the rest of his life wanted nothing to do with such wrong ideas. But at this point he fell ill and died.[1] Some of his followers confessed, repented, and found the way again, but others are in rebellion to this day.

Benjamin Kengel confessed his error.

Did not find full repentance.

[1]Andreas Ehrenpreis wrote an "Answer and refutation of the erroneous and misleading opinions of Benjamin Kengel and his followers, yet not for their sake alone but for the sake of all upright souls, as a true warning to guard against such leaven as a destructive disease of the soul so that none may miss the goal. . . . Concerning those who fell away: They do not believe in water baptism, repentance and forgiveness of sins, obedience, prayer, teaching and preaching, marriage, or martyrdom for Christ; they say they have not broken their covenant with God." See Friedmann, *Schriften*, 112 #9.

1645

On July 23 Prince Rákóczi and his whole army marched over the mountains and encamped in the fields near Karlath.[1] We were once again in great fear and danger, for our community at Sabatisch was surrounded by soldiers. From all sides they tried to force their way over fences and walls. Through God's manifold grace this was prevented, but it cost us much bread, wine, and beer.

David Lachner passed away.

On July 26 brother David Lachner, a servant of God's Word, fell asleep in the Lord at Sabatisch.

Protzka burned down. A brother murdered.

On July 27, after Protzka had been repeatedly plundered, it was burned down except for the mill and the tannery. A brother named Konrad, the head tanner, was brutally murdered.

On August 1 a big troop of imperial soldiers came from Pressburg and raided Tschäskowitz, robbing us of everything that had been left behind after the previous raid—all the horses we had managed to keep and a few oxen—and going off with everything they could find.

Uhl Tobel passed away.

On August 13 an old servant for temporal affairs, our brother Uhl Tobel, fell asleep in the Lord at Sabatisch.

About this time Prince Rákóczi again struck camp and went to Senitz with his forces. At Sabatisch Bakos Gabor remained in the fields that night. We supplied both of them with food and drink in their tents, as we had often done. They left us in peace, and apart from our terrible fear, we suffered no violence. They then returned home over the mountains.

Moved to Bodock.

Since he became ruler, Prince Rákóczi had often asked us to begin a Bruderhof at Bodock[2] on his estate. The elders had tried hard in various ways to resist, but this time it was unavoidable. The prince told them if they came voluntarily, well and good, but if not, he now had the means to make them. To prevent a dispersal of the whole community, it was agreed that they should all leave Tschäskowitz and move to Bodock. The prince's servants came with sufficient wagons and escorts for them. So on August 25 they loaded the wagons and set out in God's name, in tears and great distress. May

Set up a new community.

---

[1]Karlath Castle (Hungarian: Karlátka; Slovakian: Ostry Kamen; German: Konradstein), now a ruin, between Senitz (Senica) and Sandorf on the northern slopes of the Little Carpathians; see Beck, 471.

[2]Bodock (Sárospatak), city in the Zemplin district, northeast Hungary, at one time property of the Rákóczis. George Rákóczi I and his son and successor George II (1621–1660) were zealous Calvinists, and during their lifetime the Hutterian community at Bodock flourished. See *ME*, I, 378; Beck, 472 n.

almighty God faithfully support them and help them to build up a proper community there. *1645*

On October 17 of that same year, 1645, two brothers were chosen for the service of the Gospel and appointed for a time of testing at Sabatisch. They were Hartman Baumann, a barber-surgeon from Alwinz in Transylvania, and Erasmus Strauss, a shoemaker from Württemberg.

2 brothers chosen for the service of the Word.

On October 26 at Tschäskowitz our brother Hans Hueber, an old servant of the Gospel, fell asleep in the Lord.

Hans Hueber, a servant, passed away.

During that year the plague took a high toll in towns and villages far and wide. In November and December many died at Sabatisch also, including fine and active people.

Many died of the plague.

So the year 1645 ended in great misery and fear, and many people and animals perished. What was not stolen was lost in other ways. Once again the church was in great poverty, having little harvest from garden and field. It is impossible to describe it all. This is just a short account of the distress of these times, recorded here for the sake of our descendants. May God the Almighty grant us a better future.

1646

On April 25, 1646, brother Andreas Hiller, a servant of the Gospel, fell asleep in the Lord at Tschäskowitz.

Andreas Hiller, a servant, passed away.

On May 15 two brothers, Felix Strüby and Joseph Lercher, were chosen for the service of the Gospel at Sabatisch and appointed for a time of testing.

2 brothers chosen for the service of the Word.

On August 22 the imperial soldiers recaptured Rabensburg Castle. About the same time Korneuburg,[1] Staatz, Falkenstein, Iglau, and other places in those parts were also captured and repossessed.

On September 11 His Imperial Majesty came to the Provincial Diet at Pressburg, where Count Johann Traskowitz was elected palatine of Hungary.

This year there was an unusually wet fall, and it continued so till Christmas, making travel almost impossible.

Wet fall.

1647

On July 8, 1647, our brother Valtin Fischer, a saddler, was

Brother chosen for the service of the Word.

[1]Korneuburg on the Danube, northwest of Vienna.

1647

chosen for the service of the Gospel at Alwinz in Transylvania and appointed for a time of testing.

Hailstorm.

In that same month there was a devastating hailstorm in Moravia around Tobitschau.[1] Fifteen-pound hailstones fell, and not only birds and hares but deer and wolves were killed.

Jakob Litzenbucher, a servant, passed away.

On September 16 our brother Jakob Litzenbucher, an old servant of the Word, fell asleep in the Lord at Bodock in Hungary.

3 brothers confirmed in the service.

2 brothers chosen for service.

On September 25 the elders confirmed three brothers, Erasmus Strauss, Felix Strüby, and Joseph Lercher, in the service of the Gospel at Sabatisch with the laying on of hands. Hartman Baumann, on the other hand, was relieved of his service. On the same day two brothers, Moses Bruckner and Caspar Eglauch,[2] both shoemakers, were chosen for the service of the Gospel and appointed for a time of testing.

9 brothers chosen as servants for temporal affairs.

Besides this, nine brothers were chosen as servants for temporal affairs and appointed to the following services: Hans Schütz, Peter Kocher, Johannes Egel, Heinrich Habereuter, and Samuel Hobler, all as stewards; Michael Milder as head carpenter; Hans Nutz as head miller; Johannes Spengler as barber-surgeon;[3] Jackel Gründler as buyer.

Taxation.

In that year a heavy tax was imposed here in Hungary, and the church had to pay more than seven hundred gulden.

1648

7 horses taken.

On January 14, 1648, seven good horses were taken from us by Croatian imperial soldiers between Holitsch and Sabatisch.

On February 17 our brother Hans Albrecht, a servant of the Gospel, fell asleep in the Lord at Farkeschin.

---

[1]Tobitschau (Tovačov), approx. 10 miles south of Olomouc.

Theatrum Europaeum, VI, 301: "A destructive storm raged in July around Kremsier not far from Olmütz in Moravia. It was a terrible storm. At times the hailstones were so large that they killed birds on the wing, cattle in the field, deer in the woods, and even fish in the water. In some places the wolves ran out of the woods in fear and attacked the people. Trees were found ripped to pieces, and some houses were completely demolished." See also Beck, 475.

[2]Caspar Eglauch was to become Vorsteher in 1688. See *ME*, II, 162–163; Beck, 553; Zieglschmid, *Klein-Geschichtsbuch*, 222.

[3]About Spengler's place in Hutterian medical practice, see Friedmann, "Hutterite Physicians. . . ," *MQR*, April 1953, 133–134.

On March 11 three brothers were chosen for the service of the Gospel and appointed for a time of testing: Michael Milder, head carpenter; Johannes Rieger, a tailor; and Tobias Breunel, a miller. This took place in the large meeting at Sabatisch.

1648
3 brothers chosen as servants.

On March 28 our brother Balzer Rost, a servant of the Gospel, fell asleep in the Lord at Farkeschin.

Balzer Rost, a servant, passed away.

On April 2 our brother Dietrich Weinitz, a buyer and servant for temporal affairs, fell asleep in the Lord at Sabatisch.

Dietrich Weinitz passed away.

1649

On January 22, 1649, our brother Kuntz Porth, an old servant of the Gospel, fell asleep in the Lord at Dechtitz.

Kuntz Porth, a servant, passed away.

On January 28 our brother Hans Nutz, head miller and servant for temporal affairs, fell asleep in the Lord at Sabatisch.

Hans Nutz passed away.

On March 18 five brothers were confirmed in the service of the Gospel by the elders with the laying on of hands at Sabatisch. These were Moses Bruckner, Caspar Eglauch, Michael Milder, Johannes Rieger, and Tobias Breunel.

5 brothers confirmed in the service.

On the same day three brothers were chosen for the service of the Gospel and appointed for a time of testing: Jakob Rebstock, a barber-surgeon; Jakob Amssler, a smith; and Andreas Rosenberger, a clothmaker.

3 brothers chosen for the service.

In May our brother Samuel Hobler, a servant for temporal affairs, fell asleep in the Lord at Soblahof.

Samuel Hobler passed away.

On June 18 our brother Hans Lang, an old servant of the Gospel, fell asleep in the Lord at four in the morning at Tschäskowitz.

Hans Lang, a servant, passed away.

On June 27 our brother Valtin Fischer from Alwinz was confirmed in the service of the Gospel by the elders with the laying on of hands at Sabatisch.

A brother confirmed in the service.

On the night of August 27 at about ten o'clock, the large dwelling house at Soblahof was struck by lightning but was preserved from any great damage.

Thunderstorm.

On July 7 our brother Felix Strüby, a servant of the Word, and other brothers were sent on a journey in Transylvania. Felix Strüby became ill while traveling, and on September 8 between eight and nine in the evening he fell asleep in the Lord at Alwinz.

Felix Strüby, a servant, passed away.

1649

An Epistle to the Churches at Alwinz and Bodock
October 19, 1649

Epistle to the churches at Alwinz and Bodock from Andreas Ehrenpreis.

May grace, peace, joy, and eternal bliss be yours from the almighty, invincible, and holy God, through Jesus Christ. Amen.

Beloved brothers and sisters all, you have gone into a foreign land far from the church, with God's permission and guidance. Yet under his divine care we still have some opportunity to visit one another and exchange messages, so I do not want to miss this opportunity to send a letter of exhortation to you all, in brotherly trust and hope that it will be accepted by all the devout in good faith.

Christ our Savior and Redeemer has spoken at length of the end time and told us that the love of many will grow cold and injustice will gain the upper hand, leading even the elect astray, if that were possible. Now all this is being revealed throughout the whole world so that everything may be fulfilled. As it was in the time of the flood and when Lot left Sodom, so it will be in the last days. Therefore we have every reason to take care lest by backsliding we forfeit God's grace, bringing his disfavor and wrath upon ourselves and our children.

The Word of the Lord shall not fail, as he promised many times to Israel. Through the infinite love and grace of God they were brought out from among all people to be a crown in the hand of the Lord, a garland of honor in the hand of God, the chosen race, the royal priesthood, the holy nation, and God's own people. Through Moses and Aaron, through Joshua and many others, God the Lord performed supernatural signs and miracles among them, beyond their power to grasp or express.

Yet they could not be preserved when in their depravity they fell away from God's law. What the Lord had foretold through Moses came over them in full measure. Every calamity under the sun overtook them, as it was written, that all the curses would come upon them—in the house, in the field, and everywhere—if they did not keep all God's commandments. The Lord would visit them with the sword of the enemy and with warfare; their oxen and

1649
Epistle to the churches at Alwinz and Bodock.

sheep would be slaughtered before their eyes, but they would not get any of it to eat. The Lord would smite them with consumption, fever, inflammation, and fiery heat, and with all kinds of incurable diseases; they would have to suffer violence and injustice all their lives. His wrath would not abate until he destroyed them and wiped them out.

All this was fulfilled a hundredfold. The Lord handed them over to their enemies, into Babylonian, Assyrian, and Chaldean captivity. Thousands were cruelly murdered by these same foreign peoples. Many thousands died of hunger and perished at the hands of their enemies in foreign lands in great wretchedness and anguish. As the prophets lament: O that my head were a well of water and my eyes a fountain of tears, that I might weep day and night for the slain of my people! Would to God that I were far away from people and had a dwelling place in the wilderness which is so completely burnt and devastated that no one passes through and the lowing of cattle is not heard. Birds and beasts have fled and gone. The dead bodies of men lie in the streets like dung on the open field, like mown grass after the mower, and there is none to bury them.

In another place it is said: They did not listen, O Lord, to your voice or obey your words. Therefore you have brought upon them all that you have threatened. Now they are exposed to the heat of the sun and the cold at night. They have died in terrible pain, by sword, famine, and pestilence. And the temple is destroyed on account of the evil done by the houses of Israel and Judah.

There are many stories and piteous laments that tell of their backsliding and unfaithfulness. All these were written as a warning and example for us so that we may be on our guard not to fall into the same sin, for we must take into account Christ the Lord's earnest words: "Unless you change, you will all perish in the same way." That is exactly what we have to expect.

Therefore, dear brothers and sisters and friends, I exhort and plead with all of you who have devout and zealous hearts and still stand firm, longing for the church's well-being: do not grow weary of building and planting but

1649
Epistle to the churches at Alwinz and Bodock.

continue to warn, admonish, and discipline. Thus the innocent will not make themselves party to the sins of others, nor will the thirsty be swept away with the drunken. As the Lord said to Israel: "No longer will I lead you to pasture. What is to die, let it die; what is to be lost, let it be lost."

We have to see and hear that not only the world lies in sin and evil. It is not only in the world that wickedness increases. Even in the church, especially among the young, many are bent on worldly ways and delight in wickedness. Some even loathe and oppose the order of the church. They lose the fear of God and tenderness of conscience; they despise diligence and honest hard work. It is terrible when this happens.

Believers should be spurred by their consciences to be diligent and faithful. The Lord meant every word when he said, "Open the gates so that a God-fearing people who strive for fidelity and truth may enter in." On the great day of judgment the Judge of the living and the dead will turn only to those who have been faithful and honest with all their hearts and say, "O you good and faithful servant and handmaid of the Lord, you have been trustworthy in small things." Faithfulness, diligence, and integrity are needed for salvation.

But all those who are lazy, unwilling, and unfaithful will be set at the left hand like the slothful, foolish virgins and the useless servant. They will be shut out and cut off from eternal joy and salvation. There is no denying that every tree that does not bear good fruit will be cut down and thrown into the fire. We must therefore do our utmost in our temporal as well as in our spiritual life and conduct to reaffirm our calling and election, for whoever is not faithful, honest, and zealous in small things will certainly not be so in great things.

It is dreadful when the punishment we spoke of comes to a people because of such backsliding—when war, murder, looting, burning, and all kinds of terror and suffering overtake them for their sins. Yet, however dreadful and horrible this may be, eternal punishment and damnation are many thousands of times more dreadful. All temporal suffering comes to an end, but damnation

1649
Epistle to the churches at Alwinz and Bodock.

never ceases. It will go on eternally, in that place where the smoke goes up for ever and ever and where men will long for death but will not be able to find it, for death will fly from them.

For this reason, all men who loved God have had an earnest concern to teach and warn of future punishment and torment, although these laborers for the Lord have all received small thanks from the world. The plain facts show that many of them were stoned to death or slashed to pieces; they were tortured or died by the sword. Christ the Lord himself laments over this when he says, "O Jerusalem, Jerusalem, you kill the prophets and stone those who are sent to you!" Hardly any died a natural death. Stephen asks, "Was there ever a prophet whom your fathers did not stone? They killed those who proclaimed the power and the future coming of Jesus Christ, and you have now betrayed and murdered him." Hatred of the true witnesses of God was so intense in the Israel of former times and still works with such effect in the world today that, as John says, "The scarlet woman of Babylon is drunk with the blood of the saints and witnesses to Jesus."

Only a few are left who witness to the pure truth and admonish the ungodly with God's Word. God the Lord has done what the world wanted. He has taken away the righteous and filled the world with false prophets of all kinds—black, gray, white, piebald—who now preach to the whole world and teach what it wants to hear. They say hypocritically, "We are all poor sinners, but God willing, we will all be saved." As a result, men continue in unrighteousness and are therefore robbed of eternal life.

I write this to you, most beloved brothers and sisters in the faith, because I have been informed that even among you some have so given way to their fallen nature and to unwatchfulness that they despise the service of the Gospel and its servants, thinking and speaking mockingly and disrespectfully about them. These people no longer treasure their salvation or the guidance given, and their indifference is a sure sign of decline. The same was true for Israel. First they accepted the bread from heaven joyfully and ate it with thanksgiving to God; later they

1649
Epistle to the churches at Alwinz and Bodock.

tired of it and grew dissatisfied. As soon as this happened, fiery serpents, the sword, and pestilence descended upon them, and many thousands perished.

Therefore we warn each one to put every effort into rooting out such thorns and thistles, first from his own heart and mind, then from the church. It is helpful to take as an example the men who loved God in their day. For instance, in the time of Joshua, when the people chose him as leader, they gathered round him and said, "As we obeyed Moses, so we will obey you. Where you send us, there we will go; what you command us, we will do. Whoever disobeys your words shall die." The virtuous, praiseworthy Judith also spoke to the elders of Bethulia in this sense: "You are the venerable elders of God's people (whose lives are in your hands), and you are the ones to whom the people look."

Those of old who loved God with devout hearts all held that teaching, counsel, and discipline are needed, with constant care and watchfulness. Without this, a people will certainly perish, as many examples prove. In Paradise, when God the Lord left Adam and Eve for a short time, the serpent was immediately there and misled them in the most evil way, bringing the wrath of God and their destruction upon them. And while Moses, the servant of the Lord, was away from the people of Israel for only a few days on Mount Sinai, what an appalling horror the tempter produced among them with the golden calf! And as long as Paul was with the people at Corinth and in Galatia, how holy and devout they were! But when he was away, how corrupt they became! They fell away and went utterly astray.

There are many examples, more than can be mentioned in a short space. They all show why the services and those who hold them should not be disregarded and despised, for the Lord Jesus says, "Whoever hears your words, hears me; whoever despises you, despises me; and whoever despises me, despises him who sent me." That was what Moses meant when he said to Israel, "You murmur not against us, but against the Lord," and Paul, when he says, "Whoever despises, despises not a man but God, who has sent his Holy Spirit in us." This is how

1649
Epistle to the churches at Alwinz and Bodock.

the matter stands. That this is true and that so much depends on it is clearly shown when God says to Moses, "Let me alone to vent my anger upon them so that I may consume them to a man." Who would have saved them if Moses had not pleaded for them? They would all have had to die. It was the same when they wanted to choose other leaders and return to Egypt. Had Moses not pleaded for them they would certainly all have been destroyed. Would not Miriam have had to remain a leper her life long if Moses had not pleaded for her?

Now what do God and Christ the Lord do in our time? God does not set temporal death aside, but he does something much greater: "If you forgive the sins of any, they are forgiven; if you retain the sins of any, they are retained" (RSV). For these compelling reasons, no one should be so impudent and ungodly as to despise the service and order God has given.

It was because of such despisal that Korah and his fellow rebels had to go down alive into hell, wailing and screaming. In the same way, forty-two good-for-nothing boys were torn to pieces by two fierce bears for mocking the man of God and calling him "baldhead." Do you not think that the same avenging God still lives and will punish such things in his own time? Even though the Lord delays for a time, yet his Word cannot fail. Anyone who attacks the anointed of the Lord attacks the apple of his eye. David, who refused to lay hands on Saul, the Lord's anointed, was granted the throne of the everlasting kingdom for his charity. He spared him, although Saul was his sworn enemy and relentlessly sought his life. David surely had thousandfold reason as well as the means and opportunity to avenge himself on Saul, yet he would neither take vengeance himself nor allow his warriors to offend Saul in any way.

From the beginning of the world, God's decree and order has been shown through Noah, Lot, Abraham, Moses, Joshua, the judges, and all the prophets, and later through Jesus Christ and the beloved apostles as well as the elders and Vorsteher of all churches to this very day. No flock has ever been able to remain on the right way without a shepherd. This has always been regarded as

1649
Epistle to the churches at Alwinz and Bodock.

good and necessary, and it remains so. A shepherd is as necessary as a schoolmaster for the young. Without discipline and order children turn out to be useless, irresponsible men and women, but through discipline and correction they become respected individuals. And so, most beloved brothers and sisters in the Lord, for all these reasons, it is right to demand that justice and order be upheld and that in the fear of God all efforts be made to show respect.

To begin with, those who have the leadership and pronounce judgment should speak with humility, clarity, and kindness. They should not interrupt each other but each should wait his turn and then speak plainly from a clear discernment so that after all have spoken, a just and sound judgment may be given. Thus in all things self-control and the fear of God should come first.

Now if those who are appointed to judge must strive to be trustworthy, orderly, and humble, how much more should those who deserve judgment for their mistakes and failures do the same! By rights they should await judgment in fear and trembling and not in any spirit of resentment or dissension. It is a sin and disgrace when someone who has done wrong persists in thinking he was right, when he argues in self-justification while being judged—still more so when he is standing before the church. That should never happen and should not be tolerated.

Is it not entirely out of place and disgraceful for two or three to argue and quarrel with each other when facing judgment? The apostle rightly says in a similar case, "Will they not say you are all mad if you all speak at once," each one of you shouting and vehemently trying to defend his own position? Christ our Lord does not teach us this, but says, "Blessed are they who hunger and thirst for righteousness." In this connection his words mean that if there is a quarrel between brothers or some wrongdoing that should come up for judgment, the matter is to be brought forward humbly. Those sitting in judgment must hear both sides and should be experienced in matters of judgment. The accusers and the accused must relinquish the judgment and let those who are impartial decide who

1649
Epistle to the churches at Alwinz and Bodock.

is right and who is wrong. All arguing should stop, and both sides should accept the judgment. The guilty one should admit his guilt willingly, and no one should be unwilling to let a guilty party be acquitted or continue to quarrel and so burden his soul with wrongdoing unto his own harm.

The law of the Lord certainly does not condone this. It is written: "If a controversy arises, go to the priests and to the judge in office and consult them. They will give you the verdict, and you shall do all that they say to you. You shall not turn aside from it either to the right or to the left. The priest or judge stands there in place of the Lord your God, and anyone who presumes to disobey him shall be stoned to death. All the people shall hear of it and be afraid and not act presumptuously anymore." No one should think that these affairs and disputes are recorded for nothing, but on the day of judgment and reckoning everything will be examined, and evildoers will be punished. It is easier for heaven and earth to pass away than for one letter or one iota to pass from the Word of God.

Further, I want to mention that I have now heard several times, both verbally and in writing, that some are causing unnecessary distress to those who with much pain and sadness have parted from us to join you, out of obedience leaving the community here [at Sabatisch] and their friends and relatives, only to be called "newcomers" by some who have no fear of God. What is worse, some even tell them, "If you had been worth anything, you would not have come here; you would never have been sent." How can it be good or right to add grief to those who are already grieving! Nor is there any truth in such remarks. We find it distressing enough to part with our people, and besides, we could use them very well ourselves. This kind of talk should stop, but if it takes place it should be dealt with immediately. If those concerned had any fear of God in them and thought of the Lord's words that at the last judgment people must give account for every idle word they have spoken, they would guard their tongues better. They should carefully consider the teaching of the Lord Jesus Christ: "Whatever

1649
Epistle to the churches at Alwinz and Bodock.

you wish men would do to you, do so to them." And Tobit teaches his son: "Do not do to anyone what you yourself would hate" (NEB).

Now since it is hard even for the righteous to be saved and, as Christ teaches, the way is so narrow that few find it, we have every reason to watch over and protect each other, and every believer is responsible to stand firm until death. That is why I am writing this appeal and admonition to you who belong to the church of God—to comfort the true and sincere of heart and to warn all who may be burdened by such temptations and errors. I write in love and trust, for my only longing is that we may all together reach the appointed goal in peace and joy. What I am saying is no different from what we here [at Sabatisch] teach daily by instruction and admonition, to help us improve and go forward on the way to eternal blessedness, since our weak human nature still hampers us poor creatures as long as we are in this earthly frame.

Because of my office and service, I wanted to write all this with my own hand to you, my most beloved brothers and sisters, who are entrusted to me and are most precious to my heart. I write with the confident hope and my heart's longing that should we not see each other face to face on this earth anymore, we may yet do so in eternal joy in the promised heavenly fatherland, in the presence of all holy and devout souls who fell asleep in the Lord long since and have gone before us. This I wish for us all from God through Jesus Christ. Amen.

With this letter I greet you all—every one of you—many times from the bottom of my heart with the peace of our Lord Jesus Christ. I commend you to God and to the Word of his grace. May he keep you and us, together with all those spread abroad under heaven, in his gracious protection at all times, and may he take you at his hour from this vale of tears into his heavenly peace. Amen. Amen.

Sabatisch, October 19, 1649

Andreas Ehrenpreis
Your brother in the Lord

In this same year, 1649, on December 10 between eleven and midnight, brother Ulrich Amssler, an old servant of the Word, fell asleep in the Lord at Kesselsdorf.

1649
Ulrich Amssler, a servant, passed away.

That year prices were very high. A peck of wheat cost two gulden and a peck of rye one and a half. At Sabatisch more than fifty of our children died of smallpox or measles.

Famine and disease.

1650

In the year 1650 on the night of March 14 between twelve and one o'clock our brother Georg Gaul, a servant of the Word, fell asleep in the Lord at Soblahof.

Georg Gaul, a servant, passed away.

On March 20, Oculi Sunday, two brothers were chosen for a time of testing in the service of the Word at Sabatisch: Andreas Binder, a Swiss sickle-maker, and Moses Würz from Moravia, a cooper.

2 brothers chosen for the service.

After many years of unfruitful negotiations between His Imperial Majesty and the Crown of Sweden, peace was finally restored in June and July of this year. The long-drawn-out, devastating war, about which we have reported a great deal, finally came to an end. On July 8 the Swedes withdrew from Olmütz and other fortresses, which they had held for eight years and four days.[1] They had taken considerable goods and precious things from these strongholds.

Peace made between the Holy Roman Emperor and Sweden.

On July 24 our brother Valtin Fischer, a servant of the Word, fell asleep in the Lord at Alwinz.

Valtin Fischer, a servant, passed away.

In November of this year our brothers who were working for lords in Moravia were once again expelled by the Provincial Diet at Brünn.

Our people moved out of Moravia.

[1]The Peace of Westphalia, which officially ended the Thirty Years War, was concluded on October 24, 1648, by two simultaneous treaties negotiated between the emperor and the imperial Estates at Osnabrück, and between representatives of the emperor and France and Sweden at Münster. That this chronicle records the restoration of peace two years later reflects the state of war that still prevailed.

1651–1665: Difficult Times Continue

1651

On March 15, 1651, the elders confirmed three brothers—Andreas Rosenberger, Jakob Rebstock, and Jakob Amssler—in the service of the Gospel with the laying on of hands at Sabatisch.

3 brothers confirmed in the service.

On the same day four brothers were chosen for the service of the Word and appointed for a time of testing. They were Christoph Adler, a head miller; Tobias Bersch, a weaver; and Jakob Kettenacker, a tailor; these three were from Moravia. The fourth, Christoph Baumhauer, a shoemaker, was from Silesia.

4 brothers chosen for the service.

On May 11 our brother Georg Geher, an old servant of the Gospel, fell asleep in the Lord at Alwinz in Transylvania. He was seventy-two years old and had been a servant for thirty-three years.

Georg Geher, a servant, passed away.

On May 17 our brother Joseph Stamler, a weaver from Moravia, was chosen for the service of the Word and appointed for a time of testing.

In addition, two brothers—Uhl Schauffelberger and Melchior Kleger—were chosen for the service for temporal affairs and appointed at Alwinz.

This year and continuing into the next, prices rose so high in Upper Hungary in the area of Bodock that a peck of grain sold for eight or nine gulden. The community here [at Sabatisch] and at Alwinz had to give so much help to our brothers at Bodock that all three communities were impoverished.

Famine at Bodock.

1652

On March 14, 1652, the elders confirmed two brothers, Andreas Binder and Moses Würz, in the service of the Gospel with the laying on of hands at Velké Leváre.

2 brothers confirmed in the service.

1652
Heavy rainfall.

In July there were unbelievably heavy rains in Hungary and Moravia.[1] Many people and much livestock drowned, and the hay and some crops rotted in the fields.

Fruitful year.

But the grain, grapes, and fruit did well, and a cask of wine sold for one gulden. The fall was very dry and continued so until Christmas.

Melchior Kleger passed away.

In November brother Melchior Kleger, a servant for temporal affairs, fell asleep in the Lord at Alwinz.

From December 10 until December 16 a comet with a scarcely visible tail was seen rising in the southeast, continuing its course westward and toward the north.[2] God alone will reveal its meaning.

1653

4 brothers confirmed in the service.

On March 16, 1653, four brothers—Christoph Adler, Tobias Bersch, Jakob Kettenacker, and Christoph Baumhauer—were confirmed in the service of the Gospel by the elders with the laying on of hands at Sabatisch.

Joseph Stamler confirmed in the service.

On June 2 brother Joseph Stamler was confirmed in the service of the Gospel by the elders with the laying on of hands at Alwinz.

Georg Leopold, a servant, passed away.

On August 7 an old servant of the Gospel, our brother Georg Leopold, fell asleep in the Lord at Dechtitz between two and three o'clock in the morning.

Moses Rapertshauser, a servant, passed away.

On December 26 brother Moses Rapertshauser, a servant of the Gospel, fell asleep in the Lord at Soblahof.

1654

Daniel Zwicker joined the church.

On May 31, 1654, a medical doctor named Daniel Zwicker came to Sabatisch with three other men from Danzig. There had already been correspondence with Zwicker, dealing largely

[1]*Theatrum Europaeum*, VII, 319: "It was no better in Moravia. . . . From July 18 to 22 there was unbelievably heavy rain, after which there was such a flood on July 23 that the whole countryside was under water. Houses and villages were swept away; people and cattle, even the reapers in the field, were drowned. And then, although the land was flooded for a whole week, the water ran off as quickly and suddenly as it had come. Within an hour no water was to be seen anymore, but after it had gone, there was the horrible sight of drowned people in the villages around. Masses, . . . in all a thousand people, were found dead." See also Beck, 484.

[2]*Theatrum Europaeum*, VII, 318: "The new, unusual star. . . lasted from December 19, 1652, to January 3, 1653." See also Beck, 484.

with points of faith. These four men traveled around the communities for ten days, asking many questions about every aspect of our life. Daniel Zwicker read the church's confession and the five articles of our faith. He saw that it was all truly Christian, accepted it, believed it, and confessed to it. He was then taken into the church by the elders with the laying on of hands and became our brother. *1654*

Since he was a learned and zealous man, the service of the Gospel was laid on him, and he was confirmed in it. He was to go to Prussia and Poland and wherever the Lord would show him an opportunity to visit the zealous, gather people for the Lord, and be fully used in this service as a faithful worker for men's salvation.[1]

Hailstorm and earthquake.

On July 10 between four and five in the morning, there was a severe hailstorm at Alwinz, Transylvania. The grain fields and vineyards were badly damaged. At the same time there was also a big earthquake.

Community begun at Mannheim in the Palatinate.

In October of this year we received word that it might be possible to start a community in the Palatinate, whereas in Hungary in many places we were not allowed to accept more people. So two brothers were sent to the count palatine in Heidelberg, and he received us in a friendly way.[2] Following

---

[1]Dr. Daniel Zwicker, born 1612 in Danzig, originally a Socinian (anti-Trinitarian) who had met Hutterite missioners in Prussia between 1648 and 1650. About correspondence between Andreas Ehrenpreis and Zwicker (1649, 1650, 1654), see Friedmann, *Schriften*, 112 #10 a, b. After failing in his attempt to unite the Polish Brethren (who held Socinian beliefs) with the Hutterian church, Zwicker moved to Holland in 1657 and devoted himself to writing. He died in Amsterdam in 1678. See *ME*, IV, 1051; Beck, 487–492; Leonard Gross, "The Hutterian Brethren and the Polish Brethren: Rapprochement and Estrangement," *The Proceedings of the Unitarian Universalist Historical Society*, Vol. 20, Part 2 (1986), 46–53.

[2]The two brothers sent to Heidelberg to the count palatine Karl Ludwig were Johannes Rieger and Heinrich Habereuter, both from Sabatisch. The following year, on September 8, 1655, two more brothers from Sabatisch, Jakob Amssler and Christoph Baumhauer, were sent to Heidelberg to conclude a contract which enabled them to start a community at Mannheim, Germany. For details of the contract, dated October 8/18, 1655, see Beck, 492 n. The community at Mannheim existed until 1684; *ME*, III, 469.

The description of "Hungarian Anabaptists," in Grimmelshausen, *Simplicissimus*, Book V, ch. 19 (not included in Goodrick's translation, *The Adventurous Simplicissimus*), is evidence of the writer's acquaintance with Hutterite community life. Elizabeth Bender, in "Grimmelshausen and the Hutterites," *Mennonite Life* (Oct. 1963), 187–189 (which contains a partial translation of said chapter 19), supports Zieglschmid's conclusion that Grimmelshausen must have known the Mannheim Hutterites. See also Zieglschmid, "Die ungarischen Wiedertäufer bei Grimmelshausen," *Publications of the Modern Language Association*, LIV (Dec. 1939), 1031–1040; Robert Friedmann, "Grimmelshausen," *ME*, II, 583–584.

1654

this, we were offered a place in the city of Mannheim, which we accepted, and then we began to build. May God the Lord bless the work and make it fruitful to his praise.

Hans Kern passed away.

On November 9 brother Hans Kern, an old servant for temporal affairs, fell asleep in the Lord at Velké Leváre.

1655

Hans Gebhart passed away.

On January 3, 1655, at one o'clock in the afternoon, brother Hans Gebhart, a servant for temporal affairs, fell asleep in the Lord at Kesselsdorf.

Johannes Hilscher chosen for the service.

On March 21 of that year brother Johannes Hilscher from Moravia, who was responsible for the millers, was chosen for the service of the Gospel and appointed for a time of testing at Sabatisch.

2 brothers chosen for the service.

On April 20, also at Sabatisch, two brothers, Andreas Winter and Heinrich Wiser, were chosen for the service of the Gospel and appointed for a time of testing. Both were tailors from Moravia.

270 of our people died.

During the month of September a terrible epidemic swept through the land, causing many deaths.[1] At Velké Leváre our people suffered great pain and misery, and about two hundred and seventy died a pitiful death. One of them was brother Klaus Messner, a servant of the Word and elder there. He fell asleep in the Lord on October 20.

Klaus Messner, a servant, passed away.

1656

3 brothers confirmed in the service.

On November 5, 1656, three brothers—Johannes Hilscher, Andreas Winter, and Heinrich Wiser—were confirmed in the service of the Gospel by the elders with the laying on of hands at Sabatisch.

1657

Uhl Schauffelberger passed away.

On January 6, 1657, brother Uhl Schauffelberger, a servant for temporal affairs, fell asleep in the Lord at Alwinz in Transylvania.

Johannes Egel passed away.

On April 11 our brother Johannes Egel, a servant for temporal affairs, fell asleep in the Lord at St. Johannes.

---

[1]Beck, 494; *Theatrum Europaeum*, VII, 1029–1030.

Around New Year, 1657, Prince Rákóczi set out from Transylvania with a large army to assist the king of Sweden against the Poles. But the king of Denmark came on the scene, with the result that the Swedes were forced to stop fighting the Poles and went to fight against Denmark. Prince Rákóczi was defeated by the Poles and the Tartars. Most of his army, including their general Janos Kemeny, were led as prisoners into Tartary. Prince Rákóczi himself fled from Poland and returned home utterly defeated.[1]

1657
War.

1658

On February 13, 1658, a servant of the Word, our brother Christoph Adler, fell asleep in the Lord at Sabatisch.

Christoph Adler, a servant, passed away.

On March 1 two brothers were chosen for the service of the Gospel and appointed at Alwinz for a time of testing: Benjamin Poley, a potter, and Christel Lerch, a tailor. And on May 7 Jakob Weiss, another potter, was also appointed at Alwinz to the same service.[2]

3 brothers chosen for the service.

Around Whitsun of that year, a colonel of the imperial army, Count Sternberg, entered Hungary with an army of five thousand German soldiers. They did great damage in the Schütt Islands. There they ruined many crops in the field, with the result that the people had no harvest and could neither sow nor plant in the fall. Toward winter the troops went back into Moravia; why they had come into Hungary no one ever found out.

During the same year, the principality of Transylvania was overrun by Turks and Tartars. With their pillaging, burning, and massacring, they did terrible damage. They took thousands of lives, led off countless numbers of people and animals, and devastated the land. At this time Alwinz, where our people

Transylvania overrun with soldiers.

---

[1]George Rákóczi II, Prince of Transylvania (1648–1660); see Beck, 494–495.

[2]In the "1581" codex of this chronicle, "March 1" was covered over and "May 5" written in; "Alwinz" was also covered over.

Wolkan, *Geschicht-Buch*, 645, gives the date for Benjamin Poley and Christel Lerch as March 5 and the place as Sabatisch.

Beck, 495 b, reads in translation: "On March 31, 1658, at Sabatisch three brothers were chosen and appointed to the service of the Word for a time of testing: Benjamin Poley, a potter; Christel Lerch, a tailor (both born in the community); Balzer Wallner, a tailor; and on May 7 at Alwinz Jacob Weiss, a potter from Moravia. Balzer, however, was relieved of the service at Tschäskowitz half a year later, at his earnest request.

1658

were living, was set on fire and our community almost completely burned down. Just before the attack, the brothers had brought in their grain crops and hastily threshed and stored about one hundred pecks. The hay and straw went up in flames along with everything else. Our people fled to the castle. Eternal praise and thanks to God the Lord, who so graciously protected and saved them. He kept them together so that not one was taken prisoner and led away by these evil people. Besides this fear and misery that weighed on them, our people had to pay 115 gulden in taxes.

Brothers fled to the castle.

1659

Hans Friedrich, a servant, passed away.

On December 10, 1659, at ten in the morning our brother Hans Friedrich,[1] an outstanding servant of the Gospel, fell asleep in the Lord at Kesselsdorf. He had faithfully served the church for nineteen years as servant of the Word.

During the year, Prince Rákóczi made war on his enemies in Hungary as well as on the Turks and Tartars who invaded Transylvania.[2] With the help of the Turks, Barcagoss[3] was trying to seize the principality from Prince Rákóczi by force, and the country was in extreme danger. Barcagoss was defeated, but he escaped into Turkey and returned with several hundred Turks, set himself up in Hermannstadt, and defended himself with their help. Thereupon Prince Rákóczi came with a large army and laid siege to the city from Christmastime right into the spring. But then the Turks arrived with such a great force that he had to raise the siege. Meanwhile the community at Alwinz was attacked yet again by Hungarian soldiers and robbed and plundered. Ten horses were taken and the grain and hay used up as fodder. Although several brothers remained at the place, not one of them was harmed; the others had all fled to the castle. The brothers had to pay five hundred imperial talers in taxes.

Alwinz plundered several times.

---

[1]Hans Friedrich Küntsche, servant of the Word since 1641 (p.736 above), wrote a large number of teachings still extant and used by the Hutterian Brethren today, e.g. on Isaiah 58 (1658), Acts 2 (1659), and Romans 8 (1656). See Friedmann, *Schriften*, 167–169; *ME*, III, 259–260; Beck, 496.

[2]About the Turkish invasion of Transylvania, see *Theatrum Europaeum*, VIII, 1007; Beck, 496–497.

[3]Protégé of the Turks, who made him a prince; see Beck, 496.

1660

1660

On March 4, 1660, two brothers, Christel Lerch and Benjamin Poley, were confirmed in the service of the Gospel by the elders with the laying on of hands at Sabatisch. Johannes Milder,[1] a tailor, was appointed for a time of testing.

2 brothers confirmed, 1 brother chosen for the service.

On May 2 Jakob Weiss of Alwinz was confirmed in the service of the Gospel at Sabatisch.

1 brother confirmed in the service.

In May, General de Souches[2] entered Hungary with the imperial army. There was much talk and speculation as to why they came south, but their purpose never became clear. They camped all summer and fall in fortifications not far from Tokaj[3] by the Tisza River, where many of them died a wretched death. Rumor had it that they were bitten to death by poisonous snakes that appeared among them and by large horseflies that swarmed up from the Tisza. Those who were left returned sick and miserable to Moravia.

In June Prince Rákóczi attacked the Turks in the decisive battle of Klausenburg.[4] He fought valiantly and with knightly heroism for the fatherland, striking down a number of Turks with his own hand, but in the end he lost his own life.[5]

Prince Rákóczi met his death.

Soon after Prince Rákóczi's death, the Turks marched with a large army of fifty thousand men on Grosswardein and laid siege to it, but all their attacks were repulsed. As those in the fortress had no hope of help or relief, and as the hordes of Turks continually increased and fired unremittingly from heavy guns, they were forced to make an agreement to surrender. On August 27 the Turks took them with three hundred loaded wagons under convoy as far as Debritz. Thus the fortress of Grosswardein fell into Turkish hands.

---

[1]Johannes Milder was to succeed Johannes Rieger as Vorsteher in 1687. He passed away on March 28, 1688. See Zieglschmid, *Klein-Geschichtsbuch*, 222; *ME*, III, 687.

[2]Ludwig Raduit de Souches (1608–1683), Austrian field marshal, who won the battle of Lewenz (Levice, approx. 23 miles southeast of Nitra), July 19, 1664 (p.789 below). See *Allgemeine Deutsche Biographie*, XXXIV, 698–700; Beck, 497, 516.

[3]Tokaj, east Hungary, near the confluence of the Bodrog and the Tisza rivers.

[4]About Prince George Rákóczi II and the battle of Klausenburg (Cluj, Romania), see *Theatrum Europaeum*, VIII, 1388; Beck, 497.

[5]George Rákóczi II was succeeded by Francis Rákóczi I (1645–1676), who converted to Catholicism and delivered the Hutterian community at Bodock (Sárospatak), Hungary, into the hands of the Jesuits. From then on little is reported about the Hutterites at Bodock (see entry for May 1662, p.773 below), whereas the Hutterian Bruderhof at Alwinz, Transylvania, existed until about 1764.

1660
Heinrich Wiser, a servant, passed away.

On August 3 our brother Heinrich Wiser, servant of the Word, was traveling from Kesselsdorf to Sabatisch. On his way home through the mountains he was badly beaten by a robber, and on August 8 at one o'clock in the morning, he fell asleep in the Lord at Kesselsdorf.

Johannes Spengler passed away.

On September 5 at two o'clock in the morning, our brother Johannes Spengler, a servant for temporal affairs, fell asleep in the Lord at Tschäskowitz.

Michael Milder, a servant, passed away.

On December 6 between two and three in the afternoon, our brother Michael Milder, a servant of the Gospel, fell asleep in the Lord at Kesselsdorf.

2 brothers imprisoned for their faith.

On August 8 two brothers, Georg Schultes and Moses Würz, traveled from Mannheim in the lower Palatinate to the church to seek advice. On August 18 they left for home, but on the way they were taken prisoner for the sake of their faith at Vilshofen in Bavaria. They were held in harsh conditions and their captors intended to torture them, but since they had a pass from His Serene Highness the Elector, issued at Heidelberg, inquiries were sent to the government at Munich, and at the end of ten days' imprisonment the order came for their release. Thus God delivered them from prison. They were, however, escorted for twelve miles through Bavaria by the constable and had to submit to that.

They were set free.

1661

In the year 1661 a comet with a dim, pointed tail above it was visible from January 23 to February 10, moving ahead of the morning star.[1] It was seen every day at Sabatisch from four o'clock in the morning until daylight.

Brother confirmed in the service.

On March 13 brother Johannes Milder was confirmed in the service of the Gospel by the elders with the laying on of hands at Sabatisch.

2 brothers chosen for the service.

On the same day two brothers were chosen for the service of the Word and appointed for a time of testing; they were Hansel Esdras, a clerk born in Moravia, and Andreas Kuen, a cutler born in Hungary.

On May 6, sixteen thousand German soldiers from the imperial army advanced over the Little Carpathians into

[1]Beck, 498; *Theatrum Europaeum*, IX, 319.

Hungary. They cost the church much in bread, wine, beer, salt, oats, and gifts for the bodyguards. *1661*

On May 29 two regiments of dragoons crossed the Little Carpathians, following the previous troops. Once again, the church suffered. On June 7 yet another army of several thousand German imperial soldiers marched over the Little Carpathians into Hungary, again costing the church huge quantities of beer, wine, bread, oats, and cooked food. In addition there was the cost of the special food consumed by the officers who moved into our community. These three contingents cost our community at Sabatisch seventy-eight gulden in ready money for the bodyguards alone; the contribution of knives amounted to seventy gulden more, not counting pottery and other articles.

Great expense for the church.

In July a Turkish pasha led a large army into Transylvania, and they camped on the brothers' fields at Alwinz, not far from our houses. But with the help of God our people fled to the fortress, taking most of their belongings with them. Some of our brothers were still in the yard with three wagons when the enemy arrived, but God the Almighty made it possible for them to get the three laden wagons onto the bridge, and in this way they blocked the enemies' pursuit. While the Turks unharnessed the animals and pushed the loaded wagons into the Maros River, our brothers made their escape. Meanwhile our community, which had only just been rebuilt, was set on fire in several places; not only house, stable, and barn were burned but also the precious grain. Nearly all the grain had been cut, and a good part (about four hundred stooks) carried from the fields across the stream to the fortress. The brothers did not want to risk bringing it to our place and hoped it would be safe there. But it was all burned and ruined, not only in the fields but everywhere. Not even a handful of grain was left.

Enemy came to Alwinz.

Grain was burned.

During this raid, one brother was killed, and two others taken prisoner. One, however, regained his freedom and returned to the church community. So through God's help, not more than one soul was carried off. Praise be to God in all eternity that in spite of everything, he gave us such protection. But our people had to remain in the fortress, miserable in their worry and poverty. An epidemic broke out, and the best of our craftsmen died. In all we lost 150 people during this time.

1 brother killed, 1 carried off.

150 people died of plague.

1661
Took the community's livestock.

In October of this year the Turkish forces withdrew and returned home, causing tremendous damage wherever they passed. They discovered such animals as we still had—cows and sheep—and stole them even from quite near the fortress. So our people lost all their livestock and were left with nothing. That fall they could neither plant nor sow but had to remain in the fortress. We may well grieve over such misery, but nonetheless we should thank God for keeping our people together; no one was taken away.

On October 31 another force of a thousand German imperial soldiers, the Götz regiment, crossed the Little Carpathians from Hungary and made their way to Skalitz and then on to Moravia and Silesia. Again the church had to bear the exorbitant cost of provisions and other things.

On December 31 General Spurk, who had marched into Hungary with an army three thousand strong, returned over the Little Carpathians with a wretched little band of 180 men. Many soldiers had frozen to death in the snow and perished miserably. And again the church could not avoid the cost of provisions.

So this year 1661, which had brought the church much fear and anxiety, ended in grief. Yet God the Almighty stood by us and protected us. To him alone be all honor and glory.

1662

Hans Schütz passed away.

At midnight of February 10, 1662, brother Hans Schütz, an old steward and servant for temporal affairs, fell asleep in the Lord at Protzka.

Joseph Lercher, a servant, passed away.

On March 7 between seven and eight in the evening, brother Joseph Lercher, a servant of the Word, fell asleep in the Lord with a peaceful heart at Dechtitz.

Andreas Binder, a servant, passed away.

On March 19 at four o'clock in the morning, brother Andreas Binder, a servant of the Word, fell asleep in the Lord at Farkeschin.

Earthquake.

On March 20 at about three in the morning there was a terrible earthquake at Vienna, which lasted half an hour.

That same day there was a bad storm at Korneuburg. The sexton, who was supposed to be warding off the storm by ringing the bells, was struck by lightning and killed. God alone knows what this means.

On May 16, the same year, a cold spell set in with strong winds, snow, and frost. This lasted until May 23. Although the grapes, fruit, and berries had looked very promising and the grain in the fields was mostly in flower and as fine as one could wish, in many places everything was frozen and ruined. So the cold was followed by a time of famine. Three gulden fifteen groschen and more had to be paid for a Senitz peck of wheat, two gulden sixty groschen for rye, two gulden for barley, and fifteen groschen and more for oats. A cask of wine cost five gulden and more. The church community was badly affected, for at Velké Leváre, Protzka, and St. Johannes they had nothing but empty straw to harvest.

1662
Frost and cold.

Prices rose.

In May of this year the Hungarian nobility met at Pressburg for a Provincial Diet, and His Majesty the Emperor arrived on May 23 to attend it.

Emperor attended the Provincial Diet at Pressburg.

During this month there were two earthquakes at Bodock that were severe enough to shake the buildings. This was surely sent by God for some purpose.

2 earthquakes at Bodock.

On June 14 there was a very bad hailstorm at Sabatisch. Hailstones as big as pigeons' eggs fell down, and lightning struck a neighbor's mill, burning it to the ground with the house and the stables.

Hailstorm at Sabatisch.

During June and July, large numbers of German soldiers again came north out of Hungary. They were quartered in the villages on both sides of the mountains and had to be supplied with provisions for a long time, and the church was expected to contribute. In addition, the soldiers did considerable damage.

Many soldiers came from Hungary.

On August 1, 1662, at a quarter past nine in the morning, our dear, faithful brother Andreas Ehrenpreis fell asleep in the Lord at Sabatisch with a peaceful heart and clear conscience. He was a loyal, devout, and zealous servant of the Gospel and Vorsteher of the whole church of God.

Andreas Ehrenpreis fell asleep in the Lord.

On July 28, four days before his death, he spoke the following words to the elders who had come to visit him on his sickbed:

"Dear brothers, the time has come when I feel and hope that the Lord will soon release me, for I am very weak.

"So first of all I want to declare to you that to the best of

Andreas Ehrenpreis's last words.

1662
Andreas Ehrenpreis's last words.

my knowledge I stand before God the Lord with nothing burdening my soul, in spite of the weaknesses with which I, like everyone else, have had to struggle. From the moment I surrendered myself to God, I strove at all times and in every matter to serve wholeheartedly, especially when I was a servant of the Gospel and when I was entrusted with the burden of caring for the whole church. In matters that came up for judgment, I have tried to deal justly with everyone. I know of nothing between myself and anyone else that I am not at peace about or that was not cleared up with the brotherhood. If it was sometimes necessary to speak sharply to this one or that, I did it for his good so that each would be mindful of his or her calling.

"With regard to you, my fellow servants, who have assisted me in the service of the Word and often taken counsel with me about the community's needs, I ask your forgiveness for any time I have hurt you. Please do not hold it against me if I spoke too curtly or with irritation, which could very easily have happened. I am well content with each one of you, without exception, and I thank you for the obedience and loyal support you have shown in serving with me.

"Above all, my beloved brothers, I commend to you the faithful care of the church. Watch over her and neglect nothing, keeping steadfastly to the teaching. You can see that corruption is spreading in the community. Do not let the way be lost completely and the old boundary stones moved!

"See to it that the true Ordnungen of old are observed so that the church is firmly grounded and sustained in peace, for it has been sealed by the blood of many martyrs, and beyond a doubt the foundation is well laid. If we follow the path taken by our devout forefathers, none of us will come to shame.

"I beg you, dear brothers who carry the service of the Gospel and are appointed as shepherds and teachers for others, beware of quarrels and division so that no disunity arises among you, which could lead to rebellion among the people, causing strife and separation. As soon as you notice any sign of a disturbance, try to overcome it before it gains ground.

"I greatly fear that there will be a serious split in the community. Keep careful watch over the young and inexperienced so that they do not rush headlong to their own ruin. Seek to root out what is evil in them and implant what is good.

1662
Andreas Ehrenpreis's last words.

"Look after the sick and old, widows and orphans, and all the afflicted.

"Again and again it has been painfully evident how the enemy and tempter of the human race concentrates all his powers on sowing noxious weeds in profusion throughout the Lord's church. Therefore be on your guard and turn to God continually in prayer, for if ever there was a time when prayer was needed, it is now, especially when we see how powerfully evil has increased in these last perilous days.

"The Lord is often moved by diligent prayer to send his help and show us mercy, so it is essential not to slacken in prayer when wickedness is gaining the upper hand, not only outside our communities but inside as well.

"Now with the hands of my heart I take leave of you all and entrust you to the mighty hand of God. May he help you to be true fighters until your blessed end.

"I ask you to say farewell on my behalf to everyone in the church, including those who are on lonely outposts, serving on manorial estates, for they serve in the fear of God out of obedience to the church and, as far as it is fitting, to the authorities. May the Lord in heaven reward them!

"Accept my sincere thanks for all the kindness and loyalty shown me by everyone.

"Lastly, greet all the dear brothers and sisters a thousand times with the peace of Jesus Christ. May he in his mercy take you all into his gracious protection. I do not need to suggest anyone to take my place in the leadership when I am gone. Choose the one God shows you. It is much more profitable and reassuring for you to choose by making a unanimous witness.

"The Lord will surely respond to your fervent prayers and provide you with another faithful shepherd. This I wish you from God the Almighty through Jesus Christ. Amen."

Then the brothers who had gathered around him in his last illness responded to his words and testified that he had done his utmost to lead the church in the fear of God as long as it had been entrusted to him. May the Lord in his steadfast love reward him on the last day.

With tears in their eyes, the brothers expressed their deep gratitude and blessed him with the peace of Christ.

1662

Then dear brother Andreas spoke once more: "As we will not see each other again on this earth, may the Lord grant that we may see each other in the kingdom of grace. Amen."

Thus, as has been recorded, he fell peacefully asleep in the Lord at a quarter past nine on the morning of August 1.

Only two hours earlier he had called together all the elders and servants of the Word who had come to Sabatisch to stand by him during his illness. He declared that he stood before God with a good conscience and was at peace with all brothers and sisters, and he commended the church to their care. His mind remained clear until the end.

He was seventy-three years old and had faithfully carried out the service of the Gospel for forty-one years. He had led the church with great dedication as a true shepherd and elder for twenty-three years, giving teaching, admonition, and discipline.[1]

Since God the Almighty, according to his loving will, had released dear brother Andreas from this vale of tears, and the church could not be left long without a shepherd, the elders (servants of the Word and servants for temporal affairs), stewards, storekeepers, work distributors, and many other trusted brothers, gathered as soon as possible at Sabatisch. In the fear of God the Almighty, they prayed that he would show us another devout and faithful shepherd.

Johannes Rieger became elder.

By unanimous testimony this service of leading and serving the church as a faithful shepherd was entrusted to dear brother Johannes Rieger on August 8.

Hailstorm.

On August 14, 1662, there was a terrible hailstorm at Auspitz in Moravia that killed many deer, sheep, hares, and other animals.

Our people at Alwinz left the fortress.

That same month things were quiet in Transylvania as far as the Turks were concerned, so our people at Alwinz had some respite. On August 21 they left the fortress and returned to their homes, where they lived in huts that they put up between the burned-out walls.

The Turkish pasha gave them a letter safeguarding them from marauding Turks. God in his mercy provided help throughout this time. To him alone be praise.

---

[1]About Andreas Ehrenpreis, see above, p.682 n.; Beck, 502–503.

On August 18 the Provincial Diet ended its session at Pressburg, and the nobles from Transylvania returned home, greatly dissatisfied because nothing had been accomplished. *1662* Diet ended its session at Pressburg.

On October 3 one thousand German imperial soldiers came through Hungary, crossed the Little Carpathians, and went on to Skalitz. They did great damage everywhere, emptying the poor people's underground stores and starting fires in several villages when they did not get what they wanted. This brought further loss to the church. Soldiers.

On November 10 at three in the morning a bloodred sword was seen in the sky by many people in Sabatisch and the surrounding villages. Its point was toward the west and its hilt toward the east. God knows its meaning. Bloodred sword in the sky.

That same month another thousand German imperial soldiers, coming from Transylvania, crossed the Little Carpathians. Although many of them met a miserable death, they caused great damage all around. Soldiers.

So this year of 1662 ended in widespread terror of the troops moving back and forth. The soldiers were meant to be fighting the Turks, but all they achieved was to ruin the country. They left famine and hunger in their wake among the poor population; for instance, near Bodock one peck of grain cost seven or eight gulden. Famine.

1663

On January 6, 1663, in the bitter-cold weather, 1500 German imperial soldiers crossed the Little Carpathians to Skalitz. Many froze to death in the snow; forty were found dead along a half-mile stretch of road in a field at Tyrnau. Still, great damage was done wherever the soldiers passed. 40 soldiers frozen to death in the snow.

On February 25 two brothers, Hansel Esdras and Andreas Kuen, were confirmed in the service of the Gospel by the elders with the laying on of hands at Sabatisch. 2 brothers confirmed in the service.

On May 18 in the early morning, before sunrise, the semblance of a pillar was seen in the sky ahead of the sun. It stood above the sun and was of three colors—red, green, and yellow. This was a foreboding of approaching disaster. Pillar in the sky.

In the same month, work on the fortification of Vienna was continued. Many beautiful gardens and pavilions were torn down. A space had to be cleared to the distance of a musket shot from the city walls, so everything was demolished. Fortifications at Vienna.

1663

The town crier announced that all inhabitants of the city must stock enough provisions for a year. Anyone unable to do so must leave the city and move elsewhere.

The citizens were ordered to raise a huge sum of money, up to 100,000 gulden, and to provide food and lodging for a garrison of 60,000 men in the city, which would mean bringing in something like 60,000 bushels of rye and oats.

Imperial mass levy.

On June 7 His Imperial Majesty called for a mass levy from all Estates in Hungary to fight the perennial foe, emphasizing that this kingdom had been the first to be attacked as it was closest to these cruel enemies.[1] For the last two hundred years they had fought with dauntless valor to defend themselves and all Christendom, risking life and limb for the cause. So His Imperial Majesty did not doubt that they would do the same for their dear fatherland, for house and home, for wife and children—indeed, for their own lives and liberty—and give their utmost for this purpose.

Ring around the sun.

On June 8 a ring of many colors was seen around the sun from twelve o'clock until after three. Around the periphery of the sun, inside the ring, there appeared to be a dark cloud as if threatening rain. Many people wondered at the sight and took it for a special sign, as it was visible around the sun right in the middle of the day. It was more frightening than anything within living memory. God knows the meaning.

On July 7, all lords, nobles, and landowners were called up and required to supply one foot soldier for every twenty men to fight against the perennial foe, the Turks. The recruits marched to Neutra for the mustering and were a considerable burden on the church community. May God have mercy on devout Christians and on all oppressed souls.

Hungarian estates mustered at Sered.

On July 8 the Hungarian levies from the Branc estates, on their way to the muster at Sered or Schindau, passed through our community at Dechtitz, causing great disturbance to our people in the yard and knocking down doors as if it were a full-scale robbery. Suddenly God sent such a violent storm that the ruffians fled in terror.

---

[1]From this point on (at fol. 560v; Zieglschmid, *Chronik*, 873), a number of leaves of the "1581" codex are damaged in varying degrees. Zieglschmid supplies detailed footnotes explaining the damage and restoration of text (in at least one case leading to repetition; see below, pp.780–781), which he indicates with brackets. This translation follows his reading (which coincides with Beck, 505–511 passim) but dispenses with brackets. Ellipses indicate missing text that has not been restored.

1663
Flight from Farkeschin. Everything lost.

In August 1663, when the imperial troops were moving back and forth around Schindau our people from Farkeschin also took flight, some making for Tyrnau and others for Bibersburg Castle. They had to clear out their community completely and leave, fleeing to Kesselsdorf with their oxen, cows, and sheep. They stayed there until the enemy attacked Kesselsdorf and made off with their animals as well as other people's.

After Farkeschin was sacked and plundered, our houses there were burned to the ground. Hardly any of our people from Farkeschin survived; they were lost in the unending warfare. Most of them died on the continual flights. So we lost our community at Farkeschin. Everything was gone—people and goods and chattels.

On August 7 the Hungarians attacked the Turkish camp near Parkan but suffered a devastating defeat. The loss was estimated at four thousand men.

When the Turks had driven back Count Fargasch[1] and his men and buried most of them on the battlefield at Parkan, the way was clear for them to attack the fortress at Neuhäusel, which they had wanted to do for a long time. So they advanced with their whole army, estimated at 70,000 men or more (including 10,000 Tartars, 6000 Walloons, and 4000 Moldavians), bringing 130 pieces of artillery with them.

Troops.

On August 17 Neuhäusel was in plain sight of the whole Turkish army. They laid siege to it and started a heavy attack on the fortress, drawing up a battery and bombarding the walls with cannon fire. The Tartars waged an even fiercer battle throughout the Neuhäusel district and the neighboring area, burning to the ground every hamlet and village as far as the Waag River. They killed every living thing they met except for the women, whom they kept as slaves. That was the first thing they did. And since the Turks had razed everything to the ground for miles around Neuhäusel and had left very little for themselves to live on, they looked for an easy route to cross the Waag and March rivers into Moravia.

Freistadt taken.

On September 2 the enemy attacked Freistadt with robbery, slaughter, and burning.

---

[1]Probably Count Adam Forgács (1601–1681), who defended Neuhäusel against the Turks and was defeated. About the battle of Parkan (Štúrovo) on the Danube (opposite Esztergom), see *Theatrum Europaeum*, IX, 947–948.

1663

After the brutal murderers had encamped, to recover a bit from their strenuous expedition, hunger drove these Tartar hordes to start out again for the Waag and see how the Moravian pastures would agree with their stomachs.

Enemy crossed the Waag.

There was a traitor, however, who offered to show them a shallow place where their horses could swim across, and they forded the river at once in a mighty swarm on September 3.[1]

The fear, misery, desperate flight, and death caused by this Tartar invasion in Hungary, Austria, and especially in Moravia, defy description. All one could see from a distance was fire everywhere. The whole country was reduced to ashes and blood by these murderous evildoers, who killed young and old men alike. They dashed helpless children against the walls, raped the women, high- and lowborn alike, and took great crowds of them naked into captivity. They threw them over their horses' backs and roamed far and wide across the land until they met with resistance. By taking another direction they managed to carry many thousands of Christians out of those countries into the wretchedness of slavery.

This terrible wave of fear, misery, and death also struck the church of the Lord with great force. Our farms and houses on the other side of the mountains were attacked and pillaged without warning.

35 souls carried off from Dechtitz.

On September 3 the Turks and Tartars quite unexpectedly invaded the country on this side of the Waag and swept down on Dechtitz at half past ten in the morning. . . . Thirty-five people from our community there, men and women, boys and girls, were taken into captivity in foreign lands, among them brother Christel Lerch, a servant of the Word, and his wife Catharina Rupertshauser. Two brothers, the head weaver Christoph Engelhart and the potter Solomon Stauder, were struck down and killed. Then the buildings were set on fire, and all household supplies, tools, and grain stored inside were burned. The grain remaining in the fields was ruined, and all our cattle, sheep, and hogs were stolen. All the following brothers and sisters were struck down and killed: Johannes Bletscher, a tailor's apprentice; Klaus Bletscher, a smith's

[1]About this incident the town clerk of Schässburg (Sighisoara), Romania, Georg Kraus (*Fontes Rerum Austriacarum*, Script. IV. 2), reports: "A scoundrel named Jacob Nitzai, a man from Tyrnau and a border hussar, who had become a real Turk, led the enemy into Moravia, showing them all the passes and all the highroads and byroads." See Beck, 507.

1663

apprentice; Hansel Miller, a shoemaker's apprentice; Heinrich Schmidt and Jakob Miller, both potter's boys; Andreas Gans, from the school; Marie, the school seamstress; Marie, the cook; Katharina, the children's nurse; Katharina, the weaver; Katharina, the herdsmaid; Susanna Wollman; Solomon Stauder, a potter from Sabatisch. Abraham, a potter from Sabatisch, was carried off.

A total of thirty-five people were either carried into captivity by the enemy or killed. Then the buildings were set on fire, and all household supplies, tools, and grain stored inside were burned. The grain remaining in the fields was ruined and all the cattle, sheep, and hogs were stolen and driven off: 25 head of cattle, 250 sheep, 40 hogs, and 6 horses. Some were taken by the Croatians in the imperial army and others by the Turks in the course of this autumn.

Loss of livestock.

Those of our people who stayed at Gutwasser Castle suffered intense fear and distress. Eighteen people, old and young, died a miserable death there. Then the cold of winter drove us from the castle back to the shacks still standing on the site of our burned-out homes. That winter we had to endure much fear and distress, abuse and robbery, from the marauding Hungarian mercenaries and hussars. There was no protection to be found anywhere, and people suffered terrible hunger, misery, and death.

Raid on Kesselsdorf.

Exactly the same happened on that same day at our community in Kesselsdorf. Between ten and eleven in the morning some of our people who were in the yard were attacked quite unexpectedly by the Turks and Tartars. Most of our people were at home, hoping to bring the rest of the grain and other stores to the castle. They ran to the pond in an attempt to escape, but in their terror some did not know where to go. They ran out into the fields toward the castle to save themselves from the dreaded enemy, but they could not run fast enough.

Stoffel, the head wheelwright, and an old sister Asanath, who cared for the school children, were killed. The following were carried off into captivity: Brother Andreas Winter, two children, his oldest daughter Esther, and... Esther Tuchschneider (a clothcutter's wife) and her youngest daughter.... Anna Kretz was murdered at Gertwellisch. Johannes Lochmair, the head potter from Farkeschin, was also murdered at Kesselsdorf; his

1663

Marie Toblin was captured. Heinrich, the head miller from Farkeschin, was killed.

At Kesselsdorf 46 people fell into the enemy's hands. Various goods as well.

Within fifteen minutes these pagan tyrants had laid hands on forty-six of our people, who were carried off in misery or murdered. They stole the livestock in our yard, namely 8 horses, 24 head of cattle, and 450 sheep and many good household supplies which cannot all be listed, quite apart from the grain we had grown, which was partly on the threshing floor, partly in the barn.

Anything they could not take away, they burned along with the whole place on September 6. Not only did the church repeatedly have to bear the heartbreak of brothers and sisters being carried off into captivity, but they also had to endure the crippling losses of livestock and other movable property.

Even before the raid on September 1, three of our horses had been unharnessed and driven off by roving imperial soldiers.

Kesselsdorf destroyed and abandoned.

Our place at Kesselsdorf was now completely destroyed and deserted. The few remaining people sought refuge at Bibersburg Castle for a year and several weeks, but it was a miserable existence.

26 people died.

Then, as they no longer had food for the community, the elders decided that the people must go into the neighboring villages to look for provisions. Since about twenty-six people had died during that time, a group of old brothers and sisters, with widows and orphans, went to the community at Sabatisch to find help. Several, however, went their own way in those troubled times and left the church community. It was not until the following year, 1665, that our people moved together again, which will be recorded later.

On that day, September 3, 1663, the enemy had fanned out on many roads and byways and also raided our community at Tschäskowitz. They stole whatever was still left and took what they wanted—they took all our livestock including the horses.

A schoolboy fell into the enemies' hands.

As our people had already fled to the castle, they were saved. Only one fell into the enemies' hands—a schoolboy who was late because he was fetching water from the well; he was taken captive to a foreign land. May God have mercy on him.

The miller, a Bavarian, also disappeared, nobody knew where. He was not in his right mind, and we had to put him in a grain cellar just before the raid because he was dangerous, and after the raid he was gone. God alone knows what happened to him. *1663*

Apart from this boy, none of our people fell into enemy hands. Praise be to God in heaven who protected his people.

After the plundering, the whole place was set on fire on September 6, all except the mill and the washhouse. As it was not safe for our people to stay there any longer, they had to abandon the place and find shelter here and there on the estate, getting food however they could.

Brother Caspar Eglauch with his wife and children also had to make do with what they could in their poverty, from September 3, 1663, until 1665. When he went to Count Nádasdy at Pottendorf,[1] the count gave him a letter ordering the judge to allow him free passage. So on July 23, 1665, he and his wife and children left the castle at Schächtitz and set out for Sabatisch.

The ruthless enemy burned to ashes not only our communities and the villages and market towns on the other side of the mountains, but on the same day they came over the mountains from Freistadt and the Waag River to Senitz, Skalitz, and even as far as the March River. They were ruthless wherever they went, sacking, slaughtering, and burning.

So the terror and distress swept over our communities on this side of the mountains too, especially over Sabatisch, Protzka, and St. Johannes.

Early in the morning of September 4 the perennial foe raided our community at Sabatisch, robbing us of whatever they wanted—a tremendous loss for the community. Most heartbreaking, however, was that seventeen of our people fell into the hands of the enemy. In the turmoil of this swift raid, some were killed, some were carried off, and some lost their lives in other ways. Raid on Sabatisch. 17 people seized by the enemy.

First Paul Turk, head clothmaker, was killed.

Jockel Walte, assistant cobbler, was killed.

Kilian, the cobbler, was burned to death in the sickroom.

Lorentz, the potter and an invalid, was killed.

Marie, the Bavarian miller's wife, was murdered.

[1]Pottendorf, Lower Austria, approx. 20 miles south of Vienna, property of Count Nádasdy; see Beck, 510.

1663

Katharina, the sister in charge of the women's bath house, died near the camp in Branc.

Marie, the wife of Dionis, and Sara, the wife of Balthasar, were burned.

Hansel Freund, head miller from Gunowe, and his apprentice Tobias were carried off.

The barber-surgeon Andreas Zobel, his wife Maria, their little son, and Johannes Ram's little daughter Asnath fell into the enemy's hands between Koválov and Skalitz and were carried off.

Joseph Lochmair and Wilhelm Bachman, both young potters, and Georg, the Bavarian miller's apprentice, were captured.

Raid on Protzka.

The same day the enemy pillaged our community at Protzka and then crossed the March River, moving on to Landshut in Moravia. Some of our people had fled to the woods near Landshut, hoping to escape, but instead they ran straight into the enemy's hands and were carried off to foreign lands.

. . . the treasurer's wife and her two children were carried off.
. . . . the buyer's two daughters, one named Esther
. . . . . the other was still unmarried.
. . . . . . Bärbel, the veil-weaver's wife, and her
. . . . carried off.

Brother Hans Blesing's daughter Marie, the barber-surgeon's wife at Schossberg, was trying to escape to Skalitz when she was caught not far from the town and abducted.

The enemy reached Landshut and moved on as far as Auspitz, wreaking havoc everywhere. The roads and paths were so overrun by the enemy that on this same 4th of September the community at Velké Leváre was overcome with terror and our people had to leave the place and flee. They went to the peasants' camp below the castle at Blasenstein.[1] At first the people there filled seventeen tables; later it was usually twelve tables.

Velké Leváre lost 200 sheep.

Here they had to stay for nine weeks, barely making ends meet. The fear and hardship they endured can well be imagined. Because they were on an estate belonging to a different lord, things did not work out at all well and they suffered severe losses, including two hundred sheep and nearly all their hogs.

[1]Blasenstein Castle (Plavecký Hrad), at the foot of the Small Carpathians east of Velké Leváre, now a ruin; see Beck, 511–512.

The rest of the people from Velké Leváre fled to Schossberg and Branc where they also met with great misfortune. They were moving their belongings and a large supply of goods to Sabatisch in many wagons when disaster suddenly overtook them and everything was stolen or went up in smoke. That was a heavy blow for the Velké Leváre community. Praise be to God who guarded them from further calamity and heartbreak, for the enemy never did reach Velké Leváre. *1663*

On September 5 another horde of Turks and Tartars came to Sabatisch. First they set fire to our barn and then to all the buildings. In the end only one was left standing on the whole place. As can well be imagined, this meant another crippling loss for the church. Goods to the value of many thousand gulden were destroyed: every kind of grain in barn and mill, flour, various kitchen supplies, wool, cloth, linen, hemp, bed linen and underwear, valuable tools, besides the well-built houses. We had to leave the matter in God's hands and look on patiently, accepting what was done. Sabatisch burned down.

Even where it was possible to save something, we had to be careful not to be seen by the enemy, who were always about.

On September 6, when the Turks and Tartars were returning from Auspitz with an enormous amount of booty, they first looted our community at Protzka and then set it on fire and burned it to the ground. All the cattle and sheep were seized and driven off. There were 14 oxen, 40 milk cows, 40 head of young cattle, 350 sheep and lambs; so the raiders went off with rich spoils. Protzka burned down. Livestock stolen.

Meanwhile they had reached our place at St. Johannes. They looted wherever they wanted and took everything they found. Four of our people were caught by the enemy: Leonhard, the head weaver, and Michael, the head tailor, were killed; Hansel Donner, the potter's apprentice, and Matthias, the potter, were taken captive. St. Johannes was plundered.

Our people, trying to save a few provisions, had taken some of their grain and flour to Sabatisch, hoping to live on it in an emergency; but disaster struck so suddenly that they could not bring it to safety. The little they had was lost in the robbery and the fire, along with the rest of the community's property.

Our poor people at St. Johannes had to do without it and suffered great privation and hunger as a consequence.

On September 18 the Turks and Tartars returned and again

1663
Turks took the fortress at Neuhäusel.

inflicted tremendous harm with arson, murder, and abduction.

At four in the afternoon of September 26 the fortress of Neuhäusel surrendered on terms agreed to by the Turks, who allowed the defenders to withdraw to the fortress at Komárno[1] with a convoy of one thousand janissaries and a strong detachment of cavalry. Among those who retreated were 2472 Germans who were unhurt and well-equipped, taking with them four pieces of artillery and their baggage, lock, stock, and barrel, as well as a large number of sick and wounded.

In the fortress, however, they left behind thirty thousand musket bullets made of tin and window lead, seventy hundredweight of gunpowder and over sixty of their best pieces of artillery, seven hundred barrels of flour, three hundred casks of wine, and a hundred bales of cloth for clothing.[2]

Quite a number of the Hungarians remained in the fortress when they were offered pay to fight for the Turks, but these were later sent down to Turkey as men who could not be fully trusted. According to the Christians' report, the siege of Neuhäusel had cost the lives of twelve thousand men, but the Turks would not admit to more than a few thousand.

Such an outcome to this seven-weeks' siege of Neuhäusel made the whole of Asia and Europe hold their breath, for it meant that another great cornerstone had fallen from the bulwarks of Christendom.

In their first surprise attack on Moravia the Turks had crossed the Waag River and the March River and raided Nikolsburg, Rabensburg, Göding, Brünn, Ungarisch Ostra, Holleschau, and other places to within three miles of Olmütz.

The whole country was burned bare; everyone over forty was strangled. Many young women were carried off, one on each soldier's horse; little children were put in ragged sacks and slung behind the saddles like baggage. In this way twelve thousand people either lost their lives or their freedom, which amounts to the same.

Woods and mountains were scoured, and the poor people hiding there found little safety from the enemy, who used traitors as guides and interpreters to mislead and deceive those

---

[1]Komárno, at the confluence of the Vah River with the Danube.

[2]*Theatrum Europaeum*, IX, 956: ". . . about 700 barrels of flour, 300 casks of wine, 100 bales of material for clothing, 70 cwt. of powder, and 60 to 70 pieces of the finest artillery"; see also Beck, 513.

in hiding by speaking in German, Bohemian, Hungarian, or Slovakian. *1663*

The passes were no difficulty to the invaders. The abovementioned traitors showed them every crack and cranny, every bridge and byway. If any Tartars were captured, they could not be made to say a single word—they acted as if dumb and would rather be killed than give information. Very rarely did they let themselves be caught, preferring to plunge under water and drown.

Most of them carried flint and steel and all kinds of material for starting fires so that they could rapidly set hamlets and villages ablaze.

They drove their prisoners off like a herd of cattle. No one was daring enough to rescue the poor, groaning Christian prisoners, though it could easily have been done with a few thousand cavalry. There were only about four thousand of the brutal, naked marauders, and these were very poorly armed. Not one in a hundred had a pistol; in fact, only here and there one of them had a rusty little saber, a spear, or perhaps an arrow. How easily they might have been routed can be seen by the fact that near Drösing twenty well-armed peasants repulsed five hundred of them, and eighty men were killed.

On October 5 the Turks and Tartars attacked our community at Soblahof, sacking it and burning it to the ground. All the cows, sheep, and horses were taken.

Soblahof burned down. 12 people taken by the enemy.

Twelve of our people were ruthlessly murdered or taken captive. Jockel Binder and Hans Heinrich, the head smith, were killed. The other ten were carried into captivity: Johannes Birn, the schoolmaster, and his Hannah; Johannes Teuringer, a clothmaker; Michael Tuchmacher (a clothmaker); Joseph Aberle, a saddler, and his wife; Tobias Aberle, a young saddler, and his sister Christina Aberle; Johannes Stahl, a weaver's apprentice; and Zipora Gerber (the tanner's wife).

In all, 122 people from the church were taken in bondage to foreign countries or murdered by the perennial foe, the Turks and Tartars.

122 taken captive or murdered.

Only three of this number were released. Apel Berg, a sister from Dechtitz, died in captivity at Parkan. When Lewenz was won back by the Germans [in 1664], Tobias Harhacker, a miller's apprentice, was freed from the enemy and came into German hands. Then his father paid a ransom for his release.

1663
1665 Sarah Weber returned to the church from Turkey.

Sarah Weber came back from Turkey [in 1665] with the imperial ambassadors, all the way from Constantinople to Vienna, and from there she returned to the church. The Lord be praised!

Earthquake.

At noon on October 9, 1663, there was an earthquake at Gutwasser Castle that shook the walls and rocks.

When the siege of Neuhäusel was over and the Turks realized that winter was at the door, they planned to finish off [their campaign] by getting spoils from the Christians for the way home. So they swam the Waag River once more, raided all the way into Silesia, captured several thousand people, and brought them to their camp. Some assert that in three raids, quite apart from those murdered, they swept more than forty thousand Christians into perpetual bondage.

On October 17 the Turks planned to invade the Schütt Islands and break up the council of imperial generals assembled there. But nothing came of it; the attack backfired on them.

4 companies of cavalry at Velké Leváre.

On November 17 four companies of imperial cavalry came to Velké Leváre and camped in the market place. The sergeant major in charge and a cavalry captain with fifty horses took up their quarters in our community. They had about thirty people with them and cost the community more than thirty gulden, not counting what was taken secretly. Although our people were already going hungry and living in the poorest, most wretched conditions, they were now forced by the soldiers to run into debt.

German regiment at Velké Leváre.

On December 1 another regiment of German soldiers, who had withdrawn from the fortress of Neuhäusel, made their way to Velké Leváre and stayed for two nights. They had over fifty oxen and horses with them. Their stay cost the community at Velké Leváre about sixty gulden.

The year 1663 drew to an end with misery, terror, and death on all sides, with much heartache, groaning, and weeping. The land was laid waste, and men and cattle perished. Anything that had not been robbed was lost in other ways.

The whole church was again brought into utter poverty and ruin, for they could harvest hardly any field or garden crops.

What happened at that time was so dreadful, inhuman, and unchristian that it defies description. This is only a brief report, included here for the sake of our descendants. May God the Almighty grant a better future.

1664

1664

Neutra regained by agreement.

In the spring of 1664 the imperial field marshal Count de Souches advanced to Neutra and opened fire on the town. The perennial foe surrendered the city and fled into the castle, but the imperial forces attacked so strongly that the Turks asked for free passage to withdraw, which for some reason was granted.

So the Turks left Neutra and ceded it to the Christians. They had to abandon the ammunition that was in the castle but were escorted to Neuhäusel with all their goods and people, even their camp followers. The same happened at Lewenz, also taken by Field Marshal de Souches. He opened fire and stormed the place, and when the attack went in his favor and the enemy saw he was in earnest, they agreed to surrender the town.

In March and April there was still hope of getting something into the ground and seeding the fields at Dechtitz. Then the marauding hussars returned and took two of our horses straight from the plow in the field.

In spite of the great danger and loss, our people managed to sow and raise some field crops until harvest time, though in these months they had to flee from their houses several times, not from the Turks but from the imperial troops. Just at harvest, when they were looking forward to enjoying some of it and most of the hay and grain had been carried home, the imperial forces again invaded the country.

First of all a regiment came through Dechtitz and stole whatever they found. They stripped and beat up any brothers they caught. They carried off a mass of booty, threw the sick people out of their beds, and stole the bed linen. Our people had to abandon Dechtitz for the summer and autumn, and the little they had left in house, garden, field, and vineyard was stolen from them day after day in countless raids.

2 cows taken from Dechtitz.

Even the two cows still left after the Turkish raids were now seized and carried off by the Germans.

Neu Serinwär taken.

On June 30 Neu Serinwär in Croatia was stormed and taken by the Turks. From the seventeen thousand men in the fortress not five hundred escaped with their lives.

Soldiers from Saxony at Senitz.

On August 13 a force of about five hundred Saxonian infantry arrived at Senitz and camped on the Branc estates for eleven weeks. They were a great drain on our community at Sabatisch and caused us much trouble.

1664
1000 German and French soldiers raided Gutwasser.

On September 28, when the imperial camp was moved near Dechtitz, a thousand German and French soldiers suddenly came into the village of Gutwasser, robbing and plundering at will, taking grain, hay, and whatever else they could find. They emptied people's underground store places and drove off with loads of hay that the community at Dechtitz had hauled to this village. Five of our horses were stolen from behind the castle, where we had thought they would be safe. The soldiers beat the wagoner cruelly and carried him off for some distance but then let him go again.

From this time on until almost winter, our community at Dechtitz was continually being plundered, and no one dared be seen by the Germans. There were so many instances of cruelty that it is impossible to remember them all now. Afterward, our poverty-stricken people came back to the empty, burned-out, and ruined houses. Those who survived the enemy suffered bitter hardship and great hunger.

On October 11 Colonel Nikolaus and Sergeant Major Stang took up quarters in our place at Velké Leváre with fifty-five horses and a large number of people. We had to give them twelve pecks of oats daily and enough hay and straw too. We had to buy old wine for them, paying twenty pennies the half measure. This went on for a week. Counting all the extra gifts, it cost the community over a hundred gulden.

On October 17, no sooner had the Germans left than the French arrived. The people in Velké Leváre were preparing to hold the evening prayer meeting but had to break off and flee. When the soldiers found hardly any of our people there, they plundered and did a lot of damage in the community, amounting to several hundred gulden.

On October 18 the Saxon artillery horses were stabled at Sabatisch, costing us a great deal. Seven stable hands with fourteen horses stayed at our place for seventeen days.

The same day a cavalry regiment arrived under the command of Count von Nassau. They remained until October 22 but were no particular burden to us, praise God, except for the gifts we gave them out of good will. Then they went on to Schossberg.

War losses to the church.

On November 6 the Rabicksh regiment came to Velké Leváre. No one was quartered with our people except one cavalryman as a bodyguard, but that cost the community more than twenty-three gulden.

On November 5 the Saxonian soldiers left the country and returned home. We had to pay the sergeant major twenty-five gulden and fifty pennies for the lieutenant colonel's lodging, since he did not lodge with us. We also had to pay the quartermaster three gulden for the seven stable hands and fourteen artillery horses. With the food, drink, and fodder that was used, the cost came to nearly forty-six gulden. *1664*

One hour before midnight on December 24, a comet was seen that was visible for several nights afterward. It had also been observed earlier in various places for many nights. Its significance is known to God alone. Come

1665

On January 4, 1665, at six in the evening another comet appeared.[1] It had a pointed tail and turned toward the east. It was visible for two weeks. Only God knows the meaning of this.

On March 26 at two o'clock in the afternoon a fire broke out in our community smithy at Sabatisch as a result of carelessness. Not only the smithy burned down, but also the sicklesmiths' and wheelwrights' shops, the saddlers' and wheelwrights' huts, as well as a few little sheds between the burned-out walls of the shoemakers', blacksmiths', and cutlers' shops. The floors, however, were saved. None of the peasants' houses were burned down. Fire at Sabatisch.

This meant another serious loss for the community at Sabatisch, as the two buildings housing the sicklesmiths and wheelwrights were still new. The community, poor as it was, had just put much effort and labor into building them.

At three in the morning of April 5 a comet with a long tail was seen by a number of people and was visible for several days. Comet.

After the great fear and poverty we had endured during the oft-reported, sudden, and terrible war with the Turks and Tartars, misery and ruin had fallen on the whole church of the Lord, as well as on many thousands of other people in the land, high- and lowborn alike. On April 7 we met at Sabatisch in our great poverty, as we had done several times before, to Church took counsel.

---

[1]*Theatrum Europaeum*, IX, 1484; Beck, 518–519.

1665

take counsel on how to feed and care for our poor widows and orphans, many of whom had been brought there from the other communities during this difficult time.

We unanimously agreed to appeal for help to the [Mennonite] churches in the Netherlands.

2 brothers sent to Holland, Zeeland, Flanders, and Friesland to get support.

We counseled together before the Lord and in reverent fear of God decided that the two brothers, Christoph Baumhauer and Benjamin Poley, both servants of the Word of God, should be sent from Sabatisch on April 21 on this mission for the Lord's work. In great fear of God and under divine protection, they went to Mannheim in the Palatinate and from there to Amsterdam. They traveled in Holland, Zeeland, Flanders, and Friesland.

By word of mouth and in a letter from all the elders of our church, we asked the congregations in the Netherlands for help and support, telling them how we had come into such extreme poverty and misery. God the Lord moved their hearts to help his church and send a good contribution to support us. Glory, honor, and praise be to God the Almighty to all eternity. Amen.

To the Congregations in Holland

To our very beloved friends and brothers in the Lord

Letter to the congregations in Holland.

May the grace, love, and compassion of our great God, the true peace of our Lord Jesus Christ, and the living strength of the Holy Spirit be with you and remain in you and in all those who love and fear God in their hearts, wherever they may be scattered in these dangerous and disturbed times.

As a Christian brother, that is what I wish for all the elders, for all deacons in the Word of God, and for all brothers and friends, as our beloved benefactors in Christ Jesus our Lord, from God the Almighty in heartfelt love. Amen.

Especially to you whom our hearts hold in high esteem, dear friends in God and beloved brothers in the Lord—from us simple, unworthy, poor, and lowly servants, elders, and Vorsteher of the church of God, the totally destitute brotherhood in upper and lower Hungary.

First of all, needy, poor, and unworthy as I am in these trying and fearful days in which the good Lord has placed me, I, brother Johannes Rieger, turn to you together with my fellow elders and servants of the Word of God, and with the church of God which has been razed to the ground, ruined, and made destitute by the terrible cruelty of the Turks and Tartars. In our present state of fear and distress we do not wish to—in fact, we cannot—hold back from telling you, our beloved friends, brothers and sisters in the Lord, about our great poverty.

1665
Letter to the congregation in Holland.

Since we are reduced to extreme need and poverty, we are urged to tell you, our beloved friends, our brothers and sisters in the Lord, about the crippling losses, the privation, and the great distress we suffer. God the Lord has allowed this to fall on us wretched people and on thousands more in this country during the past year as a just punishment. This came upon us suddenly through fire, sword, robbery, and devastation. All our houses and goods were burned to ashes together with all the livestock. Within one day, September 3, 1663, practically everything was gone. Far worse than this is the anguish that cuts us deeply, making our hearts groan and weep day and night. Our dear brothers and sisters, 122 people of our own flesh and blood, young and old, have been murdered or taken prisoner and carried off to foreign countries, into barbarous slavery. We fear that they are being beaten and cruelly treated and that they are in great terror and distress.

Except for two people who got free and returned home and a sister who died in the Lord while in captivity at Parkan, we do not know for certain what has become of them all.

We thank the Lord, who helped the three in their great need and rescued them from their grief and captivity. May the almighty God and heavenly Father comfort with his divine presence those still in bonds and captivity and revive them in their misery. Each day we pray for them in grief of heart; we intercede for them in our communal prayer.

In all our meetings we ask God with loud weeping and groaning that he in his mercy may come to their help, deliver them, and enable them to overcome, so that with him to comfort and uphold them, whatever they must

1665
Letter to the congregation in Holland.

suffer (against their consciences) will not hinder their eternal salvation. We wish them this from the bottom of our hearts through Jesus Christ. Amen.

We have the Christian hope and confidence that when people in both near and distant provinces hear of the terrible suffering in this land, there will be great sympathy. We believe that wherever God the Lord has faithful followers whose hearts and minds are moved by Christian compassion for these poor people, they will wrestle and strive in deep and humble prayer for them, never doubting that the Lord will hear. They will certainly grieve over the hurt done to Joseph and lament with the daughter of Zion in her bereavement.

These hardships that have overtaken us bring sad and anxious days on account of our widows and orphans and our many helpless little children, a good number of whom have lost members of their family through the evil marauders. It takes hard work and painful efforts to support them as well as ourselves with our insufficient and dwindling means, our meager food supplies and cramped living quarters. But may God in heaven be thanked that in his great mercy, love, and compassion it is his will to let his blessed peace look down from heaven and his sun of grace shine again. We cannot thank him enough for this nor honor and praise him enough for upholding us so wonderfully through his divine protection in very evil times. The Lord still grants the rich grace of his divine blessing every day. Otherwise where would we be? Oh, you dear friends, brothers and sisters in the Lord, in the natural order of things many of us should already have starved to death during these times of want because we were so poor. Those of us who are healthy, praise God, work hard from sunup to sundown to till our fields and ply at least some trades, yet it brings us very little profit, for the land is impoverished and ruined, a deserted wilderness, and this has caused a steep rise in prices.

Yet the almighty God in his immense love and rich mercy has looked down on us from his holy heaven with eyes full of compassion. He has lifted from us the intolerable burden of war.

1665
Letter to the congregation in Holland.

Ever since His Majesty the Emperor made his long-negotiated peace settlement, all military forces have been ordered to leave the country. So, to all appearances, there is hope for twenty years of peace in our land, and for this we have good reason to give unceasing thanks to the Lord most high. We implore God in fervent prayer that he may comfort all people with true and lasting peace, to the praise and honor of his divine glory for ever and ever.

Most dear and esteemed friends and brothers in the Lord, we well remember the Christian charity and generous gifts from brothers and sisters in the Lord and other well-wishers who were concerned for the Lord's work in Germany. You brothers may have noticed that these contributions, which were intended for a good purpose and given and received in Christian love, were not used rightly in the ways that you and we had intended. This grieved us very much and still does, so we want to apologize here in all humility and Christian friendship. Nevertheless, we are continuing in our efforts, working as steadily and devotedly as we can to bring community life into true Christian order and nearer perfection in both spiritual and temporal affairs, setting it on its feet and establishing a work pleasing to the Lord. Even in extreme poverty we have never given up communal living in this country. By the grace and gift of God we hold to our life in common, sharing the little we have with one another after the example of the first apostolic church in Jerusalem. In our smallness and simplicity, God the Lord grants each one of us his gifts to the glory of the divine majesty in Christ Jesus. So we are resolved to live and die in the light of true community and to remain steadfast in this to the honor of God and for the salvation of our souls in Christ Jesus.

Our dear friends and beloved brothers and sisters in the Lord, because of all this we make our urgent appeal to you in friendship, especially to the elders, servants for temporal affairs, and all sympathetic and kindhearted souls who are stewards and administrators of God's gifts. We could not do otherwise than send our two dear brothers to you. All the elders in our communities came to the

1665
Letter to the congregation in Holland.

united decision to send these two, Christoph Baumhauer and Benjamin Poley, as our dear fellow workers and servants of the Word of God. They bring verbal and written messages to you and your congregations. We will receive whatever is given with great thankfulness as a generous support and gift from God through you, our dear brothers and sisters. We will use your loving services to support the poor and needy in the communities of the Lord, for we are all poor and needy now. Your generous response and gift from the Lord will be used with gratitude to make a start in rebuilding our burned-out houses and flour mills. We will use it in the building up of God's church, also for those who are still far away but whom God the Lord may call. Through his grace may we become a bride, sanctified and purified in every way, prepared in and for Christ in this trouble-filled world, until he leads us home with him to the royal wedding feast in heaven and to the great Supper of the Lord. May God grant this through Jesus Christ for us and for all hearts that love him. Amen.

Dear friends and beloved brothers and sisters in the Lord, you can easily imagine how hard it is for us poor people to take pen in hand to burden you dear ones in this way. Especially in these difficult and evil war years, you have enough people overrunning and disturbing you without us. Now our extreme distress and poverty has brought us to this, something our dear forefathers and brothers in the faith were spared. Although they had to face every kind of hardship and adversity, they had ample means through God's leading, since well-to-do people accepted the faith and united with them in true surrender. They helped to alleviate the need, and we did not have to burden others. When persecution against us began in Moravia and help was offered by our friends and brothers in Prussia, we thanked them in a warm and friendly way but did not accept it.

Now the harvest is over, it is finished, and we stand alone as people who live in the end time. Yet we live in the sure hope and confidence that you, dearly loved friends, brothers and sisters in the Lord, will not take this urgent appeal amiss, coming from us poor and needy

1665
Letter to the congregation in Holland.

people. Rather, let your hearts and minds in love to God be tender, compassionate, Christian, and brotherly, and then you will see that your generosity is repaid a thousand times over (as our dear Lord and Savior Jesus Christ promises), and after this life you will receive ineffable bliss for your souls through our dear Lord Jesus Christ. We will receive what you share with us in great thankfulness as a gift from the Lord. Many hundreds of those who love him will thank the Lord most high a thousand times in the depths of their hearts for moving others to care for them in their distress, to feel the weight of the burden that crushes them, and to help them up. They will pray to the Lord for those who have felt the hurt done to the whole body, and they will take deeply to heart this compassion of one member for another. This will certainly be done for the joy of your salvation, that you may become citizens of the heavenly Jerusalem, and that we all, as we wished above, may be made perfect in one spirit and one body. May God the Almighty help us through Jesus Christ. Amen.

Previously we did not know you, but now we have come especially close to you and have experienced the Christian compassion that characterizes you, the warm affection, the unity of love with which all of you receive needy, distressed, and grieving strangers and reach out a hand to help and comfort them. We know you are responsive to the divine influence that inspires you to help us, for we are indeed the poor, weak children of the woman in the desolate wilderness, and the dragon would swallow and drown some of us.

Moreover, we are never completely safe from the bloody sword and have no one but God to protect us. We are the harmless doves, constantly despised and persecuted by the bird of prey, and we must always be ready to flee.

Nonetheless, we had hoped and still hope, with God's grace, to live under a loved and respected government that is well-disposed toward us. Zeal for God brought us together from many places in different lands—some of us by wonderful and amazing ways—and we found refuge under such a government. We gained our livelihood

1665
Letter to the congregation in Holland.

honestly by the sweat of our brow. Through toil and hard work we earned our daily bread, for which we praised and thanked God with all our hearts. Although the times were not without disturbances and deprivations, we always pulled through and recovered with God's help and blessing.

But now we are completely at a loss. Many different reasons and circumstances have contributed to this. Even though we still have houses and land, our food supply has become totally insufficient.

Now beloved friends and brothers and sisters in the Lord, with innermost devotion in our daily prayer, both communal and personal, we commend each one of you to the protection of the most high God, in the tender love of Jesus Christ. We pray that through the prompting and strength of the Holy Spirit we may become new creatures in Christ and may remain so for all eternity. Amen. Amen.

Poor and unworthy as we are, yet trusting that we are chosen by God and called, appointed, and confirmed by his church, we elders and servants of the church in lower Hungary and especially I, Johannes Rieger, greet you on behalf of the whole church community. We offer the hand of our hearts and the loving kiss of our Prince of Peace, Christ Jesus, to all venerable elders and the Vorsteher, servants of the Word of God and their congregations in Holland and the Netherlands, also to all deacons, assistants, and servants for temporal affairs, and to all brothers and sisters without exception. We greet you in the Lord a thousand times as those who also belong to the bride of Christ, fellow heirs of the promise of an eternal inheritance, heavenly glory, and the future kingdom of Christ.

Written in lower Hungary, April 20, 1665

Your lowly fellow servant of the Word of God
and brother to you all, Johannes Rieger[1]

Moses Bruckner, a servant, passed away.

On June 18 of this year, 1665, at four o'clock in the morning, brother Moses Bruckner, a servant of the Word, fell asleep in the Lord at Trentschin.

[1]Johannes Rieger became Vorsteher in 1662, after the death of Andreas Ehrenpreis; see above, p.776; *ME*, IV, 328; Friedmann, *Schriften*, 123, "Riecker, Johann."

1665
Count Nikolaus let us take over his house.

On August 8 Count Nikolaus Palffy gave us his deserted house in the market place at Schattmansdorf[1] so that we could rebuild it and move in. It was to be a place for the remnant of our people from Kesselsdorf[2] to gather and live in community again. May the dear Lord grant his grace for this and grant lasting peace.

2 brothers returned home.

On October 28 the two brothers, Christoph Baumhauer and Benjamin Poley, returned home safely from their long journey to Holland and other places. They arrived in peace and under God's protection, having completed their task. God be praised for bringing them safely there and back.

Prices rose.

During the two years of 1664 and 1665 all grain prices were very high. A Senitz peck of wheat cost three gulden and more, a peck of rye cost two gulden and fifty kreuzer, a peck of barley was two gulden, a peck of oats was sixty kreuzer, and a peck of peas cost over three gulden. The price of a pair of raw oxhides was ten gulden.

---

[1]Schattmansdorf (Častá) approx. 5 miles northeast of Modra on the highway from Bratislava.

[2]About the destruction of Kesselsdorf, see above, pp.781–782.

APPENDIX 1

Political and Economic Context

At the beginning of the sixteenth century, while national states were emerging in northern and western Europe, southeastern Europe was in the hands of the Ottoman Turks. After two centuries of gradual conquest the Turks were still forcing their way westwards, and their raids and wars continued to endanger central Europe for two centuries more. Their victory at Mohacs in 1526 added two-thirds of Hungary to their possessions. That same year Ferdinand, hereditary archduke of Austria, became king over Bohemia and Moravia and over what remained of Hungary, claiming these countries by inheritance, although traditionally the crowns were elective. As a member of the Hapsburg dynasty, Ferdinand was elected Holy Roman Emperor in 1556 to replace his brother Charles V. His rule now extended over the multiplicity of German-speaking states which formed the empire. Successive Hapsburgs held the same lands and titles, some, like Ferdinand, becoming simultaneously archduke of Austria, king of Bohemia, king of Hungary, and Holy Roman Emperor.

The movement of reform associated with Martin Luther and directed against the Roman Catholic Church began in the German territories in the first quarter of the sixteenth century. It spread rapidly throughout and beyond the empire, soon fragmenting into many groups, since varying interpretations of the Bible and of Christianity arose.

Conflicting religious views soon led to armed confrontation. Between 1524 and 1525 the Peasants' Revolt broke out in Germany, the peasants appealing to biblical justice to reinforce their demands for redress of grievances. Fear became widespread among the governing powers that freedom of conscience among the lower classes would lead to insurrection and anarchy. The movement was condemned by Roman Catholic and Protestant leaders alike and was ruthlessly crushed.

1525 It was within this context of social upheaval that in early 1525 the Anabaptist movement was born in Zurich. In 1534 a radical Anabaptist group seized the town of Münster and enforced community of goods; it was notorious for its excesses. Although harshly suppressed, this violence resulted in long-lasting horror and distrust of Anabaptists, especially of any communal group, however peaceful.

Three main church organizations, Lutheran, Zwinglian, and Calvinist, had now developed among the reformers and were frequently antagonistic to each other as well as to any more radical group. In many parts of Germany and in Bohemia, Moravia, Hungary, and the adjoining state of Transylvania, people turned to the Protestant churches. The emperors, with the exception of the more tolerant Maximilian II, remained staunchly Roman Catholic and were eager to purge their lands of all but their coreligionists. Fighting broke out between the rival creeds in Germany and continued until 1555 when the Treaty of Augsburg assigned to each ruler the right to choose the religion his state was to follow.

In the four countries on the eastern borders of the empire, reform took strong root, combining with the traditional independence of the nobility to maintain resistance to the emperor's policy. Bohemia and Moravia had been deeply affected by John Huss's teaching of a more biblical Christianity and by his appeal for religious reform. Moravia early became
1528 a haven for radical believers fleeing from intolerance. It was here, in 1528, that the Hutterian movement was given its birth. Although there was persecution throughout the country in 1535 and again in 1545–1551, political and religious freedom was possible here for decades afterwards. Over a hundred Hutterian communities flourished during this time, scattered throughout Moravia and Slovakia.

Emperor Rudolf (ruled 1576–1612) was determined to gain full control of his eastern possessions and to re-catholicize them. His efforts were strengthened by the Counter-Reformation, a widely successful endeavor to revitalize the Roman Catholic

Church and win back the ground lost to the Protestants. Foremost in the movement were the Jesuits, a body of men known as the Society of Jesus, who strove with great dedication but often with extreme cruelty to make Roman Catholicism worldwide. Highly trained for their task, they organized education and opposed what they considered heresy, assisting in cross-examinations. As they found almost any method acceptable if it achieved their ends, the Jesuits were seen as cunning and dreaded agents of imperial policy.

Near the turn of the century economic change and embittered political rivalry brought increasing oppression and war, plunging Moravia and the adjoining lands into misery. A principal cause of economic oppression was the change in land usage fostered by the expansion of commerce. In western Europe with its growing towns, the demand for agricultural products was increasing and prices rose accordingly. In eastern Europe, where towns were few and land was the main resource, the nobles were eager to profit from the favorable market. Manors or estates which had been merely self-sufficient now had to be intensively cultivated for cash crops. In Bohemia the most important item was beer; in Hungary, wine. Where possible, landlords took over peasant holdings and enlarged the acreage at their own disposal, but they could not readily increase the supply of workers. They therefore tried to squeeze additional labor from the existing peasantry, whom they exploited with ever greater inhumanity. At a time when manorial control of the peasantry was almost at an end in western Europe, the once relatively free peasants of eastern Europe were reduced to serfdom, tied by law to the land and oppressed with heavier and heavier dues and compulsory labor.

Over this harshly subjected peasantry broke long and terrible wars as the political rulers pursued their irreconcilable purposes. Hapsburg determination to establish control of eastern territories resulted in the Turkish Wars of 1593–1606 and the Bocskay rebellion of 1604–1605, when Hungarian nobles allied themselves with the Turks against the emperor.
In 1618 the devastating struggle of the Thirty Years War began. 1618
At first the emperor had great success against rebellious nobles who elected a Calvinist king of Bohemia in defiance of imperial claims. Success of one ruler, however, provoked a counter-alliance of others to check his mounting power. Alliances

shifted, Roman Catholic joining Protestant to oppose Roman Catholic, and Protestant opposing Protestant, in a power struggle that lasted thirty interminable years.

Six armies, German, Danish, Swedish, Bohemian, Spanish, and French, marched and fought across central Europe. The soldiers and their leaders were mostly mercenaries, fighting on either side for pay, and expected to live from the lands where they were campaigning. Quartered on the country people, they looted, raped, and murdered at will, often setting homes to the torch. Desperate peasants resorted to banditry.

1648 The Thirty Years War was brought to an end in 1648, but there was scarcely any interval of peace in eastern Europe where Poland, Russia, Sweden, Brandenburg, Denmark—and even Transylvania in 1657—struggled for aggrandizement. The Hapsburg powers were confronted both by uprisings among the Hungarian nobility in defense of traditional liberties and by renewed Turkish thrusts into central Europe. Not until the end of the century, after the Turks had besieged Vienna a second time, were the forces of Leopold I and his allies able to repulse the enemy so decisively that in 1699, at the Treaty of Karlowitz, Austria gained possession of Hungary and Transylvania. Transylvania had been under Turkish suzerainty for over a century and a half and permitted considerable toleration for all creeds. Soon after the Turkish defeat of 1683 the Transylvanian Diet negotiated with Leopold I and accepted his suzerainty. The Diet insisted on the emperor's confirmation of some religious toleration, but only two religions were now
1700 permitted: the Roman Catholic and the Lutheran. After 1700, pressure from a centralizing imperial power became increasingly effective, while the Jesuits were zealous to eradicate any non-aligned religious group. Between 1759 and 1767 ruthless persecution suppressed the few Hutterian communities left in Hungary and reduced those in Transylvania to a handful of people who refused to give in. The Hutterites, consequently, again became a remnant, a people on the move, migrating with much suffering to Walachia, then to the Ukraine, and—to complete our story—in the 1870s, to North America.

Appendix 2

Subsequent History

After 1665, events in the Hutterian Church were recorded intermittently but not gathered into a single volume. It was not until 1793 that the continuation of the story was taken up by Johannes Waldner, Vorsteher from 1794 to 1824. He patterned his chronicle after the first volume, which he condensed as the first part of his work. Then he used other available sources to fill in the years following 1665 and went on to relate the events of his own time until 1802.

From his account we learn that the story of suffering continued. Community of goods—so characteristic and so vital—was abandoned by one Bruderhof after another as a result of spiritual decline, severe economic hardships, and continued persecution; by 1699 this practice had been 1699
abandoned altogether, also in Transylvania.

Fifty years later a movement of hearts in Carinthia (Austria) led to an event of great significance for the preservation of the Hutterian Church. There was a revival among a small section of the population which had been secretly Protestant for almost two centuries. In an effort to rid Carinthia of so-called heretics, Empress Maria Theresa enforced their migration to Transylvania (Romania) in at least fourteen groups. One of these, sent in October 1755, consisted of 270 souls. Through the providence 1755
of God, several of these newcomers, while looking for work, encountered a remnant of the brothers and sisters who still read the old Hutterian writings even though they were no longer living in community of goods. As a result of the encounter, some of the Carinthian immigrants were baptized and began to live in full Christian community of goods at

Kreuz in Transylvania. One of these, Johannes Kleinsasser, was confirmed as a servant of the Word in 1763 by the two Hutterian elders Martin Roth and Joseph Kuhr. Some of the Hutterites from Alwinz joined them, and thus the Hutterian Church survived.

Persecution, especially by the Jesuits, continued and even increased. Of the two Hutterian elders at Alwinz, Martin Roth succumbed to Catholic pressure and Joseph Kuhr (a brother filled with the fire of the Spirit) was banished from the land along with a certain Johannes Stahl. Just as the Catholics were making arrangements to put all the Bruderhof children into a Catholic orphanage, these two brothers returned secretly. In
1767 1767 they led the whole community in winter and under dangerous conditions over the Transylvanian Alps to comparative safety in Walachia (southern Romania). They set up a community not far from Bucharest. (A few brothers and sisters were left behind in prison at Hermannstadt in Transylvania.) Three years later, because of the ravages of the war between Russia and Turkey, they accepted an offer by the Russian field marshal Count Peter Alexandrovich Rumiantsev to settle on his land at Vishenka in the Ukraine. Here they were granted freedom of religion and freedom from military service.

At that time the Hutterian Brethren came close to losing their first chronicle. One of the two manuscripts we have today (see Introduction p.xvi) had been in the keeping of the elder Martin Roth, who became a Roman Catholic. At his death it passed into the possession of his son, not a Hutterian brother. His mother-in-law, however, sold it to the brothers imprisoned in Hermannstadt, and on their release in 1772 or 1773 they brought the book safely back to the brotherhood in the Ukraine. This is the book we now call the "1581" codex. Where the other copy (the "1580" codex) was we do not know, but Johannes Waldner wrote in his chronicle (which came to be known as *Das Klein-Geschichtsbuch der Hutterischen Brüder*) that the record of their history had been lost to them until the brothers arrived from prison with a copy.

1819 In 1819 disunity among the servants of the Word and inner decline led to the abandonment of community of goods for the second time. Yet the spark did not go out. The brothers and sisters held together as congregations, faithfully reading the old Hutterian writings. German-speaking Mennonites living in the Molotschna district of southern Ukraine helped the Hutterites obtain good farmland there. The entire group moved in 1842 and built up five Hutterian settlements: Huttertal, Johannesruh, Hutterdorf, Neu-Huttertal, and Scheromet. In 1859 Michael Waldner, a blacksmith, set up a small Bruderhof 1859 with full community of goods in one of these settlements, the beginning of the group known today as the Schmiedeleut or Smith People. A year later Darius Walter established another community, later called the Dariusleut.

Since 1770 the brothers had been enjoying the freedoms granted them in Russia, but in 1870 these privileges were annulled by the government. The brothers and sisters soon decided to emigrate, and in 1874 and 1877 they all moved to 1874–1877 South Dakota in the United States. There a third group reestablished community of goods under the leadership of Jacob Wipf, a teacher; hence the group was called Lehrerleut. These three groups continued communal living in the United States.

Some fifty years later, however, their stand against any form of military service brought harassment and persecution once more. In 1918, during World War I, two of their young married 1918 brothers, Michael and Joseph Hofer, died in prison as a result of cruel mistreatment by the United States military. For this reason nearly all the Hutterian Brethren moved from the United States to Canada, though many later returned to the United States.

In 1920 a new Christian community began in Germany, led in their search for radical discipleship by Eberhard Arnold, who knew the history of the Anabaptists and of the Hutterian Brethren but did not know of their continued existence in North America. The new community, founded on the Sermon on the Mount and formed in the Spirit of the early church, attracted many who were looking for a new society to end war and its evil consequences. When Eberhard Arnold read about the two young Hutterian brothers who had died in prison in 1918, he realized that Hutterian communities still existed. But it was not until 1926 that he obtained their address from Dr. Robert Friedmann of Vienna, who was doing research on Anabaptist history under Professor Wolkan. Eberhard began corresponding with the brothers in North America, especially with Elias Walter Jr. at the Stand Off Colony, Alberta. At their invitation he visited all thirty-three Hutterian colonies in 1930 and 1931.

He found that the brothers, after four hundred years, were still united in their basic faith and trust in God and in their practice of adult baptism; they shared their goods, work, and life; they made a life commitment to the church as the body of Christ; they promised lifelong faithfulness in marriage; they exercised church discipline; and they were united—to the last member—in their refusal to do military service. All this convinced the community in Germany, grown to a hundred souls, that they should join the Hutterian Brethren, not merely for their own sake but as a witness to the unity among his disciples that Jesus asked for in his last prayer (John 17). So while Eberhard Arnold was still in America, they were united with the Hutterian Brethren, and he was appointed servant of
1930 the Word by the elders in December 1930.

He returned to Germany with enthusiastic plans to publish Anabaptist writings. The most important of these was the manuscript of *Das Klein-Geschichtsbuch der Hutterischen Brüder*, consisting primarily of Johannes Waldner's work, in which he had condensed and continued the first chronicle. Work on this publication was stopped by the rise of National Socialism in Germany, and it was never resumed because of the death of Eberhard Arnold in 1935. The Rhön Bruderhof was dissolved by the Gestapo in 1937 and after settling first in England, then in Paraguay, the brothers and sisters made another home in the United States.

At the request of the Hutterian Brethren in North America, A. J. F. Zieglschmid (editor of the 1943 edition of the first chronicle) arranged for the publication of the second volume of the chronicle in the German language by the Carl Schurz Memorial Foundation, Philadelphia, Pennsylvania, in 1947. *Das Klein-Geschichtsbuch der Hutterischen Brüder* is treasured by the Hutterian Brethren today. It is to be hoped that one day it will also appear in English translation.

The twentieth century has seen another sign of God's Spirit at work: a second group to join the Hutterian Brethren. In the mid-1950s a group of eleven Japanese Christians, led by Rev. Isomi Izeki, began to search for a life of commitment in discipleship as described in Acts 2 of the New Testament. They looked for a body of believers which they might join.

After some years of living in community and sharing their possessions, they read of the Hutterian Brethren—in their own language—and realized that they stood on common ground. They visited colonies in Alberta and united with the Hutterian Brethren. In May 1977 Izomi Izeki was appointed servant of 1977
the Word by the elders of the Hutterian Brethren. In 1986 the community numbers around twenty-five souls, adults and children. They are called the Christian Community of New Hutterian Brethren, Owa Colony, and live on a farm about 150 miles north of Tokyo. The task of translating significant works into Japanese continues strong within the Owa community.

Today, in 1986, there are over three hundred Hutterian 1986
communities with about thirty thousand souls, living in Canada, the United States, England, and Japan. We are thankful for the freedoms we enjoy in these countries, where we are able to offer a life of Christian brotherhood to all people.

APPENDIX 3

Current Place Names with German Equivalents

(See index for German place names with current equivalents.)

Alba Iulia: Karlsburg, Romania
Alexovice: Alexowitz, Moravia

Beckov: Betzkow, Moravia
Bohuslavice: Bohuslawitz, Moravia
Bohutice: Bochtitz, Moravia
Bořetice: Boretitz, Moravia
Borský Sv. Jur: St. Georgen, Slovakia
Bratislava: Pressburg, Slovakia
Břeclav: Lundenburg, Moravia
Břežany: Frischau, Moravia
Brno: Brünn, Moravia
Brodské: Protzka, Slovakia
Brtnice: Birtnitz, Moravia
Bučovice: Butschowitz, Moravia
Budkov: Budkau, Moravia
Bulhary: Pulgram, Moravia
Bzenec: Bisenz, Moravia

Celje: Cilli, Yugoslavia
Cheb: Eger, Bohemia
Chtelnica: Echtlnitz, Slovakia
Cífer: Ziffer, Slovakia
Cluj: Klausenburg, Romania
Čachtice: Schächtitz, Slovakia
Čáslav: Tschaslau, Bohemia
Častá: Schattmansdorf, Slovakia
Častkov: Tschätschowe, Slovakia
Částkovec: Tschäskowitz, Slovakia
Čejč: Tscheitsch, Moravia
Čejkovice: Tscheikowitz, Moravia
Čermákovice: Tschermakowitz, Moravia
Černá Hora: Tschernahor, Slovakia
Červený Kameň: Bibersburg Castle, Slovakia
Český Krumlov: Böhmisch Krumau, Bohemia

Dambořice: Damborschitz, Moravia
Dechtice: Dechtitz, Slovakia
Děvín: Mayberg, Moravia
Dívčí Hrady: Maidburg Castle, Moravia
Dobrá Voda: Gutwasser Castle, Slovakia
Dojč: Toytsch, Slovakia
Dolné Orešany: Deutsch-Nussdorf, Slovakia
Dolní Dunajovice: Dannowitz, Moravia
Dolní Kounice: Kanitz, Moravia
Dubnica nad Vahom: Dubnitz, Slovakia

Elblag: Elbing, Poland
Esztergom: Gran, Hungary

Gbely: Egbell, Slovakia
Gdańsk: Danzig, Poland

Heršpice: Herspitz, Moravia
Hevlin: Höflein, Moravia
Hodonín: Göding, Moravia
Holešov: Holleschau, Slovakia
Holíč: Holitsch, Slovakia
Hrabětice: Grafendorf, Slovakia
Hrubšice: Hrubschitz, Moravia
Hruškу: Birnbaum, Moravia

Hrušovany: Rohrbach, Moravia
Hustopeče: Auspitz, Moravia

Iváň: Eibis, Moravia
Ivančice: Eibenschitz, Moravia

Jankov: Jankau, Slovakia
Jarohněvice: Jermeritz, Moravia
Jaroslavice: Joslowitz, Slovakia
Jemnice: Jamnitz, Moravia
Jevišovice: Jaispitz, Moravia
Jihlava: Iglau, Moravia

Kamnik: Stein, Yugoslavia
Kobylí: Kobelitz, Moravia
Kopčany: Gopschän, Slovakia
Koper: Capodistria, Yugoslavia
Košice: Kaschau, Slovakia
Kostolné: Kesselsdorf, Slovakia
Kowálov: Kowalowa, Slovakia
Kraśnik: Krasnikow, Poland
Křenovice: Krenowitz, Moravia
Křepice: Krepitz, Moravia
Krnov: Jägerndorf, Bohemia
Kroměříž: Kremsier, Moravia
Krumvíř: Grünwies, Moravia
Kubšice: Gobschitz, Moravia
Kunov: Gunowe, Slovakia
Kurdějov: Gurdau, Moravia
Kúty: Gätte, Slovakia
Kyjov: Gaya, Moravia

Ladomir: Vladimir-Volynsky, Poland
Lanštorf: Rampersdorf, Moravia
Lanžhot: Landshut, Moravia
Lednice: Eisgrub, Moravia
Letonice: Lettonitz, Moravia
Levice: Lewenz, Slovakia
Ljubljana: Laibach, Yugoslavia
Lužice: Luschitz, Moravia

Mackovice: Moskowitz, Moravia
Merano: Meran, Italy
Mikulčice: Mikultschitz, Moravia
Mikulov: Nikolsburg, Moravia
Milonice: Milonitz, Moravia
Milotice: Milotitz, Moravia
Modra: Moder, Slovakia
Moravský Krumlov: Mährisch Kromau, Moravia
Moravský Sv. Ján: St. Johannes, Slovakia
Morovice: Marowitz, Moravia
Moutnice: Mautnitz, Moravia
Mulhouse: Mühlhausen, France
Mušov: Muschau, Moravia

Napajedla: Napajedl, Moravia
Násedlovice: Nasselowitz, Moravia
Němčany: Niemtschan, Moravia
Němčičky: Klein Niemtschitz, Moravia
Nikolčice: Nikoltschitz, Moravia
Nitra: Neutra, Slovakia
Nosislav: Nuslau, Moravia
Nové Mesto nad Váhom: Neustadt, Slovakia
Nové Mlýny: Neumühl, Moravia
Nové Zámky: Neuhäusel, Slovakia

Olbramovice: Wolframitz, Moravia
Olomouc: Olmütz, Moravia
Oradea: Grosswardein, Romania
Ostrožká Nová Ves: Neudorf, Moravia

Pasohlávky: Weisstätten, Moravia
Pavlov: Pollau, Moravia
Perná: Pergen, Moravia
Petrova Ves: Petersdorf, Slovakia
Pezinok: Bösing, Slovakia
Plavecký Hrad: Blasenstein Castle, Slovakia
Plzeň: Pilsen, Bohemia
Podivín: Kostel, Moravia
Pohořelice: Pohrlitz, Moravia
Polehradice: Polehraditz, Moravia
Popice: Poppitz, Moravia
Popudinské Močidlany: Popodin, Slovakia
Pouzdřany: Pausram, Moravia
Praha: Prague, Bohemia
Přibice: Pribitz, Moravia
Prostějov: Prossnitz, Moravia
Prštice: Pürschitz, Moravia
Prušánky: Pruschanek, Moravia
Púchov: Buchau, Slovakia
Purkmanice: Bogenitz, Moravia

Rakšice: Rakschitz, Moravia
Rakvice: Rakwitz, Moravia
Rijeka: Fiume, Yugoslavia

Rohatec: Rohatetz, Moravia
Rosice: Rossitz, Moravia
Rovensko: Rabenska, Slovakia

Sárospatak: Bodock, Hungary
Sedlec: Voitelsbrunn, Moravia
Senica: Senitz, Slovakia
Sibiu: Hermannstadt, Romania
Sighisoara: Schässburg, Romania
Silandro: Schlanders, Italy
Skalica: Skalitz, Slovakia
Skalice: Gallitz, Moravia
Slavkov u Brna: Austerlitz, Moravia
Smolinské: Schmalenz, Slovakia
Soblahov: Soblahof, Slovakia
Sobotište: Sabatisch, Slovakia
Sopron: Ödenburg, Hungary
Sovinec: Eulenberg, Moravia
Stará Břeclav: Altenmarkt, Moravia
Starnice: Starnitz under Lassling, Moravia
Strachotín: Tracht, Moravia
Stráže: Sdräse, Slovakia
Strážnice: Strassnitz, Moravia
Světlov: Swetlau, Moravia
Székesfehérvár: Stuhlweissenburg, Hungary
Šakvice: Schakwitz, Moravia
Šala: Schella, Slovakia
Šaštín: Schossberg, Slovakia
Šintava: Schindau, Slovakia
Štúrovo: Parkan, Slovakia
Šwidnica: Schweidnitz, East Germany

Tasovice: Tasswitz, Moravia
Tavíkovice: Teikowitz, Moravia
Telnice: Tillnitz, Slovakia
Tovačov: Tobitschau, Slovakia
Třebíč: Trebitsch, Moravia
Trenčianske Teplice: Teplitz, Slovakia
Trenčín: Trentschin, Slovakia
Trnava: Tyrnau, Slovakia
Trstěnice: Stiegnitz, Moravia
Tvrdonice: Turnitz, Moravia
Týnec: Teinitz, Moravia

Uherské Hradiště: Ungarisch Hradisch, Moravia
Uherský Ostroh: Ungarisch Ostra, Moravia
Uhřice: Urschitz, Moravia

Vacenovice: Watzenowitz, Moravia
Valtice: Feldsberg, Moravia
Velká nad Veličkou: Welka, Moravia
Velké Bílovice: Bilowitz, Moravia
Velké Němčice: Gross Niemtschitz, Moravia
Velké Pavlovice: Pawlowitz, Moravia
Velké Štarvice: Gross Steurowitz, Moravia
Venezia: Venice, Italy
Veselí nad Moravou: Wessely, Moravia
Věstonice: Wisternitz, Moravia
Veveří: Aichorn, Moravia
Vičkovce: Farkeschin, Slovakia
Vintu de Jos: Alwinz, Romania
Vipiteno: Sterzing, Italy
Višňové: Wischenau, Moravia
Vištuk: Wystock, Slovakia
Vlasatice: Wostitz, Moravia
Vracov: Fraitz, Moravia
Vrbovec: Urbau, Moravia
Vyškov: Wischau, Moravia

Zaječi: Saitz, Moravia
Znojmo: Znaim, Moravia
Žabčice: Schabschitz, Moravia
Žadovice: Schadowitz, Moravia
Ždánice: Steinitz, Moravia
Želovice: Klein Seelowitz, Moravia
Židlochovice: Gross Seelowitz, Moravia

APPENDIX 4

Maps

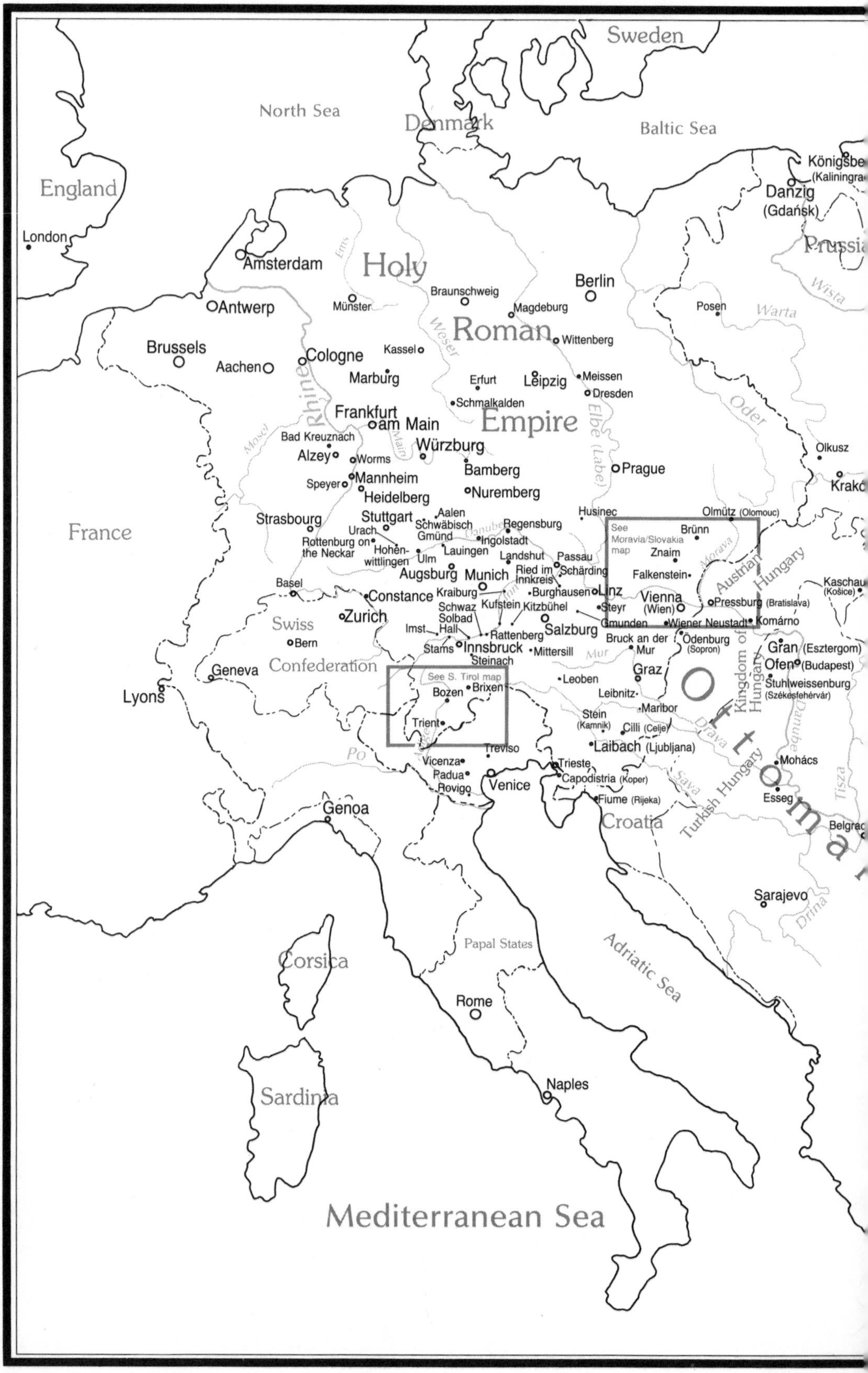

Sweden
North Sea
Denmark
Baltic Sea
England
London
Königsberg (Kaliningrad)
Danzig (Gdańsk)
Prussia
Amsterdam
Holy Roman Empire
Berlin
Braunschweig
Magdeburg
Münster
Antwerp
Brussels
Aachen
Cologne
Kassel
Wittenberg
Posen
Warta
Wisła
Marburg
Erfurt
Leipzig
Meissen
Dresden
Schmalkalden
Frankfurt am Main
Rhine
Weser
Ems
Elbe (Labe)
Oder
Mosel
Main
Bad Kreuznach
Alzey
Worms
Würzburg
Bamberg
Prague
Olkusz
Kraków
Speyer
Mannheim
Heidelberg
Nuremberg
France
Strasbourg
Stuttgart
Aalen
Schwäbisch Gmünd
Urach
Rottenburg on the Neckar
Hohenwittlingen
Ulm
Lauingen
Ingolstadt
Regensburg
Danube
Husinec
Olmütz (Olomouc)
See Moravia/Slovakia map
Brünn
Znaim
Falkenstein
Morava
Landshut
Passau
Schärding
Ried im Innkreis
Augsburg
Munich
Kraiburg
Burghausen
Linz
Basel
Constance
Zurich
Swiss Confederation
Bern
Geneva
Lyons
Schwaz
Solbad Hall
Kufstein
Kitzbühel
Steyr
Gmunden
Vienna (Wien)
Pressburg (Bratislava)
Wiener Neustadt
Komárno
Austrian Hungary
Kaschau (Košice)
Imst
Rattenberg
Salzburg
Stams
Innsbruck
Steinach
Mittersill
Mur
Bruck an der Mur
Ödenburg (Sopron)
Kingdom of Hungary
Gran (Esztergom)
Ofen (Budapest)
Stuhlweissenburg (Székesfehérvár)
See S. Tirol map
Bozen
Brixen
Trient
Graz
Leoben
Leibnitz
Maribor
Stein (Kamnik)
Cilli (Celje)
Laibach (Ljubljana)
Drava
Sava
Treviso
Po
Vicenza
Padua
Rovigo
Venice
Trieste
Capodistria (Koper)
Fiume (Rijeka)
Croatia
Turkish Hungary
Mohács
Esseg
Tisza
Ottoman
Belgrade
Genoa
Sarajevo
Drina
Corsica
Papal States
Adriatic Sea
Rome
Sardinia
Naples
Mediterranean Sea

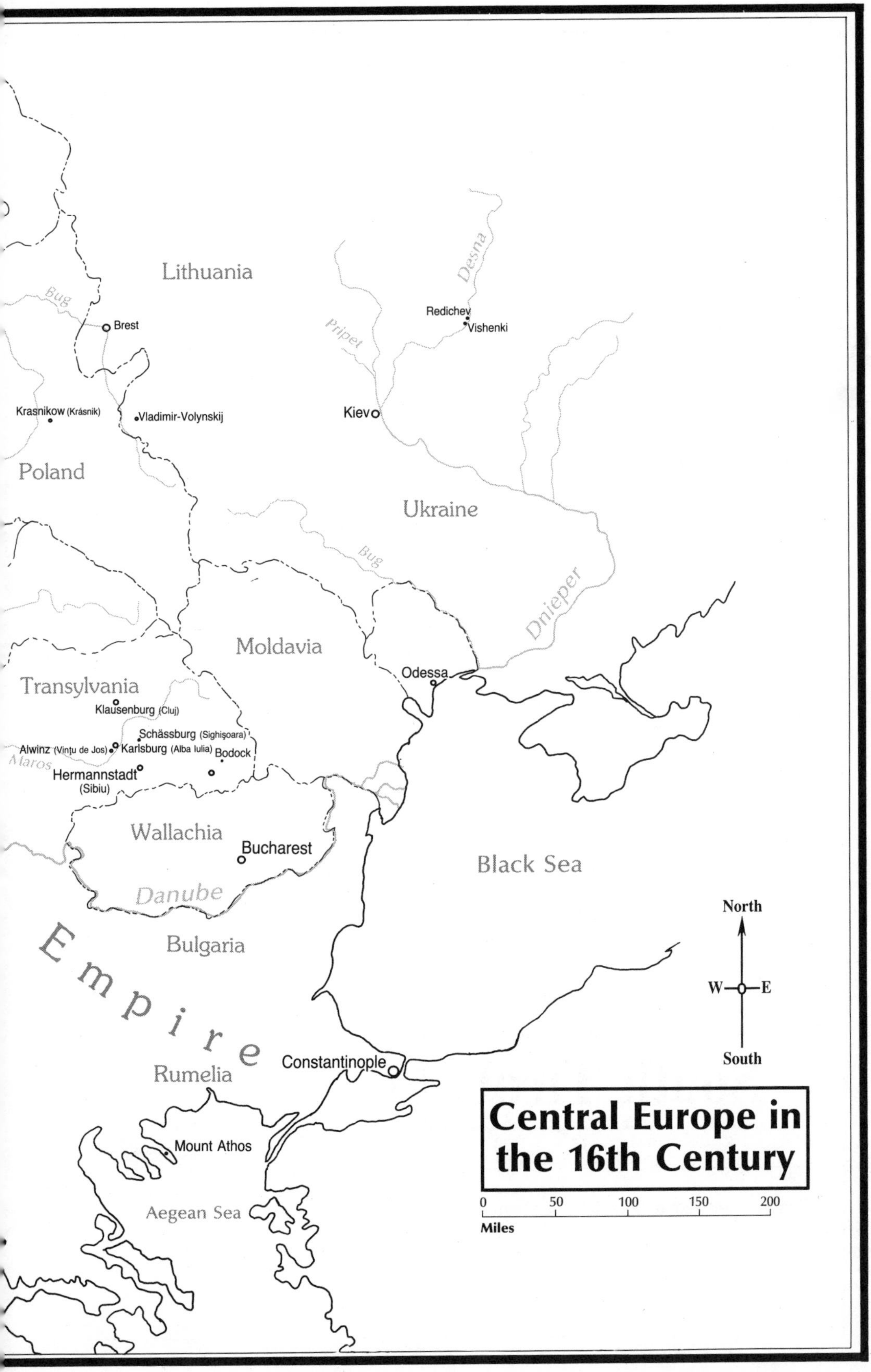
Lithuania
Desna
Bug
Brest
Redichev
Vishenki
Pripet
Krasnikow (Krásnik)
Vladimir-Volynskij
Kievo
Poland
Ukraine
Bug
Dnieper
Moldavia
Odessa
Transylvania
Klausenburg (Cluj)
Schässburg (Sighişoara)
Alwinz (Vinţu de Jos)
Karlsburg (Alba Iulia)
Bodock
Maros
Hermannstadt
(Sibiu)
Wallachia
Bucharest
Danube
Black Sea
Bulgaria
Empire
Rumelia
Constantinople
Mount Athos
Aegean Sea
North
W
E
South
Central Europe in the 16th Century
0
50
100
150
200
Miles

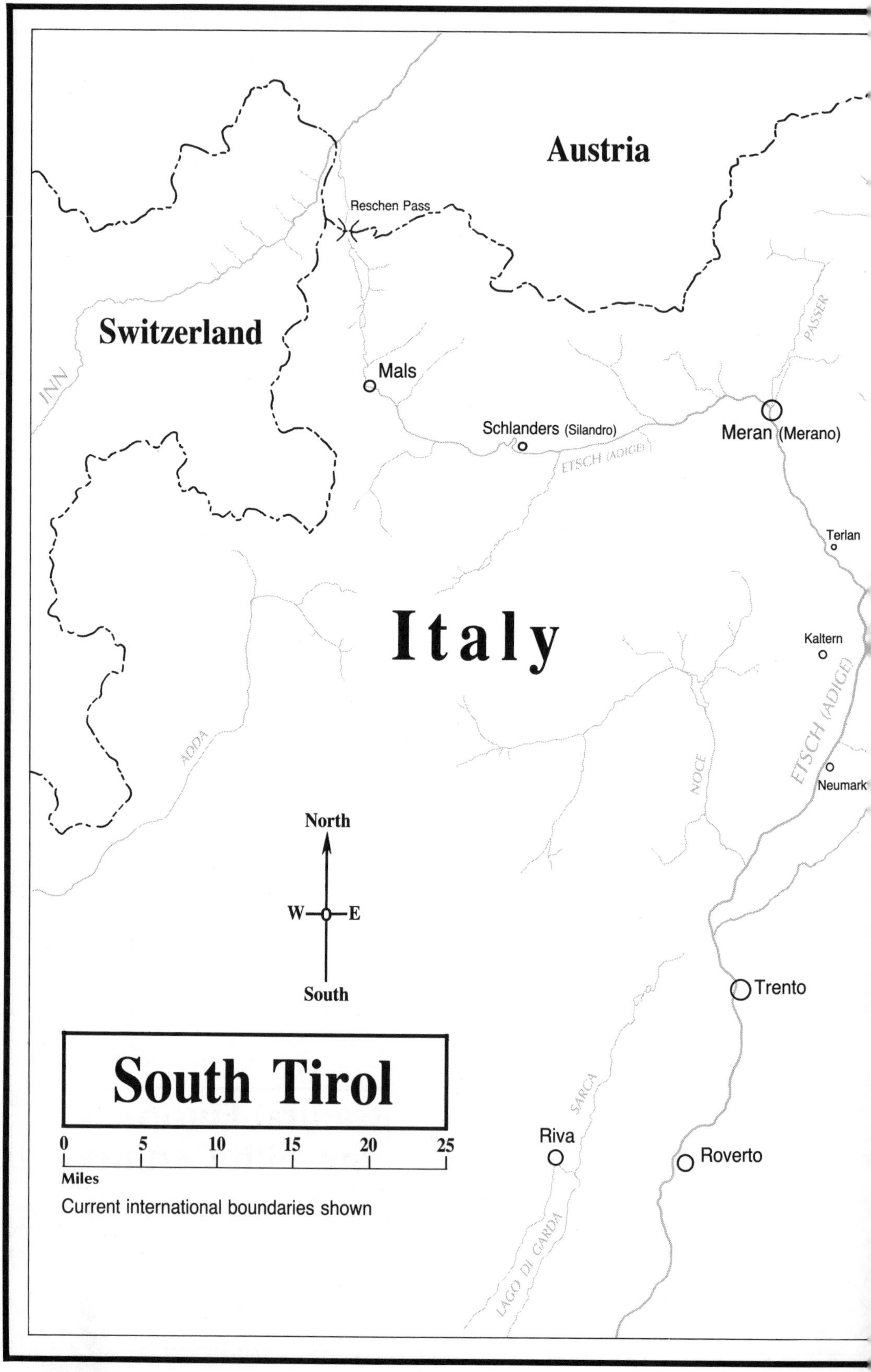
Austria
Reschen Pass
Switzerland
INN
Mals
Schlanders (Silandro)
ETSCH (ADIGE)
Meran (Merano)
PASSER
Terlan
Italy
Kaltern
ETSCH (ADIGE)
Neumark
NOCE
ADDA
North
W
E
South
South Tirol
0 5 10 15 20 25
Miles
Current international boundaries shown
Trento
SARCA
Riva
Roverto
LAGO DI GARDA

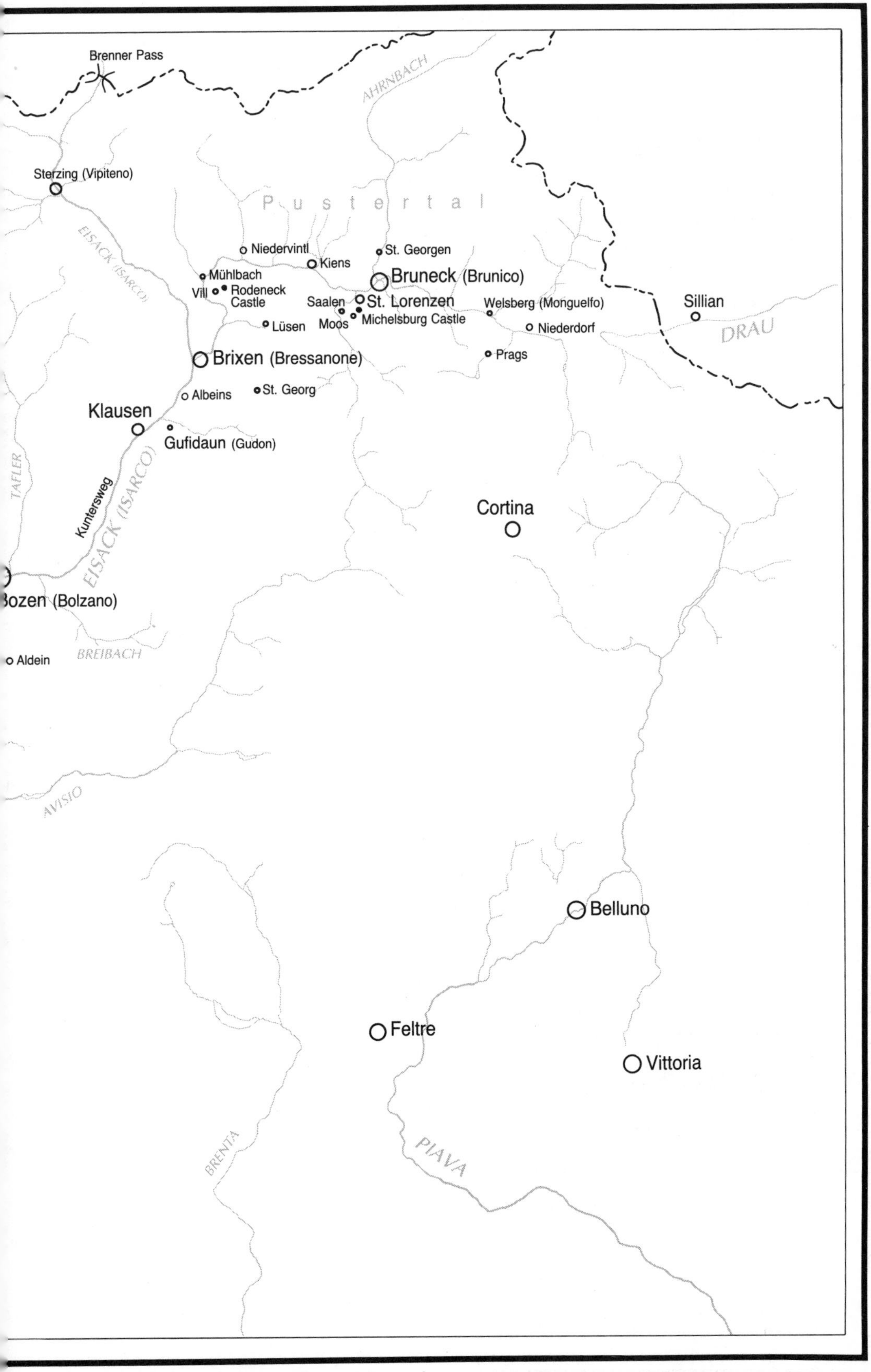
Brenner Pass
AHRNBACH
Sterzing (Vipiteno)
P u s t e r t a l
EISACK (ISARCO)
Niedervintl
Kiens
St. Georgen
Bruneck (Brunico)
Mühlbach
Vill
Rodeneck Castle
Saalen
St. Lorenzen
Welsberg (Monguelfo)
Sillian
Moos
Michelsburg Castle
Lüsen
Niederdorf
DRAU
Prags
Brixen (Bressanone)
Albeins
St. Georg
Klausen
Gufidaun (Gudon)
TAFLER
Kuntersweg
EISACK (ISARCO)
Cortina
ozen (Bolzano)
Aldein
BREIBACH
AVISIO
Belluno
Feltre
Vittoria
BRENTA
PIAVA

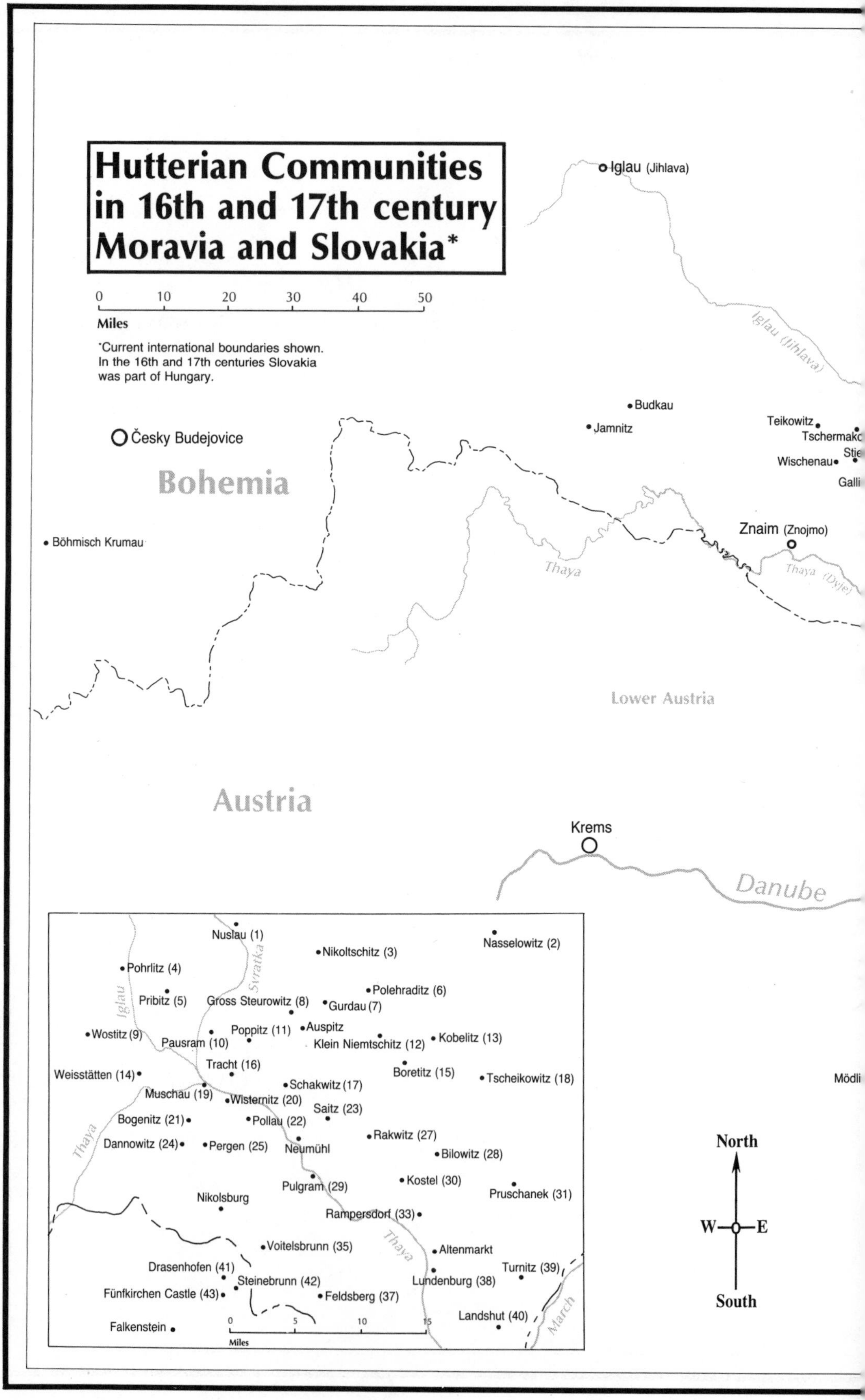
Hutterian Communities in 16th and 17th century Moravia and Slovakia*
0 10 20 30 40 50
Miles
*Current international boundaries shown. In the 16th and 17th centuries Slovakia was part of Hungary.
Iglau (Jihlava)
Iglau (Jihlava)
Budkau
Jamnitz
Teikowitz
Wischenau
Česky Budejovice
Bohemia
Böhmisch Krumau
Znaim (Znojmo)
Thaya
Thaya (Dyje)
Lower Austria
Austria
Krems
Danube
Nuslau (1)
Nasselowitz (2)
Nikoltschitz (3)
Pohrlitz (4)
Pribitz (5)
Polehraditz (6)
Gurdau (7)
Gross Steurowitz (8)
Wostitz (9)
Pausram (10)
Poppitz (11)
Auspitz
Klein Niemtschitz (12)
Kobelitz (13)
Weisstätten (14)
Boretitz (15)
Tracht (16)
Schakwitz (17)
Tscheikowitz (18)
Muschau (19)
Wisternitz (20)
Bogenitz (21)
Pollau (22)
Saitz (23)
Dannowitz (24)
Pergen (25)
Neumühl
Rakwitz (27)
Bilowitz (28)
Pulgram (29)
Kostel (30)
Pruschanek (31)
Nikolsburg
Rampersdorf (33)
Voitelsbrunn (35)
Altenmarkt
Drasenhofen (41)
Steinebrunn (42)
Lundenburg (38)
Turnitz (39)
Fünfkirchen Castle (43)
Feldsberg (37)
Falkenstein
Landshut (40)
Iglau
Svratka
Thaya
Thaya
March
0 5 10 15
Miles
North
W E
South

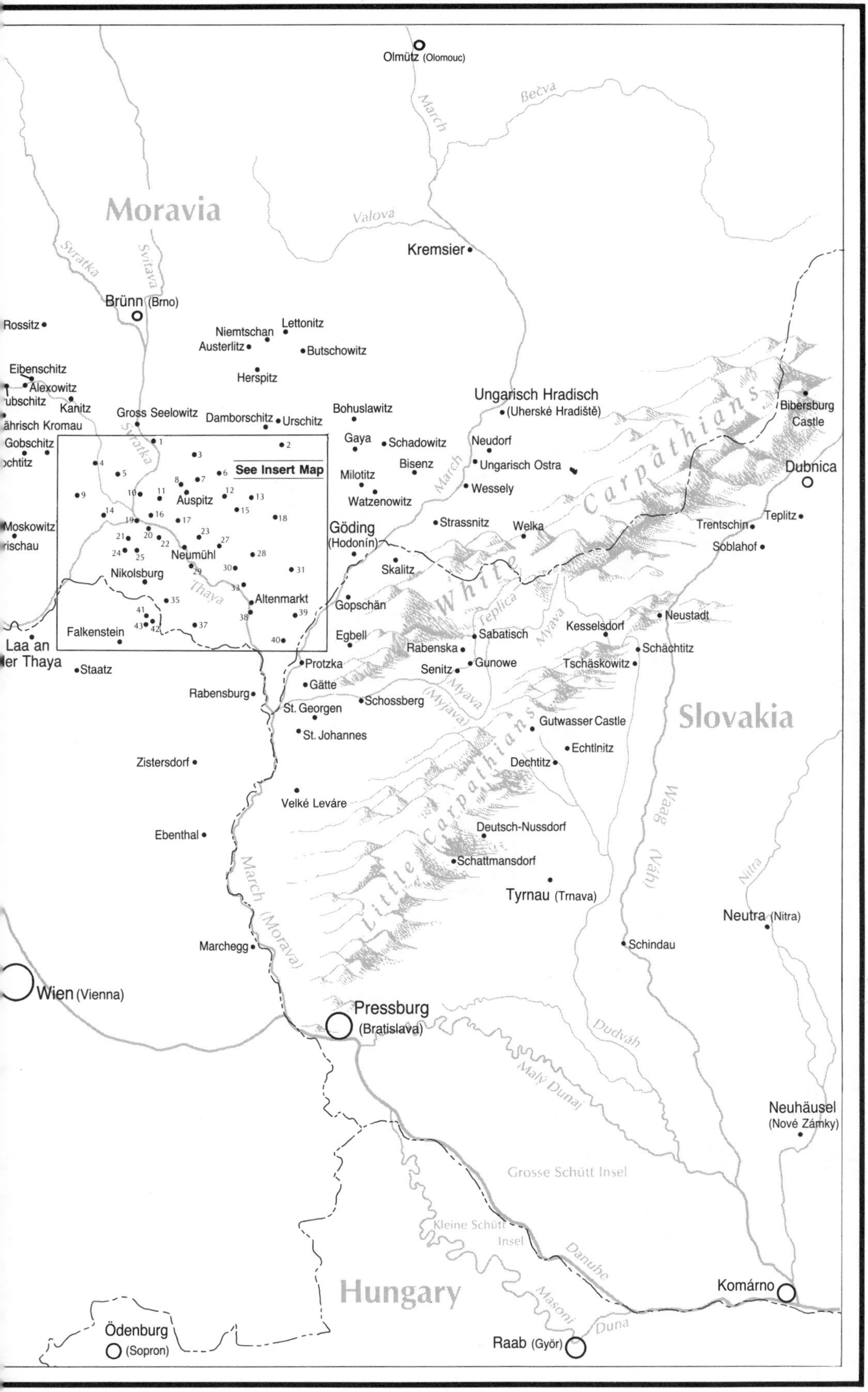

Olmütz (Olomouc)
March
Bečva
Moravia
Valova
Kremsier
Svratka
Svitava
Brünn (Brno)
Rossitz
Lettonitz
Niemtschan
Austerlitz
Butschowitz
Eibenschitz
Alexowitz
Herspitz
Kanitz
Gross Seelowitz
Damborschitz
Urschitz
Bohuslawitz
Ungarisch Hradisch
(Uherské Hradiště)
Bibersburg
Castle
Gobschitz
Gaya
Schadowitz
Neudorf
See Insert Map
Bisenz
Ungarisch Ostra
Dubnica
Milotitz
Auspitz
Wessely
Watzenowitz
Carpathians
Moskowitz
Strassnitz
Welka
Trentschin
Teplitz
Göding
(Hodonín)
Soblahof
Neumühl
Skalitz
White
Nikolsburg
Thaya
Teplica
Altenmarkt
Gopschän
Myjava
Neustadt
Kesselsdorf
Falkenstein
Egbell
Sabatisch
Schächtitz
Laa an
der Thaya
Rabenska
Tschäskowitz
Staatz
Protzka
Senitz
Gunowe
Gätte
Rabensburg
Schossberg
St. Georgen
Slovakia
Gutwasser Castle
St. Johannes
Echtlnitz
Zistersdorf
Dechtitz
Velké Levàre
Waag
Deutsch-Nussdorf
Ebenthal
(Váh)
Little Carpathians
Schattmansdorf
Nitra
Tyrnau (Trnava)
March (Morava)
Neutra (Nitra)
Schindau
Marchegg
Wien (Vienna)
Pressburg
(Bratislava)
Dudváh
Malý Dunaj
Neuhäusel
(Nové Zámky)
Grosse Schütt Insel
Kleine Schütt
Insel
Danube
Hungary
Komárno
Masoni
Ödenburg
Duna
(Sopron)
Raab (Györ)

Lochy in Moravia

Diagram of an underground hiding hole

Chambers differ in size, the largest ones measuring as much as 50 by 100 feet, with heights varying from standing room to the height of three men; tunnels afford crawling space only. Earth shelves on sides and corners of chambers were used for fugitives' belongings.

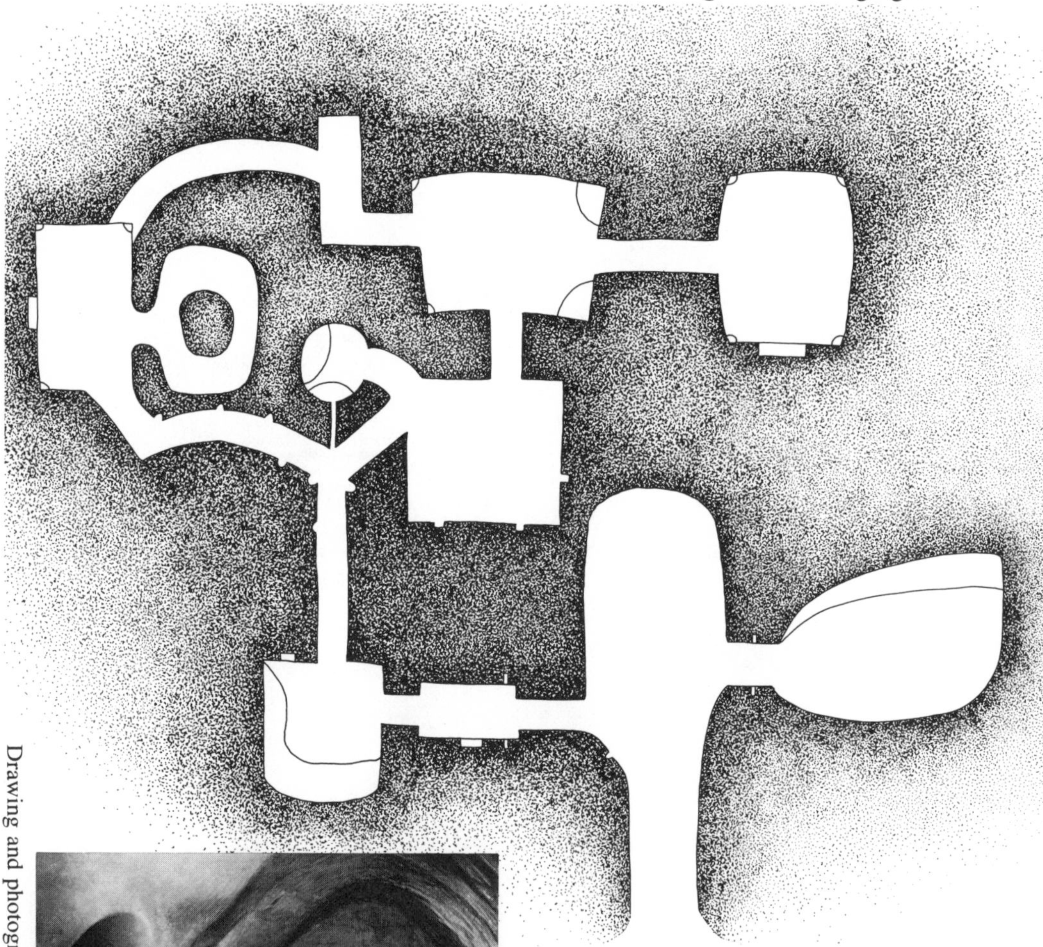

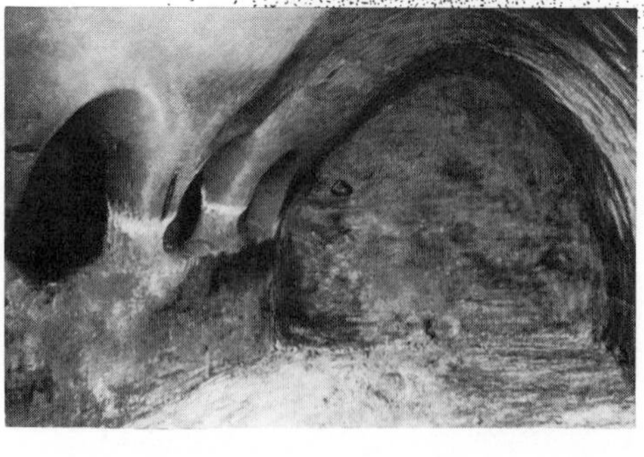

A small chamber

Drawing and photograph by Jan Gleysteen

Appendix 6

Facsimiles of the “1580” and “1581” codices

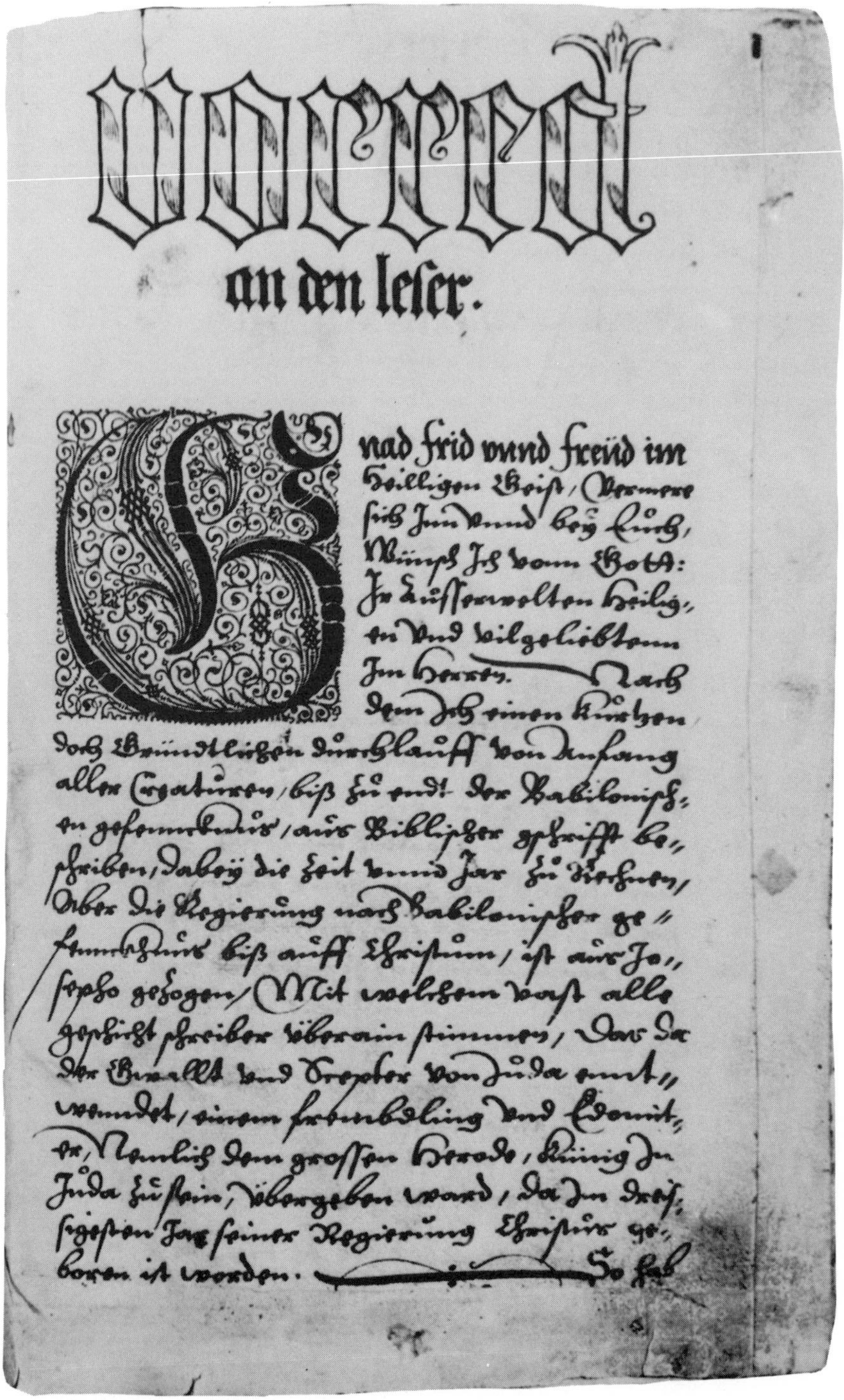
Vorred
an den leser.

Gnad frid vnnd freünd im Heiligen Geist, Vermere sich In vnnd bey Euch, Wünsch Ich vom Gott: Ir außerwelten heilig-en vnd vilgeliebten Jn Herrn. Nach dem Ich einen kurtzen doch Gründtlichen durchlauff von Anfang aller Creatüren, biß zu endt der Babilonisch-en gefencknüs, aus Biblischer gschrifft be-schriben, dabey die zeit vnnd Jar zu rechnen, über die Regierung nach Babilonischer ge-fencknüs biß auff Christum, ist aus Jo-sepho gezogen, Mit welchem vast alle geschicht schreiber überain stimmen, Das da der Gwallt vnd Scepter von Juda ent-wendet, einem frembdling vnd Edomit-er, Nemlich dem grossen Herode, König In Juda zu sein, übergeben ward, da In dreis-sigsten Jar seiner Regierung Christus ge-boren ist worden. So hab

Plate 1: Preface to the Reader
"1580" codex

Vorrede an den Leser.

Gnad/ Frid vnd Freid im Heilligen Geist/ Ver-mert sich Inn vnd bej euch/ Wünsch Ich vom Gott/ Ir Außerwelten Heiligen vnd vilgeliebten im Her-ren. Nachdem Ich einen kurtzen, doch gründtlichen durchlauff von Anfang aller Creaturen/ bis zu der Babilonischen gfencknis/ aus Biblischer schrifft beschriben/ dabej die zeit vnd Jar zu rechnen/ Aber die Regierung nach Babilonischer gfenknis biß auff Christum ist aus Josepho gezogen/ Mit welchem fast alle geschicht schreiber übereinstim-men/ Das da der gewalt vnd Zepter von Juda entwandet/ einem frembdling vnd Idomiter Nämlich dem grossen Herode/ König In Juda zu sein/ übergeben ward/ da im dreissigsten Jar sei-ner Regierung Christus geboren ist worden.

So hab Ich mir vndter dem/ vnd vorhin offt-mals gedacht/ Gott würde etwa dermallen

G j

Plate 2: Preface to the Reader
"1581" codex

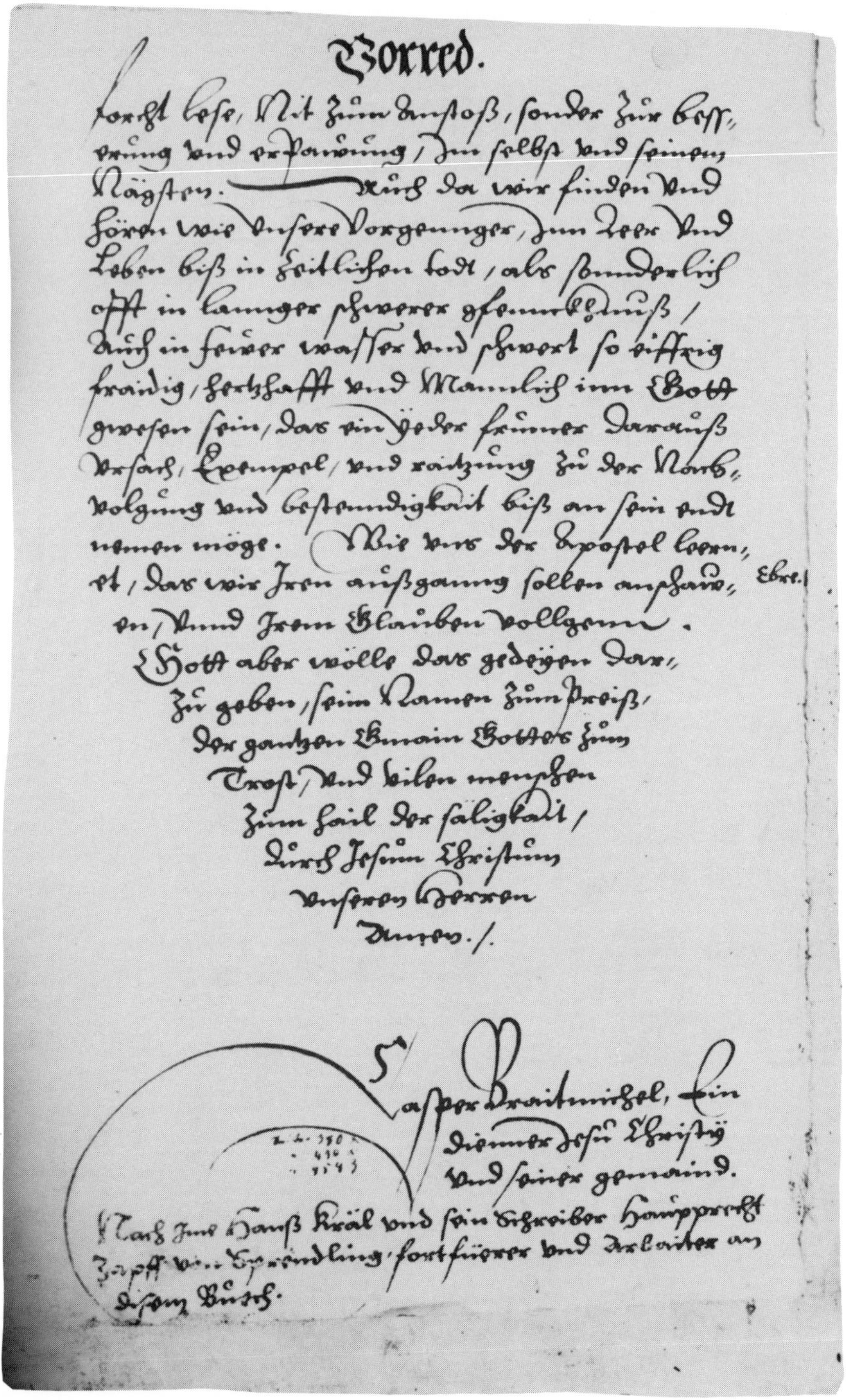
Vorred.

forcht lese, Nit zum anstoß, sonder zur bess-
erung und erfarung, im selbst und seinem
Nägsten. Auch da wir finden und
hören wie unsere Vorgenger, im leer und
leben biß in zeitlichen todt, als sunderlich
offt in langer schwerer gfencknuß,
auch in feuer wasser und schwert so eiffrig
fraidig, hertzhafft und Mannlich imm Gott
gewesen sein, das ein yeder frummer darauß
Ursach, Exempel, und raitzung zu der Nach-
volgung und bestendigkait biß an sein endt
nemen möge. Wie uns der Apostel leeret, das wir Iren außgang sollen anschau-
en, Und Iren Glauben vollgen. Ebr.
Gott aber wölle das gedeyen dar-
zu geben, sein Namen zum Preiß,
der gantzen Gmain Gottes zum
Trost, Und vilen menschen
zum hail der säligkait,
durch Jesum Christum
unsern Herren
Amen./

Caspar Braitmichel, ein
diener Jesu Christi
und seiner gemaind.

Nach Im Hanß Kräl und sein schreiber Hauprecht
Zapff von Sprendling, fortfürer und Arbaiter an
disem Buch.

Plate 3: Preface to the Reader continued
"1580" codex

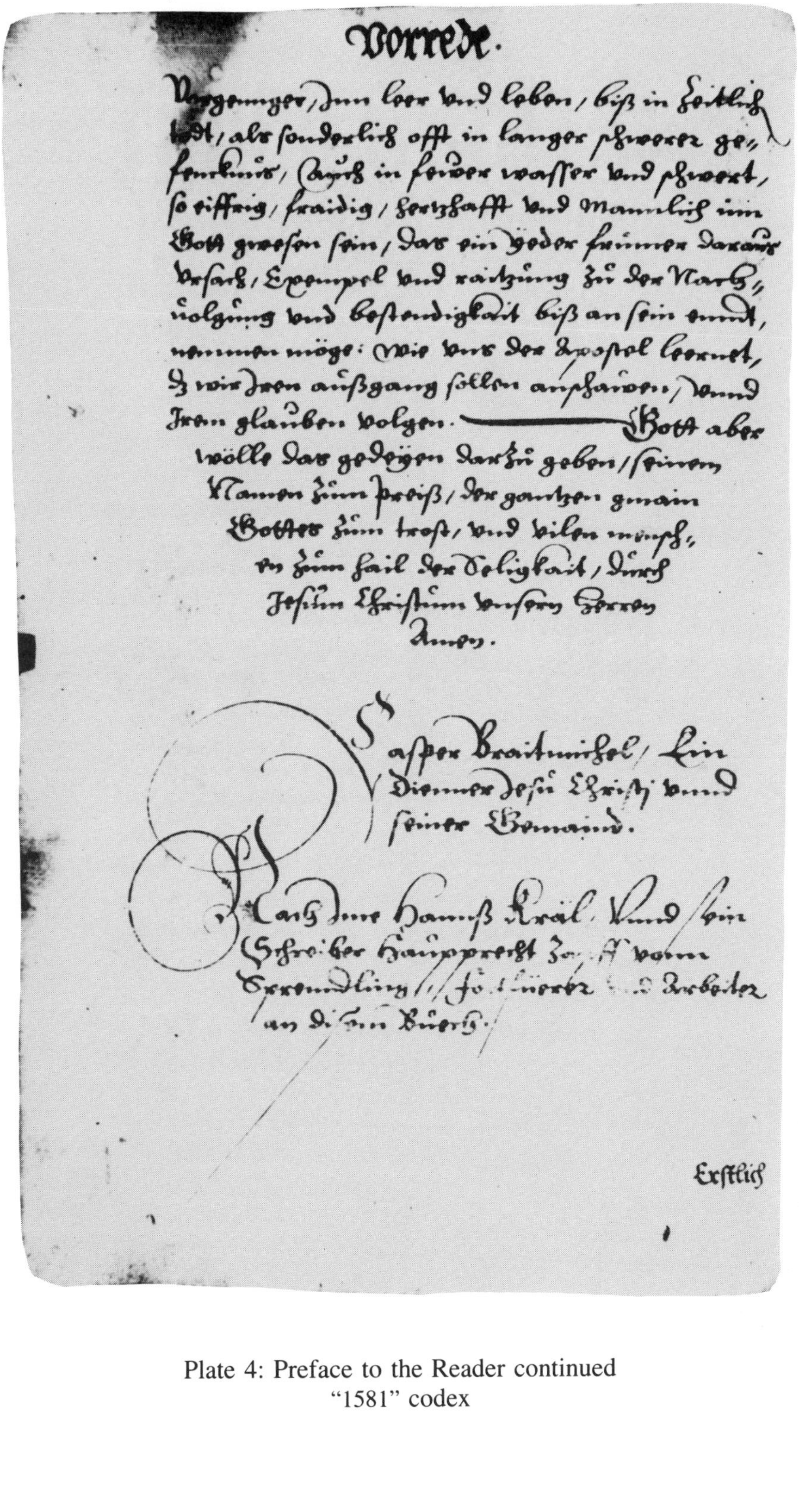
Vorrede.

Vorgennger, Irer leer vnd leben, biß in Zeitlich
todt, als sonderlich offt in langer schwerer ge=
fencknüs, auch in feuer wasser vnd schwert,
so tifferig, fraidig, hertzhafft vnd Mannlich vmb
Gott gewesen sein, das ein yeder frumer daraus
Vrsach, Exempel vnd raitzung zu der Nach=
uolgung vnd bestendigkait biß an sein endt,
nemmen möge: Wie vns der Apostel leeret,
daß wir Iren außgang sollen anschauen, vnnd
Iren glauben volgen. —— Gott aber
wölle das gedeyen dartzu geben, seinem
Namen zum preiß, der gantzen gmain
Gottes zum trost, vnd vilen mensch=
en zum hail der Seligkait, durch
Jesum Christum vnsern Herren
Amen.

Caspar Braitmichel, Ein
Diener Jesu Christi vnnd
seiner Gemaind.

Nach Ime Hanß Kräl, vnnd sein
Schreiber Hauprecht Zapff vom
Veremdling, // Fortfüerer vnd Arbeiter
an disem Buech.

Erstlich

Plate 4: Preface to the Reader continued
"1581" codex

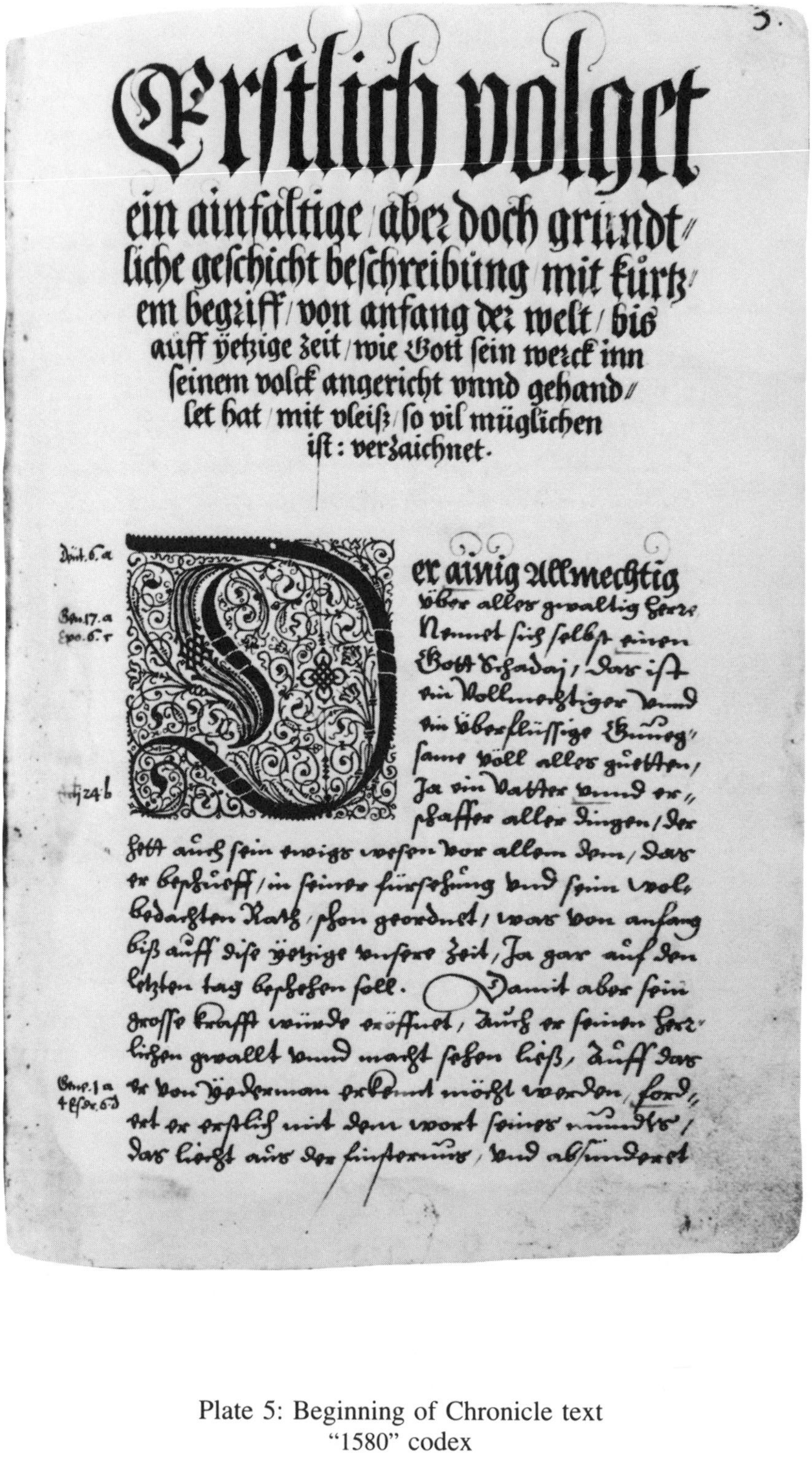
5.

Erstlich volget
ein ainfaltige / aber doch grundt//
liche geschicht beschreibüng mit kürtz//
em begriff / von anfang der welt / bis
auff yetzige zeit / wie Gott sein werck inn
seinem volck angericht vnnd gehand//
let hat / mit vleiß / so vil müglichen
ist: verzaichnet.

Deut. 6. a Der ainig Allmechtig
über alles gewaltig Herr,
Gen. 17. a Nennet sich selbst einen
Exo. 6. e Gott Schadaj, das ist
ein Vollmechtiger vnnd
ein überflüssige Genug//
sam voll aller güetten,
Actu 24. b Ja ein Vatter vnnd er//
schaffer aller dingen, der
hatt auch sein ewigs wesen vor allem dem, das
er beschüeff, in seiner fürsehüng vnd sein wol//
bedachten Rath, schon geordnet, was von anfang
biß auff dise yetzige vnsere zeit, Ja gar auf den
letzten tag beschehen soll. Damit aber sein
grosse krafft würde eröffnet, auch er seinen herr//
lichen gwallt vnnd macht sehen ließ, auff das
Gen. 1. a er von yederman erkent möcht werden, ford//
4 Esdr. 6. d ert er erstlich mit dem wort seines mundes,
das liecht aus der finsternus, vnd absündert

Plate 5: Beginning of Chronicle text
"1580" codex

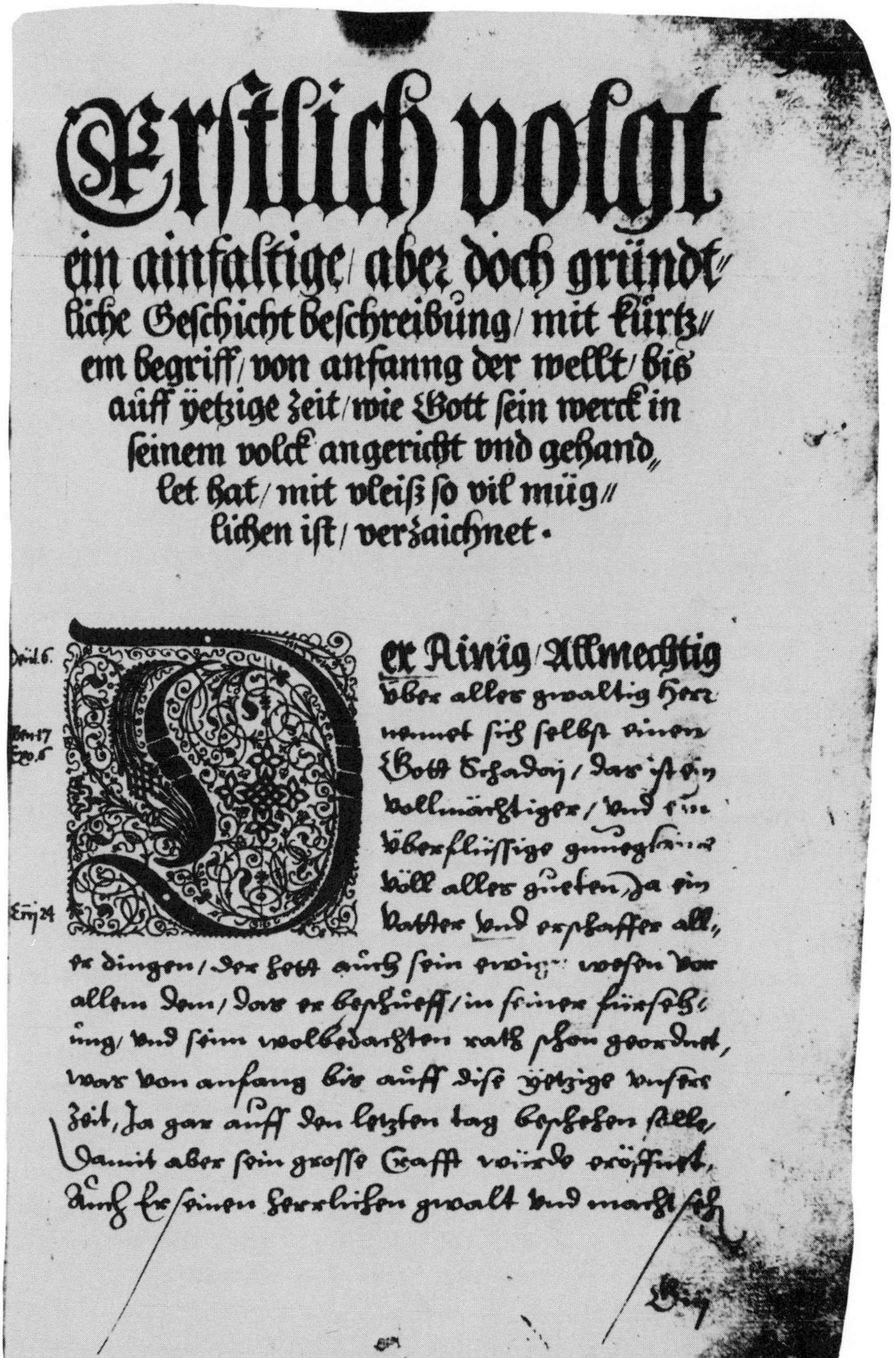
Erstlich volgt
ein ainfaltige/ aber doch gründt//
liche Geschicht beschreibung/ mit kürtz//
em begriff/ von anfanng der wellt/ bis
auff yetzige zeit/ wie Gott sein werck in
seinem volck angericht und gehand//
let hat/ mit vleiß so vil müg//
lichen ist/ verzaichnet.

Der Ainig/ Allmechtig
über aller gwaltig Herr
nennet sich selbst einen
Gott Schaddaj/ das ist ein
vollmächtiger/ und ein
überflüssige gnuegsame
voll alles gueten/ ja ein
Vatter und erschaffer all//
er dingen/ der Gott auch sein ewiges wesen vor
allem dem/ das er beschueff/ in seiner fürsehung/
und sein wolbedachten rath schon geordnet/
was von anfang bis auff dise yetzige unsere
zeit/ ja gar auff den letzten tag geschehen solle/
Damit aber sein grosse Craft würde eröffnet/
auch er seinen herrlichen gwalt und macht sich

Plate 6: Beginning of Chronicle text
"1581" codex

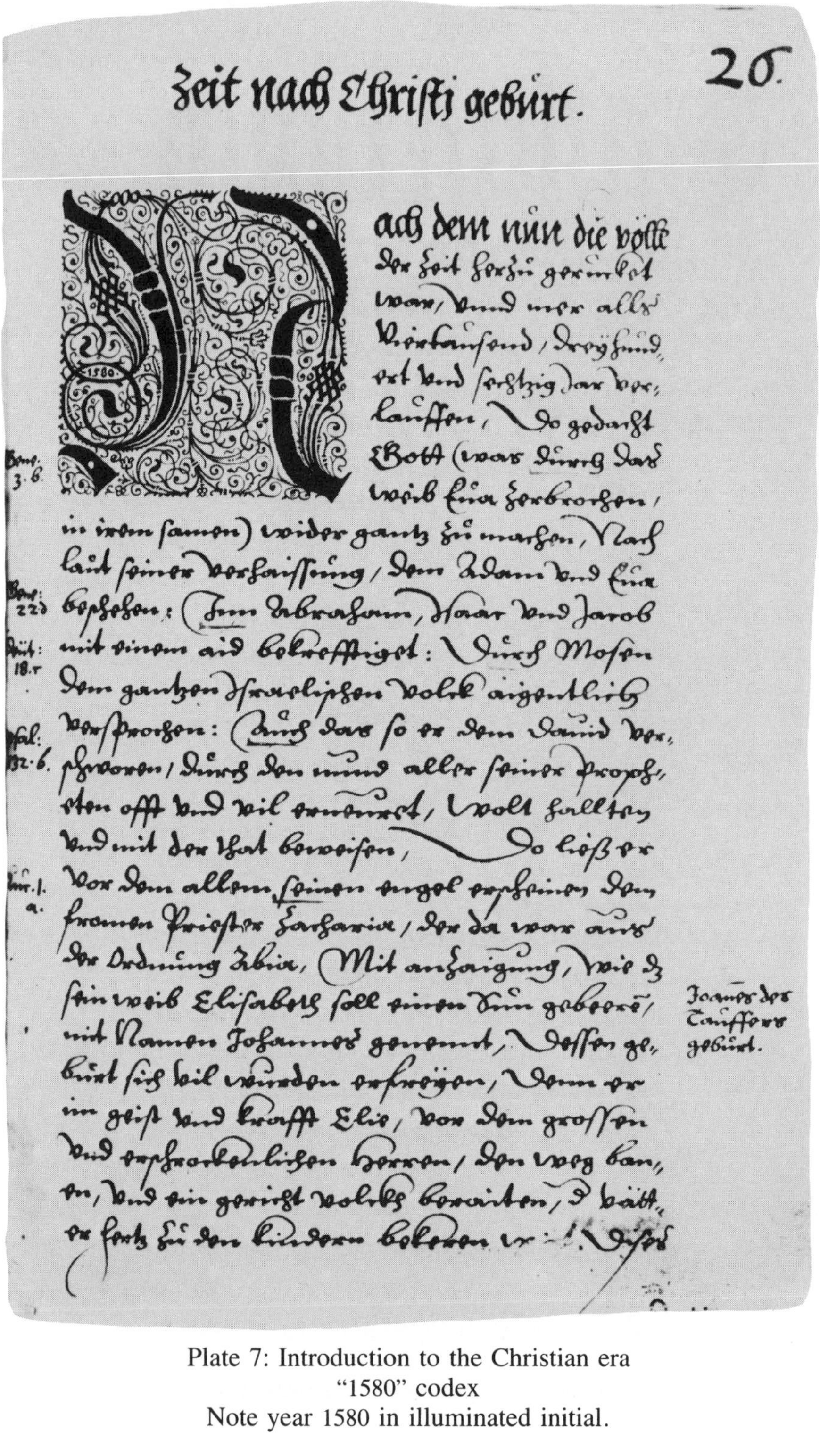

Zeit nach Christi geburt. 26.

Nach dem nun die völle der zeit herzu genahet war, und nun alle Viertausend, dreyhundert und sechtzig Jar verlauffen, Do gedacht Gott (was durch das weib Eua zerbrochen, in irem samen) wider gantz zu machen, Nach laut seiner verhaissung, dem Adam und Eua beschehen: Dem Abraham, Isaac und Jacob mit einem aid bekrefftiget: Durch Mosen dem gantzen Israelischen volck aigentlich versprochen: Auch das so er dem David verschworen, durch den mund aller seiner propheten offt und vil erneuert, wolt hallten und mit der that beweisen, Do ließ er vor dem allen seinen engel erscheinen dem fromen Priester Zacharie, der da war aus der Ordnung Abia, Mit anzaigung, wie dz sein weib Elisabeth soll einen Sun gebere, mit Namen Johannes genent, Dessen geburt sich vil wurden erfreyen, Dann er im geist und krafft Elie, vor dem grossen und erschrockenlichen Herren, den weg banen, und ein gericht volcks beraiten, d hätt er hertz zu den kindern bekeren [illegible]. Diser

Gen. 3. b. — Gen. 22 d — Deut. 18. c — Psal. 132. b. — Luc. 1. a.

Joannes des Tauffers geburt.

Plate 7: Introduction to the Christian era
"1580" codex
Note year 1580 in illuminated initial.

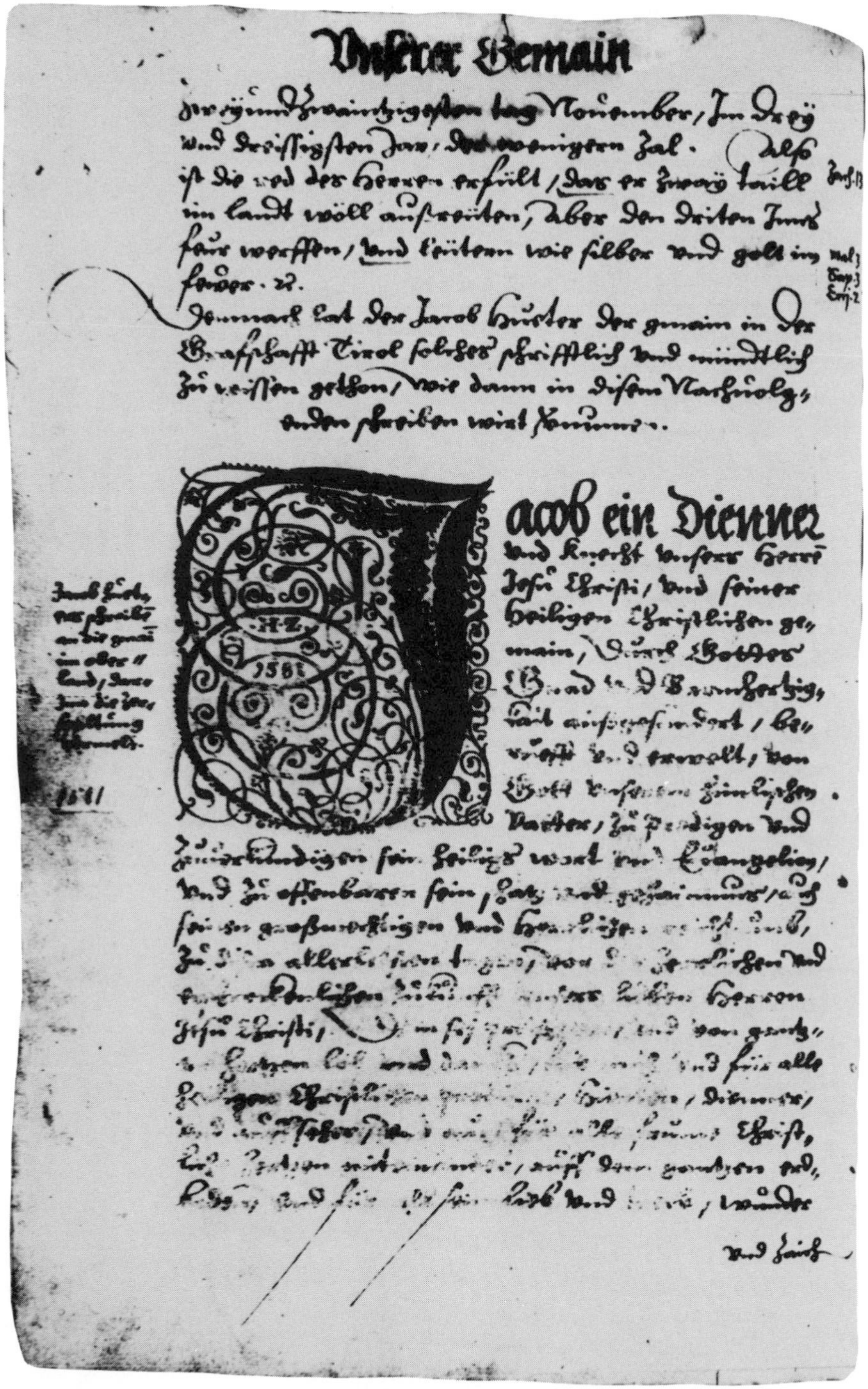

Plate 8: Beginning of Jakob Hutter's letter to the church in Tirol
"1581" codex
Note initials H.Z. (Hauptrecht Zapff) and year 1581
in illuminated initial.

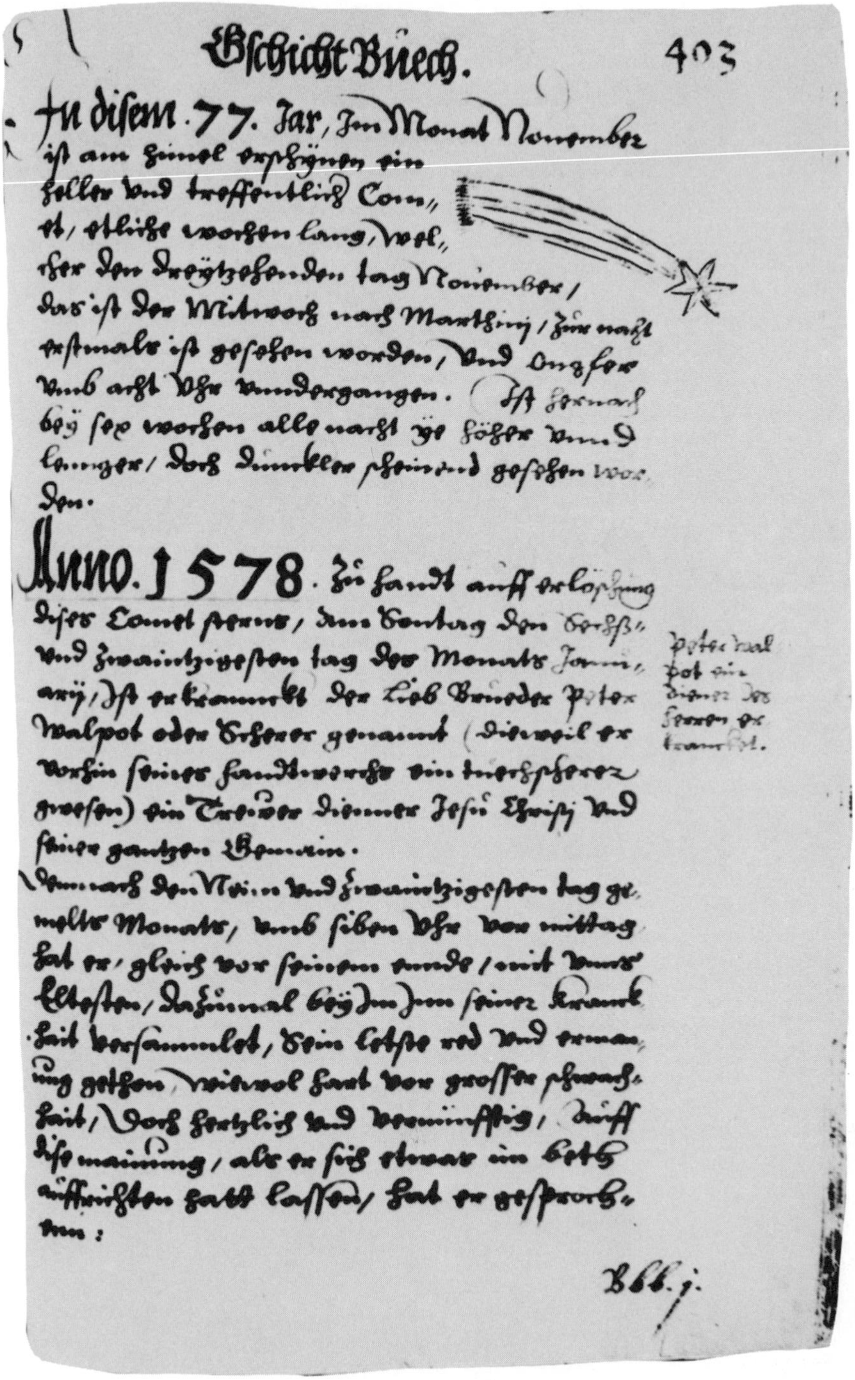

Gschicht Buech. 403

In disem 77. Jar, Im Monat November
ist am himel erschinen ein
heller und treffentlich Comet, etliche wochen lang, welcher den dreyzehenden tag Novembers,
das ist der Mitwoch nach Marthinj, zur nacht
erstmals ist gesehen worden, und ungfer
umb acht Uhr undergangen. Ist hernach
bey sex wochen alle nacht ye höher und
lenger, doch dunkler scheinend gesehen worden.

Anno. 1578. Zu handt auff erlöschung
diser Comet sterns, den Sontag den sechs-
und zwaintzigesten tag des Monats Janu-
arij, ist erkranckt der lieb Bruder Peter
Walpot oder Scherer genannt (dieweil er
vorhin seines handtwerchs ein tuechscherer
gwesen) ein Treuer diener Jesu Christj und
seiner gantzen Gmain.

Peter Walpot ein diener des Herren erkranckt.

Dennach den Nein und zwaintzigesten tag gemelts Monats, umb siben Uhr vor mittag
hat er, gleich vor seinem ende, mit den
Eltesten, dazumal bey dem im seiner kranck-
heit versammlet, sein letste red und ermanung gethon, wiewol hart vor grosser schwach-
heit, doch hertzlich und vernünfftig, auff
dise mainung, als er sich etwas im beth
auffrichten hatt lassen, hat er gesproch-
en:

Bbb. j.

Plate 9: Illustration of comet seen in November 1577
"1580" codex

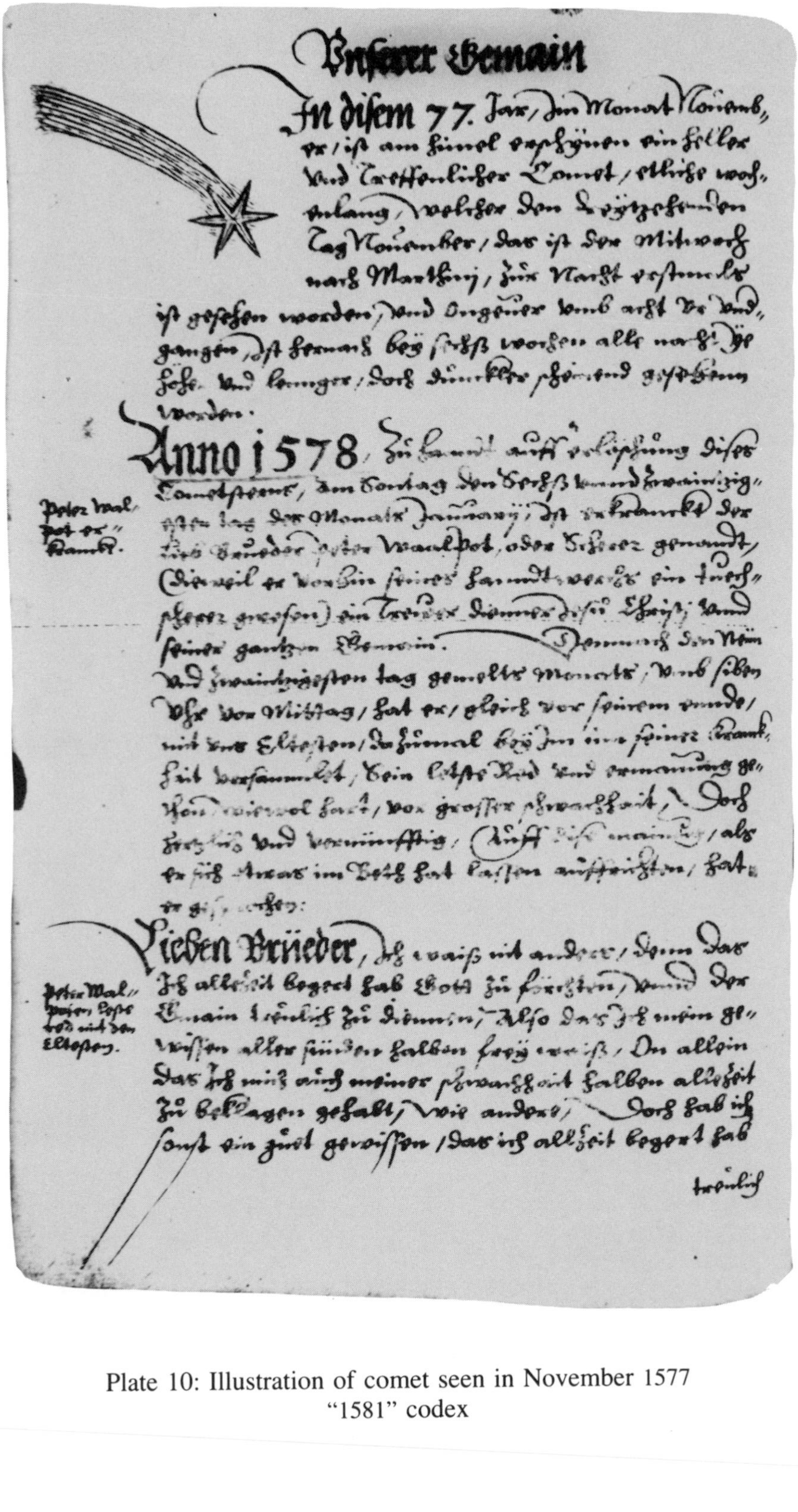
Unserer Gemain

In disem 77. Jar, im Monat November, ist am Himel erschinen ein heller
und schröckhlicher Comet, etliche wochen lang, welcher den vierzehenden
Tag November, das ist der Mitwoch
nach Martini, zur Nacht erstmals
ist gesehen worden, und ungefer umb acht Ur und-
gangen, ist hernach bey sechs wochen alle nacht in
hohe und lenger, doch dunckler scheinend gesehen
worden.

Anno 1578. Ist bald auff erlöschung diser
Cometstern, am Sontag den sechs und zwainzigsten tag des Monats January, ist erkrankt der
lieb Bruder Peter Walpot, oder Scherer genandt,
(dieweil er vorhin seines handtwerckhs ein tuchscherer gewesen) ein treuer diener Christi, und
seiner gantzen Gemain. Darnach den Neun
und zwainzigsten tag gemelts Monats, umb siben
Uhr vor Mittag, hat er, gleich vor seinem ende,
mit den Eltesten, so dazumal bey im in seiner Kranck-
heit versamlet, sein letzte Red und ermanung gethon, wiewol hart, vor grosser schwachait, doch
hertzlich und vernunfftig. (Auff dise maynung) als
er sich etwas im Bett hat lassen auffrichten, hat
er gesprochen:

Peter Walpot erkrankt.

Lieben Brüeder, Ich waiß nit anders, denn das
Ich allzeit begert hab Gott zu förchten, und der
Gemain treulich zu dienen, Also das Ich mein gewissen aller sünden halben frey waiß, On allain
das Ich mich auch meiner schwachait halben allzeit
zu beklagen gehabt, wie anders, Doch hab ich
sonst ein gut gewissen, das ich allzeit begert hab

Peter Walpots letzte Red mit den Eltesten.

treulich

Plate 10: Illustration of comet seen in November 1577
"1581" codex

GLOSSARY

BRUDERHOF. Literally: place of the brothers. The community (communal buildings, dwellings, workshops, children's houses and school) inhabited by families and single persons who are committed to share fully in the communal life.

GELASSENHEIT. Literally: a letting-go. The trusting yieldedness to God's will, abandonment of self (including private property), and joyful acceptance of suffering for Christ's sake.

ORDNUNG. (pl. ORDNUNGEN). A set of codes or regulations (also called "discipline," as in "Barber-Surgeons' Discipline") that grows out of the unity of the gathered church, to ensure orderliness in all areas of the communal life both for the group as a whole and for the individual within the group.

SERVANT FOR TEMPORAL AFFAIRS. Leader or manager of the economy of a Bruderhof, appointed by the brotherhood and made responsible for the practical concerns and outer well-being of a community.

SERVANT OF THE WORD or SERVANT OF THE GOSPEL. The brother chosen by the whole church to care for the inner and outer well-being of the community as a whole and of the individual members; usually appointed on trial, he is later confirmed by the elders with the laying on of hands. His tasks include preaching the Gospel and teaching the assembled brotherhood, counseling, acting as spokesman for the brotherhood, and undertaking mission journeys by unanimous decision of the members.

VORSTEHER. The leading elder or servant of the Word, who carries the main responsibility for the church.

Selected Bibliography

Ammann, Hartmann

1896 "Die Wiedertäufer in Michelsburg im Pusterthale und deren Urgichten." *Programm des k. k. Gymnasiums zu Brixen* 46: 3–52. Bressanone, Italy.

Aussbund Etliche schöne Christliche Geseng, wie die in der Gefengnus zu Passaw im

1564 *Schloß von den Schweitzern, und auch von anderen rechtgläubigen Christen hin und her gedicht worden: Allen und jeden Christen, welcher Religion sie auch seyen, unparteilich und fast nützlich zu brauchen.* 13th ed. Lancaster County, Pa.: 1973.

Beck, Josef

1883 Ed., *Die Geschichts-Bücher der Wiedertäufer in Oesterreich-Ungarn, . . . 1526–1785*. Vienna. Reprint: Nieuwkoop, Netherlands: B. de Graaf, 1967.

1899 "Georg Blaurock und die Anfänge des Anabaptismus in Graubündten und Tirol." Posthumous edition by Johann Loserth. In *Vorträge und Aufsätze der Comeniusgesellschaft* 7. Berlin.

Bender, Harold S.

1931 Ed. and trans., "A Hutterite School Discipline of 1578 and Peter Scherer's Address of 1568 to the Schoolmasters." *MQR* 5 (October): 231–244.

1936 "Conrad Grebel, the First Leader of the Swiss Brethren." *MQR* 10 (January): 5–45; (April): 91–137; (July): 151–160.

1938 "The Theology of Conrad Grebel." *MQR* 12 (January): 27–54; (April): 114–134.

1944 *The Anabaptist Vision*. Scottdale, Pa.: Herald Press.

1950 *Conrad Grebel, c. 1498–1526: The Founder of the Swiss Brethren Sometimes Called Anabaptists*. Goshen, Ind.: Mennonite Historical Society.

Bender, Harold S., and Ernst H. Correll

1926 "Conrad Grebel's Petition of Protest and Defense to the Zurich Council in 1523." *Goshen College Record Review Supplement* 27 (January): 23–32.

Benrath, Karl

1885 "Wiedertäufer im Venetianischen um die Mitte des 16. Jahrhunderts." *Theologische Studien und Kritiken* 1: 37–67.

Bergmann, Cornelius

1916 *Die Täuferbewegung im Kanton Zurich bis 1660*. Vol. 2 of *Quellen und Abhandlungen zur Schweizerischen Reformationsgeschichte*. Leipzig: Verlag von M. Heinsius Nachfolger.

Blanke, Fritz

1953 "The First Anabaptist Congregation: Zollikon, 1525." *MQR* 27 (January): 17–33.

1961 *Brothers in Christ: The History of the Oldest Anabaptist Congregation Zollikon Near Zurich, Switzerland.* Scottdale, Pa.: Herald Press.

Bossert, Gustav, ed.

1930 *Quellen zur Geschichte der Wiedertäufer: Herzogtum Württemberg.* Vol. 1 of *Quellen und Forschungen zur Reformationsgeschichte.* Leipzig: M. Heinsius Nachfolger Eger & Sievers.

Braght, Tieleman Jansz van

1660 *The Bloody Theatre, or Martyrs Mirror of the Defenseless Christians. . . .* Translated from the Dutch by Joseph F. Sohm. 13th ed. Scottdale, Pa.: Mennonite Publishing House, 1982.

Clasen, Claus-Peter

1972 *Anabaptism: A Social History, 1525–1618, Switzerland, Austria, Moravia, South and Central Germany.* Ithaca, N.Y.: Cornell University Press.

Conrad Grebel's Programmatic Letters: 1524. Translated by J. C. Wenger. Scottdale, Pa.:

1524 Herald Press, 1970.

Cooper, J. P., ed.

1970 *The Decline of Spain and the Thirty Years War, 1609–48/59.* Vol. 4 of *The New Cambridge Modern History.* Cambridge University Press.

Correll, Ernst H.

1927 "Anabaptism in the Tyrol." *MQR* 1 (October): 49–60.

DeWind, Henry A.

1954 "Italian Hutterite Martyrs." *MQR* 28 (July): 163–185.

Durnbaugh, Donald F.

1970 *The Believers' Church: The History and Character of Radical Protestantism.* New York: Macmillan Company.

Dyck, C. J., ed.

1962 *A Legacy of Faith.* Newton, Kans.: Faith and Life Press.

Egli, Emil

1878 *Die Züricher Wiedertäufer zur Reformationszeit.* Zurich: Friedrich Schulthess.

1879 *Actensammlung zur Geschichte der Züricher Reformation in den Jahren 1519–1533.* 3 vols. Zurich.

Ehrenpreis, Andreas

1650 "An Epistle on Brotherly Community as the Highest Command of Love." In *Brotherly Community: The Highest Command of Love: Two Anabaptist Documents of 1650 and 1560.* Translated and edited by the Hutterian Brethren, 1–77. Rifton, N.Y.: Plough Publishing House, 1978.

d'Elvert, Christian

1845 *Die Schweden vor Brünn.* Brno, Czechoslovakia.

Erhard, Christoph

1589 *Gründliche kurtz verfaste Historia Von Münsterischen Widertauffern: Und wie die Hutterischen Brüder so auch billich Widertauffer genent werden, im Löblichen Marggraffthumb Märhern, deren über die sibentzehen tausent sein sollen, gedachten Münsterischen in vilen ähnlich, gleichformig und mit zustimmet sein.* Munich.

Estep, William R.

1975 *The Anabaptist Story.* Grand Rapids, Mich.: Eerdmans.

Fast, Heinold, ed.

1962 *Der linke Flügel der Reformation: Glaubenszeugnisse der Täufer, Spiritualisten, Schwärmer und Antitrinitarier.* Vol. 4 of *Klassiker des Protestantismus.* Bremen: Carl Schünemann Verlag.

1973 *Quellen zur Geschichte der Täufer in der Schweiz* 2: *Ostschweiz.* Zurich: Theologischer Verlag.

Felbinger, Klaus

1560 "Confession of Faith Addressed to the Council of Landshut." In *Brotherly Community: The Highest Command of Love: Two Anabaptist Documents of 1650 and 1560.* Translated and edited by the Hutterian Brethren, 83–133. Rifton, N.Y.: Plough Publishing House, 1978.

Fischer, Christoph Andreas

1607 *Der Hutterischen Widertauffer Taubenkobel. . . .* Ingolstadt, Germany.

Fischer, Hans

1956 *Jakob Huter: Leben, Frömmigkeit, Briefe.* Newton, Kans.: Mennonite Publication Office.

Franck, Caspar

1576 *Catalogus Haereticorum Das ist: Warhafftige erzelung der namhafften Irrthumb und Ketzer, welche von anfang der Welt biß auff unsere zeit entstanden. . . .* Ingolstadt, Germany.

Franck, Sebastian

1531 *Chronica, Zeytbuch und geschychtbibel von anbegyn bisz inn disz gegenwertig M.D. XXXI jar. . . .* Strasbourg.

Franz, Günther, ed.

1951 *Wiedertäuferakten, 1527–1626.* Vol. 4 of *Urkundliche Quellen zur hessischen Reformationsgeschichte.* Marburg: N.G. Elwert'sche Verlagsbuchhandlung.

Friedmann, Robert

1927 *Die Habaner in der Slowakei.* Reprint from *Wiener Zeitschrift für Volkskunde* 32, nos. 3, 4. Vienna.

1931 "Eine dogmatische Hauptschrift der Huterischen Täufergemeinschaften in Mähren." *Archiv für Reformations-Geschichte* 28 (1931): 80–111, 208–240; 29 (1932): 1–18.

1942 "The Schleitheim Confession (1527) and other Doctrinal Writings of the Swiss Brethren in a Hitherto Unknown Edition." *MQR* 16 (April): 82–98.

1943 "Adventures of an Anabaptist in Turkey, 1607–1610." *MQR* 17 (April): 73–86.

1945 "Reason and Obedience: An Old Anabaptist Letter of Peter Walpot (1571) and Its Meaning." *MQR* 19 (January): 27–40.

1948 "The Encounter of Anabaptists and Mennonites with Anti-Trinitarianism." *MQR* 22 (July): 139–162.

1953 "Hutterite Physicians and Barber-Surgeons (Additional Notes)." *MQR* 27 (April): 128–136.

1955 "Christian Sectarians in Thessalonica and Their Relationship to the Anabaptists." *MQR* 29 (January): 54–69 (addenda, January 1956: 30–78).

1957 "A Notable Hutterite Document Concerning True Surrender and Christian Community of Goods." *MQR* 31 (January): 22–62.

1958 "The Philippite Brethren: A Chapter in Anabaptist History." *MQR* 32 (October): 272–297.

1959 "Leonhard Schiemer and Hans Schlaffer: Two Tyrolean Anabaptist Martyr-Apostles of 1528." *MQR* 33 (January): 31–41.

1959 "The Oldest Known Hutterite Codex of 1566: A Chapter in Anabaptist Intellectual History." *MQR* 33 (April): 96–107.

1960 "Jakob Hutter's Last Epistle to the Church in Moravia, 1535." *MQR* 34 (January): 37–47.

1961 *Hutterite Studies: Essays by Robert Friedmann: Collected and Published in Honor of His Seventieth Anniversary*. Edited by Harold S. Bender. Goshen, Ind.: Mennonite Historical Society.

1961 Ed., "A Newly Discovered Source on the Transmigration of the Hutterites to Transylvania, 1621–1623." *MQR* 35 (October): 309–314.

1967 Ed., *Glaubenszeugnisse oberdeutscher Taufgesinnter 2*. Vol. 12 of *Quellen zur Geschichte der Täufer*. Gütersloh: Gerd Mohn.

1970 "Peter Riedemann: Early Anabaptist Leader." *MQR* 44 (January): 5–44.

1973 *The Theology of Anabaptism: An Interpretation*. Scottdale, Pa.: Herald Press.

Friedmann, Robert, and Adolf Mais

1965 *Die Schriften der Huterischen Täufergemeinschaften: Gesamtkatalog ihrer Manuskriptbücher, ihrer Schreiber und ihrer Literatur, 1529–1667*. Vienna: Hermann Böhlaus Nachfolger.

Füesslin, J. C.

1741 *Beiträge zur Kirchen- und Reformations-Geschichte der Schweiz*. Zurich.

Gardiner, Samuel R.

1969 *Epochs of Modern History: The Thirty Years' War, 1618–1648*. New York: Greenwood Press, Publishers.

Geiser, Samuel Henri

1971 *Die Taufgesinnten Gemeinden im Rahmen der allgemeinen Kirchengeschichte*. 2d. ed. Courgenay, Switzerland: Christian Schmutz.

Gingerich, Ray C.

1980 *The Mission Impulse of Early Swiss and South German-Austrian Anabaptism*. Ann Arbor, Mich.: University Microfilms.

Gleysteen, Jan, comp.-ed.

1975 *The Drama of the Martyrs*. Engravings by Jan Luyken (1649–1712). Lancaster, Pa.: Mennonite Historical Associates.

Goertz, Hans-Jürgen, ed.

1982 *Profiles of Radical Reformers*. English edition edited by Walter Klaassen. Scottdale, Pa.: Herald Press.

Goeters, Gerhard
1955 "Ludwig Haetzer, a Marginal Anabaptist." *MQR* 29 (October): 251–262.

Gratz, Delbert
1953 *Bernese Anabaptists*. Scottdale, Pa.: Herald Press.

Grimm, Harold J.
1965 *The Reformation Era: 1500–1650*. New York: The Macmillan Co.

Grimmelshausen, Hans Jakob Christoph von
1668 *Der abenteuerliche Simplizissimus*. Various editions. English translation by A. T. S. Goodrick: *The Adventurous Simplicissimus*. Lincoln, Nebr.: University of Nebraska Press, 1962.

Gross, Leonard
1969 "Nikolaus Geyersbühler, Hutterite Missioner to Tirol." *MQR* 43 (October): 283–292.
1970 "Dialogue Between a Hutterite and a Swiss Brother." *MQR* 44 (January): 45–58.
1975 "Leonard Dax's Encounter with Calvinism." *MQR* 49 (October): 284–334.
1980 *The Golden Years of the Hutterites: The Witness and Thought of the Communal Moravian Anabaptists During the Walpot Era, 1565–1578*. Scottdale, Pa.: Herald Press.
1986 "The Hutterian Brethren and the Polish Brethren: Rapprochement and Estrangement." *The Proceedings of the Unitarian Universalist Historical Society*. Vol. 20, Part 2: 46–53. Chicago, Ill.

Harder, Leland, ed.
1985 *The Sources of Swiss Anabaptism: The Grebel Letters and Related Documents*. Scottdale, Pa.: Herald Press.

Hege, Christian
1908 *Die Täufer in der Kurpfalz: Ein Beitrag zur badisch-pfälzischen Reformationsgeschichte*. Frankfurt am Main: Kommissionsverlag von Hermann Minjon.

Heimann, Franz
1952 "The Hutterite Doctrines of Church and Common Life: A Study of Peter Riedemann's Confession of Faith of 1540." *MQR* 26 (January): 22–47; (April): 142–160.

Hershberger, Guy F., ed.
1957 *The Recovery of the Anabaptist Vision: A Sixtieth Anniversary Tribute to Harold S. Bender*. Scottdale, Pa.: Herald Press.

Horsch, John
1914 "Ein Sendschreiben Hans Kräls an einen Märtyrer." *Familien Kalender* 45: 32–35. Scottdale, Pa.: The Mennonite Publishing House.
1931 *The Hutterian Brethren, 1528–1931: A Story of Martyrdom and Loyalty*. Goshen, Ind.: The Mennonite Historical Society.
1939 "Strassburg, a Swiss Brethren Center." *MQR* 13 (January): 21–27.

Hostetler, John A.
1974 *Hutterite Society*. Baltimore: The Johns Hopkins University Press.

Hostetler, John A., Leonard Gross, and Elizabeth Bender
1975 *Selected Hutterian Documents in Translation, 1542–1654*. Philadelphia: Temple University.

Hrubý, František
1935 *Die Wiedertäufer in Mähren*. Leipzig: Verlag M. Heinsius Nachfolger.

Hulshof, Abraham
1905 *Geschiedenis van de Doopsgezinden te Straatsburg van 1525 tot 1557*. Amsterdam: J. Clausen.

Hutter, Jakob
1530-35 *Brotherly Faithfulness: Epistles from a Time of Persecution*. Translated and edited by the Hutterian Brethren. Rifton, N.Y.: Plough Publishing House, 1979.

Jones, Rufus M.
1909 *Studies in Mystical Religion*. Reissued, New York: Russel & Russel, 1970.

Kalesný, František
1981 *Habáni na Slovensku*. Bratislava: Tatran. Translation of Contents and Summary: "Anabaptists in Slovakia." *MQR* 56 (April 1982): 189–195.

Kann, Robert A.
1977 *A History of the Habsburg Empire, 1526–1918*. Berkeley: University of California Press.

Keller, A., C. Calvert, and A. W. Gruner
1928 *A Hangman's Diary: Being the Journal of Master Franz Schmidt von Nürnberg*. New York. Reprint: 1973.

Keller, Ludwig
1882 *Ein Apostel der Widertäufer*. Leipzig: S. Hirzel Verlag.

Klaassen, Walter
1978 *Michael Gaismair: Revolutionary and Reformer*. Leiden: E. J. Brill.
1981 Ed., *Anabaptism in Outline: Selected Primary Sources*. Kitchener, Ontario: Herald Press.
1981 Ed., *Sixteenth Century Anabaptism: Defences, Confessions, Refutations*. Translated by Frank Friesen. Waterloo, Ontario: Conrad Grebel College.

Klassen, Herbert C.
1959 "The Life and Teachings of Hans Hut." *MQR* 33 (July): 171–205; (October): 267–304.

Kosary, Dominic G.
1971 *A History of Hungary*. New York: Arno Press.

Kot, Stanislas
1957 *Socinianism in Poland: The Social and Political Ideas of the Polish Antitrinitarians in the Sixteenth and Seventeenth Centuries*. Translated by Earl Wilbur. Boston: Starr King Press.

Die Lieder der Hutterischen Brüder
1914 Scottdale, Pa.: Die Hutterischen Brüder. Reprints: Winnipeg, Manitoba, 1953; Cayley, Alberta, 1962, 1974.

Liliencron, Freiherr von
1875 *Zur Liederdichtung der Wiedertäufer*. Munich.

Loserth, Johann
1884 "Zur Geschichte der Wiedertäufer in Mähren." *Zeitschrift für allgemeine Geschichte, Kultur-, Litteratur- und Kunstgeschichte* 1.
1892 "Deutschböhmische Wiedertäufer." *Mittheilungen des Vereins für Geschichte der Deutschen in Böhmen* 30, no. 4. Prague.
1892 *Der Anabaptismus in Tirol*. Vol. 78 of *Archiv für österreichische Geschichte*. Vienna.
1893 *Doctor Balthasar Hubmaier und die Anfänge der Wiedertäufer in Mähren*. Brno, Czechoslovakia.
1894 "Zur Geschichte der Wiedertäufer in Steiermark." Reprint from *Zeitschrift des historischen Vereines für Steiermark* 17: 118–145. Graz, Austria.
1894 *Der Communismus der mährischen Wiedertäufer im 16. und 17. Jahrhundert: Beiträge zu ihrer Geschichte, Lehre und Verfassung*. Vol. 81 of *Archiv für österreichische Geschichte*. Vienna.

Macartney, C. A.
1962 *Hungary: A Short History*. Edinburgh: University Press.

Macek, Josef
1965 *Der Tiroler Bauernkrieg und Michael Gaismair*. Translated from the Czech by Eduard Ullmann. Berlin: Deutscher Verlag der Wissenschaften.

Mais, Adolf, ed.
1974 "The *Hausbuch* of Neumühl 1558–1610: The Oldest Land Register of the Hutterian Brethren." Translated by Elizabeth Bender. *MQR* 48 (April): 215–236.

Mecenseffy, Grete
1964 *Österreich, I. Teil*. Vol. 11 of *Quellen zur Geschichte der Täufer*. Gütersloh: Gerd Mohn.
1967 "Probleme der Täuferforschung." *Theologische Literaturzeitung* 92, no. 9: 641–648. Leipzig.
1972 *Österreich, II. Teil*. Vol. 13 of *Quellen zur Geschichte der Täufer*. Gütersloh: Gerd Mohn.
1983 *Österreich, III. Teil*. Vol. 14 of *Quellen zur Geschichte der Täufer*. Gütersloh: Gerd Mohn.

The Mennonite Encyclopedia
1955-59 Scottdale, Pa.: Mennonite Publishing House. Four volumes; vol. 5 forthcoming.

Mennonitisches Lexikon
1913-67 Frankfurt am Main and Karlsruhe. Four volumes.

Meyer, Christian
1874 "Zur Geschichte der Wiedertäufer in Oberschwaben. I: Die Anfänger des Wiedertäufertums in Augsburg." *Zeitschrift des historischen Vereins für Schwaben und Neuburg* 1: 207–253. Augsburg: J. A. Schlosser.

Moore, John Allen
1984 *Anabaptist Portraits*. Scottdale, Pa.: Herald Press.

Müller, Ernst

1895 *Geschichte der Bernischen Wiedertäufer*. Frauenfeld, Switzerland: J. Hubers Verlag.

Müller, Lydia, ed.

1938 *Glaubenszeugnisse oberdeutscher Taufgesinnter* 1. Vol. 20 of *Quellen und Forschungen zur Reformationsgeschichte*. Leipzig: M. Heinsius Nachfolger.

Muralt, Leonard von, and Walter Schmid, eds.

1952 *Quellen zur Geschichte der Täufer in der Schweiz* 1. Zurich: S. Hirzel Verlag.

Neubaur, L.

1912 "Mährische Brüder in Elbing." *Zeitschrift für Kirchengeschichte* 33: 447–455. Gotha: F. A. Perthes.

Nicoladoni, Alexander

1893 *Johannes Bünderlin von Linz und die oberösterreichischen Täufergemeinden, 1525–1531*. Berlin: R. Gaertner.

Oyer, John S.

1985 "Gegenwärtiger Stand der Huttererforschung." In *Die Hutterischen Täufer: Geschichtlicher Hintergrund und handwerkliche Leistung*. Mennonitische Forschungsstelle Weiherhof, Germany.

Packull, Werner O.

1977 *Mysticism and the Early South German-Austrian Anabaptist Movement, 1525–1531*. Scottdale, Pa.: Herald Press.

Penner, Horst

1949 "West Prussian Mennonites Through Four Centuries." *MQR* 22 (October): 232–245.

Polišenský, J. V.

1971 *The Thirty Years War*. Translated from the Czech by Robert Evans. Berkeley: University of California Press.

Polišenský, J. V., and Frederick Snider

1978 *War and Society in Europe 1618–20*. Cambridge: Cambridge University Press.

Rideman, Peter

1565 *Rechenschaft unserer Religion, Lehr und Glaubens, von den Brüdern, so man die Hutterischen nennt, ausgangen 1565*. English translation by the Hutterian Brethren: *Confession of Faith: Account of our Religion, Doctrine and Faith Given by Peter Rideman of the Brothers Whom Men Call Hutterians*. Rifton, N.Y.: Plough Publishing House, 1970. Modernized English edition forthcoming.

Roth, Friedrich

1900 "Zur Geschichte der Wiedertäufer in Oberschwaben." *Zeitschrift des historischen Vereins für Schwaben*, 1–45.

1901 *Augsburgs Reformationsgeschichte von 1517–1530*. 2d. ed. Munich.

Runzo, Jean

1978 *Communal Discipline in the Early Anabaptist Communities of Switzerland, South and Central Germany, Austria, and Moravia, 1525–1550*. Ann Arbor, Mich.: University Microfilms.

Ruth, John L.

1975 *Conrad Grebel: Son of Zurich*. Scottdale, Pa.: Herald Press.

Saxby, Trevor

1987 *Pilgrims of a Common Life: Christian Community of Goods Through the Centuries*. Scottdale, Pa.: Herald Press.

Snyder, C. Arnold

1984 *The Life and Thought of Michael Sattler*. Scottdale, Pa.: Herald Press.

Sommer, John L.

1953 "Hutterite Medicine and Physicians in Moravia in the Sixteenth Century and After." *MQR* 27 (April): 111–127.

Stayer, James M.

1965 "Hans Hut's Doctrine of the Sword: An Attempted Solution." *MQR* 39 (July): 181–191.

1973 *Anabaptists and the Sword*. Lawrence, Kansas: Coronado Press.

Steinberg, S. H.

1966 *The Thirty Years War and the Conflict for European Hegemony, 1600–1660*. New York: W. W. Norton & Co. Inc.

Stella, Aldo

1983 *Genesi del comunismo evangelico hutterita: Storiografia e nuove interpretazioni*. Reprint from *L'uomo e la storia: Studi storici in onore di Massimo Petrocchi* 1, 207–228. Rome.

Theatrum Europaeum. 21 vols. Frankfurt am Main, 1627–1738.

Thomson, S. Harrison

1953 *Czechoslovakia in European History*. Princeton, N.J.: Princeton University Press.

Tumbült, G.

1899 "Die Wiedertäufer." *Monographien zur Weltgeschichte* 7. Leipzig.

Vedder, Henry C.

1905 *Balthasar Hubmaier, the Leader of the Anabaptists*. New York: G. P. Putnam's Sons.

Völker, Karl

1930 *Kirchengeschichte Polens*. N.p.

Wackernagel, Philipp

1870 *Das deutsche Kirchenlied von der ältesten Zeit bis zu Anfang des XVII. Jahrhunderts*. 5 vols. Leipzig.

Waltner, Gary James

1975 *The Educational System of the Hutterian Anabaptists and Their Schulordnungen of the 16th and 17th Centuries*. Master's thesis. University of South Dakota.

Wappler, Paul

1913 "Die Täuferbewegung in Thüringen von 1526–1548." *Beiträge zur neueren Geschichte Thüringens* 2. Jena, Germany.

Wedgwood, C. V.

1961 *The Thirty Years War*. Garden City, New York: Doubleday & Co., Inc., Anchor Books.

Wenger, John Christian

1945 Trans., "The Schleitheim Confession of Faith." *MQR* 19 (October): 243–253.

1949 Trans., "Letter from Wilhelm Reublin to Pilgram Marpeck, 1531." *MQR* 23 (April): 67–75.

1949 *Glimpses of Mennonite History and Doctrine*. Scottdale, Pa.: Herald Press.

Wiedemann, Hans

1963 *Die Wiedertäufergemeinde in Passau 1527–1535*. Passau, Germany.

Williams, George Huntston

1957 Ed., *Spiritual and Anabaptist Writers*. Vol. 25 of *Library of Christian Classics*. London: SCM Press Ltd.

1962 *The Radical Reformation*. Philadelphia, Pa.: Westminster Press.

1983 *La Reforma Radical*. Augmented edition, translated from English by Antonio Alatorre. Mexico City: Fondo Cultural Económico.

1986 "Stanislaw Budziński (c.1530–c.1595): The First Historian of Unitarianism." *The Proceedings of the Unitarian Universalist Historical Society*. Vol. 20, Part 2: 77–88. Chicago, Ill.

Williams, George Huntston, and others

1987 *Stanislas Lubieniecki, the History of the Polish Reformation (Amsterdam, 1685) and Related Documents*. Vol. 34 of *Harvard Theological Studies*. Philadelphia, Pa.: Fortress Press.

Wiswedel, Wilhelm

1937 "Michael Sattler, ein Opfer seltener Glaubenstreue." *Der Wahrheitszeuge* 59, nos. 13–18. Kassel, Germany.

Wolkan, Rudolf

1903 *Die Lieder der Wiedertäufer: Ein Beitrag zur deutschen und niederländischen Litteratur- und Kirchengeschichte*. Berlin.

1918 *Die Hutterer: Oesterreichische Wiedertäufer und Kommunisten in Amerika*. Vienna.

1923 Ed., *Geschicht-Buch der Hutterischen Brüder*. Macleod, Alberta, Canada: Hutterian Brethren.

Wolný, Gregor

1850 *Die Wiedertäufer in Mähren*. Vol. 5 of *Archiv für die Kunde der Oesterreichischen Geschichtsquellen*. Vienna: Kaiserliche Akademie der Wissenschaften.

Yoder, John Howard, trans. and ed.

1973 *The Legacy of Michael Sattler*. Scottdale, Pa.: Herald Press.

Zeman, Jarold K.

1967 *Historical Topography of Moravian Anabaptism*. Reprint from *MQR* 40 and 41 (October 1966, January & April 1967). Goshen, Ind.: The Mennonite Historical Society.

1969 *The Anabaptists and the Czech Brethren in Moravia, 1526–1628: A Study of Origins and Contacts*. The Hague: Mouton & Co. N.V. Publishers.

Zieglschmid, A. J. F.
1940 "Die ungarischen Wiedertäufer bei Grimmelshausen." *Zeitschrift für Kirchengeschichte* 59, 3rd ser., no. 10.
1940 "An unpublished 'Hausbrief' of Grimmelshausen's Hungarian Anabaptists." *Germanic Review* 15: 81–97.
1941 "Unpublished 16th Century Letters of the Hutterian Brethren." *MQR* 15 (January): 5–25; (April): 118–140.
1943 Ed., *Die älteste Chronik der Hutterischen Brüder*. Philadelphia, Pa.: The Carl Schurz Memorial Foundation, Inc.
1947 Ed., *Das Klein-Geschichtsbuch der Hutterischen Brüder*. Philadelphia, Pa.: The Carl Schurz Memorial Foundation, Inc.

Zuck, Lowell H., ed.
1975 *Christianity and Revolution: Radical Christian Testimonies, 1520–1650*. Philadelphia: Temple University Press.

Bibliographical Works

Bainton, Roland H., and Eric W. Gritsch
1972 *Bibliography of the Continental Reformation: Materials Available in English*. 2d ed. Hamden, Conn.: The Shoe String Press, Inc.

"A Chronological Bibliography of the Writings of Robert Friedmann." *MQR* 35 (July):
1961 243–247.

Hillerbrand, Hans Joachim
1962 *A Bibliography of Anabaptism: 1520–1630*. Elkhart, Ind.: Institute of Mennonite Studies.
1975 *A Bibliography of Anabaptism: 1520–1630: A Sequel*. St. Louis: Center for Reformation Research.

Riley, M. P.
1965 *The Hutterite Brethren: An Annotated Bibliography with Special Reference to South Dakota Hutterite Colonies*. Brookings, S. Dak.: University of South Dakota.

Springer, Nelson P.
1952 "Mennonite Quarterly Review Cumulative Index: Volumes 1–25 (1927–1951)." *MQR* 26 (January): 65–91.
1956 "Mennonite Quarterly Review Cumulative Index: Volumes 26–30 (1952–1956)." *MQR* 30 (October): 81–288.
1966 "Mennonite Quarterly Review Cumulative Index: Volumes 31–40 (1957–1966)." *MQR* 40 (October): 298–318.
1976 "Mennonite Quarterly Review Cumulative Index: Volumes 41–50 (1967–1976)." *MQR* 50 (October): 313–334.
1987 "Mennonite Quarterly Review Cumulative Index: Volumes 51–60 (1977–1986)." *MQR* 61 (January): 89–118.

Springer, Nelson P., and A. J. Klassen
1977 *Mennonite Bibliography, 1631–1961*. 2 vols. Scottdale, Pa.: Herald Press.

Index of Bible References

General Index

Towns marked with an asterisk could not be identified with the maps available to the editors. Some may no longer be in existence.